9⁵⁰

AMERICAN CIVIL-MILITARY DECISIONS

AMERICAN CIVIL-MILITARY DECISIONS

A Book of Case Studies

Edited by HAROLD STEIN

A TWENTIETH CENTURY FUND STUDY

Published in Cooperation with

THE INTER-UNIVERSITY CASE PROGRAM

by UNIVERSITY OF ALABAMA PRESS, 1963

CONTRIBUTORS

MARVIN D. BERNSTEIN, Assistant Professor of History
State University College at Fredonia, New York

ALBERT A. BLUM, Associate Professor, Social Science Department
and Labor and Industrial Relations Center
Michigan State University

PAUL Y. HAMMOND, Research Associate
Washington Center of Foreign Policy Research
The Johns Hopkins University

MARTIN LICHTERMAN, Executive Secretary, New England Board
of Higher Education
Winchester, Massachusetts

FRANCIS L. LOEWENHEIM, Associate Professor of History
Rice University

THEODORE J. LOWI, Assistant Professor of Government
Cornell University

LAURENCE W. MARTIN, Associate Professor of European Diplomacy,
School of Advanced International Studies and Research Associate,
Washington Center of Foreign Policy Research
The Johns Hopkins University

ROBERT J. QUINLAN, Assistant Editor
The Encyclopedia Americana

MICHAEL D. REAGAN, Assistant Professor of Political Science
Maxwell School of Citizenship and Public Affairs
Syracuse University

FOREWORD

This volume of case studies constitutes the second and concluding portion of the Twentieth Century Fund project on Civil-Military Relations. Inaugurated after careful discussions in 1953, the project represented a significant departure from the economic research in which the Fund had previously concentrated. It seemed in line, however, with the kind of problems basic to the twentieth century as it advanced into its second half.

A first study in this area, *Arms and the State* by Walter Millis with Harvey C. Mansfield and Harold Stein, was published by the Twentieth Century Fund in 1958. This volume presents a general survey of civil-military relations in the United States since the 1930s. Work on the cases presented here was then already far advanced. The cases provided Mr. Millis and his associates with an important part of the substance of their account. The publication of the cases themselves will not only provide relevant and often hitherto inaccessible infor-mation but also serve as an aid to students and teachers in a field which is increasingly attracting attention in the universities.

The final editing of the cases has been delayed by numerous personal and technical problems, including the necessity in one significant instance of getting clearance of a manuscript from the military authorities. The Fund is now glad to have them completed and on their way. For their publication it has welcomed the co-operation of the Inter-University Case Program and the University of Alabama Press, which are experienced in the distribution of comparable material. It remains only to express a word of appreciation to the Director of the project, Harold Stein, Professor of Public and International Affairs at the Woodrow Wilson School of Princeton University, whose vision guided the original formulation and who has worked through many years, and over a period of serious illness, to bring it to completion.

AUGUST HECKSCHER, *Director*
The Twentieth Century Fund

41 East 70th Street, New York
February 1962

CONTENTS

CONTRIBUTORS   v

FOREWORD   vii

INTRODUCTION   HAROLD STEIN   1

THE FAR EASTERN CRISIS OF 1931-1932: STIMSON, HOOVER
AND THE ARMED SERVICES   MICHAEL D. REAGAN   27

THE HELIUM CONTROVERSY   MICHAEL D. REAGAN   43

BIRTH AND DEATH OF THE M-DAY PLAN   ALBERT A. BLUM   61

AID TO RUSSIA: THE FIRST YEAR
     MARVIN D. BERNSTEIN AND FRANCIS L. LOEWENHEIM   97

THE UNITED STATES FLEET: DIPLOMACY, STRATEGY AND
THE ALLOCATION OF SHIPS (1940-1941)   ROBERT J. QUINLAN   153

THE ITALIAN ARMISTICE   ROBERT J. QUINLAN   203

DIRECTIVES FOR THE OCCUPATION OF GERMANY: THE
WASHINGTON CONTROVERSY   PAUL Y. HAMMOND   311

SUPER CARRIERS AND B-36 BOMBERS: APPROPRIATIONS,
STRATEGY AND POLITICS   PAUL Y. HAMMOND   465

TO THE YALU AND BACK   MARTIN LICHTERMAN   569

THE AMERICAN DECISION TO
REARM GERMANY   LAURENCE W. MARTIN   643

BASES IN SPAIN   THEODORE J. LOWI   667

INTRODUCTION

HAROLD STEIN

PROFESSOR OF PUBLIC AND INTERNATIONAL AFFAIRS

WOODROW WILSON SCHOOL OF PUBLIC AND INTERNATIONAL AFFAIRS

PRINCETON UNIVERSITY

CONTENTS

I Case Studies in Civil-Military Relations   3

II The Context of the Case Studies   5
    A. Mutations in Attitudes   5
    B. Organizational Developments—Military and Semi-Military   5
    C. Changes in Economic Mobilization Methods   7
    D. Growth of Foreign Economic and Military Aid and Controls   9
    E. Scientists and the Armed Forces: The Military and Politics   11
    F. Locus of Power: The President and Congress   14
    G. The Strategy of Containment   18
    H. Diplomacy and Strategy   20

III The Future Direction of Civil-Military Relations in the United States   24

I. CASE STUDIES IN CIVIL-MILITARY RELATIONS

A case study of the kind included in this volume is a detailed account, from the perspective of a somewhat hypothetical neutral observer, of a series of events that illuminate the process by which a decision—or group of decisions—is made by both civilian and military public administrators. The studies show the administrators (almost all American in these cases) interpreting the factual material available to them, applying their own concepts of national objectives as they move toward decisions. In this process, they are always surrounded and affected by other administrators, frequently those in other government agencies; they are moved in various ways by legislators, by our allies and enemies in war and peace, and by that indefinable, amorphous but not negligible mass—the general public. Because these are case studies of civil-military relations, the administrators they describe are those who are concerned with problems in that field, and the studies are distinguished in that way from many other public administration case studies.[1]

There is no need here to attempt a precise definition of the phrase "civil-military relations." Not so many years ago the term would have referred almost entirely to relations within government of civilian and military officials, but the real and presumed sharp distinctions between the two have long been dwindling. There are, always will be, differences in occupational habits and ethos between the groups,

but, as Janowitz has pointed out, there are important overlaps, too. And the old issues of civilian control and the like have become academic, indeed largely irrelevant. The character of our civil-military relations is now dominated by sharper official awareness of the interplay between military means and diplomatic, economic, and political ends. Above all, we are far more conscious in our dealings with the world of both our power and its limitations than we were before World War II.

Awareness of the uses and limitations of power has caused a series of profound changes in the relationships of the civil and military officers of our government and equally profound changes in the weighing of factors of power and objectives in forming national policy.

Our government's willingness to face the distasteful facts of international power relations and to do so without relinquishing our ideals or our sense of purpose represents a major shift. We have come to this uneasy equilibrium belatedly, necessarily imperfectly; the enlarged ambiguity and amorphousness of the phrase "civil-military relations" represent our own enlarged sphere of concern with the use and restraint of force in world affairs.

The Twentieth Century Fund's decision to embark on the Study of Civil-Military Relations reflected a growing interest in the field. The publication of the case studies in this volume[2] is designed to enlarge public understanding of the new and complex processes by which decisions are reached which bear on the formation and maintenance of public policy in both its civil and military aspects. The case studies represent a discontinuous historical se-

[1] Each study in this volume is accompanied by my "Editorial Comments," which are not to be construed as coming from the hypothetical Neutral-Observer-Historian. The actual observer-historian is, of course, not without his own preconceptions. For an extended discussion of the problems inherent in the case method, see Harold Stein, "On Public Administration and Public Administration Cases" in *Essays on the Case Method in Public Administration and Political Science,* Edwin A. Bock, ed. Brussels, 1962.

[2] Two additional case studies were prepared for but are not included in this volume: one, "Demobilization and Postwar Planning" by Michael D. Reagan, has been omitted because the author was not allowed to make use of certain

quence and thereby illustrate the obvious fact that the processes currently in operation have been developing over the past thirty years. In each of the case studies there are civilian officials and officers of the armed services; in most of the cases they are working together harmoniously; what is usually at issue is the devising of a policy or program, the making of a decision or group of decisions in which military strength or use or needs is put in some sort of balance with judgments on economic needs, diplomatic ends, popular acceptance, and a host of other elements of explicit or implicit judgment that cannot or should not be overlooked in governing a democracy.

The character of the case studies is such that they are not solely illuminative of civil-military relations. Each of these cases is also of potential interest to readers not specially or exclusively interested in that field, but generally concerned about the operation of our national government, for all provide a view of American public administration as both politics and process seen under a microscope —a low-powered microscope to be sure, but in comparison with most comparatively telescopic studies of American government in action, a microscope nonetheless. Each of the cases is presented as a self-contained whole. Actually, in the seamless web of governing there is no such thing as a "self-contained whole." The limits of each study have been set not by the events themselves, but by the author and, to some extent, the editor. To them at least, the inclusion of much more detail (assuming it is obtainable) or more information about matters that seem to them only vaguely related to the central issues would strain the concept of relevance beyond the breaking point. Unless the reader can readily perceive how the various actions point up questions of significance, the case study would no longer serve its avowedly utilitarian function. The story of Jim Blaine and his grandfather's ram in *Roughing It* is wonderfully entertaining but it does not increase the sum of organized knowledge; it

has no focus, even though every sentence has a linkage with its predecessor and successor. What begins with "Grandfather fetched him from Illinois—got him from a man named Yates—Bill Yates—maybe you might have heard of him" ends magnificently with "sacred to the memory of fourteen yards of three-ply carpet containing all that was mortal of William Wheeler." But the "more bullier old ram" disappeared in the first sentence!

Each case study, because of its form of presentation, can stand on its own feet, so to speak; yet the more knowledgeable the reader, the easier it is for him to perceive nuances of action and relationships that might otherwise confuse or elude him. The previous volume prepared for the Twentieth Century Fund's Study of Civil-Military Relations, *Arms and the State,* is intimately connected with the case studies in this volume; but in order to make sure that this volume can be read separately, the next section of this introduction is designed to provide a context for the case studies in it.

What follows is based in large part, but not wholly, on the material in *Arms and the State.* The two accounts are not identical. This one is divided into topics, an approach which is presumed to be more useful to a reader of the cases seeking background in a very succinct account rather than the more conventional general historical technique used in *Arms and the State,* appropriate for the full-sized volume. The introduction covers a longer time period; although the most recent cases, like the account in the previous volume, go no further than the early days of Eisenhower's first term, this introductory sketch carries on toward the end of Kennedy's first year in office. There seemed to be a value in setting the cases in a contextual framework which covered a wider span of time than the cases themselves. Finally, a reader who wishes to take the trouble to compare this with *Arms and the State* will observe certain differences between the present introduction and that volume. Probably most of the differences are differences of emphasis arising from the Procrustean needs of a brief introduction; some no doubt come from judgments in which my conclusions diverged from those of Harvey C. Mansfield, whose collaborator I was in Part I of *Arms and the State;* some from those of the chief author of that volume, Walter Millis; some from changes in my own thinking.

---

files of documents essential for a full account; the other, "Conference for the Reduction and Limitation of Armaments—Geneva, 1932" by Arthur S. Olick, was dropped because the chronological focus of the studies was shifted to a somewhat later period than originally planned.

II. THE CONTEXT OF THE CASE STUDIES

A. MUTATIONS IN ATTITUDES

After World War I public attitudes in the United States about the use of force and arms and the role of the military in our government went through a regressive phase, a reverse of the process in which the public had travelled from Wilson's neutrality-without-favoritism through preparedness and into all-out war "to make the world safe for democracy." Force, it seemed, had proved to be a failure, and our future happiness would depend on our refusal to be drawn into quarrels on other continents. After 1933 this phase of American public sentiment went through a laborious process of reversal, involving profound fissions in public opinion, until the Japanese and the Germans settled our internal disputes for us.

After World War II the regressive phase was brief and uncertain. The bipartisan and wide acceptance of the United Nations and of our role in it showed that this time prewar "normalcy" was not accepted as a guide for our future. The 1948 presidential election campaign bore no resemblance to the campaign of 1920. Whoever the winner, there would be no return to isolation. Whatever the mistakes of the future, the American people had decided not to repeat the errors of the past.

No doubt there were many causes for this striking difference in postwar attitudes. Two are foremost:

First, after World War I, and for a long time thereafter, Americans had no clear vision of an enemy. Germany seemed permanently vanquished; Italy was our friend; and outspoken distrust of Japan was looked on by many as merely a trick employed by big-Navy lobbyists. Russia was an unknown quantity, and the European dictators had not yet emerged. Hate and fear of the Axis developed slowly, coming to a climax only when war approached.

On the other hand, the seeds of post-World War II suspicions were sown early. There were some public evidences of Communist animosity and faithlessness even before the end of the war, and Stalin's postwar acts piled up American distrust and hatred with remarkable speed. Churchill's Fulton speech, only a few months after V-J day, seemed shocking at the time, but its thesis was basically incontrovertible, and the Truman Doctrine message followed soon thereafter. By 1948, as Wallace's rejection by the voters showed, any widespread hope that American friendliness could by itself prevent Russia from becoming a dangerous enemy had disappeared.

Secondly, after World War I, and on through the 1930's, it was not possible to convince any large segment of the American people that we were or would ever be in serious danger of physical attack by any other nation no matter how hostile. After World War II the potentialities of our atomic bombs and our long-range bombers were known to all; in time Russia would also possess bombs and bombers and thereby the ability to attack not only our friends in their neighborhood, but us as well. Even the "Fortress America" doctrine supported mostly by former isolationists (who were frequently Asia Firsters as well) did not rely on our ability to stay out of war, but rather on our assumed ability to fight a war with the Communist powers solely with our own military forces and solely from our own country and island possessions. And "Fortress America" never had the profound and widespread appeal of "America First."

B. ORGANIZATIONAL DEVELOPMENTS—MILITARY AND SEMI-MILITARY

The striking contrast between the ideas that

were dominant in the 1920's and 1930's and those that had broad acceptance in the 1950's and 1960's might suggest that during or soon after World War II there was a scrapping of both the organizational devices and the methods that President Roosevelt had used during his first two terms in office. This assumption has a superficial plausibility but does not accord with the facts.

Organizationally progress has been primarily incremental and constructive. Besides the Army and Navy, both duly reorganized for the purpose, and the semi-autonomous AAF, the key military agency for the conduct of the war was the Joint Chiefs of Staff, created by the President as the "American Side," so to speak, of the Combined Chiefs of Staff, which was proposed by Churchill and agreed to by Roosevelt at the ARCADIA conference in Washington soon after Pearl Harbor. Much of the groundwork for JCS had been laid in the old Joint Army-Navy Board, particularly after it had been transferred to direct Presidential control by Roosevelt's Military Order in 1940.

One crucial difference between the Joint Board and JCS was Army Air Forces membership. (Actually General Arnold had been given a seat on the Board a few months earlier.) Autonomy of the Air Force had been the goal of air power enthusiasts at least since World War I, but Roosevelt was the first President and Marshall the first Army Chief of Staff to move strongly in that direction. Ironically enough, Douhet's theory, on which the aspirants relied so heavily, proved unreal for six long years from 1939 to 1945. During that period, the airplane's most perfect successes were in combat at sea (largely by carrier-based planes), in tactical air support, as in the Normandy landings, and in strategic attack on selected economic targets like synthetic oil plants and transportation. Not until the closing days of the war, with massive annihilation by atomic bombs, did the psychological impact, on which Douhet's theory had been based, prove consequential. The postwar Air Force, which had no need to prove the appalling destructiveness of air power, was in the process of creation from 1940 on, and the sharing of power with the other services has continued; what has changed most notably has been the spectacular growth of its own relative importance.

The other striking characteristic of JCS was

its power of command and sense of independence from all but the President, a fact augmented by its "closed" staff system, as has been pointed out by Hammond in *Organizing for Defense.* Furthermore, it reported directly to the President and not through the Secretary of War and the Secretary of the Navy. JCS represented an important improvement over its predecessor, the Joint Board, though the degree of its success is debatable.

There are other aspects of postwar defense organization that began before or during the war. With the shift in strategy that led to the inclusion of hemisphere defense among the military essentials, the need for coordination of strategy and diplomacy became more evident; the acceptance of force as a potential reality meant that the profound, almost complete, dichotomy of the Hoover days was obsolete. The first modest organizational product was the Standing Liaison Committee. It lapsed when the interests of the services turned more and more toward the Western Pacific and the Eastern Atlantic. Hull was too cautious to commit himself and his department to direct participation in entangling alliances, and the marriage of negotiation and power; the committee of the three secretaries proved no more than a place to exchange some information. Substitutes for SLC proved fruitless until the State-War-Navy Coordinating Committee and a revivified Committee of Three, late in the war, essentially Stimson-McCloy creations, started the government on the path towards the National Security Council, for which Forrestal provided the lead. The NSC, which followed, seems here to stay; but in the decade and a half since it was founded, the habit of working together by military and civilian officers has seemed at times even more important than the formal organizational structure for cooperation. In any event, both the habit of cooperation and the NSC committee structure have helped to open up the closed circuit of JCS and bring it into the governmental forum of diplomacy and strategy.

There are two more striking novelties in postwar organization, one pressed for by Forrestal, the other originally a plan that he distrusted. The one he desired was the Central Intelligence Agency. It had a partial wartime antecedent, the Office of Strategic Services. OSS could not have been created before the war started, partly because the collection, dissemination and coordination of intelligence were looked on with distaste, even more because covert operations were unthinkable. The CIA has picked up, formalized and enormously extended all the OSS activities. It sits in the center of government, whereas OSS was on the periphery. Perhaps the most dramatic of its innovations has been its gift for making many of its super-secret operations completely public. This is an unusual habit for any Deuxiéme Bureau, but perhaps equally unusual and more important has been the active participation of CIA leaders in the making of policy.

The second key postwar creation has been the Department of Defense—a creation that Forrestal wanted to avoid or minimize. The National Security Act of 1947 required the establishment of a single defense budget, and caused thereby the creation of a single committee in both houses of Congress supplanting the old military and naval affairs committees. The need for a single rather than multiple committees was predictable enough; what was not anticipated was that the formal consolidation of the three service budgets would serve as an exhilarating stimulant of inter-service rivalries.

The existence of the new Department has caused or facilitated the creation of combined commands (a further development of World War II practice) and of various functional agencies and operations leading to new weapons systems which are not the exclusive property of any one service. The service organizational pattern that has been emerging, as Huntington has said, is strikingly like the wartime reorganization of the War Department in 1942. Each of the three services is largely limited to the same kind of functions that were performed by the Army Ground Forces and the Army Service Forces. The three service secretaries are largely displaced from the stream of strategic planning and action much as Stimson and Knox were during the war; strategic planning and action are now carried on by JCS and other groups not directly within the ambit of the three service organizations. Simultaneously, the Secretary of Defense has emerged as a cabinet officer with very substantial control over JCS, a control formerly exercised only by the President. Unanticipated beneficiaries of the change are the Secretary of State and other agency heads who no longer are confined to a choice of usually fruitless appeals to the JCS, that corporate mili-

tary body, or to a busy President. There is no evidence that unification has resulted in what many of its proponents as far back as the 1920's had urged as its sole or chief virtue: i.e., reduced expenditures. Some real savings no doubt are demonstrable, but they represent no more than a picayune bit of the defense budget. And surprisingly enough Secretary MacNamara in 1961 admitted publicly that the basic function of budgetary control is to obtain the optimal use of defense funds, not to save money. Forrestal in his last months in office had showed some awareness of this concept; four of his six immediate successors did not, and the two who did—Lovett and Gates—were unable or unwilling to articulate their aims with MacNamara's clarity.

C. CHANGES IN ECONOMIC MOBILIZATION METHODS

The machinery of economic mobilization used in World War I was promptly and easily dismantled after Armistice Day. The structure was relatively simple and the procedure largely voluntary, for the degree of mobilization was limited: at the end of the war no limitation whatever on automobile production had yet been put into effect. The problems of immediate postwar reconversion and inflation were painful but brief.

The public at large soon forgot economic mobilization, and the academic community had never become much interested. The subject did not die, however; Bernard Baruch and a few of his wartime assistants kept preaching the gospel. Detailed planning of a sort was pursued by the Assistant Secretary of War and a few Army officers under the responsibilities assigned by the National Defense Act of 1920. Then in 1940, when Roosevelt initiated economic mobilization, he used the NDAC (National Defense Advisory Commission), an accidental survivor of the last war, and discarded the plans of Baruch, of the military, and of the Stettinius Board, set up by Assistant Secretary Johnson to start mobilization. The mobilization agencies spawned by NDAC expanded quickly in size and number. Some of the ideas fathered by Baruch and the Army were put into practice, but both organization and procedures required for World War II were infinitely more complex and far-reaching than the planners had anticipated. The one area in which civil-military contentions were most strident was industrial production. Until late 1943, the inevitable gap between production and requirements was the core of the controversy; but the organizational problems were also real. The basic solution, however partial, had not been thought of by the Army planners and their industrial advisers, nor by Roosevelt's organization planners who went to work in 1939 and 1940. Essentially it consisted of a "Presidential agency," first the Office of Economic Stabilization, later the Office of War Mobilization, an agency close to the White House, headed by a distinguished politician and unhampered by the massive detailed operational responsibilities of the production, price control and other economic mobilization agencies. The Office of War Mobilization, headed by Justice Byrnes, former Senator, former member of the Supreme Court, took the burden of decision off the President and found reasonably satisfactory methods for keeping the civilian and military teams in tandem.

By 1947 most of the wartime structure had disappeared, but in the same year the new National Security Act established the National Security Resources Board, designed to provide a center for all peacetime economic mobilization planning and activity. The Act contemplated a world in which the distinction between war and peace was the distinction between black and white. In the gray zone of cold war, NSRB led an uneasy existence. Starting in the Pentagon, it was shifted by Presidential action to the Executive Office of the President. Here, too, NSRB was unsuccessful, perhaps in part because it never realized that men of action, particularly businessmen, may prove unsuited for planning, and also because even then the vague apprehension of an atomic war with unpredictable consequences and needs cast a doubt on planning for a war resembling the obsolete model of World War II.

The Korean War was the end for NSRB; it reached for central control of economic mobilization, and failed. After hesitations, prodded by Congress, the Administration set up an overelaborate group of agencies that followed World War II patterns; these proved unsatisfactorily adaptable to limited war. Control of prices and wages was a failure, largely because of statutory defects, enhanced by the Administration's refusal to make any use of the Federal Reserve's monetary powers until March 1951, when the big wave of inflation was coming to an end anyway. The bitter conflicts over Korean War economic controls left the services relatively untouched. Their budgetary ceilings were temporarily lifted and price increases were annoying rather than a serious impediment. The only domestic event that greatly aroused the Department of Defense during the two-and-a-half-year period of active operations was the steel strike of 1952. Convinced that a strike would cause a steel shortage great enough to deprive our forces in Korea of artillery shells and other necessities, the Secretary of Defense urged the President to take whatever action was necessary to prevent the strike, and in this the mobilization agency chiefs concurred. It is unnecessary to repeat here the tale of what the President did, how it failed, how the strike came and caused no damage. In retrospect, it is hard, at least for a mere outside observer, to believe that the joint military-civilian warnings of disaster, however sincere, were justified in fact; but in our country, at least during wartime, no satisfactory method of controlling or avoiding excessive military fears of shortages has been found.

With the coming of the Eisenhower Administration, and the Korean armistice, any remaining need for complex economic controls vanished and the elaborate structure was dismantled. The top agency, the Office of Defense Mobilization (similar to wartime OWM-OWMR), remained and inherited the remaining operational powers of the control agencies, such as the issuance of rapid amortization certificates, and a voice in making export license policy. It also absorbed the planning functions of NSRB and that agency's seat on NSC. Finally, the neglected orphan of the whole defense system, before, during and after the Korean War, Civil Defense, was also assigned to ODM, which was accordingly renamed OCDM. OCDM never became a very visible landmark, but it set up a large series of arrangements with industries for the prompt adoption of control plans, for the borrowing of executives for wartime agencies, and for other devices designed to put into effect operations much like those of World War II but without painful delay. It also made some effort to provide substitutes for standard procedures like banking, in case of catastrophic bombing of centers like Washington and New York. Whether these well-laid plans would "gang agley" in case of nuclear war, no one can say.

Large-scale civil defense, unlike mobilization planning, can be provided for effectively only by the expenditure of large sums of money. Neither the people, nor the Congress, nor the states, nor the municipalities had shown the slightest desire to spend more than a pittance. Up to 1961, the results were negligible. There was no widespread agreement on what an ideal or even a "moderately" useful and "reasonably" expensive civil defense should consist of, nor any public sense of urgency. Without these, civil defense will make no significant progress. In 1961 civil defense was transferred to the Department of Defense; this move opened up the prospect of more energetic and more expensive activities, but confusions about public and private responsibilities, needs and values continued.

D. GROWTH OF FOREIGN ECONOMIC AND MILITARY AID AND CONTROLS

The use of economic means to support diplomacy and strategy is no new phenomenon in our government. It has been intermittently important and its importance has been relatively little affected by organizational and procedural changes. Historically, the foreign policy of the United States has not often made use of economic tools. Export embargoes and tariffs, quotas and other import controls have been used occasionally and sporadically for our own policy objectives, far more often merely to serve domestic interests without regard for their impact on other nations; but as far back as Jefferson there has been some awareness of the significance of economic warfare.

In the 1930's, export controls were used primarily to support the neutrality program, and were slowly modified at President Roosevelt's urging so that they could be employed as a discretionary tool, to permit aid for our friends, to deny it to our enemies, spectacularly, for example, in the embargo of oil exports to Japan, or in heterodox fashion in the denial to Germany of the opportunity to purchase helium. Postwar export controls have, with a few exceptions, been used as a weapon in the cold war. The results have been apparently far less significant than the proponents had hoped for, and

the various organizational devices have never prevented the inevitable arguments about what kind of shipments should be allowed to whom. Export controls are relatively easy to administer, and the difficulties arise in judgments on prohibited or limited items and areas. In considerable part, postwar export controls have been based on assumptions that have frequently overlooked three facts: (1) huge continental nations like Russia and China cannot be strangled like the industrial island nations—England and Japan; (2) at least since the completion of the Marshall Plan and the resurgence of the Communist empire, even in cold war the United States has had no monopoly of basic supplies; and (3) the United States has no monopoly of technology and scientific discovery.

The great new development of prime importance of the last fifteen years both to the Department of State and to other parts of the government like Treasury and Commerce has been the reverse of the coin of export controls—postwar foreign aid. The contemporary system or systems had their origin in Roosevelt's awareness of England's desperate shortage of dollars in the winter of 1940-41 and his painful memories of the miscalled war debts that bedevilled the administrations of Harding, Coolidge and Hoover, and did not recede completely into the past until the end of his own first term. It was Roosevelt who invented Lend-Lease, and it was the acceptance of the Lend-Lease concept that set the stage for massive wartime and postwar foreign aid—aid by which many billions of dollars of economic and military assistance have been dispensed to support foreign policy or military policy (or both) and never with a commercial return as their objective.

An astonishing variety of methods and a multiplicity of organizations have been used for carrying on foreign aid programs; they have also had a startling mixture of results. The Marshall Plan was a brilliant economic success, aid to Greece a clear-cut if not total military success, and Lend-Lease to Britain a great success both as military and economic aid. At the opposite end of the scale has been aid to countries like China and Cuba, where our efforts failed and much of the aid ended up in enemy hands.

The organizational arrangements have been extraordinarily varied. We have used temporary international organizations like UNRRA and permanent ones like the International Bank for

Reconstruction and Development; permanent U. S. agencies like the Treasury (for the British loan), temporary ones like ECA, ICA and the rest, and a government bank (established long before for commercial purposes) like the Export-Import Bank. Military aid has been almost entirely within the control of the armed forces, who have created their own agencies like the Military Assistance Advisory Groups. They have also handled economic aid for liberated and occupied areas using Lend-Lease (sometimes over their own protest) in the first case and GARIOA (Government and Relief in Occupied Areas) in the second. In Korea, object since 1950 of both U. S. and UN aid, there have been agencies of both, and our armed forces have served under both masters.

The two chief persistent problems are the balance between economic and military aid, and the useful application of aid to underdeveloped areas. The question of balance is a difficult one, with no fixed point of equilibrium. One of the first postwar aid programs was Greek-Turkish aid, and this was specifically military in objective, and largely military in content. It was followed, a few months later, by the Marshall Plan, limited by statute to civilian goods and economic reconstruction. Since then aid to ever-enlarging sectors of the world has been a mixture of the two, with military aid generally more acceptable to Congress than economic aid; indeed, at one stage economic aid when coupled with military aid was labelled "defense support" to increase its Congressional palatability. The correctness of the label was indisputable in many countries, for the armed forces created to use American military equipment were too large to be supported by the nation's own economy.

For several years the pendulum swung more and more toward military and away from economic aid. In Europe, for example, as the Marshall Plan reached its climax, the build-up of NATO began; in Asia, the Korean War inspired a surge of concern for the defense of the countries that border on China and for the means to put down Communist insurrections. In many places, most notably at the moment in Laos and Viet-Nam, the problems persist, and military aid continues. Yet we are also responding to the ever-widening demand for economic and technical assistance created by the emergence of new nations, of new social

pressures and aspirations in many of the older nations, indeed throughout the vast majority of the world's population who have begun to believe that poverty and subjugation are not permanent and immutable.

The proportions of military and economic aid will no doubt continue to vary but there is no end in sight for either. Both the arming of NATO and European recovery had effective terminal dates. NATO deficiencies now are not caused by any lack of American dollars, and the economy of Western Europe is booming. But in Asia, Africa and Latin America there is no visible end. Communist incursions and insurrections will continue. And in countries like Bolivia and India, our aid will be needed for many years before they can achieve a level of economic growth which will be capable on its own momentum of increasing *per capita* production of goods over an exploding birth rate.

For the United States, the technical problem of making the $16 billion of Marshall Plan aid effective was negligible; essentially as long as the dollar gap was filled, the European nations could be counted on to go through the dramatic process of reconstructing their economies and rebuilding their internal and international trade. Our technical assistance was desirable, but hardly more than a fringe benefit: the high level of development of government, education, organizational experience, and the other elements that constitute advanced industrial society meant that if we supplied the dollars, the nations themselves could supply the knowledge and the know-how.

For the underdeveloped areas of the world, in varying degrees, the model of the Marshall Plan has been misleading: unguided dollars lead to no good end. The complementary aims of economic and military strengthening, feasible in Western Europe, have proved to be exceedingly difficult elsewhere. The civil-military balance has frequently been awkward, and our growing desire to support peaceful social revolution has tended to weaken the control of the existing government over its armed forces. Solutions equally satisfactory to our civil and military representatives in dozens of our missions are not attainable. The inherent friction has, of course, been reflected in similar friction in Washington, in both the Executive Branch and Congress, and among the media of public communications. The frustrations, the errors, the inherent conflicts so visible in economic development have invited repeated tinkering with the governmental machinery; and on the uneasy question of the civil-military balance in aid there is constant disequilibrium in Washington as well as abroad.

In all these intertwined matters there is no clear division between the civilians and the military. There is a natural tendency among all those deeply involved in particular programs to seek more support for their own activities, whether they include more tractors or more tanks: each mission head tends to be propelled toward requesting an increase in both. This is particularly true when the military, for example, agree that the kind of armed forces they seek to establish can only be maintained if the country receives substantial economic aid; but it is also true that when the budgetary requests use different channels budgetary competition is avoided and cooperation encouraged: a single country mission budget enforces competition for limited funds.

E. SCIENTISTS AND THE ARMED FORCES: THE MILITARY AND POLITICS

The use of scientists is no novelty for the armed forces. Up to World War I the armed forces concentrated most of their scientific interest on the applied sciences including engineering. West Point was for a long time the only professional engineering school in the United States, and to this day the Army Corps of Engineers is as distinguished for its dam construction and other "civil functions" as it is for its notable military engineering feats. The Navy, too, has had its own engineers, uninvolved in civil functions, largely devoted to engineering problems of ships but also founders and supervisors of the Seabees in the last war. Both services have from the beginning been concerned with ordnance, and later, in the case of the Army, with chemical and biological warfare. The Navy has always been involved in marine engineering, an interest shared periodically by the Army. Both services have established useful relations with industrial scientists and technologists—and manufacturers as well. Similar developments at a highly accelerated pace have followed in the Air Force and its predecessors.

Beginning primarily in World War I, with slightly increased tempo in the inter-war period, and ever faster and with ever greater magnitude, the services have come to rely on physicists, chemists, biologists, astronomers, and other physical scientists, as well as anthropologists, psychologists, economists and other social scientists, and even on historians, linguists and other scholars in the humanities. The interests and skills of these varied scholars (the great majority of course being physical scientists) have ranged from the purest basic science to applied science that merges with technology.

The most spectacular military achievement of the scientists has been atomic fusion and fission, and no doubt the enhanced status of the physical scientists, and, on a less exalted plane, other scholars in or associated with the Pentagon, was a by-product of the research that took off, one might say, from Einstein's General Theory, culminated in rudimentary practical form at Alamogordo, and has proceeded ever since.

The multifarious effects of these developments cannot be spelled out here, but a few may be noted in passing. (1) The attitudes of many of the officers, especially of senior generals and admirals and of Washington staff officers of all ranks, have been affected, usually broadened, by frequent contact with scientists and other civilian professionals. (2) The sharp boundary line between government, especially the Department of Defense and the Atomic Energy Commission, and private activities, both industrial and academic, in military research has been irretrievably blurred. (3) The deepening and strengthening of research that was so noticeable in World War II in the War Department, with the effective collaboration of Stimson, Vannevar Bush and OSRD (Office of Scientific Research and Development), has now been highly formalized within the Department of Defense and its components, as well as in the National Science Foundation and elsewhere.

Men with the same scientific qualifications that appeal to the Department of Defense have long been sought by American industry. The tremendous technical developments of the last half-century (like synthetics) have almost all been the products of imaginative research with a solid scientific base; perhaps Edison was the last of the great inventors who could rely almost entirely on hunch and ingenuity. Military inventions like radar in England and the proximity fuse in this country, both brought to fruition in World War II, had been perfected by highly trained professionals. Furthermore, sooner or later, mass production of most military weapons has depended almost entirely on industry. More than ever before, effective preparations for national defense require constant and effective collaboration between American industry and government. In the nature of the case, many military officers, many civilian officials like the members of the Atomic Energy Commission, and many important industrialists have common interests, reinforced and bonded even more firmly by the scientists who pursue the same objectives by the same scientific means whether employed by government or industry or, for that matter, by universities carrying on government contracts.

There is thus in fact a military-scientific-industrial grouping. It has been described by the late C. Wright Mills in rather romantic fashion as "The Power Elite" and some of his dark forebodings were reflected (certainly not consciously) in one of Eisenhower's last statements before he left the White House. The American tradition fortunately encourages such admonitions. Obviously Big Business allied with respected senior military officers and with equally or even more notable scientists constitutes some kind of locus of power and no democracy should forget the existence of such loci. But it is also important to place this development in the larger framework of an enormously wealthy republic with 180,000,000 citizens and with a clumsy but extraordinarily vigorous political system. The Air Force ever since the war has had wide popular support and presumably is one of the energetic leaders in the "power elite," yet each time that a responsive Congress has voted more funds for the Air Force, the President has impounded the money, and each time the President has won. The annual defense budget now runs from $50 to $60 billion; this is a tremendous sum of money, but it is only about 10 per cent of our gross national product.

Developing bonds between the military and the social scientists have come about somewhat differently. The serious study of international relations as problems in politics rather than merely a question of law or morals is rather new in this country. In the last twenty years, with the great mutation of public attitudes suggested above, there has been a great and very useful efflorescence of teaching and research inspired by our awareness that we are part of a complex and dangerous world in which there is no hiding place.

During World War II, besides the physical scientists, many other men from the academic community—particularly social scientists, but humanists as well—were brought into government service; their interest in the application of their professional skills to the development of public policy was quickened thereby. The notable part played by economists and lawyers in the New Deal was being repeated by them and by other scholars from diverse disciplines throughout the war and postwar years. From 1946 until the coming of the Kennedy Administration there was no great and widespread search for academicians (except for the physical scientists) to serve in full-time responsible government positions, but both on the campus and as consultants, they turned with a new vigor to questions of international politics and notably to problems of direct concern to the military. Some were affiliated with a new set of institutions, quasi-governmental, quasi-academic like RAND, but many long-established universities were almost equally active in research in such matters as geopolitics and national security. Recently, there has been a great proliferation of model-building in areas of inquiry like disarmament, deterrence and the like; what the ultimate net consequence of this latter activity (conducted in sizable part by economists) will be, no one can yet say. Already it can be said that since the academicians cover the whole ideological spectrum, it would be a sorry four or five-star general or admiral who could not find a scholar willing and able to construct an elegant model illustrating with precision the correctness of the officer's views on strategic bombing, guerilla warfare, or any other strategic matter of military concern. That the models frequently convert other admirals and generals seems doubtful. Even the politicians—executive and legislative—who hold the keys to promotion and power are usually successful in securing only obedience from officers who disagree, not concurrence. Obviously model-building in the social sciences has its uses; the unsettled question is the utility of the process in projecting the political behavior of individual politicians like presidents and premiers. It will be men like Kennedy and Khrushchev who will make the crucial decisions on action, and they will not use computers as their shepherds.

The turn of the academicians toward the professional fields of interest of the military has been accompanied by a parallel turn of some of the military toward politics, international and domestic.

The American professional officer of the armed services has long taken pride in his avoidance of public display of partisan political preferences until retirement from the service. There have been exceptions like McClellan and MacArthur, but they are rare; and there have been no important instances of generals or admirals actively attempting the role of Boulanger. This tradition has never applied to retired officers, as the long list of war-hero presidents illustrates. Furthermore, avoidance of public display of partisan preferences has never meant abstention from political involvement. The great majority of the graduates of West Point and Annapolis and now the Air Force Academy, the men who hold almost all the key positions in the services, were appointed to the academy in each case, with few exceptions, in the first place by a member of Congress. Service in command posts within the United States is normally involved in some degree with local political issues. More important still, the senior officers in Washington in staff positions inevitably find themselves deeply involved in important political issues, sometimes used by professional politicians for partisan ends, sometimes not.

Obviously when officers are involved in politics they are dealing with civilians, both professional politicians and a host of others—scientists, industrialists, the general public of a community or of the whole nation. (A parallel process is at work with officers stationed abroad in important posts: Eisenhower and MacArthur are merely the most visible examples.) This process is not new but the depth and breadth of involvement are far greater than they used to be.

There are several reasons for this change. The most obvious is the impact of sheer magnitude: men who are largely responsible for persuading Congress to appropriate some fifty billion dollars or more and responsible for its expenditure live in a highly charged political atmosphere even when civilian control by the President, the Secretary of Defense and several thousand other civilians is exercised with a very strong hand. Another crucially important spur to military involvement in politics has been the dropping of isolation and the consequent merging of the military and diplomatic spheres of concern. A coalition like NATO is a political instrument; each member government's military representatives have innate political responsibilities in addition to their military tasks. These responsibilities must also be borne by our officers in Washington who defend the coalitions before the committees of Congress and the public at large. Indeed, the responsibilities are even broader than merely standing up for military needs, for over and over the State Department and other agencies have called on the officers to act as highly respected spokesmen for non-military programs, above all foreign aid, and to act also as defendants for presidential strategy, as in the case of Korea and NATO.

There is one further aspect of the military in politics, also not new but more notable than has been customary, that deserves mention. It has two principal manifestations, both greatly stimulated by the fighting in Korea. The Korean War was highly frustrating for the military forces engaged in combat and even more for their professional officers. It offered none of the emotional satisfactions that came to the Allies with the total destruction and surrender of the Axis forces in North Africa—to take a single example. Perhaps it was even more frustrating than inevitable defeat by overwhelming force, as in 1942 in the Philippines. In purely military terms Korea was neither defeat nor victory; just two and a half years of miserable bloodshed.

This kind of frustration has some resemblance, fortunately only a very minor one, to the postwar frustration of the French armed forces which in their case has even led to mutiny and rebellion. The frustrated American officers have followed classic lines—search for a scapegoat and search for a panacea. Brought up in a conservative tradition, their scapegoats have tended to be the civilian politicians and the democratic political process, and for some also our allies and our system of alliances. A reinforcing sentiment has been the theory of conspiracy as the primary source of malevolent action. The panacea has been double-headed: a political process of sufficiently authoritarian character, and a shift of strategic concentration from the actual or potential battlefield to the enemy within. The officer's responsibility for understanding his enemy and for using that understanding in the defense of his country therefore shifts to educating the people to deal with the internal danger which consists of all groups of the "left," ranging from members of the Communist Party to Eisenhower. Some of the military—perhaps only a very small number—thus become theoreticians of the new geopolitics and active in promoting and participating in anti-Communist seminars, and themselves giving lectures not on military defense but on internal subversion.

Naturally the same sense of conviction that leads to a desire to educate businessmen, students and other civilians also leads to a desire to educate the soldiers, sailors and airmen. The tragic tale of the behavior of a good many American prisoners-of-war in Korea (tragic, even though only a handful defected at the end, compared with many thousands of Koreans and Chinese) was the cause of widespread concern. There were various explanations; some emphasized the lack of discipline, identification with organization, and strictly military training in the hastily assembled troops who were first sent to Korea; others attributed the troubles primarily or exclusively to a lack of "indoctrination" in the nature and goals of American democracy and the nature and goals of communism. President Eisenhower accepted the second explanation and all the services thereupon, in varying degrees, set up indoctrination programs—all the services, that is, except the Marine Corps. That organization had sent a division to Korea apparently bereft of indoctrination, mentally equipped only with a strong sense of esprit de corps, a thoroughly established command structure, and vigorous preparation for physical hardship. Perhaps more than any of the other UN contingents except the Turks, the Marines had withstood the extreme sufferings of forced retreat, the brutalities of the Communist POW camps and Communist brainwashing. They have continued to rely on their ability to train professional fighting men and have left indoctrination to the other branches of our armed forces.

There is no clear distinction between ideological indoctrination and propaganda. There is some evidence that the enlisted men and draftees subjected to indoctrination during the past decade have been remarkably impervious to what they considered mere propaganda. At times, the serious efforts of dedicated commanders who have assumed the role of Messiah have backfired. They have preached panaceas that have not only irritated their captive audiences, but have edged into the forbidden zone of partisan politics. Here the civilians have entered in and have induced, in one way or another, repudiation.

A related problem has been created by speeches to civilian audiences made by high-ranking officers. Forrestal and all his successors have struggled with the effort to bring harmony into the relations between military orations and the current needs and objectives of military and foreign policy. It is not easy for generals and admirals who, like their civilian counterparts, hope for a spirited audience response, to restrain their ghost writers, who may have no knowledge of relevant matters like pending negotiations, from drafting something that will upset a delicate balance. On the whole, the need for some kind of censorship—usually called "coordination" by its advocates and "muzzling" by its opponents—has been accepted, although individual acts by the censors have often been irritating. Sometimes an officer has ignored or bypassed his instructions, as MacArthur did; more often the dissatisfied officers have awaited retirement before publishing their dissident views of military and foreign policy. The problem of making wise use of officers in public relations and public education is a peculiarly American one; our many allies who have parliamentary systems like the British expect their officers to share the same cloak of anonymity and silence that covers their civil servants. Yet even the British, where that tradition is very strong, have their troubles too; once Montgomery became famous on the field of battle, no one succeeded in muzzling him.

F. LOCUS OF POWER: THE PRESIDENT AND CONGRESS

Franklin Roosevelt is always and necessarily classified as a "strong" President. Leadership while he was in the office both in war and peace came primarily from him, not from Congress. Most of the important things he wanted, he got, either by exercise of the powers of his office or by persuading the Congress to take the steps or to grant the additional powers he asked for. But most is not all, even with strong Presidents.

When Roosevelt was inaugurated, he, like the rest of the country, was almost completely immersed in the problems of the depression; his concern with foreign (and military) policy was largely restricted to economic issues. However, Roosevelt's field of vision was always wide; it was not just for the fun of it that he encouraged military use of relief funds. Here he had one of his first checks, for Congress soon forbade the use of PWA funds for the construction of naval vessels. He also did not succeed in his attempt to have Congress restrain the Nye Committee; the work of that Committee was perhaps partly the cause for Congress' refusal to grant him discretionary power in the Neutrality Act of 1935, which otherwise had his approval. The inherent Congressional distrust of any President with strong personal drive was enhanced in Roosevelt's case by his own frequent willingness to circumvent Congressional limitations by ingenious devices. The same suspicion helped to keep the Neutrality Act as a fetter until after the outbreak of war in Europe. Similarly when Roosevelt started to transfer arms to Britain and France, the Congress tacked on an amendment to a naval appropriation bill prohibiting such transfers without certification from the Army Chief of Staff or the Chief of Naval Operations: in Congressional eyes, certification from the Commander-in-Chief would not suffice.

Direct Congressional limitations on Presidential action in military and foreign policy were thus ever present from 1933 to Pearl Harbor; but apart from the serious restrictions imposed by the Neutrality Act, they were bearable. How much faster and further the President might have moved without the anticipation of such limitations cannot be divined. In view of public hesitations and the deep fissure in public attitudes in the late 1930's, it is doubtful that the President would have dared to do much more than he did even if Congress had been more amenable to his pleas. Furthermore, during the whole period, budgetary requests for the military were treated with reasonable generosity by Congress. Roosevelt, using the advice of the Army and Navy, and his own intuitions, set both the totals and the major components. As war approached, he rejected Marshall's carefully balanced proposals, probably because he looked on the Army budget as a cover for Lend-Lease as well as for our own needs.

During the war, Roosevelt benefited from the cloak of secrecy that necessarily covered most military activities; and for appropriations, the sky was the limit. For example, the function of the Manhattan District, producer of the A-bomb, was not revealed even to Sam Rayburn, Speaker of the House, but the funds were provided nonetheless. There were occasional rumblings during the war from MacArthur's idolaters who wanted to give war with Japan priority. There was an outcry when many Texans were killed in a single battle in the dismal Italian campaign in the winter of 1943-1944. Now and then Congressmen and Senators offered contributions to strategy. Yet the military conduct of the war did not fall within the jurisdiction of any Congressional committee, and the Commander-in-Chief, the JCS and the services had a free hand. The freedom extended even to appointments and organization; indeed Roosevelt himself abstained from interference, and directly exercised his constitutional discretionary appointive power only with respect to the Chief of Staff, Chief of Naval Operations, the Commanding Generals in Europe and the Pacific, and one or two other key posts. Interestingly enough, even his worst enemies have never questioned his soundness of judgment in these appointments.

Economic mobilization was another matter. Here Congressional investigation was common, though generally, as in the case of the Truman Committee, prudent and usually helpful. Congressional pressures caused or hastened organizational changes in mobilization organization; Congress stepped in in a flat-footed way only two or three times, as in creating the Office of War Mobilization and Reconversion, an amplified version of Roosevelt's own OWM. Roosevelt got most of the powers he asked for, even over prices, though Congress did much to protect the farmers' prices and manpower. The draft exemptions for farm workers were looked on with dismay by the Army and in 1944 both the Services were shocked by Congressional refusal to pass the Austin-Wadsworth "work or fight" bill; but Roosevelt made no serious effort to persuade or threaten.

During the war diplomacy and coalition warfare were intertwined and Congressional intervention was limited. Congress put some brakes on Lend-Lease, but entangling alliances that were insufferable in peacetime were accepted in the war. Even aid to Russia, though subject to the general intermittent complaint that we were depriving our own men of what they needed, was not actively opposed. There was a good deal of public disapproval of our Vichy policy, our acceptance of Darlan's leadership in North Africa, and with Walter Lippmann usually in the lead, our overt official disapproval of De Gaulle and the Free French. Eisenhower for very practical and sensible reasons dealt with Darlan in November 1942, since it was obvious from the moment of the North African landings that the State Department's hand-picked leader of the North African French, Giraud, was, to use the slang word, a dud. A year and a half later it was Eisenhower again who pleaded for the recognition of De Gaulle as head of a provisional government when France was liberated, and again he did so for practical and sensible reasons; this time the State Department joined with him, and it was the President alone who remained recalcitrant up to the last minute. In fairness to Roosevelt, it should be noted that his position was apparently based not solely on his own understandable annoyance with De Gaulle and notions about popular choice of postwar governments but also on a mass of misinformation about De Gaulle supplied largely, it was said, by the staff of the Department of State. The question of our French policy, though of no great and lasting importance, is spelled out here because Congress played no significant part in this prolonged and quite public debate.

With the end of the war and the coming of Harry Truman to the White House, it might have been expected that the Presidential-Congressional balance in dealing with civil-military problems would be upset. Truman and his successors did have to deal more warily with Congress than Roosevelt did in wartime, and loud Congressional outcries have been common, but the basic determination of foreign-military policy, of military expenditures and organization, and of weapons has been made by civilians in the Executive Branch, usually with the President in active control. Congress has exercised an occasionally restraining but never a guiding hand on any major issue.

The overall success of the Executive Branch has been somewhat reduced in magnitude by a tendency on the part of high-level civilians and officers of the services to make their own guess as to what Congress would or would not permit and then to attribute refusal or parsimony to a Congress that had not been approached, or approached only on minor and technical aspects of the vital issues. Thus hasty demobilization was considered a Congressional requirement, but the lamentations over the effect of the procedure were almost exclusively confined to the inner circles of the Truman Administration; perhaps if the Secretary of State had been willing to tell the nation and Congress that, in his opinion, our diplomacy was suffering, a slowdown in demobilization would have been acceptable. (The phrase "in his opinion" is used advisedly; unless we were willing to go to war over Poland, for example, it is hard to see how the maintenance of our full armed strength would have changed the line of the Iron Curtain, or the 38th Parallel, or modified the chain of events in China. Presumably Stalin would have risked destruction to retain Poland and other neighbor-satellites; but he could not look on a possible war for any lesser cause with equanimity, no matter how small our armed forces. We possessed the atomic bomb and he did not, as Churchill pointed out on more than one occasion.)

The creation and organization of the Department of Defense has constituted a central problem for postwar administrations, but the chief area requiring persuasion has been the Pentagon rather than Capitol Hill. In spite of all the eloquent flow of words about the horrors of the German general staff and the dangers of over-centralization, there is now not only a chairman of the JCS but a chairman with power; there is now a powerful Secretary of Defense with a huge civilian staff; the service secretaries have been downgraded, and the operations of the traditional departments are superseded in large part by combined commands and other specialized groups. In all this shifting, and a good deal more, the Congress has, step by step, accepted the President's lead; the only fully privileged sanctuary has been the Marine Corps.

On the size of military expenditures, it is always the President who has called the tune; the Congress has made no cuts of consequence, and its efforts to increase Air Force expenditures have been coldly shelved. So, too, Selective Service has been enacted and re-enacted at the President's request, and whenever he has asked for special powers to call up the Reserves and the like, he has received them. There are two matters of this kind where Congress has been a stumbling block: first, repeated demands for UMT have died on the vine; the rationale has never been made clear, and the suitability of UMT for an age of highly technological warfare has come to seem improbable to most men. Second, the National Guard has remained what it always has been—an organization with deep political roots in the states and thereby more intimately affiliated with Representatives and Senators than with Presidents. Presidential efforts to reduce the National Guard have made no great progress.

The President has retained the wartime power to set strategy. Twice under Truman there was what was loosely called a "Great Debate," first in the Taft-Wherry efforts to secure for Congress control over the sending of American troops to Europe in support of NATO, second in the MacArthur hearings and their aftermath. In the first, even the Congress came to the embarrassing conclusion that the Founding Fathers were right—that command over armies must rest with the Commander-in-Chief, not with the legislative body. In the second, MacArthur won the popularity contest hands down, but Truman's Far Eastern strategy held firm.

The further from the actual center of visibly military problems, the less the President can count on Congressional support. Ever since the Marshall Plan, economic aid has had rougher treatment in Congress than military aid, to take the most obvious case; and the witnesses who are most persuasive in the hearings are generally the military themselves. The Senate has consented to all treaties involving civil-military matters and both houses have been willing to pass the implementing legislation in the form requested when the objective seemed military; the contrast afforded by the steady Congressional downgrading of Trade Agreements legislation is striking.

Perhaps the sharp controversy in 1946 about the atomic energy bills constitutes an exception, for the President's desires were largely met. In retrospect, the controversy takes on an unreal air; in the decade and a half that followed, the great developments in the military application of atomic energy have been the consequence in large part of promotion activities by scientists and other civilians, and the President has not been called on as umpire between civilians and the military. The special committee on the hydrogen bomb appointed by Truman made a unanimous report to him recommending immediate action by AEC; the members were Acheson, Lilienthal and Louis Johnson, all civilian, only one of whom might be considered a spokesman for the military. If President Kennedy decides to have AEC invent and develop (if it can) the neutron bomb, there is no doubt that his major advisers will be civilians. Furthermore, in all these developments the Joint Committee on Atomic Energy has played an important part, yet over all they and the President have generally sought the same objectives.

During the past year or two a debate has gone on about the neutron bomb. One of the most vocal proponents of such development has been Senator Dodd of Connecticut. He has endeavored to enlighten his fellow-citizens by explaining just what such a bomb would accomplish, even stating that besides being ideal for anti-missile use, it would cost far less than an equivalent H-bomb. No one can accuse Senator Dodd of an undue concern for secrecy; few men are willing to disclose the future cost of a product that has not yet been invented. And more generally, the frequently expressed conviction that our society is cursed with imposed secrecy by or on behalf of the military is hard to understand. All the interested world knew in a rough-and-ready way that the proposed H-bomb would, if created, be a weapon of enormous destructive power. The pro's and con's of creating it were widely debated. President Truman decided to go ahead and refused to argue the point—but the basic decision was no secret. Conceivably, the protestants would have preferred a formal Congressional debate on the decision, though Congress would undoubtedly have supported the President. Or perhaps they had an inarticulate desire for a plebiscite or wanted the President to explain why he said "yes." But presidential decisions of this kind are unavoidable unless our whole curious system of government is to be cast aside, and presidential explanations constitute presidential choices. In this country there is no point in even trying to keep secret the fact that AEC has been directed to proceed toward the manufacture of an H-bomb or an N-bomb; but the military aspects of the President's rationale are presumably of greater value to the Russian government than to the American people. One would assume that strategic planning is entitled to some shield of secrecy.

G. *THE STRATEGY OF CONTAINMENT*

From Wilson to Hoover, strategic planning was the serious concern only of the military. The various color plans were prepared, revised and filed; but neither Wilson nor Harding nor Coolidge nor Hoover showed any interest in the plans or the problems. Even Hoover, who was in a position to see the rising storm across the Pacific, considered the Japanese aggression no business of ours, whatever happened; and his sole active anxiety about the turmoil in Western Europe lay in its possible financial consequences for the United States.

During Roosevelt's first term, he too concentrated his attention and his Administration's attention on domestic affairs. He early showed his faith in Army and Navy officers by using them in various normally civilian tasks; and he showed his desire, based possibly on little more than hunch, to increase the strength of the armed forces. By the beginning of Roosevelt's second term, his concern about foreign policy, about our future fate in the world, and hence about strategy was heightened.

Roosevelt's attention to foreign policy, and thereby military policy, was made vividly public in his "quarantine" speech on October 12, 1937. Its extremely unfavorable reception led him to lie low for the next two years; but his interest remained, and he did what he could or dared. He backed the plans for a 20 per cent naval increase to be included in the budget for the fiscal year of 1939, reflecting his belief that we would need a two-ocean navy, as he soon suggested in his message to Congress on January 28, 1938. Meanwhile, he had known all about and approved the Ingersoll Mission to London at Christmastime 1937. Ingersoll's mission was the first step toward combined Anglo-American strategic planning and the first apoc-

alyptic sign of combined planning for combined operations. The impact of the Ingersoll Mission was quickly reflected in strategic planning when Plan ORANGE was modified to take account of a potential Anglo-American alliance.

In all these developments Roosevelt was involved, overtly or covertly. The State Department stayed clear, even though it had set the stage for Ingersoll's trip in the exchange of letters between our Ambassador Davis and Foreign Secretary Eden after Japan walked out from the disarmament conference of 1936. However, in April 1938 Hull requested the establishment of what became, with Roosevelt's blessing and modification, the Standing Liaison Committee, described above. Here Welles collaborated with the Chief of Staff and Chief of Naval Operations on taking steps to counter the Nazi (and Fascist and Japanese) penetration of Latin America. These discussions led the two chiefs to revise their strategic planning to include Latin America in our defense perimeter, which Roosevelt himself soon enlarged to include Canada. Once the Navy and the Army widened their perspectives in this way it became obvious to them that war plans must cover war with Germany and Italy in addition to Japan.

From here on the State Department left the center of the stage. Hull had no part in making or commenting on Admiral Stark's Plan DOG in November 1940—"a strong offensive in the Atlantic and a defensive in the Pacific"—and refused to commit himself on its follow-up, the national estimate prepared by Marshall and Stark. After the conclusion of the Anglo-American military conversations in Washington in March 1941, Hull refused even to look at the two agreed papers, ABC-1 and ABC-2. Until the end of the war strategic planning was thereafter carried on by the two chiefs, subsequently by JCS, under the very active supervision of the President.

The components of the strategic plans were classic: victory would finally be won by massive land armies. They would be assisted by strategic and tactical bombing, and supplemented by special campaigns like island-hopping in the Pacific. The Navy would carry on active sea warfare and naval protection of commerce, supplies, and transport in both oceans.

The "undeclared war," that very limited but active war in the Atlantic in 1940-1941 and the simultaneous cold war of military posture and diplomacy in the Pacific, can be looked on as antecedents to the kind of global war that followed. While there were disputes about the strategy pursued during the prewar period, the cunctatory tactics of the Secretary of State happened to fit in with the military plans, i.e., to defer fighting until the arms buildup was completed. As matters worked out, U. S. pressures, particularly against Japan, increased, with the President seeking to maintain a kind of equilibrium that would lead the American people toward readiness for war, reduce Japan's accumulation of war supplies, and still avoid combat. Perhaps one can best say that the immediate prewar economic, military and diplomatic moves were tactical rather than strategic in character. Strategic action was deferred until the outbreak of full-scale war.

The wartime strategy was set before Pearl Harbor, and while it underwent a constant series of modifications, the general outline never changed. The shift from the defense to the offense in the Pacific came long before V-E day, but Germany did fall before Japan, and many more millions of men were massed in the final attack in Europe than were then involved in war and direct preparations for war in the Pacific. In retrospect, it is obvious that the efforts to bring Russia into the war against Japan were unnecessary; but one shudders at the thought of our fighting Hitler with only the British and our other allies in the West and without Soviet pressure from the East.

Postwar strategy is without parallel. The general rationale for our actual strategy of cold and limited war was first defined and described by George Kennan. The definition of "containment" has varied from time to time: the Truman Doctrine, the Eisenhower Doctrine, "massive retaliation," and many of the promises to stop any further "nibbling," have said or implied that we were imitating Custer's Last Stand. In fact, however, unlike Custer, we have had and made many choices: we helped to deter Russian advances to the Mediterranean by military and economic aid, without intervention; we abandoned Tibet with expressions of moral regret; we relied largely on diplomatic means to protect Iran; in Indo-China we finally assented to Mendès-France's plan and accepted half a loaf; in Korea we sent in our own troops and ultimately settled on the 38th Parallel where the

invasion had started. We watched with dismay the collapse of China but were quite unwilling to get involved in that huge morass: if Chiang could not preserve his regime with our aid, it would have to be abandoned. As if in partial recompense, we have contained the Chinese Communist drive against Formosa by our own powerful Seventh Fleet, our Far Eastern Air Force and by subsidizing the large Chinese Nationalist armies, together with their air force and naval patrols based on Formosa and the off-shore islands.

Along the periphery of the Communist empire, in essence, we have applied the policy of containment as best we could, depending substantially on the will and the power of the countries we have helped to defend. It is notable that in Europe the line of the Iron Curtain still holds. Austria, now free of occupation troops, though technically neutral remains completely western in its orientation (a breakthrough of value for the West); Finland without tangible help from us has somehow remained at peace with Russia without being devoured. And as of this writing, Western Berlin is still free, though the Iron Curtain has now descended within the city.

As for the countries on the eastern side of the Iron Curtain, we have consistently proceeded on what might be described as reverse-containment. We have been in vocal sympathy with the uprisings in East Germany, Poland and Hungary, but we have given help only to the rebels who escaped. What we might have done about Czechoslovakia if the coup had come a year or so later when our commitment to containment was much firmer, no one can say; at the time of the coup, we did nothing. Our acute struggle with Yugoslavia when that country seemed to be part of Stalin's empire ended peacefully; ever since Tito's break with Stalin, Yugoslavia with our aid has retained its independence in spite of its Communist sympathies. However, Yugoslavia and East Germany are the only two of the six major Eastern European states that share no boundary with Russia; Russian anger would change to aggression if a Tito arose in Poland or one of the others. In the case of East Germany, Communist control has been maintained only by the continued presence of a large Russian army.

The problem of containment has also arisen in areas beyond the Communist periphery; the results have been mixed, and the degree of our success is differently measured if the variegated hues of neutralism are looked on as black, as they seemed to Dulles, or as imperfect but not generally displeasing, as they seem to the Kennedy Administration. On the whole, containment in this area lies beyond military strategy: the tools have been diplomacy, both classic and through the new international organizations, propaganda, economic aid, and CIA's covert but generally not secret operations. The armed services have not been totally uninvolved; the Sixth Fleet has steamed majestically into the Eastern Mediterranean on a number of occasions, sometimes to reinforce Turkey, on the assumption that the "show of strength" would "deter" Russia. (Because of this action, or possibly for some totally different reason, Russia did not move into Turkey.) More often the Fleet has moved to restore peace or encourage stability in the Middle East. At the request of the government of Lebanon, the Fleet's show of strength was reinforced by the landing of a substantial body of American troops designed presumably to calm the bloodless civil war in Lebanon and to discourage the revolutionaries in Iraq (whose rebellion had astonished our government) from linking up too closely with the Communists. Elsewhere we have supported containment, usually successfully, by devices ranging from bribery to para-military action. The one spectacular failure was Cuba.

Containment formed the framework for postwar strategy and strategic planning. It is no accident that it was formulated in the Department of State. George Kennan's prediction of Russia's future course of conduct, to which containment was the proposed response, struck a responsive chord, notably with Forrestal, then Secretary of the Navy. Kennan brought to bear both his knowledge of Russian imperialism and his understanding of Communist tactics. Kennan was not the only American who could foresee the dangers of the future, but he had the advantages of his position—counsellor of Embassy at Moscow—and of his gift for a prose style that is rare indeed in official government documents, or even in learned journals or serious magazines like *Foreign Affairs*.

The essence of Kennan's strategic advice can be stated quite simply: whenever, wherever the Communists push forward, resist them with whatever minimum means will suffice and with-in the limits of feasibility. Inherent in this advice was the unspoken admonition that large moral outcries would serve no useful end, and that all-out war would be an exceedingly dangerous and unwise solution.

The strategic problem that containment presented was complex and new in its prospective ever-continuing rebuttal of ever-continuing enemy probes. The strategy of World War II had involved the offensive in the Atlantic, and a defensive containment of Japan in the Pacific until V-E Day; containment was then to be superseded by a Pacific offensive, so that the need for containment would disappear in the process and be buried after V-J Day. But peacetime strategy set in the light of continuing containment was an unanticipated and new policy for the United States. Furthermore, besides containment, the armed services still had to anticipate the possibility of all-out war and be prepared to meet it. (In some indeterminate degree, the deterrent effects of readiness for total war constituted *per se* an important support of containment policy.) In one way the strategy of containment was a far simpler problem than military policy had faced immediately after World War I: the enemy, imminent and prospective, was Russia with its Communist ally-satellites: there was no need for the foreseeable future for alternate color plans. The scope of the Communist areas was dramatically enlarged in 1949 with the Communist conquest of China. Thus once again the strategic planners had to prepare for the possibility of global war, but at least for some time to come, global war under Russian leadership.

H. DIPLOMACY AND STRATEGY

Up to the outbreak of fighting in Korea, the gap between containment as a national though undeclared strategic objective and actual military means was unbridgeable. Military aid, economic aid, diplomacy had been used with much success, but Truman's budget policy left the armed forces too stripped of materials and men for any very significant planning that was at all related to military actualities. The Air Force had some planes, but not their 70-group goal, and some atomic bombs, and confined almost all their energies and thinking to strategic bombing plans against Russian targets. The Navy spoke in public mostly about protection of the sea lanes and anti-submarine warfare, and privately was planning to participate in strategic bombing. The Army could do little more than continue its occupation responsibilities and maintain cadres on which it could build large armies.

There were some efforts to strengthen our position besides the repeated plaintive pleas by each service for larger appropriations. Both Air Force and Navy were seeking bases abroad. The Army was supporting the plans that led to NATO. Civilians in the Atomic Energy Commission (which had been placed under civilian control to prevent military domination and inattention to non-military applications of the atom) were effectively promoting and supporting programs to produce better A-bombs, and later the H-bomb. After the Russians demonstrated their capacity to produce nuclear fission, in 1949, our government swung into active planning. The result was NSC-68, a key study which served as a rough outline for the dramatic change in military planning and actual power that followed the invasion of Korea. It was the product of civil and military cooperation, but the chief lead came from the State Department rather than the Department of Defense. Indeed the cooperative undertaking could never have got off the ground if it had not had Acheson's wholehearted support and, in response to his earnest plea, Truman's direct instructions to Johnson to permit the military to proceed. While the drafting of NSC-68 was in response to the first Soviet atomic explosion in September 1949, the actual carrying out of many of the NSC-68 recommendations was triggered by the Communist attack on the Republic of Korea on June 25, 1950.

Korea was the battleground of our first limited war in the twentieth century. The concept of limited war was not new; the possibility of our involvement in such a war had not been totally ignored. Kennan in July 1949 was probably the first one to urge the Joint Chiefs in formal fashion to prepare specifically for limited war. However, at that time, none of the services was really able to think of any future responsibility except total war: funds that were utterly inadequate for such an eventuality could not be diverted to other ends. The possibility of limited war was picked up in NSC-68, though limited war as early as 1950 and specifically in Korea was not envisioned. The first

half-year of the Korean War brought home to the Administration with crushing force the conviction that unconditional surrender (however defined) or "total victory" (whatever that means) is not always worth the price. In Korea, we returned to our original objective—the repelling of aggression—and were deeply relieved when the Chinese also decided to settle for the 38th Parallel.

The Korean settlement came early in Eisenhower's first term, and it greatly increased his prestige. It was particularly welcome to him because it justified or encouraged some reduction of military expenditures, though not nearly enough to satisfy him. Actually there had been considerable levelling off of the upsurge of defense expenditures under the Truman Administration; Marshall, as Secretary of Defense, had set a "plateau" as his objective, and his successor, Lovett, had carried on the same process and had made clearer than ever the abandonment of 1953 as the "target date" for total readiness, as one might say. The process thus begun was carried forward by Eisenhower's first Secretary of Defense, Wilson, acting harmoniously under the guidance of Humphrey, Secretary of the Treasury, and maintained thereafter by Wilson's successors, McElroy and Gates.

The Eisenhower Administration felt that it was aided in its program by the availability of the H-bomb (the first test of a nuclear fusion explosion had been successfully executed in November 1952). In Wilson's words, he would provide "a bigger bang for a buck," and the new lower plateau and greater, almost total, reliance on nuclear arms became known as "The New Look."

The New Look needed a political rationale; and two of the essential elements were supplied by Eisenhower himself and by his Secretary of State, John Foster Dulles.

During the election campaign, appealing naturally to the universal desire for an end to the Korean War and for an avoidance of any further distasteful activities like it, Eisenhower emphasized the importance of more attention to Asia, and evoked, somewhat incongruously, the rallying cry of "let Asians fight Asians!" Eisenhower's Asian policy was doubly welcome to Taft and the other advocates of Fortress America. It had its moment of glory in the inaugural address when Eisenhower announced the "unleashing" of Chiang Kai-shek. Soon, however, Chiang was back on the leash; and not long thereafter Eisenhower decided with somewhat accidental consistency not to permit an atomic strike at Dien Bien Phu. He also accepted the logical consequences of his refusal when he decided, as Dulles learned to his horror, that Mendès-France's compromise was better than a war the French could not continue and we would not enter.

Admiral Radford was picked as Eisenhower's first chairman of JCS, partly because he was an Asia-Firster; partly too, no doubt, because he was quite willing to reverse his previous stand against strategic bombing (particularly of cities) and had become an advocate of the use of nuclear weapons (if by Air Force *and* Navy) as perhaps the only important function of the armed forces. The rationale was expressed by Dulles, who relied on the deterrent effect of "massive retaliatory power," when he announced that in the future we would meet Communist probes "at places and with means of [our] own choosing." Massive retaliation was equally welcome to the three heads of the great departments: State, whose Secretary made the statement, Treasury and Defense, though the latter two probably interpreted the phrase with rather less predictive content. It was a recasting of the "bigger bang for a buck" in the form of a ringing homily. It probably had a special appeal to its author Dulles, because he believed in the value of dire threats —a form of diplomacy later described as brinkmanship. The actual effectiveness of threats is hard to estimate. Dulles said that he ended the Korean War by asking Nehru to have Pannikar, the Indian Ambassador in China, tell Chou En-lai that we would drop atomic bombs on Chinese cities if the armistice negotiations did not soon reach fruition. Nehru later said that he remembered no such conversation and that in any event he would never have sent such a message to Pannikar. Perhaps the Chinese were moved by other matters: the death of Stalin, the new leaders in the Kremlin, the urgent Chinese need to use their limited resources in more fruitful ways than in continued fighting in Korea where combat was certainly not leading to victory.

The third major element in Eisenhower's military policy was also a Dulles creation. It might be called containment-by-alliance. When Dulles took office NATO was very much a going concern. Truman had sent American divisions to Europe, SHAPE was headed by an American, and the defense of Western Europe, while far from certain, was no longer a mere fiction. We also had our special alliances with three Commonwealth nations—Canada, Australia and New Zealand—and with the Philippines. Finally, the new Administration inherited a far-flung established air and naval base program, ranging from Okinawa to the Caribbean islands, from Alaska to Iceland, from Western Europe to Turkey and the Arabian peninsula. Most of the bases were either on our own territory or that of our NATO and Commonwealth allies, some on territory of other nations by agreement or compact. The development of bases reached its climax about 1955; thereafter the number declined. The urgent need for bases was gradually reduced as we developed more long-range bombers, as we started to produce IRBM and ICBM missiles and, later on, Polaris and Polaris submarines. Regardless of the need, our rights as tenants of the bases proved to be impermanent, particularly with the rise of new nations like Morocco.

NATO, ANZUS and the bases did not satisfy Dulles. He wanted and obtained on paper a ring around the Soviet Union, and around China in Southeast Asia. The ring was *pro forma* the global military solution of the problem of containment, and by the same token a bastion against neutralism—regarded by Dulles as immoral. The Baghdad Pact in the Middle East, which we created and blessed without joining, and to which we secured Britain's adherence, was composed of an odd miscellany of nations, and was converted into CENTO when Iraq withdrew. There was an odd composition, too, in SEATO, which contained such dissimilar and widely scattered members as the United States and Thailand (though NATO too had a diversified and, in part, widespread membership).

What Dulles had in mind is not entirely clear; perhaps he thought that the membership of other nations warned the Communists that we would automatically come to their support. Apparently he also expected that Communism would not leap over our allies to infiltrate more distant spots. How welcome this *cordon sanitaire* was to the Joint Chiefs is uncertain. The alliance members constituted a drain on our military resources, for obviously an alliance designed to provide mutual defense must be able to count on the armed forces of all the allies. In both CENTO and SEATO almost all the arms plus much of the military guidance and training had to come from the United States. The establishment of the MAAG's (Military Assistance Advisory Groups) *per se* produced a series of sincere and alarming reports about the inability of various nations to repel attack. Putting armed strength first meant some degree of neglect of the profound political, social and economic problems that beset those countries. And the existence of alliance membership forbade the political exploitation of nationalistic neutralism—regarded by Dulles and by the Vice President as anti-American as well as immoral. Finally, since all the members of CENTO and SEATO except France, the United Kingdom and the United States have been Asian countries, perhaps Dulles and Eisenhower felt that the alliance system was an implementation of the "let Asians fight Asians" policy.

The defection of Iraq from the Baghdad Pact in 1959 cast doubt on the utility of this kind of alliance: unstable governments make dubious allies. The subsequent inability of SEATO to deal with Communist infiltration and civil war in Laos and Viet-Nam showed little hope for consensus and action in that organization. Perhaps, too, the idea of multi-nation alliances except under special circumstances and with at least a majority of solidly democratic political systems as in NATO and ANZUS is a visionary one, particularly when one of the motivating desires is the creation of a barrier. Communist interpenetration with varying degrees of success in countries like Guinea, The Congo, Guatemala, Cuba, and Egypt shows that defense by land and by sea is irrelevant when the Communist probing is directed toward the dozens of underdeveloped countries throughout the world now full of the pangs of new-born independence, or pressure for independence, and other growing aspirations. The governmental instability inherent in these situa-

tions makes both alliances and formal ideological affiliations undependable.

Since President Kennedy took office, two shifts in strategic thinking have begun to emerge. One is a broader and deeper reliance on the support of economic and social development, the other is the strong effort to improve our non-nuclear armed capabilities in spite of the concomitant enlargement of government expenditures. It was thus no accident that Kennedy's military adviser was General Taylor, who had made very public his conviction that strategic alternatives were practically ruled out by the New Look; it was also no accident that Eisenhower during the Berlin crisis of 1958-1959 said at a press conference that defense of Berlin by conventional forces was hopeless, while Kennedy had used the Berlin crisis of 1961 as the take-off point for requesting and getting a substantial improvement in our non-nuclear strength and had affirmed the feasibility of a very substantial defense without using nuclear weapons, though he did not deny the possibility of using them as a last resort. Truman's approach in 1948 forms an interesting contrast: trying to avoid the use of any arms, he quickly found the airlift as an alternative. In Truman's case, the Russians finally gave in; in Eisenhower's case, the Russians agreed to lift the deadline in return for our invitation to Khrushchev to visit America and for our agreement on a summit conference; in Kennedy's case the outcome still lies ahead, though the sealing of the border within Berlin is perhaps a kind of solution. It seems to represent Russia's abandonment of any hope for an all-Communist or neutral Berlin, and for any Communist German Republic able to withstand the appeal of the West. As long as the door between the two Germanys remained open, the preference of the East Germans for Western democracy was blatantly apparent, and the flight to the West of skilled and professional workers was depleting the East German economy. The closing of East Berlin was proof of Allied success, but it also constituted a loss to the West. And the problem of access to Berlin still remains.

III. THE FUTURE DIRECTION OF CIVIL-MILITARY RELATIONS IN THE UNITED STATES

National policy is an undefined phrase used for multifarious purposes not the least of which is the propensity of political scientists for minatory polemics. It can, however, be used more pragmatically as a convenient device for describing that great miscellaneous series of active or consciously inactive steps taken by our president and Congress and the rest of the national government over a given period of time. In this sense national policy includes in some fashion such diverse areas of action as Berlin, revision of the tax laws, housing, civil rights and anti-missile-missiles. So conceived, the spectrum represented by the vast number of miscellaneous components constantly shifts. Items invisible or barely visible at the edges move to the center and shine with far more incandescence; items that formerly constituted narrow separately identifiable bands become elements within a much larger definable collocation of merging bands.

This kind of imaginary description lends itself rather handily to the developments of civil-military relations within the United States government during the last three decades. In the early 1930's each of the two military arms represented a narrow band at the edge of the national policy spectrum not closely interrelated and even less articulated with any of the other aspects of national policy. In the 1960's the situation is strikingly different. The three services are intimately interrelated and on them is superimposed the additional elaborate and militarily all-encompassing functions of the Department of Defense. Here then is a single broad band with minor shiftings in hues within it. Equally important, this military band is intense, and in the center of the spectrum. A very high proportion of the President's time and energy (to take a useful indicator) is devoted to military problems. Finally, defense is

now no longer clearly separable from the other elements of national policy; it is inextricably intertwined with foreign policy, as the phrase goes, and with national economic policy. In these terms, probably a very major part of the President's time and energy go to problems and policies in which the effect of various alternate actions or inactions on our military position in the world and the role of our armed forces inevitably looms large. This direct effect does not include many other matters like the influence on our position abroad of racial discrimination in restaurants on U. S. 40 in Maryland on the main highway from Washington to New York.

The enlarging of the civil-military band on the national policy spectrum has resulted in a simultaneous enlargement of the responsibilities and concerns of both the military and the civilians. The Secretary of State, indeed the President, himself, find it necessary to take into account in their speeches the limits of our military power. How to do this is not easy, and a variety of devices have been used and will continue to be used. Dulles tried dire threats, or rather implied threats, that may well have terrified our allies more than they did the Soviet Union. Acheson tried frankness in saying that the Republic of Korea lay outside our defense perimeter, but that it could count on UN support; after June 25, 1950 he was widely blamed for having invited the Communist attack, but MacArthur had already announced the limits of the perimeter and had not suggested that the UN might serve as a shield. Both Truman in the Truman Doctrine and Eisenhower in the Eisenhower Doctrine—both dealing with specific problems in the Eastern Mediterranean—had given vague promises that would only be fulfilled when specific circumstances warranted specific action. For the future, one can only be sure that no panacea will be found. Basically, foreign policy which ignores military power cannot be effective; equally, foreign policy that is constricted by military preferences for ideal combat conditions is fruitless and defeatist. Korea was a bad place to fight, but without our willingness to risk defeat there, not only would the Republic of Korea have been absorbed by the Communist imperium, but our role as leader of a great alliance would have been seriously damaged. This necessity for a never-ceasing series of choices that are never optimal from any single standpoint is now widely recognized by both military and civilian officers, especially those who have had the sobering experience of working together in Washington where neat, final, total solutions prove evanescent. The presence of foreign service officers in the National War College and of Army and Air Force officers in graduate studies at universities gives promise that for the immediate future this development will continue. It is wise to remember, however, that a man with the kind of temperament and kind of role in the Army of a General Patton (and, at the other pole, his opposite number in the Foreign Service) will always be restive under the restrictions imposed by his more sophisticated superiors.

The change in attitudes is reflected in parallel developments in organization and procedure across the whole band where civil and military factors enter into the process of making decisions. Neither organization nor procedure is static in our kind of government; obviously the forms of 1962 will undergo modification and in a fashion that is unpredictable. Yet save for massive disarmament or total war or a total shift in our position in the world, it can be said with assurance that there will be no

dramatic reversal of present practices. The title of the chairman of the Joint Chiefs can be changed, but there is no prospect for perhaps the next decade, or even longer, that he or his equivalent will cease to have at least the position of *primus inter pares.* What is now the Agency for International Development may well have a new name; it may be officially closer to or farther from the State Department, but surely there will be an agency dealing with economic development constantly trying to juggle the balls of long-term and short-term interests, diplomacy, military needs and desires, Congressional preferences and presidential guidance. Our diplomacy will still be affected by the glare of publicity, by our need for operating both in the style of the classic diplomats and as a member of the United Nations and several dozen other multi-member international agencies on which our representatives serve.

The assumption that underlies this suggestion of developments in the next decade or two is that our present road leads neither to Heaven nor Hell, but to a protracted continuation in that appallingly unpleasant realm, Purgatory. This is an assumption that is condemned by the modern Manicheans, and as in other dangerous periods in history, the present stresses invite the revival of the Manichean heresy. It can only be said that there seems to be no prospect that either of the opposite kinds of absolute solutions propounded by Lord Russell in England and General Walker in this country will be adopted. Apparently the dangers that seem to be inherent in an attempted rapid escape from Purgatory act as an effective deterrent. We can only hope that we, and both our friends and our enemies, will continue to accept our unpleasant fate.

THE FAR EASTERN CRISIS OF 1931-1932: STIMSON, HOOVER AND THE ARMED SERVICES

MICHAEL D. REAGAN

ASSISTANT PROFESSOR OF POLITICAL SCIENCE

MAXWELL SCHOOL OF CITIZENSHIP AND PUBLIC AFFAIRS

SYRACUSE UNIVERSITY

CONTENTS

The Far Eastern Crisis of 1931-1932   29

Bibliographic Note   38

Notes   39

Editorial Comments   41

THE FAR EASTERN CRISIS OF 1931-1932

On September 9, 1931, Secretary of State Henry L. Stimson wrote to a friend that Manchuria was "the vital danger spot of Asia" because

three great differing nationalities, mutually suspicious and hostile, are impacted in a single geographical area. The peace machinery which Western nations have hammered out does not fit these three governments much better than a stovepipe hat fits a naked African savage.[1]

Nine days later that machinery suffered a breakdown when forces of the Imperial Japanese Army seized several towns along the South Manchurian Railway. The series of events now referred to as the Far Eastern crisis had begun.

China quickly appealed to the League of Nations and to the United States for condemnation of the Japanese action as a violation of the League Covenant, the Pact of Paris and the Nine-Power Treaty. Secretary Stimson and President Hoover were thus confronted with the problem of upholding treaties calling for the peaceful settlement of disputes, against a major power, a signatory to those treaties, which chose to settle its claims by force.

Before the alternative types of action could be explored, however, there were some questions to be answered regarding the scope of Japan's intentions: Was the Manchurian attack a local eruption, or part of an expansion planned in Tokyo? If the latter, had the plan the approval of the Prime Minister, or was it a military plot of which the civilian government had no foreknowledge? The importance of these questions lay in Stimson's assumption that if the civilians had not participated in the action, then support of them might help them to control the belligerent Army leaders. But if the presumably peace-oriented civilian government had in fact approved the Army action, then American policy would have to take a firmer line. There were other alternatives, but, as will be seen, these were the ones recognized by the Secretary.

The Secretary's sources of information included the American Minister in China, Nelson T. Johnson; American consuls in the Manchurian cities of Harbin, Mukden and Dairen; military and naval attachés in the Far East; and his departmental staff, particularly Under Secretary William R. Castle and Dr. Stanley K. Hornbeck, Chief of the Far Eastern Division. The Washington headquarters offices of military and naval intelligence supplied State in considerable volume with daily action reports from Asiatic stations. No attempt was made in Washington, it appears, to determine the strategic significance of these reports. Nor was there any machinery for systematic inter-agency correlation of diplomatic and military intelligence.

There was actually an impediment to such correlation by staff officials because of Secretary Stimson's desire to retain close personal control over such affairs, and because of the primacy he attributed to the office of the Secretary of State. When he desired consultation, his normal mode of operation was to call the civilian Secretaries or uniformed heads of the services to his office. It has been said that Secretary of the Navy Charles Francis Adams once complained that Stimson treated him like an office boy to relay orders to the Navy.[2] Apparently Stimson's relations with the uniformed heads of the services were excellent, and the Chief of Naval Operations at this time, Admiral William V. Pratt, once wrote to Stimson that during the latter's tenure as Secretary of State "there has resulted the closest cooperation between the State and Navy Departments that has ever existed since I entered the service."[3] But with the civilian Secretaries of the War and Navy Departments, his relations were less cordial. Undoubtedly there was some interchange on the lower levels in the three departments, but apparently nothing of a systematic, profound or continuing nature.

In Stimson's first tentative interpretation of the news from Manchuria, he came to the conclusion that the affair had not been planned in Tokyo, or that at least it had been planned without civilian approval and would be brought under control by the liberal government of which Baron Shidehara was Foreign Minister. Reports from the attachés and in the newspapers indicated that a sizable military operation was in progress, but these reports shed no light on Japan's ultimate goals. The only definite judgment received in the State Department during the early weeks was contained in a telegram from Johnson dated September 22, 1931, presenting the Minister's view that

the forceful occupation of all strategic points in South Manchuria . . . is an aggressive act by Japan apparently long planned . . . I find no evidence that these events were the result of accident nor were they the acts of minor and irresponsible officials.[4]

Along the same line, but more specific in fixing responsibility, was Hornbeck's analysis of September 29, asserting that the action of the Japanese Army "cannot have come as a surprise to the civil authorities, including the Foreign Office, in Tokyo."[5]

Stimson apparently accepted Johnson's estimate of planned aggression wholeheartedly,[6] but remained noncommittal about the implication of civilian responsibility in Hornbeck's memorandum. The Secretary thought it best to assume that the liberal civilians might be able to reverse the aggression if supported by the United States. The resultant policy was a calculated forbearance from even an expression of condemnation in the belief that such forbearance would help the liberal element in Japan. Stimson feared that strong action might hurt Japanese pride and lead public opinion there to support the military element, which had a constitutional position surpassing that of the civilian government. It was not a final decision, but a wait-and-see policy, and it was necessarily ambivalent in practice, because hesitant in conception.

As early as October 8, Stimson began to doubt the wisdom of his policy of restraint. The same day that he rather ambiguously informed the Chinese chargé, Yung Kwai, that we "were playing no favorites, but that we were backing

up the League of Nations," he also expressed the fear that "we have got to take a firm ground and aggressive stand toward Japan."[7]

Stimson's faith in the efficacy of public opinion as a weapon of statecraft reasserted itself on October 13 and 14. He then thought that American public opinion, as expressed in his notes to Japan, was making the Japanese government more conciliatory,[8] and told Walter Lippmann, in writing of Polish affairs, that "public opinion is getting its own way on that subject as on all others."[9] In the Secretary's conception, public opinion served the policy maker primarily as a tool to be exploited in support of official policy rather than as an ingredient in the determination of that policy. This view was evident when he withheld the diplomatic exchanges with Japan from the public until he had abandoned the policy of conciliation in favor of non-recognition and wanted the American public to support a moral judgment against Japan.

Without consulting Navy Secretary Adams, Stimson and Castle on October 13 acted to get Admiral Pratt, Chief of Naval Operations, to pull back to Shanghai the Asiatic Squadron submarines whose crews were then on autumn shore leave at Chefoo, so as to avoid any incidents[10] and also to counteract a story in the *New York Graphic* asserting that the submarine force had been sent there in anticipation of immediate war.[11] Pratt was not asked his opinion; he was told what to do.[12]

The Secretary's opinion that the situation was a grave one now began to conflict with the President's lack of concern. Hoover apparently agreed that Japan's actions in Manchuria were a blow to the treaty-built peace structure, but he was too immersed in the deepening economic crisis at home to pay much attention to foreign affairs, nor did he believe that the Sino-Japanese issue affected America. Discerning that financial matters were then all-important to the President, Stimson tried to call his attention to the Manchurian situation by pointing out to the President at a Cabinet meeting on October 9 that "if Japan runs amok, Congress will never let him cut a single dollar off on navies."[13] Even on this practical basis the Secretary apparently thought his appeal had failed, for he wrote of the President's reaction:

I don't think he realizes what it means to him in his administration to have Japan run amok and play havoc with its peace treaties, so his main proposition in this conference was not to allow under any circumstances anybody to deposit that baby on our lap; and second not to get ourselves into a humiliating position.[14]

At about the same time, Hoover called in his military advisers, presumably Pratt and the Army Chief of Staff, General Douglas MacArthur. To the President's questions regarding our preparedness for becoming involved in the Far East, they replied that although we could win a war against Japan it would involve the temporary loss of the Philippines, five years of preparation, and four to six years of fighting. If we had the aid of the British fleet, this time might be cut to two years.[15]

This information could have been the basis for an intensive military buildup, had Hoover thought that there really was a possibility of war. But since he saw no threat to American interests, he went right ahead with the largest naval budget cuts in the nation's history.[16]

A few weeks earlier Secretary Adams had announced plans for new construction in line with a reported Administration policy of a navy second to none. But it was revealed on September 29 that the Budget Bureau, acting under Presidential orders, planned to cancel all proposed naval construction appropriations for the fiscal year 1933 and to halve the destroyer allocation of the previous year. Five of the eleven destroyers appropriated for in the budget for the fiscal year 1932 were allowed to remain in the schedule only because complete cancellation would have caused shipyard unemployment. On the same day it was reported that Secretary Stimson was in favor of a naval holiday.[17]

In mid-October, at the same time that the sharply revised naval budget was being taken up in Budget Bureau hearings, Congressman Britten of Illinois, Chairman of the House Naval Affairs Committee, was quoted in protest over the cuts:

This certainly is no time to tinker with the first arm of the national defense. . . . It makes me shudder to think of the Pacific fleet manoeuvering with skeleton crews and one-fifth of its ships decommissioned for lack of proper personnel. . . . The years of 1914 and 1915 in the Atlantic might easily be duplicated in the Pacific in 1932, when it would be necessary for us to conduct our neutral commerce with Asia by show of force, or to accept the military dictates of Japan. . . . If the United States is to become an unofficial but highly important member of the Council of the League of Nations in the settlement of the Manchurian clash, then we had best be prepared to defend ourselves from the attacks of those who meet with the League's disfavor.[18]

In December, Hoover expressed his conviction that "If the world is to regain its standards of life, it must further decrease both naval and other arms."[19] The Naval Bill reported out by the Appropriations Committee in April 1932 topped the President's economies with further cuts totalling $15 million. The reduced budget was for $326 million,[20] indicating that a majority of the Committee agreed with the President's prescription.

The only action affecting our naval strength in the Pacific during the tense autumn and early winter of 1931 was a routine adjustment in the operating plan (quite the opposite of Britten's "show of force") by which six destroyers were withdrawn from the Asiatic Fleet and sent to Mare Island, California.[21]

Economic sanctions as a means of compelling Japanese respect for treaties were apparently mentioned by Stimson (though not advocated) in early discussions with the President. Hoover, who believed sanctions to be impossible unless Britain joined in their imposition, asked Treasury Under Secretary Ogden Mills to phone a friend in London to get a British reaction to the idea of sanctions and, if these were to fail, of war. The reaction was negative as apparently Hoover had anticipated without regret. Hoover also has recorded that he informed his Cabinet in mid-October that we could not go along with sanctions even if other nations initiated them.[22]

Stimson seems not to have disagreed with his chief on this subject until after the fall of the government in Japan in late November. Yet as later events made clear, Stimson did disagree with Hoover on the wisdom of revealing or concealing our unwillingness to risk war to save the treaties. The Secretary of State favored the bluffing course; the President feared reprisals unless it was made clear to Japan that she had nothing to fear from us.

Where Stimson saw humiliation (and possibly war) if we let treaties be violated with impunity, Hoover seems to have decided that the involvement of American lives and property in Manchuria was too unimportant to warrant entanglement. Neither Hoover nor Stimson received or requested military advice on these points.

Coordinated consideration of the problems of joint political and military interest had been the object of a visit paid by Admiral Mark W. Bristol, Chairman of the Navy General Board, to Secretary Stimson on October 15. Bristol suggested cooperative Navy-State discussions on Asiatic matters and broached the possibility of having a man from State sit with the Joint Army-Navy Board.[23] Nothing came of these proposals, perhaps because of Stimson's conviction of the primacy of his own department. This was not, of course, from any dislike of military men. He cherished the memory of his service in the Army, and he respected the office of Secretary of War, an office in which he himself had been proud to serve. He enjoyed his relations with Army and Navy officers and had an Army captain as his personal aide. Nevertheless, as has been explained above, his concept of his role tended to discourage close relations among officers of the three departments.

By November it had become inescapably apparent that our initial policy of mild suggestions to Japan was having no deterrent effect on her armies. Occasional intelligence reports, forwarded to State through Johnson in Peiping and passed on to the services from there in accord with established routine, spoke of the ever-widening scope of the action. In the light of this knowledge Hoover and Stimson discussed eventualities on November 7, without reaching any new decisions. Even at this point, they remained in agreement on policy; Stimson told Hoover that embargoes led to war.[24]

Later that day the Secretary received advice from Major General William Lassiter, who came in on a personal call. The General, who had at one time visited Manchuria, thought an embargo would only provoke the Japanese. In his view, Japanese pride and patriotic sentiment would foreclose any possibility of persuasion by show of force, which would instead have an inflammatory effect.[25] The Secretary appreciated this opinion; it coincided with current policy and supported him against doubts arising in several quarters. Hoover thought him too belligerent; his assistant, Allen Klots, thought him too soft; and Secretary of the Army Patrick J. Hurley scoffed at note-exchanging diplomacy.

At a Cabinet meeting on November 13 Hurley remarked that force alone could stop Japan;

that if we weren't willing to use it we were making a mistake to involve ourselves at all, since Japan was going to seize Manchuria anyway and we were simply letting the United States in for a rebuff and a loss of prestige. In his own mind, Stimson dismissed this opinion as evidently coming from the generals over whom Hurley presided.[26] To the Cabinet, Stimson asserted that American policy was to rely only on moral force, for the nation had rejected sanctions as an instrument of statecraft when it rejected the League Covenant with its provisions for sanctions.[27] Some measure short of force had to be found, for Stimson was unwilling to drop the matter completely.

Despite their unwillingness to end the note-writing campaign, obviously Hoover and Stimson did not really expect to succeed in stopping Japan, for they and Hurley agreed a few days later that even if Japan set up puppet governments in Manchuria we would not have suffered a diplomatic defeat so long as the province was not formally annexed.[28] Perhaps Hoover had in mind a letter from Admiral Montgomery M. Taylor, Commander in Chief of the Asiatic Fleet, to Admiral Pratt, which the latter had let Hoover and the State Department see. In this, Taylor expressed the opinion that Japan would not give up her control of Manchuria except under extreme pressure.[29] This the President was unwilling to apply.

On November 19 a new estimate of the situation was made, Stimson concluding that since the Japanese government was now "in the hands of virtually mad dogs," it was impossible to continue to expect that the liberal civilians would regain control of the rampaging army.[30] The policy of forbearance was now reversed and eventually only Presidential objections kept Stimson from using a boycott in an attempt to stop Japan. He informed the League that while we could not join that body in imposing an embargo we were anxious not to discourage such action and "would not allow our fleet to do anything to oppose it or to interfere with them in their attempts."[31] The President, he felt, was now ready to "go the whole thing,"[32] and Stimson soon pressed for reconsideration of the decision against an embargo. If it were a joint action with other nations signatory to the violated treaties he thought it would soon prove effective.[33] But Hoover, who later expressed the opinion that his Secretary of State was at times more a warrior than a diplomat,[34] refused to gamble. Again the views of Pratt and Mac-Arthur were not requested.

The officers of the State Department were now urging stronger action if anything was to be accomplished. On December 5 Hornbeck submitted a major memorandum in which he presented three alternatives for effective action: public denunciation of Japan as a lawbreaker, non-recognition, and an economic boycott.[35] With the latter alternative definitely eliminated by Presidential decision, non-recognition came to the fore as a measure which would be acceptable to the President and at the same time perhaps have some effect on Japan. At least it would achieve one of Stimson's aims: to register dissent from Japan's acquisition of territory by force.

On January 7, 1932, the Secretary handed to the Japanese and Chinese ambassadors in Washington a note stating that the United States would not recognize the legality of any *de facto* situation or any agreement which violated the territorial integrity of China, the open-door policy, or the Pact of Paris.[36] This was intended to be a final step, the climax of the American response to Japanese aggression. To gain public support, the note was published the next day after careful briefing of the senior members of the press corps in Washington in an effort to obtain proper perspective in the handling of the news.

On January 10, three days after this decisive action was taken, Stimson called in Admirals Pratt and Bristol to discuss the situation from a naval standpoint. Their conversation embraced the general conditions of the fleet, but centered on what we would do if Japan blockaded the Chinese ports. There is no record of the admirals' reply, except that they considered such an attempt unlikely.[37]

Also at this time, Stimson received a memorandum containing Hornbeck's politico-strategic recipe for avoiding war with Japan. On the political side, he advised that we not stand conspicuously ahead of other powers in advocating principles which Japan might not allow to stand in the way of her territorial objectives; his military course was to be always stronger than Japan on the sea.[38]

Since Japan was by now in complete control of Manchuria, the time for discussion of means to stop her had passed. Problems of the Dis-

armament Conference soon to start at Geneva came to the fore again while the Manchurian situation quieted down. But on January 24 a Japanese naval force moved toward Shanghai, where American lives and property were substantially involved. Foreign Service officers there immediately called for naval protection and vessels to be used for evacuation if necessary. Stimson feared Japan would declare war to justify a blockade of all Chinese ports.[39]

Thoroughly alarmed by the possibility of a major Far Eastern conflict, on January 25 the Secretary suggested to the President a strong note of protest and the dispatch of some of the Asiatic Fleet from Manila to Shanghai. He also explained to the British Ambassador that he did "not intend any threat against Japan; our Asiatic Squadron was not large enough to constitute a threat but I thought it might have a beneficial effect to send that Squadron . . . provided the British would do the same."[40]

The Secretary of the Navy and the Chief of Naval Operations visited Stimson that same day. But their visit concerned some fears respecting disarmament rather than the tense situation developing at Shanghai. The Secretary of State

turned the conference into a talk on Shanghai and went through the matter pretty thoroughly with them. They were not alive to the situation but soon became so after the talk got on.[41]

The next day there was a "real discussion" at the Cabinet meeting.

I brought up the situation which had developed in Shanghai . . . Hurley followed me by another statement along the line that he had made once or twice before to the effect that he was convinced that Japan would proceed definitely with her onslaught on the Chinese boycott just as she had in Manchuria; that she was determined to do it and that nothing short of force would stop her. He then said that he, therefore, did not believe in any words at all, and he was afraid that my efforts apparently in that direction might simply lead to a clash . . . I said that of course I realized the importance of having Japan fear this country. For that reason I was glad, though we had nothing to do with it, that the Fleet was going to have its battle practice this time off Hawaii. Then the President [said that] he felt that the mere size of China, 350,000,000 as he expressed it, always had succeeded and would succeed in throwing off the efforts of other nations like Japan to penetrate it and dominate it. . . . He had no doubt, however, that Japan was going ahead now as Hurley had stated. He pointed out strongly the folly of getting into a war with Japan on this subject; that such a war could not be localized or kept within bounds, and that it would mean the landing of forces in the Far East which we had no reason or sense in doing. He said he would fight for Continental United States as far as anybody, but he would not fight for Asia.[42]

Here the divergent responses to the Japanese threat were clearly stated. Hurley presented the choice as being force or nothing, and suggested the latter. Hoover agreed with both the analysis and the prescription. Stimson alone insisted that there were some things we could do short of all-out use of force. One alternative in his mind was to bluff: "to rely upon the unconscious elements of our great size and military strength; that I knew Japan was afraid of that, and I was willing to let her be afraid of that without telling her that we were not going to use it against her."[43]

Some action was obviously needed at the end of January. Japan had bombed Shanghai, violated the International Settlement, and begun ground action against Chinese forces in the city. A war scare hit the Washington planners. Stimson initiated a series of conferences with Army and Navy officials after asking at the Cabinet meeting on January 29 that "there should be no talk or action by anyone which would indicate that we were not going to use any weapon that we might have, whether it be the fleet or the boycott."[44]

The next morning, January 30, he conferred with Pratt "to ascertain where our ships were and how many more Marines we had and what vessels we had in the Far East which could transport any soldiers if necessary to Shanghai in addition to the Marines."[45] That afternoon, Hoover, Stimson and Castle conferred, the President favoring a note from himself to the Japanese Emperor as the suitable action.[46]

Action reports from Shanghai brought about a full-dress but impromptu discussion of military action on the next day, January 31. Attending were Hoover, Stimson, Hurley, Adams, Pratt, MacArthur, Castle and Hornbeck. The decision was to send the cruiser *Houston* and six destroyers to Shanghai, plus the Army's 31st Regiment and 1,000 men, and 400 Marines. Total American troops in the International Settlement would then number 2,800.

Some sixty vessels and 200 planes left California the next morning, February 1, for maneuvers at Hawaii[47]—by fortuitous decision of the previous year made without reference to the international political situation.[48]

Surprisingly stubborn resistance by the Chinese forces had stalled the Japanese attack and on January 31, Japan sought the "good offices" of the United States to end the fighting. Stimson was quickly convinced that Japan "has got the bear by the tail and . . . is trying to get help to get out of the situation without losing too much face."[49] He conferred at his home with Pratt and MacArthur on February 3, the service representatives agreeing that Japan had gotten into a bad fix by biting off more than she could chew. A review of the situation led to further agreement that it was necessary to guard the Settlement with troops in order to protect American lives.[50]

The fighting slowed down in early February, but State-War-Navy discussions continued concerning Shanghai and our general position vis-à-vis Japanese strength. Stimson still was both unimpressed and annoyed by Hurley's repeated assertions that the Japanese would not be stopped by diplomatic wrist-slapping—a judgment Stimson had earlier slightingly referred to as "the General Staff point of view."[51] At a "redhot" Cabinet meeting on February 9 Stimson was obviously irritated by Hurley, whom he recorded as having "butted in on his usual line of discrediting everything that we did by mere representations or notes and giving his sketch of what the Japanese were really doing according to his military advisers, which by the way was not very accurate."[52] (The significance of the side remark is unclear; presumably Hurley's chief adviser was the Chief of Staff, General MacArthur, who was also relied upon by Stimson.)

Stimson's faith in the sufficiency of public opinion as a sanction was evidently rudely disturbed by Japan's failure to respond to American admonishments. His diary for February 18 contains this passage:

The whole situation is beginning to shake me up and get me back to a little bit nearer my old view that we haven't yet reached the stage where we can dispense with police force; and the only police force I have got to depend upon today is the American Navy. Pretty soon I am going to tell the President so.

When the Japanese launched a heavy attack on February 20 Stimson asked Pratt for a naval résumé and estimates of our naval strength and that of the Japanese fleet in the Shanghai area. At this time his department was also receiving daily copies of all messages sent the Navy Department by its commanders in the troubled area.[53] Four days later a long talk with MacArthur seemed to Stimson a useful exploration of what he called "eventualities."[54]

Despite Stimson's gnawing doubts about the efficacy of public opinion, he made one more attempt at rallying it on the side of international morality through the device of a public letter to Senator William Borah on February 23, 1932, stating the case against Japan with reference to the Nine-Power ("Open-Door") Treaty of 1922. The letter was directed not only at American public opinion but also at Japan, as a warning, and for this purpose it included a "military bluff" (to use Stimson's own descriptive phrase). The bluff consisted of reminding Japan that the

willingness of the American government to surrender its then commanding lead in battleship construction and to leave its positions at Guam and in the Philippines without further fortification, was predicated upon, among other things, the self-denying covenants contained in the Nine Power Treaty, which assured the nations of the world . . . against the military aggrandizement of any other power at the expense of China.[55]

There is no record that Stimson consulted the military leaders about this implied threat to fortify Guam and the Philippines, presumably because it was pure bluff, on which Stimson felt certain the United States would not be called by Japan. The bluff came near being upset almost immediately, but by Hoover rather than by Japan, for when Stimson went over to show the President the latest cables two days after publication of the Borah Letter, he found that Hoover was "proposing to tell the people of the United States that under no circumstances would we go to war."[56] Nor was this the last time that the President's desire to avoid any semblance of belligerence was to "play ducks and drakes" (as the Secretary of State often expressed it) with Stimson's equally strong desire to bluff the Japanese.

Another strong attack on March 1 was coupled with Japanese appeals for peace proposals. Stimson found this combination diffi-

cult to reconcile, but decided it was probably "the same old story of an inability on the part of the regular government to control the action of their military."[57]

The fighting in Shanghai ended on March 3 but the momentum built into Stimson's discussions of our general Far Eastern position kept those conferences going several months longer. Stimson had apparently abandoned the thought of using sanctions[58] but did desire to bluff Japan and was therefore concerned lest Hoover make public his unwillingness to use sanctions.[59] Of more immediate importance was the necessity to decide how much of a fleet to keep in Pacific waters, when to withdraw the 31st Regiment, and whether the Japanese action of the past half-year required strengthening our own fleet as a long-range measure of protection.

Stimson's disillusionment regarding the efficacy of moral suasion had led him to sudden concern over the weakness of our Navy. During March and April he may have become acquainted with the strategic premises of Admiral Pratt, whom Stimson liked and thought sensible; he certainly was familiar with them in May. These premises were (1) that peace is maintained by possession of sufficient strength to swing the balance of power in any desired direction; and (2) that the United States might remain neutral in a European war but would be the main belligerent in an Asian conflict.[60] Heretofore, the General Board of the Navy, Stimson knew, had not considered him a friend; but later on, after his espousal of their cause during the spring and summer of 1932, they became "more conciliatory" toward him and began to look on him as a defender of naval strength.[61]

In March he had been much concerned about possible additional adventures on the part of the Japanese forces. Talking over the situation with Pratt, he warned the latter to be on his guard against any possible surprise attack; the Admiral replied that they were on guard, that the battleships were being kept between Hawaii and the Pacific Coast and were eventually to rendezvous at San Francisco, where they would be out of harm's way.[62]

As a pro-Navy man, Stimson was drawn further apart from the President. When he had told Hoover at a Cabinet meeting on March 8 that he had had occasion to go into the question of the Navy's strength and had found it even more unequal than he had thought to meeting Japan, the President observed that that "was all the more reason for not having an offensive Navy." Stimson's diary continues:

I said I wasn't talking about an offensive but a defensive Navy. After the Cabinet Meeting was over I went into his room and showed him the figures that Pratt had given me, and repeated very earnestly that I thought we were down to the danger point, and that one of our first things to do would be to build up the Navy.[63]

The following month he wrote of his divergence from the President in this manner:

. . . when the President gets warlike, he is inclined to feel the old Quaker urge and say something disclaiming warlike activities which plays right into the hand of Japan, who is watching for just that sort of thing. So today I told him that while I did not want him to say anything warlike, I hoped that he would not announce publicly in any way that he was unarmed. He would be quite ready to withdraw our diplomatic representatives from Japan in unison with the other powers as a next step of showing disapproval. . . .[64]

Apparently Hoover would not have agreed with Walter Lippmann's earlier advice to Stimson that all measures short of force but in that direction, such as withdrawing ambassadors, should be avoided, "for gestures of that kind are effective only if the nation making them is prepared to go the limit if necessary";[65] or, more probably, Hoover did not consider withdrawal of ambassadors as a move in the direction of force.

At the Cabinet meeting two days later, April 5, the President was still unpersuaded that the Japanese were any threat to the United States. When Stimson, with the backing of Adams and Hurley, warned that the President had better keep his powder dry, the latter "said something about phantasmagoria."[66] From April 7 to May 14 Stimson was in Europe, his trip primarily concerned with disarmament and only incidentally with Far Eastern affairs. On his return he learned that his hopes that Hoover would refrain from public acknowledgment of America's unwillingness to employ economic sanctions against Japan had been quashed by two speeches made by Castle at Hoover's insistence. The President, who had recently told the Congress that nothing was more necessary than balancing the budget, said frankly to Stimson that he was so absorbed with the domestic situation that he couldn't think very much now of foreign affairs. When he had gotten nervous about the feeling in Japan and feared "that it might lead to some attack on us," as he explained to his Secretary of State, he had "thought the best way to prevent it was to come out and say that we were not going to boycott them."[67]

Also awaiting Stimson upon his return was the problem of allocating our naval forces in the Pacific. Adams and Pratt had held up a decision regarding the removal of the Scouting Force until they could get Stimson's reaction. Believing that the presence of our fleet was the sole stabilizing factor in the Far East and the biggest asset he had had at Geneva, Stimson strongly urged that the fleet not be returned to the States. To the great relief of all of them, the President, when the recommendation was brought to him, said that "he believed in keeping the Fleet altogether in the Pacific at this time even if it cost money."[68]

Parenthetically, it is worth noting that some confusion about the composition of our naval forces in the Pacific seems to have existed in the minds of both Hoover and Stimson. Both spoke of the Asiatic Fleet as if it were synonymous with certain other forces then in the area. In fact, our naval strength in Pacific waters had been temporarily augmented by Battle Force maneuvers in February and by the annual fleet concentration from March 23 to May 28, held near San Diego. In addition to the group of vessels designated as the Asiatic Fleet, the Battle Force, the Scouting Force and the Submarine Force had participated in the concentration. But by September the Scouting Force was the only reinforcement remaining. This was something less than "keeping the Fleet altogether in the Pacific."

Encouragement from his chief apparently raised hopes in Stimson's mind that Hoover was coming around to a more militant viewpoint. Such hopes were dashed with finality on May 24 when the President sprang his disarmament proposal on the Cabinet. This plan, calling for the abolition of carriers, submarines, combat aviation and tanks, was to Stimson just a "proposition from Alice in Wonderland."[69] A few days later he was surprised to learn that the Army Chief of Staff, Douglas MacArthur, favored the abolition of military aviation, mainly because of the tremendous bite it took out of the Army budget.[70]

Meanwhile the 31st Regiment had become a temporary source of friction between the services and the State Department. The Commander of the Asiatic Fleet, Admiral Taylor, having been assigned with State Department approval—as was standard practice for naval officers who also had diplomatic functions—was normally encouraged to consult with Foreign Services officers in his area. This he conscientiously did during the Shanghai crisis, keeping Consul General Cunningham informed of his actions and of the deliberations of the multi-nation military council.

On March 9, however, the State Department felt that the Admiral and the commander of the 31st Regiment, Colonel Lorenzo D. Gauer, had gone beyond the proper role of military commanders when they forwarded a message to State through the Consul General recommending that the 31st Regiment be withdrawn, rather than referring the message to the Minister for transmittal. When State received word from the Navy Department that Taylor had sent another message, this time directly rather than through any diplomatic representatives, Hornbeck was disturbed by this interference in what he considered primarily a diplomatic concern, and especially at the attempt by a military man to shortcut diplomatic channels. He sent a memorandum to Stimson on March 11 expressing his surprise that the recommendation had been made in this manner and suggesting that the Secretaries of War and Navy be advised to inform their officers in Shanghai that the Administration wanted to keep the regiment there temporarily and that such recommendations should only be made through the American Minister in China.[71] Stimson acted immediately and sent a wire to Cunningham and Taylor advising them that withdrawal was a delicate matter not to be decided without diplomatic consultation with other interested powers, and directing that "any recommendations which any American authorities in China may desire to make in relation to this subject be communicated confidentially through the American Minister for the consideration here of the three departments concerned."[72] The next day, MacArthur came to Stimson's office to discuss the withdrawal of the 31st Infantry. The two men agreed that withdrawal would be inexpedient at the moment. MacArthur expressed the opinion that the pressure for withdrawal "was the political work of Thompson, the Chief of Staff of the Regiment, and that he would fix that by sending a telegram to Hines, who is in command at Manila."[73] The Regiment remained in Shanghai until Stimson arranged for its withdrawal on a transport leaving the end of June.

The summer of 1932 saw no change in American policy, no affirmative decision regarding Japan other than the President's continued refusal to permit economic or military sanctions. After the fighting stopped, Stimson's main concern reverted to what the League might do. On March 11 the League Assembly had unanimously voted a resolution of non-recognition of settlements violating the League Covenant or the Kellogg-Briand Pact. The Lytton Report, unequivocally condemning Japanese actions in Manchuria, was published on October 1. On February 24, 1933, it was endorsed by the League and Japan withdrew from membership in protest. Japan retained the territory she had gained by force; the faith of the American Secretary of State in the efficacy of public opinion was shaken severely; and the President retained his belief that the politics of Asia were of no concern to us.

The Far Eastern Crisis had passed, for the moment. We later learned that for us it had only begun.

BIBLIOGRAPHIC NOTE

The essential source is the Henry L. Stimson Collection at the Sterling Memorial Library of Yale University. For use of the Stimson Diary and other papers the author is grateful to the Yale library staff. Use has also been made of the State Department documents and of material in the Navy Section, War Records Branch, National Archives.

Other studies which were particularly useful, either for additional information regarding actions taken or for the judgments of those involved, include the following:

Bundy, McGeorge, and Stimson, Henry L. *On Active Service in Peace and War,* Harper, New York, 1948.

Current, Richard N. "The Stimson Doctrine and the Hoover Doctrine," *American Historical Review,* April 1954, pp. 513-542.

Ferrell, Robert H. *American Diplomacy in the Great Depression: Hoover-Stimson Foreign Policy, 1929-1933,* Yale University Press, New Haven, 1957.

Foreign Relations of the United States, Japan: 1931-1941, Department of State, 1943.

Hoover, Herbert. *The Memoirs of Herbert Hoover,* Vol. II, *The Cabinet and the Presidency, 1920-1933,* Macmillan, New York, 1952.

Morison, Elting E. *Turmoil and Tradition: A Study of the Life and Times of Henry L. Stimson,* Houghton Mifflin, Boston, 1960.

Smith, Sara R. *The Manchurian Crisis, 1931-1932: A Tragedy in International Relations,* Columbia University Press, New York, 1948.

Information was also obtained by interviews and correspondence with participants. Responding to a request for confidentiality, the names of those consulted are not mentioned here; the author is grateful, nonetheless.

NOTES

1. Letter to Fred R. Coudert, contained in Henry L. Stimson Collection, Sterling Memorial Library, Yale University, New Haven (hereafter referred to as HLS Papers).

2. Confidential source.

3. HLS Papers; letter dated May 19, 1932.

4. State Dept. Doc. 793.94/1838.

5. State Dept. Doc. 793.94/2134.

6. Henry L. Stimson and McGeorge Bundy, *On Active Service in Peace and War* (Harper, New York, 1948), p. 227.

7. Diary for October 8, 1931. Stimson's diary, part of the collection at Yale, will hereafter be referred to as HLS Diary.

8. HLS Diary, October 13, 1931.

9. Letter, HLS to Walter Lippmann, October 14, 1931, in HLS Papers.

10. HLS Diary, October 13, 1931.

11. Confidential source.

12. HLS Diary, October 13, 1931.

13. *Ibid.*, October 9, 1931.

14. *Ibid.*

15. *The Memoirs of Herbert Hoover,* II, *The Cabinet and the Presidency, 1920-1933* (Macmillan, New York, 1952), pp. 367-368.

16. *New York Times,* October 16, 1931, p. 1.

17. *Ibid.,* September 29, 1931, p. 1.

18. *Ibid.,* October 17, 1931, p. 7.

19. *Ibid.,* December 9, 1931, p. 21.

20. *Ibid.,* April 20, 1932, p. 1.

21. *Annual Report of the Navy Department,* 1932, p. 9.

22. Hoover, *Memoirs,* II, pp. 367 and 370.

23. HLS Diary, October 15, 1931.

24. *Ibid.,* November 7, 1931.

25. *Ibid.*

26. *Ibid.,* November 13, 1931.

27. *Ibid.*

28. *Ibid.,* November 17, 1931.

29. Letter, Taylor to Pratt, in Navy Section, War Records Branch, National Archives.

30. HLS Diary, November 19, 1931.

31. *Ibid.*

32. *Ibid.*

33. *Ibid.,* November 27, 1931.

34. Hoover, *Memoirs,* II, p. 366.

35. State Dept. Doc. 793.94/3117.

36. State Dept. Doc. 793.94/3437b.

37. HLS Diary, January 10, 1932.

38. State Dept. Doc. 793.94/3610-3/5.

39. HLS Diary, January 25, 1932.

40. *Ibid.*

41. *Ibid.*

42. *Ibid.,* January 26, 1932.

43. *Ibid.*

44. *Ibid.,* January 29, 1932.

45. *Ibid.,* January 30, 1932.

46. *Ibid.*

47. *New York Times,* February 1, 1932, p. 1; February 2, 1932, p. 17.

48. HLS Diary, January 26, 1932.

49. *Ibid.,* February 1, 1932.

50. *Ibid.,* February 3, 1932.

51. *Ibid.,* January 29, 1932.

52. *Ibid.,* February 9, 1932.

53. *Ibid.,* February 20, 1932.

54. *Ibid.,* February 24, 1932.

55. Full text of the Borah Letter is found in Department of State, *Foreign Relations: Japan, 1931-1941,* 1943, I, pp. 83-87. See also the excellent account of the circumstances leading up to the letter, and the reactions to it, in Robert H. Ferrell, *American Diplomacy in the Great Depression: Hoover-Stimson Foreign Policy, 1929-1933* (Yale University Press, New Haven, 1957), pp. 178-188. This also includes the text of the Letter, pp. 188-193.

56. HLS Diary, February 25, 1932.

57. *Ibid.,* March 1, 1932.

58. Letter, HLS to Henry P. Fletcher, February 27, 1932, quoted in Ferrell, *American Diplomacy in the Great Depression,* p. 187.

59. HLS Diary, January 26, February 25, April 3, 1932.

60. Cf. William V. Pratt, "Our Naval Policy," in *U. S. Naval Institute Proceedings,* July 1932, LVIII, pp. 953 ff.; HLS Papers, Letter, Pratt to Stimson, May 19, 1932.

61. HLS Diary, September 16, 1932.

62. *Ibid.,* March 2, 1932.

63. *Ibid.,* March 8, 1932.

64. *Ibid.,* April 3, 1932.

65. Letter, Walter Lippmann to HLS, December 22, 1931, HLS Papers.

66. HLS Diary, April 5, 1932.

67. *Ibid.,* May 16, May 19, 1932.

68. *Ibid.,* May 20, 1932.

69. *Ibid.,* May 24, 1932.

70. *Ibid.,* June 3, 1932.

71. State Dept. Doc. 793.94/4762.

72. State Dept. Doc. 793.94/4645.

73. HLS Diary, March 10, 1932.

EDITORIAL COMMENTS

Today, in the third quarter of the twentieth century, an earlier world in which our sole responses to imperialist aggression were efforts to secure moral condemnation by public opinion and by bluff, seems far removed. Yet in the early 1930's, the wave of revulsion over the ill-starred and ill-managed slaughter of World War I, the distasteful revelation of secret treaties, the great swing of the pendulum in the form of revisionist histories created a public response that left little else to rely on.

Today, that world in which the Army Chief of Staff welcomed a cut in the Army's appropriations as a necessary cure for depression, and looked forward to the quelling of domestic riots of the unemployed as one of the Army's most important tasks, is strange indeed. Yet this was the world in which Hoover and Stimson, Hurley and MacArthur, Adams and Pratt lived and whose limits they did not dream of transcending.

When this background is recalled, the actions of the major participants in the Washington debates about the Far Eastern crisis fall into place in a logical pattern. A major employment of American military force was conceived of solely for defense against direct attack —possibly only direct attack on the continental United States, though no firm decision of this sort was made. (The willingness to use military force to protect American lives and property in far places was a very limited exception to the general rule.) America had no military alliance, would make none. Participation in the League of Nations was strictly confined to modest and informal cooperation. Economic sanctions, a potential tool for policy, were forbidden—and no American statesman was allowed to threaten war.

What, with this state of mind, would Hoover allow, what could Stimson ask for? An appeal to the moral forces in the world, non-recognition as a device for showing Japan our disapproval, the modest bluff of keeping much of the Navy in the Pacific, the more successful bluff or minor action of stationing a few troops in China. With our friends—friends, not allies —we helped to discourage the Japanese from taking over the International Settlement in Shanghai. But the Japanese drive for what Japanese statesmen later called the Greater East Asia Co-Prosperity Sphere was neither halted, delayed, nor even discouraged.

In retrospect, Stimson's dark forebodings showed prescience; equally, however, Hurley's distasteful mockery of Stimson's attempts to mobilize world opinion and to bluff a little was based on practical political judgments. Both men were aware that our potential military power was not mobilized and that the President and the people alike refused to take any action that might induce war. Linked with this premise lay the widely though not universally shared assumption that sanctions other than moral aid constituted an inducement to war, as, of course, did any serious involvement even for defense with friendly nations or with the League of Nations.

In this climate, why endeavor to provide machinery for military-political-economic consultations within our government? Why concern oneself with the military implications of a diplomacy confined to international morality? Why interview the Chief of Naval Operations if he had no fleet capable of major war, and no expectation that he would be allowed to use what he had except to protect, as far as he could, American lives and property in a very few localities, or to defend the United States itself in the event of an almost unimaginable attack?

The hollow negative that constituted the inevitable response to questions like these essentially reflected a belief that war was an avoidable evil and that the United States could live happily and virtuously alone in a sinful world. Effective military preparations, effective civil-military relations had to await the modification of this belief. In 1931, Stimson could lay great stress on his role as Secretary of State, *primus inter pares,* to the annoyance of Adams and Hurley; he could call on the Chief of Staff and the Chief of Naval Operations and their aides for technical information. Yet his primacy in the Cabinet added no strength to his persuasive powers with the President; he had no need to concern himself with possible military opposition to his policies, but by the same token, his policies could not be based on military support, either as spear or shield.

THE HELIUM CONTROVERSY

MICHAEL D. REAGAN

ASSISTANT PROFESSOR OF POLITICAL SCIENCE

MAXWELL SCHOOL OF CITIZENSHIP AND PUBLIC AFFAIRS

SYRACUSE UNIVERSITY

CONTENTS

The Helium Controversy   45

Bibliographic Note   55

Notes   56

Editorial Comments   58

THE HELIUM CONTROVERSY

Thirty-six persons died as a result of the explosion of the German dirigible *Hindenburg* at the U. S. Naval Air Station, Lakehurst, New Jersey, on May 6, 1937. Official investigations of the airship tragedy disclosed that these deaths would have been averted had the *Hindenburg's* lifting power been provided by non-inflammable helium rather than the highly flammable hydrogen.

Why Deutsche Zeppelin Reederei, G.m.b.H., the German Zeppelin company, had not used helium was an easily answered question: hydrogen's greater lifting power significantly improved the payload capacity of the airship. The company was, of course, also aware that the United States had a world monopoly of helium, and that since World War I the Congress had put into law a policy of strict conservation and no exportation without Army, Navy and Commerce recommendation and Presidential approval.[1] The legislation making export extremely difficult for any purpose and impossible for commercial airship use was apparently based on the unexamined assumption that the demonstrated utility of airships in World War I would hold true in future wars also.

The German Zeppelin company, fearing that the *Hindenburg* disaster would destroy public confidence in airships unless safer travel could be assured for the future, promptly got in touch with the Secretary of the Interior, Harold L. Ickes, to request that they be permitted to purchase 10 million cubic feet of helium from the United States to inflate the *LZ-130* then under construction.[2] (The production and sale of helium were under the jurisdiction of the Bureau of Mines, which was a unit within Ickes' department.) Ickes raised the matter at a Cabinet meeting on May 14. The Cabinet members were simultaneously sympathetic to the German request for humanitarian reasons and hesitant because fearful that if we began to sell helium to foreign countries it might be used for war purposes. At Ickes' suggestion, President Roosevelt appointed an *ad hoc* committee of the Secretaries of Interior, War, Navy and Commerce—but not State—to consider what the Government's policy ought to be.[3]

A policy report was returned a week later favoring export for commercial use provided satisfactory safeguards could be devised to assure that such helium would not be diverted to military use. The Committee members were aware of pending helium legislation then under consideration by the Senate and House Committees on Military Affairs.[4] These bills provided for government purchase of the only important private producer of helium and also for the commercial export of helium by the government; the goals were to aid in the development of commercial airships and to increase the production of helium so that its price could be reduced and its benefits become available to the medical profession. The War, Navy and Commerce Departments favored this legislation,[5] the Interior Department had helped draft it, and the Bureau of the Budget had cleared it.[6] Fortuitously, government policy applicable to the request of the German airship interests was already in the process of receiving legislative sanction.

The *ad hoc* Committee's report, submitted by the President to the Senate and House Committees on Military Affairs on May 25, put the approval of export sales on a basis of moral obligation and public relations.

With adequate safeguards against the military use [of helium] . . . it would appear to be the duty of this country as a good neighbor to share any unneeded surplus . . . thus promoting good will.[7]

It was suggested that adequate controls could be simply arranged. By estimating airship replenishment needs, the supply could be cut off in times of stress, thus quickly grounding all airships.

The stated motivation in the report was not the only operative consideration in the situation, for the services had recently come to favor the export of helium in sufficiently large quantities to supply commercial airship needs. Requests for commercially useful quantities had been steadily rejected during the early 'thirties. In 1934, for example, Secretary of the Navy Claude Swanson had recommended to Ickes that a French request for 7 million cubic feet to be delivered over a period of five years be denied. The expressed reasons were that

Helium is a military asset which gives this country an advantage over all others if we continue to monopolize its possession. To give our commercial competitors the advantage of using helium in the future development of commercial lighter-than-air transportation seems inadvisable.[8]

Behind the first of these statements lay the assumption that European nations would make airships a part of their military arsenal if they had helium. Actually, when conscious re-evaluation of helium policy was undertaken in 1937 doubts arose concerning both the dependence of military airships on helium and their value to nations other than those (such as the United States) with long coast lines to guard. It should also be noted that the Navy Secretary's regard for commercial airship development was not an unusual concern, but an expression of the Navy's traditional peacetime role of protector and promoter of American trade and industry.

In 1935 a similar request originating from Japan had been rejected by the Secretary of War with the statement that

Helium is a military asset which gives to this country an advantage over all others. Even though it is to be used for a commercial airship, such a craft is perfectly capable of being used for military reconnaissance as well as being used by this foreign nation as a rival to our aerial commerce.[9]

The 1937 report of the *ad hoc* Cabinet Committee thus represented a sharp shift in policy. The argument for embargo on grounds of military necessity was abandoned in favor of mere restrictions against the military use of exports; the argument based on commercial rivalry evaporated.

The rationale given in the earlier period should not be taken entirely at face value, however, at least with respect to the Navy De-partment, the agency with direct concern. The reasons given are rather to be explained in large part as *pro forma* answers for public consumption.[10] The key to the change in Navy Department policy is to be found in the substantial change in the production of helium.[11] During the early 1920's, when the Bureau of Mines was the only producer, the cost was prohibitively high and the quantity insufficient even for the Navy's purposes alone. The jibe was thrown at the Navy that it was over-ambitious in trying to run two airships with helium for one. In 1926 the *Shenandoah* was lost and the Navy's supply-demand situation came into temporary balance. At about this time, a commercial producer came into existence, and from 1929 to 1932 the Navy had an adequate supply, though no excess, by using the commercially produced helium. In 1933 the *Akron* was lost, and in 1935, the *Macon*. With an increased supply and no ships left to use the gas, the airship enthusiasts in the Navy began to favor commercial utilization and development of airships by other nations, which in effect meant Germany. Their only hope of seeing technical progress in airship construction lay in encouraging the German interests and gaining their technical knowledge as a *quid pro quo* exchange for helium.[12] The improved supply situation made this a feasible proposition. (The tie-in with Germany extended back to the delivery to the United States of the *Los Angeles* in 1924 as a reparations ship, and to the construction of the *Akron* and *Macon* by the Goodyear Corporation, which imported German technicians for the purpose.)

The Chief of Naval Operations in 1937, Admiral William D. Leahy, and Secretary Swanson did not share the enthusiasts' belief in the large airship's utility for naval purposes;[13] they therefore had no military grounds for objecting to airship development by other nations, and came to the same liberal viewpoint on the export of helium as had the airship supporters —although by the opposite route.

Navy policy on dirigibles at this time was unsettled. The General Board had recommended experimental development of rigid airships in 1923, 1926, 1931, 1933 and 1934. Naval Air operating policy as formally enunciated in the latter year contained this provision: "To build and operate rigid airships as necessary to determine their usefulness for naval and other governmental purposes and their commercial value."[14]

On January 21, 1937, Admiral Leahy told an Appropriations subcommittee that the General Board was then considering its dirigible policy, and that action toward airship construction was being held in abeyance pending the Board's report.[15] Apparently the report never materialized, or else it had little effect, for a year later—February 8, 1938—Leahy testified that naval policy was "not fixed."[16] And Rear Admiral Arthur B. Cook, Chief of the Bureau of Aeronautics, stated that he had not yet seen a General Board report on the subject.[17]

Under questioning about the merits of dirigibles as had been set forth in the testimony of Lieutenant Commander Charles E. Rosendahl, Leahy said:

The consensus of opinion of the high command of the Navy has been that up to the present time rigid airships have not been particularly useful, and while there is quite a reasonable possibility that Commander Rosendahl may be correct in his estimate of their value for naval purposes, the Navy Department up to the present time has not felt it correct to expand our limited naval appropriation for construction of rigids, particularly in view of the fact that no other nation is developing rigid airships for naval use.[18]

Leahy did not object, however, to inclusion of a rigid in the experimental section of the then pending expansion bill.[19]

The most vocal enthusiasts, Commander Garland Fulton and Lieutenant Commander Rosendahl, defended the military value of airships by arguing that the United States could make good use of them in coastal patrol work, spotting submarines particularly, and possibly as aircraft carriers; but that for Germany and the European nations the Zeppelin would not be a military asset: with short sea coasts and close borders easily penetrated by airplanes, the airship would lack utility and would be subject to maximum vulnerability.

Throughout these years, the Navy Department was the only government agency concerned with airships, being responsible both for the development of rigid airships, and also for demonstrating their utility for commercial purposes. The Army had abandoned rigid airships after the burning of the *Roma* in 1924 and in 1930 dispensed with all airship activity with the exception of some captive observation balloons. The War Department was thus not particularly interested in helium on its own account and to some extent may be presumed to have suited its own policy on helium gas to that of its sister-service.

The first signs of a shift in the attitude of the Navy Department came in a letter of August 27, 1936 to Ickes regarding a request by the Girdler Corporation, the only important commercial extractor of helium, for a blanket export license. The Acting Secretary of the Navy, Admiral Standley, said that the exportation of small quantities of helium, say up to 100,000 cubic feet in any one year, could have no military significance.

He also suggested that quantities of 10,000 cubic feet or less, and up to 100,000 cubic feet a year to any one country, might be handled by the Bureau of Mines without the necessity of obtaining Presidential approval as was then the case even with the export of one liter for medical or experimental purposes. Export licenses for quantities larger than the suggested limits, and even small quantities, if they seemed destined for military purposes, should be issued only after consultation with the War and Navy Departments.[20]

The War Department, replying to Ickes' submission of the Girdler proposal a few days earlier than the Navy, had recommended on August 18, 1936 that no blanket export permits be granted, regardless of how small the quantity of helium involved.[21] But the Adjutant General's office, noting the divergence of Army and Navy views, asked the Chief of the Air Corps, Major General Oscar Westover, for an opinion. The general agreed with the Navy view and on September 22, 1936 suggested a control board composed of representatives of the State, War and Navy Departments, and the Army Air Corps and Navy Bureau of Aeronautics.[22] He recommended that the board adopt as policy the expressed attitude of the Navy Department. G-4 also sent a memorandum on the subject to the Chief of Staff, on September 29, urging that the "adoption of this less restrictive policy will benefit the commercial companies and increase their output with a subsequent reduction in the selling price of helium. This in turn would open up new fields, both scientific and commercial, and generally benefit all concerned."[23]

In fact, the Navy had benefited directly from

the ten trans-Atlantic flights made by the *Hindenburg* during 1936, for two Navy officers had been aboard on each flight as guests of the German Zeppelin company.[24] By these developments, the ground was being prepared for prompt approval of the German Zeppelin company's request after Roosevelt signed the enabling legislation on September 1, 1937, four months after the loss of the *Hindenburg*.

Under the statute[25] as finally enacted, the Secretary of the Interior had sole authority and responsibility for the production and sale of helium; but export control was held jointly by the National Munitions Control Board and the Secretary of the Interior.

On October 20, Hull, in his capacity as statutory chairman of the NMCB, formally advised the members (War, Navy, Commerce and Treasury) and Ickes of the German request, which was now for 17.9 million cubic feet to cover one year's scheduled operations between Germany and the United States. Favorable replies were quickly received from all the departments concerned, Commerce and Interior basing their approval on the advice of the Navy Department that the quantity requested was not of military importance. (Regulations adopted by the NMCB on September 3, 1937, to interpret the responsibilities of the new law made this finding a prerequisite to export approval.[26]) On November 23 the executive secretary of the NMCB, Joseph Green, who was also Chief of the State Department's Office of Arms and Munitions Control, informed American Zeppelin Transport, Inc., agents for the German company, that the request had been approved and invited application for a license covering the initial shipment desired.[27] The first license, for 2.3 million cubic feet, was issued by the State Department on January 31, 1938.[28]

All that remained to complete the transaction was for Ickes to sign a contract for the sale. Then the fun began.

Much has been written about the temperament and political propensities of the Secretary of the Interior, not least by Ickes himself. One of the first prominent government officers in the United States to take seriously and publicly the Nazi threat to Western values, he was by early 1938 suspicious of anything Germany did. In late February the Lakehurst tragedy had receded from his thoughts and he was becoming less concerned about humanitarian aid to German aviation than about possible use of any helium we might supply to support the German military machine. Accordingly, he instructed his solicitors to "stiffen up considerably" on the contractual terms, and to put in safeguards to prevent military use of helium.[29]

On March 12 Hitler invaded Austria. From that point on, Ickes adamantly refused to approve the sale to Germany since he doubted whether it was right, in view of Germany's "ruthless and wanton invasion of Austria,"[30] to supply the aggressor with what he believed to be an important item of military material. His humanitarian sympathies had shifted focus from passengers on German airships to the victims of Nazi aggression.

His statutory authority over the sale of helium gave the Secretary a convenient means by which to thwart the approval already given to the German request. While export regulations were established by the NMCB, he alone could set rules to govern the conditions of sale. On March 14 he used this authority to amend regulations he had previously established by instituting, with Presidential approval, a requirement of "liquidation damages" in the form of a penal bond, the amount of which in this case he suggested be set at $500,000.[31] Apparently he anticipated that the prospective purchaser would refuse to comply with this new requirement.

Although the regulation was promulgated by Ickes alone and without prior consultation with other departments, it did involve the Secretaries of War, Navy and State by requiring their concurrence in setting the amount of the bond. This unilateral imposition of additional duties was not appreciated by the secretaries concerned (Cordell Hull for State, Claude A. Swanson for Navy, and Harry H. Woodring for War). They reacted immediately and on March 15, before Ickes had formally requested their concurrence in the suggested amount of the bond, they jointly sent a counter-proposal suggesting a formula for much less severe penalties:

Although the administration of Section 3 of the Helium Act would appear from the terms of that Act to be a matter exclusively within your jurisdiction, this amendment will require the concurrence of the Secretaries of State, War, and the Navy in connection with every contract for the purchase of helium which is to be used for airship inflation and exported within the meaning of the

Act. In order to fulfill the obligation placed upon us by this amendment to the regulations of the Department of the Interior, we propose that the amount of the liquidated damages to be prescribed in each contract be fixed in advance at such definite figure between 100 per cent and 150 per cent, inclusive of the sales value of the helium to be purchased as your judgment may dictate, and that the figure so fixed by you be used in every case in determining the amount of the liquidated damages to be prescribed.[32]

This proposal, signed by Hull, Swanson, and Assistant Secretary of War Louis Johnson, would have worked out to maximum damages of $32,000 in the contemplated purchase for the *LZ-130.*

Ickes received the letter on March 18 and decided to raise the question at the Cabinet meeting that day. The President thought that we were under a moral obligation to complete the sale and this feeling was shared by Hull. Ickes did not give way and in the end Roosevelt suggested that the matter be held in abeyance until he returned from a ten-day trip to Warm Springs, which he was to begin the following Tuesday.[33]

Ickes did not choose to let the matter rest there. The next day he wrote to Hull, Woodring and Swanson submitting the latest draft of the contract for their consideration, the draft including provision for damages of $500,000. Ignoring the existence of the March 15 counterproposal, he explained that he thought the very substantial amount of the penalty was needed "to deter any departure from the Act or regulations with respect to use in military operations."[34] The battle lines were clearly drawn now. Without waiting for the comments he had requested from the other secretaries, Ickes went to Roosevelt on March 22—before the President left for Warm Springs—and reportedly received Presidential approval for rejection of the guaranties which the German company had so far offered.[35]

In the War Department, a memorandum was prepared by G-4 on March 30 to brief the Chief of Staff on Ickes' request for comments on the liquidation damages provision. After pointing out that the Department had not been consulted in advance and recalling the March 15 proposal of 100-150 per cent damages, G-4 remarked that the Secretary of the Interior "is unduly alarmed . . . the military importance

of the quantity of helium concerned is not sufficiently great to represent jeopardy to the National Defense." Germany *could* use helium in war, but it was not believed any illegal use would be made of it during peace. A cash bond, the Assistant Chief of Staff suggested, would not be an effective deterrent anyway, since a nation planning war would not worry about costs. This memorandum was used almost intact as the Secretary of War's reply to Ickes on April 4. At about the same time similar letters asserting that $500,000 was unreasonably high for the penalty bond were sent to Interior by State and Navy.[36]

Undaunted, Ickes tried a new angle to defend his high bond. In a letter of April 16, he protested that the sales value to form the basis for the suggested 100-150 per cent damages formula could not be determined unless a dollar figure could be placed on the military value of the helium. The gas would be sold at cost for non-military purposes, but if used for war, its value would obviously be greater than its cost price, said Ickes. He would appreciate advice from the Army and Navy regarding the cash value of helium used militarily.[37]

At this point it should be noted that Ickes never accepted—or even showed cognizance of —the Navy Department's distinction between the military importance of helium, which it felt was nil, and that of rigid airships, which, as we have noted, was at least hoped by certain enthusiasts in the Department to be considerable. The distinction rested on the conviction that, for military purposes, the inflammability of hydrogen as a lifting agent was not an effective deterrent to its use because safety is not a paramount consideration in war; that consequently it could not be said that supplying or withholding helium had any bearing on the military use of airships.

The Navy distinction was not contained in the legislation under which Ickes operated. There it was assumed that helium itself was important militarily inasmuch as airships inflated by this means could be used for military purposes. (Of course Ickes in citing the law was in effect citing his own authority, since Interior had drafted it.) In addition, the Navy had not pressed its distinction earlier; on the contrary, it had sublimated its concern over the small quantity previously available for its own purposes by citing the military advantages of helium as its reason for turning down foreign commercial requests. These rationalizations from the earlier period now proved embarrassing when the gas was in excess supply and the Navy wanted to encourage German commercial development.

While the other departments were preparing their replies to his letter, Ickes saw the President again on April 18. Since service experts had testified before the House Committee on Military Affairs that dirigibles had a useful role to fulfill in war, and since the Navy Department was itself trying to get an appropriation for a new dirigible, he told the President that he would be violating his duty if he approved the German contract when operating under a statute which forbade export of helium in quantities of military importance. Roosevelt was "quite open-minded" about Ickes' assertion, which rested on the assumption that the military values of airships and the gas by which they might be inflated were identical. In characteristic fashion, Roosevelt suggested that Ickes drag the matter along a while longer.[38] A few days later, on April 21, Ickes was again in the President's office and took the opportunity to mention that support for his position had been expressed by Senator Sheppard, Chairman of the Senate Military Affairs Committee. Sheppard had also told Ickes that a bill introduced by Senator Vandenberg prohibiting all export sales of helium would probably pass the Senate if given a chance, but he hadn't taken it up yet because he hoped the administration would take the leadership in the matter.[39]

In the War Department, developments were quite different. General Westover was asked to comment on the Ickes letter of April 16. His memorandum to the Assistant Chief of Staff, G-4, stated his belief that no country "lacking a supply of its own would set up a military program which would be dependent upon the securing of this particular item." He assumed that any military program for airships in a country not possessing helium (i.e., any country but the United States) would use locally obtainable hydrogen so that there could be no supply difficulty.[40] The Secretary of War's reply to Ickes on April 27 contained additional arguments:

It is the opinion of this Department that the intent of the Congress by its passage of the Helium Act was that helium, a natural commodity of which the United States has known resources greatly in excess of its own domestic needs, should, for humanitarian reasons, be made available to other nations for commercial uses. . . . Helium in itself is not a weapon but is merely a commodity that possesses certain value when used in connection with certain types of aircraft. In this respect, it is comparable to other commodities such as gasoline when used in connection with bombardment airplanes or tanks. The only known military use for helium is for the inflation of lighter-than-air craft. The military value of such craft, other than possibly that of captive observation balloons, has never been established either in this country or abroad. On the other hand, the military value of heavier-than-air craft has been definitely established. The ever increasing efficiency and wide ranges of use of the latter are causing them to supplant all other means for aerial operations. The War Department has definitely abandoned the idea of employing airships in military operations. . . . The diminishing military value of helium is evident. . . . While hydrogen is highly inflammable . . . its greater buoyancy gives a craft added lifting power and greater maneuverability. Even though helium is non-inflammable, it is still debatable as to which of the two gases possesses the greater value for military operations. Regardless of the inflating agent, however, lighter-than-air craft are highly vulnerable to gunfire and their destruction is a comparatively easy accomplishment.[41]

The War Department, therefore, was doubtful that any nation but the United States would base its military airship program on helium, or that helium was more valuable than hydrogen for such a program. In any event (contrary to Ickes and to some Navy officers), even if the value of helium was tied to the value of the airships in which it was used, they considered this value negligible for they saw no important role for dirigibles in future conflicts. It was at this time, in fact, that the Army was trying to turn over to the Navy even the minor developmental work in which it was then engaged regarding airships. They requested the transfer in order to make more funds available for heavier-than-air development,[42] current appropriations for the latter being considerably below departmental wishes.

Still another rationale for approving the sale of helium was contained in Cordell Hull's somewhat acid letter of May 6 in reply to the same Ickes missive. The Secretary of State, unlike the War and Navy Departments and like Ickes, was willing to relate the military value of helium to the value of airships and apparently thought this value to be considerable. But he believed the regulations approved by the NMCB and the Secretary of the Interior provided "ample safeguards of the nature of those which the amendments to the sales regulations are apparently designed to afford." He pointed out that it was not proposed that the total quantity allotted to the American Zeppelin Transport, Inc., be exported at one time; that the schedule of exports was "carefully considered by the military and naval experts designated to advise the NMCB"; and that

should there be any reason to suppose that there was any disposition on the part of the German company or the German government to put the airships to any uses other than those specified, no further export licenses would be issued under the allotment, all outstanding licenses would be immediately revoked, and with the unavoidable dissipation of the helium already on hand the operations of the airship would necessarily have to be discontinued in short order or hydrogen substituted for helium.

Additional considerations, apparently aimed at Ickes' self-appointed role as foreign-military policy maker, were presented in Hull's letter:

I am not interested in the commercial exploitation of helium but solely in carrying out the duties relating to the exportation of helium delegated to me by the Helium Act, and, in the case of the particular proposed shipment to Germany to which your letter refers, in avoiding, if possible, any action on the part of this Government which might unnecessarily jeopardize American interests in Germany or give rise to any well-founded charge of bad faith on our part. . . . [The liquidation damages amendments to the sales regulations] would appear to impose unnecessarily onerous burdens upon prospective purchasers so that their application might operate to defeat the intent of the Helium Act in respect to the advancement of commercial aviation by airships and the policy of this Government as indicated by the letter signed by the Secretaries of State, War, the Navy, Commerce, and the Interior which was transmitted by the President to the Chairmen of the Military Affairs Committees of both Houses of Congress with an expression of his approval; by the granting of an allotment of 17,900,000 cubic feet of helium to American Zeppelin Transport, Incorporated, with the unanimous approval of all the members of the NMCB and the Secretary of the Interior; as required by the provisions of the Helium Act; by the action of the Department of Commerce in approving the proposed schedule of flights by the *LZ-130;* and by the action of the Navy Department in leasing terminal facilities at Lakehurst for that airship. In view of these facts, would it not seem that these amendments are both unnecessary and undesirable?

Furthermore, these amendments might be held to constitute an encroachment on the jurisdiction of the National Munitions Control Board. . . . The effect of the amendments would apparently be to control, and perhaps even to prevent, the exportation of helium although the responsibility for the control of exportation rests, under the terms of the act, upon a group of six Cabinet officers rather than upon one alone.

You may agree with me that it would be advisable to submit the question raised by this apparent conflict of jurisdiction to the Attorney General for his decision. If, however, you find, after further consideration, that my position in regard to this matter is well-founded, it is possible that you may wish to recommend to the President that the amendments be rescinded. . . .

I am transmitting copies of this letter to the President and to the members of the National Munitions Control Board for their information.[43]

It should be recalled that at the date of this letter the State Department's public attitude toward Germany was conciliatory; Hull was endeavoring to maintain formally amicable relations. He was consequently fearful that helium, under Ickes' handling, might precipitate diplomatic difficulties which could not be justified by the minor military potentialities of the gas. Both the Department and the American Ambassador in Germany, Hugh Wilson, were also concerned that German irritation over the helium matter would make vain their efforts to intercede with the German government on behalf of refugees.

These fears were not without foundation. On April 13, 1938, just before Ickes sent the letter that provoked Hull's acrid reply, Wilson had cabled to Hull a report on the acute displeasure felt by Prince Bismarck of the German Foreign Office over Ickes' regulations of March 14 calling for a heavy bond to insure that helium would not be used for military purposes. The American Ambassador went on to say:

Unless a prompt solution can be found in this matter I believe that so deep a resentment will be created not only among Party men but among Foreign Office men . . . that it would be difficult to obtain effective protection and fair treatment for American individuals and interests in the many cases that we are obliged to bring before the Foreign Office.[44]

And on May 14, 1938, Wilson wrote to Under Secretary of State Sumner Welles that

this is a period in which the need for friendly requests is continuously apparent, particularly in relation to non-American persons in Vienna in whom we may be interested. We have been able, through the police authorities, to bring unofficial help in a great many cases and I had hoped that this would continue. I very much fear, however, that for the time being it will be exceptionally difficult to get any favor extended.[45]

On the general relationship between the U. S. and Germany another message from Wilson on April 29 put the situation in a very serious light:

In a conversation last night Goering raised the matter of helium. He spoke with deep emotion and bluntness. He said that every German felt that after the *Hindenburg* disaster and the engagement to permit the sale and export of helium which had been more favorable, the reversal of policy could only mean deliberate unfriendliness on the part of the American Government. Relations between Germany and the United States had been brought to the lowest possible point and this over a matter of minor importance to both nations. . . . If it was impossible to get helium the German people would not forget America's attitude but it would not give up thereby the use of airships and would continue them with hydrogen.[46]

Thus Hull's suggestion in his letter that the United States might suffer from a possible charge of bad faith was vindicated. Hull had taken the position because he believed that the original approval of the German allotment in November 1937 had created a moral obligation to complete the transaction. Despite his query concerning the conflict of jurisdiction, the *sale* of helium was under the sole authority of the Secretary of the Interior. Hence Hull could do nothing about the overlapping functions, though overlapping unquestionably did exist.

The strength of ill-feeling between Interior and State, generated by the affair, is suggested by a comment made by Joseph Green in a letter of May 3, 1938, to Ambassador Wilson:

As the controversy has developed in acrimony, there is a tendency even on the part of some of the responsible officers in the Department to feel that it will be easier to deal with an irate and distant Germany than with an irate Secretary of the Interior at hand.[47]

The epistolary phase of the controversy had now ended without decision. The dispute moved to the Presidential level.

On May 10 Roosevelt had a meeting on helium attended by Ickes, Solicitor General Robert H. Jackson, General Malin Craig, Army Chief of Staff, and Admiral Leahy. Roosevelt argued, "quite effectively" (according to Ickes' account) that the helium desired by the German Zeppelin company did not have military importance. He was supported in this by Craig and Leahy. Ickes countered with the assertion that experts of both services had testified that helium did have military value and called attention to the provision for a Zeppelin contained in the Naval Expansion Bill of 1938. "If helium has no military importance," he demanded, "why is a Zeppelin authorized for our own Navy?" Here again, his argument rested on the assumption that the effectiveness of airships depended on helium and that if airships were useful to the United States they must also be of value to Germany. He added a political argument that the sentiment of the country as expressed in the "great number of letters" received by him made it politically inadvisable to export this helium, and that the President "had a perfect out in letting me carry the responsibility." It was finally agreed that Roosevelt would issue a statement saying that he had no authority in the matter, Jackson having made the point that authority lay with the NMCB.[48] Ickes felt that this settled the dispute. Such was not the case.

At the Cabinet meeting on May 12 Hull raised the question again, maintaining that the letters of approval from the six Cabinet members concerned constituted an estoppel. Ickes took issue with this. Hull said there was no use calling another meeting of the National Munitions Control Board if Ickes was going to hold out against the sale. According to Ickes' account, Roosevelt strongly favored the sale, but when he referred to the Army and Navy disavowal of military importance, the Secretary replied that he could not "put my conscience in the hands of the Army and Navy." Roosevelt then asked if he would be satisfied with a letter from the Commander in Chief of the Army and Navy saying that this helium was not of military importance, to which Ickes countered that if Congress had wanted the question to be determined by the Commander in Chief, Congress would have said so.[49] The debate ended inconclusively, which favored Ickes: no decision, no sale.

Ickes now passed the ball to Congress, saying that "If Congress amends the Act and makes more lenient the interpretation of the law, I would not stand in the way of a sale. . . ."[50] He was perhaps aware when he made this statement that Congressional sentiment was swinging toward his own view, as evidenced in a Senate debate on May 14 when Ickes was praised by Senators King, McKellar and McCarran. They, like Ickes, wanted to withhold helium from Germany as a slap at Hitler.[51]

Captain Eckener arrived in this country again on May 7 to plead his case. On May 14 he had an interview with Ickes, which the latter found "somewhat painful" because he had a high opinion of Eckener and did not relish having to disappoint him. He did not doubt Eckener's conviction that a Zeppelin would never be used for military purposes, but questioned whether Hitler might not use airships regardless of any obligations entered into by Eckener.[52] There was no effective way for Eckener, who apparently had a strong dislike for Hitler, to counter this argument.

Under Secretary of State Sumner Welles entered the dispute on May 24 by way of a speech in which he remarked that the cause of world peace is "not furthered by our participation in international polemics and recriminations over internal policies of other nations regarding which we have no rightful concern." The press interpreted this speech as an effort to soothe the ruffled feelings of Axis countries over attacks from high quarters in the United States.[53] Ickes' refusal to sell helium was, of course, neither polemic nor recrimination, but it was linked with such speeches as part of the anti-Nazi movement.

Much more irritating to Ickes was the opposition to his position publicly expressed by Rosendahl, then Commandant of the Lakehurst Naval Air Station and a leading naval expert on airships. In July, Rosendahl visited Germany to attend a celebration in honor of the Zeppelin's inventor and was honored at Friedrichshafen in a gesture symbolizing the close professional ties of United States and German airship men. Upon his return he reiterated his opinion that dirigibles had no importance in European armament and that

the helium sale to Germany should be made.[54]

Ickes immediately countered with a charge that Rosendahl had changed his mind after being wined and dined in Germany. He remarked that "It seems a curious thing that an officer in the United States Navy, in view of his country's refusal to sell helium abroad, should suggest it violates the law laid down by Congress."[55] This exchange did not enhance the cordiality of interdepartmental relations. The impasse continued.

It was apparent to his opponents that Ickes would not be budged from his position, even by the President (who perhaps was enjoying the "family argument" and may not have been greatly concerned over the outcome or perhaps was even in unspoken agreement with Ickes). Since Ickes would not sign the contract of sale, the matter appeared to have been settled by inaction. The allotment of 17.9 million cubic feet expired on November 1, 1938.[56]

On November 22 the result was formalized further by a letter from Ickes to the president of American Zeppelin Transport, Inc. This informed the firm that its purchase application (based on the export license granted by State in January) was being rejected, at least *pro tem,* because the exportation requested required a determination that the quantity involved was not of military importance, and that, since the regulations failed to define this quantity, he was unwilling to assume responsibility for approving the sale.[57] In mid-December a German freighter that had brought 200 steel bottles to Houston, Texas, in January to pick up the then-expected helium was recalled to Germany.[58]

By this time, the diplomatic atmosphere had clouded over and Hull himself was no longer following the conciliatory policy which had governed earlier State Department actions. The change was indicated when, in December, Germany made sharp protest to the State Department over an Ickes speech condemning the Nazi government for its racial policies. Welles, in contrast with his apologetic remarks of the previous May, quoted earlier, this time abruptly rejected the German complaint with the countercharge that it came with ill grace from a country whose government-dominated press was making vile attacks on the President of the United States.[59]

When Germany attacked Poland in September 1939 Ickes felt that his position had been vindicated by events. He was not disputed by Hull. And in the Army and Navy, except for a handful of enthusiasts like Rosendahl, no one seriously cared.

BIBLIOGRAPHIC NOTE

The Secret Diary of Harold L. Ickes, Vol. II, *The Inside Struggle, 1936-1939* (Simon & Schuster, New York, 1954).

Conservation of Helium Gas, Hearings on S. 1567, Senate Military Affairs Committee, 75th Cong., 1st sess., 1937.

Conservation of Helium Gas, Hearings on H. R. 4415 and H. R. 7494, House Military Affairs Committee, 75th Cong., 1st sess., 1937.

Third Annual Report of the National Munitions Control Board, H. Doc. 92, 76th Cong., 1st sess., January 9, 1939.

Foreign Relations of the United States, Diplomatic Papers, 1938, Vol. II, *The British Commonwealth, Europe, Near East and Africa* (U. S. Government Printing Office, Washington, 1955).

War and Navy files in War Records Branch, National Archives; State Department files in Departmental files.

Materials from the files of Hugh Wilson, U. S. Ambassador to Germany in 1938.

The author is grateful for informative interviews with Vice Admiral Charles Rosendahl and Captain Garland Fulton, and for their comments on an earlier draft of the study; and also to Mr. Hugh R. Wilson for making available materials from his father's files.

NOTES

1. 43 Stat. 1111 (1925); 44 Stat. 1388 (1927).

2. This was not the first time that purchase of helium had been considered. Captain Hugo Eckener, German Zeppelin developer and President of Deutsche Zeppelin Reederei, testified on May 26, 1937 (while on a visit to the United States to plead for helium) that he had discussed the question with "Washington authorities" eight years ago. *Conservation of Helium Gas,* Hearing on S. 1567, Senate Military Affairs Committee, 75th Cong., 1st sess. (1937), p. 115.

3. Harold L. Ickes, *The Secret Diary of Harold L. Ickes,* II, *The Inside Struggle, 1936-1939* (Simon & Schuster, New York, 1954), entry of May 15, 1937, p. 143.

4. *Conservation of Helium Gas,* Senate Hearings; *Conservation of Helium Gas,* Hearings on H. R. 4415 and H. R. 7494, House Military Affairs Committee, 75th Cong., 1st sess. (1937).

5. *Conservation of Helium Gas,* Senate Hearings, pp. 12, 13, 18.

6. *Ibid.,* p. 10.

7. Department of State Press Releases, XVI, No. 402 (1937), pp. 397-398.

8. Letter, October 17, 1934, Swanson to Ickes, Navy files JC 1/L14-2, War Records Branch, National Archives.

9. Letter, June 19, 1935, Woodring to Ickes, quoted in letter, July 2, 1935, Acting Secretary of the Interior T. A. Walters to Swanson, Navy files JC 1/L14-2.

10. Interview with Captain Garland Fulton, USN (Ret.), October 8, 1954.

11. *Ibid.*

12. *Ibid.,* and interview with Vice Admiral Charles E. Rosendahl, USN (Ret.), November 1954.

13. Rosendahl interview.

14. Quoted by Rosendahl in Hearings on *Naval Expansion Program* (H. R. 9218), House Naval Affairs Committee, 75th Cong., 3d sess. (1938), p. 307.

15. *Navy Appropriation Bill, 1938,* Hearings before the House Appropriations Committee, 75th Cong., 1st sess. (1937), p. 34.

16. *Establish the Composition of the United States Navy* (H. R. 9218), Hearings before the House Naval Affairs Committee, 75th Cong., 3d sess. (1938), p. 2079.

17. *Ibid.,* p. 2699.

18. *Ibid.,* p. 2090.

19. *Ibid.*

20. Letter, August 27, 1936, Acting Secretary of the Navy W. H. Standley to Ickes, A.G.O. file 400.3295, War Records Branch, National Archives.

21. Letter, August 18, 1936, Woodring to Ickes, A.G.O. file 400.3295.

22. Memorandum, September 22, 1936, Westover to AC/S, G-4, A.G.O. file 400.3295.

23. Memorandum, September 29, 1936, AC/S, G-4 to C/S, A.G.O. file 400.3295.

24. Letter, Leahy (Acting Secretary of the Navy) to American Zeppelin Transport, Inc.

25. 50 Stat. 885 (1937); P. L. 411, 75th Cong., 1st sess.

26. *Third Annual Report of the National Munitions Control Board,* H. Doc. 92, 76th Cong., 1st sess. (January 9, 1939), pp. 102, 106.

27. A.G.O. file 400.3295.

28. *Third Annual Report of the National Munitions Control Board,* p. 108.

29. Ickes, *The Secret Diary,* II (February 23, 1938), pp. 324-325.

30. *Ibid.* (March 19, 1938), p. 344.

31. *Ibid.*

32. Copies in State Dept. files and Navy file JC 1/L14-2.

33. Ickes, *The Secret Diary,* II (March 19, 1938), p. 344.

34. Letter, March 19, 1938, Ickes to Hull, Woodring and Swanson, A.G.O. file 400.3295.

35. *New York Herald Tribune,* March 23, 1938.

36. Woodring's letter, G-4 memorandum and State and Navy letters are in A.G.O. file 400.3295.

37. A.G.O. file 400.3295.

38. Ickes, *The Secret Diary,* II (April 21, 1938), pp. 372-373.

39. *Ibid.* (April 21, 1938), pp. 375-376.

40. A.G.O. file 400.3295.

41. *Ibid.*

42. *Conservation of Helium Gas,* House Hearings, p. 161.

43. State Department file CA 811.659, Helium—American Zeppelin Transport, Inc./76.

44. State Department file CA 811.659, Helium–American Zeppelin Transport, Inc./101, quoted in *Foreign Relations of the United States, Diplomatic Papers, 1938,* II, *The British Commonwealth, Europe, Near East and Africa* (U. S. Government Printing Office, Washington 1955), p. 458.

45. From materials supplied to the author by Hugh R. Wilson, son of the Ambassador.

46. State Department file CA 811.659, Helium–American Zeppelin Transport, Inc./120, in *Foreign Relations,* II (1938), pp. 459-460.

47. From materials supplied to the author by Hugh R. Wilson, son of the Ambassador to Germany.

48. Ickes, *The Secret Diary,* II (May 12, 1938), pp. 391-393; *New York Times* (May 11, 1938), p. 11 and May 12, p. 9.

49. Ickes, *The Secret Diary,* II (May 15, 1938), pp. 396-399.

50. *New York Times* (May 13, 1938), p. 10.

51. Ibid. (May 14, 1938), p. 1.

52. Ickes, *The Secret Diary,* II (May 15, 1938), pp. 396-399; *New York Times* (May 15, 1938), p. 28.

53. *New York Times* (May 25, 1938), p. 1.

54. *Ibid.* (July 9, 1938), p. 1; (July 19, 1938), p. 10.

55. *Ibid.* (July 22, 1938), p. 9; Ickes, *The Secret Diary,* II (July 23, 1938), pp. 427-428.

56. *Third Annual Report of the National Munitions Control Board,* p. 108.

57. Copy in State Department files.

58. *New York Times* (January 2, 1938), XI, p. 7; (December 17, 1938), p. 8.

59. *Ibid.* (December 23, 1938), p. 1.

EDITORIAL COMMENTS

One of the American government's unique characteristics—and it has many unusual qualities, for better or for worse—is the attempted precise assignment by Congress of functional responsibilities to various departments and agencies and to their titular heads. Precision in functional assignment is a more complex problem than is easily visible to legislative draftsmen. Thus the assignment in the Helium Act of responsibility for fixing the terms of sale for helium to the Secretary of the Interior seemed reasonable at the time. Similarly, assigning responsibility for the regulation of helium exports to an interdepartmental committee including the Commerce, Treasury, War and Navy Secretaries, acting under the chairmanship of the Secretary of State, the President's right hand in foreign affairs, seemed reasonable too. What was overlooked was the possibility that neither power-nexus could force the other to act, or to act in a certain way, and that disagreement meant inaction, save for extra-statutory pressures arising from some source capable of generating them—public opinion in some tangible way, a committee of Congress, a pressure group enjoying a forcefully symbiotic relationship with one of the departments, or the President if in a position to exert his powers of persuasion without undue sacrifice, and with a desire to do so.

These commonplace comments on our governmental structure and procedure are applicable with great neatness to the controversy over helium. True enough, Ickes was always delighted with a fight while Hull had a distaste for combat, except perhaps within his own department. Obviously, regardless of the formal statutory powers, Roosevelt could have succeeded in bringing Ickes into line—if he felt the action important; but one may guess that on this as on many other occasions, Roosevelt smilingly permitted an Ickes, a Morgenthau, a

Stimson to carry forth a role in foreign policy that he personally approved but that he could not personally sponsor without serious diplomatic consequences. Partly for worse, and partly for better, the impact of such actions on the functioning of the Department of State left Roosevelt unconcerned.

And where were the War and Navy Departments in this struggle? Hardly in effective counterattack. Essentially perhaps the position is best described as one in which the War Department no longer cared, for it had abandoned all interest in dirigibles, and one in which the Navy's interest was sustained only by an embattled few. In other words, Ickes was not interfering with basic objectives like battleships, tanks, 240 mm. guns or airplanes. As for the Department of State, it found itself in the inevitably distasteful and unpopular position of trying to maintain a "correct" diplomatic relationship with a widely hated nation. It was no love of Hitler that led Hull to seek the sale of helium to the Zeppelin company, but he could not expect universal official support for his policy. The nature of our government precludes the operation of a cabinet with a single voice, and a Secretary of State must anticipate or at least learn to endure the growth of different foreign policies among governmental leaders as well as in the House, the Senate, and the nation's press.

Perhaps the helium controversy can best be taken as an illustration of the great force of public opinion in our democracy. Perhaps too it illustrates the great difficulty of conveying to the public the justification for the subtle use of diplomatic techniques in dealing with dictators, or the assumed military advantages of helping a potential enemy to carry forward experimentation that the United States' armed forces could not then perform. Both professional diplomats and professional men-of-arms might well argue that the need to convince is a sign of democratic weakness. In retrospect, however, Ickes' organizational blockade might be considered an advantage in this instance. Presumably with Roosevelt's connivance, Ickes held out early for a policy that Hull and the others later came to accept. Within certain limits, an adroit leader of a democracy can use apparent obstacles to his own advantage. Quite possibly Roosevelt was deviously acting to his own satisfaction both as Commander in Chief and maker of foreign policy. In any event, the helium controversy hardly demonstrated the weakness of our democracy.

BIRTH AND DEATH OF THE M-DAY PLAN

ALBERT A. BLUM

ASSOCIATE PROFESSOR, SOCIAL SCIENCE DEPARTMENT

AND LABOR AND INDUSTRIAL RELATIONS CENTER

MICHIGAN STATE UNIVERSITY

CONTENTS

I Organization for Industrial Mobilization Planning   63

II Planning for Economic Mobilization, 1920-30   65

III Planning for Economic Mobilization, 1931-39   66

IV Role of Louis Johnson, Assistant Secretary of War   71

V Industrial Mobilization Plan, 1939 Revision   73

VI Appointment of the War Resources Board   74

VII The President's Plan for Economic Mobilization   79

VIII Last Efforts of the War Resources Board   84

IX The President Inaugurates Economic Mobilization   88

Bibliographic Note   90

Notes   91

Editorial Comments   95

I. ORGANIZATION FOR INDUSTRIAL MOBILIZATION PLANNING

The "M-Day Plan" was the somewhat dramatic title given to the schemes for economic mobilization that were developed during the 1920's and 1930's for use in the event of war. The formal title was "Industrial Mobilization Plan," but this too was inadequately descriptive of the content of the plans, for they included provisions not only for priorities and other strictly industrial controls but also for such other diverse types of governmental activity as price controls, the direction of employment, war finance, and public information.

The planning itself was an outgrowth of our experiences in World War I.

Many people, and chief among them Bernard Baruch, claimed that the lack of planning for industrial mobilization before 1917 had led to much confusion during the war and delay and waste in the production of military goods. The claims were incontrovertible. In March 1918, President Wilson, noting the confusion, appointed his friend, Bernard Baruch, to head the War Industries Board to coordinate and direct wartime industrial production.

The early weaknesses in industrial mobilization during World War I and the improvements effected by the War Industries Board convinced the War Department and others that in order to prevent a similar wastage of time and resources during any future war, planning for industrial mobilization must be perfected during peacetime. As a result, the National Defense Act of 1920, enacted at a time when the future involvement of the United States in war seemed extremely remote, included industrial mobilization planning provisions—Section 5A. This gave the Assistant Secretary of War responsibility for planning industrial mobilization. His planning functions were twofold: "The first is to arrange in detail for the production of Army munitions in war. . . . The second task of the

Assistant Secretary of War is to develop broad plans for the mobilization of national industry to meet the country's complete industrial needs in War."[1] This study is concerned with the second task of the Assistant Secretary of War.

The assignment of responsibility to the Assistant Secretary for this second function under Section 5A seemed clear; yet some confusion existed within the Army because the members of the General Staff also believed that such planning was a function of their office. The confusion was resolved, or largely resolved, by a decision of a board headed by General James G. Harbord. The Harbord decision gave to the General Staff the responsibility for developing strategic war plans and plans for the mobilization of manpower while the Assistant Secretary of War was given jurisdiction over the plans for the mobilization of industry, including the establishment of all agencies necessary for the exercise of all needed controls.[2]

To assist him in this planning function, the Assistant Secretary of War established a Planning Branch. This Branch, made up only of Army officers, did most of the planning for the Assistant Secretary. To assist him further, the Army Industrial College was set up in 1924. The College's job was to train men to handle and to make plans for Army procurement. It was a small school; by 1940, a total of 804 officers of the regular Army, Navy, and Marine Corps had received training at the institution. Most of the work of the students consisted of a group of studies which were often published and used as a basis for planning.[3]

The focus of training at the Industrial College is indicated by the selection of the persons who lectured there. During the 1930's for example, business leaders, particularly the heads of the nation's largest corporations and executives of trade associations, made up by far the largest single group of lecturers. Practically no economists or professional social scientists other than business school economists were invited, and only a handful of the four hundred and fifty lectures were given by anyone who would have been publicly thought of as a New Dealer, even after the advent of the new administration in 1933. John Frey, then Secretary of the Metal Trades Department of the American Federation of Labor, an Army reserve officer, was the only labor union official to speak at the College.[4]

The third agency involved in planning was the Army–Navy Munitions Board, created in 1922. Its duties were those of "coordinating the planning for acquiring munitions and supplies required for the Army and Navy Departments for war purposes or to meet the needs of any joint plans." The ANMB did very little during the first decade of its existence but by 1931 the Army and the Navy had begun to use it to work out their different ideas about mobilization planning. Actually, the Navy was not as much concerned as the Army. First, by law, this was the Assistant Secretary of War's responsibility. Secondly, the Navy, unlike the Army, did not contemplate a need for a rapid expansion of industrial production to meet its needs after war began, and had been far less hampered by shortages than the Army during the course of World War I. Consequently, throughout the whole period between World War I and World War II, it was the Army which did most of the work on the IMPs, though from about 1931 on the Navy's participation increased notably.[5]

II. PLANNING FOR ECONOMIC MOBILIZATION, 1920-30

During the 1920's, the Assistant Secretary of War and his associates started to formulate plans for industrial mobilization. They were urged on by Baruch and other private citizens, especially those who had dealt with problems of industrial mobilization during the war.

For the first few years, the Army planners concentrated their energies on the problems of Army procurement, and neglected the broader questions of industrial mobilization. Indeed, their first essays in the wider field were characterized by vagueness and naïveté, as in an initial attempt to foresee legislative needs: "Upon the declaration of war, the President of the United States is hereby authorized to assume control of and utilize the resources of the nation, by such orders as he may deem necessary, until the termination of the war."[6] Even the British DORA was not quite so loose!

Gradually the planners sharpened their focus and in so doing reflected attitudes widely current at the time. In 1928, for example, there was a proposal for a labor blacklist, and another one for war service committees—"super trade associations"—voluntarily established and without official status, which would "control and police" the industries that supply Army needs.[7] Such proposals were hardly surprising since consultation outside the Army was largely limited to industry and—rather specially—the American Legion.

There was also enhanced concern with government organization for economic mobilization. The planners consistently held the belief that the regular departments and agencies were not suited for new and arduous wartime tasks. It would be necessary to establish emergency organizations; as early as 1922 and 1924, there was some talk in the plans of "superagencies," and the proposal was reaffirmed in 1925. The Army concepts were flexible at that time. Early Army planners were not prepared to fix the number or type of superagencies that would be required, but they believed that some would have to be created and that their activities must be coordinated. The President would have this "supreme authority" of coordination. The 1925 Army planners suggested that the President "may appoint an Executive Assistant who reports directly to him, who will be the authority in regard to all questions relating to industrial mobilization and who will coordinate the work of the various agencies under him,"[8] but this suggestion disappeared in later plans.

During all this period Baruch kept in touch with developments.[9] In 1925, Major General H. E. Ely, Commandant of the Army War College, wrote a reply to a letter from him in which he had criticized the lack of Army plans for a superagency. General Ely claimed that Army plans "do contemplate the organization of a super-agency that will be charged with the supervision of labor, materials, capital, etc., but, to my knowledge, this is planned to go into operation after the emergency is known to exist or to be imminent and no nucleus thereof is planned for in time of peace."[10]

Actually, full-scale plans had to await the coming of Brigadier General George Van Horn Mosely to Washington. He helped prepare the "Plan for Governmental Organization for War," which, because it was finished in 1929 when Patrick Hurley was Assistant Secretary of War, became known as the Hurley Plan. The Hurley Plan had as its unique feature a proposed Cabinet Department of Munitions which would handle and coordinate all military needs. The plan was sent out to be discussed by others. Baruch attacked the idea of a Department of Munitions. He argued that "requirements of the Army and Navy alone are by no means the sole demands upon a nation's resources in war." Because of such criticisms, a Munitions Department was omitted in all future plans.[11]

III. PLANNING FOR ECONOMIC MOBILIZATION, 1931-39

The mobilization planning of the 1920's was in no sense secret, but the successive revisions of the plans were not published and there was little general interest in them. All this was changed in 1930 when Congress established a War Policies Commission to "consider amending the Constitution to provide that private property may be taken by Congress for public use during war and methods of equalizing the burdens and to remove the profits of war, together with a study of the policies to be pursued in the event of war."[12]

For some time the Army had desired a public review of its mobilization plans and now the opportunity was at hand. The 1930 Plan was subjected to intensive revision and presented by Chief of Staff General Douglas MacArthur to the Commission in a public hearing in the spring of 1931. This 1930-31 Plan was the first of a series of four revisions; others followed in 1933, 1936, and 1939. All were duly published and open to public scrutiny and criticism. All four dealt in detail with a variety of specific operating problems like Army procurement; but they all also treated the larger questions of over-all planning for industrial mobilization and governmental organization for the task. In this connection, they developed proposals for dealing with existing governmental agencies, for superagencies, and for steps to be taken in the transition from peace to war.

Under all four plans, existing governmental agencies, like the various Cabinet departments, were practically excluded from responsibility for industrial mobilization. Thus, in the 1933 Plan, the War Department planners stated:

The existing Cabinet departments are not adaptable to the performance of (War) duties. Their functions are specifically defined by law and custom and are not directly related to any of the activities which must be undertaken by the central industrial control in war. In general, they are overburdened by their normal peacetime functions. Several of the more important departments (like the Department of Labor) exist to serve particular classes, both in peace and war. It would be unfair to expect them to exercise restrictive control over the people that they were created to serve. The changes required in our institutions to make use of the Cabinet departments . . . would be immensely greater than those necessary if a temporary organization is created especially for the emergency.

The controls and functions under discussion are not and should not be exercised in peace. The emergency organization would automatically terminate after the war. If these controls were exercised by a Cabinet department, they might be continued after the end of the war to the great detriment of the country.

The greatest objection to the use of Cabinet departments for war control is the difficulty of collecting all the scattered agencies and authorities into a focus and directing them toward the accomplishment of a definite purpose.[13]

Almost the same formula was used in 1931 and 1936; the same point was made, in fewer words, in 1939.

The 1930-31, 1933 and 1936 Industrial Mobilization Plans were all basically similar in their approach to the concept of superagencies. There were differences in name and number, but no basic alteration was made until 1939. To General Mosely, as to others, the superagencies were the "most important part" of the industrial mobilization plans. General Mosely gave his reasons to the War Policies Commission in 1931. He stated that under the IMP

the Army has its procurement activities in war, as has the Navy. These are coordinated under this superstructure, but that is not all. You have certain demands . . . that might come from such activities as the Shipping Board, from the railways, from Welfare organizations . . . —as well as the continuing demands from civil life. Those agencies all head up to this super organization and are coordinated by it and that is a very important thing for us to bear in mind, because even if the War Department had a fine plan and the Navy Department had a fine plan in itself, if they were not directed through one agency by the President of the United States, the system would fail.[14]

In the plan offered by the War Department to the War Policies Commission in 1931, the superagencies would have two functions: an advisory one as members of the President's Advisory War Council and an executive one as active war agencies. Four superagencies were to be organized: Director of War Industry, Director of Selective Service, Director of Public Relations, and Administrator of Labor. Provision was also made for National Service Corporations, authorized to conduct business-type activities like War Trade, War Finance, and Shipping. The key superagency was to be the Director of War Industry which was to handle requirements, priorities, and facilities, and coordinate industrial expansion and production through war service committees.

The 1933 Plan made certain changes in the superagencies. A War Trade Administration was added as a superagency to be on the Advisory Defense Council. The name of Director of War Industry was changed to War Industries Administration. Two independent boards were proposed: the Price Control Committee and the Capital Issues Committee (to handle stock market operations). Several National War Service Corporations were also suggested.[15]

In the 1936 IMP certain other changes were made. No longer were provisions made for National War Service Corporations or for independent boards. Instead, the number of superagencies was increased. The War Industries Administration became the War Resources Administration. Other superagencies were War Trade, War Labor, Public Relations, Selective Service, Price Control and War Finance Control.[16] In nearly the same words as the 1933 IMP, the 1936 IMP described the key role of the War Resources Administration (War Industries Administration in 1933):

The War Resources Administration is the pivot about which the wartime industrial control turns. It is the most powerful arm of the President for converting the industries into war uses. It is the meeting point of the war machine and industry. It is the first national superagency established and can operate to a limited degree under the wartime

powers of the Government and existing legislative authority until additional legislation is secured to cover the full control powers herein set forth. It will clear requirements for the Government war agencies, industry, and the civilian population, allocate to manufacturing units suitable portions of the requirements of the armed forces and of the civilian population, apportion to such facilities proportionate parts of existing stocks of available production of raw materials or of finished parts subsidiary to the manufacture of primary items, assign priority of production and delivery to war materials, curtail nonessential production, eliminate wasteful production by various restrictions, and collaborate with other governmental agencies in controlling prices.[17]

Though the War Resources Administration in the 1931, 1933, and 1936 Plans, no matter what its specific name, had these important powers and was the main superagency, it was not superior to the other superagencies and had to coordinate its program and policies with the others.

The problem of transition from peace to war concerned the Army in its planning activities. In testimony before the War Policies Commission, General MacArthur outlined a proposed procedure. After the beginning of an emergency, the President would probably call the chairmen of the superagencies and their assistants to Washington. Lists of names of those qualified for such positions would be kept current by the Army. Until the operation of these agencies could get into full swing, Army officers, who had been studying the problem, would be assigned as the temporary nuclei of the new organizations.[18]

In the 1936 Plan, the Army-Navy Munitions Board was made responsible for handling the transition from peace to war. When war appeared imminent, the ANMB was to undertake the duties of the War Resources Administration. The War Resources Administration was to be the first agency to be organized. Once organized, it was to take over all of the duties of the superagencies from the ANMB until the other superagencies could operate.[19]

Despite the Army's quasi-total responsibility for mobilization planning, and despite its plan for military responsibility during the transition period, the War Department asserted and desired that industrial mobilization be handled by civilians. It reiterated this assertion regularly and with genuine sincerity.[20]

All three plans so far described, 1930-31, 1933, and 1936, were published during a period in which anti-war feeling reached a peak. During the depression, disillusionment about World War I and our part in it greatly increased. The belief spread that it had not been a war to end war but rather one to increase the riches of a few. Revisionist historians attempted to shift the onus for starting the war from the Germans or the Central Powers to the Allied powers, abetted by the United States, and led by the "Merchants of Death" or the arms manufacturers, or more generally, to a sinister international arms conspiracy. Revelations about the admitted attempts of representatives of interested industries to prevent international agreements on arms reductions aided the Nye Committee, investigating the arms manufacturers, in impressing the public with a conveniently simple explanation of the causes of war. Conventional economic dogmas of the period stressed government economy as the basic cure for the depression; military budgets were an obstacle to recovery. And Marxist notions, though never popular in America, received some impetus from the depression: "capitalism" was the cause of both war and depression.

President Roosevelt, unhappy about the Nye Committee and uncertain about what to do, set up a committee to formulate plans for mobilization legislation. The chairman of the committee was Bernard M. Baruch, who had urged its formation, and most of the members were Cabinet officers; but the committee's brief efforts were fruitless. The need for mobilization legislation had almost no supporters.[21]

The anti-war feeling found expression in various forms—international declarations outlawing war, reduced expenditures for defense, and loudly expressed objections to military planning of all sorts. It is no wonder then that such phrases as "Blueprint for Fascism," "Iron-Heel Dictatorship," and "unblinking Frankenstein monster" were used to describe the industrial mobilization plans.[22]

The climate of opinion was unfavorable; but the Army's procedures were not well calculated to change it. The plans of the 1930's were published, but there was no active attempt to educate people generally to their significance and rationale. Furthermore, during this period there was loss of contact with one increasingly important segment of American society—organized labor.

During the 1920's there had been intermittent consultation with the American Federation of Labor on the Army's plans for industrial mobilization. John Frey represented labor in dealing with Army plans, and was commissioned a lieutenant colonel in the Reserve Corps. Despite this, relations remained generally unsatisfactory. The blacklist provision, so offensive to labor, was omitted after 1928, but was not forgotten; and there was a sharp difference of opinion over the Army's consistent views that certain types of protective legislation, like the child labor laws, would have to be suspended in wartime.

For a brief period there seemed to be a prospect of harmony. The Army Chief of Staff, General Charles P. Summerall, believed that the AFL should be asked to cooperate with the military,[23] and as early as March 1931, while the War Policies Commission was still in session, a former union man, Lieutenant Colonel C. B. Ross of the Planning Board, was working on a new labor section for the next revision of the IMP. In his draft, the AFL was mentioned by name and "organized labor" was to be represented on the Labor Administration's advisory council.

In 1932, Ross submitted the proposed labor section containing these provisions to the AFL for comment. President William Green replied that the executive council of the AFL had expressed themselves "as finding nothing objectionable in the plan submitted." G-1, on the other hand, did find the place accorded "organized labor" and the AFL objectionable. One officer wrote that the plan was "developed for the purpose of protecting the interests of labor." Another argued that it gave "Union Labor an opportunity to be the controlling factor." The plan was consequently revised and the plan favored by G-1 won out. All references to the AFL (this was before the organization of the CIO) and organized labor were omitted from the plan. The 1933 IMP further described the qualifications of the War Labor Administrator as one who "should be an outstanding *industrial* leader." Organized labor attacked this provision. From 1933 until shortly before the start of the war in Europe in 1939, organized labor was not consulted about the IMPs, while business groups continued to be. In 1939, John

Frey along with the Secretary of the NAM was consulted concerning the labor provisions of the 1939 IMP. The War Department, however, did not discuss the plan with the CIO. John L. Lewis, the President of the CIO, first saw the 1939 IMP on September 21, 1939, by which time it had been made clear that the IMP would not be implemented. Union leaders remained prominent among the critics of the IMPs during all of the 1930's.[24]

The War Department also failed to consult with the Department of Labor concerning the 1933 plan. General Hugh Johnson later wrote that "if Madam Secretary [Frances Perkins] ever read the proposed War Labor Administration, she would hit the ceiling." What Miss Perkins did do in January 1935 was to ask the Secretary of War to permit a representative of the Department of Labor to keep the War Department informed of labor trends. The Secretary of War agreed. But little came of this.[25] In 1938, Miss Perkins again protested the lack of labor representation in the planning. She wrote the President that she believed the Labor Department should be involved in the plans from the beginning "and that it [the Department] will deal with the labor people on their behalf and see that the original programs are adequately thought out to protect and satisfy all the needs of labor." The then Assistant Secretary of War, Louis Johnson, agreed to the suggestion but again no practical consequences ensued.[26]

This reluctance to consult with organized labor and the Department of Labor was in sharp contrast to the willingness, even eagerness, to consult with business. The Assistant Secretary of War's office, from 1933 through 1940, continually submitted the IMPs to business representatives for their suggestions. The IMPs themselves continued to include provisions for consultation with the leaders of private industry via war service committees "which were to serve on [business'] behalf as a point of contact with the Government" on such matters as price control. These committees, among other things, were to formulate plans for increasing production while assuring the equitable distribution of supplies of material among the various industrial establishments.[27]

The plans for war service committees with their neglect of any anti-trust implications, the failure to consult labor, the ready acceptance of business judgments, and the War Department's ideas concerning the personnel to handle economic mobilization as shown by its 1933 suggestion for a War Labor Administrator all illustrate the wide gulf which existed between the War Department and organized labor over the IMPs. This gulf grew wider during the 1930's, just when organized labor was growing in strength and when trade unions claimed the President and many of his Cabinet as their friends.

But the alienation from the strong currents of contemporary American life was far more complete than this. After the first year or two of his first term, Roosevelt, and the New Deal he led, engaged in an increasingly bitter struggle with important segments of American society of which business leaders were perhaps the best organized and most articulate. Roosevelt was the focus of strong feelings, favorable and unfavorable. Even though his following declined after his triumphal victory in 1936, it still was large and much of it was intensely devoted. Roosevelt's chief lieutenants in the government and best-known supporters outside were also deeply, and publicly, engaged in this struggle.

Naturally the Army-Navy planners took no official cognizance of the New Deal–anti-New Deal fight; but in two critical ways they were inevitably lined up with the opponents of the New Deal. First, all of their plans were posited on administration of economic mobilization generally, and not just industrial mobilization in the limited sense, exclusively by business leaders, a proposition that was as offensive to men like Ickes and Wallace and Jackson as it was to the heads of the AFL or the CIO. Second, the planners failed, apparently deliberately, to consult with the heads of the departments and agencies and their staffs. The absence of consultation was not total (at Secretary Hull's request, the State Department was added to the advisory council of the War Trade Administration),[28] but it was marked. It was hardly likely, therefore, that the rest of the government would be predisposed to look with favor on the planners' handiwork; this prejudice was all the more serious because of the latent pacifism of the old progressive tradition that helped to form the attitudes of a fair number of the chief New Dealers, who were opposed to anything as "militaristic" as IMP.

Thus, while the successive revisions of IMP toned down or removed provisions that were most likely to offend New Deal sensibilities, the strong suspicions were not allayed.

The failure to consult had another consequence that perhaps should be mentioned here, though the comment anticipates later events. The absence of contact made it impossible or extremely difficult, apparently, for the planners and, from 1937 on, their chief spokesman, the Assistant Secretary of War, to be sensitive to the President's desires. Many another man misunderstood Roosevelt on many an occasion, but the downfall of the planners' hopes in 1939 would at least not have come as a shock if the Army and Navy had not been so far removed from the flow of action and thought that centered in the White House.

IV. ROLE OF LOUIS JOHNSON, ASSISTANT SECRETARY OF WAR

Whatever the planners thought about domestic politics, the urgency of their task increased with the rising threat of Germany and Japan. They redoubled their efforts and finally found active leadership in the person of Louis Johnson, who was appointed Assistant Secretary of War in June 1937.

The appointment of Louis Johnson signalled a basic shift in mobilization planning. For a decade, Army officers in the ANMB, the Army Industrial College, and the Planning Branch had been responsible not only for the detailed work but for most of the initiative as well. The abandonment of labor consultation, for example—while not opposed by the civilian heads—was essentially a decision of the officers. With the appointment of Johnson, and the evident imminence of a world crisis, mobilization policy became an issue for the Cabinet, the President, and other civilians, even while the responsible officers continued their detailed studies. What had been a technical, almost academic problem for years—despite labor and other criticism—now blossomed forth as a political issue. Diatribe and invective, as will be seen, became the mode of argument.

Johnson came to his new post while Harry Woodring was Secretary of War. They had violently opposing views on the need for rapid industrial mobilization in the face of the threat from abroad. Johnson favored full-scale mobilization aimed at our participation in the coming war, while Woodring, whom Johnson categorized as a "sincere pacifist," was much more hesitant.[29] Johnson expected our direct involvement; Woodring, on leaving the government in 1941, became an active member of America First, an organization devoted to preventing our entry into war. The new Assistant Secretary gave the major part of two years, from 1937 to 1939, to the fight for the accept-ance of the industrial mobilization program, and made over four hundred speeches during that period.[30] In his Annual Report of 1938, Johnson described his activities:

I have visited industrial plants, Government arsenals, air fields, and airplane factories from coast to coast, and I have presented the problems of industrial mobilization and war-time procurement planning in 77 speeches to widely disparate groups—industrial, patriotic, military, and social—in practically every section of the country. This activity has required over 50,000 miles of travel. . . . As a result of this effort, I believe the purposes and objectives of industrial mobilization . . . are more widely and more clearly understood.[31]

In October 1937, not long after his appointment as Assistant Secretary of War, Johnson wrote to Baruch proposing the appointment of an advisory board to study the Industrial Mobilization Plans. "Plans of such magnitude and importance should be analyzed by a disinterested group of citizens who can not only pass upon the merits of the plan but whose review will carry sufficient prestige to be convincing to the country at large." Johnson said that he wanted Baruch to be a member but that he also wanted younger men. In Baruch's reply, he advised that as many members of the old War Industries Board as possible be appointed, with younger men serving as their alternates. "Thus," Baruch told Johnson, "you would have a trained personnel as the older men passed out of the picture."[32] A month later, Johnson spoke with President Roosevelt about setting up a review board. Roosevelt's answer was to tell Johnson to check and see if the Council of National Defense was still a legal entity and if it might be possible to appoint the Council to do what the advisory board could do.[33] As we shall see, the President's suggestion reflected a previous concern with the subject and formed the basis of the plan he ultimately adopted.

The matter again arose in the summer of 1938 at a talk between Baruch and the President. They discussed the need to appoint a committee to make recommendations for a defense program. Roosevelt sketched the idea on a pad. He called the proposed board the Defense Coordination Board. He wrote down a proposed starting date of September 1, 1938 and a reporting date of December 1st, with Baruch as chairman. Baruch again suggested to Roosevelt that the old-time War Industries Board members be appointed to such a board. The idea was dropped, possibly because the former members included such vocal critics of the President as George Peek, Alexander Legge, and Hugh Johnson. When Baruch renewed his plea for prompt mobilization action on his return from Europe in September 1938, Roosevelt refused to set up a Defense Coordination Board but did urge Baruch to repeat his advocacy of preparedness measures to the reporters on the White House steps.[34]

V. INDUSTRIAL MOBILIZATION PLAN, 1939 REVISION

By May 1939, the Army, spurred on by Johnson, completely revised the IMP. This revised IMP was much shorter, kept much of the material in secret annexes to permit frequent revisions and to prevent criticism, and proposed a different concept of organization of the war effort. In the earlier plans, as has been mentioned, the War Department contemplated the organization of a group of superagencies, all separate, with all their activities coordinated by the President. The War Industries Administration, under any name, might have been the leading and most important superagency but it was not formally superior to the other agencies. Army planners by 1939, however, had become convinced that the main defect of the earlier plan had been the fact that they "lacked a coordinating head and depended entirely upon the President, who will be too busy to coordinate the details of our industrial war effort." Instead, the 1939 Plan contemplated the creation of a War Resources Administration which would not only have broad operating powers of its own but would also be superior to and coordinate the activities of most of the other superagencies. WRA would itself handle facilities, commodities, power and fuel, and transportation; it would "coordinate" War Finance, War Trade, War Labor, and the Price Control Authority; Public Relations, Selective Service and "other administrative agencies" were to report directly to the President.[35] However, the over-all dominant role of the WRA was unmistakable; as a member of the Planning Branch put it: "The main difference [between earlier

plans and the 1939 Plan] is that the War Resources Administration . . . has been placed between the other administrations and the President for purpose of coordination, acting as his executive assistant."[36]

Although in the 1939 Plan this "line type of organization" was advocated, there was recognition of the possibility that the President might not be willing to delegate such extraordinary powers to the head of the War Resources Administration. In this case, the War Resources Administration might be placed in a "staff capacity" in its relations with the other superagencies with no jurisdiction over them other than the power to issue statements of policies. But the IMP draftsmen argued that this solution would place "too great dependence on the degree of cooperation which established agencies are expected to accord the Administrator of War Resources."[37]

The 1939 Plan also more clearly envisioned the problems attendant upon a gradual transition into war. It made note of the fact that there might not be a sudden M-Day. The Plan suggested that the War Resources Administration be immediately appointed whenever war appeared imminent. If there were any delay in the appointment of the War Resources Administration, the ANMB should handle mobilization. To the Army planners, conditions in Europe appeared so dangerous that in one of the annexes they stated that it was "highly essential that a War Resources Administration be established immediately." Louis Johnson agreed and attempted to convince Roosevelt.[38]

VI. APPOINTMENT OF THE WAR RESOURCES BOARD

The President was thoroughly aware of the dangers of explosion in Europe and the Far East. Many observers even thought that the United States itself would soon be at war; conceivably the President shared that view.[39] Johnson decided that this was an opportune moment to implement the IMP. The 1939 IMP had just been completed and reviewed by a group of armed services and business leaders. A number of them had expressed the fear that the plans might be scrapped in an emergency if civilian leaders were brought in who had had no previous acquaintance with the planning. They suggested that if the plans were reviewed by a "powerful civilian advisory committee, composed of men of the type from which the administrators would be chosen, there would be less chance of their being scrapped later on."[40]

In approaching the President, Johnson had in mind (as his subsequent conduct showed) (1) the appointment of a review board; (2) substantial approval of the IMP by the board; and (3) transformation of the board into the War Resources Administration, or its equivalent. Roosevelt agreed to the appointment of a review board, but that is all he agreed to.[41] He had earlier accepted the idea of a review by a board of private citizens in his conversation with Baruch in 1938, specifying at that time that the board complete its work in three months. There is no evidence that in 1939 he was prepared to have such a board become an executive agency like WRA, and considerable evidence, as will be seen, that he had no desire for blanket approval of the main provisions of the IMP.

Whether the divergence of views between Roosevelt and Johnson was clear to either is unknown. Johnson first made his proposal for the appointment of a board at a Cabinet meeting on August 4, and at the following meeting, on August 8, the first step was agreed to. Roosevelt directed Johnson to set up a review board. The President also appointed Edward R. Stettinius, Jr., Chairman of the Board of U. S. Steel, as his "confidential intermediary" in selecting members of the board.[42]

To the Army, the choice of members, and more important, the choice of chairman of the board, was of the utmost importance. In a staff memorandum submitted at this time to the Assistant Secretary by members of his staff, this feeling is clearly expressed. "Any members appointed to the War Resources Board," this memorandum advised, "will be difficult to get rid of for many years if not the right type, hence should be carefully chosen. Since, in the interest of prompt action in an emergency, the final decision on all matters will rest with the Chairman of the Board, he especially should be carefully chosen."[43]

Many Americans who had considered the subject thought that Baruch was the man most likely to be appointed chairman. Yet Roosevelt did not choose him for the post although he had considered him for a similar position a year earlier. In fact he specifically opposed the appointment of Baruch.[44] After a conference with Johnson, he remarked: "In thinking about men for the job, don't overlook Ed Stettinius."[45]

Some of the reasons for the President's preference are not far to seek. Stettinius was a big businessman but one who was not known for his criticism of the New Deal. He had worked with the New Deal during the days of the National Recovery Administration. Moreover, as Chairman of the Board of U. S. Steel, he had made a good impression on Roosevelt and his associates by helping to end the open shop in Big Steel. The appointment was well received, but there were critics who pointed out that Stettinius did not have the prestige of

Baruch, that he had had no specific experience in the field of industrial mobilization, and that he was fairly generally thought of as a "J. P. Morgan man"—at the time, a term of opprobrium.

On August 9, Johnson held a meeting on plans for the board, attended by Assistant Secretary of the Navy Charles Edison, Chief of Staff General George C. Marshall, two officers of the Army's Planning Branch, Colonels James Burns and Harry Rutherford, and Stettinius. Stettinius was promptly chosen chairman of the new War Resources Board. The discussion then turned to the choice of the other members of the Board. Stettinius suggested thirty persons as possibilities for the Board. The Army also brought forward a list of suggested names which it had kept current since 1937. Both lists consisted mainly of industrialists like Edsel Ford and Charles E. Wilson of General Motors. Johnson and Edison finally chose five: John Pratt, a director of General Motors; Walter S. Gifford, President of the American Telephone and Telegraph Company and Executive Director of the Council of National Defense during World War I; Robert E. Wood, head of Sears, Roebuck and Quartermaster General for the Army during World War I; Harold Moulton, President of Brookings Institution; and Karl T. Compton, President of the Massachusetts Institute of Technology. Two of the five had had extensive experience with World War I mobilization. The committee first asked Under Secretary of State Sumner Welles for his approval of these choices, which he gave. They then called President Roosevelt by telephone. The President approved the choices, but told Johnson and his associates to consult Baruch and other old-time members of the War Industries Board. Later, in September, the President also appointed John M. Hancock, an intimate friend of Baruch's and a partner of Lehman Brothers, a prominent New York investment banking firm;[46] Hancock had had substantial experience with Navy procurement during World War I.

On the same day, August 9, on which the membership of the Board was decided, Johnson and Edison issued a joint press release, prepared by Colonel Rutherford, telling the public what the WRB would do. They said the Board would have the duties "of advising with the Army-Navy Munitions Board on policies pertaining to the mobilization of the economic resources of the country in the event of a war emergency and in reviewing and perfecting the [industrial mobilization] plans already under preparation by that agency."[47]

On the surface, the review of the IMP appeared to be the main function of the newly created WRB, and indeed this was all that Roosevelt had authorized; but Johnson planned to give it greater duties and powers. The 1939 IMP had visualized the creation of a War Resources Administration which would control the economic emergency agencies and activities of any future war. In Johnson's plans, the WRB was to become that agency in the event of war, and the Assistant Secretary believed that war would come to America shortly. Johnson and Edison declared in the same press release that "in an emergency, the War Resources Board would become an executive agency of the Government with broad powers similar to those of the old War Industries Board. In this event, the Board would report directly to the President as the War Resources Administration."[48]

Almost immediately after his appointment as chairman, Stettinius telephoned Baruch, as Roosevelt had requested. The Board too was anxious to benefit from the counsel of those active in industrial mobilization during World War I. Baruch eventually did appear before the WRB and gave his ideas as did such other members of the old War Industries Board as Hugh Johnson, J. Leonard Replogle, Frank A. Scott, and Charles K. Foster. Other prominent leaders during World War I also appeared before the Board.[49]

While the Board was anxious to gain the benefit of the World War I experience of all these men, it had naturally a particular interest in the views of the most prominent of them— Bernard Baruch. General John J. Pershing had written Baruch that he was "mighty surprised" that Baruch had not been chosen as head of the WRB; many Americans shared this belief. One member of the Board in fact believed that Baruch had been so bitter about his not being appointed that he "set about systematically to undermine Stettinius"; but certainly no actions of this sort came to public attention and Baruch himself denied the charge. When Baruch came before the Board, he gave his strong support to the IMP. He declared that with some reservations "it is practically what I have been preaching for twenty years."[50]

General Hugh Johnson also appeared before the Board. An intimate friend of Baruch and one who was occasionally referred to as Baruch's spokesman, he had from the very beginning been critical of the WRB. Two days after the creation of the Stettinius Committee, Johnson took to his syndicated column to attack the Board's membership. He wrote that while the men were excellent, they had little experience. Moreover, most of them had one basic defect. They failed to live up to the premise that "no man can step into the dictatorial Federal direction of competitive industry when he himself is the head of, or heavily interested in, a competitive unit of that industry." To Stettinius, in two personal letters, Hugh Johnson continued his complaint. He told Stettinius that Stettinius was being used much the same as his father had been in 1918 and that "apparently experience is the last thing to be discussed." "Do you suppose," Johnson asked Stettinius, "the present pack of semi-Communist wolves intend to let Morgan and Dupont men run a war? It is either Louis Johnson's incomparable dumbness or somebody's downright Machiavellianism. Anyway you look at it, you, Pratt, and Bob Wood are sure to be the goats."[51]

Johnson's warning showed insight. While the first newspaper reactions to the appointment of the WRB tended to be favorable, the attacks were not long in coming—attacks on both the personnel of the Board and the contents of the IMP.

As early as two days after the creation of the WRB, Secretary of Labor Frances Perkins wrote to President Roosevelt that since the old WIB had had labor representation, she believed that a trade union representative should be appointed to the WRB "before labor has an opportunity to protest this seeming omission." She suggested Sidney Hillman and Daniel Tobin for the post. Roosevelt wrote a note which he attached to this letter: "Perkins: Labor, Women etc. later."[52]

The *American Federationist,* the official organ of the American Federation of Labor, argued that the awful powers that the WRB would wield during war should be in the hands of persons "above suspicion of self-interest." It further insisted that the WRB ignored a basic principle of the first World War—"namely, the resources of a country are first its citizens and secondly its materials." Consequently, public confidence would not be placed in any wartime organization, like the Stettinius Committee, which did not include representatives of both men and materials.[53] Joseph Curran, President of the National Maritime Union, CIO, asked that six labor representatives be added to the Board.[54] The WRB itself felt the need for broader representation and suggested that the representative from labor be the well-known Commissioner of Labor Statistics—Isador Lubin. The President however did not act upon this suggestion,[55] undoubtedly because of reservations about any immediate enlargement of WRB, not because of any doubts about Lubin.

More violent protests came from those further to the left. The Labor Department of the National Council for Prevention of War warned that the IMP meant dictatorship. If the War Resources Board gained power,

Industry, labor and agriculture would be at the mercy of a small group of men in Washington. The powers delegated to the War Resources Administration are as drastic as any of the controls exercised by dictatorship governments.[56]

Agricultural interests also asked the President to appoint an agricultural leader to the Board. Edward A. O'Neal, head of the Farm Bureau Federation, was suggested as a possible appointee. Roosevelt in replying to one such request, said that a farmer representative might be appointed to the Board at some later date.[57]

Small businessmen also demanded that their voice be heard. General "Pa" Watson, Roosevelt's aide, replied to one such request that Karl T. Compton and Harold G. Moulton would represent the independent businessman and that the whole Board would keep the interests of the small businessman in mind.[58]

There were still other groups that demanded representation but the only new appointment made, that of John Hancock, did not change the nature of the membership of the Board. As a result, even more vehement than the attacks on the WRB because of the groups which were not represented were the attacks on it for the groups which it supposedly did represent.

On August 31, Cyrus S. Eaton, a Cleveland businessman and supporter of Roosevelt, wired the President that all of the Democratic Party's international policies were in danger because of the three "Morgan members"—Stettinius, Gifford and Pratt. He warned that "one of these financial camels might pass through the needle's eye of middle western public opinion, but hardly the whole herd." In a similar vein, another New Deal supporter wrote to Senator Josh Lee to protest that the Administration's move "to make the Morgan group industrial and financial dictators of the nation in wartime is disheartening to sincere New Dealers everywhere."[59]

One of the most outspoken of the New Dealers, Harold Ickes, also joined in. In his diary, Ickes relates how he and others like Robert Jackson, Thomas Corcoran, and Benjamin Cohen grew concerned over the inroads "Wall Streeters and economic royalists" were making in Washington. Ickes agreed with Eaton's criticism of the Board's members. He feared that Roosevelt might make the same mistake Wilson did during the first World War and turn the government over to big business. Wilson's foolish action, Ickes believed, caused the liberals to lose twenty years. He consequently warned Roosevelt: "You are much abler and smarter than Wilson and you have had the advantage of having had experience in the world war but the same thing could happen now." Ickes continued fearful because he further confided in his diary that "the situation is something for the liberals in the Administration to be anxious about."[60]

Ickes did not keep his attack on the WRB within the Administration. He went on the radio to debate with Hugh Johnson at Town Hall. He launched into a bitter attack on the Board as the nucleus of an "extra-legal autocracy which, in war, would destroy both American democracy and the social reforms of the New Deal."[61] Ickes used the vernacular of the New Deal to oppose the WRB. But there were practical as well as theoretical reasons for his opposition. The creation of new agencies, controlled by businessmen, and worse, "super-agencies," would impair the jurisdiction of the New Deal agencies, old-line and new, Interior Department and Federal Works, for example. Thus John Carmody, Administrator of the Federal Works Administration, wrote to the President at the end of August that his agency was ready to "wheel into war preparations."[62] Secretary of Agriculture Henry A. Wallace also

sought to have a wartime Food Administration under the Department of Agriculture's control. His Agricultural Advisory Committee asked the President not to let the WRB handle agricultural problems.[63] Other persons active in the opposition to the WRB and in favor of having the existing agencies take charge of the war effort were Corcoran and Cohen—two stalwart New Dealers.

Corcoran, far more outspoken in his fight against the WRB than Cohen, early became convinced that the fight against the Board was a "last-ditch" struggle to prevent big business from taking over the war effort. He continually alerted the President to what he believed to be the dangerous fault of the Board. He cautioned Roosevelt about Hancock's appointment by pointing out to Roosevelt that Hancock had once opposed Roosevelt on some issue. Corcoran's attacks on the Board became so well-known that one newspaper editorial referred to the demise of the WRB as "WRB sacked by Palace Guard" of Corcoran and Cohen, while one of the organizers of the Board believed that Corcoran "was the powerful 'bête-noire' in scuttling the WRB's efficiency."[64]

Ironically enough, the criticism directed at the WRB did not rise to its height until after August 30 when, as will be seen, the Board members knew that the President was not accepting Johnson's plan. Thus, for example, Ickes' radio debate occurred long after he knew of the President's decision—indeed his knowledge may have incited the bitterness of his attack; but others made their complaints in ignorance of the President's action. Such, presumably (though not certainly) was the case with Lauchlin Currie, the President's economic adviser, when he wrote to the President on September 5 to protest the use of the Brookings Institution as the research arm of the WRB and to urge that he be made the clearing house for all its economic research. Roosevelt agreed without hesitation and so instructed the WRB.[65]

All this was in the future—though perhaps foreseeable when Hugh Johnson published his first criticism of the Board on August 11. At that time, the Board answered Johnson's attack by stating that it would be impossible to man the WRB without using men intimately associated with business. When Board members had to make any decisions involving their own business, a neutral member would be called in to review the decision.[66] This reply did not satisfy Johnson who continued to attack. Nonetheless, after Baruch spoke with him, Johnson did comment favorably on the IMP over the dinner table with the Board members and his attack on the Board abated. But he asked Stettinius, "How much of the long and intense experience of 1917 and 1918 do you think can be conveyed at a dinner?"[67]

The WRB spent many dinners and many hours evaluating World War I experience. Particular attention was given to two organizational problems:

1.   Is it feasible to operate efficiently with a whole series of independent boards, each of which reports directly to the President? If not, what boards, or agencies, should be included under the War Resources Administration and what ones should still be outside?

2.   Should the war organization be independent of government departments concerned with normal, peacetime policies?

World War I experience caused the WRB to come to the unanimous view that, with reference to question one, the whole mobilization effort during the first World War had been "substantially stalled by the log jam at the White House." Further, with reference to the second question, it was the unanimous view that maximum efficiency could not be achieved by agencies mainly concerned with peacetime problems and whose personnel had been chosen for peacetime activities.[68]

Not only were World War I experiences studied, but the Stettinius Committee also hoped that some lessons might be learned from the British experience in the field of industrial mobilization. The Board asked the Brookings Institution to make a study of the subject (as well as a study of the IMP itself), which it did. Aside from the Army Planning Branch, only Brookings was called in to do research for the WRB. The Navy, though represented at the Board, had little to do with its actual work.

In the belief that it would have operating responsibilities in an emergency, the Board started to make ready a list of individual experts in the field of industrial mobilization who could be called upon to take important defense jobs. In addition, the Board discussed or had studies made on such potentially important matters as price control, strategic materials, industrial bottlenecks, plans for plant and stockpile increases, educational orders, organization of war service committees, and the supply and training of skilled workers.[69]

Though all of these subjects of study were important, the key issue facing the Board was not the details of procedures to be used in case of emergency but rather the problem of basic organization for industrial mobilization.

The 1939 Industrial Mobilization Plan proposed in substance a pyramidal organization to run economic mobilization. At the top of the pyramid would stand the War Resources Administration, which would control the organizations below (with certain exceptions) while acting simultaneously as an operating agency with large powers and duties of its own. At the pinnacle of the pyramid stood one man, the War Resources Administrator, who, subject only to the President, would have the final word to say on all matters pertaining to economic mobilization. It was this plan that the WRB had to study.

The Board's first reactions to the proposals were favorable. Accepting the over-all organizational plan, they spent most of their time discussing matters like price control and personnel for key positions. Stettinius told Moulton that he was slated to be the price administrator. Members of the Board assumed that Dr. Compton would be the "key man" in science and that John Pratt would supervise the "over-all operation of the administration." Though the Board was less than a month old, the members must have felt that they were making progress. Right or wrong, on August 30 at their first meeting with the President, they suddenly learned of his opposition to the IMP which had been the base of all their planning.[70]

The President had decided on an alternative procedure for the beginnings of America's industrial mobilization. To understand his decision, it is necessary to turn back to events which had occurred some years earlier.

VII. THE PRESIDENT'S PLAN FOR ECONOMIC MOBILIZATION

In 1936, with the first rush of New Deal activities out of the way, Roosevelt turned his attention to over-all problems of administration, and determined to make major improvements in the organization and procedures of the federal government. Accordingly, in March 1936, he established the President's Committee on Administrative Management: the chairman was Louis Brownlow, the other members Professor Charles E. Merriam and Dr. Luther Gulick. This committee made a notable study of governmental organization and by the fall of the year was ready to discuss its conclusions with the President.

A few days after the election, Brownlow had a long talk with Roosevelt. During the course of the talk, they reminisced about World War I days, when Brownlow was a Commissioner of the District of Columbia and Roosevelt Assistant Secretary of the Navy. They chatted about the War Industries Board and swapped judgments about who did receive and who should have received credit for its accomplishments and shortcomings. Reverting to the problems of November 1936, and the forthcoming reorganization of the government, Roosevelt raised the possibility of establishing under the direct supervision of the White House some sort of agency to handle economic mobilization. (This was five years before Pearl Harbor, but during 1936 the Japanese had withdrawn from the naval disarmament agreements and entered the Anti-Comintern Pact, Hitler had occupied the Rhineland, and civil war had broken out in Spain.) He finally told Brownlow to find out from Judge Townsend of the Assistant Solicitor General's office if there were any World War statutes still valid that might serve the purpose.

Brownlow made the inquiry and discovered *inter alia* that the U.S. Code in Force January 3, 1935 included an Act of August 20, 1916 establishing a Council of National Defense. Although various substantive powers formerly possessed by the Council had been repealed, the Council itself, composed of the Secretaries of War, Navy, Interior, Agriculture, Commerce, and Labor, was still legally in existence, and still had the power to nominate, for appointment by the President, an Advisory Commission consisting of not more than seven persons, "each of whom shall have special knowledge of some industry, public utility, or the development of some natural resource, or be otherwise qualified."[71] Their function, as the title implies, was advisory, not executive.

Brownlow carried this information back to the President, but no further move was made at the time.[72] The President's general proposals for government reorganization, submitted to Congress in January 1937, were caught in the backwash of the acrid dispute over his plans for the Supreme Court, and were temporarily shelved. The reactivation of the Council was put aside, but not forgotten; the President was still thinking of the Advisory Commission in his conversation with Louis Johnson in November 1937,[73] but he bided his time. Actually, the President, who had a capacious memory, quite probably had the Council and its advisory Commission in mind when he sent Brownlow to the Department of Justice.

In 1939, with the new Congress, the reorganization program prospered. The Reorganization Act of 1939 became law on April 30. Besides its general authorization of reorganization by the President—subject to legislative review—the Act permitted the President to employ six administrative assistants.

During the spring, Brownlow was back in Washington, working out the detailed blueprints for reorganization. He frequently consulted with the President, who, despite—and in part, because of—the pressure of world events, retained his vivid interest in effective governmental organization—above all in the proposals for improving the operations of the President's staff, of which the provision for administrative assistants was merely the first step. The next step, embodied in sections of Reorganization Plans Nos. 1 and 2, effective July 1, 1939, was the transfer to the "Executive Office of the President" (created thus by reference, as it were) of the Bureau of the Budget and the functions of the National Emergency Council. On the same day, by military order, the President transferred the ANMB and the Army-Navy Joint Board to his own supervision.

The precise form and scope of the Executive Office remained unsettled; Brownlow addressed himself to this problem. By the end of August, the process of drafting an executive order establishing the organization of the Executive Office was on the way to completion. With war on the horizon in Europe, the President wanted to get his house in order.

On August 29, Brownlow had a long talk with Roosevelt. They reviewed plans for the proposed executive order, which contemplated an Executive Office of the President in six divisions: White House Office, Bureau of the Budget, National Resources Planning Board, Liaison Office for Personnel Management, Office of Government Reports, and Office for Emergency Management. The first four divisions would carry on permanent functions and activities; the Office of Government Reports would assume certain functions of the National Emergency Council, particularly suited to crises, economic or military. Division 6 was left without specific content; in the phrase subsequently adopted, the order merely provided that there would be "in the event of a national emergency, or threat of a national emergency, such office for emergency management as the President shall determine." The Office for Emergency Management was to be a holding company, at the moment without operating subsidiaries, but available as a legal framework to contain and put within easy reach of the President's control such mobilization agencies as might be established.

After reviewing these general conclusions, the President turned to more specific problems —the Industrial Mobilization Plan (1939 model), the War Resources Board, and Louis Johnson's proposal to convert the Board into the War Resources Administration when the signal was given.

It is doubtful that the President had read the 1939 IMP, but there is no doubt that he was familiar with the tenor of its recommendations, and, as he made clear to Brownlow, unalterably opposed to them. Above all, he was determined not to accept a plan under which the War Resources Administration would control and stand between the President and the agencies administering such critical and varied activities as labor, prices, and public relations. (Actually, as has been noted, Public Relations was proposed as an independent agency, but the Army planners no doubt did expect it to receive guidance from the WRA.) The inclusion of public relations in the jurisdiction of the WRA he found especially outrageous. He referred to his constitutional responsibilities and said that these "fellows" wanted him to "abdicate."

Nor was this all. He did not want to turn over this great power, or any large segment of the government to big business and to the military. Whether or not he understood or remembered that the Army and Navy had no desire whatever to operate the mobilization agencies is not known. In any event, he did know that the WRB had been established on the recommendation and under the auspices of the Assistant Secretary of War, and was advisory to the ANMB and that the Assistant Secretary of War and the WRB expected the WRB to become the WRA. Apparently he also knew of the proposal that the ANMB, a specifically military agency, take charge of civilian mobilization if the establishment of the WRB were delayed.

The answer to all this was a flat "no," and Roosevelt then proceeded to sketch his own ideas on a couple of sheets of White House stationery. (See Charts I and II.)

These sketchy charts require no great comment. In Chart I, Roosevelt was spelling out assignments for four of his administrative assistants. The chart was drawn on the spur of the moment, but the ideas it represented were neither new nor lightly abandoned. To illustrate: in due course, Lauchlin Currie was given the listed assignment, as was Lowell Mellet (with direct administrative responsibility for the OGR). The President had already talked

CHART I

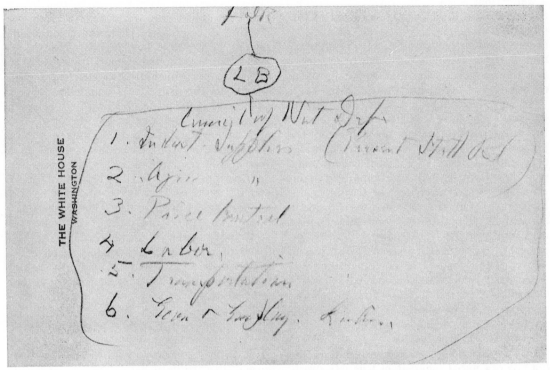

Reproduced by permission of the Harvard College Library.

CHART II

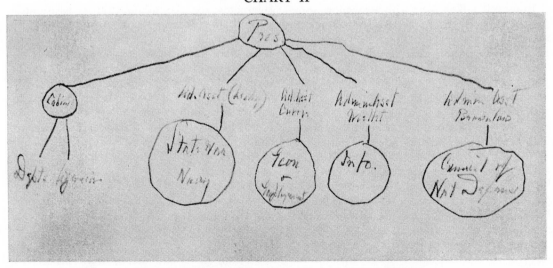

Reproduced by permission of the Harvard College Library.

to Leahy about needing his services "if we have a war,"[74] but when Leahy finally was recalled to Washington, it was as the President's Chief of Staff. For better or worse, the idea of co-ordinating War, Navy and State was dropped, though Harry Hopkins did come to execute a function in these fields that would have left no room for a mere administrative assistant.

The President repeated orally the offer to Brownlow that was indicated on both charts: Brownlow refused, politely but definitely. The job itself was discussed: it was to be the bridge between the Council of National Defense, and more practically its Advisory Commission (this would be the actual content of the Office for Emergency Management) and the President, but without administrative control over either the Council or the NDAC. In the formal language later adopted, the Liaison Officer was to "serve as the channel of communication between the President, on the one hand, and the Council of National Defense and its subdivisions, on the other." In the course of time, this position, as thus defined, was created; it was filled by W. H. McReynolds.

The "Council of National Defense" in the last box of Chart I signified, as Chart II clearly shows, the Advisory Commission to the Council of National Defense: when the NDAC was finally reactivated its organization was approximately what the President indicated on August 29, 1939.

Roosevelt talked over with Brownlow some possible appointees to the NDAC; some of those proposed eventually were appointed, Leon Henderson for price control, for example. The two listed appointments deserve a word. Lubin never was appointed formally as commissioner, though he had much to do with the work of the NDAC. The notation of "Present Stett. Bd." as the nominee for commissioner of industrial supplies was an accurate indication of the distance that separated Roosevelt and Louis Johnson. In the outcome, as will be seen, Stettinius was appointed, the board disappeared; the thought that the whole board might be retained in this limited capacity was perhaps a reflection of the embarrassment that might be caused by the dismissal of such prominent men.[75]

Embarrassing or not, Roosevelt made his dissatisfaction with the IMP quite clear when he met with the members of the WRB the next day, August 30. Not that the President specifically criticized the IMP. Rather, he first talked about the threatening world situation, and the need for us to prepare. Then, still doing all the talking, he began to describe his views on organization for economic mobilization. As in his talk with Brownlow, he sketched a plan similar to the Advisory Commission of the Council of National Defense with six or seven advisers, each reporting to the President, and each having equal power. He himself was to be coordinator, and he rejected the proposal for a War Resources Administration. He also told the Board that the Council of National Defense was still on the statute books and that he was not sure of the dividing line between the functions of the Council and those of the Board. He said that in view of this uncertainty he had asked the Director of the Budget to have the WRB describe in detail its functions before granting the WRB any additional funds to continue its work.[76]

The meeting lasted fifteen minutes. The board members left, hardly having uttered a word, to begin their task of defining their functions. Brownlow also went to work to put into formal style the President's decisions on organization of the White House and the Executive Office. After consultation with Judge Townsend, he drafted an executive order setting up the six-divisional structure of the Executive Office (without reference to the specific assignments for the administrative assistants), and orders governing the organization and procedures of the Office for Emergency Management and the Council of National Defense. These orders showed little departure from the ideas Roosevelt had outlined on August 29. The only change of some consequence was in the organization of the NDAC; it now contained seven, not six, divisions, as follows: Industrial Supply Service, Agricultural Supply Service, Price Stabilization Service, Labor Supply Service, Economic Coordination Service, Transportation Service, and Consumer Protective Service. In a parenthesis following the words "Industrial Supply Service" were the words "now known as the War Resources Board."[77]

Events, large and small, were proceeding apace. On September 1, the day after Roosevelt's talk with the WRB, Hitler invaded Poland. At a Cabinet meeting that afternoon the

President talked of calling a special session of Congress to amend the Neutrality Act, and reaffirmed his views on organization for economic mobilization. On Sunday, September 3, England and France declared war. On Monday there was a special Cabinet meeting at which the President talked of a declaration of national emergency and action under the Neutrality Act. On Wednesday, September 6, Brownlow finished his work on Executive Order 8248 governing the organization of the Executive Office; President Roosevelt signed it two days later, and it went into effect on September 12.

VIII. LAST EFFORTS OF THE WAR RESOURCES BOARD

Meanwhile, the WRB was formulating a statement of its functions, as Roosevelt had requested on August 30. On September 6, it sent a list of functions to the President. In this memorandum, it noted first that Baruch and others had approved the IMP and that therefore the Board could do work of great value in "reviewing and perfecting these plans." The WRB further suggested that its functions would be (1) to review plans of the Army-Navy Munitions Board for the procurement of munitions and to determine how the War Resources Administration might help in carrying out such plans, (2) to render advice concerning the best national economic policies to be adopted during a major war, (3) to recommend procedures which would make these proposed policies effective, (4) to establish the *"nucleus of an adequate War Resources Administration, through which the President may, in an emergency, coordinate his war control over the industrial, material and economic resources of the nation"* and (5) to arrange for the cooperation of other government agencies.[78]

The inconsistency of the WRB's organizational proposal on September 6 with the views expressed by the President on August 30 and duly recorded in the Board's own minutes is obvious. The inconsistency is even more marked in an organization chart prepared by the WRB on September 6, but not sent to the President; this was based directly on the IMP. Why the Board proceeded along these lines after meeting with Roosevelt is unknown.[79]

Whatever the reason, the President's position was unchanged, clear, and determined. He refused to approve the WRB memorandum. And on the same day, he reaffirmed to Ickes his intention to reconstitute the Council of National Defense in case of war and told Ickes that he would appoint additional members to it—Jesse Jones, Federal Loan Administrator;

John Carmody, Federal Works Administrator; and Paul V. McNutt, Federal Security Administrator—all heads of new agencies with quasi-Cabinet status. He further stated that the "Stettinius committee would not be endowed with any authority and would have no direct access to the President." And he went on to say that he had been planning for some time to reconstitute his Cabinet: in the shuffle, two prominent Republicans would be brought in, and, among other changes, Woodring and Johnson would be dropped.[80]

On September 7, at a Cabinet meeting, Roosevelt again stated his intention of not working through the WRB. He referred to the WRB memorandum of September 6 as a "very comprehensive blueprint from which it would appear that this committee was prepared to take over all functions of the government." Roosevelt added that "he had no intention of permitting this and that he would not approve this blueprint." He suggested to Woodring that Stettinius come in to see him.[81]

On September 8, Roosevelt issued a declaration of limited national emergency. The way was clear to proceed with his plans for the Office for Emergency Management, including the reactivation of the Council of National Defense and its Advisory Commission; and many people would have thought this a propitious moment to make the Cabinet shifts. Nothing happened; perhaps because of a desire to avoid entanglements with Congress in its special session, perhaps for other reasons, the plans were shelved—shelved, but not forgotten. The President's attitude toward the WRB remained unchanged; on the same day, he cut their funds from the $125,000 requested by Johnson to $50,000; he also told Johnson that he had heard that the WRB was considering someone as railroad coordinator and that "it was none of their [WRB's] affair."[82]

On September 14, the President met with Johnson and Edison in the morning and then with Stettinius in the afternoon. Roosevelt again repeated his views concerning the organization for control of industrial mobilization. He told them that the WRB would remain advisory though he thought we might be at war shortly. He further told them (as he had already told Brownlow) that the WRB's only function would be that of industrial production and that probably the Council of National Defense with the Cabinet officers inactive would handle economic mobilization.

On the following day, Johnson, Edison and Stettinius met together to discuss their meetings with the President. Stettinius then reported the previous day's discussions to the WRB. The Board members were all in agreement that the President's plan was inadequate but they still hoped that all might work out well if one man, with sufficient authority, was placed between the President and the Council of National Defense. The WRB discussed this possible alternative as late as October but nothing came of the idea. After September 14, the Board at last took heed of the President's words and began to work on an organization plan that followed Roosevelt's ideas more closely though not until a second definition of the Board's objectives proposed by Moulton and Hancock was also turned down by the President.[83]

James A. Farley, Postmaster General and Chairman of the Democratic National Committee, also had a session with the President on September 13. In his account, written many years later, he tells that the President planned to shelve the WRB because it was dominated by the "Morgan crowd." He also reports that the President was favorably impressed by Farley's suggestion of himself as coordinator; however this may be, the Postmaster General's name never reappeared in connection with this position.[84]

On September 21, Congress convened in special session to revise the Neutrality Act. By then, the partition of Poland was virtually complete, and the power of the Nazi war machine evident. The need to avoid disputes with Congress was accepted by the Administration leaders. Five days after the convening of Congress, after a Cabinet meeting, Roosevelt announced at a press conference that the WRB would submit its report and then disband. He further

stated that the WRB would not be called back "for the same thing. . . . In other words, they have graduated." To this remark, the Secretary of War, Harry Woodring, who was present at the press conference, added his amen and stated that the "War Department is not setting up any permanent war boards and war machinery and I hope never will."[85] Roosevelt neither accepted nor rejected Woodring's supplement.

Actually, at the Cabinet meeting of September 26, Woodring took the opportunity to attack his Assistant Secretary of War. Woodring and Johnson differed about their approaches to the war—Johnson was pushing toward, and preparing for, our ultimate involvement in the war; Woodring was holding back. They differed also over the War Resources Board. Johnson had organized the Board without consulting Woodring, who, at the time, was in Panama. Woodring had angrily complained to the Cabinet on September 6 that Stettinius had never been in to see him. The first WRB meeting with Woodring did not take place until September 21.[86] Now, on September 26, at the Cabinet meeting, Woodring found an opportunity to hit back at Johnson. Leo M. Cherne, then Executive Secretary of the Tax Research Institute of America, had written a book called *Adjusting Your Business to War* that had been published on August 30. Cherne, in this book, made an exhaustive study of the industrial mobilization and other War and Navy plans in order to warn business of what would take place during a war. He had received the cooperation of the Army and Navy in writing the book. More important, Louis Johnson wrote the foreword to the volume. It therefore came to be viewed as semi-official, and headlines like "U. S. to Regiment All People in Case Nation Goes to War" greeted its publication.[87]

At the Cabinet meeting, Woodring joined in Secretary of Labor Frances Perkins' attack on Johnson's endorsement of the Cherne book. Miss Perkins had strongly opposed the industrial mobilization plans as involving a semi-fascistic control over labor and she took this opportunity to attack both the volume and the Industrial Mobilization Plan. Following the meeting, at the press conference where he announced the WRB's "graduation," Roosevelt declared that Cherne's book did not "represent officially" government war plans. Roosevelt further told the reporters that he had not heard of the book until the Cabinet meeting three-quarters of an hour before, when the Secretary of War told him about it. He added that "there is no book on the Army, Navy or military prognostications which has the . . . imprimatur . . . of the administration."[88]

Three days later, Roosevelt again had the opportunity to try to separate his Administration from any "war" plans during this period when the Administration amendments to the Neutrality Act were being debated. At a press conference, a newspaper man asked him if he would make the 1939 IMP and WRB report public. Roosevelt replied that the War Department had been making these plans regularly and he did not see any reason to make them public: "After all we are not in the war and I don't think we are going into the war and therefore I don't think it is a matter of great public interest." He went on to say that the report was not a "frightening document." He described what the report would contain:

There was a report on the possibilities of necessary industrial expansion—and that check up is made from time to time—as to the location and stepping up of industry, as to the relationship of increased production with transportation, the relationship of stepped-up production with additional power facilities, and down the line, various forms of administrative handling of stepping up industry, the relationship of industry to agriculture—a dozen different things.

He added that "there is no story in it except to make a controversy out of it and there isn't any controversy."[89]

Roosevelt's fears concerning the reaction to the Administration's association with the Industrial Mobilization Plan and with Cherne's book proved justified. In October, a two-day debate took place in Congress over the Cherne book. Senator Bennet Champ Clark used the book and the IMP as a fulcrum to attack any plans for American mobilization and intervention in international affairs. Presumably this debate was exactly the kind of opening for the opposition that Roosevelt feared when he attempted to disassociate his Administration from the Cherne volume.[90]

On October 12, the War Resources Board met and approved its report.[91] The final report, prepared mainly by John Hancock, was rather short. It attempted to predict the various stages prior to a full-scale mobilization. The first, or

the "paper-planning" stage, would take place during peacetime when the Army and Navy would draw up plans. The second stage would be the transition period when war appeared imminent. At that point, the previously made paper plans would be brought down to reality by the men who were to execute the final program. The third and last stage would be war itself when the men brought in during the transition period would put the whole program into operation.

The report emphasized the fact that "final responsibility for policies and for coordination of the war program must be vested in the President" and that the number of emergency agencies set up be kept at a minimum so as to simplify the President's task. The administration of these agencies could be handled in two ways:

(1) Through the creation of a superagency which would have under its direction a number of agencies, each handling individual powers, the coordination of their activities to be effected through the superagency which would thus have almost complete control of the economic life of the nation, or (2) Through the creation of a limited number of agencies, each exercising a delegated war power, but with provision for their coordination among themselves, leaving to the President the problem of decisions, only when they do not agree.

The WRB reported that it favored the second method, though it had favored the first, or superagency, approach until the members became convinced that the President opposed it. The second method though not in accord with the President's ideas was much closer to his wishes than the rejected superagency approach. The WRB listed four advantages of the second method:

1. The problem of transition from normal peacetime procedures to the requirements of war is simplified. Even after the declaration of war, normal peacetime procedures should be followed so far as possible and departures should be made only as requirements indicate.

2. The problem of demobilization at the end of war is similarly facilitated since the emergency agencies automatically disband.

3. By relying upon coordination of separate agencies it will be possible to use the existing organization of both industry and government.

4. Personnel to supervise wartime agencies can be obtained from men in civil life whose experi-

ence and records will inspire confidence and co-operation.

Concrete proposals were then presented to carry out this approach. Unlike the 1939 IMP, where only Public Relations and Selective Service were to be independent of the WRA, the Stettinius Committee recommended that the War Labor Board, the War Finance Board, the Food Administration (to be set up "if necessary," and not mentioned in the 1939 IMP), and the Price Control Board be independent of the WRA. First, "their separation would avoid an undue and unnecessary concentration of power within the War Resources Administration." Second, this division would prevent the WRA "from becoming too large and cumbersome." Third, the WRA could function without control over these agencies. Coordination could be achieved by having a WRA representative at each of these independent agencies.

Though the WRA was shorn of its controls over the other agencies, the War Resources Board did plan to have it established as a strong operating organization. It was to be the "central agency concerned with industrial mobilization—coordinating America's productive capacity with the requirements of the Army and Navy and of the civilian population." It still would have the operating powers proposed under the IMP; it would no longer have the coordinating powers. The War Resources Administration therefore would handle such vital matters as controls over raw materials and manufacturing facilities, priorities, power and fuel, transportation and technical research; war trade, set up as a separate subordinate agency in the 1939 Plan, was also to be a division of the WRA. This control over these important facets of our economic life would be coordinated with the military who were to have representatives at key places throughout the organization.

After making suggestions for further study, the WRB concluded its report by stating that by making this study it had done what it had been appointed to do. Since the United States was not engaged in a war, the WRB had neither power nor executive responsibility. The Stettinius Committee ended its report by declaring that if desirable, it would be happy to advise the Army-Navy Munitions Board on the ANMB's continuing work on preparedness plans.[92]

Johnson delivered the report to Roosevelt in November.[93] While the report was in Roosevelt's possession, some members of the WRB still thought that the Board might continue in existence. On November 8, General Robert Wood, a member of the Board, wrote to Colonel Rutherford, its secretary, that the hands of the WRB were "tied" until the members knew whether "we will be permanently dissolved or will remain in an advisory capacity." A week later, Rutherford still expressed the hope that the Board would be kept on in an advisory capacity. Most of the Board members however had lost much of their interest in the WRB after they had become aware of the President's attitude toward their work.[94]

On the face of it, Rutherford's and Wood's hope that the WRB would be kept on in an advisory capacity was fulfilled by Roosevelt's announcement of November 24th. In a letter of that date to the Board members, Roosevelt said that since the WRB had completed its report, it had done the job for which it had been created. Since the United States was not at war, the Stettinius Committee had no further authority. Preparedness plans would be carried on by the Army-Navy Munitions Board. Roosevelt hoped that the members of the Board would advise the ANMB. Later, he announced to the press that the WRB is "still keeping on in an advisory capacity." But they were never again called upon for advice.[95]

Roosevelt thereupon "pocket-vetoed" the report. He took no action on it, and refused to make it public, perhaps because he clearly opposed the ideas contained in the report, or perhaps because he wanted to "play down" the idea that we were preparing for war, or—most probably—both. In fact, he marked it classified and ordered that it be kept secret, which it was until after the end of the war.

The fall of Poland was followed by the winter of the "Sitzkrieg," the "phony war." In fact, the wave of alarm that had paved the way for the revision of the Neutrality Act had largely abated by the time the WRB filed its report. Public acceptance of large-scale mobilization activity would have been reluctant. There was much uneasiness, even more uncertainty.

IX. THE PRESIDENT INAUGURATES ECONOMIC MOBILIZATION

The period of uncertainty came to a sudden and dramatic end with Hitler's invasion of Denmark and Norway in April 1940. Even more effective in arousing the American people was the invasion of the Low Countries in May. Prominent persons in both parties began to call for action. Some suggested the use of the Industrial Mobilization Plan but members of the White House staff urged Roosevelt not to accept the suggestion. They told the President that the IMP was based on 1914-18 experience and did not pay enough attention to the changed nature of war. Particularly in the field of price control, they believed that Army planners had thought in terms of World War I. Moreover, the IMP appeared to them to be concerned with supplies for military forces and not with civilian supply. They also told the President that the needs of the military were arrived at under the IMP by the "most elementary rule-of-thumb" methods by Army officers "after a half-a-day lecture on statistics." In fact, the White House advisers stated that many of the war plans are "nothing more profound than student exercises, worked up in a few hours or days as a problem in a brief Army Industrial College course."[96]

Republican party leaders like Alfred M. Landon and Thomas E. Dewey urged that the War Resources Board be recalled; but Roosevelt reiterated his objection to the WRB. He told members of the Department of Commerce Business Advisory Council on May 23 that he would not set up a War Resources Board or a War Industries Board and turn over the war effort to "complete outsiders who don't know anything about running government. It would be unconstitutional; the final responsibility is mine and I can't delegate it." Any men whom he called down would be "dovetail[ed]" into existing organizations.[97]

But Roosevelt while refusing to adopt the IMP, was not refusing to act. In a memorandum dated May 21, 1940, Brownlow had suggested activation of Division 6 of the Executive Office of the President, the Office for Emergency Management, and the Council of National Defense. He reminded Roosevelt that the Office for Emergency Management could be activated under existing law, that it could use existing government personnel, that it would require very few new organizations, and practically no new legislation. The OEM, moreover, would operate directly under the President and thereby relieve him of the "inevitable friction" if a wholly new organization was set up outside of existing government agencies. The OEM would not be an operating agency and therefore would give the President flexibility in working out the solution of mobilization problems. Lastly, the President could liquidate the OEM "at a moment's notice." This memorandum was generally based on ideas that the President himself had begun to cherish at least four years earlier. The work set aside in September 1939 was finding fruition.[98] So too with personnel: in June Roosevelt did drop Woodring and Johnson, as he had told Ickes he was planning to do on September 6, 1939, and he did also appoint the two prominent Republicans—Stimson and Knox.

On May 25, Roosevelt organized Division 6 of the Executive Office of the President, the Office for Emergency Management. Four days later, he reactivated the Council of National Defense and appointed an Advisory Commission to the Council (NDAC). Seven advisers were appointed to the NDAC. They were Chester C. Davis as Adviser on Farm Products; William S. Knudsen as Adviser on Industrial Production; Leon S. Henderson as Adviser on Price Stabilization; Ralph Budd as Adviser on

Transportation; Sidney Hillman as Adviser on Employment; Miss Harriet Elliott as Adviser on Consumer Protection; and Edward R. Stettinius, Jr., again on the scene, this time as Adviser on Industrial Materials. William H. McReynolds served as the link between the Office of Emergency Management and the Council of National Defense and NDAC. McReynolds was appointed Liaison Officer of the OEM and Secretary of the Council of National Defense and the NDAC. Furthermore, the NDAC was told that it "would deal with the Council solely through the President himself or his Administrative Assistant (McReynolds)." Since the NDAC was also informed that the Council was a "paper thing"—the Cabinet under a different name—the NDAC would handle mobilization problems. The President also warned the NDAC that he would be the "boss." The NDAC was given permission to appoint a chairman, but it never did and Roosevelt remained "boss."[99]

Actually, there was a brief flurry of argument over where to place the NDAC. Edward J. Noble, Under Secretary of Commerce, probably with the approval of Harry Hopkins, then Secretary of Commerce, wanted it placed in his department. But Roosevelt wanted it under the Office for Emergency Management.[100]

The appointment of the NDAC generally received a good press, but persons like Baruch, who were committed to the concept of the IMP, were critical. After the war, Baruch told a Senate investigating committee that when the IMP was brought forward before the war, "we were told this was a different kind of war and none of that 'old World War stuff' was wanted." Instead, we started World War II with the Council of National Defense which "we had gone over twenty-five years before and had thrown in the ashcan." And who had led the President into making such a mistake? "Some so-called experts or professors on organization," Baruch answered.[101]

What Baruch wanted, and what the WRB and the Army planners wanted, was to have our economic mobilization handled by a newly created agency with tremendous powers. What Roosevelt wanted, as he made clear to the NDAC, was to be boss. Though it is true that the complex evolution of agencies to handle economic mobilization from the NDAC clear down to the end of the war did pass through stages that were reminiscent of the IMP, there were significant variations. One variation stands out: all roads led to the White House, not to a War Resources Administrator. And the final resolution of the organizational problem, with Byrnes' OWMR at the top, Vinson's OES as an adjunct and both closer to Roosevelt than to the operating agencies, had never been foreseen by Baruch or by his opponents.

Furthermore, the Army planners by restricting their scope of consultation, indeed their whole horizon, also failed to satisfy a President who was at least as sensitive to public acceptance as he was to administrative imperatives.

BIBLIOGRAPHIC NOTE

A host of people, some now deceased, gave their time either through correspondence or through personal interviews to tell me or the Editor of their recollections concerning the M-Day Plan. Our thanks go to Bernard M. Baruch, Louis Brownlow, Major General J. H. Burns, Leo Cherne, Benjamin V. Cohen, Thomas G. Corcoran, Charles Edison, Harold Epstein, John P. Frey, Walter S. Gifford, Louis Hunter, Eliot Janeway, Louis Johnson, Harold G. Moulton, Frances Perkins, Major General H. K. Rutherford, R. Elberton Smith, Henry A. Wallace, and Harry H. Woodring.

I had the opportunity to go through several collections of papers for this case study: the National Archives; President Franklin D. Roosevelt's papers at Hyde Park; Bernard M. Baruch's files; and some of the material, such as the Yoshpe files, at the Office of the Chief of Military History.

In addition, the study has benefited from the written works of others. Two volumes in the *United States Army in World War II* series (Washington) on which I had the pleasure of working proved of great help; R. Elberton Smith's *The Army and Economic Mobilization* (1959) deals with the industrial side of the story; Byron Fairchild and Jonathan Grossman's *The Army and Industrial Manpower* (1959) deals with manpower. Other studies discussing the military aspects of M-Day planning are Harold W. Thatcher, *Planning for Industrial Mobilization, 1920-1940* (Q. M. C. Historical Study, Washington, 1943); Harry B. Yoshpe, *Plans for Industrial Mobilization, 1920-1939* (Industrial College of the Army, ♯R 56, Washington, 1945); and Robert H. Connery, *The Navy and Industrial Mobilization in World War II* (Princeton University Press,

Princeton, 1951). The activities of the War Production Board are discussed in *Industrial Mobilization for War* (Washington, 1947). Professor James O. Morris in his *Conflict within the AFL* (Cornell University, Ithaca, 1958) tells the story of the increasing lack of contact between the labor movement and the War Department as the decades between both wars progressed.

Personalities played a major role in the mobilization story. About Roosevelt's role, we have read the writing of others: Harold L. Ickes, *The Secret Diary of Harold L. Ickes, Volume II, The Inside Struggle, 1936-1939* (Simon and Schuster, New York, 1954); William D. Leahy and William W. Whitehill, *I Was There* (Whittlesey, New York, 1950); James A. Farley, *Jim Farley's Story* (McGraw-Hill, New York, 1948); and Robert Sherwood, *Roosevelt and Hopkins* (Harper, New York, 1948). Many books have been written about Bernard Baruch. Chapter XV of the second volume of his autobiography—*The Public Years* (Holt, New York, 1960)—deals with this period. William L. White's *Bernard Baruch: Portrait of a Citizen* (Harcourt, New York, 1950) and Margaret L. Coit's *Mr. Baruch* (Houghton Mifflin, Boston, 1957) give some of the flavor of Baruch's personality and his role in this story. Eliot Janeway's *The Struggle for Survival* (Yale University Press, New Haven, 1951) places Baruch in the central role in the dispute over the War Resources Board.

All of these authors and all of those interviewed are responsible for much that is interesting in this report; they are, of course, not responsible for any of the errors or the interpretations.

NOTES

1. Cited in Harold W. Thatcher, *Planning for Industrial Mobilization, 1920-1940* (Q.M.C. Historical Study No. 3, 1943; reprinted 1948) (OQG, Washington, 1943), pp. 12-13.

2. *Ibid.*, pp. 6-10.

3. *Ibid.*, pp. 15-42.

4. Interview, Frey with author, September 8, 1954; letter and attachments, Hunter to author, November 4, 1954.

5. Thatcher, *Planning for Industrial Mobilization*, pp. 42-56; Robert H. Connery, *The Navy and Industrial Mobilization in World War II* (Princeton University Press, Princeton, 1951), pp. 32-33, 37-39.

6. Thatcher, *Planning for Industrial Mobilization*, p. 113.

7. *Ibid.*, pp. 72-73, 79.

8. *Ibid.*, p. 80.

9. See, for example, letters from Baruch to ASW Dwight Davis, March 6, 1923, and Baruch to Major General H. E. Ely, October 29, 1925, in Baruch's files. Much additional material about Baruch's activities of this kind is available in articles and biographies; see, for example, William L. White, *Bernard Baruch: Portrait of a Citizen* (Harcourt, New York, 1950); Margaret L. Coit, *Mr. Baruch* (Houghton Mifflin, Boston, 1957); and particularly the second volume of Baruch's autobiography, *The Public Years* (Holt, New York, 1960), Chap. XV.

10. Letter, Major General H. E. Ely, Commandant, Army War College, to Baruch, October 30, 1925, in Baruch's files.

11. Thatcher, *Planning for Industrial Mobilization*, pp. 84-90.

12. Public Resolution No. 98, 71st Cong., 2d sess., cited in *ibid.*, pp. 138-139.

13. Industrial Mobilization Plan, revised 1933, GPO, Washington, 1933, p. 13.

14. U. S. War Policies Commission, *Hearings before the Commission Appointed under the Authority of Public Resolution No. 98*, March 5 to May 22, 1931, 71st Cong., 2d sess., 1935, p. 393.

15. IMP, revised 1933, pp. 14-16.

16. IMP, revised 1936, pp. 14-16.

17. *Ibid.*, pp. 17-18.

18. U. S. War Policies Commission, *Hearings*, p. 370.

19. IMP, revised 1936, pp. 17-18.

20. Thatcher, *Planning for Industrial Mobilization*, p. 154, and forewords of the IMPs of 1930-1931, 1933 and 1936.

21. Baruch, *The Public Years*, pp. 267-268.

22. Thatcher, *Planning for Industrial Mobilization*, pp. 258, 259.

23. Letter, Frey to Stein, March 15, 1955.

24. See Jonathan Grossman's MS on *Labor Planning in the War Department between Wars* at the Office of the Chief of Military History, also Thatcher, *Planning for Industrial Mobilization*, pp. 201-203, and Connery, *The Navy and Industrial Mobilization in World War II*, p. 51; interview, Frey with author, September 7, 1954; for other relations between the AFL and the War Department, see James O. Morris, *Conflict within the AFL* (Cornell University, Ithaca, 1958), pp. 71-81.

25. Thatcher, *Planning for Industrial Mobilization*, pp. 245-246; Grossman, *Labor Planning in the War Department between Wars*, passim.

26. Letter, Perkins to Roosevelt, December 2, 1938; memorandum, Roosevelt to Johnson, December 7, 1938; letter, Johnson to Roosevelt, December 8, 1938; letter, Roosevelt to Perkins, December 8, 1938, in Franklin D. Roosevelt's papers in Hyde Park (hereafter cited as Hyde Park files).

27. IMP, 1936, pp. 25-26.

28. Thatcher, *Planning for Industrial Mobilization*, p. 244.

29. *Investigation of National Defense Program*, Hearings before Special Senate Committee Investigating National Defense Program, 80th Cong., 1st sess., 1948, Pt. 42, p. 25669.

30. *Ibid.*, pp. 25661-25662.

31. Cited in Thatcher, *Planning for Industrial Mobilization*, p. 265.

32. *Ibid.*, pp. 296-297.

33. Memoranda, Roosevelt for Johnson, November 26 and December 17, 1937, in Hyde Park files.

34. Photostat with attached note by Harold

Epstein, November 14, 1952; letter, Baruch to George Peek, March 17, 1939, in Hyde Park files; see also Baruch, *The Public Years,* pp. 272-276.

35. IMP, Revision 1939, pp. 6-8.

36. Cited in Thatcher, *Planning for Industrial Mobilization,* p. 272; and letter, Lieutenant Colonel Charles Hines, Sec., ANMB, May 22, 1939, attached to the proposed 1939 IMP, in National Archives (hereafter cited as NA).

37. *War Trade Annex to Industrial Mobilization Plan, 1939,* pp. 87-88.

38. *Ibid.,* p. 25, and IMP, Revision 1939 with Annexes, *passim.*

39. Memorandum, Charles W. Wiltse to James W. Fesler, July 19, 1946, Subject: Interview with Harold G. Moulton, President of Brookings Institution, on the WRB, in NA (hereafter cited as the Moulton Interview).

40. Civilian Production Administration, *Industrial Mobilization for War* (GPO, Washington, 1947), p. 6.

41. Letter, Rutherford to Stein, March 20, 1955.

42. War Dept.—Navy Dept. Joint Release, August 17, 1939 and WRB Minutes, August 17, 1939, in NA; interview, Rutherford with author, September 8, 1954.

43. Cited in Eliot Janeway, *The Struggle for Survival* (Yale University Press, New Haven, 1951), p. 53.

44. Letter, Edison to author, November 23, 1954; interview, Moulton with author, September 8, 1954.

45. WRB Minutes, August 17, 1939, in NA; Janeway, *The Struggle for Survival,* p. 57; Letter, Johnson to author, October 19, 1954.

46. WRB Minutes, August 17, 1939, in NA; *Investigation of National Defense Program,* Senate Hearings, p. 25661 War Dept.—Navy Dept. Joint Release, August 9, 1939, Subject: Formation of WRB, in NA; interview, Rutherford with author, September 8, 1954.

47. War Dept.—Navy Dept. Joint Release, August 9, 1939, Subject: Formation of WRB, in NA; letter, Rutherford to Stein, March 20, 1955.

48. Memorandum for William D. Hassett, August 10, 1939, in Hyde Park files; War Dept.—Navy Dept. Joint Release, August 9, 1939.

49. Letter, Rutherford to Stettinius, August 12, 1939; WRB Minutes, August 17, 1939; letter, Stettinius to Replogle, August 17, 1939; letter, Replogle to Stettinius, September 7, 1939; remarks of Crowell at WRB Meeting, August 31, 1939; letter, Ayres to Stettinius, September 5, 1939; letter, Scott to Stettinius, October 3, 1939; WRB document—WWI—Experience Studies, all in NA; letter, Moulton to Stein, March 15, 1955.

50. Letter, Pershing to Baruch, August 26, 1939, in Baruch's files; letter, Baruch to Stettinius, with attachments, August 30, 1939, in NA.

51. *Washington News,* August 11, 1939; letters, Hugh Johnson to Stettinius, August 21 and 28, 1939, in NA.

52. Memorandum, Frances Perkins for President, August 11, 1939 and attached note, in Hyde Park files.

53. *American Federationist,* September 1939, p. 418.

54. Janeway, *The Struggle for Survival,* p. 60.

55. Letter, Moulton to Stein, March 15, 1955.

56. Cited in Thatcher, *Planning for Industrial Mobilization,* p. 292.

57. Letter, Representative Clarence Cannon to Roosevelt, September 4, 1939; letter, Roosevelt to Cannon, September 18, 1939, in Hyde Park files.

58. Letter, John W. Fitzpatrick, President Smaller Business Association of New England, September 18, 1939; letter, Watson to Fitzpatrick, September 19, 1939, in Hyde Park files.

59. Telegram, Eaton to President, August 31, 1939; letter, E. J. Royan to Senator Josh Lee, September 3, 1939 and forwarded to President, in Hyde Park files.

60. *The Secret Diary of Harold L. Ickes,* Vol. II, *The Inside Struggle, 1936-1939* (Simon and Schuster, New York, 1954), pp. 710, 716, 719 and 721.

61. *New York Times,* October 6, 1939.

62. Letter, Carmody to President, August 31, 1939, in Hyde Park files.

63. Letter, Wallace to President, August 26, 1939, in Hyde Park files; letter, Wallace to author, June 28, 1954; *New York Times,* September 21, 1939.

64. Editorial, *Milwaukee Sentinel,* no date, in Hyde Park files; *Newsweek,* October 9, 1939; interview, Janeway with author, June 23, 1954; interview, Corcoran with author, September 8, 1954; letter, Edison to author, November 23, 1954.

65. WRB Minutes, August 17, 1939, in NA; memorandum, Lauchlin Currie for President, September 5, 1939; memorandum, Roosevelt for Secretary of War and Acting Secretary of Navy, September 6, 1939, all in Hyde Park files.

66. WRB Minutes, August 23, 24 and 25, 1939, in NA.

67. Letter, Johnson to Stettinius, August 21, 1939, in NA; interview, Rutherford with author, September 8, 1954.

68. Letter, Moulton to Stein, March 15, 1955.

69. WRB Minutes, *passim,* and memorandum, Rutherford for Stettinius, September 6, 1939, in NA; interview, Rutherford with author, September 8, 1954; letter, Johnson to author, October

19, 1954.

70. See below, p. 82; Moulton Interview; WRB Minutes, August 30, 1939, in NA; interview, Moulton with author, September 8, 1954; letter, Moulton to Stein, March 15, 1955; Baruch's guesses about the reasons for Roosevelt's decisions are outlined in *The Public Years,* pp. 280-281.

71. U. S. Code of Law in Force, January 3, 1935, Title 50—War, Chap. 1.

72. Information on Roosevelt–Louis Brownlow conversations, 1936, from Brownlow interview with Stein, December 3, 1954.

73. See above, p. 71.

74. William D. Leahy and William W. White-hill, *I Was There* (Whittlesey, New York, 1950), p. 4.

75. Information on Roosevelt–Brownlow conversations, 1939, from Brownlow interview with Stein, December 3, 1954.

76. WRB Minutes, August 30, 1939, in NA; Moulton Interview; letter, Moulton to Stein, March 15, 1955.

77. Memorandum, EMW (Col. E. M. Watson) for President, September 5, 1939, and two attachments: (1) Administrative Order Calling into Existence the Liaison Officer for Emergency Management of the Executive Office of the President and Prescribing Regulations Covering Its Activities; (2) Rules and Regulations, Council of National Defense, in Hyde Park files.

78. WRB Minutes, September 6, 1939; memorandum, prepared by WRB for Johnson's and Edison's signature for submission to President, September 6, 1939 (italics supplied), both in NA.

79. Interview, Rutherford with author, September 8, 1954.

80. Ickes, *The Secret Diary,* II, pp. 719-720.

81. *Ibid.,* p. 720.

82. Connery, *The Navy and Industrial Mobilization in World War II,* p. 47; memorandum, Director of the Budget Harold D. Smith, September 8, 1939, in Hyde Park files; interview, Rutherford with author, September 8, 1954.

83. WRB Minutes, September 13, 14, 1939, in NA; Moulton Interview; Connery, *The Navy and Industrial Mobilization in World War II,* p. 47; interview, Rutherford with author, September 8, 1954.

84. James A. Farley, *Jim Farley's Story* (McGraw-Hill, New York, 1948), pp. 199-200.

85. Press Conference, September 26, 1939, in Hyde Park files.

86. John Hancock, *Achievements and Failures in Industrial Mobilization* (January 15, 1946, ICAF), p. 13; Ickes, *The Secret Diary,* II, pp. 716, 719; WRB Minutes, September 20, 21, 1939, in NA; interview, Rutherford with author, September 8, 1954.

87. Telephone conversation, Cherne with author, August 7, 1954; *Washington News,* September 23, 1939; *Boston Globe,* September 3, 1939.

88. Press Conference, September 26, 1939, in Hyde Park files; telephone conversation, Cherne with author, August 7, 1954; *Washington Star,* October 8, 1939; *New York Times,* September 27, 1939.

89. Press Conference, September 29, 1939, in Hyde Park files.

90. Telephone conversation, Cherne with author, August 7, 1954; *Congressional Record,* 76th Cong., 2d sess., Vol. 85, pp. 550, 1183-1189.

91. WRB Minutes, October 12, 1939, in NA.

92. The report is available in several forms; the most convenient edition is in *Investigation of National Defense Program,* pp. 25957-25971. In his account of this episode, Janeway, *The Struggle for Survival,* p. 57, states that Hancock presented the report to WRB for formal approval and that it was a product of collaboration by Baruch, Hancock, Louis Johnson, and the Planning Division; this is possible but doubtful with respect to Baruch's participation; of course, Hancock was familiar with Baruch's ideas on the subject. Distinctly unconvincing is the statement, *ibid.,* p. 75, that Roosevelt agreed "in advance to accept" this "second" Baruch Plan; the further assertion that "Baruch was beginning to bid for the job of administering whatever organization he and Roosevelt could agree to form" may be a correct statement of Baruch's position. The implication of all this is that Roosevelt and Baruch talked together in September and October. This is possible, though apparently undocumented, but it is hard to avoid the further inference that if Baruch did dicker with Roosevelt, he did not understand Roosevelt's decision to use NDAC for the first stage of economic mobilization.

93. Memorandum, WDH (William D. Hassett) for [Stephen T.] Early, November 15, 1939; memorandum, STE for President, November 22, 1939, in Hyde Park files.

94. Letter, ASW to E. C. Byers, November 7, 1939; letter, Wood to Rutherford, November 8, 1939; letter, Rutherford to Hancock, November 15, 1939, in NA; interview, Moulton with author, September 8, 1954.

95. *New York Times,* November 24, 1939; Press Conference, November 24, 1939, in Hyde Park files.

96. Comments on Industrial War Plans (read and returned by President, May 20, 1940) in files of Currie, Rowe, Forrestal and McReynolds at Hyde Park.

97. Herman M. Somers, *Presidential Agency, OWMR* (Harvard University Press, Cambridge, 1950), pp. 9-10; Press Conference, May 21, 1940

and President's Conference with members of the Business Advisory Council, May 23, 1940, in Hyde Park files; *Washington News,* May 25, 1940.

98. Memorandum, Brownlow for President, May 21, 1940, in Hyde Park files; Louis Brownlow, *The President and the Presidency* (Public Administration Service, Chicago, 1949).

99. Conference on National Defense with NDAC, May 30, 1940, in Hyde Park files; Ellen St. Sure, "The TVA Ammonia Plant," in Harold Stein, ed., *Public Administration and Policy Development: A Case Book* (Harcourt, New York, 1952), pp. 395-397.

100. Robert Sherwood, *Roosevelt and Hopkins: An Intimate History* (Harper, New York, 1948), pp. 158-159.

101. *Investigation of National Defense Program,* pp. 25740, 25762-25763, 25749-25750, 25752. Baruch has not changed his mind; see *The Public Years,* p. 282.

EDITORIAL COMMENTS

Planning for war is far more difficult for a nation that hopes to avoid or prevent war than for one that has already picked a time and a place and a method for starting war. Planning is particularly difficult in a democracy where the mere existence of war plans is frequently construed as planning to go to war, to attack, and to subjugate democracy at home.

In the United States, widespread distrust of planning for action in war *per se* has abated in the last decade, though the burning desire to avoid or prevent war is perhaps stronger than ever. There has been a shift in the form of the debate and of course a renewal of hope in international agencies and international agreements. Yet today planning for necessary action if war should come is regarded as normal rather than abnormal, as a matter of concern for the whole government, rather than merely for the military, and for all groups in society rather than for selected elites. There are still prophets of doom, who perceive a steady encroachment of a powerful handful of military, scientific and industrial leaders on all the sources of power in our democracy. There is also widespread debate on all matters connected with atomic bombing and testing; but planning for action in case of war as such is no longer the focus of the attack of those who fear and dislike what they construe as the military, or militarism. At least, except for those pacifists who wish us to beat all our swords into ploughshares *instanter,* the cry is not for a total abandonment of military planning but for a reassignment of responsibility for the making of plans away from the military and their scientific and industrial supporters.

Matters were quite different in the 1920's and 1930's. For various reasons it was assumed that only the military should be charged with any responsibility for constructing plans on action during a war. The assumption was natural enough, because the United States constituted a nation with widely-shared beliefs that it, at least, could avoid future wars. If there was to be no war, why should the President and the civilian departments and agencies concern themselves with the distasteful consideration of what to do if there was a war? Yet such faith, however profound, was never total. Congress, for example, felt free to cut deeply into proposed appropriations for the services (as did the Bureau of the Budget and the President), but there was no serious proposal to abolish the Army and the Navy. By the same token, there was a limited grudging admission that planning for the management of a wartime economy deserved some consideration—consideration, however, that did not befit any civilian agency. These ambivalences, doubts, unwillingness to face unpleasant facts frontally were reflected in the National Defense Act of 1920 in which the Assistant Secretary of War was assigned responsibility (1) for arranging in detail "for the production of Army munitions in war," and (2) for developing "broad plans for the mobilization of national industry to meet the country's complete industrial needs in war." (Perhaps the omission of the Navy represented the Navy's own faith that, given an Assistant Secretary as energetic as Franklin D. Roosevelt, the Navy could look after itself.)

The assignment of planning for economic mobilization to the War Department in 1920 had a number of now predictable though unanticipated consequences. Since the Department was at that period rather an orphan in our national government, alienated from most of the main currents of American life, the achievements were of exceedingly limited value. Even its active participation in the doings of the War Policies Commission (established by Congress in 1930 primarily to remove the profits from war on the assumption that without profits there would be no war) failed to alter its motivation. Throughout the two decades the Army's planning relied on the cooperation of two groups: Army officers and industrialists, particularly representatives of large well-established manufacturing and financial enterprises. Almost completely absent were representatives of labor and other groups in our society, as well as economists, scientists and other professional experts, the Cabinet, and the President himself. The value of broader representation became clear during World War II, even if some of the old distaste for labor and other groups is again visible. For in a democracy, possibly also in autocracies as well, large-scale industrial mobilization requires broad acceptance of the war, and willing and broad participation in war mobilization by the vast majority of the nation's citizens. Such participation would have been hard to secure with the Army's planning techniques and under its plans.

Contrary to many popular notions at the time, the Army had no desire to run the economic mobilization agencies in case of war. No doubt they were aware that such abnegation, eagerly desired by them, was also a *sine qua non* for approval of their plans by their Commander in Chief. What they failed to realize, and here the political ignorance of the officers was reinforced by the insensitivity of Assistant Secretary Louis Johnson, was that President Roosevelt had definite ideas about organization for economic mobilization. He wanted to retain control in his own hands and he had definite ideas about the participation of leaders who were not exclusively businessmen, and definite ideas about timing, for he did not want a premature establishment of mobilization organizations. The Army forgot to ask for Roosevelt's guidance. As a result of their forgetfulness, they happily gave birth to an M-Day Plan which the President promptly killed. In this process Roosevelt was showing his sharp awareness of his own supreme responsibility as Commander in Chief, in this case in relation to the development of war plans and the waging of war as part of the total political life of the nation.

One other aspect of governmental action or inaction characteristic of the twenties and thirties, obsolete today, also deserves mention.

The generic name for these efforts (including M-Day planning) was preparedness, and throughout the period between the wars its chief proponent and advocate was Bernard M. Baruch. Basically Roosevelt and Baruch were in agreement on the need for rearmament, for both agreed even during Roosevelt's first administration that large-scale war was imminent in Europe and in the Far East, and both later agreed that those distant wars, after they started, would become perilous to the United States. However, while both men agreed on the need for measures of rearmament, they disagreed, naturally enough, on ways and means and timing: the perspectives of the President were different from the perspectives of the Adviser of Presidents.

The differences became quite marked over questions of government organization in mobilization planning, a matter of importance because Baruch's ideas were eagerly sought by the Army planners and by the Stettinius Committee. Baruch felt that after being courted he was rejected, that there was a deliberate desire not to use him because he had been chairman of the World War I War Industries Board and not to use his old and trusted associates and advisers for the same reason. Baruch still believes that he was right in his mobilization ideas and the President wrong, and he assumes that Roosevelt's errors were based largely on bad advice and bad administrative habits. This study reveals that right or wrong, Roosevelt's decisions were very much his own and were based on a definable rationale. Indeed, the actions that led to the reactivation of NDAC were carefully planned and were the first steps in Roosevelt's very vigorous assumption of his role of Commander in Chief.

How applicable the actions that surrounded the birth and death of the M-Day Plan are to the problems of today is quite uncertain. The domestic strategy for an all-out atomic war would be utterly unlike the control systems of World War II; and those systems seemed too elaborate for the significant but different problems of limited war, as the Korean War showed. Still certain, however, is the profound need to have the planning suited to the character of American society and fully acceptable to the Commander in Chief.

AID TO RUSSIA: THE FIRST YEAR

MARVIN D. BERNSTEIN

ASSISTANT PROFESSOR OF HISTORY

STATE UNIVERSITY COLLEGE AT FREDONIA (NEW YORK)

AND FRANCIS L. LOEWENHEIM

ASSOCIATE PROFESSOR OF HISTORY

RICE UNIVERSITY

CONTENTS

I   Russian Aid: The First Phase—From the Nazi Attack to the Harriman Mission   99

II   The Negotiation of the First Protocol   112

III   Problems in Fulfilling the First Protocol   121

Bibliographic Note   139

Notes   141

Editorial Comments   150

I. RUSSIAN AID: THE FIRST PHASE—FROM THE NAZI ATTACK TO THE HARRIMAN MISSION

1. THE ATTACK ON RUSSIA AND WASHINGTON'S RESPONSE

Early on Sunday morning June 22, 1941, Nazi Germany attacked the Soviet Union. The outbreak of hostilities came as no surprise to London or Washington. The possibility of war had been discussed publicly for months; indeed, as far back as December 1940, "authentic" intelligence reports of a forthcoming German invasion of Russia had reached Washington and been transmitted by Under Secretary of State Welles to Constantine A. Oumansky, the Russian Ambassador.[1] The Russians, however, seemed to shrug off the information, as well as later intelligence reports to the same effect.[2] British efforts to prepare for joint action once the attack occurred came to nothing.[3]

Now that war between Germany and Russia had actually broken out, what would London and Washington do? Churchill, for one, was all prepared; the night hostilities opened he went on the radio to declare:

We have but one aim and one single irrevocable purpose. . . . We are resolved to destroy Hitler and every vestige of the Nazi regime. . . . Any man or state who fights on against Nazism will have our aid. . . . It follows, therefore, that we shall give whatever help we can to Russia and the Russian people. We shall appeal to our friends and allies in every part of the world to take the same course and pursue it, faithfully and steadfastly to the end. . . .[4]

Washington's course was far less simple and clear. While Great Britain had been at war with Germany since September 1939, the United States was formally a neutral, or, at least, a non-belligerent; and if public opinion was no longer as divided as it had been in 1940, it was still far from united even on all-out support of Britain (short of war); much less

was it prepared for such assistance to the Soviet Union.[5]

Still, the Nazi attack on Russia was a fact, and the question inevitably arose whether Washington would now follow the lead of London and declare its full support of the Soviet war effort. And if the United States were to extend aid to the Russians, what sort and amount of aid would it be, and on what basis? In particular, would the United States now extend aid to Russia on the newly established basis of Lend-Lease? (The Lend-Lease Act had been signed on March 4, 1941; the British aid program was still in its formative stages.)

Several factors seemed to operate against the chances of immediate and substantial American support. First of all, of course, the United States was not at war with Germany; there was still a deep public division on foreign affairs and foreign aid; almost two years of the Nazi-Soviet pact had left a bitter taste (not least in President Roosevelt's mouth). Besides, the United States had its hands full getting its own defense program into high gear, and doing what it could, within its resources and the vague limits of neutrality, to assist Great Britain. Above all, there was—and continued to be—active doubt in the minds of high civil and military officials in Washington whether the Soviets could and would hold out against the ferocious Nazi onslaught. Obviously, if the Soviets were going to make still another deal with the Nazis, or were to be defeated by them, any American aid would be wasted—or worse yet, would wind up in German hands, most likely to be used in an all-out offensive against Great Britain the following spring.[6]

The immediate need of course was for nothing more than a general statement of the American position, and about that there was never to have been any question. Actually when our

Ambassador, John G. Winant, had left Washington a month earlier, on June 13, to return to his post in London, he had been instructed to report to Churchill *inter alia:* "in the event that the Germans struck at Russia the President promised an immediate supporting statement following any announcement the Prime Minister might make welcoming Russia as an ally."[7] As soon as Hull received word of the Nazi attack, he phoned Roosevelt "advocating an early declaration of support for the Soviet Union"; after that he called Welles and a number of other associates in the State Department "to emphasize to them the same point of view," to make sure that the State Department knew that he, the President and Welles were all of one mind on the subject.[8] Then Hull left Washington for White Sulphur Springs for a short rest to recover from a stubborn cold, leaving Welles, as Acting Secretary of State, to carry on. The next morning Welles, after a transatlantic telephone conversation with Churchill, and conferences with Hopkins and Lord Halifax, the British Ambassador in Washington, went to the White House to get the President's approval for a statement to be issued at a State Department press conference. Roosevelt read Welles's draft, sitting up in bed, and approved it, adding what became its final sentence. In part, it declared:

In the opinion of this Government . . . any defense against Hitlerism, any rallying of the forces opposing Hitlerism, from whatever source these forces may spring, will hasten the eventual downfall of the present German leaders, and will therefore redound to the benefit of our own defense and security. Hitler's armies are today the chief dangers of the Americas.[9]

This was of course only the most general of declarations; in fact it committed the United States to nothing whatever (except perhaps sympathy and good will) and left entirely unclarified the question whether the United States would in fact extend aid to the USSR. Roosevelt, at his press conference on Tuesday the 24th, shed some but not much light on the subject. Asked about the situation, he replied that not only were Russian needs not known but help to Great Britain would come first in any case, and Russian aid would be effective only in the event of a long war. He did say that he would send as much aid as possible to Russia, but he refused to answer any questions

about possible Lend-Lease aid or whether the defense of Russia was vital to the security of the United States. (The Lend-Lease Act required such a finding by the President before aid was granted.[10])

The same day the Treasury Department announced that it had formally released to Amtorg, the official Soviet trading agency in the United States, some $39 million in frozen Soviet assets;[11] and at the State Department a group under the direction of Sumner Welles began to sift a list of impounded Russian goods with a view to seeing which could now be released for export.[12] The next day, June 25, the White House announced through Welles that the President was not invoking the Neutrality Act to cover the area of the Nazi-Soviet war, ostensibly because American interests and citizens were not affected, the practical effect of this action being to leave various Russian ports open to American ships.[13]

Despite Roosevelt's comments at his press conference, and Welles's statement to the press on the 26th, that the U. S. was in no hurry to act[14] pending the development of Russian resistance to the Nazi attack, rumors and inquiries continued to mount at the State Department. What kind of aid was going to be extended to the Russians? But there was no hard news to be had—for the simple reason that no decision had yet been made. Actually no formal decision was ever made. For no one, not even the President, seems ever to have issued an order specifically starting aid to Russia.[15]

For about a week no one had any idea what the Russians might want. But at once the pressure began to build up around the President to go slow in extending aid. The day war broke out, Welles told Halifax that for the time being the best course for the United States and Britain would be to recognize that Germany and Russia were at war but not to go beyond that. Welles feared that Japan would sooner or later also attack Russia, and that if Great Britain and Russia were allied, this would involve Great Britain in a war in the Far East.[16] The President's military advisers urged him to exploit the opportunity through all-out aid to Britain; Stimson called the Nazi attack on Russia an "almost providential occurrence."[17]

It was not anti-Soviet prejudice that was back of such military opinion (especially was this true of Secretary of War Stimson, who throughout the period of the Nazi-Soviet Pact had expressed a considerably more tolerant view of the Soviet position than had, for instance, the President himself);[18] it was simply that the best military opinion in Washington gave the Russians at best only about three months to survive. Though publicly Secretary of the Navy Knox was more optimistic about the Russian situation, he wrote to the President that "the best opinion" he could get was that "it will take anywhere from six weeks to two months for Hitler to clean up on Russia."[19] But Roosevelt, not for the first or last time, dissented from the best military opinion, and chose instead to go along with the view of the former U. S. Ambassador to Russia, Joseph E. Davies.[20] Davies told the President that before long the Russian Army would amaze the world. The President was willing to be shown, and meanwhile to do what little could be done to help the Russians.

At first, of course, as has been said, no one in Washington, including Roosevelt, had any idea what the Russians might want or need; not even the Russian Ambassador knew, as he admitted to Welles on the evening of the 26th.[21] On June 29, a week after the Nazi attack, conversations concerning American aid were formally begun in Moscow between U. S. Ambassador Steinhardt and Foreign Minister Molotov,[22] and the following day, June 30, Oumansky appeared at the State Department with the first Russian list, which, instead of listing specific Soviet requirements, simply named nine general categories of materials that the Russians wished to be supplied with: fighter planes, anti-aircraft guns, short-range bombers, anti-tank guns, airplane factory equipment, cracking plants for aviation gasoline, machinery for tire manufacture, and rolling mills for light alloys.[23] The State Department was careful to note the emphasis on manufacturing equipment, which it interpreted as evidence of Soviet determination to continue in the war. Welles also took this as a good sign and asked Oumansky to return as soon as possible with a more specific list. Oumansky agreed to this and asked Welles whether such supplies might be financed by a five-year credit rather than through Lend-Lease, which might be difficult to arrange. Welles promised to take the matter up with the Treasury Department.[24]

2. THE CURTIS COMMITTEE

In this first phase of American-Soviet dealings it was the State Department which handled all Russian approaches as well as American policy. Thus Charles P. Curtis, Special Assistant to Sumner Welles, drew up a "Memorandum on Organization and Policy for the Export and Production of Articles for Russia," which Welles approved on June 30.[25] It recommended the establishment of a special committee to act as a central agency for clearing and expediting requests from Amtorg and the Russian Embassy. Curtis himself was to be chairman of the new committee, assisted by representatives of the State Department, the Division of Defense Aid Reports, the Administrator of Export Control, the Office of Price Administration and Civilian Supply, the Office of Production Management, the Army-Navy Munitions Board, and the Maritime Commission. (DDAR was the predecessor of the Lend-Lease Administration; OPM was in charge of defense production generally and was in due course succeeded by the War Production Board.) The State Department was to provide the secretariat.

The major function of the Curtis Committee was to route Russian requests to the appropriate agencies for their consideration. Requests for military goods thus would go to the DDAR; requests for aircraft to the Joint Aircraft Committee; requests for raw materials and civilian goods were to be considered by the Curtis Committee itself on the basis of information "on the purpose to which the article is to be put." Shipping plans were also to be considered an important factor. Once a request was approved, the Office of Export Control would issue an export license for the particular item. The Curtis Committee was also to be authorized to issue immediate export licenses for goods already completed under previous Russian orders (unless there were sound reasons to the contrary); to approve the production of specific articles (unless this would take up capacity needed for items for the defense of the U. S. or other countries actively opposing aggression); to approve new Russian orders to be booked on a similar basis, provided these articles could be transferred for use by American forces or a country the U. S. was aiding in its defense against aggression. Requests for petroleum products likewise would be approved so long as the quantities requested did not interfere with American needs.

Almost at once, however, it became evident that the Curtis Committee would not be able to do the job. For one thing, all it was really authorized to do was to issue export licenses and to accept the booking of orders; it could do nothing about the matter of financing these purchases (the Russians would still have to find an acceptable way of paying for what they got). Moreover, the setup of the Curtis Committee allowed—indeed required—every participating agency to scrutinize the Russian requests, with an eye to seeing that none constituted a charge against the needs of the U. S. or other friendly powers; Soviet need, in other words, definitely was secondary as of that time. Indeed Curtis' original memorandum foresaw that the new Committee would not be a central, policy-making group:

Russia is fighting against the same aggression against which we are helping other countries to fight and against which we are preparing. The determination of which military aid is to be given is not the function of this committee. The President will decide as between Russia's need for aircraft and for military equipment and such needs here and in those countries. Russia's other needs will be handled by this committee along the lines of policy stated here and in the statement of the Acting Secretary of State on June 24th. Wherever it is possible without immediate and grave prejudice to our own defense or economy or our aid to those other countries, Russia should be permitted to maintain and fortify her internal economy by purchases in this country. This committee and the procedure above set forth is established to expedite the handling of those purchases.

The operation of the Curtis Committee reflected the cautiousness of its sponsor as well as the special interests of its members. It accepted, that is, it sent to the President for final approval, the meager recommendations of the various procurement agencies for Russian shipments; it did so of course because it was composed of the representatives of the very agencies passing on the Russian requests—agencies which, it must be remembered, were already engaged in a struggle with the British over the distribution of America's all-too-limited war production.[26]

On July 18 Welles brought to the President the Curtis Committee's recommendations on the shipment of articles on the Russian list. The original Russian requests were estimated to total $1,845,668,000, plus an additional $10,-261,000 in impounded goods. Individual items on the Russian list included 3,000 pursuit planes, 3,000 bombers, 20,000 anti-aircraft guns, 50,000 tons of toluol (for the manufacture of explosives), large quantities of aviation gasoline and raw materials, and some $50,000,-000 worth of industrial plants and equipment.[27]

Relying on the Curtis Committee report, Welles recommended "only very modest, not to say insignificant, assignments to the Soviets, even over a period of a year."[28] The President laid Welles's report before the Cabinet. The items recommended for immediate shipment were approved; indeed the entire Russian list was also "approved," presumably for eventual shipment under Russian financing. This "approval" of the entire Russian list was used by the White House to reopen with the appropriate procurement agencies discussion of the items requested by the Russians but not recommended for shipment in the Curtis Committee report.[29]

3. RUSSIAN AID TRANSFERRED TO DDAR

The Curtis Committee continued on its cumbersome and essentially ineffective way of dealing with the Russian requests. Roosevelt, however, from the beginning had had no faith in its capacity for significant action. Shortly after July 1 the President remarked to his military aid, General E. M. Watson, that he was dissatisfied with the slowness with which supplies were moving to Russia,[30] (actually the Russian request had not been presented until June 30), while former Ambassador Davies was pressing the President (through Hopkins) to make a clear-cut statement to Stalin that the United States was in fact willing to extend all-out aid to the Soviet Union. Such assurance, Davies believed, would help preclude any attempts on the part of Stalin to make peace with the Germans, and would encourage the Soviets to hold out even if they were driven back beyond the Urals.[31] Real pressure in fact soon came from the Russians themselves: Oumansky promptly began to complain to Welles of the lack of good faith on the part of the American government. Welles thereupon arranged for Oumansky to have his first interview with Roosevelt at the White House on July 10.[32]

In the presence of Hopkins and Welles, Roosevelt assured Oumansky that the U. S. would rush all possible aid to Russia by the first of October.[33]

Energetic administrative action was thus clearly called for and even while the first Curtis Committee report was still being prepared, Hopkins and Welles began looking for a new way to take care of Russian aid. At the beginning of the second week in July, they reached an agreement by which the State Department would turn over responsibility for Russian aid to the DDAR; Hopkins, it may be noted, exercised continuing oversight of that agency. On July 10 Welles drafted a series of letters for Roosevelt to sign, notifying Stimson, Knox and William S. Knudsen (head of OPM), of the change and asking them to cooperate with Brigadier General James H. Burns, the official head of DDAR. The draft letters reached the White House on July 18, appended to Welles' report on the Curtis Committee recommendations.[34]

Hopkins and Welles were not the only ones to have the idea of assigning responsibility for Russian aid to DDAR. On July 12, just before he left for England to make the final arrangements for the forthcoming Atlantic Conference between Roosevelt and Churchill, Hopkins had lunch with General Burns and informed him of his (and Welles's) plan.[35] Burns in turn told Hopkins that he had already started to lay plans to have DDAR take over the Russian supply program. Shortly after the first of July, Burns said, General Watson—"Pa" Watson—the President's physician and friend, had told him of Roosevelt's dissatisfaction with the state of the Russian aid program and had suggested that DDAR might handle it more expeditiously. Burns went on to say that he had then discussed the matter with his two assistants, Brigadier General Sidney Spalding and Philip Young, and that they had decided to create a special division to handle the Russian program. Exactly who should head the new division remained a vexing question, but it would have to be someone (Burns later recalled saying) with enough faith and sympathy for the Russians to put his whole heart into the unpopular task.

Hopkins told Burns to go ahead and appoint someone he thought suitable. Burns thereupon returned to his office for further consultation with Spalding and Young. Spalding suggested

Colonel Philip R. Faymonville, the War Department's Russian "expert," who had been military attaché at Moscow for four years, part of the time under Ambassador Davies, and had only recently returned to the United States. In Russia he had had the unique distinction of being an American who had gained the confidence of the Red Army leaders. Faymonville had learned much about the Red Army, thought highly of it, and believed its staying power was tremendously underestimated. Burns had never met Faymonville but had heard good reports of him and was willing to accept him. Hopkins also did not know Faymonville, but was likewise agreeable to his appointment. On the morning of July 14, Faymonville presented himself at General Burns's office to start his work; one of his first acts was to call in as his assistant Professor John N. Hazard of Columbia University, an old friend of his and an expert on Soviet law.[36]

A few days later, on July 18, the meager recommendations of the Curtis Committee reached the White House, and the following day, Saturday, July 19, Roosevelt signed and sent to Stimson and Knox the letters drafted by Welles, informing them of the transfer of the Russian aid program to DDAR. On Monday, July 21, Roosevelt sent a letter to Burns officially notifying him that DDAR would henceforth be responsible for obtaining "immediate and substantial" shipments of supplies to the USSR. Roosevelt requested Burns to see that these were started before winter set in, and he informed Burns that Welles had notified the Army of the President's promise of concrete help to Oumansky, at their interview on July 10. Roosevelt further ordered Burns to review the entire Russian list with representatives of the Army, the Navy, and OPM, and to have ready in 48 hours, by July 23 that is, a list of items to be shipped in the "immediate future." The remaining items on the Russian list were then to be reviewed and delivery dates set for them as well, which were to be communicated to the Russian Ambassador. Roosevelt sent Knudsen a copy of his letter to Burns with a covering note telling Knudsen of the vital importance of helping Burns carry out his job, and asking that all OPM officials be instructed to cooperate in every way in starting shipments to Russia promptly.[37]

This revamping of the administrative structure improved the situation somewhat, but not very much. Responding to the Presidential order transferring authority for Russian aid to DDAR, a meeting was held late on the afternoon of July 22 in the office of Brigadier General Charles B. Hines, Executive Officer of the Army-Navy Munitions Board, to review the Russian requests. Present were Colonel Faymonville and Dr. Hazard, who made up the Russian supply division of DDAR, representing Burns; Curtis for the State Department; and several representatives of the Army and of the Priorities Division of OPM. The group began its deliberations after noting that the list of Russian requests attached to Welles's letter of July 18, had "come back approved" following the Cabinet meeting of July 19 (as well as the modest Curtis Committee recommendations), the Welles memorandum thus in effect constituting a Presidential order for action. Nevertheless the group meeting in General Hines's office again rejected a number of requests for immediate delivery, though it did also grant a number of others. Among the requests it granted were those for gasoline and lubricants, steel tanks, drill pipe, an aviation lubrication oil plant, crude oil distillation, cracking and stabilization plants, and a tire plant. Among the items it rejected for immediate delivery were an aluminum rolling mill, a catalytic cracking plant, and a high octane gasoline plant. The group further recommended that aviation gasoline be sent instead of the aviation gasoline plant requested, and that a great number of Soviet contracts for immediate production which had been cancelled by official United States order be reinstated. The Curtis Committee's restrictions on machine tools were left unchanged.[38]

Despite the efforts of Faymonville and Hazard, therefore, which were reflected in some increase in the items recommended for immediate shipment, the Soviet request for the delivery of their entire list within twelve months was not met. The majority at the July 22 meeting thus appeared to be following the same policy as the Curtis Committee, giving export priority to finished products but turning down Russian requests for plants, machine tools, and raw materials which the United States needed urgently itself and which, if delivered, might quite possibly fall into German hands. The decision therefore was to approve only $21,-940,000 out of the initial request of $1,845,-668,000 for purchase and export by October 1; also approved for later shipment were items worth $50,603,000, while others totalling $41,-065,000 were specifically disapproved. Not acted upon were items amounting to $1,754,-000,000, including $1,050,000,000 worth of aviation and $700,000,000 of ordnance plants and equipment.[39]

4. *THE PRESIDENT BEGINS TO TAKE A HAND—AND THE AID SNARL CONTINUES*

The next day General Burns reported the group's recommendations to the President, noting that "Pursuit planes and bombers which are considered by the Soviet ambassador to be of prime urgency are not included in the list, as these items are understood to be receiving the personal attention of Mr. Welles."[40] Instead of satisfying the President's desire for action, the report only increased his impatience. On the face of the Burns report the President scribbled this note to his military aide:

July 25, 1941. To take this up this morning with the Secretary of War, Acting Secretary of State (if the latter is involved) and get the thing through because there is some mixup on it and I would like the thing gotten through by tonight.

"The thing [exactly what it was is still not clear] went through that night," Stettinius later wrote, "and procurement of those items on the list not already in warehouses was begun immediately."[41] On Sunday, July 27, Welles communicated to Oumansky the action that had thus been taken.[42]

Despite this Presidential intervention—and President Roosevelt's note of July 25 continued to be cited later on whenever requests for Soviet aid seemed to be bogging down for one reason or another—the questions that energetic good will alone could not solve were only beginning to be faced. There was the considerable problem of how the Soviets were going to pay for the aid that was now beginning to be extended to them; that question seemed to cause less trouble at the moment, however, than the fact that in certain principal—and so far as the Russians were concerned crucial—categories, the amount and character of the aid remained to be determined. What, in particular, was the U. S. going to do about supplying the Soviets with aircraft? The War Department took the position that there just weren't any bombers available for transfer to the Soviets, and in all probability not more than 50 fighters could be provided over and above what the British were willing to yield from the total of planes currently on order for them.[43] Just at this time, on July 26, a Soviet military mission arrived, under Lieutenant General F. I. Golikov, which did much to change the situation. The Russians exuded confidence; this improved their chances of obtaining substantial aid. Russia, they insisted over and over again, would hold out against the Nazis and even launch a winter offensive. After conferring with Marshall and Stimson, the Russians went to see the President, Welles, Knox, and Knudsen. Daily conversations were held by them with officials of the State Department, and their optimism finally inspired even Stimson to promise a squadron of fighter planes, beyond the 150 which had already been crated and shipped to Britain, for eventual delivery to Russia.[44]

Still, at the end of the first month of this informal Russian aid program, the actual movement of supplies to Russia was proceeding at a snail's pace. This was natural enough in view of the practical difficulties, but Roosevelt was impatient and insistent. His first drastic move came at his Cabinet meeting on August 1. There he devoted most of an hour to lecturing his Cabinet on the need for prompt and substantial assistance to the Soviets. Secretary Morgenthau noted in his diary that the President had gone "to town in a way I never heard him go to town before. He was terrific. He said he didn't want to hear what was on order; he said he wanted to hear what was on the water."[45] Only Harold Ickes, who was also serving as Petroleum Coordinator at the time, could cite a definite achievement of his own: the first shipments of petroleum products were on their way to Siberia. Roosevelt's sharp language therefore was directed chiefly at Stimson. The Secretary of War was not inclined to take the President's criticism lying down. He had long been "the most severe critic of the 'uncorrelated organization' for handling supply problems"; and the fact was, he told the President, he had heard nothing whatever so far of Russian needs beyond the request for planes, which had been considerably complicated by the Russians' senseless insistence on their shipment by way of Vladivostok (the Russians having, some time before, demanded that even planes which were already in England or on their way there be rerouted back to the U. S. for shipment to Russia by way of the Pacific). Roosevelt, however, was in no mood for long discussion. "Get 'em," he told Stimson, "even if it is necessary to take them from [United States] troops." Stimson was naturally much angered by all this. In his *Diary* he wrote: "This Russian munitions business thus far has shown the President at his worst. He has no system. He goes haphazard and he scatters responsibility among a lot of uncoordinated men and consequently things are never done."[46]

The President's next step came on the following day. Whether to introduce "system," as Stimson wanted, or merely to create another source of pressure, on August 2 he moved to set up (reportedly at Welles's suggestion) a "Top Committee" to deal with Russian aid.[47] As its members he appointed Harry Hopkins (at the moment in Moscow) to be represented by Burns; Arthur Purvis, the head of the British Purchasing Mission in the United States, to be represented by Jean Monnet; and Oumansky; Faymonville was to be the Committee's executive secretary. At the same time Roosevelt addressed a letter to Wayne Coy, who had been brought into the Office for Emergency Management—a deliberately amorphous unit within the Executive Office—as a trouble shooter, assigning him the task of expediting matters while Burns was away at the forthcoming Atlantic Conference (due to begin August 9):

Personal and Confidential

August 2, 1941

Memorandum for Wayne Coy:

I raised the point in Cabinet on Friday that nearly six weeks have elapsed since the Russian War began and that we have done practically nothing to get any of the materials they asked for on their actual way to delivery in Siberia.

Frankly, if I were a Russian I would feel that I had been given the run-around in the United States.

Please get out the list and please, with my full authority, use a heavy hand—act as a burr under the saddle and get things moving!

The enclosed [Memo from General Marshall to the President re Transfer of Air Material to Russia, August 2] comes in just before I leave. In regard to bombers, we should make and the British should make small token deliveries. In regard to

P-forties, it is ridiculous to bring back here from England by steamer through the submarine zone and we should expedite 200 of them via Fairbanks from the total number now in this country.

I have told the Russians that I am dividing things into two categories—first, material which can be delivered on the Russian western front in time to take part in battle between September 1 and October first—and secondly, those materials which physically could not get there before October first. I have chosen that date because after October first, we all doubt if there will be very active operations in view of rain, snow, frost, etc. and that if Germany can be held until then, Russia is safe until the Spring.

Step on it!

F. D. R.[48]

The new "Top Committee" proved to be ill-fated from the very start. In its nature it could be no more than a forum for negotiation or coordination: as an international group, it could give no orders to U. S. or British agencies. Secondly, British cooperation was only to be had by continual recourse to London, since British help on the matter of expediting aid to Russia had to consist not only of giving up expected American goods but actually contributing matériel turned out or available in the British Isles. Then, too, Oumansky proved anything but cooperative by constantly asking for information of all sorts without providing any in return. When Oumansky once asked the U. K. representative on the Committee, Monnet, for full information on the British financial and industrial position to determine how much aid the United Kingdom could send to Russia, Monnet was momentarily nonplussed and then angrily told Oumansky that he could not release such information to him. Burns told the Russian the same thing when asked about American production, and in turn queried Oumansky about Soviet production. Oumansky said he had no such information. The Committee met only once during the entire month of August, and then dissolved when it became apparent that it would succeed neither as a coordinating nor an expediting group.[49]

Nor, in fact, were Coy's efforts any more successful—though the problem he encountered was far more real and difficult. For the problem of U. S. production shortages was simply not soluble by administrative reorganizations and Presidential directives. These shortages were to continue for a long time and to make for con-

siderable difficulty both in our relations with the Soviets and for smooth relations within the government in Washington. On August 6 Coy wrote to Knudsen, head of OPM, enclosing a copy of the President's letter of August 2, and asking Knudsen to take in hand personally the very serious shortages of machine tools, tire plants, and aluminum.[50] Knudsen referred the letter to an assistant, John D. Biggers, and on the basis of his investigation replied on August 9. The Russians, Knudsen wrote to Coy, were already inspecting tire plants for second-hand machinery or possible dismantling. As for machine tools, 138 would be delivered by December, and 29 more could be sent if "logical substitutions" were acceptable. The rest would have to wait until "the forepart of 1942." The aluminum was on the New York docks waiting for a priority after which the Priorities Division of OPM would approve its shipment. In general, Knudsen continued, the aluminum and machine tools could be used in our own defense program, and their shipment to Russia would delay the bomber program "on the urgency of which the President has placed so much emphasis."[51]

Knudsen reiterated his position at a meeting of the Council of the OPM three days later. Remarking that Faymonville had concurred with the Russian military mission in its demand for a large shipment of machine tools, Knudsen said flatly that he would not clear those tool orders which would affect the bomber production program, "until he had an opportunity to bring to the attention of the White House the effect of so doing and received definite instructions."[52]

There the matter rested until Roosevelt returned from the Atlantic Conference with Churchill, and not only approved General Burns's second list of delivery dates for items to be shipped to Russia but also announced an Anglo-American pledge of assistance to the Soviet Union and the promised dispatch of a mission to Moscow to place Russian aid on a long-term basis. This last decision had a history of its own that throws interesting light on the civil-military background of Russian Lend-Lease.

The Anglo-American promise of assistance to the Soviet Union announced by the President on August 21 was not the first statement of its kind issued in Washington. As early as August

2, the day after Roosevelt had so vigorously lectured the Cabinet on the subject of Soviet aid, the State Department and the Soviet Ambassador had exchanged notes in which it was announced that

the Government of the United States has decided to give all economic assistance practicable for the purpose of strengthening the Soviet Union in its struggle against armed aggression. This decision has been prompted by the conviction of the Government of the United States that the strengthening of the armed resistance of the Soviet Union to the predatory attack of an aggressor who is threatening the security and independence not only of the Soviet Union but also of all other nations is in the interest of the national defense of the United States.[53]

In addition the Soviet Government was assured that unlimited export licenses would be granted them, that all possible American shipping would be made available to them, and above all that their orders henceforth would enjoy priority status equal to that of Great Britain.

5. THE HOPKINS MISSION TO MOSCOW

Almost at the very moment the United States was thus publicly pledging all possible aid, negotiations were being carried on in Moscow between Harry Hopkins and the top leaders of the Soviet Union. It was as a result of Hopkins' trip to Moscow,[54] July 29 to August 1, that the President became convinced, beyond all question, that the Russians not only could but would hold out against the Nazi onslaught and that therefore all possible military assistance should be extended to the Soviets to help them achieve the objective of stopping and, ultimately, throwing back the Nazi invader.

Hopkins, as it happened, had never planned to go to Moscow at this time. He had left Washington for Great Britain on July 13, to lay the groundwork for the Atlantic Conference scheduled for August. During his first week in London, however, he became aware of the difficulties imposed upon joint Anglo-American strategic planning by the absence of any concrete and reliable information concerning the extent to which the United States and Great Britain could depend upon the Russians.[55] Hopkins therefore decided that if he made the journey to Moscow, he might be able to garner valuable military information and re-endorse to Stalin personally the pledge of all-out support that Roosevelt had first made privately to Oumansky on July 10. Churchill at once approved the idea; and on July 25 Hopkins cabled his plan to Roosevelt, saying that his object was to do what could be done to help Stalin maintain a permanent front even if the immediate battles went adversely, and to let Stalin know "in an unmistakable way that we mean business on a long term supply job." Roosevelt replied the next day that both he and Welles highly approved the idea of the trip.[56]

The details of Hopkins' arduous journey are vividly set forth in Robert E. Sherwood's biography, and need not therefore be repeated here at length. Hopkins arrived in Moscow on the morning of July 30, and had his first interview with Stalin the same evening. Hopkins expressed to Stalin "the President's belief that the most important thing to be done in the world today was to defeat Hitler and Hitlerism. [He] impressed upon [Stalin] the determination of the President and our Government to extend all possible aid to the Soviet Union, at the earliest time."[57] The question of aid to the Soviet Union, Hopkins told Stalin, was divided into two parts. "First, what would Russia most require that the United States could deliver immediately and, second, what would be Russia's requirements on the basis of a long war?" Stalin replied that his most immediate need was for anti-aircraft guns of medium calibre, together with ammunition (approximately 20,000 pieces of artillery, large and small); and he added that he also needed large-size machine guns for the defense of cities, and one million rifles.[58] So far as long-range needs were concerned, Stalin asked first for high octane aviation gasoline, second, for aluminum for the construction of airplanes, and third, for the other items already on the list presented in Washington. At one point Stalin burst out: "Give us anti-air-craft guns and the aluminum and we can fight for three or four years."[59]

The following evening Hopkins had another three-hour conversation with Stalin at the Kremlin.[60] Stalin reviewed the military situation, admitting the temporary inferiority of the Red Army, but insisted that it would have recovered its full strength by the spring of 1942 and would then face the Germans with new divisions. Stalin also gave Hopkins numerous figures on current

Russian war production, with hopeful estimates of production figures to be reached within a few months. "He expressed great confidence that the [battle] line during the winter would be in front of Moscow, Kiev and Leningrad—probably no more than 100 kilometers away from where it is now." Stalin then repeated the specific Russian needs he had first outlined to Hopkins the previous evening.

Hopkins thereupon proposed a plan he had discussed earlier that day with Sir Stafford Cripps, the British Ambassador in Moscow, calling for a meeting of the representatives of the three powers—the United States, the United Kingdom, and the Soviet Union—to coordinate strategy and supply. Hopkins told Stalin that the decisions relating to long-range supply problems could only be resolved if the government in Washington had "complete knowledge, not only of the military situation in Russia, but of type, number and quality of their military weapons, as well as full knowledge of raw materials and factory capacity." Such a conference, Hopkins suggested, should not be held however until after the Russian front was stabilized. He proposed therefore that the date be set for some time after October 1; Stalin agreed, requesting only that the conference be held in Moscow.

Hopkins had another reason for wanting such a conference, for once in Moscow he learned quickly what it was like to deal with the Russians. "There is," he wrote Roosevelt, "literally no one in the whole Government who is willing to give any important information other than Mr. Stalin himself. Therefore, it is essential that such a conference be held with Mr. Stalin personally. I believe he would give this conference his personal attention. My suggestion is that the conference be not held prior to October 1, but not later than October 15."[61]

After his three days in Moscow, Hopkins flew back to Scotland, and almost immediately started on his voyage across the Atlantic on the *Prince of Wales en route* to the Atlantic Conference. He was Churchill's guest on board, and the two spent much time together. Hopkins also used the occasion to prepare long and detailed written reports for the President; he sent copies of these reports to the Secretaries of State, War and Navy, except for one report describing how Stalin had urged that the United States declare war on Germany. (Hopkins' report on his first conversation with Stalin may have encouraged

the President to speak as he did at the Cabinet meeting of August 1.[62])

Hopkins' written reports made a strong impression and his oral reporting, first to Churchill and then to Roosevelt, seems to have had a decisive impact. For Hopkins had reached the conclusion—which now came to be shared by the President and Churchill—that if Stalin discussed the unfavorable aspects of the Soviet situation with such candor and optimism, he was a man who could be trusted to stick it out. Hopkins further believed that the figures given him by Stalin were substantially correct, and that reports of Russian weakness had been greatly exaggerated. He was also much impressed with the morale and steadfastness of the Russian people—comparable, he felt, to that of the British in their darkest hour. The Red Army, Hopkins told Roosevelt and Churchill, was still organizationally intact, with excellent communications and a working supply system, which meant that a disaster on the scale of the French and Polish defeats was definitely not in the making.[63] From then on, therefore, Hopkins tended to discount the pessimistic reports of the American military attaché in Moscow, Major Ivan Yeaton, and to accept instead the considerably more hopeful estimates of former Ambassador Davies[64] and of Yeaton's predecessor, Colonel Faymonville—a matter of considerable importance so far as the President's continuing position was concerned, particularly since Yeaton continued to send dolorous forecasts of Russian collapse (reporting as late as October 10 that "he considered it possible that the 'end of Russian resistance is not far away' ").[65]

Roosevelt and Churchill had always been more hopeful of Russian survival than their military advisers. Now, conferring together in the Atlantic Conference at Argentia, they had Hopkins' report to justify further and more far-reaching action. As a result they began for the first time to include Soviet Russia as a permanent factor in Anglo-American war and supply plans. (General H. H. Arnold, one of the high American military officers at the conference, wrote later on: "It was a new concept to me; the only information we had received concerning the Soviet campaigns indicated the Russians were having serious troubles."[66]) Secondly, Churchill now proposed, and Roosevelt accepted, the Hopkins-Cripps plan for a joint U. S.-British mission to Moscow to confer with the Russians on long-term supply problems. A message to this effect was delivered by the American and British ambassadors on September 13.[67] Thus originated the Harriman Mission, which journeyed to Moscow in late September and concluded the First Protocol, the formal basis of all U. S. Lend-Lease aid to Russia.

6. *ROOSEVELT RETURNS FROM THE ATLANTIC CONFERENCE*

But this is to anticipate. When Roosevelt returned to Washington on August 16, he found new difficulties compounding the old. The Atlantic Charter was generally well received, though some of the Senate isolationists were bitter and vindictive in their attack on the statement and on Roosevelt.[68]

In spite of this evidence of a divided nation, the President proceeded on his course. One of the urgent matters was, of course, aid to Russia, which had made little progress during the President's absence. Roosevelt could hardly view with much satisfaction the figures on the total amount of aid actually shipped to Russia during July: $6,521,912! The fact of the matter was that, while all the right and necessary public statements had now been issued (except that Russia was still not included under Lend-Lease; this was not to be done until October 30), the actual movement of war matériel continued to be impeded by serious domestic shortages as well as unsolved administrative problems. Time and again the President had to intervene to keep the ball rolling. It was not to be an easy matter; and the fact that any new aid program inevitably attained its momentum slowly was no comfort. Roosevelt undoubtedly knew that he was frequently asking for too much too soon, but he was also convinced, with much reason, that by setting high goals, he would get more than the pessimists thought possible.

7. *HOW TO FINANCE RUSSIAN AID?*

The first problem Roosevelt had to deal with was that of financing Russian aid.[69] This was not a new problem, of course, for it had been evident, ever since the first Russian requests for aid came in, that the Soviet Government lacked anything like the dollars required to pay for what they needed to carry on the war. The American public had no idea of the tremendous amount of money that would be required to finance Russian arms purchases, nor that Soviet requests submitted since early July amounted to almost two billion dollars. While Congress was considering the second Lend-Lease Appropriation bill, the President sought to keep up the impression that the Russians would indeed be able to pay for their own military purchases.[70] Much publicity was given to the "defrosting" of $39 million in Amtorg funds; and Welles, Hopkins, Morgenthau and Jesse Jones, head of the R.F.C., made statements to the press declaring that the Soviet Union's credit standing was excellent and that it possessed sufficient dollar and gold reserves to finance its war program.[71]

The President sought to emphasize Russia's excellent credit standing by placing the problem of Russian finances in Jones's hands. Both in the Congress and among wide sections of the public, Jones enjoyed a tremendous reputation as the one truly sound businessman in the New Deal. Negotiations between Jones, the R.F.C., and the Russians were not however progressing very well. At the beginning of July when Oumansky delivered the first Russian list, Welles had suggested that Russia pay for American munitions with shipments of raw materials; Oumansky, in turn, asked for a "credit arrangement."[72] The Russian request for a $500 million credit was then referred to Jones, but a snag developed over the legal requirement for adequate security.[73] On July 22 Jones told reporters that he had had conversations with Oumansky during the past week concerning Russian shipments of raw materials, especially chrome and manganese ores, in return for American machine tools. Nothing definite however was agreed upon between the two, and Russian purchases could continue only by virtue of U. S. Treasury advances of $10 million for ninety days against gold receipts.[74]

Oumansky's talks with Jones dragged on while Roosevelt was away at the Atlantic Conference.[75] On September 11, however, at a meeting at the White House, Oumansky finally asked the President for a direct credit.[76] If such was not forthcoming, the Soviet Union would press for Lend-Lease aid. Roosevelt was not yet prepared to go so far. He countered therefore with a suggestion, first made by Hopkins, that the Russians submit a complete list of their assets and gold—as the British had done—plus a statement that barter could be carried on between the two countries. Roosevelt offered to purchase, on a deferred delivery basis, all the chrome, manganese, and other commodities needed by the United States and available for export in Russia. In order to tide Russian aid over the next few months, the President offered a credit-barter arrangement of $75 million through the R.F.C.[77] (Roosevelt had already mentioned the possibility of an R.F.C. loan at his press conference of August 18, in order to explain why the new Lend-Lease Appropriation bill did not contemplate expenditures for Russian aid.)

On September 11, in a report to Congress on the progress of Lend-Lease, the President repeated the statement that Russia would be able to purchase munitions with her own funds.[78] The following day he sent to Jones his recommendation that Russia be extended dollar credits through loan and barter arrangements. On September 16 Jones announced that the R.F.C. was considering asking Congress for authority to lend the Russians "several hundred million." (What sort of security would the United States want for a Russian loan, Jones was asked once, late in August: "Oh, I guess a promissory note," he is said to have replied.[79]) Such action through the R.F.C. would do away with the necessity of financing Russian purchases out of Lend-Lease appropriations. The amount would have to be large, Jones said, since the Russian requests were understood to be over a billion dollars. Commenting on Jones's statement, the *New York Times,* which was dubious about Russian aid, said that Congress might well approve such a loan if Jones did.[80]

The next day, September 17, Jones announced the signing of a raw-materials purchase-agreement with Andrei Gromyko, under which the Defense Supplies Corporation, an R.F.C. subsidiary, was to buy $100 million worth of Soviet manganese, chrome, arsenic and platinum ores for delivery over two or three years. Pending delivery, the Russians would be advanced $50 million. In making the announcement, Jones remarked that this money would meet Russian dollar needs for weeks because of existing shipping shortages and the small amount of munitions available for immediate export. Meanwhile he would ask the Congress to approve an R.F.C. loan.[81] The same day the second Lend-Lease Appropriation bill was introduced in Congress.[82] The problem of financing Soviet aid had been taken care of temporarily, but far more drastic action would be necessary to finance future needs.

8. *THE CATHOLIC PROBLEM AND THE TAYLOR MISSION TO ROME*

One reason why the President (and his advisers) had to go slow in accepting or proposing the idea of including Russia under Lend-Lease was simply that any aid to Russia remained objectionable to wide and vociferous sections of the public. Among the military, at least at the very top, to be sure, opposition to Russian aid in principle, was by this time dead or dying; in the first two months of war the Russians had suffered terrible defeats, but they had not collapsed. The chief opposition to Russian aid therefore, except for the still sizable isolationist bloc, came mostly from a highly vocal sector of Catholic opinion, and Roosevelt sought to pacify these objectors in several ways. Very possibly it was the President who inspired Supreme Court Justice Frank Murphy to make certain remarks before the Supreme Council of the Knights of Columbus, on August 19.[83] Justice Murphy sought to "explode the idea that the Nazi attack on Soviet Russia was a crusade against communism." He spoke at some length of the violent anti-Christian dogmas and policies of the Nazis, and concluded that under present circumstances "any nation resisting the might and aggression of Nazi Germany is, whether intentionally or not, advancing our interest as well as its own."

Roosevelt also sought to handle this particular problem more directly, with distinctly variable results. First of all, he sent Myron C. Taylor on a mission to the Vatican to enlist the personal support of Pope Pius XII.[84] The President apparently wished the pontiff to issue a statement reinterpreting the strongly anti-Communist encyclical of Pius XI, *Divini Redemptoris,* so as to make it easier for devout Catholics to accept and support the idea of supporting "godless Communism" against Nazi Germany. Taylor first met with the Pope on September 9, and presented to him a letter Roosevelt himself had written. Taylor had drawn the President's attention to Article 124 of the Soviet Constitution, which provided for freedom of religion; and the President therefore now wrote to Pope Pius, in part, as follows:

In so far as I am informed, churches in Russia
are open. I believe there is a real possibility that
Russia may as a result of the present conflict
recognize freedom of religion in Russia, although,
of course, without recognition of any official intervention on the part of any church in education
or political matters within Russia. I feel that if this
can be accomplished it will put the possibility of
the restoration of real religious liberty in Russia on
a much better footing than religious freedom is
in Germany today.

. . . I believe that the survival of Russia is less
dangerous to religion, to the church as such, and
to humanity in general than would be the survival
of the German form of dictatorship. Furthermore,
it is my belief that the leaders of all churches in
the United States should recognize these facts
clearly and should not close their eyes to these
basic questions and by their present attitude on
this question directly assist Germany in her present objectives.[85]

The pontiff seemed not unsympathetic to
the President's letter and to Taylor's own views.
Indeed the Pope did send to the Apostolic
Delegate in Washington a reinterpretation of
Pius XI's encyclical, with the result that official
(and soon private) Catholic opposition to Russian aid declined considerably.[86]

Other efforts of the President to deal with
the religious issue were less successful. While
Taylor was at the Vatican, Roosevelt raised the
matter with Oumansky in Washington. The subject came up at their meeting at the White
House on September 11, at which Oumansky
asked the President for Lend-Lease aid directly,
for the first time. Replying to Oumansky's request Roosevelt told him frankly of "the extreme difficulty of getting the necessary authority from Congress on account of the prejudice
and hostility to Russia and the unpopularity of
Russia among large groups in this country who
exercise great political power in Congress."
Roosevelt therefore suggested to Oumansky that
if Moscow "could get some publicity back to
this country regarding the freedom of religion
during the next few days . . . it might have a
very fine educational effect before the next
Lend-Lease Bill comes up in Congress." Oumansky agreed to take the matter up with his
government, but nothing ever came of Roosevelt's request.[87] Nor was the President any more
successful when he raised the subject of religious freedom in Russia at a news conference
on September 30.[88] A shower of criticism at
once descended on the President, even though
he had made it very clear that he was doing his
best to secure acceptance of the idea of religious
toleration in the Soviet Union.[89] Even the
Harriman Mission failed to extract satisfactory
assurances from the Soviet leaders.[90] Fortunately for Roosevelt the subject seemed soon
to lose its political explosiveness; other more
dramatic subjects claimed public attention and
the President's hands were freed.[91]

II. THE NEGOTIATION OF THE FIRST PROTOCOL

1. PREPARING FOR THE HARRIMAN MISSION TO MOSCOW

Financing Soviet aid on an interim basis and removing the religious issue were anything but easy matters for the President and his advisers to handle. Yet they were now confronted with a number of still more difficult problems. There was the matter of sending the promised mission to Moscow to negotiate a long-term supply agreement with the Soviets; there was the matter of producing and actually shipping out the supplies thus promised; and there was, finally, the matter of financing the large-scale aid that might well have to be extended to the Russians if they were to be kept in the war, as a powerful factor in the ultimate defeat of Nazi Germany.

So far as the forthcoming mission to Moscow was concerned—its formal title was "The President's Special War Supply Mission to the Union of Soviet Socialist Republics"[92]—the first requirement was the appointment of its members. This was handled in Hopkins' office.[93] Since this was to be a joint civil-military mission, the question arose as to who should head the mission. Hopkins was too ill to undertake a second trip to Moscow, so Averell Harriman, then head of Lend-Lease in London, was appointed chairman of the mission as a whole, with Lieutenant General Stanley D. Embick, a General Staff Corps expert on logistics and strategy, as the ranking military member. There was also the problem of finding military men of sufficiently high rank to impress the Russians with their importance—and sufficiently prominent civilians who could maintain balance in the mission as a whole. The President therefore chose Admiral William H. Standley, a former Chief of Naval Operations and a close personal friend of his, to represent the Navy; General Arnold named Major General George H. Brett to represent the Air Corps (he was later replaced by Major General James A. Chapey). General Burns was selected to represent DDAR and to take charge of administrative details and communications; he was also given the task of representing the Army when the mission arrived in Moscow. On the civilian side, Hopkins chose William L. Batt, former president of SKF Industries and currently Director of Materials for OPM. In addition, the Harriman Mission also included a number of lower echelon experts. The most important of these were Douglass V. Brown of OPM and Faymonville, who was to remain in Moscow because of his excellent contacts. Faymonville's appointment ran into some difficulty, since Army Intelligence, judging him to be pro-Russian, objected to his assignment. Hopkins however overruled them in short order: "You might as well get his papers ready, because he's going over."[94]

The relations of the Harriman Mission to the White House were clearly defined at the outset; all communications were to be sent directly to the President or Hopkins, not through the State Department or the military, though of course the actual messages went through established channels—probably naval.[95] About other preparations for the Harriman Mission nothing specific is known, though Sherwood glances at the heart of the matter in *Roosevelt and Hopkins:*

The preparations for the departure of the Harriman Mission to Moscow were immensely complicated, involving exhaustive negotiations and some heated arguments with the Army and Navy, the production and shipping authorities, and British representatives in Washington, over the long list of items which might be pledged to the Soviet Union.[96]

Shades of things to come!

2. GENERAL BURNS AND THE VICTORY PROGRAM

While the Harriman Mission was being selected, another development was coming to a climax. Ever since the inception of the Lend-Lease program, General Burns, a long-time advocate of industrial as well as military preparedness, had been much disturbed by the lack of basic American production goals and had been pushing, though without much success, the idea of an over-all American production program.[97] Burns sought to attain his objective in two ways: by operating through "channels" (meaning through his immediate War Department superior, Under Secretary of War Robert P. Patterson), and by direct contact with Hopkins and the President himself. Thus on April 18 Patterson signed and sent to Stimson a memorandum, drawn up by Burns,[98] which declared that despite existing programs, American production facilities in actual use were far below the real munitions capacity of the country. And Patterson therefore asked for a "production effort necessary to achieve victory on the basis of appropriate assumptions as to probable enemies and friends and theaters of operations."[99] Stimson referred Patterson's memorandum to the Joint Board, where it rested until the President himself took up the matter on July 9.

The President's action came in the form of a letter to Stimson and Knox, based on a memorandum Burns had sent to Hopkins. (Burns, evidently, believed that the time had come for vigorous White House action on the production issue, and so had sent Hopkins a draft memorandum on the subject, to be issued over Hopkins' signature. Hopkins, however, believed that the matter was so important that he personally redrafted Burns's memorandum, keeping much of the original language, and then submitted it to the President for his signature.) In the letter Roosevelt asked Stimson and Knox "to explore at once the overall production requirements required to defeat our potential enemies. . . . I am not suggesting a detailed report, but one that, while general in scope would cover the most critical items in our defense and which could then be related by the OPM into practical realities of production facilities." "It seems to me," the President said,

"we need to know our program in its entirety, even though at a later date it may be amended. I realize that this report involves the making of appropriate assumptions as to our probable friends and enemies and to the conceivable theaters of operation which will be required."[100]

Though the President set no time limit for the preparation of the report, his letter had (as Burns had hoped) "a galvanic effect upon both War and Navy Departments."[101] What came to be known as the "Victory Program" soon absorbed the energies of numerous top staff planners both in this country and in Britain, and became a major project of the Army General Staff.

While the President was away at the Atlantic Conference, the White House did not press for the report. Toward the end of August, however, Burns, who in his capacity as Executive Secretary of DDAR was most cognizant of the prospective value of this study for a future coalition war, managed to convince Hopkins of the priceless opportunity the forthcoming Harriman Mission afforded of obtaining badly needed data from both the British and the Russians. The British, in fact, had already cabled their desire for a high echelon supply meeting. Hopkins liked the idea, and he and Burns at once began to sketch the necessary organizational steps.

Once back from the Argentia meeting, the President, too, wanted speedier action on his letter of July 9. On August 29 (a Friday) General Burns phoned the War Plans Division to announce that "the President is getting very impatient concerning the delay in submission of the report on ultimate requirements." Burns added that "the President would expect the report to be submitted to him complete by September 6, 1941," and asked the War Plans Division to notify the Navy Department to this effect.[102]

The very next day the President himself took action to speed the report he wanted, as well as to increase its scope. Hopkins was spending the weekend with him at Hyde Park, and Hopkins' trip to Russia was apparently among the subjects they discussed. Perhaps as a result of these conversations, on Saturday, August 30, the President sent to Stimson and Knox a memorandum (again, it appears, drawn up by Burns) which went considerably beyond his letter of July 9.[103] The President informed

Stimson and Knox that, as a result of Hopkins' visit to Moscow, and his subsequent report to the President and Prime Minister, it had been decided to send a joint Anglo-American mission to Russia, before October 1, to formulate a definite munitions aid program. And the President continued:

I deem it to be of paramount importance for the safety and security of America that all reasonable munitions help be provided for Russia, not only immediately but as long as she continues to fight the Axis Powers effectively. I am convinced that substantial and comprehensive commitments of such character must be made to Russia by Great Britain and the United States at the proposed conference.

It is obvious that early help must be given primarily from production already provided for. I desire that your Department . . . submit to me by September 10 next your recommendation of distribution of expected United States production of munitions of war, as between the United States, Great Britain, Russia and the other countries to be aided—by important items, quantity[,] time schedules and approximate values for the period from the present time until June 30, 1942. I also desire your general conclusions as to the overall production effort of important items needed for victory, on the general assumption that the reservoir of munitions power available to the United States and her friends is sufficiently superior to that available to the Axis Powers to insure the defeat of the latter.

*   *   *

After the above reports and recommendations are submitted, I propose to arrange with the Prime Minister of England for a conference of high military officials, for the purpose of discussing the above two recommendations as well as the aid to be provided by England to Russia. In view of the date on which the conference is to be held in Russia, it is important that the recommendations resulting from this British conference reach me not later than September 20th next.

With the knowledge of these recommendations, and after further consultation with the Prime Minister of Great Britain, I will be able to instruct the mission going to Russia as to the aid which will be supplied by this country. Should adjustments to this program of assistance be necessary, they will be recommended to me by the mission to Russia after due consultation with the Russians and the British on the spot.

Franklin D. Roosevelt.

Attached to the President's letter was a list of Russian requests received up to that time, which Hazard had compiled at Burns's direction.[104]

3. THE RUSSIAN REQUESTS AND HOW TO MEET THEM: THE MILITARY DISSENT AND THE PRESIDENT INTERVENES AGAIN

While plans for the "Victory Program" were thus being laid, work was going forward on current Russian aid. The President continued to press for action, and on August 18, after his return from the Atlantic Conference, approved a further list of Russian aid valued at $145,-000,000, delivery of which projected considerably into the future. The items approved were mostly semi-finished military materials—armor plate, field telephone wire, field radio receivers, aviation gas and lubricants, and toluol—the export of which might well serve to retard U. S. defense preparations or previously scheduled Lend-Lease shipments to other countries.[105] And though the war continued to go against them, the Soviets, at least as far as their military orders were concerned, never acted for a moment like a power on the brink of military disaster or total defeat. Throughout July and August their requests continued to include large quantities of raw materials, industrial machinery, and semi-finished goods, though naturally they also asked for very sizable amounts of finished war material: 3,000 pursuit planes and 3,000 bombers, 10,000 anti-aircraft cannon and 10,000 anti-aircraft machine guns, 1,000 light and 500 medium tanks, 5,000 anti-tank guns and 5,000 anti-tank machine guns, 20,000 submachine guns, and unspecified amounts of .30 calibre rifles and infantry mortars.

The top military officials in Washington were aghast at such requests. Where was all this material to come from? From the very beginning of Russian aid, the military (even those who were not actively opposed) had never been enthusiastic about it, not only because they wondered whether Russia could (or would) hold out, but because they felt—as the President had originally—that the best way to aid Russia was to speed all possible aid to Britain. Gradually, however, the military had begun to make concessions, agreeing first to the export of some of the semi-finished materials mentioned above,[106] then commencing to negotiate for the procurement of materials that fell under the jurisdiction of the War Department.[107] On August 4 General Marshall agreed to token releases of .30 calibre ammunition and aerial bombs (declared surplus) on an exchange contract, and on August 18 he approved the transfer of 1,000 Thompson submachine guns and still more bombs. Beyond such releases, however, he was unwilling to go, insisting that any additional military equipment for Russia come out of aid already allotted to Great Britain. This was also the line taken by Major General Richard C. Moore, Assistant Chief of Staff, G-4, in conferences with other government officials who suggested that some war material had to go to Russia even if there were shortages at home.[108] General Marshall was especially pained by the transfer of planes to the Russians, since these represented a particularly heavy sacrifice; on August 29 he protested to Stimson:

If any criticism is to be made in the matter [of Russian aid], in my opinion it is that we have been too generous, to our disadvantage, and I seriously question the advisability of our action in releasing the P-40's at this particular time. I question this even more when it only results in criticism, and I think the President should have it clearly pointed out to him that Mr. Oumansky will take everything we own if we submit to his criticisms.[109]

The background of Marshall's protest seems to have been as follows: The Soviets were certainly desperately short of planes (bombers and pursuit types), as well as aircraft engines and anti-aircraft guns, from the very beginning of the war—shortages reflected in their heavy demands for them in Washington; yet of all the lags in the American defense programs, the shortages of planes and anti-aircraft guns likewise were two of the most critical weaknesses. Actual negotiations concerning aircraft deliveries had started on a preliminary basis early in August. The U. S. negotiators in Washington were willing to offer the Russians only forty P-40's (fighters) and five B-25's (medium bombers). General Arnold was at the Atlantic Conference when this information reached him and he conferred with the President about the problem. They finally agreed to offer the Russians about 75 fighters during September, October, and November, and five B-25's a month during the same three months; these were small amounts, hardly likely to satisfy the Russians, who were themselves producing thirty fighters a day, yet such an offer constituted a heavy sacrifice for both the U. S. and Great Britain.

General Marshall's position was thus natural and understandable, and was shared by Stimson. Under the circumstances it was clearly necessary for the President, if he wanted to maintain his policy, to intervene once more with a powerful affirmation of the principle of all possible aid to Russia. This, of course, the President was determined to do and the following day—August 20—he sent to Stimson (as well as to Knox) the vigorous memorandum already mentioned.[110] The President now called on the War Department to increase its offerings of available material beyond the 20 per cent of current production it had previously been agreed should go for foreign military aid—the increase presumably to be offered to the Russians.[111] (The 80-20 formula referred to here had been devised in June 1941, before the Nazi attack on Russia, as the most equitable division of current production between U. S. military needs and foreign military aid.[112])

On September 6 the Army offerings were sent to the White House. The War Department list, as originally drawn, had been very modest indeed but Hopkins had managed to exert enough pressure to have the list considerably increased by the time it reached the President. In order to make more war material available to the Russians, American requirements were now counted on a new formula. All U. S. base and task forces were to be equipped 100 per cent by June 30, 1942, forces in training 50 per cent; commitments already made to the British and Chinese were left intact. The surplus over and above these requirements was to be offered to the Russians. The Army list thus included 152 90 mm. anti-aircraft guns, 991 37 mm. antitank guns, 540 81 mm. mortars, 595 60 mm. mortars, 20,000 submachine guns, 729 light tanks, 795 medium tanks, 234 sound locators and searchlight units, and 250,000 kilometers of field telephone wire. No decision was made on the number of jeeps to be offered, pending notice of Russian requirements; ammunition (which was particularly short at the time) was to be furnished "on the best possible scale" to accompany the weapons transferred, bombs on a monthly basis, depending on the number of planes actually handed over.[113] Only in two categories—submachine guns and field telephone wire—were the Russian requests met; and where the Russians had asked for 3,000 pursuit planes and 3,000 bombers, the Air Force was able only to offer 1,200. The OPM list of available and industrial materials was likewise quite low, though in this case there seems to have been a misunderstanding to the effect that Russian requests were to be filled not only after American and other allied military needs but after normal domestic American civilian demands had been met.

4. *THE HARRIMAN MISSION IN LONDON*

The Harriman Mission arrived in London on September 15, and held its first meetings with Lord Beaverbrook and other British representatives the same day.[114] The London meetings were to deal with two subjects: the Anglo-American offerings to the Soviet Union at the forthcoming Moscow conference, and agreement on a combined Anglo-American Victory Program. On the latter subject agreement was not difficult; on the matter of Russian aid, however, the British and American representatives were far apart, and it took long and arduous negotiations—as well as the personal intervention of the President—to fashion the program to be proposed to the Russians.

For one thing, the Americans quickly discovered that initial British enthusiasm for the Russians had lessened somewhat since late June. Continued Russian suspicion of the British seemed to have led the latter to take a second look at their new ally; Churchill, who had earlier greeted the "arrival of Russia as a welcome guest at a hungry table," was beginning to find Stalin's postwar objectives unpalatable, the tone of his communications surly and grasping. More important yet, the British military were anything but anxious to share with their new ally the Lend-Lease aid they needed so desperately themselves—and which was very definitely in limited supply. They took the position, for the most part, that the best way to take advantage of the German attack on Russia was to increase American aid to Britain. Beaverbrook therefore proposed that the U. S. make an over-all allocation to the British, out of which they would then, with American advice, make sub-allocations to the Russians.[115] The British realized of course that any aid to Russia would tend to cut down on the amount they would receive, but Beaverbrook's method would limit their losses

and adjust them in the best possible way—for the British.[116] The possible political implications of this proposal were presumably not overlooked.

It was not that the British proposed cutting down on the aid they would send the Russians; they had already themselves promised the Soviets 200 pursuit planes and 250 medium tanks a month—what they counted on was American assistance to make up their losses. Both Harriman and General Embick, however, rejected Beaverbrook's proposal emphatically, and it was finally agreed that both countries should make separate offers to the Russians at the forthcoming meeting, the size to be agreed upon before the Anglo-American mission left for Moscow. The conference in London then broke up into a series of subcommittees—on ground, air, navy, raw materials and transport—which were to make detailed recommendations on what aid the two countries were to offer the Russians. The struggle over allocation of Lend-Lease continued in these various subcommittees, the British finding, to their utter dismay, that the Americans not only proposed to give to the Russians aid that they had themselves expected, but that the total "pie" from which they would receive their slice—that is, total American production—was now estimated to be considerably smaller than what they had anticipated.[117]

On two items—planes and tanks—it was impossible to produce agreement, and Washington had to intervene. So far as planes were concerned, the U. S. proposed to send to Russia 1,200 planes that the British had expected to receive; in addition the U. S. proposed to send the Russians all types of planes (that is, heavy, light and medium bombers, as well as pursuit planes). The Russians had originally asked for 400 planes a month for nine months, so that even what the U. S. was willing to offer amounted to less than half what the Russians had requested. The British, however, objected to giving the Russians any heavy bombers at all, and suggested instead that the U. S. compensate Britain with heavy bombers to make up for the lighter types they were sending to Russia themselves. Though Beaverbrook ultimately yielded somewhat on the issue, the final decision (from Washington, after the Mission had left for Moscow) was, in part at least, a victory for the British. On September 26 Hopkins cabled the delegation in Moscow that the President had decided to send no heavy bombers to Russia, but instead to increase their total allotment to 1,800 planes, the additional increase to come out of U. S. Army allocations, not from British Lend-Lease.[118]

The matter of tank allocations caused even more difficulty.[119] The fact was that the American delegation in London had to negotiate on the basis of tank production schedules considerably below those presented to the President in July (production on the proposed schedules having fallen behind). Indeed, tank production was sagging dangerously at the very time when Russian demands were beginning to make a considerable increase in production an absolute necessity. The American proposal therefore was to send to Russia 729 light and 795 medium tanks before June 30, 1942, this to be accomplished by ceasing all tank shipments to Britain during the first four months of 1942 (for the remainder of 1941 the British were to continue to receive tanks as previously allotted). Even so, the equipping of several American armored divisions would have to be considerably delayed.

The British were naturally flabbergasted to learn that the U. S. proposed to send 795 medium tanks to Russia over the next nine months, and only 611 to Britain. On September 19 the President himself intervened.[120] In short order he directed the Under Secretary of War to double tank production by next June 30, with delivery on the existing production schedule to be speeded up 25 per cent. The President stood on this order even after it was pointed out to him that the current priority of A-1-d was insufficient to achieve such production. Once the President had acted, it was up to the Army to figure out ways and means of producing more tanks; and Hopkins cabled Harriman the same day that the number of tanks available for export would be considerably greater than the figures originally given the American delegation. Given these revised estimates the London conference went on to decide that 500 tanks a month should be offered to the Russians, half of these to come from the U. S., half from Britain.

At home both the Navy and the Army were dissatisfied; the Navy was vigorously opposed to increasing the priority rating on tanks (but most of the tank program was nevertheless given

an A-1-a priority in November); all the Army could foresee was that if production fell behind, the British and Russians would receive their tanks, and the U. S. Army would have to do without.[121]

5. *THE HARRIMAN MISSION IN MOSCOW*

To Moscow! On September 22 the Anglo-American Mission (remembering perhaps Lord Kitchener's tragic fate) set off for Russia in two parts: Harriman, Beaverbrook and the British Mission traveling by cruiser from Scapa Flow by way of the Arctic Sea to Archangel, and from there by air to Moscow; the rest of the American Mission flying in two B-24's, over much the same route Hopkins had taken late in July.[122]

The conference in Moscow lasted four days, September 28 to October 1.[123] During that time Harriman and Beaverbrook met three times with Stalin—on the evenings of September 28, 29 and 30, for a total of about nine hours; meanwhile separate meetings were held by the subcommittees on army, navy, air force, raw materials, transportation, and medical supplies. Little or nothing, however, was accomplished in these meetings; as Hopkins had learned on his trip to Moscow,[124] the Harriman Mission quickly discovered that effective negotiations or discussions of any sort could be carried on only with Stalin. After their last meeting with the Soviet leader, Harriman wrote: "There can be no doubt that Stalin is the only man to deal with in foreign affairs. Dealing with others without previous instructions from Stalin about the matters under discussion was almost a waste of time."[125]

Yet even the negotiations with Stalin were far from smooth. At their first meeting Harriman presented him with a letter from the President, which said in part:

Harry Hopkins has told me in great detail of his encouraging and satisfactory visits with you. I can't tell you how thrilled all of us are because of the gallant defense of the Soviet armies.

I am confident that ways will be found to provide the material and supplies necessary to fight Hitler on all fronts, including your own.

I want particularly to take this occasion to express my great confidence that your armies will ultimately prevail over Hitler and to assure you of our great determination to be of every possible material assistance.[126]

This helped to get the talks off to a good start. Stalin first gave Harriman and Beaverbrook a frank statement of the military situation, stressing that German superiority lay in planes, tanks, and divisions. He then went on to give Harriman and Beaverbrook a list of the items most urgently needed: tanks, he ranked first, followed by anti-tank guns, medium bombers, anti-aircraft guns, armor plate, fighter and reconnaissance planes. Harriman discussed with Stalin the matter of the Siberian airports, and the possibility of sending American planes to Russia via Alaska. This particular idea, however, seemed not to Stalin's liking, perhaps because he wished to take no chances on Japanese reaction—perhaps for other reasons. Nevertheless Harriman considered their first meeting a success. Both "Beaverbrook and I," he wrote, "considered the meeting had been extremely friendly and were more than pleased with our reception."[127]

The second meeting, the following night, was something else again. Somehow the entire atmosphere had been transformed. This time, instead of being cordial, Stalin was cold and brusque. "The evening," Harriman wrote, "was very hard sledding."

Stalin seemed discourteous and at times not interested, and rode us pretty hard. For example, he turned to me once and said, "Why is it that the United States can only give me 1,000 tons of armor plate steel for tanks—a country with a production of over 50,000,000?" When I tried to explain the length of time required in increasing capacity of this type of steel he brushed it aside by saying, "One only has to add alloys."[128]

Neither Harriman nor Beaverbrook was able to explain the sudden change in Stalin's demeanor; perhaps he had just received word of some particularly alarming Nazi advances (this, says Sherwood, was their likeliest guess); perhaps it was part of Soviet conference strategy. At any rate, this second meeting dragged on listlessly while the Russian requests were gone over again, item by item. Stalin's manner changed only once—when Harriman mentioned that the United States might be able to supply 5,000 jeeps, and Stalin asked if he could have more than that. But when Harriman went on to inquire if Stalin was also interested in some ordinary armored cars, Stalin retorted that

armored cars were death traps and that he wanted none. About the only agreement reached was to meet again the next evening.[129]

Meanwhile the subcommittees were making no progress either. Admiral William Standley, later American Ambassador to Russia, thus recalled his own experience:

Certainly, the Naval Committee, which I headed for the American delegation could get nowhere at all. We made various proposals for a program of naval supplies but Admiral Nikolai Kuznetsov, Commissar for the Navy and my opposite number in the Russian delegation, wouldn't even comment. I never felt that this indicated a lack of desire to cooperate as much as a lack of information and indecision. If we had had specific weapons and supplies to offer, the Russians *might* have told us where they were to go. Admiral Kuznetsov had the further disadvantage that he was also charged with defense of the Coastal Area and he probably just couldn't say where the items intended for shore stations would be used.[130]

Harriman and Beaverbrook spent most of the next day (September 30) conferring with Ambassadors Steinhardt and Cripps, as well as with General Burns and other members of the Mission, discussing the Russian requests and deciding in detail what Stalin might be offered at the final meeting that evening. Despite the very large and urgent Soviet requests, it was apparently agreed that the military offerings planned at London could not be changed, but that, to show the Russians the good will of the U. S. and Britain, the industrial offerings should be increased considerably over what had been planned.

At 6 P.M. Harriman and Beaverbrook arrived back at the Kremlin, and once more the whole atmosphere was dramatically different—this time back to the cordiality that had marked the opening meeting on September 28.

Beaverbrook went through a memorandum listing everything that the Russians had asked for, stating those on which the Americans and British could not meet the demands immediately, and then a long list of items which could be met in full with even some extras thrown in. Beaverbrook asked Stalin if he was pleased with the list. Stalin replied that he had received the list with enthusiasm.

Litvinov, who was acting as interpreter, "bounded out of his seat and cried with passion, 'Now we shall win the war.'"[131]

Stalin, in the course of this last meeting, emphasized once more the Russian need for the largest possible number of jeeps and American three-ton trucks. The war, he said, would be decided by the gasoline engine: the side with the greatest output of engines would win the war. Harriman, for his part, told Stalin to feel free to communicate personally with the President on any matter he felt was important; the President, said Harriman, would welcome such direct contact—as he welcomed it with Churchill. "The meeting," Harriman wrote, "broke up in the most friendly fashion possible. Stalin made no effort to conceal his enthusiasm. It was my impression that he was satisfied that Great Britain and America meant business. . . . I left feeling that he had been frank with us and if we came through as had been promised and if personal relations were retained with Stalin, the suspicion that had existed between the Soviet Government and our two governments might well be eradicated."[132]

All that now remained was for the agreement to be signed, and this was done the following afternoon, October 1. The document, which came to seven pages, was impressively titled: "Confidential Protocol of the Conference of the Representatives of the United States of America, the Union of Soviet Socialist Republics, and Great Britain, which took place in Moscow from September 29th till October 1st, 1941," and included more than seventy main items as well as over eighty items of medical supplies of various kinds. The Protocol consisted chiefly of three columns: the first column listed all the items either asked or promised—the items ranging all the way from airplanes and tanks to gasoline, army boots, and wheat; the second column gave the specific size of each Russian request; and the third column gave the U. S.-British offer, either in the form of a definite promise to deliver a certain quantity of a particular item, or a promise to investigate the available supply.[133]

The United States and Britain promised to deliver these goods "at the centers of production," and in roughly equal monthly installments between October 1, 1941 and June 30, 1942.[134] While the Protocol specified that transportation was to be the responsibility of the Russians, for practical purposes the United States and Britain were bound to do all they could to expedite and protect the shipments. Since the Soviet merchant marine and navy were both small, the promised matériel would either have

to be delivered in British bottoms (which were likewise in very short supply) or the ships or shipping tonnage would have to be provided under Lend-Lease. Moreover, while only the amounts specifically promised by the U. S. and Britain were to be considered as binding obligations, the two countries pledged, if possible, to meet the Russian requests in full.

Looking over the Protocol, the major commitments made by the U. S. and Britain appear very large compared to what they could afford to send. In the case, for instance, of the most important single item—aircraft—General Arnold's estimate of what the U. S. could spare had already been discarded in London, and in the end the U. S. promised to deliver by June 30, 1942 not 1,200 planes but 1,800. (This decision, as mentioned above, was made in Washington after the Harriman Mission had left London for Moscow, and was cabled ahead by Hopkins, who was taking a leading position in the behind-the-scenes negotiations.[135]) The Russians thus were now to receive 400 planes a month, 200 fighters from Britain and 100 bombers and 100 fighters from the U. S. In the matter of aluminum, so important in the earlier Hopkins-Stalin talks, Britain promised Russia 2,000 tons a month from Canadian production, and the U. S. promised an equal amount, plus 500 tons of rolled "duraluminum," a "hard aluminum" used in military aircraft. The idea was for Britain to supply most of the raw materials, the U. S. the semi-manufactured items, chemicals, and aviation gasoline. And though this was not specifically stated, the July 25 and August 18 lists prepared by General Burns, approved by the President, and transmitted to the Russian Ambassador by Welles were likewise now accepted as binding agreements. This was important, for the U. S. thus also promised to make good Soviet requests for various types of industrial plants not mentioned in the October 1 Protocol.

Though the promises made in Moscow were, as has been said, very considerable in view of Anglo-American needs and capacities, in the main these promises did not go beyond decisions already reached in London; only in a few cases, where the Russians were especially insistent, were larger offerings made, and in several other instances all that was promised the Russians was "further study of the subject." In some cases, then, the Moscow Protocol satisfied Soviet demands; in others even the "paper agreement" fell far short of these requests. Thus for instance while Stalin had vigorously demanded 10,000 tons of armor plate, all that he was tentatively promised was 1,000 tons; where the Russians had asked for 4,000 tons of toluol a month the U. S. promised only 1,250 tons.[136] In the last analysis, it was not the paper promises that mattered; the important question was, would the U. S. and Britain be able to make and deliver the goods? For as Washington was soon to learn, agreeing to and signing a Protocol—even with the Russians— was a small matter compared with making good its terms.

With the signing of the Protocol on the afternoon of October 1, the official business of the Harriman-Beaverbrook Mission was practically completed. Only some technical reports remained to be written, and there was a whole round of entertainments and sight-seeing. Finally early on Saturday morning, October 4, the Harriman-Beaverbrook Mission left Moscow, as it had arrived, in two parts. It reassembled briefly in London to discuss the commitments the two countries had undertaken in the Protocol. On October 18 the Harriman Mission arrived back in Washington. The first phase of Russian aid was over: a plan for action had been drawn; the problem now was action itself!

6. POSSIBLE POLITICAL USE OF RUSSIAN AID

One parenthetical note may perhaps be in order at this point. Much has been written about how the United States blundered in not demanding a specific written guarantee from Stalin about post-war Europe or indeed the whole post-war world, either during Hopkins' trip to Moscow or during the Harriman-Beaverbrook Mission.[137]

Contentions of this sort, and counter-contentions, open up a large and very debatable subject—a subject that would be out of place in this study. All that can properly be said here is that the failure to seek a political agreement with Stalin in the summer and fall of 1941 was an act of policy—policy strongly supported by both Hull and Roosevelt. On December 5, 1941, for example, a cable from Hull to Winant, the American Ambassador in London (a cable approved by Roosevelt), said: "In our considered opinion it would be unfortunate for any of the three governments . . . to enter into commitments regarding specific terms of the postwar settlement. . . . Above all, there must be no secret accords . . . the constitutional limitations to which this Government is bound must be kept in mind."[138] This cable was read to Eden just prior to his departure for Moscow, where he sought post-war agreements and found Stalin eager to make a deal—but a deal that the British could not possibly accept, and this at a time when Moscow was still under German siege.[139]

It has been argued that Roosevelt's failure to use the Hopkins and Harriman Missions for political ends was a blunder; it was certainly not an oversight.[140] And so far as is known, Churchill, who strongly approved the Hopkins Mission and shared responsibility for the other mission, also made no effort to attach strings to the Anglo-American offers of all-out military assistance.[141]

III. PROBLEMS IN FULFILLING THE FIRST PROTOCOL

1. ADMINISTRATIVE CHANGES AND RUSSIAN AID: FROM DDAR TO OLLA

The Harriman Mission returned to Washington on October 18, 1941. During its absence, the American defense program had been growing steadily, as had Lend-Lease and other foreign aid and control programs. New goals and scarcities had led to new administrative arrangements. Two of these proved particularly consequential for the Russian aid program.

For several months in 1941, the central priorities authority and direction of industry were vested in the Office of Production Management (OPM). During the summer, however, owing to a variety of complications and difficulties, it was decided that OPM was inadequate: OPM remained in existence but on August 28 was made subject to guidance from a newly created policy body, the Supply, Priorities and Allocations Board. SPAB, as it was known, included in its membership the four members of the OPM Council—Knudsen, Hillman, Stimson, and Knox—as well as Vice President Wallace (chairman), Price Administrator Leon Henderson, and Hopkins. Donald M. Nelson was appointed Executive Director of SPAB. Partly perhaps by temperament, largely by occupational responsibility, the SPAB was far more sympathetic to Russian aid than the OPM Council had been.

The other organizational change was still in process when the Harriman Mission returned. It will be recalled that originally the administration of Lend-Lease was deliberately played down. The Division of Defense Aid Reports, headed by a mere Executive Secretary, General Burns, had no very authoritative ring; and Hopkins had been designated merely to "advise and assist" the President on Lend-Lease affairs. All this served to reduce the importance of Lend-Lease in the public eye—and kept the program under the very direct control of Roosevelt and his alter ego, Hopkins.

The growth of Lend-Lease, notably the British program, made this shadowy arrangement unsatisfactory. The first step towards putting the program as a whole on a permanent basis was the appointment of Edward R. Stettinius, Jr., as Special Assistant to the President for Lend-Lease, in late August 1941. In his letter appointing Stettinius the President wrote: "Harry Hopkins is, of course, familiar with the administration of lend-lease, and I hope you will consult with him and with me where matters of major policy arise."[142]

Such was the situation when the Harriman Mission returned. Ten days later, on October 28, the final step was taken: the Office of Lend-Lease Administration was created with Stettinius as Administrator. Under the new setup, OLLA absorbed and superseded DDAR.

2. THE HARRIMAN MISSION RETURNS TO WASHINGTON AND THE WHEELS BEGIN TO TURN—OR DO THEY?

Once the Harriman Mission was back in Washington, the next problem was to make good on the commitments made at Moscow. On the evening following the Mission's return, Stettinius asked its members to dinner at his apartment; also present were Vice President Wallace, General Marshall, Secretary Knox, Secretary of Commerce Jones (who was also head of the R.F.C.), Under Secretary of the Navy Forrestal, Assistant Secretary of War for Air Robert A. Lovett, Donald Nelson and William Knudsen—all of them men vitally concerned with the progress of foreign military aid. After dinner—Stettinius was later to write—the group "settled down to discuss how the promises of the Protocol could be translated into an effective production and shipping program. Harriman and the others gave us the full story of the trip and the negotiations in Moscow. I remember they repeatedly used the words 'tough,' 'realistic,' and 'good traders' in describing the Soviet officials but they did not think the Moscow requests were unreasonable. They had been greatly impressed by Stalin and by what they had seen of the manufacturing techniques and equipment in Russian factories."[143]

The problem now before the authorities in Washington was threefold: to produce, or to find in existing and already assigned stock, the materials promised the Russians; to transport these items to the Soviet Union; and to find a way to finance the materials so handed over.

Fulfillment of the Protocol was to prove a very difficult matter indeed, as could be foreseen from the beginning. Realizing this, Roosevelt took the position that the Protocol was a binding obligation; fulfillment of the Protocol would be looked on by the Russians as the acid test of American good faith. Both positions were repeatedly used by those who—like Hopkins—strove for vigorous action on Russian aid, in order to counteract the arguments of dissenters. The Protocol, it may be remarked, was a unique Lend-Lease agreement in its specificity; for all the others dealt in general principles, not with specific commodities and amounts. Russian aid as defined in the Protocol thus had something approaching absolute priority.

The Protocol posed a number of problems at the very outset. For one thing, the Russians had revealed little about the state of their industrial and military supplies. In some cases they were reluctant even to discuss specifications for fear of revealing the nature of their equipment—to their Allies! General Burns, for one, wrote off this attitude as part of "Russian secrecy" and accepted it as such. If he thought a specific Russian request unreasonable he rejected it; and knowing that it was useless to press the Russians for details they were determined not to give, Burns used American capacity as a yardstick to measure Russian requests. Though he was perhaps more than any other individual responsible for the acceptance of the "Victory Program" idea, Burns, too, had to accept the failure of all attempts to gather Russian statistics for the projected over-all Allied Victory Program; even a request

Hopkins made to the Russian embassy late in September was only politely acknowledged, forwarded to Moscow, and never heard of again.[144]

In a memorandum for his files in 1943, Batt, who had struggled with the problems of Russian aid since 1941, thus described the situation that obtained at the beginning of the program:

From the outset of our relationship with the USSR, I have felt that this government should have had a stronger policy with them. When most materials were in short supply and what we sent them represented a sacrifice for us and the British, I thought we had every reason to insist that they make some kind of case before we gave them what they asked for. When we negotiated the First Protocol in Moscow, we got a little information from them in connection with the more critical materials. They would give some round figures of their production, and as it was always small, it was obvious that their request of us added to their own resources didn't leave much for any army of 300 or more divisions. Between ourselves, the wonder always was how they managed to get along.

After our return, it seemed to me desirable that we continue the practice of pressing them for more information so that we could make a wiser decision, but the President and Mr. Hopkins took the larger view that it seemed to irritate and that the risk wasn't [great—] generally underneath 10% of total supply, and that seemed a small amount to make available to an Ally yielding so much in wartime returns.[145]

The First Protocol produced still other difficulties. The delivery schedules of the Protocol, for instance, were set up on a fiscal year basis, while the Army placed its orders on a calendar year basis. Moreover, the division of United States-British commitments into equal monthly installments was a highly artificial procedure, since in many cases this arrangement disregarded the lead-time necessary to prepare for the manufacture of items having a long production cycle, such as machine tools and heavy military and industrial equipment. Later on, this problem was partially solved by a complicated arrangement which allowed the Russians to place orders for such material even before subsequent Protocols had been signed.

Also, numerous items had been agreed to at Moscow in general terms, but when the specific Russian requests arrived, they turned out to be unreasonable. Thus, for instance, the Russians had been allowed a large amount of "wire" in the belief that what they wanted was commercial grades of wire and wire rope. When the actual Russian requests arrived, however, they called for a fantastic amount of highly specialized carbon steel and music wire to be used in making gun-trigger springs. But this lack of specificity in the First Protocol also cut two ways. In some categories such as machine tools, only a certain number of "pieces" of a given dollar amount were promised. The actual types delivered therefore were juggled so that, while the total number of machine tools actually sent met Protocol requirements, no tools were sent which were critically needed in the United States.

It was clear, too, that from time to time the Soviets would make certain extra-Protocol requests to meet special, unforeseen conditions. Such requests were provided for by "elastic clauses" in the Protocol, which permitted the Soviets to order "general items" up to a certain dollar limit; or they could simply submit a request for a specific item as being "extra-Protocol." Naturally such requests only added to the problem of meeting Protocol commitments already made.

3. ADMINISTRATIVE DISAGREEMENTS OVER THE PROTOCOL

The chief obstacle in the way of speedy, efficient and complete fulfillment of the First Protocol (as of later Protocols) was, it goes without saying, a shortage of the items requested by the Russians as well as a lack of shipping to transport such materials to the Soviet Union. But the complexity of the administrative machinery in Washington—not to mention of course the rival claims of the American military services—hardly made for the speediest and most successful handling of Soviet aid.

The complexity of this administrative process, which was largely the result of the burgeoning American war economy, is well illustrated by what happened to the Protocol once the text of it arrived in Washington. This occurred on October 10, and on October 13 the text was transmitted by OLLA to OPM.[146] Though much of the aid scheduled under the Protocol was to be procured by the Army and Navy, contract coordination and production sched-

uling had still to be taken care of by OPM.[147]

The Protocol was therefore taken up in the Council of the OPM (composed of Knudsen, Hillman, Stimson, and Knox) on October 14, and immediately threre began to be visible the stresses and strains, the conflicts of interest, that were to mark the Washington struggle over Russian aid throughout the entire war. This was not, it must be said at once, a struggle between the civilians and the military; it was far more a struggle between those civilians who sought to safeguard what they considered basic American needs and interests (while giving whatever aid possible to the Russians) and those civilians who believed in the necessity of all possible aid to the Russians, within broad limits that seemed to others almost regardless of American requirements. To this latter group —headed by William Batt, General Burns and Harry Hopkins, and supported all the way by the President—maintenance of the Russian front and continued good relations with the Soviets were the overriding object. It was between these two groups, essentially, that the struggle over the size of the Russian aid program now began to be contested.

At the October 14 meeting of the OPM Council Knudsen remarked at some length about the very large Russian requests for critical tools and machinery, including aluminum, steel plate and machine tools. Using as a point of departure Knox's report that Russian dock and transport facilities could only handle 15,000 tons a month, Knudsen promised "to scrutinize very carefully" the Russian requests.[148] Knudsen, it was thus clear, was one of those who believed in first taking care of American needs. Almost at once, however, jurisdiction was taken out of the hands of the OPM Council; the following day, October 15, Hopkins personally addressed the Supply, Priorities, and Allocations Board (SPAB). Hopkins emphasized the seriousness of the deficiencies in the supply of materials and equipment promised, and spoke of the necessity for immediate all-out aid to Russia and Britain.[148a] SPAB decided to make a survey forthwith of the United States' ability to meet its commitments under the Protocol. (The staff work on the survey was to be done by OPM officials, since SPAB had no separate staff of its own.)

While Batt, as head of the Materials Division of OPM, began to circularize all OPM divisions

to gather the necessary figures on possible deliveries of "open" items, as well as opinions
on how the "absolute" commitments could be
met, Knudsen began to move to try to reduce
the commitments already made, recommending
reductions of up to 66 per cent in steel and
machine tool commitments. When the list of
OPM recommendations finally reached Stettinius' office, however, he was anything but satisfied and at once wrote to Hopkins that he was
turning the list over to General Sidney Spalding, to pursue the matter further with Batt—
even top officials of the same agency, evidently,
were divided over how much material should
actually go to Russia.[149]

Knudsen, having thus failed to reduce American steel and machine tool commitments, did
succeed in getting the OPM Council to establish a new machine tool distribution formula.
Back in September Knudsen had reluctantly
agreed to the Russians' purchasing 350 machine tools to set up a rifle and machine gun
production line.[150] Now he was confronted with
new Russian requisitions for 1,200 machine
tools a month in addition to the 2,100 tools a
month already promised the British. The formula agreed to by OPM on October 21 therefore stipulated that no more than 25 per cent
of the production of any type of machine tool
should be released for export in any given
month.[151] While under this policy, which was
continued throughout the entire war with only
slight changes, the shipment of machine tools
was limited, by the same token the allies were
assured of a definite portion of American production. Knudsen's victory had its compensations for the recipients of Lend-Lease.

On October 29 SPAB met to hear and
consider Batt's report. With Hopkins and Harriman sitting in to lend weight to Batt's position,
the latter argued that the Russian requests were
really modest compared with their war effort
and our capacity, and that therefore the U. S.
should be able to make good on its commitments under the Protocol. Batt asked the Board
to grant its general approval for immediate action (despite some sacrifices that would admittedly have to be made by the American armed
forces as well as the civilian economy) so that
the United States would be able to match British aid to Russia and begin the planning of
immediate shipments. Hopkins spoke up, warning that the Russians would doubtless make

additional requests which would also have to be
favorably considered, and that the Board would
have to prepare itself to deal with increasingly
difficult problems. SPAB then went on to approve the list Batt had submitted, endorsing
prompt action upon it: "It is the sense of the
Board. . . ."[152] Events were to show, however,
that a SPAB decision was one thing; getting
action was a different and far more difficult
matter.

4. TO LEND-LEASE OR NOT TO LEND-LEASE

The next thing, indeed the first thing, that
needed to be done now was to have Russia
made eligible for Lend-Lease. The possibility
of this had been discussed of course as far
back as the outbreak of the Nazi-Soviet war,
in late June. But at that time the Administration either refused to entertain the idea or at
least to discuss publicly the possibility of it.
One reason for this was that the Congress was,
about that time, engaged in debating the second
Lend-Lease Appropriation bill, and from the
course of these debates the Administration had
good reason to believe that inclusion of Russia
in Lend-Lease at this time would only make
a difficult task—that is, passage of the pending Lend-Lease appropriation—more difficult
still.[153] The aim of the Administration therefore
was to block any amendments that would have
specifically banned all Lend-Lease aid to Russia, while disavowing the possibility of Russia's
immediate eligibility. The issue, of course, was
deeper than the immediate problem of Russian
aid: Roosevelt wanted no limits set on his discretion to determine national eligibility for
Lend-Lease aid, other than the standards set
by the original Lend-Lease Act. Stettinius, testifying for the Administration before the House
Appropriations Committee, urged that the
President's discretion be left unimpaired:

A prohibition in this appropriation bill against
lend-lease aid to the Russian Government would
be a terrific blow to Russian morale. "No matter
how bravely you fight" it would say to the Russian
people, "no matter how much your resistance
means to our defense, we won't help you!" Personally I see no reasons why we should not extend
lend-lease aid to anyone who contributes to our
defense by fighting Hitler. Personally I see no reason why we should not extend lend-lease aid to
Russia right now. But this is a high policy decision

that must be made by the President and the Secretary of State and the other ranking officials of the Government. The one thing I am sure of is that we shouldn't tie the hands of the President in protecting the interests of our own defense, when world events move as fast as they do today.[154]

On October 10 the matter came to a test on the House floor, and an amendment specifically banning all Russian Lend-Lease was defeated by a vote of 162 to 21.[155]

Even so, the opponents of Russian Lend-Lease were by no means finished. The subject came up once more when Stettinius testified before the Senate Appropriations Committee on October 14. The opposition clearly suspected that the President would use the first opportunity to deal Russia in on Lend-Lease (and many, if not most, were opposed to Lend-Lease itself). The Harriman Mission had just returned to Washington and it required no special insight to perceive that large-scale aid to Russia would inevitably mean Lend-Lease for Russia. When the second Lend-Lease Appropriation came before the Senate, there was not even a formal amendment put to ban Lend-Lease aid to Russia.[156]

This was welcome news for the President, for it had become clear that something would soon have to be done to finance the huge amount of aid that was to go to Russia under the new agreement. On October 29 Harriman submitted to the President his official report on the Mission's trip to Moscow, summarizing all that the Russians had been promised in military aid, food and raw materials. There too in black and white was the price tag: almost $1 billion for the next nine months.[157] How was it all going to be paid for? The Russians, Harriman informed the President, had been able to finance their October shipments themselves, but only with the help of R.F.C. and Treasury loans; it was "impossible for Russia to continue to finance the full program." Harriman therefore recommended to the President "that the use of lend-lease funds be authorized at the earliest possible moment." The Mission is convinced, Harriman added, that "Russia can make very effective use of the latest types of American equipment and that Russia will continue to fight even in retreat."

The President no doubt took comfort in Harriman's judgment of Russian resistance. For weeks he had been subjected to conflicting opinions on whether the Russians would or would not be able to hold out in the face of desperate and successful Nazi drives. Continually pessimistic reports were coming from the American military attaché in Moscow, Major Ivan Yeaton. On October 10, for instance, he had sent word that he considered it possible that "the end of Russian resistance is not far away," adding "the grim thought that American shipments via Archangel might be destroyed or lost or seized by the Germans." On the other hand, the very next day, word came in from Colonel Faymonville, who had stayed behind in Moscow after the Harriman Mission's return, that the Soviet General Staff believed that the encirclement of Moscow could be prevented and that, while the situation in the South was indeed serious, it was by no means hopeless.[158] It was known of course that Yeaton had long been very critical of the Soviets, and Hopkins wrote Stimson a letter saying that Yeaton had insisted, even while Hopkins was in Moscow ten or twelve weeks before, that the Russian capital would fall at any time.[159] On the other hand, there had been protests to General Marshall about Faymonville's "judgment and impartiality wherever the Soviets are concerned" —an opinion sustained, Marshall informed Hopkins, by men like Bullitt and Loy Henderson of the State Department's Division of European Affairs, who had at one time served with Faymonville in Moscow.[160]

5. THE ANSWER IS LEND-LEASE

Whom to believe? That was the question. That had been the question once before, of course, at the very outbreak of the war when the overwhelming military opinion in Washington had been most bearish on the Russian chances for survival. Then the question had been whether to give the Russians any aid at all; now the question was whether to include them under Lend-Lease. For weeks, as Robert Sherwood tells us, the argument went on in Washington; and Harriman's report gave the President a welcome reassurance that the use of Lend-Lease financing for Russia would not boomerang.[161]

The President now moved swiftly. The following day, October 30, he cabled Stalin that he was including the Soviet Union under Lend-Lease, that he had approved all the items promised in the First Protocol, and that America was "going to bend every effort to move these supplies to the battle lines." Roosevelt informed Stalin that he had ordered "that shipments up to the value of one billion dollars be financed under Lend-Lease and that 'no interest be charged on the indebtedness resulting from these shipments,'" with payments by the Soviet Government to "begin five years after the war and continue for a period of ten years thereafter"—this arrangement being conditioned on Soviet agreement of course. Roosevelt hoped Stalin "would make special efforts to facilitate the purchase in the U. S. S. R. of such raw materials and commodities as were available and of which the United States might be in desperate need." Roosevelt concluded by saying how much he appreciated the way the Moscow Conference had been handled and that he hoped Stalin would "not hesitate to communicate directly with me" whenever he thought the circumstances required it.[162]

On November 4 Stalin replied to Roosevelt's message.

Your decision, Mr. President, to grant the Soviet Union a loan in the amount of one billion dollars subject to no interest charges and for the purpose of paying for armaments and raw materials for the Soviet Union is accepted with sincere gratitude by the Soviet Government as unusually substantial aid in its difficult and great struggle against our common enemy, bloodthirsty Hitlerism.

I agree completely, on behalf of the Government of the Soviet Union, with the conditions which you outline for this loan to the Soviet Union, namely that payments on the loan shall begin five years after the end of the war and shall be completed during the following ten-year period.[163]

On November 7 the Roosevelt-Stalin exchange was published, and Russia was officially included under Lend-Lease.[164] A brief cry of opposition went up on Capitol Hill and elsewhere, chiefly from the isolationist opposition.[165] Then all was silence. One reason for the smallness of the outcry may have been the form of the U.S.-Russian Lend-Lease agreement, which was in effect a loan with generous repayment terms. This was a unique arrangement; the following June, under a master Lend-Lease Agreement, Russian Lend-Lease was put on the same financial basis as Lend-Lease to the other Allies, and the billion-dollar credit annulled.

Another reason for the mildness of the reaction may well have been the serious situation on the Russian front; for by now the Nazis were within thirty miles of Moscow. It was as though the American people sensed at last, even before Pearl Harbor, that whatever their differences, the U. S. and Russia were in fact allies in the great struggle against the Nazi tyranny.[166]

Putting Russian aid under Lend-Lease took care of one problem posed by the Moscow Protocol—how to finance all the assistance promised the Soviets. But two other problems remained: how to produce or otherwise obtain all the material promised, and how to transport it to Russia. These problems continued to occupy Washington for months, indeed years, until almost the end of the war.

6. *A NEW PRIORITY POLICY IS SET*

With Russia's inclusion under Lend-Lease, over-all priority and production policies had necessarily to be reconsidered. As early as November 3 the President, at Hopkins' suggestion, wrote to Knudsen, Stimson, and Knox, requesting them to make a study of the entire machine tool situation in the light of the new Lend-Lease needs,[167] and six days later Stimson and Knox replied, proposing a definite new formula for setting aside tools to be sent to Russia.[168] On November 7 Hopkins prepared letters for the President instructing the War Department to meet the commitments on the war material for whose procurement it was responsible under the new Protocol,[169] and on November 19 the President sent a letter, prepared by General Burns, instructing Admiral Emory S. Land, Chairman of the Maritime Commission, to provide adequate shipping for aid going to the Soviet Union.[170]

Meanwhile, on November 12, Donald Nelson, Executive Director of SPAB, held a meeting to determine the priority to be given future Russian aid. Present at the meeting were: General Spalding of OLLA; General Hines of ANMB; C. E. Rhetts, assistant to Batt; and A. C. C. Hill, Jr., assistant to Nelson. After first agreeing in general to give Russia a priority equal to that given the British and American armed forces, the group agreed to establish a distinction that was to mark the Russian program throughout the war. The priority for

Russian aid, it was decided, was not the need for any given article, but the need to meet the Protocol and shipping dates. It was further agreed that OLLA should break down the Protocol commitments and pass them on to OPM with the appropriate delivery and shipping dates. OPM was then to grant priorities commensurate with the urgency of the shipping deadline, even if this meant giving some items greater priority than was given them for delivery to American armed forces. Such priority was to be given on OLLA request. However, if shipping for such special priority items was not available at the time they were delivered, they were to be released for use by British or American forces.[171]

All these meetings and agreements helped but action still lagged behind. Between September 4 and October 1, for instance, OPM approved only $4,920,000 in Russian orders. The fault lay partly with the OPM industry divisions, which were not pressing the matter, and partly with the Russians, who were tardy in submitting their specifications and in placing their requisitions and approving contracts, and who had delayed while waiting for eligibility under Lend-Lease.[172] The Russians of course complained constantly (more will be said of this later); for example, they said on November 25 that while they required from 15 to 17 ships a month the Maritime Commission had allowed them only 10, and only 5 of these had actually turned up, one of them unseaworthy.[173] Hopkins and General Burns spent much time trying to open up the shipping bottleneck, but despite all their efforts only a fraction of the already small amount of available supplies left the United States in the next few weeks.

7. *AID CONTINUES TO LAG AND THE PRESIDENT MAKES A DRAMATIC PROPOSAL*

The President continued to look upon fulfillment of the Protocol as a task of supreme importance, and he was willing to contemplate desperate measures to speed up aid. Thus on October 31, after discussing the matter with Hopkins, the President wrote to Admiral Stark, Chief of Naval Operations, suggesting that the Navy use one of its carriers to transport a load of Army planes from the West Coast to Basra on the Persian Gulf, from where they could be flown to Russia. This five weeks before Pearl Harbor! The Navy seems to have studied the proposal at length, for there was no reply until the end of November. Then the Navy rejected the idea[174] (which was a suggestion, not an order); and on November 25 Hopkins wrote to the President:

I gather that what is really behind this is that in the light of the whole strategic situation as it is in the world today the Navy feels it would be unwise to send a carrier. Hence, unless you decide otherwise, we are going to move these planes at once by merchantship, although, as I have told you, the Maritime Commission is having a good deal of difficulty getting enough ships.

This was surely a remarkable understatement. The President returned the memorandum to Hopkins with a brief penciled comment:

H.L.H.
OK but say to them from me: Hurry, hurry, hurry!

F. D. R.[175]

Thus, to sum up, the end of October and beginning of November 1941 marked a turning point in the Russian aid program. On October 29 SPAB approved the Moscow Protocol; on November 7 the Roosevelt-Stalin Lend-Lease loan agreement was signed, and on November 12, at the meeting in Nelson's office, agreement was announced on priority policy for Protocol items. Yet such agreement in principle did not solve all practical problems, nor in fact even all questions of general policy.

8. *THE PROBLEM OF "JUSTIFICATIONS"*

One general policy issue concerned the furnishing of "justifications" for the export of items in short supply. This was to remain a painful subject throughout the war, for the representatives of other governments believed that American officials were being too fussy, while some American officials held that the Allies were making exorbitant demands on our supplies. The problem with Russia, however, was a special one, and it came to a head early in November.

The Moscow Protocol had just been approved by SPAB, when the Army and Navy began to press their general opposition against releasing to the Russians materials badly needed for the American defense effort. Stimson, and even more so Knox, continually forced the other members of SPAB to reaffirm the White House directives for all-out aid to Russia. Knox led the attack in SPAB. Already under fire on account of charges of Navy "waste" and "hoarding," Knox counter-attacked by challenging the Russian program on three counts. First of all, he said, many of the materials destined for Russia were needed in this country; secondly, many of these materials had been earmarked for the British who had ordered them to meet their own production requirements; and finally, the Russians were demanding a lot of tools without submitting adequate justification.[176]

The last point in particular touched a sore spot. For, as the competition for critical materials and tools became increasingly keen in the summer and fall of 1941, American and British planners sought to gear their productive capacities by determining which country could more effectively use a given lot of machine tools or raw materials. As donor, the U. S. was able to require the British to file long detailed justifications along with their requests for aid. These justifications were then scrutinized by OPM and the armed services and accepted or rejected in accordance with the above formula.

In the case of Russian aid, the problem of justification was more complicated and the yardstick adopted different—necessarily so, perhaps, if the program was to be successful. There was, first of all, the Russian penchant for secrecy. Neither Hopkins nor the Harriman Mission had been able to learn very much about the state of Soviet industrial and military production, the Soviets being apparently unwilling to discuss their equipment for fear of revealing exact details of it.[177] Even without such secrecy, however, it might well have been difficult to obtain the sort of justification from the Russians that was required from the British. For the fact was that Soviet industrial and war production were much too dislocated for such justification to be easily or effectively worked up. Large parts of the Russian industrial machine were by this time in German hands, and many other plants had hurriedly been moved east of the Urals. There was also some question whether the Soviet bureaucracy could actually produce the sort of figures wanted in Washington. For while the Russians were loath to admit it, they were plagued by a severe shortage of competent clerical help, and could probably not have produced the large volume of supporting statistics normally considered essential by American control agencies. Moreover, the requests sent to the U. S. emanated from the Soviet Ministry of Foreign Trade. This meant that any question about these requests had to be sent back to Russia and traced through the labyrinth of the administrative hierarchy until the actual originator of the request could be found; and as those who had negotiated with the Russians in Moscow knew, the complexity of Russian "channels" far surpassed even the complexity of our own intricate production control system.[178]

Confronted with this problem of justifications, Hopkins decided, with the President's approval, that as a matter of policy, Soviet requests should be accepted at face value since the alternative would produce infinite irritation and bickering, and no dependable information. The only check to be used was to be American capacity to deliver the goods. This decision coincided of course with official Soviet policy, which was that if Russia asked for anything, the request was itself *prima facie* evidence of Soviet need. The U. S. did not, however, commit itself to supplying everything the Soviets asked for. But so far as the items it did promise were concerned, the U. S., in the end, did very well in its deliveries. Although the cry for Russian justifications was raised continually by the War and Navy Departments, as well as by some sections of the War Production Board (the post-Pearl Harbor successor to SPAB and OPM)—and also by the British— Hopkins never wavered. At times the War Production Board would pigeonhole a particularly difficult Russian request by insisting that the Soviet Purchasing Commission submit a justification. If the case was not important enough to merit an appeal to the White House, the Russians would usually withdraw the requisition rather than submit a justification.

In the end, the ever-present shortage of shipping facilities served to hold down the more extravagant Russian demands. If, for instance, the Soviets requested a power plant whose use appeared to Washington to be remote from the war effort, the Russians were told that they could have the power plant but only at the cost of leaving behind vitally needed food or munitions shipments. The choice, then, was up to the Russians, though the United States would promise that if it could deliver the power plant, it would. American policy was to allow the Russians considerable latitude in determining their needs and listing these in priority order of their own choosing. The United States would promise to make available all it could, according to Soviet-determined priority. The Russians could use the material as they saw fit: if they wasted their deliveries, they were no better or worse off than any other country at war. They had to stand the loss, however, since shipping shortages always limited the amount of aid they could expect to receive. This, in effect, was the reasoning behind official White House policy, but few officials in charge of procurement, as well as many others connected with the Russian aid program, seemed ever to understand or to agree with this policy.

9. THE PROBLEM OF MACHINE TOOLS

Among the specific problems posed by the Russian aid program, one of the most difficult was the problem of machine tools. These had been a bone of contention as far back as the Welles-Oumansky conversations in the summer of 1940, and continued to be so throughout the summer and fall of 1941.[179] In fact, the argument over machine tool exports continued even after SPAB had approved the Moscow Protocol, late in October. Thus, for instance, at a meeting of SPAB on November 26, Knox protested vigorously that too many critical tools were being released to Russia, without the necessary justification. Batt replied that in the case of people actively resisting invasion, as the Russians were, some of the requirements of the British aid program had to be relaxed. In any event, Batt said, of the $33 million in tools thus far allotted to Russia, only $10 million had actually been released and only a few of these were considered critical tools. Wallace, chairman of the meeting, then asked that the question be carried over until another time when Hopkins himself could be present.[180] The next meeting of SPAB took place on December 2, Isador Lubin representing Hopkins. Hopkins sent a message that, in conformity with Presidential policy, prompt action in the matter of machine tools was essential, and Lubin and Batt went on to stress the strategic necessity and moral obligation to fulfill the promises made to the Russians. Knudsen admitted that the shipment of few of the tools on the list would interfere with deliveries for the Navy's programs. Knox, however, again repeated his call for Soviet justifications, and questioned whether the tools could actually be delivered because of the ice-bound condition of the Russian ports. In the end Knox was voted down once more, and SPAB authorized OPM to release to Russia 2,031 machine tools, presses, hammers and forging machines valued at $28,833,070.[181] Shortly thereafter Britton reported to Knudsen that between June 30 and December 6, the United States had shipped to Russia $3,150,865 in machine tools, $70,360 in electric furnaces, and $1,220,889 in other machinery including presses and forging equipment.[182] How much of this material was impounded machinery released by the Curtis Committee in July was not noted; probably, however, this constituted a considerable portion; and the total amount was not of massive proportions.

The struggle over the delivery of machine tools to Russia continued throughout the first half of 1942. Whenever the Ordnance Department of the United States Army was the prescribed procurement agency for placing Russian orders,[183] the first delivery date cited by the manufacturer was "frozen," meaning that no matter what the priority of any other work, the manufacturer was under an absolute obligation to deliver the Russian tools by the promised date. Following Pearl Harbor when the machine tool situation became even more acute, delivery dates were placed too far ahead to be of much use to the Russians. The War Production Board therefore informed manufacturers that 10 per cent of their production of any desired type was to be allotted to Russian aid.[184]

This figure of 10 per cent became the subject of bitter disagreement between Ferdinand Eberstadt, chairman of the Army-Navy Munitions Board, and Donald Nelson, Chairman of the newly established War Production Board (successor to OPM and SPAB).[185] While Eberstadt was quite willing to set aside 25 per cent of American machine tool production for civilian and Lend-Lease use, he insisted that Russia be required to justify her requests in order to receive her share of the 25 per cent. As if to emphasize his position, Eberstadt on March 5, 1942 requested Nelson to hold up a shipment of automatic screw machines that were critically needed for munitions production at home, citing Soviet inability to state how the machines would be used as the reason for his request. In this, as in other instances, OLLA finally prevailed upon Nelson to release the machines anyway; and OLLA, in turn, was backed by the President's personal pledge to Stalin and his direct order to all procurement agencies to meet the Protocol at all costs. Though many machine tools originally destined for Russia were eventually diverted for use by American industry, mostly for lack of shipping, Eberstadt continued to feel that Nelson was letting him and the Army-Navy Munitions Board down.[186] Nelson, on the other hand, was taken to task by General Belyaev of the Soviet Purchasing Commission for making promises which were not being kept. On July 7, 1942 Nelson answered Belyaev that while the gist of his complaint was true, some of his figures were none too accurate, and Nelson went on to say that he thought the 25 per cent rule would, in the long run, be the most equitable for all concerned.[187]

Machine tools continued to be a trouble spot in Russian aid almost throughout the entire war. Being heavily dependent upon outside sources of supply, the Russians never ceased to press the United States for more tools; but even when the tool situation in this country began to improve toward the end of the war, the War Production Board never granted the Russians all they asked for. All the same, there was still another side—quite unpredicted—to the machine tool picture. Batt expressed it when he wrote, once, in the spring of 1945: "It should be noted that in this instance [that of machine tool production], as in many others during the past three years, the Russian program has proved of incalculable value to our own military. [For] on numerous occasions diversions of finished or largely finished Russian items has enabled one or another of the Armed Services to overcome an emergency which otherwise might have proved very costly."[188]

10. THE PROBLEM OF ALUMINUM

Another vexing and persistent problem in Russian aid was the problem of aluminum supply. Fortunately aluminum is (for technical reasons) more easily allocated and controlled than are machine tools. Then, too, it was much easier, in the case of aluminum, to recognize the marginal nature of the Russian requests. For while the shipment of a certain percentage of American aluminum production might cut down the size of a particular domestic program, the effect would be nothing as compared with a missing type of tool. As a result, while the armed forces opposed the aluminum provisions of the Protocol, as they opposed its machine tool provisions, they were much less successful in diverting Soviet-ordered aluminum to their own needs, however pressing.

The Russian need for aluminum was most urgent. Sixty-five per cent of the Soviet's 1940 aluminum capacity had been destroyed in the first weeks of the war, and only a small percentage of this loss had been made good.[189] One of Amtorg's earliest requests therefore was for an export license for 1,200 tons of aluminum on the New York docks.[190] This metal had originally been fabricated into sheets and rods on a metric scale for export to France in 1940, and despite Knudsen's reluctance, its export to Russia was now approved. A great factor in the expediting of this shipment of aluminum was Stalin's plea to Hopkins, in late July; for Stalin was painfully aware of the heavy threat the prevailing aluminum shortage posed to Russian aircraft production.[191] In this country, meanwhile, Amtorg was frantically attempting to place aluminum orders, but found its way blocked at every turn by prior commitments to the Army and Navy.

In the Moscow Protocol the U. S. had agreed to deliver to Russia 2,000 tons of aluminum and 500 tons of duraluminum monthly for nine months. With Britain delivering an equal amount, and counting her own remaining production, Russia would therefore have as much aluminum as she had produced domestically before the war. The Protocol stipulated that 5,000 tons of aluminum already delivered at the time of signing would be exempted from the Protocol commitment. Batt, however, interpreted this clause to mean aluminum delivered from Britain and insisted that the 5,300 tons of sheet, tube and rod aluminum Russia had ordered in the United States prior to the signing of the Protocol be regarded as part of the American commitment.[192]

Though the export of aluminum to Russia was to cause a great deal of difficulty in Washington, the actual size of the Russian commitment was rather small. This was revealed by an analysis of the Soviet request made by the Aluminum and Magnesium Branch of OPM: the 2,000 tons of aluminum promised the Soviets monthly were only 7 per cent of the total of U. S. production while the 500 tons of duraluminum were only 2 per cent of total U. S. production.[193] Added to this was the fact that both U. S. and Canadian production of aluminum (Canada being the main source of British supply) rose very rapidly in 1941-1942, U. S. production from 280,000 tons to 473,000 tons, Canadian from 194,000 to 308,000.[194] The combined Anglo-American commitment amounted to only 60,000 tons in 1942.[195]

Nevertheless, before long the aluminum issue came up at a meeting of SPAB and produced angry disagreement. On November 26 Batt went before SPAB to report that Russian aluminum requests came to 6,600,000 pounds of sheet, 1,500,000 pounds of tubing, and 3,500,000 pounds of rod. Batt noted that while all the rod and part of the tubing order could be sent without any difficulty, the export of the sheet aluminum would apparently delay U. S. aircraft production. In fact, Batt said, the Joint Aircraft Board wanted no sheet aluminum whatever sent abroad until March 1942. At this point, Knox (who also attacked the machine tool shipments at this meeting) rose again to challenge the way the whole Russian aid program was being conducted. He objected to the delivery of aluminum sheet on the ground that there was no evidence to indicate that the Russians could use the aluminum to build any more airplanes in the same time than we could, not counting the time it would take to deliver the aluminum. Knox questioned moreover that the aluminum could be delivered promptly at all, and emphasized that numerous Soviet industrial regions were threatened by military invasion. Knox then suggested, somewhat over-optimistically no doubt, that it would take only a week to get the necessary data indicating how promptly the ordered aluminum would be sent. Knox's arguments had their effect, for Batt now proposed, by way of compromise, that only a token shipment of sheet should be sent "as a gesture of good will"; further authorization would have to await the arrival of more adequate information. The Board then

went on, Knox dissenting, to approve the release of 500,000 pounds of tubing; 3,500,000 pounds of rod; and 1,000,000 pounds of aluminum sheet.[196] The Board did not, however, place any time limits on these exports, so that Batt and Frank Cliffe, of the Aluminum and Magnesium Branch of OPM, interpreted the release to cover only the time until the end of September (amounting then to about what had been promised under the Protocol).[197] After that the Board could be approached again.

Further military reaction was not long in coming. The day following the SPAB meeting, General H. H. Arnold, acting in his capacity as chairman of the Joint Aircraft Board, wrote to Knudsen, setting forth the Air Force position:

The Joint Aircraft Committee strongly recommends that the amount of aluminum sheet available for export should be only the excess production over the domestic requirements for national defense and other export commitments established previous to the Russian request. It is requested that steps be taken to reduce the amount of aluminum alloy sheet available for export to Russia so that the aircraft industry will not be faced with a serious shortage of aluminum sheets. . . .[198]

Batt thereupon took the matter up with Hopkins, who intervened once more against the military and in favor of the full Protocol commitment. Accordingly, on December 2 Batt asked SPAB to approve the export to Russia of an additional 3,000,000 pounds of common aluminum sheet to go with the 1,000,000 pounds of hard sheet previously approved. Both Knox and Knudsen sat silent, and the request was granted.[199]

11. LEND-LEASE AFTER PEARL HARBOR: THE STATE OF THINGS AND THE IMMEDIATE OUTLOOK

Then Pearl Harbor! The actual entry of the United States into the war was bound, of course, to complicate the whole problem of foreign aid—including Russian aid. First of all, there was a period of considerable confusion—confusion well illustrated in aluminum supply. For instance, just after the Japanese attack, a Quartermaster officer, because of the temporary suspension of all Lend-Lease shipments, requested the Reynolds Metals Company to withhold shipments for a period in December: Reynolds interpreted this as an order to stop production altogether and several days' output of fabricated aluminum was lost.[200] Then, too, the armed services began once more to press for diversion of aluminum for their own needs. The Aircraft Scheduling Unit at Dayton, Ohio, for instance, wired the Joint Aircraft Board in Washington asking it to divert 800,000 pounds of hard aluminum being processed at Alcoa from Russian aid to American manufacturers. Since it appeared that the February 1942 allotment from Alcoa to American manufacturers would be 5,000,000 pounds short of the original estimates, such a transfer would have been of great help to American military production. The request, however, was turned down by Frank Cliffe, of the OPM Aluminum and Magnesium Branch, who had turned down similar requests before, and who was again sustained by his superiors.[201] Still the military pressure continued. On December 19 James Forrestal, Acting Secretary of the Navy in Knox's absence at Pearl Harbor, wrote to Henry Wallace, chairman of SPAB, asking for a reconsideration of the December 2 decision (to send another 3,000,000 pounds of common aluminum sheet to Russia) in the light of the United States' actual entrance into the war. Forrestal argued that this decision prejudiced American production and that a serious domestic shortage of aluminum was immediately ahead. He asked therefore for a review of the situation so that the aluminum now destined for Russia should be used to keep up American production. Wallace passed Forrestal's letter on to Nelson, who in turn gave it to Batt with a request to prepare an answer for the December 23 meeting of SPAB.

Batt's "answer" consisted of a memorandum from Cliffe, dated December 20, 1941, reporting an incident which, whatever its exact reason, tended to put both Army and Navy air in a somewhat unfavorable light. Cliffe reported that on December 11, 1941, a Major Bonner, a subordinate of Major Benson, the Air Corps representative in the Aircraft Scheduling Unit at Dayton, Ohio, had over the signature of the administrator of the Unit ordered the Reynolds Metals Company to divert any aluminum already produced by it or in process for Russia or any other foreign country to unfilled orders of the Air Corps or the Navy's Bureau of Aero-

nautics. Whether this had been done in deliberate disregard or in ignorance of the agreement reached on November 13 between Nelson and General Spalding for the effective implementation of the Protocol as approved by SPAB, Cliffe could not say. As it was, OPM did not hear of the order for several days, and when it finally contacted its representative on the Scheduling Unit, he replied that the order had been sent out without his knowledge. As a result, Reynolds suspended work on the Russian orders until Cliffe, on December 19, sent word from Washington to ignore Major Bonner's "order." By the time that Reynolds resumed work, almost one third of a month's production for Russia had been lost. However, after submitting Cliffe's letter to the Board, Batt reassured it that the available supplies of hard aluminum were still sufficient to back up its authorization of November 26. In any case, Cliffe's report of the incident seems to have dashed all hopes of the Air Force and the Navy to get SPAB to reverse its previous decision, which in fact the Board then went on to reaffirm: the aluminum provision of the Protocol was to be met in full.[202]

Still the Army-Navy Munitions Board did not give up; it still sought to block the export to Russia of 1,000,000 pounds of hard aluminum. On December 26, therefore, Captain James Boyd of the ANMB visited the Aircraft Scheduling Unit headquarters to gather specific statistics on the effects aluminum shipments would have in terms of retarding aircraft production, especially the output of B-17 bombers. His findings seem not to have been very significant, since the record shows that the total Russian commitment amounted to only 6 per cent of the sheet aluminum available.[203]

As it turned out, the Aluminum and Magnesium Branch of OPM did not quite meet its objective of catching up with Protocol shipments by December 31. In January 1942 therefore the President summarily ordered that all arrearages in Protocol shipments be made up by April. Once again Batt went before SPAB to plead the case for Russian aid. He told the Board that 8,300 metric tons of ingot and 1,110 metric tons of fabricated aluminum would be needed for shipment during the first quarter of 1942, and that 2,000,000 pounds of hard alloy sheet would be needed to meet the fabricated aluminum requirements. The million pounds of hard aluminum sheet, he said, could be furnished in January if non-aircraft military items were redesigned to eliminate aluminum. Nelson, who was acting as chairman of the meeting, turned to Knox with the suggestion that the Navy use light steel tubing instead of aluminum tubing in bedposts and furniture. Nelson said that the Division of Materials of OPM, which was headed by Batt, had requested a report on this matter from the ANMB, and that a list of shipments of aluminum for Navy work showed that about 130,000 pounds were specified for furniture; Knox replied that it was difficult to change the weight on the decks of combat ships. The Board thereupon agreed to release the 1,000,000 pounds requested for Russian aid in January and ordered the War and Navy Departments to eliminate at once as much aluminum as possible from non-aircraft uses.[204]

By mid-April 1942, Cliffe was able to report that, in accordance with the President's instructions, aluminum shipments to Russia would be in line with or in excess of Protocol commitments by April 30. Although some ingot would still be missing, the percentage of fabricated aluminum had been raised from 20 to 30 per cent so that the total weight of aluminum assigned to the Russians equaled the amount called for in the Protocol.[205]

While energetic efforts were thus being made both in machine tools and aluminum to carry out the American promises made at Moscow, other parts of the Protocol were doing anything but well. This was not due to any lack of earnest attempt to see the bridge of supplies to the Soviets established (for that matter, Lend-Lease to Britain continued to fall below expectation and need); it was rather that, as a whole, Russian Lend-Lease was still bogged down in domestic shortages and administrative tangles. The attack on Pearl Harbor naturally only intensified problems which had already existed before the attack came.

The first action taken by Washington, once the U. S. herself was actually in the war, was to suspend temporarily all foreign aid shipments until future policy could be decided upon and the American armed forces had had an opportunity to repossess any items they required for their own immediate use.[206] On December 24 Harriman reported that while the British were 100 per cent on schedule in

meeting their over-all Soviet commitments, the U. S. had shipped only 25 per cent of the material it had promised.[207] Actually, the Army's total task was virtually impossible, because it was called on to furnish Lend-Lease not only to Russia, but to Britain and other countries as well, and simultaneously to build a tremendous U. S. Army. It was not surprising that on December 23 Stettinius complained to Hopkins that, of the five Lend-Lease procurement agencies, the War Department had rendered the smallest amount of aid, though its required allocations were twice those of any other department.[208]

12. THE PRESIDENT INTERVENES AGAIN, AND THINGS BEGIN TO MOVE ONCE MORE—SLOWLY

Hopkins thought it was time to take a direct hand. On December 28 therefore the President signed a letter, drawn up by Hopkins, ordering all the services as well as OPM to resume shipment to Russia by January 1—and to make good all existing deficits in Protocol deliveries by April 1. Roosevelt pressed home his determination to see the Russian program fulfilled in the most vigorous language:

The whole Russian program is so vital to our interests I know that only the gravest consideration will lead you to recommend our withholding longer the munitions our Government has promised the USSR.

I wish, therefore, that all items go forward promptly after January 1, unless I authorize the specific amendment.[209]

The President's new order pumped fresh life into Russian aid. On January 7 Batt transmitted the order to all OPM Branch Chiefs. In his covering letter Batt noted that Russian failure to submit the necessary specifications in time, or to hold to standard American specifications, had contributed to the present low state of the program, but he held, rightly, that the American administrative machinery was also at fault. He therefore asked each branch to submit within twenty-four hours an estimate of the status of their deliveries and the possibility of their meeting President Roosevelt's order.[210]

For the next six months Batt consistently and vigorously pressed the WPB division chiefs to meet the Russian aid program. In his original letter of November 27, 1941 notifying each of the OPM branches of its obligations under the Protocol, Batt had remarked that U. S. official policy had now been set and that there was to be no more questioning on that score. As we have seen, Knox and other representatives of the War and Navy Departments (civilian and military) did continue to raise questions, and so did officials of WPB and other agencies. In January 1942 Batt had difficulties over policy with the Chief of the WPB Chemical Branch.[211] A much more serious difficulty arose at the same time over the lag in iron and steel shipments. For this the Russians themselves were largely to blame, having delayed in filing requisitions and then submitting large and erratic requests.[212] As a result, by the end of January 1942 the Iron and Steel Branch of OPM had only managed to obtain a total of 26,147 tons for Russian aid, as against a monthly commitment in the Protocol of 67,000 tons.[213]

On the other hand, War Department and Army deliveries of military equipment, which had earlier been lagging badly, were now beginning to pick up. Thus on February 17 Stimson was able to inform the President that while anti-aircraft matériel was still so short at home that none could be supplied the Russians, the promised number of tanks would actually be delivered by June 30, and that while only 553 planes had been delivered to the Soviets by January 31, beginning in February deliveries would meet the set quota of 212 planes a month. The chemical situation, particularly TNT, was improving, while the Army's truck allotment to Lend-Lease was outrunning the available shipping space (the lack of which Stimson emphasized as a critical factor throughout his report, and about which more will be said later). In field telephone wire, shoe leather, and army cloth deliveries, the Protocol quotas also would be met during the spring. Only machine tools continued to be in short supply, with only some $52 million worth being available for Russian aid by June 30.

Stimson's letter was more a prediction of a better future than a statement of actual accomplishments. Given the lag it was not surprising that administrative wrangling soon broke out again, and the President was forced to take a hand once more. In late February and early March an acrimonious exchange took place between Nelson and Secretary Morgenthau, whose Treasury Procurement agency had the task of actually purchasing the steel. Having been reproached by Morgenthau because the steel aid program was continuing to fall behind, Nelson replied that despite a huge increase in Soviet requests over original Protocol commitments, the Iron and Steel Branch would, by tremendous effort, have the program all caught up by May. This seems not to have satisfied Morgenthau, who thereupon took up the matter with Roosevelt. On March 11 the President gave Morgenthau a handwritten memo saying: "This is *critical* because (a) we must keep our word, (b) because Russian assistance counts *most* today." Armed with the President's memorandum Morgenthau's Treasury Procurement began to interfere directly with the WPB Iron and Steel Branch. Nelson and Batt objected vigorously to this procedure, and decided that they would henceforth deal only with OLLA, not with Treasury Procurement. Wishing, however, to avoid any future incident of this kind, which might lead to still more White House intervention, the War Production Board sent telegrams to all the steel companies ordering them to make certain that all Russian orders were delivered on schedule —as demanded by the Commander in Chief.[214] The telegram seems to have had the desired effect; for while steel deliveries for Russian aid had amounted to only 119,000 tons in March and April, by May it rose to 281,951 tons a month. As a result, it was possible to make up the cumulative arrearages on the Protocol, as well as to fulfill even some of the Russian extra-Protocol requests. All programs have their price, however, and this one was no exception: official pressure for steel for Russia had finally to be reduced when it became apparent that the Presidential order, rigidly applied, was playing havoc with essential Army and Navy programs.[215]

13. SOME REASONS FOR CONTINUING DELAY

While the steel program thus was joining the machine tool and aluminum programs in at least being brought up to date, the President's directive that the Russian Protocol as a whole be on schedule by April 1 was far from being fulfilled. It became apparent that the loss of production in October 1941, while the Russian aid program was being organized, and the renewed delays after Pearl Harbor, not to mention all sorts of serious domestic shortages and administrative tangles, were well-nigh insurmountable obstacles to complete fulfillment of the President's order, and of the Moscow Protocol.[216] It soon became apparent, too, that if real progress was to be made, more was required than a strongly worded directive—what was needed was an absolutely overriding priority. The key to the proclamation of such a priority was the overriding strategic importance of the Russian front.

Though a considerable number of Army and Navy officers, from General MacArthur on down, and a goodly section of the American public clamored for a quick offensive in the Pacific, the United States and Britain had long been agreed that Europe was the decisive theater of operations, and that victory in Europe would soon be followed by collapse of the Japanese. Certainly all combined Anglo-American planning had stressed the primacy of the European theater. After Pearl Harbor, however, a costly holding operation became necessary in the Pacific, and this consumed huge quantities of supplies and shipping that might otherwise have been devoted to British and Russian aid. The mobilization and training of the U. S. Army on an actual war footing likewise demanded huge stocks of supplies. Thus despite the recognition by the top strategic boards that Russia was the anvil upon which the Nazi armies would eventually be smashed, finding the necessary supplies for Russia became an increasingly difficult task. Under these circumstances, it was easy to see American procurement officers giving priority to U. S. needs. And Russian surliness, compounded by the difficult conditions they imposed (such as their minute inspections of everything destined for Russia), did nothing to inspire the American officials to exert themselves all-out on behalf of the Soviet war effort. As the official history of the War Production Board says: "By March of 1942, protocol commitments were on the way to being swamped by other pressing war programs. Protocol shipments to Russia had fallen far behind schedule and protocol commitments were placed in preferential lists that put them below the preferences accorded other requirements."[217]

14. THE PRESIDENT'S IMPERATIVE NOTE OF MARCH 17, 1942, AND ITS EFFECT

Something was clearly going to have to be done if the Russian aid program as a whole— not just a few important parts of it—was to be saved from complete failure. And something *was* done. In March, while Stettinius, the head of Lend-Lease, was in the hospital undergoing an operation, Thomas B. McCabe, temporarily in charge of OLLA in Stettinius' absence, drew up for the President a clear, indeed sharply worded note, addressed to Donald Nelson, head of WPB, and thus in charge of all war production. The theme was ACTION, and the note, which the President signed on March 17, concluded:

I wish that all material promised under the Protocol be released for shipment at the earliest possible date regardless of the effect of these shipments on any other part of our war program.

Franklin D. Roosevelt,
C-in-C[218]

A similar note was sent to Admiral Land of the Maritime Commission.[219] Two days later McCabe informed Nelson that he and Batt had already made substantial progress toward preparing new schedules for deliveries.[220]

On March 24 Nelson read the President's letter to the War Production Board, and Batt then reviewed for the Board the entire situation. A major cause of trouble, Batt pointed out, was the vagueness of certain items in the Protocol. The promises made at Moscow to deliver "various industrial equipment" had given the U. S. no idea of the types of equipment the Russians actually wanted. In the case of machine tools, the Russians had asked for 1,200 pieces a month; the U. S. had promised only to do its best, with the result that between October 1, 1941 and March 1942 only 200 tools had actually been sent. Meanwhile the Soviets had said that the delivery of 2,000 tools by June 30 was a matter of prime importance. Their electric furnace and forging equipment requests had likewise proved entirely impossible of fulfillment; and meeting their extra-Protocol requests on airplane and tank bearings would have completely disrupted the American war effort. Batt also noted that the Russians had submitted many "extra-Protocol" items, which had not been considered at

Moscow, while at the same time passing over many items which had originally been offered in the Protocol. As a result of Hopkins' directive to SPAB at its meeting of October 29, 1941, it had been agreed to accept orders for extra-Protocol items wherever feasible, in certain cases with the reservation that deliveries would have to await their turn. Under the President's latest directive, however, such items might also have to be considered as meriting preferential treatment. Nelson asked Robert P. Patterson, the Under Secretary of War, to name a man to work with Batt on the machine tool problem, while he personally took up with the President the question of over-all priorities for Russian aid.[221]

On April 1 Nelson wrote the President asking for a decision on the priority of extra-Protocol items. Nelson did not question the overriding priority of regular Protocol items. The question he raised was essentially the same one Batt had raised at the WPB meeting—how to treat extra-Protocol items, particularly those upon which the Russians placed greater emphasis than on Protocol items, and how to treat the vague commitments in the Protocol which were to be filled only within the limits of American capacity to produce.[222] On the same day Nelson released a letter to all WPB officials, the Army-Navy Munitions Board and all procurement agencies, citing the President's directive of March 17 and the sorry state of the Russian aid program. In order to remedy the situation, Nelson announced that he was naming Batt to coordinate the work of the War Production Board and all other interested agencies. If necessary to meet Protocol obligations, all existing priority ratings and preferences could be altered and allocated materials re-scheduled. A board was to be set up composed of representatives of the Secretary of War, the directors of the Production and Material Divisions of WPB, the Executive Director of the ANMB, and one person from the Industry Branches Division and one from the Division of Priorities of WPB. Batt was to direct the group "in expediting within their respective organizations all matters pertaining to non-munitions items of the Russian program." The recipients of Nelson's letter were put on notice: "The President's directive leaves no doubt as to the policy of the United States on this matter."[223]

As for Nelson's letter to the President, of April 1, it was given to Thomas McCabe of OLLA, who in turn contacted Nelson and Batt, and it was agreed that difficult extra-Protocol items should in the future be discussed with OLLA before a final decision was made. On April 14 the President signed a letter to Nelson, drafted by McCabe, reaffirming the Administration's desire to send everything possible to Russia including extra-Protocol items, if this could be done. In the case of non-Protocol items, the priority to be given Russian orders was to be the same as that given American military orders, except where it would result in "extraordinary interference" and "thus cut down on the number of finished munitions that we can ultimately send to Russia." Cases of "extraordinary interference" were to be evaluated by a meeting between Nelson, Batt, and Stettinius. "In very exceptional cases," the President wrote Nelson, "where you both [meaning Nelson and Batt] deem it advisable, please take the matter up with Mr. Harry Hopkins."[224]

There seems no question but that the boost given Russian aid by the President's vigorous personal attention helped immeasurably to bring the program out of the doldrums, indeed save it from possible complete collapse. Even though it now became necessary to squeeze what had been a nine-months commitment into three months of production, the final delivery record on the First Protocol reflected a tremendous final spurt in the production of Russian aid.

15. THE SHIPPING PROBLEM

No account of the first year of Russian aid would be complete without some mention of the shipping problem—a problem that soon overshadowed the questions of supply and that continued to plague Anglo-American relations with the Soviet Union long after most production problems of Russian Lend-Lease had been successfully disposed of. The full story is long and complex; all that can be done here is to indicate some of the key issues.[225]

There was, first of all, the question of which route to use. This was an issue from the beginning: the U. S. favored the Pacific route, but the question of Japan's attitude and the problem of hauling vast quantities of goods across the Pacific tied up ships for months, and ice conditions closed Soviet Far Eastern ports during a good part of the year. Nevertheless, considerable aid passed over this route from the very beginning;[226] indeed, even after Pearl Harbor, under a curious Russo-Japanese *modus vivendi,* Russian as well as U. S. Lend-Lease ships continued to make the run, bringing in thousands of tons a month, though it was understood that only food, raw materials, gasoline, and some industrial machinery were to be shipped via the Trans-Siberian Railroad.[227]

The Persian route, on the other hand, was comparatively safe, if also exceedingly long. At first the land facilities in Persia were most inadequate; but they were slowly built up by the Russians in the north and by the British, and later the Americans, in the south. It was not, however, until early summer 1942 that the shipments over the Persian route began to be significant.[228]

The ideal route for Russian aid seemed at first to be the Arctic run. It was much shorter than the others, and the Soviet Arctic ports fed the materials much more efficiently into the Russian transportation system (though of course the ports were ice-bound in the winter). This was also the route the Russians were urging the U. S. and Britain to adopt as their main supply route. During the summer and fall of 1941, and the early spring of 1942, all went well. By March 1942, however, the Germans were starting to attack the Arctic convoys not only with submarines and airplanes, but also with some of their capital ships stationed in Norwegian bases. There were serious losses of both merchant ships and escorting vessels. The responsibility for providing convoy escorts fell in the main on the Royal Navy, though the U. S. Navy also assigned two battleships, a carrier, and two heavy cruisers to Scapa Flow, for service under British command.[229]

In general, it may be said that Roosevelt urged Churchill to do his best to keep up the convoys, and that Churchill pushed the Admiralty as far as he possibly could. Admiral Sir Dudley Pound, First Lord of the Admiralty, and Admiral Ernest J. King, Chief of Naval Operations, consulted on the problem in the spring of 1942, at the President's request.[230] The Northern convoys were maintained until the end of June 1942; then, chiefly because of a tragic error in intelligence or tactics, the final June convoy lost 22 out of its 37 ships,

14 of the ships sunk being American.[231] This was too great a price to pay and the Northern convoys were temporarily suspended; the announcement of the cancellation evoked an outburst of peculiarly arrogant and ungenerous ill will from Stalin, who informed Churchill that his "naval experts" considered the reasons for the cessation of the Northern convoys "wholly unconvincing."[232] But these events took place during the program's second year.

More pervasive still than the question of routes was the question of ships. There had been some shipping shortages in the fall of 1941; but after Pearl Harbor they began to have an almost strangulating effect. The global demands for shipping increased tremendously,[233] and the German submarine campaign flourished. Everyone suffered in the competition. Until February 1942 the inherent difficulties were accentuated by inadequate U. S. administrative control of shipping. On February 7 the War Shipping Administration was created with Admiral Land as its head and Lewis P. Douglas as his energetic deputy. From then on, there were fewer shipping problems caused by inefficiency or wasteful use of ships.

Another shipping problem in the early days of Russian aid was the choice of an East Coast loading port. At first the Army chose New York, then switched to Boston, and finally settled on Philadelphia—all with great publicity. At Philadelphia, affairs were so bungled that goods were damaged by weather while ships were returned to the shipping pool for lack of cargo. Not until the spring of 1942 was the Philadelphia situation finally straightened out.[234]

One point about the shipping problem deserves special emphasis. Although delivery of goods to Russia was not guaranteed in the Moscow Protocol, both Roosevelt and Churchill placed a high value on delivering the goods, regardless of the lack of legal obligation. It was they who intervened time and again to do all that could possibly be done. It was Roosevelt who pressed Churchill to continue running the Northern convoys "if there is any possibility of success, in spite of the great risk involved."[235] It was Churchill who induced the Admiralty to keep the convoys going through June 1942. And it was Roosevelt and Churchill together who, on certain occasions, accepted naval advice and stopped the Murmansk convoys because the losses were too great or because other enterprises, such as the North African landings, required all the shipping the U. S. and Britain could possibly put together.

16. ACHIEVEMENT UNDER THE FIRST PROTOCOL

When the books were closed on the First Protocol on June 30, 1942, it was found that the United States had not met its original commitment on all items. This was understandable. There was the initial delay in carrying out the provisions of the Protocol; then the confusion of the Pearl Harbor period; the cumbersome reorganization of American industry in early 1942; and finally the shipping and convoy crises. Nor were these all the obstacles that had stood in the way: there were—to recall but briefly—the domestic shortages and the administrative tangles in Washington; the struggle between the armed forces of the United States and those of foreign countries for a maximum share of military supplies; and, finally, the delays in Russian requests or the submission of impossible specifications. Considering all these difficulties, it is amazing that early Russian aid did as well as it did—and not surprising at all that British shipments to Russia (the British being better organized, having been in the war since September 1939) surpassed American deliveries until the beginning of the second Protocol, in the summer of 1942.[236]

It is quite impossible to estimate qualitatively the American contribution to the heroic and successful Russian struggle in 1941-1942, but we are not without quantitative evidence of the amount of aid actually given. On August 18, 1942 Stimson reported to the President that in most categories the terms of the First Protocol had been met. The Army, Stimson made clear, had done a fine job of providing the Soviets with planes, tanks, jeeps, cargo trucks, telephone equipment, armor plate, toluol and TNT, chemicals, shoes, cloth, submarine guns, and rubber floats. On a number of important items, however, the Army had fallen short, notably on 90 mm. anti-aircraft guns and 37 mm. anti-tank guns as well as—and these were the most conspicuous shortages—machine tools (though 3,253 tools had been delivered), forging and pressing equipment, tractors and battery charging sets.[237]

The War Production Board likewise reported to the President that, with respect to materials, equipment, and machinery, the United States had, in over-all terms, fulfilled its obligations under the First Protocol. While total American commitments under the Protocol amounted to 922,000 tons, the U. S. had made available at the centers of production 764,000 tons (or 82 per cent) which had been supplemented by 391,000 tons of "various other kinds of materials, equipment, and machinery," bringing the total of American aid to Russia to 1,-155,000 tons.[238]

In all, a record to be proud of.

BIBLIOGRAPHIC NOTE

This study is based in considerable part, on the official records of one government agency most immediately connected with the development of Russian Lend-Lease aid—the files of the War Production Board. We have also been permitted to use the essential Roosevelt and Hopkins files at the Franklin D. Roosevelt Library at Hyde Park. For the rest of our material we have drawn, for the most part, on the pertinent documents published by the Department of State, on a number of official histories containing information on the history of the Russian Lend-Lease program, as well as on accounts by a number of prominent contemporaries, and on some of the outstanding works by historians and political scientists. Two of the individuals closely connected with the Russian Lend-Lease program assisted us by furnishing us a substantial amount of information in interviews; these were General James H. Burns and Mr. Averell Harriman, to both of whom warm thanks are due.

Although there is no official account of the origins and history of the Lend-Lease program, a number of official histories contain considerable material on its background and development. These include Richard M. Leighton and Robert W. Coakley, *Global Logistics and Strategy, 1940-1943* (Washington, 1955); T. H. Vail Motter, *The Persian Corridor and Aid to Russia* (Washington, 1952); Mark S. Watson, *Chief of Staff: Prewar Plans and Preparations* (Washington, 1950); and Kent Roberts Greenfield (ed.), *Command Decisions* (New York, 1959)—all volumes in the official history of the War Department and the United States Army in the second World War. We have also used the work of Robert H. Connery, *The Navy and Industrial Mobilization in World War II* (Princeton, 1951); Samuel Eliot Morison, *The Battle of the Atlantic, September 1939–May 1943* (Boston, 1947); the volume *Industrial Mobilization for War* issued by the Civilian Production Administration (Washington, 1947), and two other documentary publications of the Civilian Production Administration, *Minutes of the Office of Production Management* and *Minutes of the Supply Priorities and Allocations Board* (both Washington, 1946). The text of the first Soviet Lend-Lease Protocol, the basis of all Lend-Lease assistance to Russia during the period covered by this study, is printed in *Wartime International Agreements: Soviet Supply Protocols* (Department of State Publication 2759, Washington n.d. [1942]). We have drawn heavily on some of the volumes of the years 1940 and 1941 in the series *Foreign Relations of the United States* (Washington, 1959, 1958), also published by the Department of State, which contain most of the basic diplomatic documents on American-Soviet relations during this period, including the record of Hopkins' and Harriman's conversations with Stalin between late July and October 1941, some of Ambassador Laurence Steinhardt's important reports on the military situation in Russia, records of the conversations held in Washington in 1940 and 1941—before and after the Nazi attack on the Soviet Union—by Constantin Oumansky, the Soviet Ambassador to the United States, and ranking members of the Department of State, including Secretary Hull and Under Secretary Welles, as well as some of the basic directives of the President on the subject of Russian Lend-Lease, and memoranda on a number of important conferences held at the White House on the subject. Events in 1942 are covered in *Europe,* Vol. III, pp. 684-757; this volume was published too late (Washington, 1961) for use in this study, but it contains nothing new of great significance.

Among the works of the principal participants, the most valuable for this study have been Winston S. Churchill's *The Grand Alliance* (Boston, 1950) and *The Hinge of Fate* (Boston, 1950), both volumes in his *History of the Second World War,* and Robert E. Sherwood, *Roosevelt and Hopkins* (New York, 1948). There is material of interest also in the autobiographical account of Edward R. Stettinius, Jr., *Lend-Lease: Weapon for Victory* (New York, 1944); John R. Deane, *The Strange Alliance: The Story of Our Efforts at Wartime Co-operation with Russia* (New York, 1947); William H. Standley and Arthur A. Ageton, *Admiral Ambassador to Russia* (Chicago, 1955); Sumner Welles, *The Time for Decision* (New York, 1944); Henry H. Arnold, *Global Mission* (New York, 1949). Unfortunately both *The Memoirs of Cordell Hull* (New York, 1948; 2 vols.) and Henry L. Stimson and McGeorge Bundy, *On Active Service in Peace and War* (New York, 1947) contain rather little information on the background and history of Russian Lend-Lease. There are, however, a few choice bits in *The Secret Diary of Harold L. Ickes,* Vol. III: *The Lowering Clouds, 1939-1941* (New York, 1954). A little information is also supplied by Jesse H. Jones in his *Fifty Billion Dollars: My Thirteen Years with the RFC* (New York, 1951). Some additional documentary material is provided by *F. D. R.: His Personal Letters, 1928-1945* (New York, 1950), Vol. II.

The outstanding account of American foreign policy in the years immediately preceding the entry of the United States into the second World War is, of course, the two-volume work of William L. Langer and S. Everett Gleason, *Challenge to Isolation, 1937-1940* (New York, 1952) and *The Undeclared War, 1940-1941* (New York, 1953), and we have drawn heavily on the latter. There is pertinent material also

in Herbert Feis, *The Road to Pearl Harbor* (Princeton, 1950); William H. McNeill, *America, Britain and Russia: Their Cooperation and Conflict, 1941-1946* (London, 1953); Hanson W. Baldwin, *Great Mistakes of the War* (New York, 1950); William C. Bullitt, *The Great Globe Itself* (New York, 1946); Forrest Davis and Ernest K. Lindley, *How War Came* (New York, 1942); and Eliot Janeway, *The Struggle for Survival* (New Haven, 1951).

We have profited too from a number of volumes in the official British series, *History of the Second World War,* especially W. K. Hancock and M. M. Gowing, *British War Economy* (London, 1949); H. Duncan Hall, *North American Supply* (London, 1955); H. Duncan Hall and others, *Studies of Overseas Supply* (London, 1957); and S. W. Roskill, *The War at Sea,* Vol. I: *The Defensive* (London, 1954) and Vol. II: *The Period of Balance* (London, 1956).

Passing reference is made in the text to certain other books, articles, Congressional hearings, etc., which need not be listed here. Of great importance, however, and frequently cited are the *New York Times* and the *New York Herald Tribune.*

The valuable work of Professor Raymond H. Dawson, *The Decision to Aid Russia, 1941* (Chapel Hill, 1959), appeared just as this study was completed. Professor Dawson's emphasis is on Congressional and public opinion; his volume therefore serves as a complement to this study whose main emphasis is on administration. Where the two overlap, Dawson's conclusions are, generally, much the same as those of the present study. His account of the development of official policy is useful, and the work also contains a valuable bibliography on the background and early history of Russian Lend-Lease.

NOTES

1. William L. Langer and S. Everett Gleason, *The Undeclared War,* New York, 1953, p. 337.

2. For the details of these warnings and the Russian Ambassador's reaction, see Department of State, *Foreign Relations of the United States,* I, 1941, Washington, 1958, *passim* (hereafter cited as *Foreign Relations,* I, 1941).

3. Langer and Gleason, *The Undeclared War,* pp. 529 ff.; Winston Churchill, *The Grand Alliance* (Vol. 3 of *The Second World War),* Boston, 1950, pp. 358-359 and 367.

4. Churchill, *The Grand Alliance,* p. 372.

5. For a good account of American opinion of the Soviet Union before the Nazi attack, see Raymond H. Dawson, *The Decision to Aid Russia, 1941,* Chapel Hill, 1959, pp. 41-42.

6. For an account of American opinion of the Nazi attack on the Soviet Union and the Soviet Union's ability to resist, see *ibid.,* pp. 64-109.

7. John Gilbert Winant, *Letter from Grosvenor Square,* Boston, 1947, pp. 202-203.

8. Forrest Davis and Ernest K. Lindley, *How War Came,* New York, 1942, p. 238; Cordell Hull, *Memoirs,* II, New York, 1948, p. 967.

9. Langer and Gleason, *The Undeclared War,* p. 541. "The President approved the text as prepared, but added what is perhaps the most salient point in it, the final sentence, in his own handwriting." Sumner Welles, *The Time for Decision,* New York, 1944, p. 171.

10. *New York Times,* June 25, 1941; *New York Herald Tribune,* June 25, 1941. Interior Secretary Ickes said that the President's statement "indicated a state of mind rather than an active policy." *The Secret Diary of Harold Ickes,* III: *The Lowering Clouds, 1939-1941,* New York, 1954, p. 550.

11. *New York Times,* June 25, 1941.

12. Edward R. Stettinius, Jr., *Lend-Lease: Weapon for Victory,* New York, 1944, p. 122.

13. *New York Times,* June 26, 1941; Langer and Gleason, *The Undeclared War,* p. 541.

14. *New York Times,* June 27, 1941.

15. There is no official history of American military assistance to the Soviet Union during the second World War. Some of the basic documents on the background and first year of American

Lend-Lease to Russia are printed in *Foreign Relations,* I, 1941, pp. 786-866.

16. Langer and Gleason, *The Undeclared War,* p. 540.

17. *Ibid.,* pp. 537 and 538.

18. See, for instance, William L. Langer and S. Everett Gleason, *The Challenge to Isolation, 1937-1940,* New York, 1952, pp. 726-727.

19. Quoted in Langer and Gleason, *The Undeclared War,* p. 538.

20. *Ibid.,* p. 546.

21. For the text of Welles's conversation with Oumansky, see *Foreign Relations,* I, 1941, pp. 769-772. Oumansky did tell Welles—as he had already informed the State Department—that the Soviet Union now welcomed the immediate appointment of an American naval attaché and staff, which the Navy Department had been interested in sending to Moscow for some time. When Oumansky first telephoned the State Department on the morning of June 23 to inform the Department of the Russian position, Mr. Loy W. Henderson, then Assistant Chief of the Division of East European Affairs, told him that the Navy Department was concerned about finding proper housing for the attaché in Moscow. Oumansky replied: "At this time we should think of important things first and not concentrate on minor matters such as housing, and so forth" *(Foreign Relations,* I, 1941, pp. 885-886).

22. *Ibid.,* pp. 774-775.

23. Langer and Gleason, *The Undeclared War,* p. 545; *Foreign Relations,* I, 1941, pp. 789-791.

24. Langer and Gleason, *The Undeclared War,* pp. 544-545; *New York Times,* June 25, June 27, June 30, July 2, 1941.

25. Unsigned memorandum, no office of origin, "Memorandum on Organization and Policy for the Export and Production of Articles for Russia, June 30, 1941," in WPB file 113.2: Exports, January-June 1941; Langer and Gleason, *The Undeclared War,* p. 545. WPB files are to be found in the National Archives. The text of the memorandum is printed in *Foreign Relations,* I, 1941, pp. 775-778.

26. Langer and Gleason, *The Undeclared War,*

p. 558.

27. On the Curtis Committee, see also Dawson, *The Decision to Aid Russia,* pp. 130-131.

28. Langer and Gleason, *The Undeclared War,* pp. 558-559.

29. *Ibid.;* "Minutes of Meeting" held on July 22, 1941, dated July 23, 1941, unsigned, in WPB file 135.6: Reqs-Russia, July-December 1941. See also Civilian Production Administration, *Industrial Mobilization for War,* Washington, 1947, pp. 130-131.

30. Interview with General Burns.

31. Robert E. Sherwood, *Roosevelt and Hopkins,* New York, 1948, pp. 306-308; Langer and Gleason, *The Undeclared War,* pp. 540n., 545-546, 559; Davis and Lindley, *How War Came,* pp. 199-200, 208-210.

32. At Hyde Park, Pres. Franklin D. Roosevelt's Official File (hereafter cited as O.F. 220: Russia 1933-42, Box 1).

33. Langer and Gleason, *The Undeclared War,* p. 546. Roosevelt had said practically the same thing to Welles on July 9; T. H. Vail Motter, *The Persian Corridor and Aid to Russia,* Washington, 1952, p. 21. For a summary of the President's remarks to Oumansky, see Welles's conversation with Halifax in *Foreign Relations,* I, 1941, pp. 781-789.

34. See opening sentence of letter, President to General James H. Burns, July 21, 1941, in WPB file 135.6. A note on the drafting of the letters is on the copy in O.F. 4117: Harry Hopkins, 1940-1945.

35. Sherwood, *Roosevelt and Hopkins,* p. 308; interview with General Burns. See also Dawson, *The Decision to Aid Russia,* pp. 151-152.

36. Interview with General Burns; Stettinius, *Lend-Lease,* p. 122.

37. Letter, President to General Burns, July 21, 1941, and other documents in WPB file 135.6; O.F. 4117: Harry Hopkins, 1940-1945; Langer and Gleason, *The Undeclared War,* p. 559 (who believe the initiative came from Welles, not Hopkins); and *Industrial Mobilization for War,* p. 130.

38. "Minutes of Meeting" cited in note 29, and other references in same note above. See also Stettinius, *Lend-Lease,* pp. 122-123, and Langer and Gleason, *The Undeclared War,* p. 559.

39. For figures see "Summary of Russian Requests and Action Thereon, June 30 to July 30, 1941," compiled by the OPM's Branch of Research and Statistics, dated July 28, 1941 in WPB file 135.6: Reqs-Russia, Oversize.

40. Letter, General Burns to the President, July 23, 1941, in WPB file 135.6. See also *Industrial Mobilization for War,* p. 131; Stettinius, *Lend-Lease,* p. 123.

41. Stettinius, *Lend-Lease,* p. 123.

42. *Industrial Mobilization for War,* p. 131;

Langer and Gleason, *The Undeclared War,* p. 559.

43. *Ibid.,* p. 559.

44. *Ibid.,* pp. 559-560; Stettinius, *Lend-Lease,* pp. 123-124. While Stimson, as already noted, was one of the staunchest supporters of all possible assistance to the Soviet Union, he was nevertheless concerned by what he felt were evident Russian attempts to elicit military secrets from the United States in the process of obtaining military assistance. There was also considerable resentment in Washington at this time over Russian refusal to allow American observers either in the war zone or at Vladivostok. See the memorandum of Assistant Secretary of State A. A. Berle, Jr. to Welles, *Foreign Relations,* I, 1941, pp. 798-799.

45. Quoted in Langer and Gleason, *The Undeclared War,* pp. 560, 561; Stettinius, *Lend-Lease,* p. 124; Herbert Feis, *The Road to Pearl Harbor,* Princeton, 1950, p. 262; Eliot Janeway, *The Struggle for Survival,* New Haven, 1951, pp. 262-263; *New York Times,* August 15, 1941. For a more detailed account of the background of this meeting and its aftermath, see Dawson, *The Decision to Aid Russia,* pp. 151 ff. Ickes' account suggests that the chief bottleneck was in "Harry Hopkins' organization" because it was equipped to deal only with Lend-Lease supplies (Ickes, *The Secret Diary,* III, pp. 592-593); Ickes normally assumed that Hopkins was at fault whenever Hopkins' name was associated with error in any way.

46. Langer and Gleason, *The Undeclared War,* pp. 560-561.

47. To judge from Oumansky's conversation with Welles on July 24th—in which Oumansky reported his government's approval of such a committee—Roosevelt must have thought up and proposed the plan some time before. See *Foreign Relations,* I, 1941, p. 795.

48. At Hyde Park, President's Secretary's File, Russia folder, 1941, Knox 77, printed in *F. D. R.: His Personal Letters, 1928-1945,* II, New York, 1950, pp. 1195-1196, and in Wayne Coy, "Get Things Moving—FDR," *New Republic,* April 15, 1946, pp. 546-547.

49. Interview with General Burns. This committee is mentioned by Stettinius, *Lend-Lease,* p. 124, but he gives no detailed account of its actions. It is likewise mentioned in Langer and Gleason, *The Undeclared War,* p. 561, and Motter, *The Persian Corridor,* p. 21, neither of whom discuss the committee's work or document their source of information. There is no further mention of the operations of this group in the 1941 *Foreign Relations* volumes.

50. Letter, Wayne Coy to William S. Knudsen, August 6, 1941, in WPB file 135.6.

51. Memorandum, Knudsen to Coy, August 9,

1941, in *ibid.*

52. Minutes of the Council of the OPM, August 12, 1941, p. 50, item 2.

53. Langer and Gleason, *The Undeclared War,* p. 561. The text of these notes is printed in *Foreign Relations,* I, 1941, pp. 815-817.

54. For detailed accounts of Hopkins' trip to Moscow, see Sherwood, *Roosevelt and Hopkins,* pp. 323-348, and Langer and Gleason, *The Undeclared War,* pp. 563-567.

55. Sherwood, *Roosevelt and Hopkins,* pp. 309-317; Churchill, *The Grand Alliance,* pp. 424-425.

56. Sherwood, *Roosevelt and Hopkins,* pp. 318-319 and 321-322; Langer and Gleason, *The Undeclared War,* pp. 563-564. The correspondence on this topic between Hopkins and the White House is reprinted in the *Hearings of the Joint Committee on the Pearl Harbor Attack,* 79th Cong., 1st sess., Part 20, pp. 4384, 4373.

57. Sherwood, *Roosevelt and Hopkins,* p. 327.

58. *Ibid.,* p. 328.

59. The text of Hopkins' report on his first conversation with Stalin is in *Foreign Relations,* I, 1941, pp. 802-805. It was transmitted by Roosevelt to Secretary Hull on September 5, 1941. Cf. p. 802, note 52. The original copy of this report was found in the Roosevelt files at Hyde Park, and it is not clear whether the President ever transmitted a copy of it to the War and Navy Departments. For Hopkins' report on his conversation with Foreign Minister Molotov on the afternoon of July 30, see *Foreign Relations,* I, 1941, pp. 802-805.

60. The only other persons present at Hopkins' first interview with Stalin were Ambassador Steinhardt and G. Frederick Reinhardt, then Third Secretary and Vice Consul at the Moscow Embassy, who acted as interpreter. At the second meeting, the only other person present was former Foreign Minister Maxim Litvinov, who acted as interpreter on this occasion. A few months later, Litvinov was appointed Soviet Ambassador to the United States—an appointment highly welcomed in Washington.

61. The full text of Hopkins' memorandum to the President on his second conversation with Stalin is printed in *Foreign Relations,* I, 1941, pp. 805-814. It was on this occasion that Stalin said that he would welcome American troops on Soviet soil. Hopkins replied: "I told him that I doubted that our government, in the event of war, would want an American army in Russia but that I would give his message to the President."

62. See p. 105 above.

63. Sherwood, *Roosevelt and Hopkins,* p. 335.

64. Concerning Joseph E. Davies' influence on the President, see Richard H. Ullman, "The Davies Mission and United States-Soviet Relations, 1937-

1941," *World Politics,* IX, 1957, pp. 220-239; and Dawson, *The Decision to Aid Russia,* pp. 139-141.

65. Sherwood, *Roosevelt and Hopkins,* pp. 395-396. Concerning Major Yeaton's position, see Dawson, *The Decision to Aid Russia,* pp. 210, 256.

66. Henry H. Arnold, *Global Mission,* New York, 1949, p. 254.

67. Langer and Gleason, *The Undeclared War,* p. 668. The text of the message is printed in *Foreign Relations,* I, 1941, pp. 822-823.

68. *New York Times,* August 20, 1941. Senators Hiram Johnson, Bennett Champ Clark, and Robert A. Taft went so far as to charge that the President had made a secret alliance and was planning to send an expeditionary force to invade Europe.

69. See Dawson, *The Decision to Aid Russia,* pp. 161-171, for a general account of the financial background of Russian military assistance.

70. Langer and Gleason, *The Undeclared War,* p. 560.

71. *New York Times,* July 2, July 3, July 23, July 27, July 31, August 2, August 19, August 21, September 19, September 23, October 15, 1941.

72. Langer and Gleason, *The Undeclared War,* p. 545.

73. *Ibid.,* p. 791; *New York Times,* July 23, 1941.

74. Langer and Gleason, *The Undeclared War,* p. 791.

75. *New York Times,* August 21, 1941. See for instance Oumansky's conversation with Welles and Hull, August 24 and September 4, 1941, *Foreign Relations,* I, 1941, pp. 824, 827.

76. For Hull's memorandum on this conversation, see *ibid.,* pp. 832-834.

77. Memorandum, Hopkins to the President, September 5, 1941, in President's Secretary's file, Russia folder, 1941, Box 77; Hull, *Memoirs,* II, p. 977; Langer and Gleason, *The Undeclared War,* p. 791.

78. *New York Times,* August 19, August 24, 1941; Motter, *The Persian Corridor,* p. 24.

79. *New York Times,* August 21, 1941.

80. *New York Times,* September 17, 1941.

81. *New York Times,* September 17, September 18, 1941; Jesse H. Jones, *Fifty Billion Dollars: My Thirteen Years with the RFC,* New York, 1951, p. 381. Commenting on this agreement, Jones writes: "Though slow, the Russian deliveries turned out to be sure. We got our money back with interest, a not too common occurrence in government—with government deals . . ." *(ibid.,* p. 383). General Burns recalls Gromyko coming to his office at one time to ask for $50,000,000. Gromyko refused to answer any questions regarding the disbursal of the money, saying: "I don't know." Burns finally informed Gromyko that

OLLA disbursed only materials, and financing would have to be arranged through other agencies (interview with General Burns).

82. *New York Times,* September 19, 1941. For an account of the Congressional history of the second Lend-Lease bill, see Dawson, *The Decision to Aid Russia,* pp. 269 ff.

83. Langer and Gleason, *The Undeclared War,* p. 793. For the role of Catholic opposition to military aid to Russia, and the President's efforts to cope with this opposition, see Dawson, *The Decision to Aid Russia,* pp. 258-263.

84. Langer and Gleason, *The Undeclared War,* p. 794.

85. The full text is printed in *F. D. R.: His Personal Letters,* II, pp. 1204-1205.

86. Langer and Gleason, *The Undeclared War,* p. 797.

87. *Ibid.*

88. For text of the President's remarks see *Foreign Relations,* I, 1941, p. 1000.

89. Press release, October 2, 1941, O. F. 220: Russia, 1933-42, Box 1; Frederick R. Sanborn, *Design for War,* New York, 1951, p. 339; Langer and Gleason, *The Undeclared War,* pp. 816-817; O. F. 220A: Russia 1933-45, Box 6, contains much material on American public opinion and the Russian attitude toward religion.

90. Sherwood, *Roosevelt and Hopkins,* p. 392. Harriman took up the matter of religious freedom with Stalin at their meeting on October 3rd. See *Foreign Relations,* I, 1941, pp. 1001-1002. This was followed several days later by an official statement, couched in highly general terms and evidently designed to appease the President's wishes, reaffirming the formal right of freedom to worship, under Article 124 of the Soviet Constitution of 1936 (*Foreign Relations,* I, 1941, pp. 1002-1003).

91. It might be noted that the matter of religious freedom in the Soviet Union had been of interest to the State Department for some time, and continued to be after the issuance of the official Soviet statement in November. See, for instance, *Foreign Relations,* I, 1941, pp. 995-999, 1003-1005.

92. The name of the mission was later simplified by the omission of the words "War Supply." See *ibid.,* pp. 828-829.

93. Interview with General Burns.

94. Davis and Lindley, *How War Came,* p. 212.

95. Interviews with W. Averell Harriman and General Burns.

96. Sherwood, *Roosevelt and Hopkins,* p. 384.

97. For an account of Burns's efforts to stimulate American industrial mobilization, see Mark S. Watson, *Chief of Staff: Prewar Plans and Preparations,* Washington, 1950, pp. 115, 128, 174-176,

182.

98. *Ibid.,* p. 339.

99. *Ibid.,* pp. 332-333.

100. *Ibid.,* pp. 338, 339.

101. *Ibid.,* p. 339; for further details on the effect of the President's letter, see Richard M. Leighton and Robert W. Coakley, *Global Logistics and Strategy, 1940-1943,* Washington, 1955, pp. 127 ff.

102. Watson, *Chief of Staff: Prewar Plans and Preparations,* p. 347.

103. For the complete text, see *ibid.,* pp. 348-349, also note 56, p. 349, and *Foreign Relations,* I, 1941, pp. 826-827. Part of the same letter is printed in Leighton and Coakley, *Global Logistics and Strategy,* p. 99. Here the letter is dated August 31st.

104. Interview with General Burns; Watson, *Chief of Staff: Prewar Plans and Preparations,* Chap. XI; Leighton and Coakley, *Global Logistics and Strategy,* pp. 98-99; Langer and Gleason, *The Undeclared War,* p. 737; Watson fails to bring out Burns's work in tying together the Harriman Mission and the Victory Program. See also WPB file 135.6 under date August 30, 1941. The text of the President's letter to Stimson, printed in *Foreign Relations,* I, 1941, pp. 826-827, is taken from a photostatic copy obtained from the Roosevelt files at Hyde Park. The *Foreign Relations* volume makes no mention of any attached list.

105. Leighton and Coakley, *Global Logistics and Strategy,* p. 97.

106. See pp. 107 and 114 above.

107. Leighton and Coakley, *Global Logistics and Strategy,* pp. 97-98.

108. *Ibid.,* p. 99.

109. Quoted in Watson, *Chief of Staff: Prewar Plans and Preparations,* p. 329.

110. The President's memorandum is printed in full in *ibid.,* pp. 348-349.

111. Leighton and Coakley, *Global Logistics and Strategy,* p. 99.

112. *Ibid.,* p. 93.

113. *Ibid.,* p. 99; WPB file 135.6 for documents after August 30, 1941.

114. For a detailed account of the Harriman Mission's stay in London, see Leighton and Coakley, *Global Logistics and Strategy,* pp. 99-100; see also Dawson, *The Decision to Aid Russia,* pp. 213-216.

115. Interviews with W. Averell Harriman and General Burns; Leighton and Coakley, *Global Logistics and Strategy,* pp. 99-100.

116. *Ibid.*

117. *Ibid.,* p. 101.

118. *Ibid.;* Dawson, *The Decision to Aid Russia,* pp. 214-215.

119. On the tank problem at London, see

Leighton and Coakley, *Global Logistics and Strategy,* pp. 100-101; also Dawson, *The Decision to Aid Russia,* pp. 214-215.

120. Leighton and Coakley, *Global Logistics and Strategy,* p. 100.

121. *Ibid.,* pp. 100-101.

122. Sherwood, *Roosevelt and Hopkins,* p. 385.

123. For detailed accounts of the Moscow Conference, see Sherwood, *Roosevelt and Hopkins,* pp. 387-395; Langer and Gleason, *The Undeclared War,* pp. 810-815; see also William H. McNeill, *America, Britain, and Russia, 1941-1946,* London, New York, 1953, pp. 23 ff. See also Dawson, *The Decision to Aid Russia,* pp. 249 ff. Some dispatches of the Harriman Mission are printed in *Foreign Relations,* I, 1941, pp. 836-843.

124. Sherwood, *Roosevelt and Hopkins,* p. 330.

125. *Ibid.,* p. 391.

126. *Ibid.,* p. 386. The complete text is printed in *Foreign Relations,* I, 1941, p. 836.

127. Sherwood, *Roosevelt and Hopkins,* p. 388.

128. *Ibid.*

129. *Ibid.,* p. 389. It is interesting to note that in Harriman's telegram of September 30 *(Foreign Relations,* I, 1941, p. 839) reporting on his conversation with Stalin the previous evening, there is no hint of the unpleasantness mentioned in his subsequent report, quoted by Sherwood.

130. William H. Standley and Arthur A. Ageton, *Admiral Ambassador to Russia,* Chicago, 1955, p. 67.

131. Sherwood, *Roosevelt and Hopkins,* p. 389.

132. *Ibid.,* p. 390.

133. Stettinius, *Lend-Lease: Weapon for Victory,* pp. 126-127.

134. The official text is printed in Department of State, *Wartime International Agreements: Soviet Supply Protocols,* Washington, n.d. [1942], pp. 1-12.

135. See above pp. 116-117. See also Dawson, *The Decision to Aid Russia,* p. 252, note 7.

136. Leighton and Coakley, *Global Logistics and Strategy,* pp. 101-102.

137. See especially William C. Bullitt, *The Great Globe Itself,* New York, 1946, pp. 11 ff.; Hanson W. Baldwin, *Great Mistakes of the War,* New York, 1950, pp. 9 ff.; McNeill, *America, Britain and Russia,* pp. 24-26. If the subject of getting political commitments from the Russians in return for the aid promised them was ever discussed by the Harriman Mission, there is no indication of it in Sherwood, *Roosevelt and Hopkins,* or in Admiral Standley's memoirs, nor is such a possibility mentioned by Churchill.

138. Quoted in Sherwood, *Roosevelt and Hopkins,* pp. 401-402. The text of this telegram is printed in *Foreign Relations,* I, 1941, pp. 104-105.

139. For an American account of Stalin's conversation with Eden, see *Foreign Relations,* I, 1941, pp. 200-201.

140. If there was any formal discussion within the State Department looking to the attachment of specific political conditions to any military assistance granted the Russians, there is no record of it in the 1941 *Foreign Relations* volumes.

141. The subject of the potential political aspects of military aid to Russia has hardly been raised in any of the British writing on the second World War, including those works most critical of general allied strategy, such as Chester Wilmot's *Struggle for Europe* and the memoirs of Lord Alanbrooke. There is no mention of the matter, either, in the memoirs of Lord Halifax or those of John G. Winant. Churchill does not mention the matter in *The Grand Alliance.*

142. Stettinius, *Lend-Lease: Weapon for Victory,* p. 106. Stettinius writes that until his own appointment as Lend-Lease Administrator, "Mr. Roosevelt had personally signed every Lend-Lease allocation order and transfer letter."

143. *Ibid.,* p. 127, contains a brief account of this dinner.

144. Letter, Gromyko to Hopkins, September 30, 1941, in Hopkins Papers, Book VI: Aid to Russia. Hopkins' request was sent on September 22, 1941.

145. William L. Batt, Memorandum to File in WPB file 135.6; Russia-Reqs—3rd Protocol, July-December 1943.

146. Letter of R. J. Lynch to G. Smith, October 13, 1941, WPB file 135.6.

147. Memorandum of W. B. Ballis to C. E. Rhetts, October 27, 1941, subject: Soviet Priority Problems, WPB file 142.52: Preference Ratings—Extension to Russia.

148. Minutes of the Council of the OPM, October 14, 1941, p. 66, item 5.

148a. Minutes of SPAB, October 15, 1941, p. 18, item 10.

149. Letter of Edward R. Stettinius, Jr. to Hopkins, October 23, 1941, in Hopkins Papers, Book VI: Aid to Russia, OEM, DDAR.

150. Memorandum of Mason Britton to Knudsen, September 17, 1941, in WPB file 481.038; Machine Tools—Allocations Foreign, and Knudsen's handwritten note to Hazard, c. September 23, 1941, in WPB file 135.6.

151. Minutes of the Council of the OPM, October 21, 1941, p. 68, item 4.

152. Minutes of SPAB, October 29, 1941, item 2; Letter of William L. Batt to SPAB, October 29, 1941, WPB file 135.6.

153. On the subject of the "Russian issue" during the Congressional debate on the second Lend-Lease Appropriation bill, see Dawson, *The Decision to Aid Russia,* pp. 271 ff.

154. Hearings before the subcommittee of the Committee on Appropriations, House of Representatives, 77th Cong., 1st sess., on the Second Supplemental National Defense Appropriation Bill for 1942. Part I, Defense Aid—Lend Lease, p. 27. Similar testimony came from—among others—Secretary Stimson and General Marshall, who said: "Whatever we do to keep the Russian army in the field aggressively resisting the Germans is to our great advantage. It would increase the chances of a successful end to the war, it would hasten the early conclusion." (Quoted in Dawson, *The Decision to Aid Russia,* pp. 275-276.)

155. *Congressional Record,* House of Representatives, 77th Cong., 1st sess., LXXXVII, Part vii, p. 7823. As Dawson (*The Decision to Aid Russia,* p. 281, note 113) points out, Langer and Gleason, *The Undeclared War,* p. 818, erroneously reports the vote on the amendment in question as 217 to 162, thus giving a rather exaggerated picture of Congressional opposition to Russian aid, which—by this time at least—was far more vociferous than it was numerically substantial.

156. Dawson, *The Decision to Aid Russia,* p. 282.

157. Report of W. A. Harriman to the President, October 29, 1941, in President's Secretary's file, Russia folder, 1941, Box 77.

158. Sherwood, *Roosevelt and Hopkins,* p. 395.

159. *Ibid.,* p. 396.

160. *Ibid.,* p. 395; Standley and Ageton, *Admiral Ambassador to Russia,* p. 237.

161. The text of Harriman's report to the President is printed in *Foreign Relations,* I, 1941, pp. 849-851.

162. *F. D. R.: His Personal Letters,* II, pp. 1226-1227. The text of the President's cable is also in *Foreign Relations,* I, 1941, pp. 851-852.

163. Sherwood, *Roosevelt and Hopkins,* p. 397. The complete text of Stalin's reply as handed to Ambassador Steinhardt in Kuibyshev by Mr. Vishinsky, then Assistant People's Commissar for Foreign Affairs, is printed in *Foreign Relations,* I, 1941, pp. 855-856. The original text—a paraphrase of which was published to protect existing codes—varied slightly in phraseology. Stalin also wrote the President that he shared the President's desire for a meeting and was ready to do everything "to make this possible."

164. On November 7, 1941 the President also sent a message of congratulations to President Kalinin of the Soviet Union on the anniversary of the Soviet revolution of November 1917. No such message had been sent for the previous two years, but—as the editors of the 1941 *Foreign Relations* volume note—"in consideration of the wartime changes in relations, a telegram of felici-

tations was now deemed appropriate." Mr. Roosevelt's telegram concluded significantly: "I wish to assure you of the desire of the government and people of the United States to do everything possible to assist your country in this critical hour." (*Foreign Relations,* I, 1941, p. 654.) Significantly the President quoted this sentence again at the beginning of his letter to Stettinius, dated the same day, informing him that he had declared the Soviet Union eligible to receive Lend-Lease assistance, and directing Stettinius to transfer defense matériel to the Soviet Union, in accordance with the President's previous letter to Stettinius, dated October 30, 1941. See also *ibid.,* p. 857.

165. For the collapse of opposition to Russian military aid under Lend-Lease, see Dawson, *The Decision to Aid Russia,* pp. 284-289.

166. Sherwood, *Roosevelt and Hopkins,* p. 398. "The overwhelming sentiment in the United States," Sherwood writes, "was that the Russians richly deserved and would know how to use every scrap of help that we would give them." At about this time the President decided to send General Burns to Moscow as United States Ambassador to the Soviet Union. On November 5, Roosevelt wrote to Steinhardt asking him to obtain immediate Russian *agrément* to Burns's appointment. This was obtained the day after Steinhardt delivered the President's request. Burns, however, was never actually appointed. By January 1942 the President had decided that his services would be more valuable in Washington, and instead sent Admiral William H. Standley, former Chief of Naval Operations. See *Foreign Relations,* I, 1941, pp. 852-853.

167. O. F. 4117: Harry Hopkins, 1940-42.

168. Letters of Secretary Stimson and Secretary Knox to the President, November 13, 1941, in *ibid.*

169. Letter of the President to Secretary Stimson, November 7, 1941, in *ibid.*

170. Letter of General Burns to the President, November 19, 1941, and attachments, in *ibid.*

171. Minutes of meeting in WPB file 135.6. Also see letter of Donald M. Nelson to SPAB, November 25, 1941, in *ibid.*

172. Memorandum of William Batt to All Branch Chiefs, OPM, January 7, 1942, Re: Status of Russian Aid Program, WPB file 135.6.

173. Memorandum, signed A. G. (Andrei Gromyko), no addressee, November 25, 1941, in President's Secretary's file, Russia folder, 1941, Box 77. See also, for instance, Assistant Secretary of State Acheson's memorandum of November 19, 1941, printed in *Foreign Relations,* I, 1941, pp. 862-863.

174. Sherwood, *Roosevelt and Hopkins,* p. 398.

175. *Ibid.*

176. Minutes of SPAB, November 26, 1941, p. 30, item 2; Robert H. Connery, *The Navy and Industrial Mobilization in World War II,* Princeton, 1951, p. 105.

177. Interviews with W. Averell Harriman and General Burns; see also WPB files, especially memoirs of William Batt; Minutes of the President's Soviet Protocol Committee; General John R. Deane, *The Strange Alliance,* New York, 1947; and McNeill, *America, Britain and Russia,* pp. 24-25.

178. See note 176 above.

179. On the Welles-Oumansky conversations in 1940 and 1941, see *Foreign Relations,* I, 1940 and I, 1941, *passim.*

180. Minutes of SPAB, November 26, 1941.

181. Minutes of SPAB, December 2, 1941, p. 33, item 2; Connery, *The Navy and Industrial Mobilization,* pp. 105-106.

182. Memorandum, Mason Britton to William S. Knudsen, December 19, 1941, WPB file 481.0132: Machine Tools—Exports.

183. See correspondence between Robert P. Patterson, Donald M. Nelson, and Edward R. Stettinius, Jr., January-February 1942, in *ibid.*

184. On the general subject of ordnance deliveries to the Soviet Union after late 1941, see also Constance McL. Green, Henry C. Thompson and Peter C. Roots, *The Ordnance Department: Planning Munitions for War* (volume in *United States Army in World War II*), Washington, 1955, pp. 77-80.

185. See correspondence between Colonels Becker and Reimel, and between Donald M. Nelson and Ferdinand Eberstadt, March and April 1942, in WPB file 481.038: Machine Tools—Allocations—Foreign.

186. Connery, *The Navy and Industrial Mobilization,* pp. 166-167.

187. Letters of Belyaev to Donald M. Nelson, June 24, 1942, and Nelson to Belyaev (prepared by C. E. Rhetts, Batt's assistant), July 7, 1942, in WPB file 481.038.

188. Memorandum of William L. Batt to J. A. Krug, April 9, 1945, WPB file 960: Reconversion to Civilian Economy, January-May 1945.

189. WPB Requirements Comm Document No. 826, September 1, 1942, USSR Sec., WPB file 523.28: Aluminum—Reqs—Foreign, 1940-42.

190. Letter of Lombard to Lynch, August 7, 1941, in WPB file 523.132: Aluminum—Exports.

191. "Give us anti-aircraft guns and the aluminum and we can fight for three or four years," Stalin told Hopkins at their very first meeting on July 30. See *Foreign Relations,* I, 1941, pp. 804, 811.

192. "Memo of Discussion," December 6, 1941, WPB file 523.433: Aluminum—Deliveries.

193. Memorandum of T. E. Covel to A. H. Bunker, October 14, 1941, WPB file 523.28.

194. American Bureau of Metal Statistics, *Yearbook, 1947,* p. 88.

195. F. B. Cliffe, "History of Aluminum Supply to Russia," April 21, 1942, WPB file 523.28.

196. Minutes of the SPAB, November 26, 1941, p. 31, item 5; Connery, *The Navy and Industrial Mobilization,* p. 106.

197. See notes 192 and 195 above.

198. Letter of General H. H. Arnold to William S. Knudsen, November 27, 1941, WPB file 523.132.

199. Minutes of SPAB, December 2, 1941, p. 33, item 1; Connery, *The Navy and Industrial Mobilization,* p. 106.

200. See note 195 above.

201. TWX, Dayton to Richardson, December 10, 1941, WPB file 523.132.

202. Letter of James Forrestal to Henry A. Wallace, December 19, 1941, Document 19, SPAB meeting, December 23, 1941, WPB file 523.38; memorandum of Donald M. Nelson to William Batt, December 22, 1941, WPB file 523.7638: Aluminum Sheet, Strip and Plate Allocation—Foreign; memorandum of F. B. Cliffe to William Batt, December 20, 1941, WPB file 523.38; Minutes of SPAB, December 23, 1941, p. 48, item 1.

203. Memorandum of A. O. Pierrot to A. E. Lombard, December 26, 1941, subject: Aluminum for USSR, WPB file 523.7638.

204. Minutes of the SPAB, January 15, 1942, p. 66, item 4.

205. Memorandum of F. B. Cliffe to William Batt, April 14, 1942, WPB file 523.433: Aluminum—Deliveries; F. B. Cliffe, "History of Aluminum Supply to Russia," April 21, 1942, WPB file 523.28.

206. Stettinius, *Lend-Lease: Weapon for Victory,* pp. 154-155; Leighton and Coakley, *Global Logistics and Strategy,* p. 247.

207. Leighton and Coakley, *Global Logistics and Strategy,* p. 115; on the problem of British deficiencies, see Winston Churchill, *The Hinge of Fate,* Boston, 1950, p. 843.

208. Memorandum marked "Received from Mr. Stettinius, 12/23/41," in Hopkins Papers, Book V: Aid to Russia.

209. Copy in WPB file 140.31: Deliveries of Material—Foreign. The complete text of the letter (as addressed to Stimson) is printed in *Foreign Relations,* I, 1941, p. 865.

210. Memorandum of William Batt to All Branch Chiefs, OPM, January 7, 1942, Re: Status of Russian Aid Program, WPB file 135.6.

211. Memoranda of E. W. Reid to Clements, January 31, 1942; William Batt to E. W. Reid,

February 19, 1942; Reid to Batt, March 12, 1942, WPB file 135.6.

212. Report of P. F. Schucker to C. E. Adams, January 2, 1942 and memorandum of H. Mc-Kenney to P. F. Schucker, March 20, 1942, WPB file 512.38: Steel—Allocations—Foreign, January 1941-May 1942; P. F. Schucker, "The Lend-Lease and Other Export Steel Program," June 30, 1943, WPB file 122.2: Lend-Lease, Purchase Negotiation Reports. See also P. F. Schucker, "Report on the Position of the Russian Lend-Lease Program," January 24, 1942, WPB file 512.28: Steel—Requirements—Russia.

213. Memorandum of P. F. Schucker to C. E. Adams, March 5, 1942, "Report on the Position of Russian Lend-Lease Program as of March 4, 1942," WPB file 512.38; see also William Batt's pencilled comments on P. F. Schucker's report of January 24, 1942 cited in note 212 above; and Schucker's report of June 30, 1943, cited in note 212 above.

214. Correspondence in WPB file 135.6 beginning with letter of Secretary Morgenthau to Donald M. Nelson, February 19, 1942, and ending with telegram of C. E. Adams to steel company executives.

215. Report of P. F. Schucker of June 30, 1943, cited in note 212 above.

216. See Leighton and Coakley, *Global Logistics and Strategy,* pp. 102-116.

217. *Industrial Mobilization for War,* p. 348. See the excellent study of Louis Morton, "Germany First: The Basic Concept of Allied Strategy in World War II," in Kent Roberts Greenfield (ed.), *Command Decisions,* New York, 1959, pp. 3-38.

218. Letter of the President to Donald M. Nelson, March 17, 1942, WPB file 135.6.

219. Letter of the President to Admiral Land, March 17, 1942, in *ibid.*

220. Letter of Thomas B. McCabe to Donald M. Nelson, March 19, 1942, in *ibid.*

221. Minutes of the WPB, Washington, 1946, March 24, 1942, p. 34, item 3.

222. Letter of Donald M. Nelson to the President, April 1, 1942, WPB file 135.6.

223. Letter of Donald M. Nelson to All Division Directors, All Branch Chiefs, ANMB, and All Procurement Agencies, April 1, 1942, in *ibid.*

224. Letters of Thomas B. McCabe to William L. Batt, April 9, 1942; McCabe to the President, April 13, 1942; the President to Nelson, April 14, 1942, in *ibid.*

225. For a general account of the shipping problem in the first year of Lend-Lease to Russia, see Leighton and Coakley, *Global Logistics and Strategy,* especially pp. 113-115; Samuel Eliot Morison, *The Battle of the Atlantic, September*

1939-May 1943, Boston, 1947, Chap. VII. Further enlightenment is provided by W. K. Hancock and M. M. Gowing, *British War Economy,* London, 1949; S. W. Roskill, *The War at Sea: The Defensive,* I, London, 1954 and *The Period of Balance,* II, London, 1956; H. Duncan Hall, *North American Supply,* London, 1955; H. Duncan Hall and others, *Studies of Overseas Supply,* London, 1957; Motter, *The Persian Corridor* and, of course, Churchill, *The Grand Alliance* and *The Hinge of Fate.*

226. See the figures in Motter, *The Persian Corridor,* p. 481.

227. *Ibid.,* pp. 419, 433. On the subject of Russo-Japanese relations after the Nazi attack on the Soviet Union, see *Foreign Relations,* 1941, I and IV, *passim.*

228. See the figures in Motter, *The Persian Corridor,* pp. 481, 482.

229. For an account of the Arctic route, its trials and successes, see Churchill, *The Hinge of Fate,* Chap. XV; Ernest J. King and Walter Muir Whitehill, *Fleet Admiral King: A Naval Record,* New York, 1952, p. 392; Roskill, *The War at Sea,* I, Chap. XXII and II, Chap. V.

230. Churchill, *The Hinge of Fate,* pp. 258-259.

231. *Ibid.,* pp. 262-266. On the fate of Convoy PQ-17, see also Roskill, *The War at Sea,* II, pp. 136-146; and also the dramatic account of this episode in Morison, *The Battle of the Atlantic,* pp. 179-192. Morison speaks of the fate of the PQ-17 as "the grimmest convoy battle of the entire war." The Germans called it "Convoy Slaughter in the Arctic Sea."

232. See the telegram of Stalin to Churchill, printed in *The Hinge of Fate,* p. 270.

233. Letter of Admiral Land to the President, January 22, 1942, in Hopkins Papers, Book VII: Russian Requests; memorandum of P. F. Maguire to D. C. MacKeachie, February 7, 1942, in WPB file 112.2: Stockpiles—Shipping Priorities List.

234. *New York Times,* October 23, October 24, October 26, 1941. The State Department also complained about the Maritime Commission's attendant publicity because it implied that the Vladivostok route was being abandoned and that the U. S. was giving ground to Japan. See also letter of General Burns to Hopkins, and Hopkins to Gousev, January 16, 1942, in Hopkins Papers, Book V: Aid to Russia; letter of Thomas B. McCabe to Secretary Morgenthau, April 2, 1942 in Hopkins Papers, Book VI: Aid to Russia; and Leighton and Coakley, *Global Logistics and Strategy,* pp. 556-557.

235. Quoted in Churchill, *The Hinge of Fate,* p. 272.

236. Hancock and Gowing, *British War Econ-*

omy, p. 363.

237. Leighton and Coakley, *Global Logistics and Strategy,* pp. 559-560.

238. Memorandum of J. D. Coppock to William Batt, October 16, 1942, and R. M. Shepherd to Coppock, October 21, 1942, WPB file 135.6.

EDITORIAL COMMENTS

The first year of aid to Russia serves as an illustration of the slow but dramatic transition from peace-of-a-sort to outright war. Again, as in other cases, we see President Roosevelt preparing the way for attaining his objectives by a series of cautious maneuvers—the Taylor mission to Rome, the use of R.F.C. loans to postpone a decision about the designation of Russian eligibility for Lend-Lease aid, and the muting of comment about Russia's financial needs.

In this case, unlike his long postponement of all action on plans for war mobilization, the President's reticences and apparent hesitations were accompanied from the very beginning by decisive and determined action. Roosevelt was convinced that somehow an unwilling nation and an unwilling Congress could be persuaded to support or at least accept the Russian aid program. (His task of political persuasion lies outside the scope of this study.) Roosevelt also clearly had faith that he would be able in time to solve the problem of financing shipments to Russia, eventually under Lend-Lease (again by political persuasion), and in the meantime he was determined to get the aid program started. The Lend-Lease Act had been signed on March 4, 1941 and Roosevelt knew quite well on June 22, 1941, the date of the German attack on Russia, that Lend-Lease aid for Britain was still composed almost entirely of goods ordered by Britain before March 4 and taken over by Lend-Lease merely to save Britain the dollar outlay. He therefore knew all too well how slow the Lend-Lease process was at best; aid for Russia needed his urgent and full support if it was to make any progress at all.

The degree to which Roosevelt maintained his personal intervention in promoting aid to Russia throughout the first year is extraordinary. No President, least of all Roosevelt, wants to over-commit himself on a single issue, especially an unpopular one; Roosevelt's willingness to devote so much of his precious time and energy, and of his reservoir of persuasive power, to the Russian aid program was, one might almost say, uncharacteristic. Perhaps the earnestness of his conviction is demonstrated by his signing of a forceful letter on Russian aid on December 28, only three weeks after Pearl Harbor, in the middle of the ARCADIA Conference, with Churchill a guest in the White House; but perhaps Churchill, also a vigorous proponent of aid to Russia, was pressing the President for ever more energetic action during their talks.

It is not easy to tell exactly why Roosevelt felt almost from the first day that the Russians would survive the German attack and why he thought substantial aid and strict fulfillment of Protocol agreements were so important. Roosevelt would not (quite wisely, in the event) accept the advice of the professional purveyors of intelligence in the War, Navy and State Departments about Russia's capacity to fight on. One may guess that he surmised the truth, i. e., that many of the Russian experts and their superiors permitted their deep suspicions and hatred of the Soviet Union to unbalance their judgment of the regime's stability under fire. Indeed as Army attitudes toward Colonel Faymonville illustrate, any officer who asserted his faith in the Red Army was *ipso facto* suspect. Faymonville's successor as military attaché in Moscow, Major Yeaton, was praised, as it were, for his thoroughly bad advice.

Roosevelt's initial optimism about Russia's capabilities was reassured by a number of his civilian friends and advisers: by Davies (who, as Ullman has pointed out, probably reached the right conclusions for the wrong reasons), by Hopkins (with the greatest impact), by Harriman and *ab initio* by Churchill. Furthermore, the material loss if Russian resistance collapsed before the end of 1941 would be slight, and we and the British would gain from the stimulus given to defense production by proposed but still undelivered aid to Russia. Roosevelt could and did point this out to his military advisers who feared that our aid would fall into German hands. And after the successful defense of Moscow, Roosevelt could and no doubt did also point out that American aid would cause German losses on the battlefield in Asia if not in Europe. These were the hedges that protected Roosevelt's ventures and encouraged his apparently very real optimism about Russian survival.

Roosevelt could have been optimistic, and yet unwilling to insist on large-scale aid for Russia. Why did he do so? Any answer must be partly speculative. Certainly, like Churchill, he believed that there was an inherent advantage in aiding any nation that forced a division and reduction of German military power. Even before Pearl Harbor, aid to Russia could reasonably be construed as aid to a nation in defense of the United States. The advantages to Eisenhower's armies three years later given by German battles in the East prove the point that Russian Lend-Lease did aid our national defense.

There seems to be more to the matter than this. The great emphasis Roosevelt placed on the complete and prompt fulfillment of our Protocol commitments, his determination to avoid quarreling about minor points, no matter how irritating the Russians' unjustified suspicions, surliness, and unwillingness to cooperate, indicate a concern that was more comprehensive than the immediate overwhelming task of defending America and, presently, winning the war. So far as is known, Roosevelt did not disclose his objectives and his hopes either to the military (whose opinions on political matters did not interest him) or to the State Department, in which he had little faith. Yet one may presume that he hoped then as he did later that by the confidence and gratitude engendered by our wartime actions, Russia could be drawn into some kind of cooperative relationship in the task of helping to govern the postwar world. Such an objective clearly underlay many of Roosevelt's actions at Teheran, and Yalta. His sharp repudiation (and that of Hopkins acting for him) of anti-Russian

sentiments expressed by officials both civil and military indicated a concern not only with interference with the aid program but also with our long-term relations with Russia. And Churchill here again shared the desire and, to some extent, the hope for postwar cooperation.

Churchill's hearty approval of our aid for Russia never precluded his hearty objections to whatever he deemed an excessive transfer of supplies from Britain to Russia. And of course the same problem, the same anguish, arose again and again in connection with the diversion of military material from our own under-armed forces. It was particularly in this context that aid to Russia constituted one more step in Roosevelt's assumption of his full powers as Commander in Chief and *pari passu* of the acceptance of his command by the Chief of Staff of the Army and the Chief of Naval Operations. Marshall and Stark, later King, were more cautious about aiding Russia than their civilian chiefs, the two secretaries; initially they urged a step-up in aid to Britain instead. And on more than one occasion they (joined by the secretaries) spoke out from the depths of their hearts about what seemed to them excessive raids on their scanty treasuries of arms. Never, however, did they dispute Roosevelt's basic decision, and never did they question his right to make the specific decisions that disturbed them so deeply.

Perhaps one reason why Roosevelt won so much acceptance with relatively little debate was the curious gift that he and Hopkins, his alter ego in this work, had in making the best use of men both within and without the formal organizational framework in which they were officially placed. Hopkins himself, the chief mover of Lend-Lease affairs, was never Lend-Lease Administrator; he was a special assistant to, a special representative of the President. During the ARCADIA Conference he was appointed by Roosevelt and Churchill chairman of the Munitions Assignments Board, technically a subcommittee of the Combined Chiefs of Staff; he also served as a member of SPAB. And in all these positions, and outside their formal limitations, and on his trips abroad, he pursued relentlessly the objectives that were in the forefront of his chief's concern.

Another illustration of Roosevelt's gift for making flexible use of men is found in General Burns—executive director of DDAR (Lend-

Lease's predecessor agency) working under Hopkins and simultaneously executive assistant to Assistant Secretary of War Patterson. The very wording of paragraphs of a memorandum from Burns to Hopkins (or Patterson) might turn up later in a letter from Roosevelt to Stimson and Knox, or a memorandum from Patterson to Marshall. Seen in this light the difficulties of disorderly organization can be overlooked, and wisely so; for in time all the major difficulties were overcome. During the long period in which organizations were expanding at great speed and constantly shedding one chrysalis after another, the advantages of this constant interplay of devoted men were obvious. The same men, the same relationships that worked to carry out Roosevelt's Russian program helped him to set forth and send on its way the Victory Program. What seemed to some the outrageous demands of the First Protocol led to what some described as the outrageous objectives of the Victory Program—key to successful mobilization planning; and in due course both were fulfilled.

One final point concerning Roosevelt's deliberate choice of odd administrative devices and names deserves comment. In 1936, in the establishment of an agency to administer some undetermined portion of the new $4.25 billion work-relief program, the President denominated it the "Works Progress Administration," suggesting to the public that Hopkins, its administrator, might be more concerned with statistics than with work-relief projects. By this device, Roosevelt hoped to avoid some of the political criticism he feared and he also postponed the inevitable decisions on the allocation of powers among Hopkins, Ickes and the other rivals. The establishment of the "Division of Defense Aid Reports" in 1941 represents an almost perfect parallel: the political opposition was confused, the bureaucratic division of spoils postponed. And Hopkins was even better protected by being given, under the President's own direction, all the real, and none of the formal, power. Finally, in both cases, though for different reasons, much of the operational leadership was provided by Hopkins working happily with Army officers. This relationship in the mid-thirties proved to be an admirable training for joint action when we entered World War II.

THE UNITED STATES FLEET:
DIPLOMACY, STRATEGY AND THE
ALLOCATION OF SHIPS (1940-1941)

ROBERT J. QUINLAN

ASSISTANT EDITOR

THE ENCYCLOPEDIA AMERICANA

CONTENTS

Introduction   155
  Historical Background (to May 1940)   155
  Expansion and Allocation   155

  I   The U. S. Fleet Stays in Pearl Harbor (May-October 1940)   157

  II   Strategic Conferences and Plans (Winter and Spring 1941)   163
  Fleet Reorganization   166
  Rainbow V   167

  III   Pacific Maneuvers (Winter and Spring 1940-1941)   169

  IV   Pacific Defense vs. Atlantic Operations (Spring 1941)   177

  V   The Atlantic Fleet in Action: The Pacific Fleet Holds Fast
(Summer 1941)   186

  VI   Prelude to Pearl Harbor (August-December 1941)   191

  Bibliographic Note   193

  Notes   194

  Editorial Comments   199

INTRODUCTION

HISTORICAL BACKGROUND (TO MAY 1940)

During the ten years preceding Pearl Harbor, the U. S. Fleet was located in the Pacific. Several factors were responsible for this state of affairs: (1) The United States had a one-ocean Navy or, to be more precise, a one-ocean combat Fleet. Individual ships or squadrons might be, and were, stationed in other places but there was only one Fleet. (2) The Fleet was located in the Pacific because (a) the British Navy had traditionally served as a "protective shield" for the United States in the Atlantic, reducing to a minimum the need for United States naval power in Atlantic waters, and (b) Japan had for some years been considered a potential threat to American interests and the general balance of power in the Pacific. In the Pacific, the Fleet was normally based on coastal ports like San Diego, San Pedro, and San Francisco in California and occasionally on northern ports like Bremerton, Washington. By 1940, a small division of the Fleet, known as the Hawaiian Detachment, was normally based on Pearl Harbor. There also existed a force known as the Asiatic Fleet (primarily for prestige reasons since it was no more than a squadron in size) based on the Philippines and operating separately from the U. S. Fleet.

The international situation in the ten years preceding May 1940 had made these traditional allocations of naval strength increasingly unsatisfactory. Japan's conquest of Manchuria in 1931 and invasion of China a few years later made her a much more positive than potential threat in the Pacific. The rise of Nazi Germany and Fascist Italy simultaneously created a threat from the other side of the world. By May 1940, the precise nature of these threats and their actual power had become much more clear. The war in Europe between Germany on the one side and England and France on the other posed an immediate threat to America's traditional "protective shield," the Royal Navy, and a more general threat to the U. S. itself should Germany emerge victorious in Europe. Additions to German strength by alliance or by conquest would clearly worsen the situation. At the same time, the European situation was making more threatening the situation in the Far East where the preoccupation of the great colonial powers, Britain, France, and the Netherlands, provided a "divine wind," a golden opportunity for Japanese dreams of expansion to the southward.

EXPANSION AND ALLOCATION

The reaction of the United States to these threats from both East and West took two principal forms so far as the Navy was concerned: expansion and allocation. Beginning in the early 1930's and intensifying each year, a naval construction program was undertaken. The gradual rate of build-up may be seen by the number of new ships commissioned in each of these pre-war years: in 1934, 4 cruisers and 1 destroyer; in 1935, 1 cruiser, 6 destroyers, and 1 floating drydock; in 1936, 1 cruiser, 2 destroyers, and 4 submarines; in 1937, 1 cruiser, 24 destroyers, 2 gunboats, 6 submarines, 1 cargo ship, and 3 fleet tugs; in 1938, 2 aircraft carriers, 5 cruisers, 12 destroyers, and 6 submarines; in 1939, 4 cruisers, 8 destroyers, 4 submarines, 2 minesweepers, 1 cargo ship, and 1 fleet tug.[1] In the summer of 1940, the decision was reached to create a two-ocean Navy, with a combat fleet in both the Atlantic and the Pacific, and to put an end to reliance on moving the Fleet from one ocean to the other via the Panama Canal.[2]

But this two-ocean Navy would not, even under an intensified building program, be in actual existence before 1944 or 1945. This provided no immediate answer to the threats of 1940 and 1941. American response to these threats had to be based on naval strength *in being*. The vital question, therefore, became: How should U. S. naval strength be allocated to protect American interests from foreign threats? Answers to this question had a double nature: on the one hand, political; on the other, military. Had the two been in agreement on both objectives and methods, there might not have been a situation of interest to the student of civil-military relations. But civilian and military authorities did not in fact agree and therein lies the basis for this study of the United States Fleet.

I. THE U. S. FLEET STAYS IN PEARL HARBOR (MAY-OCTOBER 1940)

War games had long been a traditional spring exercise for the U. S. Fleet. Elements assembled in some area of one of the oceans, there to carry out previously specified tasks and to be judged on their performance, and also to permit the officers and men to become acquainted with the weather, tides, geography, and general conditions in the area selected. In the spring of 1940 the war games were scheduled for Hawaiian waters. The bulk of the U. S. Fleet, at this point based on various ports along the California coast, moved out to sea. "Divided into two task forces representing opposing fleets . . . [they] . . . conducted a war game and various exercises and then united with the Hawaiian detachment and proceeded to the Hawaiian area . . ." arriving there during the first week in April 1940.[3]

According to the plans for these Fleet exercises, all units with the exception of the Hawaiian detachment were scheduled to leave Hawaiian waters on May 9 and return to the regular base ports on the coast of the mainland.[4] No secret was made of this scheduled return; rather it appears to have been common knowledge of all the officers and men in the Fleet and presumably of any interested civilian. That an interested foreign power would be aware of this schedule seems more than likely. Everyone knew the Fleet was in Hawaiian waters for a specific purpose and only temporarily.

On Saturday, May 4, however, the Commander in Chief of the U. S. Fleet, Admiral J. O. Richardson, received from the Chief of Naval Operations, Admiral Harold R. Stark, this brief dispatch:

It looks probable but not final that the Fleet will remain Hawaiian waters for a short time after May 9. Will expect to apprise you further Monday or Tuesday next.[5]

On Tuesday (May 7) came Stark's expected further communication, containing a somewhat startling order:

CINCUS make immediate press release instructions as follows:

"I request permission to remain in Hawaiian waters to accomplish some things I wanted to do while here. The Department has approved this request."[6]

Stark went on to make these new plans more specific:

Delay Fleet departure Hawaiian area is for about two weeks prior to the end of which time you will be further advised regarding future movements. Carry out regular scheduled overhauls of individual units, movements of base force units at your discretion.[7]

But when the further instructions arrived (in a letter from Stark to Richardson dated May 7), they contained a more ominous hint of future arrangements which would constitute an even greater departure from the normal operational pattern:

When the fleet returns to the Coast (and I trust the delay will not be over two weeks, but I cannot tell) the President has asked that the Fleet schedule be so arranged that on extremely short notice the fleet be able to return concentrated to Hawaiian waters. This will present somewhat of a problem in lugging around more oil with you perhaps than usual and keeping more provisions on board, because if action is wanted it will be wanted quickly. As far as I can see, your proposed schedule meets this requirement, and unless you hear to the contrary, you may assume it is O. K.[8]

Richardson had not personally requested the retention of his command in Hawaiian waters. Nevertheless, as one would expect, he proceeded to issue the specified press release, and the Fleet stayed in Hawaiian waters. Stark's predicted period of delay ("not . . . over two weeks") was drawing to a close when Richardson, puzzled and apparently somewhat irritated as well, wrote him a long letter, the central theme of which was well expressed in this paragraph:

As you no doubt well appreciate, I now must plan the Fleet schedule, and employment for the next few months. To do this intelligently, however, it is necessary to know more than I know now about why we are here and how long we will probably stay. I realize that the answer to the second question is largely dependent upon the first, and probably also upon further developments, but nonetheless I should have something to go on. For instance, carrying out even a curtailed gunnery schedule will require wholesale movements of targets, tugs, utility planes, etc., from the Coast.[9]

Richardson then went on to raise what seemed to him pertinent questions:

(a) Are we here primarily to influence the actions of other nations by our presence, and if so, what effect would carrying out of normal training (insofar as we can under the limitations on anchorages, airfields, facilities and services) have on this purpose? . . .

(b) Are we here as a stepping-off place for belligerent activity? If so, we should devote all of our time and energies to preparing for war. This could more effectively and expeditiously be accomplished by an immediate return to the West Coast, with "freezing" of personnel, filling up complements, docking, and all the rest of it. We could return here upon completion.

As it is now, to try and do both (a) and (b) from here and at the same time is a diversification of effort and purpose that can only result in the accomplishment of neither.

If we are here to develop this area as a peacetime operating base, consideration should be given to the certain decrease in the efficiency of the Fleet and the lowering of morale that may ensue, due to inadequate anchorages, airfields, facilities, services, recreation conditions, for so large a fleet. If only peacetime training is involved, should the Bureau of Navigation and I not be advised so we may remove restrictions on officer details?[10]

In answer, Stark declared in a letter written some five days later:

Why are you in the Hawaiian area?

Answer: You are there because of the deterrent effect which it is thought your presence may have on the Japs going into the East Indies. In previous letters I have hooked this up with the Italians going into the war. The connection is that with Italy in, it is thought the Japs might feel just that much freer to take independent action.

We believe both the Germans and the Italians have told the Japs that so far as they are concerned, she, Japan, has a free hand in the Dutch East Indies.[11]

The Japanese indeed appeared to have a free hand in Asia. The end of the period of the "phony war" in Europe had been rapidly followed by spectacular German successes in all directions. When the Nazi blitzkrieg overran the Netherlands early in May and then subjugated France (an armistice was concluded on June 24), it seemed as if Japan's golden chance, her "divine wind," had come. The riches of the Indies—oil, rubber, tin, quinine—lay before her; neither the Netherlands nor France could effectively gainsay Japanese ambitions and demands.

In his letter to Richardson, Stark presented the U. S. position:

. . . suppose the Japs do go into the East Indies? What are we going to do about it? My answer to that is, I don't know, and I think there is nobody on God's green earth who can tell you. I do know my own arguments with regard to this, both in the White House and in the State Department, are in line with the thought contained in your recent letter.

I would point out one thing, and that is even if the decision here were for the U. S. to take no decisive action if the Japs should decide to go into the Dutch East Indies, we must not breathe it to a soul, as by so doing we would completely nullify the reason for your presence in the Hawaiian area. Just remember that the Japs don't know what we are going to do, and so long as they don't know, they may hesitate or be deterred. These facts I have kept very secret here.[12]

Out of this welter of uncertainty, there appear several reasonably clear points. The basic U. S. policy, agreed upon however reluctantly by the White House, the State Department, and the military, appears to have been *improvisation,* improvisation dictated by circumstances. However shrewd its appraisals of the current world situation and whatever its guesses may have been, Washington could not be absolutely sure in the spring of 1940 whether the Italians would enter the war. And even if the Italians did enter, there was even greater uncertainty as to what the Japanese course of action would be. Italy had at this point, according to most estimates, a Navy of some real power. Addition of this potent force to the more limited forces of the Germans would pose a definite and immediate threat to Britain, France and the Netherlands. Their limited naval forces would be needed to defend the homelands and, in the case of the British, to keep open both the Atlantic and the imperial lifeline through the Mediterranean. In any case, they simply would not have the naval forces to spare for a defense of their interests and possessions in the Far East against Japanese aggression. And the Japanese knew it.

So far uncommitted in all this jockeying for position was the U. S. Fleet. The possibility that it might be employed actively in the Pacific was a factor to make the Japanese pause. U. S. officials, and especially those in the Navy, knew how weak and woefully unprepared for combat the Fleet was. How much the Japanese knew was another question. But it was a reasonably safe assumption that they did not know *all*. The result was the decision to keep the Fleet at Pearl Harbor for the present. No one, as Stark had so vividly said, knew what the U. S. would do if the Japanese moved. But the continued presence of the Fleet at Pearl Harbor seemed to be keeping them guessing, and pausing in making any moves southward. For example, when in April, only a few weeks earlier, Secretary Hull declared that armed intervention in the Netherlands East Indies "would be prejudicial to the cause of stability, peace, and security" in the whole Pacific area, the Japanese confined their expansionist desires to increasingly arrogant demands but took no positive action: Hull's remark may or may not have affected Japanese policy, but it seemed to do so.[13] So long as the Fleet's presence (like Hull's remark) had this apparent result, it was looked on as performing a useful function, as playing a vital role in world-wide diplomacy. Concerning this role, Admiral Stark told Richardson:

This will answer the question "why you are there." It does not answer the question as to how long you will probably stay. Rest assured that the minute I get this information I will rush it to you. Nobody can answer it just now. Like you, I have asked the question and also—like you—I have been unable to get the answer.

You ask whether you are there as a stepping-off place for belligerent activity?

Answer: Obviously it might become so under certain conditions, but a definite answer cannot be given as you have already gathered from the foregoing.

I realize what you say about the advantages of returning to the West Coast for the purpose of preparation but preparation at this time is out of the question. If you did return, it might nullify the reasons for your being in Hawaii. This very question has been brought up here.[14]

However vital the role of the Fleet in worldwide diplomacy, its position and role were risky, and just how risky its Commander in Chief knew only too well. The precariousness and uncertainty of the Fleet's position led him to undertake a trip to Washington in July 1940.

Richardson's instructions had given him some leeway, not about relocating the Fleet, but about moving individual ships to and from the California coast for replenishment, overhaul, and recreation for its men.[15] These duties had brought the admiral himself, along with about one-third of the battleships in the Fleet, to the mainland in the latter part of June. There he received instructions to go to Washington.

Apparently Richardson had hoped to visit Washington earlier. On June 22, a letter to him from Stark had noted:

Your trip to Washington was held in abeyance because of uncertainty as to the movement of the Fleet in the immediate future. Tentatively, decision has been made for the Fleet to remain for the present where it is.[16]

After his arrival in California he actually started out, but the fall of France on July 4 produced another postponement. Finally, however, he arrived on July 8 and met with the President at luncheon. Their conversation lasted for some two or three hours, and was devoted, according to Richardson,

primarily to find the thought back of our retention in Hawaii, to explore and endeavor to ascertain, if possible, the duration of our stay and, from my point of view, stress the necessity of increasing the number of men in the Navy. . . .[17]

According to Richardson's recollection, it was the latter subject that occupied the greater part of the conversation. During his three-day visit, Richardson also discussed these same subjects with Secretary of State Cordell Hull, in the presence of Under Secretary Sumner Welles.

He also saw Army Chief of Staff General George C. Marshall and Dr. Stanley Hornbeck, principal State Department adviser on Far Eastern Affairs.

In Richardson's words:

Mr. Hull in a very complete and comprehensive manner presented to me his views of the relationships, relations between the United States and Japan. He felt that we should take a very strong position with respect to Japan and that the retention of the fleet in Hawaii was a reflection of that strong attitude.

I did not receive this impression from Secretary Hull, and I cannot state with certainty how I received it, but I left here with the distinct impression that there was an opinion in Washington that Japan could be bluffed.[18]

Further recounting his Washington impressions, Richardson was of the decided opinion that, if he had been "uninfluenced by other considerations,"[19] Stark would have agreed with Richardson on the desirability of basing the Fleet on the West Coast of the United States instead of in Hawaii. But these "other considerations" were, for the moment at least, in the ascendant, and the Fleet continued to remain at Pearl Harbor.

The passage of time, however, did not alter Richardson's views. Early in September Secretary of the Navy Frank Knox made a visit to the Fleet at its anchorage at Pearl Harbor. Richardson was interested in having Secretary Knox talk to many different Fleet officers. Basically, however, Richardson desired to impress upon the Secretary his views about the undesirability of retaining the Fleet at Pearl Harbor. He prepared a written memorandum setting down in detail his position. Having summarized a number of occupational, logistical, and tactical factors tending to render unsatisfactory retention of the Fleet in the Hawaiian area, the Admiral went on to consider the broader strategic and political issues at stake:

If the disposition of the fleet were determined solely by naval considerations the major portion of the fleet should return to its normal Pacific Coast bases because such basing would facilitate its training and its preparation for war.

If factors other than purely naval ones are to influence the decision as to where the fleet should be based at this time, the naval factors should be fully presented and carefully considered, as well as the more probable effect of the decision on the readiness of the fleet. In other words, is it more important to lend strength to diplomatic representation in the Pacific by basing the fleet in the Hawaiian area, than to facilitate its preparation for active service in any area by basing the major part of it on normal Pacific Coast bases?

In case our relations with another Pacific nation deteriorate, what is the State Department's conception of our next move? Does it believe that the fleet is now mobilized and that it could embark on a campaign directly from Hawaii or safely conduct necessary training from the insecure anchorage at Lahaina which is 2,000 miles nearer enemy submarine bases than our normal Pacific Coast bases?[20]

But no immediate result came of the Knox visit and the general atmosphere of uncertainty continued. In October 1940 Admiral Richardson made a second trip from Hawaii to Washington. His motives for this trip have not been made entirely clear, in part, one suspects, because they may well have been mixed. His principal purpose was undoubtedly a reconnaissance mission, to try to discover the future status of the Fleet at the final source of decision-making. Whether he also hoped to be able, by discussion with the authorities in Washington, to influence that policy, is not clear.

Admiral Richardson arrived in Washington on October 7. This time, in contrast to the trip of the preceding July, Richardson came in response to a summons from Secretary Knox. The principal point at issue, he discovered, was not retention of the Fleet at Pearl Harbor but a possible transfer of elements from the Fleet to reinforce Admiral Hart's tiny detachment, the Asiatic Fleet. Although Richardson had lengthy discussions with Stark, Admiral Nimitz, and Knox, and a luncheon meeting with Dr. Hornbeck, the position of the Fleet in Hawaii was apparently not a topic. In reply to questions at the Pearl Harbor Hearings, Richardson explained this situation by pointing out that he had, only a short time before, presented a written memorandum to Secretary Knox and given him as well an oral exposition of his views. A copy of this memorandum had also been given to Admiral Stark and a copy of part of the memorandum to Dr. Hornbeck at the State Department, both of whom had as well been made aware of, and in Admiral Stark's case "thoroughly familiar" with, Richardson's position.

The matter of reinforcing the Asiatic Fleet was settled in a brief and rather perfunctory manner. In the course of a luncheon at the White House, where the President's guests were Admiral William D. Leahy[21] and Richardson, which was devoted primarily to matters concerned with Puerto Rico, the President asked Admiral Leahy for his opinion about strengthening the Asiatic Fleet. According to Richardson's recollection, "Admiral Leahy said that whatever you send out will be lost, therefore I would send the least valuable combatant ships we have, the 7,500 ton cruisers."[22] Richardson recommended that no ships be sent at all. As a result of these rather unenthusiastic recommendations, the proposal to send out reinforcements met a prompt death. However, the position of the Fleet came to the fore in this conversation in a much more immediate and impressive way. Richardson, now that he was face to face with the President, took direct action. At the Pearl Harbor Hearings, he recounted what happened:

I took up the question of returning to the Pacific coast all of the fleet except the Hawaiian detachment.

The President stated that the fleet was retained in the Hawaiian area in order to exercise a restraining influnce on the actions of Japan.

I stated that in my opinion the presence of the fleet in Hawaii might influence a civilian political government, but that Japan had a military government which knew that the fleet was undermanned, unprepared for war, and had no train of auxiliary ships without which it could not undertake active operations. Therefore, the presence of the fleet in Hawaii could not exercise a restraining influence on Japanese action.

I further stated that we were more likely to make the Japanese feel that we meant business if a train were assembled and the fleet returned to the Pacific coast, the complements filled, the ships docked, and fully supplied with ammunition, provisions, stores, and fuel, and then stripped for war operations.

The President said in effect, "Despite what you believe, I know that the presence of the fleet in the Hawaiian area has had, and is now having, a restraining influence on the actions of Japan."

I said, "Mr. President, I still do not believe it, and I know that our fleet is disadvantageously disposed for preparing for or initiating war operations."

The President then said, "I can be convinced of the desirability of returning the battleships to the west coast if I can be given a good statement which will convince the American people and the Japanese Government that in bringing the battleships to the west coast we are not stepping backward."[23]

This in effect put an end to the matter: the Fleet remained at Pearl Harbor. And, in the light of this decision, two subsequent developments can properly be mentioned here, even though they took place several months later.

One highly important by-product of keeping the Fleet at Pearl Harbor is summarized by Morison:

. . . the mere fact of having the Fleet there from May 1940 meant that this Hawaiian port was immensely improved as a fleet base and infinitely better prepared for hostilities. In one year from June 1940 the civilian force of the Pearl Harbor Navy Yard was more than doubled and naval personnel augmented many times; hundreds of acres of land were purchased for enlargement; housing facilities for naval and civilian personnel were constructed; a new dry dock was started; foundries were equipped to turn out castings of any size, and complete machine and toolshops were set up, rendering the Yard almost independent of the mainland. How much if any of this would have been done if the Fleet had been withdrawn to the West Coast, is still a matter of opinion.[24]

This eventuality was recognized at the time. As Stark wrote to Richardson on May 27, 1940: "You were not detained in Hawaii to develop the area as a peacetime operating base, but this will naturally flow to a considerable extent from what you are up against."[25]

The second important development was of a different character. For reasons explained below, on February 1, 1941, the classification of "U. S. Fleet" was abandoned. Simultaneously, an Atlantic Fleet and a Pacific Fleet were created as major divisions of the U. S. Navy, with the status of the Asiatic Fleet remaining unchanged. The Atlantic Fleet[26] comprised all combatant ships in commission in the Atlantic Ocean except those operating directly under the Chief of Naval Operations. The Pacific Fleet comprised "all the ships in the Pacific Ocean that were not part of the Asiatic Fleet and were not operating directly under the Chief of Naval Operations."[27]

Among the several factors responsible for this development[28] was undoubtedly the decision to keep the Fleet at Pearl Harbor. Coincident with this reorganization of the Fleet,

Richardson was relieved of his command, with Admiral Husband E. Kimmel becoming Commander in Chief of the Pacific Fleet and Admiral Ernest J. King of the Atlantic Fleet. Whether Richardson's removal from his command and his replacement by an officer apparently not in conflict with the policy of keeping the Fleet at Pearl Harbor is more than a coincidence cannot be stated with absolute certainty. But the "coincidence" certainly deserves notice.

These developments, establishing finally that the Fleet in the Pacific was to be based on Hawaii and not returned, even temporarily, to the West Coast of the United States, settled the first great issue of this narrative. From this point onward, the focus shifts to the role of the Fleet at Pearl Harbor in the light of international developments. To understand the pressures and counter-pressures exerted upon the Fleet in the succeeding months, it is desirable first to sketch briefly the development of U. S. strategy and especially naval strategy during the winter of 1940-1941.

II. STRATEGIC CONFERENCES AND PLANS (WINTER AND SPRING 1941)

On a grey bleak day in late January 1941 the great new British battleship, *King George V,* entered Chesapeake Bay at the end of its voyage from England. At Annapolis President Roosevelt went aboard to greet the new British Ambassador to the United States, Lord Halifax. Amid all the official ceremonies, however, a small group of men remained in their cabins. They were the principal British delegates to the forthcoming Washington Staff Conferences, the first formal attempt to produce joint plans between the United States and the United Kingdom.

The nucleus of the British delegation consisted of the four representatives of the British Chiefs of Staff who had come on the *King George V.* Dressed in civilian clothes, they were to all outward appearances technical advisers to the British Purchasing Mission. At the conference the quartet was joined by two other officers, both then stationed in Washington. Representatives of the three dominions of Canada, Australia and New Zealand also were represented in the British delegation although they were not present at the meetings.[29]

Major General Stanley Embick headed the U. S. delegation. Not only did his rank qualify him to meet the British Army representative on equal terms but he was regarded as an able and experienced planner.[30] Embick was also considered an expert on Far Eastern affairs. The Navy section was headed by Admiral Ghormley, who had returned from his duties as Special Naval Observer in London. Admiral Richmond K. Turner of the Navy War Plans Division and Captains A. G. Kirk, C. M. Cooke, and DeWitt Ramsey were other Navy participants. Other Army representatives were Brigadier Generals Sherman Miles and L. T. Gerow, and Colonel J. T. McNarney.

At first it was intended to make Under Secretary of State Welles a member of the U. S. delegation at the first meeting with the British. The suggestion, originated by the Joint Army-Navy Planning Committee, was vetoed by the President.[31]

The initial session of the Washington Staff Conferences convened on January 29, 1941. General Marshall and Admiral Stark addressed the delegates, both emphasizing the need for secrecy. As Sherwood has observed, the real fear was not of leakage to Axis spies, but of American publicity:

It is an ironic fact that in all probability no great damage would have been done had the details of these plans fallen into the hands of the Germans and the Japanese; whereas, had they fallen into the hands of the Congress and the press, American preparation for war might have been well nigh wrecked and ruined as, indeed, it came perilously close to being when the House of Representatives voted on the extension of Selective Service.[32]

And since unfavorable publicity might have adversely affected the fate of the Lend-Lease bill, still pending in Congress, the consequences of any publicity might well have proved to be disastrous.

President Roosevelt and Secretary Hull did not have complete trust in the arrangements for secrecy; for similar reasons they were exceedingly anxious not to be open to the accusation that they had made a secret deal with the British. The President, to protect himself and his Administration, not only joined with Secretary Hull in avoiding any meeting with the British delegates, but also, as has been noted, vetoed the Joint Army-Navy Planning Committee's suggestion that Under Secretary Welles, who was chairman of the State-War-Navy Liaison Committee, attend the opening session of the conference.

Admiral Stark made the U. S. government's position quite clear in his opening statement, and there is no doubt that the official position had been set by Roosevelt himself. Whatever military agreements might be reached would have to remain contingent upon future political action by the two governments.[33] Absence from the conferences of "political" officials as distinguished from "technical" military personnel would, all this implied, keep the President free of commitment and would give the conferees more freedom to explore alternatives than if they were committed to authoritative Presidential views on strategy.[34] The British also declared that any results of the deliberations must be contingent upon approval not only by their Chiefs of Staff, but by the Government as well. And Churchill, however eager to reach agreement with Roosevelt, knew that staff understandings alone constituted a bold move on Roosevelt's part, beyond which he could not go.

The ABC Meetings (American-British Conversations) continued until March 29, fourteen sessions in all. Virtually unanimous agreement existed among the conferees on the primacy of Germany and the Atlantic Ocean. At the opening session, the British delegates presented three propositions of general strategic policy. The first two were:

The European theatre is the vital theatre where a decision must first be sought.
The general policy should therefore be to defeat Germany and Italy first, and then deal with Japan.[35]

These propositions neatly coincided with several of the cardinal points of American defense policy, as the U. S. delegates proceeded to outline them. This opening statement was based upon the recent formulation of U. S. national defense policy by the Army-Navy Joint Board, which had been approved by the President on January 26.[36] Two of its basic features were (a) the determination to keep the Western Hemisphere secure from attack and (b) the provision of maximum material assistance to the British in their war against Germany. Therefore, upon the basis of these principles, it seemed self-evident that the United States, should it become an active participant

in the war, would satisfy both its own interests and those of Great Britain if the basic American effort were exerted in the Atlantic and "naval-wise"[37] in the Mediterranean.

Over the third aspect of a possible war situation, no such high degree of unanimity existed. The area of disagreement may be summed up in one word: Singapore. Concentration of Anglo-American effort in the Atlantic and European theaters had obvious implications for the other side of the world: prevention of war with Japan by all possible means, and, if this effort failed, keeping operations in the Pacific subordinate to the main effort in the Atlantic. With this principle both sides agreed; upon the method of holding a defensive posture in the Pacific there was no such agreement.

The British position was clearly expressed in the delegation's third proposition:

The security of the Far Eastern position, including Australia and New Zealand, is essential to the cohesion of the British Commonwealth and to the maintenance of its war effort. Singapore is the key to the defence of these interests and its retention must be assured.[38]

The Americans had no objections to this basic British belief in the vital importance of their Far Eastern position and of the security of Australia and New Zealand. But they "doubted the premise" that "Singapore is the key to the defense of these interests."[39] Since they doubted the premise upon which it was based, it is scarcely surprising that they were rather less than enthusiastic about the naval strategy proposals which were based upon it.

As a corollary to their review of strategy the British proposed that American naval forces, after making necessary provision for the defense of the Western Hemisphere, should make their main effort in "the Atlantic and European theatres," and that American naval dispositions in the Pacific should nevertheless be such as to "ensure that Japanese operations in the Far East cannot prejudice the main effort of the United States and the British Commonwealth in the principal theatres of war." Read in the light of British views on grand strategy, this declaration amounted to a proposal that the United States should underwrite the defense of Singapore.

The British representatives frankly explained their position. As they pointed out, the United Kingdom, the Dominions, and India "must maintain dispositions which, in all eventualities, will provide for the ultimate security of the British

Commonwealth of Nations." It was a "cardinal feature" of British policy to retain "a position in the Far East such as will ensure the cohesion and security of the British Commonwealth and the maintenance of its war effort"—the naval base at Singapore. It was, therefore, the aim of the British to persuade the Americans to recommend the adoption of this feature of British strategic policy as a feature of Anglo-American strategic policy and to agree that the United States, in recognition of the importance of holding Singapore, should send to Singapore four heavy cruisers and one aircraft carrier, together with planes and submarines.[40]

The debate over Singapore and the naval strategy based upon its defense continued throughout the staff conferences.[41] The British argument did not rest, to any important extent, upon the value of Singapore as a naval base in a possible war with Japan. Offensively, it would not be necessary to hold Singapore in order to protect Australia and New Zealand or to conduct operations against Japanese naval forces in the Indian Ocean. "An American fleet in the Pacific, actively threatening the Japanese left flank, would be enough to prevent the Japanese from extending their operations so far from home."[42] Defensively, Singapore in British control would not prevent the Japanese from operating against British communications in the Indian Ocean; Camranh Bay or Batavia could serve this purpose equally well.

The British delegates accepted these criticisms of the value of Singapore as a military base. Instead, they rested their case upon (a) the economic, political and symbolic importance of Singapore and (b) the virtual impossibility of Britain's conducting offensive operations against Japan even after the defeat of Germany without Singapore as a jumping-off point. These two arguments need not be elaborated here.[43] Singapore did indeed constitute a vital symbol of British power—both political and economic —in the Far East.

The American delegates did not deprecate these arguments. They could well appreciate the British position; nevertheless they refused to alter their original stand. The vital common concern of both countries, already agreed upon by the delegates, was the defense of the British Isles and the attainment of the security of the North Atlantic. The Americans could, of course, make no objection to the British making unilateral efforts to defend their Far Eastern

interests, just as the United States was doing. So far as joint operations were concerned, however, the American delegates refused to agree to a Pacific strategy based upon the defense of Singapore, and its tactical corollary, the reinforcement of Singapore by units of the U. S. Pacific Fleet. They summed up their position in a statement, "The U. S. Military Position in the Far East," delivered at the meeting of February 19. In part, this statement read:

The objective of the war will be most effectively attained by the United States exerting its principal military effort in the Atlantic or navally in the Mediterranean regions . . .

The United States Staff Committee agrees that the retention of Singapore is very desirable. But it also believes that the diversion to the Asiatic theater of sufficient forces to assure the retention of Singapore might jeopardize the success of the main effort of the Associated Powers.[44]

Moreover, the U. S. delegates had a number of important objections to Singapore itself, considered purely as a base. Should Japan seize airfields in Indo-China within bombing range of Singapore, the base could not be defended. Singapore itself was highly deficient in men and material, although this limitation was one which might have been overcome had the United States elected to underwrite its defense.[45] Finally, there was the oft-cited factor that Singapore was almost defenseless from land attack (its great guns were all permanently fixed pointing out to sea), a factor which the Japanese were later to find extremely useful.

Not only did the American planners object to sending units of the Pacific Fleet to Singapore; they also rejected the alternate proposal, that of reinforcing the U. S. Asiatic Fleet based on Manila. Such division of the Pacific Fleet would, it was argued, open up the possibility of defeat by attrition. Secretary Knox had made this specific in announcing, early in January, that the Asiatic fleet would *not* be reinforced.[46] The conferees did agree on a statement of stalemate:

It was agreed that for Great Britain it was fundamental that Singapore be held; for the United States it was fundamental that the Pacific Fleet be held intact.[47]

Many other topics made their appearance at the conference table but they lie outside the scope of this inquiry. At the final meeting, approval was given to the ABC-1 Staff Agreement, usually referred to simply as ABC-1.[48]

The main elements of the plan, as bearing on American strategy and obligations (in contemplation of possible war against Germany and/or Japan), were:
1. That the principal American military effort was to be exercised in the Atlantic Ocean and in Europe, since Germany was the predominant member of the Axis and these were the decisive theaters of combat.
2. That the United States would increase its forces in the Atlantic and Mediterranean areas so that the British Commonwealth would be in a position to release the necessary forces to defend British territories in the Far East.
3. That the tasks assigned to the American Pacific Fleet were in the main defensive—the protection of Hawaii, the Philippines, Guam, Wake, etc. But it was counted upon to undertake a diversion towards the Marshall and Caroline Islands, in order to relieve pressure on the Malay Barrier, and to attack Japanese communications and shipping (mainly a task for submarines).[49]

The later history of ABC-1 can be summarized briefly: It was read and approved by Admiral Stark and General Marshall and then by Secretaries Knox and Stimson. Hull preferred not to know the details of the agreement. The President's course of action was identical with his behavior during the conversations themselves: tacit but not formal approval when, in June, ABC-1 was officially presented to him. This action was intended to indicate clearly that actual implementation of ABC-1 was contingent upon American entry into the war.[50]

It may be useful to summarize at this point the main results of the ABC Meetings, so far as the Pacific Fleet was concerned: First, they provided for agreement on strategy without political commitments. Admiral Stark's opening statement to the conferees (in which he spoke with the approval of both the President and General Marshall) was carefully followed. Whatever military agreements were reached must be contingent upon future political action by the two governments.[51]

At the same time, the value of this tentative planning cannot be underestimated. As Sherwood accurately observed,

These staff talks, and the complete interchange of expert opinions as well as facts that they pro-

duced, provided the highest degree of *strategic preparedness* that the United States or probably any other non-aggressor nation has ever had before entry into war.[52]

This situation provided a sharp contrast with that prevailing in Belgium when, in the winter of 1939-40, the King, through an over-scrupulous regard for neutrality, refused to discuss joint defense plans with the French and British. Specifically, it was possible, in the terms of ABC-1, to allocate existing resources in preparation for the eventualities called for in the plan, of special importance in view of the passage of the Lend-Lease Act on March 11, the same day as the conclusion of the conference. Thus plans for greater responsibility of U. S. naval forces in the Atlantic could be prepared for operation, and warnings could be sent to the Fleet at Pearl Harbor that some of its units might be ordered to the Atlantic in line with these plans. There were, of course, other consequences of the ABC plan, among them provision for joint military missions which eventually formed the basis for the Combined Chiefs of Staff. But these were of broad and long-range significance. Of more immediate consequence for the Fleet in the Pacific were the reorganization of the U. S. Fleet and the development of RAINBOW V.

FLEET REORGANIZATION

The reorganization of the U. S. Fleet and the creation of an Atlantic Fleet and a Pacific Fleet on February 1, 1941[53] were the result of a number of factors.[54] Chief among these were the threatening world situation, the decision to keep the Fleet at Pearl Harbor rather than return it to the West Coast, the development of the program of a "two-ocean Navy," and especially the entry into active service of increasing numbers of newly completed ships, and the enlarged role being assigned to U. S. naval forces in the Atlantic theater. Of considerable significance also was the development of war plans which called for concentration of effort in the Atlantic while retaining a defensive posture in the Pacific. These plans were raised to the level of joint Anglo-American strategy at the ABC Conferences in Washington during January and February of 1941. Thus, while it is not true that the reorganization of the U. S.

Fleet came as a result of the ABC Meetings, it is true that the naval strategy which keynoted the conference was also largely responsible for this basic change.

Admiral Ernest J. King, who had been appointed to head the Patrol Force (the old Atlantic Squadron) on the 17th of January, was made Commander in Chief of the new Atlantic Fleet. King was designated full Admiral—symbolic of the growing importance of the Atlantic force.

It was this newly created naval division—the Atlantic Fleet—whose mission and strength were to be the subject of ever-increasing debate during the months to come, debate which centered primarily around the Fleet at Pearl Harbor.

RAINBOW V

Shortly after the adjournment of the Washington staff conferences, as has been described above, the product of the delegates' efforts—ABC-1—was given the approval of the Chief of Staff and the Chief of Naval Operations. On this basis, the Joint Board proceeded to order the drawing up of a strategic plan embodying the agreements of ABC-1. This plan was also to include the provisions of ABC-2, the Joint U. S.–Canada War Plan 2, then in the process of being drafted. This new plan was entitled RAINBOW V, since it was designed to fit a situation closely resembling that envisioned in the RAINBOW V plan of 1939.[55]

The primary assumption of the new RAINBOW V was the existence of a state of war between the Associated Powers (the United States, the British Commonwealth (less Eire), the Netherlands East Indies, Greece, Yugoslavia, the Governments-in-Exile, China, and the Free French) and the Axis Powers. The Axis was presumed to include Germany, Italy, the Balkan satellites and, either actual or potential, Japan and Thailand. A subsidiary provision assumed that the republics of Latin America would remain in a non-belligerent status but would make their territories and waters available to U. S. forces.

The content of RAINBOW V was essentially the development of the general agreements of ABC-1 into more precise U. S. strategic plans. Primary effort would be directed toward the defeat of Germany; the basic policy would be centered around the security of the Western Hemisphere, the defense of the United Kingdom, and the ultimate security of the British Commonwealth. Among the main points of the strategy contained in RAINBOW V (and also in its parent, ABC-1) were these:

(1) Application of economic pressure by naval, land, and air forces.

(2) The employment of air, land, and naval forces of the Associated Powers, at every opportunity, in raids and minor offensives against Axis military strength.

(3) The capture of positions from which to launch the eventual offensive.[56]

Assuming that enemy operations in the Western Atlantic area would be limited to air and naval raids and that primary U. S. efforts should be devoted to building up large land and air forces for eventual "major offensive operations against the Axis powers," the specific role to be played by U. S. military forces envisaged these activities:

(a) Reducing Axis economic power to wage war, by blockade, raids, and a sustained air offensive;

(b) Destroying Axis military power by raids and an eventual land, naval, and air offensive;

(c) Protecting the sea communications of the Associated Powers;

(d) Preventing the extension in the Western Hemisphere of European or Asiatic military powers; and

(e) Protecting outlying military base areas and islands of strategic importance against land, air, or sea-borne attack.[57]

For the U. S. Navy, these plans involved the performance of a number of specific tasks: In the Atlantic area, the Navy was charged with the protection of sea communications of the Associated Powers,

. . . destroying Axis sea communications by capturing or destroying vessels trading directly or indirectly with the enemy, . . . protecting and routing shipping in the coast zones, and for preparing to occupy the Azores and Cape Verde Islands if such an operation became necessary.[58]

Naval forces (including Marines) would operate in conjunction with the Army in the defense of the territory of the Associated Powers, the protection of Latin America, and the various bases throughout the theater. In British home waters, U. S. naval units, operating under CINCWA (British Commander-in-Chief Western Approaches), would be responsible for escort-of-convoy and also for raiding operations in the Mediterranean.

In the Pacific, the Navy would also be assigned to protect sea communications and destroy those of the Axis powers. Support would be given to Royal Navy units in the area south of the equator and west to longitude 155°. The Navy was charged with the defense of Midway, Johnston, Palmyra, Samoa and Guam. Operations in the Marshall Islands and raiding of enemy ships and positions were designed to divert enemy strength from the Malay Barrier, with eventual achievement of control over both the Marshalls and the Carolines. All this was in line with the much asserted U. S. policy of using the Pacific Fleet for operations against the Japanese left flank. Thus subordination of Pacific activities to those of the Atlantic theater did not mean purely defensive operations for the U. S. Fleet.

The Navy contemplated no reinforcement of the Asiatic Fleet, just as the Army had no plans for strengthening its forces in the Philippines. So long as it was feasible, the existing Army and Navy units were to cooperate in defending the Philippines. After that, the Fleet was to move south to aid in defending the Malay Barrier.

During the ensuing weeks RAINBOW V was considered and accepted (by the Army and Navy) as the foundation upon which U. S. military planning and activity would be based. On April 30, it was submitted by the Joint Planning Committee to the Joint Board which, at a regular meeting on May 14, gave its approval to both RAINBOW V and ABC-1. Two weeks later it was approved by the Secretary of the Navy and on June 2 by the Secretary of War.

The two plans were then forwarded to the White House for Presidential action. In their covering letter, Stimson and Knox informed the President that ABC-1 had received the provisional approval of the British Chiefs of Staff and had been submitted by them to the British government.[59] Roosevelt read both documents and, on June 7, returned them to the Joint Board with no comment. The President's military aide, Major General Edwin M. Watson, explained this action:

The President has familiarized himself with the two papers; but since the report of the United States-British Staff Conversations, ABC-1, had

not been approved by the British Government, he would not approve the report at this time; neither would he now give approval to Joint Army and Navy Basic War Plan—Rainbow No. 5, which is based upon the report ABC-1. However, in case of war the papers would be returned to the President for his approval.[60]

Meanwhile, ABC-1 received the approval of the British government, and Roosevelt, through Under Secretary of State Welles, was so informed by Lord Halifax on June 5. Even without formal Presidential approval (it was clear that Roosevelt had no objections), the Army and Navy went ahead with action based upon RAINBOW V.[61]

At this point, it is interesting to note the fate of RAINBOW V's four predecessors:

Rainbow 2 and 3—providing for American concentration in the Pacific in the event of war— were cancelled at the Joint Board meeting of 6 August 1941. Rainbow 1 and 4—the hemisphere defense plans—were not formally cancelled until May 1942. Rainbow 4 supplanted Rainbow 1 in the spring of 1940 and, although its assumptions were actually superseded by events, it continued to serve for some purposes of hemisphere defense planning until 7 December 1941. Such long-range planning as the Army did in 1941 for future military operations was done under the assumptions of Rainbow 5.[62]

The Anglo-American Staff Conversations in Washington (ABC Meetings) during January, February, and March of 1941, the joint agreement on war strategy which the conference produced, ABC-1, and the American war plan, RAINBOW V, which made ABC-1 specific and direct so far as U. S. military and naval forces were concerned—all were of great and immediate significance for both the Pacific and the Atlantic Fleets. Despite the fact that approval (and even then not final approval of the President) did not come until the summer months, it was within the framework of these plans and agreements that the debate over the Pacific Fleet—occupying much of the spring and early summer of 1941—took place.

In the meantime, events in the Pacific had not been at a standstill. The debate over transfer of the Pacific Fleet units into the Atlantic takes on even greater significance when preceded by an account of other powerful pressures being exerted upon the command at Pearl Harbor—pressures being exerted in a quite different direction—toward the Far East.

III. PACIFIC MANEUVERS (WINTER AND SPRING 1940-1941)

While conferences and planning were going on in Washington, the Pacific was not entirely peaceful during the winter of 1940-41. Neither was there a dearth of Anglo-American interest and activity in that area.

At the ABC Meetings the British had drawn attention to Singapore, emphasizing the vital need for its defense and the role that they hoped the U. S. Fleet would play in a naval strategy based on its defense. But the ABC Meetings were not the first time that the Americans had heard of Singapore in connection with the U. S. Fleet. A visit to Singapore by units of the Fleet was proposed by the British during October 1940. But the proposal got nowhere. A recommendation in the negative by the State-War-Navy Liaison Committee was accepted by the President. Moreover, no mention of the proposal was made by Roosevelt in his conversation with Admiral Richardson on October 8. Whether this shows that the President viewed the proposal as neither feasible nor desirable, as Langer and Gleason are inclined to suspect, remains uncertain.[63]

But the idea of a Pacific maneuver apparently remained in the President's mind, one more card in the hand for possible use in the game he was playing with the Japanese leaders. During early October, the possibility that Japan might reply to the re-opening of the Burma Road with "drastic" action was an ever-present reality. On the afternoon of October 10, only a few days after the British proposal had been rejected, Roosevelt discussed the Far Eastern situation with Secretary Knox. Almost immediately thereafter, Knox reported the conversation to Admirals Stark and Richardson, together with their aides, in a meeting in his office.

. . . The President was concerned as to the Japanese reaction to the British on the reopening of the Burma Road scheduled for October 17. In the event the Japanese took drastic action, he, the President, was considering shutting off all trade between Japan and the Americas, and to this end was considering establishing a patrol of light ships in two lines extending from Hawaii westward to the Philippines, and from Samoa toward the Dutch East Indies.[64]

Someone observed that such a step, especially if it included interference with Japanese ships, would be an act of war. The President, said Knox, had not indicated whether he was contemplating a declaration of war. Richardson's reaction to this proposal of a naval patrol in the Pacific was similar to his response to the decision to base the Pacific Fleet at Pearl Harbor: amazement and objection. Again, too, the grounds for his response were both logistical and strategic.

The Fleet was not prepared, he told the group of high-ranking naval officials, to undertake such a patrol nor war if it followed. In that case, moreover, loss of many of the ships in this long thin line was highly likely. In any case, interference with their trade was likely to cause trouble with both South America and Japan. Other officers joined in the discussion as to this important effect. Why, it was asked, if cutting off Japanese trade was the objective, would it not be more effective as well as practical to do this at the source by the blockade of certain important ports?

The Secretary, Richardson recalled, was not pleased with the direction the conversation was taking and finally observed: "I am not a strategist; if you don't like the President's plan, draw up one of your own to accomplish the purpose."[65]

And so they did. An outline plan of action, based on the assumption of positive Japanese action following the re-opening of the Burma Road, was drafted by the two commanders with their war plans officers. A basic feature of this plan involved the transfer to the Pacific Fleet of additional strength, namely, "additional patrol planes, an aircraft carrier, some destroyers, and possibly a cruiser or two."[66] Where but from U. S. naval strength in the Atlantic could these additional forces be obtained? But Atlantic forces were woefully inadequate for their own duties. Here was a dramatic example of the awkward position into which the United States was being driven, facing a two-ocean war with a one-ocean Navy.

In view of the situation in the Atlantic, it is not surprising that Admiral Stark informed Richardson that he (Stark) could not at the moment approve the proposed transfers. Decision must await the President and Secretary Knox, currently out of Washington. Richardson returned to the Pacific Coast on his way to rejoin his command and, a few days later, pursuant to instructions from Admiral Stark, sent to Hart at Manila a statement of the international situation and the proposed Fleet dispositions based upon it. At this point, however, the plan died, except as some portions of it were incorporated into other and succeeding plans. This marked the end of what might be entitled, broadly speaking, the first definite plan to send units of the Pacific Fleet into Far Eastern waters.[67]

It was not, however, the end of the idea, which had important adherents within the United States government. Welles, Stark, and Marshall, the three members of the Liaison Committee, were, it will be recalled,[68] opposed to the proposal, as was Hull, who agreed with Welles's view that a Japanese trap might be involved. Hornbeck, as Richardson reported, was an active proponent, urging not only that the defense of Singapore constituted a national interest of the United States, but even that the crux of the whole international situation lay in the Far East.

Secretary Stimson, who emerged at this time as a vigorous advocate of reinforcing Singapore, was apparently greatly influenced by his friend Hornbeck's arguments.

An American naval force at Singapore, he emphasized, would strengthen British morale and establish command of the Japanese sea lanes: "By closing those lanes and, at the same time, cutting off all American commerce with Japan, we should eventually reduce that country to comparative impotency." China would be strengthened and could provide air bases for possible operations against Japan. Australia, New Zealand and the French Pacific Islands would be safeguarded.[69]

Following the collapse of the proposal for a patrol, attention was again drawn to the original idea of sending a U. S. naval detachment to Singapore. Apparently the President discussed the idea with Under Secretary Welles, along the lines of a plan in the interests of national security.[70] Following further consultation with naval advisers, however, the specific plan was temporarily laid aside.

To the British, however, the visit of an American naval detachment to Singapore remained a matter of vital and pressing importance. Information reaching London from reliable sources in Japan indicated that the General Staff favored a drive southward in the immediate future. Apparently the Japanese generals believed that the United States would do nothing before the approaching Presidential election. Afterward, if presented with a *fait accompli,* the Americans would also remain quiescent. The Japanese Navy, however, did not share the Army's confidence and, indicated the source, the project would be killed if an American naval squadron visited Singapore. However, the sense of urgency over Singapore which characterized official circles in London was not shared by their counterparts in the American capital. In Washington, the proposal was deferred.[71]

But the idea itself remained; Stimson's Singapore proposals especially continued to hold considerable weight for the President. The realization of many demands and few resources with which to supply them tempered, it would seem, the President's planning, as it was to do so many times in this period. Apparently he expressed this willingness to settle for something less if it could accomplish something of the desired result.

On October 23 Knox reported to the President that he had talked with Stimson about the latter's proposal to dispatch a naval force to Singapore and that he had "gathered the impression that he (Stimson) was satisfied that a demonstration in that quarter in less strength than he suggests would meet all requirements."[72] As it developed, however, this "demonstration in less strength" involved, not the sending of a naval detachment to Singapore, but the reinforcement of the Philippines.[73] The basic objective, in Stimson's mind and perhaps that of the President as well, remained Singapore.[74]

Secretary Hull summarized the American position in a conversation with the Australian Minister, Richard Casey, on November 12. Hull wrote:

The Australian Minister called to ascertain whether this Government contemplated sending a good will naval mission to Australia and to other countries in the southern area. I replied by reviewing all of the steps we have taken thus far to deal with the Far Eastern situation, including any threatened movements by Japan to the south, and then added that for the present we had other plans in mind than a good will mission.[75]

There was also discussion of increasing the number of planes at Singapore. The British had approximately a hundred planes there; the Australians had agreed to send fifty. Despite increases in Australian plane production, Casey did not know of further shipments to Singapore. Hull continued:

I emphasized more than once about the importance of a substantial number of planes being stationed at Singapore, and pointed out that we have assembled at Manila all of our ships in the Far East, including a number of submarines, as well as some airplanes.[76]

These two developments, British reinforcement of Singapore and American reinforcement of the Philippines, seem to have pleased everyone as at least a step in the right direction. "At least we have got this far with regard to that vital point of defense, Singapore," Stimson recorded in his diary.[77]

News of these developments was carefully calculated to produce the proper effect upon the Japanese. Hull protested to the President against a public announcement of reinforcements for the Philippines.

I said to the President that we at the Department felt that a formal announcement giving numbers and types of ships would be susceptible of misconstruction both in Japan and in some quarters here. It might be misrepresented as a deliberate waving of a big stick and might easily be sensationalized by the press.

The Japanese higher authorities, I pointed out, would obtain knowledge of our moves by their own methods. By letting the public obtain information piecemeal and gradually, there would be public knowledge of the moves we made, but several possible varieties of agitation might be avoided. Doing it quietly would facilitate the present movement of forces and possible similar operations in the future. We had already convinced the Navy Department of the wisdom of this course. The President agreed.[78]

Apparently Hull was right. The effect of this series of positive military actions was not lost upon the Japanese. Combined with strong and positive language from Churchill, in his speech of October 8 announcing the re-opening of the Burma Road, and Roosevelt, in his Columbus Day address, their effect upon the Japanese was quite visible. Apparently convinced that their hour had not struck, the Japanese backtracked. The Tri-Partite Pact was really a pact of peace, they announced, and Foreign Minister Matsuoka even invited the United States to join.

General satisfaction was voiced, both in and out of official circles. Secretary Stimson, moreover, believed that the time was propitious for "bold and affirmative action in the Pacific."[79] Such action would seemingly include the dispatch of an American naval squadron to Singapore. But the President remained passive; perhaps he was right. Langer and Gleason analyze the situation in this way:

To send the Fleet farther West, or to impose an embargo on oil, might well provoke Japan to action and result in the loss of the Dutch Indies. Above all, it might involve the United States as well as Britain in hostilities in a theater which, by common consent, was regarded as secondary to Europe. It seemed best to leave well enough alone, to gain what time was possible, and to wait and see whether the deflation of the Tri-Partite Pact might lead to a change in Tokyo's policy. If any weight is to be given statements by the Japanese Foreign Minister, the President's decision was probably a wise one. Early in November Matsuoka remarked to the British Ambassador that the possibility of war could be dismissed unless the United States should enter the war or give some serious provocation such as would be involved if a powerful American squadron were to visit Singapore.[80]

But the situation in the Far East did not remain static. On November 25, Lord Lothian, just returned from leave in London, informed Secretary Hull that a Japanese attack upon Singapore was likely in the near future. Hull noted:

He gave me the opinion of some naval experts that, if the American Navy should largely make its base at Singapore, this would safeguard the entire situation in the Orient. He expressed the view that our fleet, if stationed at Singapore, could reach Japan much sooner than a Japanese fleet could reach the South Pacific, and therefore there would be no risk involved. I merely remarked that this was a matter for experts to pass upon.[81]

This conversation was apparently coincident with a planned reinforcement of Singapore by Australian and New Zealand troops. Sir Dudley Pound was talking in a similar vein to the American naval mission in London:

... it was essential to hold Singapore at all costs. With the American fleet, or a substantial part of it based on Singapore, Japan, he argued, would be much less likely to risk war and if war came the Japanese fleet could be contained north of the long chain of islands comprising the Dutch East Indies.[82]

The British problem was undeniably serious. With all available forces over-committed in the Atlantic and the Mediterranean, there was nothing to oppose Japanese designs in the Pacific—nothing, that is, except assurances of American support. Without such assurances it was indeed difficult to maintain a firm opposition to Japanese pressures.

On the American side, Dr. Hornbeck, a constant proponent of keeping the Fleet in the Pacific, also endorsed the Singapore proposal. In a memorandum for the Secretary of State on December 9, Hornbeck "argued at length that the loss of Singapore would mean severance of the life lines between the United Kingdom and the Pacific Dominions, and would entail a serious weakening of the British position in the critical eastern Mediterranean area. Thus it would gravely jeopardize Britain's chances of withstanding the Nazi attack and by derivation would imperil America's first line of defense."[83] It is scarcely surprising that the requests, in one form or another, continued.[84] When Harry Hopkins arrived in London in January, the question of U. S. policy in the Far East was raised almost immediately. But neither Hopkins nor the officials in Washington could predict American reaction if the Japanese moved south.[85]

The ABC Conferences, meeting in Washington during January and February of 1941, also reached a stalemate over Singapore. Admiralty representatives were again balked in their efforts to have a detachment of the Pacific Fleet permanently assigned to the defense of that base. British concern grew when, in early February, reliable information pointed toward an impending Japanese attack upon Singapore.[86]

The United States government and especially the Far Eastern specialists in the State Department remained unconvinced that there was immediate danger. Yet while refusing to take positive action as the British requested, the Administration resorted to the use of what Feis has described as "signals," "signals of possible later action; signals that would seem to be clearer than they were, that would be studied more intently in Japan than in the United States."[87] One very important "signal" was the employment of the Pacific Fleet.

It was proposed to send naval vessels into the threatened areas—even to Singapore. Cruises, rather than more permanent dispositions, were suggested. Secretary Hull and the State Department now supported these proposals, but the Navy was scarcely enthusiastic. Its position remained constant; weakness and commitments in the Atlantic combined to cause opposition to any enlarged role in the Pacific. The Navy's position is clearly evidenced by these excerpts from a letter written by Admiral Stark to Admiral Kimmel, the new Commander in Chief of the Pacific Fleet:

I continue in every way I possibly can to fight commitments or dispositions that would involve us on two fronts and to keep from sending more combatant ships to the Far East. I had a two hour struggle (please keep this absolutely secret) in the White House this past week and thank God can report that the President still supports my contentions. . . .

I had another hour and a half in the White House today and the President said that he might order a detachment of three or four cruisers, a carrier and a squadron of destroyers to Phoenix and Gilbert or the Fiji Islands, then reaching over into Mindanao for a short visit and on to Manila and back.

I have fought this over many times and won, but this time the decision may go against me. Heretofore the talk was largely about sending a cruise of this sort to Australia and Singapore and perhaps the N. E. I. Sending it to the Philippines would be far less objectionable from a political standpoint but still objectionable. What I want you to do is to be thinking about it and be prepared to make a quick decision if it is ordered.[88]

These were the general positions of the two departments, to which they usually adhered. Less than a month later, however, there occurred events which produced—temporarily—an almost complete reversal of the opposing positions of the Navy and the State Department.

During March and early April a series of informal negotiations were conducted between U. S. representatives and Japanese emissaries. The arrival in Washington in February of the new Japanese ambassador, Admiral Nomura, provided an opportunity for semi-official conversations. At his first meeting with Nomura on March 14 Roosevelt made the suggestion that the Admiral should meet from time to time with Secretary Hull—to discuss pending issues. Eventually these conversations got under way. They were hardly decisive, however, since neither side was willing to make any significant changes in its already obvious position. In fact the talks were scarcely more than an exchange of generalities.[89]

Simultaneously, meetings were being held in New York between two former American missionaries to Japan and a Japanese banker. These negotiations had a slightly official character, but like their higher-level counterpart, they produced no result of any genuine importance. In fact, their primary claim to fame lies in the fact that from them resulted a series of topics for the Hull-Nomura talks.[90]

These two sets of negotiations, however fruitless in their impact on U. S.–Japanese relations, are worth noting because of their influence upon naval strategy. So long as there existed even the slightest chance of obtaining some positive result from these negotiations, Secretary Hull was unwilling to endorse any step which might interfere with their progress. Hull was even more desirous of treating Japan with caution until the consequences of a trip by Foreign Minister Matsuoka to Germany and the Soviet Union were ascertained. Matsuoka, temperamentally unstable and violently pro-German, could scarcely be expected to do anything which would accrue to the benefit of the United States. It was also quite apparent to American observers that Matsuoka enjoyed the confidence of few of his Japanese colleagues. Accordingly, it was thought, there was no point in provoking Japan and thus strengthening Matsuoka's position—so long, at any rate, as there existed any opportunity for the moderates to

exercise any influence over Japanese policy.[91]

These two factors—the Japanese-American conversations and the mission of Matsuoka to Europe—were the main determinants of Hull's change in attitude toward possible Fleet maneuvers in the Pacific. As we have seen, Hull had at first been an active proponent of the plan to send detachments of the Pacific Fleet on cruises into threatened areas, including Singapore itself. In this policy, he had met the stubborn opposition of the admirals, as demonstrated in the Stark-Kimmel correspondence of early February and the earlier Richardson reaction.

Australia, however, was different from Singapore. In March, the President, acting upon the advice of the State Department, ordered a naval cruise to Australia and New Zealand by a detachment of the Pacific Fleet. Four cruisers, the U. S. S. *Chicago, Portland, Brooklyn, Savannah,* with an accompanying destroyer squadron (Number 3),[92] constituted the detachment. The purpose of the cruise was ostensibly to demonstrate the good will of the United States toward these distant and somewhat neglected parts of the British Commonwealth. In addition, the cruise provided excellent training for the units involved, although apparently Admiral Stark at first objected that the cruise would upset naval training schedules.[93]

The real objective, at least so far as the President and the State Department were concerned, was to aid U. S. diplomacy in its relations with Japan. A further demonstration of American solidarity with the British Commonwealth was worthwhile. At the same time, if the cruise helped to keep the Japanese guessing as to American intentions, this was certainly not undesirable. In the first of these objectives, the cruise met with great success. Spontaneous and enthusiastic receptions greeted the bluejackets in the ports of Australia, New Zealand, Fiji, and Tahiti.

Reports of the visit to Australian ports demonstrate the kind of response engendered by ships which visited other areas:

On the morning of March 20, two cruisers, the *Chicago* and the *Portland,* and five destroyers, the *Clark, Cassin, Conyham, Downes,* and *Reid,* commanded by Rear Admiral John H. Newton, sailed into Sydney Harbor. The reception accorded the visiting American bluejackets was more than a polite welcome; a wave of enthusiasm swept over the Australians. The U. S. chargé d'affaires reported to the State Department:

I need hardly say that the visit of these naval vessels was hailed as implementation of United States promises to "aid the Democracies" by gestures which instill confidence in them and consternation to their adversaries as well as by material aid in the form of loan, lease or transfer of implements of war. The Navy was greeted as if it were their own returning from a great victory.

. . . The Australians definitely looked upon the detachment as their saviors. They link the visit with the passage of the Lease or Lend Act, and with the President's speech of March 15; and some even go so far as to believe that Washington had timed this visit with the Japanese Minister's arrival and first week in Australia. If such a thing had been planned, it could not have been better timed,[94] both in respect of effect upon the Australians and the Japanese. . . .[95]

An official expression of Australian gratitude was sent to the President by the Acting Prime Minister, Mr. A. W. Fadden. But even more meaningful were the expressions of approval which appeared in the columns of Australian newspapers. The following excerpt from the Sydney _Daily Telegraph_ of March 19 is indicative:

This impressive demonstration of American naval power in the Pacific is particularly intended for foreign consumption.

It shows that the effective range of the United States Navy extends far beyond Hawaii.

It gives point to the blunt warning of the U. S. Naval Secretary (Colonel Knox) that "in the Pacific the United States has the most powerful and hardest-hitting fleet afloat."

Potential trouble-makers will also note that Australia and New Zealand welcome the Americans not as strangers, but as kinsmen.

In other words we shall not be far wrong if we interpret the visit of the American warships as practical evidence of Anglo-American cooperation in the Pacific.

We can be very certain that this welcome showing of the American flag in the south Pacific will have a sobering effect upon politics in this high-tension zone.[96]

The effect on the Japanese was less easily discernible, although it is now clear that the cruise added to Japanese fears of "encirclement."[97]

"Keeping the Japs guessing" apparently commended itself to the President. Perhaps, he announced to Admiral Stark, it would be a good idea to send out more ships—"to keep them popping up here and there, and keep the Japs guessing." The Chief of Naval Operations was alarmed at this proposal, which he described as "childish." He remained fairly constant in his objections to use of the Navy for "popping up purposes in aid to diplomacy." The Australian cruise did not, however, constitute any real threat to Stark's "vital interests." He continued to regard as dangerous the sending of U. S. ships to Singapore or any substantial weakening of the Fleet at Pearl Harbor where it constituted an ever-present threat to Japanese movements southward.[98]

Stark regarded the State Department as responsible for this suggestion to send out ships to "keep the Japs guessing." He therefore decided to propose a step which he hoped would "give the State Department a shock which might make them haul back." Plans were drawn up to send a carrier force northwestward from Hawaii. The plan had the desired effect on the State Department, which reversed its earlier position and evidently persuaded the President to abandon the policy of further naval cruises designed to "keep the Japs guessing."[99]

Admiral Stark was not completely opposed to naval cruises _per se._ When, in a letter to his chief on March 4, Admiral Hart suggested a cruise through the Netherlands East Indies by ships of his command, Stark was well disposed toward the idea. Hart's suggestion involved sending his own Asiatic Fleet from its base in the Philippines through Netherlands East Indian waters. This proposed cruise was, Stark observed in a letter to Admiral Kimmel at Pearl Harbor, "about the most positive move we could make." Moreover, "it is in line with our war plans, so if war were to break, we would be with our surface ships where we want them." Here apparently was an opportunity for agreement between the Navy and the State Department. But this was not to be. Paralleling Stark's change of position, the State Department executed an about-face. Japanese talks with the Dutch on economic questions were currently in progress. These, combined with the contemporary U. S.–Japanese negotiations in New York and Washington, were enough to inspire caution. Above all, both admirals and diplomats alike awaited the results of Matsuoka's mission to Moscow and Berlin.

The result was State Department opposition to Hart's projected cruise.[100]

Hornbeck summed up the State Department's position in a memorandum for Under Secretary Welles on April 4:

It is my understanding that all who participated in the discussion of this matter in the Secretary's office yesterday were of the opinion that a trip to the N. E. I. by contingents of our Asiatic Fleet while the economic negotiations now being carried on at Batavia are in progress would not be advisable; and that at any time in the near future when such a trip is being seriously considered, consultation should be had with the Netherlands authorities before a decision to make such a trip is proceeded with.[101]

This meeting on the afternoon of April 3, referred to in Hornbeck's memorandum, dealt the death blow to the projected cruise. Stark, who had originally favored the idea and had supported it in a memorandum to the President on March 28, retreated. At the meeting, it was decided to abandon the whole project, as not being advisable just then. And there the matter rested.

The British did not, even then, give up hope entirely. The signing of the Russo-Japanese pact on April 13 provided a new danger and a new argument for the visit of American naval units to Singapore. In this they were supported by the Dutch and the Australians. Moreover, the proposed visit was to occur simultaneously with a joint Anglo-American statement warning the Japanese of the determination of the two countries to resist aggression. U. S. Ambassador to England John Winant summarized the situation in a telegram for Hull on April 19:

This afternoon Eden asked me to see him and told me in detail the Foreign Office information relating to the Russo-Japanese action to the south. He also told me that Lord Halifax had given to you all the British information on the subject. His object in sending for me was to ask that I support the request he said Lord Halifax had made to you in regard to a statement by us. I think he thought that in this way he could emphasize the importance he places on our Government agreeing to their request.

I have clearly in mind the conversation I had with the President, with you, and Dr. Hornbeck in relation to Singapore. Although Eden did not ask directly that I request strengthening of our naval forces at Manila, he pointed out the weak-

ness of a Japanese movement south from Formosa and Hainan. He did say that he hoped our navy would not limit its consideration of Singapore to a purely tactical approach, but would also recognize all efforts (*) very real importance.[102]

But Hull's attitude had not changed; he was opposed to any U. S. naval maneuver (beyond the Australian cruise of March, which he believed had served as a warning) as being overly provocative to the Japanese.

On the other hand, the U. S. government did not entirely refuse to accept the possibility of a Japanese move south or of possible measures to counteract it. Another outgrowth of the ABC Meetings in Washington was an attempt at combined planning in the Far East. While ABC-1 provided for primary Anglo-American effort to be concentrated in the Atlantic, strategy in the Pacific was not to be entirely a holding operation.

Late in April (the 21st) a group of high-ranking military officers assembled at Singapore under the chairmanship of the British Far Eastern commander, Air Marshal Sir Robert Brooke-Popham. With delegates from Australia, New Zealand, India, Burma and the Netherlands, there was also present an official U. S. representative, Captain Purnell of the Asiatic Fleet.[103]

The result of the conference, known as the ABD (American, British, Dutch) Plan, was little more than "a combined operating plan of local defense forces."[104] Its details need not be covered here; perhaps its most vital provision was the drawing of a line beyond which Japanese penetration would be considered disastrous to Allied defenders. When it was submitted to Washington, Admiral Stark and General Marshall gave the ABD Plan an unfavorable reception. Its political implications were more than the United States was willing at the time to accept. Yet, as Feis correctly observes, it was this line which, in December, General Marshall and Admiral Stark recommended to the President as the line between war and peace, should U. S. possessions in the Pacific not be directly attacked.[105]

So far as the sending of U. S. naval units to Singapore, however, no real change had occurred to alter either the American or the British position; the stalemate continued. More-

---

*Apparent omission.

over, by April of 1941 the whole idea of sending a U. S. naval detachment to the Far East was becoming more and more restricted by significant developments in the Atlantic theater, around which was centered the forthcoming debate.

IV. PACIFIC DEFENSE VS. ATLANTIC OPERATIONS (SPRING 1941)

Since the United States had decided that its own security demanded British survival, and since Britain could be saved only by maintaining a reasonably secure life line across the North Atlantic, the logic of the situation seemed to demand that the American Navy enter the Battle of the Atlantic.[106]

Developing American strategy had emphasized more and more the Atlantic as the primary theater of operations. Plan Dog had crystallized pro-Atlantic sentiment during the late fall of 1940; the ABC Meetings turned it into joint strategy; and RAINBOW V (which was essentially completed by late April 1941) made it specific and concrete. Strategic planning on paper was spurred on, during the early spring of 1941, by an immediate and monstrous problem.

During these weeks the attacks of German submarine wolf packs on transatlantic shipping bound for Britain reached a new pitch of intensity. Moreover, the attacks became more widespread. In the unprotected areas around Iceland, there was especially good hunting. On the night of April 3-4, for example, one convoy lost ten of twenty-two ships. As Admiral Stark observed:

The situation is obviously critical in the Atlantic. In my opinion, it is hopeless except as we take strong measures to save it. The effect on the British of sinkings with regard both to food supply and essential material to carry on the war is getting progressively worse.[107]

Thus, motives for more active American participation in the Battle of the Atlantic became increasingly compelling. There were several basic factors that predisposed leaders on both sides of the Atlantic toward operations in that area. Most fundamental was the belief that both the United States and Great Britain had more to fear from Germany than from any other enemy, actual or potential. In addition, American emphasis on Atlantic operations was consistent with Britain's over-all war strategy. As British forces in the Atlantic theater were reinforced or replaced by American contingents, opportunities might then arise for strengthening the British position in the Middle East and even in the Far East. Thus immediate threats to both countries from German operations in the Atlantic reinforced a basic Anglo-American predisposition toward U. S. action "in areas which are most accessible . . . namely in the general area of the Atlantic."[108]

American military leaders, both Army and Navy, had another reason for desiring Atlantic operations: the problem of relations between U. S. and British commands would be greatly simplified. In a statement to the Seventh Meeting of the Washington Staff Conversations on February 14, Rear Admiral Turner had made clear the American position:

. . . it is not the intention of the United States to agree to any breaking up and scattering of United States forces into small groups to be absorbed in the British commands. . . . The United States proposes to accept full responsibility for operations in certain definite areas, or for executing specific tasks in areas of British responsibility. . . . In brief, United States' forces are to be under United States' command, and British forces under British Command. . . .[109]

Only on this basis could the American staff hope to minimize the vexing problems resulting from the gradual intrusion of American forces into areas in which Great Britain had, and the United States did not have, a large political and economic stake and a clearly formulated policy, together with control of communications, a monopoly of intelligence, and long experience in dealing with the civil authorities.[110] These were some of the basic factors that reinforced the strategic considerations which, as we have already seen,[111] produced the development of ABC-1 and RAINBOW V.

Another factor reinforcing American predisposition toward Atlantic operations was a more subtle one: the attitude of Franklin Roosevelt. While it was always difficult to assess the real bent of the President's feelings, certain propositions may be advanced with some claim to validity. The President's personal interests were definitely maritime; his love of the sea was famous. He had moreover served as Assistant Secretary of the Navy during World War I. Despite his active interest in the rapidly expanding Army, in Lend-Lease, and in industrial production, the President could be described as a "Navy" man. His concepts of immediate strategic needs at this time were primarily "naval," in the sense of securing sea lanes and beachheads, rather than in the movement of massed armies on a continental scale. These concepts fitted in well with his acute political awareness of the willingness of the American people to accept naval extensions, and their unwillingness to condone troop movements of any size. Moreover, Roosevelt's knowledge of specific naval matters was confined largely to the Atlantic; the Pacific he tended to leave to the admirals, although it was he and not the admirals who kept the Fleet in Hawaii. Evidences of these Rooseveltian predispositions (although they were certainly predispositions and never absolutes) may be seen in the ensuing months of 1941.[112]

In the case of other high Administration officials, the U-boat campaign reinforced a long-standing desire to give more help to Britain. Stimson and Knox had both been outspoken exponents of a more active American role in the Atlantic war before their appointment to the Cabinet in the summer of 1940. Ickes had expressed similar views from his post within the Administration. There were others whose voices came to be heard during these critical weeks. But basic to the "great debate" over the roles and sizes of the two Fleets were these three general factors: (a) over-all strategy, as expressed in Plan Dog, ABC-1, and RAINBOW V, then almost completed, (b) the immediate pressure created by the intensified submarine campaign, and (c) the views of certain leading American officials which led them to intervene strongly in the shaping of naval strategy.

With U. S. leaders, both civilian and military, in substantial agreement on a policy of concentration on the Atlantic while remaining on the defensive in the Pacific, the Navy proceeded during the first three months of 1941 to put specific plans into operation.

The crux of the matter concerned the protection of shipping bound for Britain. The "escort-of-convoy" question had been actively discussed and action agreed on in the Washington staff conferences of the preceding winter. One vital provision of ABC-1 which did not require a formal declaration of war to bring it into operation was this:

Owing to the threat to the sea communications of the United Kingdom, the principal task of the United States naval forces in the Atlantic will be the protection of shipping of the Associated Powers, the center of gravity of the United States' effort being concentrated in the North-western Approaches to the United Kingdom.[113]

As Morison correctly observes, "this meant that the United States Navy would take over the prime responsibility for protecting transatlantic merchant convoys, as soon as the Atlantic Fleet was in a position to do so."[114]

The Navy lost no time in preparing for this new responsibility. The creation of the Atlantic Fleet on February 1 was followed soon after by the development of an escort force.[115] The crucial point at issue, however, was just how far the Navy should go in the protection of shipping bound for Britain. Full-fledged escort-of-convoy into British home waters would be most effective but it would scarcely meet with the enthusiastic approval of the Germans; the risk of war was definitely present. But if the Navy could not go all the way, then there was the problem of deciding where to draw the line.

The Navy planners for some time had been devoting attention to the entire matter of U. S. policy in the Atlantic. Two Hemisphere Defense Plans had been drawn up. Plan 1 provided for full naval escort of merchant shipping in the Atlantic as far as the twenty-sixth meridian of longitude. Vessels and aircraft of Axis nations were to be met with force if they entered the waters of the Western Hemisphere. Plan 2 was less forceful. The American Navy was still to assume that entry of Axis craft into the waters of the Western Hemisphere was motivated by a possible "unfriendly intent." But they were not to shoot on sight, merely to follow the Axis ships, reporting their movements to British warships, and protecting U. S. flag vessels from attack without shooting first.[116]

The passage of the Lend-Lease Act, combined with the coincident opening of the spring submarine offensive, made a decision as to the Navy's role a pressing one. The proponents of all-out action, led by Secretary Stimson, had been urging full escort-of-convoy. But such a step would provide too great a burden upon the Atlantic Fleet's infant Support Force. The whole of the newly created Atlantic Fleet was woefully inadequate to conduct the patrolling operations of Plan 2, not to mention full escort-of-convoy envisioned in Plan 1. The Fleet consisted of a division of old battleships, *Texas, New York,* and *Arkansas,* two aircraft carriers, *Ranger* and the new *Wasp,* one division of cruisers, and two destroyer squadrons.[117] If the President undertook a naval commitment in the Atlantic along the lines of Hemisphere Defense Plan 1, it was incumbent upon him to provide the means to ensure its success. The need for escort vessels was accentuated when the President concluded an agreement with the Danish Minister in which we agreed to defend Greenland.[118] And, also early in April, he issued a directive calling for outright naval escort of merchant shipping as far as longitude 26°.

The obvious answer to the deficiency in the Atlantic was to provide reinforcements from the Pacific Fleet. Following conferences with Stark on April 2 and 3, Roosevelt gave his consent to the transfer of three battleships, an aircraft carrier, four cruisers and two supporting destroyer squadrons from the Pacific Fleet into the Atlantic.[119]

Thus it seemed that with Presidential acceptance of Hemisphere Defense Plan 1 and the ordered transfer of substantial fleet units, the proponents of a strategy of Atlantic operations had triumphed.

The triumph was of short duration. Army and Navy planning had been proceeding without participation by the State Department, largely because of Hull's caution, so vividly illuminated by his refusal to look at ABC-1. Presidential action, however, did provide the State Department with basic information and did bring the question of action in the Atlantic sharply to their attention. Their concern then suddenly reached a peak when the signature of the Soviet-Japanese Neutrality Pact was announced on April 13. Naturally Hull's persistent worry about the status of the Pacific Fleet now called for action.

This was not a propitious moment, Hull argued, to transfer Fleet units from Pearl Harbor. Such a move might easily be interpreted by Japanese Foreign Minister Matsuoka as a sign of weakness. Now that the potential threat to Japan from the North had been removed by means of diplomacy, the Japanese might well regard this as a good opportunity to turn their war machine south against the Netherlands East Indies and Singapore. While predictions as to the course which Matsuoka's curious mind might take were always of doubtful validity, Hull's argument was forceful.

Moreover, this April period was also a critical moment in the Hull-Nomura negotiations, which had been going on since March 8. Two major proposals were under consideration at just this time: on April 9 the "unofficial draft" had been submitted to Hull and on April 16 Hull had given Nomura his "four points" memorandum. While neither set of proposals appeared to have much promise, nevertheless all hope of future agreement on some form of peaceful settlement was not yet gone. At the same time, State Department officials believed that whatever chance did exist for a Japanese retreat from expansionist policies would scarcely be improved by a display of weakness on the part of the United States. And a reduction in American naval strength in Pacific waters might well appear to the Japanese as a sign of American weakness.[120]

Roosevelt was also worried by the Pact and by a report that the U. S. S. *Diblock* had depth-bombed a German submarine. He summoned a meeting at the White House on April 15. Here a final choice had to be made—whether operating orders should be given to the Navy to carry out full escort-of-shipping duties within the confines of the Western Hemisphere as recently defined by Hemisphere Defense Plan Number 1—or whether alternative orders (recently prepared by Admiral Stark) calling only for intensified naval patrolling (Plan Number 2) should be adopted instead. The meeting was a long and lively one.

In general, the War and Navy Departments fought vigorously for a more positive naval role in the Atlantic, transferring units from the Pacific Fleet to make such action effective.

The service chiefs wanted the main fleet in the Atlantic not only because they wanted to make the patrol system more effective but also because they thought the United States might have to undertake expeditionary tasks in the very near future that would require strong naval protection —probably in the southern Atlantic, where Anglo-American naval power would be more impressed by an American Navy in action in the Atlantic than by an idle fleet held in the eastern Pacific.[121]

Secretary of War Stimson reiterated his earlier arguments in favor of providing naval escort and of transferring Pacific Fleet units. Moreover, he asserted, the decision should be made public by the President and the reasons for it presented to the American people. (This latter argument was, of course, part of the general concern with "psychological warfare" which several members of the Cabinet had long felt to be of vital concern.[122]) Treasury Secretary Morgenthau counselled against secrecy as being impossible to achieve and being undoubtedly productive of future embarrassment. He too favored the escort policy. Although Admiral Stark wavered, Secretary Knox also advocated a strong stand. Not only did he support the position of the service chiefs but he declared with some conviction that "if the Navy were turned loose, they would clean up the Atlantic in thirty days." Harry Hopkins, vitally concerned as he was with the newly created Lend-Lease program (the Act had been passed on March 11), added his support to the program which would ensure greater aid to Britain.

Secretary Hull's views remained unchanged. His earlier arguments in favor of caution had been reinforced by the course of events in the Pacific. Hull's counsel was reinforced on this occasion by a new participant in these top-level strategy sessions, General Stanley Embick. This was the same General Embick who was a chief War Department planner and who had only recently concluded several weeks of conversations with the British mission in Washington. Thus his advice was not to be taken lightly. Embick and Hull, with somewhat hesitant support from Stark, carried the day. Apparently General Embick's primary purpose was to advise the President of the real capabilities of the Army and the consequent effect on possible strategy. The Army view was that

it could protect the Western Hemisphere, including Iceland, but would prefer to postpone entry into the war unless the security of the British Isles was threatened. Army forces would not be ready for action until fall.[123] Embick's counsels, added to those of Secretary Hull, and to Stark's hesitations, apparently persuaded the President that a naval policy in the Atlantic which might well provoke war should be avoided, at least for the moment. Of course, as in many situations in which Roosevelt was involved, it may be argued—perhaps with much truth—that the President's mind was already made up.

On the following week-end (April 19-21), Roosevelt stayed at Hyde Park, where he went to receive the visit of Canadian Prime Minister MacKenzie King. While there he summoned Admiral King and countermanded his early April directive calling for outright naval escort of merchant shipping as far as longitude 26°. Instead, Roosevelt told the Atlantic Fleet commander that operations were to be conducted in accord with Hemisphere Defense Plan 2.

This plan, as has been noted above, envisaged an American naval patrol of Atlantic waters in an effort to detect the presence of German vessels. These were to be reported to the British for action. While the U. S. Atlantic Fleet was prohibited from shooting first, it could within that limitation make German operations as hazardous as possible. This new directive went into operation on April 24.[124]

Thus was born the curious problem of distinguishing "patrolling" from "convoying." On the following day, the President raised this question at a Cabinet meeting, insisting that there existed a legal distinction between the two. Roosevelt and the majority of his Cabinet chose to regard "patrolling" as an essentially defensive measure, a sort of "reconnaissance." When he conferred with Roosevelt and Secretary Knox on the preceding day (April 24), Stimson noted this trend of thought and protested against it.

He kept reverting to the fact that the force in the Atlantic was merely going to be a patrol to watch for any aggressor and to report to America. I answered there, with a smile on my face, saying, "But you are not going to report the presence of the German Fleet to the Americas. You are going to report it to the British Fleet." I wanted him to be honest with himself. To me it seems a clearly hostile act to the Germans, and I am prepared to take the responsibility of it. He seems to be trying to hide it into the character of a purely reconnaissance action which it really is not.[125]

In the weeks that followed, the system of "patrolling" underwent continued expansion.

It has been developed from statements by President Roosevelt and Admiral Stark that American naval vessels are patrolling way into the Atlantic, in some instances as far as two thousand miles or perhaps even more. The American policy seems to me to patrol as far as in its judgment it thinks it ought to patrol. We have definitely adopted the policy of patrolling Greenland and beyond, probably as far as Iceland.[126]

Ickes was led to believe that such a system of "patrolling" was more effective than the usual practice of convoying.[127] Whether or not he was correctly informed, the proponents of vigorous Atlantic operations were convinced that it was inadequate. For example, when, at the Cabinet meeting on April 25, Roosevelt finished describing the system of "patrolling," he observed, "Well, it's a step forward." Stimson said at once:

"Well, I hope you will keep on walking, Mr. President. Keep on walking."

The whole Cabinet burst into a roar of laughter which was joined in by the President.[128]

This whole matter of "patrolling" vs. "convoying" became increasingly technical and complex. This brief résumé suggests the lines which the controversy took. Of greatest importance here is the fact that, although Roosevelt apparently had retreated somewhat from his more ambitious project of outright escort-of-convoys, the concept of "patrolling" as it finally developed was an operation of considerable magnitude. In terms of the number and kinds of vessels and men needed to make it effective, it can be argued that there was no great difference from "convoying." The demands made upon the Atlantic Fleet were almost equally great.[129]

The general argument about the roles of the two Fleets continued throughout the period when "patrolling" vs. "convoying" was being debated. As has been noted, early in the month, on April 7, Roosevelt had approved the transfer of substantial naval units from the Pacific Fleet into the Atlantic. But then the mood of caution, induced in part by the Japanese threat

in the Pacific, heightened by the announcement of the Japanese-Soviet Pact on April 13, asserted itself. As in the case of the Hemisphere Defense Plans, the President, having issued an order, changed his mind. Instead of the sizable detachment ordered into the Atlantic only a short time earlier, Roosevelt, on about April 18, limited the transfer, for the time being at least, to one aircraft carrier and one destroyer squadron.[130] The three battleships, the four cruisers, and the second destroyer squadron were to stay in the Pacific.

In a letter to Admiral Kimmel at Pearl Harbor on April 19, Stark presented the motive behind this rather abrupt change of plan, one which left the Atlantic Fleet with no real ability to carry out fully even the more restricted operations of Plan Number 2.

The reason for the change was that the President did not want, at this particular moment, to give any signs of seriously weakening the forces in the Pacific, and it is my opinion that this will hold until there is some further clarification, incident to Matsuoka's return to Tokyo and thus further illumination on the Russo-Japanese Treaty. Don't interpret this in any sense as a change in the general idea of Plan Dog which the President again recently reiterated to me, and which still holds. He does not, however, even while adhering to that Plan, want to give Japan any encouragement or lead right now as to our intentions. I am telling you, not arguing with you.[131]

Admiral Stark's letter showed a very real understanding of Roosevelt. Roosevelt never abandoned the basic Atlantic strategy first set forth in Stark's Plan Dog in November, crystallized in ABC-1 in late March, and at this time being put in final operating form for the American forces in RAINBOW V, which would be adopted a month later. However, Roosevelt's acceptance of the Atlantic strategy did not mean for him (or really even for Stimson and Knox) a total abandonment of the Pacific. In essence, therefore, the President's decision to reduce the number of ships to be transferred was not a change of policy but of tactics. The debate that followed during the next three weeks was thus essentially a debate on degree and on timing, not a debate on strategy.

On April 22, Roosevelt raised an additional objection to the transfer of units of the Pacific Fleet: there was always the problem of the defense of Hawaii. On the following day at a meeting at the White House, General Marshall in return argued that Hawaii was impregnable even without the presence of the Fleet. In this judgment Secretaries Knox and Stimson both concurred. Roosevelt also raised again his suggestion that the Pacific Fleet could usefully send out units on occasional cruises, "to keep the Japanese guessing." Yet at the same time, the President admitted to Stimson that "there was not going to come much good to the British in the patrol with the number of ships available (in the Atlantic)."[132]

Furthermore, additional duties were also being proposed for the over-extended Atlantic Fleet. German submarines were becoming active in the unprotected Newfoundland region. And Churchill, anticipating German pressure on Spain and Portugal for bases in their Atlantic island possessions, was informing Roosevelt on April 23: "It would be a very great advantage if you could send an American squadron for a friendly cruise in these regions at the earliest moment."[133]

The possibility that the United States might have to undertake operations in the southern Atlantic was a direct reflection of current German successes in both the Atlantic and the Mediterranean during the preceding weeks. There was a genuine possibility that German forces might soon make their appearance at Dakar or in the Azores. This was not only a threat to British shipping but to the safety of the Western Hemisphere as well.

Admiral Stark foresaw what was coming and, typically, attempted to prepare Admiral Kimmel at Pearl Harbor:

Washington, April 26, 1941

Dear Mustapha: This is just to get you mentally prepared that shortly a considerable detachment from your fleet will be brought to the Atlantic.

You will recall from my last letter what that detachment was and what the President cut it to, but only for the time being, awaiting some further clue to the Japanese situation.

Not only do I anticipate the reinforcing of the Atlantic by the 3 BBs, 1 CV, 4 CLs and 2 squadrons of destroyers, but also by further reinforcements.

King has been given a job to do with a force utterly inadequate to do it on any efficient scale.

I am enclosing a copy of his last order which implements the changed Hemisphere Defense Plan No. 1 and is now known as Hemisphere Defense Plan No. 2 or WPL-49.

Even the Press and those who wanted to go all out in the Pacific are now rounding to and clamoring for an all out in the Atlantic. You know my thoughts with regard to this which were set down in my Memo about what is now known as Plan Dog and which will shortly be covered by RAINBOW 5.

Action on the above, that is transfer to the Atlantic, may come at any time and in my humble opinion is only a matter of time.

No other news for the moment and this letter is the result of a long conference yesterday in the White House. . . .

Sincerely
(S) Betty[134]

Admiral Stark's warning that the dispute over the transfer of ships from the Pacific was not ended no doubt took into account the fact that Stimson, Knox and Marshall showed every sign of continuing the struggle vigorously; he himself was of two minds.

During the two weeks that followed Stark's letter to Kimmel, Stimson and Knox used every available opportunity and every available resource to bring the President around to their view, and, as a result, to have him reverse his most recent orders to the Pacific Fleet. Their basic argument was largely military. There was stationed at Pearl Harbor a large fleet which was currently inactive. Even if war were to break out, U. S. war plans called for the maintenance of a defensive position in the Pacific. Thus, argued the two secretaries, retention of a heavy preponderance of U. S. naval strength in the Pacific was futile.[135]

Their chief stumbling block appeared to be Secretary Hull, whose attitude varied, depending usually on the state of his negotiations with the Japanese. Meeting with Stimson and Knox on the morning of April 29, "Hull pleaded for time—only one day—while he was waiting to hear important news from Tokyo which might close an agreement which he thought would hold up the Japanese."[136] Despite their skepticism, the activists like Stimson and Knox usually felt obliged to agree to Hull's delays.

Another factor to be considered was the British position. Initially the British seemed to agree with Hull to a large extent. According to Stimson:

It was like a game of chess. The British wish enough ships kept in the Pacific Ocean to act as a makeweight against the Japanese going too freely down to Singapore. They could send ships themselves from the Mediterranean but not unless we sent ships over from the Pacific to the Atlantic . . . in no event did they want us to go below holding six capital ships in the Pacific.[137]

Again, on May 5, the two service secretaries had a long conference with Hull, presenting to him what seemed to them the essence of the situation, that

. . . our force in the Atlantic now is insufficient to do the work that it is ordered to do under the new arrangement and there is likelihood of emergencies coming up there, particularly in the Azores and at Dakar at any moment.[138]

Further, noted Stimson, the effect of the existing policy

. . . is to neutralize the Fleet in the Pacific, where it is well known that we don't intend to use it actively against the Japanese, and to keep it from its real function in the main theater of operations in the Atlantic.[139]

The outcome of the conference at first appeared to Stimson to be favorable to his cause. However, at a full-scale meeting with the President at the White House on the following day (May 6), attended by Hull, Morgenthau, Stimson, Knox, Marshall, Arnold, and Stark, the pendulum swung back.

Not only did Hull stand out for his old position but, to my utter surprise, Stark switched around and trimmed on the subject and was only for moving three ships . . . three capital ships.[140]

On the same day, Secretary Stimson delivered a radio address, the text of which the President had seen and approved. He called for an expansion of patrolling into outright escorting of convoys. This step of course implied additional reinforcement of the Atlantic Fleet. Any other course, argued the Secretary of War, would mean that the United States would be obstructing the success of its own Lend-Lease program. A few days later he and Knox openly declared for removal of the neutrality legislation—a move that would certainly not reduce the need for ships to patrol in the Atlantic.

At the same time, Roosevelt, while not acceding to the requests for a large or publicly announced transfer of ships, still abided by the basic Atlantic strategy. In a telegram to Churchill on May 4, he had asserted: ". . . I believe the outcome of this struggle is going to be decided in the Atlantic and unless Hitler can win there he cannot win anywhere in the world in the end."[141]

Meanwhile, Stimson and Knox were continuing their all-out efforts and they ". . . enlisted the services of all and sundry who seemed likely to exert influence upon their stubborn State Department colleague: old personal friends of Mr. Hull, like Norman Davis, as well as Dean Acheson, Robert Sherwood, Harry Hopkins and others."[142]

When old friends seemed to be unable to persuade the President, Stimson and Knox turned to the British. Roosevelt had asserted that the Pacific Fleet should not be diminished without their acquiescence. The problem had first been submitted to British naval representatives in Washington. The British were of two minds with the need to protect the life-sustaining convoys in the Atlantic balanced by the basic strategic commitment to safeguard Singapore. At first the second consideration triumphed. The Royal Navy representative, after consulting with Australian and New Zealand experts, replied to the American request that the United States should keep at least six battleships (and appropriate supporting forces) in the Pacific at all times.[143]

However, the issue was then submitted to Prime Minister Churchill. Churchill and the Defense Committee of the Cabinet over-ruled their subordinates and agreed that the transfer of substantial elements of the Pacific Fleet into the Atlantic would be most advantageous for the British cause.[144] The British hoped nevertheless that some U. S. naval units would be retained at Pearl Harbor. This declaration by Churchill appears to have come at a crucial time. A few days later, on May 12, an answer to Hull's four-point proposal reached Washington from Tokyo. While the reply contained little that was positive, nevertheless its tone was conciliatory. In fact, its tone was sufficiently conciliatory to induce Secretary Hull to modify—at least for the time being—his stubborn resistance to any Fleet transfers.[145]

While waiting for word to come in from Churchill (and the Japanese) the proponents of a more active—and public—Atlantic policy had kept up their efforts. A dramatic illustration is the Stimson-Knox-Ickes conference of May 12. (Although Ickes was not himself a member of the "War Cabinet," he nevertheless took an active interest in many phases of military planning and preparation.) Ickes recorded the story in his diary:

I really fussed a good deal yesterday about the state of the nation, or what might better be described as the comatose state of the nation. As a result of some thoughts exchanged between Felix Frankfurter and me, I tried to get Stimson, Jackson, and Knox into my office at four o'clock. What I wanted to propose was that the four of us join in a representation to the President emphasizing two or three points that ought particularly to be emphasized. I felt that Stimson, Knox, and I could probably agree, but I was not sure of Jackson.

Stimson could not come but offered to send McCloy. Knox was in Chicago. Jackson was due at four o'clock but he got held up by an outside conference and when he called back shortly before four I told him not to come. When McCloy came in at four, I told him what I had in mind and he said that he shouldn't sit in at such a meeting. In the end, McCloy and I agreed that the thing should go over until Monday and I have called a meeting for Monday morning at eleven o'clock. Subsequently, Stimson called me to express his interest and to say that he would be in my office on Monday. I have had similar assurances from Knox's office and from Jackson . . .

McCloy told me that Stimson was beginning to worry very much about the situation and Stimson later confirmed this by telephone. People are really getting into a bad state of mind . . .

If Stimson, Knox, and I can agree on a course of action Monday, we will then give the other members of the Cabinet a chance to sign up too. However, with the possible exception of Jackson, I do not see any forthcoming signatures . . .

. . . I do not believe that Britain can hold out indefinitely. I do not even believe that she can hold out at all unless we quickly do something drastic. And if England falls, probably the English fleet will be sunk or surrender and we would be left alone on this continent to face a hostile world with not a single ally in sight . . .

. . . Stimson wants us to bring practically all of our Pacific Fleet through the Panama Canal into the Atlantic. He thinks that this would have a fine effect on our own people and would be encouraging to England while at the same time having a depressing effect on Germany and Italy. Stimson thinks that we cannot defend the Philippines anyhow if Japan should attack and that it is foolish to have the major part of our fleet in the Pacific where it will neither attack nor be reached by the Japanese fleet.[146]

At eleven o'clock on Monday morning (May 12), Ickes, Stimson, Knox and Jackson met in Ickes' office in the Interior Building. A principal topic on the agenda for discussion was the Pacific Fleet.

Stimson has been urging the President to issue an order that would bring the fleet now in the Pacific, except the minimum required to assure against any successful assault by Japan, through the Panama Canal into the Atlantic. He felt that this was the one thing that we ought to concentrate on, and it was agreed that at the next Cabinet meeting we would all support this proposal.[147]

This conference drew attention to two problems rather than one, or perhaps to a second facet of the single basic problem. The central issue remained the desirability of a physical transfer of substantial units of the Pacific Fleet into the Atlantic. But the psychological aspect of this transfer was also of major significance. Time and again attention had been drawn to the important propaganda value of the presence of the Fleet at Pearl Harbor; it constituted, as we have seen, a principal reason for sending the Fleet to Hawaii in the first place and for continuing to keep it there, though it is true that there were other factors involved.

Thus according to Stimson, Hull also feared that, in the event of a British defeat in the Mediterranean and then in the Far East, the United States Navy would not be available to meet the Japanese advance.[148]

Nevertheless, the main concern of Hull throughout was the psychological effect on the Japanese of keeping the Fleet at Hawaii. In this Roosevelt concurred, though he also was extremely sensitive to the possible effects of a transfer on the American public.

With this background, the three secretaries decided to play the same game. They concluded that the psychological value of properly emphasizing the transfer of units to the Atlantic could be very great:

Someone disparagingly remarked that probably the President would allow ships from the Pacific Fleet to trickle through the Panama Canal unannounced, and Frank Knox admitted that some ships had already gone through. What we want is something dramatic, something that will arrest the attention of the world and give courage, not only to our own people but to the British as well, by serving warning on Germany and Italy and raising a question in the mind of wavering France.[149]

On May 13, the day after the conference in

Ickes' office, Roosevelt finally came to a decision. How much weight he gave to the Japanese letter, how effective he considered the arguments of Stimson, Knox and Ickes, how much he listened to Churchill, no one can say. He did finally move. Characteristically, he gave less than had been asked for, but it was still a substantial transfer.

He gave formal approval to the transfer of three battleships, an aircraft carrier, four cruisers, and supporting destroyer squadrons.[150] This was precisely the force whose transfer had been approved in early April, approximately one month before and then cancelled. Temporarily postponed was a further proposal to transfer an even larger segment of the Pacific Fleet into the Atlantic. Nevertheless the ships actually transferred represented about one quarter of the total force stationed at Pearl Harbor. They constituted a welcome addition to the hard-pressed forces of Admiral King, when they reached Atlantic waters toward the end of May.[151]

Stimson and the others, however delighted with the President's decision, were still eager to have him make the move a psychological as well as a military gain—as they saw it. They realized, however, that the value on the world scene of properly publicizing the transfer of Fleet units could well be offset by its effect in the United States. Isolationist sentiment could easily seize upon this in their campaign of opposition to the President's limited program of aid to the Allies. To avoid this, only ten day later (May 24-26) Secretary Stimson suggested that a strong statement on the transfer of Fleet units might well be included in a major Presidential address scheduled for May 27. Similarly Ickes argued for announcing to the world "that all our Pacific Fleet had been ordered to go into the Atlantic."[152] But the President rejected the proposal, after receiving the advice of Secretary Hull. Perhaps the state of Congressional feeling (the Tobey Anti-Convoy Resolution had only recently been defeated) may have been influential here.[153] Roosevelt was merely continuing the policy that he had been following for six weeks. One might say that he was trying to deter Japanese aggression by use of the Pacific Fleet as a diplomatic tool, while actually using men-of-war in action in the Battle of the Atlantic.

V. THE ATLANTIC FLEET IN ACTION: THE PACIFIC FLEET HOLDS FAST (SUMMER 1941)

The U. S. Navy patrol of the Atlantic waters provided some help to hard-pressed Britain. But it was no real solution. The plight of Britain grew worse; May and June of 1941 were perhaps Hitler's closest approach to victory. One reverse after another befell British forces in the Middle East. More important was the devastating toll exacted on Atlantic shipping by Nazi submarines and surface raiders, climaxed by the sinking of H.M.S. *Hood* by the *Bismarck*. The danger to the United States was not, however, merely indirect. There was a clear and present danger of German attacks upon Dakar, the Azores, Iceland, even Greenland and South America.

The German campaign in the Balkans had been terrifyingly successful. After advancing into Yugoslavia, the German divisions had over-run Greece, forcing evacuation of the small British Expeditionary Force. This was immediately followed by the astonishingly decisive German air victory over the strategic island of Crete. Even more dismal was the news from North Africa where Rommel had forced the British back into Egypt and was threatening the Suez Canal. With the single important exception of Secretary Hull, all of the President's civil and military advisers favored a positive policy on the part of the United States, positive even to the extent of an outright declaration of war against Germany.[154]

The President was faced with a critical dilemma. The disastrous British position certainly argued for increased American assistance, especially toward combatting the Nazi terror in the Atlantic. At the same time, their successes in North Africa made it quite possible for the Germans to undertake offensive operations in Africa and then in South America. Provocation of the Germans might induce Hitler to throw all his weight into the struggle in the West, a possibility that might easily be accompanied by Japanese intervention in the war. Thus increased assistance to Britain could bring worse disaster upon the Anglo-American cause. Under these circumstances, "it was certainly the part of wisdom to avoid all provocative moves, to hold the policy of supporting Britain to established procedures, and at the same time to do everything possible to prepare defensively against all conceivable German moves in western Europe and the Atlantic."[155]

On June 6, the President was able to announce at a meeting with Secretaries Hull, Stimson and Knox what course of action was to be followed. The principal decision was American occupation of Iceland, replacing the British forces that were currently stationed there. This plan had been originated at the ABC Meetings.[156] Ambassador Winant, who left Washington to return to his post in London on June 13, was told to report the decision to Churchill. He also was instructed to report that there would be a further extension of our patrols in the Atlantic. The actual public announcement of both decisions was delayed until July 7.[157]

At about this time it was proposed by the Army-Navy Joint Board to send a substantial U. S. force (some 9,300 men) to Brazil to help defend that area against anticipated Nazi attack.[158] Both moves obviously required substantial naval support, which the Atlantic Fleet, still vastly under strength despite its recent reinforcement from the Pacific, could scarcely provide.

As a result, a tentative decision was also reached on June 6 further to reinforce the Atlantic Fleet by transferring a second quarter of the Pacific Fleet from Pearl Harbor into the Atlantic.[159] But the plan was very tentative, and less than two weeks later, on June 18, the decision was reversed.

Secretary Stimson was decidedly upset and wrote a letter of protest to the President which said in part:

. . . we are confronted with the immediate probability of two major moves in the Atlantic (Iceland and Brazil) without sufficient naval power to support them . . . recent news from North Africa makes it very clear that we must act immediately to save the situation in Brazil . . . the menace of Germany to South America via Dakar-Natal requires that the hold by American seapower upon the South Atlantic should be so strong as to be unchallengeable.[160]

Stimson's views were as usual supported by Secretary Knox, but the President, apparently with the difficulties of the simultaneous German-Japanese threats in mind, rejected their pleas. His action probably was also affected by the views of "the Admirals," most of whom were more interested in the Pacific than in the Atlantic.[161]

On June 22, 1941, however, a totally new situation developed: on that day occurred the German attack upon Soviet Russia. To many American leaders, this seemed to provide a golden opportunity. One of the more outspoken recommendations which were showered upon the President was one presented by Admiral Stark:

Within forty-eight hours after the Russian situation broke, I went to the President, with the Secretary's approval, and stated that on the assumption that the country's decision is not to let England fall, we should immediately seize the psychological opportunity presented by the Russian-German clash and announce and start escorting immediately, and protecting the Western Atlantic on a large-scale; that such a declaration, followed by immediate action on our part, would almost certainly involve us in war and that I considered every day of delay in our getting into war as dangerous, and that much more delay would be fatal to Britain's survival. I reminded him that I had been asking this for months in the State Department and elsewhere, etc., etc., etc. I have been maintaining that only a war psychology could or would speed things up the way they should be speeded up; that strive as we would it just isn't in the nature of things to get results in peace that we would, were we at war.[162]

Secretary Stimson, who had been an outspoken proponent of all-out action in the At-

lantic from the beginning, reported to the President his reaction and that of his Army advisers:

For the past thirty hours I have done little but reflect upon the German-Russian war and its effect upon our immediate policy. To clarify my own views I have spent today in conference with the Chief of Staff and the men in the War Plans Division of the General Staff. I am glad to say that I find substantial unanimity upon the fundamental policy which they think should be followed by us. I am even more relieved that their views coincide so entirely with my own.

First: Here is their estimate of controlling facts:

1. Germany will be thoroughly occupied in beating Russia for a minimum of one month and a possible maximum of three months.
2. During this period Germany must give up or slack up on
   a. Any invasion of the British Isles.
   b. Any attempt to attack herself or prevent us from occupying Iceland.
   c. Her pressure on West Africa, Dakar and South America.
   d. Any attempt to envelop the British right flank in Egypt by way of Iraq, Syria or Persia.
   e. Probably her pressure in Libya and the Mediterranean.

Second: They were unanimously of the belief that this precious and unforeseen period of respite should be used to push with the utmost vigor our movements in the Atlantic theater of operations. They were unanimously of the feeling that such pressure on our part was the right way to help Britain, to discourage Germany, and to strengthen our own position of defense against our most imminent danger.

As you know, Marshall and I have been troubled by the fear lest we be prematurely dragged into two major operations in the Atlantic, one in the northeast and the other in Brazil, with an insufficiency of Atlantic naval and shipping strength and an insufficient demonstrated superiority of American seapower to hold politics steady in South America. By getting into this war with Russia, Germany has much relieved our anxiety, provided we act promptly and get the initial dangers over before Germany gets her legs disentangled from the Russian mire . . .

Germany's action seems like an almost providential occurrence. By this final demonstration of Nazi ambition and perfidy, the door is opened wide for you to lead directly towards the winning of the battle of the North Atlantic and the protection of our hemisphere in the South Atlantic, while at the same time your leadership is assured of success as fully as any future program can well be made.[163]

Ickes continued the attack. In a letter to the President on the same day (June 23), he presented what was perhaps the essence of interventionist thinking:

It may be difficult to get into this war the right way, but if we do not do it now, we will be, when our turn comes, without an ally anywhere in the world.[164]

Speaking at Hartford three days later, Ickes made public his position: "If America does not go quickly all out for Britain, she may find herself all in without Britain."[165]

Secretary Knox followed this with a quite frankly belligerent address to the Conference of Governors on June 30:

For the first time since Hitler loosed the dogs of war on this world, we are provided with a God-given chance to determine the outcome of this world-wide struggle . . .

While his back is turned, we must answer his obvious contempt with a smashing blow that can and will change the entire world perspective. If, while Hitler is assaulting Stalin, we can clear the path across the Atlantic and deliver, in safety, the weapons our factories are now producing, ultimate defeat for Hitler is certain.[166]

Within eight days after Hitler's divisions crossed the border into Soviet territory, nearly all of the President's principal civil and military advisers had come out—openly or in private —for direct action in the war against Hitler. Further, there was almost equally unanimous agreement on the immediate policy to be adopted, outright escort-of-convoys in the Atlantic. Such action would not constitute a break in American policy; it was simply the logical outcome of all the partial steps which the United States had already taken. That such action would lead to open war was an eventuality recognized and accepted, even desired, by those who thus were arguing for direct action.

All this had clear and direct consequences for American naval strategy, and especially for the Pacific Fleet. Its strength reduced by about one-fourth as a result of the May transfer of ships to the Atlantic, Kimmel's command remained at Pearl Harbor. Now that even its function of occasional cruises to "keep the Japs guessing" had been abandoned, the Fleet's role in world strategy was largely one of acting

as a pawn in the diplomatic maneuvers of the Washington and Tokyo governments, of serving as a symbol of American strength.

Now Roosevelt agreed with Stimson that relaxation of German pressure throughout the West—on Great Britain, Iceland, West Africa, and South America—provided a great opportunity "to push with the utmost vigor our movements in the Atlantic theater of operations." On July 2, the President examined, and tentatively approved, Hemisphere Defense Plan 3. This plan, designed to replace Plan 2, which had been in operation since spring, had as its central feature full escort-of-convoy by U. S. vessels from the Halifax-Newfoundland area to the longitude of Iceland. The plan was to go into effect as soon as American forces landed in Iceland, an eventuality soon to occur (on July 21).[167]

While this new U. S. policy would undoubtedly provide real assistance to the British, the Churchill government's decision to aid Russia (reached immediately after the Nazi attack), followed soon after by our own, brought about new pressures upon the already overtaxed forces of the Royal Navy. As Sherwood, perhaps with the difficult years that followed in mind, described it:

. . . the supplying of Russia involved considerable extension of the convoy routes—and the route from Britain to Murmansk was by all odds the most terrible of the whole war, subject as it was to attack not only by U-boats but by surface raiders darting from Norwegian fiords and bombing planes from Norwegian air bases. The British Navy, stretched tenuously over all the lifelines of the North and South Atlantic and the Mediterranean and Indian Ocean, could not possibly take on this new and expensive assignment unless they were relieved of some of their responsibilities elsewhere.[168]

The pressure upon the Anglo-American naval forces in the Atlantic was thus greatly intensified by the two decisions to aid Russia.[169] Withdrawal of British ships for convoys to Russia would seriously deplete the number of ships engaged in convoy duty in the Atlantic. This alone would seriously overburden the U. S. Atlantic Fleet even if it adhered to its patrol duty. This was especially true because even after substantial units of the Pacific Fleet reached Atlantic waters at the end of May, King still lacked adequate forces to maintain an effective patrol system. Moreover, as Secretary Ickes had correctly estimated late in April, the range of U. S. patrol activity had been extended to the waters around Iceland. (It was at this time that Roosevelt drew on a map of the Atlantic a line separating the Eastern and Western Hemisphere, a line which swung sharply east above 60° of latitude to include Iceland in the Western Hemisphere.[170])

Now, if the President acceded to the many demands that the United States seize upon the invasion of Russia as an opportunity to replace patrolling by outright escort-of-convoy, the additional commitment would make the burden upon existing U. S. naval forces in the Atlantic an almost impossible one. Without substantial reinforcement, the Atlantic Fleet could scarcely hope to undertake these additional duties effectively.

The result: a repetition in mid-summer of the debate of April and May, although perhaps not on so great a scale. The same cast of characters recited essentially the same lines: Stimson, Knox, Ickes and the service chiefs on the side of direct action and transferring to the Atlantic the bulk of the Fleet remaining at Pearl Harbor; Hull and the State Department cautious, watching the ominous black spectre across the Pacific; the President of two minds, beset from both sides. Little need be said of this second debate; except for its final outcome it paralleled its predecessor too exactly. A few incidents will serve to highlight its progress.

The great degree of pressure exerted on the President to transfer the Pacific Fleet and its apparent near success can be seen in the concern of the Governor of Hawaii. As Secretary Ickes recorded it,

Governor Poindexter, of Hawaii, called at noon on Wednesday. He was worried lest our fleet be withdrawn from the Pacific. I felt it necessary to admonish him that while Hawaii is important, it is not as important as the mainland, particularly the Atlantic Seacoast, and that it was in the Atlantic that this war would be won or lost. I insisted that the fleet ought to be where it would be of the greatest protective use to the greatest number, but I expressed the belief that enough ships, in any event, would be left in the Pacific to make it highly venturesome on the part of Japan to attack Hawaii.[171]

After the adoption of Hemisphere Defense Plan 3 (as well as the other plans discussed above), the President announced to Stimson on July 5 that he was again planning reinforcement of the Atlantic Fleet. The contingent which had been scheduled in late June to be detached from Admiral Kimmel's command at Pearl Harbor was now to be given orders to move.[172] Stimson of course was delighted, and felt vindicated. He soon recorded in his diary (as evidence of further vindication) the following report:

. . . through authentic channels of something that Matsuoka in Tokyo had been telling Ribbentrop— about how well they had been fooling the Americans into keeping our Fleet in the Pacific. This was the last straw to me in proof of the futility of the . . . late efforts of the State Department.[173]

Thus, for a short time at the beginning of July, it seemed as if the President would give in to the insistent demands of Stimson, Knox, Ickes and company. He had agreed that operational plans for escort-of-convoy duties by the U. S. Atlantic Fleet should go into effect on July 11. Instructions were about to be given to the Navy Department to order the transfer to the Atlantic of a second substantial segment of the Pacific Fleet.[174] But the high point of the months of efforts to effect a transfer of Fleet units had come.

Once again, however, Roosevelt recalculated the balance and withdrew the offer. His attitude is reflected in this paragraph from a letter which he wrote to Ickes.

I think it will interest you to know that the Japs are having a real drag-down and knock-out fight among themselves and have been for the past week—trying to decide which way they are going to jump—attack Russia, attack the South Seas (thus throwing in their lot definitely with Germany), or whether they will sit on the fence and be more friendly with us. No one knows what the decision will be but, as you know, it is terribly important for the control of the Atlantic for us to help to keep peace in the Pacific. I simply have not got enough Navy to go around— and every little episode in the Pacific means fewer ships in the Atlantic.[175]

At this very time there came to Washington ominous and disturbing news from East Asia. Some of it was contained in various pronouncements of the Japanese government and its officials; other pieces, not designed for American consumption, were discovered by intelligence reports and by the successful breaking, by U. S. cryptographers, of the secret Japanese diplomatic code. In brief, U. S. officials learned of the Japanese decisions, following the German attack on Soviet Russia, to continue their advance into southeast Asia, with full recognition of the probability of war with the United States and the United Kingdom.[176]

The effect of this information upon the President and his advisers was the realization that war with Japan was probable and possibly imminent. A shift in plans followed swiftly.[177] No longer would it be possible to intensify American activity in the Atlantic while hoping that Japan would remain quiet in the Pacific. The plans so recently drawn up for more effective protection of shipping bound for Britain were postponed. Plan 3 was replaced by Hemisphere Defense Plan 4, a more modest plan for escort-of-specific-convoys to Iceland. (Ostensibly to supply American troops stationed on that island, these convoys might be "voluntarily" joined by ships bound for Britain.) At the same time, the President postponed the projected reinforcement of the Atlantic Fleet by units from the Pacific. This "postponement" soon became "cancellation"; after July 1941 there was no real question of moving the Pacific Fleet into the Atlantic. The Japanese threat had become too strong and too immediate.[178]

VI. PRELUDE TO PEARL (AUGUST-DECEMBER 1941)

The ensuing months may be scanned very briefly. Preparations went steadily forward at an ever-increasing pace to prepare the United States for the war drawing closer each day. As rapidly as possible, men and materials were allocated to the various units of the U. S. Navy. Joint planning continued between the United States and Britain, in accordance with ABC-1.

As the summer months of 1941 drew to a close, so too did the long debate come to an end. The often bitter conflict over transferring ships from the Pacific Fleet to help Admiral King's embattled forces in the Atlantic ceased. The end of the conflict was clear and decisive, although it was not immediately known to most of the people who participated in it. Occasional recurrences of the same arguments took place as the Japanese threat grew ever more ominous in the fall months of 1941 and the American policy of mingled negotiation and threat of force—military and economic—continued to be based in large part upon the Pacific Fleet, while the German threat continued on the Atlantic side of the world. It was met by increased action on our part: the "shoot-on-sight" order on September 11 and escort-of-British-convoys on September 16. But the principal issues concerning the build-up of the Atlantic Fleet had been resolved.

First, the Pacific Fleet was to remain based on Pearl Harbor; it was not to return to the Pacific Coast. Second, after the transfers of the spring of 1941, the Pacific Fleet was to remain essentially intact. The Atlantic Fleet continued to grow; in fact at the time of Pearl Harbor the Pacific Fleet had only two-thirds as many ships as the Atlantic Fleet.[179] But this growth resulted mainly from new construction. By a combination of luck and foresight, Roosevelt saw to it that the cream of the American Navy was quite out of the reach of Japanese threats.

Third, the course of events, which had finally caused the abandonment of attempts to transfer units of the Pacific Fleet into the Atlantic, also saw the end of the great pressure on the Pacific Fleet from the other direction. At the Atlantic Conference between Roosevelt and Churchill, with their respective staffs (August 1941), the British finally gave up their efforts of many months to have U. S. naval units stationed at Singapore. ABC-1 had provided that, upon American entry into the war against Germany, U. S. ships would be ordered into the Atlantic and the Mediterranean area to relieve British forces.[180] (Retention of some units at Pearl Harbor would, it was hoped, continue to deter the Japanese from entering the conflict.)

Accordingly, the British were now going forward with plans for the creation, from Task Force H in the Mediterranean, of a Far Eastern Fleet. When relieved by U. S. units, this detachment would proceed from the Mediterranean to the Indian Ocean and Singapore. Apparently the intention at the Washington conferences had been that the British should initially send a battle-cruiser and an aircraft carrier to Singapore. Later, when several U. S. battleships arrived in the Mediterranean, five more battleships should be dispatched to the Far East from Task Force H. Major losses among their capital ships kept the British from actually undertaking these plans until late summer. Even then, without active American support in the Mediterranean, the project was recognized as no easy one.[181]

Some discussion of these plans apparently took place at Argentia. At any rate, British plans for their Far Eastern Fleet were completed during August,[182] and the Americans were so informed. Some ships arrived in early November. Others, including the great battleship *Prince of Wales,* arrived shortly thereafter.

As a result, the ABD plans, which had never

satisfied U. S. military leaders,[183] were placed aside. Plans were now made for American and British commanders in the Far East to work out new operational plans. Accordingly, the British Commander in Chief at Singapore, Air Marshal Brooke-Popham, visited Manila early in October (the 5th) to confer with Admiral Hart and General MacArthur.

Similar talks continued during October and November. On December 6, Army and Navy officials in Washington received the final report of the arrangements concluded among Hart, MacArthur, and the commander of the British Far Eastern Fleet, Sir Tom Phillips. Local plans for resisting the imminently expected Japanese attack were not only completed but, on the evening of the 6th, Hart began to put the plans into effect. To Phillips, Hart said: "I have just ordered my destroyers at Balikpapan to proceed to Batavia on the pretext of rest and leave. Actually they will join your force."[184]

But the time for planning had ceased. A few hours later, several thousand miles away, Japanese bombs fell on Pearl Harbor. The event about which had been centered these preceding months and years of discussion and planning, of preparation and maneuver, had happened. In a sense, war had brought solution to many great problems described in these pages, while creating new and far greater ones of its own. For the Pacific Fleet, months of uncertainty had passed: war had come to Pearl Harbor.

BIBLIOGRAPHIC NOTE

Manuscripts

Kittredge, Tracy S. *United States-British Naval Cooperation, 1939-1942* (manuscript study of the Office of Naval History).

Papers of Secretary of the Navy Frank Knox, located in the custody of the Division of Manuscripts, Library of Congress, Washington, D. C.

Papers of Secretary of the Navy Frank Knox, located in the Naval Archives, National Archives, Washington, D. C.

The Roosevelt Papers, located in the Franklin D. Roosevelt Library, Hyde Park, New York.

Records in the custody of the Department of State, Washington, D. C. (cited as State Department Files).

The Henry L. Stimson Diary (MS), in the custody of Sterling Memorial Library, Yale University, New Haven, Connecticut.

Publications

Churchill, Winston S. *The Grand Alliance* (Vol. III of *The Second World War*), Houghton Mifflin, Boston, 1951.

Conn, Stetson, and Fairchild, Byron. *The Framework of Hemisphere Defense* (Vol. I of subseries, *The Western Hemisphere*, in the series *United States Army in World War II*), Office of the Chief of Military History, Department of the Army, Washington, 1960.

Feis, Herbert. *The Road to Pearl Harbor: The Coming of the War between the United States and Japan*, Princeton University Press, Princeton, 1950.

Hull, Cordell. *The Memoirs of Cordell Hull*, Vol. I, Macmillan, New York, 1948.

Ickes, Harold L. *The Lowering Clouds, 1939-1941* (Vol. III of *The Secret Diary of Harold L. Ickes*), Simon and Schuster, New York, 1954.

King, Ernest J., and Whitehill, Walter M. *Fleet Admiral King, A Naval Record*, W. W. Norton, New York, 1952.

Langer, William L., and Gleason, S. Everett. *The Undeclared War, 1940-1941*, Royal Institute of International Affairs, London, 1953.

Matloff, Maurice, and Snell, Edwin M. *Strategic Planning for Coalition Warfare, 1941-1942* (volume in series *U. S. Army in World War II*), Office of the Chief of Military History, Department of the Army, Washington, 1953.

Morison, Samuel E. *The Battle of the Atlantic, September 1939-May 1943* (Vol. I of *History of United States Naval Operations in World War II*), Little, Brown, Boston, 1955.

————. *The Rising Sun in the Pacific, 1931-April 1942* (Vol. III of *History of United States Naval Operations in World War II*), Little, Brown, Boston, 1954.

Pearl Harbor Attack: Hearings before the Joint Committee on the Investigation of the Pearl Harbor Attack, 79th Cong., 1st sess. (39 volumes), Government Printing Office, Washington, 1946 (cited as *Pearl Harbor Hearings*).

Roosevelt, Elliott, ed., assisted by Joseph P. Lash. *F.D.R., His Personal Letters, 1928-1945* (Vol. II), Duell, Sloan and Pearce, New York, 1950.

Sherwood, Robert E. *Roosevelt and Hopkins, An Intimate History*, rev. ed., Harper, New York, 1950.

Stimson, Henry L., and Bundy, McGeorge. *On Active Service in Peace and War*, Harper, New York, 1948.

Winant, John Gilbert. *Letter from Grosvenor Square*, Houghton Mifflin, Boston, 1947.

NOTES

1. Data from Samuel E. Morison, *The Rising Sun in the Pacific, 1931-April 1942* (Vol. III of *History of United States Naval Operations in World War II*), Little, Brown, Boston, 1954, p. 31, note 20. (Years specified are fiscal years, ending June 30.)

2. Provision was made "for 1,325,000 tons of new construction in battleships, battle cruisers, carriers, cruisers, destroyers, and submarines." Samuel E. Morison, *The Battle of the Atlantic, September 1939-May 1943* (Vol. I of *History of United States Naval Operations in World War II*), Little, Brown, Boston, 1955, p. 27.

3. Testimony by Admiral J. O. Richardson, *Pearl Harbor Attack*, Hearings before the Joint Committee on the Investigation of the Pearl Harbor Attack, 79th Cong., 1st sess., I, p. 255 (hereafter cited as *Pearl Harbor Hearings*).

4. Morison, *The Rising Sun in the Pacific*, p. 43.

5. *Pearl Harbor Hearings*, I, p. 260.

6. *Ibid.* "CINCUS" was the abbreviation for Commander in Chief United States Fleet.

7. *Ibid.* See also Morison, *The Rising Sun in the Pacific*, p. 43.

8. *Pearl Harbor Hearings*, I, p. 259.

9. *Ibid.*

10. *Ibid.*

11. Letter from Stark to Richardson, May 27, 1940, in *ibid.*, p. 261.

12. *Ibid.*

13. Morison, *The Battle of the Atlantic*, p. 43.

14. *Pearl Harbor Hearings*, I, p. 261.

15. "As a compromise, however, you have authority for returning ships to the Coast for docking, taking ammunition, stores, etc., and this should help in any case." (Stark to Richardson, May 27, 1940, in *ibid.*)

16. *Ibid.*

17. Richardson testimony, *ibid.*, p. 269.

18. Richardson testimony, *ibid.*, p. 282.

19. *Ibid.*

20. *Ibid.*, p. 264.

21. Admiral Leahy was a former Chief of Naval Operations and was at the time serving as Governor of Puerto Rico.

22. *Pearl Harbor Hearings*, I, p. 265.

23. Richardson testimony, *ibid.*, pp. 265-266.

24. Morison, *Rising Sun in the Pacific*, p. 47.

25. *Pearl Harbor Hearings*, I, p. 261.

26. An Atlantic Fleet had existed during World War I but it had ceased to exist in the years of the more limited naval activity which followed the war. See Ernest J. King and Walter M. Whitehill, *Fleet Admiral King, A Naval Record* (W. W. Norton, New York, 1952), especially p. 319.

27. Richardson testimony, *Pearl Harbor Hearings*, I, pp. 283-284.

28. See pp. 166-167.

29. Documentation and a much more detailed account of the ABC Meetings may be found in the following: William L. Langer and S. Everett Gleason, *The Undeclared War, 1940-1941*, Royal Institute of International Affairs, London, 1953, pp. 285-290; Maurice Matloff and Edwin M. Snell, *Strategic Planning for Coalition Warfare, 1941-1942* (volume in series *U. S. Army in World War II*), Office of the Chief of Military History, Department of the Army, Washington, 1953, pp. 33-42; Herbert Feis, *The Road to Pearl Harbor: The Coming of the War between the United States and Japan* (Princeton University Press, Princeton, 1950), pp. 165-169; Morison, *The Battle of the Atlantic*, pp. 45-49.

30. General Embick was also experienced in international planning: he was the Army representative on the Permanent Joint Board of Defense (Canada-U.S.).

31. Feis, *The Road to Pearl Harbor*, p. 165, note 2.

32. Robert E. Sherwood, *Roosevelt and Hopkins, An Intimate History*, rev. ed. (Harper, New York, 1950), p. 274.

33. *Pearl Harbor Hearings*, XIV, p. 1422, paragraph 3.

34. For a fuller discussion of this problem, in connection with Army planning, see Matloff and Snell, *Strategic Planning for Coalition Warfare*, p. 32.

35. Statement by U. K. Delegation, U.S.-Br. Stf Convs, January 29, 1941, B.U.S. (J) (41) 1, quoted in *ibid.*, p. 34.

36. This detailed memorandum, "National De-

fense Policy," was the final version of "Plan Dog." See also Langer and Gleason, *The Undeclared War,* p. 222, note 21, p. 286, note 81.

37. The wording "naval-wise" was one of three emendations made by President Roosevelt in the original text; see *ibid.,* p. 286.

38. Statement by U. K. Delegation, U.S.-Br. Stf Convs, January 29, 1941, B.U.S. (J) (41) 1, quoted in Matloff and Snell, *Strategic Planning for Coalition Warfare,* p. 34.

39. Morison, *The Rising Sun in the Pacific,* p. 50.

40. Matloff and Snell, *Strategic Planning for Coalition Warfare,* pp. 34-35; quotations are taken from various statements made by the British delegation.

41. Simultaneously with this expression in the staff conferences, the British (through Lord Halifax) submitted the substance of these views to Secretary of State Hull. The United States delegation protested this action as an attempt to bring political pressure into a non-political conference. See Matloff and Snell, *Strategic Planning for Coalition Warfare,* pp. 35-36 and notes; Feis, *The Road to Pearl Harbor,* p. 166, note 4.

42. Matloff and Snell, *Strategic Planning for Coalition Warfare,* p. 36.

43. *Ibid.,* pp. 36-37.

44. *Ibid.,* p. 38.

45. Morison makes much of this liability in note 3, p. 50 of *The Rising Sun in the Pacific.*

46. See Langer and Gleason, *The Undeclared War,* p. 287.

47. Minutes of the Washington Staff Conferences, February 10, 1941, quoted in Morison, *The Rising Sun in the Pacific,* p. 50.

48. "The documents . . . consisted of (a) the Joint Letter of Transmittal to the United States and British Chiefs of Staff; (b) the basic report—Short Title ABC-1; (c) five annexes to ABC-1, of which Annex 3 was the 'United States-British Commonwealth Joint Basic War Plan.' " Feis, *The Road to Pearl Harbor,* p. 167, note 7.

49. *Ibid.,* pp. 167-168.

50. See Langer and Gleason, *The Undeclared War,* p. 288.

51. *Pearl Harbor Hearings,* XIV, p. 1422, and Morison, *The Rising Sun in the Pacific,* p. 50.

52. Sherwood, *Roosevelt and Hopkins,* p. 273.

53. See above, p. 164.

54. See also Morison, *The Battle of the Atlantic,* pp. 14, 51, 61, 82.

55. See p. 161 above.

56. Incl A to rpt, JPC (General McNarney and Admiral Turner) to JB, April 30, 1941, sub: Jt Bsc War Plan—Rainbow 5 and Rpt of U.S.-Br. Stf Convs, March 27, 1941, JB 325, ser 642-5, quoted in Matloff and Snell, *Strategic Planning*

for Coalition Warfare, p. 44 (which see for the full text).

57. *Ibid.*

58. *Ibid.,* p. 45.

59. Of course the British had no direct concern with RAINBOW V, which was a purely U. S. plan designed to implement ABC-1.

60. Memorandum, Col. Scobey for CofS, June 9, 1941, sub: JB 325, ser 642-5—Jt A & NBsc War Plan—Rainbow 5 and Rpt of U.S.-Br. Stf Convs—ABC-1, JB 325, ser 642-5, quoted in Matloff and Snell, *Strategic Planning for Coalition Warfare,* p. 46.

61. This question was raised at a meeting of the War Council in Secretary Stimson's office on July 10. General Marshall observed that, even though the President might make changes at a later date, his failure to voice disapproval permitted positive action.

Matloff and Snell, upon whose work this section is largely based, provide a far more detailed analysis of RAINBOW V and its development than is given here. See their *Strategic Planning for Coalition Warfare,* pp. 43-48. Footnotes on pages 46-47 detail the action taken on RAINBOW V after its completion.

(The "War Council" referred to above was an informal weekly meeting of Secretaries Hull, Stimson and Knox. As Langer and Gleason, II, p. 693, comment, it "was the nearest approximation to a clearing house for national security problems which the Administration could offer.")

62. Matloff and Snell, *Strategic Planning for Coalition Warfare,* p. 47, note 54.

63. Langer and Gleason, *The Undeclared War,* p. 42.

64. *Pearl Harbor Hearings,* I, p. 305. See also Feis, *The Road to Pearl Harbor,* pp. 126-127.

65. *Pearl Harbor Hearings,* I, p. 306.

66. From Richardson's statement in *ibid.*

67. This summary is drawn largely from Admiral Richardson's account in *ibid.,* pp. 306 ff. and 316 ff.

68. Chapter II above.

69. Langer and Gleason, *The Undeclared War,* p. 42. The quotations are from the Stimson Diary and from a Stimson letter to Roosevelt of October 12.

70. Langer and Gleason, *The Undeclared War,* p. 43.

71. Feis, *The Road to Pearl Harbor,* p. 105.

72. Letter of Knox to the President, October 23, 1940, quoted in Langer and Gleason, *The Undeclared War,* p. 43.

73. Faith in the B-29's led to a basic change of American strategy with regard to the Phillippines in August 1941.

74. The President continued to be interested

in sending U. S. naval units to Singapore as late as November 29, according to the Morgenthau Diaries. See Langer and Gleason, *The Undeclared War,* p. 309, note 47.

75. Memorandum of conversation between Hull and Casey, November 12, 1940, State Department files.

76. *Ibid.* See also Cordell Hull, *The Memoirs of Cordell Hull,* I (Macmillan, New York, 1948), p. 914. Hull apparently favored the dispatch of a squadron of cruisers to southern Philippine ports, but the idea was not accepted by the President. See Feis, *The Road to Pearl Harbor,* p. 140. Roosevelt had raised a similar possibility in his conversation with Admirals Richardson and Leahy on October 8. See above, p. 161.

77. Stimson Diary (MS), November 12, 1940; see also Langer and Gleason, *The Undeclared War,* p. 44.

78. Hull, *Memoirs,* I, p. 915.

79. Stimson Diary (MS), October 12, 1940; see also Langer and Gleason, *The Undeclared War,* p. 45, for similar expressions by Knox and Morgenthau.

80. Grew Diary, November 11, 1940, quoted in Langer and Gleason, *The Undeclared War,* p. 46.

81. Hull, *Memoirs,* I, p. 914.

82. Feis, *The Road to Pearl Harbor,* p. 137, note 8.

83. Langer and Gleason, *The Undeclared War,* p. 309.

84. Feis, *The Road to Pearl Harbor,* p. 138, reports a proposal by the Australian Ambassador on December 3.

85. *Ibid.,* p. 154; Sherwood, *Roosevelt and Hopkins,* pp. 258-259.

86. See Feis, *The Road to Pearl Harbor,* pp. 154-155, for reports by the British Embassy in Washington and the British Chiefs of Staff, as well as by Ambassador Grew, who stated:

"It is axiomatic that an ounce of prevention is worth a pound of cure . . . I have expressed the opinion that the principal question before us is not whether we must call a halt to the Japanese southward advance, but when . . . The moment when decisive action should be taken, if it is ever to be taken, appears to us to be approaching."

87. *Ibid.,* pp. 155-156.

88. *Pearl Harbor Hearings,* XXXIII, pp. 1196-1197. During this conference at the White House, Stark's position was supported by Secretary Stimson. For a more detailed account of the February "war scare," see Langer and Gleason, *The Undeclared War,* pp. 322-323.

89. *Ibid.,* p. 465 ff.; Feis, *The Road to Pearl Harbor,* pp. 171-179, 199 ff.

90. Langer and Gleason, *The Undeclared War,* pp. 464 ff.; Feis, *The Road to Pearl Harbor,* pp. 174-179.

91. Langer and Gleason, *The Undeclared War,* pp. 468-470.

92. Morison, *The Rising Sun in the Pacific.* p. 56, note 19.

93. *Ibid.,* p. 56.

94. This was not entirely accidental. An unsigned memorandum of March 14, 1941, in the files of the Department of State, records that the visit of a U. S. naval detachment to New Zealand was cleared, through the British Embassy in Washington, with the British Government, including the timing of publicity.

95. Report of the U. S. Ambassador to Australia to the Secretary of State, March 31, 1941, Department of State files.

96. Clipping in Department of State files.

97. "On the Formation of the anti-Japanese Joint Encirclement by Great Britain, United States, and the Netherlands," a memorandum prepared in April 1941, by the Japanese Foreign Office, attributes to U. S. Fleet movements a major source of its fears. *Tokyo War Crimes Documents,* Defense Document No. 1739; Langer and Gleason, *The Undeclared War,* p. 472.

98. *Ibid.,* p. 471.

99. Morison, *The Rising Sun in the Pacific,* pp. 56-57; *Pearl Harbor Hearings,* XVI, pp. 2163-2164.

100. Langer and Gleason, *The Undeclared War,* p. 471.

101. Memorandum, Hornbeck for Welles, April 4, 1941, State Department files.

102. Telegram from Winant (London) to Hull, April 19, 1941, State Department files. See also Langer and Gleason, *The Undeclared War,* p. 485.

103. There had in fact been an earlier meeting in February which Captain Purnell attended as observer. This meeting had, however, not been able to agree on a plan to meet possible Japanese aggression.

104. Morison, *The Rising Sun in the Pacific,* p. 55.

105. Feis, *The Road to Pearl Harbor,* p. 170.

106. Stetson Conn and Byron Fairchild, *The Framework of Hemisphere Defense,* (Vol. I of subseries *The Western Hemisphere,* in the series *United States Army in World War II*), Office of the Chief of Military History, Department of the Army, 1960, p. 104.

107. Quoted in Morison, *The Battle of the Atlantic,* p. 56, which see for a more detailed account of the serious situation in the Atlantic.

108. Statement by United Kingdom Delegation, January 29, 1941, B.U.S. (J) (41) 2, quoted in Matloff and Snell, *Strategic Planning for Coalition Warfare,* p. 40.

109. Min, 7th MTG, BR-US Stf Convs, February 14, 1941, B.U.S. (J) (41), 7th Mtg, quoted in *ibid.,* p. 40. Areas of British and of American responsibility were agreed upon and specified in Annex 2 of ABC-1.

110. *Ibid.,* p. 41.

111. See Chapter II above.

112. Conversations of the author with Dr. Stetson Conn at OCMH, July 27-28, 1955.

113. Quoted in Morison, *The Battle of the Atlantic,* p. 50.

114. *Ibid.*

115. The Support Force (the name given to the escort force) was formally constituted on March 1, 1941. *Ibid.,* p. 51.

116. Langer and Gleason, *The Undeclared War,,* pp. 444-446.

117. Morison, *The Battle of the Atlantic,* p. 14.

118. John G. Winant, *Letter from Grosvenor Square* (Houghton Mifflin, Boston, 1947), pp. 255-256.

119. *Pearl Harbor Hearings,* XVI, p. 2163; Tracy S. Kittredge, *United States-British Naval Cooperation, 1939-1942* (MS, Office of Naval History), 14, 375 and 15, Appendix A, 312-314; and Conn and Fairchild, *The Framework of Hemisphere Defense,* p. 105.

120. Langer and Gleason, *The Undeclared War,* p. 445 and Chapter II above.

121. Conn and Fairchild, *The Framework of Hemisphere Defense,* p. 109. For further material on the April 15 meeting, see Langer and Gleason, *The Undeclared War,* p. 445; Feis, *The Road to Pearl Harbor,* p. 197, note 1.

122. See Langer and Gleason, *The Undeclared War,* passim.

123. Matloff and Snell, *Strategic Planning for Coalition Warfare,* pp. 51-53.

124. Langer and Gleason, *The Undeclared War,* pp. 445-446; Feis, *The Road to Pearl Harbor,* p. 196.

125. Stimson Diary (MS), entry for April 24, 1941; also in Henry L. Stimson and McGeorge Bundy, *On Active Service in Peace and War* (Harper, New York, 1950), pp. 368-369.

126. Harold L. Ickes, *The Lowering Clouds, 1939-1941* (Vol. III of *The Secret Diary of Harold L. Ickes*), Simon and Schuster, New York, 1954, entry for April 26, 1941, p. 492.

127. *Ibid.,* pp. 491-492.

128. Stimson Diary (MS), entry for April 25; also in *On Active Service in Peace and War,* pp. 370-371.

129. During the final week in April, news of the new activities of the Atlantic Fleet began to be conveyed to the American public, although in cautious terms. See the references to speeches by Knox and Hull in Langer and Gleason, *The*

Undeclared War, p. 448.

130. *Pearl Harbor Hearings,* XVI, p. 2163; Kittredge MS, 15, 408-409.

131. *Pearl Harbor Hearings,* XVI, p. 2164.

132. Stimson Diary, entry for April 23, 1941, in Feis, *The Road to Pearl Harbor,* p. 197, note 4. Marshall's estimate was based largely on confidence in the Flying Fortresses which had just arrived in Hawaii. See also Conn and Fairchild, *The Framework of Hemisphere Defense,* pp. 109, 110.

133. Telegram to the President, Winston S. Churchill, *The Grand Alliance* (Vol. III of *The Second World War*), Houghton Mifflin, Boston, 1951, pp. 143-145. See also Langer and Gleason, *The Undeclared War,* p. 447.

134. *Pearl Harbor Hearings,* XVI, p. 2165.

135. Langer and Gleason, *The Undeclared War,* p. 450.

136. Stimson Diary (MS), April 29, 1941.

137. *Ibid.*

138. *Ibid.,* May 5, 1941.

139. *Ibid.*

140. *Ibid.,* May 6, 1941.

141. Elliott Roosevelt, ed., assisted by Joseph P. Lash, *F. D. R.: His Personal Letters, 1928-1945* (Vol. II, Duell, Sloan and Pearce, New York, 1950), p. 1149.

142. Langer and Gleason, *The Undeclared War,* p. 451. For specific details, see Stimson Diary (MS), May 7, 8, 1941.

143. See pp. 182-183 above.

144. Stimson Diary (MS), May 2, 1941, May 8, 1941.

145. Feis interprets these events differently, apparently from the same primary source, the MS Stimson Diary. He asserts that Churchill at first supported transfer of the bulk of the Fleet; then, after consultation with Dominion leaders, requested the retention of at least six capital ships at Pearl Harbor. See Feis, *The Road to Pearl Harbor,* p. 198, and Langer and Gleason, *The Undeclared War,* pp. 451 and 475-477 for the conflicting interpretations. See also Conn and Fairchild, *The Framework of Hemisphere Defense,* pp. 109 ff., in support of the Langer and Gleason interpretation, which this author believes to be correct.

146. Ickes Diary, entry for May 10, 1941, III, pp. 509-510. See also Stimson Diary (MS), May 9, 1941.

147. Ickes Diary, entry for May 17, 1941, III, pp. 512-513.

148. Entries in Stimson Diary (MS), May 5, 13, 14, 1941; see also Feis, *The Road to Pearl Harbor,* p. 198 and note 6.

149. *Ibid.*

150. The ships involved were the battleships

Idaho, Mississippi, and *New Mexico,* the carrier *Yorktown,* light cruisers *Philadelphia, Brooklyn, Savannah,* and *Nashville,* and destroyer squadrons 8 and 9. Morison, *The Battle of the Atlantic,* p. 57. See also Stimson Diary (MS), May 13, 14, 1941.

151. For the events of these May days, see Langer and Gleason, *The Undeclared War,* pp. 450-451, and Feis, *The Road to Pearl Harbor,* pp. 196-198.

152. Letter from Ickes to the President, May 24, 1941, in Langer and Gleason, *The Undeclared War,* p. 458.

153. See *ibid.,* pp. 458-459.

154. See pp. 179-180 above.

155. Langer and Gleason, *The Undeclared War,* p. 515.

156. *Ibid.,* pp. 522 ff.; Conn and Fairchild, *The Framework of Hemisphere Defense,* p. 124; Stimson Diary (MS), June 6, 1941, p. 2. The Icelandic move was contingent upon an invitation by the government of the island, a move which required considerable diplomatic maneuvering.

157. Winant, *Letter from Grosvenor Square,* pp. 202-203.

158. Langer and Gleason, *The Undeclared War,* pp. 518-519.

159. Conn and Fairchild, *The Framework of Hemisphere Defense,* p. 124.

160. Draft of a letter from Stimson to the President, June 19, 1941, in the Stimson Diary; see also Conn and Fairchild, *The Framework of Hemisphere Defense,* p. 126. This letter was never sent, but the views contained in it were presented to Roosevelt when the Secretary and General Marshall conferred with him on the same day.

161. "Knox told me that the cancellation of the movement of the second quarter of the fleet was over his objection and under pressure of the Admirals, probably aided by the Commander of the Pacific Fleet who had been on here." Stimson Diary (MS), June 20, 1941.

162. Letter of Admiral Stark to Captain Charles M. Cooke, Jr., U.S.N., July 31, 1941, *Pearl Harbor Hearings,* VI, p. 2175.

163. Letter from Stimson to Roosevelt, June 23, 1941, quoted in Sherwood, *Roosevelt and Hopkins,* pp. 303-304. See also Conn and Fairchild, *The Framework of Hemisphere Defense,* p. 127.

164. Letter of Secretary Ickes to the President, June 23, 1941, quoted in Langer and Gleason, *The Undeclared War,* p. 538.

165. Quoted in *ibid.*

166. Quoted in *ibid.,* p. 539.

167. Conn and Fairchild, *The Framework of Hemisphere Defense,* pp. 129 ff.

168. Sherwood, *Roosevelt and Hopkins,* p. 308.

169. The German invasion of Russia also had a more direct effect on the Pacific Fleet. One of the immediate results of the decision of the United States and Great Britain to provide all possible assistance to Russia was mentioned in Stark's letter of July 25 to Admiral Kimmel at Pearl Harbor:

"I forgot to mention to you yesterday that you may be called upon to send a carrier load of planes to one of the Asiatic Russian ports. I don't know that you will, but the President has told me to be prepared for it, and I want you to have the thought." *(Pearl Harbor Hearings,* XVI, p. 2174.)

The contemplated plan came to nought; it did, however, constitute another of the many cross-pressures upon the Fleet at Pearl Harbor.

170. Sherwood, *Roosevelt and Hopkins,* pp. 308 and 310; illustration of map on p. 310.

171. Ickes Diary, II, entry for July 5, 1941, pp. 561-562.

172. Conn and Fairchild, *The Framework of Hemisphere Defense,* p. 129; see pp. 186-187 above.

173. Stimson Diary (MS), July 5, 1941.

174. Stimson Diary (MS), July 5, 1941.

175. Ickes Diary, III, entry for July 5, 1941, p. 567.

176. See Langer and Gleason, *The Undeclared War,* pp. 625, ff., especially pp. 631-637, for a detailed exposition of these events.

177. Stimson attributed this reversal of plans primarily to Hull, who he believed had "gotten at" the President again. Stimson Diary (MS), July 8, 1941.

178. Conn and Fairchild, *The Framework of Hemisphere Defense,* pp. 129 and 131-132. Formally, the question was never settled, but was left "up in the air" until Pearl Harbor. Presumably, a change in circumstances (such as a relaxation in Japanese pressure in the Far East or the British reinforcement of their Far Eastern Squadron) might have permitted consideration of transferring additional Fleet units into the Atlantic. (Conversations of the author with Dr. Stetson Conn at OCMH, July 27-28, 1955.)

179. Statement by Rear Admiral T. B. Inglis, *Pearl Harbor Hearings,* I, p. 122.

180. See the provisions of ABC-1, printed in *Pearl Harbor Hearings,* XV, pp. 1455-1550, especially pp. 1526-1527.

181. Matloff and Snell, *Strategic Planning for Coalition Warfare,* pp. 32-41; *Pearl Harbor Hearings,* XV, pp. 1485-1550; Feis, *The Road to Pearl Harbor,* p. 301.

182. Churchill, *The Grand Alliance,* pp. 588-590 and 854-859.

183. See above, p. 175.

184. Morison, *The Rising Sun in the Pacific,* p. 157.

EDITORIAL COMMENTS

Historically navies have seemed more useful tools of diplomacy than armies in international conflict of the kind nowadays referred to as cold war. There was an active cold war between Japan and the United States at the time the U. S. Fleet arrived in Pearl Harbor in April 1940; and the Fleet was kept in Pearl Harbor as an instrument in the cold war from then until the Japanese bombs started to fall on December 7, 1941. All questions about the size, the location, and the use of our Pacific Fleet were therefore debated largely in diplomatic terms.

In the Atlantic, on the other hand, beginning in the early spring of 1941, there was limited hot war, or, to use the felicitous phrase of Langer and Gleason, undeclared war. It was largely to serve this end that an independent Atlantic Fleet, of equal status with the Pacific Fleet, was created on February 1, 1941. But the limited hot war was not designed to persuade or dissuade Germany from further conquest, except against possible action in Latin America. Its primary function was to provide physical aid for Britain in its hour of trial, and, after June, for Russia too. Here the diplomats had little to say other than to remind the services that sufficient provocation might lead Germany to declare war on us.

Throughout the months of 1941, the decisions on the two Fleets (too small to be fully effective in either ocean) were burdened with a weighing of imponderables—the allocation of scarce resources between the needs of diplomacy in the Pacific and the needs of undeclared war in the Atlantic. The decisions were made no easier by the views of our tormented friend and potential ally, England; they too wanted a program of visible deterrence in the Pacific, and even in the Western Pacific, but they desperately wanted naval support in the Atlantic.

The problems of decision were further complicated by continual concern over publicity and the effect of publicity on nations. Obviously diplomacy would gain nothing if our moves in the Pacific were unknown to the Japanese; obvious also was the fact that the degree and type of publicity were likewise relevant. The same questions emerged in the Atlantic and here there was partial agreement, partial disagreement on the consequences of publicity. In the protracted debates, stirring declarations about action in the undeclared war were looked on by all as likely to cause a German declaration of war—a consequence strongly favored by some, strongly disapproved by others.

Two other issues were among those debated in the long arguments: the effect of action or inaction on the people of the United States and their discordant political leaders, and the relation of all decisions to what would be needed if, as most assumed, full-scale declared war swept the two partial wars from the board. This year and a half was, after all, the period in which the basic Anglo-American wartime strategy was hammered out and approved. It was also the period in which the production of implements of war began to rise. Decisions on what to do were affected although not settled by these factors.

Individual judgments on all these complex matters were largely—not wholly—set by the perspective of the speaker. Admiral Richardson, for example, made his recommendations about moving the Fleet back to California in definable practical terms: facilities of every type were better there, the Fleet could be readied for war duties more quickly, there would be less danger of attack. (Actually, in one conversation at the White House, Richardson went so far as to tell the President that the presence of the Fleet in Hawaii would *not* act as a deterrent on the Japanese—but this is only one example among many of the use of any stick to beat a dog when the direct professional arguments fail to convince.) Admiral Richardson's successor, Admiral Kimmel, continued the struggle with the President, though on different matters since the President remained immovable on keeping the Fleet in Hawaii. With the aid of his superior, Admiral Stark, he sought to prevent diversionary moves of contingents from his Fleet to the Western Pacific—successfully, except for the one voyage to Australia. Naturally, inevitably, he was horrified by the transfer of any units of his all-too-small Fleet to the Atlantic.

Except on this last point, Admiral Stark backed his subordinates. Knowing Roosevelt better, he stopped fighting sooner when he knew that the Presidential mind was made up, and perhaps too, stationed in Washington, he was more responsive to the arguments for keeping the Fleet in Hawaii. Yet on the diversionary tactics he did his best from start to finish. On the vital question of the transfer of units from the Pacific to the Atlantic he was of two minds. As CNO he was equally responsible for both the Pacific and the Atlantic Fleets, equally aware of the deficiencies of both for their assigned and ever-increasing tasks. Beyond this he was the first fully effective proposer of the Germany-first strategy in his Plan Dog and a hearty supporter of its successors, ABC-1 and RAINBOW V. During World War I, Stark had served in England and established happy relations with the British Admiralty and had become convinced of the desirability of Anglo-American cooperation. For these more personal reasons, less fully *ex officio,* he strongly favored an active friendly alliance with the British, an alliance that first and foremost had to be centered in the Atlantic.

The role of Stimson in all these events was considerably colored by his temperament. Throughout the year and a half from his taking office up to Pearl Harbor he felt deeply frustrated by the indecisiveness of the American people and by Roosevelt's super-caution—as he looked on it. Acting, as he made quite clear, in his role of Presidential adviser, he sought action: first in the Pacific; later, and permanently, as it were, in the Atlantic. Even General Marshall seems to have been unable to restrain Stimson's frank willingness to provoke a war that he expected would occur anyway. Marshall himself stayed out of these arguments except on two points: he did not want to ship troops

to Iceland and Brazil or anywhere else without proper naval escort, and he wanted to delay war until he had an army which was ready to fight.

This second point was one in which all the officers of both services joined. General Embick was a successful advocate of caution in the Atlantic; Stark was most reluctant to see wars start for which both Fleets were unprepared; and Richardson and Kimmel both sought preparations in the Pacific, not action.

Stimson had allies in his activism. His vigorous acceptance of the Plan Dog strategy had no opponents: at least in the available records of those concerned with decisions about the U. S. Fleet, there appears to have been no MacArthur, no Nimitz; Richardson and Kimmel tried to preserve and improve the Pacific Fleet, but they uttered no pronunciamentoes about where a war, *the* war, would be won. Stimson was strongly backed by Knox (who averred that he had no knowledge of strategy) and by Ickes acting in his role of self-made diplomat. (Ickes was picking up, so to speak, where he had left off in the controversy about helium, while Stimson was still the impatient frustrated Secretary Stimson of the Far Eastern crisis.)

To Stimson and Knox the stumbling block seemed to be Hull. Hull, patiently trying to avoid crises, to persuade if possible, to use the Fleet as a tool of diplomacy delicately and quietly, kept shifting his position with changes in events. He wanted to have the Fleet stay in Hawaii acting—in spite of its inadequacy— like the gun-in-the-closet. He resisted the blandishments of Hornbeck, his Far Eastern adviser, who naturally wanted ships to be moved to the Western Pacific. He wanted Britain to be aided, but with the least obvious "provocative" action (to use the currently popular phrase). With rare exceptions, he preferred the quiet channels of diplomacy to the noise of speeches and public threats. Thus Hull's deliberate passivity had a rationale; yet how much his hesitations and delays were based on his rationale and how much on excessive caution and undue diplomatic optimism, no one can say.

Roosevelt of course had to consider all the matters on which his subordinates tended to specialize. His great preoccupation, never to the exclusion of other factors, was the psychological impact of word and action both abroad and at home. Characteristic is his statement to Admiral Richardson:

I can be convinced of the desirability of returning the battleships to the west coast if I can be given a good statement which will convince the American people and the Japanese government that in bringing the battleships to the west coast we are not stepping backward.

In the light of this statement, Roosevelt's hesitations, delays, reversals of policy prior to action, also fit within the framework of a comprehensible rationale. Perhaps he too was at times unduly uncertain, almost fickle. Yet in essence he never forgot that he was Commander in Chief, responsible for the well-being of all the armed forces; he never forgot his role as maker of foreign policy—policy with our friends as well as with our enemies; and he also never forgot that he was the elected president of the American people, with a duty to lead, but without power to command.

THE ITALIAN ARMISTICE

ROBERT J. QUINLAN

ASSISTANT EDITOR

THE ENCYCLOPEDIA AMERICANA

CONTENTS

Note on Time   205

Foreword   205

I   The Casablanca Conference (January 1943)   206

II   Policy Disagreements   209

III   The Invasion of Sicily   215

IV   The Fall of Mussolini   218

V   The Badoglio Peace Feelers and the Allied Reactions   220

VI   The First Quebec Conference (QUADRANT) (August 14-24, 1943)   245

VII   Castellano at Lisbon   253

VIII   The Armistice of Cassibile   257

IX   The Surrender and Afterwards   267

Appendix A   278

Appendix B   280

Acknowledgments   285

Bibliographic Note   286

Notes   289

Editorial Comments   308

NOTE ON TIME

The areas of the Mediterranean theater (including Italy) covered in this narrative were designated Zone "Baker" (B); its time was two hours later than Greenwich Civil Time, seven hours later than Eastern Standard Time in the United States, and six hours later than Eastern War Time. The eastern United States was designated Zone "Z."

The time given for each event is that of the theater in which the event took place. Thus a telegram despatched from AFHQ, Algiers, at 1017B on a given date was sent at 10:17 A.M. Mediterranean time. It was then 8:17 A.M. in London and 3:17 A.M (EST) in Washington, D. C.

The footnote citations for a number of telegrams contain the time of their despatch and receipt, each in the appropriate zone's time.

FOREWORD

At 6:30 on the evening of September 8, 1943, this announcement was heard over the United Nations radio from Algiers:

Here is an important announcement from the commander-in-chief:

This is General Dwight D. Eisenhower, commander-in-chief of the Allied force. The Italian government has surrendered its armed forces unconditionally. As Allied commander-in-chief, I have granted a military armistice, the terms of which have been approved by the governments of the United Kingdom, the United States, and the Union of Socialist Soviet Republics. Thus, I am acting in the interests of the United Nations. The Italian government has bound itself to abide by these terms without reservation. The armistice was signed by my representative, and the representative of Marshal Badoglio, and it becomes effective this instant. Hostilities between the armed forces of the United Nations and those of Italy terminate at once. All Italians who now act to help to eject the German Aggressor from Italian soil will have the assistance and the support of the United Nations.[1]

This proclamation was heard by British and American troops about to begin an assault on the Italian mainland at Salerno. It was heard by units of the Royal Navy off Sardinia awaiting the appearance of the Italian battle fleet. It was heard by a weak Italian government in Rome living in deadly fear of the Germans. It was heard by German military leaders already suspicious of their Italian partner. Finally, it was heard by an astonished and delighted world which now knew that the first member of the Rome-Berlin-Tokyo Axis had fallen. A short time later a similar broadcast was made from Rome by Marshal Pietro Badoglio, head of the Royal Italian Government.

Behind these brief announcements lay months of preparation, bitter military conflict and dangerous, complicated negotiation. The story of the Italian surrender of September 8, 1943 was kept a secret from the world until its completion. Although the general course of events has long since been made public, the following study is the first attempt to trace in detail the activities of the allied politicians, soldiers, and diplomats who took part in the process in Portugal, Spain, North Africa, Sicily, and Rome, in Washington, London and Quebec.

I. THE CASABLANCA CONFERENCE (JANUARY 1943)

Italy first made her appearance as an objective of immediate Allied war strategy at the Casablanca Conference. January 1943 was a crucial time in the early post-Pearl Harbor stages of World War II. A great Russian offensive against the German eastern front relieved the siege of Leningrad and threatened Kharkov and Rostov. The bitter battle of Stalingrad ended with the surrender of all the German besiegers. Allied air attacks continued to devastate German cities and installations.

British and American forces under the command of General Dwight D. Eisenhower had landed on the shores of North Africa in November 1942. By the end of January French Morocco and Algeria had been secured and major gains were being made in Tunisia. The British Eighth Army under Montgomery had reached Tripoli in its drive to join Allied forces in Tunisia.[2] It was during this time that President Franklin D. Roosevelt and Prime Minister Winston S. Churchill, together with their military chiefs, met at Casablanca.[3]

DECISION: WHAT NEXT?

On the assumption that we are going to drive the Germans out of Africa it became clear to me that there was no agreed-upon plan as to what to do next. We had to strike somewhere—across the Channel, at Sardinia, Sicily or through Turkey. But where?

Furthermore I told the President that the next major strategic move should not be made without consultation with Stalin. Twice Stalin refused the urgent invitation of the President to meet with himself and Churchill. The Russian Front was too urgent. The next best thing was a meeting between Churchill, Roosevelt and their respective staffs. And the President wanted to meet in Africa. Churchill agreed. The Army had found a safe place outside Casablanca. And we are off to decide where we shall fight next.[4]

These notes of Presidential adviser Harry Hopkins set the keynote for the conference: What next?

Roosevelt arrived by plane on the afternoon of January 14. Churchill and the members of the Anglo-American Combined Chiefs of Staff had preceded him. During the following week the entire course of the Allied war effort was reviewed and military strategy laid down for the early months of 1943. The American chiefs —General George C. Marshall (Army), Admiral Ernest J. King (Navy), General H. H. Arnold (Air Force), and Admiral William D. Leahy, Chief of Staff to the President (Leahy was ill and did not attend)[5]—were strongly committed to a cross-Channel invasion of the European continent at the earliest possible date.[6] After lengthy discussion, the Americans finally agreed, however, that the cross-Channel operation, eventually given the code name OVERLORD, was not possible in 1943. Allied strength was not yet sufficient and it was doubtful that the Tunisian campaign would end before May. A build-up of men and material in the United Kingdom was, however, to go forward with all possible speed. Meanwhile, the question remained: After North Africa, what next? What would be the next objective of Allied forces in the Mediterranean theater? Considerable debate developed over which specific operation might be selected: Sardinia, Sicily, Crete, Rhodes, the Dodecanese Islands, or the mainland of Greece.

The Casablanca Conference produced two major policy developments toward Italy, one military, the other political. After eleven days of meetings, the Combined Chiefs of Staff presented a full report to a plenary session of political and military leaders on the afternoon of Saturday, January 23. In an eleven-page memorandum, the Combined Chiefs laid down their military objectives for the coming months of 1943. Third on the list of projected plans was the conquest of Sicily, scheduled for a favorable date in July. Thus the decision was made at Casablanca to carry the war into Italy.[7]

The decision to undertake Operation HUSKY was reached primarily, as Marshall put it,

. . . because we will have in North Africa a large number of troops available and because it will effect an economy in tonnage which is the major consideration. It is estimated that possession of the North coast of Africa and Sicily will release approximately 225 vessels which will facilitate operations in Burma, the Middle East, and the Pacific.[8]

Conquest of Sicily would deprive the Axis of its most strategic base for attacking Allied shipping in the Mediterranean and, conversely, give the Allies a major base from which to protect their shipping. In addition,

. . . because of the relatively small size of the island its occupation after capture would not absorb unforeseen amounts of Allied strength in the event that the enemy should undertake any large-scale counteraction. This reason weighed heavily with General Marshall—moreover, this decision, in January 1943, avoided a commitment to indefinite strategic offensives in the area. Successful attack would advance our bomber bases still farther, but we would not necessarily be drawn into a campaign that would continuously devour valuable resources.[9]

A more distant objective, also noted by Marshall and strongly favored by the British, was "the possibility of eliminating Italy from the war."[10]

"UNCONDITIONAL SURRENDER"

A second major result of the Casablanca Conference was the declaration to the world of the principle of "unconditional surrender." It was to play an important role in setting Allied policy toward Italy.

Sunday, January 24, was the last day of the Casablanca Conference. A news conference was scheduled for noon. The Casablanca meeting had been kept a closely guarded secret. As the noon hour approached, the garden before the President's villa was filled with newsmen and photographers. They had been flown from Algiers on the day before. Suddenly before their astonished eyes Franklin D. Roosevelt

and the Prime Minister appeared. No one had even known they were in North Africa. Pictures were taken first—to be released later.

Then the President began to talk. An official communiqué had been prepared early that morning. Hopkins had drawn up the initial draft which had later been revised by Churchill and the President.[11] Roosevelt gave a background statement, speaking carefully from prepared notes—although his talk was not for quotation. His only important addition to the official communiqué was the announcement that the United Nations were determined to accept nothing less than the unconditional surrender of Germany, Italy, and Japan. This was the first declaration to the world of the principle of "unconditional surrender."[12] Churchill followed the President's remarks with a comprehensive statement of the military situation. He concluded by asserting that he and the President were in complete agreement.[13]

Much controversy has arisen about this announcement of the "unconditional surrender" principle. The various criticisms and defenses have no place here. However, it seems clear that "unconditional surrender" had been discussed at the meetings of the Combined Chiefs of Staff and was mentioned in the notes from which Roosevelt spoke.[13a] Moreover, "unconditional surrender" had been discussed at a meeting at the White House of the American Joint Chiefs of Staff with the President on January 7, 1943, in preparation for the impending Casablanca Conference.[14] Even earlier, at meetings held during the summer and fall of 1942, a subcommittee of the State Department's Advisory Committee on Post-War Foreign Policy had agreed that "as between a negotiated cessation of hostilities or armistice on one hand and an imposed unconditional surrender on the other . . . , nothing short of unconditional surrender by the principal enemies, Germany and Japan, could be accepted, though negotiation might be possible in the case of Italy."[15]

Nevertheless, the President's own account is interesting and relevant to subsequent developments.

We had so much trouble getting those two French generals together that I thought to myself that this was as difficult as arranging the meeting of Grant and Lee—and then suddenly the Press Conference was on, and Winston and I had had no time to prepare for it, and the thought popped into my mind that they had called Grant "Old Unconditional Surrender," and the next thing I knew I had said it.[16]

While the President's statement was no doubt half-jesting, the Civil War reference, connecting the harshness of "unconditional surrender" with the generous *post-surrender* terms which Grant conceded, symbolized one of Roosevelt's serious and abiding convictions about dealings with defeated enemies.

Churchill, despite his genuine surprise at Roosevelt's addition to the communiqué, was also not wholly unprepared. Following the proposal of the "unconditional surrender" formula by the President at luncheon on January 19, he had included in a longer message to Deputy Prime Minister Attlee and the War Cabinet the following paragraph:

We propose to draw up a statement of the work of the conference for communication to the press at the proper time. I should be glad to know what the War Cabinet would think of our including in this statement a declaration of the firm intention of the United States and the British Empire to continue the war relentlessly until we have brought about the "unconditional surrender" of Germany and Japan. The omission of Italy would be to encourage a break-up there. The President liked this idea, and it would stimulate our friends in every country.[17]

The War Cabinet's reply came on January 21:

Deputy Prime Minister and Foreign Secretary to Prime Minister
The Cabinet was unanimously of opinion that balance of advantage lay against excluding Italy, because of misgivings which would inevitably be caused in Turkey, in the Balkans, and elsewhere. Nor are we convinced that effect on Italians would be good. Knowledge of all rough stuff coming to them is surely more likely to have desired effect on Italian morale.[18]

As a result, "unconditional surrender" was not included in the communiqué issued at the end of the conference. As Churchill himself said in 1949,

It will be seen that the opinion of the Cabinet was not against the policy of unconditional surrender. They only disapproved of it not being applied to Italy as well. I did not want this because I hoped—and hope has not been unfulfilled—that Italy, free from Mussolini's dictatorship, might fight on our side, which she did for several years of the war with lasting beneficial results to the state of Europe.

I have the strong feeling that I cooled off on the point because I did not want to bring Italy into this sphere; and I think that that would influence the President too. This is borne out by the agreed *communiqué* which was drafted by the Combined Chiefs of Staff and approved by both of us, and it contains no mention of unconditional surrender.[19]

In addition, Secretary of State Cordell Hull has recorded in his Memoirs that:

President Roosevelt and I believed almost from the time of Mussolini's declaration of war against the United States, four days after Pearl Harbor, that we should draw a distinction between the Italians on the one hand and the Germans and Japanese on the other. [They concluded that] . . . it might be possible to withdraw Italy from the war before the surrender of Germany and Japan, and that this withdrawal would in fact hasten that surrender. Italy's retirement, we felt, would be accelerated if we were to adopt an attitude toward the Italians different from that toward the Germans and the Japanese.[20]

In another connection, Hull observed:

I thought that our principle of surrender should be flexible. In some cases the most severe terms should be imposed. I had Germany and Japan in mind in this connection. In other cases we would have preliminary informal conversations that would result in substantial adjustments away from the terms of unconditional surrender. Here I had in mind Italy and the Axis satellite states, Rumania, Hungary, Bulgaria, and Finland.[21]

These background data have important meaning for the later course of Allied policy toward Italy. They indicate that even at this early state there was considerable sentiment in favor of excluding Italy from "unconditional surrender."

II. POLICY DISAGREEMENTS

Casablanca had produced plans of both military and political strategy; the following months witnessed developments in both. Despite their close inter-connection, it will be useful to review first the development of military strategy and second of political strategy. The period before the invasion of Sicily and the fall of Mussolini was a time of many decisions, decisions of crucial importance to the settlement of an Italian armistice.

MILITARY STRATEGY

At the Casablanca Conference in January, it was decided that Allied forces should proceed from the conquest of North Africa to the invasion of Sicily. The question: After Sicily, what next? was not answered at Casablanca. Since Allied occupation of that large Italian island would clear shipping lanes through the Mediterranean, it was quite possible that this action would conclude the campaign in the Mediterranean theater, with subsequent Allied efforts being concentrated entirely on a cross-Channel invasion.[22]

Against this there were weighty considerations. To cease heavy attacks would eliminate all threat to the Germans on the southern front and would allow the enemy great freedom of action. In Europe, Allied ground forces would be completely unengaged from the summer of 1943 to the early summer of 1944. We badly wanted the fine airfields of southern Italy. Finally, we wanted to keep up the pressure in the belief that Italy would soon crack and quit. Such an outcome would denude the Balkans of Italian garrisons and so force Germany to extend her forces still further.[23]

The question, however, remained unsettled. The great victory at Tunis (May 13) which closed the African campaign gave to it a sense of urgency.

Another conference of the President and the Prime Minister, together with the Combined Chiefs of Staff, was accordingly convened in Washington on May 12 and lasted until the 25th.[24] At TRIDENT, as the meeting was called, a number of lines of military strategy were discussed and appropriate plans and recommendations were made. There was, however, one significant omission. Nothing was said directly about the invasion of Italy in the final report of the Combined Chiefs.[25]

The American military chiefs, with their strong allegiance to OVERLORD, were not enthusiastic about following up the conquest of Sicily by an invasion of Italy.[26] In fact, May 1, 1944 was selected as the date for the invasion of northern France and the decision was made to transfer four American and three British divisions from the Mediterranean to the United Kingdom after November 1, 1943. However, although the primacy of OVERLORD in time and manpower was thus established, a considerable interim remained. Churchill was opposed to a period of idleness for the very large land, sea and air forces in the Mediterranean theater. At TRIDENT's opening session,

He made a convincing argument for a strong effort during 1943 to force Italy out of the war, citing three positive advantages, namely: (1) the psychological effect of a definite break in the Axis conspiracy; (2) the effect of withdrawal of Italian troops from countries in the Near East; and (3) the influence it would have on the future alignment of Turkey.[27]

Moreover, this was a powerful argument for putting into operation a basic part of British strategy. The British Chiefs of Staff were convinced that conquest of Sicily should be followed by an immediate invasion of the Italian mainland in the region of the toe and the heel. They hoped "to knock her [Italy] out of the war and so force the Germans to fill the vacuum in southern Europe with their strategic reserve."[28] More explicitly, "if the Allies should seize the great prize now waiting in the Mediterranean, the Italian Fleet and the twenty-six divisions with which Italy was garrisoning the Balkans would be lost to Germany, Turkey might be brought into the war to open the Dardanelles to supplies for Russia, and the British Mediterranean Fleet would be released for amphibious operations in the Bay of Bengal in support of Wavell's Eastern Army."[29]

At TRIDENT, while no specific plans respecting Italy were formulated, the following resolution was agreed upon:

That the Allied Commander-in-Chief, North Africa, will be instructed, as a matter of urgency, to plan such operations in exploitation of HUSKY as are best calculated to eliminate Italy from the war and to contain the maximum number of German forces. Which of the various specific operations should be adopted and thereafter mounted, is a decision which will be reserved to the Combined Chiefs of Staff.[30]

Thus General Eisenhower was to conclude Allied operations in North Africa, proceed to the conquest of Sicily as planned at Casablanca, and meanwhile "to plan such operations in exploitation of HUSKY as are best calculated to eliminate Italy from the war."[31] Emphasis was placed upon securing the Foggia airfields and also the city of Naples as a supply port for Allied forces.

Churchill, accompanied by Generals Marshall and Brooke, flew from Washington on May 26 for a conference at Algiers with Eisenhower (May 28-June 3). It was Churchill who wanted Marshall's presence, because Marshall was the foremost opponent of an Allied campaign in the Mediterranean. Churchill again presented his argument that the Allies should exploit their Mediterranean successes by an invasion of Italy.[32] Eisenhower reminded the Prime Minister that his opportunities were somewhat limited by the demands of OVERLORD. Seven divisions under his command had to be available for return to the United Kingdom after November 1.

The vast theme of Anglo-American war strategy, and particularly the long-standing conflict between OVERLORD and action in other theaters, is outside the scope of this study. Nevertheless, the actual policies adopted were major determinants in bringing about an Ital-

ian surrender, shaping its actual form, and deciding Allied policy toward Italy after the signature of the Armistice. A brief and very general statement on strategy is therefore appropriate here, one which will provide a frame of reference for later developments within the scope of this study.

There were at this time (late spring, 1943) three basic courses of action:

(a) an all-out offensive in the Pacific, with the war in Europe being confined to a holding operation until the defeat of Japan. This strategy was favored by Admiral King, much of the U. S. Navy, and some, possibly a large, segment of American public opinion;

(b) the defeat of Germany by means of a direct and major assault across the English Channel and a drive through France into Germany itself. All other operations, both in Europe and in the Pacific, would be secondary, holding operations. This was the favorite strategy of Secretary of War Stimson and General Marshall;

(c) the clearing of North Africa and the Mediterranean of Axis forces, followed by attacks on southern Italy and other points of the exposed "soft under-belly" of the European continent, with the objective of tying down large German forces away from the area of a cross-Channel invasion, and also from the Russian front. Such a strategy might not eliminate but might well delay a cross-Channel invasion; yet it would presumably make such an attack easier and more successful. This was the view espoused by General Brooke and usually adhered to by Churchill.

Advocates of (b) often accused the proponents of (c) of trying to avoid OVERLORD altogether, and of fighting an "imperialist," "dead-end" war in the Mediterranean. The interaction of personalities, the great limitations imposed by the shortages of equipment, especially shipping, and newly developing conditions in the war—these gave the arguments over strategy a constantly shifting appearance.

The principal motive of Churchill and Brooke at TRIDENT and at their conferences with Eisenhower was to secure further exploitation of alternative (c). Marshall, however, feared they were drawing back from OVER-

LORD altogether. Eisenhower, while generally committed to Marshall's view, nevertheless was becoming increasingly aware of the benefits, both immediate and also indirectly to OVER-LORD, of continued operations in the Mediterranean theater.[33]

At the Algiers conference, Eisenhower agreed with Churchill's view that, if possible, the conquest of Sicily should be followed up.[34] He declared that the actual progress of the Sicilian campaign would play a large part in determining his future plans. If the fighting proved easy, he would plan to follow up his advantages with an invasion of the Italian mainland. A stubborn defense would tie down Allied forces and make further operations difficult. "It was simply too early, he emphasized, to make a firm commitment now, but like the PM, he didn't want to lose any opportunity for exploitation that presented itself."[35] Invasion of Sicily was thus a temporary solution to the conflict between a suspension of Mediterranean activity in favor of OVER-LORD on the one hand and a full-scale invasion of Italy on the other. Upon the outcome of the battle for Sicily largely depended Allied policy in the Mediterranean theater. The American military chiefs in Washington looked with disapproval or at least suspicion upon any operation which might interfere with OVER-LORD.[36] Churchill, on the other hand, was scarcely in favor of permitting some thirty-six Allied divisions, most of them British, to remain idle from August or September until the following May. In addition, speaking with a characteristic surge of optimism, he considered it unlikely . . .

(a) that the Germans will attempt to fight a major battle in Sicily, or (b) that they will send strong forces into the leg of Italy. They would be wiser to fight only delaying actions, stimulating the Italians in these regions and retiring to the line of the Po, reserving their strength to hold the Riviera and the Balkans, which (latter) are of value as a supply area. If the battle goes against them in Russia and if our action upon or in Italy is also successful the Germans may be forced by events to withdraw to the Alps and the Danube, as well as to make further withdrawal on the Russian front and possibly to evacuate Norway. All these results may be achieved within the present year by bold and vigorous use of the forces at our disposal. No other action of the first magnitude is open to us this year in Europe.[37]

The Theater Commander, Eisenhower, was inclined to support Churchill's immediate view, although not his long-range strategy. Thus Allied military strategy awaited the result of Operation HUSKY.

POLITICAL STRATEGY: THE MAY MEMORANDUM

The Allied victories during the early months of 1943 gave a new look to the war and opened new horizons to Allied leaders. As the tide of conflict turned in favor of the United Nations, a new type of problem began to receive attention. Thus far, the paramount consideration had been meeting and defeating the Axis threats. With the first Axis defeats, Allied leaders began to direct their attention to the problems presented by defeat of Axis forces and occupation of Axis territory.

Allied political policy could not be directed solely toward surrender and occupation. The bombing offensive in Europe was accompanied by psychological warfare which in turn was dependent on political decisions. Thus in January 1943 there was an exchange of cables between Hull and Eden that laid the foundation for the propaganda offensive. There was substantial agreement between the two positions.

Neither side had any great hope that Mussolini could be overthrown, but they did believe that the Italians could be led to passive resistance and sabotage. This might grow to such proportions that the Germans would be forced to occupy Italy and thus make Italy a constant drain on Germany's resources. The Allies would attempt to persuade the Italian people that all their troubles came from the Fascist regime (and the Germans). The sole divergence was on the place of threats in the propaganda line: the British preferred a firm line, stressing warnings of destruction by bombing unless the Italian people cooperated. Hull wanted to limit bombing to military objectives and to play down its importance as a propaganda theme, and wished to assure the Italians that Italy would survive as a nation.[38]

But an agreed policy adequate for propaganda accompanying a bombing campaign would hardly suffice for the problems of surrender and occupation. These came up for discussion when Foreign Secretary Anthony Eden made a visit to the United States in mid-March for conferences with American leaders. During his visit references were made to policies of major significance toward Italy. At a luncheon in the President's study at the White House on March 22, Roosevelt made more precise his meaning of the principle of "unconditional surrender." To Eden, Hopkins and Secretary of State Cordell Hull,

. . . the President stated that he wanted no ne-gotiated armistice after the collapse; that we should insist on total surrender with no commit-ments to the enemy as to what we would or would not do after this action.[39]

The need for a concrete policy following Axis defeat was recognized at this time. At a tea on March 17, at which Eden, Hopkins, and Hull were Roosevelt's guests, the discus-sion turned to post-victory policies. Hopkins remarked that without prompt and positive Allied action a defeated Germany would go Communist or a state of anarchy would de-velop. This was true for Italy also. A formal agreement on Allied policy was needed, Hop-kins declared. He believed that the State De-partment should work out a specific plan with the British and the agreed plan should then be discussed with the Russians. Roosevelt agreed with these suggestions.[40]

Accordingly, consideration of the problem in general was suggested by the President in this letter to Secretary Hull on March 23:

Dear Cordell:-
Apropos of our conversation the other after-noon, I wish you would explore, with the British, the question of what our plan is to be in Germany and Italy during the first few months after Ger-many's collapse.
I think you had better confer with Stimson about it too.
My thought is that if we get a substantial meet-ing of the minds with the British that we should, then, take it up with the Russians.[40a]

The imminent invasion of Sicily focused at-tention upon the specific case of Italy. Ameri-can thinking was based primarily upon military defeat and occupation of Italy. The possibility of internal revolution within Italy seemed, in the spring, a remote one. In response to the President's suggestion, the State Department prepared a lengthy memorandum on post-victory Allied policy in Italy. The memorandum represented a development of the issues set forth in Hull's cable of the previous January.

When it reached the White House, it did not meet with unquestioning acceptance. On a carbon copy of the memorandum, Roosevelt made a number of revisions in ink. Additional revisions in pencil were made by Hopkins. A study of this memorandum with its revisions indicates both broad lines of United States policy toward Italy and also areas where there were differences in policy among individuals and agencies within the United States govern-ment. The revisions indicate clearly two cardi-nal points of Roosevelt's Italian policy: (a) complete opposition to Fascist party members on any level, and (b) a lack of support for the House of Savoy. Two sections of the revised memorandum are indicative of the general tenor of its contents.

State Department version:

On the basis of unconditional surrender the entire fascist party leadership ("hierarchy") from local party secretaries to the top should be removed from any posts of government.

The Roosevelt-Hopkins version made this provision far more sweeping:

On the basis of unconditional surrender, the entire fascist party membership from the highest to the lowest should be removed from any post of gov-ernment authority.

The State Department believed that local professional and technical officials, as well as certain administrators, were but nominal party members. Therefore, it advised that they con-tinue to perform their functions under the supervision of Allied military officers. The Roosevelt-Hopkins version permitted the use of such officials only if they were "free from fascist associations." Both versions of the May Memorandum agreed that prefects, or provin-cial governors, were to be replaced by military officers of the occupying powers.

Another section of the May Memorandum is even more significant since later on it proved to be controversial. Section II, article nine of the original State Department version of it specified:

9. The prerogatives of the Crown should be considered as suspended. The moral power of the Crown among the Italian people and the army may require some special treatment of this ques-tion as the situation develops.

Roosevelt accepted the first sentence, the rest he deleted. In place of the cautious reservation about the possible use of the "moral power of the Crown," he wrote an Italian "Bill of Rights," including "freedom of religious worship," "freedom of speech and the press" (consistent with military necessities and "factual truth"), abrogation of all previous restrictions on civil liberties, and the release of all political prisoners.[41]

It is unnecessary and probably fruitless to explore Roosevelt's motivation in making the changes, but one strand in his thinking is known and should be noted. Some months earlier, during the North African landings, Eisenhower had recognized the authority of Admiral Jean Darlan. The decision was approved by Roosevelt and Churchill as essential for the conduct of military operations, but Darlan symbolized the Fascist regime in Vichy to many people in the United States and Britain. There was a violent outcry about dealings with Fascists, and a good deal of bitterness remained even after Darlan's death in December.[42]

Progress toward the restoration of democracy in North Africa was slow under General Giraud, Darlan's successor, and it was not until June that De Gaulle, the symbol of French resistance, joined a new French government in Algiers.

The difficulties in North Africa and the painful domestic repercussions were very much in Roosevelt's mind, and it may be assumed that in amending the May Memorandum he wished to forestall similar difficulties in Italy. In a later cable to Churchill, Roosevelt further clarified his position:

I feel that in the initial stages of HUSKY we should avoid all risk of implications that would arise from any possible use of Italians in high positions such as Mayors of large towns and prefectures. I believe that it is highly preferable to remove any Italians from these positions as they are all prominent fascists. We should replace them with army officers for the time being and thus avoid stirring up Italian factions and producing repercussions at home.[43]

It may be added that the King of Italy was also not free from the Fascist taint; acceptance of the "moral power of the Crown" would not be well received in America. Roosevelt's sensitivity to possible reactions at home, of course, merely reinforced his strong antipathy to Fascism in all its manifestations.[44]

POLITICAL STRATEGY: THE BRITISH POSITION

The American position, as expressed by the President's statements and the Roosevelt-Hopkins version of the May Memorandum, contrasted with the Italian policy of the British partner in the Grand Alliance. Months earlier, on November 25, 1942, Prime Minister Churchill had drafted a memorandum on the "Position of Italy." He observed

It is in my opinion premature to assume that no internal convulsion in Italy could produce a Government which would make a separate peace.

Increased military pressure on Italy combined with propaganda efforts to provoke the fall of Mussolini should be Allied policy. The theme—"One man alone is the cause of your sufferings—Mussolini"—was to be impressed.

This, observed Churchill, would present to the Italian people a choice

. . . between, on the one hand, setting up a Government under someone like Grandi to sue for a separate peace, or, on the other, submitting to a German occupation, which would merely aggravate the severity of the war.

When a nation is thoroughly beaten in war, it does all sorts of things which no one would imagine beforehand. The sudden, sullen, universal, simultaneous way in which Bulgaria—Government, Army and people alike—cut out in 1918 remains in my memory. . . . Therefore, I would not rule out the possibilities of a sudden peace being made by Italy, and I agree with the United States policy of trying to separate the Italian people from their Government.

Finally, Churchill observed

. . . We are under no obligation to offer any terms to the vanquished, should they sue for them. That decision must be taken when and if we are offered their surrender, and in the meanwhile we certainly ought not to make promises, as some of the American propaganda leaflets have seemed to do.[45]

The Prime Minister recognized that Allied military conquest might not be the only way of removing Italy from the war. If, as he believed was entirely possible, Mussolini were overthrown and another government established, he had no objections to dealing with that government. Moreover, a deep-seated belief of Winston Churchill had important relevance to the Italian situation. The Prime

Minister was firmly convinced that the strongest and most stable form of government for a European state was a constitutional monarchy.[46] Thus he was firm in support of the House of Savoy; years later he referred to Victor Emmanuel as "the taciturn, cautious-minded constitutional King"; the last adjective is significant.

There were thus divergences of attitude within and between both British and American governments. Churchill did not see eye to eye with his cabinet on the application of "unconditional surrender" to Italy. Roosevelt differed from Hull on the possible retention of the House of Savoy and on the depth of the purge of Fascist officials. There was some divergence on bombing policy between Eden and Hull. These divergences and ambiguities foreshadowed possible difficulties in the future.[47]

"Unconditional surrender" might, for example, delay or prevent an armistice or surrender, with all its great military advantages. The use of army officers as mayors and the like would constitute a drain on military resources—a point given emphasis by Hull. Furthermore, "unconditional surrender" might help to pave the way for the removal of the King and even of the royal family, and the extensive use of military government would also facilitate the abolition of the regime. *Per contra,*

dealing with the King and certainly retention of Fascist officials would be bitterly resented in England and the United States, and abroad. The effects on the morale of the French and others suffering under Nazi occupation might be serious, and our good faith in declaring that we would eradicate Fascism might be called in question by the Russians and other allies.

Late in July, the Combined Chiefs of Staff began consideration of a paper proposing surrender terms for Italy. However, at the time of the fall of Mussolini, these prospective dilemmas had not been resolved; there was no definite Allied program for Italy.

By contrast, the Germans had a quite positive program: Italian defection would be followed by an immediate German military occupation. In fact, on the very suspicion of possible Italian disloyalty, the Germans had already begun to strengthen their forces in Italy:[48]

In the course of July, their High Command prepared plans for disarming the Italians and for deploying German divisions in their place, for seizing control in Rome, and for guaranteeing communications with Germany and with the east. . . . these were given precedence over similar plans for the Balkans after the 25th, and the preparatory deployment then got under way.[49]

III. THE INVASION OF SICILY

AFHQ lost no time in beginning to plan for Operation HUSKY, the conquest of Sicily. Shortly after the close of the Casablanca Conference, an outline plan was received from England and, on February 10, a combined planning headquarters was set up at Algiers. Complications began to develop almost immediately. General Sir Harold Alexander, commander of the troops involved in HUSKY, and his deputies, Generals Patton and Montgomery, were actively engaged in the Tunisian fighting. Other commanders were scattered at various points in the Mediterranean theater. As a result, immediate and careful attention to the planning of HUSKY was, to say the least, difficult.

Several times the original plan was developed, modified, and then scrapped altogether, to be replaced by a new plan, reflecting changing tactical considerations. More than once the planners seemed to have arrived at a state of virtual deadlock.[50] Yet from the very beginning, the importance of speed in planning was stressed. Both the President and the Prime Minister pressed strongly for an attack in June instead of July.[51] As the North African campaign drew to a close, Marshall urged Eisenhower to launch the attack on Sicily quickly. He emphasized the importance of surprise.[52] Unfortunately, the ever-present shortage of landing craft and other vessels was a major delaying factor.[53] Finally, on May 13, the day preceding the Axis surrender in Tunisia, a firm outline plan was agreed upon. The final defeat of the Axis in North Africa intensified preparations for HUSKY. A secluded mountaintop was, during May and June, the scene of intensive planning of the multitude of complicated details which had awaited completion of the master plan.[54]

It was during this period of final preparation that the Combined Chiefs directed Eisenhower to prepare plans for possible exploitation of HUSKY. Also at this time Prime Minister Churchill came to Algiers to argue for an invasion of Italy to follow the conquest of Sicily. There were no serious differences between Eisenhower and Churchill on this plan. The Allied commander, however, preferred to withhold his approval until the Sicilian campaign had indicated the nature of Italian resistance and German reactions. If the Axis defense of the island were strong and prolonged, it might be wiser to limit post-Sicilian operations to minor enterprises like the capture of Sardinia or Corsica.

On June 23, final preparations for HUSKY were completed. Favorable weather predictions had led to the selection of July 10 as target date. Beginning before 3 A.M., the first waves of troops went ashore to begin the invasion of Sicily. Some 160,000 men were involved in the initial operation, along with some 600 tanks and nearly 3,000 vessels of all kinds.

As the troops moved ashore, leaflets were showered down upon the Sicilian towns and villages. Many contained the text of a proclamation by Eisenhower which declared in part:

Allied forces are occupying Italian territory. They are doing so, not as enemies of the Italian people, but as an inevitable part of their war to destroy the German overlordship of Europe. Their aim is to deliver the people of Italy from the Fascist regime which led them into the war, and when that has been accomplished, to restore Italy as a free nation.

Allied forces have no intention of changing or undermining the traditional laws and customs of the Italian people. They will take necessary steps, however, to eliminate the Fascist system in whatever territory they occupy.[55]

On the same day (July 10), Eisenhower had received an important message from the Combined Chiefs of Staff, Eisenhower's military superiors in his capacity of Allied commander.

The message told Eisenhower that he was to be prepared to release a Joint Declaration to the Italian people from the President and the Prime Minister. Early in June, the President had prepared a first draft of the Declaration. His draft had been amended in several minor respects by Churchill, who proposed that the announcement be withheld until the success of the Sicilian operation was assured.[56] The revised draft, now sent to Eisenhower, read as follows:

ROOSEVELT-CHURCHILL APPEAL TO THE ITALIAN PEOPLE

This is a message to the Italian people from the President of the United States of America and the Prime Minister of Great Britain.

At this moment the combined armed forces of the United States and Great Britain, under the command of General Eisenhower and his Deputy, General Alexander, are carrying the war deep into the territory of your country. This is the direct consequence of the shameful leadership to which you have been subjected by Mussolini and his Fascist regime. Mussolini carried you into this war as the satellite of a brutal destroyer of peoples and liberties. Mussolini plunged you into a war which he thought Hitler had already won. In spite of Italy's great vulnerability to attack by air and sea, your Fascist leaders sent your sons, your ships, your air forces, to distant battlefields to aid Germany in her attempt to conquer England, Russia, and the world. This association with the designs of Nazi-controlled Germany was unworthy of Italy's ancient traditions of freedom and culture —traditions to which the people of America and Great Britain owe so much. Your soldiers have fought, not in the interests of Italy, but for Nazi Germany. They have fought courageously, but they have been betrayed and abandoned by the Germans on the Russian Front and on every battlefield in Africa from El Alamein to Cape Bon.

Today Germany's hopes for world conquest have been blasted on all fronts. The skies over Italy are dominated by the vast air armadas of the United States and Great Britain. Italy's seacoasts are threatened by the greatest accumulation of British and Allied seapower ever concentrated in the Mediterranean. The forces now opposed to you are pledged to destroy the power of Nazi Germany, which has ruthlessly been used to inflict slavery, destruction, and death on all who refuse to recognize the Germans as the master race.

The sole hope for Italy's survival lies in honourable capitulation to the overwhelming power of the military forces of the United Nations. If you continue to tolerate the Fascist regime, which serves the evil power of the Nazis, you must suffer the consequences of your own choice. We take no satisfaction in invading Italian soil; but we are determined to destroy the false leaders and their doctrines which have brought Italy to her present position. Every moment that you resist the combined forces of the United Nations—every drop of blood that you sacrifice—can serve only one purpose: to give the Fascist and Nazi leaders a little more time to escape from the inevitable consequences of their own crimes. All your interests and all your traditions have been betrayed by Germany and your own false and corrupt leaders; it is only by disavowing both that a reconstituted Italy can hope to occupy a respected place in the family of European nations.

The time has now come for you, the Italian people, to consult your own self-respect and your own interests and your own desire for a restoration of national dignity, security, and peace. The time has come for you to decide whether Italians shall die for Mussolini—or live for Italy, and for civilization.

Roosevelt
Churchill[57]

The Declaration, it will be noted, had the same tenor as the psychological warfare offensive that had gone on for so many months; it distinguished sharply between the Italian people and the Fascist leaders, and placed all the blame for Italy's unhappy position on Mussolini and his associates, and on the Germans. It called on the Italians to capitulate to the Allies and to repudiate Mussolini and Hitler, and promised that by so doing Italy would regain a respected place in the family of nations. There was no mention of "unconditional surrender," nor had there been any in Eisenhower's earlier message. The Declaration did, moreover, contain the phrase, "honourable capitulation."[58]

Eisenhower promptly advised General Marshall that he would inform the Combined Chiefs when Allied operations in Sicily presented a favorable moment for the release of the Declaration. Intensive preparations were made by the psychological warfare units of the Mediterranean Command. The Joint Declaration was actually announced on July 17.[59] It was broadcast to Italy by all available radio transmitters, including some recently established on the north coast of Africa. Millions of leaflets containing the proclamation were dropped by Allied aircraft on Rome and other Italian cities.[60]

The TRIDENT conference had directed Eisenhower to prepare plans for exploiting a successful Sicilian operation. These plans were to be subject to the approval of the Combined Chiefs.[61] Not long after the initial landings in Sicily, Eisenhower began to concern himself with post-HUSKY plans. No matter what plan he proposed, it was subject to important restrictions. Not only had OVERLORD been given priority on men and equipment but at the TRIDENT conference it had been decided to transfer additional landing craft and air units to India.

On June 28, Eisenhower had submitted to the Combined Chiefs of Staff alternative plans: either an attack on the heel and toe of Italy, or conquest of Sardinia. Rapid progress in Sicily, however, plus reports of internal disintegration in Italy made a landing on the peninsula appear possible and advantageous to AFHQ.[62] The British Chiefs of Staff Committee came out strongly in favor of this proposal. Not only did they favor a landing on the toe and/or heel but they advocated the far bolder plan of an amphibious assault on the Naples-Salerno area. Despite the shortages of material, Eisenhower also began to favor this plan.[63]

The British leaders, enthusiastic about the possibilities of removing Italy from the war and of providing air bases closer to the heart of Germany, argued persuasively for AVALANCHE (the proposed Salerno landing). Marshall and the other Joint Chiefs had agreed upon an attack on Italy provided that the Sicilian operation ended quickly, making further operations possible without interfering with the build-up for OVERLORD. When these conditions seemed on the way to being satisfied, the JCS continued to be willing to go along with plans for an invasion of Italy. In fact, in the hope of ending the Mediterranean campaign quickly, Marshall also approved the bolder course, AVALANCHE. But JCS approval of the Italian campaign had one important proviso: they remained obdurate in refusing their sanction to any further diversion of resources to Italy. Nothing should be permitted to interfere with OVERLORD. The British therefore decided to provide whatever additional air and naval assistance lay at their own command.[64]

By the end of July, these plans had been drafted: Once Messina had fallen, Allied troops would proceed across the Straits to the Italian mainland (BAYTOWN). Additional landings on the toe and heel of the Italian "boot" would include an amphibious attack in the Naples-Salerno area (AVALANCHE). The object: to remove Italy from the war with all possible speed.[65]

The story now shifts away from Sicily. Nevertheless it may be useful to sketch briefly the conclusion of the battle for Sicily.

The British Eighth Army, faced by fierce German resistance and difficult terrain, moved slowly up the east coast of the island. Meanwhile General Patton's American Seventh Army executed a brilliant sweep around the western end. The British took Catania on August 5. American troops proceeded along the north coast to Cape Orlando, which they secured on the 10th. Three days later, the enemy broke contact and rushed headlong for the Straits of Messina and escape. Messina was taken on August 16 and by 10 A.M. the following morning all resistance had ceased. The conquest of Sicily was accomplished in thirty-eight days. Unfortunately, the Axis commanders were able to adhere to a carefully prepared evacuation plan. Almost the entire German garrison, together with most of their equipment, were carried across the Straits of Messina, to fight again in Italy. The Italians, too, were able to ferry across substantial numbers of men and quantities of supplies, although many Italian soldiers did surrender to the advancing Allied troops.

On August 17, British and American forces stood poised on the shores of the Straits of Messina. Only a few miles distant lay the mainland of Italy, where events of crucial importance had been occurring since July 25.[66]

IV. THE FALL OF MUSSOLINI

July 25, 1943 was a quiet summer Sunday at Shangri-La, Franklin D. Roosevelt's hideaway in the Maryland hills. The President, with the aid of Judge Samuel I. Rosenman and Robert E. Sherwood, was completing work on a radio speech to be delivered on the following Wednesday evening. Late in the afternoon, the telephone rang. Presidential Secretary Stephen Early announced that an important news flash had just been heard in Washington. The Rome radio had proclaimed the resignation of Benito Mussolini, dictator of Italy for twenty-one years. King Victor Emmanuel had assumed personal command of the Italian armed forces and had appointed Marshal Pietro Badoglio as Prime Minister and Commander-in-Chief. Badoglio, conqueror of Abyssinia, had been in retirement since the disastrous Italian campaign in the Balkans during 1940. The report was a correct one: Mussolini had indeed been dismissed by the King.[67]

The circumstances of Mussolini's downfall are of more than general historical interest. They provide important clues to Italian behavior during the negotiations for an armistice.

The first six months of 1943 were unhappy ones for Italy. Defeat followed defeat in Russia and North Africa. Internal distress and demoralization grew with the destruction created by Allied air bombardment. Italy's position in the German alliance grew steadily weaker. Dissension spread throughout Italy as the course of the war changed.

Blame for Italy's reverses centered on Mussolini who, as dictator, was clearly responsible for Italian policy. He sought to alter defeat by making changes in his military and civil chiefs. These changes opened the door to opposition forces—forces whose loyalty centered around the aged King. In the monarch lay the best, perhaps the only opportunity for immediate change, since under the dictatorship all more "liberal" avenues were blocked. Two key officials were General Ambrosio, Chief of the Italian High Command, and the Duke of Acquarone, Minister of the Royal Court.[68] For some time they had been seeking means to accomplish the overthrow of Mussolini. Other groups sought the same end. Many of the important anti-Mussolini forces and probably the most effective, were loyal to the House of Savoy, and their dependence upon it for their continued existence proved to be a crucial factor in the later armistice negotiations with the Allies.

Appeals to the King had begun as early as late 1942. They came from sources ranging all the way from members of the Royal Court to Ivanoe Bonomi, underground leader of a union of left-wing parties.[69] There was widespread belief that in the monarch lay Italy's best opportunity for change.[70] Victor Emmanuel had, however, turned a deaf ear to all appeals.

The climax came during July 1943. It was in part produced by the successful and speedy conquest of the island of Sicily. This was no far-distant part of some recently conquered empire; it was an integral part of the Italian homeland. Invasion of the homeland was a fact which could not be made light of nor camouflaged from the Italian people.

Two separate forces combined, partly by accident, partly by design, to secure the final result. The Royalist conspiracy had continued for some time. The King had found in Marshal Badoglio a satisfactory leader to direct conduct of the state. Specific plans were made for General Ambrosio to undertake the arrest of Mussolini on July 26. The Royalist forces were unwittingly aided by members of the Old Guard of the Fascist party. Hoping to improve Italy's deteriorating situation without losing power themselves, they induced Mussolini to convoke a meeting of the Fascist Grand Council for July 24. On July 22, Dino Grandi, former Fascist foreign minister and Ambassador to the United Kingdom, arrived in Rome. In an interview with Mussolini, he informed his chief that he intended to propose that the King resume command of the armed forces.

The actual overthrow was a joint product of the King and the Italian High Command aided, apparently inadvertently, by certain leaders of the Fascist party. The meeting of the Fascist Grand Council convened at 5 P.M. on July 24. Mussolini presented his case, taking full responsibility for the war but declaring that he still possessed the means of repelling the violators of Italian integrity. Grandi, however, moved a resolution that the Crown assume more power and that the King come out of obscurity to take over his responsibilities including "effective command of the armed forces."[71]

A long and heated debate followed. It was after 2 A.M. when the final vote was taken. Grandi's motion was adopted 17-9, with two abstentions.[72] The impact of the vote was clear. Mussolini himself declared: "You have provoked a crisis of the regime."

Meanwhile, under the direction of Ambrosio and the Duke of Acquarone, trusted police officers took over telephone exchanges, police headquarters and other key positions. At five o'clock on the afternoon of Sunday, July 25, Mussolini was summoned before the King. Victor Emmanuel reviewed Italy's plight and the results of the Council meeting, and stated that Mussolini was the most hated man in the country. The King indicated that Il Duce would be replaced as head of the Government by Marshal Badoglio but that Mussolini could be assured of Royal protection.

As the former dictator left the Royal villa, he was taken in charge by police and driven off in an ambulance. A few hours later, Badoglio was directed by the King to form a new cabinet of civil and military chiefs.[73] That same evening the King and Badoglio broadcast to the world the news of Mussolini's dismissal. (Two days later Mussolini was interned on an island off the Italian coast.[74]) At the same time, Badoglio announced dissolution of the Fascist party, released many political prisoners, placed Italy under martial law, and declared a prohibition of all political activity until the end of the war.[75]

Badoglio's first public statement declared "the war goes on"; there was no indication that Italy would seek a separate peace with the Allies. However, it was becoming increasingly clear that the Italians were more than anxious to get out of the war and that the statement was made mainly to placate the Germans. Reports of a forthcoming armistice began to circulate almost immediately.

After contemplating immediate seizure of the King and the Badoglio government, the Germans eventually decided to "move as many troops as possible into Italy while the Badoglio government still pretended to be an ally, and to be ready to occupy the country and seize the fleet at a moment's notice."[76]

V. THE BADOGLIO PEACE FEELERS AND THE ALLIED REACTIONS

PREPARATIONS— EARLY ALLIED POLICY[77]

Reaction of Roosevelt and Churchill to Mussolini's Downfall

Q. Mr. President, what is your reaction to the change in the Italian government? [the sudden resignation of Benito Mussolini on July 25]

The President: Reaction?

Q. Yes, sir.

The President: I never have reactions. I am much too old [laughter].[78]

But as Roosevelt parried the reporter's question at a White House news conference on July 27, he had already reacted swiftly and concretely to the new situation which had arisen in Italy.[79]

The draft for the President's radio address on which he had been working on July 25 was revised to present views on the new situation in Italy. There was no apparent change in Roosevelt's position: the speech, delivered on the evening of July 28, declared:

Our terms to Italy are still the same as our terms to Germany and Japan—"Unconditional Surrender."

We will have no truck with Fascism in any way, shape, or manner. We will permit no vestige of Fascism to remain.

Eventually Italy will reconstitute herself. It will be the people of Italy who will do that, choosing their own government in accordance with the basic democratic principles of liberty and equality.[80]

However, within a few hours of receiving the news of Mussolini's downfall, he had telegraphed to Churchill, indicating his views and suggesting joint consultation. This telegram was not so uncompromising as the speech. He hoped to achieve a settlement "as close as possible to unconditional surrender." This should be fol-

lowed by "good treatment of the Italian people." He wanted to be certain of the immediate military objectives, i.e., "the use of all Italian territory and transportation against the Germans in the north and against the whole Balkan peninsula, as well as use of airfields of all kinds." In addition, he also wanted the surrender of the "Head Devil," Mussolini, and his "chief partners in crime." There was no question in Roosevelt's mind as to where policy was to be made. "In no event should our officers in the field fix on any general terms without your approval and mine," he told the Prime Minister. Churchill, in a telegram which crossed the President's message in transit, also urged consultation for joint action to meet the expected Italian overtures for peace.[81]

The hours following the news of Mussolini's dismissal had been busy ones for the Prime Minister. Realizing the importance of Allied policy toward Italy for the whole course of the war, he drafted a lengthy statement of his views. It is a comprehensive statement of Allied aims, written before a clear picture of the internal situation in Italy was available. Thus it invites comparison with the eventual Italian settlement.[82]

THOUGHTS ON THE FALL OF MUSSOLINI

By the Prime Minister

1. It seems highly probable that the fall of Mussolini will involve the overthrow of the Fascist regime, and that the new Government of the King and Badoglio will seek to negotiate a separate arrangement with the Allies for an armistice. Should this prove to be the case, it will be necessary for us to make up our minds first of all upon what we want, and secondly, upon the measures and conditions required to gain it for us.

2. At this moment above all others our thoughts must be concentrated upon the supreme aim,

namely, the destruction of Hitler, Hitlerism, and Nazi Germany. Every military advantage arising out of the surrender of Italy, should that occur, must be sought for this purpose.

3. The first of these is, in the President's words, "the use of all Italian territory and transportation against the Germans in the north and against the whole Balkan peninsula, as well as use of airfields of all kinds." This must include the surrender to our garrisons of Sardinia, the Dodecanese, and Corfu, as well as of all the naval and air bases on the Italian mainland as soon as they can be taken over.

4. Secondly, and of equal importance, the immediate surrender to the Allies of the Italian Fleet, or at least its effective demobilization and paralysis, and the disarmament of the Italian air and ground forces to whatever extent we find needful and useful. The surrender of the Fleet will liberate powerful British naval forces for service in the Indian Ocean against Japan, and will be most agreeable to the United States.

5. Also, of equal consequence, the immediate withdrawal from, or surrender of, all Italian forces in Corsica, the Riviera, including Toulon, and the Balkan peninsula—to wit, in Yugoslavia, Albania, and Greece.

6. Another objective of the highest importance, about which there will be passionate feeling in this country, is the immediate liberation of all British prisoners of war in Italian hands, and the prevention, which can in the first instance only be by the Italians, of their being transported northward to Germany. I regard it as a matter of honour and humanity to get our own flesh and blood back as soon as possible and spare them the measureless horrors of incarceration in Germany during the final stages of the war.

7. The fate of the German troops in Italy, and particularly of those south of Rome, will probably lead to fighting between the Germans and the Italian Army and population. We should demand their surrender, and that any Italian Government with whom we can reach a settlement shall do their utmost to procure this. It may be, however, that the German divisions will cut their way northward in spite of anything that the Italian armed forces are capable of doing. We should provoke this conflict as much as possible, and should not hesitate to send troops and air support to assist the Italians in procuring the surrender of the Germans south of Rome.

8. When we see how this process goes, we can take a further view about action to be taken north of Rome. We should, however, try to get possession of points on both the west coast and east coast railways of Italy as far north as we dare. This is a time to dare.

9. In our struggle with Hitler and the German Army we cannot afford to deny ourselves any assistance that will kill Germans. The fury of the Italian population will now be turned against the German intruders, who have, as they will feel, brought all these miseries upon Italy and then have come so scantily and grudgingly to her aid. We should stimulate this process in order that the new, liberated, anti-Fascist Italy shall afford us at the earliest moment a safe and friendly area on which we can base the whole forward air attack upon South and Central Germany.

10. This air attack is a new advantage of the first order, as it brings the whole of the Mediterranean air forces into action from a direction which turns the entire line of air defences in the West, and which furthermore exposes all those centres of war production which have been increasingly developed so as to escape air attack from Great Britain. It will become urgent in the highest degree to get agents, Commandos, and supplies by sea across the Adriatic into Greece, Albania, and Yugoslavia. It must be remembered that there are fifteen German divisions in the Balkan peninsula, of which ten are mobile. Nevertheless, once we have control of the Italian peninsula and of the Adriatic, and the Italian armies in the Balkans withdraw or lay down their arms, it is by no means unlikely that the Germans will be forced to withdraw northward to the line of the Save and Danube, thus liberating Greece and other tortured countries.

11. We cannot yet measure the effects of Mussolini's fall and of an Italian capitulation upon Bulgaria, Rumania and Hungary. They may be profound. In connection with this situation the collapse of Italy should fix the moment for putting the strongest pressure on Turkey to act in accordance with the spirit of the Alliance, and in this Britain and the United States, acting jointly or severally, should if possible be joined or at least supported by Russia.

12. The surrender of, to quote the President, "the Head Devil, together with his chief partners in crime," must be considered an eminent object, and one for which we should strive by all means in our power short of wrecking the immense prospects which have been outlined in earlier paragraphs. It may be however that these criminals will flee into Germany or escape into Switzerland. On the other hand, they may surrender themselves or be surrendered by the Italian Government. Should they fall into our hands, we ought now to decide, in consultation with the United States, and, after agreement with them, with the U. S. S. R., what treatment should be meted out to them. Some may prefer prompt execution without trial except for identification

purposes. Others may prefer that they be kept in confinement till the end of the war in Europe and their fate decided together with that of other war criminals. Personally I am fairly indifferent on this matter, provided always that no solid military advantages are sacrificed for the sake of immediate vengeance.[83]

On the following day (July 26) the British War Cabinet considered the paper and gave it their full approval. Churchill immediately forwarded it to the President, observing

I don't think myself that we should be too particular in dealing with any non-Fascist Government even if it is not all we should like. Now Mussolini is gone I would deal with any non-Fascist Government which can deliver the goods. The goods are set out in my memo herewith. My colleagues also agreed with this.[84]

Within twenty-four hours of the fall of Mussolini, the Prime Minister and the President had drafted statements of broad policy toward Italy. Churchill's position was well-defined; Roosevelt's, expressed only in a few words in his radio address and cable, was not so clear. One strain of difference emerges: Churchill was definitely committed to retention of the Badoglio government, if it could be useful. Roosevelt apparently was leaning toward the policy of dealing with no central Italian government after surrender, merely with local governmental authorities through military government—a policy that he later attempted to maintain in dealing with the French until after the Normandy landings. Furthermore, Churchill chose to describe the King and Badoglio as heading a non-Fascist government—a conclusion that Roosevelt evaded. The one suggestion of compromise on Roosevelt's part lay in his phrase "as close as possible to unconditional surrender." He too was anxious to reap all possible military benefits from the new government.

These differences were not entirely motivated by political considerations; strategy was also an important factor. The British preference for Allied attacks in Italy and possibly the Balkans, to draw German forces away from northern France and OVERLORD, would be substantially assisted by Italian cooperation with the Allies. The vigorous opposition of the American JCS to any Mediterranean "adventures," on the other hand, might lead them to look with suspicion on any dealings with the Italian government.[85]

Churchill was apparently sensitive to the divergence between himself and the President. In a speech in the House of Commons on July 27, he said:

It would be a grave mistake, when Italian affairs are in this flexible, fluid, formative condition, for the rescuing Powers, Britain and the United States, so to act as to break down the whole structure and expression of the Italian State.

It is the interest of Italy, and also the interest of the Allies, that the unconditional surrender of Italy should be brought about wholesale and not piecemeal.[86]

However, in his correspondence with Roosevelt at this time, he said nothing of this; and Roosevelt replying to Churchill merely suggested a few minor amendments to the "Thoughts."[87] These Churchill accepted and incorporated in the document which then received War Cabinet concurrence on August 2. Even before this (on July 31), he reported to Roosevelt:

I have not had time to consult my colleagues but I have no doubt whatever that our joint draft as amended expresses in perfect harmony the minds of our two Governments on the broad policy to be pursued. It seems to be a case of "two hearts that beat as one."[88]

AFHQ: Objectives and Policies

General Eisenhower received the news of Mussolini's dismissal before breakfast on Monday, July 26. Transcripts of the radio addresses delivered by the King and Marshal Badoglio were forwarded to him shortly after 2 A.M. About an hour later further reports arrived in Algiers from General Marshall. These messages were slightly delayed by having to be transmitted from Algiers to Eisenhower at the advance command post of La Marsa on the Tunisian coast. Shortly after breakfast, Harold Macmillan, British Resident Minister at Algiers, arrived to discuss the new situation. The reaction of AFHQ, like that of Washington and London, was immediate and concrete. This reaction was a direct product of the views and objectives of AFHQ in the Mediterranean theater. A brief examination of these views is necessary. If the military men in the field simply endorsed the objectives of their political superiors at home, few difficulties would be produced beyond those already implicit in the vaguely impending Roosevelt-Churchill disagreement. However, if they envisioned different objectives and policies, a third major element might well be introduced into the making of policy toward Italy.

Eisenhower's discussion of possible AFHQ policy toward Italy with his British political adviser, Harold Macmillan, but not with the U. S. political representative on his staff, Robert D. Murphy, deserves brief comment. Essentially, in late July 1943, the arrangement was an informal one.

Murphy had been appointed Chief Civil Administrator, Allied Forces, when the Allied armies invaded North Africa. He was "charged with the direction of political and economic affairs as a member of the staff of the Commander-in-Chief."[89] As such, he specialized almost exclusively in French and French North African affairs, especially in the complex relations existing between the partisans of General De Gaulle and those of General Giraud. Macmillan, on the other hand, was a member of the British Cabinet, appointed Resident Minister at AFHQ in December 1942. He was not, strictly speaking, a member of Eisenhower's staff, although he worked closely with both Eisenhower and Murphy. His original appointment was designed to keep the British government informed on political matters and to supervise British civilian personnel in the area. Shortly after Macmillan's appointment, in January 1943, a Political and Economic Council was established at AFHQ, "for the purpose of advising the Commander in Chief, Allied Force, on political and economic matters. . . ." Murphy and Macmillan were both appointed full members, thus providing a medium of official collaboration between the two. In addition, Macmillan was, in February, officially invited to "associate himself closely" with Murphy in his functions as Chief Civil Administrator.[90]

In May, the Foreign Office informed the State Department that the British government felt that Macmillan

. . . should be recognized as the channel between General Eisenhower and His Majesty's Government on all political matters, in which capacity he would whenever necessary be called into consultation and entitled to offer advice.[91]

The word "all" meant French *and* Italian prob-

lems. Both the U. S. War and State Departments were opposed to this step. As Assistant Secretary of War McCloy stated in a memorandum for Harry Hopkins:

The State Department opposes the introduction of Macmillan in the HUSKY scene. They are not using Murphy for anything except North Africa and do not wish or intend to place any political representative in the field. They want to deal in the initial stages entirely through the Combined Chiefs of Staff.

The English counter with the statement that Macmillan has no official position, is merely on the ground so that his government may get the benefit of his first-hand impressions which they would want to get in any case by reason of his ability and experience. They say that all they ask is that he should be able to look at all the cables as they come and go and communicate his thoughts to his Government or to Eisenhower as may seem desirable. While this is all they ask, it is a great deal, because you simply cannot have a Cabinet Minister on the ground, particularly one of Macmillan's character and ability, without his taking part in the play. . . .[92]

But when this position was cabled by Roosevelt to Churchill, the Prime Minister in his reply urged that the happy relations between Macmillan and Murphy and Eisenhower in the North African campaign be continued in Sicily and Italy. He stressed the desirability of the informal report of the two political representatives to their chiefs not as a substitute for but a complement to the formal communications via the CCS. He added that he thought Eisenhower would be pleased with such a statement on Roosevelt's part. Roosevelt concurred in Churchill's recommendation.

This was the way matters stood during the summer of 1943 when the negotiations for the Italian armistice were taking place—an informal arrangement. Murphy devoted most of his time to French and French North African affairs.[93] Eisenhower consulted Macmillan on Italian affairs, not because of his position (although this was obviously of some importance) but because of his experience, ability, and general background. Later on, of course, with the establishment (following the signature of the armistice) of the Allied Control Commission for Italy and Murphy's appointment to it,[94] all this became official and Murphy was given formal responsibilities for advising on Italian problems. But during these intervening weeks Eisenhower simply availed himself of the expert advice which, on an informal basis, Macmillan was able to provide for him; no doubt he would have turned to Murphy if Macmillan's help had been insufficient.

Returning to Eisenhower's views on Italy, it should be recalled that the Allied command in North Africa was, of course, operating under the directives of the Casablanca Conference to "knock Italy out of the war." Yet it was clearly recognized that this operation was subordinate to OVERLORD. To pin down German divisions, away from the Russian front or away from the projected cross-Channel assault, it would be necessary for Allied forces to operate on the Italian peninsula. An Italian surrender would certainly facilitate Allied plans. No political commitments were involved in these considerations. It would not matter what Italian group the Allies dealt with, so long as that group was effectively able to bring about a surrender of the Italian military machine.[95]

The appraisal of Italy's position by AFHQ at the time of Mussolini's surrender is well illustrated by the G-2 Weekly Intelligence summary for the week ending July 31. Fascism, the report stated, has been overthrown in Italy. The new government of Marshal Badoglio is a military dictatorship. Its major objective is to keep itself in power. It has done so thus far by a relaxation of certain controls in the name of democracy as well as by strong action to curb riots. However, it is evident that the new government must make peace or it will be unable to prevent Italy from falling into riots and anarchy. The report also recognized Italy's delicate position vis-à-vis the Germans. German troops occupied most of Italy and would not hesitate to oust the Badoglio government and replace it with a pro-Fascist quisling regime should Italy make the attempt to switch sides.[96]

This was the background of Eisenhower's thinking at the end of July. Anxious to deal with the new situation effectively and promptly, he proposed a concrete plan of action designed to achieve his military objectives. This plan was drafted into more precise terms by Macmillan, following the conference with Eisenhower and his aides on the morning of July 26.[97] In essence, the General proposed to employ political strategy to achieve his military objectives, beginning with a rapid advance onto the Italian mainland. His program to exploit the new situation in Italy was centered around two means: psychological warfare and a simple set of armistice terms.

In addition, Eisenhower's reaction also included some military planning. After a conference with his commanders in Tunis on the 26th, he proposed to the Combined Chiefs of Staff employment of alternative plans, BUTTRESS (attack on the toe of Italy) or AVALANCHE (landings in the Naples-Salerno area), depending upon the "military significance of recent political changes in Italy." A sudden seizure of Naples by a small Allied force was contemplated, in the event of an Italian collapse or a German withdrawal from southern Italy.[98] The Combined Chiefs of Staff in reply asked Eisenhower to prepare his plans for AVALANCHE, urged him to proceed as rapidly as possible, and told him that the Admiralty would furnish one heavy carrier and four escort carriers for air support.[99] But these military measures were distinctly subordinate to the more ambitious political strategy.

A Radio Appeal

The Allies had developed an active psychological warfare unit in North Africa. Its radio broadcasts and leaflets dropped by airplane were reported to have a concrete effect upon Italian morale. Eisenhower proposed to use this apparatus, to intensify its appeals to the Italian mainland. To remove Italy from the war and then to use Italian territory in the war against the Germans, Eisenhower proposed, in effect, a two-step plan. While in fact these steps are intricately related parts of the same project, an attempt must be made to separate them. Not only does this facilitate clear understanding, but the second of Eisenhower's proposed steps constitutes an early stage in the development of a set of armistice terms—a story to be taken up at a later point. Attention must therefore be directed to the first of Eisenhower's proposals—a broadcast to the Italian people. This broadcast would be directed to them via the facilities of the psychological warfare apparatus. Its object would be to build Italian public opinion to encourage the new government to despatch an emissary to open negotiations. Eisenhower would offer to the

Italians a quick and honorable escape from the war.

Under the General's direction, Macmillan prepared the text of a proposed radio message. Addressed to the Italian people, it commended them and the House of Savoy on getting rid of Mussolini, Hitler's tool. It told them that the sole remaining stumbling block in the way of an immediate and honorable peace was the German army in Italy. The Allies would liberate Italy if the Italians stopped giving any assistance to the Germans. Occupation would be as mild and beneficent as it had been in Sicily. All Italian prisoners-of-war would be released and in the ultimate peace settlement, Italy would be blessed with the protection of the Atlantic Charter and the Four Freedoms. In closing, the message called on the people to stop aiding the Germans and instructed the King to get in touch with Eisenhower.[100]

The message was significant in four respects. First, it recognized the continuing sovereignty of the King. Second, it made no reference to "unconditional surrender."[101] Third, despite the assurance of ultimate peace terms on the basis of the principles laid down in the Atlantic Charter and the Four Freedoms, the message was concerned primarily with an immediate military armistice. Fourth, the final sentence emphasized Eisenhower's conviction that AFHQ would be a principal in any armistice negotiations. The Allied commander was quite unaware of Roosevelt's intention that he and Churchill, not officers in the field, would make the final decisions.

Eisenhower regretted the existence of modern communications. He wished to be free to negotiate a quick military armistice with Italy on his own initiative and authority. If he were back in the days of sailing vessels, the General believed that he could arrange a speedy and advantageous settlement. The delay involved in communicating with Washington or London and waiting for instructions or approval was costly in his estimation. It was, however, the twentieth century and Eisenhower knew his responsibilities. At 5 P.M. on the same day (July 26) he despatched to the Combined Chiefs in Washington and to the British Chiefs of Staff Committee in London telegrams containing the text of his proposed radio message to the Italian people and requesting authority to pursue his plan.[102] The telegrams emphasized

the need for haste, on the rather odd theory that otherwise the King might inherit Mussolini's unpopularity.[103]

In Washington the message was considered by the American Joint Chiefs of Staff. They deleted any reference to the Atlantic Charter and the Four Freedoms, together with the entire concluding paragraph, which would have given Eisenhower the power to negotiate an armistice. However, the praise of the House of Savoy was allowed to remain and peace under honorable conditions was not superseded by "unconditional surrender." On the following day (July 27) Roosevelt forwarded the amended message to Churchill in London. Meanwhile, upon his reading of Eisenhower's draft, Churchill was struck by this provision:

Your men will return to their normal life and their productive avocations, and hundreds of thousands of Italian prisoners now in our hands will return to the countless Italian homes who long for them. The ancient liberties and traditions of your country will be restored.[104]

This was too high a price to be paid. Eisenhower's promise involved more than he apparently realized. Accordingly, Churchill promptly telegraphed a revision of this section to Roosevelt.

Former Naval Person to President Roosevelt
27 July 43

There are 74,000 British prisoners in Italy, and there are also about 30,000 Yugoslavs and Greeks. We cannot agree to any promise to release "hundreds of thousands of Italian prisoners now in our hands" unless our men and Allied men are saved from the horrors of German captivity and restored to us.

2. Moreover, apart from Italian prisoners taken in Tunis and Sicily, we have at least a quarter of a million Italians captured by Wavell two years ago and parked about the world. We think it is too much to offer the return of such a large plurality of prisoners arising from earlier phases of the war, nor do we think it necessary. We are ready, however, to agree to all Italian prisoners taken in Tunis and taken or to be taken in Sicily being traded against the British and Allied prisoners mentioned above.

3. Accordingly we suggest that Eisenhower's message at this point should read as follows: "Your men will return to their normal life and to their productive avocations, and, provided all British and Allied prisoners now in your hands are restored safely to us and not taken away to Germany, the hundreds of thousands of Italian prisoners captured by us in Tunisia and Sicily

will return to the countless Italian homes who long for them," etc.

Otherwise, we cordially agree with the message and to save time, I am repeating this telegram to Eisenhower, making it clear that he should not act till he has your okay.

Since writing the above, I have received Eisenhower's NAF 302 of July 27, setting forth proposed armistice terms. This meets our point about prisoners and seems otherwise satisfactory to us. It is being immediately examined. The broadcast, however, which is coming out before they have asked for an armistice, should still surely be amended as suggested above.[105]

Roosevelt concurred in a telegram to the Prime Minister on the following day (July 28).

. . . I have authorized Eisenhower to make an announcement to the Italian people incorporating therein your paragraph in regard to the return of Italians to their normal life, etc. . . . It now appears possible that by skillful handling of the situation we may be able to get Italy out of the war without the sacrifice of large numbers of our soldiers and sailors.[106]

Accordingly, General Marshall, acting for the Combined Chiefs, sent this message:

To Eisenhower:

Replying to your NAF 266, the following announcement by you to the Italian people is approved by the President:

"Message from Allied Headquarters to the Italian people. We commend the Italian people and the House of Savoy on ridding themselves of Mussolini, the man who involved them in war as the tool of Hitler and brought them to the verge of disaster. The greatest obstacle which divided the Italian people from the United Nations has been removed by the Italians themselves. The only remaining obstacle on the road to peace is the German aggressor who is still on Italian soil. You want peace. You can have peace immediately and peace under honourable conditions which our governments have already offered you. We are coming to you as liberators. Your part is to cease immediately any assistance to the German military forces in your country. If you do this we will rid you of the Germans and deliver you from the horrors of war. As you have already seen in Sicily our occupation will be mild and beneficent. Your men will return to their normal life and to their productive avocations and, provided all British and Allied prisoners now in your hands are restored safely to us and not taken away to Germany, the hundreds of thousands of Italian

prisoners captured by us in Tunisia and Sicily will return to the countless Italian homes who long for them. The ancient liberties and traditions of your country will be restored."[107]

This radio message was beamed to Italy, beginning on Friday noon, July 30.[108] It was, however, as had been noted, a considerably revised version of Eisenhower's original proposals. There was no mention of specific armistice terms (either immediate or ultimate) nor of the Atlantic Charter. Proposals for return of Italian prisoners-of-war were modified to insist upon the return of Allied prisoners, as Churchill had advocated. Despite this watering-down, this broadcast from North Africa was, according to Italian General Rossi, the straw that broke the back of Italian resistance to an armistice.[109]

Eisenhower's Armistice Proposals

A radio appeal to the Italian people was but the first step in Eisenhower's plan.[110] On the afternoon of July 27, the day before approval of the radio appeal, a proposal for a set of armistice terms reached Washington and London from AFHQ.

In the event that the new Italian government should in the immediate future request a military armistice, we must be prepared to announce at once the conditions under which such a general armistice would be granted by the Commander in Chief. It is important that the broad outline of the prescribed measures be approved in advance by the Combined Chiefs of Staff with the understanding that further details would be amplified and carried out by the Allied Armistice Commission which would be set up in Italy to operate under my general supervision. This particular matter has *not* been discussed in detail with my several Commanders in Chief.

It is to be understood that the conditions recommended below would be applicable only in the event that the Italian government asks for a general armistice *before* any actual invasion of the Italian mainland takes place. On and after such a date, the armistice with respect to German formations, now in Italy would involve the unconditional surrender of all German formations, at least those in contact with the Allies. It is considered that if the Italians should attempt to make a general surrender now, they would deem it completely dishonourable to attempt to turn definitely against their former Allies and to compel the surrender of German formations now in the mainland of Italy. Moreover they would not be getting the only thing in which they are interested, which is peace. Consequently, to insist on the particular point might prevent us from obtaining great advantages.

The conditions that I believe should be imposed are as follows:

1. Immediate cessation of all hostile activity by the Italian armed forces with disarmament as dictated by the Commander in Chief, and a guarantee by the Italian government that German forces now on the Italian mainland will immediately comply with all provisions of this document applying to German formations.

2. All prisoners or internees of the UNITED NATIONS to be immediately turned over to the Commander in Chief, and none of these may, from the beginning of these negotiations, be evacuated to Gemany.

3. Immediate transfer of the Italian fleet to such points as may be designated by the Commander in Chief Mediterranean, with details of disarmament and conduct to be prescribed by him.

4. Immediate evacuation from all Italian territory of the German Air Force.

5. Immediate beginning of the evacuation of German Land Forces from Italian mainland on phase lines to be so prescribed by the Allied Commander in Chief that the evacuation from all Italy will be complete within one month. German forces in Sicily are *not* affected by this armistice and will either surrender unconditionally or will be destroyed.

6. Immediate surrender of Corsica and of all Italian territory, both island and mainland to the Allies, for such use as operational bases and other purposes as the Allies may see fit.

7. Immediate acknowledgment of the overriding authority of the Allied Commander in Chief to establish military government and with the unquestioned right to effect, through such agencies as he may set up, any changes in personnel that may seem to him desirable.

8. Immediate guarantee of the free use by the Allies of all airfields and naval ports in Italian territory, regardless of the rate of evacuation of the Italian territory by the German forces. These ports and fields to be protected by Italian armed forces until this function is taken over by the Allies.

9. Immediate withdrawal of Italian armed forces from all participation in the current war from whatever areas in which they may be now engaged.

10. Guarantee by the Italian government that if necessary it will employ all its available armed forces to insure prompt and exact compliance with all the provisions of this armistice.

The above ideas are submitted in the hope that they may serve as a basis for an immediate directive to me by the Combined Chiefs of Staff.

My further idea in this connection is that the terms of this armistice are such that they could be immediately broadcast to the Italian population and, together with the message previously recommended to the Combined Chiefs of Staff on this general subject, would present to the Italian population such a promise of peace under honorable conditions that no Italian government could remain in power if it refused to request an armistice.[111]

Eisenhower's proposals apparently left nothing to chance. If he were approached with an Italian offer of an armistice, the Allied commander wished to be prepared. If the Italians were so uncooperative as not to make an offer, he proposed a propaganda campaign to persuade them to the proper course of action.

Several provisions in this set of terms are significant in their implications. Not only were the Italians themselves to carry out the provisions of the armistice but they were also to guarantee compliance by the Germans. This all too hopeful condition was presumably based upon the then current estimate that German forces in the peninsula consisted of only eight to ten divisions, and the further assumption that the Italian army could persuade even eight or ten German divisions to depart from Italy. Secondly, the terms did not envisage Italian cobelligerency in the war against Germany. Eisenhower considered such a "switch" to be dishonorable—a remarkably naive idea, in the light of what actually happened. Moreover, no references were made to "unconditional surrender." In contrast to Eisenhower's draft of the radio appeal, no mention was made of the Atlantic Charter and the Four Freedoms.[112]

Eisenhower's telegram, setting forth his proposal for armistice terms, received careful scrutiny in Washington and London. Roosevelt's initial reaction was one of cautious approval, expressed in a telegram to Churchill:

I am in agreement with you that Eisenhower's NAF 302 of July 27 seems satisfactory and will appreciate early information as to the results of your further examination of his proposed conditions for an armistice.[113]

Eisenhower's stated objectives were very similar to those contained in Churchill's earlier "Thoughts." A copy of the "Thoughts" was received in Algiers very shortly after the despatch of Eisenhower's proposals to the Combined Chiefs; thus the two documents were prepared independently. Their similarity indicates the substantial area of agreement between Allied political and military leaders on aims in the campaign against Italy. However, there were differences—and it is largely with them that Allied policy makers were concerned during the ensuing weeks.

Upon receipt of Churchill's "Thoughts," Eisenhower sent a cable to the Prime Minister which usefully summarizes some of the similarities and differences:

When your 4116 arrived, I had just dispatched a message to the CCS on the same subject. My purpose was to suggest to my two governments the general principles upon which an armistice should be granted if requested by the new Italian Government *prior* to any Allied invasion of the Italian mainland. My idea is that the terms should be so written that they could be broadcast to the Italian people. Such a broadcast together with that recommended by us yesterday to the CCS would hold out to the Italians such a hope of fulfilling their desires on an honourable peace that no government could deny it to them and remain in power. Details of the armistice would be worked out and administered by an Allied body that would be set up in Italy. I am delighted you have started discussion of the same subject.

I find that the points I made in my recommendation paralleled yours throughout except as to your paragraph 7. I think our different views on this point probably stem out of an expression you use in your paragraph 9, which is "the fury of the Italian population." It is my conviction that there is no fury left in the population unless it is aroused by desperation. The people are tired and sick of the war and want nothing but peace. Aside from this, the population would probably like to have a formula which would allow it to save face to some extent. Consequently, in approaching the item mentioned in your paragraph 7, I had confined my requirements to immediate evacuation of the whole peninsula by all German forces. However, I excluded German forces in Sicily which should either surrender unconditionally or be destroyed. If the terms of the armistice should present to the Italian population only an immediate choice as to partners in the war, we must not forget that they are under daily domination by the hostile troops they see in their midst. Consequently, the incentive to surrender will not be the same as if the whole population is given

the promise of peace. On the other hand, it is my belief that since we would require the entire Italian army to be available for execution of the exact terms of the armistice, there would certainly arise incidental conflict between Italian units and the German troops attempting to evacuate the country, and the conditions you visualize would probably come about spontaneously.

I should make it clear that these particular thoughts represent my side of a personal discussion and are merely those of myself and Macmillan.[114]

One underlying difference, although apparently small, was highly significant. Churchill was more willing to accord limited sovereignty to an Italian government which would take effective action against the Germans, providing, of course, it surrendered control over Italian armed forces and especially the fleet. Eisenhower not only wished full sovereignty over the Italian government—a position with which Churchill agreed—but the right to establish nationwide Allied Military Government if necessary. Both significantly also assumed not only that the Italians were free agents to negotiate and to put into effect an armistice, but also that they possessed the power to make the Germans obey.

The Prime Minister had a more fundamental objection to Eisenhower's plan. He vehemently disagreed with the whole idea of broadcasting armistice terms. Before taking up Churchill's objections, however, it would be useful to examine Eisenhower's basic position. The General's enthusiasm for a political offensive was increased by the disappointing military news from his planning staff. In the first hours following receipt of the news of Mussolini's overthrow, Eisenhower had inclined toward a bold policy. According to Butcher, he

felt inclined toward rushing a division into Naples area for capture of an airdrome three miles from the beach. Felt this was a time to take great risks as the enemy is upset, off balance, and excited. So little to be gained by pursuing BUTTRESS, which means merely getting a toehold on Italy, when a bold kick in the shins might cause Italy to give up the fight.[115]

But lack of landing craft and carriers simply made it impossible to launch an attack on the Italian mainland until early September.

At this time also (July 27), Eisenhower was visited by Secretary of War Stimson who was concerned with OVERLORD, and the effect upon it of further Mediterranean operations. Believing Churchill's position to be one of opposition to the cross-Channel invasion, Stimson wished to be able to present Eisenhower's estimate at the forthcoming Quebec conference.

Ike was confronted with a difficult situation: if he fails to exploit what now appears to be a rapidly approaching victory over Italy, history will say that he "missed the boat," yet our own government seems to want to slam on the brake just when the going gets good.[116]

Eisenhower's estimate was essentially the same as he had earlier presented to Churchill.[117]

He had always been for ROUNDUP or SLEDGE-HAMMER, provided the British would support it wholeheartedly, but there was much to be said, he thought, for exploiting our anticipated victory over Italy. By causing withdrawal of Italian troops from the Balkans, where there are said to be some thirty divisions, and others from France, we embarrass the Germans greatly because they will have to substitute troops for the arduous policing tasks. Mr. Macmillan had told us that commanders of five Italian divisions in Yugoslavia had informed British secret-service agents that they wished to surrender. And, over all, loss of Italy to the Axis would be a psychological shock to the Germans and an uplift to the peoples of the occupied countries.[118]

Three possible developments might theoretically occur on the Italian scene: (a) military conquest of Italy, or some part of Italy, by the Allies and imposition of "unconditional surrender"; (b) a tentative offer for a military armistice either by the Badoglio government itself or by a local Italian commander; (c) no offer from the Italians combined with Allied inability to impose military conquest, at least for the present time. The report of Eisenhower's planners removed the first alternative from the immediately possible. The Italians had made no move. This left the Allies with the necessity of devising a policy to fit the third possibility. The answer proposed by Eisenhower and Macmillan was the broadcast of terms to the Italian people.

The terms proposed by AFHQ were simple, comparatively informal, and comparatively lenient. They would provide for an honorable capitulation by the Italians and some latitude in negotiation over specific points. Moreover, a reasonable opportunity would be given the German forces in Italy to escape (on the assumption that they had any such desire). The underlying idea was, in effect, to make of the whole of Italy an "open city." When the Italian people knew the terms of surrender, Eisenhower believed, they would force their government to get out of the war. He did not envisage Italian co-belligerency in the war against Germany, but simply a withdrawal from the conflict.

Churchill was not impressed with this proposal from AFHQ, despite a personal plea from Eisenhower on the 27th.[119] After careful consideration of Eisenhower's telegram, he wired back:

Prime Minister to General Eisenhower (Algiers)
29 July 43

There are obvious dangers in trying to state armistice terms in an attractive, popular form to the enemy nation. It is far better that all should be cut and dried and that their Government should know our full demands and their maximum expectations. We are sending our alternative draft to your Government, and will no doubt reach agreement with them in plenty of time for any negotiations which you may have to conduct or which we shall be handling.[120]

At the same time, Churchill expressed his position in more detail to President Roosevelt:

Former Naval Person to President Roosevelt
29 July 43

4. The War Cabinet are quite clear that we ought not to broadcast armistice terms to the enemy. It is for their responsible Government to ask formally for an armistice on the basis of our principle of unconditional surrender. Then I suppose envoys would be appointed and a rendezvous fixed. Our version is already in your hands. As you will see, it follows the main lines of Eisenhower's draft, but is more precise and is cast in a form suited to discussion between plenipotentiaries rather than a popular appeal. There are great dangers in trying to dish this sort of dose up with jam for the patient.

5. We also think that the terms should cover civil as well as military requirements, and that it would be much better for them to be settled by envoys appointed by our two Governments than by the general commanding in the field. He can of course deal with any proposals coming from the troops on his immediate front for a local surrender.[121]

Roosevelt agreed with the position of Churchill and the War Cabinet that Eisenhower should not be permitted to broadcast armistice terms.[122] AFHQ received appropriate instructions late in the evening of July 29.[123] Thus Eisenhower's ambitious plans for achieving an Italian settlement through the medium of psychological warfare were disallowed by Roosevelt and Churchill. Both of them were opposed to military negotiation of an armistice and Roosevelt apparently also concurred in Churchill's belief that attempted negotiation by publicity would create difficulties in later dealings with the Italians. Aside from a passing reference in Churchill's cable of July 30, they failed to think of the possible danger in German reaction to a radio announcement that was designed to welcome Italian defection from the Axis. With or without a radio announcement, one essential problem remained clear: what should be the terms of a settlement with Italy? The other problem—what promises would the Italian government in fact be able to carry out—had not yet been recognized.

Short Terms vs. Long Terms

Work had begun on a concrete set of armistice terms for Italy within hours of the downfall of Mussolini. The issue raised by Eisenhower's proposal to broadcast the terms was in effect subordinate to the major problem at hand: the need for agreement on a comprehensive set of terms. This problem was obscured for a few days by the furor excited by the Eisenhower proposal; it came to the fore once that proposal had been rejected by his political superiors.

Shortly after Churchill's lengthy "Thoughts on the Fall of Mussolini" was received by the President, he referred it to the service chiefs for their study and recommendation. The document was reported back to the President as meeting their approval provided that several changes were made. Most of these suggestions were of a relatively minor character, such as the change of the conditions to be imposed upon the Italian fleet and air forces from "surrender" to "demobilization." All reference to surrender of the "Head Devil," originally proposed by Roosevelt himself, was deleted. One change, however, concerned a matter of vital importance. Paragraph nine concerned possible Allied relations with the King and Badoglio.

9. In our struggle with Hitler and the German Army we cannot afford to deny ourselves any assistance that will kill Germans.

This entire paragraph was deleted. Whether this change represented a reflection of Roosevelt's "no truck with Fascism" or merely cautious preference for military government over any dealings with a *de facto* Italian government, or perhaps something else, is not known.[124]

On the 30th, the President gave Churchill's revised recommendations his endorsement. "Your message," he cabled the Prime Minister, "expresses generally my thoughts of today on the prospects and methods of handling the Italian situation, with which we are now confronted."[125] Certain minor alterations suggested by Roosevelt were made in the document. Three days later, this amended statement of broad policy was approved by the War Cabinet as a draft joint directive to the Combined Chiefs from both governments.[126]

A fortnight earlier, there had arrived in Washington a lengthy document containing full military, political and legal terms for an Italian armistice settlement. It had been prepared by the British to put into effect the broad recommendations of the Prime Minister's "Thoughts." The proposal, entitled "The Draft Instrument of Surrender of Italy," was placed before the Combined Chiefs.

This comprehensive document, usually referred to as the "Long Terms,"[127] covered fully the following subjects and many more:

Unconditional surrender of the Italian Armed Forces, immediate cessation of hostilities, delivery of the Italian Fleet.

Delivery of merchant shipping and other property to the Allies.

Use and control of Italian territory and waters by Allied Forces.

Obedience of Italian officials in occupied territory to Allied instructions.

Obedience of Italian government to Allied instructions. Provision of Italian currency for Allied Forces. Subjection of Italian foreign relations to Allied control.

Seizure and delivery of Axis personnel and property. Apprehension and surrender of Mussolini and other war criminals.

Dissolution of Fascist organizations and repeal of discriminatory legislation.

Release and delivery of war and political prisoners, compliance with instructions on restitution.

Establishment of a Control Commission to supervise execution of the terms.

The Long Terms were soon challenged by a rival instrument of surrender. Eisenhower vigorously advocated a separation of military from political terms. In a telegram to General Marshall in Washington on July 29, he presented his reasons:

I am grateful that you obviously appreciate the dilemma in which I might well be placed in the absence of an advanced directive or grant of authority to act in the event of the Italian High Command seeking an armistice. What had worried me in this particular situation is the possibility that there might occur a vast but possibly fleeting opportunity to accomplish all that we are seeking in the Italian peninsula. I am perfectly aware of the fact that there are many implications and corollaries that far transcend military considerations as well as my own authority. My suggestions as to armistice terms were therefore limited to military problems. Actually of course the contingency mentioned may never occur. However, I deem it of the utmost importance that the two governments authorize me, subject to such general or specific instructions as they may wish to include, to act decisively. . . . While then waiting for all such proposals to be discussed at home, the Germans might possibly take effective military or other measures to eliminate the opportunity. It must not be forgotten that our only real opponents in the theater at the moment are the Germans and if through Italian cooperation we could seize a spot that would put the Germans into an indefensible position, this whole campaign might come to a successful conclusion very quickly, and this would save the maximum number of troops for other commitments. It is for the reasons hastily sketched above that I have asked the governments to give me some directive that will allow me to act promptly and quickly in the event that an authoritative representative of the Italian government should ask me for a military armistice. I request that you inform the President that it is only with military contingencies in mind that I seek advanced instructions in this matter. I feel that all economic and broader political problems can be handled by the two governments at their own convenience, and it is for this reason that the armistice terms I recommend stated with respect to military government only that it must be accepted by the Italian authorities.

The Prime Minister sent me a long telegram on this subject and I answered him along the lines indicated in this message. Since I already have a specific recommendation before the Combined Chiefs of Staff I will merely wait orders.[128]

To secure an immediate military armistice, Eisenhower needed to speak precisely and authoritatively. Therefore an approved set of military terms was necessary at once. A separation of military and political terms would, he believed, permit him to put an end to the Italian campaign. This ambitious plan sharply contrasted with the views of Eisenhower's political superiors, both British and American. In general, they believed that the Allied commander should possess authority only to accept a local military surrender of troops facing his armies. The negotiation of an armistice with an enemy government was the task of political leaders and diplomats, not generals in the field.

Nevertheless, after the receipt of his telegram to Marshall, Eisenhower's draft of military terms[129] was submitted to the Combined Civil Affairs Committee on July 29.[130] This committee (CCAC) was established by the Combined Chiefs of Staff in the late spring of 1943 and met for the first time in July. Its purpose was to "recommend civil-affairs policies for enemy or enemy-held areas that were occupied by combined operations and to coordinate military and civilian agency interests in such matters."[131]

The Chairman was an American civilian, John J. McCloy, Assistant Secretary of War. American membership consisted of representatives of the Army (Major General J. H. Hilldring), the Navy (Captain H. L. Pence), and the State Department (James C. Dunn, Political Adviser on European Affairs). British members were a representative of the Foreign Office (Sir Ronald Ian Campbell),[132] two members of the Joint Staff Mission in Washington (one of whom was Lieutenant General G. N. Macready) and one civilian expert.

The immediate task of the CCAC was to consider what instructions should be given to Eisenhower by the Combined Chiefs of Staff in effecting an Italian surrender. Sir Ronald Ian Campbell of the Foreign Office presented the British position: The Long Terms defined in detail both civil and military surrender terms. If Eisenhower were approached by the King or Badoglio, either or both of whom were considered acceptable as signatories of an unconditional surrender, he should be authorized to obtain the signatures. He should not, however, be permitted to negotiate. If, on the other hand, there existed *no responsible civil authority* with which to deal, the Allied commander should then be authorized to obtain signature to a purely military document embodying unconditional surrender.

The American members objected that the Long Terms did not make any plans for the disposition of German troops in Italy nor did they contain the principle of "unconditional surrender." John J. McCloy, civilian chairman of the Committee, pointed out that the President had emphasized the necessity to require an "unconditional surrender," as opposed to a negotiated armistice.[133] Moreover, the document made frequent use of the term, "United Nations." Mr. Dunn questioned this, pointing out that "an unconditional surrender could be accepted by the United States and British governments without consulting the other United Nations." The British replied that in preparing the draft of the Long Terms in London they had consulted representatives of United Nations present there and they assumed the United States would act similarly with regard to the countries of the Western Hemisphere. McCloy reminded the committee that Roosevelt and Churchill were discussing the matter, so that he and his American colleagues would have to wait until they heard from Roosevelt or Admiral Leahy. The Committee accordingly decided to wait for decision on the highest level—the President and the Prime Minister.

Roosevelt had agreed to the British refusal to permit Eisenhower to broadcast the Italian armistice terms.[134] At the same time, he again urged that Eisenhower be given authority to state conditions for an armistice on military terms, when and if the Italian government asked for an armistice, using the terms set down in his original proposal of July 27. "I am," said the President, "convinced that it is necessary in order to avoid unnecessary and possibly costly military action against Italy." At the same time, Roosevelt informed Churchill that Eisenhower

. . . should be directed to inform the Italian Government that details of the military and the civil requirements will at a later date be discussed and settled by envoys appointed by the interested parties. In any event Eisenhower should submit any change or changes in armistice terms to you and me.[135]

Accordingly, on July 30, the British War Cabinet reconsidered its position and agreed that Eisenhower should have authority to accept a general instead of a local surrender. These powers were to be used only in one specified situation. In the event that AFHQ were suddenly approached by an Italian envoy, Eisenhower "should have precise terms embodying the principle of unconditional surrender which he could immediately use as the basis for granting an armistice."[136] To the British, a general surrender meant surrender on the basis of comprehensive military *and* political terms. In other words, Eisenhower was to negotiate on the basis of the Long, not the Short, Terms.

The entire question appeared rather academic in British eyes. It was highly unlikely, they believed, that *any* approach would be made to AFHQ. As Churchill pointed out, Eisenhower's forces were in contact with the enemy only in Sicily, where the opposing forces were German. It appeared much more likely that Badoglio would attempt to negotiate through the Vatican, the Swiss, or through the Turks.[137]

Negotiations on the basis of military terms alone seemed risky in British eyes. So many important issues would be left in doubt. There was no guarantee that the Italians would sign a second document. Moreover, it appeared likely that there would be adequate time to work out a comprehensive set of surrender terms.[138] Why, then, settle for half measures when the affair might be handled properly? The Americans, however, continued to support Eisenhower's position that a separation of military from political terms was advisable and that an immediate military armistice should be arranged, on the basis of the Short Terms.

During the course of these conferences, a barely perceptible but quite significant change had been occurring in the nature of the proposed surrender terms. Originally, as McCloy had pointed out in the CCAC meeting on the afternoon of July 29, the President had insisted upon an unconditional, not a negotiated, surrender (as he had stipulated in the radio speech of July 28). Moreover, although he had not specifically reaffirmed the position of the May Memorandum on the House of Savoy, the President had not said that he would deal with the King. However, Roosevelt was greatly impressed with Eisenhower's program for achieving great military gains at small cost, specifically: the separation of military from political terms, the immediate use of these simple surrender terms to remove Italy from the war, and the postponement until later of a formal political surrender.

The President was gradually developing a position which differed a little, at least in emphasis, from his original attitude. Now he was willing, like Churchill, to deal with the King and Badoglio but not, as the British advocated, on the basis of a comprehensive political and military surrender. Instead he tended to favor Eisenhower's program of an immediate *military* armistice, to be arranged by Eisenhower rather than his political superiors. As a result, Roosevelt had accepted the possibility of a qualified unconditional surrender (as expressed in his cable to Churchill of July 26) and indicated a limited willingness to deal with the House of Savoy as represented by the King and Badoglio. While this position was developing, it is unclear how much the President's subordinates knew of his changing attitude, as indicated by McCloy's emphasis on Roosevelt's insistence on the principle of unconditional surrender at a time when the President himself was moving away from this idea.

However, doubt about the President's views on dealing with Badoglio and the King was removed on the following day, July 30, at a press conference:

Q. Mr. President, there has been some discussion as to whether we ought to deal with the [Marshal Pietro] Badoglio government, or with the King [of Italy], and so forth; and I wonder whether you might think it useful to clarify that point?

The President: Steve said you would ask that question. [laughter] I said to him it reminds me a good deal of the old argument—I could go on and have an argument about it—as to which came first, the chicken or the egg.

When a victorious army goes into a country, there are two things—two essential things that they want to meet, in the first instance. The first is the end of armed opposition. The second is— when that armed opposition comes to an end— to avoid anarchy. In a country that goes into a state of anarchy, it is a pretty difficult thing to deal with, because it takes an awful lot—it would take an awful lot of our troops.

I don't care who we deal with in Italy, as long as it isn't a definite member of the Fascist government, so long as they get them to lay down their arms, and so long as we don't have anarchy. Now

his name may be a King, or a present Prime Minister, or a Mayor of a town, or a village.

We have a great big objective. The first thing is to stop the fighting, and the second thing is to avoid anarchy. Now mind you, that is only the very first step.

You will also remember that in the—I think it was the Atlantic Charter, something was said about self-determination. That is a long-range thing. You can't get self-determination in the first week that they lay down their arms. In other words, common sense.

And I don't think that any controversy is either called for or advisable, because it puts the thing, at this stage of the game, into the "which comes first, chicken or egg" category.

Q. Mr. President, you wouldn't consider General Badoglio as the Fascist, then?

The President: I am not discussing personalities. It was only a columnist . . . who went on the air the other night that did that. [laughter] Gave his own personal views.[139]

The President's reference to the columnist was to Samuel Grafton, who had spoken of "the moronic little King" in a broadcast. The Office of War Information, lacking any guidance other than the President's speech, assumed the Allies would not deal with the King, and had rebroadcast Grafton's statement.[140]

The President had already sharply repudiated OWI's action in a news conference:

Q. Mr. President, could you say whether the broadcasts of the O. W. I. which have attacked the King of Italy were authorized by you or by the State Department?

The President: Neither of us. Nor by Bob Sherwood [O. W. I. Overseas Director]; and I think Bob Sherwood is raising Hell about it now. It ought never to have been done.

Mr. Early: He is, and it was a slip.[141]

All this was embarrassing and likely to cause much complaint from the same people who had objected to Allied dealings with Darlan in Algiers.[142] The President took note of this in a cable to Churchill on the same day:

President Roosevelt to Prime Minister 30 July 43

There are some contentious people here who are getting ready to make a row if we seem to recognize the House of Savoy or Badoglio. They are the same element which made such a fuss over North Africa.

I told the press today that we have to treat with any person or persons in Italy who can best give us, first, disarmament, and, second, assurance against chaos, and I think also that you and I after an armistice could say something about self-determination in Italy at the proper time.[143]

Thus, by July 30, Roosevelt's own position was clear. Military necessity would compel him to negotiate with the King and Badoglio despite these "political" complications. Later Italy would be entitled to "self-determination."[144] With this view Churchill apparently agreed:

Former Naval Person to President Roosevelt
                                        31 July 43

My position is that once Mussolini and the Fascists are gone, I will deal with any Italian authority which can deliver the goods. I am not in the least afraid for this purpose of seeming to recognize the House of Savoy or Badoglio, provided that they are the ones who can make the Italians do what we need for our war purposes. Those purposes would certainly be hindered by chaos, Bolshevisation, or civil war. We have no right to lay undue burdens on our troops. It may well be that after the armistice terms have been accepted both the King and Badoglio will sink under the odium of surrender and that the Crown Prince and a new Prime Minister may be chosen.

I should deprecate any pronouncement about self-determination at the present time, beyond what is implicit in the Atlantic Charter. I agree with you that we must be very careful not to throw everything into the melting-pot.[145]

There was, however, a fundamental difference between the effects of self-determination in the minds of the two leaders. The King and Badoglio might be removed, Churchill agreed, but the House of Savoy would remain. To Roosevelt, self-determination meant a complete political reconstruction of Italy as laid down in his revision of the May Memorandum. The fate of the House of Savoy would be in the hands of the Italian people. Dormant under military necessity, these differences were to come to the surface at a later time.

Following Roosevelt's proposal and Eisenhower's plea, the British War Cabinet reconsidered the issue of Short Terms vs. Long Terms. In a telegram to Roosevelt on July 30, Churchill accepted Eisenhower's draft proposals[146] with several modifications. He wanted the specific terms about the removal of German troops from Italy deleted, for the very sensible reason that any such promises would be unenforceable, and proposed instead that there be a general provision that the Italians would do their best to deny aid to the Germans.

He wanted general powers over all Italian government activities retained by the Commander-in-Chief in addition to the powers of military government. Finally, he wished the document to include specific provisions with respect to disarmament, war criminals and merchant shipping.

The President agreed to Churchill's very practical proposals, with one exception. In an answering telegram, he observed:

It is my opinion that the question of war criminals should not be brought up by General Eisenhower in a statement of his terms for an armistice. The war criminal problem can be taken up later, and I believe that all demands by the Allied Nations that are not essential at the present time should be postponed with the purpose of getting Italy out of the war at the earliest possible date.[147]

This was a rather important change for Roosevelt who had once emphasized the surrender of war criminals as an essential of any set of terms. He realized that an insistence upon the surrender of Mussolini might prove a major stumbling block to the conclusion of a quick armistice. Roosevelt observed further:

. . . I am in agreement that it is more likely Italy will negotiate for peace through neutral diplomatic channels but believe it necessary for Eisenhower to have precise terms of an armistice agreement which he may use in the event of his being suddenly approached by the Italian Government with a proposal to cease hostilities between the Italian forces and the United Nations forces.[148]

This exchange of messages was reported to Eisenhower by General Marshall, for the Allied commander's information.[149] No action could be taken by him, of course, until a formal directive from the Combined Chiefs of Staff had been issued. The text of the Short Terms upon which Roosevelt and Churchill agreed was this:

1. Immediate cessation of all hostile activity by the Italian armed forces.

2. Italy will use its best endeavors to deny to the Germans facilities that might be used against the United Nations.

3. All prisoners or internees of the United Nations to be immediately turned over to the Allied Commander-in-Chief, and none of these may from the beginning of these negotiations be evacuated to Germany.

4. Immediate transfer of the Italian fleet to such points as may be designated by the Allied

Commander-in-Chief, with details of disarmament to be prescribed by him.

5. Agreement that Italian merchant shipping may be requisitioned by the Allied Commander-in-Chief to meet the needs of his military-naval program.

6. Immediate surrender of Corsica and of all Italian territory, both islands and mainland, to the Allies, for such use as operational bases and other purposes as the Allies may see fit.

7. Immediate guarantee of the free use by the Allies of all airfields and naval ports in Italian territory, regardless of the rate of evacuation of the Italian territory by the German forces. These ports and fields to be protected by Italian armed forces until this function is taken over by the Allies.

8. Immediate withdrawal of Italian armed forces from all participation in the current war, from whatever areas in which they may now be engaged.

9. Guarantee by the Italian Government that if necessary it will employ all its available armed forces to ensure prompt and exact compliance with all the provisions of this armistice.

10. The Commander-in-Chief of the Allied Forces reserves to himself the right to take any measure which in his opinion may be necessary for the protection of the interests of the Allied forces or for the prosecution of the war, and the Italian Government binds itself to take such administrative or other action as the Commander-in-Chief may require, and in particular the Commander-in-Chief will establish Allied military government over such parts of Italian territory as he may deem necessary to the military interests of the Allied nations.

11. The Commander-in-Chief of the Allied forces will have a full right to impose measures of disarmament, demobilization, and demilitarization.[150]

The Prime Minister accompanied this approval with an emphatic statement that the Short Terms were, of course, only an emergency arrangement, to be used when and if the Italian government suddenly requested an armistice. If, as Churchill confidently expected, more time should be involved, diplomatic channels would be used for armistice negotiations. Then the British-proposed Long Terms would have to be the basis for settlement. What about the Long Terms? he telegraphed to the President on July 31:

We hope . . . that you will also urgently have our Instrument of Surrender examined, so that we reach full agreement on it. There are several points in this not dealt with in the emergency terms, and it is couched in a precise, formal, and legal vein, on which much thought has been bestowed here. We are rather puzzled to know why you never refer to this document, as it seems to us to be in fact only a more careful and comprehensive version of the emergency armistice terms. We should be very grateful if you would let us know how you feel about it. We ought certainly to have it, or something like it, ready as soon as possible.[151]

Churchill held to his original view that "any statement made to the Italian people should be agreed formally both by the Americans and ourselves and not merely put out by Allied Headquarters at Algiers, and anyhow it was very much better for the generals to go on with the military operations and to keep the armistice terms till they were asked for."[152]

However, in a message to Foreign Secretary Eden, Churchill declared that use of the Short Terms and then the Long Terms might be a sound policy.

Prime Minister to Foreign Secretary   31 July 43

Many things in life are settled by the two-stage method. For instance, a man is not prevented from saying, "Will you marry me, darling?" because he has not got the marriage contract, drawn up by the family solicitors, in his pocket. Personally I think the terms which Eisenhower may now offer are much more likely to be understood by an envoy, and thus be capable of immediate acceptance, than the legal verbiage of the Instrument of Surrender, and they will look much better if published. If we get emergency terms it means that the Italians will have given themselves up to us, lock, stock, and barrel. There would be nothing improper in our requiring them to hand over the pull-through and other cleaning materials afterwards.[153]

For some reason Churchill soon abandoned this neatly stated position.

Following the Roosevelt-Churchill agreement, the approved text of the Short Terms, together with authorization to use them, was forwarded to Eisenhower by General Marshall on August 1.

In case the Italian Government asks for an armistice, you are authorized to prescribe conditions contained in President's 332 of 30 July to PRIME (as contained in our 3824 July 30) with the following conditions:

In paragraph 4 of Conditions after the words "Italian fleet" add the words "and Italian aircraft."

The conditions will NOT be made public without prior approval of our two governments.[154]

Thus Eisenhower now possessed an approved set of military terms should Badoglio wish to negotiate an armistice.

Despite this agreement on the Short Terms, Washington and London were quite unclear on what to do with the Italian government after the Short Terms. Roosevelt was unwilling to endorse the British Instrument of Surrender (Long Terms). He approved its language but doubted the advisability of its use. "After all," he telegraphed to Churchill on August 2, "the terms of surrender already approved and sent to Eisenhower ought to be all that is necessary. Why tie his hands by an instrument that may be oversufficient or insufficient?" He preferred to let Eisenhower meet each new situation as it arose.[155] Nevertheless the President did instruct the Joint Chiefs in consultation with the State Department to re-examine the Long Terms.[156]

Accordingly, the American Joint Chiefs of Staff met on August 3 to re-study the British-proposed Long Terms. During the preceding twenty-four hours the British had made some slight alterations in their original draft proposal, presumably in response to the objections made by the Americans in the CCAC meeting of July 29. Despite these changes and the length of time since the Long Terms were first considered (at a meeting of the CCS on July 16), the Allies were no closer to agreement. The Joint Chiefs reiterated the earlier American objections and proceeded to advocate what they believed to be Roosevelt's views. The British draft, they objected, did not contain a statement of the principle of "unconditional surrender."[157] Apparently, the Joint Chiefs were still not aware of the President's changed position. Roosevelt had expressed to Churchill his desire to come "as close as possible" to "unconditional surrender." The securing of military objectives was, however, primary. The President was thus willing to negotiate a settlement with the King or Badoglio.

The American Chiefs had other objections to the British draft, among them its lack of consideration of the presence of German troops in Italy. Moreover, there was reference to a "Supreme Command of the United Nations"— a title which did not exist. Further, the document provided ". . . for implementing its terms by a 'Control Commission' under the authority of the United Nations, rather than by Eisenhower under the authority of the United States and British governments through the CCS."[158]

The Americans then proceeded to make further revisions of the British draft, with two objectives in view: (a) to satisfy the American objections and (b) to make the military provisions of the Long Terms identical with the Short Terms already furnished to General Eisenhower. Suggestions for a re-wording of the text came from the Civil Affairs Division and the Operations and Plans Division of the War Department.[159]

Both the Joint Chiefs of Staff and the State Department agreed that the revised document met all of their earlier objections. Yet the Americans were still not satisfied. In a memorandum submitted by Admiral Leahy to the president, this concluding recommendation may be found:

The Joint Chiefs of Staff and the Secretary of State agree with the view expressed in your message yesterday, i.e., to allow Eisenhower to act to meet the situations as they arise and to use as he sees fit the terms of surrender already furnished to him.[160]

In other words, disagreement no longer centered over the *substance* of the Long Terms but over making *any* political instrument at this time.

The difference in Anglo-American policy was clear and fundamental. Churchill advocated negotiations by accredited diplomatic envoys —negotiations based on a comprehensive set of terms, military, political and economic. Eisenhower might, however, obtain the signature of a responsible Italian political authority, in the rare case that AFHQ should be approached. On the other hand, *if no civil authority existed,* Eisenhower might obtain Italian signature to a purely military document, the already approved Short Terms.

Roosevelt had somewhat altered his original position of insistence upon military conquest and "unconditional surrender." He was now willing to have an armistice signed that contained the substance but not the phrase itself. Moreover, the President preferred to reach an immediate military settlement, meeting other problems as they arose. This change had been wrought primarily by Eisenhower's argument that such a policy might produce vast military gains at little cost.

The underlying reasons for the continuing disagreement over the Long Terms were never made entirely clear. It seems possible that Roosevelt feared that signing of the Long Terms would tend to confirm the status of the Italian government and prevent or hinder the Italian people from determining their own future. And he may well have wished to retain the possibility of disavowing the House of Savoy. The same line of reasoning would, of course, have pushed Churchill in the opposite direction. Whatever the validity of this speculation, in fact the Americans, under Roosevelt's direction, continued to delay approval of the Long Terms.

On August 5, the Combined Civil Affairs Committee met for the fourth time. This was the third session at which terms for an Italian surrender were considered. Since their last meeting on July 29, the President and the Prime Minister had, in effect, settled the problem of military terms by furnishing General Eisenhower with the Short Terms on the basis of which he could accept an Italian surrender. McCloy opened the discussion by pointing out that the Short Terms contained no clause empowering Eisenhower to impose additional *political* conditions, should he find it desirable to do so. The Committee perceived the importance of this comment and recommended insertion of such a "saving" clause.

Moreover, McCloy stated, such additional conditions to the Short Terms should be drawn up immediately. British General Macready asserted that the amended version of the Long Terms would satisfy this need since it contained *both* political and military terms. General Hilldring said that the President and the Prime Minister had already decided on a military armistice but that additional terms should be drafted immediately. The Prime Minister, replied Mr. Hayter of the Foreign Office, regarded the military (Short) Terms only as an emergency measure and continued to prefer use of the comprehensive terms. Dunn, representing the State Department, stated that it appeared desirable to prepare two documents, (1) an agreed version of the Long Terms and (2) a directive to General Eisenhower telling him how to implement the Long Terms.

The Committee decided to follow these suggestions and agreed that a cable should be drafted (subject to the approval of CCS and the Prime Minister and President) informing Eisenhower that the Long Terms were under consideration and that if the Short Terms were used, the Italians should be informed that a more comprehensive surrender instrument would follow.

This proposal was adopted by the Combined Chiefs of Staff on the following afternoon (August 6), and an appropriate order was sent to Eisenhower. He was instructed to add to the original military terms a new one, clause twelve:

12. Other conditions of a political, economic and financial nature with which Italy will be bound to comply will be transmitted at a later date.

The text of the Short Terms was now complete.[161] The addition of this clause preserved the substance of "unconditional surrender" in the Short Terms, even though the phrase itself was not included.

Thus, by August 6, the text of the Short Terms had been completed and in the form actually used later on in the first negotiations with the Italians at Lisbon on August 20. A considerable number of officials had shared in the development of the text from the original ideas of Churchill and Eisenhower. These included: Churchill, Eisenhower, Roosevelt, the British War Cabinet, the Foreign Office, the State Department, the Combined Chiefs of Staff, the American Joint Chiefs of Staff, the Combined Civil Affairs Committee, and, in a minor role, the Civil Affairs Division and the Operations and Plans Division of the War Department.

On August 6, despite the uncertainty surrounding the Long Terms, AFHQ was prepared to meet any peace feelers from the Badoglio government. The feeler never came. Or rather, it had already come, but not to AFHQ. Three days earlier, the Allies had had their first direct contact with the Badoglio government.

PRELIMINARY FEELERS

Disputes about Bombing and the First Italian Peace Feeler

The Allied bombing of targets in Italy and

particularly of Rome constitutes a topic in its own right. Nevertheless the execution of the bombing program in the summer of 1943 became involved in Allied endeavors to induce the surrender of Italy and led to the first "peace feeler" put out by the Badoglio government. Thus for a brief period, the two tales overlap.

Rome was an important cog in the Axis war machine. Not only was it a major headquarters of the German and Italian armies, but it was an all-important communications center. Through its marshaling yards passed men and materials on their way to battle with Allied forces in North Africa and Sicily. In fact, "all rail traffic between northern and southern Italy, with the exception of that routed direct from Bologna to such east coast points as Foggia and Bari, passed through Rome's two large marshaling yards, the Littorio and the San Lorenzo."[162] Obviously it presented a vital target for Allied bombers. Yet, before July 19, 1943, it had never been subjected to air bombardment.

During the early stages of the war, the British had used Rome as a sort of "hostage." They had prevented the bombing of Cairo and Alexandria by a constant threat to bomb Rome if the two Egyptian cities were attacked by the Axis. The strategy was successful. By June 1943, the situation had changed radically. Axis forces were no longer in a position to attack Egypt. Rome constituted a key link in the Axis defenses against Allied invasion of Italy. The tactical advantages in attacking military installations in Rome, especially the marshaling yards, were obvious. Moreover, attacks on Rome had definite political advantages. They might exert a tremendously depressing effect on Italian morale, might help to drive a wedge between Mussolini and the Italian people, and as a result would further Allied efforts to remove Italy from the war.

The Italian capital was, however, the site of many historical and cultural monuments. Damage to the city would be a matter of world-wide concern. Perhaps more important, within Rome lay Vatican City, world headquarters of the Roman Catholic Church. Any threat to its safety would be looked on with alarm, and might well be violently protested, especially by Roman Catholic leaders. This was of special importance in the United States, unscarred by the blitz, and with its millions of Roman Catholic citizens. The bombing of Rome was, therefore, a ticklish problem. At the Churchill-Eisenhower conversations at Algiers on June 2 and 3, bombing of the marshaling yards

. . . was agreed as essential in the air campaign to break up Italian communications. The recommendation that such bombings be laid on is being carried by the Prime Minister to the British War Cabinet and by General Marshall to the United States Chiefs of Staff, with a view of getting authority from the U. S. and British governments authorizing Ike to order the bombings. In this connection, Anthony Eden said at the meeting that Rome, like Naples, is on the supply line to Sicily. As the marshaling yards are on the opposite side of the river from Vatican City, and as the accuracy of our daylight bombing has been demonstrated, it was felt the Vatican would be safe from damage. Naturally, all are concerned with the possible political repercussions. . . . The Prime Minister had assured the President, after seeing Archbishop Spellman, that we would not bomb Rome for the present, but the Prime Minister now felt there was no tenable objection, as the marshaling yards are proper military objectives.[163]

After long discussion, and a careful appraisal of both the military and political considerations involved, it was decided to go ahead. In mid-June 1943, Eisenhower was authorized by the Combined Chiefs to bomb the marshaling yards but cautioned to avoid all harm to the surrounding city. The psychological warfare branch began to make plans to preclude unfavorable repercussions and warnings were dropped on Rome on July 3 and 18. On July 19—shortly after the invasion of Sicily—the Twelfth Air Force, carefully briefed, made its first raid. The raid, involving some 500 bombers, was successful, being directed primarily against the railroad yards through which the Germans were sending reinforcements to their armies in the south, but one church, the Basilica of San Lorenzo, was badly damaged. The Pope issued a mild statement regretting the action and hoping it would not be repeated but there was surprisingly little world-wide expressed resentment, except by German propagandists.[164]

The raid had a further impact, of great though indirect military significance. It seems to have been one of the events that shook the regime and helped to precipitate the dismissal of Mussolini. It happened to coincide with a

Hitler-Mussolini conference designed to plan the expulsion of the invaders and served as a demonstration of Mussolini's inability to protect his country.[165]

During the following week, the bombing of other Italian targets continued, but there was no further attack on Rome. On July 31, after a three-day lull in all bombing for operational reasons, a proclamation was broadcast in Eisenhower's name. It stated: "Italians, you know that on July 25 we let up on the aerial bombardment of Italy. We hoped thereby to give Italy a breathing space in which to unite for peace and freedom." This is intended to provide an opportunity ". . . for the new government to avoid further destruction in the country by accepting without delay our demands for unconditional surrender of their entire armed forces."[166] The proclamation went on to say that since the Badoglio government had failed to use the time advantageously, the bombing would be resumed. This proclamation was picked up in London and read by Churchill, who "construed the propaganda statement as emphasizing that the Allied forces had purposely laid off bombing of Italy after Mussolini's fall while Badoglio was forming his new government."[167] He was greatly annoyed that generals in the field should meddle in political affairs and make political pronouncements. He sent off a sharply critical message to Hopkins, objecting to the "anonymous and unauthoritative proposals pumped out by the machines."[168]

Eisenhower, informed by Washington of Churchill's complaint, was also disturbed. As it happened, he had not seen the proclamation, which had been duly approved by the appropriate British and American officers, civilian and military, at AFHQ. It was part of the general propaganda plan for inducing an Italian surrender. However, Eisenhower felt that Churchill's criticism might impair his own ability to take advantage of such opportunities as might occur. As Butcher reports:

Ike is more interested in getting the two home governments, through the Combined Chiefs, to give a broad outline of propaganda policy under which his staff for psychological warfare can operate. This will avoid undesired or virtual commitment of the home governments beyond the terms of the directive. He has sent this suggestion to General Marshall for the information of the President.[169]

The result was the formation of a combined committee with full authority over all Allied propaganda.

Meanwhile, at a conference with Eisenhower on the 31st, the Allied air commander, Air Marshal Tedder, reported that

. . . Badoglio was actively trending to the Germans and wanted permission to resume the heavy aerial bombardment of Italy, particularly of Naples and of the marshaling yards at Rome. Ike gave his assent.[170]

The bombing was resumed though Rome was not a target in the first few days. Meanwhile the new Italian government and the Vatican had not been idle. On August 2, Archbishop Cicognani, Papal Delegate in the United States, sent a letter to Under Secretary of State Sumner Welles. In it, he asked conditions for making Rome an "open city."

My dear Mr. Welles,
His Eminence, the Cardinal Secretary of State, has just informed me that, continuing its previous efforts to spare Rome the destruction occasioned by aerial bombardment, the Holy See has made representations to the present military government of Italy in order to have Rome recognized as an open city.
Subsequently to these representations, the new Italian government advised the Cardinal Secretary in writing, on July 31st, that it has decided to declare Rome an open city. It has furthermore requested His Eminence to ascertain the essential conditions which will be imposed by the Allies before the aforesaid declaration will be accepted. I shall be honored to transmit the reply of the United States government to this inquiry.[171]

Upon receipt of the letter, Secretary of State Hull telephoned its contents to General Marshall at the War Department. A few minutes later, Welles forwarded the document itself to Marshall, noting

When the War Department has determined the reply that should be made, if you will have it sent to me personally, I shall be glad to communicate it at once to the Apostolic Delegate for transmission to Rome.[172]

Work began immediately upon the preparation of a statement of conditions.[173] The letter appeared to be (and probably was intended as) a tentative peace feeler from the Badoglio government through the Vatican. It had, however, a more immediate effect—cancellation of the second bombing of Rome which had been originally scheduled for the night of August 3.[174]

Marshall despatched the news of Cicognani's letter to Eisenhower at Algiers. His telegram also contained this recommendation:

. . . This is for your information only. Pending further instructions it would appear desirable to refrain from air activities against the city of Rome proper. I am taking this up with the Combined Chiefs of Staff but meanwhile pass this view informally on to you. You certainly should continue to strike at such airfields in the vicinity of Rome as give evidence of being used by either the Germans or Italians.[175]

Scarcely had this advice been despatched when a message arrived in Washington from AFHQ announcing that the second bombing of Rome would take place within a matter of hours. The two telegrams had crossed in transit.[176] Marshall had to move quickly. A second message was despatched to AFHQ advising cancellation, at least until further instructions.[177] Hurried conferences were held with British and American members of the Combined Chiefs of Staff. At 5:30 on that same afternoon, August 2, Marshall telegraphed to Eisenhower a positive order. He was to refrain from air activities against the city of Rome proper, although strikes might be made against nearby airfields.

This policy had scarcely been agreed upon when a sharply discordant note was heard. Marshall received a telephone call from Churchill, asserting that he and the British Cabinet believed that the bombing should proceed as originally planned. It would be difficult to explain to the much-bombed people of London that the Allies were refraining from bombing such an important military target as the Italian capital.[178] The Prime Minister then promptly telegraphed his views to Roosevelt.

Marshall again had to act swiftly. The Combined Chiefs immediately sent Eisenhower authorization to proceed with the bombing if he so desired. This order, Marshall advised Roosevelt a few minutes later, could still be revoked by the President if he acted quickly.[179] Thus the final decision apparently rested in Roosevelt's hands. Early the following morning he sent this message to Churchill:

I consider it unwise in the time available to interfere with the military plans of General Eisenhower to attack with bombs today the marshaling yards and airfields in Rome.

However, I believe further raids should not continue pending outcome of Vatican efforts.[180]

In the event, Rome was not attacked on August 3. Marshall's first message reached Algiers about midnight of the preceding day. Eisenhower was asleep but General Bedell Smith, Chief of Staff of AFHQ, immediately took action to cancel the raid. By the following morning the entire series of messages from Washington and London reached AFHQ. Operating under the discretionary powers finally granted him by the Combined Chiefs of Staff, Eisenhower restricted air operations in the Rome area to nearby airfields which displayed enemy activity.

Meanwhile in Washington a memorandum was prepared by the War Department embodying the necessary conditions for making Rome an "open city." After approval by the President and concurrence by the British Chiefs of Staff the conditions were forwarded by the State Department to Vatican authorities for transmission to the Badoglio government. All agencies of the Italian government directly concerned in the conduct of the war must leave Rome. All military personnel and equipment must be removed from the city and all military movement prohibited within its borders. Provision was made for neutral inspection to ensure compliance with the conditions.[181]

Rome was bombed for the second time on August 13, under Eisenhower's discretionary powers. Two purposes were involved: the raid was undertaken to check enemy military activity in the area and it was also designed to increase the pressure upon the Badoglio regime.[182] On the seventeenth, however, orders came from the Combined Chiefs to suspend bombing pending settlement of Rome's status as an "open city." This problem continued until long after the declaration of the Italian armistice, and thus is not part of this story. However, the original contacts initiated by Archbishop Cicognani do represent the first—although tentative and indirect—peace feeler from the Badoglio government, and the brief flare-up over Eisenhower's policy on bombing was part of the continuing attempt to define his role in securing the surrender of Italy.

D'Ayeta: A Plea for Time

The first direct contact between the new

Badoglio government and the Allies was almost simultaneous with Archbishop Cicognani's appeal. On August 3, the Marquis D'Ayeta, newly arrived Counsellor of the Italian Legation, contacted the British Ambassador in Lisbon. D'Ayeta, a veteran Italian diplomat and statesman, had American relatives and was an acquaintance of Under Secretary of State Sumner Welles. He had just arrived in Lisbon and, in requesting a meeting with Sir Ronald Hugh Campbell, hinted that he was the bearer of a communication from his government. Badoglio thus used a diplomatic appointment—one of the few opportunities open to him to contact the Allies without German knowledge.

D'Ayeta's action had been authorized by a conference on July 31, where the King, Badoglio and other principal ministers had decided to negotiate with the Allies.

At Guariglio's request Cardinal Maglione of the Vatican staff relayed this news to the British Minister at the Vatican. Since the Germans knew his code he could not communicate with London. The American representative was in the same position and it was decided, therefore, to send emissaries to make personal contact with the Allies at Lisbon and Tangier.[183]

On the day following D'Ayeta's request, (August 4), Sir Ronald Hugh invited D'Ayeta to the Embassy. The Italian diplomat brought no specific peace proposals. His concern was to explain the position of his government: the King and the Marshal wanted peace. Action now, however, would simply mean destruction of the Badoglio government by the Germans and the establishment of a puppet Fascist regime. A pretense of collaboration with the Germans in the war must therefore be kept up. The purpose of D'Ayeta's remarks was largely to explain to the Allies the meeting of Italian military and diplomatic chiefs with their German counterparts, to take place on August 6.[184]

D'Ayeta's mission was immediately reported to the Foreign Office and to the Prime Minister. In communicating the news to Roosevelt on August 5, Churchill observed:

Fascism in Italy is extinct. Every vestige has been swept away. Italy turned Red overnight. In Turin and Milan there were Communist demonstrations which had to be put down by armed force. Twenty years of Fascism has obliterated the middle class. There is nothing between the King, with the patriots who have rallied around

him, who have complete control, and rampant Bolshevism. The Germans have an armoured division just outside Rome, and will march in if there is any sign of Italian weakening. . . . As many Italian troops as possible have been concentrated round Rome, but they have no stomach for fighting. They have practically no weapons, and are no match for even one well-equipped German division.

In these circumstances the King and Badoglio, whose first thought was to make peace, have no alternative but to put up a show of going on with the fight. . . .

D'Ayeta never from start to finish made any mention of peace terms, and his whole story, as you will have observed, was no more than a plea that we should save Italy from the Germans as well as from herself, and do it as quickly as possible.[185]

Berio: A Request for Terms

Two days after the D'Ayeta-Campbell conversations, a more positive proposal was made. On August 6, Signor Berio, another Italian diplomat, approached the British representative in Tangier. He too asserted the Italian need for time, but announced that he possessed direct authorization from Badoglio to open armistice negotiations.

It was clear from the tenor of Berio's communication that Badoglio was feeling out Allied willingness to negotiate on terms. The Italians were aware of the principle of "unconditional surrender." There was, however, doubt as to the real meaning of this phrase when it came to an actual armistice. Eden reported this new contact to Churchill, then at sea *en route* to Quebec:

We are entitled to regard it as an offer by the Badoglio Government to negotiate on terms. . . . Should we not then reply that, as is well known, we insist on unconditional surrender, and the Badoglio Government must as a first step notify us that Italy surrenders unconditionally? Subsequently, at a later stage, if the Badoglio Government were to do this, we should then inform them of the terms on which we should be prepared to cease hostilities against Italy.[186]

Upon receiving this report of Berio's proposal, Churchill noted on the telegram: "Don't miss the bus" and also "If they surrender immediately we should be prepared to accord conditions as acts of grace and not as a bargain."[187] These two marginal notes put into capsule form the Prime Minister's conception of what Allied policy should be. It was obvious that the opportunity to obtain an Italian surrender should not be missed. Nevertheless the surrender should be a genuine one; Italy must not be permitted to forget that she was a conquered enemy.

The Prime Minister then sent this reply:

We agree with the course you have taken. Badoglio admits he is going to double-cross someone, but his interests and the mood of the Italian people make it more likely Hitler will be the one to be tricked. Allowance should be made for the difficulties of his position. Meanwhile, the war should be carried forward against Italy in every way that the Americans will allow.[188]

Arriving in Canada for the QUADRANT conference, Churchill made his position more precise in a telegram to Eden at the Foreign Office.

Prime Minister to Foreign Secretary
9 August 1943

Badoglio must state that he is prepared to place himself unreservedly in the hands of the Allied Governments, who have already made it plain that they desire Italy to have a respectable place in the New Europe.

Reference should also be made to General Eisenhower's offer of the return of Italian prisoners of war taken in Tunisia and Sicily, provided Allied prisoners are speedily set free.

2. The object of the above is to convey to the Italian Govenment the feeling that, while they have to make the formal act of submission, our desire is to treat them with consideration, so far as military exigencies allow. Merely harping on "unconditional surrender," with no prospect of mercy held out even as an act of grace, may well lead to no surrender at all. The expression "Honourable capitulation" has also been officially used by the President, and I do not think it should be omitted from the language we are now to use.[189]

On the basis of these comments, Eden drafted a reply to Berio:

Badoglio must understand that we cannot negotiate, but require unconditional surrender, which means that Italian Government should place themselves in hands of Allied Governments, who will then state their terms. These will provide for an honourable capitulation.[190]

The draft continued along the lines laid down in Churchill's message of August 9.[191] Following approval by the President and the Prime

Minister, the British representative in Tangier was instructed to make an appropriate reply to Berio. However, this approach, like the two which preceded it, was tentative. It was superseded, this time by Badoglio's most important "feeler."

Allied leaders expected peace feelers from Italy as soon as reports of the fall of Mussolini were confirmed. They were not disappointed. Il Duce was dismissed on July 25. In the ensuing twelve days three preliminary contacts were made. These were followed on August 15 by the official and definitive bid for an armistice.

CASTELLANO'S MISSION

Cicognani, D'Ayeta, and Berio were but preliminaries to the appearance of the Badoglio government's formal bid for peace. On August 15 an official representative of the Italian High Command, Brigadier General Giuseppe Castellano, appeared in Madrid, empowered to speak with the full authority of the Badoglio government.

Castellano's entire mission was full of secrecy and drama, in the best traditions of cloak-and-dagger diplomacy. With Rome occupied by Germans who were already suspicious, the Badoglio government had to exercise great care in despatching this important envoy. An opportunity presented itself during the middle of August when a diplomatic group was being sent to Lisbon, there to meet on August 20 or 21 and escort to Rome the returning Italian ambassador to Chile.[192] Castellano, attired in civilian clothes and carrying a false passport, was added to the group.[193]

Shortly after their arrival in Madrid (*en route* to Lisbon) at noon on Sunday, August 15, Castellano managed to slip away (2 P.M.) from his companions. He took with him an interpreter, Major Montanari.[194] Together they went to the British Embassy. Most of the foreign diplomatic corps, including the U. S. Ambassador, had deserted Madrid for the summer retreat of the Foreign Office at San Sebastian.[195] Fortunately, the British Ambassador, Sir Samuel Hoare, was in residence. When Castellano produced a letter of introduction from Sir D'Arcy Osborne, British Minister at the Vatican, Hoare had the two Italians admitted.[196]

Castellano identified himself as Chief of Staff to General Ambrosio, Chief of the Italian General Staff, and announced that he came officially and with full authority from the King and Marshal Badoglio. He presented a vivid picture of an Italy weary of war and anxious to remove herself from the German alliance. But Italy was not a free agent; the country was thoroughly under the domination of occupying German forces. Castellano argued that Italy's primary desire was to fight the Germans. She was prepared to accept any peace terms which the Allies wished to impose if she could enter the war against Nazi Germany. However, the strength of the German occupation forces and Italian weakness made it imperative that Italy could not openly break with Germany until the Allies landed on the peninsula. Italian strength did not match Italian willingness.

In answer to questions put to him by Hoare, Castellano declared in effect: "We are not in a position to make any terms. We will accept unconditional surrender provided we can join the Allies in fighting the Germans." He declared that no proposal had been made to the United States government or any other quarter, that this was "the first official proposal." He explained that the Lisbon mission was his government's first chance to escape from German scrutiny to propose an armistice. Provided he could rejoin his mission by August 20, Castellano reported that he would be ready to fly to London. Again and again he emphasized the great need for urgency. He also said that although his mission was a military one, he was authorized to speak for the whole of the government.

Castellano seemed prepared to conclude an immediate agreement with the British Ambassador. Once this was completed, he was willing to furnish detailed information about German military strength and dispositions in Italy, together with proposals for Italian cooperation with the Allies in Sicily and with guerrilla forces in the Balkans.[197] When Sir Samuel Hoare protested that he had no authority to conclude any armistice nor, indeed, any agreement that Italy would join the Allies as soon as they landed on the Italian mainland, Castellano was obviously surprised and disappointed. He offered to talk with the Embassy's military aide, but Hoare assured him that his own lack of authority extended to all members of his staff. All that he could do, Sir Samuel asserted, was to inform the Foreign Office in London and await their instructions.

This was scarcely what Castellano had hoped to achieve. In his view, time was of the essence. The disparity between German power and Italian weakness in his homeland was growing.[198] He himself was part of a diplomatic mission which was soon to return to Rome. Castellano, like Eisenhower three weeks earlier, would seemingly have been happier in the days of sailing ships. Then agreements might be reached on the spot, without the delays imposed by communicating with far distant capitals. Castellano had to face reality. He asked if General Eisenhower could send to Lisbon a senior officer to participate in the forthcoming talks with the British Ambassador? This new proposal was dictated largely by the change of conference sites and consequently of the personnel involved. Badoglio knew Hoare personally, as a result of the Ambassador's earlier military service in Italy, and thus had hoped for talks in Madrid.

In his long conversations with Sir Samuel, the Italian envoy also added details to his picture of an Italy desirous of peace and cooperation with the Allies but entirely under the heel of the Germans. In sum, what the Italians wanted was to switch sides, provided the Allies landed on the mainland and protected them from the Germans. Castellano seems to have looked on the armistice itself almost as a mere technical agreement among friends.

Hoare of course immediately transmitted all this information to the Foreign Office, which promptly forwarded it to Churchill. Decisions regarding Castellano's proposals and the overall problem of the Italian surrender thus passed to Roosevelt and Churchill, and their advisers, assembled at Quebec. One topic on the agenda of the Quebec Conference was Allied strategy for eliminating Italy from the war by *military* action. Accidentally, by the course of events in distant Madrid, Quebec became the place in which a political and military armistice for Italy was decided.

The Badoglio government's peace feelers had come through diplomatic channels, as Churchill had predicted, and not to AFHQ. This fact alone was enough to prevent the fulfillment of Eisenhower's hopes for a quick armistice achieved in the field. Whether the modifications imposed upon Eisenhower's plans by his political superiors seriously impaired their chances for success is merely a subject for speculation. Certainly the plan had small chance of success even with complete Allied backing. The weak and war-weary Italian people, living in constant fear of the occupying Germans, were unlikely to rise up in a great demand for peace. Yet despite the failure of his overly ambitious plans, Eisenhower's role had not been without importance. His propaganda campaign, his success in Sicily, and the bombing of Rome had helped to speed the downfall of Mussolini and Badoglio's moves toward surrender.

The separation of Allied diplomatic and military channels made difficulties in keeping everybody informed and in harmony. Eisenhower had learned promptly enough about Archbishop Cicognani's letter. However, no word of the approaches by D'Ayeta and Berio reached AFHQ.[199] The isolation of AFHQ continued during the early reaction to Castellano's mission. On August 15, Castellano was ready and willing to provide extensive information on German troop movements and dispositions in Italy. This information did not reach AFHQ. Allied planning in the Mediterranean theater continued to be made on the basis of outmoded and imperfect data.

But the delay was not prolonged. It was only two days later (on the afternoon of August 17)[200] that a report of Castellano's mission (including the military information furnished by him) was sent to Eisenhower by Churchill. The message was forwarded by the United States European Theater commander in London, Lieutenant General Jacob L. Devers—a routine procedure.[201]

The locus of decision and action now passed to Quebec, where a major Anglo-American conference had opened on August 14.

VI. THE FIRST QUEBEC CONFERENCE (QUADRANT) (AUGUST 14-24, 1943)

From the close of TRIDENT, Allied leaders had generally agreed upon another major Anglo-American conference to follow the successful conclusion of Operation HUSKY. A meeting had been tentatively planned for late August or early September.[202] Events soon dictated that it be held at an earlier date.

The very rapid changes on the several fronts and, in particular, the overwhelming success of the Sicilian campaign made it imperative to hold the meeting earlier. The degeneration of Italian resistance and the possibility of complete Italian collapse, greatly increased by the unexpected fall of Mussolini on July 25th, gave birth to new problems only faintly foreseen in the spring. . . . The Prime Minister pressed for a very early date in August but the President replied that he would be unable to arrive in Quebec earlier than August 17th.[203]

At the President's suggestion, The Citadel, ancient fortress overlooking the Canadian city of Quebec, was chosen as the site for the conference.

The principal objective of the conference was the formulation of Allied strategy for the second half of 1943 and early 1944.[204] Military strategy was the primary concern. In addition, circumstances decreed that this meeting should determine the final policies for the surrender of Italy.

The British and American Chiefs of Staff began to arrive at Quebec late in the week of August 9. Their first meeting took place in The Citadel on Saturday, August 14, and talks continued through the following week. Actually, QUADRANT consisted largely of a series of technical staff conferences. The President and the Prime Minister met with their military chiefs in two plenary sessions to survey the results of the technical conferences.

The *Queen Mary* docked at Halifax on August 9, bringing Churchill and a large staff. While these exploratory meetings were getting under way, Churchill journeyed to Hyde Park, arriving at the Roosevelt estate on Thursday, August 12. For two days he and the President conferred informally. Hopkins was also present.

Following his informal conversations with Roosevelt, Churchill returned to Quebec on Saturday, August 14. On Monday morning four telegrams arrived from Eden in London, reporting Castellano's meetings with the British Embassy at Madrid and containing a full account of the Italian peace proposals.[205] Churchill outlined a reply to Castellano in a telegram to the President. This was Roosevelt's first report of Castellano's mission.

Like the previous Italian feelers (D'Ayeta, Berio), information had gone through British diplomatic channels: Ambassador to Foreign Office to Prime Minister. In each case, Churchill immediately informed Roosevelt.

Churchill's draft reply to Castellano is significant. He sharply rejected the basic Italian request:

We note the statement of Italian envoy: "We are not in a position to make any terms. We will accept unconditional surrender, provided we can join as allies in fighting the Germans." We, the Allies, for our part cannot make any bargain about Italy changing sides, nor can we make plans in common at this stage.[206]

Thus the draft took note of Badoglio's acceptance of "unconditional surrender," but did not stress the point and made no mention of Short Terms nor of Long Terms. Churchill's basic point was simple: By taking action against the Germans (by direct military action, by sabotaging German communications, by aiding Allied prisoners, by furnishing military information to the Allies, and by aiding guerrillas in the Balkans), Italy would gain Allied favor.

Thus, by taking action against the common enemy, the Italian Government, Army, and people could without any bargain facilitate a more friendly relationship with United Nations.

These provisions were based upon two important assumptions: (a) a willingness of the whole Badoglio government and of the Italian people to work *actively* to save themselves, combined with their ability to do so, in other words, taking Castellano's views at their face value, (b) a belief that a strong hint of better things to come could properly accompany unconditional surrender.

At the close of his telegram to Roosevelt, Churchill noted:

Eden should be here tomorrow, and we can discuss the whole position together. I send you this budget in order that you may see the way my mind is working.

The Chiefs of Staff are considering the practical steps and timings required to make an Italian turnover effective.[207]

Now, for the first time, AFHQ was informed of the Italian moves. A telegram was despatched to Eisenhower containing, for his information only, the four reports which had been sent from Madrid to the Foreign Office and thence to Churchill. "These telegrams," noted the covering message, "are being studied at QUADRANT and decisions may be taken tomorrow night, Tuesday, August 17."[208]

Eisenhower discussed the cable with Macmillan and with his G-2, Brigadier K. W. D. Strong. He then sent a cable to Washington (for immediate transmission to the Combined Chiefs at Quebec) declaring:

I have seen messages Number Concrete 231, 232, 233, and 234 from the Foreign Secretary to the Prime Minister. I have the following suggestions to offer. First, if the CCS should direct me to send a staff officer to Lisbon, I believe he should go with the following general instructions: (a) to collect information and check it against that already in his possession; (b) to inform General Castellano that the Allied force here makes *no* promise in advance but that if the Italian Army is really anxious to speed up the date when an Allied force lands in Italy, it should proceed at once with widespread sabotaging operations, particularly directed against all communications, airfields and public utilities useful to the Germans; (c) that the Italian government and army have no recourse except to depend upon the

decency and sense of justice of the Allied governments when once we have arrived in Italy.

My second suggestion is that if I am *not* directed to send a staff officer to Lisbon that the British military attaché at that place be directed to secure every possible item of information he can from General Castellano and forward it to this headquarters by early cable.

If I am directed to send a staff officer to Lisbon, the individual will be Brigadier Strong of the British Army, head of my intelligence division. He will travel in civilian clothes with passport duly issued by the local British consulate.[209]

Eisenhower's telegram arrived at Quebec while decisions regarding Italy were under discussion.

Following his meeting with Churchill at Hyde Park, the President returned to Washington for last-minute conferences with his advisers. With Hopkins, he arrived at Quebec on Tuesday, August 17. Eden and Brendan Bracken flew in from London on the same day to take their places at the conference.

On the 19th, QUADRANT's first full session convened. In their preliminary meetings, the military chiefs had drawn up a comprehensive report on the war strategy for the remaining months of 1943 and early 1944. A principal concern of QUADRANT was the approval of plans for Operation OVERLORD, the projected cross-Channel invasion (target date, May 1, 1944). One section of the final report of the Combined Chiefs of Staff, presented on the 24th, specified:

As between Operation "Overlord" and operations in the Mediterranean, where there is a shortage of resources available, resources will be distributed and employed with the main object of ensuring the success of "Overlord." Operations in the Mediterranean Theatre will be carried out with the forces allotted at "Trident," except in so far as these may be varied by decision of the Combined Chiefs of Staff.[210]

These provisions, together with the setting of a fixed target date, alleviated at least temporarily American fears that the British were attempting to postpone OVERLORD indefinitely or to divert its resources into a Mediterranean "sideshow."[211] The essential point at this time was, however, British insistence that, for OVERLORD to be successful, several preconditions must be met. Among these was

. . . the opposition on land must not exceed a given figure during the first nine days of the operation nor must it be reinforced beyond a further figure for the first two months of the campaign.[212]

More specifically, in addition to holding the German forces in the projected landing area below a certain total, the Allies must also ensure that

the Germans should not be in a position to transfer to France from other fronts in Europe more than fifteen divisions of the first quality during the first two months of the campaign.[213]

These preconditions could be met only by operations in other areas, designed to attract and keep committed German forces which might otherwise be free to defend against OVERLORD. The only area in which such operations could be effectively undertaken was the Mediterranean, principally Italy. "But such operations in turn must not attract Allied forces which might otherwise be devoted or added to 'Overlord' itself."[214] The critical point at issue between the Allies was that ". . . where the British feared that 'Overlord' would fail without larger diversionary operations in the south, the Americans feared that those operations would grow so large that 'Overlord' would fail."[215] These issues of over-all strategy of course played a vital role in the development of Allied policy toward Italy.

Several immediate results of these policy decisions were not welcomed at AFHQ. As Butcher records it,

Yesterday Ike stewed because the Combined Chiefs had ordered that the three groups of American bombers sent here to bomb the Ploesti oil fields and the Vienna fighter factories return to England. Ike feels most strongly that because of the higher percentage of good weather for bombing activities in the Mediterranean and because we need the groups here to help take Italy, the Combined Chiefs of Staff have made an unwise decision. He is combatting it. General Spaatz said that weather in the Mediterranean permits more bombing operations in one month than are permitted by the bad flying weather in the U. K. in three months.[216]

Similar objections were raised to the Combined Chiefs' refusal of a temporary loan of LST's on their way to India.

In addition, the Combined Chiefs of Staff reaffirmed their decision to withdraw seven divisions —four American and three British—from this theater starting November 1.

Ike has felt that his bosses have already dis-

counted an Italian victory and, consequently, are stripping his fighting force prematurely and not taking sufficient notice of the rapid build-up of German forces in Italy, which has now reached some fifteen divisions. It is becoming increasingly apparent that the Germans intend to defend their European Citadel as far from Germany as possible and will make Italy a battleground whether the Italians co-operate or not.[217]

Churchill expressed hope, in a memorandum dated August 17, that Allied operations plus disintegration in Italy would permit establishment of a line as far north as Leghorn and Ancona by November. Thereafter, with good ports in Allied hands, landing craft would not be needed (except for a few minor efforts) in the Italian theater and could be sent to England for OVERLORD.[218] He thus hoped to "have the best of both worlds." Whether his plan would have worked, in the light of later events, is highly doubtful.

On August 17, two days earlier than this important determination of policy, the Chiefs of Staff at Quebec having considered Eisenhower's recommendations,[219] agreed upon the objectives of the campaign in Italy. These were made specific in the final report:

OPERATIONS IN ITALY

(a) First phase. The elimination of Italy as a belligerent and establishment of air bases in the Rome area, and, if feasible, further north.

(b) Second phase. Seizure of Sardinia and Corsica.

(c) Third phase. The maintenance of unremitting pressure on German forces in Northern Italy, and the creation of the conditions required for "Overlord" and of a situation favourable for the eventual entry of our forces, including the bulk of the re-equipped French Army and Air Force into Southern France.[220]

Approval was given at the full session of the conference on August 19.[221] As Marshall expressed it in his later *Report,*

Compelling reasons had developed for the invasion of the Italian mainland. The operation . . . would enable us to capitalize on the collapse of Italian resistance; it offered a field of engaging German divisions which otherwise might operate against the Red Army and later against the forces in France; it would provide airfields from which the German homeland and the Balkans could be bombed from substantially shorter range; it would complete Allied control of the Mediterranean.[222]

These plans were based upon two fundamental assumptions: (a) an Italian surrender; (b) a withdrawal of the Germans northward. The fall of the Rome area as a minimum result of these two factors was also assumed. Therefore no plans were made independently to conquer Rome and southern Italy. However, the presence of sixteen German divisions in Italy, with an additional twenty in France from which reinforcements could be drawn, made such prospects dim for Eisenhower's limited forces. Indeed, the falsity of the second assumption of German withdrawal rendered the correctness of the first of limited value; and Rome proved to be no ripe plum.

In addition, the Combined Chiefs made no plans concerning the Italian armed forces. This was not considered necessary. The members knew about the Italian offer to surrender, delivered by General Castellano at Lisbon two days earlier. Moreover, the Quebec Conference had already formulated a positive course of action in response to Castellano's proposals for an Italian armistice. This course of action took the form of two directives, the Quebec Memorandum and the Long Terms.

THE QUEBEC MEMORANDUM

At their morning meeting on August 17, the Combined Chiefs of Staff drafted a memorandum entitled "Suggested Action on Italian Peace Feelers." It was based upon

a. the "unconditional surrender" formula
b. Churchill's draft reply to Castellano
c. the approved text of the Short Terms
d. knowledge of the still pending Long Terms
e. a very imperfect realization of the internal situation in Italy and its effect upon Allied military strategy
f. the detailed accounts from Madrid of Castellano's information and proposals, especially for a Lisbon meeting, and, before their drafting was completed,
g. Eisenhower's cable of August 17.

This memorandum, prepared by the Combined Chiefs of Staff for submission to the President and Prime Minister, was completed late on August 17. Following their approval, it was forwarded to Eisenhower.[223]

18 August 1943
The President and Prime Minister to General Eisenhower:
The President and the Prime Minister having

approved, the Combined Chiefs of Staff direct you to send at once to Lisbon two Staff Officers, one United States and one British. They should report upon arrival to the British Ambassador. They should take with them the agreed armistice terms which have already been sent to you. Acting on instructions, the British Ambassador in Lisbon will have arranged a meeting with General Castellano. Your Staff Officers will be present at this meeting.

2. At this meeting a communication to General Castellano will be made on the following lines:

The unconditional surrender of Italy is accepted on the terms stated in the document to be handed to him [i.e. the Short Terms]. (He should then be given the armistice terms for Italy already agreed and previously sent to you. He should be told that these do *not* include political, economic, or financial terms, which will be communicated later by other means.)

These terms do *not* visualize the active assistance of Italy in fighting the Germans. The extent to which the terms will be modified in favour of Italy will depend on how far the Italian Government and people do in fact aid the United Nations against Germany during the remainder of the war. The United Nations, however, state without reservation that wherever Italian forces or Italians fight Germans or destroy German property or hamper German movement they will be given all possible support by the forces of the United Nations. Meanwhile, provided information about the enemy is immediately and regularly supplied, Allied bombing will so far as possible be directed upon targets which affect the movements and operations of German forces.

The cessation of hostilities between the United Nations and Italy will take effect from a date and hour to be notified by General Eisenhower.

Italian Government must undertake to proclaim the armistice immediately it is announced by General Eisenhower, and to order their forces and people from that hour to collaborate with the Allies and to resist the Germans.

The Italian Government must, at the hour of the armistice, order that all United Nations prisoners in danger of capture by the Germans shall be immediately released.

The Italian Government must, at the hour of the armistice, order the Italian Fleet and as much of their merchant shipping as possible to put to sea for Allied ports. As many military aircraft as possible shall fly to Allied bases. Any ships or aircraft in danger of capture by the Germans must be destroyed.

3. General Castellano should be told that meanwhile there is a good deal that Badoglio can do without the Germans becoming aware of what

is afoot. The precise character and extent of action must be left to his judgment, but the following are the general lines which should be suggested to him:

General passive resistance throughout the country, if this order can be conveyed to local authorities without the Germans knowing. . . .

Germans must not be allowed to take over Italian coast defense.

Make arrangements to be put in force at the proper time for Italian formations in the Balkans to march to the coast, with a view to their being taken off to Italy by the United Nations.[224]

The content of this directive follows familiar lines; the only new turn is the decision to authorize Eisenhower, through his staff officers, to negotiate with the Italian emissary. Roosevelt and Churchill had both been emphatic about the desirability of excluding soldiers from diplomatic negotiations, yet they now accepted this proposal, apparently without demur. The basic reason for adopting this procedure was the situation which had arisen in Lisbon. Castellano, a representative of the Italian High Command, had proposed military conversations, a proposal seconded by Eisenhower. Moreover, and perhaps most important, the Lisbon mission appeared to be the principal and (given the watchfulness of the Germans) perhaps the only opportunity available for armistice negotiations with the Badoglio government. In addition, the Short Terms were ready for immediate use, while the political, economic, and financial terms were not yet even agreed upon.

On August 18, Roosevelt and Churchill cabled Stalin about Castellano's proposal and about their own instructions to Eisenhower.[225] They continued to keep Stalin informed of progress and invited Russian participation in the armistice, even though Stalin replied to one of the messages with suspicion and great discourtesy.[226] But the course of Russian relations in connection with the events in Italy lies outside the scope of this narrative.[227]

With the question of immediate action settled, the conferees at Quebec could turn to longer-range problems—the Long Terms.

THE "LONG TERMS" AT QUEBEC

In the interval between August 6 and the opening of the Quebec Conference, much had happened in the controversy of Long Terms vs. Short Terms. While the center of the stage had been occupied with the series of Italian peace feelers, negotiations on Allied policy had proceeded.

Roosevelt and Churchill had on July 31 agreed by telegram on the Short Terms. Roosevelt was satisfied. Churchill accepted the Short Terms only as an emergency matter, in the rare case that no civil authority existed in Italy; otherwise comprehensive terms should be employed. (This was a reversal of the position that Churchill had taken in his cable to Eden on July 31.[228]) The British members of the Combined Civil Affairs Committee therefore continued to urge political and economic terms. On August 6, Eisenhower had been directed to indicate, if he used the Short Terms, that additional conditions would be imposed later. The form of these additional terms was not clear to the members of the Combined Civil Affairs Committee. They might be a list of purely political and economic terms, *supplementary* to the Short Terms. On the other hand, they might constitute a single comprehensive document (like the British "Draft Instrument of Surrender") to *supersede* the Short Terms.[229]

At their fifth meeting on the afternoon of August 12, the CCAC began examination of the much-revised British draft of comprehensive terms. General Hilldring, speaking for the United States members, said that the President, who had been satisfied with the Short Terms, might be hesitant to have it superseded by the British Long Terms. Yet there should be a comprehensive instrument if the Italians offered to surrender to the British, or United States, government rather than to Eisenhower. Therefore, the Committee should prepare a statement of supplementary non-military terms to be forwarded to Eisenhower via the CCS. The Committee should also prepare a directive for Eisenhower telling him how to implement either the Short or Long Terms.

Sir Ronald Ian Campbell reiterated Churchill's position that the Short Terms were to be used only in an emergency. Moreover, the British continued to hope that there would be sufficient time to approve a comprehensive document. In their view, not only was this desirable, but there was difficulty in separating military from non-military terms to create two separate sets of terms. And in any case the military provisions of the Long Terms covered their respective areas more fully and precisely than the equivalent provisions of the Short Terms.

The proposal was then advanced by General Hilldring that, in effect, the President and the Prime Minister themselves decide the issue. Alternative documents—one comprehensive, the other containing non-military provisions to supplement the Short Terms—would be presented to the Combined Chiefs for submission to the two leaders at the QUADRANT Conference.

Dunn approved this suggestion, merely noting that the two documents should be accompanied by a statement of the views of the CCAC members. Campbell also concurred but suggested that, to satisfy the view of his government that the Short Terms needed amplification, additional and supplementary military terms be drafted as well.

The Committee finally agreed to follow these suggestions, in order to have ready a comprehensive set of terms and also a document containing the political, economic, and fiscal conditions (as well as additional military terms) to supplement the military terms already furnished to Eisenhower. They also agreed to draft a directive for Eisenhower to use in effecting the surrender terms. Thus the Committee decided to prepare for either course of action, leaving the final decision up to Roosevelt and Churchill at the Quebec Conference.

Preliminary drafts of these three documents were prepared at a special meeting of several Committee members on Friday morning, August 13. Then, at a special full session on the 21st, these drafts were examined. With two minor alterations, the first document, "The Draft Instrument of Surrender of Italy" (Long Terms), was given approval.[230]

In discussing the second draft, the Additional Conditions to be sent to Eisenhower as a supplement to the Short Terms if the Long Terms were not used, the recurrent Anglo-American disagreement over the House of Savoy reared its head.[231] J. Wesley Jones, acting for Dunn as representative of the State Department, pointed out a major inconsistency between the Additional Conditions and the third document, the draft Directive to Eisenhower. The Directive provided for suspension of all prerogatives of the Crown; no such provision was incorpo-

rated in the Additional Conditions. R. E. Barclay of the Foreign Office stated that even if the prerogatives were suspended in occupied areas, his government would not agree to any such suspension in unoccupied areas.

Since the official position of the British government on these two new documents had not yet been received by the Committee members, it was decided to postpone decision on this point until further word from London was received. However, recognizing the need for speedy action, the Committee decided to combine into one memorandum to accompany the documents the differing views of the British and United States delegates.

In further discussion of the Directive to Eisenhower for putting the armistice terms into effect (Directive of Military Government of Continental Italy and Sardinia), British representative Barclay stated that his government favored use of the HUSKY Directive for those portions of Italy occupied by Allied troops. However, the British believed that "additional guidance" should be furnished for unoccupied areas. With these views the Committee was in agreement.

As a result, the three documents, together with a statement of the British and American views on the advantages and disadvantages of each, were submitted to the Combined Chiefs at Quebec. This briefly summarizes the history of the Long Terms up to the opening of QUADRANT.[232]

Shortly after the arrival of Secretary of State Hull at Quebec on August 20, Eden brought up the matter of the Long Terms. Hull consulted Roosevelt and learned that Roosevelt had been discussing the question with Churchill. There was no change in the President's attitude. Negotiations were to proceed on the basis of the Short Terms as held by Eisenhower, with the understanding that additional political, economic, and financial terms would be imposed later following imposition of the military terms. Hull neither recommended nor objected to the Long Terms. He merely informed Eden (and the President as well) that the non-military matters in the Long Terms were entirely satisfactory to the State Department.

Churchill and Eden then secured some sort of approval from Roosevelt that the Long Terms should be substituted for the Short Terms. On August 23, Sir Alexander Cadogan of the Foreign Office informed Dunn of the Roosevelt-Churchill agreement on the Long Terms. Cadogan added that on the basis of this agreement the British were instructing their ambassador at Lisbon to use the Long Terms instead of the Short Terms in future dealings with Italian emissaries.

But the Foreign Office was still not sure of Roosevelt. Cadogan requested Dunn to clear the matter with the President and have the Combined Chiefs of Staff telegraph Eisenhower to use the Long Terms in place of the Short Terms. Dunn declined to take the initiative. He declared that this was outside the province of the State Department and suggested that Cadogan take it up with the British Chiefs of Staff.

On August 26, back in Washington, the British secured full concurrence from Roosevelt on the Long Terms. Eisenhower was directed to use the Long Terms and not the Short Terms in subsequent dealings with Badoglio. Similar instructions were sent by Foreign Secretary Eden to British Ambassador Sir Ronald Hugh Campbell at Lisbon.[233]

Dunn and Sir Ronald Ian Campbell reported to the Combined Civil Affairs Committee (at its regular meeting on the same afternoon), that Roosevelt and Churchill had agreed on the Long Terms and had instructed the Combined Chiefs to communicate the provisions of the comprehensive document to Eisenhower.

Accordingly, on the following day (August 27), the Combined Chiefs wired the text of the Long Terms to Eisenhower. The Long Terms reached AFHQ in time to be available at the signing of the armistice at Cassibile the following week.

The State Department forwarded a copy of the Long Terms, together with a summary outline, to the governments of Russia, the British Dominions, Brazil, Ethiopia, Greece, and Yugoslavia, and to the French Committee of National Liberation. The step produced considerable dissatisfaction at AFHQ which feared possible "leaks" to the enemy.[234]

Thus Roosevelt and Churchill decided the immediate issue which had arisen in the CCAC. The Additional Conditions were not used, nor was the Draft Directive to Eisenhower. In their place was the brief telegram of instructions of August 27, specifying use of the Long Terms. The more fundamental cause of disagreement,

the role of the House of Savoy, was not settled, merely avoided, at this point. It remained, and grew more troublesome in the weeks that followed.

QUADRANT: *The Results*

Partly by intention, partly by a response to outside developments, the Quebec Conference (which ended on August 24)[235] devoted much attention to the Italian situation. The results lay along three main lines: (a) military policy, (b) immediate reaction to Castellano's approach, (c) long-term policy for an Italian surrender. Each of the three was closely dependent upon the other two.

In setting down the objectives of the military campaign in Italy, the Combined Chiefs acted on the basis of information available to them. They approved Eisenhower's plans for landings on the Italian mainland across the Straits of Messina (BAYTOWN) and in the Salerno-Naples area (AVALANCHE).[236] The immediate objectives were the port of Naples, the Foggia airfields, and Rome. Attainment of these goals was immediately possible only if successful Allied landings were combined with the surrender of Italy. Moreover, the plan assumed (a painfully false assumption) that the Badoglio government was sufficiently strong to help turn over these objectives to the Allies. The limited forces and landing craft available to Eisenhower were not in themselves enough to secure them.[237] The Germans did not appear too dark a spectre on the scene, at least in the eyes of the planners at Quebec. They would voluntarily withdraw north of Rome, or their obedience could be enforced by the Italians, or, by a series of bold moves, combined with fortuitous circumstances in Italy itself, the Allies themselves might succeed in making these gains.[238]

In effect, the attainment of these Italian objectives was dependent upon (a) Eisenhower's success in arranging an Italian surrender and (b) the willingness and ability of the Badoglio government to carry out its terms.

The consequences [of an Italian surrender] could not yet be judged, for both the German and the Allied measures would depend on the event itself and on the manner of its accomplishment. Meanwhile, the Allies prepared to assault the Italian peninsula as soon as fighting ended in Sicily, so as to assist or exploit the surrender of the Italian Government.[239]

Eisenhower's task was largely prescribed for him by his superiors at Quebec. Negotiations began on the basis of the Short Terms and the Quebec Memorandum. The Long Terms were completed and forwarded to AFHQ at a later date. Their effect upon the negotiations was an unknown quantity.

Obviously, the Quebec plans were based on available information about the Italian situation. The picture was not, however, all that it seemed to be. Castellano had hinted to Sir Samuel Hoare at Madrid the actual state of affairs—the growing power of the Germans, the weakness of the Italians. Shortly after the close of the Quebec meeting, an ominous warning arrived.

G-2 of AFHQ had by this time acquired an accurate picture of German strength in Italy. On learning of the Long Terms, Macmillan protested against their immediate use. In a telegram to his superiors at Quebec (August 26), he warned them that because of the military difficulties in AVALANCHE, there was an inestimable value in concluding an armistice and announcing it before the landing. Unless removed from the battle by an armistice, the Italian forces might give the Germans the additional strength necessary to push the Allies back into the sea. Additional terms might cause the Italians to think twice about an armistice. Moreover, any delay produced by further negotiations would give the Germans more time to increase their strength and thus their ability to offer even tougher resistance.[240]

It is now necessary to turn back from Quebec to Eisenhower's headquarters and to the steps that he and his aides took in response to the instructions from his superiors.

VII. CASTELLANO AT LISBON

About 10:30 on the evening of August 17, only a few hours after his own message to Washington, Eisenhower received a cable from CCS telling him that Roosevelt and Churchill were preparing a directive for him and instructing him to have two staff officers in readiness to go to Lisbon to confer with Castellano as soon as the directive arrived.

In response to this message, Eisenhower decided to send his Chief of Staff, Major General Walter Bedell Smith, in addition to Brigadier Strong, whom he had already selected. About 4 A.M. on the 18th, Eisenhower's instructions (the Quebec Memorandum)[241] arrived from Quebec and events then proceeded rapidly.

Smith had to be recalled from Sicily but as soon as he arrived (around noon on the 18th), the two officers set out. They were first flown to Gibraltar. There they donned civilian clothes and were issued British civilian passports. (The Portuguese visa officer at Gibraltar lacked authority to authorize the transit visa for Smith's American passport.[242]) As Mr. Kenneth Strong and Mr. Walter Smith of 20 Grosvenor Square, London (the old address of U. S. military headquarters in London), the two generals boarded a civilian plane for Lisbon.[243] On Thursday evening, August 19, the Allied emissaries secretly met Castellano and his interpreter Montanari at the British Embassy in Lisbon. Also present were Sir Ronald Hugh Campbell and George F. Kennan, American chargé d'affaires.[244]

Smith, following the instructions prepared by the Combined Chiefs at Quebec, announced that he was prepared to accept the unconditional surrender of Italy.[245] He then presented to Castellano a document containing the specific surrender terms. (These were, of course, the Short or military terms.)[246]

The Italian emissary was again surprised by the Allied position. His primary purpose, he emphasized, was to arrange for joint Italian-Allied operations against Germany. If this were done, there would be no objection to unconditional surrender. However, this would really be unconditional surrender in principle, but not in reality. A nation which would enter the war as a fighting ally could scarcely be treated as a conquered enemy. Castellano's position was understandable. He represented a government which wished to remain in power. As an Italian, he wished to save his country from conquest. His proposals had as their object an Italian escape from both German occupation and from "unconditional surrender," or, perhaps, more explicitly, from Allied occupation. The Allies insisted upon unconditional surrender (whatever the phrase might mean), with the promise of better treatment for Italy in return for aid against the Germans. This was something quite different from Castellano's hopes.[247] Actually, what bothered Castellano was not the phrase "unconditional surrender" but the Allied unwillingness to accept instantaneous Italian co-belligerency.

The Allied officers listened but could provide no solution to the Italian dilemma. A flexible diplomatic negotiation was not possible. They were charged with the delivery of inflexible terms. No other course was open to them. Castellano realized the hopelessness of his position. The Allies would make no alterations in the terms of surrender. However, Smith also communicated to the Italians the text of the Quebec Memorandum,[248] which did promise favorable modification of the armistice in return for Italian aid in the war against Germany. Castellano decided that the best, perhaps the only, course open to the Badoglio government was to put its trust in the Allies. Co-belligerency might be achieved soon, if not immediately.

Throughout the night Castellano and the Allied officers continued their discussions. The

Italian general posed one question after another. Realizing that opposition to the Allied terms was hopeless, he attempted to clarify the tersely worded document which had been presented to him. He was concerned with the treatment of the Italians; even though the words "unconditional surrender" were omitted, the status of the Italian government and people was left uncertain. Smith pointed out the humane record of AMG in Sicily. Castellano, a Sicilian himself, had heard good reports of fair treatment of the island's inhabitants and of their friendliness for the Allies.[249] He was reassured.[250]

This is an example of the skill displayed by the Allied emissaries in their negotiations with the Italians. Officially, their attitude was stern and uncompromising. On an informal, personal basis, however, a change took place. Another instance occurred during a ten-minute intermission proposed by Smith. He was remarkably friendly and praised some Italian military actions during the war. The effect of this attitude on the Italians was spectacular.

Above all, Castellano was concerned with Allied plans for the campaign in Italy. He repeated to Smith and Strong the picture of his country which he had drawn for Sir Samuel Hoare in Madrid. The dominant characteristic of this picture was the weakness of Italy in contrast to constantly increasing German strength throughout the peninsula. He declared that fifteen German divisions had reached Italy, with reinforcements streaming through the Alps. When, he asked the two officers, would the Allies land on the Italian mainland? Smith assured Castellano that an attack would be made, but refused to disclose dates or locations.

During their all-night session, Castellano gave an account of the overthrow of Mussolini. His version gave almost all credit to officers of the Italian High Command. The King and the members of the Fascist Grand Council were described as mere tools of the military clique.[251]

The Italian emissary displayed bitter hatred for the Germans. He drew a map indicating the dispositions of German and Italian forces in Italy. Castellano was closely questioned by Brigadier Strong to substantiate further the information available to Allied Intelligence.

Finally, the conference drew to a close, about 7:30 in the morning. Castellano was given a short-wave radio transmitter concealed in a small suitcase, and an appropriate Allied code. A special radio channel would permit the Badoglio government to contact AFHQ.[252]

Castellano had hoped to return to Rome immediately. However, the ship carrying the returning Italian ambassador was delayed in passage across the Atlantic. The diplomatic mission of which the General was ostensibly a member did not set out for home until August 23 and did not arrive in Rome until August 27.[253] Castellano was to report to his home government. Then a further meeting with the Allies was planned for August 31, this time in Sicily.[254] The island had been completely occupied by Allied forces by August 20.

Having carried out their instructions to deliver the terms of military surrender, Smith and Strong returned to Algiers on Friday evening, August 20, and reported to General Eisenhower about 6:30.[255]

A very different and disturbing picture of Italy was beginning to impress itself upon Allied planning. The Allies had not anticipated an offer of surrender based on Castellano's proposal of co-belligerency. The original plans for invasion of the Italian mainland had been designed to force the Italian government to sue for peace. This was a central assumption of both the broad strategy of the Combined Chiefs of Staff and Eisenhower's more immediate and specific plans. Castellano's report confirmed earlier Allied suspicions that this concept was a false one. Italy was not a free agent, to make war or peace of her own volition. This had been partially true for some time before July 25—Mussolini's position as an equal of Hitler had steadily deteriorated. After the Duce's fall, Italy rapidly began to resemble a conquered province. German occupation forces were large and steadily increasing. German agents occupied most of the key positions in the government and defense of the peninsula.

Now it appeared that an Allied landing in force would be necessary, not to *force* the Italian government to surrender, but to *permit* it to surrender. In this sense, the precise nature of the surrender—unconditional or not—was immaterial. This was the reason for Castellano's desire for joint action against the Germans. Above all, it accounted for his insistent and repeated attempts to learn the time and place of the Allied landing in Italy.

Eisenhower's review of the situation emphasizes the curious position of the two sides:

The Italians wanted frantically to surrender. However, they wanted to do so only with the assurance that such a powerful Allied force would land on the mainland simultaneously with their surrender that the government itself and their cities would enjoy complete protection from the German forces. Consequently they tried to obtain every detail of our plans. These we would not reveal because the possibility of treachery could never be excluded. Moreover, to invade Italy with the strength that the Italians themselves believed necessary was a complete impossibility for the very simple reason that we did not have the troops in the area nor the ships to transport them had they been there.

Italian military authorities could not conceive of the Allies undertaking this venture with less than fifteen divisions in the assault waves. We were planning to use only three with some reinforcing units, aside from the two that were to dash across the Messina Strait.[256]

An interval of some ten days occurred at this juncture, since Castellano could not leave Lisbon until August 23 and reach Rome for several more days. The Allies, in full possession of Sicily, waited for the response of the Badoglio government to the terms delivered through Castellano. Full-scale preparations went forward for BAYTOWN and AVALANCHE, the projected initial landings on the Italian peninsula. An exchange of telegrams between Churchill and General Alexander in Sicily indicated the need for haste:

Prime Minister (Quebec) to General Alexander (Middle East)   19 August 1943

. . . Our greatest danger is that the Germans should enter Rome and set up a Quisling-Fascist Government under, say, Farinacci. Scarcely less unpleasant would be the whole of Italy sliding into anarchy. I doubt if the Badoglio Government can hold their double-faced position until the present date fixed for "Avalanche," so that anything that can be done to shorten this period without endangering military success will be most helpful.

General Alexander to Prime Minister (Quebec)
                              20 August 1943

. . . Everything possible is being done to put on "Avalanche" at the earliest possible date. We realise here very clearly that every hour gives enemy more time to prepare and organise against us.[257]

Meanwhile, the Badoglio government, apparently disturbed over Castellano's lengthy absence,[258] sent out another emissary. On the morning of August 26, there appeared in Lisbon General Giacomo Zanussi, principal assistant to the Chief of the Italian General Staff (Roatta).[259] He was accompanied by British General Carton de Wiart, who had been released from an Italian prisoner-of-war camp for the purpose. Zanussi had been instructed by Badoglio to try to reach London, there to urge an Allied landing on the Italian peninsula north of Rome.[260]

Allied discussions had already begun with General Castellano. Therefore, it was decided at the British Embassy in Lisbon to send Zanussi to AFHQ to meet General Eisenhower. At first, Zanussi wished to return home to report the failure of his mission to London. Later he acceded to the Allied plan and was forthwith sent to Algiers.

Zanussi was met upon arrival by General Smith, who reported the new mission to Eisenhower on Saturday evening (August 28). Officers at AFHQ were rather uncertain of Zanussi's status and purpose. There was some suspicion that he might represent a pro-German faction and had come to discover the extent of the Badoglio government's relations with the Allies. It was therefore decided that the negotiations with Castellano should be kept secret until some word came from Rome. Zanussi was to remain in Algiers while a check was made on his status via the secret radio contact. He, too, was questioned on the internal situation in Italy.

By August 30, however, word came to Algiers confirming the proposed meeting with Castellano in Sicily, to take place on the following day.[261] Thus the Zanussi mission was of no real value. It was significant, however, in again demonstrating the persistent desire of the Badoglio government to conclude an armistice with the Allies. One envoy after another was sent out until success was assured.

Meanwhile, final Allied preparations for the armistice negotiations were underway. Eisenhower had been furnished with the Short Terms on July 31. Following the approach from Castellano, the Quebec Conference had sent Eisenhower instructions to use the Short Terms, while at the same time informing the Italian emissary that comprehensive terms would follow. This had been done at Lisbon on the evening of August 19-20.

On August 27, eight days later, the Long Terms were approved in Washington. Copies of the text were sent to AFHQ and to the British Ambassador at Lisbon. After Castellano had departed from Lisbon on his return trip to Rome, the Allies did not know where future contacts with the Badoglio government might take place. Smith and Strong had proposed a meeting in Sicily and had furnished Castellano with a wireless transmitter and appropriate code for confirming this arrangement. At the same time, there was also the possibility that the Italians might return to Lisbon. Therefore preparation was made for either eventuality. Furthermore, the appearance of General Zanussi presented a third possible means of contact, and he was about to be on hand in Algiers.

On August 26, Macmillan, acting for Eisenhower, informed his government (and ours) that the text of the Long Terms had not yet reached Algiers. Since the negotiators would have to be in Sicily on August 28, they were expecting to use the Short Terms, employing the final draft that included the article about the subsequent imposition of the comprehensive instrument. If they received the Long Terms in time, they would try to secure Italian acceptance. But again, Macmillan pointed out the difficulties involved, and urged that the negotiators be authorized to use the Short Terms instead if necessary. He again reminded his government that it was a matter of great importance to secure acceptance of an armistice and to announce the fact so as to coincide with AVALANCHE. Finally, he noted that probably the Italians would not send an envoy, but merely a notice of acceptance, and this would of course apply to the Short Terms.

When Macmillan's message reached London, Churchill and Eden were still abroad. Attlee replied and told Macmillan that he had asked the British Ambassador in Lisbon to give Zanussi a copy of the Long Terms and have Zanussi fly back to Rome with it. Therefore the Italian envoy in Sicily might be able to give his government's official reaction to the document. He agreed—reluctantly—that if the Italian emissary was not commissioned to deal with the Long Terms, and if signature of an armistice seemed militarily essential, the Short Terms could be used. However, the significance of Article 12, concerning the comprehensive instrument, should be made clear.

Attlee's hope that the Italian government would have an opportunity to study the Long Terms before August 28 came to nought. During this interchange of telegrams, Zanussi was requested to proceed to Algiers instead of returning to Rome. As the time of the Palermo meeting drew near, the situation was this: Castellano had been furnished only with the Short Terms and the information that Long Terms would be forthcoming. Since he was the only contact, this was the only information possessed by the Badoglio government. Zanussi had been informed of the Long Terms but he was in Algiers.

Just before his departure for Sicily, Macmillan received final instructions from Eden in London. Eden in substance reaffirmed what Attlee had said. He recognized the probability that Castellano would not be authorized to sign the Long Terms, but emphasized the importance of making Castellano realize the import of Section 12 to preclude any subsequent annoying bargaining attempts by the Italian government. Eden's slight modification of Attlee's position was of course the result of his knowledge that Zanussi was in Algiers and that the Italian government had not seen the Long Terms.

Thus circumstance largely determined the final location and nature of the armistice negotiations. This was the situation on the eve of the meeting at Cassibile.

VIII. THE ARMISTICE OF CASSIBILE

THE NEGOTIATIONS

At nine o'clock on the morning of Tuesday, August 31, an Italian plane landed at Termini Imerese airfield near Palermo in Sicily.[262] It carried General Castellano and his interpreter, Major Montanari. They were met by Brigadier Strong and taken to the headquarters of the 15th Army Group at Cassibile, a few miles west of Syracuse. General Walter Bedell Smith had arrived at Cassibile a short time earlier for this meeting which had been planned at Lisbon. He had brought with him from Algiers General Zanussi, who informed Castellano in a brief meeting that the Long Terms had been made available.[263]

By the time of Castellano's arrival in Sicily, actual responsibility for securing Italian acceptance of the armistice terms had been given to AFHQ. The Allied political leaders and the Combined Chiefs of Staff had agreed upon objectives and the policies designed to achieve them. These had been set down in the Short Terms, in the Quebec Memorandum and, finally, in the Long Terms. In essence, Eisenhower's course of action, in terms of both objectives and specific policy, had been prescribed, save for the timing of the announcement of surrender.[264] Now he was authorized to carry these instructions into effect. Nevertheless, the President and the Prime Minister, now both at the White House in Washington,[265] continued to receive full reports through the Combined Chiefs. Their approval was of course necessary for any major change of plan, as in the case of GIANT TWO, described below.[266] The War Cabinet in London played a similar role.

Their initial greetings over, the Italian emissaries and their Allied hosts sat down to a general conference.[267] Besides Smith and Strong, the Allied delegation included General

Sir Harold Alexander, commander of the Allied ground forces, and high naval and air officers of the Mediterranean Command. The sole question was at once raised by General Smith: Had the Badoglio government empowered Castellano to sign the Short Terms? The Italian general replied in the negative and proceeded to read a memorandum prepared by his government.

The Italian government, it stated, was not free to sign and carry out the armistice terms. German strength had continued to increase since the Lisbon meeting and Italy was now completely under German control. Therefore the government could not agree to the condition that the armistice be announced *in advance* of the main Allied landing. The Italian army, suffering from a lack of ammunition and equipment, would be destroyed by superior German forces. Thus it could not guarantee the security of Rome, where the King and his government were situated. The Germans could then turn, unimpeded, to face the Allied invasion of the peninsula. The Allies must make their main landing north of Rome, with a force of at least fifteen divisions. The announcement of the armistice could then be made. The Badoglio government wished to cooperate with the Allies; it must, however, be protected from destruction by the Germans.

Smith's answer was blunt: The Italian proposals were unacceptable. The armistice terms, including the timing of the armistice announcement, must be accepted in their entirety or refused. The decision must be made before midnight of September 1/2.

In reality, General Smith was not himself a free agent. His instructions did not permit freedom to negotiate. General Eisenhower's latitude of action had been carefully circumscribed in the instructions from Quebec, and on the one undetermined point—the timing of the armistice announcement—his decision was already made,[268] and Smith could not bargain on that. Nevertheless, Smith made a firm and clear reply to Castellano. In essence, he pointed out that Italy was in no position to bargain. An end to the negotiations would leave Italy a passive element in the coming campaign and a conquered country, at the mercy of the conquerors, at the end of the war.

Smith declared that General Eisenhower had only with great difficulty secured authorization from the Allied governments to negotiate a military armistice. The terms of the Quebec Memorandum provided Italy with a means of salvation. Under them, General Eisenhower had been empowered to modify the surrender terms in return for Italian aid given to the Allies during the remainder of the war. Eisenhower had decided that the armistice must be proclaimed on the day of the main Allied landing (AVALANCHE). Proclamation by the Italian government must be simultaneous with the Allied announcement. Under the terms of the Quebec Memorandum, Italian failure to comply would put an end to negotiations for a military armistice.[269]

Castellano's basic program of military collaboration with the Allies was tied to a military armistice. Unless Italy collaborated in the war against the Germans, the preservation of the Royal government and the eventual mitigation of the armistice terms would seem to be doubtful possibilities.

Moreover, the Allies would not guarantee a landing of fifteen divisions north of Rome. If, said General Smith, a landing in such strength were planned, no armistice need be offered. He declared that the Allies would land in Italy with or without Italian support. The role which the Italians should play and, in turn, much of the severity of the campaign itself were left for the Italians themselves to decide.

This conference had a clear resemblance to the one in Lisbon some ten days earlier. Again each side stated its position. Again Castellano was told that there could be no modification of Allied terms, including the vital point that the armistice be announced simultaneously with the main Allied landing. Again Castellano tried to secure information as to the date and place of the main Allied landing. Again he was unsuccessful. He attempted to alter the terms of the surrender of the Italian fleet by threaten-

ing that otherwise it might be used against Allied convoys. Smith replied that failure to agree to the armistice would leave Italy a bloody battleground and a conquered enemy. Castellano at length declared that he would again have to consult his government.

The morning conference ended inconclusively. Quite clearly, the Italians were faced with a cruel dilemma. Refusal to accept the armistice terms, with the prospects they held out of military collaboration and eventual modification of the terms themselves, might well mean the end of the Royal dynasty and the Badoglio government. Acceptance would bring German seizure of Rome and probably of the government unless Allied protection was guaranteed. The Allied officers feared that the Italian government would lack the courage to sign and announce the armistice unless convinced of strong Allied landings to protect Rome.[270]

A luncheon conference improved the situation. Here, as at Lisbon, Smith displayed diplomatic skill. Firm, sometimes harsh, in official conversations, he was courteous and friendly when the formal sessions adjourned. Castellano again pointed out that his government was willing to accept the armistice. It merely asked for postponement of the announcement. Moreover, the Italian armed forces could not save Rome from the Germans without Allied support. General Smith then asked Castellano to make a specific request for Allied aid in securing the capital. Castellano did so, specifying an armored division to land at Ostia and an airborne division in the vicinity of Rome. After conferring with other Allied commanders, Smith stated that it might be possible to furnish one airborne division, provided the Italians were able to furnish appropriate airfields. This presented no difficulty, declared Castellano, but, if a full armored division could not be allocated, at least a few anti-tank batteries should be landed at the mouth of the Tiber on the same day as the airborne landing. Smith promised to study this possibility.[271]

Later in the afternoon a summary of the conference was drafted:

1. The Italian Government may accept or may refuse the conditions of armistice, but if it accepts it must accede to the methods desired by the Allies for the official declaration;

2. The Allies will effect the secondary landing

with five or six divisions; during this landing the Italian troops cannot avoid offering resistance;

3. After a certain period of time (one or two weeks?) there will be the main landing south of Rome. The total force employed in both landings will equal, if not exceed the fifteen divisions regarded as necessary by Badoglio. Simultaneously there will be effected the landing of the paratroop division in the vicinity of the capital and that of 100 antitank guns at the mouth of the Tiber;

4. Acceptance on the part of the Italian Government shall be made by radio within twenty-four hours of September 2. In the negative case no communication will be made.[272]

Castellano, Zanussi and their interpreter then flew back to Rome, reaching the capital about 7 P.M. The conferences with the Allied officers had given them a clear understanding of Allied plans, even though they had not learned the date of the main Allied landing. Perhaps the most important point was this: the Allies would not make their main landing north of Rome to save the capital and the Royal government. They had, however, offered assistance to the Italian government in defending itself.

On the following morning (September 1), Castellano made a complete report at a meeting with Badoglio and his military and civil chiefs. The general view seemed to be that no course was available other than complete acceptance of the Allied terms. However, General Carboni, commander of the Italian forces around Rome, spoke in decided opposition. He declared that his forces lacked supplies to withstand a German attack; moreover, the oral Allied promises were not to be trusted.

Despite this opposition, Badoglio reported to the King. Late on the same day, the Allies were notified via secret radio that the armistice terms were acceptable.[273] General Smith then sent a radio message requesting Castellano to return to Sicily on the following day and assuring Badoglio that plans for airborne aid to Rome were being studied. This was dependent upon a guarantee that

the armistice is signed and announced as desired by the Allies; that the Italians should seize and hold the necessary airfields and stop all anti-aircraft fire; that the Italian divisions in the Rome area would take action against the Germans.[274]

Castellano returned to Sicily on the morning of Thursday, September 2.[275] It had been agreed at Lisbon that acceptance of the armistice would be made by radio. Uneasy over the

indecision prevalent in Rome, the Allied officers now demanded that Castellano formally sign the armistice. The Italian general declared that he lacked powers to sign. He was permitted to radio to Rome a request for such powers. Not until the afternoon of September 3, did the authorization reach Castellano in Sicily.[276]

At dawn on Friday morning (September 3), the invasion of the Italian mainland began. Two divisions of Montgomery's Eighth Army crossed the Straits of Messina with negligible opposition. The advance up the boot began, delayed more by difficult terrain and demolition than by actual fighting. The Germans had apparently pulled back and Italians were surrendering everywhere.

In the meantime in Sicily, plans for the airborne operation were begun. Following a conference with the Italian officers and an all-night meeting of Allied planners, an outline plan was completed by early Saturday morning, September 4. In a message on the evening of September 2, the Italian High Command had said that airfields were available. Castellano presented detailed information on the disposition of German and Italian forces around Rome. He also promised a number of specific aids to be furnished by the Italians to the incoming force, the 82nd Airborne Division. Specifically, the airfields at Guidonia, Littorio, Cerveteri, Centocelle, and Furbara were to be made ready to receive the paratroopers and the troop carrier planes on the nights of September 8 and 9. The Italians would protect them against the Germans and have transportation, supplies, including 355 trucks, 12 ambulances, and 11,000 rations, and extra fuel stationed at the fields.[277] Castellano again emphasized that the Italians did not lack men but were in desperate need of anti-tank guns.

[American] . . . General Rooks mentioned that consideration was being given to running two or three ships up the Tiber with ammunition and supplies, and Commodore Dick, Chief of Staff to Admiral Cunningham, asked if the swing bridges could be opened. Castellano stated that the bridge at Fiumicino could be kept open, and this would permit the ships to go as far as the Magliano airport where supplies could be landed along the banks. As far as Littorio field the Tiber was thirty feet deep.[278]

The operation was given the code-name GIANT TWO.

Eisenhower received approval of this plan from the President and the Prime Minister in Washington:

We highly approve your decision to go on with AVALANCHE and to land an airborne division near Rome on the conditions indicated. We fully recognize military considerations must be dominant at this juncture.[279]

The situation is summarized in a joint Roosevelt-Churchill telegram to Stalin, sent on September 2:

We have received from General Castellano statement that the Italians accept and that he is coming to sign, but we do not know for certain whether this refers to short military terms, which you have already seen, or to more comprehensive and complete terms in regard to which your readiness to sign was specifically indicated.

2. The military situation there is at once critical and hopeful. Our invasion of the mainland is beginning almost immediately, and the heavy blow called "Avalanche" will be struck in the next week or so. The difficulty of the Italian Government and people in extricating themselves from Hitler's clutches may make a still more daring enterprise necessary, for General Eisenhower will need as much Italian help as he can get. The Italian acceptance of the terms is largely based on the fact that we shall send an airborne division to Rome to enable them to hold off the Germans, who have gathered Panzer strength in that vicinity, and who may replace the Badoglio Government with a Quisling Administration, probably under Farinacci. Matters are moving so fast there that we think General Eisenhower should have discretion not to delay settlement with the Italians for the sake of the difference between the short and long terms. It is clear that short terms are included in long terms, that they proceed on basis of unconditional surrender, placing the interpretation in hands of Allied Commander-in-Chief.

3. We are therefore assuming that you expect General Eisenhower to sign short terms on your behalf if that be necessary to avoid the further journeying of General Castellano to Rome and consequent delay and uncertainty affecting military operations. We are of course anxious that Italian unconditional surrender be to Soviet as well as to Great Britain and the United States. The date of surrender announcement must of course be fitted in with the military stroke.[280]

There were two ways in which the GIANT TWO operation could be useful from a military viewpoint:

Italian acceptance of an armistice might be contingent upon Allied aid in Rome against German reprisals; at the cost of one diverted division he [Eisenhower] might secure Italian help in retarding the movement of German reinforcements and thus insure the success of AVALANCHE.[281]

The actual signature of the text of the Short Terms took place at Cassibile shortly after five o'clock on the afternoon of September 3.[282] General Castellano signed on behalf of Marshal Badoglio. General Smith signed for the Supreme Allied Commander, ". . . acting by authority of the governments of the United States and Great Britain and in the interest of the United Nations."[283] Eisenhower flew from Algiers to witness the ceremony.[284] He later reported the conclusion of the armistice to the Combined Chiefs, announcing that signature of the Short Terms made possible joint military planning with the Italians.[285] (The actual proclamation of the armistice would await a predetermined time, immediately preceding the Salerno landings, a time not yet disclosed to the Italians.) Formal signature of the Long Terms, he assured his chiefs, would await a convenient time in Allied operational plans.[286] The armistice was to remain a secret until a code message was sent to Badoglio from AFHQ. At that point Badoglio would announce the armistice simultaneously with General Eisenhower.

The hopes of the Allied leaders at this time were expressed in a telegram which Churchill sent to Stalin on September 5, two days later:

General Castellano, after a long struggle, signed the short terms on September 3, and he is now working out with Generals Eisenhower and Alexander the best way to bring them into force. This will certainly lead to immediate fighting between Italian and German forces, and we are going to help the Italians at every possible point as effectively and speedily as we can. The next week will show a startling development. The invasion of the toe has been successful and is being pressed, and Operation "Avalanche" and the airborne venture are both imminent. Though I believe we shall get ashore at "Avalanche" in strong force, I cannot foresee what will happen in Rome or throughout Italy. The dominant aim should be to kill Germans and make Italians kill Germans on the largest scale possible in this theatre.[287]

At this time, Eisenhower expressed considerable dissatisfaction with the Short Terms, referring to the signature of the document at Cassibile as a "crooked deal." According to

Butcher's report, "Ike feels that the terms of agreement are unduly harsh . . . [he] had hoped to handle the negotiations with Italy, as a purely military matter, as he did the Darlan affair, so that his objective would not be complicated with a variety of demands from all the belligerents against Italy."[288]

Shortly thereafter, General Smith presented to Castellano a copy of the Long Terms, "The Instrument of Surrender of Italy." A brief note declared that this document:

Contains the political, financial and economic conditions which will be imposed by the United Nations in accordance with paragraph 12 of the Armistice terms. The military conditions of the Armistice are contained in the document which we have just signed. The attached paper is identical with the one handed to General Zanussi by H. M. Ambassador in Lisbon.[289]

The text of the Long Terms provided another painful surprise for General Castellano. The initial clause stated coldly:

The Italian Land, Sea and Air Forces wherever located, hereby surrender unconditionally.

Castellano's basic objective had been to obtain for Italy a status which was not consistent with the words "unconditional surrender." The phrase itself was contained nowhere in the Short Terms. Moreover, such a declaration seemed totally inconsistent with the joint military planning then underway. Castellano protested against this Allied procedure. Allied officials in the Mediterranean theater were not happy over the Long Terms either. British political adviser Harold Macmillan had protested over their use on August 26. Apparently, Eisenhower and Smith were not pleased with this order from the Combined Chiefs. Probably none of them knew that Roosevelt had planned to set the Long Terms aside, but had finally given in to British urging.

In addition to opposition to the actual provisions of the Long Terms, Eisenhower also feared effects which might stem from their publicity.

He suspects that our home governments want to make a propaganda Roman holiday by publicizing to the entire world the stern restrictions of the surrender—the terms which will be formalized at a later ceremony. Already London and Washington have sent messages to the United Nations, asking for their concurrence in the terms. This

Ike regarded as extraordinarily risky to AVALANCHE, as the news, undoubtedly, will leak from some capital. The negotiations in Sicily may have set the public announcement of the armistice only five hours before the actual launching of AVALANCHE, scheduled for 3:30 A.M. Tuesday, September 9. A leak in the meantime seems almost inevitable and will probably cost us heavily in lives, as the Germans will begin taking over Italy and certainly will replace Italian coastal units which manned pillboxes and shore batteries with their own German troops. This will make the landing even more hazardous.[290]

Castellano expressed doubts that his government would agree to these additional terms. When Smith reminded him of the modifications promised by the Quebec Memorandum, the Italian general pointed out that these were only general promises. What recourse was open to the Italian government if these assurances were not fulfilled? The Italians apparently did not share President Roosevelt's recollections of Grant's generosity at Appomattox. At this point, General Smith wrote a short note for Marshal Badoglio:

The additional clauses have only a relative value insofar as Italy collaborates in the war against the Germans.[291]

Thus without deviation from the letter of his instructions or changing a comma in the text of the surrender instrument, Smith found a way to qualify unconditional surrender.

ROME: "PASSIVE" vs. "ACTIVE"

On the afternoon of September 4, Castellano prepared his report for the Rome government. He included the signed Short Terms, the Long Terms with Smith's note, "Instructions for the Movement of Italian Warships and Shipping," an *aide-memoire* listing the general procedures to be followed by the Italian government in advance of the armistice announcement, and detailed plans for the joint military operations. These included not only GIANT TWO but also instructions for the movement of Italian ships and aircraft into Allied control as soon as the armistice was proclaimed. The documents, translated into Italian, were flown to Rome early the next morning, September 5. They were delivered to General Ambrosio, Chief of the Supreme General Staff, and by him to Marshal Badoglio.

At AFHQ, it was expected that the Italian High Command, now informed of the joint military plans, would begin preparations for joint operations to save Rome. AVALANCHE was but three days away. In fact, it did not do so. Uncertainty and timidity among the military leaders were rampant. Hesitation was promoted, indeed made inevitable by lack of clear direction from the three men in supreme authority: General Ambrosio, Chief of the General Staff, Marshal Badoglio, head of the government, and, above all, King Victor Emmanuel. The full story is long and complicated.[292] Personalities played a large role in the politics of this small group of men, leaders of a weak nation occupied by one army, about to be invaded by another. A few salient facts are clear.

Perhaps foremost was Italian fear of the Germans and lack of confidence in themselves. Another factor developed from Allied policy. Partially distrusting the Badoglio government, Allied representatives had withheld from the Italians information as to the timing and size of the main Allied attack. In fact, Castellano had been encouraged to believe that it would be mounted in far greater force than was actually planned.[293]

[This] . . . had the unfortunate effect of encouraging Badoglio and his advisers to do what they were in any case inclined to do; sit back and wait for the Allies to come and save them from the consequences of their double dealing and internal weakness. Expecting a great landing at some indefinite time in the future, the Italians allowed the days to drift past without making preparations to bring their forces to bear against the Germans.[294]

Actually, Castellano, misinterpreting a remark made by General Smith during the negotiations, estimated that the main Allied landing would come on September 12.

Also to be taken into account was the personality of the monarch. Victor Emmanuel may be described as old and timid, or as a cautious conservative monarch, clinging to the forms of a constitutional structure which no longer existed. Whichever description is accurate, the King's role was vital. Both of these factors were important in the delay in overthrowing Mussolini and in sending out peace emissaries until after the Allied invasion of Sicily.

The King's word was final; his assent had to be given to any successful policy proposal. Yet he refused to make known his wishes, leaving policy formulation to Badoglio. The Marshal often appeared bewildered by this lack of direction. Below the level of Badoglio and Chief of Staff Ambrosio, two schools of policy were in ceaseless conflict. One side, represented by Castellano, may be entitled "active"; the other, led by Carboni, "passive."

Castellano's policy was already clear: to save Italy and the House of Savoy, the Italians should engage themselves wholeheartedly on the Allied side. In contrast were the views of the older and more timid officers. They were willing to accept the armistice but only if the Allies would save them from the Germans. They themselves could, or would, do nothing. In the two days following Castellano's report to Rome, the passive policy was permitted to triumph.

The departure of Ambrosio for the north on September 6 left the field to the "passivists." Roatta, Carboni and company examined the joint plans. In their view, two things were obvious. First, the Italians were too weak to fulfill their role. Actually, they made no effort to carry it out. For example, the joint plans called for the Italians to make some 400 trucks available to the airborne division. This seemed totally impossible to Roatta.[295] Castellano's scheme of commandeering vehicles from Rome seems never to have occurred to him. On the other hand, it is not clear that gasoline was available for trucks, commandeered or otherwise. The incident is typical.

Secondly, the plans for GIANT TWO indicated that the Italians were not to be rescued by the Allies. They were instead to be assisted to defend themselves. This unpleasant fact was further strengthened by an Italian realization (from reports of Allied convoys) on September 6 that the Allied landing would come, not near Rome, but south, probably near Naples, and would be smaller than they had anticipated. These reports also showed that Castellano's guess that the landing would not take place until September 12 was wrong. The Italians realized, with a sense of unpleasant shock, that they themselves would have to defend Rome,[296] aided by only one American airborne division. To the "passivists," this was clearly impossible. If Marshal Badoglio agreed with the "passivists," the joint Allied-Italian plans—including GIANT TWO—were doomed. It may be well to note parenthetically that the plans were doomed anyway if Carboni's judgment was right; and there is highly persuasive evidence to show that by September 1943, the Italian army had no fight left in it.[297]

On September 4, General Smith had informed Castellano of Eisenhower's wish that an Italian Military Mission be attached to AFHQ. It was to be composed of army, navy and air force representatives and would be headed by Castellano. Accordingly, the Italian general requested his government to authorize and constitute such a mission.

When this request reached Rome, Carboni and Roatta were in *de facto* charge in the absence of General Ambrosio. Instead of sending a mission to facilitate the carrying out of Castellano's optimistic commitments, they determined to use it for the opposite purpose. The mission was provided with instructions designed to effect fundamental changes in Allied plans. A lengthy memorandum was prepared by the Italian High Command embodying requests to that effect. In brief, they advocated cancellation of GIANT TWO and postponement of the armistice announcement until the Allies could land in strength near Rome.[298]

In the midst of this confusion, two Allied officers arrived in Rome. They were Brigadier General Maxwell D. Taylor of the 82nd Airborne Division and Colonel William T. Gardiner of Troop Carrier. From the beginning of the negotiations at Cassibile, the Allies had been suspicious of affairs in Rome and especially of Italian ability to fulfill the commitments made by Castellano. Thus the Allied officers were sent to Rome to confirm final arrangements for GIANT TWO, which, without full Italian support, could easily end in disaster.[299]

Via a British PT boat and an Italian corvette the two were secretly smuggled into Italy on September 7. With their uniforms splashed with sea water to give the appearance of fliers shot down and rescued from the sea, they were driven in an ambulance into Rome. At nightfall they arrived at the Palazzo Caprara where (in a building opposite the War Office) they were met by Italian staff officers. An elaborate dinner had been prepared but it was apparent that no arrangements had been made for any real business to be done that night. It also became increasingly clear that the Italians did not expect the main Allied landing until the period September 10-15 and probably nearer to the 15th. At the insistence of the Americans, a conference was arranged with General Carboni about 9:30 P.M.

Carboni lost no time in presenting a "passivist" view of the situation, emphasizing the large build-up of German forces in Italy since the fall of Mussolini and especially the heavy German concentrations around Rome, as well as the shortage of ammunition and fuel among Italian units largely as a result of rationing by the Germans. He further observed:

If the Italians declare an armistice, the Germans will occupy Rome, and the Italians can do little to prevent it. The simultaneous arrival of U. S. airborne troops would only provoke the Germans to more drastic action. Furthermore, the Italians would be unable to secure the airfields, cover the assembly and provide the desired logistical aid to the airborne troops. If it must be assumed that an Allied seaborne landing is impossible north of Rome, then the only hope of saving the Capital is to avoid overt acts against the Germans and await the effect of the Allied attacks in the South. He stated that he knew that the Allied landings would be at Salerno, which was too far away to aid directly in the defense of Rome. He stated that General Roatta shared his views.[300]

On hearing Carboni's estimate, Taylor and Gardiner saw dire threats to the success of GIANT TWO; regardless of the soundness of his views, they felt "he displayed an alarming pessimism certain to affect his conduct of operations in connection with GIANT TWO."[301] They therefore requested, and were granted, an interview with Marshal Badoglio himself. The meeting took place at Badoglio's villa around midnight.

It immediately became clear to the two American emissaries that Badoglio had been converted to the "passive" estimate. The Marshal reiterated Carboni's judgment of the military situation and declared that the proclamation of the armistice would have to be postponed and GIANT TWO cancelled.

To the Allied officers, this represented a blatant disregard of the commitments agreed upon through Castellano. Badoglio replied simply that the situation had changed. An announcement of the armistice now would mean an immediate German occupation of Rome and the creation of a quisling government. The

Marshal expressed the hope that Taylor and Gardiner would explain the new situation and the changed Italian position to General Eisenhower. Upon their refusal, Badoglio accepted the responsibility himself. He prepared this message for Eisenhower:

Due to changes in the situation brought about by the disposition and strength of the German forces in the Rome area, it is no longer possible to accept an immediate armistice as this could provoke the occupation of the Capital and the violent assumption of the government by the Germans. Operation GIANT TWO is no longer possible because of lack of forces to guarantee the airfields. General Taylor is available to return to Sicily to present the views of the government and await orders.

BADOGLIO.

General Taylor drafted a message of his own for AFHQ:

In view of the statement of Marshal Badoglio as to inability to declare armistice and to guarantee fields GIANT TWO is impossible. Reasons given for change are irreplaceable lack of gasoline and munitions and new German dispositions. Badoglio requests Taylor return to present government views. Taylor and Gardiner awaiting instructions. Acknowledge.

Taylor.[302]

At eight the following morning (September 8) AFHQ acknowledged receipt of Badoglio's message.

Taylor feared that his message had not been received. Aware that the first wave of airborne troops was scheduled to take off at 6:30 that same evening, he sent off at 11:35 A.M. the simple code message "situation innocuous." This was the prearranged signal for the cancellation of GIANT TWO. It was well that he did so. Planes of the first lift were ready to take off when the order to cancel was given.[303]

Worried over Allied reaction to its change of position, the Badoglio government decided on September 8 to send an emissary to Eisenhower. His assignment was to persuade the Allied commander to delay announcement of the armistice until the success of the Salerno landing was assured. Then the Allies would be in a position to seize Rome and the Italians would join them. In the late afternoon an Italian plane set out from Rome for Tunis. In addition to Lieutenant-General Rossi and his interpreter, it carried Taylor and Gardiner

back from their hazardous mission. But events were taking place as the plane neared North Africa that made the Italian general's trip a useless one.

THE ARMISTICE DECLARATION

The Italian about-face was an unpleasant shock to the Allied command. When Badoglio's message reached AFHQ at Algiers, Eisenhower was absent on a visit to advance headquarters near Carthage. The staff radioed to the Combined Chiefs for instructions while forwarding Badoglio's message to Eisenhower.[304] Not until afternoon did he receive the messages. With the attack on Salerno scheduled to commence in less than twenty-four hours, Eisenhower had to make a quick decision. This telegram to the Combined Chiefs records his action:

8 Sept. 43

I have just completed a conference with the principal commanders, and have determined *not* to accept the Italian change of attitude. We intend to proceed in accordance with plan for the announcement of the armistice, and with subsequent propaganda and other measures. Marshal Badoglio is being informed through our direct link that this instrument entered into by his accredited representative with presumed good faith on both sides is considered valid and binding, and that we will *not* recognize any deviation from our original agreement.[305]

From Roosevelt and Churchill at Washington came quick approval of Eisenhower's course of action and a reaffirmation of their decision to leave the timing of the announcement to Eisenhower:

8 Sept. 1943

It is the view of the President and the Prime Minister that the agreement having been signed, you should make such public announcement regarding it as would facilitate your military operations.[306]

On September 6, the Badoglio government had been warned over the secret Allied radio to stand by for a message designating X-day. Subsequent messages on the 8th indicated that the Allies would proclaim the armistice that very day.[307] In answer to Badoglio's requests for postponement, Eisenhower warned the Marshal that he planned to broadcast announcement of the armistice at 6:30 on that very evening. Italian failure to make a similar proclamation according to agreement would result in an Allied publication of the story to the world. While agreeing to cancel GIANT TWO, Eisenhower asserted that Badoglio had sufficient troops around Rome to protect the city if he were willing to use them. Above all, Allied plans assumed that the Italians were acting in good faith. Failure to live up to its commitments would destroy Allied confidence in the Badoglio government and in the Italian nation. Such failure would mean the inevitable end of the Badoglio regime and the Italian nation.[308]

[The Allies] . . . were counting on the Badoglio announcement as an integral part of [the] invasion plan. The whole purpose of timing the announcements in English and Italian simultaneously that evening was to permit the news to permeate Italy and especially to filter through the Italian Army. Whatever Italian opposition there was left ahead of the Eighth Army and whatever they might have expected to find on the beaches would disintegrate, and they would have only Germans to face. More than that, they knew by now that the announcement was going to catch the Germans by surprise. The resulting consternation and hurried activity on the part of the Germans might be of help to them in making their beach-heads secure. It was imperative that Badoglio make his announcement as scheduled.[309]

At 6:30 P.M. on September 8, Eisenhower broadcast a proclamation of the armistice.[310] Immediately thereafter the text of the declaration was broadcast.[311] Badoglio followed suit a short time later. The text of Badoglio's message, released at 7:15, read as follows:

The Italian Government, recognizing the impossibility of continuing the unequal struggle against the overwhelming power of the enemy, with the object of avoiding further and more grievous harm to the nation, has requested an armistice from General Eisenhower, Commander-in-Chief of the Anglo-American Allied Forces. This request has been granted. The Italian forces will, therefore, cease all acts of hostility against the Anglo-American forces wherever they may be met. They will, however, oppose attack from any quarter.[312]

Instructions were telephoned to the various Italian naval commanders to set sail for Allied ports, according to plans concerted with Castellano at Cassibile. The first waves of troops were ashore at Salerno by 4 A.M. the following morning.[313] The Fifth Army success in a difficult landing was certainly facilitated by lack

of Italian resistance. It is reasonable to assume that without an armistice there would have been some show of Italian resistance, not serious in itself, but possibly just enough to tip the precarious balance.[314] As it happened, the Germans had disarmed the Italians and themselves fiercely defended the beaches against Allied landings; and perhaps the announcement of the armistice precipitated the German move.

Within hours of the announcement of the armistice, German forces began to encircle Rome.[315] Berlin announced the creation of a Free Italian government. Before dawn on September 9, lacking confidence in their own troops, the Royal Family, Badoglio and his chief ministers slipped out of Rome; their flight did not endear the government to the Italian underground. Two naval corvettes conveyed them to Brindisi. Here, in territory occupied by the Allied forces, an anti-Fascist government was established on September 10.

The apparent delay in the armistice negotiations provoked some criticism. To this Churchill replied in a speech to the House of Commons on September 21:

I have seen it said that forty days of precious time were lost in these negotiations, and that in consequence British and American blood was needlessly shed around Salerno. This criticism is as ill-founded in fact as it is wounding to those who are bereaved. The time of our main attack upon Italy was fixed without the slightest reference to the attitude of the Italian Government, and the actual provisional date of the operation was settled long before any negotiations with them had taken place, and even before the fall of Mussolini. That date depended upon the time necessary to disengage our landing craft from the beaches of Southern Sicily, across which up to the first week in August the major part of our armies actually engaged there had to be supplied from day to day. These landing-craft had then to be taken back to Africa. Those that had been damaged—and they were many—had to be repaired, and then reloaded with all their ammunition, etc., in the most exact and complex order before there could be any question of carrying out another amphibious operation.[316]

Wagg points out also that any delay in negotiations was the consequence of factors outside Allied control:

All during the rather protracted negotiations it was the matter of distances and arranging travel

in and out of Italy that was the principal difficulty. Time consumed in the discussions was
in itself brief. Had the two sides had ready access
to each other the whole matter would certainly
have been settled in two or three days. But concealment, the necessity of secret meetings in a
neutral country or flying across the fighting lines
from Italy to Sicily with the dangers of discovery
and the physical hazards involved, and the time
consumed in communicating secretly between Algiers and Rome, were what lengthened the negotiation period from the date of the first Lisbon
approach, August 18th, to the date of the signing
of the Armistice on September 3rd.[317]

IX. THE SURRENDER AND AFTERWARDS

Eisenhower's proclamation of the armistice was promptly followed up by Roosevelt and Churchill. From Washington, on September 10, they addressed a message to Badoglio and the people of Italy. It began with a stirring appeal for action:

It has fallen to you in the hour of your country's agony to take the first decisive steps to win peace and freedom for the Italian people and to win back for Italy an honourable place in the civilization of Europe.

You have already freed your people from Fascist servitude. There remains the even more important task of cleansing the Italian soil from the German invaders.

It ended on the same note:

Strike hard and strike home. Have faith in your future. All will come well. March forward with your British and American friends in the great world movement towards Freedom, Justice, and Peace.[318]

In the critical week following the Salerno landings, the Allies were in need of whatever assistance the Badoglio government could provide. Nor were they then aware of the full extent of Italy's collapse. As a result, Badoglio's past sins and recent hesitations were certainly being overlooked in the hope of great and immediate military gains. And at that moment Badoglio's government was indeed making a major contribution to the Allied armed forces.

In the early morning hours of Friday, September 10, a British naval squadron stood off the western coast of Sardinia. At 8:25, there hove in view a large fleet. It was the Italian battle fleet, making its rendezvous to surrender to the Allies. Two representatives of Admiral Sir Andrew Browne Cunningham, Allied naval Commander-in-Chief, boarded the Italian flagship. A short time later, the Italian ships swung into line behind the British squadron and the two fleets headed for Malta.

Early on the following morning, Admiral Cunningham sent this message to the Admiralty in London:

BE PLEASED TO INFORM THEIR LORDSHIPS THAT THE ITALIAN BATTLE FLEET IS NOW ANCHORED UNDER THE FORTRESS GUNS OF MALTA.[319]

The prize was an important one. Two battleships, five cruisers and seven destroyers were in the first contingent, which had sailed from Genoa and Spezia at 6:30 on the eighth (concurrently with the announcement of the armistice). The detachment had at first been more numerous but the flagship of the fleet, the battleship *Roma*, had been bombed and sunk by the Germans on its voyage to surrender. Among the many casualties was the Commander-in-Chief of the Italian Navy. In addition, two destroyers were sunk by German shore batteries on the Sardinian coast. Two additional battleships, with two cruisers and a destroyer, sailed from Taranto on the ninth and reached Malta safely on the following day.[320]

A cruiser and three destroyers, left to rescue survivors of the Genoa contingent, ran short of fuel and put in at the Spanish Balearic Islands.[321] Submarines and merchant ships appeared at a number of Allied ports, and later an additional battleship and a seaplane carrier, with a number of destroyers, torpedo boats and submarines, arrived at Malta.[322]

Some repercussions of an earlier omission delayed the smooth integration of Italian naval vessels into the Allied war effort. This is recorded by Cunningham:

On September 22nd I sailed from Malta for Taranto in a cruiser to clear up certain uncertainties about the Italian Navy and merchant shipping. My chief trouble was that the soldiers had produced surrender terms—the "Shorter Instrument" signed in Sicily on September 3rd—without consulting myself or any of my staff. In consequence, various important naval matters had been left unspecified. My main object was to get the Italian mercantile marine, or what remained of it, working in the Allied cause as soon as possible. I also wished to arrange for the smaller vessels of the Italian fleet, destroyers and so forth, to be used for escort work.[323]

The result was "The Cunningham-de Courten Agreement," between the Allied naval Commander-in-Chief and the Royal government's Minister of Marine, whose arrangements were, according to Cunningham, strictly carried out.[324]

The surrender of the Italian Fleet was of great importance. It removed a major threat to Allied shipping in the Mediterranean, thus releasing British (and American) seapower for use elsewhere. It added a considerable number of useful vessels to the Allied command. However, as it turned out, delivery of the fleet was the only one of the military terms of surrender which the Italians were actually able to fulfill.[325] The destruction of the battleship *Roma* was a tragic symbol of events to come. The Germans used every means at their command to deprive the Allies of any advantage from Italy's surrender. Ehrman suggests that

the uncertainties of the final events surrounding the Italian surrender prevented its purpose from being achieved. The armed forces in Italy received no warning of their Government's intentions, and the result was a fatal apathy and disorganization. Only the Fleet observed the terms of surrender to the Allies: the land and air forces found themselves surrendering instead to the Germans. The Germans indeed moved so fast near Rome and in the south that by 10th September they had disarmed all the Italian divisions, and could turn, without fear of interference, to face the Allies at Salerno.[326]

In the confusion of leaving Rome, the Badoglio government neglected to give precise instructions for the safeguarding of Mussolini. On Sunday morning, September 12, German paratroopers "rescued" the former dictator from the small mountain resort where he was held in custody. A skeleton Fascist government was established in northern Italy under the nominal leadership of Mussolini. The German army was in fact the real ruler of Italy. Its forces clamped a rigid occupation upon all of Italy outside Allied control, especially the north. On September 11, Rome was declared an open city, open to the movements of German troops.[327] In fact, as Montgomery later remarked, "the Italian armistice had not seriously prejudiced the German position in Italy."[328]

The Badoglio government sat in Brindisi, a symbol rather than an active and effective force. It possessed negligible authority outside its headquarters building.[329] Especially at the beginning, Allied Military Government took full charge of liberated territory.[330] *In toto,* the armistice gained for the Allies little beyond the almost intact Italian navy. The Germans simply prevented the Italians from accomplishing the planned surrender. With a few exceptions, Italian forces put up no resistance and surrendered meekly to the Germans.[331] Actual military gains were achieved by the hard fighting of Allied ground, air, and sea forces. Italy became a battleground, scene of some of the fiercest and bloodiest fighting of the war. Anzio, Monte Cassino—these names are reminders of the horrors of the campaign. Inch by inch, the Germans stubbornly defended Italy. Rome was not taken until June 1944.

These actual results provide a sharp contrast with the hopes of Allied leaders. In a memorandum which met approval from Roosevelt and the Combined Chiefs of Staff, Churchill indicated possible Allied plans on September 9, a time when the real situation in Italy was not known. He listed several "assumptions":

(a) that the present battle for Naples and Rome is successful and that the Germans retreat to the line of the Apennines or the Po.
(b) the release of the British Fleet from the Mediterranean for operations against Japan.
(c) The public must be gradually led to realise what we and our Combined Staffs have so fully in mind, namely, the conversion of Italy into an active agent against Germany. Although we could not recognise Italy as an ally in the full sense, we have agreed she is to be allowed to work her passage, and that useful service against the enemy will not only be aided but recompensed. Should fighting break out between Italians and Germans, the public prejudices will very rapidly depart, and in a

fortnight or so matters may be ripe, if we can so direct events, for an Italian declaration of war against Germany. The question of the Italian flag flying from Italian ships, and even some arrangement of Italians manning those vessels under British or American control, requires consideration. The whole problem of handling and getting the utmost use out of the Italian Navy requires review on a high level.[332]

Taking advantage of the German withdrawal, the Allied armies should, Churchill believed, move as far north in Italy as possible and there construct a strong defensive line, permitting them to hold down German forces while releasing troops for OVERLORD. It was believed "by Allied military intelligence as well as by some at least of those responsible for the defense of Italy at this time that the Germans, if attacked in force, might make no stand south of Rome but withdraw to the 'Pisa-Rimini' line."[333] Such a development was also the object of some wishful thinking on the part of the Italian leaders. And in fact, such a withdrawal had been one of the German plans some weeks earlier, before the great reinforcement of their troops in Italy. Thus originally this estimate was not merely a Churchillian hope; but after the landings in Sicily, Hitler had decided to fight all the way on the Italian peninsula.

American insistence upon the sanctity of OVERLORD and consequent refusal to make even the slightest alteration or postponement in the diversion of resources for it from the Mediterranean, as well as the strength of the German resistance, would perhaps have doomed these hoped-for gains from the beginning;[334] and under the circumstances, no easy victory in Italy was possible with or without the additional landing craft and divisions.

The appraisal of the developments in Italy by Montgomery is brief but accurate:

The original Allied object in invading Italy was to knock that country out of the war. This was achieved very soon after our leading troops had landed on the mainland.

Following the Armistice there had been a hope that to evict the Germans from Italy with the aid of the Italian Army would be a speedy matter. Events proved this impossible and we became involved in a major campaign lacking a predetermined plan of action. The result was that the administrative machine became unable to keep pace with the constantly widening scope of our operational commitments. We were therefore unable to exploit our advantages in September and October, when operationally a speedy advance to the Rome Line seemed still a very feasible proposition. If then we had had the resources to allow us to maintain pressure on the enemy, our superiority in armour and in the air might have enabled us to roll the enemy back to the Rome Line before the winter began.[335]

Nevertheless, all was not a lost opportunity.

The surrender of Italy and the conquest of the southern part of the peninsula brought to the Allies a number of actual and potential benefits. The first wedge had been driven into Hitler's *Festung Europa;* a heavy blow had been struck at German prestige. The elimination of thirty Italian divisions in the Balkans cut heavily into German reserves by forcing the Wehrmacht to police that area. With the Italian fleet out of the war and the Mediterranean virtually an Anglo-American lake, the Allies could release heavy naval units for service elsewhere. The prospects for a successful cross-Channel invasion were enhanced: men, material, ships, and planes could be spared for use out of the United Kingdom, and a pincer movement against the German armies in France could be planned. In the face of these threats the Germans would have to disperse further their air and ground forces.

For the air forces there were various advantages. From airfields near the Adriatic coast, heavy bombers could hit important targets in the Balkans, Czechoslovakia, Austria, and southern and eastern Germany. . . .[336]

Moreover, while the material advantages of the Italian armistice may have been limited, its symbolic advantages are not to be ignored. The defection of a major Axis partner, the downfall of the first Axis dictator—these are not to be passed over lightly. As one authority has put it, ". . . the political gains were considerable. The breakdown of Mussolini's regime had a great effect on anti-Hitler resistance all over Europe . . . [and] . . . Mussolini was reduced to a mere puppet of Hitler."[337]

Beyond that, the Badoglio government had some sort of value to the Allies. The Royal government was a group of rulers with no country to rule, sitting helpless in a small provincial town, but it was also widely accepted as the legitimate government of Italy.[338]

As against these uncertain benefits, there was a considerable though equally intangible loss.

Primary was the fact that, in part through its own hesitations and lack of positive action, the Royal government was disorganized almost to the point of non-existence. This collapse of the government probably would have made it impossible for Badoglio to fulfill most of the provisions of the armistice, even if the Germans had not reacted so swiftly and effectively. For example, had other units received as positive and precise orders as the fleet, it is possible that something more might have been salvaged for the Allies.

Moreover, there was, especially in the United States, a serious problem of political psychol-ogy. The King had maintained quasi-friendly formal relations with Mussolini throughout the twenty years of Fascist rule, and Badoglio had led the Italian armies in the conquest of Abyssinia. Allied support of such men was widely viewed with distaste and alarm, especially in the United States and England, as Roosevelt had foreseen at the end of July. Even in Italy itself there was grumbling. The repetition of the North African pattern was noted, disliked, and not soon forgotten.

The Allies had two main objectives in dealing with Badoglio—first, to get the Italians to lay down their arms; second, to prevent anarchy in Italy. The first objective Badoglio fulfilled, notably with respect to the fleet. The second was also fulfilled, with the all-important aid of Allied Military Government. It may, however, be recalled that AMG maintained order in Sicily without benefit of the King or Badoglio, although Sicily, unlike Italy and North Africa, did constitute a political "vacuum."

In bringing the story of the armistice to a close, a few details of post-armistice Italian history deserve mention. This epilogue might well be entitled—"Allied chickens come home to roost." The weeks of September and early October began to show the strains in Allied political policy for Italy. British and American differences, apparent in the spring, had been hidden by the overriding military considerations of the summer. Now they were to reappear in full flower.

The critical issue was Allied policy toward the King and Badoglio.

On September 19, after conferring with Macmillan, Eisenhower sent the following message:

My views are summarized as follows. In our future relations with Italy there are only two courses:

1. To accept and strengthen the legal government of Italy under the King and Badoglio; to regard this government and the Italian people as co-belligerents but with their military activity subject to my direction under terms of [the] armistice, and I, of course, making such military, political and administrative conditions as I may find necessary from time to time. Included in these would be the imposition by directive of such clauses of the long terms as may be necessary from the supply, shipping, economic and other points of view under the authority of Article 12 of the short terms.

2. To sweep this government aside, set up an Allied military government of occupied Italy, and accept the very heavy commitments involved.

Of these two courses, on military grounds, I strongly recommend the first. Since as [a] co-belligerent it [Italy] would necessarily declare war on Germany and on the Fascist Republic Government of Italy, for all elements desiring to fight against Fascism in Italy it will be the natural rallying point.[339]

Eisenhower backed up this view with a lengthy telegram of propaganda instructions, entitled "Propaganda for Italy." One paragraph read:

(2) Deliberately build up Badoglio Government as rallying point [for] Italian resistance, stress left parties accept Badoglio leadership.[340]

The response of the two home governments to Eisenhower's proposals indicated their differing attitudes.

THE BRITISH POSITION

When Eisenhower's telegram on Italian policy was given to Churchill, he cabled the Allied commander:

3. We are backing you up all we can about working with the Italian Government, and I am pretty sure all will go as you wish it.[341]

At the same time he noted in a speech to the House of Commons:

. . . two obvious and practical targets for us to fire at [are] Nazi tyranny and Prussian militarism. Let us aim every gun, and let us set every man who will march in motion against them. We must not add needlessly to the weight of our task or the burden that our soldiers bear. Satellite states, suborned or overawed, may perhaps, if they can help to shorten the war, be allowed to work their passage home. But the twin roots of all our evils, Nazi tyranny and Prussian militarism, must be extirpated.[342]

British policy for Italy centered on full support of the King and Badoglio, at least until the capture of Rome, expected at this point to be imminent, and of full support for the House of Savoy—though not necessarily of Victor Emmanuel—thereafter. This was Churchill's personal policy, accepted by the Cabinet, although it met with less than universal acceptance among the British people and their politicians.[343]

As Churchill made clear, he feared anarchy and Communism in Italy. These twin evils he regarded as probable or even inevitable concomitants of the removal or fall of the government, or even of any major change in its character prior to Allied entry into Rome, whether superseded by some other Italian government or by AMG's full assumption of responsibility for rule. Probably more important, and quite sufficient to negate the AMG alternative in his analysis, was his long-held conviction that constitutional monarchy was essential for the creation and survival of democratic government in Italy.

Churchill went somewhat further than this. Mussolini, "delivered" by the Germans, had set up a puppet Fascist regime in the North. Following the armistice, civil war had broken out in German-occupied areas between Germans and Italians, between pro-Mussolini Italians and anti-Mussolini Italians.[344] These anti-Fascist elements needed a focus of loyalty, a rallying point. In addition, important Italian garrisons existed on a number of Aegean islands, as well as Sardinia and Corsica. Leadership by the Royal government, especially a declaration of war against Germany, might rally the officers of these troops to support the Allies and important military gains might thus be achieved. Despite its many weaknesses, the Royal government at Brindisi was the legitimate government of Italy. Churchill considered it a rallying point, and wanted it to be the cornerstone of Allied policy.

Alternatives, in addition to AMG, soon appeared. Italian anti-Fascist leaders, long in hiding, in retirement, or in exile, came forward and demanded a place in the government. Many of them wanted a republic, some wanted or were willing to settle for a regency, none had any respect for Badoglio. The alternatives proposed by these men—a reconstructed Cabinet, with or without the establishment of a regency or of a republic—and the men themselves did not meet with Churchill's approval and were resisted by him on all occasions. This small group of party leaders, described by Churchill as "Leftish," had been in exile or underground for twenty years or more. He was convinced that they were out of touch with the realities of current Italian politics and they appeared to him more interested in assuming power themselves for personal aggrandizement than in strengthening the Royal government.[345] (That they had no desire to strengthen the Badoglio government, which they despised, seems obvious.) Churchill was not denying to the Italian people the promised right of ultimate self-determination. But only a small fraction of Italy was free from German occupation. Other considerations were paramount for the moment.

From the moment when the Armistice was signed and when the Italian Fleet loyally and courageously joined the Allies, I felt myself bound to work with the King of Italy and Marshal Badoglio, at least until Rome should be occupied by the Allies and we could construct a really broad-based Italian Government for the prosecution of the war jointly with us. I was sure that King Victor Emmanuel and Badoglio would be able to do more for what had now become the common cause than any Italian Government formed from the exiles or opponents of the Fascist regime.[346]

After all, the Badoglio government had signed the armistice and had delivered the Italian battle fleet to the Allies. No group of quarreling "leftish" party leaders could produce an accomplishment like that. (Nor could the Badoglio government repeat it, one might add.) This view of Allied policy was endorsed by the Russians, who certainly could not be accused of Royalist sympathies. Their view was accurately and colorfully expressed by the old Russian proverb, "You may walk with the Devil until you come to the end of the bridge."[347] Secretary of State Hull, who took no part in the entire affair, nevertheless supported this view in his *Memoirs.* A primary advantage to be gained from dealing with the Royal government was

. . . the direct military advantages that would accrue to the Allies from having a legitimate government in Italy. This would, of course, prohibit any question as to the constitutional legality of the surrender. Perhaps even more important, it would help to prevent a complete state of anarchy in Italy—a condition imposing heavy burdens upon the already over-taxed Allied armies.[348]

Churchill's views were well expressed in a speech which he made to the House of Commons on the twenty-first:

The escape of Mussolini to Germany, his rescue by paratroops, and his attempts to form a Quisling Government which, with German bayonets, will try to refix the Fascist yoke on the necks of the Italian people, raise of course the issue of Italian civil war. It is necessary in the general interest, as well as in that of Italy, that all surviving forces of Italian national life should be rallied together around their lawful Government, and that the King and Marshal Badoglio should be supported by whatever Liberal and Left-Wing elements are capable of making head against the Fascist-Quisling combination, and thus of creating conditions which will help to drive this villainous combination from Italian soil, or, better still, annihilate it on the spot. We are coming to the rescue and liberation of Italy. (A Member interjected: "You will not get the Italian people to rise behind the banner of turncoats.") I think the honourable gentleman may be not thinking quite sufficiently of the importance of diminishing the burden which our soldiers have to bear . . . . The Government certainly intend to pursue a policy of engaging all the forces they can to make head against the Germans and drive them out of Italy. We are not going to be put off that action by any fear that perhaps we should not have complete unanimity on the subject. Parliament does not rest on unanimity; democratic assemblies do not act on unanimity. They act by majorities. That is the way they act. I wish to make it perfectly clear that we are endeavouring to rally the strongest forces together in Italy to make head against the Germans and the Mussolini-Quisling-Fascist combination.[349]

After considering Eisenhower's recommendations, Churchill outlined specific means of implementing this broad policy in a telegram to Roosevelt on September 21:

. . . I and my colleagues in the War Cabinet have come to the following conclusions:

It is vital to build up the authority of the King and the Brindisi Administration as a Government and have unity of command throughout Italy. . . . Despite Badoglio's broadcast tonight we still feel it is essential that the King should go to the microphone at Bari, tell the Italian people he is there, and proclaim that Badoglio is carrying on the legitimate Government of Italy under his authority. This is needed, not only for the Italian people, but for the Italian representatives and garrisons abroad.

The King and Badoglio should be told that they must build up the broadest-based anti-Fascist coalition Government possible. Any healthy elements that can deliver some goods should be rallied in this crisis. It would be very useful if Count Sforza and the professors who claim to represent the six parties were willing to join in the common effort. It must however be clearly understood that none of these provisional arrangements, dictated by war needs, will stand in the way of the free choice by the Italian people of the form of democratic government which they prefer. These points should be made plain in the King's broadcast.

The question of giving the Badoglio Government an Allied status does not come into our immediate programme. Co-belligerency is good enough. On this footing we should work for the gradual conversion of Italy into an effective national force against Germany, but, as we have said, she must work her passage. Useful service against the enemy will be recognized by us in the adjustment and working of the Armistice terms. In return we expect Badoglio to continue to work for the Allies on the basis of the Armistice. Our principle will be payment by results. Badoglio should be free to declare war on Gemany, and by so doing he would at once become, though not an ally, a co-belligerent.

Badoglio can be told that it is no part of our plan to install Allied military government everywhere. If he will co-operate, we are ready to hand over territory of his Government as quickly as it is free from the enemy. This offer applies to the historic mainland of Italy, Sicily, and Sardinia. The dealings of the United Nations with the Italian Government in territories which they were allowed to administer will be carried out through a Control Commission.

It would make it much easier for us if the full instrument of surrender, even though somewhat superseded, could now be signed. It is true that many of the clauses could not be operated by the Brindisi Administration in their present situation. But as we go up the peninsula and turn over territory to the Italian Government, these questions will become real. We do not want to put ourselves in the position of having to haggle over every requirement with the Government. The longer we leave it the more difficult it becomes to get the instrument signed, so I hope Eisenhower will get Badoglio's signature to it as soon as possible on the basis suggested in the Foreign Secretary's telegrams.

This programme should be put to the King and

Badoglio at once. The first essential is that the King should make the public announcement suggested. This should not surely await final refinements of policy.[350]

This policy was tied to a military strategy of an aggressive major campaign in Italy.

THE AMERICAN ATTITUDE

British policy after the armistice was more clearly defined than the American. It was set by Churchill, with Cabinet concurrence, and was brought into sharp focus by Churchill's devotion to the legitimacy of the House of Savoy. American policy had no such unmistakable guiding star.

From important quarters, there was strong opposition to continued dealings with the King and Badoglio.

On September 20, Hopkins read a copy of the proposed agreement whereby Italy would be permitted to enter the war not as an "ally" but as a "co-belligerent," and he wrote the following memorandum and sent it to the President.

"I hope you will not encourage Eisenhower to recognize Italy as a co-belligerent. This will put them in exactly the same status as the rest of our Allies. Nor do I think there is enough evidence that Badoglio and the King can be trusted for us to arm any of their divisions. I should think that Eisenhower could quietly look the other way if some of the armistice terms are being violated, such as Italian naval ships being used to transport our troops, or Italian bombers from Sardinia fighting the Germans.

"Would it not be better in paragraph 2 to cut out the words 'to wage war against Germany' and substitute 'to assist us in the war'?

"I cannot see that a declaration of war by Badoglio gets us anywhere except a precipitated recognition of two men who have worked very closely with the Fascists in the past. I think we should get every possible advantage out of them, but I don't think we are under any obligation to them.

"I don't see why, if Eisenhower wants to use the Italian crews and Italian ships, he does not go ahead and do it, providing he thinks he can trust them. I simply hate to see this business formalized until we have had a much better look at Badoglio and the King. McFarlane, the British general's, report on them was certainly none too good.

"I would not throw out Badoglio but recognition would be an inevitable step. Could you not tell Eisenhower to keep on as he is for the present and make the decision in another week?"[351]

Two days later, probably referring to Eisenhower's proposal and Churchill's cable, Hopkins wrote again:

I have grave misgivings about both the King and Badoglio. Certainly neither of them, by any stretch of the imagination, can be considered to represent a democratic government.

It is very easy to recognize these people, but it is awfully hard to throw them overboard later.

I surely don't like the idea that these former enemies can change their minds when they know that they are going to get licked and come over to our side and get help in maintaining political power.[352]

Roosevelt's personal views are not definitely known. Some inkling of his basic attitude may be found in an unsigned memorandum, dated December 24, 1942, discovered by Sherwood in the Hopkins Papers. Sherwood considered it an "admirable statement of Roosevelt's fundamental point of view in dealing with the French problem." Portions of this memorandum are worth quoting here because there are a number of analogies to the Italian situation and also because comparisons may be drawn between it and the Eisenhower views presented above (p. 270).

The sovereignty of France rests with the French people. . . . The sympathy of the French that expressed itself for De Gaulle, reflects not a choice of De Gaulle as the future head of the French government, but the French anxiety to continue to *fight* Germany alongside of England and the United States. They would, however, certainly resist a government, even if provisional, which would owe its initial authority to foreign recognition. The basis of legitimacy which permitted Darlan to effectively bring North Africa alongside the Allies, is due to the fact that he represented what was then the existing constituted authority of Vichy. He was thus able to give orders which were followed by the local military commanders and the local administration. Indeed, while as it has been proved since, most responsible officials wanted at heart to cooperate with America and Great Britain, their action had to be determined by an order from the regular central authority. Men entrusted with authority in an orderly society are not revolutionaries, and it is to be revolutionary to act contrary to the orders of the central accepted authority. Admiral Darlan gave the order that was wished for—but the order had to be given. He alone could give it, not General Giraud at that time.

But now that this has been done, and that the various local commanders have sided with the Allies, it is important to prevent the use which Darlan made of Petain's authority from being developed into a legitimacy recognized or fostered by the Allies. Such a development in North Africa would be a denial of those conditions which alone will enable the French people to give free expression to their sovereignty.[353]

More specifically, Roosevelt was aware of Churchill's determination to maintain the monarchy as the cornerstone of stability in Italian politics. He was equally familiar with Eisenhower's wish to work with Badoglio and the Royal government as the most advantageous policy from a military point of view. At the same time, he could scarcely ignore the Fascist elements in the background of both the King and Badoglio and the bitter feelings against them in the Allied and occupied countries. Nor could he ignore the fact that the Badoglio government was looked on with contempt by a great many Italians. The inability of the Badoglio government to fulfill all the terms of the armistice provided grounds for its repudiation by the Allies.

Roosevelt's public pronouncements and, more definitely, his revisions of the May Memorandum show his strong interest in promoting the growth of democracy in Italy. This included encouraging the tiny groups with "democratic leanings" in Italian politics.

The result, perhaps typically for Roosevelt, was a compromise. The President accepted the proposition that military considerations should be predominant at first. Later on the Italian people should be guaranteed the right to choose their own government.[354]

In part at least, Roosevelt's decision stemmed from an agreement which had been arrived at by him and Churchill:

The prime factor in the development of Allied policy towards Italy in the weeks immediately after the armistice was an agreement reached privately between Churchill and Roosevelt according to which the British would take the lead in Italian affairs. This agreement was made either at the first Quebec Conference, or in the days immediately afterwards when Churchill stayed on in Washington in order to concert Italian policy with Roosevelt.[355] This arrangement was a counterpart to the agreement which had entrusted the

lead in French North Africa to the Americans, but in neither case did the agreements assign complete and exclusive control of affairs to one of the Allies. Consultation still preceded every important move.[356]

In instructions to Eisenhower (issued by the Combined Chiefs of Staff and received at AFHQ on September 23rd), which were approved by Churchill, the President stated his policy:

In view of the existing situation in Italy the earliest practicable action is important.

You will withhold long-term Armistice provisions pending further instructions.

2. On the basis of military necessity, you are empowered to make recommendations from time to time to lighten the provisions of the military armistice in order to enable the Italians, within the limit of their capacities, to wage war against Germany.

3. On condition that it declares war on Germany, the present Government of Italy should be permitted, subject to the provisions of paragraph 4 hereunder, to carry on as the Government of Italy, and as such should be treated as a co-belligerent in the war against Germany; such relationship to be based on the clear understanding that it is not in any way to prejudice the untrammeled right of the people of Italy to decide on the form of government they will eventually have, and that no final form of government of Italy will be decided upon until the Germans are evicted from Italian territory.

4. The Allied Military Government and the appropriate functions contemplated for the Armistice Control Commission will be merged as promptly as practicable into an Allied Commission under the Allied Commander-in-Chief, which shall be empowered to furnish guidance and instructions from time to time to the Badoglio Government on military, political, and administrative matters.

5. You will encourage in all practicable ways the vigorous use, under your direction, of the Italian armed forces against Germany.[357]

SIGNATURE OF THE LONG TERMS

A further result of the Roosevelt-Churchill compromise was a decision to require Badoglio to sign the Long Terms. This the Royal government did not want to do, as evidenced in part by its delay in declaring war on Germany in the hope of achieving some modification. The terms were harsh but, more important, many of them were obsolete, i.e., could not be carried out by Badoglio because of his impotence in German-occupied Italy. Additional terms could not be carried out if the Italian government was to cooperate with the Allies in the war against Germany.

Roosevelt had been reluctant to have the Long Terms signed, probably because, unlike the Short Terms which were temporary and essentially military in character, the Long Terms were political and permanent. He could defend dealing with Badoglio on the basis of the Short Terms as dictated by military requirements. A more permanent relationship such as that involved in the longer document was more troublesome and therefore to be avoided.[358]

The actual decision to require signature of the Long Terms (reached two days later on the 25th),[359] although conforming to Churchill's long-established policy and tending to strengthen the legal position of the Badoglio government, was perhaps as well a further concession to what Roosevelt conceived to be the military situation. The terms gave a little more formal legality to the *de facto* position of the Allied Commander-in-Chief in Italy and confirmed his sweeping powers over all phases of life of the Italian nation. In effect, they placed the Italian government completely under the control of the Allies through the Commander-in-Chief;[360] but this had been the position of the King and Badoglio ever since they fled from Rome.

On September 29, at a ceremony on board the battleship *Nelson* in Malta Harbor, the Long Terms were signed in person by Badoglio and Eisenhower.[361] Following the ceremony, this letter was presented to Badoglio:

The terms of the armistice to which we have just appended our signatures are supplementary to the short military armistice signed by your representative and mine on September 3rd, 1943. They are based upon the situation obtaining prior to the cessation of hostilities. Developments since that time have altered considerably the status of Italy, which has become in effect a co-operator with the United Nations.

It is fully recognized by the Governments on whose behalf I am acting that these terms are in some respects superseded by subsequent events and that several of the clauses have become obsolescent or have already been put into execution. We also recognize that it is not at this time in the power of the Italian Government to carry out certain of the terms. Failure to do so because of existing conditions will not be regarded as a breach of good faith on the part of Italy. However, this document represents the requirements with which the Italian Government can be expected to comply when in a position to do so.

It is to be understood that the terms both of this document and of the short military armistice of September 3rd may be modified from time to time if military necessity or the extent of co-operation by the Italian Government indicates this as desirable.

> Sincerely,
> Dwight D. Eisenhower[362]

Finally the Royal government, on October 13, declared war on Germany. Simultaneously, a declaration by Roosevelt, Churchill, and Stalin was released which accorded Italy the rather nebulous status of "co-belligerent."

The Governments of Great Britain, the United States and the Soviet Union acknowledge the position of the Royal Italian Government as stated by Marshal Badoglio and accept the active co-operation of the Italian nation and armed forces as a co-belligerent in the war against Germany. The military events since September eighth and the brutal maltreatment by the Germans of the Italian population, culminating in the Italian declaration of war against Germany have in fact made Italy a co-belligerent and the American, British and Soviet Governments will continue to work with the Italian Government on that basis. The three Governments acknowledge the Italian Government's pledge to submit to the will of the Italian people after the Germans have been driven from Italy, and it is understood that nothing can detract from the absolute and untrammelled right of the people of Italy by constitutional means to decide on the democratic form of government they will eventually have.

The relationship of co-belligerency between the Government of Italy and the United Nations governments cannot of itself affect the terms recently signed, which retain their full force and can only be adjusted by agreement between the allied governments in the light of the assistance which the Italian Government may be able to afford to the United Nations' cause.[363]

General Eisenhower continued to adhere to his policy of working with the Badoglio government. His primary concern was still his military objectives and he believed that Badoglio continued to offer the best means of helping the Allied command to secure these objectives. For example, at the conference at Malta on September 29, Badoglio discussed with Eisenhower several ways of furnishing greater Italian assistance to the Allies. The Marshal thought "that when he could get his troops to Sardinia, he could put eight divisions in the field against the Germans."[364]

Moreover, Eisenhower had strongly favored the declaration of war on Germany by the Royal government. Responding to pleas from the British to help hold the Dodecanese Islands,[365] Eisenhower, unwilling to subtract from his forces in Italy,

again put pressure on Badoglio and the King immediately to declare war against Germany in the hope this will crystallize the resistance of Italians on the islands and elsewhere. . . . [He] felt that declaration of war by the King would be a great psychological help because some Italian units would be induced to fight, whereas now they are just jellyfish.[366]

These assumptions may have been reinforced in Eisenhower's thinking by some suspicion of Sforza and some of the other "leftist" politicians, referred to by Butcher at the time as "professed liberals."[367] At a later point (October 28), Butcher noted: "The Badoglio government is showing its good faith by pressing for inclusion of at least one Italian division in line of combat in addition to supplying troops for labor and guard of lines of communication."[368] The contrast between the political "quarreling" of the "leftish" leaders (whatever its genuine and far-reaching importance in Italian politics) and the offer of a badly needed combat division is obvious, especially to a general concerned with military requirements and in no position to judge the military impacts of governmental change. In December, an Italian combat group was put into the line. However, as the Allies learned how great had been the disintegration of the Italian army and air force, and how great were its deficiencies in equipment and effective leadership, they became increasingly reluctant to avail themselves of Italian offers of combat troops. Despite Eisenhower's hopes, the contributions of the Badoglio government in this direction were negligible.[369]

SFORZA AND THE CONTINUING DISPUTE

Concurrently with the Royal government's declaration of war against Germany, Badoglio issued a proclamation which declared in part:

The Government headed by me will shortly be completed. In order that it may constitute a true expression of democratic government in Italy, the representatives of every political party will be asked to participate. The present arrangement will in no way impair the untrammelled right of the people of Italy to choose their own form of democratic government when peace is restored.[370]

When, however, he attempted to bring representatives of liberal and "leftish" groups into his government, Badoglio met refusal. A principal factor in the rebuff to Badoglio was Count Carlo Sforza. His entrance upon the Italian political scene at this point produced a long-drawn-out dispute between the Allies, a dispute which reflected their underlying differences over Italian policy.

Count Sforza was a prominent anti-Fascist Italian, a former Foreign Minister and Ambassador to France, in exile since Mussolini's advent to power. About the end of September, the United States decided to help him return to Italy in spite of his announced aversion to the King. Sforza did say at the time of his departure for Italy that he would work with the Badoglio government so long as it played its part and fought the Germans. However, his distaste for it was well known and it was not at all clear that his presence in Italian politics would be a means of strengthening Badoglio or the King. Sforza was, however, experienced; he had had "no truck with fascism"; and he was regarded by many as a symbol of Italian democracy.

In despatching Sforza to Italy, Roosevelt made one small concession. Sforza was returned via the United Kingdom, where Churchill would have the opportunity of persuading him to help the Allies by temporarily supporting the Royal government. Whether the President actually believed Sforza's philosophy could be temporarily altered—or cared—is debatable. The official American attitude, it is true, was one which Churchill would have approved:

Badoglio, in command of the Italian forces, recognized the relentless logic of the situation. He called on all Italians to make common front against the Nazi tyranny. Many sincere anti-Fascists have differed with the Marshal during his long career. But their best thinking was summed up by Count Carlo Sforza, who promptly and forthrightly declared that so long as Badoglio was fighting the common enemy, it would be criminal for any Italian to weaken his hand: politics and constitutional questions should be adjourned, to be dealt with after the liberation; all hands, now, must join the common front against the common enemy.

Clearly, the Italian people can be trusted to deal with the reorganization of Italy when it is cleared of invading bayonets. Today the pressing task is to mobilize every Italian from the Alps to the Ionian Sea as a mighty army to repel these modern barbarians who seek to make of Italy a Nazi gau.[371]

Nevertheless, the fact remains that Sforza's arrival in Italy immediately strengthened demands for the King's abdication, which led to extreme irritation with Sforza on the part of both Churchill and Eisenhower. Roosevelt agreed with Churchill on the principle of "self-determination." The President, however, had no burning desire to set the stage for a self-determination that would almost inevitably include the House of Savoy.[372]

As a result, when Badoglio attempted to bring representatives of liberal and "leftish" groups into his government, Sforza was prominent in their refusing the offer. Led by the Count, these groups instead demanded the abdication of Victor Emmanuel. The King refused, was supported by the British and then by the Americans, the liberals proved intransigent, and nothing came of Badoglio's efforts.[373]

The dramatic days of the Italian armistice came to an end. German resistance to Allied advances in Italy was stiff. The Anzio amphibious landing was nearly a disaster. The armistice brought no change in the central policy of the American military leaders and in agreed Allied policy: OVERLORD. During the fall of 1943 men and supplies were withdrawn from the Italian peninsula to take part in the build-up in England. General Eisenhower left the Medi-

terranean Theater on January 1, 1944 to assume command of OVERLORD.

Thus Italy became a subsidiary military theater. Its status during the remainder of World War II conformed to the plans of the American Joint Chiefs of Staff, plans agreed to but not entirely liked by Churchill and the British. OVERLORD was not "impaired" by the efforts of Churchill and his aides, as the Americans had feared, and the great victories in Italy and the Mediterranean so ardently desired by Churchill never came to pass. The strategy of direct frontal assault did not give way to the strategy of peripheral attacks. British strategy fell victim not only to American insistence upon OVERLORD but also to the Germans. Hitler determined to defend the Italian peninsula inch by inch. This ruined prospects for a quick and easy campaign in Italy. Yet it was this very decision which helped to make OVERLORD viable. German troops in Italy, as Brooke and his colleagues had planned, were not free to oppose an Allied landing in France.

Allied acceptance of the King and Badoglio continued through the following months. After the failure of his attempts to form a more broadly based government, Badoglio formed a cabinet of technicians, designed as a temporary expedient until the imminently expected fall of Rome. However, as a result of the stubborn German defense and Allied unwillingness to wage a major campaign in Italy, Rome did not fall until June 1944. In the interim, Italian political dissension, centering around the future status of the King, grew more and more bitter.

The persistent issues of internal Italian politics remained a source of bitterness in Allied relations until they were finally resolved by the Italians themselves, many months after the armistice of September 1943.

APPENDIX A

THE SHORT TERMS

CONDITIONS PRESENTED SEPTEMBER 3, 1943

Fairfield Camp Sicily
September 3, 1943

The following conditions of an Armistice are presented by

General Dwight D. Eisenhower,
Commander-in-Chief of the Allied Forces,
acting by authority of the Governments of the United States and Great Britain and in the interest of the United Nations, and are accepted by

Marshal Pietro Badoglio
Head of the Italian Government

1. Immediate cessation of all hostile activity by the Italian armed forces.

2. Italy will use its best endeavors to deny, to the Germans, facilities that might be used against the United Nations.

3. All prisoners or internees of the United Nations to be immediately turned over to the Allied Commander in Chief, and none of these may now or at any time be evacuated to Germany.

4. Immediate transfer of the Italian Fleet and Italian aircraft to such points as may be designated by the Allied Commander in Chief, with details of disarmament to be prescribed by him.

5. Italian merchant shipping may be requisitioned by the Allied Commander in Chief to meet the needs of his military-naval program.

6. Immediate surrender of Corsica and of all Italian territory, both islands and mainland, to the Allies, for such use as operational bases and other purposes as the Allies may see fit.

7. Immediate guarantee of the free use by the Allies of all airfields and naval ports in Italian territory, regardless of the rate of evacuation of the Italian territory by the German forces. These ports and fields to be protected by Italian armed forces until this function is taken over by the Allies.

8. Immediate withdrawal to Italy of Italian armed forces from all participation in the current war from whatever areas in which they may be now engaged.

9. Guarantee by the Italian Government that if necessary it will employ all its available armed forces to insure prompt and exact compliance with all the provisions of this armistice.

10. The Commander in Chief of the Allied Forces reserves to himself the right to take any measure which in his opinion may be necessary for the protection of the interests of the Allied Forces for the prosecution of the war, and the Italian Government binds itself to take such administrative or other action as the Commander in Chief may require, and in particular the Commander in Chief will establish Allied Military Government over such parts of Italian territory as he may deem necessary in the military interests of the Allied Nations.

11. The Commander in Chief of the Allied Forces will have a full right to impose measures of disarmament, demobilization, and demilitarization.

12. Other conditions of a political, economic and financial nature with which Italy will be bound to comply will be transmitted at a later date.

The conditions of the present Armistice will not be made public without prior approval of the Allied Commander in Chief. The English will be considered the official text.

Dwight D. Eisenhower,
General, U. S. Army,
Commander in Chief,
Allied Forces.

Marshal Pietro Badoglio
Head of Italian Government

By: Walter B. Smith
Walter B. Smith
Major General, U. S. Army,
Chief of Staff.

By: Guiseppe Castellano
Guiseppe Castellano
Brigadier General, attached to the
Italian High Command

Present:

Rt. Hon. Harold Macmillan
British Resident Minister, A.F.H.Q.

Robert Murphy
Personal Representative of the President of the United States

Royer Dick
Commodore, R.N., Chief of Staff to the C. in C. Med.

Lowell W. Rooks
Major General, U. S. Army, Assistant Chief of Staff, G-3, A.F.H.Q.

Franco Montanari
Official Italian Interpreter

Brigadier Kenneth Strong
Assistant Chief of Staff, G-3, A.F.H.Q.

This text, taken from *U. S. and Italy,* 51-52, is identical with the text printed in the British *Documents Relating to the Conditions of an Armistice with Italy,* 3-4, and differs only in minor differences of phraseology from that in *Documents on American Foreign Relations,* VI, 161.

APPENDIX B

THE LONG TERMS

The "Instrument of Surrender of Italy," the correct original text of the Long Terms, was the document wired to Eisenhower by the Combined Chiefs of Staff on August 27 and signed by Marshal Badoglio at Malta on September 29. On November 9, 1943, a Protocol was signed by Badoglio and General Noel Mason-MacFarlane for General Eisenhower which made certain modifications in the text of the Long Terms:

The title of the Long Armistice was changed from "Instrument of Surrender of Italy" to "Additional Conditions of Armistice with Italy." In Article I the last word "unconditionally" was deleted so that it read "the Italian Land, Sea, and Air Forces wherever located hereby surrender." In paragraph six of the preamble, the word "unconditionally" was inserted to make it read, "These terms . . . have been accepted unconditionally by Marshal Pietro Badoglio. . . ."

The resulting document is the one printed below; it is taken from *U. S. and Italy,* 55-64. The correct original text is printed in the British *Documents Relating to the Conditions of an Armistice with Italy,* 4-10. The Protocol of November 9 is printed in the same collection, pp. 11-12.

Whereas in consequence of an armistice dated September 3rd, 1943, between the United States and the United Kingdom Governments on the one hand and the Italian Government on the other hand, hostilities were suspended between Italy and the United Nations on certain terms of a military nature;

And whereas in addition to those terms it was also provided in the said Armistice that the Italian Government bound themselves to comply with other conditions of a political, economic and financial nature to be transmitted later;

And whereas it is convenient that the terms of a military nature and the said other conditions of a political, economic and financial nature should without prejudice to the continued validity of the terms of the said Armistice of September 3rd, 1943, be comprised in a further instrument;

The following together with the terms of the Armistice of September 3rd, 1943, are the terms on which the United States and United Kingdom Governments acting on behalf of the United Nations are prepared to suspend hostilities against Italy so long as their military operations against Germany and her Allies are not obstructed and Italy does not assist those Powers in any way and complies with the requirements of these Governments.

These terms have been presented by General Dwight D. Eisenhower, Commander-in-Chief, Allied Forces, duly authorized to that effect;

And have been accepted unconditionally by Marshal Pietro Badoglio, Head of the Italian Government.

1. (A) Italian participation in the war in all Theaters will cease immediately. There will be no opposition to landings, movements or other operations of the Land, Sea and Air Forces of the United Nations. Accordingly, the Italian Supreme Command will order the immediate cessation of hostilities of any kind against the Forces of the United Nations and will direct the Italian Navy, Military and Air Force authorities in all Theaters to issue forthwith the appropriate instructions to those under their Command.

(B) The Italian Supreme Command will further order all Italian Naval, Military and Air Forces or authorities and personnel to refrain immediately from destruction of or damage to any real or personal property, whether public or private.

2. The Italian Supreme Command will give full information concerning the disposition and condition of all Italian Land, Sea and Air Forces, wherever they are situated and of all such forces of Italy's Allies as are situated in Italian or Italian occupied territory.

3. The Italian Supreme Command will take the necessary measures to secure airfields, port facilities, and all other installations against seizure or attack by any of Italy's Allies. The Italian Su-

preme Command will take the necessary measures to insure Law and Order, and to use its available armed forces to insure prompt and exact compliance with all the provisions of the present instrument. Subject to such use of Italian troops for the above purposes, as may be sanctioned by the Allied Commander-in-Chief, all other Italian Land, Sea and Air Forces will proceed to and remain in their barracks, camps or ships pending directions from the United Nations as to their future status and disposal. Exceptionally such Naval personnel shall proceed to shore establishments as the United Nations may direct.

4. Italian Land, Sea and Air Forces will within the periods to be laid down by the United Nations withdraw from all areas outside Italian territory notified to the Italian Government by the United Nations and proceed to areas to be specified by the United Nations. Such movement of Italian Land, Sea and Air Forces will be carried out in conditions to be laid down by the United Nations and in accordance with the orders to be issued by them. All Italian officials will similarly leave the areas notified except any who may be permitted to remain by the United Nations. Those permitted to remain will comply with the instructions of the Allied Commander-in-Chief.

5. No requisitioning, seizures or other coercive measures shall be effected by Italian Land, Sea and Air Forces or officials in regard to persons or property in the areas notified under Article 4.

6. The demobilization of Italian Land, Sea and Air Forces in excess of such establishments as shall be notified will take place as prescribed by the Allied Commander-in-Chief.

7. Italian warships of all descriptions, auxiliaries and transports will be assembled as directed in ports to be specified by the Allied Commander-in-Chief and will be dealt with as prescribed by the Allied Commander-in-Chief. (Note: If at the date of the Armistice the whole of the Italian Fleet has been assembled in Allied ports, this article would run—"Italian warships of all descriptions, auxiliaries, and transports will remain until further notice in the ports where they are at present assembled, and will be dealt with as prescribed by the Allied Commander-in-Chief.")

8. Italian aircraft of all kinds will not leave the ground or water or ships, except as directed by the Allied Commander-in-Chief.

9. Without prejudice to the provisions 14, 15 and 28 (A) and (D) below, all merchant ships, fishing or other craft of whatever flag, all aircraft and inland transport of whatever nationality in Italian or Italian-occupied territory or waters will, pending verification of their identity and status, be prevented from leaving.

10. The Italian Supreme Command will make available all information about naval, military and air devices, installations, and defences, about all transport and inter-communication systems established by Italy or her allies on Italian territory or in the approaches thereto, about minefields or other obstacles to movement by land, sea or air and such other particulars as the United Nations may require in connection with the use of Italian bases, or with the operations, security, or welfare of the United Nations Land, Sea or Air Forces. Italian forces and equipment will be made available as required by the United Nations for the removal of the above mentioned obstacles.

11. The Italian Government will furnish forthwith lists of quantities of all war material showing the location of the same. Subject to such use as the Allied Commander-in-Chief may make of it, the war material will be placed in store under such control as he may direct. The ultimate disposal of war material will be prescribed by the United Nations.

12. There will be no destruction of nor damage to nor except as authorized or directed by the United Nations any removal of war material, wireless, radio location or meteorological stations, railroad, port or other installations or in general, public or private utilities or property of any kind, wherever situated, and the necessary maintenance and repair will be the responsibility of the Italian authorities.

13. The manufacture, production and construction of war material and its import, export and transit is prohibited, except as directed by the United Nations. The Italian Government will comply with any directions given by the United Nations for the manufacture, production or construction and the import, export or transit of war material.

14. (A) All Italian merchant shipping and fishing and other craft, wherever they may be, and any constructed or completed during the period of the present instrument will be made available in good repair and in seaworthy condition by the competent Italian authorities at such places and for such purposes and periods as the United Nations may prescribe. Transfer to enemy or neutral flags is prohibited. Crews will remain on board pending further instructions regarding their continued employment or dispersal. Any existing options to repurchase or re-acquire or to resume control of Italian or former Italian vessels sold or otherwise transferred or chartered during the war will forthwith be exercised and the above provisions will apply to all such vessels and their crews.

(B) All Italian inland transport and all port

equipment will be held at the disposal of the United Nations for such purposes as they may direct.

15. United Nations merchant ships, fishing and other craft in Italian hands wherever they may be (including for this purpose those of any country which has broken off diplomatic relations with Italy) whether or not the title has been transferred as the result of prize court proceedings or otherwise, will be surrendered to the United Nations and will be assembled in ports to be specified by the United Nations for disposal as directed by them. The Italian Government will take all such steps as may be required to secure any necessary transfers of title. Any neutral merchant ship, fishing or other craft under Italian operation or control will be assembled in the same manner pending arrangements for their ultimate disposal. Any necessary repairs to any of the above mentioned vessels will be effected by the Italian Government, if required, at their expense. The Italian Government will take the necessary measures to insure that the vessels and their cargo are not damaged.

16. No radio or telecommunication installations or other forms of intercommunication, shore or afloat, under Italian control whether belonging to Italy or any nation other than the United Nations will transmit until directions for the control of these installations have been prescribed by the Allied Commander-in-Chief. The Italian authorities will conform to such measures for control and censorship of press and of other publications, of theatrical and cinematograph performances, of broadcasting, and also of all forms of intercommunication as the Allied Commander-in-Chief may direct. The Allied Commander-in-Chief may, at his discretion, take over radio, cable and other communication stations.

17. The warships, auxiliaries, transports and merchant and other vessels and aircraft in the service of the United Nations will have the right freely to use the territorial waters around and the air over Italian territory.

18. The forces of the United Nations will require to occupy certain parts of Italian territory. The territories or areas concerned will from time to time be notified by the United Nations and all Italian Land, Sea and Air Forces will thereupon withdraw from such territories or areas in accordance with the instructions issued by the Allied Commander-in-Chief. The provisions of this article are without prejudice to those of article 4 above. The Italian Supreme Command will guarantee immediate use and access to the Allies of all airfields and Naval ports in Italy under their control.

19. In the territories or areas referred to in article 18 all Naval, Military and Air installations,

power stations, oil refineries, public utility services, all ports and harbors, all transport and all intercommunication installations, facilities and equipment and such other installations or facilities and all such stocks as may be required by the United Nations will be made available in good condition by the competent Italian authorities with the personnel required for working them. The Italian Government will make available such other local resources or services as the United Nations may require.

20. Without prejudice to the provisions of the present instrument the United Nations will exercise all the rights of an occupying power throughout the territories or areas referred to in article 18, the administration of which will be provided for by the issue of proclamations, orders or regulations. Personnel of the Italian administrative, judicial and public services will carry out their functions under the control of the Allied Commander-in-Chief unless otherwise directed.

21. In addition to the rights in respect of occupied Italian territories described in articles 18 to 20,

(A) Members of the Land, Sea or Air Forces and officials of the United Nations will have the right of passage in or over non-occupied Italian territory and will be afforded all the necessary facilities and assistance in performing their functions.

(B) The Italian authorities will make available on non-occupied Italian territory all transport facilities required by the United Nations including free transit for their war material and supplies, and will comply with instructions issued by the Allied Commander-in-Chief regarding the use and control of airfields, ports, shipping, inland transport systems and vehicles, intercommunication systems, power stations and public utility services, oil refineries, stocks and such other fuel and power supplies and means of producing same, as United Nations may specify, together with connected repair and construction facilities.

22. The Italian Government and people will abstain from all action detrimental to the interests of the United Nations and will carry out promptly and efficiently all orders given by the United Nations.

23. The Italian Government will make available such Italian currency as the United Nations may require. The Italian Government will withdraw and redeem in Italian currency within such time limits and on such terms as the United Nations may specify all holdings in Italian territory of currencies issued by the United Nations during military operations or occupation and will hand over the currencies withdrawn free of cost to the United Nations. The Italian Government will take

such measures as may be required by the United Nations for the control of banks and business in Italian territory, for the control of foreign exchange and foreign commercial and financial transactions and for the regulation of trade and production and will comply with any instructions issued by the United Nations regarding these and similar matters.

24. There shall be no financial, commercial or other intercourse with or dealings with or for the benefit of countries at war with any of the United Nations or territories occupied by such countries or any other foreign country except under authorisation of the Allied Commander-in-Chief or designated officials.

25. (A) Relations with countries at war with any of the United Nations, or occupied by any such country, will be broken off. Italian diplomatic, consular and other officials and members of the Italian Land, Sea and Air Forces accredited to or serving on missions with any such country or in any other territory specified by the United Nations will be recalled. Diplomatic and consular officials of such countries will be dealt with as the United Nations may prescribe.

(B) The United Nations reserve the right to require the withdrawal of neutral diplomatic and consular officers from occupied Italian territory and to prescribe and lay down regulations governing the procedure for the methods of communication between the Italian Government and its representatives in neutral countries and regarding communications emanating from or destined for the representatives of neutral countries in Italian territory.

26. Italian subjects will pending further instructions be prevented from leaving Italian territory except as authorised by the Allied Commander-in-Chief and will not in any event take service with any of the countries or in any of the territories referred to in article 25 (A) nor will they proceed to any place for the purpose of undertaking work for any such country. Those at present so serving or working will be recalled as directed by the Allied Commander-in-Chief.

27. The Military, Naval and Air personnel and material and the merchant shipping, fishing and other craft and the aircraft, vehicles and other transport equipment of any country against which any of the United Nations is carrying on hostilities or which is occupied by any such country, remain liable to attack or seizure wherever found in or over Italian territory or waters.

28. (A) The warships, auxiliaries and transports of any such country or occupied country referred to in article 27 in Italian or Italian-occupied ports and waters and the aircraft, vehicles and other transport equipment of such countries

in or over Italian or Italian-occupied territory will, pending further instructions, be prevented from leaving.

(B) The Military, Naval and Air personnel and the civilian nationals of any such country or occupied country in Italian or Italian-occupied territory will be prevented from leaving and will be interned pending further instructions.

(C) All property in Italian territory belonging to any such country or occupied country or its nationals will be impounded and kept in custody pending further instructions.

(D) The Italian Government will comply with any instructions given by the Allied Commander-in-Chief concerning the internment, custody or subsequent disposal, utilisation or employment of any of the above mentioned persons, vessels, aircraft, material or property.

29. Benito Mussolini, his Chief Fascist associates and all persons suspected of having committed war crimes or analogous offences whose names appear on lists to be communicated by the United Nations will forthwith be apprehended and surrendered into the hands of the United Nations. Any instructions given by the United Nations for this purpose will be complied with.

30. All Fascist organisations, including all branches of the Fascist Militia (MVSN), the Secret Police (OVRA), all Fascist youth organisations will insofar as this is not already accomplished be disbanded in accordance with the directions of the Allied Commander-in-Chief. The Italian Government will comply with all such further directions as the United Nations may give for abolition of Fascist institutions, the dismissal and internment of Fascist personnel, the control of Fascist funds, the suppression of Fascist ideology and teaching.

31. All Italian laws involving discrimination on grounds of race, color, creed or political opinions will insofar as this is not already accomplished be rescinded, and persons detained on such grounds will, as directed by the United Nations, be released and relieved from all legal disabilities to which they have been subjected. The Italian Government will comply with all such further directions as the Allied Commander-in-Chief may give for repeal of Fascist legislation and removal of any disabilities or prohibitions resulting therefrom.

32. (A) Prisoners of war belonging to the forces of or specified by the United Nations and any nationals of the United Nations, including Abyssinian subjects, confined, interned, or otherwise under restraint in Italian or Italian-occupied territory will not be removed and will forthwith be handed over to representatives of the United Nations or otherwise dealt with as the United

Nations may direct. Any removal during the period between the presentation and the signature of the present instrument will be regarded as a breach of its terms.

(B) Persons of whatever nationality who have been placed under restriction, detention or sentence (including sentences in absentia) on account of their dealings or sympathies with the United Nations will be released under the direction of the United Nations and relieved from all legal disabilities to which they have been subjected.

(C) The Italian Government will take such steps as the United Nations may direct to safeguard the persons of foreign nationals and property of foreign nationals and property of foreign states and nationals.

33. (A) The Italian Government will comply with such directions as the United Nations may prescribe regarding restitution, deliveries, services or payments by way of reparation and payment of the costs of occupation during the period of the present instrument.

(B) The Italian Government will give to the Allied Commander-in-Chief such information as may be prescribed regarding the assets, whether inside or outside Italian territory, of the Italian state, the Bank of Italy, any Italian state or semi-state institutions or Fascist organisations or residents in Italian territory and will not dispose or allow the disposal, outside Italian territory of any such assets except with the permission of the United Nations.

34. The Italian Government will carry out during the period of the present instrument such measures of disarmament, demobilisation and de-militarisation as may be prescribed by the Allied Commander-in-Chief.

35. The Italian Government will supply all information and provide all documents required by the United Nations. There shall be no destruction or concealment of archives, records, plans or any other documents or information.

36. The Italian Government will take and enforce such legislative and other measures as may be necessary for the execution of the present instrument. Italian military and civil authorities will comply with any instructions issued by the Allied Commander-in-Chief for the same purpose.

37. There will be appointed a Control Commission representative of the United Nations charged with regulating and executing this instrument under the orders and general directions of the Allied Commander-in-Chief.

38. (A) The term "United Nations" in the present instrument includes the Allied Commander-in-Chief, the Control Commission and any other authority which the United Nations may designate.

(B) The term "Allied Commander-in-Chief" in the present instrument includes the Control Commission and such other officers and representatives as the Commander-in-Chief may designate.

39. Reference to Italian Land, Sea and Air Forces in the present instrument shall be deemed to include Fascist Militia and all such other military or para-military units, formations or bodies as the Allied Commander-in-Chief may prescribe.

40. The term "War Material" in the present instrument denotes all material specified in such lists or definitions as may from time to time be issued by the Control Commission.

41. The term "Italian Territory" includes all Italian colonies and dependencies and shall for the purposes of the present instrument (but without prejudice to the question of sovereignty) be deemed to include Albania. Provided however that except in such cases and to such extent as the United Nations may direct the provisions of the present instrument shall not apply in or affect the administration of any Italian colony or dependency already occupied by the United Nations or the rights or powers therein possessed or exercised by them.

42. The Italian Government will send a delegation to the Headquarters of the Control Commission to represent Italian interests and to transmit the orders of the Control Commission to the competent Italian authorities.

43. The present instrument shall enter into force at once. It will remain in operation until superseded by any other arrangements or until the voting into force of the peace treaty with Italy.

44. The present instrument may be denounced by the United Nations with immediate effect if Italian obligations thereunder are not fulfilled or, as an alternative, the United Nations may penalize contravention of it by measures appropriate to the circumstances such as the extension of the areas of military occupation or air or other punitive action.

The present instrument is drawn up in English and Italian, the English text being authentic, and in case of any dispute regarding its interpretation, the decision of the Control Commission will prevail,

Signed at Malta on the 29 day of September, 1943.

Dwight D. Eisenhower
Dwight D. Eisenhower
General, United States Army,
Commander-in-Chief,
Allied Force.

Badoglio
Marshal Pietro Badoglio
Head of the Italian Government

ACKNOWLEDGMENTS

A large number of cooperative men and women have helped to make this study possible. Most must unfortunately remain unidentified. I do, however, owe special thanks to: Major Victor L. Walker and Lieutenant Colonel William C. Pelton of the Office Chief of Information and Education, and Major Leonard Cassidy of the Adjutant General's Office, Department of the Army; Miss Wava Phillips of the Research Division of G-3, Department of the Army; Dr. Kent Roberts Greenfield, until 1958 Chief Historian of the Department of the Army and his deputy (now his successor), Dr. Stetson Conn; Mr. Herman Kahn, Director of the Franklin D. Roosevelt Library, Hyde Park, New York; Dr. Wayne Grover, Archivist of the United States; and Dr. E. Taylor Parks, Chief of the Advisory and Review Branch, the Historical Division of the Department of State.

BIBLIOGRAPHIC NOTE

Manuscripts

The following list covers all sources directly cited in the footnotes, and a few others as well. Additional information was furnished by correspondence and by other sources that cannot be cited. There are, of course, a considerable number of Italian publications that deal in some fashion with the Armistice, but aside from Villari they are of only quite tangential relevance.

Records of the Department of the Army, Washington, D. C. (cited as Army files).

The Roosevelt Papers, located in the Franklin D. Roosevelt Library, Hyde Park, New York.

The Smyth Manuscript. This includes chapters and portions of chapters by Howard McGaw Smyth, prepared for inclusion in *The U. S. Army in World War II*. The Smyth MS is in the custody of the Office of the Chief of Military History, Department of the Army, Washington, D. C.

The Weinberg Manuscript, located in the files of the Office of the Chief of Military History, Department of the Army, Washington, D. C.

Published Collections of Documents

Armistice with Italy, 1943, Treaties and Other International Acts Series 1604 (Department of State Publication 2963). Washington, D. C.: Government Printing Office, 1947. Pp. 34.

Documents on American Foreign Relations, Volume VI, *July 1943-June 1944.* Boston: World Peace Foundation, 1945. Pp. 725.

Royal Institute of International Affairs, *Documents on International Affairs, 1939-1946,* Volume II, *Hitler's Europe,* selected and edited by Margaret Carlyle, Oxford University Press, 1954. Pp. 361.

Documents Relating to the Conditions of an Armistice with Italy, September-November, 1943 (Great Britain, Foreign Office, Italy No. 1, 1945, Cmd. 6693). London: His Majesty's Stationery Office, 1945. Pp. 20.

Federal Records of World War II, Volume II,

Military Agencies (National Archives Publication No. 51-58). Washington, D. C.: General Services Administration, National Archives and Records Service, The National Archives, 1951. Pp. 1061.

United States and Italy, 1936-1946, Documentary Record. Washington, D. C.: Government Printing Office, 1946. Pp. 236, map.

U. S. Department of State Bulletin, IX, Numbers 210-235 (July 3-December 25, 1943). Washington, D. C.: Government Printing Office, 1944. Pp. 471.

————— Bulletin, XIII, Numbers 314-340 (July 1-December 30, 1945). Washington, D. C.: Government Printing Office, 1946. Pp. 1100.

The War Reports of General of the Army George C. Marshall, in *The War Reports of Marshall, Arnold, King.* Philadelphia and New York: J. B. Lippincott Co., 1947. Pp. 801, illus.

(Note: The texts of the Short Terms and the Long Terms, the Cunningham–de Courten Agreement, and several related documents to be found in *United States and Italy, 1936-1946,* were published earlier by the Department of State in *Armistice with Italy, 1943,* and in individual Department of State *Bulletins.)*

Books

Bryant, Arthur. *The Turn of the Tide (A History of the War Years Based on the Diaries of Field Marshal Lord Alanbrooke, Chief of the Imperial General Staff).* Garden City, New York: Doubleday and Co., 1957. Pp. 624, illus.

Butcher, Harry C. *My Three Years with Eisenhower.* New York: Simon and Schuster, 1946. Pp. 911, illus.

Carroll, Wallace. *Persuade or Perish.* Boston: Houghton Mifflin Co., 1948. Pp. 392.

Churchill, Winston S. *The Gathering Storm* (volume I of *The Second World War).* Boston: Houghton Mifflin Co., 1948.

—————. *The Hinge of Fate* (volume IV of *The Second World War).* Boston: Houghton Mifflin Co., 1950. Pp. 1000, maps.

——————. *Closing the Ring* (volume V of *The Second World War*). Boston: Houghton Mifflin Co., 1951. Pp. 749.

——————. *Onwards to Victory*. War speeches by the Right Hon. Winston S. Churchill, C.H., M.P., compiled by Charles Eade. Boston: Little, Brown and Company, 1944.

Cline, Ray S. *Washington Command Post: The Operations Division* (volume in series *U. S. Army in World War II, The War Department*). Washington, D. C.: Office of the Chief of Military History, Department of the Army, 1951. Pp. 413, illus.

Craven, W. F., and Cate, J. L. *Europe: Torch to Pointblank, August 1942 to December 1943* (volume II of *The Army Air Forces in World War II*). Chicago: University of Chicago Press, 1949. Pp. 897, illus.

Cunningham, A. B. *A Sailor's Odyssey*. New York: E. P. Dutton, 1951. Pp. 715, illus.

Ehrman, John. *Grand Strategy (V), August 1943-September 1944 (History of the Second World War, United Kingdom Military Series*, J. R. M. Butler, editor). London: Her Majesty's Stationery Office, 1956. Pp. 634, illus.

Eisenhower, Dwight D. *Crusade in Europe*. Garden City, New York: Doubleday and Co., Inc., 1948. Pp. 559, illus.

Hayes, Carlton J. H. *Wartime Mission in Spain, 1942-1945*. New York: Macmillan Co., 1945. Pp. 313.

Holborn, Hajo. *American Military Government, Its Organization and Policies*. Washington: Infantry Journal Press, 1947. Pp. 243.

——————. *The Political Collapse of Europe*. New York: Alfred A. Knopf, 1951. Pp. 207.

Hughes, H. Stuart. *The United States and Italy*. Cambridge: Harvard University Press, 1953. Pp. 256.

Hull, Cordell. *The Memoirs of Cordell Hull,* Volume II. New York: Macmillan Co., 1948.

King, Ernest J., and Whitehill, Walter M. *Fleet Admiral King, A Naval Record*. New York: W. W. Norton and Co., Inc., 1952. Pp. 674, illus.

Kogan, Norman. *Italy and the Allies*. Cambridge: Harvard University Press, 1956. Pp. 246.

Leahy, William D. *I Was There*. New York: Whittlesey House, McGraw-Hill Book Co., 1950. Pp. 527, illus.

Morison, Samuel Eliot. *Sicily–Salerno–Anzio, January 1943-June 1944* (volume IX of *History of United States Naval Operations in World War II*). Boston: Little, Brown and Company, 1954. Pp. 413, illus.

Roosevelt, Elliott, editor, assisted by Joseph P. Lash. *F. D. R.: His Personal Letters, 1928-1945,* Volume II. New York: Duell, Sloan and Pearce, 1950.

Royal Institute of International Affairs. *Survey of International Affairs, 1939-1946*.

McNeill, William Hardy. *America, Britain, and Russia, 1941-1946*. Oxford University Press, 1953. Pp. 819, maps.

Toynbee, Arnold and Veronica M., editors. *Hitler's Europe*. Oxford University Press, 1954. Pp. 730, maps.

Scrivener, Jane (pseud.). *Inside Rome with the Germans*. New York: Macmillan Co., 1945. Pp. 204.

Sherwood, Robert E. *Roosevelt and Hopkins, An Intimate History* (revised edition). New York: Harper and Brothers, 1950. Pp. 1002, illus.

Stimson, Henry L., and Bundy, McGeorge. *On Active Service in Peace and War*. New York: Harper and Brothers, 1947-1948. Pp. 698, illus.

Templewood, Viscount (Sir Samuel Hoare). *Ambassador on Special Mission*. London: Collins, 1946. Pp. 320.

Thruelson, Richard, and Arnold, Elliott. *Mediterranean Sweep, Air Stories from El Alamein to Rome*. New York: Duell, Sloan and Pearce, 1944. Pp. 278, illus.

Tregaskis, Richard. *Invasion Diary*. New York: Random House, 1944. Pp. 245, illus.

United States Department of State. *Postwar Foreign Policy Preparation, 1939-1945*. Washington, D. C.: Department of State, Office of Public Affairs, Publication 3580, General Foreign Policy Series 15 (edited by Harley A. Notter), 1949. Pp. 726.

Villari, Luigi. *Italian Foreign Policy Under Mussolini*. New York: The Devin-Adair Co., 1956. Pp. 396, illus.

Wagg, Alfred, and Brown, David. *No Spaghetti for Breakfast*. London: Nicholson and Watson, 1943. Pp. 231.

Wilmot, Chester. *The Struggle for Europe*. New York: Harper and Brothers, 1952. Pp. 766.

Articles

Brown, David. "The Inside Story of Italy's Surrender," *The Saturday Evening Post,* CCXVII, No. 11 (September 9, 1944) and No. 12 (September 16, 1944), illus. (Reprint of chapters, dealing with the armistice negotiations from *No Spaghetti for Breakfast*.)

Crossman, R. H. S. "Supplementary Essay," in Lerner, Daniel, *Sykewar*. Pp. 23. New York: George W. Stewart, Inc., 1949. Pp. 463.

Gavin, James M. "Airborne Plans and Operations in the Mediterranean Theater," *Infantry Journal* (August 1946), 22-29.

Graham, M. W. "Two Armistices and a Surren-

der," *American Journal of International Law,*
XL (1946), 148-158.

Kecskemeti, Paul. "The Italian Surrender September 1943," Chapter 4, pp. 71-118 of *Strategic Surrender: The Politics of Victory and Defeat,* Stanford, 1958. (This appeared after the completion of this study; it elaborates the odd thesis that "unconditional surrender" deferred the armistice and affected the Allies adversely.)

Smyth, Howard McGaw. "Armistice of Cassibile," *Military Affairs,* XII, No. 1 (Spring 1948), 12-35.

Thruelson, Richard, and Arnold, Elliott. "Secret Mission to Rome, The Complete Story of the Taylor-Gardiner Mission," *Harper's Magazine,* CLXXXIX (October 1944), 462-469. (This article forms one of a series in *Mediterranean Sweep.*)

NOTES

1. This text of the Eisenhower Declaration of the armistice is quoted from a transcript in the *Roosevelt Papers* in the Franklin D. Roosevelt Library at Hyde Park, New York (hereafter cited as the *Roosevelt Papers)*. An identical text, taken from the *New York Times* of September 9, 1943, is reprinted in *United States and Italy, 1936-1946, Documentary Record* (Washington, D. C., 1946, 50-51, n.63a, hereafter cited as *U. S. and Italy);* it is also reprinted in Wagg, Alfred, and Brown, David, *No Spaghetti for Breakfast* (London, 1943), 121; and *Documents on American Foreign Relations, VI, July 1943-June 1944* (Boston, 1945), 169. Transcripts of Radio Berlin's initial reaction and other statements released by Radio Algiers may also be found in the *Roosevelt Papers.*

2. The Eighth Army entered Tripoli on January 23. A brief but excellent picture of the latter stages in the Tunisian campaign may be found in "The War Reports of General of the Army George C. Marshall," in *The War Reports of Marshall, Arnold, King* (Philadelphia and New York, 1947), 93-98, 155-156 (hereafter cited as *Marshall's Report).*

3. A detailed account of the Casablanca Conference, together with the lengthy planning for it, is contained in Churchill, Winston S., *The Hinge of Fate* (volume IV of *The Second World War,* Boston, 1950), 660-695. This account includes the discussion of the nature of the conference, the futile attempts to make it a three-power meeting with Stalin in attendance, and the difficulties of location. For further background information, see Butcher, Harry C., *My Three Years With Eisenhower* (New York, 1946), 230, 232, 237-241; Sherwood, Robert E., *Roosevelt and Hopkins, An Intimate History* (revised edition, New York, 1950), 661-665, 668-697; Eisenhower, Dwight D., *Crusade in Europe* (Garden City, New York, 1948), 135; King, Ernest J., and Whitehill, Walter M., *Fleet Admiral King, A Naval Record* (New York, 1952), 414-415; Bryant, Arthur, *The Turn of the Tide* (Garden City, New York, 1957), 439-459; Morison, Samuel Eliot, *Sicily-Salerno-Anzio, January 1943-June*

1944 (volume IX of *History of United States Naval Operations in World War II,* Boston, 1954), 1-11 (hereafter cited as Morison, IX); Wilmot, Chester, *The Struggle for Europe* (New York, 1952), 117-127; Cline, Ray S., *Washington Command Post: The Operations Division* (volume in series *U. S. Army in World War II, The War Department,* Washington, D. C., 1951), 213-219.

4. Notes written by Harry Hopkins *en route* to the Casablanca Conference. Printed in Sherwood, 671. (A photostatic illustration of this portion of the original notes appears on p. 670.) This volume contains a number of direct transcriptions from the "Hopkins Papers," now located at the Franklin D. Roosevelt Library, Hyde Park, New York.

5. Hopkins' Notes, printed in Sherwood, 671; Roosevelt letter to Mrs. Roosevelt, January 13, 1943, in Roosevelt, Elliott, ed., assisted by Joseph P. Lash, *F. D. R.: His Personal Letters, 1928-1945,* II (New York, 1950), 1393. Leahy was left behind at Trinidad, King, 415; Leahy, William D., *I Was There* (New York, 1950), 143-144.

6. According to Churchill, Admiral King argued for first priority for the Pacific theater. See Churchill, *Hinge of Fate,* 676. This view is not fully supported by King in his memoirs; see pp. 416 ff.

7. For the text of the Combined Chiefs' directive to Eisenhower, see *Marshall's Report,* 156.

For Churchill's urgent desire to keep the Allied forces occupied, see Sherwood, 701; see also Cunningham, A. B., *A Sailor's Odyssey* (New York, 1951), 535; Churchill, *Hinge of Fate,* 678; Eisenhower, 159; Stimson, Henry L., and Bundy, McGeorge, *On Active Service in Peace and War* (New York, 1947-1948), 428; Craven, W. F., and Cate, J. L., *Europe: Torch to Pointblank, August 1942 to December 1943* (volume II of *The Army Air Forces in World War II,* Chicago, 1949), 113-114.

Tentative plans for an invasion of Sicily were being prepared early in December, with March 30 as a target date (Butcher, 218).

8. From Hopkins' notes of the conference,

quoted in Sherwood, 675.

The report of the CCS listed three objectives of the occupation of Sicily:

"(i) Making the Mediterranean line of communications more secure.

(ii) Diverting German pressure from the Russian front.

(iii) Intensifying the pressure on Italy."

Furthermore there was a desire to use large numbers of Allied troops who would otherwise be idle.

See also Morison, IX, 10.

9. Eisenhower, 160. These views coincided with those expressed by Churchill in an earlier message to Roosevelt, quoted in Sherwood, 674.

In addition, the plan fitted well with the British policy of forcing the Germans to disperse their forces. See below, pp. 210-211, 246-247.

10. From Hopkins' notes of the conference, quoted in Sherwood, 675. Marshall's concurrence was significant because he was perhaps the foremost proponent of OVERLORD at the earliest possible date.

11. The text of the official communiqué is printed in *U. S. and Italy*, 38-40. A combined military subcommittee had drafted a summary of the results of the conference for use both in a message to Stalin and in the communiqué to the press (Cline, 217).

12. A useful examination of the whole question of "unconditional surrender" at the Casablanca Conference may be found in Churchill, *Hinge of Fate*, 684-691.

13. This description of the news conference is based largely on Hopkins' notes, printed in Sherwood, 691-694.

13a. The notes included the following sentence: "This involves the simple formula of placing the objective of this war in terms of an unconditional surrender by Germany, Italy and Japan." The remainder of the relevant paragraph is printed in Sherwood, 696-697.

14. Eisenhower, 489, n. 7. See also Sherwood, 972, notes. Cline, 217, notes ". . . [the President] . . . announced for the first time the unconditional surrender formula as the proper aim of the Allied war effort, a subject on which no real military staff work had been done at all." Leahy, 145, received the impression that the matter had *not* been discussed with the *Combined* Chiefs at Casablanca.

15. "The subcommittee's calculation of the relative advantages of this policy was based in part on historical experience with international conflict, which conferred a degree of concreteness on its conclusions. The President's enunciation of the policy of unconditional surrender at

Casablanca on January 26, 1943, reflected no recommendation by the [State] Department; none had been made. He had, however, been appraised informally of the subcommittee's early thinking on this point by its Chairman [Norman Davis]." (United States Department of State, *Postwar Foreign Policy Preparation, 1939-1945*, Washington, D. C., 1949, edited by Harley A. Notter), 127. See also *ibid.*, 126, 131-132.

16. Roosevelt's statement is quoted from Hopkins' notes of the conference, in Sherwood, 696. See also Memorandum, F. D. R. to Cordell Hull, April 1, 1944, in *F. D. R.: His Personal Letters*, II, 1504. Roosevelt's memory was always elephantine, but not always accurate; Grant used the phrase in his message to General Buckner at Ft. Donelson on Feb. 16, 1862, not at Appomattox where he met Lee more than two years later; but perhaps Roosevelt was merely telescoping his recollections.

17. Churchill, *Hinge of Fate*, 684.

18. Quoted in *ibid.*, 686.

19. Portions of a foreign affairs debate in the House of Commons, reported in the *Times* of London, November 18, 1949; quoted in Sherwood, 973, notes.

20. Hull, Cordell, *The Memoirs of Cordell Hull*, II (New York, 1948), 1548.

21. *Ibid.*, 1570.

22. This short-range policy was indicated in a joint Roosevelt-Churchill communiqué to Stalin on January 26 in Churchill, *Hinge of Fate*, 742. A broader statement is contained in the same document, *ibid.*, 744.

23. Eisenhower, 167.

24. A general account of the conference may be found in Churchill, *Hinge of Fate*, 782-811.

25. The actual text of the document is printed in *ibid.*, 808-809. Sherwood, 732, contains a summary of some of these decisions.

26. For example, "although King appreciated the value of thrusts in the Mediterranean, he feared that extensive activity there might make it impossible to build up sufficient forces in the United Kingdom for the invasion of France in 1944." (King, 436-437.)

27. Leahy, 158.

28. Bryant, 494.

29. *Ibid.*, 503 and 509.

30. Printed in Churchill, *Hinge of Fate*, 810. Ehrman, John, *Grand Strategy* (V), *August 1943-September 1944 (History of the Second World War, United Kingdom Military Series)*, 58-63, carefully analyzes the advantages and disadvantages of an Italian campaign and explores the principal alternatives to it.

31. "It was at this conference that the Com-

bined Chiefs of Staff decided to extend Allied influence in the Mediterranean to the point where Italy would be forced to withdraw from the war." *(Marshall's Report,* reprinted in *U. S. and Italy,* 41.)

32. "I was determined to obtain before leaving Africa the decision to invade Italy should Sicily be taken." (Churchill, *Hinge of Fate,* 816.)

"The PM is so persistent in his desire to knock out Italy that he said that the British people would be proud to halve their already short rations for a month if the shipping thus released would contribute to cure the supply difficulty inherent in the conquest of Italy." (Butcher, 318.)

33. This statement is so brief and so general that footnotes for it are scarcely appropriate. Reference may be made, however, to the pages of Churchill, Winston S., *Closing the Ring* (volume V of *The Second World War,* Boston, 1951), Eisenhower, Sherwood, Ehrman, and Bryant. A useful brief exposition appears in McNeill, William Hardy, *America, Britain, and Russia, 1941-1946* (volume in Royal Institute of International Affairs, *Survey of International Affairs, 1939-1946,* Oxford, 1953), 261-268, and in Wilmot, 127-132.

34. According to Butcher, 317, ". . . there were no serious questions of difference between the two."

35. Butcher, 318.

36. "General Marshall was in no way hostile to these ideas [the invasion of Italy] but he did not wish for a clear-cut decision to be taken at this moment. He said that it would be better to decide what to do after we had started the attack on Sicily." (Churchill, *Hinge of Fate,* 825.) For another more positive statement, see Eisenhower, 168.

37. Churchill, *Hinge of Fate,* 824-825.

38. The development of this propaganda strategy is discussed very fully in Carroll, Wallace, *Persuade or Perish* (Boston, 1948), 160-163 ff. Carroll notes that the State Department failed to give copies of the Hull-Eden cables to the Office of War Information in Washington. Although Ambassador Winant turned over copies to the OWI office in London, there was some disagreement and delay.

39. Hopkins' notes, printed in Sherwood, 715.

40. The account of this discussion is based on Hopkins' notes, printed in *ibid.,* 714-715.

40a. There is a copy of this letter in the *Roosevelt Papers.*

41. This entire account of the May Memorandum is based upon *ibid.,* 721-724. On Sherwood pp. 722 and 723 are illustrations of actual portions of the State Department draft, together with the Roosevelt and Hopkins revisions, in addition to regular quotations.

42. As Churchill expressed it, "We have done our very best to help in the Darlan business, and continue to do so in regard to the Vichy contacts still being preserved. But the general feeling is that a brilliant military episode has been tarnished and tainted." (Churchill telegram to Eden, 2 January 1943, printed in Churchill, *Hinge of Fate,* 923.)

43. This message is printed in Sherwood, 724, but is not dated (note on 976).

44. The slightly different views of the State Department may also be seen in one paragraph of "Suggested Comments on Italy for Use by the President in a Press Conference," left with Presidential Press Secretary Early by Cordell Hull on June 9: "If I had an opportunity to speak to the Italian people . . . I would tell the people of Italy that when the German domination of their country has been eliminated, carrying with it the last remnants of Fascist authority, we will assure the Italian people their freedom to choose the kind of [non Fascist or non Nazi kind of] government they wish to establish." *(Roosevelt Papers.)*

The deletion of the word "democratic" and its replacement by the phrase "non Fascist or non Nazi kind of" may be compared with a similar State Department position in the May Memorandum. A copy of this "Memorandum for Mr. Early" (June 9, 1943) may be found in the *Roosevelt Papers.*

45. The text of Churchill's "Position of Italy" is printed in Churchill, *Closing the Ring,* 53-55. This memorandum may well have been the basis for a discussion of Allied action "in the event of a collapse of the Italian nation" which took place on board the *Queen Mary en route* to the TRIDENT conference. (Bryant, 498.)

46. Churchill's views are set down in more detail in *The Gathering Storm* (volume I of *The Second World War,* Boston, 1948), especially 10-11, and in Sherwood, 743.

47. It should be noted that, generally, Allied propaganda was designed to obscure most of these differences. For example, Churchill's instructions to Ismay (May 21, 1943) would fit both the British and American positions.

48. The Italian ambassador to Berlin, Alfieri, reported that (as of July 14) "Germany regarded Italy merely as a bastion to hold up and wear out the enemy forces as long as possible, 'thereby preventing them from menacing areas more directly connected with the territory of the Reich.' " Villari, Luigi, *Italian Foreign Policy Under Mussolini* (New York, 1956), 298.

". . . Throughout the Italian governmental structure Mussolini had permitted or had been forced to accept the infiltration of countless Germans, all of whom were ready to pounce upon the first sign of defection and to take over the Italian nation in name as well as in fact." (Eisenhower, 183.)

See also Churchill, *Closing the Ring,* 52-53.

49. Ehrman, 65; specific details of the German deployment are presented in *ibid.,* 65 ff.

50. Churchill's determination to proceed with the operation was so great that he proposed a study of an all-British HUSKY. See his telegram to General Ismay (February 19, 1943), printed in Churchill, *Hinge of Fate,* 932-933.

51. Bryant, 478.

52. Butcher, 295, 296-297. This move was interpreted by Brooke as another attempt by Marshall to liquidate the Mediterranean campaign as soon as possible. (Bryant, 493.)

53. "In addition, the Sicilian show will be some weeks in starting because we are throwing so much of our resources and energy into the current battle, and there will be time required for training of some of these same troops for amphibious operations." (Butcher, 297.)

54. Cunningham, 527 ff., presents a vivid and detailed account of the planning and preparations for the invasion of Sicily. A discussion of command and strategy appears in Churchill, *Closing the Ring,* 24-29.

55. Proclamation of the Commander-in-Chief of the Allied Forces (Eisenhower) to the people of Sicily, posted following the landing of Allied troops in Sicily, July 10, 1943, printed in *Documents on American Foreign Relations,* VI, 162-163, and in part in Carroll, 166.

56. Hull, 1548, notes that the State Department took part in the preparation of this Declaration, presumably in the preparation of the President's first draft.

The purpose of the Churchill amendments was to make the declaration a joint Anglo-American product rather than a unilateral American declaration or one emphasizing simply the United Nations. See his cable to Roosevelt (July 5, 1943), printed in Churchill, *Closing the Ring,* 44-45.

57. The entire message is printed in Churchill, *Closing the Ring,* 45-46, in *U. S. and Italy,* 42-44, and in *Documents on American Foreign Relations,* VI, 163-164.

58. At a news conference on the 16th, the President denied that the Declaration was an ultimatum. Transcript of Press and Radio Conference #909, July 16, 1943, 11:05 A.M., *Roosevelt Papers.* See also Transcript of Press and Radio Conference #910, July 23, 1943, 10:56 A.M., *ibid.*

59. Churchill, *Closing the Ring,* 46. By July

16 about one-quarter of Sicily was in Allied hands. *(Marshall's Report,* 16.)

60. Sherwood, 741.

61. See p. 210 above.

62. Butcher, 369. At this point, Eisenhower apparently believed that preparations for a landing on the mainland could not be completed before November. (Churchill, *Closing the Ring,* 35.)

63. For Eisenhower, the primary inducements were tactical. (Eisenhower, 185-186.) According to Whitehill (King, 442, n. 15), Admiral King also favored this plan.

64. This additional strength consisted in part of four escort carriers and one fleet carrier, three bomber squadrons, and a number of landing craft. (Churchill, *Closing the Ring,* 37-38; Craven and Cate, 496; Morison, IX, 232, 248.)

65. On July 27, AFHQ ordered General Mark Clark, commanding the Fifth Army in North Africa, to prepare plans for the assault on Naples. This followed approval of this plan by the CCS on July 26. (Leahy, 172.)

66. "In January 1943 the objectives of the Sicilian campaign had been described as follows: to make secure the Allied line of communications in the Mediterranean; to divert Axis strength from the Russian front during the critical summer period; to intensify pressure on Italy. HUSKY accomplished all of these objectives. It accomplished more: it required Germany to extend military commitments into southern France and the Balkans, made Sardinia untenable and threatened Corsica, forced the resignation of Mussolini on 25 July, and led to an Allied-Italian armistice on 3 September." (Craven and Cate, 487.)

67. The description of Roosevelt's reception of the news of Mussolini's downfall is based on Sherwood, 741-742. Sherwood incorrectly reports that Roosevelt's speech was scheduled for Tuesday evening.

68. Churchill, *Closing the Ring,* 43. Villari, 294-295, includes as well Marshal Badoglio, Count Ciano, Dino Grandi, and the Princess of Piedmont, but observes that they did not work together.

69. A useful description of these parties, their aims and activities, may be found in Kogan, Norman, *Italy and the Allies* (Cambridge, 1956), 14-18. See also Hughes, H. Stuart, *The United States and Italy* (Cambridge, 1953), 124.

70. ". . . the conception that totalitarian governments can be wrecked by popular uprisings shows a misapprehension of the modern totalitarian state. Only a split within the leadership or the defection of groups that can command the loyalty of substantial sections of the army, police, and bureaucracy can lead to a change of govern-

ment. Such a *coup d'état* involves immeasurable risks and is not likely to be undertaken by patriotic men unless the very existence of their nation is at stake. In Italy the survival of the monarchy under fascism gave the anti-Mussolini revolt a legal character." Holborn, Hajo, *The Political Collapse of Europe* (New York, 1951), 171.

71. The text of the resolution is quoted in Royal Institute of International Affairs, *Documents on International Affairs, 1939-1946,* II, *Hitler's Europe* (Oxford, 1954), 118, Toynbee, Arnold and Veronica M., editors (hereafter cited as *Hitler's Europe*); Villari, 298.

72. Churchill, *Closing the Ring,* 49.

73. A list of Badoglio's cabinet appointments may be found in *U. S. and Italy,* Appendix E, 219. *Hitler's Europe,* 315, notes that the make-up of the new government was dictated by the King, who would not let Badoglio appoint any representatives of the anti-Fascist parties, nor indeed any party leaders.

74. He was later moved to a mountain resort in Central Italy. Churchill, *Closing the Ring,* 116; *Hitler's Europe,* 315; and p. 268 below.

75. McNeill, 288; *Hitler's Europe,* 315; Kogan, 26, 28-31; Hughes, 127-128.

During the pre-armistice period there was tacit cooperation between the underground "leftish" parties and the Badoglio government. See Kogan, 28-31.

76. *Hitler's Europe,* 316; see also Morison, IX, 186-187; Kogan, 26-27; Wilmot, 133. This was, of course, simply an acceleration of their existing policy. See p. 214 above.

"Hitler's headquarters as early as 1 August had drawn up a plan for Operation ACHSE, to start when and if Italy surrendered. This involved the swift occupation of Genoa, Leghorn, Venice and Trieste by Marshal Rommel, now commander in northern Italy; of central and southern Italian ports by Marshal Kesselring, commander in those parts of Italy, the evacuation of Sardinia and Sicily by German troops, and a brisk transfer of German divisions to Italy." (Morison, IX, 260.)

77. In preparing Chapter V and the one following, the author received material assistance from a manuscript prepared in 1951 by Howard McGaw Smyth for the Office of the Chief of Military History, Department of the Army. Citations are to its Chapter VIII "Midsummer Allied Strategy," which in revised form is to be included in *Sicily and the Surrender of Italy,* a volume in the series *The United States Army in World War II.*

78. From Transcript of White House Press and Radio conference #911, July 27, 1943, 4:11 P.M., *Roosevelt Papers.*

79. The reaction of the U. S. State Department was summarized by Secretary Hull's comment at a news conference on July 26 that ". . . he had no information to that effect ('any change in our policy of unconditional surrender in respect to Italy as a result of the conditions that had taken place') from either the President or the War Department, who are dealing immediately with that matter. He added that he was not anticipating anything from them to the contrary." (Quoted in *U. S. and Italy,* 44; parenthetical quote from an earlier portion of the release.)

The events in Italy also induced the American JCS to approve the preparation of plans for an expedition against Naples, a proposal to which they had been rather cool before. (Leahy, 172, and p. 217 above.)

80. In the *Roosevelt Papers* are some four drafts as well as the final text of this radio address. The earlier ones, prepared before July 25, contain no mention of Italy; in the later ones may be noted gradual insertion of the paragraphs quoted above.

81. The text of the Roosevelt telegram (President to Prime Minister, #324, July 25, 1943) is printed in Churchill, *Closing the Ring,* 55. Churchill's telegram which it crossed in transit is also printed, *ibid.,* 55.

Roosevelt's reference to the Balkans was probably made, as McNeill, 289, suggests, before consultation with the JCS, who regarded such possible action as anathema.

82. Consideration of the possibility of a crack-up in Italy had taken place earlier. For example, Brooke had raised the possibility at the Churchill-Eisenhower meeting on May 29. (See p. 210 above.) See also Churchill's telegram to Eden of February 13, 1943, printed in Churchill, *Hinge of Fate,* 932.

83. The text of these "Thoughts" is printed in Churchill, *Closing the Ring,* 56-58.

84. *Ibid.,* 55-56. A copy of the "Thoughts" was also despatched (via General Devers) to Eisenhower. Telegrams #4116 and WARE 1119/3 (Army files). See also p. 228 below.

85. See McNeill, 289, for an elaboration of this theme.

86. Quotations from "Mussolini's Downfall," a speech to the House of Commons delivered by Churchill on July 27, 1943. *Onwards to Victory* (War Speeches by the Right Hon. Winston S. Churchill, C.H., M.P., compiled by Charles Eade, Boston, Little, Brown and Company, 1944), 186-187. See also McNeill, 288.

87. See p. 230 below; also Churchill, *Closing the Ring,* 59.

88. Quoted in *ibid.,* 58-59.

89. AFHQ Staff Memorandum No. 13, February 10, 1943, Weinberg MS, II, 24-25. The Weinberg Manuscript, deposited in the files of the Office of Chief of Military History, Washington, D. C., is the source for most of this discussion of the respective roles of Macmillan and Murphy (hereafter cited as Weinberg MS).

90. The Political and Economic Council was established by AFHQ General Order #4 (January 7, 1943), Weinberg MS, II, 24. The official invitation is contained in AFHQ Staff Memorandum No. 13 (10 February 1943), Weinberg MS, II, 24-25. See also Churchill, *Hinge of Fate,* 669-670.

91. Memorandum handed by Sir Ronald Ian Campbell to James Dunn (May 5, 1943), Weinberg MS, VII, 33.

92. Memorandum: McCloy to Harry Hopkins, May 25, 1943, Weinberg MS, VII, 34. This American policy also was expressed in the case of Mayor LaGuardia's projected role in Sicily (Sherwood, 725).

93. For example, Murphy's role during the negotiations for the Italian armistice was apparently limited to this field. Note his telegram to General W. B. Smith (August 3, 1943) specifying various *French* demands for inclusion in any Italian armistice settlement. Telegram in Army files.

Murphy's preoccupation with French affairs at an earlier point is illustrated in the account of the Casablanca Conference in Sherwood, 675-697.

94. "The President has appointed the Honorable Robert D. Murphy, presently in Algiers, to be the United States member on the Advisory Council to the Allied Control Commission for Italy. He will have the personal rank of Ambassador and will continue as an adviser on General Eisenhower's staff for Italian affairs." (Department of State *Bulletin,* November 27, 1943, 379.)

95. As Sherwood, 744, phrased it, ". . . the prospect of removing Italy from the war without serious bloodshed—which meant possession of the air bases on the Italian mainland and elimination of the Italian Fleet as a threat to shipping in the Mediterranean—was so overwhelmingly tempting that long-term considerations of morality were apt to be shoved aside."

96. G-2 Weekly Intelligence Summary #49, August 3, 1943 (for week ending July 31), Smyth MS, 52-53.

97. Butcher, 372. It seems possible that some thought had already been given at AFHQ to armistice terms. During the Churchill-Eisenhower meeting on May 29, "Brooke raised the possibility of a crack-up in Italy during the Sicily fighting. In that case we ought to have a scheme of action,

and he felt that General Eisenhower should give some thought to the consideration of armistice terms and how far up into Italy we should go." (Churchill, *Hinge of Fate,* 820.)

98. Telegram #NAF 300, from Eisenhower to the Combined Chiefs of Staff and the British Chiefs of Staff, July 27, 1943, sent 1252B and Telegram #4894 from Eisenhower to Devers for the Prime Minister, July 27, 1943, Army files.

99. The JCS had decided to accept the plans that they had previously opposed; see p. 217 above.

100. Telegram #NAF 266, Eisenhower to Washington for CCS and London for British C of S, July 26, 1943, Army files.

101. The general opposition of AFHQ to "unconditional surrender" is noted by Butcher, 386.

102. Butcher, 371, 372. He further reports: "[Eisenhower] . . . is for offering them peace with honor, including repatriation of Italian prisoners as rapidly as possible, provided, of course, they will complete the overthrow of Fascism and turn and fight the eight to ten German divisions on the Italian mainland. He would ask them to guarantee safe use of certain airfields and strategic points from which the Germans could be dealt with." (372.)

Here reference is being made in part to some of the points included in Eisenhower's proposed set of armistice terms, which were being drafted simultaneously with the radio appeal. See pp. 226-227 below.

103. Telegram #NAF 266, cited above.

104. Churchill, *Closing the Ring,* 59, and also pp. 224-225 above.

105. The message is printed in *Documents on American Foreign Relations,* VI, 166. Eisenhower promptly telegraphed to the Prime Minister his agreement with this proposal. At about this time, the psychological warriors in North Africa began to step up their campaign and to promise that Italian prisoners-of-war would be restored promptly to their homes. When Churchill heard of this, he was furious and he cabled Hopkins expressing his views on the "anonymous and unauthoritative low-level propaganda pumped out by the machines."

"Churchill certainly did not object to the political maneuvering, but he did object strenuously to the proffering of the olive branch on a silver platter. . . ." (Sherwood, 744; see also p. 239 below.)

See also Churchill's telegram to Roosevelt of July 29, paragraphs 2 and 3, printed in Churchill, *Closing the Ring,* 61.

106. Telegram, President to Prime Minister, July 28, 1943, Army files.

107. The message is printed in *Documents on American Foreign Relations,* VI, 166. See also Butcher, 375.

108. Butcher, 375. Butcher notes: "Immediately there was a murmur in the press corps because the message indicated permission to retain the House of Savoy."

109. Smyth MS, 65. See also Cunningham, 560.

110. Leahy, 171, makes mention of still another proposal: "One idea that came from Eisenhower's headquarters was to use a 'black radio' proclamation of an armistice in our projected offensive. Roosevelt rejected the suggestion. It would have been a dishonest kind of warfare and I agreed with the President in believing it would not be necessary."

111. Telegram #NAF 302, Eisenhower to Washington for CCS and London for British Chiefs of Staff, July 27, 1943, Army files.

112. See Butcher, 372, and p. 225 above.

113. Telegram, President to Prime Minister, July 28, 1943, Army files. Another paragraph of this telegram is quoted on p. 226 above. For Churchill's reaction, see the last paragraph of his telegram to Roosevelt on July 27 (p. 226 above).

114. Telegram #4894, Eisenhower to Devers for the Prime Minister, July 27, 1943, sent 1604B, Army files.

". . . as regards the disposal of the Italian Navy the demands fell far short of what was required. Neither myself nor my Chief of Staff, Commodore Dick, had been consulted." (Cunningham, 560.) See also pp. 267-268 below.

115. Butcher, 372.

116. Butcher, 374.

117. See pp. 210-211, 215 above.

118. Butcher, 374. For Stimson's account of this trip and his own views, principally a single-minded adherence to OVERLORD, see *On Active Service,* 429-439.

119. Telegram #4894, Eisenhower to Devers for the Prime Minister, July 27, 1943, Army files. See p. 228 above.

120. This portion of the telegram is quoted in Churchill, *Closing the Ring,* 60.

121. Printed in *ibid,* 61.

122. *Ibid.* A copy of this telegram may be found in Army files: Telegram #330, President to Prime Minister (July 29, 1943). See also p. 232 below.

123. Telegram #3648, President Roosevelt to Eisenhower, Army files. "Prime Minister and I agree: 1. No terms should be made public until Italy asks for them. 2. Important, when the time comes for publicity, to stress release of Allied prisoners and none of them to be allowed to be taken to Germany."

124. Cf. pp. 220-222 above and Churchill, *Closing the Ring,* 56-59.

The State Department was also busy:

"On three occasions the [Security] subcommittee [of the State Department's Advisory Committee on Post-War Foreign Policy] appointed special sub-committees to handle a particular task. Each was composed of a few members assisted by the research staff and functioned only for one or two weeks. The first instance was on June 17, 1943, when Admiral Hepburn [Chairman], General Strong, and Messrs. Dunn, Joseph C. Green, and Myron C. Taylor were designated to study surrender terms, with particular reference to the urgent consideration of the terms for Italy that had been drafted in the War Department and that were shortly to be presented to the Joint Chiefs of Staff. This group held three meetings with a view to recommending revisions in these terms before their final approval for presentation to the enemy. Its report was approved in meetings of the full subcommittee and sent to the Joint Chiefs on July 8." (*Post-War Foreign Policy Preparation,* 131.)

So far as can be ascertained, this was the end of the career of this particular set of proposed surrender terms, although they may have been used by the JCS in criticizing the Churchill draft.

125. Churchill, *Closing the Ring,* 58.

126. This is presumably the document referred to by Churchill in *ibid.,* 98-99. See p. 222 above, and also p. 250 below.

127. A detailed analysis of the various provisions of the Long Terms is contained in Graham, M. W., "Two Armistices and a Surrender," *American Journal of International Law,* Vol. 40, No. 1, January 1946, pp. 150-155.

128. Telegram #W6024, Eisenhower to General Marshall, July 29, 1943, Army files.

129. As contained in Telegram #NAF 302; see pp. 226-227 above.

130. ". . . the terms of surrender for Italy . . . were drawn up by the Combined Civil Affairs Committee of the Anglo-American Combined Chiefs of Staff in Washington." (Hull, 1549-1550.) In fact, the CCAC took part in but portions of the drafting.

131. *Federal Records of World War II,* II (Washington, D. C., 1951), 6. This committee continued throughout the war. See also Holborn, Hajo, *American Military Government, Its Organization and Policies* (Washington, D. C., 1947), 9. The committee's first regular meeting was held on July 15.

132. Sir Ronald *Ian* Campbell, *Minister* of the British Government in Washington, 1941-1945,

and member of the CCAC, is to be distinguished from Sir Ronald *Hugh* Campbell, British *Ambassador* to Portugal, 1940-1945, who later becomes an important figure in this narrative.

133. See also Memorandum, "Conditions for Italian Surrender," drafted by James C. Dunn for the Secretary of State, September 1, 1943, Army files.

134. See pp. 229-230 above.

135. Telegram #330, President to Prime Minister, July 29, 1943, Army files. In the same message, Roosevelt suggested elimination of a portion of paragraph 5 in the text of Eisenhower's original proposals, i.e., "on phase lines to be so prescribed by the Allied Commander in Chief that the evacuation from all Italy will be complete within one month." See pp. 234-235, 278-279 below for the final text of the Short Terms.

Presumably this was the message referred to by Leahy when he recorded: "Most of July 29 was spent preparing for the President drafts of messages for Churchill, concerning the Italian situation. In one, Roosevelt insisted that Eisenhower be authorized without delay to issue general armistice terms, whenever and if an armistice were requested by the Italian Government." (Leahy, 172.)

Upon receipt of these messages, Churchill then ". . . called the War Cabinet out of bed at half-past one in the morning of July 30th and kept them up till four." (Bryant, 558.)

136. Churchill, *Closing the Ring,* 62, where the portion of the telegram containing the proposed terms is quoted.

137. *Ibid.,* 61-62.

138. An intelligence report reaching Algiers at this time (July 30) stated that an Italian officer who arrived in Madrid on the preceding night "thinks Badoglio will need about fifteen days to replace high Fascist leaders and get firm grip on country before forming commission to sue for peace." (Report in Army files.)

139. Transcript of Press and Radio Conference #912, July 30, 1943, 10:57 A.M., *Roosevelt Papers.*

140. For an account of OWI's anti-Badoglio line, which brought them into immediate conflict with their British counterpart, and which was promptly repudiated by the U. S. government, see Carroll, 178-180.

141. Press and Radio Conference #911, July 27, 1943, 4:11 P.M., *Roosevelt Papers.*

142. See p. 213 above. For a subsequent defense by Churchill of this policy, see the portions of his September 21 speech to the House of Commons, printed in Churchill, *Closing the Ring,* 158-159.

Sherwood reports "howls of protest" against the State Department's alleged policy of "doing business" with the avowed enemy, 742-743. This criticism is especially interesting in view of the State Department's almost negligible role in the whole matter of the Italian armistice.

143. Printed in Churchill, *Closing the Ring,* 64; a copy may also be found in Army files.

144. As Sherwood, 744, phrased it, ". . . the prospect of removing Italy from the war without serious bloodshed—which meant possession of the air bases on the Italian mainland and elimination of the Italian Fleet as a threat to shipping in the Mediterranean—was so overwhelmingly tempting that long-term considerations of morality were apt to be shoved aside."

145. Printed in Churchill, *Closing the Ring,* 64.

146. See pp. 226-227 above.

147. Telegram #332, President to Prime Minister, July 30, 1943, Army files.

148. *Ibid.*

149. Telegram WD #3824, July 30, 1943, Army files. (This telegram included the full text of the Short Terms.) Churchill had also had the bulk of his Telegram #389 to the President repeated to Eisenhower.

150. This text is printed in Churchill, *Closing the Ring,* 62-63. See also p. 235 below.

151. Quoted in Churchill, *Closing the Ring,* 63.

152. *Ibid.*

153. *Ibid.,* 64-65.

154. Telegram #3974, Marshall to Eisenhower, August 1, 1943, Army files; Butcher, 378.

The addition of the words, "and Italian aircraft," to Article 4, plus two minor amendments by Churchill in Articles 3 and 5, completed the drafting of the Short Terms. The resulting text, with the addition of Article 12 (see p. 237 below), was that signed on September 3 at Cassibile.

155. The text of Roosevelt's telegram of August 2 is printed in Churchill, *Closing the Ring,* 65.

156. In *ibid.,* 63, Churchill reports that the President said "that he needed further advice from the American Chiefs of Staff and the State Department."

157. See the Dunn Memorandum for the Secretary of State, September 1, 1943, Army files.

158. Leahy Memorandum, cited below.

159. *Memo for Record,* "Surrender Terms for Italy," initialed MNH, dated August 6, 1943, Army files (hereafter cited as "Hammond Memo"). A copy of the full text of "Document A" showing the American revisions may be found in Army files attached to a memorandum bearing the label "Colonel Lincoln, OPD."

160. Memorandum for the President, "Draft Instrument of Surrender of Italy," signed "Leahy," undated (probably August 3, 1943), Army files.

161. The full text of the Short Terms is printed in *U. S. and Italy*, 51-52, and in British *Documents Relating to the Conditions of an Armistice with Italy*, 3-4. It is identical with the text quoted on pp. 234-235 above (plus additions and notes on p. 237), with the addition of Clause 12. See p. 260 and Appendix A, pp. 278-279 below.

162. Craven and Cate, 463-464.

163. Butcher, 322-323; Eisenhower, 168-169; Churchill, *Hinge of Fate*, 828-829. See the message sent by President Roosevelt to Pope Pius XII (July 10, 1943) promising that "Churches and religious institutions will, to the extent that it is within our power, be spared the devastations of war during the struggle ahead. (*U. S. and Italy*, 42.) This message was drafted by Leahy. At Secretary Hull's suggestion, the letter was made public. Similar messages were forwarded to Churchill and Eisenhower. (Leahy, 171-172.)

164. Details of the raid may be found in Craven and Cate, 463-465; Morison, IX, 186; Butcher, 371. For the propaganda efforts of both sides, see Carroll, 169. A good eyewitness account appears in Tregaskis, Richard, *Invasion Diary* (New York, 1944), 10-20; for the reaction in Spain, see Templewood, Viscount (Sir Samuel Hoare), *Ambassador on Special Mission* (London, 1946), 211.

165. See above, pp. 218-219; Churchill, *Closing the Ring*, 47; *Hitler's Europe*, 313; Morison, IX, 185-186. This raid followed by little more than 48 hours the Roosevelt-Churchill Declaration to the Italian people. See p. 216 above.

166. Eisenhower, 184.

167. Butcher, 382; see also Eisenhower, 184.

168. This quotation from Churchill's telegram, dated August 2, may be found in Sherwood, 744. See also note, *ibid.*, 977, and n. 105 above.

169. Butcher, 383. Butcher presents a detailed account of this whole episode, 381-383. See also Carroll, 171-172.

170. Butcher, 375.

171. Letter, Apostolic Delegate to Sumner Welles, August 2, 1943, included in Memorandum for General Handy, August 2, 1943, Army files.

For earlier Vatican efforts to prevent Allied bombing of Rome, see various letters and memoranda in *F. D. R.: His Personal Letters*, II, especially 1382, 1383, 1432, 1441.

Cicognani's letter to Welles of August 2 stemmed in part from Roosevelt's transmission to him (through Hull) on June 28 of the suggestion that "in order to be fair and equally just to both sides, we suggest that the Vatican try to have Rome declared an open city i.e. that all military installations, activities and personnel of Italy be removed from Rome, together with the use of all railroad facilities in and about Rome for military purposes." *F. D. R.: His Personal Letters*, II, 1433. See also Hull, 1560-1563.

172. Letter, Sumner Welles to General Marshall, August 2, 1943, included as part of Memorandum for General Handy, August 2, 1943, Army files.

173. Memorandum for General Handy from General Marshall, August 2, 1943, Army files.

174. Craven and Cate, 474, report that Eisenhower cancelled a mission scheduled for August 1 for operational reasons but make no mention of the August 3 episode.

175. This message arrived in Algiers about midnight. Butcher, 378-379. Telegram, Marshall to Eisenhower, August 2, 1943, Army files.

176. This telegram was a result of the decision arrived at in the Eisenhower-Tedder conference of July 31. See p. 239 above.

177. In fact, the raid had already been cancelled upon receipt of the first message. Butcher, 379.

178. For the British view, see Bryant, 564.

179. The details of Marshall's activities from his receipt of Cicognani's letter to his advice to Roosevelt are drawn from a Memorandum to the President from General Marshall, August 2, 1943, Army files.

180. Telegram, President to Prime Minister, August 3, 1943, Army files.

181. The full list of conditions is contained in Hammond Memo. See also Butcher, 379, 390.

182. This second raid provoked bitter complaint from the Vatican. (Butcher, 398.)

183. Kogan, 32. Kogan also notes that "Guariglio also sent Alberto Pirelli, the rubber magnate, to Switzerland to try to enlist the services of the Swiss government as an intermediary." (218, n. 19.) Guariglio was, of course, Foreign Minister in the Badoglio government.

184. Villari, 303, reports that Sir Ronald Hugh Campbell, "after hearing D'Ayeta's account of the state of Italy, declared that the country must accept unconditional surrender." This does not coincide with Churchill's cable to Roosevelt (August 5) in which he stated, "Campbell was instructed to make no comment." (Quoted in Churchill, *Closing the Ring*, 99.) However, Campbell may have merely been repeating Allied public pronouncements.

185. Quoted in Churchill, *Closing the Ring*, 99-100.

186. Quoted in *ibid.*, 101.

187. *Ibid.*

188. This telegram from Churchill to Eden, August 7, 1943, is printed in *ibid.,* 101-102.

189. This telegram is printed in *ibid.,* 102.

190. Quoted in *ibid.,* 103.

191. The full text of these instructions is contained in a telegram from Churchill to Roosevelt, August 12, 1943, printed in *ibid.,* 102-103.

192. Wagg, 123, discusses at length the very real problem of keeping the mission secret from the Germans.

193. Templewood, 213; details of Castellano's wardrobe are presented in Wagg, 122.

194. Templewood, 213, describes the interpreter as "Signor Montenaro, an official of the Italian Foreign Office." Wagg, 122, uses the spelling "Montanari," noting also that he was American-educated (Harvard, 1927) and had served as Italian Consul at Honolulu.

195. Hayes, Carlton J. H., *Wartime Mission in Spain, 1942-1945* (New York, 1945), 164.

196. A detailed account of the Castellano visit to Sir Samuel Hoare is contained in Templewood, 212-215; see also Churchill's speech to the House of Commons on September 22, quoted in Wagg, 122.

197. According to Templewood, 213, Castellano was also prepared "to undertake that the Italian armies would forthwith evacuate the Balkans and Croatia."

198. He reported 13 German divisions then in Italy (Templewood, 213, says 15 divisions) and German plans to hold a line over the Apennines and Ravenna. (Butcher, 391.)

Castellano indicated to Templewood, 214, that "a delay of a few days might mean that the Italian army would no longer be a free agent." Whether or not, even at this point, it really was a free agent is open to question.

Kogan, 27, asserts that the initial decision of the Badoglio government "to wait until Allied armies . . . in Sicily would be in a position to save the capital and the government . . . really paralyzed the Badoglio regime in its attempt to make contact with the Anglo-Americans. By August 17, Italian divisions were encircled and German troops ready to enter action at any moment."

199. See Butcher, 386.

200. *Ibid.,* 391.

201. The date of Eisenhower's reception of the news about Castellano is confirmed in Cunningham, 560.

202. Butcher, 315, 370, 380-381.

203. *The Log of the President's Visit to Canada, 16 August 1943 to 26 August 1943,* iii, *Roosevelt Papers.*

204. "The scope of the Conference comprised not only the Mediterranean campaign, now at its first climax, but even more the preparations for the cross-Channel design of 1944, the whole conduct of the war in the Indian theatre, and our share in the struggle against Japan." Churchill, *Closing the Ring,* 67.

205. *Ibid.,* 83; Leahy, 175; McNeill, 298; Bryant, 579.

206. Churchill, *Closing the Ring,* 103.

207. Telegram, Former Naval Person (Quebec) to President Roosevelt, August 16, 1943, quoted in full in Churchill, *ibid.,* 103-104.

208. Telegram #4488, Eisenhower from General Devers, London, August 17, 1943, Army files. Transmission of messages from Churchill to Eisenhower via Lieutenant General Jacob Devers, the U. S. European Theater commander, was a routine procedure. This telegram was despatched from London about 3 A.M. (0340Z) on the morning of the 17th and was received in Algiers shortly before noon (1017B). See also Cunningham, 560.

209. Telegram #W-7578, General McNarney (Washington) from Eisenhower, August 17, 1943, Army files. It was sent from Algiers at 1706B and received in Washington about 5:00 P.M.

210. Quoted in Ehrman, 9. This decision had immediate and important consequences for coming operations in the Italian area. General Smith received a message from Quebec on the 23rd which specified some of these consequences. The return of seven divisions to the United Kingdom was planned, as well as a number of landing craft. Other landing craft and several air squadrons were scheduled for assignment to India. (Telegram #118, August 23, 1943, received Algiers 0743, Army files.)

211. Note, for example, the fears expressed by Secretary of War Stimson in his Diary, *On Active Service,* 428-439. On the other hand, Churchill's own position should also be noted: "I emphasized that I strongly favoured 'Overlord' in 1944, though I had not been in favour of 'Sledgehammer' in 1942 or 'Round-up' in 1943. The objections which I had to the cross-Channel operation were, however, now removed." (Churchill, *Closing the Ring,* 84.)

212. Ehrman, 57.

213. *Ibid.*

214. *Ibid.*

215. *Ibid.,* 116. The attitude of the American Chiefs of Staff toward these "extra operations" is recorded by Leahy, 175.

216. Butcher, 393-394. This was only one of several requests made by Eisenhower for additional air strength. All were flatly turned down. (Craven and Cate, 494-495.)

217. Butcher, 398.

218. Relevant portions of the memorandum are printed in Churchill, *Closing the Ring,* 82-83.

219. See p. 217 above.

220. Quoted in Ehrman, 9-10. "Sardinia, so long thrust forward in Staff argument as the alternative to the assault on Italy, fell into our hands for nothing, as a mere bonus, on September 19, and Corsica was taken by French troops a fortnight later. (Churchill, *Closing the Ring,* 154.)

221. *Ibid.,* 85-86. At the same time Churchill drafted a comprehensive statement on the whole Allied war policy. The section on strategy in the Italian theater printed in *ibid.,* 82-83, is mentioned above.

222. *Marshall's Report,* 164.

223. At a 6:00 P.M. cocktail party given by the Governor-General of Canada, Brooke records this event: "As soon as I arrived I was roped in by the P. M. to discuss with him, the President and Admiral Leahy the wire to be sent to Eisenhower connected with Badoglio's proposals. The President altered one sentence concerning bombing, otherwise was in full agreement and we sent it off." (Bryant, 582.)

224. The cable is printed in Churchill, *Closing the Ring,* 105-106. See also Butcher, 392, who includes as well the provision that "a secure channel of communication between Badoglio's headquarters and General Eisenhower's should be provided." This memorandum placed a number of substantial limitations on Eisenhower's course of action; Smyth MS, 119-121.

225. A portion of this cable is printed in Sherwood, 745; see also note on 977. The footnote reference (958) incorrectly dates the cable August 16; it could not have been sent before the cable to Eisenhower, August 18.

226. Churchill observed: "He has absolutely no ground for complaint, as we have done no more than to hand the Italian representative the severe directions expressing unconditional surrender which had already received the cordial approval of the Soviet Government and have immediately reported all these matters to him." (Telegram from Churchill to the War Cabinet, August 25, 1943, printed in Churchill, *Closing the Ring,* 93-94.)

227. For a brief account of earlier and continuing efforts to keep the Russians informed and participating in the Italian armistice, see Hull, II, 1549 and ff.

228. See p. 235 above.

229. Smyth MS, 121.

230. See Memorandum, "Conditions for Italian Surrender," drafted by James C. Dunn for the Secretary of State, September 1, 1943, a copy of which exists in Army files.

231. Hull, 1549-1550. Earlier discussion of the Additional Conditions had centered around the inclusion of a preamble and space for signatures, provisions on strikes and currency, and, as pointed out by Captain C. K. Lloyd of the British delegation, an apparent inconsistency between Article 6, which provided for suspension of powers of the Italian government in all occupied areas, and Article 17, which provided that local administrative authorities and public services would continue to function.

232. Churchill brought with him to Quebec the final draft of his "Thoughts on the Fall of Mussolini," but apparently it was not used for anything except background material. See Churchill, *Closing the Ring,* 59, and also pp. 222, 230 above.

233. Much of the foregoing account of the Long Terms at Quebec is based on the Smyth MS, 122-123.

234. See p. 261 below.

235. See the Joint Statement released by the President and the Prime Minister, *U. S. and Italy,* 48-49.

236. Eisenhower and his commanders decided, at an August 16th meeting, "to go across the Messina Strait early in September as soon as landing craft and guns can be assembled and for the attack for Naples to be made September 9." (Butcher, 390.) These plans were approved by the Combined Chiefs, the President and the Prime Minister. (Churchill, *Closing the Ring,* 95-96.)
These plans developed from those discussed above, pp. 217, 224.

237. "The preparations could not but attract the attention of the enemy, and their success therefore depended on the achievement of strategic surprise or on the exploitation of a favourable political situation." (Ehrman, 64.)

238. The Allied landing at Taranto was perhaps the only successful case in which these hopes came to fruition. See Eisenhower, 189.

239. Ehrman, 7.

240. For example, German forces were reported withdrawing from the toe to escape being trapped by Allied landings in the Naples area. This re-grouping would make BAYTOWN easier but would add to the difficulties of AVALANCHE. (Butcher, 399-400.)
The difficulties of the military operation and the consequent need for the psychological value of the armistice announcement were emphasized by General Alexander in a meeting with the psychological warfare experts just before AVALANCHE took place. Crossman in Lerner, Daniel, *Sykewar* (New York, 1945), 326-327.

241. See pp. 248-249 above.

242. Telegram #2782, General Smith to Gibraltar, August 18, 1943, Army files.

243. Butcher, 392-393, 395.

244. The authenticity of the Castellano mission had already been confirmed to Campbell by the Badoglio government through the British Minister at the Vatican. (Wagg, 123.)

Hull observes *(Memoirs,* II, 1549) that "The State Department had little share in these discussions, which were of a military nature."

245. Wagg, 122-123.

246. According to Wagg, 124, the terms were read aloud by General Smith.

247. His aim ". . . was to jump from one side to the other without surrendering. It was to execute a classic Italian reversal of alliances." (Kogan, 33.)

248. See pp. 248-249 above.

249. For example, through AFHQ and the British and American governments, a message had been forwarded to the Pope from the Cardinal at Palermo, reporting that "he and his people were being treated with the 'utmost courtesy' and that the occupation had occurred without any 'unpleasant incidents.' " (Butcher, 377.)

250. According to Kogan, 34-35, Smith "observed that the Quebec Document apparently attenuated the rigor of the clause on disarming the navy and added that while he could put nothing in writing he could say the Italian flag would continue to fly over the ships." Smith refused, however, to comment upon Castellano's insistence that AMG must not replace Royal sovereignty.

251. Sherwood, 745. In his conversations with Sir Samuel Hoare in Madrid, Castellano had presented a similar account, although giving more credit to Count Grandi (Templewood, 214-215).

252. Details of this Lisbon meeting are drawn from Churchill, *Closing the Ring,* 107; Butcher, 394-395; Wagg, 122-128; McNeill, 298 and n.2; Kogan, 34-35.

253. Wagg, 127, who further notes that Allied bombing of the Genoa-Rome railroad was prohibited to ensure the safety of the special train on which Castellano and Montanari were traveling. See also McNeill, 299.

254. According to Templewood, 215, "it was further arranged that a code message on the Italian radio should, on August 28th and 29th, give the clue as to whether or not the armistice had been accepted by the Italian government." The message, however, was never received. Wagg, 128-130, states that the signal was to be given on the 26th. Successful contact was not established until noon on Friday, the 27th.

255. A report of their mission was immediately cabled to Washington (Sherwood, 977). The un-abashed alacrity with which the Italians proposed to switch sides created a somewhat unpleasant impression among some Allied officers, Butcher, 394, noted on the 21st.

General Smith accounted for the Castellano mission, rather than an approach to the Allies through the Vatican, by asserting "there are so many nationalities represented at the Vatican, leaks are inevitable and as the Italians fear reprisals by the Germans, they simply could not afford to take the risk," Butcher, 395. Bryant, 581, observes that the Italians were unable to establish contact with the Allies through the Vatican "because the British and American Ministers to the Holy See had not been provided with a cipher which the Germans could not break."

256. Eisenhower, 184.

257. The two telegrams are printed in Churchill, *Closing the Ring,* 106-107.

258. General de Wiart was told that "one dove had been sent out, but as it had not returned another was being dispatched." *(Ibid.,* 108.)

259. Roatta was Chief of the *Army* General Staff; Ambrosio was "Chief of the General Staff of all Italian Armed Forces, including the Army, Navy and Air Force." (Wagg, 128.)

260. Churchill, *Closing the Ring,* 107-108; Templewood, 215-216. (The spelling of the Italian general's name is here recorded as "Zanucci.")

261. For three days following Castellano's return to Rome on August 27, the Italian government debated its course of action. "Guariglia objected to the General's clear-cut offer to fight on the side of the Allies for he would have preferred this issue to be negotiated later with compensations for Italy." (Kogan, 36.)

262. A large portion of this chapter is based directly upon Smyth, H.M., "The Armistice of Cassibile," *Military Affairs,* Vol. XII, No. 1, Spring, 1948, pp. 12-35. It constitutes the first four sections of Volume II, Chapter iv, Part II, "The Campaign in Sicily and the Surrender of Italy" in the *History of the War in the Mediterranean Theater,* a part of the *Official History of the U. S. Army in World War II.*

263. Churchill, *Closing the Ring,* 108; Butcher, 403; Wagg, 132, reports that Smith and party arrived half an hour *after* Castellano, a statement contradicted by Smyth, "Armistice," 12.

264. It was scheduled (as of September 2) to be made 24-48 hours prior to the landings at Salerno, which were to take place on September 9. (Butcher, 400.)

265. Upon leaving the Quebec Conference, Churchill spent about a week in Canada, resting and working. He arrived in Washington on September 1. These plans had been largely dependent

upon the rapidly changing Italian situation. As he telegraphed the Cabinet on August 25, "It is only in the event of some unexpected development in Italy or elsewhere which would make it desirable for me and the President to be close together that I should prolong my stay." (Churchill, *Closing the Ring,* 94.) This is precisely what happened (*ibid.,* 118-123). He sailed for England from Halifax on September 14 (*ibid.,* 142).

266. Churchill described their role in this way: "The President and I . . . had directed during these critical days the course of the secret Armistice talks with the Badoglio Government, and had also been following anxiously and closely the military arrangement for a landing on Italian soil. I deliberately prolonged my stay in the United States in order to be in close contact with our American friends at the critical moment in Italian affairs. On the day of my arrival in Washington, the first definite and official news was received that Badoglio had agreed to accept the surrender terms proposed by the Allies. The strategic arrangements debated at Quebec had of course been considered in the light of the possible Italian collapse, and this aspect was our main concern in these days." (*Ibid.,* 123.)

267. About 11 A.M. (Wagg, 133.)

268. It was scheduled to precede the Salerno landings by 24-48 hours. (Butcher, 400.)

Acceptance of the Italian proposals would have involved a major re-casting of Allied plans. (McNeill, 299.)

269. "In such a case, General Smith remarked, negotiations would be taken up by the diplomatists of the Allied nations who would necessarily impose much harsher conditions than those demanded by General Eisenhower." (Smyth, "Armistice," 13.)

270. Butcher's comment is indicative: "The Italians present a pathetic picture. They are negotiating for peace with a rope around their neck. Ike said yesterday they are simply frightened to death because the Germans, undoubtedly, will wreak a fearful vengeance. However, they seem intent upon concluding a peace provided we can get our troops and other support to Italy promptly." (Butcher, 400.) See also Smyth, "Armistice," 13-14.

271. The landing of the 82nd Airborne Division was originally scheduled as part of AVALANCHE: it was assigned to capture towns northwest of the city of Naples and disrupt German communications by "destroying all crossings of the Volturno River from Triflisco to the sea and . . . holding the Volturno itself against all enemy attempts to cross." Gavin, James M., "Airborne Plans and Operations in the Mediterranean The-

ater," *Infantry Journal,* August 1946, 24. Gavin's article presents a detailed tactical analysis of both GIANT ONE and GIANT TWO.

This "drop" was cancelled on the 26th when it appeared that the problem of supply was too great an obstacle. The airborne troops thus became available for re-assignment. The original drop was rescheduled by the planners at Cassibile to take place in the Rome area; GIANT ONE thus became GIANT TWO.

In addition, Butcher reported (entry for August 10): "Admiral Cunningham has advocated to Ike a bold landing at Rome, which is relatively lightly defended. This would have effective psychological reactions in Italy, but the harbor at Rome is not nearly as useful as that at Naples. Unfortunately, Rome is far beyond the effective range of our nimblest fighters—the Spitfires. Flying from our closest airfields on Sicily, they can go only as far as Salerno, where the landings are to be made to take Naples, give air cover for only twenty minutes, and then must return to Sicily to refuel. Without air cover any landing would be a juicy target for the Jerry." (385.)

However, Cunningham did undertake the responsibility of "supplying this force (the paratroop division) by sea through the small port at the mouth of the Tiber." (Cunningham, 561.)

272. Quoted in Smyth, "Armistice," 15.

273. The message was carefully checked for authenticity, Butcher, 400, 403. It read: "The reply is affirmative repeat affirmative period In consequence known person will arrive tomorrow two September hour and place established period Please confirm." Quoted in Smyth, "Armistice," 17.

274. Quoted in Churchill, *Closing the Ring,* 106; the plan was given the personal approval of the President and the Prime Minister (Butcher, 404, and p. 260 below).

275. McNeill, 300. While Smith remained at Cassibile, Strong made an overnight trip to report to AFHQ. He returned early on Thursday morning to join with Smith in again meeting the Italian delegation. (Wagg, 135.)

See *ibid.* for the clues picked up by the press and the successful attempt to keep the Italian visits secret. Tregaskis, 95, reports one of the many rumors, partially true, that were circulating.

276. Churchill, *Closing the Ring,* 110. McNeill, 300, reports that "Badoglio first replied that the armistice terms had already been 'implicitly' accepted," then, a few hours later, changed his mind and wired the authorization.

The two telegrams are quoted in Smyth, "Armistice," 21.

277. "There were, in fact, several pages of itemized needs including such things as telephones,

picks, shovels, wire, gasoline, and civilian laborers, all of which were to be furnished by the Italian commander to the airborne troops." (Gavin, 26.)

278. Smyth, "Armistice," 20; "and Admiral Cunningham promised to send LCT's or even destroyers up the Tiber with ammunition and supplies." (Morison, IX, 239.) "The Italians had also agreed to clear the Tiber River so that there could be amphibious support for the airborne landings." (Gavin, 26.)

Paragraph three of the summary of the conference of August 31 had specified the landing at the mouth of the Tiber River in support of the main attack (see p. 259 above).

279. Telegram #6704, President Roosevelt and the Prime Minister to General Eisenhower, September 2, 1943, Army files. Covering note by General Deane stated "early morning."

The telegram is quoted in Churchill, *Closing the Ring,* 109. Churchill also notes: "The War Cabinet met in London on the same day and endorsed this view."

280. The telegram is printed in Churchill, *Closing the Ring,* 110.

281. Craven and Cate, 519.

282. The text of the Short Terms to which the signatures were appended was identical with the original eleven terms approved by the President and the Prime Minister on July 30 (pp. 234-235 above), with the addition of clause twelve (p. 237 above) and these concluding paragraphs:

"The conditions of the present Armistice will not be made public without prior approval of the Allied Commander-in-Chief.

"The present instrument shall be confirmed by the Italian Government. It will enter into force —— hours after the instrument of confirmation has been received at Allied Force Headquarters.

"This Armistice will continue until the coming into force of a treaty of peace. It may be denounced by the Allies with immediate effect if the Italian Government does not fulfill its obligations."

See *U. S. and Italy,* 51-52, and Appendix A, 278-279 below. Further materials may be found in Wagg, 138-139, and Cunningham, 560.

283. Preamble to the Short Terms, *U. S. and Italy,* 51.

284. On September 2, "Ike had a message from Generals Alexander and Beetle saying that for 'operational reasons' it may be necessary for one of them to sign the armistice agreement and 'unconditional surrender' with General Castellano, with whom they have been meeting in Sicily. Ike had previously radioed the two that under the terms by which Russia would approve the proposed agreement, only Ike was directly empowered

to affix his signature, although he preferred to delegate the responsibility." (Butcher, 405.)

Present at the ceremony, in addition to Eisenhower, Smith, Strong, Castellano, and Montanari, were Commodore Kenneth Dick, RN, Chief of Staff to Admiral Cunningham, Commander-in-Chief, Mediterranean, and Major-General Lowell W. Rooks, Assistant Chief of Staff (G-3) at AFHQ, and political advisers Macmillan and Murphy. A description of the actual ceremony may be found in Wagg, 137-138. See also Craven and Cate, 519; Wagg, 136; Butcher, 406. Somewhat later Castellano was presented to Macmillan and Murphy (Smyth, "Armistice," 21).

Hull notes, 1549: "On August 28 Admiral Standley, our Ambassador in Moscow, cabled us that the Soviet Government approved the terms and empowered General Eisenhower to sign on their behalf, a special representative of the Soviet Union not being required in this instance." (This apparently applied to both sets of terms.)

285. Telegram to Churchill from General Alexander, September 3, 1943, printed in Churchill, *Closing the Ring,* 111.

286. See Butcher, 421.

Hopkins' comments are also worth noting: "The Italian show is fantastic, but none of us know yet just what all the implications are. For myself, I think we are in for some pretty rough fighting in Italy, particularly if the Germans really decide to try to hold the northern half. We have every reason to be hopeful that we are going to get the Italian fleet intact." (Letter from Hopkins to Captain Donald Duncan, September 10, 1943, partially printed in Sherwood, 751, and n. 977.)

287. Quoted in Churchill, *Closing the Ring,* 111.

288. Butcher, 405, 406. On September 16, Butcher noted: "There will be a meeting with Badoglio in Tunisia. Ike said that the home governments are anxious to have the long-term agreement signed with appropriate showmanship. He hates the thought, but it must be done." (Butcher, 421.)

289. Smyth, "Armistice," 22.

290. Butcher, 405-406; and p. 251 above; Leahy, 181, expressed a similar view. See p. 264 below.

291. Quoted in Smyth, "Armistice," 22.

292. A good analysis appears in *ibid.,* 26-31.

293. See pp. 258-259 above.

294. McNeill, 298-299.

295. Castellano had observed at Lisbon that Roatta was pro-German.

296. "This is the essential fact which explains the contradictory and ambiguous conduct of the Italian Government during the next two days.

All along the King and the group associated with him had been unwilling to run any risks but insisted on being rescued by the Allies." (Smyth, "Armistice," 29-30.)

297. The appraisal in Craven and Cate, 520, is an accurate summary: ". . . the two officers [Taylor and Gardiner; see below] speedily became convinced that the mission would end in disaster: the Germans had built up their strength in the Rome area and had stopped the flow of gasoline and munitions to the Italian troops; the Italian military leaders had overcommitted themselves and could neither render effective aid to the airborne troops nor guarantee the security of the airfields and, disorganized and vacillating, had adopted an attitude of 'let the Allies save the Italian government and Rome.'"

298. For details of the mission and a transcript of the memorandum, see Smyth, "Armistice," 30-32.

299. Butcher, 410. One Allied appraisal of GIANT TWO is recorded by Butcher, 406: "Whether the King and Badoglio will run out of Italy depends upon the success of our paratroop division which is to be dropped near Rome the same night. There are four Italian divisions in the vicinity of Rome, but the Eyeties simply quake with fear because of the one German Panzer division in that area."

300. Quoted directly from General Taylor's report entitled, "Mission to Rome," printed in Smyth, "Armistice," 32. See also Wagg, 145-146: "Carboni said the new German units had taken control of the airfields which were to be their objectives. His Rome troops, which were to have been counted on for help, were in an almost defenceless condition. The Germans had been keeping a close grip on supplies of ammunition and fuel in the area and doling it out to the Italian Army in the smallest possible rations. His soldiers had only enough ammunition for a few hours of combat. They had almost no petrol to ensure their mobility. They could not put their hands on the supplies needed to provide hidden stockpiles for the American parachute division."

301. From General Taylor's Report, quoted in Smyth, "Armistice," 32.

302. Both messages are printed in their entirety in Smyth, "Armistice," 33. One report was that "the Germans had cut supplies of gasoline and ammunition, some Italian units having as little as twenty rounds per gun." (Butcher, 410.)

303. Details of the Taylor-Gardiner mission to Rome may be found in Churchill, *Closing the Ring,* 111-112; Wagg, 147-152; Thruelson, Richard, and Arnold, Elliott, *Mediterranean Sweep* (New York, 1944), 462-469. See also portions of

Churchill's speech to the House of Commons (September 21, 1943), quoted in Wagg, 140; Cunningham, 561; Gavin, 26-27; Tregaskis, 103-108, who quotes, apparently *verbatim,* a description of the expedition by Colonel Gardiner; Sherwood, 751.

Wagg, 154, quotes General Taylor as saying: "We believe that the whole value of our mission was that it stopped an operation which in our judgment would, under the circumstances, have been disastrous." But see also the discussion in *ibid.,* 158.

Morison, IX, 241-242, argues strongly that GIANT TWO should not have been cancelled, citing German records to assert that the Germans "had only two battalions in a position to challenge Italian control of the Roman airfields," that the Germans feared an airborne attack, and notes also that the leaderless Italian garrison did in fact hold off the Germans for two days following Kesselring's decision to occupy the city.

Gavin, 26, observes: ". . . I think the fact was that the Italians at Syracuse [i.e., Cassibile] had simply promised everything—about ten times as much as they could possibly have done. And it became fully evident that there were no guarantees of the needed support at the airfields where the regiments of the 82nd were to land, so the plans were changed almost at the last minute."

304. Eisenhower, 186; Wagg, 150-151, 155-156, attributes part of the delay to poor radio transmission.

305. The Eisenhower telegram is printed in Churchill, *Closing the Ring,* 112.

306. This telegram is printed in *ibid.*

307. Butcher, 406, reports: "It is agreed that the announcement of an armistice will be made simultaneously by the Italians and the Allies in Ike's name at 6:30 P.M. Wednesday evening, September 8." This agreement presumably was not then made known to the Italians. (Eisenhower, 186.)

308. Villari, 304; Eisenhower, 186; Wagg, 156; Butcher, 410, paraphrases most of the message.

"Any failure on your part to conduct to the finish all the obligations of the signed agreement can have very grave consequences for your country. No future action on your part can then restore any confidence in your good faith and consequently will be followed by the dissolution of your government and of your nation." (Italian translation quoted in Kogan, 39.)

In addition to Eisenhower's stern message, AFHQ came up with other measures to induce Badoglio to comply. At first there was thought of "faking" Badoglio's broadcast from Algiers. This ruse was abandoned in favor of following

Eisenhower's broadcast with an explanation of the events leading up to the surrender in the hope of "shaming" Badoglio into adhering to his prescribed role. Whether this procedure actually helped prod Badoglio into complying is not known, but it illustrates the activity of the psychological warfare specialists at AFHQ during the crucial hours preceding the armistice declaration. A good account of this is presented by Crossman in Lerner, *Sykewar*, 327-329.

309. Wagg, 156.

310. Churchill, *Closing the Ring*, 113, gives the time of Eisenhower's broadcast of the proclamation as 6:00 P.M.; Wagg, 121, as 6:15.

311. The announcement is reprinted on p. 205 above. See also *U. S. and Italy*, 50.

312. Butcher, 410; Hull, 1549; Eisenhower, 186; Thruelson, 469—all give the time of Badoglio's message as 8:00. Wagg, 121, 153, says 7:30. The text used here is taken from the *New York Times* of September 9, 1943; it is reprinted in *Documents on American Foreign Relations*, VI, 169-170, and is identical with the one reprinted in Wagg, 154.

313. Butcher, 410; Wagg, 121.

314. *Marshall's Report*, 164. Not knowing about the heavy German reinforcements in Italy, many Allied servicemen on hearing the announcement expected an easy occupation of Italy. For one account, see Butcher, 411.

Smyth, "Armistice," 35, observes: "Salerno was touch and go: had Italian troops aided the Germans the balance might have favored the defenders."

315. Scrivener, Jane (pseud.), *Inside Rome with the Germans* (New York, 1945), 1-5.

316. Churchill, *Closing the Ring*, 156.

317. Wagg, 131. McNeill's suggestion that the Sicilian campaign should have been broken off about August 1 seems highly impractical. (McNeill, 291-292 and n.1.)

318. The full text of the Roosevelt-Churchill message is printed in *U. S. and Italy*, 68; and in *Documents on American Foreign Relations*, VI, 170. A copy also exists in the *Roosevelt Papers*.

319. Butcher, 416.

320. Cunningham, 562-565, details these arrangements, observing: "We could not be certain, of course, that the Italian fleet would conform to these arrangements; but as the alternative was falling into the hands of the Germans we hoped they would." In addition, Italian Minister of Marine de Courten reported to Cunningham that "the Italian captains who had been unable to get their ships away from Spezia and had scuttled them in harbour had been summarily shot by the Germans." (Cunningham, 572.)

321. For this story and the problems of obtaining their release from internment, see Hayes, 172-173, 174-175 ff.

322. Carroll, 174, attributes the surrender of the Italian Fleet primarily to Allied propaganda efforts on the day of the armistice. In fact, however, the ships sailed in response to orders issued their commanding officers by Badoglio. See above, p. 265.

323. Cunningham, 572.

324. *Ibid.* See also Morison, IX, 244-245. This "Memorandum of Agreement on Employment and Disposition of Italian Fleet and Mercantile Marine, September 23, 1943" is reprinted in *U. S. and Italy*, 53-55, and in the British *Documents Relating to the Conditions of an Armistice with Italy*, 12-14.

325. After conferring with the King, Badoglio, and the principal ministers of the Royal Italian Government, Lieutenant-General Mason-MacFarlane reported, according to Butcher, 420, that "Outside of the acquisition of the Italian fleet we have virtually nothing to gain, certainly, from the Army, except as the soldiers may be used as labor at ports and on our line of communication. He said that they are short of boots and ammunition and have 1918 armor."

326. Ehrman, 66-67. Kogan, 40-41, observes: "After several days, of an Italian army of sixty-one divisions in Italy, France, the Balkans, and the islands, only seven were left to the Allies, ill-equipped and demoralized."

327. A vivid picture of the occupation of Rome by the Germans and life there until the city's liberation by the Allies is presented in Scrivener (pseud.), *Inside Rome with the Germans*.

328. Montgomery, 161.

329. McNeill, 303. Four small provinces in the neighborhood were turned over to the King shortly thereafter but as the rest of Italy was liberated it remained under AMG. (Kogan, 43.)

330. Churchill, *Closing the Ring*, 116-117.

331. A notable exception was in Greece and Yugoslavia where Italian surrenders to Greeks and Yugoslavs brought considerable amounts of arms and supplies to the guerrilla forces (McNeill, 303). At Salerno, Germans took over all Italian coastal guns and fieldpieces and shot the Italian commander who objected (Morison, IX, 260).

332. Churchill, *Closing the Ring*, 134-135.

333. *Hitler's Europe*, 316.

334. The theme is well developed in McNeil, 303-305.

335. Montgomery, 180-181.

336. Craven and Cate, 546.

337. Holborn, *Political Collapse of Europe*, 166.

338. One effect of Allied acceptance of the government of the King and Badoglio was to secure, in most cases, the cooperation of Italian diplomatic staffs in neutral countries like Spain. Faced with the alternatives of supporting Mussolini's puppet regime or continuing to be loyal to the Crown, they chose the latter. In addition, the Spanish government, continued diplomatic recognition of the Royal government, refusing to recognize (as the United States government feared it might) the Mussolini regime. (For these developments in Spain, see Hayes, 170-175.)

339. Telegram #502, General Eisenhower (Fairfield Rear) for personal attention of General Smith: "If you agree, pass following to Combined Chiefs of Staff in continuation of long telegram which you sent yesterday." (September 19, 1943, sent 1911B, received 2003B, Army files.) See also Leahy, 182 ("His request was relayed to Roosevelt and Churchill and to the State Department").

340. Telegram, #NAF 423, General Eisenhower to General Smith for Combined Chiefs of Staff, September 18, 1943, Army files.

A partial explanation of Eisenhower's attitude may be found in his interpretation of his experience with the French in North Africa:

"Ike is worried for fear the insistence of the President that this is a 'military occupation,' regardless of whatever sideline political fight it may represent as between the United States and Britain, may force him to say to Giraud, 'Do this, or else.' Then if Giraud replied: 'I don't choose to do this —what are you going to do about it?' Ike would be up against the man-wasting job of taking over the civil administration of the country, which General Patton reported, soon after the assault was completed, would require 60,000 soldiers in Morocco alone. The French who are guarding our line of communication to the front would be withdrawn, those actually fighting at the front would be called back to their billets around Algiers, Oran, and Casablanca and elsewhere, and we would have to more than offset their strength with Allied troops, and instead of active help from our re-created ally we would have little help, probably passive resistance a la Gandhi, or possibly French resumption of French fighting Americans and British *pour l'honneur.*" (Butcher, diary entry for January 4, 1943, 232.)

341. Telegram, Prime Minister to General Eisenhower (Algiers), September 21, 1943, congratulating him on the success of the Salerno landings. Printed in Churchill, *Closing the Ring,* 147-148.

342. Quoted in *ibid.,* 160.

343. On August 17th, returning from a trip to London, Macmillan reported (according to Butcher) that "His brother ministers of the Cabinet, particularly Sir Stafford Cripps, felt AMGOT could do more for democracy if it immediately held free and open elections in the territory we occupy in Sicily. According to Bob Murphy, Macmillan felt dejected. The British public, he reported, seems rather tired of the war but, oddly, is insistent on 'unconditional surrender.' The two simply do not fit. We can shorten the war by giving Italy honorable terms, not to mention the lives that would be saved." (Butcher, entry for August 17, 390.)

344. Fear of the disappearance of any effective and "respectable" (i.e., non-Fascist) government in Italy and a resulting state of chaos prompted the British to draft an "Omnibus" Proclamation for dealing with such a situation. It was discussed in meetings of the CCAC in early September and later, portions of the document were forwarded informally to AFHQ.

345. For a picturesque account of the "emergence" of these groups from hiding, see Carroll, 175-177. For a detailed account of their tacit cooperation with the Badoglio government during the period from the fall of Mussolini to the armistice, see Kogan, 28-31.

346. Churchill, *Closing the Ring,* 188.

347. Quoted in *ibid.* See also Holborn, *Political Collapse of Europe,* 17-18.

348. Hull argued that the principle of unconditional surrender "logically required the victor nations to be ready to take over every phase of the national and local Governments of the conquered countries, and to operate all governmental activities and properties. We and our Allies were in no way prepared to undertake this vast obligation." (*Memoirs,* II, 1570.)

Sherwood notes (*Roosevelt and Hopkins,* 756) that "Hopkins was frequently in disagreement with Hull, particularly in the interminable insistence on the sanctity of the Vichy policy which by now had been extended into Italy to cover the arrangements of 'expediency' with King Victor Emmanuel and Badoglio."

For Hopkins' position, see below, p. 273.

349. This portion of the speech is printed in Churchill, *Closing the Ring,* 161.

350. Telegram, Prime Minister to President Roosevelt, September 21, 1943, printed in Churchill, *Closing the Ring,* 189-190.

". . . the Prime Minister has unhesitatingly approved and, in fact, amplified Ike's recommendation for acceptance of the Italian forces under Badoglio and the King as cobelligerents, but adds that they must 'work their passage.' " (Butcher, 424.)

Churchill's proposals were approved by Stalin.

See the exchange of telegrams printed in Churchill, *Closing the Ring,* 192-194.

351. Sherwood, 751-752. The memorandum to
which Hopkins objected is printed on p. 274
below.

352. Hopkins' memorandum is printed in Sherwood, 744. See also the note on p. 977. Hopkins'
objection to the stand taken by Secretary Hull
has been noted above, n. 348. In his *Memoirs,*
II, 1550, Hull generally supports the Hopkins
position described here.

An incidental comment is furnished by Butcher,
writing on September 23: "Wes Gallagher, of the
Associated Press, freshly returned from the U. S.,
thinks our dealings with the King will be even
more unpopular at home than those with Darlan."
(Butcher, 424.) For a good presentation of the
case against dealing with Badoglio, see Carroll,
175-178.

353. Printed in Sherwood, 680, 681.

354. Roosevelt's recognition of military considerations is reflected in this passage in a message
which he delivered to Congress on September 17:
"Italian leaders appealed to their Army and Navy
to end hostilities against us. Italian soldiers, though
disorganized and ill-supplied, have been fighting
the Germans in many regions. In conformity with
the terms of unconditional surrender, the Italian
fleet has come over to our side; and it can be a
powerful weapon in striking at the Nazi enemies
of the Italian people." (Message of the President
[Roosevelt] to the Congress of the United States,
September 17, 1943; this quotation is taken from
an excerpt printed in *Documents on American
Foreign Relations,* VI, 170-172.)

355. Hull, *Memoirs,* II, 1557, merely says that
the agreement was made "in their (i.e., Roosevelt's and Churchill's) early discussions concerning Italy"; but it seems clear that the joint message of September 10, quoted above, was the fruit,
perhaps the first fruit, of the agreement (cf. Leahy,
I Was There, 311). Churchill himself does not
refer to any such agreement directly, but some
of the phrases in his telegrams to Roosevelt imply
it. (Churchill, *Closing the Ring,* 498.)

356. McNeill, 307.

357. Telegram, President Roosevelt to Prime
Minister (for General Eisenhower), September 21,
1943, printed in Churchill, *Closing the Ring,*
190-191. (There is, of course, no indication in
Closing the Ring of the draftsman of this cable;
one might venture the guess that it was McCloy.)
See also the Roosevelt memorandum of October
27, 1943 in *F. D. R.: His Personal Letters,* II,
1459. On September 22, a copy of the telegram
was also sent by the State Department to Robert
Murphy at AFHQ. Murphy was now acting as

American adviser on Italian affairs on Eisenhower's staff (Hull, 1550-1551). A letter emphasizing these same points was sent, about a week
later, by Roosevelt to the King (Leahy, 182).

358. Thus, at Roosevelt's request, the instructions to Eisenhower of September 23 had contained a paragraph which declared: "You will
withhold long-term Armistice provisions pending
further instructions." (See above, p. 274.) The
setting up of an Armistice Commission may also
have affected Roosevelt's decision. See the exchange of telegrams in Churchill, *Closing the
Ring,* 194.

359. "I go along with your thought about the
long set of terms if signature can be obtained
quickly, and I am so advising Eisenhower." (Telegram, President Roosevelt to Prime Minister,
September 25, 1943, printed in *ibid.*)

360. McNeill, 308; see full text of the Long
Terms in Appendix B; see also p. 230 above.

361. "I met Badoglio yesterday at Malta where
we signed the Long Term document with the
amended preamble." (Telegram, Eisenhower to
Combined Chiefs of Staff, September 30, 1943,
Army files.) For an explanation of "the amended
preamble," see immediately below and also Appendix B.

Eisenhower, Bedell Smith, Alexander, Tedder,
Cunningham, Lord Gort, Macmillan and Murphy, on the Allied side, and Badoglio, de Courten,
and Ambrosio on the Italian, were among the
participants. Cunningham, 572-573, describes the
event, noting as well that "again the question of
the disposal of the Italian fleet was not properly
faced. This omission, greatly to my disgust, had
later to be repaired by adding a clause to 'The
Cunningham-de Courten Agreement.' " (Cunningham, 573.) See also Churchill, *Closing the Ring,*
195.

362. The letter is printed in *United States and
Italy,* 64, and in the British *Documents Relating
to the Conditions of an Armistice with Italy,* 10-11.

"The first such change was the elimination of
the phrase 'Unconditional Surrender' from the
official text of the 'long' armistice. Badoglio had
particularly objected to the inclusion of these
words, and on November 9, 1943 the Allies met
his wishes while salvaging the slogan by inserting
'unconditionally' in the preamble, where it appeared in a context less obnoxious to Italian feeling." (McNeill, 308, n. 4.)

See Appendix B below.

According to Churchill, at the ceremony itself,
"Badoglio hoped to be spared the clause on unconditional surrender, but the Allied commanders
insisted that this was a formal meeting to sign
documents presented by the Allied governments

which would admit of no discussion." (Churchill, *Closing the Ring,* 195.) See also Telegram, Former Naval Person to President Roosevelt, September 24, 1943, printed in Churchill, *Closing the Ring,* 194. According to this telegram, the suggestion for the eventual change in wording apparently came from Eisenhower (Kogan, 46-47).

363. The text of this Joint Declaration is printed in *U. S. and Italy,* 71, in Churchill, *Closing the Ring,* 196-197, and in *Documents on American Foreign Relations,* VI, 178. A copy may also be found in the *Roosevelt Papers.* For some of the problems which the Declaration was designed to meet, see Churchill, *Closing the Ring,* 195-196. Villari, 308-309, castigates this Allied policy.

A "Message of Marshal Badoglio to General Eisenhower, October 13, 1943," announcing the Royal government's declaration of war is printed in *U. S. and Italy,* 69-70, and in *Documents on American Foreign Relations,* VI, 176. A copy may also be found in the *Roosevelt Papers.*

364. Butcher, 429. See also Churchill, *Closing the Ring,* 195.

365. Churchill idiosyncratically put great store on the importance of the islands; the Italian troops failed to hold them.

366. Butcher, 429.

367. *Ibid.,* 439.

368. *Ibid.,* 436.

369. Kogan, 70-75, who treats the matter with some thoroughness, attributes the continuation of failure to use Italian troops to Allied, especially British, policy. Churchill, *Closing the Ring,* 199-200, describes Allied efforts to make the fullest use possible of Italian manpower and shipping.

370. The full text of this Proclamation is printed in *U. S. and Italy,* 70, and in *Documents on American Foreign Relations,* VI, 177-178. A copy may also be found in the *Roosevelt Papers.*

371. Address by Assistant Secretary of State Berle before the Italian-American Labor Council, New York City, October 12, 1943; an excerpt from this speech is printed in *Documents on American Foreign Relations,* VI, 174-176.

372. For Churchill's position in the Sforza dispute, see Churchill, *Closing the Ring,* 197-199. The U. S. position is presented in Hull, 1551-1552; the Italian situation in Kogan, 50-52. See also Tregaskis, 181-189, and a Roosevelt memorandum of October 27, 1943 in *F. D. R.: His Personal Letters,* 1459.

373. Carroll, 183-184; Kogan, 52 ff.; and "Statement of Marshal Badoglio Regarding Future Intentions of His Government, November 13, 1943" in *Documents on American Foreign Relations,* VI, 178-180.

EDITORIAL COMMENTS

Armistice is an uncertain concept. Most commonly, it represents a concession of defeat and an agreement between victor and vanquished; but the agreement may range from abject surrender under harsh terms set exclusively by the victor to an agreement in effect *inter pares:* the Korean armistice is an extraordinary example of the latter. Theoretically an armistice sets the stage only for the brief period until a treaty of peace is signed; but in fact, even that still more ephemeral agreement, a cease-fire, can have some of the more lasting qualities of a treaty as is evidenced by Israel's territorial acquisitions under the truces set to end the first two Israeli-Arab wars. Finally, warfare involving two coalitions may lead to armistices affecting the separate vanquished members of the defeated coalition in diverse but lasting forms (as with Italy, Germany and Japan) and the diverse coalition victors too—witness the Iron Curtain and the 38th Parallel.

The famous phrase "unconditional surrender" was originally used by Grant on February 16, 1862; what he wanted was the surrender of Ft. Donelson by Confederate General Simon Bolivar Buckner together with its 15,000 Confederate soldiers, and that was what he got. This is quite different from a truce, an armistice, or a national surrender. The Civil War had a long way to go, and while Grant's victory at Ft. Donelson might be called, in Churchill's happy phrase, the end of the beginning, the terms imposed on Buckner had no connection with the reconstruction policies that followed the final victory of the Union forces more than two years later.

When Roosevelt used the phrase in his press conference at Casablanca, he apparently had in mind what he had already discussed with the Joint Chiefs of Staff and Churchill, the complete surrender of all the German and later the Japanese armed forces with their clear admission of defeat on the field of battle. The wisdom of including Italy was doubted by both Roosevelt and Churchill, but they bowed to the preference of the British War Cabinet. What both Roosevelt and Churchill seem to have overlooked were the possible implications of "unconditional surrender" when it was applied not to a single military unit, but to the surrender of a whole nation and its armies. The phrase had a dramatic appeal and, to the ultimate distress of both men, it soon began to be interpreted as the equivalent of *"Carthago delenda est."* Somewhat ironically, Roosevelt, whose subordinates took the phrase very seriously, tried for a good many weeks to avoid pressing the Italian quasi-government for signature of the Long Terms in which unconditional surrender, not even mentioned in the straight military Short Terms, was applied to an instrument of political subordination.

Refusal to bargain with Italy about the terms of surrender was looked on differently by the different actors on the Allied stage. Eisenhower, assisted by Macmillan, was interested solely in the immediate effect of armistice terms on his conduct of the war. He had no interest in any long-term consequences; he sought a cessation of fighting by the Italian troops and their assistance in protecting military installations of all types from the Germans. He wanted to ease the task of his own soldiers, to gather in and avail himself of the Italian airfields and, almost as an afterthought, secure possession of the Italian fleet and merchant marine. In political terms he had two objectives: first, to use an announcement of proposed armistice terms as a weapon in psychological warfare; and second, to keep himself free to negotiate with an Italian Darlan if such action proved desirable. His commitment to military advantage as the sole criterion was limited by his military ethics: he had no desire to ask for Italian "co-belligerency" because such action would be "completely dishonorable." (His subsequent shocked surprise at the Italians' own desire for co-belligerent status would have been avoided by a little knowledge of Italian history.) Finally, Eisenhower pleaded for authority to negotiate the armistice, partly perhaps because he looked forward to a white flag on the field of battle—or some equivalent thereof—partly perhaps because he was afraid that diplomats might make it harder to secure Italian signature by interposing non-military requirements.

Both Churchill and Roosevelt looked on armistice, save for a battlefield surrender, as a diplomatic maneuver inappropriate for soldiers because its terms would have long-term political consequences. In the outcome, the delegation of negotiatory responsibility to Eisenhower's staff officers was forced by the Italians when they sent one of their generals as their envoy. In their case the choice was inevitable for what they wanted was co-belligerency in principle and military protection in fact: what they offered were the dubious advantages of co-belligerency and, of more immediate practical value, military information. Obviously military representatives were necessary, but by then Roosevelt and Churchill had nothing to fear: the armistice terms themselves were set and the negotiators could deal only with peripheral problems.

The actual negotiations with Castellano went with remarkable speed; the three-week delay between Castellano's arrival in Madrid and the signing formalities in Cassibile was caused by problems of communications, not by diplomatic wrangling. General Bedell Smith ingeniously pacified Italian fears by promising indeterminate gains in the future in a manner that was entirely consistent with Roosevelt's and Churchill's desires. Both of them looked on Italy with a mixture of pity and contempt; they wanted some of the appearances of unconditional surrender not for the sake of punishing the Italians—now that Mussolini was deposed—but to encourage the underground movements elsewhere and to prove to the world that Allied determination would not be satisfied with anything less than victory on the battlefield.

The Anglo-American negotiation on the Short Terms (and the proposed Eisenhower announcements) prior to the delivery of the document to the Italian representatives was a curious triangular and quadrangular affair with proposals arising in Africa, Europe, Canada and the United States. There was no real dispute over the strict military arrangements except to make sure that maximum pressure was put on the Italians to ensure the freedom of the British prisoners-of-war. There were military advantages in such action but of course this was a matter of overriding domestic political concern for Churchill and his cabinet. Eisenhower and his advisers—Bedell Smith and Macmillan—did not forget about the Italian fleet and merchant marine but Admiral Cunningham made it clear subsequently that neither the soldiers, the politicians nor the diplomats had dealt adequately with problems that only a sailor could understand. Finally, the need for a saving clause in the Short Terms, which was noted by McCloy, had previously been overlooked by the military draftsmen (as it subsequently was in relation to the German armistice) and by the British Foreign Office representatives.

Unlike the Department of State the Foreign Office played some part in the proceedings, primarily to make sure that Roosevelt would not indefinitely postpone agreement on the Long Terms. The rationale for Churchill's eager desire for the Long Terms as substitute for the Short Terms if possible and at least as supplement was never clear; as has been suggested in the text, probably both Churchill and Roosevelt believed that the Long Terms would tend to stabilize and maintain the role of the House of Savoy, a consequence that Churchill ardently hoped for and that Roosevelt wanted to avoid. Roosevelt was saved at Cassibile when both Eisenhower and Macmillan stridently protested the substitution at that time of a new document for the one that the Italians were about to sign. The evident need for a signed armistice to be announced when the Allied troops landed on the mainland of Italy was conceded, but Churchill remained insistent and Roosevelt, yielding the political lead in Italy to Churchill, eventually gave up the struggle. When the Long Terms were finally signed, they had long since become out-of-date and unworkable. Actually Eisenhower had already assumed with inevitable Italian assent complete control of the liberated portions of Italy. The document was no more than a code of unreal legalisms—and Churchill's support for such an instrument was startlingly uncharacteristic.

The unreal quality of the Long Terms was a reflection of the abject failure of intelligence about the state of Italy in the summer of 1943. Throughout the preparations for the assault on Sicily, throughout the planning for the landings in Italy, and until some time after the troops had entered the peninsula, Eisenhower (and presumably his top staff officers), CCS, and the president and prime minister kept thinking in terms of military quantities in which one German division equalled one Italian division. Churchill had a single moment of insight, when he said on August 5: "Italian troops . . . round Rome . . . have no stomach for fighting . . . and are no match for even one well-equipped German division." Yet this practical wisdom was soon forgotten by Churchill himself and by the others; they all kept assuming that Badoglio had a real government and real fighting forces; this false assumption underlay the unrealities in the Long Terms and almost led to a disaster in GIANT TWO. After Taylor and Gardiner had spent a few hours in Rome, they realized that sincere or not, Italian promises were writ in water.

The benefits of the surrender, although limited, were nonetheless real. Even disintegrating armed forces are likely to show some token resistance to the enemy—even if they have no hate for the enemy country. The Italian Army in Italy was not capable of protecting itself against German onslaughts but could have been an obstruction to the Allied forces, however minor, an obstruction that might have seriously impeded the Allied advance against the Germans. The Italian Air Force was no

danger, but airmen feeling some lingering sense of responsibility might have damaged the airfields in southern Italy. The Italian occupation troops in Yugoslavia were hardly doing more than guarding themselves, but the arms they surrendered to the Yugoslavs were used to fight Germans. Finally, the most cohesive and disciplined group, the Italian Navy, would never have left their Italian ports for Malta if orders that they accepted as legitimate had not emanated from a central authority.

The other hopes about Italian surrender proved vain. Uprisings, sabotage, and all the anticipated spontaneous and semi-spontaneous reactions to the fall of Mussolini were evanescent, because the power lay not with the fragments of the Fascist government but with the Germans: the Nazis were quite capable of dealing with internal difficulties. Indeed, the failure to appreciate the real situation in Italy was probably primarily caused by the constant automatic assumption that any surrender implies the existence of only a victor and a vanquished. The presence of the ominous third party could not be learned from past histories; old habits of thought persisted.

The Italian armistice was as much a success as the situation allowed. A more realistic appraisal would have prevented the emergence of false hopes and saved a good many hours of wasted time. But without hopes true, and— if not too frequently or profoundly so—false, statesmen would not be leaders; and the archives of every government in the world are replete with the laborious products of endless hours spent in the pursuit of the impractical and the inacceptable. The Italian armistice did reflect an adequate awareness of Anglo-American political objectives, duly compromised by coalition constraints and by realistic and imminent military requirements.

DIRECTIVES FOR THE OCCUPATION OF GERMANY: THE WASHINGTON CONTROVERSY

PAUL Y. HAMMOND

RESEARCH ASSOCIATE

WASHINGTON CENTER OF FOREIGN POLICY RESEARCH

THE JOHNS HOPKINS UNIVERSITY

CONTENTS

Foreword   313

I   Initial Planning, 1942-1943   314

II   Policy for Germany: The Crystallization of State and War Department Positions (January to August 1944)   327

III   The Struggle over the Morganthau Plan (August through December 1944)   348

IV   Towards an Occupation Directive: The First Revision of JCS 1067   389

V   Completing the Occupation Directive: The Second Revision   408

VI   The Final Revision of JCS 1067   428

Bibliographic Note   444

Notes   447

Editorial Comments   461

FOREWORD

Developing a policy for the post-war treatment of Germany was inevitably a difficult problem for the United States, as for its Allies. All aspects of the problem presented difficulties, and all led to disagreements between us, Britain, and Russia, and eventually France as well. This was natural enough: no easy answers were available; crucial, and significantly divergent national interests were at stake. What was not inevitable was the process by which policy for Germany was established within our government: considering the difficulties, this is a tale of clever administrative improvisation, shrewd advocacy of policy, and skillful mediation; but it is also a tale of confusion, reversals, conniving—possibly conspiracy—and administrative incompetence, not to speak of what seem in retrospect at the very least gross errors of judgment on policy questions. This is the tale set forth in the following pages.

The primary subject of this study is the formulation of a policy directive to guide and control the occupying forces in Germany.

Originally it was hoped to secure agreement on a directive that would be equally binding on all the occupying powers. In the upshot, and only after a dismally painful birth, a directive was produced and agreed on—JCS 1067 —to govern the actions of the U. S. zonal commander. But though the production of such a directive was the primary object of concern for the opposing factions in our government, its drafting was entangled in a variety of ancillary disputes: over the demarcation and assignment of occupation zones; over the instrument of surrender; over the inter-governmental control machinery for Germany; over plans to partition Germany; over reparations; and over the organization and procedures for dealing with civil affairs and military government in the various occupied and liberated countries. On most of these matters, the disputes within the American administration were even more acrimonious than the disputes with our Allies, and they aggravated the troubles of those who were trying to formulate a policy for Germany.

I. INITIAL PLANNING, 1942-1943

A. ALLIED POLICY—ITS AMBIGUITY

1. Raising the Question of Dismemberment

Long before entering the war, the United States had made clear its own unalterable opposition to Hitler and his regime. In August 1941, in the Atlantic Charter, Roosevelt and Churchill proclaimed their aspirations for the post-war world: an abjuration of any ambition for aggrandizement, support for national self-determination, economic collaboration, and a secure peace. On Christmas Day after Pearl Harbor, in the Declaration of the United Nations, they reaffirmed these aims and pledged themselves to the destruction of Hitler and his allies. Aside from this clear but negative and limited goal, no policy for Germany was set or even adumbrated: what would happen to the Germans after defeat, what Germany's place would be in the post-war world, were unanswered questions.

At the beginning of the New Year, a more direct and concrete reference to the treatment of Germany was made in the "Allied Declaration of German War Crimes" of January 13, 1942, which announced the intention of exacting retribution for war crimes. A year later, in January 1943, the doctrine of unconditional surrender was announced at Casablanca, and subscribed to by representatives of the Soviet Union and China at Moscow in October of the same year. In March 1943, during conversations between Britain's Foreign Secretary, Anthony Eden, and President Roosevelt, it was agreed that Germany should be dismembered,[1] although it is clear that the matter was discussed only in general terms,[2] and that Roosevelt was uncertain about the concrete application of his proposal.[3] According to Harry Hopkins' notes, Eden had been relating to the President his impression of Stalin's attitude towards Ger-

many. The Russian Premier, in Eden's opinion,

has a deep-seated distrust of the Germans and . . . will insist that Germany be broken up into a number of states. The President said he hoped we would not use the methods discussed at Versailles and also promoted by Clemenceau to arbitrarily divide Germany, but thought that we should encourage the differences and ambitions that will spring up within Germany for a Separatists Movement and, in effect, approve of a division which represents German public opinion.

[Hopkins] asked what they would do if that spontaneous desire did not spring up and both the President and Eden agreed that, under any circumstances, Germany must be divided into several states, one of which must, over all circumstances, be Prussia. The Prussians cannot be permitted to dominate all Germany.[4]

A few days later, again in conversation with Eden in the presence of Hopkins and Hull, President Roosevelt reiterated his unconditional surrender views and indicated that he doubted if a peace treaty should be signed for some time after the collapse of Germany and Japan.[5]

These discussions took place on March 15 and 22; in between, on March 20, Hull had a long conversation alone with the President about the post-war treatment of Germany. But all these talks amounted to no more than an expression of attitudes and a glance at the problem rather than a step toward solid agreement or action. The one practical proposal during Eden's visit came from Hopkins, when he, Hull, and Eden had tea with the President on March 17. As Hopkins wrote in his notes:

I said I thought there was no understanding between Great Britain, Russia and ourselves as to which armies would be where and what kind of administration should be developed. I said that unless we acted promptly and surely I believed one of two things would happen—either Germany will go Communist or an out and out anarchic state would set in; that, indeed, the same kind of thing might happen in any of the countries in Europe and Italy as well. I said I thought it required some kind of formal agreement and that the State Department should work out the plan with the British and the one agreed upon between the two of us should then be discussed with the Russians. The President agreed that this procedure should be followed. It will, obviously, be a much simpler matter if the British and American armies are heavily in France or Germany at the time of the collapse but we should work out a plan in case Germany collapses before we get to France.[6]

On March 23, picking up this suggestion, the President wrote Hull:

Apropos of our conversation the other afternoon, I wish you would explore, with the British, the question of what our plan is to be in Germany and Italy during the first few months after Germany's collapse.

I think you had better confer with Stimson about it too.

My thought is that if we get a substantial meeting of the minds with the British that we should then take it up with the Russians.[7]

The State Department had, in fact, begun its consideration of the post-war treatment of Germany a year or so earlier, and Under Secretary Sumner Welles had made clear his own advocacy of German partition.[8] This letter from the President had no discernible effect on the State Department planning; if the planners devoted any particular attention to dismemberment, it was probably because of Welles's views. There was some discussion of the problem, apparently not very fruitful, with Secretary of War Stimson, and with the British.[9] And Hull talked briefly, informally, and inconclusively with Eden about partition at Quebec on August 20; each revealed that there was some support for "imposed dismemberment" within his government, and each indicated his own disagreement with the proposal.[10]

By the fall of 1943, however, whether Germany was to survive as a unit or as fragments, it was necessary for the State Department to crystallize its policies for the treatment of Germany so that Hull might have some preliminary proposals to present at the Conference of Foreign Ministers in Moscow. On October 4 and 5, prior to his departure, he had talks with the President. On the second day, when the President brought up the dismemberment of Germany, Hull was accompanied by the new Under Secretary, Edward R. Stettinius, Jr., and three officers of the department who were directly involved in planning policy for post-war Germany; Admiral Leahy, the President's Chief of Staff, was also present.[11] The President said that he favored the partition of Germany into three completely sovereign states. Hull and his assistants were well briefed in their objections to this proposal. Their argument was that the conquering powers would have to carry the burden of extensive controls if Germany were thus to be kept divided; that these controls would not make controls for enforcing economic and military disarmament unnecessary; and that, indeed, the economic and military controls would have to be so severe that they would "evoke a greatly increased resentment on the part of the German people to the serious detriment of their ultimate reconciliation with the peace settlement."[12] It is not unlikely that Roosevelt had heard this argument from Hull before, possibly the previous March, during Eden's visit to Washington. While it was based on policy papers newly prepared in the State Department, in substance it was not new; as Hull later put it, "I myself had been opposed to dismemberment from the beginning."[13]

Roosevelt took up the argument that dismemberment might only cause the German people to desire national unity more strongly. He said he thought that his listeners were inclined to exaggerate this effect, and indicated that he based his appraisal on his own personal experience in Germany. After the discussion had gone on to other matters, the President returned to the subject of Germany to point out that occupation policy would have to be one of trial and error, and that they might discover that partition did not work.[14]

2. *Moscow and Teheran*

At the Moscow Conference, in October 1943, the three foreign ministers discussed the treatment of Germany. They agreed that Germany would be returned to her pre-1938 borders, and prepared a "Declaration on German Atrocities," later signed by Roosevelt, Stalin, and Churchill.[15] But with respect to basic occupation policy, they made no great progress. Hull presented two memoranda, "for discussion purposes"; Molotov's first reaction to them was enthusiastic, though he later said that he regarded them as constituting a minimum rather than a maximum proposal.

These proposals began with an elaboration of the meaning of unconditional surrender by detailing the rights of the occupying powers. They recommended that the terms of surrender be enforced by an Inter-Allied Control Commission rather than by the three victors individually, but that Germany be occupied by British, Soviet, and American forces in separate sectors, with minimum interference with local government. "All Nazi officials would be promptly removed and every vestige of the Nazi regime uprooted." Reparations for physical damage inflicted by Germany would be set by a commission for that purpose.[16]

The proposals for demobilization and disarmament as such were clear-cut: no standing army, dissolution of the German General Staff, and the like. But these questions of security merged into questions of economic and political reorganization, and here ambiguities appeared, ambiguities that were the subject of much quarrelling later on. Thus, the possibility of voluntary dismemberment was suggested, but clouded in doubt, and the issue was described as "still under study" (although it was assumed that in the end the U. S. government would not favor dismemberment). Alternatively, it was suggested that the German threat to security might be lessened by "decentralization of the German political structure." The memoranda advocated for Germany "a broadly based democracy operating under a bill of rights." Steps toward this end would include restoration of "freedom of speech and religion, and of the press, freedom to organize political parties other than those of Nazi-Fascist doctrine, cultural associations, and trade unions," and would culminate in free elections for a central German government.

The economic proposals grew out of the demobilization plan, which provided that "arms manufacturing facilities be dismantled, importation and manufacture of arms, ammunition, implements of war, *and materials essential to their manufacture,* including all types of aircraft, be prohibited"[17] (italics added); all this would be done under a permanent United Nations inspection system.

The italicized phrase seemed to point toward the elimination of all heavy industry: Is not steel "essential" to arms manufacture and might not this vague requirement lead to differing interpretations among the Allies? Although obvious, the implication was not intended; heavy industry was to be controlled, not eliminated. The ambiguity of the crucial demobilization plan was assured by the prescription for the requirements of a viable democracy: "a tolerable standard of living; restriction of measures of control to the requirements of general security; and harmony of policy and purpose among the British, Soviet, and American governments."[18]

Hull felt that there was general agreement on his memoranda, and in fact many of the detailed proposals were later put into effect; but general agreement on the ambiguities that lay at the heart of the policy issues settled nothing. The only point that seems to have come up for concrete discussion was dismemberment. On this there was also a strange kind of unanimity; apparently the three chiefs of state all favored partition, while the three foreign ministers and their experts were against it. That question was therefore laid aside. The American memoranda were disposed of by referring them for study to the European Advisory Commission. This body, by agreement of the three ministers, was to be located in London to "study and make recommendations to the three governments upon European questions connected with the termination of hostilities."[19]

A month after the Moscow Conference, the three chiefs of state met in Teheran and here again Germany's future was discussed—discussed but certainly not decided. Stalin talked at length about Germany. He questioned the wisdom of the undefined "unconditional surrender" doctrine, and argued the need for more stringent controls than any envisaged by Roosevelt or Churchill. He expressed no great satisfaction with either of two partition proposals; Roosevelt had presented a plan for five autonomous states and three international zones, while Churchill had proposed that Prussia be detached and the southern states included in a Danubian federation. The general policy questions were left hanging, and the problem of dismemberment was referred to the European Advisory Commission. On a more practical plane, the three governments designated their representatives on that body: Sir William Strang for the United Kingdom, Feodor T.

Gusev for the Soviet Union, and for the United States, our Ambassador in London, John G. Winant.[20]

On December 15, the European Advisory Commission had an informal organizing meeting, and held its first formal session on January 14, 1944. Its mandate to "study and make recommendations" was, of course, a term of art; EAC was a forum for negotiations where the three members, duly instructed by their governments, could present and discuss formal proposals, and, in accordance with instructions received, reach agreements. The scope of the negotiations was uncertain; the British were anxious to settle as many questions as possible while the war was still on, the Americans wanted to limit the agenda to problems arising immediately out of surrender. Since unanimity was required for deciding the agenda, the Americans had an effective veto power.

For Germany, the question of scope did not arise. It was agreed that there were three problems requiring urgent consideration—occupation zones, the instrument of surrender, and the organization of tripartite control machinery. Policy for Germany would be taken up later.

The American power to prevent discussions was unlimited; but American ability to lead the way on what it considered appropriate topics was not. Leadership depended on Winant's ability to get instructions: no matter how convinced he was of the soundness of his own ideas on what to do, no matter how wise his counselors (he was soon equipped with political, naval, and military advisers, and— later on—also an economic adviser), he could present no plans, indeed he could make no decisive comments on British or Russian proposals, without instructions from Washington.

The EAC was perhaps bound to work slowly. The Russians were difficult to work with, especially so when their suspicions were aroused by leaks about EAC negotiations to the British press; we had differences with the British on all matters; the addition of a French member caused trouble later on; but most significant, at least for this account, were the delays caused by Winant's failure to receive instructions. The causes for this must be sought in Washington.[21]

The establishment of EAC precipitated the need for agreed American plans for Germany, but the need had been long foreseen and planning was well advanced. Before describing the developments of 1944, in EAC and elsewhere, it is necessary to review what had already been done in the interested agencies.

B. STATE DEPARTMENT PLANNING: 1942-1943

State Department policy with respect to the post-war treatment of Germany was, in the winter of 1943, the product of extensive consideration within the Department, mostly by experts—career officials and others—for nearly two years. Early in 1942 Under Secretary Sumner Welles assigned the subject of the possible dismemberment of Germany to the newly created Advisory Committee on Post-War Foreign Policy, an organization partly intra-departmental in membership, but with six of its fourteen original members drawn from private life.[22] In the course of considering the dismemberment of Germany the committee had its research staff, recruited in the main from among academic experts on the various countries, prepare detailed arguments for and against dismemberment, and draw up plans for dividing Germany into three, five, and seven separate states, with accompanying analyses of the political, economic, and demographic problems involved.

The argument against dismemberment, which found early support in the expert staff and among certain members of the Advisory Committee, particularly Hamilton Fish Armstrong, editor of *Foreign Affairs,* and Isaiah Bowman, President of the Johns Hopkins University, was eventually supported by the majority of the committee. During April, May, and June 1942, the committee gave careful consideration to the dismemberment question, and reviewed it from time to time over the next year and a half. As was indicated earlier, Secretary Hull, who was Chairman of the Advisory Committee, opposed dismemberment "from the first"; his views remained unchanged, as has also been seen, when he met with the British and Soviet foreign ministers a half-year later in Moscow. His stand on general policy for Germany was, perhaps, best expressed both in the clear and in the ambiguous proposals he presented there. The President also remained set in his views; he wanted dismemberment, but he obviously hoped that it would come about by voluntary action, and he tended to postpone any decision on imposed dismemberment. For the rest, his attitude toward Germany was stern, as evidenced, for example, in his persistence in the unconditional surrender doctrine, though he seems to have had no specific plans for the treatment of Germany after the war.

These divergences, especially on the subject of partition, put the Advisory Committee members in an awkward position. Apparently they had dismemberment under consideration (along with many other topics) for a long time without completing their formal report and submitting it to the President through the Secretary of State.[23] Their position was made no easier by the fact that Welles, who participated much more actively in the committee's work than did Hull, sided with the President and against Hull. Eventually, however, their strong opposition to dismemberment was recorded. They also recommended a vigorous long-range policy for preventing German rearmament, promoting democratic institutions, and reducing or controlling Germany's economic preponderance in Europe.[24]

Shortly thereafter, on July 12, 1943, the Advisory Committee on Post-War Foreign Policy was suspended by Secretary Hull "in order to enable the technical staff to carry out the work of intensive preparation for a more definitive round of discussion."[25] However, the Advisory Committee and its subcommittees were never reconvened. The end result of their work was the drafting by the technical staff of policy summaries on each of the many subjects with which the subcommittees had dealt. One of these was a 49-page document dated July 27, 1943, which strongly opposed the dismemberment of Germany. It was used in briefing Secretary Hull in preparation for the first Quebec Conference in August 1943.[26]

Within the State Department a new structure of committees was established immediately after the demise of the Advisory Committee. One of these was the Interdivisional Country Committee on Germany, composed of the staff assembled to do research for the Advisory Committee and of the "desk officers" in the operating geographic and functional divisions.[27] By September 23, 1943, this group had produced a policy-recommendation paper on "The Political Reorganization of Germany," which was used as the basis for the memoranda on Germany which Hull presented at Moscow.[28] Al-

though the policy recommendations of the Interdivisional Committee showed the influence of its predecessors (the Advisory Committee and its subcommittees), the new committee had a clear field within the Department, for Welles, the active proponent of dismemberment, left in August.[29]

During the autumn and winter of 1943-1944 the Interdivisional Committee on Germany made an intensive study of post-war policy toward Germany, partially directed toward the need for policy guidance for Ambassador Winant in his EAC negotiations. The American draft of an instrument of German unconditional surrender, which became the basis for terms agreed to the following summer in the EAC, originated here. Proposals for zones of occupation and Allied control machinery for the joint administration of Germany were also produced, and will be further considered below. Here let it suffice to note that the general policy position of the Interdivisional Committee remained as it had been in the early fall, when the committee was preparing for the Moscow Foreign Ministers' Conference. It opposed dismemberment, wished to encourage democracy in Germany through a moderate peace, and advocated decentralization of the government of Germany.[30] In spite of all the changes in planning procedures, the professional staff of the State Department remained firmly committed to the policy for Germany that they had first formulated early in 1942. Moreover, despite the President's evident opposition to leniency towards Germany, Secretary Hull had demonstrated his strong agreement with this general approach.

C. AMERICAN ARMY PREPARATIONS: 1942-1943

1. Army Doctrine and Its Uses

Military government was no novelty to the United States Army. In the Philippines, in Cuba, and elsewhere in Latin America, the Army had had long experience in administering the territory of other nations. Its doctrines were embodied in successive revisions of field manuals, and were based on the concepts of "welfare of the governed" and "military necessity."[31] As an Army manual published in 1925 put it:

International law recognized that, having overthrown the pre-existing government and deprived the people of the protection which that government afforded, it becomes not only the right but the duty of the invader to give the vanquished people a new government adequate to the protection of their personal and property rights.

With reference to military necessity, it stated:

It is decidedly to the military advantage of the invader to establish a strong and just government, such as will preserve order and, as far as possible, pacify the inhabitants.[32]

This conception of civil affairs could be traced to the venerable theory of war which held that armed conflict was an affair of state, not of individuals or the nation, and that customs, traditions, laws and government were not to be unnecessarily disturbed by occupying troops.[33]

Such was the doctrine applied by our forces in their brief responsibility for governing a very small portion of Germany at the end of World War I. The doctrine had, of course, been modified to suit the circumstances in the various occupations in the Caribbean and the Philippines—underdeveloped areas, in the modern terminology.

Neither doctrine nor experience (except that the experience in administration as such proved invaluable) furnished a sufficient guide for military government in Europe in World War II. There we had to prepare for military administration in "liberated areas" like France, where we (at least Roosevelt) expected a friendly population but no firmly established resident government. And we also had to prepare for government in "occupied areas," Germany and Italy, where we were pledged to destroy the governors and the whole basis of their government: Hitler and Mussolini, Nazism and Fascism. Later on, we would face a similar problem in Japan. And in both liberated and occupied areas, the kind of government that would eventually take over the reins from the military administrators was not a matter of indifference nor, as it turned out, a matter to be avoided up to the moment when power was actually transferred.

The possible conflicts between "military necessity," "welfare of the governed," "eradication of Fascism and Nazism," and "establishment of democracy" were not clearly seen at the beginning. The first proposed solution of these potential conflicts was to create a political vacuum as a step towards the ultimate goal of democracy. This inconsistency in civil affairs policy found its way into the revised field manual on military government issued at the end of 1943. Since the spring of 1942 the War Department had been operating a School of Military Government at the University of Virginia. There the possible incompatibility between the "welfare of the governed" and the "military necessity" doctrines, as embodied in the earlier version of the field manual, had been exposed and explored. The new manual acknowledged the triumph of the "military necessity" doctrine. It also showed a severer attitude toward enemy populations under military government. The military implications of civil disorder led it to be less concerned than was its predecessor with the eradication of Fascism. And its vagueness and generality made possible a wide range of interpretations. Dealing for the first time with economic policy, it provided for rapid reconstruction in order to alleviate the burdens upon Allied supplies, both for relief and military purposes. This revised field manual was representative of military government policy as it was understood by civil affairs officers of the Army at the time of the establishment of EAC.

2.   First Encounters with the President

The doctrines of the Army and its prospective role in the administration of occupied and liberated areas had been brought sharply to the attention of the President a year earlier in the fall of 1942, but were not resolved in any effective way until November 1943. In October 1942, Secretary of the Interior Harold L. Ickes complained to the President about the military government school at Charlottesville, which had started to operate six months earlier. In response Roosevelt wrote to Secretary of War Stimson inquiring about the school. Echoing the Ickes complaint, he stated:

This whole matter is something which should have been taken up with me in the first instance. The governing of occupied territories may be of many kinds but in most instances it is a civilian task and requires absolutely first-class men and not second-string men.[34]

Rumors of Fascists in the school prompted

the President to request information concerning the backgrounds of its trainees. Stimson defended the school vigorously and successfully. In doing so he found Secretary of State Hull a "staunch ally . . . who agreed with Stimson's view that administration in foreign lands must initially be an army responsibility, while Stimson in turn fully accepted the State Department's responsibility for the formulation of political policy."[35] But the President's critical attitude was very discouraging to the Army planners.[36]

Roosevelt's views on civil affairs were given further expression when on November 18, 1942, he delegated to the Secretary of State full authority over all economic, political, and fiscal questions concerning liberated (not occupied) areas.[37] Meanwhile, however, during the autumn of 1942, Eisenhower, commanding the invasion of North Africa, was heading into real political problems. The North African invasion had been planned in haste, and to the neglect of civil affairs. The difficulties that arose were somehow surmounted, but the need for more effective organization for civil affairs and military government was clear to all, especially the military.

It is unnecessary to pursue the complex tangles over civil affairs in Algiers and Washington, and the debates that continued thereafter: they concerned primarily dealings with future liberated areas. To a considerable extent, the Army found itself accidentally involved in controversies among the civilian agencies of the government. Its primary aim was to ensure control over civil affairs in combat and communication zones. Eventually the President came to accept this view and decreed on November 10, 1943, that the Army should have full responsibility for civilian relief (the main subject of controversy) in each area so long as the fighting continued and for six months thereafter.[38] The effects on the President of all these events and the painful dilemmas in North Africa and Italy can hardly be spelled out. His later behavior, in 1944, seems to show that while he recognized the need for Army administration of civil affairs, he was not disposed to accept advice from the Army, State Department, or any other agency on underlying policies, though this minimization of the role of the State Department had not become apparent by the end of 1943.

3. *The Establishment of the Civil Affairs Division*

The effects on the War Department can also be observed. One important consequence was the recognition at the top of the need to coordinate Army activities in civil affairs and to assign the responsibility for guiding these activities to a single new agency within the Army. The new agency was the Civil Affairs Division, established on March 1, 1943. It was created to deal in a regular and systematic way with the civil affairs problems already present in North Africa and expected to arise in areas subsequently occupied or liberated as a result of military operations. While CAD was to be a part of the War Department Special Staff, in order to assure that its work was in harmony with the regular military business of the War Department, its communications with commanders in the field were to be cleared through the Operations Division of the War Department General Staff, which was responsible for directing the key supervisory and operating activities of the General Staff on behalf of the Chief of Staff. In order further to gear its activities in with OPD, an OPD officer was detailed as a member of CAD. During most of its existence its head was Major General John H. Hilldring. A month after its establishment, the Joint Chiefs of Staff recognized CAD as the logical place to coordinate the planning and administration of civil affairs in most occupied areas. The Secretaries of War and the Navy promptly endorsed this recommendation.[39]

When Hilldring took charge of the Civil Affairs Division in April 1943, Stimson explained to him that he did not want the Army to have anything to do with the making of policy, but that as a Cabinet officer, though not as head of the War Department, he might himself become involved in policy questions. Marshall indicated that he was going into civil affairs planning and administration with reluctance. He instructed Hilldring to get into it no further than he had to. These were instructions which Hilldring took seriously: as director of a division of the War Department Special Staff, his job was to service the field commanders. The function of his particular division, the coordination of civil affairs activities, turned out to be largely administrative problems, usually concerned with civilian supply. If the fighting forces needed policy for civil affairs, he was only to see that it was provided, not make it himself. Stimson, the Cabinet officer, and McCloy, his energetic Assistant Secretary, were the only ones in the War Department properly concerned with the substance of occupation policy, and they only through Stimson's role as an adviser to the President. General Hilldring and the other military and civilian chiefs were operating on the assumption that the Army was to remain the handmaiden of policy, and that CAD was to be only the handmaiden's handmaiden. Nevertheless, the confinement of CAD to the role of coordinator of things which were presumably not policy, but only questions involving military government was not to limit CAD to a wholly passive role. One of the first tasks Hilldring undertook was to make State and other Departments realize that they would have to take second place to the War Department where military government problems were involved. By the end of May Hilldring could say that State had been brought into line with this view.[40]

For months after its establishment, CAD was largely preoccupied with organizational and jurisdictional problems within the Army, more generally with the United States government, and with the British Army, as will be seen below. It also was busy with the selection and training of civil affairs officers, with arrangements for essential supplies for liberated and occupied areas, and with civil affairs agreements with the governments-in-exile. Finally, it had to struggle with the requests for aid, information, and guidance that flowed in from General Eisenhower's headquarters as urgent practical problems arose first in North Africa and later in Italy. All this left little time for the long-term planning of policy, and aside from work done on military government handbooks and manuals at Charlottesville, the year marked little progress on German affairs.[41]

Recurrent efforts of CAD to arrange to have someone outside the War Department conduct studies on German institutions indicate the limited progress of the Army towards competence in long-term military government planning made by the end of 1943. These studies were originally conceived as an examination of Axis laws, to be conducted in the Depart-

ment of Justice. The request was soon withdrawn as the need for something broader in scope became more apparent. But by the end of the year nothing more concrete had been done than to discuss the project with two Harvard professors.[42]

At the end of November, while the chiefs of state were discussing at Teheran what to do with Germany, State submitted to CAD for its clearance the "Treatment of Germany" paper presented by Hull at Moscow. CAD specifically approved of State's intention that the surrender terms be brief, was troubled that the paper made no direct statement that military government was contemplated (it did speak of occupying forces), and objected outright to the proposal to scrap German armaments as a part of the plan to disarm Germany. CAD wanted it made clear that a period of military government was inevitable and should be provided for, and wanted to preserve German armaments in case they could be used in the war against Japan.[43] The larger issues such as economic policy, dismemberment, denazification and demilitarization, it passed over in its concern for what it considered at this time to be the only aspects of German policy which were important from a military standpoint.

D. ANGLO-AMERICAN MILITARY PLANNING FOR THE OCCUPATION OF GERMANY

The war was conducted by a Grand Alliance, but the members of the Grand Alliance were not all equally involved in the whole global conflict, nor, *a fortiori,* on all fronts. In much of the world, the Anglo-American partnership was very close and nowhere more so than in the campaigns in the Mediterranean and European theaters of operations. In the Mediterranean, from November 1942 to the end of 1943, General Eisenhower was commander of a combined headquarters, acting under the direction of the Combined Chiefs of Staff whose superiors were the President and the Prime Minister. Coalition warfare under CCS and General Eisenhower's AFHQ was found workable and successful; it established a pattern for future operations in Europe.

At the Casablanca Conference in January 1943, Roosevelt and Churchill agreed that Allied forces would invade France in 1944, and agreed further to set up an organization in England to prepare plans for the invasion. The planners, as well as the invading armies, were to be "combined," i. e., Anglo-American. In the early spring of 1943 the planning agency was established under the deliberately mystifying designation of COSSAC—Chief of Staff to the Supreme Allied Commander (designate); COSSAC himself, pending the long-delayed designation of a supreme commander and the formation of his command, was British, Lieutenant General Sir Frederick E. Morgan.[44]

General Morgan's primary concern, in his uneasy position, was the planning of the actual invasion. In time, however, he found it necessary to assign officers to civil affairs planning as well, and by an odd circumstance was forced to develop plans for the occupation of Germany almost a year before the actual invasion of France, almost two years before V-E Day.

What happened was this. Periodically, in both London and Washington, there was a sudden conviction or fear or hope that Germany would collapse. One such occasion occurred in the summer of 1943. At the end of July, Morgan was told to prepare RANKIN (Plan C), as it was called, a plan for operations if Germany did collapse, and to have it ready so that it could be presented at the first Quebec Conference which was to open on August 14.[45]

RANKIN (C) dealt with a complicated problem, involving as it did plans for the countries that would be suddenly liberated as well as for Germany itself. The plans for Germany were rudimentary, but in one respect they were specific and determinative of future controversy and action: this was the question of occupation zones. On a question of this sort, planning allows no room for ambiguity.

Morgan sought guidance from the British government, and received none. He thereupon proceeded on three straightforward assumptions: (1) British, American and Russian armies would occupy Germany; (2) the zones should be of approximately equivalent size; (3) Berlin, as capital, would be a separate enclave. On a map of Germany lines were drawn, following provincial boundaries, showing three zones fitting these assumptions. The remaining question was who would get which zone. Obviously the Russians would be in the East. The decision on the Western assignments seemed almost equally automatic, for the American

troops already in Britain were in the West; they would enter the continent, and ultimately Germany on the right flank, and would therefore arrive in the Southwest zone.[46]

RANKIN (C) was ready on August 13, and forwarded to Quebec, where it received the general blessing of CCS. From the standpoint of COSSAC, this marked the beginning of serious planning for civil affairs, but the problem of zonal boundaries had a strange life of its own.[47]

Morgan's plan for the zones was, as has been said, approved by CCS at Quebec and, though designed for the case of German collapse, soon became the plan for use after victory as well. Whether this item, one among many, was discussed at Quebec by Churchill and Roosevelt is not known, though of course CCS had reported the plan to them and they had approved the final CCS report. (There is no available evidence that either Hull or any of his assistants was told of this, but then or later they learned that there was some kind of joint Anglo-American agreement or disagreement over occupation zones.) At any rate, by mid-November Roosevelt decided that he did not like these arrangements. He was extremely eager to have no involvement with France, or any responsibility for order or for relief there, or in southern and central Europe, including Austria. He was also anxious to facilitate the redeployment of our forces to the United States and the Far East, especially since he believed that our forces of a million men could not stay in Europe more than one or maybe two years after the end of the fighting in Europe. For these reasons he was determined that we should have the Northwest zone while the British took the Southwest zone.

The President's views were expressed to the Joint Chiefs of Staff on the U. S. S. *Iowa* en route to the Cairo and Teheran Conferences. On November 19, 1943, in a discussion of RANKIN, he reiterated his desire for the Northwest zone. In what seems to have been a rather confused fashion, he linked the concept of occupation zones with the concept of dismemberment. He had in mind the creation of three German states, with the possible addition of a buffer state between Germany and France: presumably each of the three zones would later become one of the three states. Either forgetting or setting aside General Morgan's map, he took a National Geographic Society map and drew hasty pencil lines on it to show the boundaries he wanted for the three zone-states. The Joint Chiefs indicated that his plan would present certain logistic problems because the U. S. Army was and would be on the right flank of the British Army, but they said they would work out a solution.

Aside from logistic and other difficulties, it is hard to imagine that the Russians or the British would have accepted Roosevelt's zonal proposal. Morgan's plan had made three slices of Germany with almost equal divisions of population and area. Roosevelt's proposal contemplated the creation of a buffer zone or state and an assignment of a lion's share of the rest to the United States; both Britain and Russia would have seriously reduced shares. The pencil marks on the map also show that Roosevelt proposed that the U. S. and Russian zones meet at Berlin, though the minutes could be interpreted to mean that Berlin would be in our zone.[48]

Roosevelt's plans did not suit Churchill. At the second Cairo Conference, on December 3, 1943, Churchill and Eden argued with Roosevelt for the Northwest zone; Admiral Leahy, who was present, seems to have agreed with them and presumably said nothing. The issue was debated but not resolved at a meeting of the Combined Chiefs of Staff the following day.[49] They merely decided to ask General Morgan to study the possibility of devising a plan that would resemble Roosevelt's map. A later discussion between Roosevelt and Churchill—largely in terms of dismemberment —was inconclusive. Thus, when the time came to send Winant instructions, the Army had become possessor of two plans for zonal boundaries, and was also awaiting agreement by Roosevelt and Churchill on zonal assignments. Of all this, the Department of State was only generally aware. It did not know what the agreements and disagreements were.

One additional element in combined planning during 1943 needs to be noted. In July, CCS established the Combined Civil Affairs Committee to recommend civil affairs policies for occupied and liberated areas, and to coordinate military and civilian agency interests. Its chairman was Assistant Secretary McCloy, and its other American members were General Hilldring, a Navy officer, and James C. Dunn,

Director of the Office of European Affairs of the State Department. Two British members represented the Joint Staff Mission, one the Foreign Office, and one was a civilian expert.[50]

CCAC, as a subcommittee of CCS, normally prepared instructions for transmission by CCS to Eisenhower, or other heads of combined commands. Thus, though it included important civilian representation, it was not designed as a general civil-military coordinating body, as useful on the American side to the State Department as to the military; and its formal access to Roosevelt and Churchill lay only through military channels. Furthermore, it was not designed to prepare policies for areas where the Russians would join in the occupation, or for the period after dissolution of a combined command.

Notwithstanding its limitations, CCAC had a function to perform, and soon started on its task. In its early meetings it dealt largely with problems of Italy, but soon began on other matters. In the fall, it ran into difficulties. The British were eager to make London the headquarters for all civil affairs matters. From November to the end of January CCAC was deadlocked. And the U. S. Army, not pleased with what they viewed (with much reason) as an attempt by the British to dominate civil affairs, looked with disfavor on EAC (the tripartite European Advisory Commission) because of its London site.[51]

E. SUMMARY

By the end of 1943 the American armed forces had had some valuable experiences with civil affairs in North Africa and Italy, the first Big Three wartime conference had been held, and the cross-channel attack had been set for the coming spring. Occupation policy for Germany remained unsettled. Preliminary soundings at Moscow and Teheran in October and November had revealed that the three powers were not prepared to commit themselves as yet to a policy and, indeed, that there were divisions within their own governments. If the discussions at Teheran on the post-war treatment of Germany indicated anything about substantive policy, it was that the three heads of state favored some form of dismemberment of Germany.

But while policy issues remained unsettled,

some administrative machinery for settling them had been constructed—on the tripartite level the European Advisory Commission, for Anglo-American affairs, CCAC, and within the American government the Working Security Committee, described below. What any of them could accomplish remained to be seen.

The President, the State Department, and the War Department were playing the major roles at this time in the development of policy for Germany within the American government. If President Roosevelt had been a different kind of person, what he wanted might have been describable in one or more of several ways. He might by this time have had strong views about, first, the general nature of policy, and, second, specific programs for carrying out that policy. In fact, his general view (he wanted to be stern) was too general to be policy, and his only specific program, if dismemberment could be called that (and on that he was not absolutely sure), was opposed by the State Department. Third, he might have decided upon the procedure by which the American position on occupation policy for Germany was to be determined within the American government. He had already taken positions which had implications for this decision: that the War Department was to have a minimum role in policy-making, and that the State Department was to have a maximum role in the administration of liberated areas, and in the development of a tripartite policy in the European Advisory Commission. But he had allowed the War Department to handle with him the first concrete decision concerning post-war Germany, the determination of zonal boundaries; the Army's demand for behind-the-lines control in the Mediterranean was evidently going to be given liberal interpretation with Roosevelt's blessing; and the importance of EAC, and hence of State, in all of this was illusive.

Fourth, he might have decided how urgent it was for his government to reach tripartite or Anglo-American agreements on policy, and how far such agreements should go. Early in 1942 he had shown some interest in reaching an agreement with the British, and then with the Russians, on what to do with Germany in case she collapsed unexpectedly. But by the end of 1943, since the President had offered no substantial encouragement to efforts to answer the question in the meantime, it was clear

that he did not regard tripartite agreement as very urgent. Actually, both he and Hull disapproved of decisions on post-war settlements while the war was still going on. The establishment of the European Advisory Commission at the end of the year provided a basis for a new test of his sense of urgency, the results of which were not yet evident. And, as later occurrences will make clear, for better or for worse, and in accordance with what he had said on one occasion during Eden's visit, he had evidently decided to postpone policy until the actual situation in Germany could be surveyed and until more could be known about other factors relevant in the determination of long-range policy for Germany.

What Roosevelt wanted could therefore be described with the fourth alternative: that policy commitments for the treatment of Germany were not greatly urgent and should be postponed wherever possible. He had, to be sure, indicated his preferences from time to time regarding the three other approaches to policy for Germany. But only with respect to the fourth approach was he consistent in both his expressed and applied views. He had decided not to decide just yet; but he did not stifle, as we shall see, all efforts to produce policy. That would have put him under a handicap when the time came for making a decision. On the other hand, he did not encourage his subordinates to badger him with potential policy commitments; it was the pressure of their work that forced them into doing that.

The State Department position on the post-war treatment of Germany had taken shape in mid-1942, and had not changed by the end of 1943. State shared the popular desire for a stern peace: it sought demobilization, demilitarization, denazification, and restitution. But the enforcement of these programs was to be limited because of the long-term objectives of State Department policy. State Department officials believed that in order to enable Germany to develop as a peace-loving democracy (which was State's panacea for post-war international relations), post-defeat living conditions in Germany would have to be attractive enough to endear the new regime to the Germans.

In attempting to strike a balance between these two conflicting objectives, State had produced a variety of finely drawn policy papers which were careful in their statements of general policy but not particularly precise, and certainly not concrete in the spelling out of policy. For use within the Department, these papers might have been entirely adequate in their precision. But they were to prove ambiguous when subjected to hard negotiation with Treasury and War.

State accepted its position as policy-maker for the post-war treatment of Germany, but this function was performed by middle-ranking officials who received little active support from the Secretary's office. Evidently at the end of 1943 State was not willing (or perhaps able enough) to give policy-making for the treatment of Germany, or cooperation with the War Department on such matters, a priority high enough to require the Secretary's active and continuing interest.

By the beginning of the third year of overt American participation in the war it was becoming increasingly evident that the War Department's role in occupation was bound to be significant. Cooperation between the State and War Departments seemed essential. But the two departments were not finding a working relationship easy. State had been preoccupied with refining policy documents, while the War Department viewed civil affairs largely as an intrusion upon its primary responsibilities, both because these "non-military" matters seemed to threaten the involvement of the Army in politics, and because they were rivals of military requirements.

While at the end of 1943 the State Department had only begun to view the settlement of German policy as urgent, and hence cooperation with the War Department as necessary, by this time the latter had four persuasive reasons not to reciprocate. A continuing one was the security problem: the War Department, determined to protect the secrecy of its operational plans, was unwilling to share information related to them with State. Another reason was the War Department's experience with establishing the zonal boundaries for occupation which suggested that going to the trouble of clearing with or even consulting the State Department in the settlement of pressing political issues related to military operations was unnecessary. Here had been an urgent policy question which the combined planners in London had wanted settled. And to the extent that it was by 1944, it was settled through the

Joint Chiefs of Staff dealing directly with President Roosevelt.

A third reason persuading the War Department against cooperation with State had developed over the Army's struggle to prevent the British from dominating Anglo-American civil affairs. The War Department had insisted that a duplicate CCAC sit in Washington because the British seemed intent on dominating the original one in London. Since State expected to use EAC as its channel for an agreed Anglo-American policy, and EAC sat in London where the British could also (as the Army thought) dominate it, the War Department officials who had fought the civil affairs battle with the British were understandably reluctant to help State support the EAC. At the same time, the existence of a combined staff structure under CCS, and in COSSAC in London, assured the War Department of its own avenue to Anglo-American agreement which was a potential rival to the distrusted State-EAC channel.

But besides these factors which tended to persuade War Department officials to drag their heels in State-War cooperation, and to look towards military channels instead for settling policy on the treatment of Germany, the War Department's conception of its role in civil affairs as only the executor, and perhaps the coordinator, but certainly not the maker of policy, compelled it to take seriously the State Department's efforts at policy-making. As we shall see, however, not all of the above reasons were equally apparent to all War Department officials, which meant that cooperation with State was viewed differently in different parts of the War Department.

Thus the problems emerging at the end of 1943 within the American government over the establishment of policy for the treatment of Germany were less matters of substance than of procedure. No one had challenged the State Department's policy paper or, in principle, its right to make the policies involved. The major task at hand was to develop a working relationship with the War Department. But if issues of substance had not yet been joined between State and War, several important ones were nevertheless emerging. Was the Army to conduct a "neutral" administration of Germany, leaving to a later time, when the State Department would be in charge, the carrying out of American post-war objectives towards Germany? Surely this would be impractical; and yet it was the only way the Army could be kept out of policy-making. To what extent were long-term policy considerations to give way to military "necessities," real or alleged, or to the Army's judgment as to what policies were workable, during the period of Army occupation? This was the major potential conflict between the State and War Departments, and neither of them really anticipated it.

The imminent procedural problems were attributable to the inherent rivalry, so to speak, of the two policy-making channels: the Working Security Committee—European Advisory Commission channel (described below) sponsored and fostered by State, and the joint and combined military staff channel dominated by the military, especially the War Department.

II. POLICY FOR GERMANY: THE CRYSTALLIZATION OF STATE AND WAR DEPARTMENT POSITIONS (JANUARY TO AUGUST 1944)

During the first eight months of 1944 a variety of efforts, well organized though not always vigorously pressed, were made in a variety of ways to settle the emerging questions concerning the German occupation. One major effort—the one which yielded the most tangible results—concluded with the issuance of a policy directive to Eisenhower, who as commander of the combined operation across the English Channel was to open the new front in Europe and destroy the enemy forces. The directive set the policy for the administration of behind-the-lines military government by the Allied forces in Germany while the German state was still at war. Another one was the effort of the State Department to provide the American representative on the tripartite European Advisory Commission with policy guidance for negotiations over the treatment of Germany which had been cleared with the War Department, since the Army would have initial responsibility for carrying out any policies agreed to in those negotiations. As disparate as these two efforts were, both had their origins in the President's trip to Cairo and Teheran at the end of 1943, the former, in his decision at Cairo to appoint Eisenhower to command the combined Western front operation, which led immediately to a request for a combined directive on pre-surrender occupation policy; and the latter, in the decision made at Teheran to approve the Foreign Ministers' recommendation and establish the European Advisory Commission, which, *inter alia,* would serve as the forum for the negotiation of a three-power agreement on Germany. Besides these two-power military and three-power diplomatic efforts at the settlement of short-term and long-range policy, respectively, the State Department sponsored in the

spring of 1944 an inter-departmental committee intended to reach agreement within the Executive Branch of the American government on foreign economic policies. Although the committee membership did not include the War Department, it gave extended consideration to post-war economic policy for Germany. These three efforts to establish policies for the occupation of Germany led to the crystallization of the State Department's position on occupation policy and the War Department's position on its role in the occupation. These were the positions held by the two departments at the time of the intervention of the Treasury Department in the determination of our German policy in August 1944. They therefore deserve fuller treatment.

A. CCS 551: THE PRE-SURRENDER DIRECTIVE (DECEMBER 1943 THROUGH APRIL 1944)

On December 5, 1943, during the second Cairo Conference, President Roosevelt had finally decided to appoint General Eisenhower to the supreme command of OVERLORD; on January 15, 1944, Eisenhower arrived in London to take up his duties. Thereupon SHAEF succeeded COSSAC, inheriting its staff and its voluminous plans, but bringing in new officers (mostly from AFHQ), and endowing the headquarters with the command authority that COSSAC had lacked.

The time was short, since the target date for the invasion was only four months hence. COSSAC had made great progress, but its plans were incomplete and not authoritative. Eisenhower wanted major changes in the proposed initial landing operations. Changes were also soon instituted in the staff and organization for civil affairs, and officers went to work to revise the handbooks and manuals that had been prepared in COSSAC. There was no neglect of Germany. In March 1944, SHAEF had some thirty-eight studies planned or in preparation, dealing with such diverse topics as armistice terms, disarmament, and control of German courts. By the end of April, some seventy-two studies were in process.[52]

At about this time, Eisenhower asked CCS for a definitive directive on the military government of Germany. In Washington, CCS, appropriately enough, referred the request to CCAC, which replied to Eisenhower that EAC was working on a directive and program for Germany. However, since early agreement in EAC was not anticipated, CCAC agreed to initiate a directive for the pre-surrender period with the understanding that it would be subject to amendment by EAC. This directive, known as CCS 551, was approved informally by the Combined Chiefs of Staff and dispatched to Eisenhower on April 28, 1944. It was later circulated in EAC for Russian examination. Financial, economic, and relief supplements were approved by CCS in May 1944, and the financial guide was amended in August.[53]

Before turning to the substance of CCS 551, it may be useful to consider its background. Any agreements on tripartite government of Germany could not very well come into effect until the surrender, since the Russian armies in the East and the Allied forces in the West would be separated by whatever German forces and government still survived. By the same token, until the fighting was over, SHAEF would certainly continue as a combined command. Thus a single directive for the Anglo-American armies for the pre-surrender period was essential.

The War Department took the initiative in drafting CCS 551, although the initial proposals may have come from Eisenhower. On the American side the State, Treasury, and Navy Departments participated in the initial drafting and in resolving divergent views with Great Britain.[54] Quite probably the Foreign Office and State Department representatives were responsible for the careful preservation of EAC's jurisdiction. The Army, as has been noted, was suspicious of EAC, though the desire to secure Russian concurrence and to preclude any impression that the British and Americans were "ganging up" on the Soviet Union was accepted policy in JCS as well as in the State Department.[55]

Some of the foregoing is speculative, but CCS 551 itself can be analyzed directly. Entitled "Combined Directive for Military Government in Germany Prior to Defeat or Surrender," it was addressed to General Eisenhower as Supreme Commander, Allied Expeditionary Forces. It served as the basic document for Anglo-American civil affairs planning for Germany at the time of the Normandy landings, and was to remain in effect until the surrender of the German armies. In September 1944, an Interim Directive known as JCS 1067 was issued; this was designed to apply to the period immediately following surrender and was issued to Eisenhower as the commander of American troops in Europe, not as Allied Commander. CCS 551 was never rescinded. Its semi-successor, JCS 1067, was never endorsed by the British military chiefs, and applied only to the American zone in Germany and only in the post-surrender period.

The opening words of the Political Guide, Appendix A of CCS 551, were these: "The administration shall be firm. It will at the same time be just and humane with respect to the civilian population so far as consistent with strict military requirements. . . . It should be made clear to the local population that military occupation is intended (1) to aid military operations; (2) to destroy Nazism-Fascism and the Nazi Hierarchy; (3) to maintain and preserve law and order; and (4) to restore normal conditions among the civilian population as soon as possible, insofar as such conditions will not interfere with military operations." To accomplish these aims CCS 551 envisaged extensive controls over the economy. Military government would see to it that the production, control, collection, and distribution of food and agricultural produce were maintained, and that the production of food was maximized. Utilities and coal mines were to be kept in full working order, and the German industrial plant was to be protected. German regulations of wages, prices, and rationing and the German tax system (except discrimination in favor of Nazi troops) were to be continued. Exports, imports, and the inland transport system were to be controlled to aid the Allied military effort.

The political clauses were limited. The Supreme Commander was to "permit freedom of speech and press, and of religious worship, subject to military exigencies and the prohibition of Nazi propaganda; and establish local government, making use of Germans or of Allied officers. Military Government will be effected as a general principle through indirect rule." Fraternization was to be discouraged; and sweeping measures undertaken to destroy Nazism and Fascism, and the German General Staff and Supreme Command. Discriminatory Nazi legislation was to be revoked, but there was no absolute ban on the employment of Nazis. Political activity was to be forbidden or discouraged, but the Supreme Commander was to "permit the formation of a democratic trade union movement and other forms of free economic association."

The directive also covered Austria, if Allied troops entered Austrian territory. By contrast with the rule for Germany, fraternization was to be permitted, and political activity given more latitude.[56]

CCS 551 thus shows the paramountcy of military considerations. Law and order and the production of food and other goods were objectives that would contribute to Allied military success. The only major specifically political objective contemplated in the directive was the vitally significant but purely negative one of destroying Nazism.

B. INSTRUCTIONS FOR WINANT (DECEMBER 1943 THROUGH AUGUST 1944)

1. Establishing the Working Security Committee

As soon as the three members of the EAC were named at Teheran, the State Department moved to establish a mechanism for inter-departmental clearance of instructions for Ambassador Winant. It was realized that other agencies, notably the War Department, had a material and legitimate interest in the EAC actions. There was clearly need for some sort of inter-departmental committee structure, and a plan for inter-departmental cooperation was proposed. Apparently the original proposal of the State Department called for a State-War-Navy committee "at the Assistant Secretary level," to be established by the President, assisted by a drafting group with members from the same departments. But this plan was abandoned, and only the drafting group was created. Named the Working Security Committee, it was established on an "informal" basis by a letter from the Secretary of State to the Secretaries of War and Navy asking them to designate members. The chairman of WSC was James C. Dunn, the State Department representative on CCAC, but after the first two meetings his place was taken by James Riddleberger, the division chief in charge of Central European Affairs under Dunn. The "principal permanent representatives" of the State Department were, in addition to the chairman, the Chief of the Division of Territorial Studies and the Adviser in the Office of Economic Affairs; other State Department officers also attended. Sometimes as many as ten came to one meeting. The Civil Affairs Division appointed the Army representative, Lieutenant Colonel Edgar P. Allen. The Navy member was designated by the Office of the Chief of Naval Operations. He was Commander Curtis Shears, but his alternate, Lieutenant T. R. Cissel, usually sat for him.[57] In anticipation of the establishment of inter-departmental clearance procedures, State had submitted informally to CAD, as soon as the results of the Teheran Conference became known in Washington, the paper on the "Treatment of Germany" which Hull had distributed at the Moscow Conference in October, so that by the time the Working Security Committee got underway on December 9 with the formal submittal of that document to CAD, Hilldring had already taken a position on it.

In conformity with the CAD position (on which it felt it had State Department agreement) that on military government matters State was to take second place to the War Department, the CAD member who represented the War Department began—and temporarily ended—the proceedings for organizing the Working Security Committee by asserting that WSC had no jurisdiction over the surrender and occupation of Germany, since these were "a military matter," to be decided "at the military level"; necessary orders would be issued by the Combined Chiefs of Staff. This stopped all progress for two weeks,[58] until the deadlock was broken from above.

On the same day that his representative on

WSC deadlocked its proceedings, Hilldring referred the State Department paper to Stimson and McCloy. The CAD reaction to State's attempts to initiate WSC work had seemed adamant and severe, but it did not reflect major differences over substantive policy. CAD's interest in the document was confined to three matters. One was the implication that the surrender instrument should be brief; on this CAD agreed with State. A second was the role anticipated for American military government. The paper made no direct statement that military government was contemplated. CAD thought there should be a formal announcement of military government, particularly since they anticipated that American troops in Germany would encounter chaotic conditions, whether or not capitulation occurred before or after occupation.[59] Finally, CAD objected to the State Department's proposal to scrap German armaments, arguing that they might be used in the war against Japan. This initial reaction showed the protective concern of CAD for the authority and discretion of military commanders to prosecute the war whatever the surrender conditions, plans for indigenous populations (to use the Army phrase), or disarmament policies.

Eventually the deadlock was broken. The first regular meeting of WSC was held on December 21, 1943. The State Department submitted some thirty or more papers, all dealing with policy questions relating to the surrender and occupation of Germany. WSC had plenty to work on; but there were troubles ahead. Because of the State Department's view of the committee, it did not feel obligated to present a single agency position in the WSC. The several State Department spokesmen who attended WSC meetings would often take different positions, with the result that CAD could not assure the JCS staff that WSC papers represented State Department positions. On the other hand, to the State Department representatives, bargaining with CAD seemed like bargaining with the Russians, marked as it was by interminable haggling. Progress was slow at best and nil at worst.[60]

2. WSC and the State Department

State's view of the WSC function was expressed in a memorandum prepared in the Division of European Affairs:

It is our understanding that the Working Security Committee is intended to constitute a central body within this Government through which the policy recommendations of the various interested agencies on matters before the European Advisory Commission can be cleared. It is the function of the Committee to provide Ambassador Winant with draft documents stating the views of this Government for presentation to the European Advisory Commission[,] with directives to be followed by him in his conduct of negotiations, and with background material which, though not necessarily representing the definitive policy of this Government, is essential for his guidance in discussion of the various subjects before the Commission. It is likewise the duty of the Working Security Committee to take appropriate action on and reply to incoming communications from our representative on the European Advisory Commission.[61]

State saw the Working Security Committee as "an operational unit and not a body for the conduct of research and debate."

What did all this mean? "Operational unit" could not be taken in any conventional sense, for WSC was not by any stretch of the imagination engaged in operations. But operating, in administrative terms, is a relative matter, usually referring to the central day-by-day responsibilities of the agency. Surely in this sense State was justified in viewing the function of WSC, which was to provide guidance for the ambassador engaged in tripartite diplomatic negotiation, as close to the center of its immediate responsibilities, that is, as "operational." Even thus limited, this interpretation is not entirely accurate, however, for WSC was not expected to establish, or generate the establishment of "definitive policy," but to generate guidance short of final commitment by the government. The above quotation reveals the desire of the State Department that Winant's instructions be flexible enough to allow for genuine negotiation in the unusual diplomatic situation in which he found himself. No doubt this fact helps to explain why the Department did not expect to supply him with unalterably final positions for "negotiations."

Though explainable, State's conception of WSC's function was nevertheless ambiguous. And the ambiguity made working with the War Department more difficult for State.

The function of WSC was tied up with the scope of authority of the European Advisory

Commission. On this subject State was ambivalent. On the one hand, it was drawn into supporting EAC by reason of its primary responsibility for negotiations there and the possible implications of those negotiations for postwar planning. On the other, it saw EAC as a potentially permanent regional international organization which would rival the projected United Nations Organization, to which State was strongly committed. Thus, though for different reasons, the State and War Departments both distrusted EAC.[62] Evidently officials in both Departments were disturbed by the expansive views of the British regarding the purpose of the Commission. These were made public (and, probably, carelessly overstated) on December 17, 1943, when the Under Secretary of State for Foreign Affairs, George Hall, said in the House of Commons that, according to his understanding of the functions of the Commission, it was "charged to consider almost any question with regard to peace problems which might arise when war is over," and that this included the Japanese as well as the German war.[63] The State Department wished to confine the jurisdiction of the European Advisory Commission to the letter of its charter from the Teheran Conference protocol. But this included a surrender instrument and control machinery for occupation, and, by implication, agreed policies which could serve as the basis for operating the control machinery. The ambivalence of the Department toward EAC was magnified by the view, taken by "Hull, the entire State Department, . . . Winant, and his Delegation," that the "Allied Control Council for Germany could not be made to function unless the three governments provided their military commanders with a solid foundation of agreed specific and detailed policy directives to be enforced uniformly throughout Germany," a view which they shared with the British.[64]

3. Differences over the Status and Purpose of WSC

The State Department provided WSC with satisfactory support, once agreement was reached in WSC: cables to Winant agreed upon there went out without undue delay, for the committee machinery of the Department could ensure sufficiently prompt internal clearance. But the State Department officials who set up WSC were unable to provide for other necessary mechanisms, and never quite understood their relations with the War Department. There was, for example, no systematic way in which the actions of WSC could be geared into the elaborate and effective committee structure underlying the Joint Chiefs of Staff and the Combined Chiefs of Staff. There was, as has been noted, no committee superior to WSC that would permit its problems to be considered formally and regularly by State, War, and Navy Secretaries or Assistant Secretaries. To be sure, Dunn served on the Combined Civil Affairs Committee, a committee whose field of interests paralleled or overlapped that of WSC. Yet obviously neither CCAC nor its superior CCS could send instructions to Winant, although CCAC-CCS instructions for Eisenhower would be closely related to WSC instructions for the Ambassador. Possibly, since the chairman of CCAC was the Assistant Secretary of War, the use of CCAC or its "American side" to secure clearance or concurrence on WSC problems by its State Department member might have been effective. But this possibility had already been fairly well eliminated when earlier efforts to establish a Civil Affairs Committee under the Joint Chiefs of Staff failed. Indeed, the proposal of a committee of Assistant Secretaries from State, War, and Navy (described above) was an effort to correct that deficiency; and its rejection only a further sign that opposition to it still existed in the Navy and the Joint Chiefs of Staff. The major stumbling block in both instances was the reluctance of the Joint Chiefs to accept closer liaison with civilians, particularly outside their own department. Without access to JCS papers, the suggested council of Assistant Secretaries could not hope to achieve a common position for both State and the military; but the Joint Chiefs would not allow access to their papers for reasons of security. Similarly, efforts to establish a Joint Civil Affairs Committee failed because of objections raised in the War Department to having a civilian agency (State, and possibly Treasury) represented on a committee of the JCS, which was conceived as a purely military organization. CCAC represented a partial breach of the dike, and eventually—in December 1944—the impasse was removed with the establishment of the State-War-Navy Coordinating Committee, described below.

These problems appeared to be organizational and procedural, but behind them lay fundamental differences of view between the State and War Departments about their respective roles in the formulation and execution of policy. Although Hull and Stimson had reached an understanding about the functions of their respective departments, Hull evidently did not make that understanding clear to his subordinates, for a year later, in December 1943, Dunn expressed a widely held view in State in instructing George F. Kennan upon his appointment as Counselor for the U. S. Delegation to EAC. Kennan was admonished to remember that in wartime the State Department had only an advisory role, and gave advice only when it was asked.[65] The War Department's view, it should be recalled, had been made clear to Hilldring at the time of his appointment as head of CAD. Both Stimson and Marshall had told him that his agency was not to make political policy. Put together, these views would seem to produce a policy vacuum into which neither State nor the War Department was willing to move; in combination they should at least have meant mutual forebearance as each department approached issues of policy with reluctance. But both of these inferences are incorrect. War and State differed over the meaning of "policy" and the requirements of "policy guidance" for the field, so that when they denied themselves jurisdiction (and responsibility) for policy, they were talking about two different things, which they were inclined to deal with differently, anyway. Although State considered its policy role to be only secondary to the military function in wartime, it considered itself responsible for diplomatic relations and for post-war planning, a function which it took very seriously indeed. Between the pressure for policy guidance for Winant, and State's interest in anything which was likely to affect post-war conditions, its determination to give the military their head was likely to be abandoned. As we shall see, its concern with long-range, in contrast with short-run, policy could lead it to insist that nothing should be done in the short run to jeopardize long-run considerations. The War Department, in contrast, was inclined to view policy—or at least the kind of policy which it was supposed to avoid making—as something quite apart from military considerations. In its attempt to protect its own freedom of action in military affairs, and to provide Eisenhower with adequate guidance for military operations, the War Department in fact became involved in what it intended to avoid in principle, political policy determination.

For all of these reasons, the War Department and the State Department both found themselves, particularly after the civil affairs mix-ups in North Africa, leading contenders in a contest which both of them had declined to enter.

Furthermore, in its dealings with State through WSC, CAD was caught in a vacuum between its instructions to leave political policy-making to the Secretary of War and security policy-making to the Chief of Staff (or the Operations Division). Besides its operating responsibilities, CAD was to be only expediter and coordinator of policy, and not a policy-maker in its own right. Until this definition of its function was changed, its membership on an inter-departmental committee to clear policy for Winant was an anomaly. Moreover, the existence of such a committee implied co-responsibility for State and War in advising Winant. Since the War Department did not regard this to be the case, Hilldring could only treat membership for CAD on the committee as an advisory function, which implied no commitments to or responsibility for policies considered by the committee.[66] Inevitably, this was unsatisfactory to State, which had established the committee in order to get the War Department committed to its policy papers— as it turned out, often before they were cleared internally in State.

The difficulties encountered by CAD in its initial attempt to establish an appropriate relationship for itself and for the War Department as a whole with the Working Security Committee did not end with the breaking of the deadlock marked by the holding of the first regular meeting of the committee on December 21, 1943. The State Department submitted at that meeting more than thirty papers on German policy for clearance. Without objecting to the general substance of policy, CAD now found, as it had with the "Treatment of Germany" paper, much that was not in harmony with War and Navy Department thinking.[67] The changes which were needed would take time, but the time was needed anyway for clarifying the role of the War Department in guiding the United States representative to the EAC in his tripartite London negotiations.

4. The Clearance Problem

The Department of State tried to use WSC for two kinds of business: (1) replies and instructions to Winant in his coping with questions as they arose in EAC under the Moscow charter; and (2) the formulation of inter-departmental policy as a basis for Winant's instructions. With respect to the first, WSC had been assigned three "urgent" matters: an instrument of surrender, allied control machinery, and zones of occupation. The first two of these were worked out in a few months in WSC and satisfactory instructions forwarded to Winant (later vicissitudes are irrelevant here). But even they demonstrated problems of WSC clearance which plagued it until it was superseded by the State-War-Navy Coordinating Committee in December 1944.

The clearance problem can be stated simply enough: The State Department wanted War and Navy Department clearance for its instructions to Winant. But War and Navy Department clearance meant JCS clearance. Navy Department clearance was usually no problem. CAD was the principal agency in the government exclusively concerned with civil affairs matters, and this fact, along with the limited relationship between naval operations and civil affairs in Germany, assured the War Department leadership in European civil affairs. Clearance, then, meant War Department and JCS clearance.

But the clearance problem was in fact not so simple. For one thing, the Joint Chiefs would not accept for consideration anything which had not been thoroughly cleared in the State Department. For another, the requirement of War Department clearance meant interminable delays while staff divisions tried to cover themselves on matters to which they had never given much consideration. Taken together, these clearance requirements resulted in painfully protracted problems for the State Department in seeking inter-departmental clearance for EAC negotiations. At times they meant that WSC was merely an outpost through which State approached the Joint Chiefs.

The clearance problems encountered in dealing with the three urgent matters, surrender terms, occupation machinery, and zones, were not, on the whole, the central problems of WSC clearance. Initial guidance on surrender terms went through quite rapidly (although not rapidly enough to satisfy the State Department, which was not yet accustomed to the slow motion of the committee). WSC, which met almost daily in these early months, completed a detailed review of the basic document on German surrender terms in one week. Army and Navy clearance took two weeks, and JCS clearance one week. But this speed was no indication of military cooperation with the State Department. The Joint Chiefs did not clear the original document, which was a British draft in much detail, but a commentary on it which made the largely negative point that the surrender instrument should be as short as possible; besides approving this commentary they approved the appropriate substitute, i.e., a short draft instrument. As this procedure was seen in the State Department, the draft text of the German surrender instrument which was finally cleared and sent to Winant "was prepared in the War Department and . . . not communicated to the Working Security Committee until after it had been approved by the Joint Chiefs of Staff."[68]

Occupation machinery was a subject which also fared poorly in the military clearance procedures for WSC, although here again the action was relatively prompt. After some delay, WSC agreed on February 1 to a document on "Military Government of Germany" and referred it to the Joint Chiefs via General Marshall's "Command Post," OPD, the Operations Division.[69] Here, for the first time, the question of how to get JCS approval for a document which did not have full War Department and State Department clearance was faced. OPD's solution was to clear the document for referral to the Joint Chiefs only on condition that they be told that it was only a preliminary draft of the United States' views. OPD recommended that JCS only "take note" of the document and insist that Winant clear it with Eisenhower before using it in EAC negotiations.

The Joint Chiefs did not act to approve the OPD proposals until February 24. In the meantime, Winant had cabled his concern over the delay, stating that he was being pressed by the British to discuss the subject.[70] The response from Eisenhower's command came a week after

JCS approval. The document had proposed three separately occupied and administered zones following German defeat, with a tripartite control council for coordinating the administration of these zones. But SHAEF was planning for an Anglo-American combined administration of military government during the operations phase in Germany. Fearing that switching over to separate administration and occupation at the close of hostilities would prove too disruptive, Eisenhower approved the proposal for a tripartite control council, but not the separate British and American administrations for their respective zones. He thought it would be more practicable to continue the combined Anglo-American administration for the two zones, while each country would occupy its own zone with its own troops.[71] The State Department learned Eisenhower's views from Winant. The dissent which it promptly registered with CAD was based on an established premise: It was necessary to avoid going to the Russians in the EAC with a fixed Anglo-American position. CAD could add to this its knowledge that the President and the Joint Chiefs had taken a firm stand that the United States should not participate in the occupation and administration of Germany except in Northwest Germany.[72] McCloy, visiting the European Theater of Operations headquarters in mid-April, pointed out to Eisenhower that in view of the President's known position, the proposal for a combined administration of occupation zones would not be acceptable. He emphasized that the President had made up his mind on the matter and did not welcome suggestions of alternative policies from U. S. officials in or out of uniform.[73] Eisenhower withdrew his objection to the control machinery document, and in late April Winant finally had the guidance he needed to begin negotiations on that subject in the EAC.

5. The Muddle over Zones

The dispute over zones was exasperating since the Army representatives were never instructed by those in the Army who knew that the zonal boundaries and the zonal assignments had been discussed but not agreed to by Roosevelt and Churchill. If this had been explained to the State Department representatives, the subject could have been put aside, or their

proposal (which included access to Berlin by a slight rearrangement of boundary lines) might have been referred to the President (as, in a sense, it eventually was). They were aware that the Combined Chiefs had concerned themselves with the subject of zones, but did not know of the blocked negotiations in the Combined Chiefs over zonal boundaries and assignments. They could not know how their own plans did and did not fit these disagreements.

On January 15, 1944, the British presented in EAC what was in fact Morgan's proposal, but Winant, lacking instructions, could take no position on it; and when relevant instructions did arrive from WSC via the Secretary of State they only provided for a different (and quite unworkable) division of zones. This new U. S. plan for zones was simply the map that the President had pencilled on shipboard. At that time, General Marshall had turned it over to General Handy, head of OPD; somehow it had gone from him to WSC. In the meantime, Roosevelt had apparently accepted in its stead the British zonal plan (but he still rejected the Southwest zone for the United States) in a note to the Acting Secretary of State on February 21, 1944. Some months later Winant secured direct from the President permission to put aside the JCS division of zones and agree to the boundaries (so that the Russian zone could be definitely settled). In September 1944, at Quebec, the President finally gave way to Churchill and accepted the Southwest zone for the United States, though only after securing certain modifications in the two Western zones. Subsequent tangles over zones, corridors, and access to Berlin were significant, but are not relevant to the present study.[74]

Thus, guidance for Winant through WSC on zones of occupation was significant not so much for its promptness, or lack of it, or even for its reasonableness, or lack of it; but for its irrelevance. Similarly, guidance for Winant on the two other urgent matters—surrender terms and machinery for military government following defeat or surrender—did not cease to be a problem once Winant had received a document from WSC on the subject. The War Department's insistence upon a short instrument of surrender postponed the major policy questions about the treatment of Germany. (How those questions were handled by WSC will be related below.) And JCS clearance, as coveted as it was by State, could be troublesome. It could hardly be reassuring to Winant that the Joint Chiefs had "taken note of" a document. And if approval were based on numerous specific conditions, Winant's hands could be tied in his negotiations almost as effectively as if he had no instructions whatever. His military adviser, Wickersham, considered it his duty to see that Winant hewed close to the JCS position. As Wickersham interpreted his own position, he had his marching orders from the Joint Chiefs and was not prepared to give an inch on anything until they told him to do so.[75] This was precisely what happened in EAC deliberations on the instrument of surrender. The War Department view that the instrument be brief had been accepted and followed meticulously by Winant. Central to this position was the point that since the surrender would be unconditional, the instrument of surrender would have only military significance, so that the enemy could not derive from it any limitations on the authority of the victors. But when the Russians wanted to make the military nature of the instrument an explicit point in it, JCS approval had to be sought again, for the Joint Chiefs had not stated their own position in these precise terms.[76] JCS clearance could hamstring as well as expedite EAC negotiations.

6. *The First Attempt to Clear General Policy*

All of the difficulties with WSC clearance procedures either suggested or avoided by the handling of the three urgent matters for EAC came to a head in the efforts to use WSC for its second purpose, the formulation of inter-departmental policy as a basis for Winant's instructions. Agreed statements of general policy on the treatment of Germany, while not in the same sense "urgent," were nonetheless imperative. They were needed as the basis for planning the operations phase of military government, for drafting the directives to be handed to the German authorities following their acceptance of the surrender instrument, for planning the occupation which would follow, and for guiding Winant in EAC negotiations on these and related subjects. As difficulties with WSC clearance procedures continued, two additional objectives developed. Clearance of general policy was needed, first, in order to give Winant instructions which would guide

without hamstringing him; and, second, to free him from the necessity of clearing more specific agreements.

The first document on which the State Department sought War Department clearance through WSC channels, it will be recalled, was the "Treatment of Germany" paper which Hull had distributed at the Moscow Foreign Ministers' Conference in October 1943. It was at once the most general and the most authoritative statement of policy in the possession of the Department. Yet the document had never been approved by the President, its consideration at Moscow had been highly informal, and it had certainly not been given approval by Eden and Molotov.

State had submitted the "Treatment of Germany" paper to CAD before the Working Security Committee was established. Although CAD's reaction to it was quite favorable—with all the ground it covered CAD only objected to its failure to make clear the anticipated role of military government and the fact that it had ignored the possible military value in the war with Japan of captured German arms manufacturing capacity—it appeared advisable for several reasons to seek inter-departmental clearance on policy papers which were not quite so comprehensive. The most practical reason for doing so was that major elements of the paper dealt with the urgent matters of surrender terms, occupation machinery, and zones of occupation. It also dealt with two short-term matters, demilitarization and denazification; and with the long-term questions of political and economic reorganization. Demilitarization and denazification were principles on which State had every reason to expect easy inter-departmental clearance. As principles they were no more questionable than the objective of victory. Disarmament of the enemy was equally unquestionable as a principle (except in the prognosis of the British Prime Minister), but CAD had already challenged its particular meaning, as we have seen. Political reorganization had its bromidic aspects also. But the issue of disarmament had kept political reorganization unsettled as a principle, although within the State Department political decentralization rather than dismemberment had drawn virtually unanimous support since the resignation of Under Secretary Sumner Welles. The "Treatment of Germany" paper, repeating phrases drawn when Welles and the President had kept the issue alive, rejected dismemberment in favor of decentralization. The State Department officers might have pressed papers through the WSC (or tried to) which stated and clarified their position on political reorganization. They certainly had given this subject extensive consideration and felt strongly enough about it. But if anything appeared postponable, this did. Decentralization was, after all, the prelude to dismemberment. Whether that next step would be taken could be decided after occupation had begun. Besides, State had reason to leave the issue of dismemberment as dead as possible after the beginning of 1944, a tactic which it carried off with notable success, as we shall see. After the resignation of Welles and the Moscow Conference, State had reason to hope that dismemberment was no longer a serious possibility for the American position on the political reorganization of Germany. But to the surprise, and no doubt dismay, of Hull and his associates, they learned from Winant that at the second formal meeting of EAC the British representative, Strang, had introduced the subject of dismemberment and stated that British records of Teheran indicated that it should be studied and recommendations should be made on it.[77] Since the record of the Teheran proceedings had not been furnished to the Department of State, Hull was unable to know exactly what was the validity of the British claim. He had good reason to know that the President liked the idea of dismemberment. But beyond that, he and his associates could not know how much Roosevelt was really committed to it. These were uncomfortable circumstances for State. Preparing for the Yalta Conference in mid-January, its stated position was that Germany should not be forcibly partitioned. In London, at the same time, a subcommittee on dismemberment was appointed in EAC, after it was understood that agreement on establishing the subcommittee did not imply whether dismemberment should or should not occur. The subject was then buried in subcommittee.[78]

The general subject of the political reorganization of Germany, including dismemberment, was also dropped by State from its submittals to WSC in favor of the second and more pressing question of general policy. In place of the comprehensive "Treatment of Germany"

paper appeared two papers on the economic treatment of Germany entitled "Germany: Post-Surrender Problems; Control of the German Economy Immediately After Surrender; Policies Essential to Guard Against Internal Collapse" and "Germany: General Objectives of United States Economic Policy with Respect to Germany."[79] By early February WSC had approved the two documents but the obstacle of War Department clearance remained. It proved formidable.

An attempt to gain clearance of the papers by the individual action of all the offices of the War Department whose clearance the Operations Division would require before submitting them to the Joint Chiefs was soon abandoned in favor of a conference in the Civil Affairs Division with some five branches of the Department, in addition to representatives from CAD and OPD. This group welcomed the distinction of short-range and long-range objectives of American policy for Germany represented by the two documents, concurred in their general approach, and criticized them, as CAD had done of the "Treatment of Germany" paper in December, for their failure to make the defeat of Japan an objective of civil affairs policy in Germany. The group then went on to concern itself with the substance of economic policies: reparations, reconversion of agriculture and industry, and German foreign trade. German agriculture, industry, and manpower should be used for rebuilding devastated countries, and Germany should be integrated into the world economy. On these points the group wanted to go beyond the wording of the State Department's draft to clarify and to emphasize.[80]

All members of the group agreed that these papers represented the proper approach to the solution of extremely important problems and would be of great usefulness in military planning. The branches present were not the whole War Department, but their approval satisfied the Operations Division that it could refer the two papers to JCS as approved by the Department. The meeting on February 9 indicated CAD's growing concern over War Department clearance procedures, but it did not assure prompt consideration of the documents, in turn, by the Joint Chiefs. They were unwilling to commit themselves to approval "from a military viewpoint," as their phrase went, of economic policies the precise relationship of which to military strategy and operations remained unclear. JCS consideration of the two documents dragged on through the months of February and March.

7. *Guidance Without Clearance*

Meanwhile, the State Department's Division of European Affairs, faced with its responsibilities to Winant, grew more and more restive. After surveying the deadlocks and delays encountered thus far by WSC, one of the staff of the Division wrote his chief on February 19:

A considerable backlog of documents for the consideration of the Committee has now accumulated, and its dimensions are constantly expanding. This is explained by the fact that until certain of the basic documents now before the Joint Chiefs of Staff have been considered, it is not feasible for the Committee to pass on other related subjects.

It is hoped that some means may be found for speeding up the process of clearance by the Army and Navy and more prompt action by the Joint Chiefs of Staff. As a possible step in this direction, it is suggested that the appointment to the Committee of a representative of the Joint Chiefs of Staff might be useful.[81]

Not until the end of March were the two economic policy papers rescued from the Joint Chiefs of Staff, and then only by a device similar to the one used in early February to gain JCS "clearance" for the paper on occupation machinery. At a meeting on the last day of March, McCloy, Hilldring, and Colonel Edgar P. Allen, the CAD representative on WSC, met with Riddleberger, the acting chairman of the committee, and two of his assistants, and worked out an arrangement by which the documents could be sent on to Winant for his use. Although it could be said that the War Department had cleared the two economic policy papers after they had been amended to meet War Department criticisms, Major General Thomas T. Handy, the Assistant Chief of Staff, Operations Division, probably acting only after making inquiries with Marshall, had declined to refer the papers to the Joint Chiefs because military plans had not advanced to the point where economic and military considerations for the occupation of Germany could be integrated.[82] The next step, a device worked out at the instigation of OPD

and CAD, and accepted by McCloy and Riddleberger at their meeting on March 31, was to have McCloy sign a letter to Dunn, the official chairman of WSC, informing him that there was no objection to sending the two documents to Winant providing it was understood that they did not have War or Navy Department or JCS approval.[83] Thus, just two months after the economic policy papers were referred to the War Department by WSC, Winant was allowed to make use of them. But since WSC had been established at the instigation of the State Department, and in this instance the passage of two months—to say nothing of the time spent in WSC itself on the documents—had gained no commitment from the military except, in practical terms, the agreement not to complain to the President that Winant was considering economic policy for Germany as a subject for negotiation in EAC, the usefulness of WSC must have seemed negligible to the State Department officials concerned with it.

To the State Department these two documents were particularly significant because they were concerned with basic policy. Once they were approved, other documents intended for guiding Winant which were based on them could be cleared more expeditiously. The form of their referral to Winant not only meant that the two papers would be of only limited use to him, but that the prospects for clearing the many papers being held up in WSC pending JCS approval of the two basic economic policy papers remained the same, and that State continued to be interested in gaining clearance of the two papers as a device for breaking the log-jam in WSC. Within a week of learning of the Joint Chiefs' determination not to commit themselves on the economic policy papers, State had produced a new revision of the "General Objectives" paper by adding to it an introduction on the nature of the document which sought to meet the JCS refusal of clearance. First, it emphasized the non-military character of economic policies for Germany by referring to their long-run implications and their expected effect upon Germany's future position in the world and upon the peace and security of the United Nations. Second, it described the paper as a formulation of broad objectives of American policy which was not intended to prejudge decisions still to be taken regarding the form, extent, and duration of the occupation. But the effort had no effect. Neither this document nor the one dealing with short-term economic problems of the occupation was ever approved by the Joint Chiefs. As we shall see, in June the State Department took its economic policy papers to a quite different forum, the Executive Committee on Economic Foreign Policy, for inter-departmental clearance through a channel which did not involve the Joint Chiefs.

8. *Winant's Proposals*

The first six months of 1944—Winant's first half-year as the U. S. member of EAC—were painful ones for him. Aside from the problems within EAC itself, he had been bedevilled by his failure to receive prompt instructions, and by the recurring and continuing difficulties over the occupation zones. At the beginning of April, just at the time that it became known in London that the JCS had avoided clearing the two economic policy papers, Winant's political adviser, George Kennan, and his military adviser, Brigadier General Cornelius Wickersham, returned to Washington. Kennan went in search of more adequate policy guidance for the whole range of EAC issues. An appointment with the President was arranged for him. He found Roosevelt exceedingly vexed by the British demand for the Northwest zone, but obtained from him an agreement to lay aside the JCS proposal for zones so that negotiations could proceed on the basis of the British proposals in EAC which reflected the agreement on boundaries between Roosevelt and Churchill —leaving the assignment of the two Western zones still at issue.[84]

In May, Winant himself returned to Washington to discuss all EAC problems, but made no progress. The President remained firm on the need for obtaining the Northwest zone (whatever its boundaries), and Winant failed to reach agreement with the War Department on a corridor to Berlin. But, as a result of Kennan's visit to the President, Winant was able to return to London in June and present an American zonal plan in EAC which accepted the zonal boundaries proposed by the British but not the assignments. And partially as a result of Wickersham's visit, the prospects were bright for early agreement on the other organizational and procedural issues—the surrender instrument and the control machinery. So Winant began to concern himself with the substantive issues of occupation policy. In formulating his own views, he had the assistance of his immediate advisers.[85] But he did not have access to the voluminous studies prepared by SHAEF or still in process. Instead of continuing to wait for guidance from Washington, he decided to send in his own recommendations, a step that would help to ensure their consideration by the State Department and that might hasten agreement on a policy. What these papers amounted to and how they were received in Washington will be considered shortly.

Frustrations over JCS clearance of WSC papers had led one State Department officer to propose in mid-February that a JCS representative sit on the Working Security Committee. The idea was obvious and attractive, but it begged the question. The reason why JCS clearance was so hard to come by was because of the Chiefs' determination not to delegate to anyone their corporate authority, and going beyond that, not to give what a lawyer would call "advisory" opinions. A representative on WSC would have to violate one or both of these objectives. Another proposed solution to the JCS clearance impasse came from Lieutenant General Brehon B. Somervell, Commanding General, Army Service Forces, who evidently had become interested in assuring that Winant had adequate guidance in order that the supply and logistics aspects of EAC negotiations would be taken fully into account. A major War Department criticism of the State Department economic policy papers, it will be recalled, had been of their omission of the defeat of Japan as a prominent objective of occupation policies for Germany. In late March Somervell proposed to the JCS that CAD be especially charged with overseeing development of recommendations to the Joint Chiefs for United States policies covering military problems arising from disarmament, demobilization, and demilitarization of the Axis nations.[86] If his proposals had been accepted, CAD would in effect have become for certain purposes an extension of the JCS staff, with direct access to the Chiefs. The problem of War Department clearance would thus have been circumvented and the chances of JCS clearance would have been considerably increased, though not guaranteed. No doubt this would have been an extraordinary procedure, but had the Chiefs been seriously concerned over the delays in clearance of papers for Winant, they could have accepted it. But Somervell's proposal was referred to the Joint Staff Planners and forgotten, and the Joint Chiefs adopted a much more modest change in procedures in order to cope with the clearance problem. On June 6, more than four months after JCS had delayed and evaded clearance of the two economic policy papers, they set up the Joint Post-War Committee to handle post-war military problems of interest to them, and specified that the committee was to work with State on instructions to Winant on military matters, including Axis surrender terms.[87]

Although the establishment of this committee has been interpreted as an indication that the Joint Chiefs were interested in solving the problem of policy clearance for instructions for Winant, it actually demonstrated that the Joint Chiefs were more intent upon protecting their military cognizance than upon expediting WSC clearances. Creating a Joint Staff committee specifically for that purpose was likely to assure adequate consideration of the substance of policies on their merits once the propriety of such consideration had been established. But the major issues of clearance were jurisdictional and procedural, and these the establishment of another committee could not help. Moreover, the senior member of the committee, Major General George V. Strong, was an advocate of a very stern peace for the Germans. These views led him to disagree with the substance of economic and political policy papers reflecting the State Department's position in favor of a peace of reconciliation.[88] Because it did not deal with the real problems of clearance, and possibly also because of the views of the senior member of the committee, the establishment of the Joint Post-War Committee in no way helped solve the clearance problem.

In the meantime, Winant and his staff had been working on the material which they intended to submit to WSC. The bulk of it consisted of short directives which originated out of negotiations over the surrender instrument. It will be remembered that the British had begun these negotiations with a long and detailed surrender instrument draft of seventy paragraphs. They gave it up provided the sub-

jects omitted from it would be covered by proclamations and general orders which would be issued following the execution of the surrender instrument.[89] On July 11, Winant began to submit to the WSC via the State Department, drafts of these directives and general orders prepared by his staff.

The first submittal consisted of three important documents entitled "General Directive for Germany," "Principles of Allied Military Government for Germany," and "Military and Political Policies to be Followed in the Administration of Germany." After that, documents were sent at the rate of about two a week until, by the end of October, twenty-two had been received by the State Department. They consisted of brief, broad policy statements within the framework of the "unconditional surrender" policy and relevant proclamations and general orders, and it was hoped that they could be acted upon quickly in Washington by merely checking them for consistency with existing policy. Hence, copies were sent directly to JCS as well as to State.[90] But if the later documents were intended only to implement established policy, the first three unavoidably dealt with policy questions. The proposed "General Directive for Germany"[91] provided that the general mission of the occupation forces included the disarmament and demilitarization of Germany and the destruction of German's warmaking potential. The occupation was to convince the German people of their total defeat and of the futility of future wars of aggression. It was to destroy the Nazi Party and discredit its doctrines. It was to allow those Germans who were interested in peaceful international life to establish a responsible democratic government, although it was not to give its support to any particular party or movement. It was to discourage fraternization.

In view of the discussions going on at this time in Washington in the Executive Committee on Economic Foreign Policy (described below), the suggestions from London regarding the use of the machinery of government in Germany and the reconstruction of Germany's industry are of particular note. The draft directive proposed that Germany be governed indirectly by the occupying forces through the use of existing civil service staffs, after they had been purged of active Nazi leaders and other unreliables or undesirables. And the industrial system, at least by implication, was to be extensively reconstructed. The occupation was to make available to the countries that had been victimized by Germany as much of her resources as was possible for relief, rehabilitation, and reconstruction. And, in order to maximize these contributions, the occupation was to assist the German people to establish efficient administration and to develop their national economy.

The document on the principles of military government[92] was notable for three particular points: (1) The economic reconstruction of Germany should occur on a basis which would provide minimum subsistence in Germany while it furnished a maximum German contribution to the relief, rehabilitation, and reparation of the United Nations. (2) Existing administrative machinery, but not policy-making machinery, should be used for the execution of agreed policies and routine administration in Germany. (3) The tripartite control council would have considerable administrative machinery which would be able to, and would (so it was implied) assure uniform implementation of control council policies throughout the three zones. The document on military and political policies (a later version of which will be discussed more fully below) proposed economic reconstruction of Germany, along with demilitarization and denazification. Thus, all three papers dealt with major policy questions concerned with the treatment of Germany.

Winant may have hoped that somehow policy papers drafted by his assistants would fare better in inter-departmental clearance than had papers drafted in Washington. Perhaps he thought—mistakenly—that the troubles in WSC were due to the fact that the State Department had raised more policy questions than were necessary to obtain the policy guidance he needed. Whatever the reason, his own papers encountered the same snags that had stopped the State Department drafts from going through. The papers concerned merely with implementation could not be approved in the War Department or the JCS until policy was established, and the policy papers were held up because some of the matters they dealt with, and were bound to deal with, were not directly determinable on the basis of requirements for military operations. Winant's three policy documents were sent to the Working Security Committee

where they remained throughout the rest of July and most of August.[93]

9. The War Department Shift

During August, while they were under consideration by WSC, the entire situation for German policy-making in Washington changed. Beginning in early August the War Department developed into a vigorous expediter of policy guidance for Winant; and in mid-August German policy suddenly became a matter of violent inter-agency dispute. The origins and course of the dispute require separate treatment which they will receive in a later section. The reasons for the shift in War Department attitudes are also discussed below, but the extraordinary military advances in Europe underlay the rather sudden move towards a new approach. Obviously, D-Day on June 6, the capture of Cherbourg on June 27, the breakthrough at St. Lo on August 1, and Patton's subsequent drive to the East raised the problem of how to occupy Germany from the status of a dim future need to an urgent, possibly immediate, necessity.

The first sign of change in Washington of the War Department attitude towards the WSC and its purpose may have been the cable from Hilldring to SHAEF on July 1 in which he warned SHAEF that post-war policy for Germany was a responsibility of EAC, not of SHAEF, and that no agreements had yet been reached on the duration of military government or on the nature of the agency that would succeed it.[94] But beyond offering encouragement to Winant in his efforts to assemble his draft directives for clearance through WSC, the cable had no effect on Washington clearances for EAC. It was not until a month later that the change took definite shape. Over lunch with Stimson at the end of July, Harry Hopkins, the President's intimate adviser, had agreed to talk personally with Roosevelt to gain his approval of the Southwest zone of Germany for the American occupation forces. With this encouragement, McCloy was anxious to press the immediate settlement of German policy in general by telegraphing Roosevelt, who was in Warm Springs. When he showed his draft to Stimson in Stettinius' office, however, Stimson objected, fearing it would seem to press Hopkins' hand, and that it might jeopardize a favorable decision on the zones.

He did, however, show McCloy's draft to Hopkins and talked with him about it later that day. Failing in his attempt, McCloy returned to the cumbersome channels already in existence for policy-making for Germany. A letter to Stettinius, the acting Secretary of State, on August 2 mentioned the problem of speeding up policy guidance to Winant and suggested that a solution should be found.[95] The solution arrived at in the following week appeared to differ little from the vain attempts made over the previous eight months by the State Department to accomplish the purposes of WSC. Hilldring and Dunn agreed that papers under consideration by WSC would be reduced to contain only the essence of policies requested by Winant. This, it was hoped, would simplify War Department action and enable the Army to get rapid JCS clearance. But this time the "solution" was initiated in the War Department, and was regarded as important enough to involve the Assistant Secretary, McCloy. Moreover, the new arrangement went further than any of the devices attempted previously by the State Department. Informative material of a voluminous nature would go to Winant as a guide, not requiring JCS clearance, although Hilldring would examine it with a view to its acceptability from a military viewpoint.[96]

The Civil Affairs Division's change of attitude towards WSC and EAC was evidently due to a growing sense of the urgent need to have agreed EAC directives for the three Allied commanders in chief, compounded by a change in the assumptions on which military government planning was being based which exposed major policy questions theretofore avoided. SHAEF's military government planners, Winant and his advisers, the State Department, and CAD had all assumed that the collapse of the German economy could and would be avoided. The possibility of collapse was not ignored, as the economic policy papers which the State Department submitted to WSC indicated. Nor was the problem of keeping the German economy going ignored. SHAEF plans, for instance, anticipated that major reconstruction work would be needed. But the ultimate preventability of collapse had never been seriously questioned. In the summer of 1944, however, doubts on this point began to spread in the government. In June, during deliberations of the Executive Committee on Economic Foreign Policy (re-counted below), the State Department representative refused to commit himself on whether or not collapse could be prevented; yet its preventability had been an axiom of State Department policy planning for at least six months. More relevant to our interest is that these doubts developed in SHAEF at about the same time.[97]

The significance of this changed prognosis about the German economy cannot be overemphasized. In its efforts to avoid policy-making the Army had tried to work within established policies or make indisputable policy assumptions. Assuming that the collapse of the German economy could be prevented without great difficulty, Army civil affairs and military government planning for Germany was based on the fully agreed objectives of demilitarization, denazification, demobilization, restitution and reparation, the security of American forces, and the prosecution of the Japanese war. The major means for the accomplishment of the last four of these objectives were to be the continued operation and reconstruction of the German economy. Hence, a major policy question, the post-war economic treatment of Germany, was avoided by reliance on well-known American aims.

But if collapse was going to occur, despite some effort by the occupying powers to prevent it, the question arose as to whether the military should make a supreme effort to prevent it, or be prepared to accept its consequences; if so, the policy question of how to treat the German economy, which was hardly susceptible to an indisputable answer, had to be confronted directly. As a consequence, the increasing belief during the summer of 1944 that the collapse of the German economy during military occupation could not be prevented made the need for established policy guidance for the Allied commanders clear to SHAEF and to CAD in a way that it had never been before. The rapid movement of the cross-channel invading forces towards Germany only added great urgency to that new clarity.

Thus, in mid-August, when the intervention of the Treasury Department precipitated a violent dispute within the American government in Washington over its policy for the treatment of Germany, the War Department had just come to the conclusion that major policy decisions were urgently needed on these matters, and had just begun to press for them.

C. THE EXECUTIVE COMMITTEE ON ECONOMIC FOREIGN POLICY (APRIL THROUGH AUGUST 1944)

1. Establishment of the Executive Committee on Economic Foreign Policy

The Executive Committee on Economic Foreign Policy was created by Presidential letter on April 5, 1944, as an inter-departmental committee "to examine problems and developments affecting the economic foreign policy of the United States and to formulate recommendations in regard thereto for the consideration of the Secretary of State, and in appropriate cases, of the President."[98] It was established because of a growing awareness that the economic problems of foreign policy are "frequently of proper concern to other Departments as they administer laws in their respective fields," although the President acknowledged the "principal responsibility" of the State Department "for the determination of policy in relation to international problems. . . . " The committee consisted of representatives of the State, Treasury, Agriculture, Commerce, and Labor Departments, the United States Tariff Commission, and the Foreign Economic Administration. It first convened on April 18, 1944. The chairman was Dean Acheson, then Assistant Secretary of State. Harry C. Hawkins, Chief of the Division of Commercial Policy and Agreements of the State Department, was Vice Chairman.

All but one of the agencies which later played important roles in the development of policy for the treatment of Germany were represented here. Harry D. White, an Assistant to the Secretary, represented the Treasury Department. Lauchlin Currie, Deputy Administrator of the Foreign Economic Administration, sat for his agency. Acheson represented the State Department. The War Department was the agency not represented.

FEA promptly requested consideration by ECEFP of policy toward ex-enemy countries because it had an immediate concern with related problems. FEA had been created in September 1943, as a catch-all to contain the proliferation of war agencies concerned with international economic activities. Into it were put the Office of Economic Warfare and the Office of Foreign Relief and Rehabilitation Operations, the Office of Lend-Lease Administration, and the Office of Foreign Economic Coordination of the Department of State. In addition, the functions of two government agencies with respect to the procurement of food in foreign countries were transferred to FEA. Through their concern with economic warfare, FEA personnel had to be familiar with the German economy. At the same time, their responsibilities for lend-lease, relief and rehabilitation, and for the procurement of food abroad, required them to anticipate (1) what economic burden the United States, as a matter of policy, would assume for defeated Germany, and (2) to what extent and in what way Germany would be a source of supply for other countries. Such questions as the comparative standard of living in Germany and in liberated areas after surrender were clearly within its proper range of interests, and other problems, by a liberal interpretation of its charter, might also be made its concern. Furthermore, it had resources in information and staff which, in the economic area, were more extensive than those of any other agency.

The third agency represented on ECEFP which was later to play an important role in the formation of American policy on the post-war treatment of Germany was the Treasury Department. In general, by the summer of 1944 its responsibilities had not involved it in problems connected with the post-war treatment of Germany, though it was actively engaged in trying to track down hidden German assets and would eventually be concerned with the exchange rate for German marks and similar matters. It had played some part in drafting the Financial Guide, Appendix C of CCS 551, which had been issued (in its original version) just ten days before ECEFP took up the German problem.

2. Preparation of State Department Plans

The State Department's efforts to get a general position on economic policy for Germany cleared through the military for Winant's guidance had come to failure by the end of March when it was agreed that its two economic policy papers could be sent to Winant, but only if he were told that the War and Navy Departments and the JCS had not approved them. These documents had been derived from its "Treatment of Germany" paper, which had been discussed at the Foreign Ministers' Conference at Moscow in October 1943, submitted to the War Department as the first paper for clearance through WSC, and then abandoned in favor of the two economic policy papers because they were concerned with only the most urgent aspects of German policy.

The establishment of ECEFP posed for the State Department the prospect of a new avenue for the inter-departmental clearance of its economic policy papers. It would have been foolish for those in the Department who were concerned with providing policy guidance for Winant—in particular, Dunn, Riddleberger, and their associates—to conclude that they could simply outflank the Joint Chiefs by obtaining ECEFP endorsement of their papers. The military were not represented on this committee and military clearance was precisely what Winant needed. But at least the State Department officials could hope that ECEFP approval would place them in a stronger bargaining position, and possibly help them to approach the Joint Chiefs from a less subordinate position than WSC had provided.

Hopefully, in the spring of 1944, when SHAEF was preparing German studies and CCS 551 was being drafted, the Department's Interdivisional Committee on Germany revised the "Treatment of Germany" paper to abandon the ambiguity of the Moscow document on dismemberment. The new general policy statement opposed the forcible dismemberment of Germany, recommending instead the decentralization of the future structure of German government wherever practicable, and also demilitarization, the punishment of war criminals, and the control of education. Reparations to the United Kingdom, the Soviet Union and some of the other European allies were tied in more closely with economic policy, making them more moderate.[99] The new draft was then considered by the Postwar Program Committee, one of two high-level policy committees established by the Departmental reorganization of the previous January, and composed of the highest officers of the Department, with Secretary Hull as Chairman.[100] During three long meetings of the committee in early May presided over by Under Secretary Stettinius, agreement was reached on a basic policy document of some fifteen pages.[101] The two economic policy papers had undergone revision in the

State Department as late as April 10.[102] State was now prepared with current statements of its position on German policy for ECEFP. As it had anticipated, or arranged, at the weekly meeting of the committee on May 19, 1944, the representative of the Foreign Economic Administration requested, and it was agreed, that the subject of the economic treatment of ex-enemy countries would be placed on the agenda of the committee.[103]

3. *The State Department's Proposals*

On June 9 the State Department presented to the Executive Committee on Economic Foreign Policy the latest drafts of the two documents on economic policy for Germany for which it had failed to obtain military clearances in the Working Security Committee, and the following week a document on Reparation, Restitution and Property Rights. The first document proposed that our general objectives should be: to deprive Germany of the economic means for resuming hostilities; to guarantee the performance of acts of restitution and reparation; to redress the balance of economic power in Europe; and to bring about fundamental changes in German economic life so that it could, in time, be integrated into the type of world economy envisaged in the Atlantic Charter. These objectives (as the Civil Affairs Division of the War Department had insisted the previous December) were to be subordinated to the effective prosecution of the war with Japan. The means proposed for attaining them were listed as integration of Germany into the world economy, control of German materials usable for the manufacture of armaments, conversion (rather than the dismantling) of war industries, and the elimination of forms of industry and commercial organization which could threaten peace. The meaning of economic integration was explained as including full employment of manpower and resources in the production of commodities and services of a non-military character for which the German economy was well adapted. The purpose of integration was to make Germany more vulnerable to sanctions, to prevent her making use of trade as an instrument of war, and to make possible the rising standard of living necessary to reconcile the German people, under new leadership, to the peace settlement. The document stated that the United States placed great importance upon the preservation of continuity of German economic life, and therefore that the prevention of economic collapse was an extremely urgent matter. To maintain a functioning German economy it might be necessary at the beginning of the occupation to utilize existing economic organizational machinery in Germany, even purely party organizations exercising economic control functions.[104]

In two respects this treatment of the collapse problem in the State Department's objectives paper must have been unsatisfactory to CAD when the paper was under consideration there. In the first place, the prevention of collapse was put equal to or above military necessity as justification for departing from other objectives. And second, the accomplishment of an economic policy was held to be sufficient reason to expect the Army to seek the collaboration of Nazis and Nazi organizations in Germany. The problem of how to deal with possible or threatened economic collapse in Germany could not have been put in a more unattractive way to the Army.

The second document indicated what would be needed to prevent breakdown in the German financial system, inland transport, food and other essential civilian supplies, production, and foreign trade. In each case it proposed that the existing system be taken over, maintained and extended, if necessary, even if drastic action was needed to do so.[105] In view of this document's preoccupation with the administration of occupation policies, it is surprising that the State Department submitted it to ECEFP. Evidently the committee took this same view, for it laid the document aside.

The State Department's position on policy during occupation, as it was explained to the committee in two other papers, was that in principle the occupation forces should have broad powers to control, that the extent of control would depend upon the use which could be made of German administrative machinery, and that in any case Germany was to be deprived of the economic means of resuming hostilities. Specifically, this meant the control of imports and the prohibition of the manufacture of implements of war, but not a restriction on the development of heavy industry in Germany. State envisaged an occupation period of about ten years, and anticipated that these

controls, along with reparations deliveries, would last as long as the occupation.

These were the major restrictive features of the Department's plan. On the other side were its plans for a peace of reconciliation. It expected the German standard of living to be equal to the minimum living standard of the countries despoiled by Germany. And it took the view that a collapse of the German economy was extremely undesirable because it would tend to associate chaos and poverty with democratic government, a circumstance that could hardly endear democracy to the Germans. Although the Department was strongly committed to the prevention of collapse, its committee spokesman, perhaps because of growing doubts about the possibility of doing so, expressly refrained from saying whether collapse could be prevented or not.

4. Committee Criticisms and Revisions

The State Department's presentation of its views on the economic treatment of Germany was impressive for its comprehensiveness, but it was also notable for what it avoided saying. How low a standard of living would be allowed in order to meet reparations schedules, or to see that Germany was deprived of the economic means of committing further aggression? How much building up of German heavy industry would be permitted in order to meet reparations deliveries? Was there no point beyond which the further development of German heavy industry as such could be regarded as a threat to the peace? And on the other hand, how much effort would be expended in preventing the economic collapse of Germany, or in assuring a minimum standard of living? These unanswered questions, involving as they did inherent conflicts among the generalities of the State Department position, or doubts as to the relative importance of general objectives, indicate how little State policy planning had tested its major policy assumptions against the concrete problems that it anticipated would have to be faced in the occupation of Germany. An explanation of this failure is obvious. ECEFP took up the discussion of post-war policy for Germany only three days after D-Day, when Germany seemed far away; and on August 4, when it reached agreement on the revisions of two of the State Department papers, although Bradley's armies were in open country, the magnitude of his success was still uncertain.

But if the pressure of events had not forced State to face some of the harder problems connected with the post-war treatment of Germany, the committee, led by one of its members, did. The FEA representative objected to a number of points in the State Department papers when they were first presented, and he continued to challenge and suggest in the meetings which followed. From its first meeting on June 9, the ECEFP was unanimous in advocating control, not destruction, of the German economy.

The FEA position, as it developed through June and July, was that collective security and economic controls, not economic destruction, would have to be relied upon ultimately as protection against future German aggression. The ten-year reparations period envisaged by the State Department FEA thought was too long. Rather, reparations should be short term, but severe. At the same time, FEA insisted that the possibility of an economic collapse of Germany be taken into account. (State had admitted that this might occur but had not developed any policy position in case it did.)[106]

By July 5 FEA had formulated a statement of reparations policy for the committee which dealt systematically and, above all, with a sense of priority, with the major facets of the reparations problem. It was a formulation which became, and remained, the basis of U. S. reparations policy. First, FEA wanted to determine reparations on the basis of the capacity to pay rather than by the magnitude of admissible claims for damages. Its representative suggested that a minimum standard of living should be set, and that all else for the next five years— that is, all that Germany could produce with existing machinery—should go to reparations. Second, the State Department view as to what that minimum standard should be was rejected. State had originally proposed in the ECEFP that Germany should be permitted a standard of living equal to the minimum of those countries which she had attacked. Although FEA had originally accepted this proposal, it now argued that this was too low a standard, for it would affect Germany's ability to pay reparations, would result in instability, and might jeopardize the reintegration of Germany with the world economy. And third, financial repa-

rations should be avoided, since they would necessarily be paid out of the normal commercial trade of Germany, and hence would, on the one hand, build up the capacity of the German economy beyond what it needed in normal times, and on the other, develop a pattern of trade which would make other nations dependent on German exports.

On August 4, 1944, ECEFP approved two papers on post-war German policy, one on the general economic treatment of Germany, and the other on German reparations. The first was a revision of the "General Objectives" paper. Its final amendment, made that day, indicated that the committee had become heavily committed to the policy of preventing a collapse of the German economy. The new sentence emphasized the belief that one of the most important devices for preventing a collapse of employment and the disintegration of the economy would be the prompt placement of orders in the heavy industries for reparations goods.

The main objectives of the first document— the control of Germany's economic war potential, the elimination of Germany's economic domination in Europe, the eventual integration of the German economy with the rest of the world, the establishment of democratic institutions, and prevention of the collapse of the German economy—had been clarified considerably, particularly in their relation to each other. For instance, it was made clear that economic disarmament did not mean a large-scale and permanent impairment of all German industry, or of the development of heavy industry, nor was it to prevent the integration of the German economy with the rest of the world, nor the saving of the German economy from collapse.

The main part of the second document, a revised "Report on Reparations, Restitution and Property Rights,"[107] was its recommendations for a reparations agreement. Reparations should begin as soon as possible after the war and be limited to a maximum of five years. "Fairly extensive controls" would probably be needed for the collection of substantial reparations from the German economy. Pressure from nations might make it necessary to extend the period of reparations deliveries beyond five years, in which case they should be tapered off gradually. It was evident that Germany could only pay for a small proportion of the damage for which it was responsible, and certain criteria were suggested for determining the amount. The time limit should be set first; then the amount could be the maximum collectible within that period, and incentives could be provided or penalties inflicted by changing the time period. The amount was also to be conditioned by the requirement that the Germans be allowed to keep enough of their own production to maintain a certain minimum standard of living.

Reparation payments in kind were preferred over cash payment. They were to come from inventories, capital equipment, current production, and labor service, the bulk from current production.

The extent to which the industrial plant of Germany should be built up in order to maximize current production for reparations was explained in an ambiguous paragraph which, on the one hand, stated that such capital formation should be kept to a minimum in Germany, but on the other permitted reconstruction to the extent necessary to maintain the prescribed standard of living and to meet reparation schedules. The paragraph concluded by recognizing the danger of leaving Germany at the end of the reparations period with a greater productive capacity than at the beginning.

The Executive Committee on Economic Foreign Policy, in reaching agreement on the treatment of Germany by early August 1944, had secured significant, though not fundamental, modifications of the State Department recommendations. FEA had objected continually to the lack of precision in the policy proposals of State and to several specific points of substance. Other agencies raised a random series of objections to the Department's proposals. But the proceedings of the Executive Committee carried steadily through to final agreement on August 4, with each meeting showing definite progress towards the reconciliation of differences. The conciliatory and constructive atmosphere of ECEFP meetings contrasted notably with the exasperated tone which the State Department had come to take toward the meetings of the Working Security Committee and the difficulties it had with the War Department there.[108] But in one respect this atmosphere was misleading. The Treasury representative on the committee, Harry Dexter White, had regularly sent a substitute to the meetings who participated very little in its deliberations. Evidently the Treasury Department

regarded the committee as a State Department device to encroach upon economic and financial matters in which the Treasury was interested. Holding this view, it had no interest in supporting ECEFP. Illustrative of this fact was the noncommittal position taken by the Treasury representative on August 4 at the time the committee approved the two policy statements on Germany. Though he had no objections to raise regarding these two documents, and he could see no reason why the committee should not act on them, he was not at that time prepared to state definitely the Treasury's position on these matters. As will be seen, Treasury soon took a very definite position.

5. *Summary: The Establishment of Policy (August 1944)*

By mid-August 1944, certain definite steps towards an established American policy for the treatment of Germany had been taken, and certain definite obstacles had been encountered. (1) An Anglo-American military directive, CCS 551, had been issued to Eisenhower for guidance of the combined forces in Germany concerning military government prior to the defeat or surrender of the German state. This directive emphasized the paramountcy of military considerations, but at the same time provided for the destruction of Nazism, and such extensive control of the German economy that, in the absence of further guidance, the military would be in a position to do with the German economy what they wished. (2) The State Department's policy of a "stern peace with reconciliation" had reached a fairly clear formulation by the end of August, largely because of the criticisms of earlier drafts by FEA representatives in the Executive Committee on Economic Foreign Policy. (3) The State Department had not yet learned how to work with the War Department in the making of policy. Indeed, each department tended to think of its own position as that of the honest broker when it was actually promoting a particular policy. (4) Until early August the War Department had shown only indifference to cooperation with the State Department for the purpose of clearing American policy in order to expedite Anglo-American negotiations on the treatment of Germany. It seemed to be confident that what policies had to be settled could be handled the same way that establishing the occupation zones had originally been: through military channels to the President. It was highly protective of military discretion. And perhaps too it shared the President's view that policy decisions should be postponed until the condition of Germany was known.

With the demands on the War Department such as they were in this period, neglect is a poor basis for criticism. Nevertheless, the pattern of War Department indifference is unmistakable. The failure of the War Department to provide the Working Security Committee with a counterpart committee of Secretaries, or with adequate internal clearance procedures—indeed, without even attempting to do so until six months after the establishment of WSC—and the attitude of the Joint Chiefs towards WSC papers, even when they had been approved by the Secretary of State, indicate that the War Department was not disturbed about the slowness with which occupation policy on a two- or three-power basis was being made. Moreover, from the first controversy in WSC over that committee's jurisdiction to deal with policy for the surrender and occupation of Germany to the failure to obtain JCS approval of WSC drafts, the War Department seemed primarily concerned with protecting its freedom of action in the accomplishment of its mission. While it was sensitive to the military implications of other matters, it discounted the policy implications of military matters. Quite naturally, its military considerations had policy implications. Hence, its determination to be the servant of the policy-makers, which assured that it would not commit itself to overt substantive policy, did not assure that it would keep out of policy-making, or even that it would not support a definite policy. Was there any pattern, then, to the policy implications of the positions taken by the War Department on the basis of allegedly military considerations? That is to say, did the War Department, in the last analysis, have a kind of back-door policy for the German occupation? Certainly by mid-August 1944, no distinct policy approach was evident in War Department thinking about the treatment of Germany unless (as was done) one can derive an approach from the Department's insistence on the power of the occupation forces to control extensively the German economy.

III. THE STRUGGLE OVER THE MORGENTHAU PLAN (AUGUST THROUGH DECEMBER 1944)

A. INVOLVEMENT OF THE TREASURY, AUGUST 1944

1. Introduction

The Treasury Department had shown little interest in helping the State Department develop policy for the treatment of Germany in the ECEFP during the early summer of 1944, but it was neither devoid of interest nor without views concerning post-war Germany. The Secretary of the Treasury was one source of these views, for he had strong personal opinions about Germany. Another source was the general economic and financial war program of the Department. A third was the finance officers who had been recruited from the Treasury Department for Army civil affairs activities. During August 1944, all three sources were suddenly drawn upon to produce a full-blown policy for Germany. Before describing the circumstances which led the Treasury to take this step, it will be helpful to know more about these main sources of policy, particularly because they continued to play an important role in the Treasury position after its original formulation.[109]

1. Morgenthau's father had been prominent in public life, serving during World War I as U. S. Ambassador to Turkey. As the result of this experience he developed a distrust of the German nation for what he was convinced was premeditated and cold-blooded aggression.[110] Young Henry apparently shared his father's feelings, for prior to America's entrance into World War I he was anxious for intervention, both in national and personal terms. How relevant this early experience was to Morgenthau's later views is not easy to determine, but it suggests that his approach to German policy in 1943 cannot be explained simply as a re-action to the anti-Semitism of the Nazi regime, as does also the fact that the Treasury approached the fiscal and monetary problems of the Italian "liberation" with a far greater emphasis on punitive objectives than did the State or War Department officials. For Morgenthau, and for many of his associates in the Treasury, there may have been more of a disposition to try to fix the problems of foreign affairs once and for all than was characteristic of War and State Department officials both amateur and professional. An early indication of Morgenthau's views in World War II was provided by his fight with OWI in April 1943 over whether in a public speech he could refer to the "rotten bloodstained foundation" of "Germany" or of "Nazi Germany." He insisted on making it "Germany," but in the end gave in reluctantly to OWI's effort to differentiate between Germany and its current regime.[111]

2. Treasury programs related to the war could be expected to reflect Morgenthau's vigorous and determined attitude toward the war effort, but they also were characteristic of the Department's approach to economic and financial problems. On the whole, while the Treasury pursued its objectives with vigor and skill, it was not a bold innovator or user of new economic techniques. By 1944, Harry D. White was the most influential economist in the Treasury. He had an imaginative intellect which he used to great advantage in the initiation of economic objectives. But in the application of economic techniques his talents were less obvious. Perhaps partially out of inclination and personal limitation, perhaps also because his preoccupation with economic objectives had led him to neglect the rapidly developing techniques of his field of competence, he was more skilled in seeing the economic problem than in drawing fully upon

available economic tools to analyze and solve it. Professor Hart might have said of him, not that he was anti-Keynesian, for no competent economist can be that, but that he was pre-Keynesian[112]—a comparison of particular relevance since a major antagonist of White in economic policy matters often was the pre-eminent British economist of his day, Lord Keynes.

Apparently a result of White's approach to economics was a tendency to apply the meat cleaver rather than the scalpel; that is to say, to place little faith in economic controls, but rely instead more upon a favorable arrangement of economic power. In financial planning for Italy he had fought for what many people considered an unduly hard economic policy as exemplified in a low rate of exchange for the lira, a policy many considered unwise. The application of this approach in the achievement of Morgenthau's objectives with respect to Germany will be made clearer below.[113]

3. The first Treasury official to become an Army civil affairs officer was Bernard Bernstein, who was commissioned in October 1942 with the express approval of Morgenthau, and in response to a cable from Eisenhower for a Treasury official to help with currency matters in Algiers after the landing. During 1943 the need for Army finance officers, mostly in SHAEF, grew rapidly. When the Army turned to private banking as a source for these people, Treasury complained. As a result, the Army attempted, when possible, to recruit its finance specialists from the Treasury Department. It was Army policy to defer to Treasury on financial policy, and this was taken by Treasury and by the Army finance experts recruited from Treasury to mean that the latter enjoyed a special status in the Army with respect to command and communication channels, a status which they also claimed for their representatives in American embassies. They insisted that in order to carry out their assignment in the Army as financial experts, they needed to maintain direct and private contact with the Treasury Department, and that, in fact, they were representatives of the Treasury in the Army. The emphasis in military procedure upon the proper clearance of communications made it impossible for the Army to look upon this assertion with anything but hostility, and Hilldring, for one, never accepted it. But despite the strong objection of the Army, the Treasury continued to work directly with its former officials in uniform. By doing so it had a channel of communication with civil affairs planning and experience in the field which was often more direct than was that of CAD, which was usually bound by the circuitous routes of Army command channels. When the time came, Treasury could use this channel to its advantage in the formulation of its own policy position with respect to the treatment of Germany.

A final note about Treasury policy for Germany: Any administrative organization expects or hopes to count on the support of its staff for a policy, regardless of personal views, once the policy is established authoritatively. But the Treasury Department expected and got this same kind of support from its staff for non-authoritative Treasury positions. That is to say, policy discipline in the Treasury allowed for free discussion of policy within the Department but a solidarity of viewpoint outside the Department. This fact is crucial for an understanding of both the Treasury position on Germany and its sources. There were, to be sure, differences within Treasury at this time over policy, not the least of which was the question of the post-war treatment of Germany. But in dealings with other agencies the Treasury maintained a kind of "cabinet solidarity" which gave it a powerful voice in matters of its own interest, and provided the basis for maintaining control over Treasury "representatives" among Army civil affairs officers.

2. *Morgenthau's Trip*

On August 6, 1944, two days after the Executive Committee on Economic Foreign Policy had finally approved the report on economic policy for Germany, and the one on reparations, restitution and property rights, Secretary of the Treasury Henry Morgenthau, Jr., flew to London to settle some financial problems connected with the liberation of France. Traveling with him were two Assistants to the Secretary, Harry D. White and Fred B. Smith, and a Treasury lawyer, Josiah E. DuBois. During the flight White showed Morgenthau a copy of the paper on reparations, restitution and property rights the ECEFP had approved two days earlier (with White's representative taking a noncommittal position for the Treasury). Perhaps reflecting his view of ECEFP, in presenting the paper, White described it as a "State Department memorandum."[114] Morgenthau read it and listened to White's comments about it. The provision that reparations be taken out of current production from German industry over several years, White said, would cause Germany to become again the industrial heart of Europe. First, German industrial plants would have to be reconstructed; and second, after reparations were completed, Europe would be dependent on Germany, while Germany, accustomed to maintaining herself and producing for reparations account also, would not be so dependent on Europe.

After this explanation, Morgenthau expressed his sharp disagreement with the reparations document, for it failed to deal with what he thought was the basic question—the establishment of conditions which would prevent Germany from the forcible domination of Europe a third time.[115]

The following day Morgenthau and his party lunched with Eisenhower at SHAEF headquarters in southern England. Here, White pressed his views on Eisenhower also. He asserted that the Civil Affairs Division, SHAEF, was planning to get the German economy going as soon after occupation as possible, just as it was planning to do in liberated countries. (He and Morgenthau were acquainted with SHAEF plans for Germany.) Instead, he insisted, "we should give the entire German economy an opportunity to settle down before we do anything with it."[116] Eisenhower, picking up this point, indicated that he would like to "see things made good and hard for the Germans for a while."[117] However, he considered the flooding of the Ruhr coal mines "silly and criminal."[118] While White was also opposed to abandoning the mines, Morgenthau liked the idea, and may have mentioned it to Eisenhower. Despite this specific point of disagreement, Morgenthau came away from the meeting convinced that the Supreme Commander agreed with him. Eisenhower talked in general terms about holding the Germans responsible and making them sense their guilt—the kind of general objectives found in CCS 551. Accounts of his statements are confusing, and it is not clear whether he went on to say, for instance, that he wanted to prevent Germany from reconstructing her industry on her own. But he spoke of controlling industrial production

and requiring Germans to "make their own living," and this may have been enough to convince Morgenthau that Eisenhower did not support the views of his subordinates in civil affairs who expected to provide Germany with American help in order to get its economy functioning again.[119]

After a brief trip to Normandy, Morgenthau held a meeting on August 12 with several American officials in England to acquaint himself with his government's thinking about the treatment of Germany. Ambassador Winant attended, accompanied by his political adviser, Philip Mosely, an economic expert, E. F. Penrose, and Walter Radius, a State Department expert on transportation and communications. Colonel Bernard Bernstein was the only member of the armed forces in attendance. As has been noted above, he was a former Treasury official and an acquaintance of Morgenthau, and since October 1942 an Army civil affairs officer. Morgenthau's party—White and DuBois, together with two Treasury men stationed in London at the Embassy, Aarons and Taylor —were also present. Winant and his associates did not know that German questions would be discussed at this meeting and they were completely unaware, at its beginning, of Morgenthau's views. Penrose, the economic expert, was first called upon to give an account of the British views on the treatment of Germany. In response to a specific question, he expressed the belief that the British would not long seek revenge upon Germany.

An intermission followed Penrose's statement. During it he and Mosely discussed with White the two papers on Germany prepared in ECEFP. White told them that he had read neither document. At no time during the meeting or, indeed, after it, did the State Department officials suspect that White and Morgenthau were familiar with the report on reparations or that this document lay behind Morgenthau's sudden intervention; his interest in the German problem had been of long standing.

After the intermission, Morgenthau opened the discussion with a brief and unordered statement of his views. "From all the evidence I have been able to gather in both the United States and England," he has been quoted as saying, "I am not at all convinced that a realistic program is being followed which will result in Germany's inability to wage war again."[120]

Serious consideration should be given to the reduction of Germany to an agrarian economy, he stated, so that Germany would be a land of small farmers with no large-scale industry, comparable to the farm plan in Denmark. Since the United States would be unwilling to keep troops in Germany for a very long period to control her, this seemed to be the only way to prevent her further aggression.

Bernstein was asked to report on planning within SHAEF for the occupation of Germany. He indicated that the Army philosophy of "take over and control" inevitably led to assumption of responsibility for economic, financial, and social affairs in Germany, and that its desire to do a good job was leading it into plans to buttress and invigorate the German economy. Army civil affairs, he thought, was being carried away with a concern for what was good and efficient from the point of view of administration.

Winant then explained the work of the EAC, accounting for its lack of accomplishments by the lack of official instructions or authority from any of the three governments.

White then expounded in more systematic form the ideas Morgenthau had already expressed. In order to deprive Germany of the means to take aggressive action again, it would be necessary to destroy German industries. Chaos might issue from the occupation, but it should be made clear to the Germans that they alone were responsible for it, and could obtain no help from the victors in dealing with it. White opposed reparations drawn from current production of German industry. This, he pointed out, would encourage the reconstruction of industry in order to expand production. Rather than allow this he would prefer to cancel reparations deliveries.[121]

Hearing this exposition of Morgenthau's proposals, Winant's economic adviser was impressed:

Whatever might be thought of the opinions of Mr. Morgenthau, it was impossible to deny the resourcefulness of Dr. White in mastering the main points of the interdepartmental committee's report just before the meeting, and transforming the Secretary's sketchy and spasmodic exposition of his views into a clear, amplified, and well-organized restatement composed in fifteen minutes after Mr. Morgenthau had finished speaking. . . .[122]

While Morgenthau had at this meeting evidently approached the subject of his current concern with considerable restraint, in the course of the ensuing conversation he revealed the extent of his commitment to the agrarianization thesis. When confronted with the problem of what to do with the population which could not be supported by farming in Germany, he suggested dumping it in North Africa.

Although Mosely argued persistently against the Morgenthau-White thesis, during the course of the meeting Winant made little comment on Morgenthau's views; he wished to avoid personal involvement in what promised to be a nasty squabble in Washington, and he was embarrassed by the intervention of the Secretary of the Treasury in the affairs of the Department of State. His own attempt to persuade Morgenthau not to repeat certain statements to Anthony Eden seems to have had little effect.[123]

Before returning to Washington, Morgenthau also talked with British officials about his newly awakened interest. Before the conference on the 12th, he talked with the Chancellor of the Exchequer, Sir John Anderson, and the Foreign Secretary, Anthony Eden, and thought he detected a difference of opinion between them. Sir John indicated that he thought Germany should be allowed to continue manufacturing non-military items. Morgenthau suggested: "We could divide Germany up into a number of small agricultural provinces, stop all major industrial production and convert them into small agricultural land-holders."[124] Sir John did not respond. His silence was interpreted as indicating that he disagreed. Over lunch, Eden emphasized that a soft policy toward Germany would only incur the suspicion of Russia and make post-war cooperation with her more difficult.[125] At this or a later talk with Eden, Morgenthau outlined his scheme to turn Germany into an agricultural state. Eden, perhaps sensing the intra-governmental conflict brewing in American quarters, did not express objections to this plan. His silence was interpreted (almost certainly incorrectly) as indicating agreement.[126]

3. Winant's Reaction

Morgenthau's European visit apparently had almost immediate repercussions. A few days after the August 12 conference in the English countryside Winant sent a long cable to the President in an attempt to get confirmation in Washington for the agreements already reached in the European Advisory Commission. As Penrose has put it,

Winant was anxious . . . to consolidate the gains already made in negotiations on the European Advisory Council [sic], and hoped that the row would not break out in full force until the White House had confirmed the results of past negotiations.[127]

Winant's cable attempted to present his viewpoint on the problems of policy development in EAC, to indicate what agreements had already been made in EAC, and to focus attention on the policy questions still to be settled with respect to Germany. Optimistically, he pointed out that EAC had reached agreement on the terms of German surrender, that the agreement on zones could be completed as soon as Britain and the United States agreed on their zonal assignments, and that an agreement on the machinery of Allied control was imminent. What was needed, he indicated, was the content or substance of the policies to be administered. Suggesting that Russia would be eager for extensive reparations, and that these would have to come mostly from the industrial West of Germany, Winant urged the formulation of a reparations policy and the early agreement on one by the Allies. The cable was an impressive one, running to some seven thousand words. It attempted to put the German problem within the framework of a stable postwar relationship with Russia.[128]

4. Eisenhower's Reaction and CAD Response

On August 17, about the same time as the Winant cable, Eisenhower warned the War Department that the occupation of Germany might have to begin sooner than had been anticipated; by this time, the German armies west of the Seine had been decisively beaten, and hopes for German surrender were running high. Less than a week later, on August 23, he advised the Combined Chiefs of Staff that the policy directive for the occupation of Germany under which he was operating, CCS 551, was out of date and no longer applicable. In this message to the CCS, Eisenhower said that plans for the occupation of Germany were based on the pre-surrender directive which assumed conditions that no longer existed: that the Allies would have to fight their way into Germany, and that there would eventually be a general surrender of German armed forces or of a central German authority. Under these conditions, even though a main function of SHAEF would be the re-establishment of law and order behind the lines, extensive controls over the economy by SHAEF would be unnecessary since the maintenance of a functioning economic system could be made a responsibility of the surviving central government authority. However, now that it was evident that the central German government would not survive, SHAEF should be relieved of the responsibility for maintaining law and order or for controlling the economic system.[129]

In part, this cable was undoubtedly inspired by the wave of optimism nourished by the great victory and the continuing sweeping advances; it was in this sense a reaffirmation of the message of August 17. In part, too, it seems to reflect the conversation with Morgenthau a fortnight earlier. White had spoken of the German economy "bogging down in a morass of economic wreckage."[130] This conviction was apparently firmly held by him and by Morgenthau, who remarked in his talk with Winant that "chaos was inevitable."[131] But by this time it was also a view held by many within Eisenhower's own staff, notably the G-5 Division of SHAEF.[132] On the assumption that "chaos was inevitable," the responsibilities laid on Eisenhower by CCS 551 would be impossible or at least difficult to fulfill. Furthermore, an attempt to carry them out when civil order and agricultural and industrial production were no longer needed to sustain military operations in Europe would run counter to Eisenhower's stated belief: "The Germans should be permitted and required to make their own living, and should not be supported by America."[133]

In Washington, the new expectations of CAD officials that the German economy was bound to collapse before or during occupation had produced new efforts to obtain policy agreement on a longer-term basis than the pre-surrender directive, CCS 551. The War Department's first attempts in early August to unblock the Working Security Committee's efforts to provide Winant with instructions on the treatment of Germany have been described above. On August 15, two days before Eisenhower's first cabled warning of the need to reduce his responsibility for maintaining the economy of Germany, the Civil Affairs Division had requested that the Combined Civil Affairs Committee prepare a statement of general policy for SHAEF to be used in the immediate post-surrender period, in case a successor to CCS 551 was not prepared in time.[134] Thus, by mid-August new approaches were being made to existing short-term and long-term policies, all at the initiative of Army officials. Had the imminent surrender of Germany been the sole reason for concern over policy, only the second of these would have been urgent. The unavoidability of Army involvement in high political policy questions which the prospects of economic collapse had revealed to Army officials lay behind this major change in its viewpoint.

The Treasury Department had come to a change of viewpoint by a different route. By the end of July, Treasury was advocating a revision of the Financial Guide to CCS 551 which would shift the primary reliance for financial (and economic) policies from elaborate, pre-set administrative plans to the improvisation of a program on the spot because of the difficulty of anticipating important conditions.[135] The effect of this proposal would be to make not only occupation planning, but the extent of Army responsibility for the German economy more flexible. Apparently in response to Eisenhower's cable of August 23, three days later the CCS approved the Financial Guide Revision. The issue was thus side-stepped rather than settled, as an impasse in the CCS over instructions to Eisenhower directly bearing on his responsibility for the German economy later revealed.[136]

B. *MORGENTHAU IN WASHINGTON*

1. *Morgenthau Acts*

Upon returning to Washington on August 17, Morgenthau directed Harry White and two Treasury lawyers, John Pehle and Ansel Luxford, to have a draft of the Treasury's position on policy toward Germany prepared. They, in turn, enlisted the help of several others in the Department.

Morgenthau himself promptly saw Hull about the terms of reference of the EAC, a question which had come up in his conversations with Eden. To settle the question, Eden had gone over the minutes of the Teheran Conference with Morgenthau. At that conference, it had been agreed that the question of the dismemberment of Germany was to be considered by the EAC. The discussions leading up to the understanding indicated that there was only agreement to *consider* the proposal.[137] Since the EAC, after burying dismemberment in subcommittee, had proceeded immediately to consider matters which assumed a single German state, Morgenthau asserted that EAC was "blandly ignoring its instructions from Teheran." Morgenthau did not understand the workings of EAC, nor did Hull clarify the situation. EAC would only "consider" or "study" a subject if one of the three governments instructed its member to present a formal written proposal. This had not been done, and Winant had correctly proceeded with matters on which he did have instructions. Roosevelt had failed to tell Hull about the discussion at Teheran, and the State Department naturally took no steps to advocate a policy it opposed.

Morgenthau's version of the Teheran Conference minutes shocked Hull, who admitted that he had never seen them, and then went on to pour out all the exasperation which had built up in the attempts of the State Department to get instructions through the Working Security Committee to the European Advisory Commission.[138]

The following day Morgenthau tried to rouse the President by telling him that since the Teheran Conference no American officials were attempting to plan policy for Germany in accordance with his wishes, particularly in relation to dismemberment. Roosevelt did not respond. He chose to interpret this information to indicate that there was a misunderstanding between Churchill and himself—a misunderstanding which could be settled easily through direct contact.[139]

Stimson had been away from Washington for most of August recuperating from a minor surgical operation which had been slow to heal. Before that, he had traveled in the European theater. Roosevelt, in turn, had gone to the Pacific in the early summer. Consequently, when Stimson arranged to see Roosevelt on August 23rd, it was his first appointment with the President since June. Stimson had wanted to talk about the settlement of policy for Germany. His appointment was cut short, however, and all that he could accomplish was to stress the urgency of the matter, to learn of the forthcoming Anglo-American conference at Quebec where Roosevelt expected to settle with Churchill "all these questions in regard to Germany," and to make an appointment two days later.[140]

Stimson, Morgenthau, and McCloy lunched together that day. The talk was about German policy. Morgenthau recounted his story of the agreement on dismemberment at Teheran, but Stimson was able to satisfy himself that Roosevelt, Churchill, and Stalin had not committed themselves so formally and fully as Morgenthau seemed to think.[141]

There seems to have been no very clear meeting of minds between Morgenthau and Stimson and McCloy. Morgenthau continued to press his views on Germany without realizing how little support he would get from Stimson. His report to the President, upon his return from England the week before, that American officials were not planning for the dismemberment of Germany, was a general criticism, but it was most likely to reflect upon the State Department in its conduct of EAC negotiations, although the more tangible evidence Morgenthau had was concerned with Army conduct. Two days later Morgenthau called the White House and requested the first appointment that morning with the President;[142] he thought that Stimson's meeting with the President on the same day would deal only with the specialized question of the Army's responsibilities in Germany, while he would cover the whole range of German questions. Stimson and McCloy knew of Morgenthau's appointment, and Morgenthau knew of Stimson's. Neither was bothered because neither realized how profound their differences were.

To his meeting with Roosevelt Morgenthau took a SHAEF military government handbook for Germany which Colonel Bernstein had handed him in England, and a memorandum on the handbook prepared by his staff—probably after his luncheon with Stimson and McCloy.

Roosevelt was interested enough in what he saw in the memorandum to agree to read the handbook that night. He discussed the treatment of Germany with Stimson at lunch in general terms, but evidently without saying very much about the SHAEF handbook. If Morgenthau was attempting that day to arouse the President to disapprove of civil affairs planning in England, Stimson tried to impress him with the urgency of settling the policy issues about Germany and at the same time refute Morgenthau's proposals, such as he knew them. Stimson emphasized the importance of a prompt settlement of the zonal assignment question, arguing for acceptance of the British proposal on which he, Stettinius, and McCloy agreed. He explained that the British had naval interests in occupying the Northwest zone which the United States did not have. He understood, he said, that the President was alarmed at the prospects of American assignment to the Southwest zone because the lines of supply and communication to it would lie through France, where they would be in jeopardy when the revolution which Admiral Leahy had forecast occurred. No revolution would occur, he insisted, while the war was still being waged, because of the presence of so many American troops; and when it was over, there would be independent lines of communication through Germany, anyway. Furthermore, he suggested, the Southwest zone will be "a more congenial part of Germany," and it will be considerably further away from the "dirty work that the Russians might be doing with the Prussians in eastern Germany."

He went on to talk of the questions raised, or soon to be raised, by Morgenthau. While he thought that "trimming the outer edges of Germany"—East Prussia, Alsace and Lorraine, and possibly Silesia—would not be unwise, he opposed the partitioning of the whole country. Were it divided, he said, and a policy of deindustrialization followed, he feared her "excess population" of thirty million people would starve. In the long run, the destruction of the economic structure of Germany would have serious consequences. For now, he argued against a punitive exchange rate for Germany, which Morgenthau was proposing. As alternatives to Morgenthau's proposals he suggested the internationalization of the Ruhr and the Saar and individual punishment by legal methods. His "main point" at the end was that the Army was going to have to go into Germany without instructions on vital questions of policy.[143]

2. The President Responds

After lunch, Roosevelt and Stimson went into the Cabinet meeting together. There the President explained that he had been talking with Morgenthau

on the general question of the control of Germany after the end of the war. He said that he had just heard about a paper prepared by the Army and that he was not at all satisfied with the severity of the measures proposed. He said that the Germans should have simply a subsistence level of food— as he put it, soup kitchens would be ample to sustain life—that otherwise they should be stripped clean and should not have a level of subsistence above the lowest level of the people they had conquered.

At the Cabinet meeting Stimson indicated his disagreement with this view. He

pointed out that among other things Germany was a highly industrialized nation, that it would be a practical impossibility to shift large segments of the population who depended for their existence on industrial [sic] economy back to the land; furthermore, he pointed out that the products of German industry and business were needed for the rebuilding of Europe, particularly the iron and steel from the Ruhr.[144]

While the President continued with the expression of his views regardless of Stimson's opposition, he did accept a suggestion, made by Stimson during lunch that day, that he name a Cabinet committee composed of the Secretaries of State, War, and Treasury to consider the problem of how to treat Germany. Stimson had pointed out to the President that he did not really have the time to study through the problems involved and suggested that the committee of these Cabinet officers "could assimilate the work that was already being done by men on a lower level and prepare it for the President himself."[145] In announcing to the Cabinet his acceptance of this suggestion, Roosevelt instructed the committee to consider the problem of how to deal with Germany along the lines that he had just outlined.[146]

While Roosevelt had made no severe criticism of the SHAEF handbook at the Cabinet meeting (he had not yet read it), the following day, August 26, he sent a memorandum to Stimson.

This so-called "Handbook" is pretty bad. I should like to know how it came to be written and

who approved it down the line. If it has not been sent out as approved, all copies should be withdrawn and held until you get a chance to go over it.

It gives me the impression that Germany is to be restored just as much as the Netherlands or Belgium, and the people of Germany brought back as quickly as possible to their pre-war estate.

It is of the utmost importance that every person in Germany should realize that this time Germany is a defeated nation. I do not want them to starve to death, but, as an example, if they need food to keep body and soul together beyond what they have, they should be fed three times a day with soup from Army soup kitchens. That will keep them perfectly healthy and they will remember that experience all their lives. The fact that they are a defeated nation, collectively and individually, must be so impressed upon them that they will hesitate to start any new war.

.   .   .   .

There exists a school of thought both in London and here which would, in effect, do for Germany what this Government did for its own citizens in 1933 when they were flat on their backs. I see no reason for starting a WPA, PWA, or CCC for Germany when we go in with our Army of Occupation.

Too many people here and in England hold to the view that the German people as a whole are not responsible for what has taken place—that only a few Nazi leaders are responsible. That unfortunately is not based on fact. The German people as a whole must have it driven home to them that the whole nation has been engaged in a lawless conspiracy against the decencies of modern civilization.

Please let me see the revision of this and also let me have this original copy back.

[s] F.D.R.[147]

In his note to Stimson, Roosevelt quoted some twelve excerpts from the handbook which dealt with the Army's responsibility for keeping German economic and political life functioning adequately. Indicative of the tone of all of them was the first:

Your main and immediate task, to accomplish your mission, is to get things running, to pick up the pieces, to restore as quickly as possible the official functioning of the German civil government in the area for which you are responsible. . . . The first concern of military government will be to see that the machine works and works efficiently.

Thus, on his second try with the President,

the Secretary of the Treasury scored. He had been unable to raise the President's interest over the failure of the European Advisory Commission to consider the question of the dismemberment of Germany. But a demonstration that the Army had stated that the first and main task of civil affairs was to maintain or restore civil and economic life in Germany drew Roosevelt's immediate disapproval. It was indeed ironic that he aroused the President's interest in a position which the Army was already trying to abandon.

3. War Department Reaction to the President's Note

While Stimson's wish was granted by the establishment of the Cabinet Committee, Morgenthau's views on the substance of policy found in the President a sympathetic reader. Roosevelt's note to Stimson on the civil affairs handbook was copied and circulated widely in the State and Treasury Departments. Upon receipt of it, the War Department had the Combined Chiefs of Staff suspend distribution of the handbook.[148] The Combined Civil Affairs Committee then attempted to fill the gap left by that suspension. At first it was planned to tell Eisenhower to use the pre-surrender directive if Germany surrendered before he received other instructions. But the committee finally decided to notify him that he might issue pre-surrender interim directives based on directives of the Combined Chiefs of Staff. It instructed him also to block out of the handbook all directives that assumed a policy of general economic or administrative rehabilitation. For post-hostilities guidance, he was informed, a directive was under consideration.[149]

On September 15, after it had been found impossible actually to block out the offending passages, at the suggestion of CCAC the handbook was issued with a fly leaf insertion which stated that the directive would apply only to the pre-surrender period, and that its application should insure that

(1) no steps beyond those necessary for military purposes should be taken for the economic rehabilitation of Germany;

(2) no relief supplies except the minimum necessary to prevent disease and disorder that might interfere with military operations should be imported or distributed; and

(3) no Nazi sympathizer, nor Nazi organization should be continued in office for purposes of convenience or expediency.[150]

The War Department was in a difficult position to defend itself against the President's rebuke because the handbook represented a position which the Army had been in the process of abandoning for several weeks. Hilldring, writing to Eisenhower's G-5 at the end of August, stated that both he and McCloy were in complete agreement with the substance of the President's memorandum.[151] But the action of SHAEF in going ahead with the handbook and the works it represented needed and deserved defense. A draft memorandum to the President was prepared for Stimson's signature by CAD. Although it was never sent (the matter was handled informally by Stimson or McCloy), it was an important statement of CAD's position at the time:

MEMORANDUM FOR THE PRESIDENT:

The Handbook of Military Government for Germany dated August 15, 1944, referred to in your memorandum dated August 26, 1944, is a preliminary draft prepared in the Supreme Headquarters, Allied Expeditionary Forces, in London. The draft is a working paper and at the time of its delivery to you had not been approved by General Eisenhower. It has not been distributed to the Armies nor has it yet been transmitted to the War Department for approval or comment. Supreme Headquarters was immediately notified by the Combined Chiefs of Staff to defer any use of the Handbook pending further instructions.

I agree that many of the provisions which you quote seem unduly solicitous of the future welfare of Germany. The Handbook has now been reviewed by General Eisenhower's Headquarters and a new draft of it has just arrived which we have checked and believe to be in conformity with your views. Mr. Morgenthau has seen the new draft and concurs in this statement.

.   .   .   .   .   .

With respect to food and relief the directive states that "German food and other supplies will be utilized for the German population to the minimum extent required to prevent disease and unrest." There is no provision for any imports.

In other matters, I think you will find that this directive, which is the only official instructions issued to date to General Eisenhower, is entirely consistent with any long range policies this country, acting in conjunction with England and Russia, may see fit to adopt.

As to the post-surrender period, there are still no agreed tripartite policies established, but General Eisenhower's staff has been required to make plans on a tentative basis. It has always been understood, however, that these plans would be and are subject to change, in accordance with such policies as may be handed down either by tripartite agreement or by the Combined Chiefs of Staff. It was on this basis that the SHAEF staff prepared the draft of the Handbook which you saw.

In the meantime the War Department has prepared a draft of a directive dealing with the Post Surrender period and pending such time as tripartite or other instructions are given as to the long range policy for the treatment of Germany. This directive will be submitted to your Committee within the next day or two for review.

Your concern on this matter again brings forward the need for a clear understanding of our policy, which I trust the creation of the informal Committee of the State, Treasury, Navy and War Departments will expedite.

With events moving so rapidly, it is urged that such policy and guidance be furnished to the military authorities as soon as possible to the end that those who are charged with the duty of executing the terms of surrender and administering military government will have the fullest information as to the policy of the United States.

In accordance with your request, I am returning to you the draft of the Handbook which you sent me with your memorandum of August 26.[152]

4. The War and State Departments Press for Agreement

Policy instructions for Winant constituted an old subject, but at the end of August it was an old subject with a new urgency. Paris had been liberated; the Allied armies were rushing eastward; a collapse of Germany within days or weeks seemed highly possible. The need for an immediate directive was incontestable. As if this was not enough, Roosevelt's memorandum to Stimson showed that the establishment of agreed policy was likely to be even more complicated a process in the future than it had been in the past.

Meanwhile, working under the shadow of these events, the Civil Affairs Division's change of attitude toward the Working Security Committee and the tripartite negotiations in London, which reflected SHAEF's changed prognosis about the German economy and the responsibility which the occupation forces should take for it, continued to gain momentum. In early August Colonel Thomas W. Hammond,

the Assistant Military Adviser to Winant, returned to Washington to assist CAD in its efforts to improve the military clearance procedures for Winant. As Hilldring and his representative on WSC, Allen, now saw it, the slowness of WSC was due to the State Department. On about August 17, the day Morgenthau returned to Washington, Hilldring, Hammond, and Allen met with H. Freeman Matthews from State to impress upon him the urgent necessity for getting action in Washington on the draft directives which were coming in from Winant each week. They emphasized that these documents differed from earlier papers considered by the committee since they were concerned only with the implementation of policy already established, not with questions of general policies. As was noted above, this was not true of the first three papers submitted by Winant in July, for they were very much concerned with questions of general policy. In order to reach agreement on general policy so that the directives dealing with more specific subjects could be cleared for Winant, a meeting was scheduled for the following week to consider two of the three policy documents from London, the draft "General Directive for Germany" and "Principles of Allied Military Government for Germany." On August 24 the committee cleared both papers. It was expected that War Department clearance could by some special dispensation be by-passed and the papers could be submitted at once to the JCS.[153] This WSC action immediately took on new significance. The Cabinet Committee on Germany was designated the next day, and CAD learned from Winant's staff in London their view that it was unlikely that individual directives would ever be approved by the EAC, but that a broad policy directive might well receive favorable and prompt consideration.[154] The two papers dealt with broad policy, but the third was potentially the most comprehensive of them all. CAD now hurriedly brought it out of WSC, intent on speedy military clearance.[155]

The new comprehensive policy paper took into account the most recent developments. It avoided the issue on which the President had expressed such strong views by leaving out the proposals on economic reconstruction, so that no general statement on economic policy remained. In its form, it followed, in some degree, the directive, "Military and Political

Policies to be Followed in the Administration of Germany," prepared by Winant's staff and transmitted by him in July, though it was considerably more detailed. The greater detail revealed a modest denazification policy, involving only "chief Nazi associates" and "important" government officials, much like the policy of CCS 551. Also noteworthy was the failure of this directive to adjust to the changing circumstances described in the SHAEF cable to the Combined Chiefs of August 23. German administrative machinery and German personnel were to be relied upon for the execution of Allied policies and to maintain law and order, while extensive controls were to be exercised over the German civil authority. The basic policy of the directive was wholly in conformity with the expressed State Department position; its greater concreteness probably reflected War Department views. Winant had originally intended that this document only lay down general policies on the most important matters requiring tripartite agreement; evidently the War Department representative on WSC had led it into more detailed provisions.

While the pressures for expediting clearance of WSC papers now came from within the War Department instead of from State, with the appointment of the Cabinet Committee on Germany clearance again came to a standstill. Meanwhile the Operations Division held up both papers until formal concurrences by War Department agencies concerned should be received.[156] Thus rebuffed, Hilldring tried a different routing for the third paper, the comprehensive policy agreement draft. He referred it on August 28 to the Joint Post-War Committee. Although this was the usual routing, he was told to expect clearance to the JCS secretariat by September 1, in just two days. But the clearance was held up at the last minute when the appointment of the Cabinet Committee on Germany was interpreted by the JCS staff to mean that the President wanted an agreed German policy worked out in a different way.[157]

Shortly before this, on August 25, the day after the President had established the Cabinet Committee on Germany, and the Working Security Committee had cleared Winant's two policy papers for Germany, Hull had sent Stimson the two economic policy papers which State had had cleared by the Executive Committee

on Economic Foreign Policy in early August, pointing out that they had been approved by ECEFP, listing its inter-departmental membership, and requesting the views of the War Department on it before its transmittal to the President. Hull's letter also asked that an appropriate War Department officer be designated for informal discussion of the subject matter with Assistant Secretary of State Dean Acheson, the chairman of ECEFP. And, in what was almost a paraphrase of what CAD had been telling Hull's own subordinates, the letter explained that an agreed general policy statement was necessary in order to go ahead with subsidiary issues which now needed decision.[158]

5. Adjustments in the War Department Position of Policy Neutrality

CAD's determination to expedite the establishment of policy for Germany can be viewed as one retreat from an extreme position of policy neutrality—an indifference to the making of policy based on a confidence that it was not really necessary. Stimson's proposal of a Cabinet Committee was a second retreat from policy neutrality. It had been intended that the War Department be the servant of the policymakers, but not a policy-maker itself. There were bound to be two objectives for this desire to keep the Army out of politics: One was to protect America from the dangers of militarism; the other, to protect the military from the dangers of politics. By late August 1944, in the War Department the latter objective seemed to be in considerable jeopardy.

From the viewpoint of the Army, the hazards of a political role for itself rendered policymaking which was "civil" or "political" rather than "military" in character unthinkable as an Army responsibility. As we saw earlier, the major Army doctrines on military government were "military necessity" and "welfare of the governed"—one of which emphasized the military character of occupation duties, the other the service functions of the Army, while both sought to minimize the Army's involvement in policy. But in thirty-two months of war the Army had found the avoidance of involvement difficult if not impossible. With encouragement from the State Department and the President it had hoped that it would be responsible for occupying Germany for a short time only. During that time it hoped that it could carry on a kind of neutral military government and that the policy questions involved in the treatment of Germany could be postponed until the War Department's responsibility for military government had ended. But the Army had learned that its hopes had little foundation. Experience in North Africa, Sicily, and Italy had made clear that it was impossible to administer civil affairs without becoming involved in policy-making. At the same time, there was a growing expectation of longer Army control of occupation than had originally been anticipated. In an attempt to hold the line against involvement with policy-making, the War Department had established the Civil Affairs Division as a policy coordinator. Presumably, by "coordinating" policy made elsewhere, the War Department could still avoid policy-making, and at the same time provide its civil affairs people with instructions, so that they could avoid the dangers encountered in North Africa which had resulted from operating in a policy vacuum. But CAD had found it difficult to coordinate without further involvement in the making of policy. The distinction between the two functions was clever but not wholly realistic.

The Army's hopes had been pinned on what was probably the old Army tenet of "welfare of the governed," as modified under the inspiration of State Department policy positions. In the course of developing occupation plans for the Army, what at first seemed to be purely administrative devices were revealed to have significant policy implications. Many of these implications were avoidable with the reconstruction policy, for reconstruction meant in fact an economic policy for Germany, but one determined, not on its own merits, but in pursuit of some of the universal objectives of post-war policy: restitution and reparation. This was the State Department modification of "welfare of the governed." But when economic collapse in Germany began to seem probable, so that if it were to be prevented the effort required would have to be of such a scale that it could only be undertaken as a result of a clear commitment with respect to German economic policy as such, the last hope of avoiding involvement in non-military policies collapsed for the Army. Thus, in addition to entanglements with policy-making which it had found unavoidable in the administration of civil affairs, the War Depart-

ment now had to anticipate that it would be held responsible, not merely for the efficient administration of civil affairs in Germany, but also for carrying out policies with important long-term implications for American foreign policy.

The first reaction in the War Department was to see that those policies were clearly established by others. This was the point at which the Army had arrived by the end of July 1944. It accounts for CAD's change of attitude toward the Working Security Committee and the tripartite negotiations in the European Advisory Commission on occupation policies. But Stimson's move went further, for he attempted not simply to expedite but to shape the substance of policy.

The Army's new sense of urgency for agreement on military government policy was a major reason as well for this second retreat into policy-making. Whatever else the War Department's attempt to remain neutral had accomplished, it had not expedited the determination of policy. The military plans developed at SHAEF with painstaking effort had become as doubtful as had the major assumption on which they were based, that the German economic and political system would not collapse. The War Department's conflicting desire to keep out of policy-making, but make sure that policies established did not conflict with military necessity, had made it refuse to commit itself in advance to State Department position papers, thereby immobilizing the WSC and EAC. Indeed, thus far the only concrete progress made in the settlement of the major questions concerned with the occupation of Germany had been accomplished by considering the question of occupation zones as a military one and settling it through military channels. Finally, the War Department might become intent upon expediting policy guidance, but that was not enough, for the War Department did not constitute the Joint Chiefs of Staff.

When the Treasury intervention occurred it cut across the War Department's disappointments over its own role in policy-making. In the first place, the Treasury began with an attack upon a military government handbook prepared by an Army staff in London. If this kind of instruction could not be kept free from criticism for its policy content, what could? Secondly, the manner of criticism was disturbing, besides being embarrassing: the Secretary of a civilian department had gone to the President, who had reprimanded the Army in a letter which was widely circulated. Thirdly, from what could be known about the views of the Treasury, impossible demands might be placed upon the Army's civil affairs administration. And finally, even if they were not impossible to execute, occupation policies were bound to be the subject of partisan debate.

Under these circumstances the War Department was faced with an unhappy dilemma: if it left the making of policy for Germany to others, the Army was likely to become the spokesman for a partisan viewpoint, or the scapegoat of failure, or worse. The only immediate alternative seemed to be the unabashed abandonment of its neutral position vis-à-vis policy, and its active and overt participation in policy-making. However, Stimson's conception of his position as Cabinet member provided another way out. He could, not as spokesman for the War Department but as a member of the President's Cabinet, take an active part in the development of policy for Germany.[159] In this way, the fiction of the War Department's unconcern over the substance of the civil affairs policies which it administered could be preserved, and in fact the Army's active involvement could be subdued, while at the same time policies in the execution of which the Army would not become vulnerable to partisan attack could be encouraged, if not assured.

Determined now to expedite policy decisions for the occupation of Germany, but still to minimize the responsibility of the War Department for policy-making, Stimson turned to his role as a Cabinet member. It is ironic that in doing so he temporarily quashed CAD's efforts to expedite inter-departmental agreement on policy for Winant's guidance in the tripartite negotiations in London, although it may not have been unintentional. Stimson had become distressed during his recuperation at Saranac Lake by what appeared to be increased efforts by the State Department to by-pass the Secretary of War and deal directly with the Joint Chiefs of Staff. On his way back to Washington he had drafted a memorandum to Hull protesting this practice, which he delivered in person the next day. Dining that night with Dunn, McCloy, and Harvey H. Bundy, his Special

Assistant, he tried to interest them in his protest, but was disappointed in the response.[160] They had little reason to respond with enthusiasm. While he had been away, Dunn's and McCloy's subordinates, with the initiative coming from the War Department, had devised a way, or thought they had devised a way, to get JCS approval for WSC papers—by by-passing War Department clearance (including, presumably, the Secretary). It may well be that Stimson, from a distance, had mistakenly thought that these efforts were the result of State Department pressure. Whether he understood them or not, his memorandum to Hull could only jeopardize their success, for which, presumably, McCloy and Dunn were hoping. When Stimson's point, that only the President, the Secretary of War and the Secretary of the Navy had an inherent right to consult directly with the Joint Chiefs of Staff, was pressed by him later, after Stettinius replaced Hull as Secretary of State, it led to the establishment of the State-War-Navy Coordinating Committee, which proved to be a much more effective agency for the expediting of inter-departmental agreement on politico-military policies.

C. PREPARING FOR THE CABINET COMMITTEE

1. Hopkins and the State Department Position

On August 29, four days after the President had accepted and acted upon Stimson's proposal of a Cabinet Committee, at a conference in Hull's office with Patterson and Forrestal, the Under Secretaries of War and Navy, respectively, present, McCloy pressed for an early meeting of the Cabinet Committee. His immediate concern—one which must indeed have been alarming to Army financial planners—was with the President's idea of having no established rate of exchange with Germany and, by implication, no currency controls. With these notions as an impetus (for no one present liked them), plans were laid to get the committee under way. Forrestal was assured that the Navy would have access to proceedings of the committee and could be represented whenever it desired.[161]

Three days later, Harry Hopkins called on Hull to announce that the President had asked him to give the Cabinet Committee his undivided attention. Hopkins, formerly Secretary of Commerce, had taken up residence in the White House in May 1940, to become a kind of alter ego of Roosevelt, functioning as his most intimate and trusted adviser and assistant. At this time, the Roosevelt-Hopkins relationship had entered a cool phase,[162] and Hopkins was aware that he would not attend the forthcoming Anglo-American conference at Quebec.

While visiting Hull, Hopkins was shown by James Riddleberger, Chief of the Division of Central European Affairs, and H. Freeman Matthews, the studies on post-war Germany made in the State Department and in the European Advisory Commission.[163] Later in the day, Riddleberger and Matthews drew up a memorandum outlining the State Department's views on American policy for the post-surrender treatment of Germany.[164] By this time—September—negotiations in the European Advisory Commission had dealt with surrender terms, zones of occupation, and control machinery and military government. The United States had approved formally the instrument of unconditional surrender of Germany recommended by the EAC. Britain and the USSR were expected by the State Department to approve it also. Tentative, but not formal, agreement had been reached regarding the zones of occupation, but Britain and the United States remained in disagreement as to which would take the Northwestern and which the Southwestern zone. In March 1944, Britain and the United States had submitted proposals to the EAC for the machinery of occupation. The USSR had at first refused to discuss them until the surrender terms had been agreed to. By the end of August, however, they had agreed on discussions and submitted their own proposals.

The Riddleberger-Matthews memorandum noted that several important problems remained unsolved for which high policy decisions were urgently required. First, they urged acceptance of the State Department's policy of opposition to an imposed dismemberment of Germany. This view had been well established and coherently expressed by the staff during more than two years. The Department now favored a federal system which, it thought, would avoid the disadvantages of both dismemberment and the existing centralization of government in Germany. Second, it wanted the dissolution of the armed forces of Germany, of all forces re-

lated to the military; and the destruction of all military equipment. Third, it proposed the liquidation of the Nazi Party. Party members were to be excluded from political or civil activity and subjected to a number of restrictions. (Whether or not this was to apply to all party members was not made clear.) Discriminatory laws were to be abolished. Fourth, war criminals were to be held for whatever disposition was later decided upon. On all of these proposals general agreement existed within the government. Sharp differences did exist within the government on economic measures for Germany, but Riddleberger and Matthews based their position on the general policy statement approved by ECEFP on August 4, summarized above.

These views of the State Department, particularly the reassertion of its approval of the ECEFP Report on General Objectives of United States Economic Policy with Respect to Germany, reflected its awareness of opposition from the Treasury and the President. Riddleberger and Matthews undoubtedly had heard word of Morgenthau's plans for turning Germany into an agricultural country. They objected on the grounds that such actions would adversely affect the economy of Europe, and would require the liquidation or emigration of millions of Germans. Beyond that, the President's memorandum of August 26 showed them that he had strong views on economic policy; apparently Matthews and Riddleberger at this point hoped that the President might be persuaded to modify his position.

2. *Treasury Preparations*

On the same day that the State Department completed the memorandum described above, the Treasury committee which Morgenthau had appointed upon his return from England completed a draft memorandum entitled "Suggested Post-Surrender Program for Germany," which might be considered the first formal draft of what soon was widely known as the Morgenthau Plan;[165] and, indeed, while Morgenthau was not the draftsman, it was in substance *his* plan. In brief, it suggested that the position of the United States should be based on the following principles: First, the complete demilitarization of Germany. "This means completely disarming the German Army and people . . .

and the total destruction of the whole German armament industry as well as those parts of supporting industries having no other justification." Second, the partitioning, or dismemberment, of Germany. East Prussia, the southern portion of Silesia, the Saar, and the adjacent territories bounded by the Rhine and the Moselle Rivers, and all German territories north of the Kiel Canal were to be incorporated into other countries. The remainder of Germany, excluding the Ruhr, was to be divided into two states, each of which was to be decentralized by making it a federation. Third, the Ruhr, the Rhineland, and the Kiel Canal were to be made into an internationalized zone, which should be a free trade area.[166] Fourth, reparations out of current production were not to be demanded; but all reparations and restitution would have to come from existing German resources and territories, including forced German labor outside Germany. The fifth provision involved denazification. Indicative of its severity was the following provision:

Apart from the question of established guilt for special crimes, mere membership in the S.S., the Gestapo, and similar groups will constitute the basis for inclusion into compulsory labor battalions to serve outside Germany for reconstruction purposes.[167]

It further provided that all Nazi Party members, Nazi sympathizers (broadly defined), Junkers, and military and naval officers should be "dismissed from public office, disenfranchised, and disqualified to hold any public office or to engage in the journalist, teaching and legal professions, or in any managerial capacity in banking, manufacturing or trade." The final principle of particular significance concerned the German economy. It was a clear and forceful statement of the "let Germany stew in its own juice" view:

The sole purpose of the military in control of the German economy shall be to facilitate military operations and military occupation. The Allied Military Government shall not assume responsibility for such economic problems as price controls, rationing, unemployment, production, reconstruction, distribution, consumption, housing, or transportation, or take any measures designed to maintain or strengthen the German economy, except those which are essential to military operations and are indicated above. The responsibility for sustaining the German economy and people rests with the German people with such facilities as may be available under the circumstances.[168]

Once Germany was disarmed, it was expected that her neighbors (including Russia, but not including Great Britain) would take primary responsibility for policing and administering her. U. S. troops would be withdrawn "within a relatively short time."

3. Preliminary Meetings

At the request of the President, Hopkins called together several advisers of the Secretaries of State, War, and Treasury for an exchange of views prior to the convening of the three as a Cabinet Committee. Three of these meetings were held, the first two in Hopkins' White House office on September 2. Matthews and Riddleberger represented State; the Assistant Secretary of War, John J. McCloy, and the chief of the Civil Affairs Division, General Hilldring, represented War; and Harry D. White, Assistant to the Secretary, and ranking Treasury official who helped prepare the first draft of the Morgenthau Plan, was the Treasury spokesman.[169] White produced the "Suggested Post-Surrender Program for Germany," and in a lengthy interpretation of it went beyond its terms in describing the extent of the severity, especially by emphasizing that no trade from the proposed internationalized zone of the Ruhr and Rhineland be permitted to contribute in any way to the German economy.[170]

In the afternoon session the State Department memorandum prepared the previous day was presented, and Matthews and Riddleberger explained how it fitted into British and Russian ideas, as they understood them. McCloy pointed out the difficulties which would arise in attempting to carry out the plan advanced by the Treasury. He insisted that it was essential to give General Eisenhower an interim directive for the treatment of Germany to suffice until more long-range plans could be made. Hopkins thought it most important that this directive be prepared as soon as possible, and urged McCloy to hurry its completion. McCloy replied that the State and War Departments had both been working on this directive (the document completed in WSC on August 30), and that there were only minor differences between them which could be adjusted easily, but the

Treasury memorandum was in obvious conflict with some major provisions of the State-War draft.[171]

It was decided that a meeting should be held, with Treasury representation, to hasten the completion of the interim directive.[172] Riddleberger was requested by the conferees to draw up a further memorandum attempting to reconcile the views of the three Departments which their respective Secretaries might submit as their recommendation to the President.

On Sunday, September 3, Hopkins met again with State Department representatives, evidently to go over the draft Riddleberger was to prepare. Besides Riddleberger and Matthews, James C. Dunn, Director of the Office of European Affairs, attended. Dunn pressed with Hopkins the State Department theme which had been introduced the previous day in defense of its own work. He emphasized the great importance of working out with our Allies the questions involved in post-war treatment of Germany. He explained the impossibility of obtaining the concurrence of Russia and Britain in some of the principles proposed by the Treasury. He described the tripartite control of Germany envisaged in U. S. and British proposals to the European Advisory Commission for a Control Council for Germany, and indicated how extensively they would have to be modified to conform with Treasury ideas. The State Department representatives had the impression that Hopkins accepted the validity of this line of argument. He remarked, somewhat noncommittally, that he believed it essential for the President and the Secretary of State to keep in agreement on all plans that might be developed for Germany.[173] It is useful to note that Hopkins gave the same impression to the Treasury representative that he gave to State; Morgenthau believed that Hopkins was on his side.

After the conclusion of these three meetings with Hopkins, the State Department participants advised Secretary Hull that there had been agreement on demilitarization, denazification, the extensive control of communications, press and propaganda, and the educational system, and the decentralization of the German government. The points of disagreement, Hull was informed, were whether Germany should be partitioned, and what the economic policy toward Germany should be. State objected to the forcible partitioning of Germany, while Treasury wanted to divide it into two separate states and the internationalized Ruhr zone. These were the areas of explicit disagreement. But the generality of the areas of agreement hid further differences which only became evident later. With respect to economic policy, the State Department had advocated far-reaching rights of control over the German economy for the purpose of effecting restitution and reparation, forcing the conversion of the German economic capacity to non-military production, and eliminating German economic domination in Europe. The ultimate objective would be to change the fundamental organization and conduct of German economic life so that the economy could eventually be integrated into an interdependent world economy.

The Treasury, Hull was told, contended that reparations in the form of recurrent payments and deliveries should not be demanded. Restitution and reparation should be accomplished by the transfer of German resources and territories.

The general form of the statements in the State Department memorandum of September 1 had evidently prevented a clash in the preliminary meetings with Hopkins between State and Treasury over their divergent views regarding denazification. Although the State participants advised Hull that this was a point on which State and Treasury agreed, their memorandum provided that party members should be excluded from political or civil activity and subjected to a number of restrictions, while the Treasury memorandum suggested the areas of exclusion in more specific terms, and, in addition to party members, applied it to Junkers, military and naval officers, and Nazi sympathizers who by word or deed sided with or abetted the Nazi program. When denazification was later considered in more concrete terms, the differences implicit in these two statements became clearer.

4. *Morgenthau and Roosevelt*

While Hopkins was preparing the ground for the meeting of the Cabinet Committee, Morgenthau was advancing his cause with the President. Both had gone to their Dutchess County homes for the Labor Day week-end. There Morgenthau received a copy of the September 1 draft prepared by his staff. His own reaction to it was not wholly favorable. In general, it was not severe enough for him. Under the provisions of the draft, the only industry which would remain in the internationalized Ruhr area would be what survived the destruction of all armament industry and "supporting industries," and the removals of equipment for reparation. The remainder would belong to the international body administering the zone, and could never be allowed to develop in such a way as to contribute to the military potential of the Ruhr area or of Germany. How extensive the stripping of industrial plants for restitution and reparations would be was not indicated in the draft, and in any case could not be determined on the basis of general policy.

Neither was the extent of destruction through previous military action mentioned; nor could it be indicated in the draft. Certainly, however, it was believed that destruction through strategic bombing was by this time severe. Perhaps ignoring the total weight of all these factors, Morgenthau objected to this draft because it left the Ruhr "intact."[174] He preferred to see a plan for the complete dismantling of Ruhr industry, and the distribution of the Ruhr plants among the nations which had been victims of Germany. He also found the following provision on German re-education to be weak:

All schools and universities will be closed until an Allied Commissioner of Education has formulated an effective reorganization program. It is contemplated that it may require a considerable period of time before any institutions of higher education are reopened. Meanwhile the education of German students in foreign universities will not be prohibited. Elementary schools will be reopened as quickly as appropriate teachers and textbooks are available.[175]

When President and Mrs. Roosevelt drove over from Hyde Park one afternoon during the week-end for tea, Morgenthau showed him the draft. Roosevelt indicated that he regarded three things as psychologically and symbolically important. First, Germany should be allowed no aircraft of any kind. Second, Germans should not be allowed to wear uniforms. And third, there should be no marching of any kind. Prohibiting uniforms and parades would do more to impress the Germans with their

defeat, he thought, than anything else.[176] The President seems to have avoided any discussion of basic policy questions suggested by the Treasury memorandum. His strictures on parades and uniforms were, no doubt, based on recollections of a summer spent in Germany in his youth. His proposal to prohibit German aircraft had a quite different origin and significance.

Stimson returned to Washington on Labor Day, September 4, from another week of recuperation. While away he had kept in touch with McCloy by direct wire, and had formulated what he seems to have regarded as his own alternative to Morgenthau's punitive economic policy proposals, legal punishment for individuals. He wanted to intern Gestapo and perhaps SS leaders and "then vigorously investigate and try them as the main instruments of Hitler's system of terrorism in Europe."[177] When he returned to Washington he discussed his proposals with his own assistants and with Marshall. Marshall expressed particular approval of his plan to have civilians instead of Army officers man the court panels of his tribunal system, although he anticipated that the Russians would use military men.[178]

Again, as when he returned to Washington the previous week with his letter to Hull on direct State-JCS relations, Stimson seems to have been out of touch with the developing situation. While he was away the second time the breadth of the Treasury Department's onslaught against developing or prevailing policy views had become apparent, and it certainly included a far more stringent denazification policy than State or War Department officials contemplated. In the face of the Treasury proposals, as they were presented in the preliminary meetings with Hopkins, the expectation that a relatively mild denazification program, even one which was worked out in relatively concrete terms, could be a serious counterweight to the Treasury proposals was ill-founded. Yet the attention Stimson gave it before the first meeting of the Cabinet Committee suggests that he considered it a serious alternative. If he did, his illusion was short-lived.

On the evening of Labor Day, September 4, and the eve of the first meeting of the Cabinet Committee, Stimson and McCloy dined with Morgenthau and White. Stimson had become aware of the great divergences in view between himself and Morgenthau shortly before he had suggested to the President the appointment of a Cabinet Committee to consider the treatment of Germany, and had discussed them with him immediately after it. At dinner with Morgenthau the central issue was skirted, although on both sides there was an awareness of sharp differences.[179] "Morgenthau," he later observed, "is, not unnaturally, very bitter and . . . it became very apparent that he would plunge out for a treatment of Germany which I feel sure would be unwise."[180]

D. THE CABINET COMMITTEE MEETINGS

1. The First Meeting

The Cabinet Committee, consisting of Hull, Stimson, Morgenthau, and Hopkins, met for the first time in Hull's office on the Tuesday morning after Labor Day, September 5. Hull presented as an agenda for the meeting the memorandum prepared by Riddleberger at the request of the participants in the week-end meetings.[181] It should be recalled that Riddleberger was asked to attempt to reconcile the views of the three departments in a memorandum for the approval of the three Secretaries. His draft was based on earlier State Department staff studies, and took familiar and non-controversial positions on such matters as the demilitarization of Germany, the dissolution of the Nazi Party and all affiliated organizations, extensive controls over communications and the educational system, and the acceptance of the principle of reparation. He attempted to reconcile Treasury views with expressed State Department views by postponing the settlement of differences. He proposed that the question of the partition of Germany be deferred until the internal situation and the attitude of the principal Allies could be determined; but the proposal may have carried with it the hope that the idea would be dropped. A decision on reparations was also to be deferred indefinitely. This action was justified by emphasizing a preliminary statement in the Report on Reparations, Restitution, and Property Rights to the effect that the United States had no direct interest in receiving reparations itself.[182] Whereas the earlier report had gone on to assert indirect American interest in a reparations pro-

gram because it would affect the achievement of general economic, political, and security objectives,[183] the draft for the Cabinet Committee suggested that since the U. S. wanted no reparations for itself, it should take no fixed position on reparations until the views had been expressed of governments which had more direct interest.

Apparently the State Department tactic of suggesting postponement was successful, for no one raised any serious objections to the document, except to its last paragraph which was an ingenious but perhaps unfortunate restatement of economic policy. Hopkins, indeed, indicated that he approved the whole document.[184] Stimson could accept it down to the last paragraph.[185] Morgenthau seemed to agree with most of it, but refused to commit himself.[186]

The paragraph to which Stimson objected so strongly read:

h. The primary objectives of our economic policy are (1) the standard of living of the German population shall be held down to subsistence levels; (2) German economic position of power in Europe must be eliminated; (3) German economic capacity must be converted in such manner that it will be so dependent upon imports and exports that Germany cannot by its own devices reconvert to war production.[187]

Like its predecessors in State Department policy papers, this paragraph was susceptible of varying interpretations. While it followed closely the wording of such previous drafts as the two documents on Germany approved by ECEFP on August 4, the earlier phrases "minimum German economy" or "minimum prescribed standard of living" were translated into "standard of living held down to subsistence levels." Presumably Riddleberger was trying to find a definition that would satisfy the President (who had spoken of "soup kitchens") and yet avoid the Treasury's planned chaos.

Similarly, the conversion of German economic capacity to ensure dependence on exports and imports would avoid Morgenthau's proposals for drastic reparations and destruction, while conforming to Hull's own free-trade policies.

Hull was ill at this time and had had little time to study the memorandum. Surprisingly, he now momentarily abandoned the moderate views he had expressed at Moscow, and eventually supported at home. He gave an extreme interpretation to Riddleberger's last paragraph, and more or less joined Morgenthau in recommending that the Ruhr and the Saar be converted to agriculture.[188] Even Hopkins was willing to have steel production prohibited. Stimson was the only one of the four who clearly opposed the deindustrialization of Germany in this meeting. While Morgenthau argued strongly for his own views at this time, he did not present any proposal in writing. Rather, it was agreed that Hull would send his memorandum to the President and that Stimson and Morgenthau would each submit a statement of their own views on it.

After the meeting, Stimson prepared a memorandum setting forth his views on the paper Hull had presented. He sent copies to Morgenthau, Hopkins, and Hull, who forwarded his to the President. After quoting the last paragraph from Hull's memorandum, Stimson observed:

While certain of these statements by themselves may possibly be susceptible of a construction with which I would not be at variance, the construction put upon them at the discussion this morning certainly reached positions to which I am utterly opposed. The position frankly taken by some of my colleagues was that the great industrial regions of Germany known as the Saar and the Ruhr with their very important deposits of coal and ore should be totally transformed into a non-industrialized area of agricultural land.

Since this memorandum of Stimson's is one of the clearest and most direct arguments against the deindustrialization of Germany and in favor of a moderate treatment of the enemy, it is quoted here at length:

I cannot conceive of such a proposition being either possible or effective and I can see enormous general evils coming from an attempt to so treat it. During the past eighty years of European history this portion of Germany was one of the most important sources of the raw materials upon which the industrial and economic livelihood of Europe was based. Upon the production which came from the raw materials of this region during those years, the commerce of Europe was very largely predicated. Upon that production Germany became the largest source of supply to no less than ten European countries. . . .

I can conceive of endeavoring to meet the misuse which Germany has recently made of this production by wise systems of control or trustee-

ship or even transfers of ownership to other nations. But I cannot conceive of turning such a gift of nature into a dust heap.

War is destruction. This war more than any previous war has caused gigantic destruction. The need for the recuperative benefits of productivity is more evident now than ever before throughout the world. Not to speak of Germany at all or even her satellites, our allies in Europe will feel the need of the benefit of such productivity if it should be destroyed. Moreover, speed of reconstruction is of great importance, if we hope to avoid dangerous convulsions in Europe.

.   .   .   .

My basic objection to the proposed methods of treating Germany which were discussed this morning was that in addition to a system of preventive and educative punishment they would add the dangerous weapon of complete economic oppression. Such methods, in my opinion, do not prevent war; they tend to breed war.[189]

2. *Two Meetings with the President*

On the following day, September 6, a White House meeting of the Cabinet Committee was called suddenly. Hull presented his memorandum of September 4 to the President, and said that while it had not been agreed to by the other members of the committee, it might serve as a basis for discussion.[190] Instead of a statement on Hull's memorandum, Morgenthau submitted a modified version of the document he had shown the President at Hyde Park.[191] Added at the end of it as sections 12 and 13 were the President's three suggested proscriptions against airplanes, uniforms, and parading. The other changes reflected Morgenthau's views. Besides the German armaments industry, "other key industries which are basic to military strength" should be destroyed. This was to include all industry in the Ruhr, which was to be "so weakened and controlled that it can not in the foreseeable future become an industrial area." All existing industry in the Ruhr should be dismantled within a period of six months after the cessation of hostilities. Included in the new version of the Morgenthau Plan was the specific proviso that "all equipment shall be removed from the mines and the mines closed"; apparently in explaining the application of this proposal, Morgenthau said it meant that the mines would be flooded and wrecked.[192] So much for the "weakening" of the Ruhr; it was to be "controlled" by an international security organization established by the projected United Nations organization, as had been suggested in White's draft of the Morgenthau Plan.

Morgenthau's changes in the Treasury proposals were all designed to make for an even sterner peace. His "key industries which are basic to military strength" has a broader sweep than White's "those parts of supporting industries having no other justification," and his proposals to destroy all industry in the Ruhr and to shut the coal mines were drastic supplements to the earlier plan.

The President had evidently read and pondered over Stimson's memorandum of the day before. At this meeting Stimson had the impression that Roosevelt was addressing most of his remarks to him. The President reverted to his proposal in the memorandum on the military government handbook, stating that "Germany could live happily and peacefully on soup from soup kitchens." However, he did not seem to accept Morgenthau's proposal for the dismantlement of the Ruhr, but argued instead that the Ruhr could furnish raw material for the British steel industry. Stimson pointed out the incompatibility of this scheme with dismantlement. Hull had shifted his position somewhat at this meeting, and Stimson felt that he made some progress with the President. Evidently Morgenthau drew the same conclusion, for he requested another meeting. That afternoon Stimson was in touch with Hull by telephone. He suggested that McCloy might try to prepare a compromise statement of the final section of Hull's September 4 draft on which he had taken issue. Hull "heartily" agreed.[193]

On the 9th, the Cabinet Committee met again with the President, the last time until after Roosevelt's return from his second Quebec Conference with Prime Minister Churchill. Although two hours had been allotted, the President could spend only forty-five minutes with them. Both Stimson and Morgenthau had, with the aid of McCloy and White, respectively, prepared memoranda which went over much of the same ground again. Morgenthau, attempting to deal with the point raised by the President at the previous meeting that the Ruhr could furnish raw material for British industry, argued that the destruction of German industry and mines would give England the markets it needed on the continent and cure the English depres-

sion in coal mining. In support of his argument he asserted that England had enough coal to supply its present output for five hundred years. Stimson regarded this as a misstatement of fact and considered the whole argument fatuous.[194] Furthermore, he was "unalterably opposed" to any such program. These resources constituted a natural and necessary asset for the productivity of Europe, he said, and the total obliteration of them was wholly wrong when the world was suffering from destruction and from want of production. The memorandum which Stimson introduced argued to this effect.

At this meeting Stimson and Morgenthau found themselves at odds on another important issue also. Morgenthau favored the execution of an agreed list of war criminals upon apprehension. Stimson insisted on observance at least of the rudimentary aspects of the Bill of Rights, which, he thought, included notification to the accused of the charge, the right to be heard, and within reasonable limits, the right to call witnesses in his defense. He was willing, however, to characterize such a trial as "summary." He indicated that he had an open mind on partition, and evidently would go along with the State Department proposals of September 4 to postpone decision on that question. He did not, as Morgenthau consistently advocated, approve of letting France have the Saar or the Rhineland. Indeed, in preparing for this meeting he had obtained the assistance of Jean Monnet, a prominent Frenchman working with the British mission in Washington, who privately favored the internationalization of the Ruhr and the Saar.[195] But Stimson would accept with certain modifications the State Department draft of September 4, as it was introduced at the first meeting with the President. To it he wished to add a prohibition of the manufacturing, design, or use of airplanes or flying. To the section of the document proposing postponement of a decision to partition Germany, he would add the Treasury provision that East Prussia and a portion of Silesia go to Poland and Russia, but suggesting internationalization for the Rhineland, the Ruhr, and the Saar. The question of rebuilding destroyed plants in Germany he would leave to the appropriate Allied or United Nations authority. The controversial last paragraph of the document he would rewrite, leaving out the clause: "the standard of living of the German population shall be held down to subsistence levels. . . ." The President again remained noncommittal on the opposing views advanced by Stimson and Morgenthau, although evidently Morgenthau's argument that Europe did not need a strong industrial Germany quite struck his fancy. He reiterated his view that the United States should not occupy the Southwest zone in Germany because he expected, as Admiral Leahy had predicted, a revolution in France which would jeopardize American lines of communication.[196] Hull remarked to Morgenthau that he agreed with the Treasury memorandum. That night the President left for Quebec and his conference with Churchill.

The following day there was a report in the press on the Cabinet Committee meeting with the President. Morgenthau's presence was explained in terms of "the important matter of providing new Reich currency."[197]

E. THE QUEBEC CONFERENCE

1. Morgenthau's Achievements

Morgenthau was with the President when he left Washington for Quebec, and it was decided that he would go along as far as Hyde Park, where Roosevelt planned to stop off for the night. The Secretary of the Treasury could then drive on to his own Dutchess County farm—perhaps to be nearer Quebec in case the President wanted him there. That day Roosevelt had indicated to the Cabinet Committee that if the financial situation was brought up at Quebec, he would want Morgenthau at the conference. (Earlier Hull had been invited to attend but had declined, evidently because he anticipated a row between Eden and Churchill in which he did not want to become involved—a premonition which proved accurate.[198]) As the result of riding to Hyde Park with his Dutchess County neighbor, Roosevelt went on to Quebec with the draft of the Morgenthau Plan which had been presented to him that day at the Cabinet Committee meeting.

On the afternoon of the 13th, in response to the President's request, Morgenthau arrived at Quebec, where he was soon joined by Harry White. That evening at dinner, in accordance with the President's arrangements, he presented the Treasury plan to Churchill and Eden. The Prime Minister reacted immediately by heaping vituperation upon Morgenthau for his sugges-

tions. The next day Morgenthau talked with Lord Cherwell, Churchill's personal adviser on scientific problems, and occasionally on other matters as well. He learned that Cherwell was interested in modifying Churchill's position, but it is not clear whether Cherwell had ideas equivalent to Morgenthau's in mind to begin with, or whether Morgenthau persuaded him, possibly with the same argument that had earlier appealed to Roosevelt—that the agrarianization of Germany would be to the advantage of Britain in her concern for restoring her balance of payments, since Germany would be eliminated as a competitor for export markets. Cherwell, in turn, convinced Churchill.[199] Cherwell and Morgenthau were assigned the task of writing a memorandum of understanding to be signed by Churchill and Roosevelt. They were instructed orally by Churchill, who summed up the discussion which he had been having with Roosevelt in regard to the future disposition of the Ruhr and the Saar. Paraphrasing this summary, the Cherwell-Morgenthau draft read:

> . . . He said that they would permit Russia and any other of our Allies to help themselves to whatever machinery they wished, that the industries of the Ruhr and in the Saar would be shut down, and that these two districts would be put under an international body which would supervise these industries to see that they would not start up again.
>
> This programme for eliminating the war-making industries in the Ruhr and in the Saar is part of a programme looking forward to diverting Germany into largely an agricultural country.

Dissatisfied with this statement, Churchill dictated another, which was approved as dictated. It read:

> At a conference between the President and the Prime Minister upon the best measures to prevent renewed rearmament by Germany, it was felt that an essential feature was the future disposition of the Ruhr and the Saar.
>
> The ease with which the metallurgical, chemical, and electrical industries in Germany can be converted from peace to war has already been impressed upon us by bitter experience. It must also be remembered that the Germans have devastated a large portion of the industries of Russia and of other neighboring Allies, and it is only in accordance with justice that these injured countries shall be entitled to remove the machinery they require in order to repair the losses they have suffered. The industries referred to in the Ruhr and in the Saar would therefore be necessarily put out of

action and closed down. It was felt that the two districts should be put under some body under the world organization which would supervise the dismantling of these industries and make sure that they were not started up again by some subterfuge. This programme for eliminating the war-making industries in the Ruhr and in the Saar is looking forward to converting Germany into a country primarily agricultural and pastoral in its character. The Prime Minister and the President were in agreement upon this program.

O.K.

F.D.R.

W.S.C.

15 9[200]

Exactly what was meant by this document was a question which received much attention thereafter. The Treasury officials, who at first regarded themselves as the victors in this contest over policy, later come to feel that Churchill had added the word "pastoral" as a device to ridicule and discredit the whole idea of agrarianizing Germany,[201] but this is not plausible. In comparison with the draft which Churchill rejected, the one which he dictated had less of the tone of spiteful punishment than that of caution and stern justice. And its use of the phrase "metallurgical, chemical, and electrical industries," if any significance could be attributed to it at all, could be regarded as an attempt to limit the area of applicability of the policy of deindustrialization and narrow the scope of the removals program; at least it seemed to exclude the coal mines from destruction. Actually the phrase was one that Morgenthau, who had picked it up from one of his advisers, had proposed; the authorship, however, did not settle the question of interpretation. In other respects, too, the memorandum could be read as a milder restatement of the Treasury proposal; aside from the vague proposal of international control in the Ruhr and the Saar, dismemberment was not mentioned, nor were any of the rest of Morgenthau's supplementary projects, which were not discussed at Quebec. Any attempt to make precise comparisons with earlier proposals would be futile; as subsequent events showed, however clear the intentions of Cherwell and Morgenthau, Roosevelt and Churchill were quite unclear about the full implications of the document they signed.

Eden was greatly upset by Churchill's formulation of the minute on Germany. They had a "heated discussion," and Churchill asked Eden not to take up the matter with the War Cabinet until he himself returned. (Eden's opposition surprised Morgenthau.[202])

Roosevelt and Churchill turned to other important problems. Morgenthau was delighted. He had achieved his chief goal. Germany would be converted "into a country primarily agricultural and pastoral in its character." And reparations, based solely on German aggression, could well result in complete removal of all German industry. Subsequent events were to cause Treasury officials to take a second look, but Morgenthau never changed his view that Roosevelt had endorsed his policy on Germany. It was White's view too, and he returned from Quebec determined to aid the British in their precarious financial condition—a problem which he had theretofore thought unimportant. However, Morgenthau had been deeply concerned about England ever since his visit to London when he was appalled by the devastation wrought by the V-bombs.

2. Hull's Reaction

On the following day, September 16, Hull received in Washington two memoranda from Roosevelt, one enclosing a copy of the minute on Germany, the second transmitting another agreement made on the 15th. From the first Hull concluded that the President and the Prime Minister had largely embraced Morgenthau's ideas; from the second he gained a suspicion as to why. It was concerned with financial arrangements with the United Kingdom. Hull had wanted to relate the continuance of lend-lease to British concessions on trade barriers, particularly imperial preference tariffs. The British lend-lease understanding, as a consequence, keenly disappointed him. The recorded conversation stated that the President had agreed that after the defeat of Germany, and while the war against Japan went on, Britain should continue to receive munitions assistance from us to the extent of $3.5 billion, and non-munitions assistance of $3 billion. The understanding further allowed Britain to use component parts and raw materials obtained on lend-lease in her export trade.[203]

It was Hull's view that Morgenthau had arranged this concession on trade policy for the British in exchange for their endorsement of his plan for Germany. He evidently found little significance in the President's covering letter to these documents which, referring to the one on the rearmament of Germany, said: "I think you will approve the general idea of not rehabilitating the Ruhr, Saar, etc." The President's statement may have reflected what was in his mind; it certainly did not reflect the text of the agreement: "not rehabilitating" is hardly the same as pastoralizing. It seems fairly certain that Hull's conclusions about the views and motivations of Roosevelt, though not unreasonable, were wrong, but it may well be that there was some degree of mutual understanding between Churchill and Morgenthau.[204]

While the President was at Quebec, Stimson and McCloy were not idle. McCloy spent one morning in New York seeking out support for Stimson's views. Two days later he and Stimson lunched with Lord Halifax, the British Ambassador, and Sir Alexander Cadogan, who was in Washington for the monetary conference at Dumbarton Oaks. However, the British officials, their hosts were disappointed to learn, were unwilling to commit themselves, even informally, on German policy questions. On September 14, the day the papers announced that Morgenthau had gone to Quebec, Stimson telephoned Hull to suggest that the Cabinet Committee continue its work in Morgenthau's absence in view of Eisenhower's urgent need for a directive. Stimson also pointed out that the State Department was in the same position with respect to instructions to Winant. Hull delayed his response until the next day when he replied that he would send his instructions for Winant to the President through Hopkins. (He thus hoped to abandon the Working Security Committee as hopeless.) The Cabinet Committee was to await Morgenthau's return.[205]

In the meantime, McCloy had been preparing, under Stimson's guide-lines, another memorandum to send the President. Based on a broad humanitarian argument, it concluded: "The sum total of the drastic political and economic steps proposed by the Treasury is an open confession of the bankruptcy of hope for a reasonable economic and political settlement of the causes of war."[206] This paper was sent to Hyde Park, to which the President had returned after the conference. Stimson had learned of the Quebec decisions before sending his third memorandum, but decided to do so anyway.

On September 20, while Roosevelt entertained Churchill at Hyde Park, the Cabinet Committee met in Hull's office to hear Morgenthau's story about Quebec. Besides the three Secretaries, White, McCloy, and Matthews were there. Morgenthau related his story. Churchill's initial reaction to his plan, he said, was like Stimson's earlier. He ascribed the Prime Minister's subsequent reversal to his acceptance of the argument, advanced by Morgenthau, that the elimination of German commercial competition would aid Britain. Stimson had been inclined to accept this explanation from his first hearing of the Quebec decisions;[207] but he asked Morgenthau if Churchill had accepted the plan because of eagerness to get continued lend-lease assistance. Morgenthau denied this (though Hull remained unconvinced), indicating that upon his arrival at Quebec he had found the President prepared to accept the Prime Minister's views without question, and that it was he who had insisted that a committee be set up to work out the problem where a more liberal trade policy could be kept in mind.[208]

This meeting marked the first explicit change in Hull's attitude toward the Morgenthau Plan, evidently brought about both by what actually happened at Quebec and by his suspicions about what happened there. He was disturbed to see such a setback to the liberal international trade policy which he had sponsored and supported over the long span of the Roosevelt Administration. While he had not found violent objection to the Morgenthau Plan theretofore, he bitterly objected to the way this fundamental problem of foreign policy, on which State Department committees and study groups had been working diligently since the first months of the war, had been settled through the efforts of the Secretary of the Treasury at an international conference where he was not present. These had been his feelings as the meeting began, and Morgenthau's remarks only aggravated them. For the Secretary of the Treasury explained that Eden's bitter opposition to the German memorandum upon his arrival at Quebec took him by surprise because Eden had not objected when Morgenthau had presented his views to him in London the previous month. Hull found this another indication of Morgenthau's propensity to interfere with matters properly the concern of the State Department.[209] At this meeting Hull expressed his acute shock at the procedure followed in the settlement of foreign affairs at Quebec. His sense of jurisdictional outrage seems to have sharpened his views on the Morgenthau Plan.

F. THE DRAFT INTERIM DIRECTIVE

1. The Setting for Negotiation

The Quebec agreement on Germany was, as we have seen, a significantly modified version of the Morgenthau Plan; but this fact was missed in the general surprise over the agreement within government circles at the time. McCloy's immediate interpretation of that agreement was recorded on September 18, just two days after he could have learned of it, by James Forrestal: ". . . the President had decided to go along with Morgenthau."[210] All the participants at the Cabinet Committee meeting two days later seemed to agree with McCloy's conclusion, although what Morgenthau told them there about how the agreement was drafted may have led some of them to question the magnitude of the Treasury victory. But for the time being, no one challenged its completeness.

It was in this atmosphere of triumph for the Morgenthau Plan that the Draft Interim Directive for Germany was given its final form on September 22. Inevitably, it reflected to some degree the advantageous position currently held by the advocates of the Morgenthau Plan. Yet even more than the Quebec agreement, it modified significantly the Treasury position.

On September 2, a week before President Roosevelt began his trip to Quebec, in a meeting preliminary to the proceedings of the Cabinet Committee on Germany, the three assistants agreed that a Draft Interim Directive on the treatment of Germany to Eisenhower for use immediately and until a long-term policy could be determined should be hurried through to completion, regardless of the outcome of higher-level discussions. In effect, they were deciding on a temporary abandonment of the attempts to get instructions to Winant on German policy via the Working Security Committee from which tripartite agreements could be negotiated in the EAC, and which in turn would provide the basis for military government by the three occupying powers. The Interim Directive was to be first an American policy agreement and then an Anglo-American directive, like CCS 551. Perhaps in order to assure that the agreement would not be repudiated after its completion, Treasury representatives were to be added to the group of State and War Department officials who were already working on it.

From the beginning the Treasury position in drafting the Interim Directive had certain advantages derived, first, from the President's blast at the military government handbook, second, from Roosevelt's willingness to include the Treasury in the Cabinet Committee deliberations over the treatment of Germany, third, from the Quebec agreement, which came at the climax of the drafting process, and finally, from the fact that CAD was now recoiling from the State Department's position on the reconstruction of the German economy. That is to say, while Stimson and McCloy were presenting their arguments for moderation in dealing with Germany, CAD was moving in the opposite direction. It had been rudely awakened by Eisenhower's fears that Germany would collapse, and by Morgenthau and the handbook incident to the extent to which military government planning had in effect committed the War Department to the reconstructionist views of the State Department. While they were bound to avoid other such traps, and their own position in these negotiations, as elsewhere, was circumscribed by military proprieties about civil policy-making, they were nevertheless likely, if only in compensation for their previous alliance with State, to side with the Treasury now.

The tendency for CAD, even after its awakening, to drift again over into a substantive policy position had already been demonstrated before the establishment of the Cabinet Committee. In late summer an attempt was made by the Office of War Information to draft a paper for guidance on long-range propaganda for Germany, which led CAD to state its own position. The fundamental principles of War Department policy, as CAD conceived them, were (1) "nonfraternization," and (2) the impression on the Germans of their war guilt. Specifically, General Hilldring objected to OWI's statement that at the end of the war German economic, social, and cultural reconstruction would begin.[211] In a similar vein, the senior member of the JPWC had written Brigadier General Vincent Meyer, by this time Winant's military adviser, to object to the reconstructionist approach to Germany. Evidently Meyer had already abandoned reconstructionist views included in papers drafted in his own office not two months before.[212]

The Treasury position also had certain weaknesses. The handbook blast and Morgenthau's inclusion in the Cabinet Committee had both come from his questioning of the approach being taken to military government in terms of its ultimate, or long-range implications; and the Quebec agreement, if not exclusively long range, was certainly general policy. But the Interim Directive was intended only for use until long-term policy could be agreed upon. It was to embody no policy. Indeed, while its purpose was to provide SHAEF with operating objectives until policies were settled, as the directive itself finally stated, those "objectives must be of short term and military character, in order not to prejudice whatever ultimate policies may be later determined upon."[213] Because the directive was intended to provide neutral guidance only, Treasury efforts to write elements of the Morgenthau Plan into it could therefore be opposed on the ground that the directive was not intended to embody policy. The neutrality of the document, then, was a defense against the Morgenthau Plan proposals which were available to its State and War Department opponents—although the War Department's intense interest in completing the directive as soon as possible made that argument of less use to War than to State.

2. The Drafting Process Before Word from Quebec

The drafting process began promptly on September 3, when the War Department made available to the new Treasury members a draft "Interim Directive to SCAEF Regarding the Military Government of Germany in the Period Immediately Following the Cessation of Organized Resistance." The Draft Directive provided that the objectives of the military occupation were to be short-term and military in character. It avoided unsettled policy questions or questions which seemed to be under consideration at higher levels by emphasizing the discretion of the military commander. Although the War Department, particularly CAD,

where this document was under consideration, was moving rapidly away from wanting the Army to assume responsibility for German society, it should be noted that this fact was not made clear in the document. Had it done so, undoubtedly Dunn, Riddleberger, and their associates in the State Department would have objected strenuously to it. Instead, while providing for a positive function for the Army in the occupation of Germany which reflected the earlier War Department position, the wide discretion proposed to be conferred on SCAEF would allow him to avoid any responsibility for maintaining the functioning of the German economy and government.

Two days later, September 5, William H. Taylor of the Treasury Division of Monetary Research had produced a new version of the Interim Directive which reflected the views of his Department. It omitted authorization for SCAEF to make arrangements with Russian field commanders concerning the tripartite occupation of Germany. It added a provision that any infraction of occupation rules should be punished severely. And it allowed for the reopening only of elementary schools, after they had been purged, and not of secondary schools and colleges. But SCAEF was still given broad authority.

In financial and economic matters, however, the Treasury draft differed sharply from the War Department draft, which would have allowed SCAEF to control financial institutions, industry, agriculture, utilities, and transportation and communications facilities, in order to preserve a functioning economic system and prevent disease and unrest. The Treasury proposal, in contrast, simply left out the portion dealing with the control of financial institutions; and sought to limit severely the section on economic policy. It provided:

1. In the imposition and maintenance of economic controls, German authorities will to the fullest extent practicable be ordered to proclaim and assume administration of such controls. Thus it should be brought home to the German people that the responsibility for the administration of such controls and for any breakdowns in those controls, will rest with themselves and their own authorities.

2. In furtherance of the policy stated in the previous paragraph, you, as U. S. member of the Control Council, should use your efforts to see that the Allies intervene in the operation of the

German economy only for the following purposes:

a. Assuring the safety of your forces and the satisfaction of their needs.

b. Assuring the immediate cessation of production to the iron and steel, metallurgical, electrical and chemical industries, insofar as their equipment has been used for production of implements of war.

c. Assuring, to the extent that it is feasible, the production and maintenance of goods and services essential (1) for the prevention or alleviation of epidemic or serious disease and serious civil unrest and disorder which would endanger the occupying forces and (2) for further military operations to be conducted in other theaters (but only to the extent that specific directives of higher authority call for such goods or services).

d. Preventing the dissipation or sabotage of German resources and equipment which may be required for relief, restitution, or reparation to any of the Allied countries, pending a decision by the appropriate Allied governments whether and to what extent German resources or equipment will be used for such purposes.

. . . .

Except for the purposes specified above, you will take no steps (1) looking toward the economic rehabilitation of Germany, nor (2) designed to maintain or strengthen the German economy. Except to the extent necessary (1) to accomplish the purposes set out above, and (2) to assure thorough elimination of discriminatory Nazi practices in actual operation of economic controls, the responsibility for and the task of dealing with such economic problems as price controls, rationing, unemployment, production, reconstruction, distribution, consumption, housing or transportation will be left in German hands, [sic] You should, however, take such steps as may be necessary to assure that economic controls are operated in conformity with the above purposes and the general objectives of military government.[214]

Four meetings of State, Treasury, and War officials were held between September 2, when it was agreed that the drafting of an Interim Directive to SCAEF should be accelerated, and September 22, when, in an all-day meeting of State, Treasury, and War Department officials, an Interim Directive was set in the final form in which it was later transmitted to Eisenhower. Three of the preliminary meetings were held before the announcement of the Quebec agreement; the last of them was held on Sunday evening, September 17, the day after Hull and Stimson received the news from Quebec. Representing the War Department were McCloy,

his executive officer, Colonel Harrison A. Gerhardt, Adrian Fisher, an assistant, and three officers from the Civil Affairs Division: William Chanler, David Marcus, and John Boettiger, a son-in-law of the President. The Treasury sent its Under Secretary, Daniel Bell, an Assistant to the Secretary, John W. Pehle, and Ansel Luxford and Josiah DuBois. Riddleberger and Dunn represented State. Except for Bell, Boettiger, and Gerhardt, all the Treasury and War representatives were lawyers.

Since September 5, when the Treasury completed the draft quoted above, the Interim Directive had been through several revisions at the hands of Treasury and War Department officials. The Treasury had continued to insist on its clause requiring severe punishment for the infraction of military government regulations, adding to the provision which allowed the use of either military government officers or Germans in occupation administration the requirement of severe punishment for Germans thus employed who refused to comply with the instructions of the occupation authorities. From early in War Department civil affairs training and planning, an accepted, if perhaps unrealistic, principle was that no political activity would be allowed, and military government was not to become identified with any political group. The Treasury insisted that to this be added a provision empowering SCAEF to dismiss and return to his homeland any officer who violated this provision. In contrast to the severe tone of the punishment and dismissal provisions, and the restrictive character of its amendments of the economic and financial policy provisions, Treasury saw to it that the responsibilities of SCAEF for political prisoners of the Nazis, and to allied nationals and prisoners of war, were positively and clearly stated. These, then, were the major developments in War-Treasury negotiations by the time of the September 17 meeting.[215]

3. *The Meeting of September 17*

In the draft it submitted on the 17th, the Treasury continued the tactic of filling earlier War Department drafts with sterner stuff. Simultaneously, its changes connoted a concern lest the broad grant of authority to SCAEF be itself the basis for a soft occupation policy. The sterner stuff was added, as it had been earlier, through greater details in provisions; the other loophole for softness was drawn smaller by reducing the discretion allowed SCAEF in the administration of the directive —an attempt perhaps to force the compliance of an agent expected to be hostile.

In earlier proposals SCAEF would have been allowed to ignore at his own discretion the categories of people to be arrested that were set forth in the directive. The Treasury wanted to require him to report back to Washington, giving reasons why he wished to exclude any categories. Presumably he would not be allowed to ignore them without approval from Washington. Similarly, SCAEF had been empowered to make credits available to the Reichsbank or its branches, thereby establishing it as a central bank. The Treasury wanted to make it necessary for him to clear the matter with the Combined Chiefs of Staff. Finally, the statement of the aims of the occupation was to be altered by replacing "lasting peace" as an aim with the objective of preventing Germany from ever becoming a threat to the peace of the world again; and by making as essential steps in the realization of the aims of occupation the elimination of Nazism and militarism and the immediate punishment of war criminals. Thus, an attempt was made in the redrafting of the directive to reduce the discretion of the Supreme Commander even with respect to the general goals of the occupation.[216]

Though it was concerned with "details," the sterner stuff dealt with basic policy. Denazification was to be broadened from applying only to Nazis to include Nazi sympathizers and anyone in key positions. And Treasury wanted SCAEF's authority over German finances, both public and private, further reduced. All of these proposals from the Treasury Department were accepted in the September 17 draft.

As has been noted, the Quebec agreement on Germany reached Washington on Saturday, the 16th. Probably available to the drafters of the Interim Directive on the 17th, the reinforcement which it seemed to give the Treasury position in these negotiations may well account for State's acceptance on that day of all the amendments proposed by Treasury. The same amendments presumably appealed to the War Department because they were intended to reduce the responsibility of SCAEF. The War Department had attempted to withdraw from

responsibility for economic and social collapse in Germany, but, by maximizing SCAEF's discretionary powers, had tried to avoid as well a controversy over policy. There were disadvantages in this approach. Discretionary powers are authority, and authority implies responsibility—the very thing which CAD wanted to reduce. If the policy issue were to be avoided by enlarging discretion, the reduction of SCAEF's responsibility towards German society could not be clearly established. Thus the proposed limitations on SCAEF's discretionary authority had an appeal to CAD. And the Treasury, which had no inhibitions about involvement with policy, was interested in the same objective. This was the point at which Treasury and War Department interests coincided, at least as well as can be understood a decade and a half later.

The main issue raised and still left unsettled in the Sunday evening meeting was the exact wording of the statement on economic policy (in the form of the directive it was called "Appendix 'C' "). The Treasury had recommended beginning the economic directive with a statement wholly negative in tone. It provided that no steps looking toward the economic rehabilitation of Germany were to be taken unless and until further directions were given. SCAEF was not to assume responsibility, except as otherwise directed, for such economic problems as price controls, rationing, unemployment, production, reconstruction, distribution, consumption, housing or transportation, or take any measures designed to maintain or strengthen the German economy. These responsibilities, the Treasury proposal indicated, would continue to remain with the German people. It would empower SCAEF, however, to impose such economic measures and take such other action as he deemed necessary for the accomplishment of the objectives of the occupation or to prevent serious civil unrest and disorder which would endanger the occupying forces.[217]

Both War and State Department officials objected to this draft, the State representatives, however, the most strenuously,[218] for they continued to hold to the position that the German economy should not be allowed to break down, but should be used for the further prosecution of the war. (Actually to most State Department officers the long-term objective of establishing a regenerated Germany was probably equally important.)

4. *Final Agreements on the Directive*

McCloy was more concerned about getting a directive settled upon for the present than about furthering a particular viewpoint. By this date—September 17—the Allied armies were outrunning their supplies, but a collapse of German resistance still seemed possible. Indeed, on this very day, Montgomery was launching the airborne attack over the lower Rhine; if that succeeded, the road to Berlin might well be open. Under the circumstances, McCloy was under strong compulsion to get some sort of directive approved and forwarded to Eisenhower without delay. The sense of urgency was reflected in the directive when it was approved a few days later; its opening words were:

In the event that Rankin "C" conditions obtain in Germany or that the German forces are either defeated or surrender before you have received a directive containing policies agreed upon by the three governments of the U. S., U. K., and U. S. S. R.[219]

Rankin "C," it will be recalled, was the plan for action if Germany collapsed—a plan prepared by COSSAC a year before, for the first Quebec Conference in August 1943.

The need for speed limited McCloy's freedom of action. So did the Quebec agreement, for it was the most authoritative statement of the President's line of thought. And so also did the War Department's new position on the responsibility of SCAEF for the German economy. All that McCloy could appropriately seek at this point was a directive that would be consistent with his conception of military needs and responsibilities, although his own concern, like Stimson's, went further. While he favored a strong denazification program, he was convinced that Germany would have to be reconstructed. He had done much of the drafting on the three Stimson memoranda to the President. In fact, he wrote all of the third one, which took such a broad humanitarian position. Yet necessarily in his negotiations with Treasury regarding the draft directive he had conceded much to the views of Morgenthau; but he had kept in the directive most of its positive tone. Following the meeting on the 17th, he had a

draft prepared which had the effect of placing the Treasury paragraph on economic policy described above, which was designed to make sure that the German economy would *not* be controlled, as an exception to a statement of the purposes for which the German economy *would* be controlled. It read:

1. You shall assume such control of existing German industrial, agricultural, utility, communication and transportation facilities, supplies, and services, as are necessary for the following purposes:

   a. Assuring the immediate cessation of the production, acquisition or development of implements of war.

   b. Assuring, to the extent that it is feasible, the production and maintenance of goods and services essential (1) for the prevention or alleviation of epidemic or serious disease and serious civil unrest and disorder which would endanger the occupying forces and the accomplishment of the objectives of the occupation; and (2) for the prosecution of the war against Japan (but only to the extent that specific directives of higher authority call for such goods or services).

   c. Preventing the dissipation or sabotage of German resources and equipment which may be required for relief, restitution, or reparation to any of the allied countries, pending a decision by the appropriate Allied governments whether and to what extent German resources or equipment will be used for such purposes. Except for the purposes specified above, you will take no steps looking toward the economic rehabilitation of Germany nor designed to maintain or strengthen the German economy. Except to the extent necessary to accomplish the purposes set out above, the responsibility for such economic problems as price controls, rationing, unemployment, production, reconstruction, distribution, consumption, housing or transportation will remain with the German people and the German authorities.[220]

Treasury accepted this new draft, and it was sent on to the officials concerned in State.[221] They were not satisfied with it. Failing to obtain their approval, on the 19th McCloy asked them to prepare a draft of their own.[222] At a final meeting held on the 22nd—two days after Morgenthau's triumphal meeting in Hull's office—State's draft was considered. The meeting lasted most of the day, although little was done to change the draft directive, and its economic policy sections raised the only point of controversy involving the draft itself. Since the previous meeting, however, the full implications of Quebec were becoming more evident. The Cabinet Committee meeting on the 20th had left Hull outraged at Morgenthau's usurpation of State Department responsibilities, even though Hull had found little in the Morgenthau proposals to disagree with in earlier Cabinet Committee meetings. His principal assistants, who had disagreed with the substance of Treasury policy from the beginning, now had reason to expect the backing of their chief. With reference to the draft economic directive, as approved by War and Treasury, they insisted that nothing in it should be construed to mean that the War Department intended to introduce economic chaos into Germany.[223] They demanded a less ambiguous statement in the directive to this effect than it contained. (They did not get it. They settled instead for a letter from Hull to Stimson setting forth the State Department reservation on the Interim Directive. The reservation stated that nothing in the economic directive was to be interpreted as preventing the Supreme Commander from retaining or imposing such economic controls as he might deem essential to the safety and health of the occupying forces. Since this was merely the reiteration of an idea which occurred in several places throughout the directive, the State Department received little comfort or reassurance for its misgivings.)

The Treasury officials at the meeting also attempted to adjust to the new situation. State had been forced to rely on the tactics of entrenchment, but Morgenthau's assistants could advance—or foray—with confidence. According to a State Department participant, the Treasury representatives

made it altogether clear that in their opinion the Treasury Department, as a result of the establishment of the Cabinet Committee on Germany, should be consulted on all phases of German problems, including both political and economic. They participated vigorously in the discussion on the political directive and insinuated that the Treasury plan for the treatment of Germany had received the approval of the Cabinet Committee and the blessing of the President. They stated flatly that the economic documents, as approved by the Executive Committee on Economic Foreign Policy, had been repudiated both by Secretary Morgenthau and Secretary Hull and that no further attention was to be given to these papers.

[This meant, it should be noted, that they had picked up Hull's misunderstanding of Riddleberger's September 4 memorandum.] They requested that certain other confidential memoranda be transmitted to them at once and implied that henceforth all such material should be immediately made available to the Treasury Department. In general, they took the line that henceforth the Treasury must be consulted on all important matters respecting Germany and that that was the purpose of the Cabinet Committee.[224]

With the approval of the State Department secured by the inclusion of Hull's letter of reservation, on the following day (September 23) the drafting of the Interim Directive to SCAEF Regarding the Military Government of Germany in the immediate post-defeat period was completed. It was cleared with Roosevelt by Hopkins and sent to Winant in London on September 27 for background information and guidance, but not for transmission to the EAC. Winant was informed that it had been prepared by the War and State Departments and concurred in by the Treasury Department, but it had "not as yet been approved" by CCAC; it was intended to cover an interim period after the defeat or surrender of Germany and before a directive containing policies agreed upon by the U. S., Britain, and the Soviet Union had been prepared.[225]

The Interim Directive was recommended by JCS for consideration by CCS on September 24, 1944, and in that transmittal it was given the file number JCS 1067. It was sent to Eisenhower at the same time it was forwarded to Winant. Originally intended as a directive from the Combined Chiefs of Staff to Eisenhower as the Supreme Commander of the Allied Expeditionary Forces, the Interim Directive continued to be known by its JCS file number for it was opposed by the British when it was considered in the CCS on October 3, somewhat to the surprise of War Department officials, who anticipated difficulties with the British Cabinet instead. Indeed, on that same day Stimson had enlisted the President's help in gaining prompt action from Churchill.[226] Eisenhower had now been provided with stopgap policy guidance which was supposed to have the effect of keeping his administration of occupied Germany from prejudicing one way or the other the implementation of a long-term policy for the treatment of Germany, once that policy was established. But since the British would not accept JCS 1067, it did not provide policy guidance to Eisenhower as SCAEF, but only as the ranking American military commander in Europe and only with effect in the U. S. zone of Germany. In a sense, its interim nature was thereby compounded, for it could be superseded, not only by a long-term policy, but also by a short-term policy agreed to by the British and American military chiefs, and not only by a new policy for one-third of Germany, but by a policy for two-thirds, or even all of Germany.

G. THE AFTERMATH OF QUEBEC

1. Status of the Morgenthau Plan, October 1, 1944

The extent of the Treasury victory at Quebec and in the Interim Directive to Eisenhower was deceptively clear. Both State and War Department officials interpreted Quebec as a victory for Morgenthau, though the text of the Quebec agreement did moderate Morgenthau's proposals considerably. A second and equally important victory for the Treasury Department was the Interim Directive, which was drafted with the assumption that the President had endorsed the Morgenthau Plan at Quebec. But the Quebec agreement was rejected by the British Cabinet (a fact which Morgenthau would never recognize). And the Interim Directive, rejected by CCS, never received combined command status. It could be at best only a temporary and limited victory for Treasury, for it was only intended to stand as a policy guide even for the American forces until a more permanent directive could be drafted. Moreover, while it contained much of the Morgenthau Plan, the Treasury policies were weakened by qualifying and escape clauses. And beyond that, of course, since the British controlled the Ruhr, and the Russians Silesia, JCS 1067 could hardly constitute a major move toward full-scale agrarianization!

At the end of September 1944, the future of the Treasury Department position even for treatment of the United States' third of Germany could be determined by the answers to these three questions:

(1) How firmly would Morgenthau's victory at Quebec stand?

(2) How long would the Interim Directive last? and

(3) Would the War Department or any one else, carry out the Morgenthau Plan as it was contained in the Interim Directive or its successor?

Each of these questions exposed a threat to the Treasury position. The threat of the first, that Roosevelt would either clarify or withdraw his seeming endorsement at Quebec of Morgenthau's views, was compounded by the impending election and the hostile public reaction to the Morgenthau Plan. It might be minimized or eliminated by obtaining subsequent commitments to the Treasury position from the President. The threat of the second was that a longer-term occupation directive which would succeed the Interim Directive might not contain as much of the Treasury viewpoint as did the latter, which was drafted in the full flush of Treasury's alleged victory at Quebec. This threat could be countered by making sure either that the replacement of the Interim Directive be postponed or that the long-term directive not be substantially different from the Interim Directive. The third threat, that the War Department would make the occupation easy on the Germans because, as Colonel Bernstein had put it, of its desire to do things well, or would depart from the hard-peace views of the Treasury for some other reason, could be countered by ensuring that the Army authorities charged with carrying out occupation policy would be given a minimum of discretion to depart from the Treasury tenets, or, alternatively, that the occupation authorities were sympathetic to Treasury views.

The Treasury's capability of meeting the first threat was high. Morgenthau's personal relations with Roosevelt assured him an advantage over Stimson and the ailing Hull. In meeting the second threat, the Treasury could count on the force of inertia in policy-making, the attitude of the War Department, and its own strict internal policy discipline. The Interim Directive represented a settlement (on restricted terms) of a controversial problem within the American government; to try to alter it would be to reopen the controversy. Since the directive was a document of compromises, almost as much could be lost as gained by challenging the settlement it had made. And the War Department's primary explicit goal was not any particular policy, but policy determination. Army officials would view with alarm any effort to reopen the controversy. Hence, the Treasury Department could count on the War Department as an ally in the strategy of preserving the Treasury victories of September by tying the substance of subsequent occupation directives to the Interim Directive. Finally, in any test of negotiating capabilities with other departments in the Executive Branch, the Treasury Department could count as an asset its internal policy discipline, which assured it that its bargaining position would not be weakened by internal dissent.

The third threat, that the War Department would take advantage of the ambiguities of the Interim Directive, and of the discretion which it had insisted would be left to its field commanders, to fail to carry out the hard peace terms of the Morgenthau Plan as they were incorporated into the Interim Directive, could be minimized by continuing the Treasury participation in the drafting of policy papers concerned with the treatment of Germany and by direct influence upon the occupation officers themselves. The Treasury's continuing participation in the drafting of policy papers was assured, if not by the relevancy of its interest, then by its power to reopen a policy settlement with which it did not agree, as had been demonstrated in August 1944. By participating, the Treasury could work for minimizing the discretion allowed the Army in administering policy, and hence its capability of departing from policy settlements in favor of the Treasury which were made in Washington. At the same time, the Treasury Department was favorably situated to influence the actual administration of occupation policy by the War Department through the rather large number of civil affairs officers recruited by the Army from Treasury as financial experts who continued to look to Treasury for policy guidance.

2. *The Disengagement of Public Interest*

While the treatment of Germany was the subject of discussion at several levels throughout the month of September, both interdepartmentally and internationally, it was not discussed authoritatively in public until after the press brought some of this activity to public attention. To be sure, the first Cabinet Committee meeting with Roosevelt was reported with no awareness of the nature of the problem discussed, or of the personalities involved. By September 11, however, the press was able to identify the "hard" and "soft" peace split, and to single Morgenthau out as advocate of the former. In reporting the controversy over dismemberment, the *New York Times* correspondent, Turner Catledge, showed a familiarity with the official State Department position which could only indicate a pro-State leak. This was countered on September 21 in Drew Pearson's column with a strongly pro-Treasury version of the military government handbook incident of the previous month, including the President's letter to Stimson. Roosevelt was quoted, upon being presented with the handbook by Morgenthau and White, as saying that "there's not going to be any industry in Germany to control."[227] Then on Sunday, the 24th, the story of the Cabinet split came out, including a pro-Treasury version of Quebec; and the *Wall Street Journal* published a fairly complete summary of the Morgenthau Plan. While the press reaction was generally divided, both Morgenthau and the President—for he was closely identified with the Morgenthau Plan in the newspaper accounts—came in for a good deal of criticism. Like most of the government officials, the reporters had no clear realization of the fact that the Plan as such was really not adopted in Quebec. The following day, September 25, Morgenthau met with White and other assistants who had been concerned with drafting the Treasury Plan to decide what the Department should do in view of the widespread publicity. Despite strong sentiment among the group in favor of further defense of the Treasury side of the story, Morgenthau decided against it. He cancelled his press conference for the day, and insisted that his staff refrain from giving out information to the press.[228]

On the same day Hull issued a statement to the press on the post-war German situation. It did not deny the reported split, nor did it mention the Morgenthau Plan. It read:

The whole question of dealing with the post-war German situation has been receiving attention by each of the governments most interested, and that includes this government and the State Department. It would serve no purpose to say more at this time, except that the higher officials of the governments concerned will reach mutual understandings, I hope, at an early stage. It is very necessary that we wait until we know the true conclusions they reach.[229]

This statement was widely interpreted as confirmation of the Cabinet split.

On the following day Roosevelt dissolved the Cabinet Committee and issued a statement in an attempt to calm the public and editorial furor raised by publication of news of the Cabinet split and the Morgenthau Plan. The statement read:

The President announced today that the Cabinet Committee which he had appointed some time ago to advise him regarding certain aspects of the American policy towards Germany after the collapse or surrender of that country, had completed its responsibility and accomplished its purpose.

First, it had considered the American recommendation to the CCS.

Second, it had submitted its views to the President. These several memoranda will now receive the consideration of the President and the Secretary of State, and American representatives conferring with our allies in respect to the long-range policy will be advised of the position of this government at an appropriate date.

Both this statement and Hull's of the previous day are notable for their attempt to disengage public attention from the problem of post-war Germany, rather than to educate or inform public opinion, and indicative of the fact that the President particularly was unwilling to determine future policy. In further pursuance of this policy, publication of the Interim Directive to Eisenhower, planned for September 27, 1944, when the Supreme Commander received it, and already prepared for the press, was cancelled. It was not published until over a year later, during which time its secrecy was purportedly based on considerations of national security. The version that was finally published in October 1945 was the second revision of JCS 1067, issued on April 25, 1945.

At the same time, "high administration sources" were giving out information to the press that the President did not favor the Morgenthau Plan, and never really had adopted its basic philosophy.[230] The press, on September 28 and 29, carried several different reports either indicating a change of heart by the President or clarifying his position. On the 28th, Morgenthau again cancelled his press conference, but managed to send a note to the President indicating the strongly favorable response to his Plan indicated by his mail.[231] He also had a talk with Elmer Davis, head of OWI, who asked how fifteen million Germans would be kept from starving; Morgenthau arranged an appointment for Davis with White.[232]

The next day, September 29, Roosevelt made public in his press conference a letter to Leo T. Crowley, FEA Administrator. It instructed Crowley to speed up the studies that FEA had under way to determine what should be done with the German economy after surrender. These studies were intended to devise means of controlling the power and capacity of the German economy to make war in the future.[233] Asked about the Cabinet split, he replied that "every story that came out was essentially untrue in its basic facts."

The President's letter of September 29 to Crowley was his final effort to disassociate himself from the Morgenthau Plan in the public eye, and to disengage public interest in German policy. He was largely successful, except for sporadic attempts by the Republican Presidential nominee to make the Morgenthau Plan a campaign issue. The Morgenthau Plan as a campaign issue will be described later. First, however, it is necessary to go back to the period immediately following the Quebec Conference when the State Department began its efforts to modify the commitment which the President had made there to the Treasury Department's views on how Germany should be treated after the war.

3. The State Department Presses Its Case

Stimson had argued against Morgenthau's views in a series of three memoranda to the President. Then, after Morgenthau's triumphant return from Quebec, Hull, having returned to the moderate position of his own Department, assumed the mantle of advocacy. On September 25, the day his press statement was distributed, he sent to the President a memorandum which took the line of argument previously developed in State that certain specific channels had to be followed for the settlement of policy concerning Germany, since the matter had ultimately to be settled on a tripartite basis. The memorandum suggested that the United States should as the next step have the firm agreement of the British and Soviet governments on a policy for Germany—implying without saying so that this would not be the policy of the Quebec agreement.

We have thus far acted on the basis that every action followed with respect to Germany, particularly in the post-hostilities period, would be on an agreed tripartite basis. It has also been our understanding that the Soviet Government has also acted on this general assumption, and of course the European Advisory Commission, established by the Moscow Conference, was set up for the purpose of working out the problems of the treatment of Germany. We must realize that the adoption of any other basis of procedure would enormously increase the difficulties and responsibilities not only for our soldiers in the immediate military occupation period but also of our officials in the control period following.

It implied quite correctly that the British government might not stick by Churchill's commitment at Quebec on German policy: "We have not yet had any indication that the British Government would be in favor of complete eradication of German industrial productive capacity in the Ruhr and Saar." It suggested that the State Department sound out the views of the British and the Russians, either through the EAC or otherwise. Hull's assistants concerned with German affairs drafted this document,[234] and it was presumably as satisfying to them as to him.

At about the same time, Hull went to the White House with a copy of the Morgenthau Plan and the September 15 memorandum from Quebec. He made several points which, taken together, indicated the extent to which he had come to accept State Department staff work on Germany, and had departed from his brief association with Morgenthau's views. He told the President that the Morgenthau Plan was not prepared by experts on the subject. Forty per cent of the German population could not be supported just on the land of Germany, and would have to die. And he summarized the present policy of his own Department: Germany should be kept under military control until the theories of Nazism and racial superiority had been completely eliminated—possibly twenty-five or fifty years. And the standard of living of Germany should be kept below the average of neighboring populations and should be raised as German ideas on human rights,

individual liberty, freedom, and peace improved.[235]

Hull's policy still had important differences from the policies planned by State Department officials over the previous two years. They had not expected military occupation to be of very long duration. Their long-range goal was, like Hull's, democratization. But they regarded a long period of occupation and an enforced minimum standard of living as incompatible with this objective. Presumably, Hull was taking into account the President's desire for "hard" treatment of the Germans.

Hull then expressed his suspicions that the British had agreed to Morgenthau's proposals because Morgenthau agreed to help them get their $6.5 billion lend-lease arrangement from the United States. He concluded his argument by restating the reasons why the State Department should handle such negotiations, and by pointing out to the President that he would be injured politically if he were connected in the public mind with the Morgenthau proposals.

Hull noted that Roosevelt's only reply to his comments was that he had not actually committed himself to the Treasury proposals.[236]

On the day following his talk with Hull, Roosevelt dissolved the Cabinet Committee.

4. *Further Views of the President*

Roosevelt telephoned Stimson on September 27 to comment on Stimson's third memorandum. He said that he did not really intend to try to make Germany a purely agricultural country, but said that he had wanted to pull Britain out of a post-war depression, using the familiar argument of Morgenthau that Germany should be eliminated as a commercial competitor of Britain. Stimson was sure that Roosevelt felt he had made a mistake in supporting Morgenthau and was trying to get out of it, an interpretation confirmed by Robert E. Sherwood who saw a good deal of Roosevelt after Roosevelt's return to Washington.[237]

Two days later, on September 29, the President sent a memorandum to Hull. Replying to the suggestion in Hull's memorandum of September 25 that since tripartite agreement would be necessary for any policy concerning the treatment of Germany, Britain and Russia should be sounded out for their views, it read:

I do not think that in the present stage any good

would be served by having the State Department or any other Department sound out the British and Russian views on the treatment of German industry. Most certainly it should not be taken up with the European Advisory Commission which, in a case like this, is on a tertiary and not even a secondary level.

The real nub of the situation is to keep Britain from going into complete bankruptcy at the end of the war.

Somebody has been talking not only out of turn to the papers or [sic] on facts which are not fundamentally true.

No one wants to make Germany a wholly agricultural nation again, and yet somebody down the line has handed this out to the press. I wish we could catch and chastise him.

You know that before the war Germany was not only building up war manufacture, but was also building up enough of a foreign trade to finance rearming sufficiently and still maintain enough international credit to keep out of international bankruptcy.

I just cannot go along with the idea of seeing the British Empire collapse financially, and Germany at the same time building up a potential rearmament machine to make another war possible in twenty years. Mere inspection of plants will not prevent that.

But no one wants "complete eradication of German industrial productive capacity in the Ruhr and Saar."

It is possible, however, in those two particular areas to enforce rather complete controls. Also, it must not be forgotten that outside of the Ruhr and Saar, Germany has many *other* areas and facilities for turning out large exports.

In regard to the Soviet Government, it is true that we have no idea as yet what they have in mind, but we have to remember that in their occupied territory they will do more or less as they wish. We cannot afford to get into a position of merely recording protests on our part unless there is some chance of some of the protests being heeded.

I do not intend by this to break off or delay negotiations with the Soviet Government over Lend-Lease either on the contract basis or the proposed Fourth Protocol basis. This, however, does not immediately concern the German industrial future.[238]

The President's memorandum revealed more of attitude than of policy, although its readers in the State Department thought that it "modified appreciably" his views as expressed at Quebec.[239] Perhaps his reference to potential German resurgence in twenty years reflected some preference on his part for the Morgenthau Plan's promise of quick action with permanent results, just as the general tone of the plan was consistent with his clear desire for stern action, though the comment on controls in the Ruhr and the Saar points in the opposite direction. Yet, in this very personal document, it is hard not to believe that Roosevelt's key sentiment for his reaction to the specific Morgenthau proposals was expressed in the second paragraph: "the real nub of the situation is to keep Britain from going into complete bankruptcy at the end of the war." This notion stood by itself; only when he repeated it did the President link it with his desire to prevent German rearmament. But equally characteristic was his unwillingness to enter into negotiations with Russia about Germany before surrender.

Roosevelt's note was somehow delayed in transmittal. On October 1, two days after it was written but two days before it actually reached the State Department, Hull went to the President with a memorandum, also written on September 29.[240] In the opening paragraph of this paper Hull remarked that the Cabinet Committee had never reached agreement, and added that the President's memorandum of September 15 "seems to reflect largely the opinions of the Secretary of the Treasury." Then: "I feel that I should therefore submit to you the line of thought that has been developing in the State Department on this matter." (Indirectly Hull was suggesting that the President was not really committed to Morgenthau's Plan or the Quebec agreement.)

The body of the memorandum consisted of two parts. The first was a familiar recital of the status of organizational and procedural negotiations on Germany in EAC. The second dealt with the unresolved policy issues, and emphasized that "these objectives will have to be worked out with our principal Allies if they are to be applied throughout the German Reich." Then followed a restatement, with little modification, of Riddleberger's memorandum of September 4, as amended by Stimson on September 9, which set forth the State Department's position on the post-war treatment of Germany: (moderate) denazification, controls over communications and education, postponement of a decision on partition. The long-term economic objectives were "to render Germany incapable of waging war," and "to eliminate permanently German economic domination of Europe" (as in Stimson's draft of September 9). The short-term objective was reparations. The proposals for achieving these objectives were more sharply drawn than those in the early State Department papers, and reflected some of the negotiations over JCS 1067: plants incapable of conversion to peaceful uses were to be destroyed, the rest were to be converted; German economic self-sufficiency would be eliminated; controls would be established over foreign trade and key industries, while the power of the large industrialists and landowners would be reduced.

One paragraph dealt unsympathetically with reparations and another set forth the need for long-term controls. Only in the final paragraph was there any very clear reflection of the President's stern attitude. It read:

It is of the highest importance that the standard of living of the German people in the early years be such as to bring home to them that they have lost the war and to impress on them that they must abandon all their pretentious theories that they are a superior race created to govern the world. Through lack of luxuries we may teach them that war does not pay.[241]

On October 3, Stimson lunched with the President. Roosevelt by this time was willing to blame the whole mid-September furor over Germany on a "boner" committed by Morgenthau. In explaining away his own position, he now turned, not to Morgenthau's argument that Britain would be aided by having Germany eliminated as a competitor for export markets, but to a rationale with more positive implications: Britain would need German steel to keep its own manufacturing going. The rest of the products of the Ruhr would be left to Germany. Roosevelt was so affirmative in his assertions that Stimson read him parts of the Quebec memorandum of understanding, which had been marked "O.K. F. D. R." The President was frankly staggered by this and said he had no idea how he could have initialed it; that he had evidently done it without much thought.[242]

5. *The Quebec Minute Undermined*

Stimson sent Hull an account of this meeting, and Hull also had before him the President's memorandum of September 29, quoted above, which reached the State Department on October 3. Hull considered following up immediately with a request to the President for clarification of his views. He had his assistants draft a memorandum concerning the ambiguity of the President's statements regarding the treatment of German industry. It referred to the September 15 document which indicated that the Ruhr and the Saar would be "necessarily put out of action and closed down"; and later: "This programme for eliminating the war-making industries in the Ruhr and in the Saar is looking forward to converting Germany into a country primarily agricultural and pastoral in its character." The President's memorandum of September 29, however, stated: "No one wants 'complete eradication of German industrial productive capacity in the Ruhr and Saar.' " After pointing out this "ambiguity," the memorandum stated that the note left by Hull on October 1 corresponded to the views of the President's September 29 memorandum. It concluded by asking the President for his approval of Hull's note so that the confusion which had arisen could be ended.[243]

This memorandum was never sent. Instead, Hull waited patiently until two weeks later, when the President, on October 20, wrote him a reply to the memorandum he had presented in their October 1 meeting.

Roosevelt began:

In regard to your memorandum of September twenty-ninth, I think it is all very well for us to make all kinds of preparations for the treatment of Germany but there are some matters in regard to such treatment that lead me to believe that speed on these matters is not an essential at the present moment. It may be in a week, or it may be in a month, or it may be several months hence. I dislike making detailed plans for a country which we do not yet occupy.

Concerning the first part of Hull's memorandum dealing with EAC negotiations, he said:

I agree except for going into too much detail and directives at the present moment, and we must emphasize the fact that the European Advisory Commission is "advisory" and that you and I are not bound by this advice. This is something which is sometimes overlooked and if we do not remember that word "advisory" they may go ahead and execute some of the advice, which, when the time comes, we may not like at all.

Concerning the second part, the policy recommendations, he began:

In view of the fact that we have not occupied

Germany, I cannot agree at this moment as to what kind of a Germany we want in every detail. In regard to the problems involved, there are some which now are perfectly clear and which can be approved now.

He agreed with the demilitarization proposals, but stressed the prohibition of aircraft. He concurred in the recommendations on denazification, controls over communications and postponement of decision on partition. On control of education, he wrote: "I should like to talk to your experts as to just what this means." Finally, on the economic objectives, he wrote:

I should like to discuss this with the State Department in regard to some of the language. I agree with it in principle, but I do not know what part of it means. Much of this sub-head is dependent on what we and the Allies find when we get into Germany—and we are not there yet.[244]

When the President wrote his first memorandum to Hull, on September 29, the failure of the Arnhem operation was known, but there was still a fading hope of quick victory. When he wrote again on October 20, it seemed all too clear that Germany would hold out at least into the spring or summer of 1945. The President was therefore freer to indulge his predilection for, one could even say his insistence on, the postponement of decision on policy for Germany. But in the State Department this point was missed. As Riddleberger described the October 20 memorandum, "the President approved many of the proposals for the treatment of Germany made by the State Department and approved in principle the economic objectives as described by us."[245]

These two memoranda to Hull show another slight change in the President's views. The first had called for a cessation of all activity in EAC; the second indicated some willingness to have EAC continue its work, though EAC directives without details would hardly have much meaning.

Roosevelt's general desire to postpone decision on Germany was given new emphasis in a memorandum to the CAD on October 25 which "even placed in question the U. S. draft directives which had already been cleared in Washington and circulated to the EAC."[246]

H. THE TREASURY AND THE ELECTION OF 1944

Knowledge of these post-Quebec probings of Roosevelt's viewpoint was confined largely within the Executive Branch. After the President's letter to Crowley on September 29, public attention, at least as judged by press reporting, had been effectively disengaged from Morgenthau's proposals and the dispute they had caused in Washington over the post-war treatment of Germany.

Morgenthau, fearing that his role in the formulation of German policy might be made an issue in the Presidential campaign then in full swing, and also sensing the President's mood, kept out of the work on German policy which continued throughout October. His fears were well founded. On October 18, in a speech to the *New York Herald Tribune* Forum on Current Problems, Dewey, the Republican Presidential candidate, used the version which had appeared in the papers of the mix-up over post-war German policy as an example of the difficulties which resulted from Roosevelt's personal handling of diplomacy. The State and War Departments, he said, had been planning for the occupation of Germany, as was appropriate; but neither Stimson nor Hull went to Quebec. Instead, Morgenthau, "whose qualifications as an expert on military and international affairs are still a closely guarded military secret" was taken, and this resulted in the acceptance of his plan there. Later, the Morgenthau Plan was "scrapped"—as the previous State-War plan had been—and FEA was ordered to produce a new one. Dewey pointed out that the Morgenthau Plan had, upon its publication, been picked up by the German propaganda apparatus and given considerable play. The effect of these "ill-conceived Treasury proposals" he described as follows: "Almost overnight the morale of the German people seemed wholly changed. Now they are fighting with the frenzy of despair. We are paying in blood for our failure to have ready an intelligent program for dealing with invaded Germany."[247]

Undoubtedly these charges, and the press reports upon which they were based, disturbed Morgenthau personally, but he was soon looking forward to the time when he could again play a part in determining German policy. About November 1, he told McCloy at dinner ". . . that after the elections he intended to get back into the German picture in a big way."[248]

In his wind-up speech for the campaign on

the night of November 4, Dewey struck again at the Morgenthau Plan. "The publishing of this plan while everything else was kept secret," he said, "was just what the Nazi propagandists needed. That was as good as ten fresh German divisions." And in support of his claims, Dewey cited two of the several news sources which saw a connection between the publication of the Morgenthau Plan and the stopping, in mid-September, of the swift Allied advance to the German border.[249] Morgenthau was extremely sensitive to this kind of charge. Forewarned of it, he had called the White House earlier that day and talked with Stephen Early, the President's Press Secretary. Early recorded the somewhat exaggerated message which he received as follows:

Sec'y Morgenthau says: Have just been tipped off that Dewey will devote his entire speech tonight to the Morgenthau Plan and to what Morgenthau told the President at Quebec—*that this has prolonged the war.* He thinks Stimson or Marshall should stand by to issue statement of denial tonight after Dewey's speech.[250]

Morgenthau also called Stimson that evening, who agreed to have McCloy listen to the speech and then talk with Morgenthau about it, although he was anxious to keep the Army out of the campaign. In any event, Stimson and McCloy both listened to it, and agreed that from Morgenthau's point of view, as well as Roosevelt's and the Army's, it was better not to publish any reply to it. Stimson did write privately to Morgenthau to assure him that Dewey's criticism had "no basis whatever,"[251] but the letter was not published at the time. Stimson also recorded in his diary his own interpretation of the event: "I am sorry for Morgenthau for never has an indiscretion been so quickly and vigorously punished as his incursion into German and Army politics at Quebec."[252] Within Morgenthau's own office a reply was prepared to Dewey's charge. It was a re-statement of Morgenthau's views, intended to set the record straight, which was to be approved by Stimson, Hull, and the President prior to its publication. (Presumably, the approval was to be of its accuracy as a statement of Morgenthau's views, for Stimson and Hull clearly would not have approved its substance.) Like the Stimson letter, it was not published, and probably not circulated.[253]

Morgenthau was in fact involved again in German policy just before the elections were over, although in a way not likely to produce press accounts. The British, it will be remembered, had not been willing to let JCS 1067 become a Combined Chiefs of Staff document and had, in turn, submitted to CCS a draft of a policy directive for Germany which embodied the British viewpoint. It was much longer and more detailed than JCS 1067, and provided for long-term policy, rather than the interim period covered by the American document. Morgenthau had his staff prepare a memorandum on it, completed on November 1, which read in part as follows:

2. The appropriate document for immediate discussion is the American interim directive document. This document is to the large part [sic] a statement of principles which after agreement would provide the basis for the preparation of handbooks containing full details for administration. The failure of the British Government to present its views on this document is preventing further progress of combined discussions on the treatment to be accorded Germany. We are faced with the danger that the prolongation of the period in which the military directive operates will seriously prejudice the situation within Germany and limit the effectiveness of long range policies which may be found to be desirable by the three governments.

3. The following are some of the major policy issues which the British document fails to deal with adequately and which must be dealt with in any long range program:

(a) The elimination or destruction of heavy industry in Germany, specifically the metallurgical, chemical and electrical industries in Germany.

(b) Future boundaries of Germany.

(c) Partitioning of Germany.

(d) Disposition of the Ruhr through internationalization or otherwise.

(e) Restitution.

(f) Reparations, including whether there will be reparations in the form of recurring payments.

(g) A comprehensive educational program.

(h) A positive program for political decentralization.

(i) The character of controls to be employed in preventing re-emergence of a powerful industrial Germany.

(j) Agrarian reform including the breaking up of the Junker estates.

(k) The punishment of war crimes and the apprehension of war criminals.

(l) The extradition of war criminals to the scene of their crimes.

The Treasury memorandum concluded with a series of critical comments on the British proposal intended to "indicate the difference in approach." It began: "Administrative convenience is frequently placed above principle in dealing with programs of German occupation"; and went on to assert that the punishment of infractions was not severe and direct enough, that the list of persons to be detained for political and security reasons was "totally inadequate" and gave too much discretion to the Allied Commander in Chief, that "too much political freedom" would be given the Germans, that the need for a "fundamental reorientation of German educational institutions" was ignored, and that the German police were to be too heavily armed.[254]

Here was the first important indication of the Treasury position since its period of quiescence in German policy had begun following the President's dissolution of the Cabinet Committee in late September. The Treasury had by now adopted a tactic which later became a characteristic of the position taken by Bernstein in civil affairs planning in London. The original JCS 1067, the Treasury memorandum insisted, should be the basis for discussion and hence of agreement on a short-term, Anglo-American policy for Germany. This position was understandable from the American standpoint, but since the British had already rejected JCS 1067 in the Combined Chiefs of Staff, it had no more status in Anglo-American negotiations than had any British draft.

With respect to long-term policy, the Treasury position at the end of October was slightly less severe than it had been before the Cabinet crisis, and, as we shall see, wholly out of touch with views expressed by the President to the State Department since Quebec. Missing from the list of "major policy issues" which needed to be settled for any long-range program was any reference, such as appeared in the Quebec agreement, to the most important proposal raised by the Treasury: the agrarianization of the German economy. The exclusion of this issue was not by itself an indication that the Treasury position had been changed; by this time the proposal had become too sensitive an issue to be dealt with directly. But its exclusion does record a step in Morgenthau's gradual (and limited) moderation of view on the treatment of Germany.

The Treasury memorandum listed first as a major policy issue "the elimination or destruction of heavy industry in Germany, specifically the metallurgical, chemical and electrical industries in Germany." If this had ever been an accurate statement of the President's views, it was so no longer. The Quebec agreement, where the "metallurgical, chemical and electrical industries" phrase first appeared, proposed a "programme for eliminating the war-making industries in the Ruhr and in the Saar," but said nothing about industry in other parts of Germany. While this may not have been a significant exception in fact, Roosevelt made it important, for on September 29, while he was in the process of backing out of his commitment at Quebec, he seized upon this exception, saying in his memorandum to Hull: "Also, it must not be forgotten that outside of the Ruhr and Saar, Germany has many *other* areas and facilities for turning out large exports."[255] Roosevelt had begun to back out of the Quebec agreement when he talked with Stimson on the telephone on September 27, and on October 3 he clearly repudiated it while lunching with Stimson.[256] On October 20 he seemed to confirm that repudiation by his favorable treatment of the State Department's position on German policy.[257] Although the Treasury memorandum on the British document failed to take into account these later indications of the President's views, it is quite possible that Morgenthau knew of them by this time, for, even after he was sure to have known of them, the Treasury never did take cognizance of them, but continued to maintain that the President's views were most accurately expressed in the Quebec agreement, and that the Interim Directive on the treatment of Germany, which was written in its shadow, remained authoritative.

At the end of October Morgenthau showed his memorandum on the British policy draft to McCloy, who tried without success to persuade him not to give it to Lord Cherwell, who was in Washington at the time.[258] On November 1, just before Cherwell returned to England, Morgenthau gave it to him anyway. Cherwell agreed that the British proposals of long-range policy for the treatment of Germany were inappropriate at that time, and that the American Interim Directive could better serve as the basis for Anglo-American discussions. Whether he took this position because he considered himself—or his chief—to be committed to it is not clear; and whether Cherwell's agreement was as definite as Morgenthau thought is also uncertain.

I. THE TREASURY WRITES A BOOK

While State was trying to commit the President to its views, White had been supervising the writing of a book to be published under the by-line of Morgenthau as a reply to the critics of the Morgenthau Plan. The book had apparently begun as an outgrowth from the staff work done in Treasury for the Cabinet Committee discussions on Germany.[259] Following the November elections, preparation of the book became more serious, perhaps because of Dewey's charges against the Morgenthau Plan. A dozen or more people tried their hands at chapters. As was usual Treasury practice in its staff work, those who worked on the book were not necessarily expected to agree with what they produced, and many of them did not. The major part of the writing was done during November and December 1944, although before it was published in October 1945, under the title of *Germany Is Our Problem,* the book underwent substantial revision. The extensive activity involved in the book's preparation had little to do with the outcome of occupation policy, but it provided a stockpile from which to draw arguments and was a significant indication of an important development in Treasury thinking.

The clash over the treatment of Germany had been carried on at its inter-departmental points of contact with the usual personal frictions, but with little recrimination, although undoubtedly within the three departments primarily involved some dark suspicions were held by each about the other. Treasury was resented for its very involvement, suspected of double-dealing, doubted as to its veracity, and disliked for its aggressiveness. State was thought to be pro-German, somewhat inept, and impractical. War appeared as an empire builder, anxious to take over policy direction—perhaps to promote reaction, perhaps only because it preferred administrative convenience to principle. Each department saw the other dominated by a group in which it could not place its full confidence. In Treasury it was New

Deal lawyers and economists; in State, the career diplomat; in War, Republican lawyers, comparatively new to the Washington scene, but backed by the career officers.

Early drafts of Morgenthau's book indicate that by November 1944 a substantial suspicion had developed within Treasury that the real reason for most of the opposition in War and State to the Morgenthau Plan was due to a belief, which no one dared disclose, that Germany should be built up as a bulwark against Russia on the European continent. In an early December draft of Chapter 2, for example, Morgenthau's answer to the "real issues" involved in the German problem was stated for him as follows:

II. I believe that in formulating a solution to the German problem we must address ourselves to the German problem and not be shunted off into a whispering orgy of red-baiting on how to prepare for war against Russia. I do not believe that the American people are so immature about the political facts of life that they have to be kept in sheltered ignorance of the undisclosed major premise of much of the "discussion" about Germany. I believe that the Russian issue should be flung on the table and that the American people should be given the opportunity of deciding for themselves whether Germany or Russia is their real enemy.[260]

This draft paragraph was probably based on an idea set forth by Morgenthau, who had been greatly perturbed by some remarks on the subject by Churchill, as he said in one of his articles in the *New York Post.* However, the one person mentioned in connection with this argument by the staff doing the drafting was Stimson, who had opposed the Morgenthau Plan from his first hearing of it. A letter from Stimson to a Congressional committee in 1930, when he was Secretary of State, was used to illustrate the "real issue motivating many of those who are desirous of building up Germany." The letter read: "In her position in the center of Europe, Germany in good health would be a bulwark of strength against instability and communism."[261] In the Morgenthau book, a careful refutation followed: While Russia was capable of being "the greatest menace that the world has yet seen,"[262] she is anxious to return after the war to her economic development. Russia and the United States are traditional friends, and have no major conflicting interests. We can continue to be friends. But if we mistrust her, that will only lead to mutual suspicions.

If we conjured up fears against a nation which is going to great lengths to demonstrate its friendship and which has no intelligent reason for attacking or provoking us to war, we shall have to embark upon the impossible national policy of maintaining military forces to fight all the rest of the world.[263]

J. TREASURY INFLUENCE IN LONDON

While State was trying to get the President committed to its own viewpoint, the Treasury Department, in addition to working on Morgenthau's book, was watching the development of policy in another quarter. The Joint U. S. Advisors to Winant, in his capacity as Delegate to EAC, had continued preparation, in conjunction with sections of Eisenhower's U. S. Group Control Council, of a large number of draft directives for Germany which were intended for tripartite approval. Upon their approval by the Joint U. S. Advisors, they were to be submitted simultaneously to the State and War Departments. When approved by the Working Security Committee (or the new SWNCC) and the Post-War Planning Committee of the Joint Chiefs of Staff, and cleared by JCS and State, they were to be introduced into the EAC, where they would be negotiated with Britain and Russia. Ultimately, they were intended for issuance to the Commander in Chief, U. S. Army, European Theater of Operations, and to his British and Russian counterparts. Bernstein, as head of the Finance Division of the U. S. Group Control Council, was involved in the preparation of the draft directive on financial controls, and had access to the rest of the draft directives. He made them available to L. C. Aarons, a Treasury representative at the American Embassy in London, who forwarded summaries of them to White in Washington. Some of the documents had already been approved in Washington; some had not. Their summaries described to White the degree to which they conformed to JCS 1067, as the Treasury interpreted that directive. Since Bernstein was at odds with his Army superiors over the right of direct and private communication with the Treasury Department, which he claimed, White was cautioned to use this information discreetly in order to protect Aarons' source of information.

Bernstein was opposed to the very idea of drafting the directive on financial controls, for he was reluctant to have new plans for German financial matters formulated in the absence of further top-level guidance. He preferred, instead, to stand on the financial directive in the original CCS 551 (presumably letting it carry over by default from the pre- to the post-surrender period). When the American Advisors insisted that their terms of reference required them to prepare such a draft, he agreed to give his views on it. He indicated that he did not want the Control Council involved in the administration of the zones of occupation, thus taking a more extreme position on zonal autonomy than did the War Department. He also wanted a clear distinction drawn between the power of the Control Council to control German financial institutions and its authorization to do so only to the degree necessary to accomplish Allied aims. In this way, it would be clear that the clauses in JCS 1067 and previous documents which stressed the sovereign power held by the occupying powers would be responsible for all phases of German affairs. Bernstein also indicated, in his consultations with the U. S. Advisors to EAC, that any additional financial directive should strengthen the proscriptions against Nazis.

Evidently not satisfied with the way the drafting of this document was going in the American EAC delegation in London, Bernstein sent copies of it in various stages of its drafting to L. C. Aarons and other Treasury representatives assigned to the embassy, together with the background information and his own comments. These papers were copied and forwarded in turn to White and other Treasury officials in Washington concerned with German policy, who were involved in rewriting JCS 1067 as a post-surrender document. Meanwhile, Aarons was planning a trip to Washington. In the last letter on the draft financial directive, dated from London, December 28, 1944, the Treasury officials in Washington were cautioned: "Buz [Aarons] is familiar with the Draft General Order. No inquiries should be made concerning it until he arrives in Washington."[264]

With the issuance of the "Handbook for Military Government in Germany Prior to Defeat or Surrender" in December 1944, and of various technical manuals, the basic planning by SHAEF of military government for the pre-surrender was complete. By that time it was apparent to G-5, SHAEF, that the period of SHAEF's responsibility (or of British and American responsibility) would extend beyond the date of surrender, although how long beyond was not clear. The pre-surrender directives were deemed inadequate for the post-surrender period. At the the same time, it was recognized that EAC had produced little agreed tripartite policy, and, with the stalemate into which the President had thrown it as the result of his instructions of the previous September 29 and October 20, SHAEF was not hopeful of EAC action. Besides, a new obstacle to effective EAC deliberation had arisen with the addition of a French member to the Commission on November 27, 1944, following the liberation of France. The determination of the French provisional government to establish its independence in foreign affairs, and to press at all costs for ambitious objectives with respect to Germany, caused new difficulties in EAC negotiations. Furthermore, as has been noted earlier, the War Department was not likely to encourage action by EAC, a body it distrusted. CCS, the only body which could and did provide SHAEF directly with policy guidance in civil affairs, had not produced a post-defeat directive either. As a consequence, G-5, SHAEF, undertook in mid-December to prepare a post-surrender policy, with the expectation that it would be submitted to CCS as the policy which was proposed to be followed in the absence of further direction. A month earlier State and War had begun to prepare a revision of JCS 1067 for use in the European Advisory Commission.

The SHAEF pre-surrender directives to army group commanders, based on CCS 551 and issued in April 1944, contained none of the sterner stuff which was added to that document the following September in the process of turning it into JCS 1067. Since the JCS document applied only to the immediate post-defeat period, its use as a policy guide in the planning in SHAEF for Phase I (the pre-surrender period) was not appropriate, since CCS 551 was still in effect for that earlier period. But Bernstein and others who agreed with the Treasury position on the treatment of Germany consistently used it as the basis for planning in both phases. On the other hand, in Winant's EAC staff, where efforts were being made to plan for the whole of this post-surrender period, moderate State Department views predominated, and Treasury policies could make little headway. When Brigadier General Frank J. McSherry, Chief of the Operations Branch of the G-5 Division, SHAEF, undertook the development of a post-surrender policy, Bernstein, his Chief of the G-5 Finance Division, was presented with his first real opportunity to promote the Treasury thesis.

Before considering the next Treasury move, it will be useful to return briefly to the two approved—but differently approved—directives about Germany. For, since JCS 1067 was not approved in the Combined Chiefs of Staff, CCS 551 remained the only Anglo-American agreement on the treatment of Germany—although it was applicable only to the period prior to defeat or surrender, while JCS 1067 was intended to be used after defeat or surrender until a longer-range policy could be negotiated. Because the British were to insist that CCS 551 should be the basis for a longer-term policy, it will be well to review the substance of each of these two documents for the control of Germany.

IV. TOWARDS AN OCCUPATION DIRECTIVE: THE FIRST REVISION OF JCS 1067

A. INTRODUCTION

CCS 551, the Anglo-American directive on the treatment of Germany prior to defeat or surrender, which was issued to Eisenhower on May 28, 1944, had assumed that the German society, government, and economy would be substantially intact behind the lines; and that all that military government would have to do would be to purge them and supervise them. Because of this assumption, the question of whether or not, or how effectively, the occupying forces could operate and control the German state was passed over. Instead of considering this question, the officials who drafted CCS 551 concentrated their attention upon the less speculative objective of providing the responsible officers with maximum discretion and power. Eisenhower was instructed to maintain: (1) taxes, bona fide pensions, allowances, and social security, and resume service on the public debt as soon as possible; and (2) the agricultural, industrial, and production systems of Germany. At no point in the directive was the eventuality that these tasks might prove impossible given consideration.

CCS 551 stressed the paramountcy of military considerations, and to that end, the wide discretion of the Supreme Commander. For instance, he was instructed to purge Nazis from public positions; but it was up to him to decide whether other government officials were to be replaced. In combination, this broad grant of discretionary power and the assumption that the state of affairs would not inhibit the exercise of that power meant that military government would be held responsible for the operation of the entire German state. As has been shown, by August 1944, Eisenhower had become alarmed at the responsibility which CCS 551 placed upon him to maintain the operation of the German economic system, particularly since it was rapidly becoming clear that the social and economic fabric of Germany would not be able to hold together in defeat, with military government acting merely as overseer.

Even given the assumption that German society would not collapse, one major question remained unanswered by CCS 551: what criteria were to be used in settling questions which came within the discretion of the military government officials which could not be settled by the dictates of military necessity? For instance, Eisenhower was instructed to purge the German government of Nazis, but it was left up to him whether other government officials were to be replaced. To give a general answer to that question would be to draw conclusions about the relationship of the Nazi Party to the German people as a whole, and about the nature of war guilt—issues which remained unsettled in every Allied government. The alternative was a pragmatic solution which emphasized the particular facts of each situation in order to avoid the need for a general solution. But the Army could not thereby avoid responsibility for the unarticulated general policy that underlay whatever particular decisions were based on this pragmatic approach, as its first experience with occupying Germany, in Aachen, was later to demonstrate. What happened, of course, was that military necessity tended to get stretched to cover this gap. But that was an expedient solution which could never be wholly satisfactory. Maximum discretion for the military proved to have its drawbacks.

How to avoid policy-making and still have administrative discretion was not a new or a unique problem for Army civil affairs officers in 1944; nor was it susceptible of an easy or final solution. However CCS 551 might have been drawn, the problem would still have existed to some extent. Nonetheless, it was magnified by granting maximum discretion to the field commander in the accomplishment of his military objectives.

But once it was evident that German society was likely to fall apart, and that the Army would probably have to pick up the pieces, it became imperative for the Army that its responsibilities in the occupation of Germany be strictly limited. For the Army, this raised two questions: How could its responsibility be limited without its discretion being limited correspondingly? and second, how could the Army be held responsible for the occupation of Germany when it could not be in complete control of the situation?

The Interim Directive, JSC 1067, sent to Eisenhower on September 22, 1944, was, like CCS 551, a stop-gap measure, in this case to be used by the United States Army in its own zone following defeat or surrender, but only until something more long-range had been decided upon. While it was prepared by an interdepartmental committee, under the supervision of Assistant Secretaries, for the most part, and while it was concerned with a period of time during which the dictates of "military necessity" could not be so compelling as during the period covered by CCS 551, the latter document dealt more frankly with policy questions than did the Interim Directive. CCS 551 had been able to avoid policy questions by using the doctrine of "military necessity," and by its assumption that German society would remain substantially intact. But in August, Eisenhower had cabled his belief that this was a risky assumption. The deliberations of the Executive Committee on Economic Foreign Policy in June and July had already brought the assumption under close scrutiny; and in August, American officials concerned with civil affairs in both London and Washington came to doubt it. Nevertheless, it is striking that CCS 551, which was drafted by military staffs in lieu of policy settled by civilians responsible for it, delved more frankly (though not in greater detail) into some policy matters than did JCS 1067, the Interim Directive. The Interim Directive failed to settle issues of German policy because of its stop-gap purpose, and because it was a negotiated document which was acceptable to officials with widely divergent views.

Perhaps the most prominent questions which remained unanswered by JCS 1067 concerned the economic treatment of Germany. It authorized the occupation authorities to assume control of industrial, agricultural, utility, communication and transportation facilities, supplies, and services only for purposes of demilitarization, prevention of disease and unrest, prosecution of the Japanese war, and the preservation and protection of facilities and supplies for purposes of relief, restitution, and reparation. While this was clearly an attempt to make the "German authorities," rather than the American occupation, responsible for the successful functioning of the German economy, in contrast to the provisions of CCS 551, it raised questions which remained unanswered elsewhere in the text: How could "German authorities" be held responsible for anything unless they had some independence of action, which was evidently not contemplated? Here was a new problem of responsibility for the Army. How stringent would the life of the German populace be under this directive? The answer to this question depended upon the military interpretation of "disease and unrest" (which would determine how much the occupation forces would do to help) and by how much "the German people and the German authorities," with whom responsibility for any other positive actions was to rest, would be capable of doing. But how could the Germans act except with the approval and support of the occupation authorities? Undoubtedly they could not, and yet they were to be responsible for what they did or failed to do. Apparently, German efforts would have to come from local initiative, for "all dealings in so far as possible should be with municipal and provincial government officials rather than with Central government officials." But of the economic problems specifically left to the German authorities—"price controls, rationing, unemployment, production, reconstruction, distribution, consumption, housing or transportation" —most of them could be accomplished only on a national (or, as it turned out, zonal) basis. Clearly, the relationship between occupation forces and viable indigenous government remained an unsettled question.

Two other important matters also were left

unsettled by the Interim Directive, even though they were given attention in it. The categories of people who were to be arrested were fairly clear, but not what was to be done with them after arrest. Could the Army release its prisoners at its own discretion? Or were all to be tried? Or were some to be given summary punishment? Silence on these points covered real differences between the three departments. Treasury viewed arrest as the first step towards trial for war crimes, while the War Department came to see arrest as an administrative tool for keeping undesirables out of circulation.

The second matter involved the problem of political centralization in Germany. JCS 1067 looked ahead to a unified, tripartite administration of occupied Germany, while at the same time it envisaged decentralization of the political structure of Germany. How these two were to be reconciled was not indicated.

Thus, CCS 551 and JCS 1067 both avoided many of the questions involved in occupation policy. Some of these questions were questions of detail to be worked out at the proper place by the civil affairs staff of the Army. Others awaited resolution in the Cabinet Committee or by the President. For the time being, however, Eisenhower was provided with a policy statement on Germany which followed the Morgenthau Plan in some respects, but which was ambiguous enough to place in question the degree to which Morgenthau's views were to be carried out; which provided the Supreme Commander a maximum degree of discretion, and which absolved him, as best it could, of responsibility for the collapse of Germany.

B. *AFTERMATH OF THE CABINET COMMITTEE: CLEARANCE OF WINANT'S DIRECTIVES RESUMED*

McCloy and the Civil Affairs Division had struggled to get the Working Security Committee going from early August until after the appointment of the Cabinet Committee on Germany on August 25. Hilldring, indeed, had pressed on with his efforts to get War Department and JCS clearance for Winant's basic policy papers right up to the eve of the Cabinet Committee's preliminary meetings a week later. But he discontinued these efforts when he learned not only that the Joint Chiefs were now more reluctant than ever to consider policy

papers which had not been thoroughly cleared in the War and State Departments, but that the War Department, or Operations Division at least, was reluctant to present post-war matters on Germany to the JCS until the Cabinet Committee's views were known. When the committee was dissolved a month after its designation, McCloy promptly proceeded to "devise a more expeditious means of providing Winant guidance."[265] JCS 1067 could now serve as the approved general policy paper which had been anticipated for so long as the device which would break the log-jam of Winant's instructions. On September 30 McCloy met with representatives of CAD, State, Navy, and the Joint Post-War Committee of the JCS and worked out a plan whereby the twenty-two draft directives which had now been received from Winant could be processed through the Working Security Committee. In early August he had attempted to accomplish the same thing by arranging that WSC would refer for JCS clearance only a minimum number of papers which would contain the essence of policies, and that the large volume of other materials would be cleared as supporting documents without reference to the Joint Chiefs. But the hurdles of War Department and JPWC clearance had remained formidable for the policy documents, and this arrangement had never gotten underway. The new procedure was to dispatch papers worked out in the WSC directly to the Joint Chiefs of Staff for their consideration. The three departments represented at McCloy's meeting approved this arrangement, and so did the JPWC (which, however, did not "represent" the Joint Chiefs). The first two papers to be submitted under this procedure were held up by the Operations Division because they had not received formal concurrences from the appropriate War Department agencies. Marshall personally attempted to submit them to JCS and was turned down by Leahy when he was told that the documents had not been fully cleared in the War and State Departments.[266]

War Department clearance was then attempted, but State Department officials pointed out that the approval of WSC had been based on the assumption that both State and War were thereby committing themselves to approval, subject only to JCS concurrence, and that "if the War Department seeks to refer the actions of the Committee to War Department agencies with reference back to the Working Security Committee, the State Department will demand the same consideration."[267] CAD now attempted to achieve its long-desired direct contact with the Joint Chiefs by having CAD submittals cleared when necessary in the War Department *after* JCS had taken cognizance of them, and by arranging for referral from the JCS to the Secretary of State rather than back to WSC. But even as "an emergency and temporary expedient" this proposal proved unacceptable or unworkable.[268]

There were passing hopes in CAD that JCS 1067 had settled general policy, and that details could now be worked out at a military level without the need for referral to EAC. And in both London and Washington there was always the continuing hope—perhaps it was an illusion—that if only the directives were less detailed they would get over the clearance hurdles.[269] Although by this time that hope had little foundation, the War Department had good reason to indulge in it: the Army was interested in maintaining the freedom of action of its zone commander at the same time that it was interested in getting policy settled.

The impasse of ten months duration remained unbroken at the end of October 1944. The Joint Chiefs had avoided since December 1943 the approval of any long-term policy for the treatment of Germany. But it had approved a short-term policy in JCS 1067. The problem of the JCS impasse, combined with difficulties with the British over a general occupation directive, was now to turn American officials in Washington to JCS 1067 as the basis for its negotiations in EAC.

The British, it will be remembered, had rejected JCS 1067 as a Combined Chiefs of Staff document. They preferred their own more detailed draft for a long-term directive. Then, on October 12, they revealed a new and bolder strategem. Since the establishment of EAC they had pressed Winant for agreement there on German policies. The War Department and the JCS, however, had in effect denied him the instructions by which he could act. Now, however, it was clear that the Americans wanted policies settled, and that they could agree on policy intended for military channels. But the military channels—the Combined Civil Affairs Committee and the Combined Chiefs of Staff

—were in Washington, and for the moment, at least, were clogged with, what was to the British, the objectionable JCS 1067. What was needed was a way to turn the American desire for settling policy to agreement on a British draft.

The strategem adopted was revealed to McCloy when the British representative on the Combined Civil Affairs Committee called on him on October 12, the day of a regular CCAC meeting. His instructions from the War Cabinet were, he explained, not to discuss in the CCAC, even informally, the American Interim Directive. The proper place to discuss post-surrender policies was the European Advisory Commission. Anglo-American negotiations in CCS or CCAC over JCS 1067 would, he explained, prove embarrassing to tripartite efforts in EAC —a reference, no doubt, to the policy instigated earlier by the U. S. to avoid facing the Russians in EAC with settled Anglo-American positions. If the EAC did not come through with agreed policies in time, he went on, CCS 551 could be used until something else had been agreed on.

The British insistence upon the settlement of policies on the treatment of Germany through diplomatic channels in London was by this time familiar enough, but not the new use for CCS 551. If it could be carried off with the Americans, that use would give the British a decisive advantage in the EAC by eliminating the time pressures on them while the Americans were becoming more impatient. The Americans would be posed with the unpleasant alternatives of losing to the British by default, or accepting the British draft in order to achieve agreement.

McCloy responded that, as he recorded it, CCS 551 was "not only inadequate but misleading as a directive for a post-defeat period." Later he argued that negotiations in the CCS over CCS 551 would be no less embarrassing, and went on to point out the larger differences between the two documents to show how contrary CCS 551 was to the established position of his government. He placed his greatest emphasis on the economic policy implications of the two documents and on the greater responsibility which CCS 551 placed on SCAEF for the rehabilitation of German industry and the re-establishment of economic life in Germany.[270]

The British and American positions were

now in fundamental disagreement. The Americans probably would have been willing to settle their differences in the CCS, but the British clearly were not. Because it was diplomatic rather than military, because it was tripartite rather than just Anglo-American, and because it was in London, the British evidently insisted that EAC was the place to negotiate over fundamental disagreements concerning policy for Germany. And the Americans involved were in no position to argue the other way. It had been difficult enough to get the Joint Chiefs simply to concur in policy for Germany formulated anywhere in the American government; to expect it to negotiate such policies with the British would have been absurd. Instead, CAD and McCloy turned once again to EAC. At a meeting in McCloy's office on November 6, with McCloy, Hilldring, Dunn, Matthews, Riddleberger and Winant present, it was agreed that the attempt to clear Winant's directives would be abandoned, and that instead, JCS 1067 would be revised for presentation to EAC as a broad general directive for the initial government of Germany. Matters of detailed planning would then be handled by the tripartite Control Council for Germany, or on a military level.[271]

The War Department, it should be noted, had two particular reasons to be satisfied with this agreement, and both were at Winant's expense. One was that it abandoned Winant's draft directives, which were too detailed for the Army's liking. Even while supporting them, CAD had fretted over them.[272] It had insisted on keeping them out of the surrender instrument. Only three weeks earlier Winant's Military Adviser had disputed CAD's contention that the drafts were too detailed for EAC consideration. Now Winant had concurred in that view. The second reason was that while Winant was to carry on the negotiations over German policy, the reins on him were to be held as tight as policy agreement in Washington would permit. It was agreed that if the British or the Soviet Union wished to depart from JCS 1067, Winant was to submit any proposed changes in detail to Washington for approval.[273]

Both the State and War Departments, it will be remembered, were determined to minimize the importance of EAC in the determination of post-war policy. With the President's October memorandum to Hull to support these views, Winant was in no position to protest.

The third reason was that the efforts of State and Winant to negotiate in EAC on the basis of long-term policy for Germany was abandoned in favor of the short-term period envisaged in the Interim Directive. Dunn and his associates from the State Department could have been pleased with the outcome of this meeting only because it meant that agreement would be sought through Winant, not through the Combined Chiefs of Staff.

C. FEA STUDIES ECONOMIC CONTROLS FOR GERMANY

In his letter of September 29 to FEA Administrator Leo T. Crowley, the President specifically exempted the Foreign Economic Administration from his general caveat against detailed planning. To understand the circumstances under which this exception was authorized, it is necessary to go back to events in early August.

Just before Morgenthau's trip, approval of the two documents on Germany in the Executive Committee on Economic Foreign Policy (on August 4, 1944) was followed up immediately in FEA by the setting up of a program for the study of economic controls necessary in Germany during the control period. It was directed by James W. Angell, an economist on leave from Columbia University, and run on the basis of a working committee of FEA officials. The "study" was expected to outline controls, and suggest general policy in administering them and the type of machinery for doing so. These proposals would be considered by ECEFP subcommittees, set up for that purpose. Originally planned to be completed in two months, the project continued on long after that.[274] By September 1 the German Working Committee had worked out an approved policy draft entitled: "Germany: General Objectives of United States Economic Policy with Respect to Germany."[275]

The document followed closely the moderate lines laid down by the ECEFP papers. While this paper was not made available to the three departments represented in the Cabinet Committee, it did draw immediate reaction within FEA. The Assistant Director of the Northern European Division took issue with its general tone. He argued that Germany was a diseased, lethal, psychopathic and virulently contagious country, which had given no evidence that it was curable. He recommended that, rather than be operated for maximum reparations, German industry be used as replacement parts. He would prohibit airplane, synthetic oil and rubber production, and drastically reduce, through reparations, steel-making capacity.[276] This may have been the beginning of the "hard line" in FEA with respect to German policy. But as yet the agency had not accepted it. Later, in the winter of 1944, as it followed out the logic of its studies of how to control Germany (politically) through economic controls, FEA would come to identify itself with a stern, even grim, approach to the economic treatment of Germany, but it would do so only after long and sometimes bitter arguments among its staff.[277]

FEA did not get drawn into or become identified with either side in the Cabinet Committee split, at this time; it continued to object to State Department policy planning as vague, unrealistic, and incomplete; and the general sentiment of its staff supported a more assertive role for its representatives in inter-departmental work. But by mid-September it was too late to do so, for inter-departmental work was in a state of suspense pending the outcome of Cabinet Committee deliberations.[278] Aware of the Cabinet Committee split, the German Working Committee found its task to be more and more impossible. It started to work on the assumption that the ECEFP documents could be taken as setting forth settled questions of principle. It soon became apparent to the GWC staff that these documents were neither clear nor authoritative. Without any general policy from which to begin their studies, they were unable to proceed.[279]

In late September, a letter was drafted under the supervision of the FEA Executive Policy Committee for the President's signature, and addressed to Leo T. Crowley, FEA Administrator. Its purpose was to provide that agency with the minimum of policy instructions necessary for the GWC to continue its work.[280] We have already seen how Roosevelt was able to issue this letter at a time when it aided him in his efforts to disengage himself in the public eye from the Morgenthau Plan. FEA had intended to make the letter a direct authorization from the President, but in clearing the draft, State added "under guidance of the Department of State." FEA officials objected to the State amendment. They had never been entirely satisfied with the fact that their agency was under the policy guidance of State, and in this case they felt that the change in the President's letter to Crowley would only inject FEA into the dispute between Treasury, State, and War. Oscar Cox, FEA General Counsel and Deputy Administrator, who vigorously cultivated his relations with the White House, explained this point in a note to the President's press secretary, while Crowley took the matter up with Hull.[281] Neither of them was successful. However, with the release of the letter on September 29, their fears that its reference to State guidance of FEA would involve their agency in the interdepartmental row over Germany failed to materialize.

But their original plans that the letter to Crowley should clarify the work of the German Working Committee were also disappointed, largely owing to their own error. Crowley, Cox, and their immediate assistants had evidently drafted the letter without understanding the committee's problem; three days after its publication George Pettee, a GWC member, pointed out to Angell the inadequacies of the letter for policy guidance.[282]

A week later, October 12, Angell presented to the Executive Policy Committee of FEA the important policy issues which still remained unsettled, and the remaining conflicts on those that supposedly had been settled. The August agreement of ECEFP on Germany, recorded in two documents, had failed to cover several important matters: at what level German living standards should be maintained; how to handle property controls; what to do about the Nazi underground; how to dispose of Reich and Nazi Party property; and what to do about cartels, combines, and large estates. Moreover, these documents seemed no longer to be approved policy. On the other hand, the President's September 29 letter to Crowley and an earlier one which emphasized that the whole German people must feel defeat, laid down as the objectives of U. S. policy concerning the German economy (1) the elimination of German capacity to make war, (2) the eventual development of a prosperous German community without any aggressive inclinations, and (3) retribution designed to fit in coherently with the first two purposes. Since these objectives conflicted, policy guidance could not be considered adequate.[283]

The attempt to obtain adequate top-level political guidance thus having failed, the executive group decided that this was an unrealistic approach. It was agreed that, instead of trying to fill in the details of such decisions, the function of GWC should be to work up its own material based on facts, and then recommend policy. Somewhat circuitously, however, it was recognized that some assumptions had to be made prior to the gathering of facts in order to render the economic studies meaningful.[284]

It was on this basis that the GWC continued its work throughout the winter of 1944-1945. With incomplete and conflicting policy guidance, it had to turn to the amassing of facts; and in order to make them pertinent, it had to listen to the latest indications of Presidential attitudes, through gossip and his public statements. For instance, they found great significance for themselves in his campaign speech of October 21, in which he said:

. . . we and our Allies are entirely agreed that we shall not bargain with the Nazi conspirators, or leave them a shred of control—open or secret— of the instruments of government. We shall not leave them a single element of military power— or potential military power.

. . . .

We bring no charge against the German race, as such, for we cannot believe that God has eternally condemned any race or humanity. . . . But there is going to be stern punishment for all those in Germany directly responsible for this agony of mankind.

The German people are not going to be enslaved. . . . But it will be necessary for them to earn their way back—earn their way back into the fellowship of peace-loving and law-abiding nations. And in their climb up that steep road, we shall certainly see to it that they are not encumbered by having to carry guns. We hope they will be relieved of that burden forever.[285]

D. RESULTS OF THE NEGOTIATIONS OF THE FIRST POST-SURRENDER DIRECTIVE

The efforts throughout September and early October 1944 of the President, his Secretaries of State, Treasury, and War, and their assistants, to settle the pressing questions concerning the post-war treatment of Germany had pro-

duced several effects by mid-October—as had the President's move toward the postponement of settlement, beginning in late September, which has been described above.[286] Roosevelt's objection in late August to the military government handbook caused its publication to be held up while SHAEF requested more specific guidance. The Combined Civil Affairs Committee instructed SHAEF to revise the handbook along the following lines: (a) there should be no economic rehabilitation of any kind except for necessary military purposes; (b) imports should be kept to the minimum to prevent disease and unrest which might interfere with the occupation; and (c) Nazis or Nazi-sympathizers were not to be kept in office for reasons of administrative convenience. After much correspondence, the handbook was issued with an inserted flyleaf containing the three principles.[287]

The Combined Chiefs of Staff examined this "revision" of the handbook, and stated in a cable to SHAEF on October 7 that it was not yet satisfactory, and that it should be revised to embody certain principles. Most of these principles were in sympathy with the new, hard-peace line. But among them was the following instruction which seemed to hold the occupation authorities responsible for keeping the German economy from breaking down:

. . . the maintenance of existing German economic controls and anti-inflation measures should be mandatory upon the German authorities and *not* permissive as in the present edition of the Handbook.[288]

On October 9 the Assistant Chief of Staff, G-5, at SHAEF, Lieutenant General A. E. Grasset (a British officer), ruled on the basis of CCS 551 that the restoration and maintenance of law and order were to go as far as military necessity *required;* and that therefore, "in certain cases" it would be desirable to go back to the original handbook (which the President had criticized). Thus, Morgenthau's first success in hardening the heart of military government, and the President's blast at the military government handbook, were nullified in considerable part. The British had never agreed to JCS 1067, which had therefore no CCS standing; nor, as soon became clear, did they feel themselves bound by the Quebec agreement. CCS 551 remained for the British, and for Anglo-American planning, the most important policy guide. The consequences of British action were therefore apparent in CCS policy and even more apparent in SHAEF, where the G-5, Grasset, was, as has been noted, a British general. The British and Americans in CCS and CCAC continued to disagree on policy. The President's actions resulted in confusion rather than clarification in London military circles.

The effects on Winant of the events of September and October, and especially the President's decision to postpone all decision, were severe. Roosevelt's acceptance of the Southwest zone made it possible for Winant to secure agreement on an EAC zonal protocol; he was also able to push forward with the protocol on control machinery. But policy to guide the use of that machinery was held in suspense.

The effect on the Army was to make it anxious to help Winant—at least on its own terms. After another vain attempt to push German policy papers through the JCS, the War Department turned again to the European Advisory Commission, but consolidated its position around JCS 1067 by gaining an agreement from State and Winant that the Interim Directive would be revised for submittal to the Commission.[289]

The drafting of an Interim Directive (JCS 1067) to General Eisenhower, pending more definitive and long-range political decisions, had been undertaken to clarify policy for the German Country Unit, the group planning the military government of Germany under Grasset in SHAEF.[290] This objective was not accomplished. It was obvious to the American military planners in England that JCS 1067 had incorporated certain provisions of the Morgenthau proposals, as they had been published in the daily press. But to what extent the JCS document was intended to incorporate Morgenthau's views was not clear.

Colonel Bernstein, the Chief of the Finance Division of G-5, SHAEF, and the one who had shown Morgenthau the handbook, and explained to him the tendency of military government to be overly solicitous of occupied areas, became the chief spokesman of the retribution school and "representative" of the Treasury Department within military government. When, in the fall of 1944, the German Country Unit was abolished, and its American members transferred to the U. S. Group Control Council,

he was given the additional assignment of Director of the Finance Division of that organization.

On September 29 the President wrote the Secretary of War suggesting that in recruiting civilians for financial work in Germany he call upon the Treasury Department (and upon other departments and agencies for other specialists), a policy which had been followed, though not consistently, since 1942. Bernstein was thereby authorized to surround himself with people from the Treasury Department, and was provided with grounds for claiming that he and other Army finance officers had a special relationship with the Treasury which entitled them to maintain direct communication with that department (a claim which did not go unchallenged by his Army superiors).

The basis of faction was thus laid in London within the Army civil affairs organization for Germany. The Treasury "crowd," through its spokesman, asserted that the Morgenthau Plan was incorporated without modification into JCS 1067. Many of the Group Control Council officers held more moderate views regarding the treatment of Germany, and they contested this assumption. Bernstein's contacts with his former chief, the Secretary of the Treasury, gave him a great advantage in his negotiations in England.[291] On the other hand, as the CCS instructions of October 7 indicated, the moderate faction had support at high and influential places also. JCS 1067, as with the other results of the Cabinet Committee deliberations and Presidential activities of September and October 1944, did not settle or clarify policy for the treatment of Germany, but only led to further disputation within SHAEF.

Another factional split developed in the field at this time. The U. S. Group Control Council was staffed largely with officers of civilian background who had come from the German Country Unit, where they had also predominated. This civilian element had been organized originally in early 1944 in order to have a combined planning staff for each of the countries of Europe, and when it was entirely unclear as to what the relationship between Allied military commands, military government and occupation forces, and possible Allied civilian administrators in Germany would be. With the establishment of the U. S. Group Control Council in August (the British had established a

parallel organization somewhat earlier) a definite struggle developed for influence between
the Army regulars of the U. S. element of G-5,
SHAEF, constituting the civil affairs side of
military command, and the civilian-oriented
staff of the U. S. Group Control Council, which
envisaged military government as relatively independent of military command and operating
in its internal structure on a somewhat modified
conception of military command.[292]

The three civilian agencies in Washington
were affected in different ways by the events
of September. The State Department continued
its exchanges with the President in its effort
to undermine his Quebec commitment to Treasury views on German policy. But new work
required active leadership by the Secretary,
and Hull could not give it. A fresh start could
not be made until December when Hull, yielding to the bad health which had kept him from
all work since the end of October, resigned and
Stettinius, his successor, took office.

The Treasury Department staff, as has been
described, kept up the momentum of its preparation of position papers on German policy,
while it kept out of controversy on the subject
within the government during the 1944 Presidential campaign, by a collective effort to write
a book on Germany, and by producing a long
blast at a British position paper on Germany.

The position of FEA, following the drafting
of JCS 1067, was not so frustrating as it was
for State or Treasury, but that agency was left
in a confusing situation, trying to study the
German policy problem without adequate terms
of reference, turning indeed to the President's
campaign speeches for policy guidance.

E. ROOSEVELT'S VIEWS AND THE STATE DEPARTMENT

The correspondence concerning German
policy which the State Department had undertaken with the President following the Quebec
Conference had by the end of October yielded
results markedly favorable to the State Department viewpoint, although the Department officials undoubtedly overestimated the extent
to which the President agreed with them. The
President's last reply, dated October 20, had
informally commented on and raised questions
about their October 1 memorandum. Anxious
to continue this correspondence because of its

apparent success, because of the Department's
desire to settle policy questions, and particularly because JCS 1067 was now to be revised
for Winant's use in EAC negotiations, State
prepared by November 10 a new draft statement of economic policy for the treatment of
Germany which attempted to incorporate
Roosevelt's latest views. Stettinius, who was
acting Secretary most of the time now, talked
with the President on the afternoon of the 10th.
He said that Roosevelt had requested in his
last memorandum a new draft on economic
policy, which was now ready. He stressed the
importance of providing EAC promptly with
a settled American position on the treatment
of Germany so that a tripartite agreement could
be reached before occupation began. When
promised that the new draft was short, the
President agreed to read it. Stettinius sent it to
him the following day, asking for further discussion "if this draft does not accurately set
forth your views."[293]

The memorandum was an ingenious exposition of American policy on the economic
treatment of Germany in relation to British and
Soviet views which neatly refuted by oblique
reference both the Morgenthau Plan and the
only real justification the President had ever
given for accepting a portion of it at Quebec
—the protection of British markets.

Tripartite agreement on the economic treatment of Germany is urgent, it began,

because present British, Russian and American
attitudes on the question show major divergencies
which, if allowed to persist, would begin to be reflected in widely different policies at an early
state in the occupation of Germany. Such differences, in turn, would lay the basis for new European rivalries and endanger the effectiveness of
an international security organization.

With this familiar claim of the State Department reasserted, the draft described the British
and Russian positions on the economic treatment of Germany. The British intend to retain
"as large a part of the existing organization
and structure of the German economy as is
compatible with the destruction of the Nazi
regime," it stated. Their aim is to prevent economic breakdown, but retain control over the
German economy. And now State made its
oblique assault upon the argument used at
Quebec, and adopted at that time by the President, that the Morgenthau Plan would assure

Britain of markets for export. It showed that Roosevelt's and Churchill's objective of protecting Britain against German economic competition did not require Morgenthau's solution.

Furthermore Russia had "no economic interest in restraining German competition." Rather, she would want to exploit the German economy to aid Russian reconstruction and development. "It is pretty clear," the State draft concluded (underestimating the Russian demands for reparations in the form of existing plant), "that sweeping deindustrialization would be regarded by Russia as incompatible with her interest in Germany as a source of supply of industrial goods."

These divergent tendencies of policy could "seriously endanger long-run cooperation between Britain and the U. S. S. R." But the two powers do have a mutual interest in cooperation itself, and in certain economic conditions. One of these, State claimed, would be inter-zonal movement of goods, since the two zones are economically interdependent. The other was a common ground on economic treatment:

(a) Both Britain and Russia favor exercise of extensive responsibility by the occupation authorities for control of the German economy.

(b) Both countries seem to oppose sweeping deindustrialization of Germany. Agreement could probably be reached on a program of industrial dismantling—to include specialized facilities for production of munitions and aircraft and, perhaps, a few synthetic materials.

Here was the oblique assault on the Morgenthau Plan itself, for the stated area of Anglo-Soviet agreement on the economic treatment of Germany was strikingly like the position which the State Department had been taking, while the description of the British and Russian positions was intended to make clear that neither country could be brought around to accept the essential features of the Treasury position. The conclusion drawn from it was a clear challenge to the Morgenthau Plan.

A program of sweeping deindustrialization does not provide an adequate basis for sustained international security cooperation, nor does it provide a satisfactory alternative to such cooperation. A program designed to impose lasting restraint on Germany's industrial exports to Western markets also involves the danger of generating serious, new rivalries in Europe and of weakening the basis for international security cooperation.[294]

The draft concluded with a restatement of policy on the economic treatment of Germany. It referred to the familiar liberal economic objectives of the "abolition of German self-sufficiency" and the "elimination of German economic domination over Europe," as distinctly long-range. For negotiating with the British and Russians on a policy for the period of Allied control it proposed a series of six general points. The first concluded the main argument of the draft:

We shall be obliged to go along with the British and Russians in accepting large responsibilities for the guidance and reorientation of German economic life. It is altogether unlikely that a "hands off" policy would be accepted and adhered to by all three powers. Consequently, we must be prepared to take all possible steps in the initial phases of occupation to prevent development of a chaotically unmanageable economic situation, since this is a prerequisite to the exercise of effective economic control.[295]

The remaining points proposed a low initial German standard of living, disarmament, heavy reparations for a short period, and machinery to ensure inter-zonal movements of commodities.[296]

On November 15, Stettinius and two assistants met with the President. Roosevelt told them their memorandum was generally satisfactory, particularly because "it did not dot all the i's and cross all the t's,"[297] but that he feared that the proposed Control Council in Berlin would have "insufficient representation of a tough civilian point of view," since present plans were that it would be made up of "military men." The Control Council had not been mentioned in the memorandum. Apparently in accepting the main point of the memorandum—that the United States would have to accept "large responsibilities for the guidance and reorientation of German economic life"—the President had thought ahead to the execution of those responsibilities, and concluded that the military viewpoint was insufficiently "tough" because it tended to emphasize administrative convenience.[298]

Stettinius wanted a definite commitment. He asked the President if he would be willing to send copies of the memorandum to War, Treasury, and Navy for comment as a draft which he considered satisfactory. The President agreed to do so, but returned to his earlier theme. He "said he was still in a tough mood and that he is determined to be tough with Germany." But he agreed that the memorandum was "sufficiently tough." He ended by reaffirming his conviction that we could not tell what Germany would be like after defeat—hence, of course, his praise for the memorandum's failure to "dot all the i's and cross all the t's."

That day Roosevelt showed Morgenthau the memorandum at lunch. Morgenthau convinced him that the policy statement was not satisfactory, for the President subsequently indicated to the State Department that he wished to redraft it.[299]

A week later, when no new draft had come from the White House, Stettinius attempted to prod the President. "At the time you redraft the memorandum on the Economic Treatment of Germany you might find the attached memorandum useful," he wrote.[300] The "Summary of Department's Views on Economic Treatment of Germany"[301] which he enclosed was —excluding Hull's confusions in the early Cabinet Committee meetings—perhaps the greatest compromise with the Treasury position ever proposed by State. It read:

The Department of State believes:
(1) The German economy should be operated as nearly as possible *as a unit* during the occupation period.
(2) Allied occupation policy should be severe—
(a) a rock-bottom standard of living for the Germans;
(b) labor services for the rehabilitation of devastated parts of Europe;
(c) transfer of such industrial equipment and stockpiles as liberated countries can put to effective use, limited only by necessity for maintaining a minimum German economy;
(d) conversion of the German economy to peacetime production, including production for minimum German needs and for reconstruction of rest of Europe on reparation account;
(e) elimination from positions of control of those industrial and financial leaders who have been closely identified with the Nazi regime or who have derived large benefit from Aryanization or spoliation of occupied countries.

To be sure, it went on to insist that Germany could be controlled effectively only by an international security organization, and that in the long run economic inter-dependence would be an important factor—both points which throw into question the seriousness of the quoted passage. Moreover, the passage uses far less precise terminology than was available as a by-product of the nearly three months of contention over German policy. "Rock-bottom standard of living," for instance, in the light of the dispute over the German living standard, the issues raised by it, and the terms of measurement developed for it, was meaningless. It revealed no new position: only a greater concern on the part of State that some kind of long-range policy be settled.

A week later Stettinius reminded Roosevelt again that he awaited the President's revision of the memorandum on the economic treatment of Germany—this time by sending to the White House a memorandum on British views which served to reinforce the tentative description included in the November 10th memorandum.[302] The President finally responded from Warm Springs on December 4, but hardly in the way Stettinius had expected. He sent a short note to Stettinius which read:

I have yours of November 29th on the Economic Treatment of Germany. There are two things which I think the State Department ought to keep in the linings of their hats. (1) That in the Economic Treatment of Germany we should let her come back industrially to meet her own needs, but not to do any exporting for sometime and we know better how things are going to work out. (2) We are against reparations. (3) We do want restitution of looted property of all kinds.[303]

Instead of a positive policy statement, affirming State's position, the note seemed intended to correct what were regarded as misconceptions held by State. Furthermore, its first two points were in disagreement with the British position described in Stettinius' previous note. State had been trying to get the President to take into consideration the British viewpoint in order to facilitate tripartite agreement, but Roosevelt had now balked. The Warm Springs note had a tone of impatience and finality to it which may well have been intended. For, despite Stettinius' badgering of the President, the policy paper on the economic treatment of Germany was never redrafted in the White House. On March 6, 1945, after it had clearly become outdated, it was returned to the State Department.[304] The President had been led away from the Morgenthau Plan through the persistence of State, but it could not tie him down to its own position. Perhaps the key phrase in his memorandum of December 4 was: "[until] we know better how things are going to work out."

F. THE FIRST REVISION OF JCS 1067

1. The Setting for Revision

In Washington the attempt to produce a policy directive for the occupation of Germany in the post-defeat period through inter-departmental agreement had already been disrupted when Roosevelt announced at the end of September 1944, the dissolution of the Cabinet Committee on Germany. Only the pressing Interim Directive, which was an expression of United States policy only, had been completed. While SHAEF was left to wrestle over the ambiguities of the original Interim Directive, JCS 1067, and over its applicability to SHAEF planning, efforts were resumed to achieve agreement within the United States government on a longer-term policy for the treatment of Germany which would apply throughout the American occupation, and could serve as the basis of Anglo-American and tripartite agreement.

One of the difficulties in arriving at a German policy had been the lack of effective interdepartmental machinery—a lack that was not remedied by CCAC and ECEFP in spite of some successes within their particular spheres; certainly it was not solved by WSC. The problem was, of course, not confined to Germany: similar problems requiring agreement particularly among the State, War, and Navy Departments were arising all over the world.

The high status of JCS in the wartime government, as the experience of the Working Security Committee so amply demonstrated, complicated the problem of inter-departmental coordination. State had found it virtually impossible to reach the Joint Chiefs by way of WSC. Yet a direct approach to the Chiefs was resented in the Secretary of War's office. For a solution of this dilemma new machinery was developed.

Since his first letter to Hull in August about direct State-JCS relations Stimson had remained troubled over what he considered an unjustifiable intrusion on the status of the Secretaries of War and the Navy. His letter went unanswered. When he was sure it had been for-

gotten, he wrote again, on October 12.[305] In August, McCloy and Dunn had been hopeful of expediting guidance for Winant by going directly to the Joint Chiefs without War Department clearance (because of the cumbersomeness of full staff clearance, not the difficulties of clearance in Stimson's office). From their viewpoint, therefore, Stimson's suggestion that the State Department deal with JCS through the Secretaries of War and the Navy was badly timed. Two months later, however, when their joint efforts to rejuvenate the Working Security Committee were proving vain, Stimson's complaint was more timely. Hull's office (he was ill and soon to retire) responded with a sympathetic query. McCloy thereupon took the matter up with Admiral Leahy, the President's representative on the Joint Chiefs of Staff. Since Leahy had opposed having the Joint Chiefs clear papers not first cleared fully in both the State and War (or Navy) Departments, he naturally favored it, although King and Forrestal did not.[306]

On November 4, Stimson wrote the now Acting Secretary of State, Edward R. Stettinius, Jr., making his point a third time, and suggesting that communications should be jointly addressed to the two service Secretaries, who would then be responsible for consulting the appropriate military authorities and coordinating the views of the two departments.[307]

Stettinius replied with a proposal for an interdepartmental committee composed of representatives of the three Secretaries, and "charged with the duty of formulating recommendations to the Secretary of State on questions having both military and political aspects and coordinating the views of the three Departments in matters of interdepartmental interest." In effect, he intended to replace the now defunct Working Security Committee with a new committee of higher rank, such as his Department had originally intended as the mechanism for providing Winant with guidance for EAC negotiations. While Stimson's proposal was for what seemed to be another obstacle to policy clearance for Winant and other politico-military questions, it was now turned, undoubtedly with the willing cooperation of officials in both the State and War Departments who had been concerned with expediting the clearance of guidance papers for Winant, into a new effort at coordination.[308]

On December 1, which was also the day Stettinius succeeded Hull, a working committee of Assistant Secretaries which came to be known as the State-War-Navy Coordinating Committee was appointed, consisting of Mc-Cloy, Artemus Gates from the Navy, and, as chairman, Dunn from State, who by the time of the first meeting of SWNCC on December 19 had been promoted to Assistant Secretary.[309]

On the same day, and largely at Stimson's initiative, the Committee of Three, the Secretaries of State, War, and the Navy, resumed its weekly meetings. After meeting regularly for only a few months, Hull had signalled its decline into uselessness exactly three years earlier when he had announced to Stimson scarcely two weeks before Pearl Harbor that he had washed his hands of further attempts to negotiate with the Japanese, and that the problem of American relations with Japan was now in the hands of the military—Stimson and Knox and their departments.[310] Although the meetings had continued, they remained no more than a casual exchange of information, the routine probably maintained out of a felt need for, or hope that, something more could be achieved. Then, when Hull fell ill, they were discontinued.[311]

Now, with Stimson anxious to assert his Cabinet role, a new Secretary of State who wanted to improve his Department's relations with the services, a new Secretary of the Navy, Forrestal, who had become greatly interested in the developing policy implications of the war, and the three departments committed to SWNCC, an attempt was made, which proved partially successful, to rejuvenate the Committee of Three. At its first meeting on December 19 both Stettinius and Forrestal "suggested that McCloy come in as recorder to keep us in connection with the lower committee [and through it, with the JCS] and also to act in helping us to formulate and regulate our own agenda."[312]

Since SWNCC was to concern itself with matters of mixed military and political significance, if it was to be effective, it needed to be closely geared in with the Joint Chiefs of Staff, and have available for its use JCS papers. In December 1944, the Joint Chiefs were at the height of their wartime prestige and influence. They were persuaded to cooperate with the new inter-departmental committee, but only after extracting from Stimson the promise that, in order to minimize the risk to JCS security, SWNCC would be strictly limited to its three original members. The promise met an immediate test, for among SWNCC's initial tasks was completing the formulation of a directive on the treatment of Germany for negotiation in the European Advisory Commission, an activity in which Treasury would demand participation.

However, in December 1944, such demands were not likely to be pressed hard or conceded readily. Stimson had committed his Department against such a development. At the same time, State felt, on the basis of its talks and exchanges of memoranda with the President during October and November, that he had repudiated the Morgenthau Plan and all but formally ratified its own position. Moreover, the directive under consideration was for Winant's use. Treasury might have some excuse for helping to provide the Army with the policy guidance which the Army could not produce itself, but it held no favored position in policy-making for the State Department.

To the Treasury, the fact that the revision was destined for use in EAC, which had accomplished so little thus far, may have made working on that document seem unimportant, particularly since Bernstein was at that time participating under General McSherry in London in the drafting of policy papers for submittal through the Combined Chiefs which could have ultimately the same effect as would the proposed EAC agreement.

The War Department continued to try to play a neutral role, in principle; in fact, it now tended to side with the Treasury. McCloy and Hilldring, determined to keep the Army out of high policy-making, were anxious to carry out the wishes of the Commander in Chief. But what were those wishes? To the State Department Stettinius' correspondence with Roosevelt in October and November, following the Quebec Conference, had indicated that the Commander in Chief had had a change of heart on the Quebec statement on Germany, a change which State was anxious to exploit. To McCloy, the salient problem was to keep the agreement which JCS 1067 represented from disintegrating, and the salient fact, that whatever the views the President expressed, the Treasury

Department was still influential with him.

In addition, the War and Treasury Departments had coincident viewpoints concerning two important elements of German policy. For different reasons both wanted the Army clearly absolved from any responsibility for maintaining the German economic system in operation; the Treasury, because it did not want the Army to be authorized to build up the German economy, and the War Department because it did not want to have responsibility which clearly over-reached its capabilities. The other point at which War and Treasury Department views tended to coincide at this time was over denazification policy. The War Department had, as a result of its somewhat indiscriminate use of Nazis in the administration of Aachen, the first major German city it had taken, come under bitter attack in the press, and was at the time of revision of JCS 1067 developing a more strict denazification policy for the pre-surrender period.

2. *The SWNCC Revision Initiated*

The first draft of the revision of JCS 1067 was prepared in the War Department in mid-November. An *ad hoc* committee worked on it during the latter part of November and much of December 1944, holding conferences almost daily. It consisted of two of Hilldring's assistants in CAD, Colonel R. Ammi Cutter and Lieutenant Colonel Edgar P. Allen, Riddleberger and Emile Despres for the State Department, and Lieutenant Harding F. Bancroft for the Navy Department—a rejuvenated Working Security Committee, so to speak.[313] The State Department had evidently hoped to make substantial changes in JCS 1067 in transforming it from an interim policy directive to a long-range policy position paper for Winant. The War Department, on the other hand, anxious to expedite the establishment of long-term American policy, wished to avoid any changes in JCS 1067 which might lead to further inter-departmental bickering of the kind which had occurred three months earlier. The issue between them was joined in meetings of the working committee on November 24 and 25, while the State Department still hoped to nail down a repudiation by Roosevelt of his Quebec commitment to Treasury views. Riddleberger advocated substantial changes in JCS 1067 and

insisted that the Treasury need not be consulted except on matters of financial consequence, including the financial appendix to JCS 1067. Cutter stated as McCloy's view that deviations from JCS 1067 should be as slight as possible, and that, as a matter of good judgment, any substantial ones should be reported to the Treasury. Cutter defended automatic arrest as a feature of denazification policy. Both men ended up citing the strong (and divergent) views of their superiors.[314] By December 27, when the first business meeting of the SWNCC was held, the working committee had reached tentative agreement on a draft, and it had been decided that a part of it, the financial directive, should be cleared with the Treasury Department. In fact, before giving final approval to the revised JCS 1067, the whole of it was referred to the Treasury Department for comment, as Cutter and McCloy had proposed.[315]

Among other things, the Treasury insisted that the denazification provisions be made more severe by extending the arrest categories further down the pyramid of the Nazi hierarchy. War Department officials supported this change. As has been noted above, the Army was moving at this time towards a stronger denazification policy. In addition, it had come to accept a more comprehensive arrest policy because of a transformation in its own thinking about the function of arrest in military government. While it had originally seen the arrest policy proposed by the Treasury, which was intended to assure the apprehension of a maximum number of persons for punishment as war criminals, as an unnecessary burden on the Army, since in any case the War Department would insist on maximum discretion for the commander on the spot, it was an easy shift of emphasis to viewing arrest—or "security arrest," as it was called—as a technique of control for military government. Seen in this light, detention was not a burden but a necessity.[316] With War Department support, the Treasury proposals for broadening the arrest categories, and thus strengthening the denazification policy, was accepted in the SWNCC revision.

The War Department had held the initiative in its relations with State throughout the revision of JCS 1067, although perhaps only because it had strictly circumscribed its own freedom of action. It had insisted that nothing be done in the revision to alienate the Treasury, that changes from the original version be modest, and that policy provisions remain general. All of these were points with which State Department officials were inclined to disagree.

On December 27, when the draft was practically completed, Hilldring and six of his assistants gathered in McCloy's office for a final settlement of the War Department's position. The first question raised, although it was a procedural one, was in some ways the most important: whether it was necessary to obtain JCS clearance for the revised directive prior to turning it over to Winant. McCloy settled the matter promptly, for he had anticipated it. He had discussed it with General Handy, the head of OPD, who had agreed with him that no major changes of substance which had military implications—in fact, no major changes of substance at all—had been made in JCS 1067, so that JCS approval was unnecessary. Moreover, "the document must come back from the European Advisory Commission in any event for approval, when it could be submitted to the Joint Chiefs of Staff in final form."

This time, it would appear, the tables were turned on the Joint Chiefs. For a year their requirement that a matter be in its final form before they be asked to review it had held up clearance of guidance for Winant because it had not been possible to establish a final State-War-Navy position. Now that one had been reached, the fact that it was only intended as a position for tripartite negotiation, and hence, not really a final position, was used to avoid JCS clearance. Once an agreement had been negotiated between Britain, the Soviet Union, and the United States, it would be in final enough form to be reviewed by JCS. Even JCS could hardly expect to modify inter-governmental agreements.

There were other features of the revised JCS 1067 which were troublesome. Herbert Feis, a prominent State Department economist, and some of the CAD personnel were concerned about the way the economic directive prohibited the occupying authorities from interfering with the German economy for any constructive purpose. Also the attempt to set an absolute ceiling on the German standard of living was fraught with difficulties. And denazification provisions, which, according to

McCloy, represented an adjustment between the final American practice in Italy and the extreme position of the Treasury Department, were obscure, and according to some, too soft. But all objections gave way to practical considerations. The Army needed a policy, and this one would do. As it stood, it had the agreement of the State, War, and Treasury Departments, and the President. Modifying it would jeopardize that agreement and cause delay. Moreover, if the *laissez faire* philosophy of its economic policy was extreme, it was a good point from which to begin bargaining with the British, who were inclined, McCloy said, to want too much interference and control in German economic affairs. Finally, it met the Army's desire for a general directive, rather than a detailed one such as the British proposed.

At a meeting on January 6, 1945, after final consideration of the other Treasury objections to the document, SWNCC agreed to recommend to the Secretary of State that the revised JCS 1067 be sent to Winant in London as a Working Paper representing U. S. views for negotiation in EAC. This was done. The draft was also sent to Ambassador Robert D. Murphy, Political Adviser to General Eisenhower.[317]

The revision was designed to rephrase JCS 1067 (which was originally drafted in the form of a directive from CCS to the commander of a combined theater) as a directive from each of the three governments to its commander in chief in Germany. Such a redraft was necessary in order to put the directive in a form appropriate for discussion (as requested by Ambassador Winant) in EAC. It also reflected a change of policy in the winter of 1944-1945 to back-step on combined Anglo-American military government plans in order that the Russians, who might be brought into civil affairs planning in London, would not be suspicious of Anglo-American collusion. It was for this same reason that the U. S. Group Control Council had been separated from the British parallel organization shortly after their reorganization in August 1944.[318]

The first part of the January 6 revision of JCS 1067, indicating a growing concern for the provision of control machinery, differed from the original draft in that it defined the relationship between the tripartite Control Council, which was to be the central Allied organ of occupation, and the zone commanders in terms of the supremacy of the Control Council. The authority of the Control Council was to be paramount throughout Germany, and the commanders would enforce its decisions in their own zones of occupation. Throughout the rest of the document minor changes were made to carry through this provision.

Reflecting the factional fight in the field over whether the civilian-dominated U. S. Group Control Council or the Army "regulars" in G-5, SHAEF, were to dominate military government, and the earlier dispute in WSC between State and War representatives as to the relative degree of autonomy to be exercised by the Army field command, considerable discussion had occurred in SWNCC over the authority to be granted the zone commander in the revised directive. State held that cooperation with the Russians and the functioning of Germany as a whole unit were essential, and that therefore the tripartite level of occupation administration deserved strong support. The Army, in contrast, perhaps because of its earlier difficulties with the British over civil affairs planning for Germany and its skepticism of Allied cooperation through diplomatic means, in addition to its general opposition to changing JCS 1067, was reluctant to accept provisions for the establishment of strongly centralized joint occupational arrangements. Hence, the clear assertion made at one point in this document of the Control Council's authority over the zone commanders thus constituted a significant concession to the State Department viewpoint (although the draft still contained so much "separate zone" doctrine as to upset the British and Russian delegations seriously). Similarly, the economic directive in the revised JCS 1067 bore the marks of new concessions to the moderate economic view. It began by adding to the controversial first paragraph (which was, as it had been approved in September, an elaborate combination of positive and negative statements regarding economic policy) an additional positive statement. It required the commander in chief of each nation's forces to assume such control over various activities in Germany as was necessary for assuring the safety of his forces, the satisfaction of their needs, and the accomplishment of his mission, thus beginning on the note of military

necessity. It left the Control Council to deal with the problem of zonal surpluses and deficiencies.

Like the relationship of zone commander to central machinery of occupation, the length of the occupation period was dealt with more directly in the January revision of JCS 1067. To the earlier directive it added:

It is envisaged that control or surveillance of Germany will be maintained in some form for a prolonged period, and that military government will, when practicable, be replaced by other methods of control involving smaller commitment of forces.[319]

The economic directive in the January revision spelled out the deindustrialization provisions of the original JCS 1067 in somewhat greater detail. Though still ambiguous, the result was a statement of severe policy. Besides war production, all ferro-alloy, light metal, and synthetic oil and rubber production was to be eliminated, either by destruction, conversion, or removal for reparations; and all other industry was to be reduced to its 1932 level. While this was seemingly a victory for the Morgenthau Plan, another provision required the occupation authorities to exercise controls over wages and prices, and fiscal and monetary affairs in order to prevent inflation, an obligation which could easily lead to a responsibility for preventing breakdown in the German economy. One of the first indications of Treasury policy, it will be remembered, had been White's insistence, while accompanying Morgenthau on his trip to England in August 1944, that Germany should be left to "stew in her own juice."[320]

Thus, the revision of JCS 1067 had produced a tortuous draft of statements and counterstatements, of new refinements and new loopholes. To say that it favored either the Treasury viewpoint or the State Department position would be misleading. It was not a victory for State because the hard-peace provisions and the other features of the Treasury position were not eliminated—because, that is to say, JCS 1067 was not substantially modified. Nor was it a Treasury victory, for, although JCS 1067 had survived without major alteration, some definite concessions had been made to the State Department position. If anyone did emerge from this encounter as the victor, it was the War Department, but only because its objectives were modest: to expedite and to maximize its freedom of action.

While the economic directive showed few signs of new Treasury influence, the financial directive for the revision of JCS 1067 was clearly dominated by the Treasury position. Since it was not completed by January 6, the rest of the revision was sent to Winant without it, with the understanding that the missing part would follow when completed. An agreed financial directive revision was not to be completed for another month. In the meantime, Bernstein had returned to Washington from London and influenced its preparation decisively.

3. Bernstein in Washington: Revising the Financial Directive

While the revision of JCS 1067 was being completed in the State-War-Navy Coordinating Committee at the turn of the year, Bernstein traveled to Washington to carry through, in the Treasury Department, a careful survey of the Treasury position, and apply it specifically to the problem at hand in London of developing a post-surrender policy to be used by SHAEF so long as it remained responsible for the occupation of Germany. When he arrived, he found Treasury involved in similar work through another channel: the redrafting of the financial directive for JCS 1067 referred to above. Drawing from his own experience working on the financial section of a general order being prepared in London by the U. S. Group Control Council, he suggested to his Treasury colleagues that the new financial directive grant substantial police powers to the zone commanders, subject to the overriding authority of the Control Council on matters on which it agreed. He also proposed that the use of German foreign exchange to purchase imports be prohibited except where clearly and urgently needed to further occupation objectives. In London, Bernstein had had some difficulties with Winant's economist, E. F. Penrose, over the draft financial directive being prepared there, the latter insisting that the occupation authorities would have to be made responsible in some measure for public finance, since otherwise inflation would be likely to occur; and that would render taxation meaningless.[321] Bernstein, on the other hand, was

anxious that the occupation not be given powers with the constructive potentialities which accompanied a responsibility for public finance. In Washington he saw to it that, along with the suggestions mentioned above, the Treasury's draft of the revised financial directive had written into it a statement that the Germans would be responsible for taxation and public finance.

Bernstein's stay in Washington led to a flurry of meetings within the Treasury Department—seven all told from January 10 to February 3, 1945.[322] At these sessions, the central task was the preparation of the revised financial directive for JCS 1067. However, Bernstein and his associates reviewed all phases of German policy, and their discussions stimulated a variety of side activities by Treasury officials.[323]

On the day of the first meeting, January 10, Morgenthau sent a memorandum to the President on Germany after defeat in which was summarized the Treasury position at that date as it had been developed in the drafts for his book. Echoing Churchill's phrase in the Quebec minute, it said:

We are more convinced than ever that if we really mean to deprive Germany of the ability to make war again within a few years it is absolutely essential that she be deprived of her chemical, metallurgical and electrical industries. We don't think that this alone will guarantee peace, but that it is one of the steps we must take now.[324]

This conclusion was based on three premises: (1) "The German people have the will to try again." (2) "Programs for democracy, reeducation and kindness cannot destroy this will within any brief time." (3) "Heavy industry is the core of Germany's war-making potential." He went on to state to the President for the first time the suspicions which his staff had been writing about for more than two months:

The more I think on this problem, and the more I hear and read discussion of it, the clearer it seems to me that the real motive of most of those who oppose a weak Germany is not any actual disagreement on these three points. On the contrary, it is simply an expression of fear of Russia and communism. It is the twenty-year-old ideal of a "bulwark against Bolshevism"—which was one of the factors that brought this present war down on us.

The memorandum suggested that the people

who held this view were unwilling to admit it, but covered their real reason with such arguments as the following: Europe needs industrial Germany. German production is needed for necessary reparations out of production. The removal or destruction of German war materials and armament industry would effectively prevent them from waging war again. Leniency would facilitate the growth of democracy in Germany. Making Germany "a predominantly agricultural country, with light industries but no heavy industries, would mean starving Germans." He concluded:

This thing needs to be dragged out into the open. I feel so deeply about it that I speak strongly. If we don't face it I am just as sure as I can be that we are going to let a lot of hollow and hypocritical propaganda lead us into recreating a strong Germany and making a foe of Russia. I shudder for the sake of our children to think of what will follow.

Growing out of the meetings with Bernstein, Treasury officials drafted a letter to be sent to McCloy. It raised strong objections to the instructions issued from SHAEF by General Grasset on October 9, which, it said, were designed to preserve the economic structure of Nazism. It asserted that there was a great gap in the denazification program as laid down in the military government handbook, since there was no provision for removing "Nazis, Nazi collaborators and other undesirables from the important sectors of industry and commerce,"[325] and the procedure in finance provided for suspension, not removal. Specific proposed changes in the military government handbook were included.

In mid-January, Josiah DuBois of the Treasury played an active part in inter-departmental negotiations on the treatment of German war criminals. He pressed for stern and prompt action and feared that the proposed procedures left loopholes through which some war criminals might escape. The Treasury had had some measure of success in securing adherence to its views.[326]

During Bernstein's absence in Washington, his Finance Division, USGCC, continued to work with EAC political advisers on German financial policies. A draft entitled "Advanced Ministerial Control Plan (Germany)—Finance," dated January 13, 1945, was sent to him in Washington. He raised several objections to it,

criticizing most strongly the assumption of financial responsibilities in Germany by the Allied occupation. He disagreed with the assumption that public financial agencies would be in existence or reconstituted on a national basis, since it involved objectionable centralization. He thought it wrong to conclude that executive control of zonal activities would be exercised from Berlin. He pointed out that his idea of the division of functions between the Zone Headquarters and the Control Commission was that the Zone Headquarters would have the function of picking the representatives of the Ministry of Finance in their respective zones. Finally, he said that he did not "like the idea of our saying that we will coordinate our policies with the British even, in fact, if the Russians are not available."[327]

On January 24 he wrote his executive officer, Major Morton P. Fisher,[328] to this effect, and later reprimanded him for failing to insist on his interpretations of JCS 1067 as the embodiment of the Treasury viewpoint, and demand that it be the only basis for policy negotiations in EAC.

The Treasury conference on German policy was resumed for two days on February 2. The answers to several questions of occupation policy in the post-surrender period were agreed to. They included some relatively specific problems involving reparation and restitution, art objects as foreign exchange assets, the counterfeiting of AM (American Military) marks, and other matters. In more general terms, it was decided that SHAEF should not be authorized to allow exports to neutrals.

The revision of the financial directive for JCS 1067 was also considered at these meetings. Bernstein had helped Treasury officials draft a new version which was submitted to State and War officials at the end of January. In comparison with other draft revisions then under consideration, this document emphasized more emphatically the Treasury view. It stressed decentralization by authorizing the zonal administrations to carry out policies in the absence of EAC approval—perhaps copying General McSherry's tactics in London. It made the Germans, rather than the occupation authorities, responsible for public finance, and added a new paragraph which limited strictly the application of the disease and unrest formula. (Bernstein thought the British interpreted the disease and unrest formula too broadly.)

Somewhat belatedly, at these Treasury meetings on February 2 and 3, a letter to McCloy was approved which, echoing Bernstein's dispute with Penrose in London, protested a provision in the economic directive (approved January 6 along with the rest of the revision of JCS 1067) which made the occupation authorities responsible for the prevention of inflation. The Treasury letter stated that the assumption of any responsibility for inflation controls was in effect responsibility for the entire German economy—a responsibility which the Treasury did not think should be assumed.[329]

4. *The SWNCC Revision Completed*

McCloy and Hilldring, finding nothing important in the new version of the financial directive to which the Army could object, accepted it with minor modifications. But the State Department's reaction was more critical. It found the autonomy of the zones in financial policy undesirable, and the restrictive character of the policy guidance furnished unsatisfactory. In its view, the breakdown of banking and financial machinery ought not to be allowed, nor should inflation be permitted. Both would jeopardize the objectives of the occupation. Furthermore, it considered the proposals for blocking German public assets to be a technique without a policy. With Hilldring and McCloy willing to accept the Bernstein draft financial directive, State was unable to demand much alteration of it. Indeed, on February 6, after War and Treasury had cleared the document, it was Hilldring who attempted to gain concurrence from State. Eventually, State was satisfied by the addition of one of those curious paragraphs so characteristic of the original JCS 1067 which combined constructive and restrictive statements, but which indicated that the financial machinery of Germany was not to be allowed to break down. The Treasury's sweeping policy on internal blocking was also slightly modified in order to allow the use, under general licenses, of government property. The financial directive was finished on February 12, thereby completing the first revision of JCS 1067.

V. COMPLETING THE OCCUPATION DIRECTIVE: THE SECOND REVISION

A. *YALTA*

1. *Background*

The Yalta Conference was long in the making.[330] Roosevelt first proposed it to Stalin in July 1944, but eventually the earliest feasible time was found to be February 1945. The delay was irksome, and led to Churchill's meeting with Roosevelt in Quebec in September 1944, and with Stalin in Moscow in October.

To the State Department, Yalta seemed to offer great promise. Here, for the first time since the first Quebec Conference in August 1943, the Secretary of State would be present at an international meeting; indeed, this was the only wartime conference in which, it was anticipated, he would be present from start to finish and in daily, almost constant, touch with Roosevelt. Furthermore, there would be a happy absence of distracting personalities— no Morgenthau, no Stimson, no Crowley—and a happy assurance that the JCS would either stick to their own business (as the State Department viewed it) or be readily at hand for prompt decisions when their action was needed. At one time it was hoped that Stettinius would accompany Roosevelt on the *Quincy,* but this did not occur; instead, Stettinius went by air and, after conferring with Eden at Malta for a couple of days, saw the President there only briefly before the whole delegation set off for Yalta, where it arrived on February 4.

Although Stettinius was at the President's side only briefly on the voyage to Yalta, he had had some opportunity to acquaint Roosevelt with the State Department's viewpoint before leaving Washington. On January 18, five days before the President set sail, Stettinius had presented him with a briefing book which contained summaries, full statements, and sup-

plementary materials on ten points which the Department hoped to have "satisfactorily dealt with" at Yalta; and before the voyage began, Stettinius had numerous conferences with Roosevelt on topics expected to be considered at the conference including the United Nations and the treatment of Germany. In addition, the President asked to have the briefing book placed in "his cabin aboard ship." How much he supplemented his talks with Stettinius by reading on shipboard the massive State Department documentation is unknowable, but, for reasons discussed below, it is doubtful that he would have found much that was new to him in the State Department's papers on German policy.

The section in the briefing book on the treatment of Germany consisted of three papers running to some ten thousand words, and summaries with another two thousand words, to boot.[331] From one standpoint, this was the best of all the Department's policy statements on Germany. It was frank and inclusive; it tried to avoid ambiguities even on the tough questions; it was precise where other memoranda had been vague and it presented a reasonably consistent and coherent program. It evinced active awareness of British and Russian desires, and tried manfully to incorporate some recommendations embodying points on which Roosevelt seemed to have made his position clear; it was, for this reason, "sufficiently tough."

Of the three papers one was on the general treatment of Germany, one on economic policy, and one on reparations. The paper on economic policy was a clarified and elaborated version of the November 10 State Department draft on the same subject which the President had been brought to the very brink of approving and with which he was certainly familiar. The paper on reparations was substantially the same as the Report on Reparations, Restitution, and

Property Rights, which had been approved by the Executive Committee on Economic Foreign Policy on August 4, 1944—before Morgenthau had risen to challenge the developing views of his government on the treatment of Germany. It is highly doubtful that the President was familiar with this document, but he probably was familiar with its approach to reparations.

The paper on the general treatment of Germany began with one recommendation which Roosevelt carried out before the Yalta Conference convened: that the draft "Agreement on Control Machinery in Germany" be accepted by the President "without reservation." There is no reason to doubt that the President was fully conversant with this recommendation. Some of the other portions of the paper had deep roots in State Department staff work, such as its recommendation against the forcible dismemberment of Germany, which went back to the first policy papers on Germany prepared in 1943; and its proposals on public information and education policy, a summary of which the President had approved in his October 20, 1944 memorandum.

Taken as a whole, the briefing book made a conscientious effort to treat seriously the President's repeated demands that he wanted a "tough" policy for Germany. He had made it clear to all and sundry that he wanted the Germans to know that they had been beaten; he wanted all alibis removed; he wanted Germany to learn that all Germans shared Hitler's guilt. With these immediate objectives in mind (based largely on vivid memories of the aftermath of World War I), Roosevelt clung to "unconditional surrender," wanted to have the fighting end on German, not on Austrian, Hungarian or other soil, and wanted a severe though not a vindictive occupation policy.

Faced with the unpalatable alternative of having the President approve Treasury proposals, the State Department authors of the German policy papers had tried to meet his desires in their own policy drafts following Quebec. And they did so now in the briefing book in providing "policy for the period immediately following the cessation of organized resistance." They proposed that the victors should not provide more than a minimum standard of living —the standard to be determined in quantitative terms at Yalta. They proposed drastic con-

trols and general reduction of heavy industry, and even elimination of certain industries such as synthetic gasoline and aircraft during, but only during, the control period. They proposed the elimination of all Nazi laws, public institutions, and party organs, and of active Nazis from influential positions in public and private life—although they wanted to draw a sharp distinction between Nazi leaders and party members. They proposed "direct military government . . . as a means of reinforcing the reality of defeat on the German mind."[332] They rejected a provisional government of Germans, although German administrative machinery would be used for the purposes of the occupation authorities. And they made most emphatic their recommendation that the tripartite (or quadripartite) control machinery be set up and operated in a way that would assure uniform policies throughout Germany.

While these were "tough" proposals, representing in some instances modifications of earlier State Department positions to conform to Presidential wishes, the Department had drawn in its briefing papers a sharp distinction between the "period immediately following the cessation of organized resistance" and "long-range objectives and measures," and had confined its "tough" policy to the former. For the latter, all the old schemes developed in the Advisory Committee on Post-War Foreign Policy in 1942 and 1943 were applied. They envisaged a gradual improvement in the conditions of life in Germany; the development of democratic government, first on the local level; the removal of occupation controls after a period of moderate duration; and the political and economic assimilation of Germany into the liberal, free-trade world envisaged for the future. In deference to the President's expressed wishes, no details were suggested for the accomplishment of these "ultimate objectives."

2. *Briefing Book Ambivalences and Presidential Hesitations*

This sharp division in the briefing book between short- and long-range policies for Germany was an ingenious way of dealing with a situation which had grown increasingly uncomfortable for the State Department. To begin with, it had certain long-range objectives for Germany which reflected its concept of the ideal post-war world, and hence which were not easy to give up. These objectives had come under attack for their fuzziness and leniency. Then the pressure of events as they developed through 1944 created in State a sense of urgency for the establishment of policy agreements which, if they were to be of any use as agreements, must be concrete enough to apply; and State became committed, largely through its responsibilities in the European Advisory Commission, to the establishment of concrete American policies which could serve as the basis for tripartite negotiation. Then, however, the President's own reluctance to commit himself beforehand to post-war policies, plus his embarrassment over his premature commitment on post-war German policy at Quebec, made him wary of long-term policy agreements, and determined to avoid commitments to details for the future treatment of Germany. Under these circumstances, State, inspired perhaps by the tactic embodied in the Interim Directive, began talking with the President, following Quebec, about very short-term policies. By restricting the period for which the policy was to be made, State could the more easily compromise with the Treasury position without jeopardizing its own objectives, and at the same time contain a commitment from the President on enough details to make tripartite negotiation in the European Advisory Commission at least feasible.

The briefing book papers on Germany embodied this State Department tactic. The detailed proposals of policy were to apply for a period of time indefinitely short; while the long-range policy, which was of a more liberal cast, would begin as soon as that period ended. State had really turned the President's own argument against him. He had been trying to force a more pragmatic approach to post-war commitments. In doing so, he gave State an opportunity to continue advocating its own long-range policies for settlement.

The Department's basic recommendation that long-term German policy be determined prior to surrender had a well-argued rationale; and the substance of the policy was also well reasoned. Both had been, in the main, accepted by Stimson and McCloy. Morgenthau, too, wanted a prior determination of policy and he too had a rationale for his preferred policy. What neither Hull and Stettinius nor Morgen-

thau seem to have realized was that Roosevelt in preferring postponement also had a rationale. The Big Three Alliance was working remarkably well, all things considered. To raise issues of post-war policy could jeopardize it. Moreover, the unknowns of the future—the conditions in Germany, the American public temper towards continuing foreign involvements, and the fate of the Big Three coalition, to mention a few—placed a premium on the maintenance of freedom of action for Roosevelt, at least so it appears in retrospect. Occasionally Stimson and McCloy may have had some inkling of this viewpoint, though Roosevelt never made fully clear his reasons for delay on many issues. But it is interesting to observe that Churchill, in preparing for Yalta, also proposed delay as a policy and did give his reasons.[333]

Meanwhile, Winant had received in London the revised JCS 1067 (except, of course, the financial directive). On January 28, he sent Roosevelt a long letter on EAC problems, primarily to get the President to obtain tripartite agreement on certain pressing issues at the forthcoming Yalta meeting, and also as background for a meeting he expected to have with Roosevelt on the return trip after Yalta. In writing of JCS 1067 revised, he pointed out that both the British and the Russians, as far as he could tell, planned to use central German agencies (after denazification) "to carrry out their will in Germany." "This," he added, "has nothing to do with a hard or soft policy." JCS 1067 revised—as he read it—"runs counter to this policy and sets up an economic control" in each zone. He foresaw serious economic and political difficulties in this arrangement. On the same day, in a letter to Stettinius, he said that he would not introduce the document in EAC until he had seen the President.[334]

Winant made one final attempt to influence the deliberations at Yalta. On February 7, when the conference was in mid-course, he sent another message to the President. In it he spoke with some bitterness of his exclusion from the conference especially since Gusev (the Russian member of EAC) was there, as was Eden, who, while not a member of EAC, had intimate knowledge of its proceedings. He informed the President that a series of draft directives to the three commanders had been prepared in the U. S. delegation to EAC for the post-surrender period. "The directives are on broad lines without detailing and provide a groundwork for Allied cooperation in dealing with problems that affect Germany. I hope these directives will have your support."[335]

There the matter rested. Winant spent three days with Roosevelt in the Mediterranean in February on the homeward voyage; the President seemed too exhausted to concentrate on the German problem, but was apparently still determined to postpone long-term policy decisions.[336]

To return to the preparations for Yalta: Roosevelt had pretty clearly in mind what he wanted at Yalta and what he would have to deal with. During his trip across the Atlantic he held daily conferences. Admiral Leahy judged from what the President said in these talks that his two chief objectives were completion of plans for the defeat of Germany and cooperation of the Russians in establishing the UN as the key to permanent world peace. He also wanted to secure freedom for Poland; and was preparing to make a start on solving the inevitable problem of reparations possibly by establishing a reparations commission. He had decided to make a bargain with Stalin on Russian aid in the Japanese war. This last was surely a third chief objective; possibly Leahy's own disagreement with the plan led him to underestimate its importance to Roosevelt.[337]

Obviously other matters were going to arise; some would be minor, to be disposed of out of hand; some could be dealt with by temporary arrangements. But it is clear that the only long-term problem on which Roosevelt wished to move forward was the UN. The rest, it seems certain, the President was determined to postpone.

We know that Churchill,[338] and we can be quite sure that Stalin also, had ideas about what was important, what should be settled, what could or should be postponed.

In closing this section, a bit of retrospective speculation may not be amiss. Roosevelt was acutely embarrassed over the Morgenthau episode; partly, as is evident, because of domestic political complications; partly, as has been suggested, because he had agreed at Quebec to more than he clearly realized; and partly, it may be surmised, because, responding sympathetically to arguments about British welfare and German deserts, he had committed himself to

an apparently firm policy before commitment was necessary.

The State Department draftsmen might usefully have indulged in speculation of this character. Instead, anxious to wean Roosevelt away from the Quebec minute, they were too intent upon extricating from him counter-commitments to their own views to take adequate notice of those matters on which he continually avoided commitment.

A final note needs to be added on attempts to brief the President before Yalta. On January 19, the Treasury returned to the wars; their memorandum was in effect a restatement of Morgenthau's letter of January 10.[339] The War Department held its peace.

3. The Conference Negotiations

Both in anticipation and in practice the Yalta Conference consisted of simultaneous military discussions conducted by the chiefs of staff of the three nations and their associates, and political discussions conducted by the foreign ministers and their associates. The three chiefs of government concerned themselves with both areas; in reviewing the whole field they tended to discuss first one set of topics and then the other, but to them, far more than to their subordinates, the interrelationships of fighting and politics were consciously in mind; the agreement on the Far East is merely the most obvious case in point.

Germany may have bulked large in the thinking of the conferees at Yalta, but it occupied only a small place in their discussions, and in the deliberations of the foreign ministers and their aides.

One reason for this comparative brevity of the discussions on the fate of Germany was the general conviction that the three powers were not ready for final decisions. At the first luncheon of the foreign ministers, Eden said that "there had yet been no Cabinet discussions" on the treatment of Germany and added that the matter would have to be referred for further joint study. Molotov agreed. Stettinius said nothing. A little later Stettinius said in an aside to Molotov that the United States would like an agreement on economic matters; Molotov replied that the Soviet Union wanted reparations and hoped for long-term credits from the United States—a request he had earlier made to Harriman. Stettinius expressed sympathy. The discussion ended with Molotov urging agreement on "these economic questions," presumably reparations and credits.[340]

The decisions on Germany taken during the conference reflected, in a sense, this opening talk. Aside from some general affirmations in the communiqué (quoted below), only four German questions were disposed of at Yalta.

(1) Approval of EAC Protocols on zones and Control Council.[341] The tripartite zonal division had been agreed to in EAC. U. S. concurrence was finally given at Malta on February 1, 1945. Russian formal approval was relayed to EAC from Moscow just before Yalta. There still remained need for final completion of an Anglo-American military agreement on zonal transit arrangements. Marshall settled this ancient squabble with a large-minded gesture.

The protocol on the Control Council had also been agreed to in EAC and needed only formal approval by Russia. This was given.

(2) Granting of a zone and a seat on the Control Council to France.[342] On the very first afternoon, Stalin and Roosevelt discussed the question of a French zone. The French were eager to have a zone, and were supported by the British. Roosevelt was willing to go along out of "kindness," or so he said. Later Churchill pressed the matter and Stalin agreed—his own zone would be unaffected. The question of a French seat on the Control Council was harder. Churchill kept on insisting against the opposition of the other two. Eventually Roosevelt switched and Stalin fell into line.

(3) Dismemberment of Germany.[343] Stalin wanted an agreement that Germany would be dismembered; and to an agreement in principle there was no objection. It was quite obvious to all, however, that no one knew how to apply the knife, and that neither Roosevelt nor Churchill, at least, was ready for an irrevocable commitment. Roosevelt talked about provincial autonomy in the Germany he had visited forty years before, but this was no help. The problem was referred to the Anglo-Soviet-American members of EAC—not to EAC itself because French membership on that body, recently acquired, created complications. The word "dismemberment" was added to the instrument of surrender, but, largely at Eden's initiative, only permissively as a step that might be taken by

the Allies if they deemed it necessary. The terms of reference of this problem to the committee of three were an open invitation to delay: the committee was to "study the procedure" and to "consider the desirability of associating with it a French representative."

(4) Reparations.[344] This was a matter on which Stalin pushed hard. Maisky was well prepared and made a full presentation of the Russian proposal. In brief, the Russians wanted the Germans to provide Russia with $10 billion of reparations in kind. Half of the total (it was later explained) would consist of capital goods to be removed during the first two years, the balance of goods from current production delivered over a ten-year period. In principle, reparations would also go to other countries (later a sum of $10 billion was mentioned) that had suffered most and fought hardest.

Maisky also proposed that German heavy industry (steel, chemicals, etc.) be reduced by 80 per cent during the initial two-year period, and specialized industry for war purposes (airplanes, synthetic gasoline, etc.) be removed completely. He proposed the establishment of a reparations commission to sit in Moscow, and thought that after the reparations period German enterprises "which could be utilized for war purposes should be placed under international control."

The Russian request had a double rationale: First, and no doubt foremost, the Russians needed and wanted the goods. Second, they looked on reparations as a device to reduce Germany's capacity to make war.

Both Roosevelt and Churchill evinced signs of embarrassment. Both expressed sympathy —Roosevelt, who was in what he described to Stalin as a "bloodthirsty" mood, perhaps more heartily than Churchill. But both the President and the Prime Minister warned of the perils that would arise from starvation in Germany and both referred gloomily to the disastrous experience with war debts after World War I, Churchill stressing the paucity of the harvest, Roosevelt the American financing that came to German support. Churchill opposed the setting of a specific amount; Roosevelt made clear that the United States would not finance Germany for the sake of making reparations possible. Stalin wanted firm instructions for the reparations commission. He also said, in response to a question, that he was not yet prepared to discuss forced labor as a form of reparations.

The discussions went on, in plenary sessions, and in meetings of the foreign ministers. There was little talk of the relation of reparations to Germany's war potential, much about the question of the amount; the first written Russian proposal set $10 billion for Russia, $8 billion for the U. S. and U. K., and $2 billion for the rest. There were repeated questions about forced labor, but the Russians remained reticent—they had it under consideration. Undoubtedly all three knew that the British and Americans wanted to put some limits on forced labor (the briefing book had proposed that a distinction be made between "active Nazis" and others), and also knew that Stalin wanted a free hand. There was considerable discussion of the wording of the principles of allocation of reparations. The real argument was over the figure of $20 billion. An American compromise that the Reparations Commission should take it "in its initial studies as a basis for discussion" was accepted by Stalin, rejected by Churchill, and the rejection stood; this was the only formal recorded dissent in all the conference protocols. A Russian formula for priority of recipients was accepted. All questions of elimination or control of German industry were avoided in the protocol except that the plant removals, etc., to be executed in the first two years, were described as "chiefly for the purpose of destroying the war potential of Germany." Finally, "use of German labor" was listed as one form of reparations—undefined and unlimited.

Thus the issue of reparations was postponed, though the Reparations Commission was certainly not intended merely as an evasive device; there were bound to be reparations; the main question was the amount.[345]

The Yalta protocols were not published; the public document was the communiqué. With respect to Germany it read as follows:

The Occupation and Control of Germany

We have agreed on common policies and plans for enforcing the unconditional surrender terms which we shall impose together on Nazi Germany after German armed resistance has been finally crushed. These terms will not be made known until the final defeat of Germany has been accomplished. Under the agreed plan, the forces of the three powers will each occupy a separate zone of Germany. Coordinated administration and con-

trol have been provided for under the plan through a central control commission consisting of the Supreme Commanders of the three powers with headquarters in Berlin. It has been agreed that France should be invited by the three powers, and if she should so desire, to take over a zone of occupation and to participate as a fourth member of the control commission. The limits of the French zone will be agreed by the four Governments concerned through their representatives on the European Advisory Commission.

It is our inflexible purpose to destroy German militarism and nazism and to insure that Germany will never again be able to disturb the peace of the world. We are determined to disarm and disband all German armed forces; break up for all time the German General Staff that has repeatedly contrived the resurgence of German militarism; remove or destroy all German military equipment; eliminate or control all German industry that could be used for military production; bring all war criminals to just and swift punishment and exact reparation in kind for the destruction wrought by the Germans; wipe out the Nazi party, Nazi laws, organizations and institutions, remove all Nazi and militarist influences from public office and from the cultural and economic life of the German people; and take in harmony such other measures in Germany as may be necessary to the future peace and safety of the world. It is not our purpose to destroy the people of Germany, but only when nazism and militarism have been extirpated will there be hope for a decent life for Germans, and a place for them in the comity of nations.

Reparation by Germany

We have considered the question of the damage caused by Germany to the Allied Nations in this war and recognized it as just that Germany be obliged to make compensation for this damage in kind to the greatest extent possible. A commission for the compensation of damage will be established. The commission for the compensation of damage will be instructed to consider the question of the extent and methods for compensating damage caused by Germany to the Allied countries. The Commission will work in Moscow.[346]

The communiqué needs no great comment. The omission of any mention of the quasi-decision on dismemberment was by agreement. The communiqué was essentially devised for propaganda purposes. Aside from the statements on the French zone and reparations, it was expressive of general sentiments. It committed no one. Any real commitments would have been included in the protocols.

When Treasury officials learned of the decisions taken at Yalta, they concluded that the State Department had reversed the established policy of the United States, as it had been trying to do ever since the Morgenthau Plan was accepted at Quebec. They probably based their judgment on the communiqué and did not know about the protocols, though these would not have satisfied them either. But in either event, they missed the point. The President was not ready to push for the Morgenthau Plan or any other plan. Whatever his sympathies, he wanted to wait.

B. AFTERMATH OF YALTA

1. The Henderson Mission and Perkins Report

Before the President returned to Washington on February 28 from his trip to Yalta, Leon Henderson, New Deal economist and former head of the Office of Price Administration, had returned from a quite different kind of trip: a special mission to observe and report on planning in Europe for the economic control of Germany. Henderson's trip had grown out of concern in FEA over what was considered there the right-wing political views of War Department planners. Originally, Henderson had been cleared with the White House as economic adviser to Eisenhower, but when Hilldring, Murphy, and Eisenhower objected, that plan was abandoned. Then, in November 1944, it was suggested that he should be sent to Europe on a special mission for the President, sponsored by FEA, War, and State. When War and State backed out, he went under the sole sponsorship of FEA, as little welcome, apparently, as later that year was H. H. Fowler, whose trip is described below. Henderson returned after a month in London and two in Paris, disgusted with the treatment he had received and disturbed by what he had seen. The report on this trip was written by James A. Perkins, an FEA official who had accompanied him. On February 21 Henderson met with Under Secretary of State Joseph C. Grew, and other State Department officials, to tell them that the State Department was not listened to by American officials in Europe. He asserted that Robert D. Murphy, Eisenhower's political adviser, was frustrated as the Department's spokesman assigned to Eisenhower, and that the European Advisory Commission was para-

lyzed. At lunch the next day with White, Hilldring, and McCloy, he insisted that the Treasury Department had been taking advantage of the Army in order to further its own political purposes.[347]

Perkins' report on the Henderson Mission was equally to the point in its appraisal. It ended as follows:

Conclusions and Recommendations

1. The United States is not adequately prepared to discharge its responsibilities towards (a) the elimination and control of German war-making power on the economic front, (b) the handling of a system of reparations, and (c) the prevention of serious disease and unrest.

2. Present U. S. policy will, on the contrary, make it possible for the Germans to rebuild their economic potential, escape their responsibilities for delivering reparations, embroil the occupying powers in a series of misunderstandings and eventual recriminations.

3. If these results are to be avoided and if our purposes are to be achieved the U. S. Government might give consideration to the following measures.

A. JCS-1067 revised should immediately be reviewed and rewritten. The new version should contain specific reference to the basic objectives of industrial control and reparations and make provision for control machinery necessary to achieve them.

B. The negative clause in the economic appendix disavowing responsibility for the German economy should be eliminated and replaced with a positive directive indicating that Allied authorities must be prepared to supervise all aspects of the German economy.

C. It might be advisable to consider the establishment of an upper limit above which German consumption will not be allowed to go such as a percentage of consumption levels in the liberated areas or German consumption in a base year such as 1930. This directive should make clear that the Allies are not responsible for the establishment of such a level but it will positively assure that this level is not exceeded.

D. The new directive should attempt to clarify the respective functions of the Control Council and the zonal authorities. In addition to the development of agreed policy the Control Council will have to directly supervise and in some cases, participate in the administration of those controls that will have to be handled on a uniform basis. Decentralization of administration should be urged but only to the extent necessary to simplify the task of the Control Council.

E. Policy making in Washington should be developed and supervised by a new administrative arrangement. Consideration might be given to the establishment of a cabinet level committee presided over by someone appointed by the President. Under this committee there might be an interdepartmental working committee charged with the responsibility of developing the studies, guides, and draft directives necessary to present the U. S. position on matters pertaining to our administration in Germany. The Bureau of the Budget has done detailed and excellent work on this problem.

F. The USGCC (the American staff for the Control Council) should be completely overhauled. The [numbers] and quality of its personnel should be enormously increased. Immediate needs are for at least 250 officials for the Economics Division, with 750 more ready for dispatch to the theater with two weeks notice, and an additional 2000 earmarked for eventual service. Other divisions dealing with economic matters should be similarly increased such as the Manpower, Transportation and Communication Divisions. The bar against the extensive use of civilians should be lowered and if it is decided that U. S. officials should arrive in Germany in uniform then arrangements for commissioning these officials should be permitted.

G. Officials of the USGCC should be brought into direct touch with relevant civilian agencies in Washington. If the cabinet and interdepartmental committees indicated in "E" above are established then direct contact between the head of the Economics Division, USGCC and the representatives of the FEA, Department of Agriculture, etc. that are concerned with the work of the Division should not only be encouraged but made mandatory. Without such contact the USGCC will be in no adequate position to speak for the U. S. Government in its conversations and negotiations with other powers.

H. Attention should be turned both in Washington and in the USGCC to the great problem of the administrative machinery necessary to direct the German economy. To this end a group of officials should be appointed to study and develop the framework of such machinery and the way it will have to operate. These officials should have the widest experience in handling public controls in the economic sphere and should, on this problem, direct the planning of both the USGCC and SHAEF.

I. Finally, it is imperative that agreement on the revised economic policy and machinery be arrived at with the British, Russians, and French at the earliest possible moment. Agreement in advance of the establishment of the Control Council is, possibly, a condition of its future success.[348]

This critical appraisal of U. S. policy and machinery for the occupation of Germany was dated March 3, 1945. It was thus available to policy-makers in Washington shortly after the U. S. delegation returned from the Yalta Conference. Evidently the substance of it was known earlier, for a commentary on it on the same date by Eisenhower's Chief of Staff, General Walter Bedell Smith, was also available, but only to the Civil Affairs Division. Smith insisted that JCS 1067 revised was a very sound document, and that the U. S. Group, Control Council, received adequate policy direction in its work. He pointed out that he was its director and that Eisenhower was satisfied with the way it was run. He passed off the complaints of the State and Treasury people in London as something that could be ignored. But he agreed that the planning of economic controls and the size of the USGCC civilian staff should be augmented. He wanted, in short, more manpower, not more direction.[349]

2. *State Department Initiative After Yalta*

On February 28, the day he arrived back in Washington, the President wrote Stettinius that he should assume responsibility for seeing that the conclusions of the conference, except the military ones, were carried out.[350] Stettinius was away, but the State Department officials concerned with the problem of post-war Germany, under the direction of Dunn, immediately set to work to draft an entirely new directive for the treatment of Germany.

Deadwood was quickly cleared away. The revised JCS 1067 had not yet been presented to the European Advisory Commission. Joseph C. Grew, the Acting Secretary of State, had written Winant to delay its presentation because at least its economic and relief sections did not conform to the Crimean decisions. Then, upon the President's return the next day, he wired Winant that he was not to present the document at all to EAC for it had been superseded by Yalta.[351] Since the revision had not been intended for use by the Army but only in EAC negotiations, it was thus disposed of.

Evidently Dunn and his associates took seriously Henderson's charge that they were not listened to and Perkins' recommendation that JCS 1067 revised be completely revised again. Stettinius approved the completed draft of the proposed new directive on March 10, the day he reached Washington. He sent it on to the President with a covering letter which stated that such a directive was "urgently necessary," and suggested that, if the directive was approved, an informal policy committee on Germany should be established under the chairmanship of State and including representatives of War, Navy, Treasury, and also FEA.[352] The committee should serve as a central source of policy guidance for Germany and displace SWNCC on German problems. To be sure, here was the "new administrative arrangement" recommended by Perkins, but it amounted to much more than that, for it was the way out of a problem with which SWNCC had been faced since its establishment in December. SWNCC had been set up to operate with the benefit of a close relationship to the JCS staff only on condition that its membership be limited to State, War and Navy. But by early January, Treasury was a burr under its saddle, participating in fact in the revision of the Interim Directive. Treasury involvement in policy-making for Germany was inevitable, so that activity would have to be carried on outside of SWNCC, in an *ad hoc* inter-departmental committee the temporary and specialized nature of which would be emphasized in order to minimize the possibility of its becoming a rival to SWNCC. On the other hand, if SWNCC was to develop as a continuing institution—and there were people in State and War in particular who strongly believed that it should —important matters like the settlement in German policy should not be handled elsewhere. In the face of these conflicting considerations, in early March McCloy wrote Clayton to urge that any new agency dealing with politico-military affairs be brought within the orbit of SWNCC.[353]

Reflecting its dispute with Treasury, but particularly with the Army in both SHAEF and EAC staff work in London, and perhaps emboldened by the Perkins report, the State draft directive came down hard time and again

to emphasize the significance of the central administration of occupation. The inter-allied military government agreed to at Yalta was to be a central government of Germany. The authority of this central government, the Control Council, was to be paramount throughout Germany, and the zones of occupation were to enforce its decisions. In order to eradicate Nazi ideas there were to be centralized control, under the direction of the Control Council, of mass communications, and a uniform system of control over education. A substantial degree of centralized financial and economic control was declared essential, under the general responsibility of the Control Council, to carry out the economic policies proposed. In contrast, Army officers had been concerned with emphasizing the autonomy of the zone commanders, partially perhaps because they were reluctant to become too much involved in joint occupation arrangements such as the Control Council constituted, and undoubtedly also because they were concerned with a contingency which State tended to ignore: What do the zone commanders do in the event (which War increasingly thought probable) that the Control Council fails to agree on uniform policies for the zones? Indeed, this was the Army's major difference with the State Department. State, where the point of reference was policy, was determined to get accepted what it regarded as adequate policy guidance. War, on the other hand, had as its reference point the responsibility to administer in the field whatever the policy. There was no direct answer to the War Department's insistent query; it was not that State or the EAC delegation was unwilling to consider the possibility that the three major Allies would not cooperate after the war, but their preoccupation with seeing that the record showed that the U. S. was not responsible for any breakdown of cooperation made them push it into the background.[354]

The denazification provisions of the State draft directive were moderate, as compared with current Treasury and War Department views. There were the universally supported provisions for the dissolution of the Nazi Party and its affiliated and subsidiary organizations, and of Nazi public institutions and Nazi-inspired laws. But the non-political social services of these organizations which were judged desirable could be transferred to other agencies.

Active Nazis and supporters of Nazism, and other individuals hostile to Allied purposes as well, were to be eliminated from public and quasi-public office and from positions of importance in industry, trade, and finance. It was made clear that party membership by itself was not sufficient reason for such elimination.

Economic policy envisaged the elimination of production facilities which specialized in implements of war or for the production of aircraft, synthetic oil, synthetic rubber and light metals. Reparations from current production were proposed, while a minimum standard of living, defined as being sufficient to prevent disorder and disease on a scale that would make the task of occupation and the collection of reparations substantially more difficult, was maintained. The reparation period would be ten years. It was made clear that the German production would go first to maintaining the minimum standard of living, and second to reparations; and that economic disarmament would be made compatible with both.

In sum, the draft directive was based on the briefing book, modified slightly to take into account the tenor of some of the discussions at Yalta. Thus, for example, this document spoke of a ten-year reparation period (as requested by the Russians) even though the Yalta protocol set no time limit. This was policy for an interim directive, i.e., for the "control period" in which the State Department contemplated a "hard-peace" program, subject to amelioration as time went on and the Germans showed progress toward democracy.

While the State Department staff was preparing the draft directive, Stimson met the President by appointment to talk about Germany, and particularly Roosevelt's idea that the Under Secretary of War, Robert P. Patterson, should be the military governor. Stimson persuaded Roosevelt that Patterson was still needed in Washington. In a more general vein, Roosevelt spoke of the old Germany with such affection that, as Stimson reflected later that day, it "reassured me to think that at bottom he did not differ from McCloy and myself in respect to the basic reorganization to be aimed at in Germany." Stimson went on to define the issues of policy-making for Germany as he saw them. "At the end," he has written,

I impressed again the chaotic condition which existed now in Germany and the dangers of a

general break up, and I enumerated the four contradictory theories which have been variously suggested in dealing with it and the importance of having someone who would organize agreement out of this loose situation. Those four theories were (1) the British proposition to in effect merely surround Germany with bayonets and leave her alone within to sizzle in her own juice; (2) the "pastoral" proposition for Germany suggested at Quebec; (3) the medium proposition actually set out in the approved War Department post-war directive [JCS 1067]; and (4) the proposition resulting from Russia's demand for reparations which Leon Henderson reports will be given the closest kind of economic control—viz. rationing, ceilings, etc. etc.[355]

Stimson and McCloy had both hoped that SWNCC and the Committee of Three could be the instruments for settling German policy.[356] They were, however, to be disappointed. On March 15, Stettinius held a meeting attended by Morgenthau, Stimson, Crowley, and a representative of the Navy Department, at which he announced the President's approval of his proposals for an informal policy committee on Germany and presented the March 10 draft directive with the President's initials on it.[357] At this meeting the Informal Policy Committee on Germany was established. Assistant Secretary of State Will Clayton was made chairman. Stimson named McCloy as his representative, with Hilldring as alternate. Morgenthau designated White (who was now an Assistant Secretary), with V. Frank Coe as alternate. Crowley's representative was H. H. Fowler, who was supervising the German studies in FEA as Director of its Enemy Branch. The Secretary of the Navy later designated Under Secretary Ralph A. Bard and Assistant Secretary Artemus L. Gates as his spokesmen.[358]

While the committee was being organized, Clayton saw the President about the March 10 draft which he had initialed. Roosevelt repeated his familiar remarks about feeding the Germans from "soup kitchens," this time emphasizing that they should not be set up until the Germans were actually threatened with starvation. He also made a brief and enigmatic comment about the administration of German occupation which, as it was passed on by Clayton, was interpreted in various ways. He said that his idea about governing Germany would be to appoint a committee of "say, three Germans. They would be told to do thus and so, and if they didn't do it, we would take them out and shoot them and get three more Germans."[359]

3. The Development of War-Treasury Opposition

The March 10 draft directive apparently caught War and Treasury completely by surprise. Stimson was prompt in protesting such an emphasis on centralized administration. The Control Council, he asserted, "should be confined to making the policies, and the administration should be left to the respective military governors of the four zones."[360] Morgenthau, however, failed to catch the significance of the issue of centralization to the fate of his own proposals, for he left the meeting on the 15th without realizing the extent to which this draft differed from the original September and revised January drafts of JCS 1067, and how much of it was contrary to his own views. However, the same day McCloy telephoned him to point out the significance of the new draft, a copy of which Stimson had brought him. Treasury immediately prepared memoranda for the President and Stettinius. The one intended for Stettinius argued that the new draft departed from the Yalta agreements, as well as from Quebec and JCS 1067, with respect to the elimination of German heavy industry, the control of the German internal economy, and the decentralization of Germany. It recommended that the new March 10 draft directive be withdrawn in favor of JCS 1067, on which immediate approval in EAC should be sought. Then programs and policies would be worked out on the major questions in accordance with the Yalta agreements. This Treasury memorandum was not sent until it was revised in a meeting on the morning of March 20 of Morgenthau, White, Coe, McCloy, and Hilldring.

The War Department also prepared papers opposing the new State draft directive. They were in the form of a revision of the directive. Significantly, they proposed much that Treasury would never accept. Under the revision, the zone commanders would have all powers necessary to accomplish the objectives of the occupation. Their authority and responsibility were to be restricted by the existence of central control machinery only if it took positive action. The State Department definition of active Nazis was broadened. And denazification was strengthened by the addition of a statement that administrative convenience would be no excuse for retaining Nazis in any influential office at any level. Treasury officials would not object to these changes. But War's revision also permitted the use of Germans and German-staffed agencies in the administration of Germany. What was more important, it provided for reparations from current production, and eliminated the State restriction of Germans to a "minimum living standard," leaving in its stead the much more flexible and conventional military formula of disease and unrest.

Before the meeting between Treasury and War officials, Roosevelt moved to disassociate himself from the March 10 State Department draft, and Stettinius followed suit. The President told Stimson that he did not remember the document, and had not read it, to his knowledge. On the 19th, following Morgenthau's description to him of its contents, Stettinius claimed that when he returned from his trip, tired, Dunn had handed him the document, and that he had only glanced at it.[361]

The Treasury and War Department officials convened early on March 20 in Morgenthau's office. In the course of the meeting the Treasury memoranda to the President and to Stettinius were redrafted, and the War Department revision of the March 10 directive was discussed in detail. McCloy suggested toning down the Treasury note to Stettinius in its assertions that he had departed from the Yalta agreements. In the Treasury letter to the President, Morgenthau had suggested a redraft of the March 10 directive in accordance with the following principles:

1. We should avoid assuming responsibility for the functioning of the internal German economy and its economic controls. The maintenance and rehabilitation of the German economy is a German problem and should not be undertaken by us in order to collect reparations or for any other reason except the security of the occupying forces.

2. We should aim at the greatest possible contraction of German heavy industry as well as the elimination of her war potential. The occupying forces should accept no responsibility for providing the German people with food and supplies beyond preventing starvation, disease, and such unrest as might interfere with the purposes of the occupation.

3. During the period of military occupation,

policies in the separate zones should be coordinated through the Control Council, but the actual administration of affairs in Germany should be directed towards the decentralization of the political structure.[362]

McCloy agreed that if these three sentences were accepted, the basic confusion would be cleared up; but he cautioned Morgenthau, who was having lunch with the President, against getting Roosevelt's signature on them without a full hearing. White raised objections to the War Department draft revision because under it the Army would assume responsibility for internal economic conditions in Germany.

Minutes of this meeting, taken by Coe, a Treasury participant, record the following conversation on the directive of March 10: Morgenthau said that

the policies of the document seemed to be those of Riddleberger and Despres of the Department of State and of Leon Henderson (who had returned a month before from his trip inspecting military government in Germany for FEA, and was being widely quoted to the effect that the powers of the zone commander were being emphasized by the Army at the expense of the Group Control Council and its functions). They had been debated before and not been established. JCS 1067 was a long-worked over compromise but now it was abandoned, in the name of Yalta, although no chapter and verse from Yalta was cited as reasons for the change. [Morgenthau] said that he was amazed at this handling of the most important issues of the time. . . .

Mr. McCloy said that he agreed with the Secretary as to how this had happened. He said that Leon Henderson had a large share in it, for he had been talking all around town on these issues. Also Ambassador Winant had never liked JCS 1067 and was constantly working against it. He said that as far as the War Department could see, policies seemingly well established had been tossed overboard, with no consultation, and with superior officers not even reading the documents.

Morgenthau indicated that he had interested himself in the treatment of Germany again as a result of McCloy's phone call of the 15th. Now that he saw what was being done, he was determined to fight until the matter was cleared up. He wanted to know where Stimson stood on the matter. McCloy replied that

Secretary Stimson had had definite views on Germany. But he was confronted after the Quebec Conference with a policy with which he in part disagreed. Now, after Yalta, he finds a State Department policy document, initialed by the President, and with this he disagrees, in part. Secretary Stimson feels badly about these incidents. He had determined to keep quiet about basic policy and pay attention to his responsibility as head of the department which will administer the U. S. occupation. He finds, and has so told the President, that the policies of the State Department will prevent our soldiers from doing their job in Germany. In particular, the Army, which has been trained for a zone command in Germany, cannot adapt to these vague ideas of centralized administration in Berlin. Stimson wants the zone commanders to have powers to act and complete residual authority until a matter is taken over and handled centrally by the Control Commission.

Accordingly, the War Department was leaving the basic economic questions to others. It would carry out any agreed policy on these matters. At this juncture it would concentrate on the administrative feasibility of the new proposals.[363]

Thus had McCloy stated the position of the War Department at this time. It viewed with alarm the reopening of policy issues following Quebec, and the State Department determination to emphasize the powers of the Control Council at the expense of zone commander discretion. Beyond these considerations—indeed, in order not to lose sight of them—the War Department wished to avoid involvement in issues of substance, such as the explosive economic questions. Because State had seemingly reopened the issue of German policy by its Yalta Conference activities and by Dunn's March 10 memorandum, and had, in that memorandum, pressed its Control Council policies, McCloy at this time supported the Treasury position. Morgenthau apparently now regarded him as an ally. (Some of his assistants were less trustful.) Actually, any equating of the position of McCloy and his department with the views of either major protagonist was an over-simplification of that position. The War Department's concern over its responsibility for the execution of a policy for Germany simultaneous with the prosecution of the war (if not against Germany, then against Japan) had made it appear to be on every side of the issue at one time or another. For the time being it supported Morgenthau. Later it would depart from his views, as it had from the State Department's position. Since, to be sure, issues of substance did creep into the War Department position on German policy (and, most emphatically, that position always had unavoidable policy implications), its switches could be viewed as vacillation. But behind them lay a consistent rationale: it supported or opposed issues of substance or procedure in the interest of administrative feasibility—that is to say, of getting in time a policy for Germany which it could execute.

4. *The Presidential Policy Statement of March 23, 1945*

Morgenthau went on to his luncheon with the President that day (March 20) and apparently heeded McCloy's warning not to seek Roosevelt's signature on the Treasury document, for two days later the President called in officials from the three Departments to discuss a replacement of the March 10 directive. Roosevelt began by stating directly that he did not like the directive. He went on to make clear that he wanted to decentralize authority in Germany as much as was possible, consistent with the principles of the occupation. In particular, more definite authority should be given the zone commanders in relation to the Control Council. This point had been made in Morgenthau's suggested revision of the March 10 directive. The other two points in the Treasury revision had been (1) "We should avoid assuming responsibility for the functioning of the internal German economy . . . ," and (2) "We should aim at the greatest possible contraction of German heavy industry." Apparently Roosevelt ignored the first of these points. But he made it clear that he did not want to destroy Germany's industry, emphasizing the point by stating that the Germans should be permitted to maintain their own heavy industry such as heavy machine tools and locomotives. McCloy interpreted the President's remarks to mean in general that he favored a middle course between Morgenthau's earlier extreme views and the State Department's positive position as stated in the March 10 directive.[364]

The War Department then drafted a "Summary of U. S. Initial Post-Defeat Policy Relating to Germany" which was intended to, and which McCloy felt did, represent the views of the President. State and Treasury made minor changes in it. On March 23rd it was marked "O. K. F. D. R., superseding memo of March 10, 1945" and signed, at Morgenthau's insist-

ence, by the three men from each of the three Departments who were then present.[365] FEA did not participate, it should be noted. The "summary" was to be introduced into EAC (it never was), and be used as the basis for directives to the U. S. Commanding General in Germany.

This was the last policy statement on the treatment of Germany which received Roosevelt's attention; he died three weeks later.[366] It stated that the Control Council was to have paramount authority, but that the zone commander could decide policy in the absence of Control Council agreement. The administration of Germany was to be directed toward decentralization of government and the economic system

except that to the minimum extent required for carrying out the proposal set forth herein, the Control Council may permit or establish central control of (a) essential national public services such as railroads, communications and power; (b) finance and foreign affairs; and (c) production and distribution of essential commodities.[367]

In a long paragraph, the whole question of economic policy received cautious handling:

Controls may be imposed upon the German economy only as may be necessary and (a) to carry out programs of industrial disarmament and de-militarization, reparation, and of relief for liberated areas as prescribed by appropriate higher authority and (b) to assure the production and maintenance of goods and services required to meet the needs of the occupying forces and displaced persons in Germany, and essential to prevent starvation or such disease or civil unrest as would endanger the occupying forces. No action shall be taken, in execution of the reparations program or otherwise, which would tend to support basic living standards in Germany on a higher level than that existing in any one of the neighboring United Nations. All economic and financial international transactions, including exports and imports, shall be controlled with the aim of preventing Germany from developing a war potential and of achieving the other objectives named herein. The first charge on all approved exports for reparations or otherwise shall be a sum necessary to pay for imports. No extension of credit to Germany or Germans by any foreign persons or Government shall be permitted, except that the Control Council may in special emergencies grant such permission. Recurrent reparations shall not, by their form or amount, require the rehabilitation or development of German heavy industry and should not foster the dependence of other countries upon the German economy.

German authorities were to be made responsible for economic controls "to the fullest extent practicable." A series of brief statements on the Nazi Party, Nazi laws, education, war criminals, restitution, and the armed forces followed, none of them detailed enough to denote a dominant viewpoint. The statement concluded:

The German war potential shall be destroyed. As part of the program to attain this objective, all implements of war and all specialized facilities for the production of armaments shall be seized or destroyed. The maintenance and production of all aircraft and implements of war shall be prevented.

This Presidential Policy Statement, taken as a whole, settled the dispute over policy in the same manner that the original September 1944 version of JCS 1067 had done—by placing it in tenuous balance. In the case of the earlier document, the battleground had then shifted to the interpretation and comparison of its phrases and clauses. In the meetings of IPCOG to prepare the second revision of JCS 1067 on the basis of the policy statement, which began late in March and continued through April and May before agreement was ultimately reached on drafts to be sent to JCS, the same kind of bickering over the meaning of the terms —in this case the policy statement—occurred.

When he learned of the Presidential Policy Statement, the FEA Administrator, Leo Crowley, complained to Stettinius that his agency had not been consulted in the preparation of such an important statement on German economic policy. The statement contains only a limited recognition of the cardinal United States policy of industrial disarmament and destruction of the German war potential, and no reference to administrative controls, he wrote Hull:

Indeed, it seems to represent a retreat from the Yalta Agreement in which the leaders of the three governments represented stated their affirmative intention to "eliminate or control all German industries that could be used for military production."[368]

It will be recalled that the purpose of the Presidential Policy Statement was to instruct Winant in negotiating tripartite agreements on the control machinery for Germany, and to guide IPCOG in drafting new instructions on the immediate post-defeat period in Germany which would supersede the January draft of JCS 1067, since that document had supposedly been outdated by the Yalta agreements. IPCOG had originally begun the drafting of new instructions on the basis of the March 10 directive, but had quickly dissolved into a White House conference which produced the Presidential Policy Statement. Before IPCOG resumed work on the basis of its new instructions, McCloy again pressed with Clayton his objections to the establishment of an *ad hoc* committee to do work for which the State-War-Navy Coordinating Committee had been established. The prospects of another revision of JCS 1067 had posed an unpleasant dilemma for McCloy. If SWNCC were utilized, its membership would have to be broadened to include Treasury and possibly FEA, against the wishes of JCS, whose cooperation was vital to the success of SWNCC. But if the work were done outside of SWNCC, its authority would be rivaled and its function undermined.

It is interesting that McCloy was emphatic in his choice of the first alternative. FEA and Treasury, he wrote Clayton on March 27, should sit on the European Sub-committee of SWNCC, and on SWNCC itself when dealing with economic policy for Germany.[369] Clayton responded by reminding McCloy that SWNCC was to be strictly limited in its membership, and by suggesting that the SWNCC Secretariat could be utilized in order to avoid confusion and assure access to the Joint Chiefs.[370] McCloy insisted that the important consideration was to develop SWNCC as a satisfactory arrangement between the political and the military, that IPCOG would be only the first of many special committees to deal with problems which SWNCC should handle; and that FEA and the Treasury could be dropped when they were no longer needed on SWNCC. But the State Department would not concede McCloy's point. In his final answer to McCloy, Clayton mentioned his Department's fears that if SWNCC were used, it would be difficult to exclude Treasury and FEA from all its deliberations.[371]

Whatever the merits of the arguments, IPCOG was already established, so the State Department prevailed, and IPCOG continued. To carry out its task of revision, IPCOG was divided into political, financial, and economic subcommittees.

C. *IPCOG DRAFTS THE SECOND REVISION*

1. *Political Sections*

The discussions in the political subcommittee were based on a draft introduced by the Civil Affairs Division of the War Department dated March 28. It was a carefully constructed statement, skillfully utilizing earlier documents in such a way as to minimize the points of dispute. Two notable features in it were the provisions on denazification and education. Under the heading of denazification was a broad definition of the persons to be excluded and the kinds of public and private positions from which they were to be excluded. Here was a subject which had evoked little dispute. The control of education was a more debatable matter. Since Morgenthau's first examination of his subordinates' draft of the Morgenthau Plan the previous September, Treasury had been committed to a very cautious policy concerning the reopening of German schools. The CAD draft provided for the reopening of elementary schools when their personnel, curricula, and books had been purged of Nazi influence. It left to the Control Council responsibility for determining the disputed conditions under which the opening of secondary schools and universities would occur.

Four major conflicts arose in the development of this draft, one between War and Treasury, and the others between Treasury and State. (FEA did not sit on this subcommittee.) All of them came to a head on April 18, when a draft was completed for submission to the whole committee.

1. Paragraph 8 of the April 18 Revised Political Directive, dealing with the arrest of Nazis and related categories, had been changed at the request of the Army by the insertion of a sentence which granted discretion to the zone commander to postpone the arrest of certain persons if he believed it desirable in the light of conditions which he encountered, provided that he reported his reasons to JCS. Army insisted that this discretion was necessary for proper handling in the field.[372] Treasury objected to this provision, saying that it provided a loophole in the arrest provisions. "Such a provision," one of its spokesmen argued, "can easily be abused to protect prominent personalities in the political and industrial life of Germany."[373] They proposed, instead, in characteristic fashion, that a sentence be added to ensure that "special favor would not be granted to persons like Krupp and von Papen." It prohibited any differentiation in the manner of arrest or the conditions of detention by reason of wealth, or any kind of rank. The Army version won out, with the condition added that JCS could reverse the zone commander's decision.

2. Paragraph 4 (c) of the April 18 Revised Political Directive stated in general terms the objective of occupation, and the "essential steps" in its accomplishment. State had added to such "essential steps" as deindustrialization, industrial disarmament and the apprehension of war criminals, a phrase which characterized the basic approach to the treatment of Germany which it had used for over three years. It asserted as essential to the prevention of Germany from ever again becoming a threat to the peace of the world the "preparation for an eventual reconstruction of German political life on a democratic basis." Treasury officials claimed that the phrase was meaningless, and that it might afford an opportunity to reconstitute Germany. Nonetheless, it was not removed.[374]

3. Paragraph 9 (a) of the April 18 revision read:

Initially you will not permit political activities of any kind, and you will assure that your military government does not become committed to any political group.

State insisted that adherence to this direction would create a political vacuum. It proposed an amendment which restricted the prohibition to an initial period, after which certain nonobjectionable kinds of political activity would be permitted. The whole committee, instead, reverted to the language of the January revision of JCS 1067 which prohibited political activity unless authorized by the zone commander, but still required him to see that his military government did not become committed to any political group.[375]

4. State wanted the instruction that elementary schools be reopened as soon as they were denazified to include "middle and vocational" schools. The Treasury Department was determined that the German schooling be wholly reshaped before the schools were reopened. It anticipated that a long and energetic

period of denazification would be required for books, curricula, and teachers. Consequently, it continued to oppose any provision for the reopening of schools. The State Department's objective was eventually obtained because the Army supported it on very practical grounds: it had discovered in Italy the great inconvenience (at the very least) of having children running loose in the streets, and had learned that the best way to keep them off the streets was to put them in school.[376]

2. Financial Sections

The financial subcommittee used as its basic draft the revised financial directive from the January revision of JCS 1067. This directive, drafted originally by the Treasury, had included more of the Treasury views than its predecessor, and constituted the strongest statement in agreed policy of the Treasury position. In the IPCOG subcommittee Treasury officials made only a few refinements and changes based on the observations of Treasury personnel in the field. However, on two subjects there was much discussion. These were inflation control and external assets. The first was finally decided to be an economic question, and was left to the economic subcommittee for resolution. A paragraph which authorized the taking of financial measures to prevent monetary and financial disturbances which would cause disease and unrest was accordingly cut out of the directive.

The State Department suggested, while the revision of the financial directive was in progress during April, that the provision for the disposition of German external assets was too narrow because it failed to allow for the disposition of such assets in order to pay for needed German imports. Accordingly, it proposed that the provision which stated that the American zone commander should hold the German foreign exchange assets seized by him "for distribution or reparation or restitution as determined by appropriate authority" should have inserted in it after the word "restitution" "or for other purposes." State argued that it was inevitable that the United States would provide substantial supplies for Germany during the control period, so that it would be to her financial advantage to assure payment for these supplies from foreign exchange assets. Treasury

insisted that such an advantage would be purely illusory. "The United States already has claims against Germany for war costs, etc., which far exceed any amount we can possibly obtain as reparations out of Germany's external assets. Accordingly, it is merely self-deception to suggest that there is any financial gain in using German resources which are already ours by virtue of existing claims to pay for goods to be delivered to Germany during the control period."[377]

Behind this dispute lay two fundamentally different conceptions of policy. State was trying to make sure that the German economy would not be cut loose to drift without regard to the political implications of the economic floundering which might follow. State thought in terms of a "minimum living standard," and wished to guarantee that minimum. Treasury, on the other hand, no longer demanded the complete disorganization of the German economic system, but it was still prepared to deal far more sternly with Germany than was State. Hence, it was determined that no provision in the directives on the treatment of Germany should allow the possibility of lenient treatment. The Treasury was not necessarily intent on promoting economic collapse; but it was determined that nothing should allow the reconstruction of Germany. The State insertion was viewed in Treasury essentially as a loophole to a more lenient policy. The outcome of this controversy was a characteristic paragraph which laid out a carefully hedged compromise. It allowed the use of foreign exchange derived from exports to pay for imports, but required the approval of the Control Council for the disposition of other foreign exchange assets.

3. Economic Sections

The economic subcommittee became involved in a more fundamental but related clash over the imposition of controls on the German economy. Here the issue was joined on the particular question of whether the zone commanders should have the authority and responsibility to control inflation. State thought they should, since the long-range objectives of a democratic Germany would be severely jeopardized by run-away inflation, as would such short-run objectives as reparations. FEA, reflecting its own studies of economic controls, while it was not as inclined to treat Germany liberally, did want substantial economic controls established. It proposed adding to the economic draft a statement making it the aim of the zone commander, during the occupation period, to develop the basis for a permanent system of controls over industrial disarmament. While the substance of FEA policy for Germany did not differ from that of Treasury, Treasury officials opposed this suggestion because it would empower the zone commander to carry out positive acts of control. Again, it was seeking to close the loophole to leniency.

The first draft of the economic directive was prepared by FEA, and contained extensive provisions for economic controls. State was prepared to accept them, while Treasury insisted, as it had so often in the past, that the whole draft be rejected, and the subcommittee begin all over again, going back to JCS 1067. Army felt that much that was important had been left out. It requested specific language concerning the responsibility of the zone commander, decentralization provisions, and a statement making it clear that the Germans were to be responsible for their own economy. It specified several other items which needed to be dealt with, including a limitation on control measures, a provision for breaking up landed estates, and a detailed statement concerning distribution of commodities between zones.

Despres volunteered to have State redraft FEA's revision. Coe suggested that a drafting committee be appointed to help State. But Despres, with Fowler's support, rejected the proposal. State's redraft was discussed April 6. The first section of the revision dealt with controls. Coe again suggested substituting the language of the original JCS 1067 for the State revision. Despres replied that his Department objected to that language because it gave the wrong tone, and had been overruled by the Presidential Policy Statement of March 23 which, he said, authorized the taking of more responsibility for controls than JCS 1067 envisaged. Boettiger indicated that Army approved the State redraft on this point. The language on controls in the old JCS 1067, he said, was the very language which he opposed. He pointed out that the Army was already controlling prices and rationing in Aachen and other cities, and that these controls would have

to continue. He requested a specific direction on whether or not it would be the function of the Army to maintain controls, and indicated that a statement to the effect that the Germans were to be responsible was not adequate. Such a statement would indicate that the Army was to see to it that the Germans were to carry out controls properly, and the Army would thus be responsible for running the entire German economy.[378] Coe said that in the Treasury view it was not only undesirable but impossible for the Army or other occupation authorities to take any responsibility for the control of the German economy. This conflict remained unresolved in the subcommittee, and was taken up to the full committee, which sanctioned language envisaging the control of prices, rationing, wages, industry, commerce, finance, etc.[379]

In the same manner, other details were fought over. FEA continued to advocate the adoption of detailed provisions for control, which Treasury adamantly opposed. On substantive policy matters, however, these two agencies were not in real conflict. State was interested in a more lenient substantive policy, and was prepared to accept controls to get it. The Army, while it took a moderate line on policy, insisted on broad authority to impose controls in order to achieve its primary objective of the maximum of power for its commander in the field to solve problems at his own discretion. No single point of view predominated in the final draft which was approved by IPCOG.

Most of the work on the second revision of JCS 1067 had been done in the subcommittees of IPCOG, but ultimately the committee itself had to ratify this work and thrash out the questions which remained unsettled. While Clayton had been appointed chairman of IPCOG, almost all of its plenary sessions were held in Morgenthau's office, and in deference to his Cabinet rank he was, in effect, the chairman.

The new directive was intended as policy guidance for Eisenhower (or more literally, for Lieutenant General Lucius D. Clay, his deputy for military government) in administering the American zone of occupation, and in negotiating uniform policies for all of Germany in the Control Council. One important War Department demand was successful. The new version clearly provided for the eventuality of Control Council deadlock: Eisenhower was given policy guidance for the American zone in the absence of Control Council agreement on policies which should be uniform throughout Germany, or required central control. However, another important War Department demand was, at best, only partially met. It will be remembered that in the earliest efforts to draft a directive for Eisenhower, the Treasury had adopted the tactic of limiting the power of the military governor as much as it could, in order to insure that he would be unable to engage in constructive activities in Germany. The War Department, on the other hand, had continually fought for greater discretion for its military governor, as was consistent with its administrative doctrine concerning instructions to field commanders generally. One passage from the new version of JCS 1067 illustrates the extent to which the military governor's powers continued to be circumscribed. It was the revision of a paragraph granting power to control inflation which originally appeared in the second version, and was belatedly objected to by Treasury in early February.

"With due regard to paragraph 4a," it stated, referring to a list of basic objectives of military government which included making the Germans aware that they were responsible for their own "chaos and suffering,"

the Control Council should adopt such policies as are clearly necessary to prevent or restrain inflation of a character or dimension which would definitely endanger accomplishment of the objectives of the occupation. The Control Council, in particular, should direct and empower German authorities to maintain or establish controls over prices and wages and to take the fiscal and financial measures necessary to this end. Pending agreement in the Control Council you will assure that such measures as you consider necessary are taken in your own zone. Prevention or restraint of inflation shall not constitute an additional ground for the importation of supplies, nor shall it constitute an additional ground for limiting removal, destruction or curtailment of productive facilities in fulfillment of the program for reparation, demilitarization and industrial disarmament.[380]

D. FINAL CLEARANCE OF THE SECOND REVISION OF JCS 1067

On April 12, while the laborious process of revision was still going on, President Roosevelt died. The day before his death, Morgenthau stopped off to see him at Warm Springs, where he obtained the dying man's hearty approval of his proposal to write a book on how sixty million Germans could feed themselves. This last indication of Roosevelt's attitude on Germany encouraged Morgenthau and his assistants in their belief that he agreed with them.

Two weeks later, on April 26, the second revision of JCS 1067 was approved by IPCOG, and sent to JCS for clearance; JCS forwarded it to Eisenhower on April 28. However, at that time the War Department was attempting to deal with a question from Eisenhower as to whether the production of synthetic oil in Germany would be permitted. Lieutenant General Brehon B. Somervell, Commanding General of the Army Service Forces, wrote Hilldring on April 28 warning that unless German facilities for the production of synthetic rubber, synthetic oil, magnesium, and aluminum were kept intact and operated to some degree like other basic industries in Germany, it would be necessary to import these products from outside Germany, presumably the United States. In fact, he maintained, steel, iron, and heavy industry production should be maintained until requirements for a minimum German economy and for liberated areas were determined. Otherwise, heavy import burdens might result.[381] In the light of Eisenhower's inquiry and Somervell's recommendations, the Joint Chiefs recommended that the draft be changed to allow the zone commander to waive prohibition of the production of synthetic rubber and oil, magnesium, and aluminum without clearance through JCS. Morgenthau, seeing the proposal as representing an unduly liberal treatment of Germany, protested to Stimson, but to no avail.[382] IPCOG promptly accepted the amendment, which was dated May 10. The approval of President Truman was obtained on May 11 and this "Directive to Commander-in-Chief of U. S. Forces of Occupation Regarding the Military Government of Germany," known as JCS 1067/8, was issued to Eisenhower on May 14.[383]

Since President Roosevelt's approval of the Presidential Policy Statement on March 23, the pace in Europe had been swift, culminating in the German surrender on May 7. The Allied military successes and the German defeat in Europe brought with them a host of problems which were being dealt with from day to day in concrete terms by the armies while they were being debated abstractly and in general terms at the same time in the Informal Policy Committee on Germany. The question of synthetic oil production, referred to above, was one of these questions. Another was coal production. While economic policy for Germany was being haggled over in Washington, in the field it was becoming more evident than before that German coal was required to meet the critical needs of much of Western Europe. In the face of the immediate problem, FEA was willing to go along with McCloy's plans to use German prisoners of war in the mines in order to speed production. But it was not so easy to agree on general policy. Beginning in mid-February, FEA had continually attempted to obtain assurance from McCloy that the German standard of living would be kept the lowest in war-ravaged Europe. Finally, on April 3, he responded by refusing to be tied to such a formula. Later that month, on the eve of IPCOG's approval of the new version of JCS 1067, McCloy wrote General Clay that something should be done immediately for the German people in order that they would not perish during the coming winter. It would be advisable, he argued, apart from humanitarian reasons, because famine, disease and starvation know no boundaries. He suggested as a partial solution the establishment of a government-directed work force, patterned after the Civilian Conservation Corps, which would rebuild German housing.[384]

Two other events which occurred during the final drafting of the second revision of JCS 1067 serve to indicate the developing situation. While in IPCOG the question of how much control the zone commander should exercise over the German economy was being hotly argued, Lewis Douglas, the financial adviser to General Clay (who by then was Eisenhower's deputy in charge of military government for Germany), took a hurried trip to Washington to report to McCloy his fears and those of Clay concerning the German economic and financial structure and to request the power to exercise economic and financial controls in Germany.[385] And two days before the new President signed the revised JCS 1067, a twelve-man Senate delegation, returning from a tour in Europe at Eisenhower's invitation, saw Marshall and Stimson. Their individual reactions, as reported in the press, indicated uniformly strong feelings in favor of severe treatment of Germany.

Thus although the May 1945 version of JCS 1067 constituted agreement after a long struggle in Washington (and sometimes in Europe, or at least London, as well) over occupation policy for American military forces in Germany after her defeat, even as final clearance for the new directive was being completed, the lines of dispute could be seen reforming: Morgenthau obtained new support from the dying Roosevelt; FEA was at least ready to offer the facts and figures to support an economic disarmament plan for Germany; military necessity was forcing alterations in the final wording of JCS 1067; the military governor had become uneasy about the limits of his power to save Germany from collapse; McCloy, though a defender of limited responsibility for the Army in Germany, had become concerned with the problems of large-scale suffering there; and a Congressional junket had returned with strong convictions for a hard peace. Under these circumstances, policies could be agreed upon, but could not be settled.

While IPCOG had been preparing the second revision of JCS 1067, it also had under consideration a policy statement to be used by the U. S. representative on the Reparations Commission to be established in Moscow under the terms of the Yalta Protocol. Most of the issues involved in reparations policy were identical with issues concerned with the treatment of Germany, and the State Department took the position that reparations policy should be wholly subordinate to policy for the general treatment of Germany; specifically, that reparations negotiations in Moscow should not interfere with economic policy being formulated in the EAC in London. The Treasury, on the other hand, viewed the Moscow Reparations Commission, and the drafting of instructions for it, as another chance to try for the adoption of its views. Hence many of the economic questions were raised and settled twice in the course of IPCOG deliberations during April and May 1945, once in revising JCS 1067 and again in drafting instructions for the Reparations Commission. The final draft of the reparations document was completed May 21, 1945. It reflected very much the same compromises between Treasury, War, and State Department views as did the previously completed JCS 1067/8.[386]

E. *JCS 1067/8 SUMMARIZED*

As it was approved by President Truman on May 11, 1945, three days after V-E Day, the third official version of JCS 1067 (though the second version to be issued to the Army civil affairs officers) remained the official policy for the U. S. occupation of Germany for two years. A brief summary of JCS 1067/8 follows:

1. The basic objectives of military government in Germany were negative: The principal objective was to prevent Germany from "ever again" becoming a threat to the peace of the world. Another objective was to bring home to the German people that they were responsible for the chaos and suffering which they were experiencing in defeat.

2. The role of the Control Council was to administer matters affecting Germany as a whole. In the absence of Control Council agreement on these matters, the American occupation authorities were to follow the guidance of their own directives.

3. Denazification policy was drawn broadly and flexibly. The dissolution of Nazi-oriented organizations had remained from the beginning an undisputed provision. In addition, three categories of people were to be purged or removed from public office and private positions of importance: (1) Nazis and their associates, (2) war criminals, and (3) all persons who were "hostile to Allied purposes," i.e., who were deemed by the occupying authorities to pose a threat to the security of the occupation. In effect, the third category authorized the Army to remove anyone for security reasons.

4. Arrest policy also included security arrests in addition to the arrest of war criminals.

5. Educational institutions were all to be closed, with only elementary, middle, and vocational schools to be reopened when they had been denazified.

6. Demilitarization was to include the destruction of military equipment and the disbanding of military and military-type organizations.

7. Economic policy was directed towards the negative objectives of the document, as stated in number one above. Certain limitations were placed upon the Army in accomplishing those objectives. Only those economic controls could be used which were necessary; and conversely, no other steps could be taken which would contribute to the economic rehabilitation of Germany or maintain or strengthen the German economy. The German standard of living was to be kept within a minimum defined as high enough to "prevent starvation or widespread disease or such civil unrest as would endanger the occupying forces," and a maximum which would be equal to that of the neighboring United Nations member with the lowest standard of living. Industrial disarmament, which had been the central concept in the Morgenthau Plan, was to be accomplished by prohibiting the production or acquisition of war products and removing (through reparations) or destroying production facilities "especially adapted" to the production of components "specifically designed" for military use. While these provisions were not the maximum envisaged in the Morgenthau Plan, they were also not the minimum alternative which would have all industries which operated for a direct military purpose converted to non-military production, if they could be. Here, in order for an industry to become eligible for confiscation for reparations or for destruction, its military purpose did not need to be direct, nor did conversion of it to non-military production need to be impossible.

VI. THE FINAL REVISION OF JCS 1067

A. INTRODUCTION

Some of the forces which led to the revision of the occupation directive in mid-1947 had already begun to be felt by the time of its first issuance two years earlier in May 1945. The painstaking negotiations which produced JCS 1067 had been necessary because President Roosevelt was never willing to settle definitely the inter-departmental dispute which had begun in August 1944, and was still going on at the time of his death in April 1945. The occupation directive which was issued in early May 1945, just after the German surrender, had been approved by President Truman, who was, for other reasons, not in a position to act decisively. Actually, the dispute was inherent in the nature of the case and would have continued in some form, regardless of Presidential efforts at settlement. An agreement glued together like JCS 1067 with careful phraseology, by avoiding issues, or delegating their determination in the absence of agreement, was bound to come unstuck. It was also to be expected that much would be learned in the administration of occupation. To be sure, some experience had been gained already, first in the Mediterranean theater, and by May 1945, behind the lines in Germany. But the post-surrender period brought a new dimension in occupation policy, even as CCS 551 had given way to JCS 1067, the Interim Directive, and that to the occupation directive JCS 1067/8.

President Roosevelt's misgivings about premature decision on Germany proved prophetic, for, as we shall see, the experience of occupation had an enormous impact on opinions about policy for the occupation. Some of the assumptions on which JCS 1067/8 was based turned out to be inaccurate or incorrect. Some of its instructions appeared impractical or unwise to those who saw their application. The period covered between the issuance of JCS 1067/8 and its revision two years later was a period of important transition in American foreign policy; and this transition affected significantly the American conception of the relationship of Germany to the security of the United States. As America became more concerned about its deteriorating relations with its wartime ally, Soviet Russia, it came to view Germany, not in isolation, but as part of a larger pattern of strategic interests. In this new perspective, a stern peace for Germany could produce the social and economic conditions out of which Communism could grow, instead of serving just as a means of preventing Germany from becoming a military power "ever again."

The deteriorating relations of the Soviet Union with the three Western occupying powers in Germany also made invalid the assumption that Germany could be treated as a political and economic whole. The unexpected conditions which grew out of this false hope or anticipation were vital. The Control Council became virtually useless. The American zone of Germany was far from self-sufficient, and proved to be an economic burden on its occupier. Finally, the United States soon found itself in competition with the Soviet Union for the support of the German people—a popularity contest which it was not likely to win with the Morgenthau Plan, or any part of it.

We have noted the ambiguities of the occupation directive. In carrying it out considerable differences in interpreting and administering it developed. Personal conviction and administrative convenience were probably both significant causes of the divergencies in policy which occurred "in the field."

Indeed, while the final revision of JCS 1067 was significantly different from the occupation directive issued in May 1945, in view of the forces for change in policy the more pertinent question is not why the directive was changed so extensively after two years but why it was allowed to stand unchanged so long. With these pressures for change in mind, there follows a brief account of the events which led to the third revision in an attempt to indicate why it did not occur sooner.

But first, we must consider the Potsdam Protocol, an early modification of JCS 1067/8.

B. THE POTSDAM PROTOCOL

1. The Setting for the Potsdam Conference

With the surrender of Germany on May 7, 1945, the primary mission of the joint military operations directed by SHAEF was accomplished. The next phase of military responsibility was zonal occupation, for which purpose British, French, and American commands had to be re-established along national lines. At the end of March, Lieutenant General Lucius D. Clay had been appointed Deputy Military Governor, SHAEF, but only after the President, evidently still wanting a "tough" civilian viewpoint on the Control Council, had first offered the post of Military Governor to Patterson and then to McCloy.[387] Upon his arrival in Europe in mid-April, Clay was also designated Deputy Commanding General, European Theater of Operations, U. S. Army (later changed to U. S. Forces, European Theater), and Commanding General, U. S. Group, Control Council, in anticipation of the dissolution of SHAEF. By July 4, American troops had been withdrawn into the U. S. zone. SHAEF was dissolved on July 14, and General Eisenhower assumed command of all American forces in Europe the following day.[388]

As the re-establishment of national military commands was consummated, preparations were being completed in a suburb of Berlin for another meeting of the "Big Three." On July 17 the leaders of the three major Allies met at Potsdam to consider, among other things, the future treatment of Germany.

These meetings revealed a wider breach between Russia and her Western Allies on reparations policy than had been evident at Yalta, and on the German policy in general substantial differences remained even on the surface until the very end of the conference.[389]

The Potsdam Communiqué, issued on August 2 reflected in its general phraseology and counter-statements at once the unresolved differences between the wartime Allies and the policy divisions within the ranks of American officials from whose drafts it had largely been drawn. Those Americans who looked to it in the course of their work as a source of policy guidance supplementary to JCS 1067 tended to read it not for what it said, but for what it could be claimed to say.

The Potsdam Protocol[390] was the first full-scale agreed Allied instruction since CCS 551 designed to govern in some detail the occupation authorities in Germany; and the first and only tripartite document of the kind. The two sections of it dealing with occupation policy for Germany, one on the principles to govern the treatment of Germany by the Control Council and the other on German reparations, were treated quite differently at the conference. The first received negligible attention, while the second was discussed extensively. This difference was not without significance. Reparations policy had implications which were both concrete and far-ranging, while the principles for the treatment of Germany, particularly in the form in which they were discussed, were not likely to settle the major controversies with which they dealt; and there was no assurance that the Control Council would have carried them out had they done so.

2. The American Proposals for Germany

In the first plenary session of the conference on July 17, President Truman handed to Stalin and Churchill, as his second proposal for the conference agenda, a proposed agreement on principles to govern the Control Council in the treatment of Germany during the initial control period. As Truman has summarized it:

Complete disarmament of Germany and the elimination or control of all German industry that could be used for military production.

The German people should be made to feel that they had suffered a total military defeat and that they could not escape responsibility for what they had brought upon themselves.

The National Socialist party and all Nazi institutions should be destroyed, and all Nazi officials removed.

Preparations should be made for the eventual reconstruction of German political life on a demo-

cratic basis and for eventual peaceful cooperation in international life by Germany.

Nazi laws of the Hitler regime which established discriminations on grounds of race, creed,
or political opinion should be abolished.

War criminals and those who had participated
in planning or carrying on Nazi enterprises involving or resulting in atrocities or war crimes
should be arrested and brought to judgment.

Economic controls should be imposed only insofar as they were necessary to the accomplishment of these ends. Germany . . . should be
treated as a single economic unit.[391]

This document became the key draft for
both political and economic agreements reached
at Potsdam. It was drawn up as a statement
of policy towards Germany in preparation for
the conference. A version of it was included in
the Potsdam briefing book compiled by the
State Department and examined by President
Truman on the transatlantic voyage. Evidently
during the trip the decision was made to submit
the document as an agenda item at the conference, for it was transformed by State Department experts on Germany on the eve of the
first meeting of the Big Three from a statement of U. S. policy to a proposed tripartite
agreement.[392]

The proposal was largely a condensation of
JCS 1067/8, the occupation directive issued in
May. Two definite changes had been made
during its transformation. State, it will be remembered, had not wanted to consider as a
serious contingency the possibility that three-
power cooperation would not continue after
the war, insisting that the maintenance of the
wartime alliance was absolutely necessary for
post-war plans. Only at the insistence of War
Department officials was the occupation directive written to provide that in the absence
of agreement by the Control Council, the U. S.
zone commander was authorized to make his
own policies. The new proposal broadened the
freedom of action of each occupying power in
its own zone by adding that in "matters exclusively affecting" its own zone, it would "exercise supreme authority."[393]

The second change was to eliminate the
principle of a political vacuum that had such
venerable origins in War Department civil affairs doctrine. The proposed agreement stated
that "non-Nazi political parties with rights of
assembly and of public discussion shall be allowed and encouraged throughout Germany,"
and provided for local elections "as rapidly as
results of local self-government seem to warrant."[394]

Each of these changes reflected a corresponding shift in position by a Department. The first,
which amounted to further hedging against the
possibility of failure of tripartite (actually, quadripartite) rule in Germany, was acceptable in
the State Department because events of recent
months, such as the impasse reached in the
Allied Commission on Reparations in Moscow,
coupled with reports of Soviet plundering in
Eastern Europe, plus continuing difficulties
with the French in the European Advisory
Commission and elsewhere in connection with
the occupation of Germany, had made the
prospects of deadlock in the Control Council
seem very real. The second change corresponded to an alteration of the War Department's attitude about political activity under
the occupation. By the end of 1945, Clay had
become unhappy with the ban in JCS 1067
on political activity, evidently because it deprived the Germans of any incentive for taking
responsibility for their own affairs (which civil
affairs planning assumed they would do), and
because it tended to discourage the development of democratic movements and to encourage radicals of both the left and right. Robert
Murphy, the foreign service officer who was
Clay's political adviser, notified the State Department of Clay's new attitude at the end of
June, and suggested that policy on political activity could now change. As a result, State was
free to incorporate provisions for political activity in the position papers for the forthcoming
meeting of the Big Three.[395]

Both of these changes were in political matters. The economic sections of the President's
proposed agreement contained no such clearly
identifiable departures from JCS 1067. They
did state plainly what was more implicit in
the American occupation directive, that Germany should be treated as a single economic
unit; and the abbreviation of the economic provisions of the directive tended to include more
detailed affirmative than negative provisions,
although there was no indication that any
major alteration in the economic policy provisions of that directive, or for that matter,
any clarification of them, was intended.[396]

The key to economic policy, it was clear
by this time, was reparations. An annex to the

proposed agreement set forth the American position on the principles to govern a reparations agreement. The State Department had been at its best in defining the reparations issue. As early as the spring of 1944, and possibly earlier, it had identified what remained throughout ensuing disputes the two major elements of the American position on reparations: first, that the United States had no direct interest in reparations; and second, that the amount of reparations should be what was left over after the requirements for maintaining the German living standard at an agreed level were met, including exports to pay for essential imports. At Yalta, the latter principle had been jeopardized—some say it was compromised—by Roosevelt's agreement to the Soviet proposal that a total figure of $20 billion (half of which would be for the USSR) be agreed to as the basis for "discussion" in the Reparations Commission. Notwithstanding Soviet insistence that the figure had been accepted without qualification, the American position in the commission remained that no figure could be set until German needs had first been met. Consequently, the annex reiterated this principle, the passage of time and the Moscow reparations deliberations having only sharpened its meaning, and the American commitment to it.[397]

3. *The Changing Influence of State and Treasury*

The inter-departmental dispute over German policy had run on, to say the least, long and actively by the time of the Potsdam Conference. The War, State, and Treasury Departments had been the major protagonists in Washington, with their ranks joined by the Foreign Economic Administration in the spring of 1945 as it completed its studies on the economic disarmament of Germany. By mid-July, when the conference began, some major changes had occurred in the respective positions of these agencies. The State Department's star had risen, and the Treasury's was in descent. The change had begun when the mantle of the Presidency had unexpectedly fallen on Harry S. Truman on April 12, 1945. Simultaneously, the Secretary of the Treasury's special and intimate relationship with the President was eliminated and the White House began to depend more upon conventional State Department channels for the

formulation of foreign policy. The shift in position was gradual. The Treasury officials had established their competence in promoting their viewpoint; and the possibility that they would continue their special relationship with the White House could not be immediately dismissed, particularly because of the initial modest deference of the new President to the views, policies, and choice of subordinates of his predecessor. That the State Department could not be sure of its ascendant position as late as three days before the Potsdam Conference opened can be seen in an exchange of correspondence involving two Assistant Secretaries of State, Archibald MacLeish and Willard Thorp. MacLeish, perhaps overestimating the significance of Clay's interest in modifying the restrictions in JCS 1067 on political activity under the occupation, argued in a memorandum that "common agreement as to the American purpose in the occupation of Germany does not exist," that the only valid objective could be to change the German character through education, and that a treaty should therefore be reached immediately with the other occupying powers on the content of the democratic principles to be used in the reshaping of German character. Thorp's response was first to disagree with the substance of MacLeish's argument. There was not just one objective of policy, he asserted, but several which needed compromising to be made compatible with each other. He listed six, including reform, industrial demilitarization, prevention of starvation and disease, the satisfaction of reparations and restitution claims, acceptance by the American public and its officials, and the development of friendly relations with the Soviet Union. He pointed out that Clayton, the Under Secretary, as chairman of the Informal Policy Committee on Germany, was "instrumental in developing the compromises which are apparent in its directives. I am sure he endeavored to achieve as much clarification as possible." Thorp concluded that it would be unwise to reopen "the whole issue of the objective[s] of the occupation" at that time. While he obviously had his reasons for disagreeing with MacLeish's viewpoint, and he may not have wanted to reopen the major substantive questions of policy because of some underlying disagreement within the State Department staff which had emerged in recent months, it is significant to note that the question of a real alteration of the government's position on German policy came up only after the American delegation had left for the Potsdam Conference.[398]

Whether or not MacLeish's attempt to reopen major policy questions was actually connected with it or not, the State Department's position in the formulation of American occupation policy toward Germany had taken a sharp upturn relative to the Treasury Department shortly before the Potsdam Conference as the result of two events. Two weeks before the conference the appointment of James F. Byrnes as Secretary of State to replace Stettinius indicated the President's interest in providing the Department with energetic leadership. At the same time, Morgenthau resigned as Secretary of the Treasury because of his exclusion from the Potsdam Conference delegation.[399] Because the new President and his newer Secretary of State would be so dependent upon the work of the State Department staff, one would expect that Byrnes would have been in a position to obtain some major changes in the American position vis-à-vis Germany. To understand why this was not the case at Potsdam, it will be necessary to note the respective positions of War and Treasury, the other two major protagonists of occupation policy for Germany within the American government in Washington.

Before Potsdam, there were indications that the War Department's position in policy-making for Germany had improved. As much as Mc-Cloy had labored over the months that had passed to see that the Treasury position was not wholly excluded from inter-departmental deliberations over German policy, Stimson and he were relieved to learn that Morgenthau would not represent the Treasury at Potsdam. Twice before Potsdam Stimson expressed to the new President with considerable candor his version of the struggle over the Morgenthau Plan, including his view that Roosevelt had completely repudiated it. The second time had been in person, during final preparations for the President's departure for Germany. He came away thinking that Truman agreed with his position on Germany, an impression that could not have been entirely wrong, since Truman had just asked him to be on hand at the impending conference.[400] Thus while the War Department's role was becoming more significant, Treasury's was declining. These changes

naturally affected the position of the State Department in relation to policy on Germany both at Potsdam and thereafter.

4. The Position of the Military in Policy-Making

As the Potsdam Conference opened, the military presented three faces. First, the War Department was preoccupied with its responsibilities for civil affairs in the American zone of Germany. Second, Stimson was prepared to exercise his responsibilities as a Cabinet member and return to an active role as adviser to the new President. And third, unofficial views were now forthcoming on German policies from a staff committee under the Joint Chiefs. The first two faces, though not conflicting, were in sharp contrast. At the conference, and before it, Stimson restated to Truman his position of the previous September that the fate of Germany was inseparably bound up with the fate of Europe. His was a long-term view.[401] Unlike Stimson, the civil affairs people were concerned with more pressing matters: getting necessary production started in Germany, meeting emergency relief requirements, allowing Clay the freedom of action he needed to meet the many unforeseen circumstances which arose. Since the death of Roosevelt this aspect of the War Department's position had already come into conflict with the State Department on at least two important matters arising out of the economic chaos of Europe that spring.

Liberated Western Europe, intent upon reestablishing its transportation network, and desperate for rolling stock, pressed for immediate restitution of railroad equipment. The State Department took up their cause, but the War Department declined to act without more explicit formal instructions.[402] In a similar vein, it refused to spend War Department appropriations to finance the imports needed to get German coal production underway so that it could be used throughout Western Europe. In this instance, the reason given was that War Department funds had not been appropriated to be spent for supplies directly or indirectly intended for "foreign occupied zones, the benefits of which would accrue to civilians of liberated areas."[403]

Both of these cases could be seen as conflicts between the policy-making and the administering agent. At the time that State had suggested to the War Department that Eisenhower "be instructed to interpret liberally his . . . directive" on interim reparations, hearings on Capitol Hill were for the first time since the November 1944 elections interjecting the treatment of Germany into public discussion. Not responsible for policy-making, and committed to keeping the Army out of politics, War Department officials had no incentive to commit the Army to a position which was likely to prove controversial. Similarly, the State Department could readily justify the use of Army funds for initiating the extraction of German coal as the carrying out of JCS 1067, for which Eisenhower was responsible. But the War Department had to contend with the military appropriations subcommittees in Congress for its moneys, and there the State Department's arguments were not likely to be heard. Eisenhower, it was pointed out in rejoinder, might have responsibilities as American representative on the Control Council for dealing with the economic problems of Germany as a whole, or of Europe, but Army appropriations for civil relief were justified before Congress for Army purposes only.[404] It would be vain to argue that this was a device to veto a policy disliked in the War Department. McCloy, indeed, had been attempting to promote German coal production for some time, and was instrumental in obtaining the President's authorization for the use of Army funds to do so.[405] The challenge for proper authorization had been thrown down in early July by Stimson in response to pressures from the State Department on the interim reparations problem:

If the State Department will transmit to the War Department a definite policy to be followed in the administration of Germany with respect to reparations pending action by the Reparations Commission, the War Department will gladly endeavor to carry out such a policy.[406]

Besides the two faces of the War Department —Stimson's calm advice to the new President, and the stubborn efforts from within the Department to minimize the policy-making role of the Army—the Joint Chiefs of Staff provided another military face. The Joint Strategic Survey Committee, responding to a general invitation from Admiral Leahy for material useful to the President in preparing himself for the Potsdam Conference, and making plain that it was speaking for itself, not for the Joint Chiefs,

had opposed the dismemberment of Germany and the internationalization of the Ruhr and the Saar for political reasons directed against the Soviet Union.[407] This was the range, then, of the military position on Germany during the Potsdam Conference.

5. *FEA Joins the Hard-Peace Faction*

The fourth major agency involved in German occupation policy in Washington, the conglomerate Foreign Economic Administration, had intentionally kept out of the three-sided squabbles carried on in producing an interim and then an occupation directive for Germany. Three days after Roosevelt's death, while IPCOG was fighting its final battles over the occupation directive, FEA sent a memorandum to Stettinius, who was still Secretary of State, setting forth a "Preliminary U. S. Program for German Economic Industrial Disarmament." Drawing from the massive documentation which it was collecting on the German economy, FEA offered in this paper a preliminary and partial program as a specific interpretation of the agreement at Yalta to "eliminate or control all German industries that could be used for military production. . . ." Though sketchy, the FEA program indicated the direction in which its studies were carrying it. What it proposed was a program of severe economic treatment for Germany, including decentralization, deindustrialization, and close supervision. This memorandum was the first comprehensive statement of the position on the treatment of Germany that FEA made on the basis of its studies[408]—which had been undertaken to provide a factual basis for the determination of an occupation policy for Germany.

FEA's newly articulate position, and the corresponding one of the Treasury people in Army civil affairs assignments in Europe, were being given sympathetic hearings and publicity in the Senate Military Affairs Committee hearings during June 1945, while the State Department was gathering and drafting its documents for the Potsdam Conference.

Thus the Potsdam Conference was poorly timed for those who were interested in raising again the fundamental issues compromised in the drafting of JCS 1067. The War Department was preoccupied with its operating problems in Germany. Clay was willing to interpret his instructions broadly when administrative necessity required it, but not for any other reasons. The supporters of a hard peace for Germany had the ground swell of opinion seemingly with them, and FEA was now heavily committed in their front ranks; but their most effective champion, Morgenthau, was out of power. The German experts in the State Department, on the other hand, were in no position to act decisively. In their quarter, at least, the Department had been drifting without decisive leadership. First Stettinius' energies and attention were in the San Francisco Conference during June; he was then to be replaced. Under these circumstances, the State Department officials interested in doing so were incapable of moving rapidly enough even to begin the exploitation for the Potsdam Conference of the opportunity presented by Morgenthau's resignation. As we have seen, their attempts to egg the War Department into informal modifications of occupation policy without assistance from the Secretary of State were challenged by Stimson. Thus the State Department could do little more in the policy papers on the treatment of Germany which it prepared for the Potsdam Conference than restate the compromises reached in the occupation directive.

6. *The Conference Deliberations over the Treatment of Germany*

When one of these policy papers, the American proposal of an agreement on principles to govern the Control Council in the treatment of Germany, introduced by Truman at the first plenary meeting of the Potsdam Conference, was referred without discussion to the foreign ministers for their consideration, they, in turn, referred the economic questions to a subcommittee. The chief United States spokesman on the committee was the Assistant Secretary of State for Economic Affairs, William L. Clayton, who had been the chairman (at least in name) of the Informal Policy Committee on Germany which drafted JCS 1067/8 and the reparations policy of the government. Political principles were easily settled. At the third plenary session of the conference the foreign ministers presented a document which modified only slightly Truman's proposal of two days earlier and the three governments approved it.[409] But the economic principles were soon deadlocked over

issues involved in the reparations problem and Soviet interests in the Ruhr, though not until someone, probably Clayton, had gained acceptance of a significant change in his own document, the substitution of "average" for "lowest" standard of living of Germany's neighbors as the measurement for the German living standard. On the fourth day of the conference, the differences over reparations were made so clear in the economic subcommittee (the Russians wanting reparations to have prior claim on the German economy over everything else, including the needs of the occupying armies and the subsistence needs of the German people) that, at Clayton's suggestion, it referred the subject back to the foreign ministers. On the same day, a Soviet proposal for internationalization of the Ruhr and the Rhineland under four-power control was parried by the British and American representatives as a political question as well as an economic one. Ultimately, the disposition of the Ruhr was put off for the reason that France had not attended the conference.[410]

Reparations dominated the conference's entire deliberations over Germany. From the beginning, it was either the subject or the basis of dispute. On the second day, Stalin and Truman locked horns on what the boundary of Germany was as the basis for discussion, Stalin arguing that it was the 1937 boundary, minus what it had lost in the war; Truman insisting on the 1937 boundary without modification. Behind this dispute lay the question of whether German territory turned over to Poland by the Soviet Union was to count in the reparations discussions.[411]

On July 23, three days after the economic subcommittee had reached a deadlock on reparations, the foreign ministers made an effort to break it. Molotov proposed that imports and reparations be treated equally in the priority of their claim to German exports. If it was found that the German economy could not produce enough to provide the agreed-upon standard of living, to pay for necessary German imports, and to meet whatever reparations figure was finally set, then all three would be reduced proportionately as much as was necessary. Byrnes, in turn, proposed basing reparations extractions on the principle that each nation would be responsible for making the extractions from its own zone, and would have first claim to the yield. Since American estimates were that half of the German wealth was in the Soviet zone, and the USSR had asked for half of the total reparations figure which it wanted to have set, the questions of priority and German living standard could be side-stepped by simply allowing the Russians to liquidate their reparations claims in their own zone. Molotov's proposal was unacceptable to Byrnes, who insisted that the living standard and necessary imports had to be satisfied ahead of reparations. Molotov could not accept Byrnes's proposal in its entirety because the Soviet estimate of the proportion of German wealth in its own zone was considerably lower than one half, and because the USSR insisted on a fixed quantity of reparations from the Ruhr. The Byrnes proposal eventually formed the basis for the final agreement as it was set forth in the Potsdam Protocol. But for the moment, disagreements too fundamental to be settled by the foreign ministers remained. All major issues were referred to the three heads of government,[412] who, two days later, postponed discussion of the problem.[413]

The foreign ministers tried twice more in their regular meetings to break through their reparations differences, and the economic sub-committee continued its efforts, but to no avail.[414] In the closing sessions of the conference Byrnes tied together three questions which had not been settled: reparations, the western frontier of Poland, and entry into the United Nations. They were agreed upon in that order. The statement of economic principles, a deadlocked issue throughout most of the conference, was then approved as a matter of course, its disputed points having been resolved by the agreement on reparations.[415]

7. German Policy in the Protocol

The reparations agreement reached at Potsdam provided that Soviet reparations claims would be met by removals from the Soviet zone of Germany, plus 10 per cent of German capital equipment intended for reparations in the Western zone. Fifteen per cent more of that capital equipment was also to go to the Soviet Union in exchange for products from the Soviet zone.[416] Since what was available for reparations was contingent upon the achievement of certain basic conditions in the German economy—a minimum standard of living and

exports to pay for necessary imports, all of which involved judgments by the zone commander or his government—Clay was thus given wide discretion in the American zone. That discretion was enhanced by a new statement of the relationship of the zone commander's authority to that of the Control Council. JCS 1067 had provided that the zone commander was free to follow instructions from his own government in the absence of Control Council agreement on the subject. The Potsdam Declaration provided that there would be joint action on "matters affecting Germany as a whole"[417]—a considerably more restricted concept of Control Council authority than appeared in the occupation directive. Supplementing the meaning of this phrase was the provision that common policies would be established in regard to mining and industrial production, agriculture, wages, currency and banking, and several other matters (including reparations). Again, however, deference was shown the discretionary powers of the zone commanders by the additional provision that in applying common policies "account shall be taken, where appropriate, of varying local conditions."[418]

In addition to this bolstering of the authority of the zone commander over what he was granted in JCS 1067, three other differences from that document also contributed to a modest liberalizing of its provisions for the treatment of Germany. (1) Rather than prohibiting political activity except where the zone commander authorized it, as did JCS 1067, the Protocol stated that all "democratic" political parties "shall be allowed and encouraged."[419] (2) The maximum level of the living standard to be allowed Germans was to be the *average* living standard of her neighbors rather than the lowest living standard of her neighbors, as provided by JCS 1067.[420] (3) A new paragraph in the document provided:

Measures shall be promptly taken
(a) to effect essential repair of transport;
(b) to enlarge coal production;
(c) to maximize agricultural output; and
(d) to effect emergency repair of housing and essential utilities.[421]

Although only the first of these differences was definitely initiated by the State Department before the conference, evidently all can be attributed to State.

Thus, out of bargaining with the Russians

at the conference had come the enhancement of zonal commander authority and discretion, which had been a primary objective of War Department officials throughout the disputes in Washington; and out of its relative freedom of action at the conference, State had been able to achieve some of the more liberal policies for the treatment of Germany which it had so long advocated. But most important of all, the Potsdam Protocol left the treatment of Germany in fundamental ambiguity. As a report of the House Special Committee on Postwar Economic Policy and Planning observed three months after Potsdam, referring to the assumption made there that it would be possible to pay reparations from Germany and strip her industry of the future capacity to make war without lowering the standard of living below the danger point for the occupation forces:

> This general formula, . . . in the judgment of the committee, contains several self-contradictory directives to our occupying authorities.

> Large reparations from Germany and the stripping of its normal industries on the grounds that they may potentially be used for war are not compatible with maintaining a minimum standard of living for Germany and are certainly not compatible with a sound German contribution to general European recovery. The interpretation of the directive leaves a latitude which can be used to stress either the Draper-Hoover report of the experts called upon by General Clay to advise him as to the minimum standard of living for Germany, or it may stress the crippling of Germany demanded in certain quarters.[422]

The ambiguity of the Potsdam economic formula, like the enhancement of the authority of the zonal commanders, resulted from the accommodation of Big Three interests. In the former case it was a Soviet-American compromising of fundamentally different positions on the economic treatment of Germany, the United States wanting to assure a minimum residual economic capacity in the conquered country, the Soviet Union determined to extract a predetermined amount of reparations.

C. POLICY DISPUTES IN THE FIELD

The May 1945 revision of JCS 1067 and the Potsdam Declaration failed to clear up the fundamental ambiguities of earlier statements on American policy regarding the treatment of Germany, so the differences over policy continued unabated within the U. S. military government organization. During the planning phase for the occupation of Germany, with the information available for formulating policy necessarily limited, American officials had, to say the least, diverged sharply in their views regarding the treatment of Germany. As the occupation became an operating reality, the actual circumstances under which it was to be carried out were more evident, and captured documents and personnel made available a flood of information relevant to the problem of controlling German military power. The divergent groups, instead of finding grounds for agreement in the wealth of information available or in the pragmatic solution of problems, were only provided with a greater arsenal from which to draw their polemical weapons.

For some, unexpected circumstances seemed additional support for a moderate interpretation of the policy directives. It had not been anticipated while JCS 1067 was being drafted and revised that zones of occupation in Germany would become and remain separate economic units, with Russian and French intransigence (and Anglo-American red tape) preventing inter-zonal economic activity. This economic compartmentalization slowed the recovery of trade and industry in Western Germany and left the three Western zones with a food deficit, since the major food-producing area of Germany was in the East. Equally unanticipated was the massive shift of population from eastern to western Germany in the wake of the Russian conquerors and as a result of Poland's acquisition of German territory. Eight million more Germans had to be supported by Western Germany than had been expected. It is true that the need of Germany's victims for her coal was recognized early in the occupation. The first revision of JCS 1067 (approved January 6, 1945) provided that production of coal and food was to be "affirmatively and aggressively promoted." The second revision, which became the occupation directive, reflected the sterner view again by including coal production as an economic activity which was to be encouraged to the minimum extent necessary. Before V-E Day, as stern an advocate of the industrial disarmament of Germany as FEA was pressing the War Department for assurance that German coal production would be maximized. Indeed, the exportation of German raw materials would fit into the new patterns of European industry envisaged by the FEA program, which was to redistribute industrial power in Europe through the relocation of German plants in France, Belgium, Czechoslovakia, and other countries.[423] But the need for German manufactured products by her victims in the war was underestimated. Holland and Belgium were soon urging an increase in German production so that they could recover the valuable transit trade upon which their economies depended; Denmark wanted an outlet for her agricultural products and needed manufactured goods in return; and actually all the world was seeking manufactures from any source. By early 1946, the small Western European nations were advocating the diversion of more German coal to the production of soda ash and caustic soda in Germany. And officials representing several Allied countries who were concerned with transportation problems in Europe turned to Germany as the major possible immediate source of transport equipment.[424]

Eventually, it became evident that reparation through the removal of capital equipment was of only limited value to the recipient nation, a fact which worked to the double disadvantage of Morgenthau Plan proponents, for it left them with only the punitive and vengeful arguments to make, while at the same time it lent support to the policy of reparations from current production as the only workable method of obtaining reparation.

Denazification, too, provided surprises. Many of those who accepted during the planning phase the denazification provisions of JCS 1067 were not fully aware of the pressures generated by a totalitarian system like the Nazi regime to force compliance, cooperation, and active support from the citizen. Nor, indeed, did they fully anticipate the personnel problem which would be created for the occupation by the enforcement of a strict and broad denazification program.[425]

In other areas the pressure of responsibilities was inclined to work in favor of a mild application of JCS 1067; and its finely drawn provisions and numerous qualifications made strict adherence to the directive, regardless of viewpoint, difficult, if not impossible. The tendency of some who were responsible for civil affairs was to avoid or postpone the application of the punitive or disruptive provisions of JCS 1067

and the Potsdam Declaration, or to interpret them generously, either because they made the more immediate objectives of military government more difficult to achieve, or simply because they did not seem to be as pressing as the re-establishment of essential civilian services.

Thus, for some of those in military government, experience led to moderation. For others, however, new information and experience only served to confirm or convince them in a belief that the wisest course would be a radical decentralization of Germany's industrial system, an extensive reduction of her economic power, and a complete overturning of her leadership groups in public and private life. Many of these people observed with alarm the flight of German assets to neutral countries where they might be safe from the reparation schemes of the United Nations. They were incensed with the evidence uncovered of business collaboration with the Nazi regime, and of the international affiliations of German industry.[426] For them, the occupation brought new evidence that Germany could be made safe only by an extensive purge of her business leaders, as well as of her public officialdom. Though they hardly represented all who held this view, the Treasury "representatives" in the Army, because they remained close-knit, though definitely in the minority, were still its major proponents. Another identifiable group with a "severe peace" orientation somewhat different from the Treasury group's, for instance, had been recruited for economic warfare activities and for the Nuremberg trials from the Department of Justice.

Throughout most of 1945 the major spokesman of the Treasury viewpoint in the Army continued to be Colonel Bernard Bernstein, who served first as Chief of the Finance Division of G-5, SHAEF; then as Director of the Finance Division of the U. S. Group, Control Council; and finally as Director, Division of Investigation of Cartels and External Assets, OMGUS—Office of Military Government, United States.

The cohesiveness and prominence of the Treasury group in the Army, as we have seen, was based on their claim to special status as representatives of the Treasury Department, which entitled them to direct contact with the Treasury without clearance through Army channels. So long as Morgenthau was in Roosevelt's Cabinet, the Army could argue with its financial experts about the propriety of their Treasury relationship, but it could not stop those contacts. Following Roosevelt's death, however, this link with Treasury was inevitably weakened. It was fortuitously but momentarily bolstered in late May 1945, when Senator Harley M. Kilgore, the Chairman of the Senate Military Affairs Committee, gave Bernstein, who was on his way back to Washington, a letter of introduction to Truman. But Morgenthau resigned in July, shortly before Potsdam, and his successor, Fred M. Vinson, who at the time, was still widely considered as a potential candidate for the Presidency in 1948, was anxious to remove the department for which he was responsible from any unnecessary connection with the politically explosive American occupation of Germany. Throughout the summer of 1945 Bernstein constantly protested the general drift of policy application in an effort to force a more severe enforcement of occupation policies. Sometimes he met with considerable success. But in the end, without the support of the Secretary of the Treasury, he returned to Washington to protest, to fight for his views, and to resign. While other reasons were involved in his resignation, it ended the organized advocacy of the Morgenthau view in the occupation of Germany.

D. THE REVISION ATTEMPT OF OCTOBER 1945

1. Clay Promotes a New Draft

Clay had left Washington in April 1945 to take up his duties as the American military governor in Germany firmly committed to a vigorous enforcement of a "hard peace" along the lines of JCS 1067, then undergoing revision.[427] Its punitive aspects did not disturb him; but in Germany he soon came to the conclusion that its severe restriction on his authority to control the German economy was an error. When he saw the April 26 draft of the third version, which somewhat reinforced the earlier limitations on military government authority, he dispatched his political adviser to Washington to see to it that the final draft allowed more discretion.[428] The Potsdam Protocol increased his responsibilities for the German economy and, by implication, his discretionary powers.

By the fall of 1945, continuing difficulties in the Control Council had made it evident that only on limited subjects would Control Council policies supersede American policy for its zone of occupation. Consequently, JCS 1067 was becoming, by default, more of a long-term than an interim directive.

When he was in Washington in late October and early November 1945, Clay sought a revision of JCS 1067 so that it would reflect those clauses of the Potsdam Declaration which would give OMGUS broader authority to control Germany. Under Riddleberger's direction, the State-War-Navy Coordinating Committee began revision. Initially hopeful of the outcome, Clay found no difference of opinion "among the several departments in Washington charged with its preparation."[429] And Riddleberger was confident that the revised draft would be completed in a few weeks.[430]

The dispute over the role of the Treasury in the operation of military government and the substantive issues over which Bernstein had argued with State prior to his resignation had apparently shattered the inter-departmental agreement upon which was to be based the new revision of JCS 1067, for by this time strong differences had developed in State over occupation policy for Germany, caused by divergent views as to how to cope with the Soviet Union, and over many of the concrete details of occupation policy, such as the level of steel production to be allowed in Germany. Moreover, Senator Kilgore, Chairman of the Senate Military Affairs Committee, had been creating an atmosphere in Congress throughout the summer and fall of 1945 which was not conducive to a formal revision of that document by holding hearings at which he and his colleagues were able to provide a forum for "tough-peace" spokesmen and to express their own concern over the apparently lenient policy evolving in practice in the occupation of Germany.[431] Senator Kilgore made public FEA reports and accompanying testimony on them which took a strongly negative line on the economic treatment of Germany and also his own criticism of U. S. officials in Germany for their failure to follow a tough policy.[432] The following day Henry Morgenthau published his book on the Morgenthau Plan. Although as now presented, the plan was considerably milder than it had been in September 1944, it still contained the main features of the earlier Treasury position. Yet it was received with much less criticism than the earlier version.

The flurry of interest in the American occupation of Germany caused by these incidents in early October 1945 was increased by the publication of excerpts from a report on the economic situation in Germany for the U. S. Group, Control Council, by Calvin B. Hoover, at the time an economist in its Economic Intelligence Branch.[433] The Hoover report was followed a month later by the Colmer Committee report on Economic Reconstruction in Europe. This argued for a more affirmative economic policy for Germany, stressed the economic burden which Germany would be on the United States, and on European recovery, as long as the economic reconstruction of Germany were avoided, and recommended the revision of existing occupation directives where necessary.[434] The Hoover report was taken by many, including Morgenthau, as an indication that military government authorities were overemphasizing the need for reconstructing the German economy. In a lengthy interview Morgenthau presented his case to the new Secretary of War, Robert P. Patterson. The several inquiries and comments precipitated by the Hoover report led to a request from Patterson for an analysis in his department of the major economic problems confronting military authorities in Germany which could be used as the basis of discussion with the Secretary of State and the Secretary of the Navy.

Patterson's request became the occasion for abandoning the attempt at revising JCS 1067 in favor of the issuance of a statement on economic policy by the State Department. Such a statement would have the advantage of not requiring inter-departmental clearance, with all its hazards, and it would not be directly compared with the third version of JCS 1067 just published (on October 17), and used to support the charges that military government was not being severe enough. As McCloy, writing to Clay for the last time as Assistant Secretary of War, put it:

Although it is clear that in many respects JCS 1067 was modified and superseded by the [Potsdam] Protocol, I do not think the problem merely is one of making corresponding amendments in JCS 1067. In addition to the [Potsdam] Protocol there has, of course, been an almost continuous interchange of cables dealing with specific policy questions and these, too, have in effect modified or elaborated the basic Directive. The task of tying together in one streamlined Directive all the relevant policies embodied in JCS 1067, the [Potsdam] Protocol and instructions transmitted by cables to my mind really poses a very complex problem of codification, editing and renegotiation. With recollections of the difficulties we encountered in getting Governmental agreement on JCS 1067, none of us has any illusions about the magnitude of the job of agreement [on] a new comprehensive Directive. Efforts along this line might well prove to be a field day for those who have ardently criticized existing policies from divergent and extreme points of view.[435]

Furthermore, the State Department was now the appropriate agency to clarify economic policy for Germany. IPCOG was dissolved at the end of August 1945, when Truman approved a memorandum which provided that the State Department, by reason of its responsibility to the President for carrying out the foreign policy of the United States, deal primarily with the policy aspects of questions arising in the treatment of areas under military government; and that the War Department, by reason of its military responsibility for control of such areas, deal primarily with the executive and administrative aspects of such questions.[436]

2. *The State Department's Policy Statement*

The analysis requested by Patterson was referred to SWNCC with the recommendation that the State Department be requested to clarify the U. S. position on a series of points of interpretation and application derived from the Potsdam Protocol and JCS 1067. They were:

a. The level of the balanced "peace economy" in Germany which the United States envisages as the measure of the industrial plant to be left to Germany after implementation of the reparations and industrial disarmament program.

b. The criteria by which the level of such German "peace economy" is to be determined.

c. Whether or not the desired level of the German "peace economy" is to be measured by the average of the standards of living of European countries, excluding the UK and USSR, and, if so, the time period for which, and the criteria by which . . . such average [is] to be determined.

d. Whether or not it continues to be the policy of the United States that the affirmative action of military government authorities in the operation of the German economy be limited to the repair of transport, the emergency repair of housing and essential utilities, the maximization of coal and agricultural production, and the imposition of economic controls.

e. The extent to which it is desirable for military government to take affirmative steps to rehabilitate the German economy, with particular reference to: (1) the relation of the German economy to that of Europe as a whole; (2) the ceiling above which military government should not assist German economy; (3) the particular types of assistance which it is desired the military government should render the German economy; and (4) the extent to which the United States will assume responsibility for the provision of imports to support the German economy.

f. Whether or not, in determining a desired level of the German "peace economy," provision must be made for sufficient resources to enable Germany to provide foreign exchange to pay for occupation costs.[437]

It was also recommended to SWNCC that the State Department's clarification of these policy matters be published.

The State Department's answer, a 4,000-word "Statement on American Economic Policy Toward Germany," was published on December 12, 1945. The War Department had raised two general questions by its request: (1) What should the level of the German peacetime economy be, and how should it be measured? And (2) what and how much should military government do to maintain or rehabilitate the German economy? A maximum standard of living had been set at Potsdam and mentioned in the War Department's third point. What needed clarifying was whether it was to be the sole measure of the level of the economy, and how precisely was it to be determined. The statement was fairly precise about measurement, but it made three points about how the measurement was to be used which were in conflict: (1) The depression of the productive capacity of the economy to the living standard ceiling would not be necessary except to meet Germany's reparation payments. (2) At the end of the two-year reparations period, the German industrial capacity ought to be capable of producing enough to meet the standard-of-living ceiling. And (3), given the reparations program, and the problems of industrial organization, the

German economy would not be able to reach the standard-of-living ceiling "for some time" after the end of the reparations period.

What could these propositions mean, taken together? Was the maximum living standard provided for at Potsdam to be a guaranteed minimum instead? The statement implied that it might. Was it intended that the ceiling be enforced if, after reparations had been completed, the German economy could produce a higher living standard for its people than the ceiling? A careful analysis of the statement could only show that it was not. The statement was so preoccupied with the immediate problems of economic breakdown, and so gloomy about the future, that it was careless (or clever) in dealing with what seemed to be the extreme upper limits of possibility. The net effect of the State Department's policy statement was, if not to repeal, at least to render irrelevant the standard-of-living ceiling as a measure by which to set the level of the German economy.

The second general question raised by the War Department, how much the German economy should be maintained or reconstructed by military government, was dealt with in the same manner. Reconstruction was not to be limited to any specified list of economic sectors: nothing important in a peacetime economy was barred from aid. And no ceiling was set above which military government authorities should not assist the German economy.

The edifice of military government economic policy for Germany was thus reduced to industrial disarmament through destruction and reparation. Necessarily, this would be somewhat flexible, but certainly not severe. The statement indicated that German reparations obligations would be observed strictly, but that it was not intended to destroy industry "which can readily be used for permitted peacetime industrial activities."[438]

Finally, the State Department's policy statement delayed the applicability of these policy standards until 1948 when the two-year reparations period would come to an end. Until then, the prevention of "disease and unrest," an even more flexible standard, would be the basis for economic policy, including a German standard of living. As for the long term, the State Department position was familiar: Germany was to be reconstructed along democratic lines and treated without vengeance. To emphasize its position the State Department was now able to draw upon a residue from the Treasury Department's contribution to German economic policy. In order to minimize the possibility that the occupying forces would reconstruct the German economy, the Treasury, throughout its year of substantial influence on that policy, had chiseled away at the authority of the occupying forces to control the German economy. The State Department now used these limitations to its own advantage:

In planning the peacetime German economy, the interests of the United States are confined to the industrial disarmament of Germany and to the provision of a balanced economic position at the standard of living indicated. The United States does not seek to eliminate or weaken German industries of a peaceful character, in which Germany has produced effectively for world markets.[439]

E. THE FINAL REVISION

1. The 1946 Attempt

Clay made no effort to get JCS 1067 revised again until July 1946. On July 10, in the Council of Foreign Ministers, Molotov made an open appeal for German favor in a statement of Soviet policy on the future of Germany by attacking the sterner aspects of occupation policy, and referring by implication to the Morgenthau Plan.[440] The following day Secretary of State Byrnes announced that the United States was ready to fuse the U. S. zone of Germany economically with others as a step toward German economic unity. A week later, Clay suggested to the Civil Affairs Division in Washington the need for a summary statement of U. S. policy for Germany as a counter-propaganda weapon. While Germany was discussing the Molotov statement, he pointed out, our military government officials had no summarized, up-to-date statement of policy or objectives which could be used in discussions with the German people. He enclosed with his message a draft of a summary of United States policy and objectives in Germany. A general statement of objectives listed the destruction of war potential, re-education to a liberal philosophy of life and government, the establishment of democratic procedures, and acceptance on terms of equality into the United

Nations. It supported German unity with respect to economic and financial policy and the provision of essential services, and in its political structure. The Rhineland and the Ruhr would remain a part of Germany, since they were essential to the German economy. There was to be no limit in peaceful light industrial expansion or any permanent limit to industrial growth.[441]

Clay's message remained unanswered for over a month. Byrnes wanted to hold off any public pronouncement on Germany until the Council of Foreign Ministers took up the problem. He changed his mind, however, and, with Clay's encouragement, made a major speech on Germany (arranged for by Clay) at Stuttgart on September 6. In it he indicated that, in the absence of Soviet cooperation, American policy would be to strive for what German unity could be achieved in the West, and in the absence of a peace settlement, for the re-establishment of German responsibility for German affairs. Moreover, since U. S. economic policy for Germany, including the Level of Industry plan, had been erroneous in its expectation of German unity, it would have to be liberalized.[442]

Following the Stuttgart speech, CAD finally answered Clay's proposal. It informed him that SWNCC was considering the revision of JCS 1067 with the object of combining in one document the changes made by Potsdam, subsequent amendments, Byrnes's Stuttgart speech, and current proposals. Clay's views, it indicated, would be appreciated.[443] He responded immediately, suggesting that the Stuttgart speech be taken as the basis for a positive statement which should be short and concise and general enough so that it would not have to be changed soon or often. Implementing directives, he proposed, could then fill in details. They could be changed, but basic policy would stand. Clay's message was dated September 16.[444]

The following day SWNCC referred JCS 1067, together with Clay's two messages to CAD, to its European subcommittee for revision in the light of the later documents.[445] Nothing happened there for seven months.

The wide divergencies of view in the State Department, for the most part between the "desk officers" and the economists, over how to adapt to the diplomatic tactics and rising threat of the Soviet Union may have prevented action, as they apparently had a year earlier in the fall of 1945. But there were also the same external reasons for inaction. Throughout the summer and fall of 1946 Congressional hearings had tended to emphasize how much military government had departed from the "spirit" of Potsdam, and at the time of this referral to the SWNCC subcommittee rumors were rife of a possible Senate investigation of military government. After the November elections, with the first Congress organized by the Republicans in sixteen years imminent, the victorious party talked enthusiastically of investigations of Democratic misrule. The issuance of a revision of JCS 1067 might well have drawn the fire of Congress to occupation policies, although, at the end of December 1946, the Colmer Committee issued another report in which it again recommended a more affirmative policy for Germany.

2. *The Change of Climate*

By the following April, however, the situation had changed radically. When the Senate War Investigating Committee fell into Republican hands in January 1947, Administration pressure had helped forestall it from investigating military government.[446] And, determined to cut what it regarded as profligate Democratic spending, the new Congress was soon intent upon budget cutting. The State Department had asserted, in trying to fend off the proposed investigation of military government, that it would interfere with efforts being made at that time to consolidate three of the occupation zones of Germany into an economic unit.[447] The reduction which this would make possible in U. S. expenditures for its zone in Germany had already been made clear in connection with the merger of the British and American zones, then underway.[448] And the connection between economy in the budget and the German economy was underlined in the President's budget message,[449] in the reports of Herbert Hoover on his economic mission to Germany and Austria for the President,[450] and in General McNarney's report at the time of his retirement in March as Military Governor of the U. S. zone.[451] The obstacles in domestic politics to a more constructive policy directive for Germany were thus being cleared away in the spring of 1947.

At the same time, the Moscow Foreign Ministers' Conference of March 1947 helped to make perfectly clear the status of quadripartite cooperation in the administration of occupied Germany. The American officials attending the conference hoped to settle the vexing issues concerning the treatment of Germany. Some of these issues, such as reparations, had been postponed intentionally when they had been raised during the war; some of them, such as demilitarization and denazification, were thought to have been settled by earlier agreement; and others, such as the economic unity of Germany, were new problems based on unanticipated circumstances. None of them proved soluble at Moscow. When the conference ended in complete failure, demonstrating that the East-West split over Germany was likely to be permanent, the Western powers felt free to make more positive decisions.[452]

On their way back from the Moscow Conference, Clay, Murphy, and Riddleberger prepared a revision of the occupation directive. Clay had succeeded McNarney as Commander in Chief of the U. S. Forces and Military Governor of the U. S. zone on the eve of the Moscow Conference, and apparently he was determined to achieve now the revision he had so long advocated. Upon his return to Washington, Riddleberger pressed for a change in the directive. On April 11, 1947, Hilldring, who had become an Assistant Secretary of State in charge of occupation matters in 1946, moved to re-activate SWNCC deliberations. Undoubtedly, Riddleberger was the immediate moving force behind this exhumation.

Once the revision was resumed in April, it proceeded steadily, though not rapidly. On May 1, Clay issued a directive outlining the basic principles and concepts of the U. S. military government. It was his version of the revision Riddleberger had taken on to Washington. In both form and substance it satisfied his request of the previous July for a short, positively phrased document, which could be used for propaganda as well as policy guidance.[453]

SWNCC completed a draft of the revision by mid-May. Most of the changes involved no substantive amendments. The relations between the Control Council and the military government in the U. S. zone were given diminished attention, and the provisions for German self-government were made more general and more reassuring, leaving out specific references to the extent of decentralization and self-government. After clearing the new version with the Joint Chiefs of Staff and the Secretaries of State, War, and Treasury, and then laboriously re-examining it again for points of difference, at the July 10 meeting of SWNCC, with the Navy representative absent, the revision of the directive was finally approved.[454]

The following day, JCS dispatched the substance of the revision to General Clay as the Commander in Chief, European Command. In this, its final form, the directive was purged of the most important elements of the Morgenthau Plan.

BIBLIOGRAPHIC NOTE

This study is largely based on unpublished documents, particularly files of the War and State Departments and the wartime Foreign Economic Administration. War Department files for this period are now in the custodianship of the Military Records Branch of the General Services Administration, located at the Federal Records Center, Alexandria, Virginia, though access to them must be obtained through the Office of the Chief of Information and Education, Department of the Army. State Department files are accessible through the Historical Division, Department of State, which is also responsible for access to the FEA files used for this study. Citations of FEA files are all identified in the footnotes by the initials of that agency. State Department files are also designated by name, except a special group of documents which I have simply called the Potsdam collection. With two exceptions, War Department files have been identified by the Army file number, and the agency name has not been repeated. The file numbers begin with either CAD (for the Civil Affairs Division) or ASW (for the Office of the Assistant Secretary of War).

I have also drawn material from the Harry Dexter White Papers and the James Forrestal Papers at the Firestone Library, Princeton University; from Henry L. Stimson's Collection and particularly his Diary in the Historical Manuscripts Division of the Yale University Library; and from the Roosevelt Papers, Franklin D. Roosevelt Library, Hyde Park, New York, although these collections were not so extensively useful as were the agency files. The archival and other responsible officials in Washington, Hyde Park, New Haven, and Princeton have been most helpful and I gladly acknowledge my debt to them.

I have used one privately held collection of unpublished materials, the personal papers of Josiah E. DuBois, a former Treasury Department official, and have drawn from two unpublished manuscripts, Walter Dorn's "The Purpose and Scope of the Original American Purge Policy," which is part of a more general study on the American occupation of Germany, and John L. Chase's "The Development of the United States Policy Toward Germany During World War II" (Ph. D. thesis, Princeton University, 1952); I am grateful to all three for their generosity in making their documents or unpublished manuscripts available to me.

I am also deeply indebted to those who were willing to submit to personal interviews or to supply written comments. The following persons materially assisted in this way in the preparation of this study: James W. Angell, Elting Arnold, Laird Bell, Bernard Bernstein, Edward M. Bernstein, Francis L. Blewer, William C. Chanler, John L. Chase, V. Frank Coe, R. Ammi Cutter, James C. Davis, Walter Dorn, Goldthwaite H. Dorr, Francis X. Downey, Josiah E. DuBois, Charles Fahy, Merle Fainsod, Adrian Fisher, Artemus L. Gates, Harrison A. Gerhardt, Edward S. Greenbaum, Ernest Gross, David Harris, John Haskell, John H. Hilldring, Charles C. Hilliard, Hajo Holborn, R. Keith Kane, George F. Kennan, Charles P. Kindleberger, Marx Leva, George A. Lincoln, Robert A. Lovett, Ansel F. Luxford, William C. Marbury, Charles W. McCarthy, John J. McCloy, James McCormack, Jr., Philip E. Mosely, Otto L. Nelson, Jr., John H. Ohly, John W. Pehle, E. F. Penrose, James A. Perkins, Howard C. Petersen, James W. Riddleberger, Walt W. Rostow, Arthur M. Schlesinger, Jr., Walter Surrey, Albert C. Wedemeyer, Albert K. Weinberg, and Richard Wilmer.

Of official documentary publications used in this study, the most important are *Foreign Relations of the United States, Diplomatic Papers, The Conferences at Malta and Yalta,* Department of State Publication 6199 (Washington: Government Printing Office, 1955); *Foreign Relations of the United States: The Conference of Berlin* (The Potsdam Conference), Vols. I and II (Washington: Government Printing Office, 1960); and *Foreign Relations of the United States, Diplomatic Papers, The Conferences at Cairo and Teheran, 1943* (Washington: Government Printing Office, 1961). Other useful printed collections of relevant public documents are U. S. Congress, Senate Committee on Foreign Relations, *Documents on Germany, 1944-1959,* Committee Print, 86th Cong., 1st sess.; Senate Doc. No. 123, *A Decade of American Foreign Policy, Basic Documents, 1941-1949,* 81st Cong., 1st sess.; and Hajo Holborn, *American Military Government: Its Organization and Policies* (Washington: Infantry Journal Press, 1947), which also includes valuable descriptive material by the author. Some Treasury Department documents are printed in Senate Judiciary Committee, *Interlocking Subversion in Government Departments,* Hearings, Parts 29 and 30, 84th Cong., 1st sess. Henry Morgenthau, Jr.'s book, *Germany Is Our Problem* (New York: Harper & Bros., 1945), is itself a documentation of Treasury viewpoints. Some other Congressional documents which bear on the subject are House Special Committee on Postwar Economic Policy and Planning, *Economic Reconstruction in Europe,* Eighth Report, 79th Cong., 1st sess.; and Senate Committee on Military Affairs, *Elimination of German Resources for War,* Hearings, 79th Cong., 1st sess.

The official histories most important to this study are, Harley A. Notter, ed., *Postwar Foreign Policy Preparation, 1939-1945,* Department of State Publication 3580 (General Foreign Policy Series 15) (Washington: Government Printing Office, 1949); Forrest C. Pogue, *The European Theater of Operations: The Supreme Command,* and Ray S. Cline, *The War Department: Washington Command Post: The Operations Division,* volumes in *United States Army in World War II,* ed. by K. R. Greenfield (Washington: Government Printing Office, 1951 and 1954); Maurice Matloff, *Strategic Planning for Coalition Warfare, 1943-1944,* volume in *United States Army in World War II* (Washington: Government Printing Office, 1959); U. S. Bureau of the Budget, War Records Section, *The United States at War: Development and Administration of the War Pro-*

gram of the Federal Government (Washington: Government Printing Office, 1946); and Oliver J. Fredericksen, *The American Military Occupation of Germany, 1945-1953 (Historical Division,* U. S. Army, Europe, 1953).

Of a considerable number of books and articles used in this study, the most valuable were those which were based on the author's personal connection with and knowledge of his subject, such as Cordell Hull, *Memoirs,* 2 vols. (New York: The Macmillan Co., 1948); H. L. Stimson and McGeorge Bundy, *On Active Service in Peace and War* (New York: Harper & Bros., 1947); Winston S. Churchill, *Closing the Ring* and *Triumph and Tragedy,* vols. 5 and 6 of *The Second World War* (Boston: Houghton Mifflin Co., 1951 and 1953); Sir Frederick Morgan, *Overture to Overlord* (Garden City: Doubleday & Co., 1950); William D. Leahy, *I Was There* (New York: Whittlesey House, 1950); E. F. Penrose, *Economic Planning for the Peace* (Princeton: Princeton University Press, 1953); Dwight D. Eisenhower, *Crusade in Europe* (Garden City: Doubleday & Co., 1948); Harry C. Butcher, *My Three Years with Eisenhower* (New York: Simon & Schuster, 1946); Lucius D. Clay, *Decision in Germany* (Garden City: Doubleday and Co., 1950); Philip E. Mosely, "Dismemberment of Germany: The Allied Negotiations from Yalta to Potsdam," and "The Occupation of Germany: New Light on How the Zones Were Drawn," *Foreign Affairs,* XXVIII (April and July, 1950), pp. 487-498 and 580-604; Fred Smith, "The Rise and Fall of the Morgenthau Plan," *United Nations World,* I (March 1947), pp. 32-37; Henry Morgenthau, Jr., "Our Policy Toward Germany," *New York Post,* November 24-29, 1947. Holborn's work could also be included in this list, and, for all practical purposes, so can Walter Millis (ed.), *The Forrestal Diaries* (New York: The Viking Press, 1951).

Other books and articles which were particularly useful are Robert E. Sherwood, *Roosevelt and Hopkins* (New York: Harper and Bros., rev. ed., 1950); Carl J. Friedrich and Associates, *American Experiences in Military Government in World War II* (New York: Rinehart and Co., 1948); John L. Snell, Ch. II, "What to Do with Germany?" in John L. Snell (ed.), *The Meaning of Yalta* (Baton Rouge: Louisiana State University Press, 1956); John L. Chase, "The Development of the Morgenthau Plan Through the Quebec Conference," *Journal of Politics,* XVI (May 1954), pp. 324-359; Walter Dorn, "The Debate over American Occupation Policy in Germany in 1944-1945," *Political Science Quarterly,* LXXII (December 1957), pp. 481-501; Albert L. Warner, "Our Secret Deal Over Germany," *Saturday Evening Post,* CCXXV (August 2, 1952), pp. 225-304.

The future student of this subject should be able to find further documentation in the Henry Morgenthau diaries, now under the custodianship of the National Archives, and in the files of the U. S. Treasury Department, both currently inaccessible to scholars, as well as among Army records which today bear too high a security classification to be available for this study. The currently available documentation, however, is of sufficient magnitude so that major changes and additions to the account seem unlikely.

Throughout the preparation of this study I have worked under the directing hand of Harold Stein. Since his contributions to it have been both formative and substantive, he shares with me responsibility for its contents. It should be emphasized that no one else does. Neither those agencies and individuals who have allowed me the use of materials under their control, nor the people listed above who have commented and recalled for the benefit of this study, have assumed any responsibility for what I have written. The clearance for publication of this study by the Departments of State and the Army is likewise in no way intended as an endorsement of its contents.

NOTES

1. *Robert E. Sherwood,* Roosevelt and Hopkins: An Intimate History (rev. ed., Harper, New York, 1950), p. 711.

2. *Ibid.;* Harley A. Notter (ed.), *Postwar Foreign Policy Preparation, 1939-1945,* Department of State Publication 3580 (General Foreign Policy Series 15) (Government Printing Office, Washington, 1949), pp. 186 f.

3. Eden must have been expressing an off-hand judgment, for five months later he told Hull he opposed dismemberment. Cordell Hull, *Memoirs* II (Macmillan, New York, 1948), pp. 1233 f.

4. Sherwood, *Roosevelt and Hopkins,* p. 711.

5. *Ibid.,* p. 715.

6. *Ibid.,* pp. 714 f.

7. Hull, *Memoirs,* II, pp. 1284 f.

8. Philip E. Mosely, "Dismemberment of Germany: The Allied Negotiations from Yalta to Potsdam," *Foreign Affairs* (April 1950), p. 488. Welles's position on partition is published in his *The Time for Decision* (Harper, New York, 1944), pp. 439-452.

9. Hull, *Memoirs,* II, p. 1285.

10. *Ibid.,* pp. 1233 f.

11. Those accompanying Hull were: Leo Pasvolsky, Special Assistant to the Secretary and Executive Director of the Advisory Committee on Post-War Foreign Policy, which had been studying dismemberment since early in 1942, at Roosevelt's suggestion; Green H. Hackworth, a member of that committee and Legal Adviser of the Department; James C. Dunn, Director of the Office of European Affairs; and H. Freeman Matthews. All were members of the Committee on Post-War Foreign Policy. Hull, *Memoirs,* II, p. 1265.

12. Quoted from a State Department interdivisional committee policy recommendation entitled, "The Political Reorganization of Germany (September 23, 1943)," printed in Notter, *Postwar Foreign Policy Preparation,* pp. 558-560; see also pp. 554 ff.

13. Hull, *Memoirs,* II, p. 1287.

14. *Ibid.,* pp. 1265 f.

15. *Ibid.,* pp. 1287-1291.

16. *Ibid.,* pp. 1285 f.

17. "The Political Reorganization of Germany," *loc. cit.;* Hull, *Memoirs,* II, pp. 1286 f.; and Mosely, "Dismemberment of Germany," p. 489.

18. "The Political Reorganization of Germany," *loc. cit.*

19. Mosely, "Dismemberment of Germany," p. 489; and Hull, *Memoirs,* II, p. 1287.

20. Sherwood, *Roosevelt and Hopkins,* pp. 782-783, 786-787, and 797-798; Philip E. Mosely, "The Occupation of Germany: New Light on How the Zones Were Drawn," *Foreign Affairs* (July 1950), p. 582; and E. F. Penrose, *Economic Planning for the Peace* (Princeton University Press, Princeton, 1953), pp. 228 f.

21. Mosely, "The Occupation of Germany," pp. 581 ff.

22. It later grew to include "ten nonofficial members, five Senators and three Representatives, eleven members from the Department of State of whom four were *ex officio,* a member each from the War and Navy Departments and from the Joint Chiefs of Staff as a unit, and one member each from four other Departments, three members from the White House staff, one from the Library of Congress, four from the wartime agencies, and one from among the continuing agencies of the government." Notter, *Postwar Foreign Policy Preparation,* p. 72. Needless to say, the committee did most of its work in subcommittees. *Ibid.,* pp. 63-164, *passim.*

23. *Ibid.,* p. 64.

24. Mosely, "Dismemberment of Germany," p. 489. Much of the material above is drawn from this article.

25. From Hull's letter to members: Notter, *Postwar Foreign Policy Preparation,* p. 164.

26. *Ibid.,* p. 176.

27. *Ibid.,* p. 177.

28. Mosely, "The Occupation of Germany," p. 581. That this was the document used can be established by the comparison of its wording with Hull's summary of the document in his *Memoirs,* II, pp. 1285-1287; the document is printed in Notter, *Postwar Foreign Policy Preparation,* pp. 558-560.

29. Hull, *Memoirs,* II, pp. 1231, 1256.

30. See "The Political Reorganization of Germany," *loc. cit.* Policy papers in use the following spring indicated no change in this policy; Penrose, *Economic Planning for the Peace,* pp. 239 f.

31. Merle Fainsod, "The Development of American Military Government Policy during World War II," Chap. II in Carl J. Friedrich and Associates, *American Experiences in Military Government in World War II* (Rinehart, New York, 1948), p. 25.

32. *The General Service Schools Military Aid to the Civil Power* (Fort Leavenworth: The General Service Schools Press, 1925), p. 57.

33. *Ibid.,* pp. 42 ff.

34. Official File 5136, Franklin D. Roosevelt Library.

35. Henry L. Stimson and McGeorge Bundy, *On Active Service in Peace and War* (Harper, New York, 1948), p. 554.

36. Edwin J. Hayward, "Coordination of Military and Civilian Affairs Planning," American Academy of Political and Social Science, *Annals* (January 1950), p. 19.

37. *Ibid.* It is not clear what the President had in mind here, although the order was interpreted at the time as an endorsement of the narrow view of military government. But the next day, in a letter to William C. Bullitt, in the Navy Department, the President stated that "occupation is wholly a military matter and . . . only when the military authorities are ready to turn over civilian authority should be put into operation." Official File 5136, Franklin D. Roosevelt Library. Probably he was drawing a distinction between "occupied" and "liberated" areas.

38. There are various accounts of the 1943 squabbles over the administration of civil affairs, none of them definitive; see Stimson and Bundy, *On Active Service in Peace and War,* pp. 553-561, also pp. 542-551; Hayward, "Coordination of Military and Civilian Affairs Planning," pp. 19-24; U. S. Bureau of the Budget, War Records Section, *The United States at War: Development and Administration of the War Program of the Federal Government* (Government Printing Office, Washington, 1946), pp. 403-428.

39. Ray S. Cline, *The War Department: Washington Command Post: The Operations Division* (volume in *United States Army in World War II,* edited by K. R. Greenfield) (Government Printing Office, Washington, 1951), pp. 321 f.

40. Minutes, Meeting of the General Council, March 15, 1943, Office of the Deputy Chief of Staff, U. S. Army, p. 10, War Department files.

41. Cline, *The War Department: Washington Command Post,* pp. 322 f.; Stimson and Bundy, *On Active Service in Peace and War,* pp. 554 f.; Hayward, "Coordination of Military and Civilian Affairs Planning," pp. 23 ff.

42. McCloy to Biddle, July 18, 1943, in CAD 014 Germany, Sec. 1; Hilldring to Provost-Marshal General, July 30, 1943, Jones to Provost-Marshal General, August 14, 1943, all in CAD 014 Germany, Sec. 1; Schomaker to Hilldring, December 4, 1943, and Stimson directive, November 18, 1943, *ibid.,* Sec. 2.

43. Burnett memorandum, November 27, 1943, *ibid.*

44. Except as otherwise indicated, all the information on COSSAC in this study is derived from General Morgan's own admirable account: Lieutenant General Sir Frederick Morgan, KCB (COSSAC)—*Overture to Overlord* (Doubleday, Garden City, 1950). For the beginnings of COSSAC, pp. 1-2, 18-28; Winston S. Churchill, *Closing the Ring,* Vol. 5 of *The Second World War* (Houghton Mifflin, Boston, 1951), p. 70.

45. Morgan, *Overture to Overlord,* pp. 106-107.

46. *Ibid.,* pp. 112-117.

47. *Ibid.,* pp. 117, 118-122, 227-236.

48. Forrest C. Pogue, *The European Theater of Operations: The Supreme Command* (volume in *United States Army in World War II,* edited by K. R. Greenfield) (Government Printing Office, Washington, 1954), pp. 348-349, 349n.; Fleet Admiral William D. Leahy, *I Was There* (Whittlesey House, New York, 1950), pp. 197-198; Cline, *The War Department: Washington Command Post,* p. 228, 228n. A fuller and much more enlightening account is given in Maurice Matloff, *Strategic Planning for Coalition Warfare, 1943-1944* (Government Printing Office, Washington, 1959) (volume in *United States Army in World War II),* pp. 341-342; it also contains a reproduction of Roosevelt's map between pp. 340-341. The minutes of Roosevelt's discussion with the Joint Chiefs are printed in *Foreign Relations of the United States, Diplomatic Papers, The Conferences at Cairo and Teheran, 1943* (Government Printing Office, Washington, 1961), pp. 253-256, 261 (referred to hereafter as the *Cairo and Teheran Papers).*

49. Pogue, *The European Theater of Operations,* p. 349, 349n.; Leahy, *I Was There,* p. 213; *Cairo and Teheran Papers,* pp. 674, 786-787, 813-814, 879.

50. Pogue, *The European Theater of Operations,* pp. 77-78; Stimson and Bundy, *On Active Service in Peace and War,* p. 559 (where the establishment of CCAC is erroneously dated May 1943); Robert J. Quinlan, *The Italian Armistice,* p. 231 of this volume.

51. Pogue, *The European Theater of Operations,* pp. 76-78; Quinlan, *The Italian Armistice,* pp. 222-224.

52. The general transition from COSSAC to SHAEF is described in Pogue, *The European Theater of Operations,* pp. 56-60; developments in military government and civil affairs, *ibid.,* pp. 75-84, 346-347.

53. *Ibid.,* pp. 347-348.

54. Draft memorandum, Secretary of War to President, undated, ASW 370.8 Germany.

55. See letter from Admiral Leahy to Secretary Hull, May 16, 1944, printed in *Foreign Relations of the United States, Diplomatic Papers, The Conferences at Malta and Yalta* (Department of State Publication 6199, 1955), pp. 106-107n. This volume will be cited hereafter as *Yalta Papers.*

56. The text of CCS 551 is printed in Hajo Holborn, *American Military Government: Its Organization and Policies* (Infantry Journal Press, Washington, 1947), pp. 135-143. This text includes the economic and relief appendix issued on May 31, 1944, and the financial appendix in the revised version of August 1944. The information cited in the text on the dates of the appendices appears on p. 135.

57. Mosely, "The Occupation of Germany," pp. 583-584; Notter, *Postwar Foreign Policy Preparation,* pp. 225-226; Cline, *The War Department: Washington Command Post,* p. 323; Hayward, "Coordination of Military and Civilian Affairs Planning," pp. 24-25; Albert L. Warner, "Our Secret Deal Over Germany," *Saturday Evening Post* (August 2, 1952), p. 30; Fahy to Tansey and Roberts, September 29, 1944, CAD 334 EAC.

58. Mosely, "The Occupation of Germany," pp. 583-586.

59. Burnett memorandum, November 27, 1943, CAD 014 Germany, Sec. 2; Hilldring to Chief of Staff, December 9, 1943, *ibid.*

60. Mosely, "The Occupation of Germany," pp. 583-586.

61. Leverich to Dunn, February 19, 1944, CAD 334 EAC.

62. Thomas T. Hammond to Hilldring, January 10, 1944, *ibid.*

63. *House of Commons Debates,* CCCXCV (5th Series), p. 1901.

64. Walter Dorn, "The Debate over American Occupation Policy in Germany in 1944-1945," *Political Science Quarterly* (December 1957), p. 486.

65. Letter, George F. Kennan to author, October 31, 1955.

66. Warner, "Our Secret Deal over Germany."

67. Hilldring to Hammond, December 27, 1943, CAD 014 Germany, Sec. 3.

68. Leverich to Dunn, February 19, 1944, CAD 334 EAC; JCS to Secretary of State, February 5, 1944, CAD 014 Germany, Sec. 3; Hill-

dring to Wickersham, February 8, 1944, *ibid.*

69. Leverich to Dunn, February 19, 1944, *loc. cit.*

70. *Ibid.,* WS-93 (March 6, 1944), and WS-98 (March 7, 1944), *ibid.,* Sec. 4.

71. Winant to Secretary of State, March 30, 1944, *ibid.,* Sec. 5.

72. Draft Cable, Marshall to Eisenhower, April 2, 1944, *ibid.,* Sec. 5.

73. Hilldring to Laux, April 24, 1944, *ibid.,* Sec. 5.

74. Mosely, "The Occupation of Germany," tells the whole story but at the time he wrote he was unaware of the COSSAC plan and the negotiations prior to December 15, 1944; Pogue, *The European Theater of Operations,* pp. 348-351 and notes; *Cairo and Teheran Papers,* p. 261; Matloff, *Strategic Planning for Coalition Warfare, 1943-1944,* pp. 341-342.

75. Wickersham to Hilldring, March 6, 1944, CAD 334 EAC; Wickersham-Hilldring telephone transcript, February 23, 1944, CAD 014 Germany, Sec. 4.

76. Wickersham to Hilldring, March 16, 1944, *ibid.,* Sec. 4.

77. Winant to Secretary of State, January 27, 1944, CAD 334 EAC.

78. Winant to Hull, January 29, 1944, *ibid.*

79. WS-55 and WS-54, respectively, February 3, 1944, CAD 014 Germany, Sec. 3.

80. Rounds to Director, CAD, February 11, 1944, *ibid.*

81. Leverich to Dunn, *loc. cit.*

82. Handy memorandum, March 13, 1944, CAD 014 Germany, Sec. 4.

83. Hilldring memorandum, March 31, 1944, *ibid.;* McCloy to Dunn, April 5, 1944, *ibid.*

84. Interview with George F. Kennan, October 15, 1958.

85. Pogue, *The European Theater of Operations,* p. 347.

86. Somervell to Jefferson, April 6, 1944, CAD 014 Germany, Sec. 5.

87. Cline, *The War Department: Washington Command Post,* pp. 323-325.

88. Strong to Meyer, September 16, 1944, CAD 014 Germany, Sec. 9.

89. Meyer to Hilldring and Strong, October 14, 1944, CAD 334 EAC, Sec. 3.

90. Hammond to Strong and Hilldring, August 13, 1944, and Hammond to Meyer, August 16, 1944, CAD 334 EAC, Sec. 2; Hilldring memorandum, August 28, 1944, CAD 014 Germany, Sec. 8.

91. "General Directive for Germany" (July 12, 1944), CAD 334 EAC, Sec. 2.

92. "Principles of Military Government for Germany" (July 12, 1944), CAD 334 EAC, Sec. 2.

93. Memorandum by Acting Director, CAD, undated, CAD 014 Germany, Sec. 9; Hammond to Meyer, August 23, 1944 and August 25, 1944, CAD 334 EAC, Sec. 2.

94. Pogue, *The European Theater of Operations*, p. 353, 353n.

95. McCloy to Stettinius, August 10, 1944, CAD 334 EAC, Sec. 2.

96. *Ibid.*; Henry L. Stimson Diary, Stimson Collection, Historical Manuscripts Division, Yale University Library, July 31 and August 1, 1944.

97. Brigadier General Julius C. Holmes, Assistant Chief of Staff, G-5, AEF, believed that his office was the first to become aware that it would be not only dangerous but futile for the Army to attempt to prop up the rickety economic and financial structure of Germany. Holmes to Hilldring, September 11, 1944, CAD 014 Germany, Sec. 8.

98. Notter, *Postwar Foreign Policy Preparation*, p. 219, quoting letter.

99. Penrose, *Economic Planning for the Peace*, pp. 239 ff.

100. Notter, *Postwar Foreign Policy Preparation*, p. 219, quoting letter.

101. Mosely, "Dismemberment of Germany," p. 490.

102. See, e.g., WS-54d (April 10, 1944), CAD 014 Germany, Sec. 5.

103. Minutes, ECEFP meetings, May 19, 1944, FEA Box 59. Except where otherwise indicated, the following account is based on the minutes of ECEFP meetings, May 19 through August 4, 1944, *ibid.*

104. WS-54c (March 2, 1944), CAD 014 Germany, Sec. 4.

105. WS-55c (March 2, 1944), *ibid.*

106. Angell to Currie, June 21, 1944, FEA Box 97; FEA memorandum on ECEFP D-17/21 June 28, 1944, FEA Box 97; "A Report of the Interdivisional Committee on Reparations, Restitution, and Property Rights," undated [July 22-31, 1944], to ECEFP, FEA Box 59; "A Report on Reparations, Restitution, and Property Rights" (July 31, 1944), *ibid.*

107. Summarized in John L. Chase's "The Development of the Morgenthau Plan Through the Quebec Conference," *Journal of Politics* (May 1954), pp. 327 f.

108. Mosely, "The Occupation of Germany," pp. 584-589.

109. No attempt is made here to compare the features of the Morgenthau Plan with the views of Lord Robert Vansittart in Great Britain. For a discussion of this subject see Dorn, "The Debate over American Occupation Policy in Germany in 1944-1945," pp. 484-485, 493-494.

110. See, e.g., Henry Morgenthau, *Ambassador Morgenthau's Story* (Doubleday, Page, New York, 1919), *passim.*

111. Fred Smith, "The Rise and Fall of the Morgenthau Plan," *United Nations World*, I (March 1947), p. 33.

112. Albert Gailord Hart, *Money, Debt, and Economic Activity* (Prentice-Hall, New York, 1948), p. vii.

113. No attempt is made in this study to deal with Harry Dexter White's alleged connections with the Communist Party and the Soviet espionage apparatus in the United States. As the account should indicate, it is possible to explain his economic policies without the Communist thesis. On the other hand, his basic economic assumptions were not incompatible with Marxism. So too his political attitudes on the treatment of Germany served to parallel the Soviet line, but they were also held by many Americans who were neither Communists nor fellow travelers.

114. Quoting Henry Morgenthau, Jr., "Our Policy Toward Germany," *New York Post* (November 24, 1947); letter, Josiah E. DuBois to author, January 4, 1956.

115. Morgenthau, "Our Policy Toward Germany."

116. Smith, "The Rise and Fall of the Morgenthau Plan," p. 32.

117. *Ibid.*

118. Dwight D. Eisenhower, *Crusade in Europe* (Doubleday, Garden City, 1948), p. 287.

119. Eisenhower's position is not entirely clear; he certainly seemed to be leaning toward a "hard peace"; but as he himself says, he had not studied the issues involved; see Harry C. Butcher, *My Three Years with Eisenhower* (Simon & Schuster, New York, 1946), pp. 609-610; Eisenhower, *Crusade in Europe*, p. 287. Before D-Day, Eisenhower and his staff were doing everything possible to soften the unconditional surrender formula because they believed it essential to convince the Germans that they would be treated with some consideration if they surrendered prior to the invasion of Europe. Later, as the forces under Eisenhower's command were penetrating Germany, he attempted to minimize the damage done to the industrial facilities of the Ruhr. Pogue, *The European Theater of Operations*, pp. 339-343 and 439. Smith, "The Rise and Fall of the Morgenthau Plan," suggests that Eisenhower's comments on this occasion were the source of the Morgenthau Plan; but in November 1953, when the question of Harry Dexter White's connections with Communism were under intense public discussion, Smith said that White, not Eisenhower, was the source of the Morgenthau Plan, *New York Times* (November 14, 1953). It should be noted that Eisenhower could as well have agreed with his

civil affairs officers in wanting to get the German economy functioning again and still have wanted to "hold the Germans responsible." A functioning German economy was a military necessity for the security of the occupation forces and for its possible contribution to winning the war against Japan; justice for the Germans could come later, as could other long-term American objectives.

120. Smith, "The Rise and Fall of the Morgenthau Plan." Smith accompanied Morgenthau on his trip to Europe, but was not present at this meeting. This account of the meeting is based upon Smith's article and upon the following: Morgenthau, "Our Policy toward Germany," *New York Post* (November 25, 1947); Penrose, *Economic Planning for the Peace*, pp. 244-248; and an interview with E. F. Penrose (January 26, 1955).

121. Smith, "The Rise and Fall of the Morgenthau Plan," and Penrose, *Economic Planning for the Peace*, p. 246.

122. Penrose, *Economic Planning for the Peace*, pp. 246 f.

123. *Ibid.*, pp. 247-249.

124. Morgenthau, "Our Policy Toward Germany."

125. *Ibid.*

126. Hull, *Memoirs*, II, p. 1615.

127. Penrose, *Economic Planning for the Peace*, pp. 248 f.

128. As summarized in Mosely, "The Occupation of Germany," pp. 241 f. Winant himself played an active part in the drafting of this cable, with the assistance of Penrose and Mosely; conversation with Mosely.

129. Pogue, *The European Theater of Operations*, pp. 353 f.

130. Smith, "The Rise and Fall of the Morgenthau Plan," p. 32.

131. Penrose, *Economic Planning for the Peace*, p. 246.

132. Holmes to Hilldring, September 11, 1944, CAD 014 Germany, Sec. 8.

133. Eisenhower, *Crusade in Europe*, p. 287.

134. Pogue, *The European Theater of Operations*, p. 354.

135. CAD Director to the CCAC, July 31, 1944, CAD 014 Germany, Sec. 7.

136. Since the issue was side-stepped rather than settled, it would appear that both Hilldring and his British colleagues felt strongly about their respective (and divergent) views; Pogue, *The European Theater of Operations*, p. 357.

137. The British records themselves showed that dismemberment was to be considered, but had not been agreed upon. Winant to Secretary of State, January 27, 1945, CAD 334 EAC;

Churchill, *Closing the Ring*, pp. 354-356, 359-360. See also Leahy, *I Was There*, p. 353; *Yalta Papers*, pp. 611-616; James F. Byrnes, *Speaking Frankly* (Harper, New York, 1947), pp. 25-26; John L. Snell (ed.), *The Meaning of Yalta* (Louisiana State University Press, Baton Rouge, 1956), pp. 53-56; "Germany-Partition," Doc. 331, *Potsdam Papers*, I, pp. 456-460.

138. Henry Morgenthau, Jr., "Our Policy Toward Germany," *New York Post* (November 26, 1947).

139. *Ibid.*

140. Stimson Diary, August 23, 1944.

141. *Ibid.*

142. Official File 21, Franklin D. Roosevelt Library, Hyde Park. It is difficult to explain otherwise why Morgenthau arranged to see the President in such haste about a handbook which he had brought from England a week before.

143. Stimson Diary, August 25, 1944; H[arvey] H. B[undy], "Memorandum of Conversation with President," August 25, 1944, *ibid.*; Stimson and Bundy, *On Active Service in Peace and War*, p. 569.

144. Walter Millis (ed.), *The Forrestal Diaries* (Viking Press, New York, 1951), pp. 10-11. Forrestal records incorrectly that Roosevelt came in with Morgenthau. Cf. Stimson and Bundy, *On Active Service in Peace and War*, p. 569. Roosevelt during the Cabinet meeting referred to the two conversations on Germany he had just had with Morgenthau and Stimson; Forrestal's note on Byrnes's recollection of these events two years later (Millis, *The Forrestal Diaries*, p. 11) contains certain obvious inaccuracies.

145. Stimson and Bundy, *On Active Service in Peace and War*, p. 569.

146. Millis, *The Forrestal Diaries*, p. 10; Forrestal is not always dependable on details in his reporting, but this seems plausible.

147. Morgenthau, "Our Policy Toward Germany"; also *Interlocking Subversion in Government Departments*, Hearings before the Senate Committee on the Judiciary, 84th Cong., 1st sess., Part 30, pp. 2580-2582.

148. Pogue, *The European Theater of Operations*, p. 355.

149. *Ibid.*

150. *Ibid.*, p. 356.

151. Hilldring to Holmes, August 30, 1944, CAD 014 Germany, Sec. 8.

152. Memorandum for the President, undated. ASW 370.8 Germany—General.

153. Hammond to Strong and Hilldring, August 13, 1944, Hammond to Meyer, August 16, 1944, Hammond to Meyer, August 23, 1944, Hammond to Meyer, August 25, 1944, all in CAD 334 EAC, Sec. 2. A similar State Department

view (getting a general policy paper through in order to break the log-jam) is expressed in memorandum, Matthews to Hull, "Status of Negotiations and Discussions on Germany," August 22, 1944, JCS file, State Department.

154. Hilldring to Dunn, August 26, 1944, CAD 334 EAC.

155. Hilldring memorandum, August 28, 1944, and OPD to CAD, September 1, 1944, CAD 014 Germany, Sec. 8.

156. CAD memorandum, October 13, 1944, CAD 334 EAC.

157. OPD to CAD, September 1, 1944, CAD 014 Germany, Sec. 8; Fahy to Tansey and Roberts, September 29, 1944, CAD 334 EAC.

158. Secretary of State to Secretary of War, August 25, 1944, CAD 014 Germany, Sec. 8.

159. For an example of Stimson's use of this distinction, see Stimson Diary, October 19, 1944.

160. *Ibid.,* August 22, 1944.

161. "State Department Conference," State-War-Navy, File 3, drawer 2, Forrestal Papers, Princeton University Library.

162. Sherwood, *Roosevelt and Hopkins,* pp. 812-814.

163. Hull, *Memoirs,* II, p. 1604.

164. Riddleberger memorandum, "American Policy for Treatment of Germany after Surrendar," September 1, 1944, JCS file, State Department.

165. "Suggested Post-Surrender Program for Germany" (September 1, 1944), *ibid.*

166. Some of the Treasury staff work on dismemberment is printed in *Interlocking Subversion in Government Departments,* Senate Hearings, Part 29, pp. 2402-2408.

167. "Suggested Post-Surrender Program for Germany," *loc. cit.*

168. *Ibid.*

169. Riddleberger to Hull, "The Treatment of Germany" (September 4, 1944), JCS file, State Department; Chase, "The Development of the Morgenthau Plan Through the Quebec Conference," p. 338; and Hull, *Memoirs,* II, p. 1604.

170. Riddleberger to Stettinius, "Developments in the Formulation of American Policy for the Post-War Treatment of Germany," October 28, 1944, *Yalta Papers,* p. 160.

171. Hull, *Memoirs,* II, p. 1607.

172. *Ibid.,* pp. 1607 f. A slightly different account of the September 2 meetings is given in a memorandum, Riddleberger to Stettinius, October 28, 1944, *Yalta Papers,* p. 161.

173. Hull, *Memoirs,* II, p. 1608.

174. Henry Morgenthau, Jr., "Our Policy Toward Germany," *New York Post* (November 28, 1947). Cf. Dorn, "The Debate over American Oc-

cupation Policy in Germany in 1944-1945," p. 494.

175. "Suggested Post-Surrender Program for Germany," *loc. cit.*

176. Morgenthau, "Our Policy Toward Germany."

177. Stimson Diary, August 26-September 3, 1944.

178. *Ibid.,* September 4.

179. *Ibid.*

180. As quoted from the Stimson Diary in Stimson and Bundy, *On Active Service in Peace and War,* p. 569.

181. "Suggested Recommendations on the Treatment of Germany from the Cabinet Committee for the President," September 4, 1944, JCS file, State Department.

182. Chase, "The Development of the Morgenthau Plan through the Quebec Conference," p. 327.

183. *Ibid.*

184. Hull, *Memoirs,* II, p. 1609. Meeting incorrectly dated September 5, described in Riddleberger to Stettinius, *loc. cit.*

185. Stimson and Bundy, *On Active Service in Peace and War,* p. 570.

186. Hull, *loc. cit.*

187. Stimson and Bundy, *On Active Service in Peace and War,* p. 571.

188. It is possible that Hull was merely trying to take a position which was mutually acceptable to all concerned. For a statement of this interpretation see "What to Do with Germany?" Chapter II in Snell, *The Meaning of Yalta,* pp. 42-45.

189. Stimson and Bundy, *On Active Service in Peace and War,* pp. 569-573. Stimson was apparently shocked by the discussion, and he later had some doubt that his diary entry accurately reported Hull's position (p. 570n.); but it is safe to conclude that Hull at this moment was closer to Morgenthau than to Stimson. See Dorn, "The Debate over American Occupation Policy in Germany in 1944-1945," p. 491 and 491n.

190. Hull, *loc. cit.* Riddleberger to Stettinius, *loc. cit.* In cases of conflict, Stimson's version has been weighted more heavily than Hull's. While it is also based on diaries written at the time, Hull wrote his account long after the event, relying for the most part upon official documents to recall other pertinent details to his mind. This has led to a number of errors.

Examples of Hull's inaccuracies are the following: (1) Although it is vaguely stated, Hull (II, p. 1606) has Harry White arguing in favor of flooding the German coal mines at the September 2 meeting. Yet the suggestion was not in the memorandum which he introduced, and he personally opposed the idea strongly, although he knew at that time that Morgenthau's preliminary views favored it. But Morgenthau had not yet seen the memorandum, which was the result of the furious efforts of his staff under White's direction. Hence, it is more likely that, as Stimson indicates, Morgenthau himself introduced the idea orally on the 5th. (2) On the same page, Hull has his assistants refuting at their September 2 meeting a proposal advanced for the first time on the 5th, at the earliest. (3) Again (p. 1609), Hull indicates that at the September 6 White House meeting Stimson presented a memorandum which "was largely in agreement with our memorandum." Stimson did not present a memorandum that day; rather it had been forwarded to all concerned the previous day. And, rather than agreeing with the State paper, its whole purpose was to argue against one crucial paragraph in that document.

Finally, Hull's whole detailed account of this period is thrown into question by the fact, which can be fairly well substantiated (Stimson and Bundy, *On Active Service in Peace and War,* pp. 570, 571; Stimson Diary, September 6, 1944; Penrose, *Economic Planning for the Peace,* p. 253; and interview with John J. McCloy, April 12, 1956), that Hull at first sided with Morgenthau, then switched to Stimson. Yet Hull indicates that he always agreed with Stimson.

191. This document is reproduced in the front of Henry Morgenthau, Jr., *Germany Is Our Problem* (Harper, New York, 1945).

192. Hull, *Memoirs,* II, p. 1609.

193. Stimson and Bundy, *On Active Service in Peace and War,* p. 573; Stimson Diary, September 6, 1944.

194. *Ibid.,* p. 574.

195. Stimson Diary, September 7, 1944.

196. Henry Morgenthau, Jr., "Our Policy Toward Germany," *New York Post* (November 28, 1947); Stimson and Bundy, *loc. cit.;* Stimson Diary, September 9, 1944.

197. *New York Times,* September 7, 1944.

198. Hull, *Memoirs,* II, p. 1602; Stimson Diary, September 9, 1944.

199. Penrose, *Economic Planning for the Peace,* pp. 256 f.; Stimson and Bundy, *On Active Service in Peace and War,* p. 576; and Hull, *Memoirs,* II, p. 1615. Note particularly Penrose's reasoning on this point in relation to other possible interpretations.

200. As quoted in Stimson and Bundy, *On Active Service in Peace and War,* pp. 376 f.

201. Chase, "The Development of the Morgenthau Plan Through the Quebec Conference," p. 357; Winston S. Churchill, *Triumph and Tragedy,* Vol. 6 of *The Second World War* (Houghton Mifflin, Boston, 1953), pp. 156-157.

202. Memorandum for the Files, September 20, 1944, H. Freeman Matthews, *Yalta Papers,* pp. 134 f.; Memorandum for the Secretary's Files, undated [September 20-25, 1944], Harry D. White, *ibid.,* pp. 136-141. Since Matthews wrote his memorandum on the same day that Morgenthau reported on the events at Quebec, it is probably the most accurate recording of the conversation.

203. Hull, *Memoirs,* II, pp. 1601 f., and pp. 1613 f.

204. Hull was almost certainly wrong in his suspicion that Churchill accepted the Morgenthau Plan in return for favorable financial arrangements. The manner of Morgenthau's arranging the agreement on Germany does not suggest such a deal. By his own account, after encountering spontaneous objections to his proposals from Churchill, Morgenthau convinced Cherwell of the validity of his arguments, and Cherwell in turn convinced his chief. Henry Morgenthau, Jr., "Our Policy Toward Germany," *New York Post* (November 28, November 29, 1947). White's memorandum on this meeting (*Yalta Papers,* p. 137) says: "The Secretary pointed out that the memorandum on lend-lease aid was not drafted until the final day, and that Churchill had agreed to the policy on Germany prior to the final drafting of this memorandum. He explained that the President was about to approve of the request which the British made for lend-lease aid when he interposed and recommended that a committee be appointed to consider the matter. The Secretary pointed out that he was successful in getting the matter turned over to a committee though the committee would have to act in accord with the oral conversations between Roosevelt and Churchill on the matter. The Secretary said that if he had not been there the decision would have been made right there without being referred to a committee." Stimson's diary shows that at the time the Secretary of War believed Morgenthau's account. The mild tone of the President's covering letter suggests that he, at least, thought that the initialed statement was a mild one. Rather than a deal being made, Morgenthau—and the two chiefs of state—had apparently toned down the original Morgenthau proposals. If a deal had been made, it is likely that the Morgenthau proposal would have been given a stronger statement—and it is *not* likely that the whole memorandum of understanding would have been dictated by Churchill. Morgenthau's argument in behalf of his plan, though fallacious, was believable: evidently he convinced Roosevelt as well as Churchill. Certainly Roosevelt used it repeatedly thereafter with evident conviction. The President's memoranda of September 15 are described in Hull, *Memoirs,* II, pp. 1610 f. and 1613 f. Cherwell's later active participation as

Churchill's spokesman in Anglo-American Lend-Lease negotiations is described in R. F. Harrod, *The Life of John Maynard Keynes* (Harcourt, New York, 1951), pp. 586-591.

205. Stimson Diary, September 11, 13, 14, and 15, 1944.

206. Stimson and Bundy, *On Active Service in Peace and War,* p. 579.

207. *Ibid.,* p. 576.

208. Hull, *Memoirs,* II, p. 1616. The meeting in Hull's office is described in *ibid.,* II, pp. 1614-1617; in Stimson and Bundy, *On Active Service in Peace and War,* pp. 576 f.; and, in considerable detail, in Matthews' memorandum, *loc. cit.,* and White's memorandum, *loc. cit.*

209. Hull, *Memoirs,* II, p. 1615.

210. Millis (ed.), *The Forrestal Diaries,* p. 11.

211. Pogue, *The European Theater of Operations,* p. 342.

212. Strong to Meyer, September 16, 1944, CAD 014 Germany, Sec. 9.

213. *Yalta Papers,* p. 143.

214. "Draft Directive for Military Government in Germany under Phase 2." A printed version, in which the quoted passages are identical, is printed in *Yalta Papers,* pp. 143-154.

215. Treasury thinking at this time can be seen in "Program to Prevent Germany from Starting a World War III," in CAD 014 Germany, Sec. 8.

216. "Directive to SCAEF Regarding the Military Government of Germany in the Period Immediately Following the Cessation of Organized Resistance (Post-Defeat)," September 17, 1944, draft, JCS file, State Department.

217. Appendix "C," Economic Directive (September 17, 1944), draft, *ibid.*

218. Interview with Adrian Fisher, March 16, 1954; memorandum, Riddleberger to Hull, September 23, 1944, *Yalta Papers,* p. 141.

219. *Ibid.*

220. "American Draft of Directive for Germany in the Period Immediately Following the Cessation of Organized Resistance" (prepared for publication, September 27, 1944).

221. McCloy to Matthews, September 18, 1944, JCS file, State Department.

222. White memorandum, *Yalta Papers,* pp. 140 f.

223. Riddleberger to Hull, September 23, 1944, JCS file, State Department.

224. *Yalta Papers,* p. 141; see also Hull, *Memoirs,* II, p. 1616.

225. The September 27 transmittal memorandum to Winant is printed in *Yalta Papers,* pp. 142-143; see also Stimson Diary (October 3, 1944).

226. *Ibid.* The text of this version of JCS 1067 is reprinted in *Yalta Papers,* pp. 143-154.

227. *Washington Post,* September 21, 1944.

228. *New York Herald Tribune,* September 26, 1944.

229. *Ibid.*

230. Arthur Krock in *New York Times,* September 29, 1944.

231. Official File 21, Franklin D. Roosevelt Library.

232. *Interlocking Subversion in Government Departments,* Senate Hearings, Part 29, p. 2412.

233. See below, pp. 393 ff.

234. The complete text is printed in *Yalta Papers,* p. 142; see also Hull, *Memoirs,* II, pp. 1616 f.

235. *Ibid.*

236. *Ibid.,* pp. 1617 f.

237. Stimson and Bundy, *On Active Service in Peace and War,* p. 580; Sherwood, *Roosevelt and Hopkins,* p. 818.

238. Hull, *Memoirs,* II, pp. 1619-1621; the full text is also printed in *Yalta Papers,* p. 155.

239. Memorandum, Riddleberger to Stettinius, October 28, 1944, *Yalta Papers,* p. 162.

240. The delivery dates of the two memoranda are noted in *Yalta Papers,* pp. 155 and 156.

241. Hull, *Memoirs,* II, p. 1619, gives a summary of the memorandum with quotations; the complete text is printed in *Yalta Papers,* pp. 157-158.

242. Stimson and Bundy, *On Active Service in Peace and War,* p. 581. Apparently Churchill underwent a somewhat similar experience. His guarded account is given in *Triumph and Tragedy,* pp. 156-157, and his remarks elsewhere are even more conclusive; see, e.g., *New York Times,* July 22, 1949.

243. Memorandum, Hull to Roosevelt, October 5, 1944, JCS file, State Department.

244. The full text of the President's memorandum is printed in *Yalta Papers,* pp. 158-159; a briefer account is given in Hull, *Memoirs,* II, p. 1621.

245. Riddleberger to Stettinius, October 28, 1944, *Yalta Papers,* p. 162.

246. Mosely, "The Occupation of Germany," p. 596.

247. Text of speech published in *New York Times,* October 19, 1944.

248. Matthews to Stettinius, November 4, 1944, *Yalta Papers,* p. 165.

249. *New York Times,* November 5, 1944. For an account of the German stand at the West Wall, see Pogue, *The European Theater of Operations,* pp. 245 ff.

250. Note, Early to Judge Rosenman and Miss Tully, undated, Official File 21, Box 5, Treasury Department, 1940-1945, Hyde Park.

251. The full text of the letter reads:

I think that there is no basis whatever for such criticism of you as that made by Gov. Dewey.

At the time when the rumors as to the Treasury plan became public the rapid advance of the Allied armies through France had already reached their finish. The German retreat had already reached the Siegfried Line, and the Germans had begun to make their stiff defense behind those fortifications which has lasted substantially ever since.

I do not think that the use of the rumor by the Nazi propagandists made any substantial change in the situation whatever. I am very sorry that you should have been troubled by such a criticism. It is printed in Henry Morgenthau, Jr., "Our Policy Toward Germany," *New York Post,* November 29, 1947.

252. Stimson Diary, November 4, 1944.

253. Undated "Draft of Public Statement," Harry Dexter White Papers, Princeton University Library, Item No. 22, Germany.

254. Memorandum on the British Draft of Policy Directive for Germany, November 1, 1944, *Yalta Papers,* pp. 163-165.

255. See p. 380.

256. See p. 382; Stimson Diary, September 27, October 3, 1944. Evidently Roosevelt told Winant the same thing before the month was out. *Ibid.,* October 27, 1944.

257. See pp. 382-383.

258. Morgenthau to Stettinius, November 3, 1944, *Yalta Papers,* p. 163; Matthews to Stettinius, November 4, 1944, *Ibid.,* p. 165.

259. See, e.g., Memorandum, "Is European Prosperity Dependent upon German Industry?" September 7, 1944, White Papers, Item No. 22, Germany.

260. *Interlocking Subversion in Government Departments,* Senate Hearings, Part 30, p. 2704. See also *ibid.,* pp. 2707-2712, and later drafts of this chapter in Item No. 22, White Papers.

261. *Interlocking Subversion in Government Departments,* Senate Hearings, Part 30, p. 2707.

262. *Ibid.,* p. 2708, quoting from Sumner Welles, *The Time for Decision.*

263. *Ibid.,* p. 2709.

264. Letter, William M. Tomlinson, U. S. Treasury Representative, Embassy of the United States, London, to Harry D. White, December 28, 1944.

265. Fahy to Tansey and Roberts, September 29, 1944, CAD 334 EAC.

266. CAD memorandum, October 13, 1944, *ibid.,* interview with John H. Hilldring, February 7, 1956.

267. CAD memorandum, October 13, 1944.

268. *Ibid.*

269. Meyer to Hilldring and Strong, October

14, 1944, CAD 334 EAC.

270. Memorandum, McCloy to Chanler, October 12, 1944, Interim Directive Working File, ASW 370.8 Germany; McCloy to Macready, October 27, 1944, CAD 014 Germany, Sec. 9.

271. CAD memorandum, November 6, 1944, and McCloy to Matthews, November 20, 1944, ASW 370.8 Germany—General.

272. Hilldring to Strong, October 14, 1944, CAD 334 EAC.

273. CAD memorandum, November 6, 1944, *ibid.*

274. Coe to Angell, August 8, 1944, FEA Box 97.

275. German Working Committee, "Germany: General Objectives of United States Economic Policy with Respect to Germany," September 1, 1944, *ibid.*

276. Assistant Director, Northern European Division to Assistant Director, Liberated Areas Division, September 5, 1944, *ibid.*

277. FEA was in fact split by a series of disputes. Its position was peculiarly difficult to determine because of the diverse character, origins, interests, and responsibilities of its staff. Moreover, some of its officials, in particular V. Frank Coe, and Lauchlin Currie, were close friends of, and closely associated with, Harry Dexter White of the Treasury Department. During that winter (1944-1945) Coe succeeded White as Director of Monetary Research in the Treasury Department when White was promoted to Assistant Secretary.

278. FEA representative, CAC Foreign Trade Sub-Committee, to Chief, Economic Institutions Staff [Rosenberg], September 15, 1944, *ibid.*; Rosenberg to Currie, September 16, 1944, *ibid.*; Angell to Rosenberg, September 27, 1944, *ibid.*

279. Memorandum, by Angell, September 27, 1944, *ibid.*; Pettee to Angell, September 28, 1944, *ibid.*

280. Minutes, FEA Executive Policy Committee Meeting, September 25, 1944, FEA Box 55.

281. *Ibid.*; note, Cox to Early, September 25, 1944, O.F. 5430, Roosevelt Papers.

282. Pettee to Angell, October 2, 1944, FEA Box 55.

283. Minutes, Executive Policy Committee Meeting, October 12, 1944, FEA Box 59.

284. *Ibid.*

285. *New York Times,* October 22, 1944. Discussions of the relationship of economic studies to policy guidance are reported in Wainhouse memorandum, October 12, 1944, ASW 370.8 Germany—Control.

286. See Part III B, above.

287. Pogue, *The European Theater of Operations,* p. 356.

288. As quoted in Treasury Department, pro-

posed draft memorandum to McCloy, January 13, 1945.

289. McCloy to Matthews, November 20, 1944, ASW 370.8 Germany—General.

290. The German Country Unit was a combined staff attached for technical direction to the operations branch of the G-5 division. Dale Clark, "Conflicts over Planning at Staff Headquarters," Chapter X in Friedrich and Associates, *American Experiences in Military Government in World War II*, pp. 214-219.

291. *Ibid.*, pp. 224-231.

292. *Ibid.*, pp. 234 ff.

293. Stettinius to Roosevelt, November 11, 1944, *Yalta Papers*, p. 165.

294. *Ibid.*, p. 170.

295. *Ibid.*

296. *Ibid.*, pp. 170 f.

297. Memorandum of conversation by Pasvolsky, November 15, 1944, *Yalta Papers*, pp. 171-172.

298. *Ibid.* Perhaps this was his reason for originally asking McCloy to become military governor of Germany.

299. *Ibid.*, p. 172n.

300. Memorandum, Stettinius to Roosevelt, November 22, 1944, *Yalta Papers*, p. 172.

301. *Ibid.*, p. 173.

302. *Ibid.*, November 29, 1944, p. 174.

303. *Ibid.*, December 4, 1944, p. 174.

304. *Ibid.*, p. 172.

305. Stimson Diary, October 11, 12, 1944.

306. *Ibid.*, October 26, 1944.

307. U. S. Congress, Senate, Naval Affairs Committee, Committee Print, "Unification of the War and Navy Departments and Postwar Organization for National Security, Report to Hon. James Forrestal, Secretary of the Navy," 79th Cong., 1st sess., p. 54.

308. Stimson and Bundy, *On Active Service in Peace and War*, p. 563; file memorandum, State-War-Navy File 3, drawer 2, Forrestal Papers.

309. Notter, *Postwar Foreign Policy Preparation*, pp. 347-348; Cline, *The War Department: Washington Command Post*, p. 426; Senate Naval Affairs Committee, *loc. cit.*

310. U. S. Congress, Joint Committee on Investigation of Pearl Harbor Attack, Hearings, *Pearl Harbor Attack*, 79th Cong., 2d sess., Part 11, pp. 5434 f.

311. Stimson Diary, December 19, 1944.

312. *Ibid.*

313. Hall to Joint U. S. Advisers, EAC, November 23, 1944, CAD 334 EAC, Sec. 3. Memorandum of Conference in McCloy's office, December 8, 1944, Interim Directive Working File, ASW 370.8 Germany.

314. Memorandum of Meeting on Revision of

JCS 1067, November 24, 1944, ASW 370.8 Germany; Minutes of Meeting on Revision of JCS 1067, November 25, 1944, *ibid.*

315. Memorandum of Conference in McCloy's office, November 27, 1944, Interim Directive Working File, ASW 370.8 Germany.

316. This change in the War Department attitude toward arrest policy is discussed in Walter Dorn, "The Purpose and Scope of the Original American Purge Policy" (unpublished MS.), pp. 12-15.

317. Memorandum, SWNCC proposal on redraft of JCS 1067, January 8, 1945, JCS file, State Department.

318. Clark, "Conflicts over Planning at Staff Headquarters," p. 219.

319. "Directive to Commander in Chief of U. S. (U.K.) (U.S.S.R.) Forces of Occupation regarding the Military Government of Germany in the Period Immediately Following the Cessation of Organized Resistance (Post-Defeat)," January 6, 1945, JCS file, State Department.

320. *Ibid.*

321. Penrose interview.

322. The officials who attended the meetings were Glasser, Taylor, Kamarck-Gunter, DuBois, Luxford, and Joseph Friedman, Irving Moskovitz, Leonard Ackerman, C. J. Hynning, Sonia Gold, and Bella Schwartz.

323. Memorandum, "General Minutes of the Meetings with Colonel Bernstein, January 11, 12, 18, 19, 20, 1945," January 22, 1945. The account of Colonel Bernstein's Washington visit is based on this and the following documents: Memorandum, "Comments on the Memorandum of Lt. Bogdan, dated December 26, 1944, entitled: Matters requiring policy decisions or clarifications during Phases I and II," undated; Memorandum, from Andrew M. Kamarck [sic] for the Files, "Subject: Policy toward Germany (Minutes of Meeting with Colonel Bernstein, January 10, 1945)," January 10, 1945; Memorandum, Glasser to White, January 5, 1945; "Agenda on German Problem," undated; Memorandum, US Group CC Finance Division to Colonel Bernstein, "Treatment of Property of Displaced Persons," December 25, 1944, all from personal files of Josiah E. DuBois.

324. Memorandum, Morgenthau to Roosevelt, January 10, 1945, *ibid.*

325. Proposed memorandum to McCloy, January 13, 1945, *ibid.*

326. Memorandum, DuBois to Morgenthau, January 29, 1945, *ibid.*

327. "Comments Re Financial Planning for Phase Two," undated, *ibid.*

328. Bernstein to Fisher, January 24, 1945, *ibid.*

329. "Minutes of Meeting in Harry D. White's Office on the German Problems," February 2 and 3, 1945.

330. No separate annotation is attempted for general comments about the Yalta Conference. The basic source of information is the *Yalta Papers*; all the major subsidiary sources are listed in the introduction to that volume.

331. *Yalta Papers*, pp. 178-197.

332. *Ibid.*, p. 182.

333. Churchill, *Triumph and Tragedy*, pp. 359-361.

334. Winant to Roosevelt, January 28, 1945, *Yalta Papers*, pp. 130-133; Winant to Stettinius, January 28, 1945, *ibid.*, p. 133.

335. Winant to Roosevelt, February 7, 1945, *ibid.*, pp. 957-958.

336. Sherwood, *Roosevelt and Hopkins*, pp. 872-873.

337. Leahy, *I Was There*, pp. 292-293; James F. Byrnes, *Speaking Frankly*, speaks of "four or five" talks, especially about the UN.

338. Churchill, *Triumph and Tragedy*, passim.

339. *Yalta Papers*, pp. 175-176.

340. *Ibid.*, pp. 609-610. For an excellent account of the negotiations on Germany, see Snell, *The Meaning of Yalta*, pp. 52-74.

341. *Yalta Papers*, p. 175.

342. *Ibid.*, pp. 499, 573, 613, 616-619, 628-630, 634, 672, 701-702, 707, 710-711, 718-719, 936-937.

343. *Ibid.*, pp. 611-616, 624-628, 633, 656-660, 700-701, 704, 706, 709, 809, 812, 874-875, 880, 885, 936, 947, 978.

344. *Ibid.*, pp. 610, 612, 618-619, 621-624, 630-633, 702-710, 738, 741, 807-809, 812, 814, 816, 822, 843-844, 859, 874-875, 879-880, 882, 885, 901-903, 909-910, 914-916, 920-922, 927, 933, 937, 947, 971, 978-979, 982-984.

345. Sherwood, *Roosevelt and Hopkins*, p. 862, expresses the opinion that Roosevelt hoped reparations would die of "inanition" in the Reparations Commission. We do have Roosevelt's stated opposition to reparations, but it is hard to believe that, by the end of the Yalta Conference, he retained any serious hope that the Russians would ever agree to forego reparations, or be satisfied with anything but sizable amounts.

346. *Yalta Papers*, pp. 970-971.

347. Interview with James A. Perkins, February 9, 1956; John L. Chase, "The Development of the United States Policy Toward Germany During World War II" (Ph. D. thesis, Princeton University, 1952), pp. 387 ff.

348. James A. Perkins, "Planning the Economic Control of Germany," March 3, 1945 (unpublished MS. in possession of Mr. Perkins), made available to this author, and reproduced in Chase MS, Appendix, pp. 29-73.

349. Smith to Hilldring, March 3, 1945, CAD 014 Germany, Sec. 11.

350. President to Secretary of State, February 28, 1945, copy in FEA Box 68.

351. Grew to Winant, February 27, 1945, and Grew to London Embassy, February 28, 1945, ASW 370.8 Germany—Control.

352. "Memorandum for the Secretary's Files; Conference on the Treatment of Germany," Treasury Department, March 20, 1945, DuBois files; the date of Stettinius' return to Washington is taken from Edward R. Stettinius, Jr., *Roosevelt and the Russians: The Yalta Conference*, Walter Johnson, ed. (Doubleday, Garden City, 1949), p. 294.

353. Cline, *The War Department: Washington Command Post*, p. 327.

354. "Draft Directive for the Treatment of Germany," March 10, 1945, JCS file, State Department. For Stimson's view of the March 10 directive see his Diary, March 29, 1945.

355. *Ibid.*, March 3, 1945.

356. Ibid., March 7, 1945; Cline, *loc. cit.*

357. "Memorandum for the Secretary's Files."

358. Notter, *Postwar Foreign Policy Preparation*, p. 370.

359. "Memorandum for the Secretary's Files."

360. Stimson Diary, March 29, 1945.

361. "Memorandum for the Secretary's Files."

362. Draft memorandum for the President, attachment to "Memorandum for the Secretary's Files."

363. "Memorandum for the Secretary's Files."

364. McCloy to Stimson, March 26, 1945, ASW 370.8 Germany—Control. Stimson's resolution to keep out of the policy discussions on Germany weakened at this time. In an undated, handwritten letter, in *ibid.*, from the Army Ground and Services Forces Redistribution Station, Miami Beach, Florida, he wrote McCloy on about March 22:

Dear McCloy

I received the enclosed letter from Baruch just the morning I left home. Please have a copy made for yourself and give original to my Sec'y.

I think you should also see Baruch; tell him I am away; and let him read for himself all three of the memos we wrote for the President last fall when we were having the row over "Pastoral" Germany. That ought to prove to him that we did our best on that subject which he write[s] of. Tell him that if he will give me his support I am willing to take up the same subject again with the White House.

I now see (thru' Drew Pearson's column) that Leon Henderson is preparing to blast the Army for not doing what we tried to do in those memos—viz to treat Germany as an economic entity—for that was the purport of my first memo at least. I think you should see him before he gets his report off and show him our memos. If you can do these two things (See B. B. and L. H.) you will ease my mind.

Faithfully,

H. L. S.

365. *Ibid.*; "Summary of U. S. Initial Post-Defeat Policy Relating to Germany," March 23, 1945, JCS file, State Department.

366. Roosevelt wrote Morgenthau an important statement on his position on German policy on March 28, 1944, but this document has not been available to the author.

367. This agreed statement on Germany policy is reproduced in "History of Treasury Participation in Formulation of German Occupation Program" (unpublished MS.), DuBois files, pp. 12 f.

368. Crowley to Secretary of State, April 10, 1945, ASW 370.8 Germany—Control.

369. McCloy to Clayton, March 27, 1945, ASW 370.8 Germany—January '45 thru [sic].

370. Clayton to McCloy, March 28, 1945, *ibid.*

371. McCloy to Clayton, March 29, 1945, *ibid.*; Clayton to McCloy, March 31, 1945, *ibid.*

372. "History of Treasury Participation," p. 16.

373. Memorandum, White (or J. B. Friedman) to Morgenthau, April 21, 1945, DuBois files.

374. "History of Treasury Participation."

375. *Ibid.*, pp. 16 f.

376. Letter, David Harris to author, August 16, 1955.

377. White (or Friedman) memorandum to Morgenthau, April 21, 1945, DuBois files.

378. "History of Treasury Participation," p. 22.

379. *Ibid.*

380. Holborn, *American Military Government,* p. 169.

381. Somervell to Hilldring, April 28, 1945, CAD 014 Germany, Sec. 12.

382. Stimson Diary, May 8, 1945.

383. Lucius D. Clay, *Decision in Germany* (Doubleday, Garden City, 1950), p. 16, 16n.; Holborn, *American Military Government,* p. 157; Holborn reprints the text, pp. 157-172. The directive approved on April 26 was JCS 1067/6, the revised version, JCS 1067/8.

384. McCloy to Clay, April 25, 1945, ASW 370.8 Germany—Control.

385. Clay, *Decision in Germany,* p. 19; for Clay's appointment, see below.

386. "History of Treasury Participation," pp. 27-32. For complete text, see Holborn, *loc. cit.*

387. Byrnes, *Speaking Frankly,* p. 47; Stimson Diary, March 3, 1945.

388. Oliver J. Fredericksen, *The American Military Occupation of Germany* (Historical Division, U. S. Army, Europe, 1953), pp. 24, 29. The American troops in Italy had not been part of the ETO and SHAEF commands.

389. Clay, *Decision in Germany,* p. 39.

390. With respect to Germany, the Protocol and Communiqué are practically identical, for the Communiqué deletes nothing dealing with Germany from the Protocol, and only adds some explanatory introductions for publication. The text of the Potsdam Communiqué was released to the press on August 2, 1945, and has been reprinted frequently. A convenient source is Holborn, *American Military Government,* pp. 195-205. (Holborn also reprints the text of JCS 1067/6, April 28, 1945, pp. 157-172, and the Yalta Communiqué, pp. 154-156.) The Potsdam Protocol was made public March 24, 1947, and is published in Raymond Dennett and Robert K. Turner (eds.), *Documents on American Foreign Relations* (Princeton University Press, 1948), VIII, pp. 925-940. The Protocol also appears in U. S. Congress, Senate Doc. No. 123, "A Decade of American Foreign Policy, Basic Documents, 1941-1949," 81st Cong., 1st sess., pp. 34-48. The Protocol and the Communiqué are printed in Vol. II, pp. 1477 ff. and 1499 ff. of *Foreign Relations of the United States: The Conference of Berlin (The Potsdam Conference),* Vols. I and II (Washington, Government Printing Office, 1960). (These two volumes are cited hereafter as *Potsdam Papers,* I and II.)

391. Harry S. Truman, *Year of Decisions, Memoirs,* I (Doubleday, Garden City, 1955), p. 345; text in *Potsdam Papers,* II, pp. 775-778 (Doc. 852).

392. Compare *Potsdam Papers,* Doc. 327, I, pp. 435-449, Doc. 848, II, pp. 750-753 and Doc. 852, II, pp. 775-778.

393. *Potsdam Papers,* II, p. 775.

394. *Ibid.*, p. 777.

395. Murphy to Matthews, June 28, 1945, Doc. 339, *ibid.*, pp. 472-474.

396. *Ibid.*, Doc. 852, II, pp. 777-778.

397. "German Reparations," July 17, 1945, Doc. 894, *ibid.*, pp. 832-835.

398. MacLeish to Secretary of State, July 12, 1945, annex, Doc. 349, *ibid.*, I, pp. 500-503; Thorp to MacLeish, July 14, 1945, Doc. 350, *ibid.*, I, pp. 503-505.

399. Truman, *Years of Trial and Hope, Memoirs,* II, p. 327.

400. Stimson Diary, July 3, 4, 1945.

401. *Ibid.*, May 16, July 3, 15, 16, 17, 1945.

402. Grew to Stimson, June 8, 1945, Doc. 365, *Potsdam Papers,* I, pp. 524-525.

403. McCloy to Clayton, June 21, 1945, Doc. 337, *ibid.,* pp. 470-471. See also Clayton to Mc-Cloy, June 18, 1945, Doc. 336, *ibid.,* I, pp. 468-470.

404. McCloy to Clayton, June 18, 1945, Doc. 337, *ibid.,* I, pp. 470-471; Stimson to Stettinius, July 4, 1945, Doc. 342, *ibid.,* I, pp. 479-482.

405. Memorandum by E. G. Collado, "War Department Responsibility for German Interim Financing," July 18, 1945, Doc. 854, *ibid.,* II, pp. 779-780; Byrnes and McCloy, "Memorandum for the President," July 25-29, 1945, Doc. 883, *ibid.,* II, pp. 820-821; Truman to Stimson, July 29, 1945, Doc. 884, 123, *ibid.,* II, pp. 821-823.

406. Stimson to Grew, July 4, 1945, Doc. 365, *ibid.,* I, p. 526.

407. Memorandum, JSSC, "Internationalization of the Ruhr and the Saar," undated, Doc. 403, *ibid.,* I, pp. 595-596; and memorandum, JSSC, "Dismemberment of Germany," undated, Doc. 332, *ibid.,* I, p. 461.

408. FEA Enemy Branch, "A Program for German Economic and Industrial Disarmament," Forrestal Papers, Item 8.

409. Truman, *Year of Decisions,* p. 355; Leahy, *I Was There,* pp. 389 f.; Minutes, Third Plenary Meeting, *Potsdam Papers,* II, p. 117.

410. Arthur H. Vandenberg, Jr. (ed.), *The Private Papers of Senator Vandenberg* (Houghton Mifflin, Boston, 1952), p. 283.

411. Minutes, Second Plenary Meeting, July 18, 1945, *Potsdam Papers,* II, pp. 89-90.

412. Byrnes-Molotov Meeting, Bohlen Minutes, July 23, 1945, *ibid.,* II, pp. 274-275; Sixth Foreign Ministers' Meeting, Department of State Minutes, July 23, 1945, *ibid.,* II, pp. 277-281; Informal Meeting of Foreign Ministers, July 23, 1945, *ibid.,* II, pp. 295-298; Department of State minutes on Seventh Plenary Meeting, July 23, 1945, *ibid.,* II, p. 300.

413. Minutes of Ninth Plenary Meeting, July 25, 1945, *ibid.,* II, pp. 381-392.

414. See particularly Minutes, Ninth Meeting of Foreign Ministers, July 27, 1945, *ibid.,* II, pp. 428-432; U. S. Delegation memorandum, July 30, 1945, *ibid.,* II, pp. 497-499; Byrnes-Molotov Meeting, July 30, 1945, *ibid.,* II, pp. 481-482; Tenth Meeting of Foreign Ministers, July 30, 1945, *ibid.,* II, pp. 484-492; Rapporteur's Report, July 31, 1945, *ibid.,* II, pp. 500-501.

415. Minutes, Eleventh Plenary Meeting, *ibid.,* II, pp. 510-538; and Minutes, Twelfth Plenary Meeting, August 1, 1945, *ibid.,* II, pp. 565-585.

416. Holborn, *American Military Government,* p. 200.

417. *Ibid.,* p. 197.

418. *Ibid.,* p. 199.

419. *Ibid.,* p. 198. The American draft had referred to "non-Nazi" political parties. At the request of Molotov, this was changed to "democratic." See Minutes, Second Meeting of Foreign Ministers, July 19, 1945, and Doc. 856, *Potsdam Papers,* II, pp. 101, 109, 786.

420. Holborn, *American Military Government,* p. 199.

421. *Ibid.,* p. 200.

422. U. S. Congress, House, Special Committee on Postwar Economic Policy and Planning, *Economic Reconstruction in Europe,* Eighth Report, 79th Cong., 1st sess., p. 34. "Draper-Hoover Report" is: Calvin B. Hoover, *Report of Economic Situation in Germany,* July 2, 1945, War Department files.

423. John C. Campbell, *The United States in World Affairs, 1945-1947* (Harper, New York, 1947), p. 188.

424. *Ibid.,* p. 189.

425. Carl J. Friedrich, "The Three Phases of Field Operations in Germany, 1945-1946," Chapter XI in Friedrich and Associates, *American Experiences in Military Government in World War II,* p. 243; U. S. Congress, Senate, Committee on Military Affairs, *Elimination of German Resources for War,* Hearings . . . , 79th Cong., 1st sess., *passim.*

426. See, e.g., James Stuart Martin, *All Honorable Men* (Little, Brown, Boston, 1950); and Josiah E. DuBois, Jr., *The Devil's Chemists* (The Beacon Press, Boston, 1952).

427. He did not call at the State Department prior to his departure for Europe, nor did it occur to him to do so. Clay, *Decision in Germany,* p. 6.

428. *Ibid.,* p. 19.

429. *Ibid.,* p. 72.

430. *Ibid.*

431. See, e.g., the testimony of Bernard M. Baruch in Senate, Committee on Military Affairs, *op. cit.,* pp. 5 ff.

432. *New York Times,* October 4, 1945.

433. *Ibid.,* October 8, 1945. The full report is Hoover, *Report of Economic Situation in Germany.*

434. House, Special Committee on Postwar Economic Policy and Planning, *Economic Reconstruction in Europe.*

435. McCloy to Clay, November 23, 1945, ASW 370.8 Germany.

436. Gross memorandum, November 1, 1945, *ibid.*

437. *Ibid.*

438. Holborn, *American Military Government,* p. 218.

439. As quoted in *ibid.,* p. 219. Holborn reprints the full text of the statement, pp. 215-222.

440. Campbell, *The United States in World Affairs,* pp. 195 f.

441. Message, Clay to Echols, CAD, July 19, 1946, JCS 1067 Revision file, State Department.

442. *Ibid.,* pp. 196 f.; Byrnes, *Speaking Frankly,* pp. 187-191.

443. Message, Civil Affairs Division to Commanding General, USFET, September 13, 1946, JCS 1067 Revision file, State Department.

444. Message, Office of Military Governor of Germany to CAD, September 16, 1946, *ibid.*

445. The three items, referred to the subcommittee September 20, 1946, are mentioned in *ibid.*

446. *New York Times,* January 11, 13, 1947.

447. *Ibid.,* January 11, 1947.

448. *Ibid.,* January 3, 1947.

449. Text in *ibid.,* January 11, 1947.

450. See, e.g., Report No. 3, printed in *ibid.,* March 24, 1947.

451. *Ibid.,* March 10, 1947.

452. For an account of the Moscow Foreign Ministers' Conference of 1947, together with its immediate results, see John C. Campbell, *The United States in World Affairs, 1947-1948* (Harper, New York, 1948), Chapter III.

453. *New York Times,* May 2, 1947. For instance, it set forth seven "important tenets of democracy." Text in U. S. Senate Doc. No. 123, *op. cit.,* 81st Cong., 1st sess., pp. 552-562.

454. Memorandum, Hilldring to SWNCC, April 11, 1947; Working Party to SWNCC, "Revision of JCS 1067," May 16, 1947; SWNCC to JCS, May 16, 1947; SWNCC minutes, May 20, June 24, and July 10, 1947, all in JCS 1067 Revision file, State Department.

EDITORIAL COMMENTS

The problem of formulating in a single agreed document in 1944 and 1945 wise and practical directives for the three prospective occupying forces in Germany acceptable to all three was no doubt insoluble; the problem of agreeing on such a directive even for the Anglo-American forces proved insoluble too, once CCS 551, designed exclusively for the convenience of their armies, became obsolete. And the solution provided by JCS 1067, and its revisions, for General Eisenhower's, and later General Clay's American troops satisfied no one.

The difficulties were three-fold in character: In the first place, the question of the treatment of Germany was so complex and so bound up in the new problems of Cold War relations that its inherent dilemmas could not be swept aside or satisfactorily overcome. In the second place, within the American government there were sharply divergent views about the need for policy, both short-range and long-range and the relation of policy to military government. And finally, the American organizational structures involved in proposals for policies for Germany turned out to be peculiarly ill-adapted for inspiring or even permitting inter-agency cooperation in the devising of policies for Germany. The situation was further complicated by the two inter-allied organizations that were also involved.

On the first question—the intractability of the problem itself—little need be said here. All the occupying powers were in agreement that armistice, occupation, and an eventual peace treaty should prevent in some fashion a third German aggression. The agreed solution was a "democratic" Germany. And there the agreement ended. As we came to learn, rather quickly in Germany and at varying speeds elsewhere, our concept of a "democratic republic" is quite different from what this phrase means in Communist doctrine. Even within the United States

zone alone, the answers to the policy questions were sure to represent a reflection of various American needs and desires, and would *ipso facto* be partially or wholly self-contradictory. Finally, whatever the best or least unsatisfactory solution adopted for 1944 and 1945, it would be obsolescent at birth and obsolete two years later. And in fact the various policies adopted by the United States, the United Kingdom and the USSR, and presently France, were all shelved in 1947 and 1948; two German governments emerged.

The intra-governmental divergences on the tempo of policy decision and the degree of policy commitment can appropriately be outlined here with somewhat more specificity. The War Department's approach to policy was in large part an inheritance of a long tradition about the role of occupation forces. Except in dealing with the lesser breeds without the law, occupation forces were expected to leave untouched the existing structure of government, law and custom and to concern themselves solely with "law and order" and the enforcement of armistice or treaty provisions such as the disbanding of armed forces, the extraction of indemnities, and the transfer of territory from one sovereignty to another. Under these traditional circumstances, the policy directives needed for the occupying powers were so simple that the army officers involved came to the conclusion that there was no policy and that no policy was needed.

When CCS 551 was adopted in April 1944, the Anglo-American commanders seriously believed that they were avoiding the adoption of policy except what would aid the prosecution of the war; on agreeing to take steps necessary to prevent "disease and unrest," they were, in theory, merely preventing the disruption of their troops. So too, the possibility of using German governmental agencies was looked on with satisfaction as a means of avoiding the excessive involvement of British and American officers in local affairs. In all this, the possible effects of their actions on the future of Germany were looked on as irrelevant; indeed any such consideration was looked on as *ultra vires*.

The first time the military themselves faced up to some of the problems of the presumed no policy–policy dichotomy was when Eisenhower in the summer of 1944 became worried about possible economic collapse in Germany; the policy he then urged was one in which the operational responsibilities for the execution of policy would be minimized. Eisenhower's appeal for instructions coincided with Morgenthau's trip to Europe. From that time on, the military could no longer live in their ivory tower.

The Department of State was always convinced that the occupation of Germany would and should be a tool in Germany's regeneration for an honorable and peaceful place in the family of nations. As V-E Day approached, the Department also became concerned with the effects of occupation policy, procedure and organization on our future relations with Russia. In this respect, the departmental officers, particularly Winant and some of his aides, were anxious to secure approval for plans for the immediate future. Hull's main interest lay in the longer-term program; he and his more immediate associates were seeking approval for a blueprint for five or ten years. They were half-inclined to accept the Army's no-policy as a substitute for policy for a year or two, provided, of course, that prompt action was taken on the issues that could not be delayed: the zonal boundaries, the surrender instrument, the formation of an Allied Control Council.

The State Department's concern with a long-term pacific policy led it into direct conflict with the President. The President's own notions about the treatment of Germany were based partly on his moral revulsion from Hitler and the Nazi regime, partly on his conviction that Germany did not learn from World War I because defeat was not pressed home. (Hull and his associates probably based their thinking on some of the assumptions in Keynes's *Economic Consequences of the Peace*.) Thus Roosevelt wanted at least to begin with a sterner peace than Hull planned for, or than was inherent in the Army's no-policy program.

Equally important was Roosevelt's conviction that advance planning for a situation full of unknowns and unpredictables should not be given official sanction. This was a characteristic politician's political judgment. The importance that avoidance of premature commitment held for Roosevelt is neatly illustrated by his own repeated postponement of action on his own dismemberment program for postwar Germany.

Roosevelt was a cause of a further block in the path of the adoption of policy. He was, as has often been noted, both extremely open and extremely secretive. He was particularly distrustful and therefore secretive with almost all the officials in the State Department with whom he dealt; he also avoided the use of State's communications system and normally used the Navy's instead. In this case, State Department officers spent an appalling amount of energy on the question of zones of occupation in Germany because they had no knowledge of Roosevelt's acceptance of General Morgan's map at the first Quebec Conference, and of his subsequent long-drawn-out argument with Churchill about occupancy of the Northwest and Southwest zones. The Joint Chiefs, it may be added, shared Roosevelt's desire for secrecy and distrust of civilian agencies; if they and if Generals Eisenhower and Clay had been less concerned with the avoidance of any policy commitment, the possibility of guaranteed access to Berlin might at least have been explored with the Russians.

Into the policy vacuum created by the attitudes and interests of the War Department and the State Department, and the President, rushed the Treasury. The Treasury had a variety of advantages. Roosevelt and Morgenthau were old friends; Morgenthau first approached Roosevelt by showing him a copy of the Army's military government manual, a booklet that avoided any effort to force the Germans to realize beyond peradventure that they had lost the war; Morgenthau's anti-Germany policy happened to coincide with Eisenhower's preferred policy of avoiding responsibility for German rehabilitation and reconstruction. Finally, while the Foreign Economic Administration and Treasury did not share objectives, the FEA plans for the elaborate economic regimentation of Germany gave more help to the Treasury than to the others involved in the struggle.

FEA, like Treasury, wanted to fill the policy vacuum.

The organizational problems were manifold. The establishment of the European Advisory Commission was rational enough, though its actual contribution to post-war settlements proved meagre. From the standpoint of the United States, the EAC turned out to present difficulties that should have been avoided. Since the State Department necessarily provided the focus for instructions to our member, Ambassador Winant, the gap between the Department, the White House, the War Department civilians, the Civil Affairs Division of the Army and above all, the Joint Chiefs of Staff, made the task of instruction almost infinitely difficult. And beyond all this, the Army's belief that the British Army was trying to capture the control of military government intensified their suspicion of EAC, which was located in London.

The State Department's device for formulating and transmitting instructions for Winant was the Working Security Committee. The State Department's *de facto* representative on WSC had no high rank in the hierarchy and was faced by others of similar rank from the other agencies. For this reason, or largely for this reason, any effort to remove obstructions was extremely difficult. The representatives were ill informed on what was known or had been agreed to on higher levels, and in no effective position to put their case before their agency heads. This was particularly true of the military representatives, for they came from the Civil Affairs Division, rather newly established, and partly under the control of the Operations Division. OPD was General Marshall's instrument both for control of the overseas commands and for Army representation on the JCS and CCS. General Hilldring, Director of CAD, worked closely with Assistant Secretary of War McCloy, but this led away from, not towards, JCS. Indeed, when Stimson and McCloy finally moved to push for action on directives for Germany, they found it so hard to move JCS that they turned to circumvention of JCS as the wiser choice, for in those days, when there was no Secretary of Defense, JCS answered only to Roosevelt. Marshall kept Stimson informed, but JCS as a corporate body moved outside the orbit of the War Department. And the Combined Civil Affairs Committee proved to be a largely ineffective device for

McCloy's use, because as a mere subcommittee it could work only when its parent committee, CCS, and that committee's highly independent member groups, JCS and the British Chiefs of Staff Committee, concurred. Concurrence vanished after CCS 551 had been approved in April 1944.

The military tangle was not quickly unwound when OPD started to concern itself with post-war plans. Eventually they got on the right track and when the State-War-Navy Coordinating Committee was set up it was at least the harbinger of post-war civil-military cooperation. Yet for reasons peculiar to the winter and spring of 1944-1945, SWNCC could not promptly tackle the problem of directives for Germany.

The peculiar reason for the impotence of SWNCC in relation to Germany during the last winter of the war was the intrusion of Treasury into the long-drawn-out wrangle; JCS distrust of Treasury could exclude Treasury from SWNCC, but exclusion meant that policy for Germany had to be decided elsewhere. Administrative confusion was increased when the Foreign Economic Administration responded vigorously to the State Department's use of the Executive Committee on Economic Foreign Policy. The absence from that committee of the necessary and sole executor of American policy for Germany after the fighting ceased—the U. S. Army—meant that ECEFP approval was primarily an invitation to FEA to go down a blind alley.

FEA did, however, stimulate Harry White and the Treasury to move in on the German problem, and Morgenthau's interest was then spurred on by his discovery of the Army's military government manual. There is no need to recapitulate the complexities created by Morgenthau's vigor: the Quebec memorandum, promptly repudiated by both signatories, the attempts by all sides to persuade the President, the Cabinet Committee. From the Cabinet Committee emerged JCS 1067, basically unsatisfactory to both State and War Departments; its acceptance by Stimson was indicative of his decision to withdraw from his role of presidential adviser on policy. Likewise, the structure of power within the Committee was such that the State Department had to abandon its hopes —no doubt futile in any event—for a powerful Allied Control Council. Treasury opposition to the proposal was based on policy, Army opposition on their essential organizational need, the preservation of discretion for the field commander.

The administrative consequences of Treasury intervention did not end with the Cabinet Committee and the first draft of JCS 1067. The presence of Treasury men in Army uniform but still oriented toward Treasury was a continual source of annoyance for the Army. And when the Army wanted the second revision of JCS 1067, when McCloy's belated effort to include Treasury in SWNCC failed, policy was again made, or at least put in writing, not in SWNCC but in the newly created Informal Policy Committee on Germany, still another *ad hoc* device, designed to circumvent unsatisfactory inter-agency relations.

There the story ended, or seemed to end. Urgent cries for further revision of JCS 1067 went unheeded for a long time and General Clay proceeded with his business on his own terms. The final revisions of the directives for Germany were more in the nature of formal confirmation of the *de facto* situation than new orders. The future of Germany began to rest in German hands.

Thus the history of JCS 1067 represents in an exceedingly painful way the absence of effective working relations, as well as of satisfactory procedural and organizational devices, between the Army and the civilian agencies. Their absence underlay many of the supposedly substantive disputes between the Army and the State and other civilian departments: State kept overlooking the very practical problems that Eisenhower would face if he had to rely on the Control Council for instructions, the Army showed an almost total unwillingness to assist in the rehabilitation of Western Europe—even to glance, so to speak, outside the borders of the U. S. zone, and an avoidance of policy for Germany except in relation to the interests of its own armed forces. The gradual development of viable relations in the revising of JCS 1067 was a good augury of things to come.

SUPER CARRIERS AND B-36 BOMBERS: APPROPRIATIONS, STRATEGY AND POLITICS

PAUL Y. HAMMOND

RESEARCH ASSOCIATE

WASHINGTON CENTER OF FOREIGN POLICY RESEARCH

THE JOHNS HOPKINS UNIVERSITY

CONTENTS

I   The First Clash over Aircraft Roles and Missions—Military Judgments and the Fiscal 1949 Budget   467

II   The Development of the Fiscal 1950 Budget and of the Aviation Feud until the Cancellation of the Flush-Deck Carrier   484

III   The B-36 Investigation—Phase I: The Procurement Program   496

IV   Background to the Second Phase of the Hearings: The Navy Finds Silence Impossible   501

V   The Hearings on "Unification and Strategy"   514

VI   The Hearings Analysed   538

VII   The Aftermath of the Hearings   546

VIII   Concluding Reflections   552

Bibliographic Note   555

Notes   557

Editorial Comments   565

I. THE FIRST CLASH OVER AIRCRAFT ROLES AND MISSIONS—MILITARY JUDGMENTS AND THE FISCAL 1949 BUDGET

INTRODUCTION

The National Security Act of 1947, enacted in July of that year, was the first statute designed to put into effect what had come to be called "unification" of the armed services by the creation of the National Military Establishment. In addition to accomplishing the major change in military organization, and various other important but less dramatic changes, it marked the successful ending of a long struggle by the Army Air Corps for independence from the War Department, and a rather inconclusive ending of a much shorter struggle by the Navy Department to prevent "unification" from establishing a higher, central control. Since the late 1920's, the Air Corps had seen in unification its chance for separation and independence from the Army;[1] but in the same concept the Navy had, at least since 1945, seen a threat to its own independence and its functional identity. The Air Force got virtually all it wanted from unification—except perhaps its wildest dream: naval and marine aviation. The Navy suffered considerably less from unification than it had feared: its independence as an executive department was retained, though slightly curtailed by the limited direction of a military establishment, with cabinet status firmly established for the new Secretary of Defense.

Adjustments to the requirements of the National Security Act naturally constituted only part of the activities of the Air Force and the Navy at this time. Both of them had post-war, peacetime programs that reflected wartime lessons and future expectations. When the war ended, the Navy had a major construction program in progress. As in the early 1920's, in the mid-1940's the Navy expected to continue the build-up of its fleet in peacetime on the basis of these wartime undertakings. Furthermore, it expected to maintain a sizable fleet in operation to carry out the Navy's traditional role in diplomacy. It had plans for future development of naval weapons, notably naval air and undersea craft; and very soon some Navy officers were counting on Navy use of atomic bombs. The Air Force was intent upon developing the strategic independence of its forces. It set a minimum-strength goal of 70 groups, and emphasized the development of aircraft capable of strategic bombing, and to many Air Force planners strategic bombing would be atomic bombing. The Army, too, like the Navy and the Air Force, wished to maintain a large force capable of carrying on a massive mid-century war.

What were the strategic doctrines upon which these force programs of the armed services were based? During the first two peacetime years following World War II the size, if not the composition, of the armed forces was largely determined outside the military establishment, for headlong demobilization became a national policy at the same time that the services were attempting to maintain some semblance of their wartime strength and establish the elements of their own long-term force policies.

Close to their military victories in World War II, involved in adjustments to a new central organization, and demoralized by the rapid reduction in their strength, the services were inclined to regard other matters as more pressing than the re-examination of their strategic doctrine. The National Security Council had just been set up. Conceivably it could have a significant effect upon national security policy, and provide constructive leadership for integrating the functions of the three services. But it had not yet done so. In the meantime, the services suspected that any encouragement from outside the military establishment to re-examine strategic doctrine in order to update or integrate it was motivated by a desire to justify demobilization and reduced budgets. The Navy also feared that re-examination would lead to further integration of the services. All three services felt that they were faced with indifference, even at times with some hostility, from both the executive and legislative branches of the government, to any articulation of their long-range strategic plans and forces policies which came in conflict with demobilization.

On the other hand, to officials in the Bureau of the Budget and the White House, who had to weigh the demands of the military against other national requirements, the services seemed stubborn and inflexible, unwilling to re-examine the doctrines with which they had gained victory in World War II, determined to tolerate overlapping and duplication rather than work out functional accommodations with each other, and insistent that unless they were granted what they asked for, regardless of the relationship of requests to the total budget, they would not, or could not, take responsibility for accomplishing their service missions. Unable to bring the service estimates within a range which seemed at all reasonable, the President and his staff felt compelled to impose budget ceilings upon the services.

The results of this impasse were remarkably uniform from the end of World War II until the beginning of the Korean War. (The post-Korean War period is not relevant to this study.) We shall examine the latter part of this period in greater detail below. As for the earlier part of it, there is little available evidence that in either the executive or legislative budget-making processes during 1946 and 1947 military strategic plans were presented as the underlying basis for budgetary requests or taken into serious consideration during the reviews of these requests, except as they involved the immediate deployment and maintenance of forces. Apparently, the armed services, as well as almost all other interested governmental agencies and members of Congress, assumed that if war came it would be total war with the Soviet Union. In 1947 such

a war was not thought impossible, but it was generally deemed improbable, especially in the near future. This explicit or implicit assumption of no war or total war contributed weightly to the continued inadequacy of the estimates for the military establishment in the budget, an inadequacy that was first faced up to under the combined impact of the evaporation of our atomic monopoly and the Korean War.

DEVELOPMENT OF NAVY AND AIR FORCE PROGRAMS THROUGH THE FISCAL 1949 BUDGET MESSAGE

The Navy Program

The Navy emerged from World War II with, to say the least, a great enthusiasm for aircraft carriers. In the later phases of the Pacific war task force commanders recommended construction of larger carriers than the *Midway* class, so that they could handle heavier aircraft. One of these commanders, Admiral Marc A. Mitscher, who was made Deputy Chief of Naval Operations in 1945, became the chief sponsor of these proposals. In October 1945, design studies were begun in the Navy Department on the proposed new carrier.

Initially the objective had been merely to build a carrier with a larger deck than the largest wartime carrier, but very soon the proposals were aimed at a very large "flush-deck" carrier, i.e., a carrier without the "island" protruding far above the deck. The objective was to have a carrier capable of handling larger aircraft more effectively than existing carriers handled smaller aircraft.[2] And beyond that, the flush-deck carrier could handle the enormous planes then needed to transport the big A-bombs. Certainly Mitscher was eager to have the Navy participate in atomic strategic bombing.

The new, large flush-deck carrier was approved for planning purposes by the Navy Department in 1946. How soon this approval could be translated into inclusion in the Navy's budgetary requests, the President's budget, and thence the Congressional appropriations for Navy, presented a problem. The governmental budgetary mills are much like the mills of the gods: they do tend to grind exceeding fine (in some uncertain sense), and they certainly grind slow. The appropriations for the fiscal year beginning July 1, 1947 and ending June 30,

1948 (the fiscal 1948 budget) would (or should) be passed by Congress not later than June 1947; the President's budget underlying but not determining all aspects of these appropriations would have been announced at the beginning of January 1947; but the Bureau of the Budget's formal and informal reviews of departmental budgetary proposals would have preceded it by many weeks, even months, with the departments themselves starting far sooner. Thus, in general, the appropriations for the Navy made available by Congress for use in fiscal 1948 would be based, however modified, on a budgetary program on which departmental budget officers had begun work in early 1946, perhaps even in the late months of 1945.

To return to the problems of the flush-deck carrier: The approval of it in principle in 1946 would seem early enough for an appropriation request for a carrier to be included in the Navy's budgetary program for fiscal 1948. Actually the major principles of design were not settled and actual designing begun until July 1947, some time after the cycle of budget preparation for the following year, fiscal 1949, had already begun. Nevertheless, in 1946, when the principle was approved, the Chief of the Bureau of Ships, Vice Admiral Earle W. Mills, wanted to get funds for flush-deck carrier construction appropriated in the fiscal 1948 budget, the first budget since the war in which the Navy proposed new ship construction, which would be the first step in the development of a whole series of new ship types and classes. In this, its first year, the program called for the construction of the new prototype ships and the conversion of sixteen others, in addition to its continuing commitment to the completion of construction on thirteen ships begun during the war.[3] Probably because plans for it were not far enough along, the flush-deck carrier could not be included in the fiscal 1948 budget; but the Navy did not abandon its desire for the carrier.

Army–Navy–Air Force Chiefs: Civilian and Military: 1947-50

Passage of the National Security Act of 1947 marked the beginning of a period of gradual centralization in the decision-making procedures of the military establishment—a centralization which was still in progress in 1950.

In the new organization established in 1947 by the Act, James Forrestal became the first Secretary of Defense. Forrestal was a highly successful investment banker who began his career in Washington in 1940 as an Administrative Assistant to President Roosevelt. After brief service in the White House he was appointed Under Secretary of the Navy and finally, upon the death of Frank Knox in 1944, Secretary of the Navy, from which post he was elevated to the new Secretary of Defense position in 1947. Marx Leva and Wilfred J. McNeil, two of his three principal assistants in his new assignment, had held similar positions under him in the Navy, Leva as special assistant and personal legal adviser and McNeil as fiscal director of the Navy. Leva had come to that post already experienced as a government lawyer. McNeil had reached the rank of Captain during his wartime service, and was promoted upon retirement from the Navy to Rear Admiral. The third of Forrestal's principal assistants, John H. Ohly, had been assistant to Secretary of War Robert Patterson.

Until March 1949, Admiral William D. Leahy served as Chief of Staff to the Commander in Chief, a non-statutory post to which he was appointed from retirement by President Roosevelt in 1941. In this capacity he chaired the Joint Chiefs of Staff. When the National Security Act of 1947 went into effect, General Dwight D. Eisenhower was Chief of Staff of the Army, Admiral Chester W. Nimitz was Chief of Naval Operations, and General Carl "Tooey" Spaatz was Chief of Staff of the Air Force, whose independence was granted by the Act. Each had distinguished himself as a top combat commander of his service during the war—Eisenhower as Supreme Commander of the Allied Forces in Western Europe, Nimitz as Commander in Chief of the Pacific Fleet, and Spaatz in various Army Air Forces command posts in Africa, Europe, and the Pacific. Nimitz was replaced in December 1947 by Louis E. Denfeld, then Commander in Chief of the Pacific Fleet, who had served during most of the war as Assistant Chief of the Bureau of Personnel. Eisenhower's successor in early 1948 as Army Chief of Staff was General Omar N. Bradley, who had been an Army group commander in Europe during the war, and the first Administrator of Veterans Affairs after the war. General Hoyt S. Vandenberg succeeded Spaatz in April 1948. Vandenberg had been Air Force Vice Chief of Staff since October 1947, and had held a variety of command and staff posts prior to that.

Kenneth C. Royall had just been appointed Secretary of War when the title of that office was changed by legislation in July 1947 to Secretary of the Army. He was succeeded in the summer of 1949 by Gordon Gray. Royall was a lawyer who had left the Army in 1945 with the rank of Brigadier General, after service primarily as Deputy Fiscal Director of the Army Service Forces, and as a special assistant to the Secretary of War.

When Forrestal became Secretary of Defense, the Under Secretary of the Navy, John L. Sullivan, moved up to succeed him as Secretary of the Navy. Sullivan, lawyer and prominent Democrat from New Hampshire, had been Assistant Secretary of the Treasury from 1940 through 1944, then Assistant Secretary of the Navy for Air in 1945, and Under Secretary in 1946.

Upon Sullivan's resignation as a result of the cancellation of the new flush-deck carrier in April 1949, Francis P. Matthews was appointed Secretary of the Navy. Matthews was a prominent Omaha banker and lawyer and an even more prominent Roman Catholic layman who had no previous experience in government.

The first Secretary of the new separate Air Force was W. Stuart Symington, who had been serving as Assistant Secretary of War for Air for a year and a half prior to the statutory creation of the Air Force as a department. Before entering government service as Chairman of the Surplus Property Board in 1945, Symington had been a successful businessman in Missouri, and earlier in other states.

The Navy Budgetary Program for Fiscal 1949

During preliminary presentations by his staff in the fall of 1947 on the 1949 budget, Sullivan learned that the Navy intended to ask for appropriations for a new flush-deck carrier. Questioning the proposal, he was told that Forrestal had approved it when he was Secretary. Sullivan indicated that if the Navy wanted his support for the new carrier it would have to convince him of its merits. The presentation

which followed in late fall was run by Sullivan like a hearing, with cross-examination of the Navy "witnesses" by Sullivan and his Under Secretary, John Kenny, who was also a lawyer. In the end, Sullivan was convinced of the soundness of the proposal, and of the widespread support for it within the Navy. Confident that he had examined the issues involved thoroughly and critically, he became an active advocate of the new carrier. Work then proceeded on the customary task of preparing budget requests.

The procedure for preparing the first budget following the passage of the National Security Act of 1947 was not substantially different from procedures used for previous ones. One additional step, the approval of the Secretary of Defense, was required, but his staff was too small and had too many assignments to permit it to conduct a searching appraisal of the Navy estimates. In any event, Forrestal's staff knew that he favored construction of the carrier and the other ships. The construction requests for the continued building of the thirteen ships begun during the war, plus the appropriation for one flush-deck carrier, were thus approved by Forrestal's office; but then they were held up by the Bureau of the Budget. In the previous year the Navy had been willing to hold its new construction program to a minimum in order to continue with its construction legacy from World War II. But now, confronted with the possibility of even more stringent limitations on its new construction program, particularly on its highly valued new prototype aircraft carrier, a carrier capable of participating in atomic warfare—the Navy was willing to give up the birds in the hand, which its thirteen legacies from World War II represented, for the less certain gains of its future plans. Secretary Sullivan proposed to the Budget Bureau that construction on the thirteen partially built ships be halted, and that the money thus saved be used for the 1949 increment of the Navy's new shipbuilding program. The Bureau agreed on condition that the Navy sponsor the legislation necessary to make such a change. With this condition accepted by Sullivan, the flush-deck carrier and the rest of the Navy's fiscal 1949 new construction program[4] were approved by the Bureau of the Budget and became part of the President's program. At this time, neither the Secretary of Defense, nor the

Budget Bureau, nor the President asked for concurrence or for formal approval by the Joint Chiefs of Staff.

The Air Force Program

The post-war program of the Air Force was based upon a minimum-force level of 70 groups. Apparently, the program was officially established within the Air Force in late 1945, and was first presented to Congress in 1946, along with a personnel strength of 400,000 men. It served as the basis for Air Force budget estimates made in 1947 for fiscal 1948, and was assumed by Air Force witnesses before a House Appropriations subcommittee that year to be its uncontested minimum requirement.[5] But what the Air Force meant by 70 groups, or by the minimum requirement which it represented, was not clear; the estimates for fiscal 1948 which the Air Force had submitted to the Bureau of the Budget provided for the maintenance of only fifty-eight full-strength air groups, plus twelve skeletonized ones. Yet "the 70-group program as originally conceived," the Deputy Commander of the AAF, General Ira C. Eaker, told the subcommittee, "is still considered the very minimum to do the job." Whether the General meant to imply that the Air Force was submitting original budget proposals which it regarded as inadequate, or to indicate that the adequate seventy could include twelve skeletonized groups, was not stated. Seventy groups had perhaps become more a symbol of air power than a specific program.[6]

By the end of 1947, the Air Force had again tried for seventy air groups and again been cut down by the President to fifty-five.[7]

During 1947 both the executive and legislative branches of the national government instigated investigations into the air power policies of the country. (The role of the Congressional Aviation Policy Board report will be discussed below.) The President's Air Policy Commission (Finletter Committee) found considerable duplication in Air Force and Navy aviation plans, and requested that those services establish an integrated program for presentation to the committee. The Joint Chiefs of Staff complied with this wish on December 10, 1947, by agreeing to a paper which stated the forces programs of both services. Later, as the air power controversy between the Navy and the Air Force developed further, what was or was not agreed to in this paper became a matter of argument.

Although the JCS paper of December 10 was prepared specifically because of complaints of overlap in the Air Force and Navy air programs, agreement was reached between them by avoiding that issue, for the paper merely approved the statement of requirements each service presented—14,500 aircraft for naval aviation and a 70-group Air Force. The flush-deck carrier was included in a statistical summary which served as supporting data for the naval plane requirements, apparently because existing carriers could not withstand the weight of nor provide the space required by some of the new aircraft envisaged in the Navy's program.[8]

THE BUDGET MESSAGE (JANUARY 12, 1948)

The defense budget for fiscal 1949, presented to Congress following the President's budget message on January 12, 1948, was for $11 billion, divided quite evenly between the three services, and representing a hold-the-line philosophy in defense affairs. New procurement of aircraft was postponed, an action made feasible by a policy of more rapid consumption of existing aircraft. Fifty-five full-strength air groups, plus fifteen skeletonized ones, were proposed for the Air Force. Naval air strength was to be supported at a total aircraft inventory of 10,922, and the construction of new ship types (not yet including the flush-deck carrier) was to be started at the expense of older models already under construction. The Army was budgeted for a strength of 560,000 men, although the prospects were that enlistments would limit it more than would budget ceilings, for by the end of March 1948, it was 22,000 men under that strength.[9] (No Selective Service Act was in effect at this time.)

The House subcommittee on naval appropriations began its hearings on the Navy's budget for the next fiscal year on February 14, 1948. The new ship construction mentioned above, with its emphasis upon prototypes, constituted a commitment to greater strength in the years to come, at the cost of reduced naval strength in the immediate future. The naval aircraft procurement program presented in the budget, while it offered less hope for the more distant future, was equally limited in what it offered for the immediate future. Although it included an increase of 37 per cent over the previous year in money for new aircraft, and almost double the number of aircraft, the number of new aircraft was less than half the total needed each year to maintain the operating strength of naval aviation.[10] But it represented an expansion over the previous two lean years, and a definite break with previous downward trends in naval aircraft procurement. At the same time, the procurement program documented the dominant position which naval aviation had acquired in Navy plans for the future.

The naval appropriations hearings were concluded March 8, before hearings on either of the other services had begun.

About two months earlier, in January 1948, Air Force–Navy friction over their overlapping aviation functions had increased considerably as the result of a valedictory statement made by Admiral Nimitz, and widely circulated by the Navy. Nimitz spoke of bombing the heartland of Russia with naval aircraft, and of a growing fleet of super aircraft carriers. (The speech was quite similar to his retirement speech of October 1945.) His statements caused considerable suspicions of Navy motives and aspirations in Air Force circles.[11] The resulting furor came at a most inopportune time. On February 5, when the Secretary of the Navy followed up the President's budget message by announcing at a news conference the Navy's construction program for new ships, including a flush-deck, 65,000-ton carrier, he gave assurance that the Navy had no intention of taking over Air Force responsibilities of strategic bombing.[12] But, despite denials, thereafter the flush-deck, or "super" carrier, as it was called, tended to be identified with a Navy interest in strategic bombing, although it is noteworthy that this possibility received only passing attention in the naval appropriations hearings of February and early March.[13] It seems almost certain, nevertheless, that some of the Admirals were planning to share in, if not take over, strategic bombing executed with atomic bombs, although officially they spoke only of using the bombs against "naval targets."

THE CRISIS OF MARCH 1948

Throughout 1947, while the services were involved in the implementation of their own unilaterally determined force objectives, in pursuit of their self-interpreted functions, the pattern of American foreign relations was undergoing an important transformation. The Truman Doctrine was announced in March, and the Marshall Plan was proposed in June 1947. Greek-Turkish military and economic aid legislation soon implemented the first; and in pursuit of the second, by mid-summer the governments of Western Europe were energetically planning the economic cooperation program which the United States seemed willing to underwrite. Congress appropriated emergency aid for that winter, and in December President Truman laid before Congress the Marshall Plan estimates, totaling $6.8 billion for the first fifteen months, and ultimately, for more than four years, $17 billion. Naturally, when the fiscal 1949 budget was submitted to Congress in January 1948, what was perhaps the most controversial part of it consisted of the initial Marshall Plan appropriation for the first fifteen months.

While there were humanitarian and economic justifications for the Marshall Plan, the strategic importance of keeping Western Europe out of the Soviet orbit was its ultimate if not its sole justification. In strategic terms, the Marshall Plan represented a commitment of American resources to the protection of Western Europe against the expansion of Soviet influence and control. The Marshall Plan also had important military implications with respect to the types and sizes of armed forces needed by the United States. For the time being, however, these implications remained only theoretical: the Administration was too occupied with the economic elements of the Marshall Plan to implement as systematically its military implications. To the extent that it was aware of these implications, it did not find them urgent. "While in effect, the services were insisting that they had to start immediately a substantial build-up" in order to implement the military implications of the Marshall Plan, "the President was partly taking the position that they should first establish a basis, through decision as to roles and missions, as a means of proper consideration of the requirements for the build-up."[14] The enabling statute itself, the Economic Cooperation Act, made the funds available to the participating European nations only for economic, not military, support. The indirect military value of economic support was not discussed, and a phrase like "military support" had not yet been invented.

The military expansion program which developed during the spring of 1948 was thus not the result of an effort to carry out any military implications of the Marshall Plan, but a reaction to a series of events of international significance and to a popular sense of crisis which was in turn largely a result of those events. The sense of crisis began in the military establishment as early as January 1948. Public and Congressional concern began to be noticeable a month later. The Administration as a whole responded much more moderately, although it had considerably more knowledge than the general public of the need for a large increase in the means of national defense.

Within the Administration the disappointing initial results of military aid to Greece and Turkey, the success of Chinese Communist forces against the Nationalist Government in China, and the imminent need of American aid in enforcing the United Nations' partition of Palestine, all were situations where the need for immediate commitment of our armed forces seemed at least conceivable. The public was not told of the immediate considerations which posed these demands. Its growing if latent alarm had more general origins: in the East-West division of Europe which the Marshall Plan forced into the open, in the noticeable deterioration of Soviet-American relations generally, and especially in occupied Germany, and in the ominous developments in Greece and Turkey, and in China.[15]

The Communist coup in Czechoslovakia was dramatic confirmation of both the private concern of the Administration and the public sense of crisis, bridging the gap between the two, and leading to a striking foreign policy speech by the President on March 17, and a military expansion program authorized by Congress in the three months which followed. This was the spring crisis of 1948. While it thus had two origins, a general movement of events affecting the strategic position of the United States and arousing the American public, and certain specific potential demands upon the military forces to which only the executive branch was privy, in neither case was the alarm over the strength of our armed forces focussed upon the development and implementation of a broad strategic plan.

The President's own interest in universal military training, together with an alarmingly low rate of enlistment in the Army, led him to initiate consideration of Universal Military Training (UMT) by the Cabinet and the National Security Council at the end of January 1948. Following up this interest, one of Forrestal's military assistants, Major General Alfred M. Gruenther, then serving as Director of the Joint Staff of the JCS, made a presentation at a White House meeting on February 18 which compared available military strength with present and possible commitments. It underscored the great extent to which the military budget was used up in support of the overhead expenses of the military establishment, leaving little for forces in readiness. The employment of anything more than a division in any area, Gruenther concluded at one point, would make partial mobilization a necessity.[16] Although manpower was not the only limiting factor described by Greunther, UMT remained the official solution until mid-March. The chairman of the Senate Armed Services Committee, Chan Gurney, was apprised of the Administration's interest in UMT early in February, but Gurney had declined to hold hearings on it until definite cost figures were available.

On March 5, little more than a week after the Czech coup, a top-secret telegram from General Clay in Berlin added to the worries of the Administration. Clay had nothing tangible to report, only "a feeling of a new tenseness in every Soviet individual with whom we have official relations." But it led him to believe that war now might come "with dramatic suddenness." Actually, of course, it was an advance warning of the Berlin blockade which was not war but which had serious military significance. The first step towards the blockade was taken by the Russians on March 31, 1948.[17] Three days later, Forrestal and the three service Secretaries and the Chiefs of Staff met with the House Armed Services Committee. Strong criticisms were raised on budgetary grounds to the UMT proposal, but the committee unanimously decided to hold hearings on it.[18]

Key West

Later that week the Secretary of Defense retired to Key West with the Joint Chiefs of Staff to thrash out conflicts which had developed in their interpretations of the National Security Act of 1947 over the roles and missions of the respective services, and the functions of the JCS itself. The immediate impetus for this session (it lasted from the 11th to the 14th day of March) was the mounting controversy between the Air Force and the Navy over the roles and missions of their aircraft. "I shall have to make my own decisions" if agreement is not reached, Forrestal had told the press on the 10th.[19]

What the Secretary of Defense expected to accomplish with this conference is not entirely clear. He had devoted much attention to developing mutual confidence among the services, and he may have believed that talking things out would itself help to promote the understanding and agreement now so evidently needed. Or, as his press conference statements of March 10 hinted, he may have believed that he was now in a position to force acceptance of partial agreement or compromise. But his hopes were not fulfilled.

The Key West Conference was a peculiar affair, to say the least. The Functions Paper which was signed there served usefully, though imperfectly, for years as a general settlement of roles and missions. But even this limited long-range utility of its ambiguous formula was achieved at the expense of any immediate constructive effect. As we shall see, the immediate effect of the conference was only misunderstanding. It did not solve the impending problem of whether the flush-deck carrier should be built, or whether its construction required approval by the Joint Chiefs of Staff. For the answer to these questions the National Security Act of 1947 remained the only source. It charged the JCS with the duty "to review major material and personnel requirements of the military forces, in accordance with strategic and logistic plans,"[20] but these ambiguous words settled nothing.

The main concern of the conference, the settlement of disputes over roles and missions,

Forrestal himself summarized for his diaries as follows:

1. For planning purposes, Marine Corps to be limited with the inclusion of a sentence in the final document that the Marines are not to create another land army.

2. Air Force recognizes right of Navy to proceed with the development of weapons the Navy considers essential to its function but with the proviso that the Navy will not develop a separate strategic air force, this function being reserved to the Air Force. However, the Navy in the carrying out of its function is to have the right to attack inland targets—for example, to reduce and neutralize airfields from which enemy aircraft may be sortying to attack the Fleet.

3. Air Force recognized the right and need for the Navy to participate in an all-out air campaign.

And more specifically, the Navy was not to be denied use of the atomic bomb.[21]

The implementation of these general principles governing the delineation of roles and missions depended upon reaching an understanding on the functions of the JCS. In the course of clarifying the latter, a formal statement was prepared and agreed to:

The Joint Chiefs of Staff member of the service having primary responsibility for a function shall be the agent of the Joint Chiefs of Staff to present to that body the requirements and plans for the employment of all forces to carry out the function.[22]

This statement was supposed to solve the problem of roles and missions by providing a means for carrying out the delineation of functions mentioned above. But in fact it did not. This paragraph is an agreement on how Section 211 (b) (4) of the National Security Act of 1947 should be carried out. That section is concerned primarily with combat theaters, for it deals with the development and utilization of joint strategic and logistic plans. The review of "major material requirements" mentioned in the statute was to be based upon, and hence draw its meaning from, these same plans. Since such plans were non-existent in the peacetime conditions of 1948 and 1949, the pressing questions raised by the aviation controversy remained unsettled. Specifically, did the Navy's program for the construction of new prototype ships need approval by the Joint Chiefs? While at the time the Chiefs did not discuss this concrete application of the Functions Paper, apparently the services were to pick their own weapons, even though the very fact that the naval need for a flush-deck carrier prototype was considered at the Key West meetings may suggest that the contrary was the case.

Since the reason for raising the question of the carrier at Key West later became a bone of contention between the Air Force and the Navy, the circumstances under which the carrier was considered are worth noting. Forrestal announced to the Chiefs at Key West that he and the President had approved the construction of a flush-deck carrier prototype, and the Chiefs "said that they would go along with it because it was in the President's program."[23] These facts were undisputed. The question later raised was whether these actions constituted JCS endorsement of the carrier. In effect, the JCS merely noted that the President had decided to permit the Navy to build the carrier; faced with a *fait accompli,* they could neither affirm nor deny. General Vandenberg later said, with some justification, that at Key West the flush-deck carrier "was not agreed [upon] nor was it discussed for that purpose." Yet Forrestal, not to mention Denfeld, believed it had been. In reporting to the President on the day following the conclusion of the conference, the Secretary of Defense stated that among the decisions reached at Key West was approval for the Navy to proceed with the development of its new 80,000 ton carrier. Later, in a press interview on the conference, Forrestal stated that the larger carrier would not be built for strategic air war, since that was an Air Force job. He said it "might" not be justified purely for Navy roles. But its Navy function plus its possible contribution to the Air Force's job might justify the vessel, *"if so decided by the Joint Chiefs of Staff."*[24] Forrestal's phraseology seemed to imply that the question of approving the carrier was still open; but apparently he considered the matter settled, for he had already told the President unequivocally that the carrier was approved. The significance of his statement to the press is derived, not from its phraseology, but from its definite assertion that the flush-carrier could be properly justified only by an affirmative vote of the Joint Chiefs of Staff. Presumably Forrestal was proceeding on the assumption that at Key West the Joint Chiefs had approved the construction of the flush-deck carrier on its merits, and not merely in recognition of a decision already made by the President.

Thus the first application of the Key West agreement on functions revealed only disagreement among the Joint Chiefs and misunderstanding between them and the Secretary of Defense. Moreover, even the general agreement at Key West on roles and missions, which allocated strategic bombing to the Air Force but preserved the role of naval aviation within the Navy, rested upon sand. For Spaatz, and his Deputy Chief of Staff for Operations, Lieutenant General Lauris Norstad, made clear to Forrestal before the press release on the conference was issued that they could support the statement of functions of naval aviation only as an interpretation of the National Security Act of 1947, but that they disagreed with it in principle.[25] The upshot of this reservation was to nullify the whole agreement, for its practical purpose was to circumscribe the behavior of the services before the public and Congress, and there the merits of public policy, not the interpretation of existing legislation, constituted the major determinant. The Functions Paper had settled no part of the Air Force–Navy dispute, for the Air Force had never claimed that the National Security Act of 1947 had authorized the absorption of naval aviation into the Air Force; nor had the Navy made its air role claims on the basis of statutory interpretations, but like the Air Force, on the substance of the issues involved, regardless of statute.

The one thing of substance which was accomplished by the Key West Conference was only an incidental part of it. The Joint Chiefs decided while meeting there that, besides UMT, selective service would have to be enacted in order to provide for the immediate manpower requirements of the services, and that a supplemental appropriation should be requested in order to bring total armed strength more nearly in proportion to the realities of the world situation.[26]

Truman's Address to Congress, March 17, 1948

The President was apprised of the selective service recommendation from Key West before Forrestal had returned to Washington, and, by the time of their appointment late that day, had already announced his sudden decision to address Congress two days later. He had originally planned to back UMT at a St. Patrick's Day dinner in New York City, but when he learned of the Joint Chiefs' request for selective service, he decided to use a more serious and dramatic forum. There is no evidence that he was planning at this time any increase in the defense budget.

Although President Truman identified the Soviet Union as the one nation which threatened the peace, his address to Congress was a measured statement about the deteriorating situation in Soviet-American relations. The day before, the Speaker of the House, Joseph Martin, had spoken of "a grave crisis in our international relations," and of the need for a build-up in armed forces.[27] This was not an unpopular view in Congress. Truman's speech dealt with an explosive subject in a charged atmosphere. It was taken to be a strong appeal for national rearmament, although it made only three specific proposals for legislative action; these recommended enactment of (1) the Marshall Plan, (2) Universal Training, and (3) selective service. The two latter proposals were aimed at maintaining the full authorized strength of the armed services.[28] The speech made no specific recommendations for increases beyond authorized strengths or existing appropriations. Nonetheless, it was interpreted as a rearmament proposal.

THE EFFECT OF THE WAR SCARE ON BUDGET-MAKING AND THE AVIATION DISPUTE

One Month in a Policy Vacuum

Forrestal and his staff (perhaps in hope, perhaps in error, perhaps in desperation) seized upon the President's speech as a call for mobilization, and pressed ahead with budget estimates which would raise military strength substantially. Truman attempted to curb Forrestal's expectations by indicating that $1.5 billion would be enough for the anticipated supplementary appropriation requested at Key West, but Forrestal did not convey this information to the Joint Chiefs. He continued to negotiate with the President, who in the end was willing to go along further by accepting a supplementary defense budget totaling twice the amount which he had originally thought sufficient.[29] His belated change of heart only

confirmed the widely held view that his speech of March 17 had been intended to initiate a general rearmament program. While this was probably a mistaken impression (though the speech is not clear), its results were nonetheless real; an aroused Congress, left with no policy guidance from the executive branch for nine days, with no figures for its appropriations mill for another fourteen days, and with only the aircraft estimates for another month, turned to programs largely favorable to Air Force fortunes. Without new guidance from the Administration on rearmament policy, Congress and the public had to look elsewhere. The only well-known programs were those of the Finletter and Brewster Committees on air power calling for a 70-group Air Force. It was easy to conclude that rearmament should begin there.[30] The Administration, by releasing budget estimates on aircraft a month ahead of the rest of its supplementary figures, encouraged this view. Encouragement was hardly necessary. Congressional support for a stronger Air Force was deep-rooted at this time; as Millis has said, the Finletter report was no surprise— it was propaganda for a full 70-group Air Force and not a statement of a new policy.[31] It is highly doubtful that the lack of additional guidance created or permitted a crystallization of Congressional sentiment that would not have occurred anyway.

Congressional hearings had been scheduled and presentations prepared without anticipation of the President's speech of March 17, and they proceeded on schedule. Forrestal had appeared before the House Appropriations Committee the day before that speech to urge a balanced military program, and he returned the day following the speech to the Senate Armed Services Committee to testify on UMT and selective service, and to take advantage of the greater interest of the committee members in the military budget.[32] On March 25, before the House Armed Services Committee, he, and the three civilian and three professional heads of the service departments, moved beyond the President's program as outlined in his speech. They presented, in terms of the manpower involved, the broad outlines of the manpower goals envisaged by them for a limited rearmament program. Forrestal's presentation divided the new program into its short-term and long-term elements, identifying selective service with the former and Universal Military Training with the latter. He requested 349,500 more men for the services. The bulk of them— 240,000—were to go to the Army, and 11,000 to the Marines. The Air Force was to have manpower and aircraft to fill out its 55 groups. The total cost would be about $3 billion, not counting UMT, for which $600 million had already been requested.[33] Although it was presented as a balanced and agreed program, Symington did not hesitate, under questioning, to imply that the Air Force had been over-ridden in its demand for 70 groups.

The National Military Establishment witnesses could not at this time make a definitive presentation of the supplemental program, but only a statement of its manpower implications, and through the last ten days of March appropriations hearings limped along with outdated budget presentations. Prior to their appearance before the House Armed Services Committee on the 25th, Symington and Spaatz, on the 19th, just two days after the President's speech, testified at one of the appropriations hearings, using statements prepared before rearmament was expected. The result was that the committee, in an attempt to keep its efforts relevant, divided its attention between outmoded budget presentations and possible supplementary figures. It was natural for them to take 70 groups as their supplemental goal. Even after the statement on the 25th, witnesses could say nothing significant about the impending increases.[34]

While the military establishment was feverishly developing its new program, the budget hearings continued in the House Appropriations subcommittees with testimony based on the regular budget, but with conjectures on what the (as yet unknown) supplementary requests would mean. Congressional sentiment favoring the 70-group Air Force, encouraged by the continuing forceful advocacy of Air Force expansion by Symington and Spaatz, grew noticeably, though with much stronger support in the House than in the Senate. The advocates followed two lines of attack in attempting to commit Congress to the 70-group goal. One was authorization. Pointing out that the Air Force had no statute establishing its composition, Air Force supporters sought substantive legislation providing for the 70 groups, as a statement of House policy. Before the President's rearmament speech a concurrent

resolution was introduced in the House which provided for the 70 groups. After the speech, three bills dealing with Air Force composition were introduced which provided for 70 groups, and comparable strength in other elements.[35] Furthermore, these were joint resolutions, i.e., statutes, not merely statements of intent, like a concurrent resolution. One of them passed the House, but none got through the Senate. Hence, Air Force supporters had to rely upon appropriations as a means of committing Congress to their program.

On April 8, ending the period of drift in the appropriations hearings, the aircraft portion of the rearmament program was presented to the House Appropriations Committee as a supplement to the fiscal 1948 budget (rather than the fiscal 1949 budget, which was then under consideration), in order that funds could be made available as soon as possible for contracting. It was hoped that in this way there would be an early start in dealing with development, production, and allocation problems, all expected to be crucial in such a rapid expansion in aircraft production.[36] The rest of the budget was to follow later in the month. Forrestal's proposal for the Air Force was to fill out the 55 groups already planned. But by separating this portion of his balanced program from the rest of it, he only made it vulnerable to attack. As was to be expected, Symington and Spaatz repeated before the committee their assertion that 70 groups was the absolute minimum necessary for the defense of the United States. The following day Bradley, perhaps attempting to show the "balanced" equivalent of the 70-group program, reverted to the minimum Army program of 822,000 men, instead of the 782,000 to which Forrestal had pared it. But that did not help. Led by Carl Vinson, the ranking minority member of the House Armed Services Committee, the Appropriations Committee voted to add $822 million to the supplemental appropriation as the first-year cost of a five-year build-up to 70 groups, and the House accepted the bill as amended on April 15 by a vote of 343 to 3 in what was on any basis a rousing victory for the 70-group advocates, moderated only by procedural details in the bill (to be discussed later), and by their subsequent failure to carry the Air Force authorization bill through the Senate.[37]

The New Budget

Forrestal had announced $3 billion as the magnitude of the rearmament supplement, and had submitted to Congress on April 8 a specific budget for aircraft procurement appropriations. But the rest of the program remained to be put together. This was done by April 21, when it was presented first to the President, and then, with his approval, to the House Armed Services Committee. "Based solely on military considerations," the Joint Chiefs had set as a minimum a balanced force commensurate with the 70-group Air Force.[38] Although Denfeld had replaced Nimitz, and Bradley had replaced Eisenhower in the meantime, JCS views remained substantially unchanged from the previous December, when it will be recalled, the Joint Chiefs had merely accepted each other's programs. A balanced force at the "70-group level" was really just a pleasant euphemism, for the minimum-force level of each of the three services was determined by itself. The baffling questions of "balance" had been avoided. This minimum program would have cost about $9 billion. The JCS left to Forrestal any modification of this total that might be based upon considerations of impact upon the economy, and other non-military factors. Presumably taking into account these considerations, he came out with a figure of $3.481 billion, which he took to the President and Congress,[39] a figure far closer to his own announced tentative total of $3 billion than to the JCS total of $9 billion, but more than double the $1.5 billion figure which the President had originally set (and Forrestal had ignored).

In the hearings, Forrestal revealed that he was strongly concerned over two problems involving proposed solutions that were in direct conflict with each other. In 1947 and 1948 he was remarkable in his efforts to have Congress understand and face up to Russian threats to national security. Now Forrestal accepted, perhaps because he had just won a substantial budgetary concession from the President, the widely held assumption that if the peacetime national budget was not reduced to about a $30 billion level, the national economy would be placed in jeopardy. The Marshall Plan seemed to Forrestal to strain the economy so close to its limit that only modest increases were possible for the armed services. Hence, he told

the Senate Appropriations Committee he would prefer to take the military risk attendant upon a mere $3 billion increase in the defense budget, which the Joint Chiefs regarded as inadequate from a military viewpoint, to the economic risks attendant upon the $9 billion increase considered by the Joint Chiefs to be the minimum needed.[40]

Forrestal told the House Armed Services Committee, in presenting this supplemental budget request for fiscal 1949, that the Joint Chiefs had agreed to it unanimously. But, like the Key West treaty, the agreement had little meaning. We have seen that the Air Force made a vital reservation in its agreement at Key West which left it free to criticize and resist. Here, again, reservation undercut the agreement. In the final discussions of the budget between the Secretary of Defense and the Joint Chiefs, Spaatz raised for consideration as related to the discussion the appropriations for the Air Force which had already passed the House and were pending in the Senate. They included, besides the Administration's regular and supplementary budgets, $822 million in additional funds to begin a five-year build-up to 70 groups. While Forrestal undoubtedly recognized the relevance of this appropriation to the achievement of a balanced military establishment, he refused to discuss it with the JCS since the question of what Symington and Spaatz would say to the Senate committee was a matter which he most assuredly could not control.[41] Possibly Forrestal decided upon this procedure because, aware of the proviso which the Chairman of the House Appropriations Committee had inserted in the 70-group appropriation bill, which would leave its expenditure to the discretion of the President, he expected it would never be spent anyway. But with a factor so important to the Air Force budget thus ruled out of any agreement between the services and Forrestal on the budget, the Air Force commitment to the budget became meaningless. Here, Forrestal's concern with different kinds of problems and solutions was evident. Although he was an avowed admirer of the British Cabinet system, including, presumably, the secrecy and public unanimity of Cabinet proceedings, and seemed instinctively to prefer to settle matters of public policy through private negotiation outside of the political limelight, he seemed to uphold as a matter of principle the right of his own subordinates to dissent in public.[42] The effect on his own announcement that the $3.481 billion increase was approved by the JCS was striking.

As Forrestal presented the rest of the supplementary program, it represented a small increase in authorized Army manpower, but, coupled with selective service, promised a substantial augmentation in personnel. The Navy was given no budget increases for manpower, although it received proportionate budget increases in non-aircraft material. It likewise could anticipate a significant increase in personnel merely by building up to the strength provided for by its appropriations. The Air Force received the largest manpower increase, in comparison with both its actual and its authorized strength. Moreover, its force structure, which Forrestal had expected to hold to a fully manned and equipped 55 groups, he proposed to expand to 66 groups, using, as would the Air Force in its 14,500-plane program which was incorporated in the aviation supplement to the fiscal 1948 budget, obsolete and obsolescent aircraft then in storage.

The supplemental defense program which Forrestal presented on April 21 was not, strictly speaking, the President's program, although Truman had authorized its submittal to Congress. To begin with, Truman had initially wanted it to go no higher than $1.5 billion. After the detailed estimates had been presented, the Bureau of the Budget cut the amount to $3.17 billion and suggested that it ought to be cut to $2.5 billion, since it was really only the first-year increment in a program which each of the services projected over several years with steadily rising costs. The lower figure, the Director of the Bureau, James E. Webb, pointed out, would make it possible for the budget to level off at an annual defense expenditure of about $15 billion after 1950.[43] It would mean going back to the 55 air groups. Forrestal went to the White House supporting the higher figure, and Webb, the lower one. Seeking the best of two worlds, the President agreed to recommend the $3.17 billion supplement provided the services would not spend all of it. His condition was

that administratively we do not, in the next eight months, create a military structure which would require in excess of approximately $15 billion for

the next fiscal year. I do not want immediate action taken toward the activation of all of the units contemplated—and by that I mean such things as Army training camps, Naval Air stations and air groups.[44]

Aggregate manpower strength, he further indicated, should not exceed 1,539,000, which was 86 per cent of the agreed program of April 21.[45]

The President's new program, $11 billion in the original budget, plus $3.17 billion in the supplemental estimates, passed the House with $889 million cut from it. The Senate restored $530 million, and it was approved in mid-June with most of these restorations retained. The balanced program which Forrestal had advocated was upset by the $822 million appropriation for a 70-group Air Force, which passed both Houses by overwhelming votes, and by the elimination of UMT. Otherwise, the military budgets had not received any substantial alteration.[46]

The Developing Navy–Air Force Feud

Once the figures for the supplementary budget request were released, the full implications of the new budget were developed in public and private sessions in several subcommittees of the House Appropriations Committee, in the Senate Committee on Appropriations, and in the Armed Services Committees of both Houses from late May to early June. Forrestal appeared many times, stressing a balanced program, the worsening international situation, and what was widely accepted as the necessity of a severely limited arms budget.[47] Although he insisted that 70 Air Force groups would unbalance defense, he defended Symington's action in continuing to insist on them, saying that the Secretary of the Air Force had done so with his approval.[48]

Air Force witnesses, particularly Symington and Spaatz, continued to emphasize the 70-group program as the minimum essential to national security.[49] On the other hand, under the same kind of persistent questioning by Congressional committeemen which Air Force witnesses constantly faced, the Army Chief of Staff, Bradley, and the Navy Secretary, Sullivan, were each led on one occasion to propose appropriations in excess of the agreed budget and to support force levels in their own services equivalent to the 70-group goal of the Air Force. But otherwise they followed the lead given them by Forrestal—freely discussing the larger forces agreed to by the Joint Chiefs but agreeing that, everything considered, the President's program made the best sense.[50] While Forrestal had publicly acknowledged Symington's right to present his own views, the Secretary of Defense was evidently not happy with the way those views were actually presented. Twice in May he reprimanded Symington, although with no visible effect.[51] Nor was Spaatz easily controlled. He had already made clear his belief that all service aircraft should be under the control of the Air Force, and he continued to maintain this position.[52] As his retirement in June approached, he let it be known in the military establishment that thereafter he would feel even freer to voice his views.[53]

Air Force advocacy of its own expansion could, with care, have kept it from involvement in a dispute over naval aviation, although Spaatz's views made such forbearance unlikely. But the publicity efforts of both services kept their inter-service quarrel going. After Nimitz's speech of the previous January, Symington had replied to him in a magazine article, challenging the former Chief of Naval Operations' views on naval aviation. On February 13, 1948, the day before the first hearing on the fiscal 1949 budget, Forrestal announced that he had forbidden unauthorized public discussions of controversial subjects by the service Secretaries and Chiefs and their assistants. He put the budget high on his list of controversial subjects.[54]

The reports of the President's Air Policy (Finletter) Commission, published on January 13, and of the Congressional Aviation Policy (Brewster) Board, on March 1, were welcomed by Congress, and would have been welcomed even if a different policy had been stated by the President.[55] But because of the vacuum in the Administration's military policy after the President's speech of March 17, many friends of naval aviation must have been particularly alarmed. For, although the Brewster Board's proposals included a substantial expansion of naval aviation as well as of the Air Force, the Finletter Commission Report did not; and, in consequence, little of the discussion that followed dealt with naval aviation.[56] For

some reason, public and hence Congressional interest was more stirred by Finletter and the Air Force than by Brewster and naval aviation.

By the end of April, those most concerned had become aroused. A memorandum written four months earlier in the Navy Department by a strong advocate of naval aviation, Rear Admiral Daniel V. Gallery, was leaked to a syndicated columnist by someone other than its author. The memorandum was a comment on the final report of a Policies and Programs Review Board in the War Department. "I believe that the publication of the report," it read in part,

affords the Navy an excellent opportunity to present its case as being the branch of the National Defense destined to deliver the Atom Bomb. Ever since the end of the war, the Navy has been on the defensive and has been answering arguments of those who say that Navies are obsolete and useless. We have been protecting ourselves against attempts to abolish the Navy—the original merger proposal.

4. For the past two years our defense of the Navy has been based mainly in old familiar arguments about exercising control of the seas. Much has been said about anti-submarine warfare, naval reconnaissance, protection of shipping, and amphibious operations. It has been assumed, at least implicitly, that the next war will not be much different from the last one. This assumption is basically wrong, and if we stick to it the Navy will soon be obsolete. The next war will be a lot different from any previous one. It seems obvious that the next time our Sunday Punch will be an Atom Bomb aimed at the enemy capitals or industrial centers and that the outcome of the war will be determined by strategic bombing. The war will be won by whichever side is able to deliver the Atom Bomb to the enemy, and at the same time protect its own territory against similar delivery. I think "the time is right now for the Navy to start an aggressive campaign aimed at proving that the Navy can deliver the Atom Bomb more effectively than the Air Forces [sic] can."[57]

The response to the publication of this memorandum was immediate. Secretary of the Navy Sullivan, after securing the signature of the Chief of Naval Operations to a statement which denied that the Gallery memorandum represented his views, reprimanded Gallery and disavowed the memo. Spaatz announced at the same time that he would block any attempt by the Department of Defense to split the air bombing role with the Navy.[58]

The leak of the Gallery memorandum could not have been more poorly timed. The Navy budget had yet to be reconsidered by both Houses of Congress in the light of the supplemental requests. In the February hearings on naval appropriations only passing reference had been made to the flush-deck carrier. But now the flush-deck carrier could be identified with a Navy role in strategic bombing. Closely questioned in a House Armed Services Committee hearing on JCS approval of the flush-deck carrier, Denfeld contended that the Chiefs had given their approval both at the time of their meeting with the Finletter Commission and at Key West, although he carefully stated the circumstances in both cases, thereby leaving the alleged approval in doubt.[59] When Denfeld repeated his claim a month later (May 19) before a House Appropriations subcommittee,[60] Spaatz denied that construction of the carrier had ever been approved by the Joint Chiefs.[61] Denfeld promptly took the matter up with the JCS, making a formal request for approval of the carrier. The vote was three to one in favor of construction, with Vandenberg, who had now replaced Spaatz, opposing it. Although the subject had obviously been taken up before the JCS because Congress wanted JCS views, Denfeld reported to Congress that Vandenberg's negative vote was based on a procedural point, not on the substance of his judgment of the carrier. According to Denfeld, Vandenberg objected to having the Joint Chiefs pass on an individual item in one service's budget without going over the budgets of all three services in detail.[62] Vandenberg's rejoinder to Denfeld's account apparently came in a letter to the Senate Armed Services Committee which was never published,[63] perhaps because Vandenberg's vote on the carrier was quite rightly regarded in Congress as an indication of his disapproval of the proposed ship.

The confusion over this JCS vote did not end here. Seventeen months later, when its context had been forgotten, General Bradley was to claim with reference to his own vote of approval:

This apparent agreement by me at that time was based upon my understanding that it had been approved by those in authority and I accepted it as a fait accompli. Therefore, I was merely noting, in effect, a decision that had already been made by higher authority.[64]

Bradley's statement is a puzzling one. The very reason Denfeld had made a formal presentation of the carrier proposal to the JCS at that time was in order to correct the ambiguity of the action taken by the Joint Chiefs at Key West concerning the carrier. That action Spaatz had thrown into question on the grounds that at Key West the Joint Chiefs had only been asked to ratify a decision already made by higher authority, and hence had not considered the carrier on its merits. Whether Bradley actually had some curious reservation in mind, or even announced, at the JCS meeting of May 28, 1948, or whether his recollection of that meeting seventeen months later was inaccurate, is unknown. One may, however, guess that Bradley still believed, as he had at Key West, that the President had approved construction.

SUMMARY OF FACTORS AFFECTING THE NAVY POSITION IN JUNE 1948

1. In a test of political strength between the Air Force and the Navy over air-power roles as they were affected by the fiscal 1949 budget, the Air Force demonstrated that it had substantially stronger political support than the Navy both in Congress (particularly in the House) and out of it. Active support of the Air Force had been further strengthened by the growing pressure for more armed strength for less money, or, as a later administration said, "a bigger bang for a buck."

2. Despite efforts to end the rift over air power, the Navy and the Air Force were further apart at the end of June than they had been at the first of the year.

3. Nevertheless, the aviation dispute was not a direct, head-on encounter, for the direct victim of the 70-group program was UMT, not naval aviation. The naval air arm had enjoyed the same advantage accorded Air Force aviation of being considered first in the defense appropriations proceedings that followed the March 1948 crisis.

4. The Air Force enjoyed a distinct advantage over the Navy in its Congressional, public, and even executive branch relations because of the outspoken protagonism of its civilian and military chiefs. Because Sullivan and Denfeld were committed without substantial reservation to the program of the Secretary of Defense, their participation in the dispute

with the Air Force was limited. But Symington and Spaatz were effective and more highly independent spokesmen for Air Force claims. Without their constantly reiterated demands for the 70-group Air Force program Congress might have been hesitant to support it.

In contrast, there were no major spokesmen for the unmodified Navy viewpoint, and it found public expression only in two bootlegged documents written by Nimitz and Gallery, one of which was repudiated by the Secretary of the Navy, and neither of which was publicized in a favorable light.

5. There was some reason to believe that the Army high command, as well as the Air Force, was hoping for a cut in the Navy.[65]

6. The actions of the Joint Chiefs of Staff had, if anything, aggravated inter-service irritations, for their own deliberations had been a source of contention and misunderstanding, and had been used for partisan advantage. This was almost inevitable. The JCS was a political body with political stature, settling or recommending settlement of non-military issues of public policy; it was also a professional military organ protected by military secrecy and concerned with matters requiring only professional military judgment. And finally, its three members were also chiefs of their respective and competitive services. The JCS was only partly visible; and that part could give a misleading impression of the whole, as the dispute over JCS approval of the flush-deck carrier had repeatedly shown.

7. Despite the emerging political strength of the Air Force in its dispute with the Navy, the fiscal 1949 budget, while it was a qualified victory for the Air Force, was not a defeat for the Navy. Even the Army, although it did not get its UMT program, came off with selective service. Indeed, the fiscal 1949 budget was indecisive with respect to all three services, for by a combination of design and circumstances it postponed the most important budget issues. The circumstance of its being the first increment in a rearmament program left the larger expenditures, and hence the tougher decisions, to later years. The rising costs of foreign aid, and the high priority of foreign aid in the Administration's program, was another circumstance which promised greater stress for the program's later years. And by design, while Congress had recognized the long-range implications of the higher armed forces levels being proposed, it committed itself to as little of the long-range program as was possible. For instance, it passed selective service, but not UMT; and it apportioned funds for the first year's increment of a five-year, 70-group Air Force program, and for the first year of construction on a flush-deck carrier. The real pinch would come, as the Director of the Bureau of the Budget had concluded, when the costs of the new rearmament program had risen over $15 billion, as it would within three years. The President was well aware of this problem, and it undoubtedly influenced him in his avoidance of a clear decision on the defense budget program. At a defense budget meeting on May 7, as Forrestal reported it,

he pointed out that the very people in Congress who would now vote for heavy Air appropriations are those who a year from now would deny anything to the Armed Forces, and that if we permit the military budget to rise to proportions that cut too deeply into the civilian economy, the ones that will suffer in the long run will be the Armed Services.[66]

Hence, for the Navy in June 1948, its relatively satisfactory budget for the coming fiscal year offered only temporary comfort, for greater budget squeezes seemed unavoidable in the future.

8. The President's reservations on the budget, that is, his initial ceiling of $1.5 billion for expansion short of mobilization, and his decision not to spend all he requested, marked a break with Forrestal. This divergence, though slow to reach a climax, was the beginning of the split which eventually caused, in large part, Truman's request for Forrestal's resignation. Forrestal's successor was an enthusiastic supporter of the President's views on the problems of the military budget.

9. The two rather incongruous rivals, the flush-deck carrier and the 70-group Air Force, had received somewhat comparable treatment in Congress. Substantive legislation authorizing them had, in each case, been defeated; but appropriations for their first-year costs had, in each case again, been approved.[67] However, these were only superficial similarities, as the subsequent legislative history of the two weapons programs will indicate, for while the carrier and the 70 groups occupied rather comparable positions as symbols of their respective service's

aspirations, those aspirations were quite different. The Air Force sought its goal through Congressional authorization, while the Navy preferred to build its carrier under its general ship-tonnage authorizations rather than run the gamut of possible attacks on specific authorization in Congress. The 70 groups symbolized the expansive aspirations of the Air Force; while the flush-deck carrier, which the Navy was *authorized* to build anyway, provided it could get the necessary appropriations, symbolized the Navy's determination to remain autonomous in the development of weapons for the maximum exploitation of seapower. Both services wanted to change; but the Navy at this point did not want to open up public discussion of the long-run strategic implications of the carrier.

10. Forrestal and Truman, or at least Forrestal and Webb, had basically different views about the relationship of budgets to integrated organization and strategic plans. While Forrestal wanted a settlement of the roles and missions controversy, the elimination of duplication, and the development of a common strategic plan for all the services, he was willing to construct his defense budgets on the basis of combined strategic plans and existing administrative arrangements until such time as it would be possible to base them on integrated administrative and strategic plans. Webb, on the other hand, seemingly wanted to allow the military only those funds which he thought would probably be sufficient under an integrated budget. If it could be assumed that integrated planning and administration were forthcoming in the Defense Department, that budget pressures would encourage their development, and that the costs of an integrated budget could be anticipated and would total less than the sum of the individual budgets, Webb's view about the relationship of defense budgets to strategic planning and administration was eminently sound. But if any one of these assumptions did not work out, national security would face incalculable risks. Forrestal's approach sought to minimize the possibility of at least that kind of risk, but it offered little incentive to the services to integrate their functions and plans.

Which view did Truman take? If anything can be inferred from the account of the 1948 supplementary budget, he stood somewhere in between, for he began with a low figure for the supplement, but was persuaded that considerably more than that should be spent. As we shall observe below, Forrestal's successor did not share his cautious view about the relationship of strategic planning to budget-making, but was convinced he could produce a more efficient military establishment through budget pressures.

II. THE DEVELOPMENT OF THE FISCAL 1950 BUDGET AND OF THE AVIATION FEUD UNTIL THE CANCELLATION OF THE FLUSH-DECK CARRIER

THE EXECUTIVE BUDGET

The fiscal 1950 military budget was developed under a $14.4 billion ceiling imposed by the President.[68] At Forrestal's request, the Joint Chiefs had in June 1948 agreed to divide the sum among themselves,[69] but instead, they ended up dumping their aggregate estimates, totaling $30 billion, in Forrestal's lap.[70] Perhaps one reason why the Joint Chiefs were so reluctant to cut their basic post-war programs was the fear that such action might cast doubt on the validity of their original estimates and hence of any of their estimates. When they finally did cut their requests it was pointed out in justification by Admiral Radford that the cuts were based upon "unified concepts," and he implied that without these concepts reductions would not have been possible.[71] Whether all members of the JCS would have subscribed to this explanation is not known; exactly what the "unified concepts" were was left unstated.

Forrestal anticipated the failure of the Joint Chiefs to reduce their budgetary requirements and therefore had tried to set up his own budget committee, staffing it with officers of his choosing. But the JCS balked, and then deputized instead a committee, known as the Mc-Narney Board, to act in their behalf.[72] The Mc-Narney Board brought the total budget down to $23.6 billion, but could get no further.[73] Forrestal finally persuaded the Joint Chiefs to produce an "intermediate" program midway between this figure and the President's $14.4 billion ceiling. The total figure they arrived at was $16.9 billion—lower than they expected; unlike most budgetary compromises, it did not merely "split the difference." It was sent to the President on December 1. They had made clear in the course of the negotiations of November 1948 that in their estimate the President's ceiling of $14.4 billion would only allow the mounting of an air counter-attack from Great Britain, and would support nothing more. Nevertheless, when a presentation of the "intermediate" budget was made to the President on December 9, Truman indicated his unwillingness to accept any increase in the ceiling which he had imposed.[74] As a body, the Joint Chiefs would not agree to the lower figure. But Webb, the Director of the Bureau of the Budget, was able to undermine this failure to accept the President's ceiling. He met for a half day with each of the Chiefs, presenting to him directly the entire military budget (based on the President's ceiling), its relationship to the total budget, and to the budget's policy assumptions. Unwilling to question those assumptions, each Chief was unable to suggest a better course, and conceded that the $14.4 billion defense budget should be presented to the President.

Forrestal, following the logic of the gamble on the only strategic plan which the armed services believed themselves capable of executing under the President's budget ceiling, turned to a concentration on air power. On December 20 he made a desperate appeal to the President for $700 million more for long-range bomber groups. He was unsuccessful.[75] But his effort demonstrated how much his orientation had changed from what would be expected of a Secretary of the Navy to a sense of responsibility for all the roles of the military establishment.

It is noteworthy that while the fiscal 1950 budget was being planned a new burden was imposed upon the Air Force by the Berlin airlift, which started in July 1948, began to taper off in August 1949, and ended on October 1, 1949. Needless to say, the airlift taxed the freight-carrying capacity of the Air Force, rapidly aged its cargo aircraft, and incurred considerable expense for the Air Force. All of these factors could have been used to support increased appropriations for the Air Force, but little effort was made to do so.

The airlift was a major achievement in air power, though not simply U. S. Air Force air power, for approximately 25 per cent of the payload was carried by the Navy, and the RAF was an active participant also. It was studied carefully in the Air Force, but apparently its impact on the public was greater than its impact on that service, and it had remarkably little effect upon any aspect of the aviation dispute between the Navy and the Air Force. In a gesture of deference which was quite appropriate, though hardly characteristic, the Air Force left publicity for the airlift to the State Department.

Why did the Air Force thus fail fully to exploit the public relations value of the notable achievement of air power in the Berlin airlift? And why did the extraordinary and unexpected experience of the airlift have so little effect upon the developing dispute over roles and missions? Any answers to these questions must be wholly speculative, but some seem possible. The airlift was a freight-carrying operation which served to demonstrate the importance of air transport. But the Air Force has been paring its transport facilities to a minimum in order to maximize its strategic bombing forces. Supporters of strategic air power, the predominant strategic doctrine in the Air Force, might have viewed the airlift as a potential threat to the primary mission of the Air Force, and feared that airlift publicity would only give substance to the charges which had often been voiced in Army circles that the Air Force was neglecting its duty to provide air transport for Army troops. This answer to the first question suggests an answer to the second. Since the airlift was more relevant to Air Force–Army relations than to Air Force–Navy relations, and since the latter were the ones which were currently raising the inter-service issue of roles and missions, the airlift had no direct relationship to the aviation controversy then developing. Moreover, as has been indicated, boasting about the airlift could have been shared by the British

and even the Navy. Sharing of aviation responsibilities was not what the Air Force was trying to enlarge. It may be added that jurisdictional conflicts have a habit of shifting: in later years, when the Navy was happily building super carriers, atomic submarines, and Polaris missiles, it was the Army which considered itself the primary victim of Air Force expansionism.

The importance of the President's decision not to allow any increase in the defense budget ceiling would be difficult to overestimate. Certainly this was not the first budget ceiling to which Truman had held firm. But it was the first one to follow the development of "unified concepts," and, hence, the first from which could be extrapolated some over-all strategic implications. The Joint Chiefs had related strategic planning to the budget in only a rudimentary way. They had not established strategic concepts that could be fulfilled under any of the three alternative totals for the defense budget (approximately $23, $17, and $14 billion), but had only agreed upon what force levels could be supported by each total. From these they estimated the strategic capabilities of their forces.

This did not mean, for instance, that in order to come within the minimum budget to which the President held them, the Joint Chiefs conceived of a military establishment overwhelmingly concentrated upon air power, since in their judgment the minimum budget would only support an air strike on the Soviet Union based upon the British Isles. Rather, it meant that the three services were scaled down to the minimum budget on a roughly equal basis; it was then concluded that the forces thus provided for would be capable merely of mounting the air attack from Britain.[76]

For the services themselves the equalized tripartite cutting of the pie meant that their chief enemy was the Budget Bureau; soon, however, the successful pressures for "more than a third" created service enmities of even greater intensity. For in the long run, in the face of Congressional and public interest in defense policy, it was inevitable that the forces and weapons policies of the military establishment would be examined in the light of strategic needs—as, indeed, Forrestal foresaw.[77] When, in December 1948, the President set his budget ceiling for defense at $14.4 billion, and thereby restricted the military to a strategic capability of air retaliation, only the strategic bombing function of the Air Force was provided with an ultimate advantage over the major functions of the other two services in that examination. The limited advantage which the Air Force and its strategic bombing function enjoyed over the Navy and its aviation at the hands of Congress and the Chief Executive during 1949 was entirely justified by the analysis of the Joint Chiefs of Staff, given the budget ceiling established by the President.

On November 30 the Army had announced a cut in its draft quota for January 1, attributing it to the expected $15 billion budget for the next year, and pointing out that this would mean that by mid-1949 Army strength would be only 667,000 instead of the authorized 900,000. The announcement led Hanson Baldwin to observe in his column in the *New York Times*: "If the $14,400,000,000 ceiling is approved none of the services will be able to reach their July 1, 1949, goals, either in manpower, divisions, groups, or ships."[78] The Army announcement was widely thought to be an effort by the Army to bring public pressure on its side in the budget deliberations, although it had been perhaps the most cooperative of the three services in the budget discussions.[79] The President immediately issued instructions to the services cautioning them against public disclosure of fiscal matters prior to presentation of the budget, and indicating that the services were expected to support the President's budget at all times.

Two days before the President's annual budget message to Congress, Symington's first annual report for the Air Force was made public. Citing the backing of the Finletter Commission and the Brewster Board, it resumed the call for a 70-group Air Force.[80]

The President's budget message disclosed a further reduction in the defense budget of $200 million. He recommended $14.2 billion for the military establishment, excluding the stockpiling sums. This meant a further slight increase in Army manpower, and a slight decrease in Air Force and Navy personnel from existing strengths. The expansion begun the previous spring was over, and air power was in fact to decrease. The expansion towards a 70-air group program, which by January had reached 59, would be cut to 48 groups.[81] Navy ships in commission would be cut slightly, and most sharply in attack carriers. The procurement of aircraft would be cut a third, and the number of operating aircraft would be similarly reduced.[82]

THE FEUD OVER AIR ROLES FROM JUNE THROUGH DECEMBER 1948

Through the summer of 1948, with the 70-group authorization still pending in the Senate, Symington continued his strong advocacy of Air Force expansion in numerous public speeches. One of them, delivered on the West Coast on July 18, almost led to a break with Forrestal, who had telegraphed changes in the speech to Symington, and regarded the latter's failure to use them as "an act of official disobedience and personal disloyalty."[83] At dinner the next day, Symington explained his action, and Forrestal said he was satisfied with the explanation.[84] What Symington said or why Forrestal changed his mind is unknown. The larger issue of the rival publicity policies of the three services which stood behind this incident was taken up thereafter by Forrestal in a meeting with the three service Secretaries. But the four Secretaries merely agreed that the problem existed.

Air Force Day was September 18—marking the first anniversary of the new service. The Air Force made the most of it, carefully staging massed flights of B-29's over some of the major American cities, single flights of five B-36's over 103 separate cities in the United States, and a wide variety of other aircraft exhibitions. The press release for the B-36 flights described that craft as follows:

The design gross weight of the B-36 is 278,000 pounds. It is 163 feet long, 230 feet wide, and 46 feet, 7 inches high—the approximate height of a four-story building. The plane carries a crew of 15, including four relief personnel. It was designed to carry 10,000 pounds of bombs 10,000 miles, and can carry up to 72,000 pounds of bombs shorter distances.

In tests during the summer, a B-36 carried a sizeable "useful" load of bombs approximately 8,000 miles, and later took off on a flight at a gross weight exceeding 300,000 pounds and flew approximately 6,000 miles at an average air speed of more than 300 miles an hour.[85]

During the course of the celebration, several new aircraft models were made public for the first time.[86] Following up the festivities, the Air Force Association's national convention endorsed a severe attack on naval aviation, and called for unified air power.[87]

The Newport Conference

On September 20, two days after Air Force Day, Forrestal took his service chiefs once again into seclusion, this time to the Naval War College at Newport, R. I., for three days, to work out the old problem of roles and missions.[88] At Key West the functions of the services had been divided (at least to some extent), but weapons had not been. And since a single weapon (notably, aircraft) could be used for the accomplishment of more than one mission, the old conflict over the relationship of weapons and forces to missions remained unsolved. Like the Functions Paper agreed to at Key West, a "treaty" was signed at Newport. It set forth the obligation of one service to take into account, in planning to fulfill its function, the forces of the other services:

. . . The service having the primary function must determine the requirements, but in determining these requirements must take into account the contributions which may be made by forces from other services.

On the other hand,

Subject to control by higher authority, each service, in the fields of its primary missions, must have exclusive responsibility for programming and planning, and the necessary authority [to do so].[89]

What seemed to be meant by the agreement was that the material and force requirements of a service could not be questioned in the JCS, but that its plan for providing the necessary material and forces could be challenged by raising the question of who should provide them. Alternately, the agreement could be interpreted to mean that the service in charge of a role (e.g., strategic bombing) should utilize the resources of others even though their role was different (i.e., Navy bombers).

Following the conference, the Defense Department issued a release to the press which included statements of Forrestal, Bradley, Denfeld, and Vandenberg. Denfeld stated:

The words of our understanding are clear and to my mind unequivocal. They will serve if they are interpreted properly—in the spirit of "all for one and one for all." Any agreement will work only if the personnel of each service work together with sympathy and understanding and really desire to make it work.[90]

Denfeld's statement, typical of his effort to maintain harmony, was optimistic because the whole concept developed at Newport begged the question. The procedure it envisaged assumed that whenever a service's material and force plans were challenged, the material and force programs of the other two services would already be fixed. For instance, theoretically under the Newport understanding, the Navy could challenge Air Force material programming by saying: "You don't need to build the two hundred medium bombers which you undisputedly require, for we already have one hundred bombers which, taking off from carriers now in operation, could do the work of seventy-five of yours. Therefore, you will only need one hundred and twenty-five medium bombers." But as a matter of fact, at the same time the Air Force would be entering a cross-claim to perform the functions of the Navy bombers, and concluding that the Navy did not need to keep any of its fleet carriers in commission. Hence, the old controversy remained—which service should perform functions which both apparently could do. To be sure, as Denfeld stated after the Newport Conference, "Strategic Air Warfare is a primary responsibility of the Air Force";[91] but Navy facilities were to have some part in meeting that responsibility.

The Presidential campaign that fall was fought largely on domestic issues, and the special support of the Air Force given by isolationist-interventionist elements in the two major parties was never made very explicit. But the very fact that foreign affairs were slighted boded ill for national defense, for the sense of crisis which had developed in the spring of 1948, and had helped to reverse the downward trend of American military strength, had evaporated rapidly during the summer. With public attention drawn by the campaign to domestic issues, public indifference to national preparedness was encouraged.

Moreover, the Administration, under the leadership of the Secretary of State, General George C. Marshall, was preoccupied with a foreign aid program for Europe. Marshall was so alarmed at the predicament of Europe that, although he undoubtedly did not object to

Forrestal's efforts to expand the military establishment, throughout 1948 he ignored Forrestal's attempts to get him to throw the weight of his prestige behind the military expansion program.[92]

As the campaign entered its last month, and the stresses from budget-making within the defense establishment gradually increased, the air power dispute arose in another forum.

The Eberstadt Task Force Incident

The Hoover Commission, which was concerned with the reorganization of the executive branch of the government, had undertaken a "task force" study of the military establishment, holding hearings in October 1948. Consideration was given to a proposal for the absorption of naval aviation into the Air Force, made by Secretary of the Army Kenneth C. Royall. Although these proceedings were secret, the Royall proposal leaked out. On October 18, during the course of its presentation to the task force, John Nicholas Brown, the Assistant Secretary of the Navy for Air, and Vice Admiral Radford, Deputy Chief of Naval Operations, in attempting to deal with this issue, apparently attacked the capability of the Air Force to perform its own primary function. Radford gave his views on the need for a flush-deck carrier capable of launching aircraft carrying atomic bombs. Then, anticipating his testimony before the House Armed Services Committee a year later, he evidently criticized the B-36, charging that it was too big and slow to penetrate Soviet defenses, and even insisting that the Air Force did not have bombers which could reach targets in Russia.[93]

Forrestal, but not the press, learned of Brown's and Radford's testimony. Hoping to restrain the discussion, he drafted a letter to Sullivan on October 29, which stated that it was appropriate for one service to testify before a Congressional or other committee in defense of its competence to perform its own mission, but that it was not appropriate to extend that defense into an attack upon the competence of another service to perform its mission. Specifically, he wrote, in defending its own aviation the Navy should not attack "the capabilities of the bomber aircraft of the Air Force to penetrate enemy territory."[94] The letter was never sent. Two days later, at the climax of the political campaign, on October 31, Admiral Gallery delivered a widely reported speech in which he continued in the role which he had assumed the previous April, that of a Navy antagonist of the Air Force in the dispute over air power.[95] The following day Forrestal ordered the services to adjudicate their differences over proposed legislation in his office and not carry them to Congress. And on November 8 he sent a memorandum to the three service Secretaries which applied the point of his undelivered letter to Sullivan to all three services. They should, it indicated, submit to him, prior to delivery, all presentations or reports intended for an agency outside the military establishment which contained criticism of another service. And they should exercise great caution when, under questioning before an outside agency, they were asked to criticize a sister service.[96]

With this memorandum to back him, Symington charged in a letter to Ferdinand Eberstadt, chairman of the Hoover Commission Task Force, that because Navy officers had disobeyed the orders of the Secretary of Defense (he did not indicate that the order came after its violation) the country's security was put to great risk. Symington asserted that "a large part" of the testimony of Brown and Radford on October 18 was "an unwarranted attack on the Air Force." It was, Secretary Symington insisted,

based on an unsupported challenge of the ability of the Air Force to accomplish its primary mission.

The Air Force denies categorically the validity of the challenge and the propriety of such a presentation before your body. Common sense and justice would dictate that you give the Air Force an opportunity to present our answer to the serious charges against it. I do not request this at this time, because it is my understanding that military functions—roles and missions—do not come within the purview of your committee and the Air Force does not consider it in the public interest to become party to a public brawl.

Dealing in more general terms with the conduct of the Navy in its feud with the Air Force, Symington wrote:

Action must be taken to resolve the present conflict resulting from the Navy's continuous attacks, even if the solution means consolidation. In our opinion, unless somebody can stop these attacks from regular Navy officers, made directly against the instructions of the Secretary of Defense, efficient functioning of the military establishment is impossible; therefore, the security of our country is seriously jeopardized.[97]

The whole of the Symington-Eberstadt correspondence leaked to the press. It was a highly advantageous publicity break for the Air Force, particularly since no adequate account of the Navy presentation to the Eberstadt group ever was published, and most of what the public learned of it came from Symington's bitter attack.

Forrestal promised to investigate the one-sided leak. The Air Force officially denied that it had been the culprit, and nothing further was heard of the incident in public.[98]

A more permanent result, however, was the beginning of an attempt at objective inter-service evaluation of weapons in the defense establishment. In October Forrestal put to the JCS two questions raised by the latest episode in the aviation controversy which were possibly capable of objective determination. They were:

First, what are the chances of successful delivery [of atomic bombs by aircraft]? Second, assuming successful delivery, what would be the effect on the enemy war effort in physical damage and in psychological effect on the will to wage war?

Two committees were established to deal with these questions, and apparently one question was assigned to each of them. The first, which was set up by Forrestal to report directly to him, was called the Weapons Systems Evaluation Group. The proper name of the second, which was a JCS committee, was never made public; it was called the Harmon Board after its senior member.[99]

Objective evaluation (even if "objective" evaluation was actually possible) did not remove friction; and another circumstance at the same time contributed to Navy–Air Force controversy. The *Reader's Digest,* a popular monthly with a circulation in the United States of over six million, began a series of four articles on the Navy, by William Bradford Huie, which were wholly critical of naval aviation and often scurrilous in tone. It was widely believed within the Navy that the author was paid by the Air Force to write these articles. While this belief was without supporting evidence, apparently Huie had the help of some high-ranking Air Force officers in preparing his account.[100]

CONGRESSIONAL AVIATION POLICY (JANUARY TO MAY 1949)

If the President's new budget boded ill for the Air Force, the legislative program introduced by Congressional leaders on the opening of the new Congress was cause for optimism. Carl Vinson and Millard Tydings, chairmen respectively of the House and Senate Armed Services Committees, had announced, shortly after the election in November had assured their party control of Congress, that they approved enactment of authorization for a 70-group Air Force before the appropriation bills for fiscal 1950 were passed. On the first day of the new session Vinson introduced bills which authorized a 70-group Air Force and an 837,000-man Army, and which prohibited the Navy from building ships of over 45,000 tons without Congressional authorization, a provision obviously aimed at the 65,000-ton flush-deck carrier. Tydings followed suit with a 70-group authorization bill in the Senate a few days later.[101] Although he had tried unsuccessfully in the previous session of Congress to gain Congressional authorization for the 70-group Air Force, Vinson was all the more determined to accomplish it now, for in it he saw a way to prevent the President's withholding money appropriated for Air Force expansion, as had been done with $197,845,000 of the $1.5 billion appropriated for Air Force procurement the previous June.[102] (Vinson had used this strategem on behalf of the Navy in 1945.)

The Senior Officers Board of the Air Force had convened in late December to consider in closed sessions the procurement program of the Air Force in the light of (1) the existing situation in aircraft development in the Air Force, particularly the greatly improved performance of the B-36, and (2) the President's stand on the budget. Anticipating the severe cuts in existing and future force strength which the President was determined to make, the Board decided to concentrate the limited resources of the Air Force upon strategic bombing aircraft (i.e., long-range and heavy bombers), in order to make sure that the Air Force could at least fulfill what they regarded as its first responsibility, retaliatory capability. It recommended to the Secretary of the Air Force on January 6 that the procurement of medium bombers (B-45, RB-49), troop transports (C-125), and a new version of the F-86 jet fighter (F-93) be cut back and the money thus saved transferred to purchasing B-36's and B-50's.

Under a provision of the 70-group appropriation act of the previous year, which had provided these funds, purchase of additional aircraft required the approval of the Secretary of Defense and the President. Anxious to have production stopped as soon as possible on items planned for cancellation, the Air Force announced in the charged atmosphere of the day following the President's budget message that there would be a "readjustment of presently available Air Force procurement funds in line with the President's budget message, and to achieve a more effective Air Force in being with minimum delay."[103] The readjustment included the purchase of additional B-36's and the modification of B-36's and B-50's already under contract. While the announcement was accurate so far as it went, no mention was made of the fact that the additional number of B-36's had not yet been approved.[104] Two weeks passed before an official request for the procurement of 39 additional B-36's was submitted to Forrestal. He forwarded it in turn to the Research and Development Board, the Munitions Board, and the Joint Chiefs of Staff, according to established procedure. None of them objected. Before forwarding it to the President, he also consulted Dr. Karl Compton and General Eisenhower, whose continuing connection with the military establishment, particularly since December 1948, had been given more formal recognition with his appointment as principal military adviser to Forrestal on February 19.[105] Presidential approval did not come until April 8, the final delay being caused by the replacement of Forrestal by Johnson as Secretary of Defense.[106]

Vinson, pressing hard for appropriations, as well as authorization for a 70-group program, seized upon the highly vulnerable UMT proposals in the President's program as a source for funds. His plan was to transfer the $800 million requested for UMT to the Air Force for use in achieving the 70 groups.[107] The Vinson Plan was first disclosed on January 28 in House Armed Services Committee hearings on his Army and Air Force authorization bill. While Vinson's proposal was under consideration in the Appropriations Committee, the House gave the same overwhelming approval to

his authorization bill for a 70-group Air Force and an 837,000-man Army that the bill for the supplementary aircraft appropriation containing the initial funds for the 70-group program had received the previous spring.[108]

On March 30, in a long statement to the House Appropriations Committee, Vinson presented his own defense budget, prepared by the Armed Services Committee staff. It included not only the $800 million for the Air Force above what the President had requested but also lesser increases for the Army and Navy as well. Vinson sought an additional $245 million for the Army and $545 million for the Navy, to be used primarily for carriers and aircraft. The total was $16.364 billion, while the President's estimate was $14.765 billion.[109] Although Vinson had become a strong advocate of the Air Force program, he thus continued to support a general increase in the defense budget. But the Appropriations Committee reported a bill on April 9 which reduced the President's requests for the Army and Navy $214 million and $12 million, respectively, while it increased the Air Force appropriation to within $14 million of the $800 million asked by Vinson. Four days later the House passed the bill unamended.[110]

Thus, by mid-April the Air Force had won a decisive victory in the House, its 70-group program having been approved both in statutory authorization and in appropriations. The Senate was not to act upon the authorization bill until late August. In the meantime, the Army and Navy had to plan for even more severe limitations on their activities than they had the previous January. The Chief of Naval Operations had told the House Appropriations Committee in February that the budget for the next fiscal year provided such a low rate of naval aircraft procurement that "unless corrected in the future, our combat readiness will decrease at an accelerated rate." The only reason he had accepted it, he indicated, was "in order to avoid further unacceptable reductions in our operating ships."[111] But now the Navy would have to get along on even less.

THE AVIATION FEUD FROM JANUARY TO MAY 1949

Air Force Testimony before Congress

At the opening of the new session of Congress in January, the announced intention of Vinson and Tydings, the chairmen of the two Armed Services Committees, was to win a stronger commitment from Congress for the 70-group Air Force than had been gained in the previous session. Air Force spokesmen now needed only to encourage their supporters in Congress. Symington's Annual Report, published two days before the President's budget message, was clearly designed to persuade the new Congress to act in behalf of Air Force expansion. In their appearances before Congressional committees during the three months that followed, Symington and Vandenberg were usually led by sympathetic questions into reiteration of their 70-group Air Force program.[112]

Air Force Publicity vs. Navy Publicity

The public relations activities of the Air Force and the Navy were in obvious competition during these months. In mid-February the Air Force held a weapons exhibition at Andrews Field, Maryland, and the Navy conducted some exercises in the Caribbean later in the month, to which it invited government officials and the press. Both received moderate publicity, and undoubtedly had their effect within the government. The naval exercises included amphibious landings, a tactic which was believed by many important officials both within and outside of the Defense Department to be obsolete.

But the Air Force won an overwhelming public relations victory over the Navy in March 1949, with a series of three announcements. With the upturn in the Air Force evaluation of the B-36, officially recognized by the Senior Officers' Board at the beginning of the year, Air Force spokesmen began to talk with greater confidence of that weapon, and of intercontinental bombing.[113] The B-36 was now greatly exceeding earlier, though not original, expectations. And at the same time a project accelerated during the days of discouragement over the B-36, had reached fruition. In-flight refueling of the shorter range B-50, a substantially modernized version of the B-29, had been given high priority in 1948 as an alternative way of achieving intercontinental range in a bomber.

On March 1 a B-50 using the new in-flight refueling technique completed a non-stop flight around the world. Press coverage for the feat was elaborately organized by the Air Force, and was correspondingly extensive. Reaction on Capitol Hill, especially in the Senate Armed Services Committee, was highly favorable. The flight was well-timed to influence both houses of Congress favorably in their consideration of both the 70-group authorization bills and Air Force appropriations; and it seems to have had a significant effect. The flight was also well-timed in relation to the Navy's fleet exercises in the Caribbean, which were just ending, for it pushed the reports of those exercises completely out of the headlines and columns of the press.

The Air Force followed up its B-50 publicity coup a few days later with an announcement that a B-36 had flown 9,600 miles non-stop, carrying a load equivalent to an atom bomb 5,000 miles. Then, on March 14, the press carried a leaked account of a spectacular Air Force presentation to the Joint Chiefs of Staff which consisted of the earmarking of seventy strategic targets in the Soviet Union within range of B-36's on non-stop return flights from the North American continent.[114] On April 20, the presentation was repeated for the benefit of President Truman.[115]

Carl Vinson, the Chairman of the House Armed Services Committee, learning of the leak about the Air Force target program before its publication, had written Symington requesting an investigation and explanation of the leak. Symington reported in response that the leaks had not been officially inspired. Fearing that such *sub rosa* public relations activities might continue, Vinson tried to discourage them. On April 5 the House Armed Services Committee approved unanimously a statement prepared by its Chairman which was designed to serve as a warning:

The Armed Services Committee wants it clearly understood that if persons in the armed services or in their employ continue to pass statements to the press which are calculated to deprecate the activities of a sister service, and which, at the same time, jeopardize the national security, the committee will step in with a full-scale investigation.[116]

During the same four-month period in which these events were occurring, it should be remembered, William Bradford Huie's attacks on the Navy continued to be published in the *Reader's Digest*—in January, March, and

April. The major reply to these articles came from Republican Congressman James E. Van Zandt on the floor of the House.[117] Following its exercises in the Caribbean, the Navy had attempted to counter Air Force publicity by announcing that its Banshee fighters, used as carrier-based aircraft during the recent Caribbean exercises, could carry an atom bomb.

The Army was also having trouble with the Air Force and its rising popularity. Although it was not involved in the Air Force–naval aviation controversy and although it still had substantial differences with the Navy about the organization of the military establishment, the recurrent Air Force theory that air power alone could supply all needs of national defense was naturally sharply rejected by the Army. Indeed, the Army could look with sympathy, if not envy, upon the Marine Corps with its generous allotment of close-support tactical air power. The Army and the Navy had much in common in their views on tactical air power.

In February 1949, General Bradley had become so alarmed over the uncritical acceptance by the public of the claims of Air Force extremists that he undertook to explain in a series of public speeches the continuing importance of the Army in modern warfare.[118]

Louis A. Johnson Replaces James Forrestal as Secretary of Defense

On March 3, 1949, the White House issued a press release containing James Forrestal's letter of resignation as Secretary of Defense and a letter of acceptance from President Truman which praised and thanked Forrestal for his services. It also announced that his successor would be Louis A. Johnson.

Truman and Forrestal had discussed the question of Forrestal's resignation at various times since the beginning of January, and Forrestal had known since the end of January that Johnson would be, or was likely to be, his successor. Forrestal himself was torn between a desire to leave and a desire to complete his job; and he seems to have fluctuated in his judgments on the definitiveness of the President's decision both on his successor and on the date of his own resignation. (Forrestal's own exhaustion, brought on primarily by his overwork during the period discussed above, was probably a major factor in his fluctuating judgments on these matters.) The date of May 1 was at least tentatively agreed to at one point; later, the date of April 1 was fixed; and, in the end, the date was advanced at Forrestal's request and Johnson took the oath of office on March 28.[119]

There have been various explanations of these events. Forrestal took no part in the 1948 campaign because he believed that a Secretary of Defense should stay clear of partisan politics; Johnson had performed valiantly for President Truman as a fund raiser. Furthermore, by 1949 Forrestal was suffering from what one could describe as battle fatigue, and he was no longer as promptly and firmly decisive as he had been. These matters may have been taken into account by Truman. He may also have been affected by the fact that throughout 1948, as we have seen, Forrestal had become more and more at odds with the President over his defense budgets. The significance to national defense policy of Forrestal's departure later proved to lie in this factor more than in any other. As pessimistic as Forrestal had been about the economic risks attendant upon large defense budgets, his departure from the Truman Administration substantially weakened the position within the government of those who advocated a larger military budget.

Louis Johnson, the new Secretary of Defense, was a West Virginia lawyer who had helped to found the American Legion, and became its National Commander in the early thirties. He had served as Assistant Secretary of War from 1937 through July 1940 when he had fought vigorously and effectively for national defense preparations, but was eased out when Stimson became Secretary of War.

In 1948, when the Democratic Presidential campaign was in sore financial straits, Johnson took over the fund-raising tasks for his party with characteristic energy and collected the money needed to run a successful campaign. Johnson's appointment as Secretary of Defense the following spring was widely, but not necessarily correctly, regarded at that time as the payment of a political debt incurred by President Truman in the campaign.[120]

The Public Relations Policy of the National Military Establishment

In March 1949, shortly before his retirement, Forrestal had begun the consolidation of the public information activities of the three services. In June, Johnson told the services to reduce their public information staffs from 473 to 45, and to transfer 285 of surplus staff to the Defense Department public relations staff.[121] Policy was already moving in the same direction as staff. On April 14 Johnson issued his Consolidation Directive No. 1, dealing with public information policy and procedures in the military establishment. Its principal provision centralized security review procedures for the services in his own office, and was widely interpreted as a "gag" order for both active and retired regular officers.

Another indication of the trend in the public relations activities of the services was the announcement by Johnson, following the celebration of Army Day on April 6, that such observances for each service would be abolished in the future.

CANCELLATION OF THE FLUSH-DECK CARRIER

On February 19, 1949, more than a month before Johnson became Secretary of Defense, General Eisenhower, then President of Columbia University, was named principal military adviser to the President and the Secretary of Defense, replacing Admiral Leahy as unofficial chairman of the Joint Chiefs of Staff. The Joint Chiefs immediately became involved in discussions of how the fiscal 1951 budget was to be planned.[122] Planning for the new budget involved, as it had in the past, considerations of over-all strategy. On April 8, the day the President approved the purchase of the 39 B-36's announced in January, and three days after Vinson had warned the services against leaks to the press depreciatory of each other, the Joint Chiefs went to Key West to meet with Eisenhower, who was recuperating from a stomach ailment, in general discussions of service functions and strategy.[123] Johnson joined the group on the 10th, the day after the House Appropriations Committee had approved a defense budget quite favorable to the Air Force. On the 11th, with Johnson present, the flush-deck carrier was discussed, "though not in any great detail."[124]

Appropriations hearings, coupled with the impending laying of the keel of the new carrier on April 15, had raised again the question of the advisibility of its construction. At a press conference on April 12 Johnson was asked about the carrier. He replied that a statement would be made in due course.[125] On the 15th he addressed a letter to Eisenhower, who was still in Key West, with a copy to each member of the JCS, in which he asked for the individual views of the Joint Chiefs on the new carrier. Three days later, the actual date of keel-laying because April 15 was Good Friday, at the conclusion of a conference with the Secretary of the Navy on other matters, Johnson asked Sullivan his opinion about continuing the carrier, but interrupted the conversation before Sullivan could answer by saying that he had another caller waiting. On the following day, the 19th, Sullivan sent him a memorandum covering one phase of the carrier question, and asked for a further chance to state his views in person. This was never given.

Johnson, anxious to act quickly, if action were necessary, in order that money would not be wasted on unnecessary construction, was in touch with the Joint Chiefs individually on a daily basis after the 15th, and conferred several times the following week with President Truman. By Friday, April 22, he had read final drafts of the opinions of all three of the Chiefs of Staff, had shown them to the President, and had obtained his permission to stop construction of the carrier.

The JCS answers were 2 to 1 against construction of the carrier. Admiral Denfeld, according to his later account, "strongly recommended its construction, pointing out in detail its importance to the evolution of carrier aviation and naval warfare."[126] General Vandenberg stated that he thought it would cost closer to $500 million than the $189 million figure estimated by the Navy; and that its main function would be a duplication of the primary role of the Air Force—strategic bombing.[127] Bradley's views have been recounted most thoroughly, and are perhaps also the best statement of General Vandenberg's opinion at this time.

1. The fundamental purpose of the super carrier is included within a primary function of the Air Force.

2. The USSR is not a sea power, nor is it dependent upon the sea for obtaining raw materials.

3. The United States plus the British Empire have a vast preponderance of naval power already.

4. The use of carrier task force planes against land targets should be limited. The present 700-mile capability is sufficient.

5. The use of naval air forces initially in war and as a temporary reinforcement of the Air Force in performing its functions is justifiable, but not for sustained operations against land.

6. The new carrier would involve large expenditures, plus numerous accessories, including various kinds of ships. Bradley concluded that additional aircraft carriers should not be constructed, and that construction of the new flush-deck carrier should be stopped.[128]

Having read these views, Johnson decided that the flush-deck carrier was a duplication of Air Force strategic bombing efforts, and that its construction should therefore be discontinued.[129]

The next morning, Admiral Denfeld as the senior member of the Joint Chiefs, in the absense of Eisenhower, prepared a covering letter for the three opinions and delivered them in person to the Secretary of Defense. In the meantime, Johnson had inquired of Eisenhower at Key West and learned that he was also in favor of cancelling the flush-deck carrier. He had also ascertained that Vinson and Tydings, the chairmen of the House and Senate Armed Services Committee, respectively, approved cancellation.[130] At the moment that Denfeld delivered his papers, Johnson's cancellation announcement, already prepared, was being duplicated for the press. After reading Denfeld's covering letter (he had already read the enclosed opinions), Johnson telephoned the President to inform him that nothing new had developed. He then announced to the press that construction of the new carrier would be stopped "at once." Forty-five minutes after delivering the JCS documents to the Secretary of Defense, Denfeld had in his hand a mimeographed copy of Johnson's cancellation announcement.[131] Sullivan was in Texas at the time. Learning of the press release, he returned to Washington on the same day, and immediately prepared an irate letter of resignation to Johnson, in which he stated the Navy's case against both the wisdom and manner of the carrier's cancellation. The most effective summary of the Navy's developing attitude at that date, it read as follows:

My Dear Mr. Secretary:

On Saturday, April 23, without discussion with the Chief of Naval Operations, without consultation with the Secretary of the Navy, you directed the discontinuance of the construction of the [flush-deck carrier] U.S.S. *United States,* the construction of which had twice been approved by the President.

This carrier has been the subject of intensive study in the Navy Department since it was first proposed early in 1945 by the late Marc A. Mitscher whose combat experience had convinced him of its necessity. In a hearing with the Director of the Budget on December 16, 1947, with approval of the Chief of Naval Operations and the Chief of the Bureau of Ships, I volunteered to surrender $307,000,000 which was the cost to complete the approved construction of other vessels, to insure that funds would be available for the U.S.S. *United States.* Its construction was explicitly approved by the reports of the Armed Service Committees of the Senate and House on June 2, 1948, and June 9, 1948, respectively. In the Naval Appropriation Act for the fiscal year 1949 the appropriation for the first year of construction of the U.S.S. *United States* was approved by the Congress. Again on December 17, 1948, in a conference with the Secretary of Defense and the Director of the Bureau of the Budget, with the approval of the Chief of Naval Operations and the Chief of the Bureau of Ships, I abandoned construction of other vessels in the amount of $57,000,000 to insure the continuance of the carrier and other vessels. Additional funds for the continuing construction of this vessel in the fiscal year 1950 were included in the budget message which the President sent to the Congress on January 3, 1949, and were included in the National Military Establishment appropriation bill passed by the House on April 13, 1949.

Professional naval men, charged with the task of planning for a Navy adequate to the defense of America believe that the construction of the U.S.S. *United States* is so indispensable to the continuing development of American sea power that they have twice sacrificed other substantial construction because of the carrier's highest naval priority.

On Monday, April 18, while discussing a variety of subjects with you, the question of the continuance of work on the U.S.S. *United States* was raised, and my opinion was asked. I started to give my opinion, but before I had talked more than a minute you advised me that you had another appointment and would discuss this matter with me at a later date. The following day I sent you a very brief memorandum touching on only one phase of the justification of this carrier. In this memorandum I referred to my desire to resume the discussion that had been interrupted the previous day. I heard nothing about this again until Saturday, April 23, when in Corpus Christi, Tex., I was advised by long-distance telephone that you had sent me a memorandum directing the discontinuance of construction.

I am, of course, very deeply disturbed by your action which so far as I know represents the first attempt ever made in this country to prevent the development of a power weapon. The conviction that this will result in a renewed effort to abolish the Marine Corps and to transfer all naval and marine aviation elsewhere adds to my anxiety.

However, even of greater significance is the unprecedented action on the part of a Secretary of Defense in so drastically and arbitrarily changing and restricting the operational plans of an armed service without consultation with that service. The consequences of such a procedure are far-reaching and can be tragic.

In view of the foregoing I am sure you will agree with me that no useful purpose can now be served by my remaining as Secretary of the Navy. I have accordingly submitted my resignation to the President.

I deeply regret the circumstances that lead to my departure from the National Military Establishment at such an interesting and crucial period of its development.

Sincerely yours,

John L. Sullivan.[132]

Sullivan saw the President on Monday. Truman agreed to release the irate letter of resignation to Johnson on Tuesday, and they parted friends, as Sullivan's cordial letter of resignation to Truman attested. Yet the rancor in the Johnson-Sullivan relationship is unmistakable. Johnson's indication of it can be found in the Unification and Strategy hearings, discussed below. How could Sullivan have been so critical of Johnson's leadership of the Defense Department, and yet have found no quarrel with the President? Three possible answers to this question suggest themselves: (1) He might have believed that the cancellation of the carrier was a big enough issue to justify or require his resignation, but not a big enough one to expect intervention in Johnson's policies by the President. Or (2) he could have believed that Truman did not consider himself free to direct Johnson in this matter, either because of political obligations to him or because of the popularity of Johnson's economy program, or (3) because Truman believed in the important values of the economy program. Whichever answer is correct, it would seem that Sullivan, at least, did not hold Truman responsible for all of the policies initiated by Johnson as Secretary of Defense.

The personal act of Sullivan's resignation was admired, but sentiment generally ran the other way. Reaction to the carrier cancellation was mostly favorable. Vinson, who earlier had registered his objection to the carrier, lauded Johnson on the floor of the House for what he termed a courageous act.[133] Press approval was based on the belief that the carrier would have encroached upon the Air Force mission.[134] Within the Navy the carrier cancellation cast an ominous shadow over other incidents, including Consolidation Directive No. 1, centralizing the public relations activities of the services; an Army staff study proposing the transfer of Marine Headquarters to the Department of the Army; and House action on the defense budget, favoring as it did the Air Force.[135]

III. THE B-36 INVESTIGATION—PHASE I: THE PROCUREMENT PROGRAM

AUTHORIZING THE INVESTIGATION OF THE B-36 PROCUREMENT PROGRAM

A month before cancellation of the flush-deck carrier, and only a few days before Forrestal left office, Symington had informed him of Air Force plans to purchase still more B-36's.[136] Throughout April and May press leaks unfavorable to the big bomber continued, many undoubtedly provided by naval officers, but some by Air Force fighter pilots. After the Navy had recovered from the initial shock of the carrier cancellation, a new element was added to the many rumors about the B-36 by the bragging of some Navy flyers that they could shoot it down.[137] As a result the House Armed Services Committee passed a resolution proposing a Navy–Air Force duel to settle the dispute over the capabilities of the B-36.

The Origins of the So-Called Anonymous Document

Cedric Worth was at this time Special Assistant to Under Secretary of the Navy Dan A. Kimball. A former Commander in the Naval Reserve, and a professional writer of some experience, Worth had apparently become an important source of unofficial leaks from those persons in the Navy Department who were conducting a *sub rosa* publicity battle with the Air Force partisans.[138] He had worked for some time as a special assistant to the Assistant Secretary of the Navy for Air prior to his shifting over to Kimball's office; he had several contacts among the leading journalists interested in service affairs; and he seemed to have a knack for collecting information informally from within the Navy.[139]

Worth began to compile rumors about the B-36 and the Air Force in late March or early April. Shortly thereafter Congressman C. B. Deane, Democrat, North Carolina, visited his office after being referred there by the Office of the Chief of Naval Operations. Deane had become disturbed about the rumors he had heard concerning the Air Force.[140] Worth agreed to show Deane a compilation of the material he was collecting when it was finished. Worth had, at the same time, been in touch with Glenn L. Martin, an aircraft manufacturer whose main plant was in Baltimore, where contracts with the Air Force had recently been cut back as a result of the transfer of Air Force funds from lighter aircraft to the B-36. Martin was a source of some of the rumors Worth collected. When Worth had completed his document he had an impressive collection of scandalous charges, all woven cleverly together, with some authentic references to certain classified material and to some public information. The gist of his charges was that the B-36 was a "billion dollar blunder" by the Air Force which remained uncorrected because the Secretary of Defense and the Secretary of the Air Force had a personal financial interest in its continued production; and because political and personal favors were owed to Floyd Odlum, whose company was the manufacturer. This theme was developed in a series of fifty-five specific allegations. Once completed, a copy of the document was first given to Glenn Martin for delivery to Senator Millard Tydings of Maryland, a friend of Martin and Chairman of the Senate Armed Services Committee. About two weeks later, in late April or early May, Worth delivered another copy to Representative Deane in his office. On the same day he gave a copy to Congressman James Van Zandt, a Republican member of the Armed Services Committee. Van Zandt was a known spokesman for the Navy who at the time was carrying on a series of attacks in the House on the author of the anti-Navy articles appearing in the *Reader's Digest.* Congressman Deane showed his copy to Speaker of the House Sam Rayburn, who referred him to Congressman Vinson, chairman of the House Armed Services Committee.[141] Van Zandt, Martin, and others had hoped for an investigation, but neither Vinson nor Tydings would investigate the charges made in the document.[142] Thus blocked in the regular committees, Van Zandt introduced a resolution in the House on May 25 for a select committee to investigate the awarding and cancelling of aircraft contracts since May 8. And the following day, supporting his measure before the House, he stated that ugly and disturbing reports of irregularities in connection with the procurement of B-36 aircraft were being circulated. He did not specifically refer to the Worth document or to the press reports which had begun to appear on the substance of the Worth allegations. Repeating many of these allegations, however, while he emphasized their unproved nature, he insisted that they were sufficiently strong to require investigation.[143] Van Zandt's repetition of these rumors on the floor of the House led to their wider publication and alarmed Air Force officials.

The Investigation Is Forced by Van Zandt

Under House procedure Van Zandt would have been chairman of the select committee originated by passage of his resolution. Congressman Vinson apparently saw in this proposal a challenge to his own position as chairman of the House Armed Services Committee, as well as a potential undermining of the committee itself, and an opportunity for Van Zandt to give publicity to every kind of nasty rumor about the Air Force. Vinson feared the effects of such an investigation upon the military appropriations then pending in the Senate, particularly the increased sums passed by the House for the Air Force, and upon the whole unification process. Although several weeks earlier he had seen the document upon which most of Van Zandt's charges were based, he had chosen to ignore it, for it was exactly the kind of thing that he had wanted to keep from publication when on April 5 he warned the services that he would

investigate the source of any further leaks from one of them depreciatory of another. But now he had no choice. If he failed to act himself, Van Zandt would conduct the investigation.

Deciding to act, however, he had every advantage. The investigation could be shown to be within the jurisdiction of the Armed Services Committee, and the only justification for establishing a select committee to conduct it would be the failure of the Armed Services Committee to act. And within the committee, Vinson was chairman, while Van Zandt was its junior minority member. The House passed a resolution approved by the Armed Services Committee giving the full committee broad authority to conduct the investigation.[144] On June 9 the committee approved the following agenda for its investigation:

1. Establish the truth or falsity of all charges made by Mr. Van Zandt and by all others the committee may find or develop in the investigation.
2. Locate and identify the sources from which the charges, rumors, and innuendoes have come.
3. Examine the performance characteristics of the B-36 bomber to determine whether it is a satisfactory weapon.
4. Examine the roles and missions of the Air Force and the Navy (especially Navy aviation and Marine aviation) to determine whether or not the decision to cancel the construction of the aircraft carrier *United States* was sound.
5. Establish whether or not the Air Force is concentrating upon strategic bombing to such an extent as to be injurious to tactical aviation and the development of adequate fighter aircraft and fighter-aircraft techniques.
6. Consider the procedures followed by the Joint Chiefs of Staff on the development of weapons to be used by the respective services to determine whether or not it is proposed that two of the three services will be permitted to pass on the weapons of the third.
7. Study the effectiveness of strategic bombing to determine whether the Nation is sound in following this concept to its present extent.
8. Consider all other matters pertinent to the above that may be developed during the course of the investigation.[145]

With the adoption of this agenda, the investigation took on a scope far broader than Van Zandt had originally intended, for the agenda included, in addition to a consideration of the charges which were the immediate cause of the investigation, the major questions raised since the war over unification, national strategy, and the respective functions of the three services. Moreover, the sources of the charges Van Zandt had relayed to Congress were to be investigated, an inquiry hardly likely to help the Navy.

PREPARATION FOR AND IMMEDIATE BACKGROUND OF THE HEARINGS ON B-36 PROCUREMENT

Following adoption of an agenda for its investigation, the House Armed Services Committee solicited the views of the senior officers and civilians of the three service departments on the eight agenda items, and assembled a staff which carried on the investigation. Public hearings on the first two items of the agenda, involving the validity and source of the Worth charges, were begun on August 9th. A broader inquiry based upon the rest of the agenda was scheduled to open hearings on October 5. To direct the inquiry, the committee on July 7 hired Joseph B. Keenan, a Democrat with an established reputation as a criminal prosecutor during the New Deal, and more recently as a war crimes prosecutor in Japan. A Republican attorney from Bangor, Maine, James M. Gillin, was appointed as Keenan's assistant in order to counter already publicized claims that the investigation would be a "whitewash."

More than a month earlier, on June 2, the Air Force had appointed as "Coordinator-Director" of its preparation for the investigation W. Barton Leach, a reserve colonel in the Air Force and a Harvard Law School professor who had had considerable experience in the Army Air Forces during the Second World War, especially in analyses of AAF operations. Leach immediately set up a complete and comprehensive program for developing the Air Force case. He outlined it on the day of his appointment as follows:

(1) Analyse all statements hostile to the Air Force and prepare therefrom a list of charges.

(2) Prepare answers to these charges.

(3) Seek out charges based on rumors in the aircraft industry which may not yet have become general public knowledge.

(4) Prepare a detailed memorandum on JCS action on the B-36.

(5) Prepare a study on the aircraft in-

dustry so that the Secretary of the Air Force can answer the charge that he ought to nurture the industry instead of over-concentrating his orders.

(6) Prepare a memorandum on Secretary Symington's policies regarding the aircraft industry, particularly regarding the reorganization and consolidation of industries, and changes in management and in legal counsel.

(7) Collect all statements by Air Force people on the heavy bomber program. Then (a) organize them chronologically and compare them with Air Force policy at that date, and if any discrepancy is found, after consultation with the individual involved, prepare an explanation of the discrepancy; and (b) organize the statements by persons so that each will know all that he has said about the heavy bomber program.

(8) Examine and analyze the Inspector General's reports on the B-36, and prepare a justification for action taken on them.

(9) Prepare an explanation of Air Force action on the B-36.

(10) Examine correspondence with aircraft manufacturers for any incidents in which the committee may be interested.[146]

The major product of this massive preparation was a "History of the B-36 Procurement," which Vinson requested of Symington on June 13. It formed the backbone of the Air Force presentation to the committee in August, and remained the basis of the Air Force refutation of Navy charges in the October hearings. Its preparation took a large proportion of the time of four Air Force investigators, two of them highly skilled, for two months.

At the invitation of the Air Force, Keenan and his staff took over an office in the Pentagon directly across the hall from Leach's staff. The extent of Air Force cooperation was impressive, and the investigation, while it revealed that the administration of the B-36 procurement program was not free from error, found no evidence of the personal corruption implied in the Worth charges. For a considerable period, despite the Air Force's open-handedness with its material, the committee staff was apprehensive that it was being "taken in." But by August 9, when the committee hearings began, Keenan and his associates had reached the tentative conclusion that there was no substance to the Worth charges. They therefore approached the presentation of the evidence, not as convinced prosecutors, but as narrators of an episode in the development of a segment of the nation's armed forces. The Air Force was permitted to develop this narrative through its own witnesses in accordance with its exhaustive preparation. Keenan cross-examined the witnesses, as did many members of the committee.

In the meantime, the Air Force had been mending its fences. In a publicized speech at the Air University on June 17, Symington undertook to deny the public impression, so widely held by this time, that the Air Force expected to win the next war without significant help from its sister services, and that it was gambling all on long-range heavy bombers.[147]

In mid-June one of the continuing points of friction between the Army and the Air Force was bared when General Jacob L. Devers, Commander of the Army Field Forces, had come to Washington to complain that the Air Force was not providing adequate tactical air support for the Army ground forces. According to Devers, there was: (1) a shortage of troop carrier aviation, (2) insufficient training in close support of tactical aviation and ground troops, (3) no satisfactory fighter-bomber for close support of troops, and (4) too few tactical air groups in the original Air Force allocation of the 48-group program. Impressed with these claims, Bradley arranged to have Devers present them to the Air Force. Although Devers was objecting to a long-term policy which the Air Force had intentionally been following for some time, and in fact continued to follow, with at best slight temporary abatement, Vandenberg accepted the criticism so readily, and was so reassuring that things would improve, that Devers came away satisfied, only hedging enough to tell the press the whole story.[148] Although this incident might have led to a running criticism by the Army of Air Force indifference to tactical aviation, Bradley was evidently determined to avoid criticism of the Air Force at this time, perhaps for fear that the Navy would benefit.[149]

The Air Force evidently also became more temperate in its Congressional presentations that summer, as the B-36 investigation approached. A Senate Appropriations subcommittee was able to report that in closed hearings service chiefs had "unanimously" supported the President's program, including 48 Air Force Groups.[150] In public hearings, Symington's reluctance to be pinned down on the 70 groups was in marked contrast to his earlier behavior in committee hearings.[151]

THE HEARINGS ON THE CHARGES ABOUT B-36 PROCUREMENT

The first phase of the B-36 hearings, concerning the validity and source of the Worth charges, was held daily from August 9 through 12 and August 22 through 25 as full hearings of the House Armed Services Committee, with its Chairman, Carl Vinson, presiding. During the ten-day interval, a subcommittee held hearings for two days in California.

The pattern of the hearings was simple. Symington had not cared about a systematic approach and strongly desired to be the first witness;[152] but the committee adopted a different procedure. First the Air Force presented its "History of the B-36 Procurement," and then those people who figured in the episode which it recounted in such detail appeared and testified personally and in detail. Because of the careful preparation of the Air Force staff, no inconsistencies or contradictions capable of exploitation appeared in the testimony. The result was an impressive showing for the Air Force.

Two sources of information were available for determining who was responsible for the charges which Van Zandt had relayed to the House. One was the several people to whom Worth had given copies of the document: Congressmen Deane and Van Zandt directly, and Senator Tydings through Glenn Martin. They must either have known or had a strong suspicion about who wrote it, although it is clear that they might have had some doubt as to whether Worth was author or messenger. Whether or not anyone else knew about Worth through this source is unknown, for none of the recipients was willing to disclose Worth's identity, either as author or messenger. The other source was information obtained by the Office of Special Investigations in the Air Force, which was under the direction of a former F.B.I. agent, Joseph Carroll. As the hearings moved on through August, the Air Force investigators concluded that several Navy officials were involved, and that Worth was probably, though not conclusively, the main one.[153] Secretary Symington, Keenan, and Chairman Vinson knew what the Air Force knew.[154]

Of those who knew or suspected, Symington was the only one who was anxious to have the information disclosed. He believed that making it public would be detrimental to the Navy, and a justifiable rejoinder to the vicious personal charges which had been collected and spread by Navy personnel.[155] Keenan did not wish to introduce this information in the hearing because he (quite justifiably) did not regard it as conclusive.[156] Vinson avoided its disclosure in order not to distract attention from the Air Force presentation. Van Zandt, in his role of defender of the Navy, was interested in exploiting the charges, not their source. But finally, on August 24, after it had become entirely clear that the longer the hearings continued the more impressive the Air Force position would be, Van Zandt charged that Senator Tydings, Representative Deane, and Chairman Vinson of the committee all knew the identity of the author of the Worth document. Insisting that he himself did not, Van Zandt demanded that Vinson call its author to testify.[157] Keenan protested, but Vinson called Worth as a witness. Worth freely—almost eagerly—admitted authorship of the anonymous charges and denied that anyone else in the Navy Department had had a share in it. The hearings adjourned the following day until October 5, when their second phase was to begin.

IV. BACKGROUND TO THE SECOND PHASE OF THE HEARINGS: THE NAVY FINDS SILENCE IMPOSSIBLE

Phase I of the B-36 investigation was a diversion from the main issue of the respective functions of Navy and Air Force aviation in national strategy. But it was a diversion that ended abruptly. The Worth memorandum resulted from the tensions created by the controversy over functions. Had the charges in it about the personal motives of the men ultimately responsible for the development of the B-36 been proved, the House Armed Services Committee would undoubtedly have gone on with a comprehensive examination of the influence of personal profit in the development of weapons and the determination of weapons policies in the armed services. Since the charges were not only not proved but were in fact flatly and clearly disproved, this line of approach was dropped completely. Meanwhile, the basic issues involved in the functions controversy itself, which were to reach a dramatic climax in the hearings on Unification and Strategy in October 1949, had continued to develop. We have already seen how, following the House committee's vote at the end of May 1949 to investigate the armed services, the Air Force had striven to give the appearance of interservice harmony until the August hearings were held. Now we must go back again to the spring of 1949 to trace the circumstances which led a group of naval officers in late September to insist, over the objection of the Secretary of the Navy, the Chief of Naval Operations, and the Chairman of the House Armed Services Committee, that the hearings be continued. These circumstances are part of the main theme of the controversy about functions.

THE SETTING OF THE HEARINGS

National Security Act Amendments of 1949

When the Secretary of Defense announced the cancellation of the flush-deck carrier on April 23, 1949, the Tydings bill amending the unification legislation enacted in 1947 had already passed the Senate and was awaiting consideration in the House. Among the services, the nascent Air Force had been the most enthusiastic proponent of the original act, while the Navy, led by Forrestal, had been reluctant to give up any of its independence to a common military establishment. But a year and a half as Secretary of Defense had changed Forrestal's mind. The amendments now proposed, based upon recommendations made by him in December 1948, would strengthen the authority of the Secretary of Defense. Again the Navy was more reluctant to change than were the two sister services. Before the carrier cancellation, in the Senate hearings on the bill, it had shown only lukewarm support, with the Marine Corps actually opposing the bill.[158] After the cancellation of the carrier, Navy opposition in the House hearings, though still restrained, increased. On the day scheduled for the trial committee vote on the bill, Representative Van Zandt introduced into the record of the committee over the protest of the chairman a directive from the Secretary of Defense requiring the submittal of all testimony on the B-36 to his office for coordination prior to presentation to the committee. Van Zandt termed the directive an effort to deny the committee the real opinions of the military services. With this move he rallied the committee to vote 13 to 12 to postpone the final vote on the bill until the B-36 hearings were over.[159] The Senate promptly threatened as a reprisal to cut the military pay rise bill already passed by the House, and the President threatened, after a visit from Vinson, to issue an executive order which would accomplish the same results as the blocked bill.[160] The committee remained dead-locked on the measure but reported out a section of it. The whole bill was eventually restored in conference committee of the two Houses.

On August 2 both Houses agreed to the bill as amended in conference, and the President signed it eight days later.[161] The feelings generated by the cancellation of the flush-deck carrier, and perhaps by other controversies as well, had thus created such opposition in the House Armed Services Committee to the new unification act, or at least to immediate action thereon, that the committee in effect had to be bypassed in order to get the legislation approved during the first session of the 81st Congress.

Military Appropriations for Fiscal 1950

By the time of the carrier cancellation the House had completed action on appropriations for the military establishment—a reduction in Army and Navy funds, and an increase in Air Force funds in order to carry on expansion to 70 groups. In the Senate, with Johnson's encouragement, the President's original program was virtually restored by cutting $800 million from the House appropriation to keep the Air Force at 48 groups.[162] But the Senate was under intense pressure to economize,[163] and although its primary response to that pressure was to reduce the Air Force budget, the Navy could derive little comfort from that action, for in other areas the movement for economy was pointed directly at the Navy.[164]

Johnson's Economy Aims

By the summer of 1949, only two or three months after he took office, the new Secretary of Defense was feared and distrusted in the Navy. He had turned around, after cancelling the flush-deck carrier in April, to approve in June, over the opposition of the Joint Chiefs,[165] the modification of two *Essex*-class carriers, but had done nothing else to reassure the Navy, and much to worry it.[166] During this period there was much talk about his alleged political ambitions as an aspirant for the Presidency. In the unification and appropriations hearings of that summer, and in speech after speech through 1949 and the first half of 1950, he

claimed that military expenditures could be, and in fact were being, decreased simultaneously with an increase in military strength. During the spring and summer of 1949 in the hearings on the Tydings bill, the primary purpose of which was to increase the power of the Secretary of Defense, he claimed that with the necessary power he could save up to $1 billion by reorganization and management reforms.[167] But whatever the validity of his claims, or the meaning of his plans, economy to the Navy after April 23rd meant carrier cancellations.

Executive Budget-Making

Between April and October 1949 Johnson had shown in two ways what his plans for the future expenditures of the services were: first, in the preparation of the budget for fiscal 1951; and second, in reducing expenditures for fiscal 1950.

In mid-July 1949, at a White Sulphur Springs conference with the Joint Chiefs, Johnson began discussions on the fiscal 1951 budget. The ceiling was apparently set at $13 billion—a significant reduction from the budget for the new fiscal year 1950 then awaiting passage in Congress. The Navy now sought a tripartite division of the funds, with autonomy in their use, but the Army and the Air Force were determined to get away from that procedure, and so evidently was Johnson. Before the conference was over it was apparent that, while all three services would be pinched in order to fit into the reduced budget, the largest reductions were intended for naval aviation. At White Sulphur Springs, the issue was fought over the large fleet carriers, a subject which had been under discussion a month before in considering whether two more *Essex*-class carriers should be modernized. In June the Air Force and the Army had voted against the proposal, but Johnson had overruled them. Now, in planning for fiscal 1951, the Air Force wanted to have all the large fleet carriers put into moth balls, the Army was willing to have four kept active, and the Navy planned to keep eight of them in the active fleet.[168] Johnson's stand was soon made clear. He ordered a 50 per cent reduction in the Navy air arm, and cuts in other naval components. As a weekly news magazine summarized them:

1. Carriers of the [*Essex*] class to be cut from 8 to 4.
2. Carrier air groups to be cut from 14 to 6.
3. Smaller carriers of the *Saipan* class to be cut from 10 to 8.
4. Marine Corps aviation squadrons to be cut from 23 to 12.
5. Anti-submarine air squadrons to be cut from 8 to 7.
6. Patrol squadrons to be cut from 30 to 20.
7. Cruisers to be cut from 18 to 12.
8. Destroyers to be cut from 162 to 140.
9. Submarines to be cut from 80 to 70.[169]

Budget-Making and Military Strategy

The strategic implications of the frugal military budget outlook of the new Truman Administration were made clear during the summer of 1949 when the Policy Planning Staff of the State Department attempted to correlate its conception of national strategy with the strategic plans of the military establishment. The conception was, of course, centered on the problem of dealing with Communist Russia. The definition of Soviet conduct and conclusions about modes of solution had been matters of ever-increasing concern to the Department since the end of World War II. The first major statement was an extraordinary cable sent from Moscow by the U. S. Counselor of Embassy, George F. Kennan, a career foreign service officer, in February 1946. The cable had great impact not only within the State Department but elsewhere as well, notably, for example, with Forrestal, then Secretary of the Navy.[170] The first major public statement was also Kennan's, an anonymous article entitled "The Sources of Soviet Conduct" that appeared in the July 1947 issue of *Foreign Affairs*. The article advocated "a policy of firm containment."[171] The period of April to July 1947 was thus a time when much of the post-war foreign policy and the substance and background of military policy was crystallizing and in process of being revealed by the Administration to the American people: the Truman Doctrine; the Marshall Plan; and, though unofficial, Soviet Containment.

Shortly after Congress received the "Truman Doctrine" message on April 12, 1947, Kennan became Director of the State Department's newly established Policy Planning Staff, a post he held for more than two years. During that period the practical implications of the 1947 policies were in process of development. Kennan had begun by emphasizing the flexibility and patience of the Soviet method in international politics. He rejected the simple equating of hostile purpose in international politics with all-out war. The Soviet Union, he reasoned, should be contained within the perimeter of her present power by the careful application of appropriate counter-force at whatever point or points along that perimeter she sought to extend her influence and power. The counter-force envisaged did not need to be military, but if it should involve armed forces, they would be used in limited military actions for the limited political purpose of preventing Soviet expansion in a particular area. Limited war, it should be evident, was a part of the State Department conception of national strategy in the summer of 1949, though how far the Secretary and others were willing to go in active support of Kennan's views is unknown.

But limited war had no comparable place in the strategic thinking of the Joint Chiefs of Staff. During the fall of 1948, when the fiscal 1950 budget was under preparation, the Joint Chiefs had maintained that if the President's defense budget ceiling were not lifted the military establishment would be capable of only a hard air strike from the British Isles in case of war. With budget prospects even dimmer in the summer of 1949 than nine months earlier, the military establishment remained committed to this strategic plan. The full-scale retaliatory air strike, whether or not it could by itself end a war with the Soviet Union, could not be wasted upon a minor Soviet aggression. It would have to be reserved for a large-scale Soviet aggression, and might do no more than give the United States time to mobilize for total war. Furthermore, if the United States was prepared to fight only this kind of war, it would have nothing to offer a military ally in Western Europe except liberation following conquest— a prospect uncomfortably close to annihilation.

All of these facts were pointed out to the Joint Strategic Survey Committee, a strategic planning appendage of the Joint Chiefs of Staff, by members of the Policy Planning Staff of the State Department. Kennan, then Director of the Staff, argued for two highly mechanized and mobile divisions to fight the "brush fires" which he anticipated in containing Russia. Others on the staff thought that additional forces would be needed, but all stressed the needed capability of fighting limited wars to contain Russia and help protect America's allies in Europe.

The rejoinder of the Joint Strategic Survey Committee was simple and unanswerable: While the recommendations of the Policy Planning Staff were quite persuasive, and in general already familiar to the committee, the budget made their implementation impossible. Under existing and anticipated budget ceilings the only strategy which could be implemented was the existing one—primary reliance upon the deterrent effect of a strategic air strike which the United States could mount if the Soviet Union invaded Western Europe.

The Policy Planning Staff's recommendations were thus rejected, regretfully, by the Joint Chiefs; but by that time all the world knew that the balance of power between the United States and the Soviet Union was changing, for the first Russian atomic explosion occurred in September 1949. Rather than continue their discussions with the JCS, the Staff began working for authoritative approval of a thorough re-examination of national security policy. That approval finally came from the President in December 1949, and eventually led to NSC 68—a basic restatement of national security policy. Long before that, in October 1949, the strategic plans of the United States were subjected to public criticism in the hearings on Unification and Strategy.[172]

Expenditure Reductions for Fiscal 1950

Johnson had been promising Congress and the public greater armed strength for less money. On August 10, 1949, the day the new unification act was approved, he established the National Defense Management Committee, the purpose of which was to carry on a continuing program for the promotion of economy and efficiency in the Defense Department. Its members were Gordon Gray, Secretary of the Army, Dan A. Kimball, Under Secretary of the Navy, and Eugene Zuckert, Assistant Secretary of the Air Force. General Joseph T. McNarney of the Air Force, the services' leading management expert, was chairman. The curious mixture of rank among the civilians was notably due to the fact that Gray, who had been Under Secretary of the Army until a few months before,

was still the civilian most conversant with the Army budget. Associated with the McNarney Committee as an Advisory Group was a management engineering firm with experience in government reorganization, Robert Heller Associates.

The McNarney Committee was intended to develop administrative reforms which would reduce the cost of operation in the Department of Defense, as the military establishment was now called, and within two weeks it had produced a program of expenditure reductions calculated eventually to save the government expenditures at an annual rate of $500 million.[173] But its major achievement by October was to institute a reduction in armed strength during the current fiscal year in order to reduce the rate of expenditure by July 1950 to the lower rate of expenditure being planned for the next fiscal year, 1951. Under Johnson's prodding, and with his backing, the committee set figures for a total cut of $929 million from the President's budget for 1950, which at the time was still being fought over in the Senate. Reflecting the emphasis planned for fiscal 1951, the Air Force had the smallest share of the cut, $196 million, while the Navy had the largest, $376 million.[174] The Army was to be cut only slightly less than the Navy, $357 million. On September 8, two weeks after the close of the first phase of the B-36 hearings, McNarney issued a memorandum to the services informing them of the proposed expenditure cuts. The events that ensued constituted the immediate setting for the second phase of the B-36 hearings, but before recounting these, it is necessary to describe the development of the Navy viewpoint from the cancellation of the carrier on April 23 to September 8, the date of the McNarney Memorandum.

The Developing Navy Viewpoint

The last week in May 1949 was one of mounting tension in the Navy. Congressman Van Zandt lost his appeal in the House for a Navy-oriented investigation of the Air Force. At the same time, high-ranking officials in the Navy were alarmed to find themselves under what appeared to be F.B.I. surveillance. The detectives were in fact investigators for the Air Force whose function has been described above. Those who were in contact with Representative Van Zandt felt compelled to wear civilian clothes when calling upon him.[175] And on the first of June the Joint Chiefs, with Denfeld again signing and delivering the documents in the absence of Eisenhower, refused to test the B-36 against a Navy Banshee fighter in a simulated battle. The reason given for this decision was that interception was far too complicated a matter to be settled correctly merely by setting a fighter upon a bomber, a view in which Denfeld quite properly concurred.[176]

Throughout the summer Navy relations with the press remained tense. Although the Secretary of Defense suspended on June 3 the provisions of his Consolidated Directive No. 1 which had established centralized security review for all three services in his office, and within the week had retreated further from the restrictions imposed by this order upon the free expression of views by service officers,[177] he soon again imposed restrictions. Throughout the summer the public information policies of the Defense Department were in a state of turmoil which continually aroused Navy suspicion, fear, and distrust, feelings which Johnson's personal conduct made no effort to dispel. On June 21, for instance, in a speech to the National War College, he charged that Navy "partisans" had "twisted" the facts about the cancellation of the flush-deck carrier and were waging "a campaign of terror against further unification of the armed forces."[178]

While some moderate expositions of the Navy case were publicized during the summer of 1949,[179] the headline value of the more partisan statements gave them greater prominence. A contentious article by Admiral Gallery, which appeared in the *Saturday Evening Post* issue of June 25, 1949, received perhaps the widest circulation of any statement of the Navy viewpoint.[180]

Reaction within the Pentagon was also striking. Johnson and other Defense Department officials tried to prevent publication of the article, and then considered reassigning Gallery in order to get him out of Washington.[181] And in the same month the Navy League, an independent private organization committed to the promotion of Navy interests, embarked upon a $500,000 campaign designed to "establish the Navy and Naval Aviation as an essential element of National Defense."[182] Thus while the Air Force was avoiding public controversy as a prelude to the forthcoming hearings, Navy partisans seemed uninhibited.

The Navy Preparation for the B-36 Hearings

"Op. 23," Navy parlance for the Organizational Policy and Research Division of the Office of the Chief of Naval Operations, became during the summer of 1949 the center of activity for the preparation of the Navy presentation for the House Armed Services B-36 investigation. In some respects it was comparable to the office run by Leach, the Coordinator-Director of the B-36 investigation for the Air Force; but in most important respects it was not. To begin with, it was run by a prominent professional naval officer, Captain Arleigh A. Burke, who became Chief of Naval Operations six years later, while Leach was a reserve officer who was by training and experience a civilian lawyer. Second, while the sole objective of the Leach organization was preparation for the Air Force presentation, Op. 23 gave that function only secondary attention. Already carrying on other work when the hearings were planned, Op. 23 continued with its established functions, providing only a modest amount of research and writing to help those chosen to present the Navy's case. Third, Op. 23 operated in surroundings almost entirely hostile to it, while the functions of Leach and his staff were understood and appreciated by those who knew about it.

Most of the hostility which developed towards Op. 23 was of the Navy's own making. Set up for a normal and wholly legitimate purpose—to study Navy organization, and formulate Navy policy towards the organizational problems incident to unification—Op. 23 was treated by the Navy from the beginning like dirty business; and the press had soon drawn the same conclusion. Upon its establishment it was located next to the Office of Naval Intelligence, and its activities from the beginning were subject to an unusual degree of secrecy. The press was soon aware of its existence, but could obtain no satisfactory explanations from the Navy. The result was suspicion and adverse publicity. There was actually some substance to the charges leveled at it. Material circulated within the Navy on such an explosive subject as the unification controversy was bound to leak, and anyone who put out such material in any quantity should have realized that fact. Moreover, some of the circulated material was quite inappropriate for sponsorship by the Navy. And finally, some of the Op. 23 staff were personally involved in public relations activities not approved by the Secretary of the Navy. One of them, for instance, helped Admiral Gallery with his *Saturday Evening Post* article of June 25, 1949, and another was heavily involved with Cedric Worth.[183] In sharp contrast, Leach's staff in the Air Force gave no comparable cause for suspicion or distrust.

The final and perhaps major contrast between Op. 23 and the Leach staff in the Air Force lay in the relations of each with the ranking officer and civilian of that service. Although Symington and Vandenberg were too busy to devote much time to the preparation of the Air Force presentation, they gave those who were making that preparation their wholehearted support.

In the Navy, preparation had apparently begun as a rather elaborate operation, with plenty of ranking officers and skilled civilians participating. But gradually the work became less and less of a departmental effort as the Bureau Chiefs, the Judge Advocate General, other departmental officers, and their civilian assistants were withdrawn from it one by one (although some of them were able to continue their participation on a voluntary basis). Matthews eventually cut himself off entirely from the preparation, and Denfeld, who was in Europe a great deal during this time, had little to do with it either. Leadership was assumed by Admiral Arthur W. Radford, Denfeld's Vice Chief of Naval Operations until May 1949 when he became Commander in Chief of the Pacific Fleet. He was called to Washington two months later, in July, at the request of the Chairman of the House Armed Services Committee. Vinson wanted him as a kind of technical consultant to assist the committee's chief counsel in the B-36 investigation. Radford had directed the staff work for the Navy on unification in 1945 and 1946, a position roughly comparable to Burke's in Op. 23. In view of his background in dealing with the issues involved in the forthcoming investigation, it was understandable for him to take a prominent role in the Navy's preparation for the hearings. But, in effect, he was per-

forming what should have been Denfeld's duty, as Chief of Naval Operations, acting as the chief spokesman for the Navy. Denfeld's failure to play a more important role in this activity, which was so vital to the Navy was undoubtedly due to reservations held both by him and by Radford and Op. 23. Denfeld at this time was still determined not to identify himself wholly as a Navy partisan. On the other hand, his failure to take a vigorous stand with Radford and his followers was itself, on their part, a cause of an increasing lack of confidence in him.[184]

Following the dramatic conclusion of the first phase of the B-36 hearings, on August 25 the Navy instigated an inquiry into the circumstances surrounding the writing and release of the Worth document, with the primary objective of determining whether anyone in the Navy Department intentionally cooperated with Worth in the preparation of the document. A Navy fact-finding board headed by Admiral Thomas C. Kinkaid began full-scale hearings on September 6, during the course of which a number of people Worth had mentioned in his testimony before the House Armed Services Committee were called as witnesses.[185] Chief among them was Commander Thomas B. Davies, the assistant head of Op. 23, and one of two chosen by Radford to help him in his work with the House Armed Services Committee. Davies admitted that he had provided Worth with many of the rumors set down in the document, but denied that he had any prior knowledge that they would be thus used. Other witnesses took the same position, and the naval court ultimately concluded that Worth was the only one responsible for the document. Although possibly justified by its terms of reference, the court's decision was a charitable one. For while Worth's intention to produce the exact document which he did, and to use it the way he did, may not have been known beforehand by any of his associates in the Navy Department (may not, indeed, have been known by him beforehand), it is evident that some of the Navy personnel who helped him were well aware of the ultimate political purpose to which the material they collected would be put.

After trying unsuccessfully to call the Secretary of the Air Force as a witness in order to have him disclose the information which his investigators had turned up, the court suspended its hearings on September 23, until such time as the material could be obtained. Symington had previously turned it over to the House Armed Services Committee. When, in early October, the committee made it clear that the naval court would not be able to see the evidence, the court closed its proceedings entirely, happy to end the inquiry.[186]

THE IMMEDIATE BACKGROUND OF THE HEARINGS ON UNIFICATION AND STRATEGY

By September 1949, the outlook for the Navy, and particularly for its dominant branch, naval aviation, was ominous. The Army, as well as the Air Force, had demonstrated its interest in reducing substantially the size of naval forces, and the Secretary of Defense was actively engaged in a program to cut naval aviation in half, a program which, because it was reinforced by the broadly attractive appeal of economy in the national budget, had solid, although not unanimous, outside support. Congress, in its infinite variety, had provided a modest measure of encouragement to Navy hopes; but a bold appeal for stronger support had only backfired. For Navy partisans, the situation was alarming.

Those, like Radford, who were alarmed, could find little comfort in trusting to the leadership of the Secretary of the Navy, Francis P. Matthews, a soft-spoken lawyer from Omaha who took the job Sullivan gave up over the carrier cancellation. By his appointment Matthews was a Johnson man. In his five months in office the Navy partisans had never found reason enough to give him their full confidence.

If the professional leader of the Navy, Louis Denfeld, the Chief of Naval Operations since December, 1947, had ever enjoyed the full confidence of the Navy partisans, by September 1949, it had been withdrawn from him. His role as senior member of the Joint Chiefs in the carrier cancellation recommendations, and in the decision not to hold a contest between the B-36 and a Navy fighter, had been misunderstood within the Navy. He had remained silently in office when Sullivan resigned in a blaze of naval glory. And when in the August hearings the Air Force related the times he, as a member of the Joint Chiefs, had

approved the B-36, the misunderstanding grew. In mid-September, after Matthews had decided to renominate him for a second two-year term as Chief of Naval Operations, a rumor was circulated which was revelatory of Denfeld's reputation within the Navy (although it was almost certainly incorrect). He had been reappointed, the rumor went, on condition that he would de-emphasize naval aviation and emphasize anti-submarine warfare and surface vessels.[187] Actually, he was both a submariner and a battleship admiral, and by temperament a conciliator. For various reasons his appointment was not looked on with favor by the naval aviators, and in office he was not a popular or articulate leader. Whether or not one more colorful than he could have taken the moderate course which he did without serious loss of support within the service is uncertain. In any event, Navy partisans had come to feel that he was not an adequate spokesman for their cause.

When the Defense Management Committee notified the Navy Department on September 8 that it proposed to reduce naval expenditures during the current fiscal year by $353 million, there was a sharp reaction throughout the top ranks of the Navy. Matthews remained confident that the matter could be worked out satisfactorily with the Secretary of Defense, even though he opposed the cuts. He awaited the outcome of Navy budget studies which would show how the cut would have to be taken. The studies were not complete until the end of the month. Meanwhile a Navy revolt had overtaken him.

Captain John G. Crommelin, a distinguished naval aviator, at that time serving on the staff of the Joint Chiefs of Staff, had been named as a witness in the naval inquiry into the Worth document, and had prepared a statement for use before the court. On September 9, the day after the Navy had officially learned of the proposed cut in its budget, the Navy Court of Inquiry recessed. Crommelin, fearing that he would never be heard by it, called reporters to his home on September 10 and issued a statement which attacked unification as a terrible mistake, and claimed that the Navy was gradually but intentionally being eliminated by the Joint Chiefs and the Secretary of Defense. His prepared statement was strongly worded, and Crommelin elaborated upon it orally with still stronger and more colorful language. Crommelin had testified three years earlier against the establishment of a separate air force when the unification legislation of 1947 was under consideration; he was still challenging the basic organizational and strategic policy of the defense establishment, and of the Administration. He made quite clear to the press his realization of that fact. He told them it was his intention to "blow the whole thing open," and that he was violating official orders, and would probably get a general court martial.[188]

Because Crommelin's outburst came so immediately after the Defense Management Committee's notification of a $353 million cut in Navy Department funds, and because Crommelin's outburst monopolized publicity, many within the Navy who rallied to his support were not aware of this latest move in Johnson's economy drive. Crommelin received a flood of messages approving his action and agreeing with the views he had published. Retired Fleet Admiral William F. Halsey, after lunching with him, announced that he had shown "wonderful courage" and "deserves the help . . . of all naval officers." Two Rear Admirals, Austin K. Doyle and Hugh H. Goodwin, soon added their public endorsements to that of Halsey.[189]

Congressional reaction to Crommelin's statements was more measured. The Navy Captain had appealed for a new Congressional inquiry into the Air Force-Navy feud, but press inquiries on Capitol Hill indicated that it would not be forthcoming. However, Vinson announced that Crommelin would be called to testify in the second phase of the House hearings on the B-36 investigation scheduled to begin October 5. The Judge Advocate of the Naval Court of Inquiry also announced that Crommelin would be called as a witness when the proceedings which he was conducting reopened on September 21.

Within the Defense Department reaction was varied. Johnson avoided involvement in the matter. Matthews told the press that by his partisan act Crommelin had "obviously disqualified himself" for his job on the Joint Staff, but he did nothing about it. Denfeld's reaction was to ignore the unpleasant affair. He neither supported Crommelin, nor initiated any effort to reprimand or discipline him. It was the Under Secretary, Dan A. Kimball,

who established the Department's position with respect to Crommelin. Three months earlier Kimball had prevented the banishment of Admiral Gallery from Washington for his highly partisan article in the *Saturday Evening Post*,[190] and Worth, it will be recalled, worked in Kimball's office. Now Kimball moved to protect Crommelin. Arguing that Crommelin had made clear that he was stating his personal views, which he had a constitutional right to do, and that he had criticized no specific individual within the military establishment, Kimball proposed that no disciplinary action be taken against Crommelin. After obtaining the concurrence of Denfeld, he announced his proposal to the press as the position of the Navy.[191]

Faced with this accomplished fact, Matthews accepted it,[192] but still expected to have Crommelin transferred from his assignment on the Joint Staff to a post not involving the other services. His proposed reassignment came early on September 15. As a distinguished senior captain with expectations of promotion to flag rank, his assignment to a post vacated by a Rear Admiral would, under normal circumstances, have been regarded as not extraordinary, but nevertheless as a definite "break" for him. When Crommelin was transferred to a Rear Admiral's billet, Matthews, suspecting that the Navy high command was trying to reward him, promptly intervened and had him given an assignment where he would serve under a Rear Admiral.[193]

Aware of the widespread feeling throughout the Navy reflected in and aroused by Crommelin's public statement, Matthews issued a communication to the Navy on the 16th, carefully constructed so that it could not be interpreted as an order, which requested naval officers to cease their public criticisms of defense plans and send them instead through channels to the Navy Department, where they would be put to good use in the second session of the B-36 hearings. It read:

Please take steps to insure that the following is made known to responsible officers of your command:

The recent series of public statements beginning with and resulting from Captain Crommelin's statement, all of which appear to have been inspired largely by apprehensions concerning the future of naval aviation, have from the standpoint of successful unification and maintenance of harmony among the services been a source of embarrassment to the Navy Department.

While there is no intent to impair your right of free expression of views, I believe a more appropriate and effective procedure would be to transmit them to me through channels in accordance with Article 1245 Navy Regulations. This is particularly pertinent, bearing in mind the announced intention of the House Armed Services Committee to examine next month many of the issues now receiving attention in public print.

The views so transmitted will, I assure you, be used in support of the integrity and efficiency of the naval service. The cooperation of all personnel affected by the foregoing will be greatly appreciated.[194]

A Pacific Fleet officers' conference was held at Monterey, California, on September 21, 22 and 23. Following the policy of the Department as expressed a few days before in Matthews' communiqué, Kimball, the Under Secretary, addressed the conference, encouraging his listeners to express their criticisms of Louis Johnson's economy measures—but to do so through channels. Vice Admiral Gerald F. Bogan, Commander of the First Task Force of the Pacific Fleet, had come to the conference with a draft of a reply to the Secretary's communiqué. To send his letter through channels to the Secretary of the Navy, Bogan required the endorsements of Radford, the Commander in Chief of the Pacific Fleet, and Denfeld, the Chief of Naval Operations. There at the conference he sought Radford's endorsement. But Radford had taken a dim view of Matthews' communiqué. Evidently interpreting it as an effort to assume the role of the Navy's chief spokesman in the October B-36 hearings, a role which Radford had been carrying on since July, the Pacific Fleet commander had already wired Washington that he thought it was a mistake to ask naval officers to send their complaints to the Secretary. "I felt this would invite a mass of colored criticism," he later explained.[195] Nevertheless, he endorsed Admiral Bogan's reply to the Secretary. His endorsing letter refrained from judging the merits of Bogan's arguments.

Meanwhile Matthews had become involved on another front in his fight to contain within channels Navy opposition to Johnson's economy policies. Upon receipt on September 8 of the Defense Management Committee's proposed reduction in naval expenditures for the current fiscal year, several of the ranking naval officers, apparently again led by Radford, resolved that they should immediately take their complaints about it before a Congressional committee. Although he also objected to the cuts, Matthews felt that "our first duty, under the unification act, was to protest the proposed cuts in a hearing before Secretary Johnson. I pointed out that, if we lost there, we could then legitimately make our complaint to Congress."[196]

While Matthews was trying to hold down the Department from running to Congress and to channel Navy complaints through his office rather than through the press, Vinson was preparing to cancel the scheduled October hearings. On September 27 two investigators for the House Armed Services Committee visited Matthews, saying that they had come on their own initiative, but were confident that what they had to propose reflected the view of the committee. They then persuaded Matthews to order that naval officers were not to mention the B-36 in their presentations to the committee.[197]

The following day (probably the same day that Matthews issued his order) Admiral Denfeld endorsed the Bogan correspondence and forwarded it to Matthews. As it reached the Secretary of the Navy on September 28, 1949, the Bogan correspondence read as follows:

[BOGAN'S LETTER]

Commander
First Task Fleet
United States Pacific Fleet
Flagship of the Commander
A7-1/00 WGT
20 September 1949.
Serial: 0183
From: Vice Admiral Gerald F. Bogan, U. S. Navy, 9628
To: The Secretary of the Navy.
Via: (1) Commander in Chief, U. S. Pacific Fleet
        (2) The Chief of Naval Operations.
Subject: Comment on statement of Capt. John G. Crommelin. U. S. Navy, 57979.
Reference:
  (A) Secnav dispatch
  (B) Article 1245, U. S. Navy regulations.
My Dear Secretary:
At the beginning it is proper for me to state that in no manner have I, to date, endorsed or condemned Captain Crommelin's statement be-

cause no one has asked me to do so. Had such been the case honest necessity and conscience would have required hearty and complete agreement with the affirmations made in his release to or interview with the press.

Your dispatch, which prompts this letter, is surprising in its interpretation of the motive in the basic statement. It avers that the Crommelin statement and subsequent public utterances have embarrassed the progress of unification and harmony and the Navy Department. It further states that these remarks have been inspired by apprehensions concerning the future of naval aviation.

Mr. Secretary, while realizing that this is your honest belief, that interpretation of the genesis of Crommelin's release is the most superficial gloss and does not remotely touch the heart of the question. The basic reason behind all of it is a genuine fear in the Navy for the security of our country if the policies followed in the Department of Defense since the National Security Act became law are not drastically changed, and soon.

It is necessary for me to assert now to you that I opposed the act as written and passed and so testified before the committee. My reasons for opposition and suggestions for other methods of achieving ultimate unity in the military establishment were given at that time 1 July 1947. I forecast much of what subsequently occurred. Records of that testimony are available.

The creation of three departments or sub departments where formerly there were but two is not unification. Under the present law it can be made to and does operate effectively in the field. But it would be sheer balderdash to assume that there has been anything approaching it among the Secretariat, the Joint Staff, or the high command of all three services. Knowing that honest differences of opinion must constantly be present, bickering is still the rule; unanimity is nonexistent.

SITUATION HELD DETERIORATING

The morale of the Navy is lower today than at any time since I entered the commissioned ranks in 1916. Lowered morale, to some degree, may be expected to follow any war during the readjustment to the organization for peace. In my opinion this descent, almost to despondency, stems from complete confusion as to the future role of the Navy and its advantages or disadvantages as a permanent career.

Optimistic letters and plans issue from Washington. And concurrently the situation deteriorates with each press release. The younger men are necessarily concerned with their future security. We of greater age, and, we hope, more mature judgment, are fearful that the country is being,

if it has not already been, sold a false bill of goods.

Junior officers in large numbers, whose confidence I enjoy, have come to see me asking advice on their future course of action. I have invariably encouraged them to enhance their professional ability against the day when the troublesome questions now paramount would be equably resolved. It is becoming increasingly difficult for me to do this honestly.

If the adequate military or defense establishment could be achieved without a navy and naval aviation, I would gladly advocate using funds now expended to maintain that service, on the procurement of the best other necessary weapons and equipment. Not even the United States can support indefinitely, during peace, the tragically large military budgets we are devouring.

There is no cheap quick victory possible between any two nations or groups of nations each having strong even if relatively unequal power. Yet at a time as potentially critical as ever existed during our history, the public has been lured into complacency by irresponsible speeches by advocates of this theory. The result could be a great national and world-wide catastrophe.

I have been informed that when the [House Armed Services] committee hearings resume in October the Navy will be afforded the opportunity to state its case completely on the items comprising the agenda. Since Captain Crommelin's press statement, I am more optimistic than before that such will be the case.

But the agenda does not cover the fundamentals of our national security. It embraces a total of eight items, all pertinent but by no means the complete whole. It is my earnest hope that at some time in the near future this vital subject may be thoroughly explored with no consideration being given to the reputations nor politics of the witnesses who appear. It is bigger than personalities, broader and deeper than politics. It is our country.

Respectfully,
C. F. Bogan.

[RADFORD STATEMENT]
Commander in Chief,
U. S. Pacific Fleet
22 September 1949

First Endorsement on Vice Admiral C. F. Bogan's ltr ser 0183 of 20 September 1949.

From:　　Commander in Chief, U. S. Pacific Fleet
To:　　Secretary of the Navy.
Via:　　Chief of Naval Operations.
Subject:　Comment on statement of Captain John G. Crommelin, U. S. Navy, 57979.

1. Forwarded.

2. Vice Admiral Bogan is an officer of great ability and wide experience in naval aviation and naval warfare. There is no question of his sincerity and high principles. I know that the writing of his letter was motivated by sincere patriotism.

3. Rightly or wrongly, the majority of officers in the Pacific fleet concur with Captain Crommelin and with the ideas expressed by Vice Admiral Bogan above. Most will avoid any statements to that effect and they would probably question the propriety and timing of such public statements. Nevertheless, it would be a grave mistake to underestimate the depth and sincerity of their feelings.

4. Because of my conviction that this letter is representative of a general feeling, I commend it to your attention. .   A. W. Radford.

[DENFELD STATEMENT]

28 September 1949

Second endorsement on Vice Admiral C. F. Bogan's ltr. ser. 0183 of 20 September 1949

From: Chief of Naval Operations
To: Secretary of Navy
Subject: Comment on statement of Capt. John G. Crommelin, U. S. Navy. 57979.

1. Forwarded.

2. I concur in the endorsement of Commander in Chief, Pacific Fleet. Naval officers have faith in the Navy and a knowledge of the aggressive role it plays in the defense of the country. They are convinced that a Navy stripped of its offensive power means a nation stripped of its offensive power.

3. I believe that Fleet Admiral [Ernest J. I.] King in October 1945 summed up the present Navy-wide concern when in a report he stated: ". . . Seapower will not be accorded adequate recognition because the organization contemplated would permit reduction of that sea power by individuals who are not thoroughly familiar with its potentialities, as has happened in several other countries.

"France never used her Navy to good advantage. The German General Staff failed, in two wars, to appreciate the potency of sea power. The absorption of Britain's crack Royal Navy Air Service into an independent Royal Air Force and the consequent withering of her naval aviation, left her, in 1941, a second rate Navy.

"Another significant fact is that Japan's collapse was coincident with the reduction of her sea power—at the end of the war she was stronger on the ground and in the air than at the start, but her Navy was practically eliminated. It follows that if the Navy's welfare is one of the prerequisites to the nation's welfare—and I sincerely believe that to be the case—any step that is not good for the Navy is not good for the nation."

Louis Denfeld.[198]

On the 1st of October Matthews wrote Johnson requesting a hearing on the proposed $353 million cut in current naval expenditures, claiming that the cuts could not be arranged. Later that day he talked with Johnson on the phone. Johnson assured him that the Navy would be given a full hearing.[199] On the same day Crommelin appeared on a "Meet the Press" broadcast where he declined, on the grounds that he had been given a direct order, to discuss any inter-service differences.[200]

On the afternoon of October 3 Navy Department officials, including Matthews, Denfeld, and Radford, met with Vinson and his staff. Perhaps because it now seemed hopeless to expect that the Navy's witnesses could be kept from talking about the B-36, Vinson was now anxious to postpone the hearings, which were scheduled to begin two days later. He listened with sympathy to Matthews' argument for postponement. Matthews indicated that he was willing to go up to the Hill later to fight, but that he wanted first to take the Navy's case to Secretary Johnson. Denfeld agreed with him on postponement, indicating that it would give him the chance, which he had not yet had, to study the material prepared in the Navy for presentation. Evidently Vinson accepted these arguments. It was agreed that he would recommend to Congress that the B-36 hearings be adjourned until Congress returned in January, at which time an investigation of the results of unification would be the initial business of his committee.[201] To the Navy partisans, concerned as they were with the pressure of immediate reductions in expenditures for the current fiscal year, the promise of hearings in January seemed to offer little hope. By January—halfway through the fiscal year—the Navy's immediate dispute with the Defense Department would certainly be settled, and probably not in favor of the Navy. Radford had arrived late for the meeting. Although the other naval officers present had been willing to go along with postponement, he insisted that the matter be reopened. Eventually, he convinced Vinson that the hearings should proceed immediately.

That afternoon Captain Crommelin turned

copies of the Bogan correspondence over to representatives of the three wire services, stipulating that his name not be used and that the material not be released until seven o'clock that evening.[202] The following day this material, together with the manner of its release, received wide coverage in the press.

The publication of the Bogan correspondence had several immediate results. One most hoped for by the Navy partisans had undoubtedly been the shattering of Vinson's plans to postpone the hearings. Actually Radford had already persuaded Vinson to abandon postponement a few hours before Crommelin published the Bogan correspondence. The release of the letters merely provided Vinson with a convenient excuse for reversing himself. With the papers before them the House Armed Services Committee decided on October 4 to proceed with the hearings as planned, giving the Navy an opportunity to express every aspect of its discontent.[203]

A second (and actual) result was apparently the first indication to Denfeld of Matthews' dissatisfaction with him. Until Matthews had seen the Bogan correspondence, the two of them had appeared to be in complete harmony, both trying to accommodate the Navy viewpoint with the views of its sister services and of the office of the Secretary of Defense. In mid-July, in response to an invitation from the House Armed Services Committee to express their views on the agenda items that the committee was preparing to investigate, Denfeld and Matthews had sent substantially identical replies, Matthews' letter being little more than an abbreviation of Denfeld's. Both had been slightly conciliatory about the cancellation of the flush-deck carrier, although expressing concern about the future development of naval aviation as a result. Both had described the general advantages of short-range carrier-based bombers over long-range heavy bombers. Both had agreed with the Secretary of Defense that no service was entitled to "exclusive judgment" and "autonomous control" of funds allocated to it, but insisted that each service should develop its own weapons.[204]

Early in August Matthews had faced the question of who should replace Denfeld as Chief of Naval Operations when his two-year term expired in December, and decided that Denfeld should succeed himself. A month later,

when, following its confirmation by the Senate, Denfeld's commission was unofficially delivered to him, Matthews was evidently still his enthusiastic supporter.[205]

According to Matthews' later account, after reading the Bogan correspondence, with Denfeld's endorsement of it, Matthews summoned Admiral Forrest P. Sherman to Washington to see if he was willing to be the next Chief of Naval Operations. But it was not until the Bogan letter and its endorsements were published that Matthews told Denfeld "that I feared his usefulness as Chief of Naval Operations had terminated."[206] What Matthews meant by this statement is unclear, for although it sounded final, when Matthews talked to the President about Denfeld's replacement the next day he gave no indication that he had decided upon it.

And Denfeld evidently did not take his interview with Matthews very seriously. Still concerned lest he become identified with the Navy partisans (and at the same time refuting the principal grounds Matthews later claimed for dissatisfaction with him) Denfeld issued a statement denying press reports that his endorsement approved the views expressed by Bogan. It read in part:

Vice Admiral Bogan's letter to the Secretary of the Navy was an expression of his personal opinion, written in keeping with the Secretary's directive of Sept. 14. It was forwarded through official channels, via the Commander in Chief, United States Pacific Fleet, and the Chief of Naval Operations, from each of whom, by Navy regulations, a forwarding endorsement is required.

Such an endorsement does not mean approval.

Admiral A. W. Radford's forwarding endorsement specifically did not concur in the view Vice Admiral Bogan expressed. My forwarding endorsement concurs with Admiral Radford.

And it concluded with an avowal of loyalty to unification.

Unification of the armed forces of the United States is the law of the land, the principles and objectives of which I have wholeheartedly endorsed and am striving to make effective. In this effort I am fully supported by a large majority of naval personnel.[207]

Denfeld immediately ordered an investigation into the Bogan correspondence leak. But the next day Crommelin announced that he had done it, thus rendering the inquiry unnecessary. Had he chosen to remain silent, it is likely that a Naval Court of Inquiry investigation as unbecoming to the Navy as was the inquiry into the Worth memorandum would have ensued. As it was Crommelin had obtained maximum publicity for his leak, provided Vinson with a perfect excuse for not postponing the hearings, and then squelched an inquiry into what he had done—and, of course, jeopardized his career.

The engagement was won. With the hearings underway their outcome still seemed hopeful to the Navy. But a major battle had been lost, for the Navy Department entered the hearings with the Secretary potentially at odds with the Chief of Naval Operations, and both of them isolated from the support of the main body of naval officers.

The naval officers involved in the hearings nevertheless had reason to approach them with confidence. Two of the Navy's ablest officers, Burke and Radford, had helped prepare the presentations, and would themselves testify. A third, Oswald S. V. Colclough, the Navy's Judge Advocate General who, though a career naval officer, was a skilled lawyer in his own right, had helped select and groom the witnesses. Considerable effort had gone into the Navy's presentation. Characteristic of Navy staff work, preparation was oriented around the individuals making the presentation. Each witness prepared his own testimony. While all the statements were read over and criticized in common by the witnesses, each was expected to decide for himself what he was to say. As we shall see, in at least one case this led to considerable difficulty.

Matthews was invited to the conference at which individual statements were examined by the group. He declined to come. The final effort to gain his cooperation was to request that he be the last Navy witness, in hopes that as the hearings progressed he would come to realize that the dissidence within the Navy did not come from just a few rebels. Matthews insisted on being the first witness.

V. THE HEARINGS ON "UNIFICATION AND STRATEGY"

Between October 6 and October 21, 1949, the House Armed Services Committee held twelve days of hearings with an average of three and one-half hours a day on the general subject of "Unification and Strategy." For the first seven of those days (October 7 through October 13) the Navy presented its case. On the eighth day, in a brief morning session, the two senior officers of the Marine Corps appeared. As the committee report described it,

Almost the entire high command of the United States Navy appeared—the Secretary of the Navy, three of the four fleet admirals of the Navy, six admirals and two generals of the Marine Corps, one vice admiral, three rear admirals and a brigadier general of the Marine Corps, supplemented by a number of captains and lower-ranking officers and civilians of the Department of the Navy.[208]

On the ninth day of the hearings Stuart Symington, the Secretary of the Air Force, was the only witness. He was followed the next morning by the Air Force Chief of Staff, General Hoyt S. Vandenberg. He shared what was the longest day of open hearings with General Omar N. Bradley, the recently appointed Chairman of the Joint Chiefs of Staff. Two Army generals[209] and a civilian management consultant testified on the eleventh day—only one of them, the Army Chief of Staff, appearing as an Army spokesman. On the final day the former Secretary of State and wartime Army Chief of Staff, General George C. Marshall, the Secretary of Defense, Louis Johnson, and former President Herbert Hoover testified briefly.

Unlike the August hearings on B-36 procurement, the questioning of the witnesses was carried on entirely by members of the House Armed Services Committee, who had decided to conduct this phase of the hearings under the general investigatory powers of the committee rather than under the special authorization which it had been given by the House resolution.

The hearings explored the subject of national defense policy. They took place shortly after the first Russian atomic explosion, but no assessment of defense needs had yet been stated, and almost no mention was made of this event. There were six identifiable groups of protagonists, three distinguishable positions among, and sometimes within, these groups, and a wide variety of issues. The protagonists were, in order of appearance: (1) the House Armed Services Committee, (2) the Secretary of the Navy, (3) the Navy, (4) the Office of the Secretary of Defense, (5) the Air Force, and (6) the Army. (Obviously, a phrase like "the Navy" is shorthand for a coherent group of naval officers, etc.) In terms of positions taken, the Navy stood alone, except that its Secretary stood with it on some important matters; the Office of the Secretary of Defense, the Air Force, the Army (in each of these the Secretary was in agreement with the senior officers) and sometimes the Secretary of the Navy stood together (though not always closely); and the House Armed Services Committee, while it was not in complete agreement internally, contained a single and distinct view within it. Briefly, the Navy was antagonistic to certain developments under unification, among them the power which the Secretary of Defense had exercised in determining weapons policies, and a unified and reduced defense budget. The position of the rest of the military establishment was favorable to unification and its implications, and less alarmed at the prospects of a unified and reduced defense budget.

The Armed Services Committee was favorable to unification, doubtful about a unified, and opposed to a reduced, defense budget. The numerous issues given consideration during the course of the hearings ranged in nature from the highly technical question of whether a Navy Banshee fighter could intercept and shoot down an Air Force B-36 to the political-administrative issue of whether Congress was playing a sufficiently active role in the formulation of the defense budget. (Needless to say, the committee could not decide the former question; and its witnesses from the armed services could not decide the latter.)

Secretary of the Navy Francis P. Matthews was the first witness. He appeared on the morning of October 6. In introducing him, the committee chairman, Representative Carl Vinson, stressed the responsibilities of Congress under the Constitution towards the armed services, a theme which he continually emphasized throughout the hearings.

Before Matthews read his prepared statement he made a final effort to keep the conclusions of the Navy partisans from being made public. He urged the committee to hear Admiral Radford's statement in executive session as well as any other testimony which "should be classified." He had read Radford's statement, he said, and regarded it as capable of having "a definite effect upon the national security of our country," not because it contained "technically classified material," but because a disclosure of serious differences within the military establishment would have an effect which would be beneficial to our enemies.[210]

Vinson rejected Matthews' plea for closed hearings and suggested that Radford might first be heard in executive session in order to see if any portions of his statement should not be made public. (This procedure was later followed.)

Matthews' formal statement seemed to anticipate the committee's attitude towards publicity. Its general objective was to minimize dissatisfaction within the Navy. The whole problem, he said, was naval aviation. The naval air arm had expanded immensely during the Second World War and had come to expect favored treatment. When it was cut back after the war along with the rest of the Navy and the other services, he explained, it was more keenly dis-

appointed by the cuts than any other branch within the Navy. Some of its officers "voiced their protests quite frantically." In addition, a number of naval aviators spoke "vigorously in opposition" to the National Defense Act of 1947 during Congressional hearings and these people roused their fellow fliers. Two of these witnesses were identified: Admiral Bogan and Captain Crommelin. "I can find little that is new in what they say now," Matthews told the committee, "as compared with their testimony before the Hoffman committee on July 1, 1947."[211] The tone of Matthews' statement can be observed in the following passage:

The spectacle of distinguished naval aviators, holding high office in the Navy, denouncing a law offered to the Congress by the President of the United States and twice overwhelmingly approved by the Congress, could hardly be expected to be utterly without effect upon some members of the Navy personnel among whom they are numbered. However, the fact that they have seen fit, in the exercise of their discretion, to speak out so sensationally and in such an un-Navy-like manner, against a law which they can be rightly expected to support does not in any sense justify a conclusion that the morale of their portion of the Navy personnel which is not involved in their forensic manoeuvers is all shot to pieces.[212]

Matthews thus attempted to attribute the whole disturbance within the Navy to spoiled and die-hard aviators. He later claimed that by this time he had concluded that he could no longer count on loyal support of Admiral Denfeld, but he would hardly have tried to isolate the naval aviators if he had any substantial doubts as to whether his Chief of Naval Operations, a submariner and battleship admiral, would support the "aviators." Furthermore, while Matthews had turned down Denfeld's offer to help prepare this statement, and while he did not accept Denfeld's suggestions for changing it (nor, for that matter, the Judge Advocate General's suggestions), nevertheless he continued to expect Denfeld to support his position. His refusal to take into account Denfeld's suggestions and proposals for changes had, as will be seen, unfortunate consequences.

In the questioning of Matthews which followed, Vinson rebutted the Secretary's contentions about Navy discontent, arguing that it was a legitimate reaction to a severe cutting of all naval forces.[213]

Two other matters received special attention. First, Matthews was questioned closely about his reason for marking "confidential" the communiqué from his office to which Admiral Bogan had responded. Here, as in his comments to the committee before reading his statement, he candidly admitted his belief that the security classification regulations could be interpreted to include matters which involved efficiency as well as security. Second, Vinson's questioning brought out the fact that Matthews did not approve of the August 8 proposal of the Defense Management Committee to cut the Navy's fiscal 1950 budget, and that he had objected to it.

Since Matthews' statement was his last attempt to keep the Navy's quarrel from the public, it was not easy for the naval officers who read it to appreciate the middle position which he was trying to take. In telling the committee of his disapproval of the proposed new cut in the fiscal 1950 budget, he expressed his belief that the Air Force plans were "unbalanced in favor of strategic bombing."[214] But he said much to offend the many regular Navy officers who were in no mood to understand halfway loyalty to their views. His attack upon Crommelin was particularly severe, and his attribution of Navy discontent to spoiled aviators and die-hard critics of unification, while couched in moderate language, hardly displayed an understanding of the attitudes of most of the senior naval officers, and, of course, of their juniors as well. Indeed, in view of the officers' feelings, the more reassurances he gave the committee about Navy morale, the more certain were they that their own Chief did not understand them. And finally, Matthews, with one exception (the pending reduction in current expenditures), strongly supported the actions of his Chief, Secretary of Defense Johnson, in whom these officers had lost all confidence. To the aroused professional men of the Navy, a man loyal to Johnson could not be loyal to their service. The explosiveness of these feelings was made apparent on the first day of the hearings when Matthews, at one point in the question period, was asked by Congressman Porter Hardy, Jr., of Virginia:

Now, in the services, of course, you have certain prescribed regulations which military personnel must follow in expressing themselves. I would like to inquire as to what avenue a conscientious believer that a change is necessary in the interest of national security has to make his views known if he runs into a stone wall within his own department or if he gets blocked in the Department of Defense and can't make his position known.[215]

Matthews replied, "I don't know how he could become blocked."[216] There followed "a loud and jeering laugh of disbelief from his audience of naval officers."[217]

Matthews concluded his testimony before lunch on the first day of the hearings. The assumption upon which much of his testimony was based—that his Chief of Naval Operations would stand by him—was immediately, if temporarily borne out. At the conclusion of the session Denfeld disclosed to the press that he had supported Matthews in his effort to keep Radford's statement from being made public: "I told Mr. Vinson that the [Radford] statement would just continue to keep up the interservice fight, cause continued bickering and be of aid and comfort to any possible enemy."[218]

That afternoon, following Matthews' testimony, the committee held an executive session which lasted for two hours, at which Admiral Radford read his statement. It was agreed by a vote of 9 to 6 to hear the Admiral's presentation in the public session scheduled for the following day.

On the same day, Matthews directed Denfeld to place "appropriate charges" against Crommelin;[219] and the Navy gave General McNarney a preview of the effects of the $353 million budget cut for the Navy proposed by the Defense Management Committee. At the conclusion of the preview it was decided that further analysis was needed so that the effect of the cut upon naval forces, procurement, and the naval shore establishment could be shown more clearly.[220] Also on the opening day of the hearings the President signed the $5.8 billion Foreign Aid Appropriation Act and the $1.314 billion Mutual Defense Assistance Act.[221]

On the next day Admiral Radford was principal witness before the House Armed Services Committee, this time reading his statement and answering questions in open session for more than four hours. As the first spokesman for the Navy officers, he introduced their other witnesses, and then went on to speak in general terms of national strategy, weapons policy, and roles and missions, laying out the major arguments of the Navy's case. In conclusion, he summarized his statement as follows:

1. The B-36, under any theory of war, is a bad gamble with national security. Should an enemy force an atomic war upon us, the B-36 would be useless defensively and inadequate offensively. The plane itself is not so important as the acceptance or rejection of the theory of atom blitz warfare which it symbolizes. It is fortunate that honest doubts as to the adequacy of the B-36 have served to bring this more vital issue before the country.

2. I do not believe that the threat of atomic blitz will be an effective deterrent to a war, or that it will win a war. I do not believe that the atomic blitz theory is generally accepted by military men. However, if, after careful study of all sides of the question, the retaliatory atomic blitz were to become the determined and studied policy of the United States, then, we must have a much more efficient weapon than the B-36 to deliver the blitz. We are today capable of procuring more effective and more efficient planes for the task than the B-36.

3. Development in the Air Force of planes suitable for tactical and fighter missions has suffered by overemphasis on the heavy bomber. This is apparent by inspecting the proportions for each category—not in terms of numbers of groups and planes—but in terms of money, men, and materials. Less than 6 percent of Air Force research and development funds is earmarked for tactical and fighter types. The lack of adequate fighters may have grave consequences for future security of our bases and our homeland. It is not only wasteful, but may be disastrous to spend our scarce budget dollars on large, expensive planes dedicated to an unsound theory of warfare.

4. The unusual procedures used to push the B-36 program to its present status were not justified. They undermine all unification; they prevent progress toward mutual trust, understanding, and unified planning; they short-cut the vital and proven procedures developed through experience for safeguarding the security of our country.

5. Any service must be permitted to bring an experimental weapon through the development, test, and evaluation stages. On the other hand, any service must be prevented from procuring any weapon in quantity until it has passed these stages.

6. We should develop weapons capable of maximum effectiveness from all land and sea areas which we can control. We should push research and development of weapons to this end. We should not, however, base our war plans on such weapons, nor should we procure them in quantity, until they are proven. Our defense bud-

get should not be used for unproven weapons. American taxpayers cannot afford billion-dollar blunders. Nor can they afford expensive military procurement on a stop-and-go basis involving costly cancellations for which our country receives nothing.

7. Strategic bombing should be a primary role of the Air Force. However, the United States is not sound in relying on the so-called strategic bombing concept to its present extent. This concept is symbolized by the B-36 delivering the atom blitz. In the minds of our citizens this fallacious concept promises a short cut to victory. Our citizens must realize that its military leaders cannot make this promise—that there is no short cut, no cheap, no easy way to win a war. We must realize that the threat of instant atomic retaliation will not prevent it, and may even invite it. We must realize that we cannot gamble that the atom blitz of annihilation will even win a war. We must realize if war is forced upon us, we must win it, and win it in such a way that it can be followed by stable, livable peace.[222]

As this summary indicates, in the foreground of Radford's argument stood the B-36. He objected to it for its performance capabilities (i.e., its ability to carry out a strategic bombing plan), for the emphasis the Air Force was giving its production, for the manner in which its procurement was handled, and for the strategic concepts which its development and expected use assumed. The Navy witnesses who followed Radford mounted a well-organized and detailed attack upon the performance capabilities of the B-36, made some persuasive arguments against what they considered to be the strategic implications of the B-36 (i.e., exclusive reliance upon the "atomic blitz"), and claimed that the Air Force emphasis upon the B-36 was unjustified, that the Air Force intended to eliminate naval aviation by "nibbling it to death." Radford himself presented support for his general assertion that "the unusual procedures used to push the B-36 program to its present status were not justified." Later his assertion was supported in detail by Admiral Denfeld, who claimed that twice within the year (in January and April) the Air Force had decided to concentrate even more of its budget upon procurement of B-36's without consulting the Defense Secretary or the Joint Chiefs.

He insisted that at the time of these increments in the Air Force's commitment to the B-36, its prototypes had not been adequately tested and that no results were available from the joint studies undertaken in the fall of 1948 to evaluate all aspects of strategic air warfare.[223]

Here Radford was speaking as an exponent of unification, and of the powers of the JCS in the determination of forces for each of the armed services. He insisted that the Air Force should have obtained approval from the JCS before it thus altered its procurement program so extensively. He thus attacked the principle of service autonomy with respect to weapons-procurement. The Navy had invoked the same principle in its criticisms of the cancellation of the flush-deck carrier the previous April. But Radford drew a distinction between these two situations which remained an important (though not unquestioned) element in the Navy's case throughout the remainder of the hearings. A weapons-policy consists of two phases, he stated:

First, the development of weapons, and, second, the procurement of proven weapons and their assimilation into current war plans.

During both phases, each of the armed services has a valid interest in action proposed by any other service. The effect upon final decisions which that interest has, however, differs in the two phases.

In the pure development of weapons—in other words, in the design, production, and testing of prototypes—it is fundamental that each service must be free to carry through the prototype state any proposed weapon which that service feels will contribute to the execution of its primary mission. In developing such prototypes, due regard must be had to the views of the other services and other agencies such as the Munitions Board and the Research and Development Board. Other services and agencies must not, however, have the power to veto in the development stage. Had we not followed this general principle in the past, many valuable weapons would have died on paper.

When the issue becomes one of large fiscal obligations for quantity procurement of specific weapons, the three services should become partners in striving for sound decisions. They approach the problem with an interest comparable to that which they have in joint war planning.[224]

This was in fact the established procedure, Radford indicated, and quoted from the Key West agreement the stated intention "that an individual service is to be permitted to carry through the development stage any material improvement program or new weapon development program" it considered essential, while "the ultimate application and utilization of the product of such a development program" was to be subject to JCS recommendations.[225]

This distinction between the development and use phases of a weapon was generally accepted, so it is understandable why it was never challenged by either Congressmen or service men. But its application by Radford to the flush-deck carrier was not so clear, and Vinson challenged this:

Chairman VINSON. Admiral, when have you classified the building of any particular type of ship as a prototype? For 20 years we have sought to get two similar ships and every time we laid down a building program of three ships, the last one has been entirely different than the first one.

Admiral RADFORD. Yes, sir.

Chairman VINSON. And so you are not trying to put yourself in the position to say that you were advocating the building of a supercarrier as a prototype to have other ships built along that line. You wanted that carrier of a particular kind and it is not a prototype, it is building a ship.

Admiral RADFORD. Mr. Vinson, times have changed. Under this unified organization, and being for unification, the Navy is required to make this new procedure effective. Mr. Forrestal determined that we would build one as a prototype, completely evaluate it and then the question of additional ones would come up.

Chairman VINSON. That would have been left up to Congress.

Admiral RADFORD. Beg pardon?

Chairman VINSON. Congress would determine whether to carry on a shipbuilding program of that character.

Admiral RADFORD. I thought that the Joint Chiefs of Staff would have to recommend it to Congress under the new procedure.

Then Congressman Paul J. Kilday, Democrat, a senior committee member from Texas, joined the questioning:

Mr. KILDAY. But your whole statement, Admiral, is based on the point that as a prototype the individual service should have been permitted to continue, so that you did regard it as a prototype?

Admiral RADFORD. That is correct.

Mr. KILDAY. Having built your prototype, if the Navy had come to the conclusion that it was the proper weapon, wouldn't you then have felt just as badly about being refused permission to go ahead with additional carriers as you do now on the cancellation of the prototype?

Admiral RADFORD. I had hopes, Mr. Kilday, that by the time that ship was finished, which would have been 1952, that we would have a much better mutual understanding between the services and that we wouldn't run into these snarls.[226]

With doubt thus thrown upon Radford's effort to classify the construction of the flush-deck carrier as solely a weapons-development project, it should be understandable why the House Appropriations Committee had insisted the previous May on knowing whether the Navy had JCS authorization for the flush-deck carrier (applying the procedure provided for procurement-for-use rather than for weapons-development) even though the Navy called its new ship a prototype.

While this distinction in the Key West agreement was basic to his argument, Radford did not rely upon it exclusively to ground his criticism of the carrier cancellation, or of the B-36 procurement increases of January and April 1949. The carrier was cancelled, he asserted, without an adequate appreciation of its place in the defense team,[227] thereby including in his argument the merits of the decision, as well as the procedure in making it. As for the new B-36 orders, in addition to claiming that they should have been submitted for approval by the JCS because they involved phase two of a weapons policy, he insisted that they should not have been approved because they had not been adequately evaluated, and because an adequate evaluation would show them to be undesirable as the major bomber type of the Air Force.

Finally, there were issues on which Radford took no position. He did not question the total budget ceiling of the Defense Department, nor the limitation of strategic plans to the assumption that if war came it would be total. While thus avoiding any criticism of the adequacy of the total defense budget, and the wisdom of Johnson's new economy drive, he did, of course, question the proportion of each which fell upon the Navy. Indeed, he might also have shown that some important aspects of the air power strategy which he was criticizing had been accepted out of necessity because of the low defense budget ceilings of the past two fiscal years. His avoidance of any challenge to total defense expenditures was presumably due to a belief that these were not matters which he could properly raise in public.

But his failure to mention the possibility of limited war, which the United States would not be prepared to fight, is not quite so easily explained, particularly in light of his striking challenge of the "atomic blitz" plans of the Department of Defense. And, it may be added, it is hard to conceive of any limited war in which the Navy would not have an important role. Yet it seems quite probable that Radford, while aware of the needs of limited war, felt that Congress would appropriate money for carriers only if convinced that carriers would be an important tool in blitz warfare.

The committee's questioning of Radford following his prepared statement brought out his strong difference with Matthews, who had minimized the importance or extent of low morale in the Navy. Navy morale, Radford contended, was low for legitimate and serious reasons.[228] And his comments on Navy morale led into a recurrent theme in his testimony and in the statements of subsequent witnesses: that the Navy lacked confidence in the intentions, actions, and, most particularly, judgments of the other members of the unification team.[229]

On the day following Radford's presentation of the Navy's master statement of its case to the House Armed Services Committee, a team of technical experts from the Navy was originally scheduled to give detailed testimony in support of his denunciation of the B-36 for its performance capabilities and for the strategic assumptions upon which its planned use was based. But before calling these people, the chairman of the committee arranged to have Rear Admiral Herbert G. Hopwood, the Budget Director of the Navy, and W. J. McNeil, the Comptroller of the Department of Defense, testify concerning the cut in defense expenditures for the current fiscal year which the Defense Management Committee was attempting to make.[230]

Two days before, while Secretary Matthews was testifying, Vinson interrupted his questions about Navy morale to state his belief that Navy morale was low because of the severe reductions being made in its budget. Now Vinson, in introducing the two budget officers, one from the Defense Department and one from the Navy, outlined the reductions with which the Navy was or would be faced by comparing the fiscal 1950 budget (then in conference committee) with its predecessor, and indicating what he understood was being planned for fiscal 1951. He also described what he knew about the expenditure reduction program of the Defense Management Committee. Summarizing, he stated:

It would appear that the Congress intended to let Navy aviation wither on the vine by failing to give enough aircraft to maintain the required number of operating aircraft. And it would also appear that the leaders in the Pentagon in the other services and in the Office of the Secretary of Defense are themselves out of sympathy with naval air power for it was their recommendation that persuaded the Congress to take the action as stated.[231]

The questioning of the two witnesses made public for the first time the significant features of the Defense Management Committee's activities, which have been described above.[232] From the questions of the Congressional committeemen, and their stated reactions to the answers they received, many of their attitudes about the defense budget were revealed, attitudes which were repeatedly expressed throughout the remainder of the hearings, particularly by the Committee Chairman, Carl Vinson.

The committee displayed deep resentment that the Secretary of Defense was, in effect, trying to cut the fiscal 1950 defense budget by reducing expenditures in his Department, at the same time that he was encouraging passage of the budget at a level of appropriations which ignored his planned cuts. Vinson explicitly denounced this procedure as a usurpation of the functions of Congress. As he put it,

Now, what disturbs me, members of the committee, is this: The basic question is whether or not Congress has a voice in this matter or whether it is to be entirely set by the Secretary of Defense. That is the basic thing. That is fundamental. Here it is after months of hearing by one of the most distinguished groups of men in the Congress, who reach a decision. And I will tell you that when an appropriation committee composed of Mr. Mahon, Mr. Engel, and Mr. Sheppard, Mr. Plumley, and Mr. Sikes give you an appropriation it is certainly justified. Now, they reach a decision. Then Mr. Johnson, without the slightest information as to what effect it is going to have, sets lower figures and tells these departments to disprove them. The country must know what is going on in the Pentagon. It is time Congress knows what is going on.[233]

The committee also revealed a disposition to be hostile to cuts in any of the services. On the other hand, it never lost sight of the neces-

sity, whether political or economic, for economy measures.[234]

Throughout this episode with the budget officers, the committee members took a strongly pro-Navy line in their questions, denouncing the Defense Management Committee and interpreting its economy plans as fixed and definite directives, a position which later Navy witnesses took, despite denials from Johnson's spokesmen.[235]

With what Vinson regarded as the fiscal background for the hearings thus presented to the committee, the team of Navy witnesses resumed their testimony on the day scheduled (October 8). Radford had been led to say, under questioning, that he did not believe the committee was competent to judge the B-36 as a weapon. But in his written statement he had expressed the hope that the "testimony [of the Navy witnesses who followed him] will assist you in an evaluation of the B-36 as a weapon."[236] And he had laid out a series of contentions concerning the capabilities of the B-36 which were so general and fundamental that a determination of their accuracy would go far towards a thorough evaluation of the B-36. Following Radford, a group of technical experts from the Navy testified in support of the Admiral's claims about the B-36 and strategic bombing in general. The qualifications and major lines of argument of these witnesses were, in brief, as follows:

(1) Captain Frederick M. Trapnell led off for the Navy experts, taking up the remainder of the third day of the hearings (October 8). A senior and distinguished Navy test pilot then in command of the naval air test center at Patuxent, Md., he talked about "the over-all aspects of the interception of heavy bombers by jet fighters." The unescorted B-36 can be found, intercepted, out-maneuvered, and shot down, all without great difficulty, he asserted,[237] and went on to discuss in general terms the capabilities of radar and of Navy jet fighter aircraft. He concluded with this challenge:

It is impossible to reconcile the publicity in favor of the B-36 with the reluctance to engage in joint comparative tests with the Navy. This employment of the equipment would be the most valuable possible training for both services.

I believe, however, that it will result in cancellation of any further B-36 production.[238]

On the following Monday (October 10) six Navy experts testified:

(2) Lieutenant Commander Edward W. Harrison, a specialist in electronics who was then a member of the Radar Panel of the Research and Development Board, and an adviser in a similar capacity to the JCS, was supposed to talk about "the technical aspects and capabilities of radar" as used both in the interception of the B-36 and in strategic bombing by the B-36. However, he devoted all of his attention to the interception problem, stressing how easy radar detection of large, slow, high-flying bombers was, and the availability of most radar technology to the Soviet Union.[239]

(3) Commander William N. Leonard, a Banshee fighter squadron commander and former test pilot, discussed daylight interception problems and fighter performance at 40,000 feet and above. "Navy jet fighters," he said,

currently operate freely and effectively in the regions above 40,000 feet. They have proved their ability to intercept, overtake, and shoot down targets that are much faster and more difficult than the B-36 class of bomber could be at its best.

In the face of current world-wide jet fighter capabilities, a bomber with performance no better than the ultimate attainable in the B-36 has a negligible chance of survival.[240]

(4) Commander William Martin, an "outstanding night-fighter and all-weather" pilot, gave testimony about nighttime interception of bombers. He mentioned the newest night-fighter developed, or under development, by the Navy, reiterated the advantage of fighters over bombers of the big, slow type, and went on to emphasize the many hours of daylight through which B-36's would have to fly to reach Moscow, and the few hours of darkness at 40,000 feet.[241]

(5) Commander Alfred B. Metsger, an aeronautical engineer who held the "key position in the development of modern Navy fighter aircraft" from 1945 until early 1949, summarized "the interception problem as it affects fighter design, and the vulnerability of the [B-36] bomber to the guns, rockets, and missiles which the fighter can shoot." He described studies which he said showed conclusively "that two Banshees are more than a match for the large long-range bomber." He mentioned evidence which indicated that Russia had fighters which in "combat ability are equal to or better than the best in our country today."[242] And he concluded with a reaffirmation of what had already been claimed by the lead-off man, Trapnell. He said:

Bombers, even these superb modern jet bombers, remain utterly dependent on their fighter escort. Lacking such support, a large bomber operating at long range over enemy territory cannot expect to get by without disastrous losses, neither night nor day.[243]

(6) Mr. Abraham Hyatt, also an aeronautical engineer and then head of the Design Branch of the Navy's Bureau of Aeronautics, talked about the maximum performance characteristics of the B-36. He presented an elaborately reasoned argument to show that the B-36 would suffer unacceptable losses in an unescorted run over Russian territory.[244]

(7) Commander Eugene Tatom, an aviation ordnance specialist then in charge of research and development of aviation ordnance for the Navy, spoke of the difficulty of accurate bombing at high altitudes, and the limited destructive effects of atomic bombs. Tatom proved to be one of the most colorful of the Navy witnesses. High altitude bombing is difficult and inaccurate, he asserted, and radar bombing can never be as accurate as visual bombing, which, even under ideal conditions, at 40,000 feet is of questionable accuracy. Yet radar must be used for high-altitude night bombing. Hence, he concluded that high-altitude night bombing is necessarily quite inaccurate.[245]

The use of atomic bombs does not help in this situation, for atomic bombs have a limited destructive area and are very expensive. Accuracy with them is therefore even more important than with conventional bombing. On the basis of this reasoning he concluded:

To have a reasonable assurance of destroying a particular installation from 40,000 feet, at night or in daylight, we must send enough planes to saturate the area with bombs, after allowing for expected operational losses and combat losses of aircraft before the target is reached, even when using atom bombs.

And he ended his statement with a direct refutation:

Just let me assure you, gentlemen, that precision bombing of military targets deep in enemy territory from 40,000 feet at night or in daylight is a myth.[246]

In the course of Tatom's testimony on the power of atomic bombs he made a statement which he had added to his presentation at the last minute, after it had been checked over by fellow witnesses. He said:

You could stand in the open at one end of the north-south runway at the Washington Airport, with no more protection than the clothes you now have on, and have an atom bomb explode at the other end of the runway without serious injury to you.[247]

The hearings were hastily adjourned at noon, following the completion of Tatom's statement, in order to allow committee members time to attend to other business, but not before Vinson had forewarned the witness that the committee would want to question him the following morning, especially concerning his last-quoted statement.[248] That evening and the following morning the press gave wide coverage to Tatom's remarkable claims regarding the limited destructiveness of atomic bomb explosions.

Late that day (Monday, October 10), following a speech before the AFL national convention at which he repeated earlier charges that the Navy was waging a "campaign of terror" against unification, the Secretary of Defense released to the press a letter which he was sending to Vinson as a reply to the latter's continuing criticisms in the hearings of the methods and motives of Johnson's economy program. Johnson recalled in his letter that Vinson had said the previous week that Congress ought to be advised of the money requests made by each service as well as the final budget recommendations made by the Department of Defense. Johnson claimed that on January 26, 1949, Vinson had received from Forrestal "complete information" for the entire current military budget, and he attached a copy of the Forrestal communication. Johnson's letter went on to say, "I would greatly appreciate an opportunity to appear before your committee," and to suggest that Vinson invite as witnesses former President Hoover, Generals Eisenhower, Bradley, Vandenberg, and Collins, and Admiral Denfeld.[249]

Until he saw this letter, Vinson fully expected that the hearings would be closed at the end of that week, when the Navy witnesses had completed their testimony, and would re-open, as he had originally planned, as an inquiry into the results of unification the following January. But when Vinson learned from reporters of Johnson's letter to him, he announced at once that Johnson, and "anybody else who will help us out," would be called as witnesses.[250]

Tatom returned as the first witness the next morning (October 11). He read a supplementary statement in which he presented the basis for his claims about atomic bomb destructiveness. He showed them to be based upon findings of the Medical Division of the United States Strategic Bombing Survey, as published in "The Effects of Atomic Bombs on Health and Medical Services in Hiroshima and Nagasaki." Representative Paul J. Kilday of Texas challenged these figures by quoting from a document issued by the Manhattan District, the wartime Army command which produced the atomic bomb, and forced Tatom to admit that the two sets of figures did not agree. Democratic committee member Melvin Price, also a member of the Joint Atomic Energy Committee, emphasized the obsolescence of Tatom's data:

Mr. PRICE. Mr. Chairman, I would like to bring out one further point. While we are talking about the Hiroshima bomb, that was constructed and built in 1945—not in 1949, isn't that true?
Commander TATOM. That is right, sir.
Mr. PRICE. That is all I have, Mr. Chairman.[251]

But Price had more to say to the press after the hearing. Then he declared that the Navy high command had displayed "surprising ignorance" of the effectiveness of the atomic bomb.[252]

That day Tatom's claims were denied on the floor of both Houses of Congress and disclaimed by the Secretary of Defense. Emerging from a conference with the President on the Navy–Air Force row, Johnson emphatically denied to the press that Tatom had spoken officially in his estimate of the atomic bomb.[253] Brien McMahon, speaking as its leading authority on atomic energy, told the Senate that "the statements made in yesterday's hearing were untrue. It is dangerous to overemphasize the importance of the atomic weapon, but God knows it may be fatal to under-emphasize it."[254] Following the line of unofficial Air Force charges against the Navy, McMahon further contended that the Navy had wanted a super carrier in order to deliver the atomic bomb, but "now when the issue of the super carrier had been decided adversely the Navy finds the atomic bomb of small destructive force." And, anticipating one of Symington's charges in his statement to the House Armed Services Committee a week later, McMahon, who had conferred with Symington just prior to taking the floor of the Senate, expressed the hope that "this kind of action would stop before irreparable harm is done to our national security."[255] And on the floor of the House, Representative Chet Holifield, a member of the McMahon Atomic Energy Committee, denounced Tatom's testimony as dangerous and apparently based on an evaluation of the obsolete bombs dropped on Japan.[256]

In the Vinson Committee hearings on that morning, Representative George Bates had attempted to rescue Tatom's main point, which had been lost sight of in the furor:

I believe the point the commander is trying to bring out here is the effect of the bomb within a certain radius or what we might call precision bombing. And unless that bomb is dropped within, say, a mile of the target that it is aimed at, then, it will have practically no effect . . . the bomb must be a precision hit in order to be effective on the target of the B-36.[257]

But Congressman Bates did not discuss the coverage and hence the lesser need for precision in the use of the new powerful atomic bombs.

(8) Following brief questioning of Commander Tatom, Captain John H. Sides, a specialist in ordnance and weapon-systems, who was then responsible for guided missile development for the Navy Department, described to the committee how highly vulnerable the B-36 would be, in comparison with fighters, to anti-aircraft guided missiles then developed or under development, and argued that Russia was not likely to be backward in these developments.[258]

(9) Rear Admiral Ralph A. Ofstie, a naval aviator who had been a senior naval member of the United States Strategic Bombing Survey in its studies of air warfare against Japan, and subsequently a member of the JCS evaluation group for the Bikini atomic bomb tests, then presented a systematic denunciation of strategic bombing as a military technique. His views were assertedly personal but representative.

He presented his case against strategic bombing on the basis of the following theme: "Any military weapon or technique has to be measured by at least three yardsticks. Will it work? Will it contribute to military victory? Will it support the national policies and objectives?" He assumed that the first question had already been answered (in the negative), and went on to the second and third. He interpreted the second as inquiring whether "successful delivery of the bomb [would] destroy the enemy capacity and will to resist" and cause him to surrender. It could be best answered with the results of strategic bombing in World War II, and with an analysis of a prospective enemy's vulnerability to strategic bombing. For strategic bombing results he drew from the United States Strategic Bombing Survey and the British Bombing Survey Unit the conclusions that the "strategic bombing campaign against essential war production did not have a decisive effect on the outcome of the war," but that, in the case of Germany, "the campaign against transportation targets [which he classed as tactical bombing] . . . so reduced the mobility and logistic supply of the German armies that the offensive on land was immeasurably assisted." Yet, he insisted, "the import of this lesson has not been incorporated into the current theory of strategic bombing."[259]

For an appraisal of the prospective enemy's vulnerability to strategic attack, Ofstie referred the committee to "a recent report on this subject to the Joint Chiefs of Staff," apparently speaking of the Harmon Board report of the results of the studies undertaken the previous autumn at the request of Forrestal, to determine whether atomic bombs could be delivered to targets of strategic significance.

He then turned to his third yardstick for measuring a military weapon. As applied to strategic bombing, it was: "Does the concept of strategic bombing effectively support the policies, objectives, and commitments of the United States?" He related war to national objectives: "War is an instrument of national policy; consequently the method of waging war must effectively support national policy. Military aims must be consonant with political aims." And by this standard he judged that "the greatest defect of the present concept of strategic bombing . . . [is] its contradictory relation to fundamental ideals, policies, and commitments of the United States."

These ideals, policies, and commitments of the United States Admiral Ofstie listed as follows:

1) The defense of Western Europe, which, if defended by strategic bombing, would only be destroyed.

2) The bombing of urban areas, which he held to be technologically unavoidable, is "contrary to our fundamental ideals."

3) We are committed to the maintenance of the physical structure of civilization, on humanitarian grounds, and in order more effectively to oppose communism.

4) The concept of "instant retaliation" has encouraged "bomb-rattling jingoism," and led us to over-commit ourselves in relation to our military strength. "In recent weeks we have been made aware of the fact that we are not alone in our possession of the atomic weapon, which had been the basis of this illusory strength."[260]

Having thus disposed of strategic bombing on the grounds that its basic characteristics were in conflict with our policies, objectives, and commitments, Ofstie then turned to the argument that the "present emphasis on strategic bombing" failed to contribute to "the essential requirements for the security of the United States." This was a particularly bold assertion, since the most telling argument in favor of the 70-group Air Force had been that, whatever else was needed, the first priority belonged to the instrument which could deter by providing effective, instant retaliation.

Ofstie, following a line of reasoning strikingly similar to the one taken by the Policy Planning Staff in the State Department in its dealings with the Joint Strategic Survey Committee, listed as the essential requirements of our military forces for minimum security:

1. The defense of Western Europe.

2. The defense of Allied bases against disastrous air attack.

3. Attack on the vulnerable elements of enemy strength (which he held to be military forces and their supply lines, requiring tactical air attack).

4. We and our Allies must maintain control of the sea, because of our commitments in Western Europe.

Referring to the recent disclosure of the first atomic explosion by Russia, and pointing up the inconsistency between America's foreign aid commitment to Western Europe and its alleged reliance upon the B-36, he said:

The present concept of strategic bombing is in most urgent need of review at this time, not alone because of the recent information from abroad but also in its relation to the European military aid program.[261]

Pursuing this same point, he concluded his statement by insisting that national security required that we have "forces which can meet the actual demands of the current situation—which can add the most strength to the military power of the democracies in the critical years immediately ahead."

While Admiral Ofstie won high praise from the committee for the quality of his statement,[262] no heed was paid in the questioning which followed to the fundamental questions which he had raised regarding the relationship between the weapons and forces policies of the military establishment on the one hand and the diplomatic, economic, and military alliance of the United States with Western Europe on the other hand.

(10) Brigadier General Vernon E. Megee, USMC, Assistant Director of Marine Aviation in the Office of the Chief of Naval Operations and the last technical expert, was the next Navy witness.[263] He appeared as the major authority among the Navy team on tactical aviation. He emphasized the importance of tactical air power for the success of German and Japanese forces in the early phases of World War II, and for Soviet successes later. He spoke of the difficulties of obtaining adequate tactical support from the Air Corps by the Army ground forces during World War II. He argued that Russia would continue to place its faith in tactical aviation as the basic concept for the employment of aircraft in battle. He insisted that the then existing ratio of tactical air units in the Air Force to ground troops in the Army was much too small; and that "tactical air force exists largely on paper —at least that part of it which is earmarked for Army support." He referred for support of his assertions to the recently publicized

charges about the Air Force by General Devers.

Admiral William H. P. Blandy, Commander in Chief of the Atlantic Fleet, was the next witness. Since he was not an aviator, his testimony served as an illustration of the inaccuracy of Secretary Matthews' claim that the whole trouble was due to naval aviators grown spoiled during the war. He spoke with special authority because during the war he was one of the chief developers of amphibious warfare in the Pacific and since then he had been in command of the Bikini Atoll atomic bomb tests.[264]

As a fleet commander he was concerned with the functions of the Navy and the adequacy of its forces to perform those functions. He presented a calm and persuasive case for better treatment of the Navy, emphasizing its necessary minimum requirements, in view of its responsibilities, and explaining its value in terms of the versatility of its weapons. But he concluded his presentation with a warning in reference to the carrier cancellation: "Should the day come when the United States Navy can no longer improve its weapons and techniques in accordance with its own ideas of its needs, it will signal the end of our command of the sea."[265]

Blandy's rank and moderation evoked considerably more questions from the committee than had been put to any of his predecessors since Admiral Radford opened the Navy's presentation.

But he was nonetheless firm. Under questioning he told the committee that the cuts in the current Navy budget would reduce the operating forces of the Navy "dangerously below the minimum estimate of forces I have submitted to the Chief of Naval Operations as needed at the beginning of a war."[266]

Retired Fleet Admiral William F. Halsey was the first witness to be heard on the following day (October 12). He threw the weight of his authority behind the Navy presentation, introducing nothing new in evidence or argument, but restating most of the Navy's contentions.

Once this got him in trouble. He spoke generally against strategic bombing as the airpower extremists described it. When asked who in the Air Force was advocating it, he said he had read it in the paper, and then that he had heard a letter of Symington's quoted in the hearings.[267] Radford thereupon handed Vinson the following extract from a speech Symington had made in February to the Catholic Club, Norwalk, Connecticut:

A B-36 with an A-bomb can take off from this continent and destroy distant objectives which might require ground armies years to take and then only at the expense of heavy casualties. The B-36 can do the job within 16 hours after taking off from this continent and then return nonstop to its home base, all this at the risk of 16 American lives.[268]

Halsey had actually read this paragraph in the highly partisan pamphlet entitled "The Strategic Bombing Myth," which had circulated widely in Washington by this time, and which all the Navy witnesses had evidently read. Radford, quickly realizing that fact, handed Vinson the pamphlet itself in order to show him the quote. Vinson promptly read it into the record, thinking at the time that he was quoting from Radford's statement. Later that day the Defense Department gave reporters at the hearings a document which quoted Symington's speech further as follows:

Of course, it [the B-36] could not replace the other members of the team. The Air Force has never claimed that a strategic air offensive alone could win the next war.

And the following day Vinson had the whole speech entered on the record of the hearing.[269]

Following Halsey's appearance, a statement by the wartime Chief of Naval Operations, retired Fleet Admiral Ernest J. King, was read, after explanations were made that he was ill. Then Captain Arleigh A. Burke, who had risen to fame as a commander of destroyers, now Assistant Chief of Naval Operations, in charge of the Organizational Policy and Research Division (Op. 23), proceeded to give the most systematic and complete defense of the flush-deck carrier recorded in the hearings. The argument was already familiar so long as he talked of the next step in the development of carriers, and of the problems of handling heavier aircraft. But he did go on to some new ground for support. As weapon advancements of the enemy occur, he argued, the flush-deck carrier will eventually become necessary for command of the sea, although it is not now necessary. Moreover, a greater flexibility in range and aircraft types will be possible with the flush-deck carrier.

Burke summarized his argument as follows:

1. Our country is a maritime nation and will always need to command the sea. A Navy will be required to obtain and exercise command of the sea. A Navy will need to take advantage of the technical progress in weapons. It will need to utilize aircraft of improved characteristics.

2. The new carrier U. S. S. *United States* would have enabled the Navy to speed progress in the design of aircraft of better performance characteristics without the hampering restrictions on plane design necessitated by the physical characteristics of the present carriers.

3. The U. S. S. *United States* would have been a most useful component of the fleet, in performing other naval missions, and to support the Army and Air Force, because of the types of aircraft she could carry, the versatility possible in the composition of her air group and the large number of planes she could carry.

4. It takes several years to design and build a new carrier. She is usable for 20 or more years. Consequently, a new carrier must be capable of operating planes foreseeable within her lifetime.

5. A prototype of any weapon is desirable to evaluate new methods of tactics, operations, and equipment. When the need for several of these carriers becomes apparent later on, there may not be time for evaluation of one carrier before the others need to be built.

6. Aircraft are presently the most powerful weapons of the Navy. The United States needs a new prototype carrier. That carrier should have the improved characteristics of (a) flush-deck, (b) greater hanger-deck height, (c) greater capacity to operate heavier and faster aircraft.[270]

Admiral Thomas C. Kinkaid, another non-aviator who had been a cruiser division and task force commander in the Pacific in the Second World War, as the next witness, then proposed to discuss the nature of war, past, present and future. He pointed out that unescorted bombing stopped in 1943 after the Ploesti oil refinery and Schweinfurt raids of August and October, respectively, and claimed that the war proved area bombing inconclusive. He attacked strategic bombing as irrelevant in the defense of Europe against Russian aggression.

Turning to a defense of the flush-deck carrier, he told the committee:

It may be difficult for men who served in the European theater to realize the essential part played by carrier air power in the great majority of amphibious landings which our forces made in the last war and which will be necessary in a future war.[271]

And he went on to describe the capabilities of a fast carrier task force.

He made no attempt to refute the skepticism of future amphibious operations then prevalent in Air Force and Army circles. This skepticism, which came out so strongly in rebuttals to Navy testimony,[272] was based on the anticipated dispersion of forces made necessary by atomic bombs. Indeed, Kinkaid's testimony gave the impression that the future necessity or possibility of amphibious operations was beyond dispute. (Parenthetically it may be noted that eleven months later Inchon seemed to substantiate Kinkaid's conclusion—at least for limited war; but, on the other hand, Hiroshima and Nagasaki had been attacked by unescorted bombers.)

The next witness, Captain John S. Thach, who was on the staff of the Chief of Naval Operations, talked of fast carrier task forces and their fire control. Like Kinkaid, he constantly referred to the use of the carrier in the last war. He made no attempt to link up the requirements for defeating Russia with his argument. While he made some reference to the flexibility of Navy weapons, and the advantages of that flexibility,[273] he made no reference to the enemy or to the nature of the threat.

Admiral Richard L. Conolly, Commander in Chief, Naval Forces, Eastern Atlantic and Mediterranean, testified that in his official capacity he found that he had not enough ships, particularly carriers, to perform his responsibilities. He reported that representatives of allied governments had frequently voiced their concern over United States air support.[274]

Vice Admiral Robert B. Carney, Deputy Chief of Naval Operations (Logistics), and Chairman of the JCS Budget Advisory Committee, told the Vinson committee that:

(a) The strategic air force cannot be maintained modern and ready in its present strength on its present allocation of funds for procurement.

(b) The allocation of funds for strategic bomber procurement cannot be increased to insure maintenance of the present strength without further disastrous cuts in other areas.[275]

The cost of "strategic bombing on a scale intended to be a decisive factor" would be so great that it would have to assure decisive results, he said. And "of all methods of conducting strategic bombing the intercontinental method would be by far the most costly."[276]

These cost implications of Air Force weapons policy, it should be remembered, had a parallel in both Army and Navy plans, for all three services had gone to Congress in April and May of 1948 with supplements to their original budgets which represented in their eyes only the first step in the building up of their forces and weapons to adequate levels.

Vinson's interest in developing as an issue the efforts of the Secretary of Defense to take credit for cutting the budget was made evident on the second day of the hearings during the questioning of Radford, and the following day in his calling of two special witnesses to testify on the defense budget. Thereafter he questioned witnesses regarding the budget whenever their testimony revealed the slightest possibility of their having personal knowledge concerning the Defense Management Committee and its expenditure reduction plans. Carney was the first since McNeil and Hopwood who was at all conversant with these facts, and a few references to them by him, in response to questions from Vinson, gave the latter an opportunity to repeat his criticism of Johnson. "Here, during this week we are fighting for what the nation needs," he explained, referring to disputes over the long-delayed military establishment appropriations bill for fiscal 1950, then in conference committee,

and the departments have justified every item. Then Mr. Johnson, to make his record of saving $800,000,000 says Congress is giving more money than he needs and he lets Congress go along and do it and then he says "I will cut it out and it will reflect credit on my great ability to save the taxpayer's money."

Vinson's plain words brought applause from the packed hearing room. Encouraged, he went on:

Congress is not going to be led into a position of appropriating money and then have some bureaucrat, it makes no difference who he is, say, "I won't do that. I want to make a record of my own. I want to show up the Congress."[277]

The following day Rear Admiral Luis de Florez and Admiral Raymond A. Spruance testified, a statement by Fleet Admiral Chester W. Nimitz was read, and Admiral Denfeld concluded the Navy presentation. De Florez, an aeronautical engineer, presented a moderately stated brief for diversified weapons develop- ment, including the B-36 *and* the flush-deck carrier, and followed that with a statement in favor of carrier development, based on World War II data. Spruance, talking about grand strategy for the next war, assumed that we would have allies, that Russia would have some too, and that Russia would start the war. He insisted that we would want to "liberate" Russia's allies, but that this could not be done with strategic air power. He then turned, as had previous witnesses, to a commentary on the successes of the U. S. Navy in the Pacific ocean during World War II.[278]

Nimitz's statement assumed that war would be global in scope "almost from beginning." Hence command of the sea would be necessary. He did not think the B-36 could be evaluated "short of its test in war."[279] The rest of what he said the committee had already heard many times.

In retrospect, the dramatic focus of these hearings was on Denfeld, the final witness for the Navy who summed up its presentation. From the first day of the hearings, when Matthews' split with his senior officers over the public presentation of Radford's statement became evident, and Denfeld supported the Navy Secretary in his effort to keep the controversy from the public, it appeared that the Chief of Naval Operations would stick by the civilian head of the Navy, and refuse to side with his fellow officers who were determined to lay their fears, suspicions, criticisms, and accusations before Congress and the public. Matthews later claimed that he entertained grave doubts about Denfeld's willingness to stick by him, in view of Denfeld's endorsement of the Bogan correspondence. But the endorsement by itself, as Denfeld explained at the time, did not imply approval. By adding his endorsement to Radford's on the Bogan letter, and then opposing Radford's efforts to take the Navy's case to the public, Denfeld had lent support only to an effort to have Navy complaints considered through channels within the Defense Department, or at the most, privately with Congress. Matthews and Denfeld had seen eye to eye in July on the agenda items for the hearings, and Matthews' statement to the committee was based on the assumption that Denfeld would back him up, though he had rejected Denfeld's proposed emendations. But evidently once the statement had been made Matthews came to wonder whether Denfeld would stand by him. During the week's lapse between their appearances before the committee, Matthews asked his Chief of Naval Operations several times what he was going to say, indicating that he hoped Denfeld would "get him off the hook" with the press. And Matthews gave no public indication following his speech of hope or expectation that Denfeld would support him in the end, although his optimistic boss, Louis Johnson, was evidently quite free with his assurances throughout the hearings that Denfeld would repudiate his Navy colleagues and "toe the Johnson economy line."[280]

That week of hearings on the Navy's presentation was a difficult one for Denfeld. His immediate reaction to Matthews' testimony was automatic: he announced to the press that he had supported Matthews in his efforts to keep Radford's testimony secret. But he had soon concluded, in the light of Matthews' testimony, that he could no longer play the role of conciliator. He gave Radford and his group to understand that when he testified as the final Navy witness, he would not avoid taking sides, and would definitely support them. To Matthews' queries about what he would say, he responded that he had not yet prepared his statement. It was in fact written the night before he testified. Working with him were officers who had helped the Radford group prepare their statements. (Perhaps significantly, none of them were witnesses, and none aviators.) About two days before Denfeld was to testify, he was telephoned by Vinson, who advised him to take a strong stand alongside his fellow naval officers. Since he was not a flyer, Denfeld did not regard it as his responsibility to restate and defend in detail the contentions of the naval aviators, and in the preparation of his testimony he carefully avoided any such presentation. Although this self-limitation kept him from total support of Radford and his partisans, Denfeld, and those who helped him prepare his testimony, believed that he was placing his naval career in jeopardy by making public his differences with Matthews and Johnson.

Denfeld's opening words to the committee were without exception interpreted to mean that he had gone over completely to the side of Radford and his supporters:

As the senior military spokesman for the Navy [he said,] I want to state forthwith that I fully support the *broad conclusions* presented to this committee by the naval and marine officers who have preceded me.[281]

The limitation of his endorsement to the "broad conclusions" of the previous witnesses was lost to public notice, perhaps because it was vague and seemed, to anyone who stopped to notice it, so feeble. But a careful examination of the testimony which followed indicates that it was not devoid of meaning. Denfeld proceeded with accurate summary of what the rest of his statement would deal with:

I shall summarize the arguments you have heard from the naval service for a balanced national defense, utilizing the best weapons of all the armed services. I shall further discuss the role of the Navy in our defense team and what it needs to discharge its responsibilities. Finally, I shall relate certain facts and trends which I, as Chief of Naval Operations and the Naval member of the Joint Chiefs of Staff, am best qualified to offer in the Navy's presentation.[282]

As this précis indicates, Denfeld did not reiterate the attacks on the B-36 as a bombing weapon or the identification of the views of air power extremists with Air Force policy. He gave most of his attention to a criticism of the methods of administration in the Department of Defense, centering his attack upon the manner of approval of the two additional orders of B-36's, and the manner of cancellation of the flush-deck carrier. He also gave considerable attention to the budget cut the Navy was facing. These three were the major points of his statement, and his general conclusion was that unification was not really being followed, in the sense of a coordinate operation of the Defense Department based upon mutual respect and trust, but rather that in its operation the Defense Department was excluding Navy counsel. Although Denfeld's statement was a vigorous one, there was an underlying tone of self-restraint in it. He was bitterly ironic about the hair-splitting in the hearings when he insisted that the Navy's morale was not low "if by morale you mean enthusiastic loyalty to the nation and to the service."[283] Although cautiously phrased, his allegation that Bradley reneged on his original support of the super carrier was not entirely relevant to his argument. Nor was his account of the consultations leading up to the carrier cancellation much more than partisan history. There were, indeed, some colorful and contentious passages in his testimony.

The real moderation of Denfeld's statement can only be seen when it is compared with Radford's testimony in introducing the Navy case, for Denfeld was moderate not in what he said so much as in what he did not say. He did not, as Radford had, present a wholly negative view of the B-36 as a weapon. And his assertions about the fallacies of strategic bombing were strongly qualified. Instead of chopping away at Air Force weapons and plans, as so many of the previous witnesses had done, he presented instead an appreciation of naval power as an integrated and organized force. This is the real focus of his testimony and at the same time a measure of its moderation.

If Denfeld had hoped to maintain any semblance of his former position as a conciliator between the Navy group (the most visible of whom were the Navy witnesses and the personnel in Op. 23, all led by Radford) and the Secretary of the Navy, his hope soon evaporated. As the hearings closed for the day, following his testimony, Secretary Matthews, visibly flushed, hurriedly left the committee room, while naval officers in attendance crowded around the Chief of Naval Operations to congratulate him. The press interpreted his statement as a complete identification of Denfeld with the position most strikingly presented by Radford; and messages of congratulation immediately began to pour in to Denfeld from all over the Navy. He was now regarded as one of the partisans.[284]

With the Navy presentation to the committee completed on Friday, October 13, the hearings were adjourned until the following Monday. Over the week-end it was learned that General J. Lawton Collins, the Army Chief of Staff, had been recalled from his trip to the Far East in order to testify.[285] On Saturday, the Navy court of inquiry which was investigating whether anyone collaborated with Cedric Worth in the collection and dissemination of the disproved charges regarding the B-36 procurement program, adjourned after the House Armed Services Committee had refused its request for documents submitted to the committee by Symington. In justification of its refusal the House committee claimed that the Air Force documents in its possession gave little or no information not already available to the court.[286]

On the same day, a Gallup Poll was published which indicated that a vast majority—74 per cent—of the American public believed that the Air Force "would play the most important part in winning" another World War.[287]

The Marine Corps had its day before the House Armed Services Committee on Monday, October 17. The major spokesman was General Clifton B. Cates, the Commandant. Following his appearance, General Alexander A. Vandegrift, the retired former Commandant, gave a very brief statement in which he spoke of the ability of Congress to make positive contributions to defense policy.

The case for the Marine Corps, as General Cates presented it, resembled a portion of the Navy case, but was not a cross section of it. Parts of the Navy case were concerned with tendencies which could not be measured carefully or documented with dates and specific events. They were tendencies of decline, of nibbling away; of the accomplishment through budget cuts of objectives which Congress could not be persuaded to allow; of circumventing by a gradual process the intentions of Congress in the unification act. This is a theme which came up continually in the Navy testimony. It was the dominant theme of Marine Corps testimony.

The Marines, General Cates told the committee, were gradually being eliminated. He was disturbed with what he saw in the fiscal 1950 budget with respect to the future of the Corps; but he was even more apprehensive about planning underway for fiscal 1951.

The two other major points which the Commandant made corresponded with Admiral Denfeld's references to unification procedures and their misuse. First, he said, the Marine Corps deserved more adequate representation in the higher councils of the Defense Department, although he did not ask for complete equality with the other three services. In this connection he insisted that Congress had set up the Marine Corps, not as a subsidiary of the Navy comparable to a Navy Bureau or an Army Corps, but as a separate service. Secondly, he argued that the Marine Corps should be allowed autonomy in deciding how to spend the money allocated it.[288] This point was made specifically in connection with his implication that higher authority wanted to cut the combat strength of the Marine Corps more than the budgetary cut made necessary.

He made constant references to the Army General Staff and its intentions to take over the amphibious functions of the Marine Corps. At one point he described a proposal of the Army General Staff which would transfer amphibious operations, a function of the Marine Corps, to "another agency" and provide that "Marine forces will not be appreciably expanded in time of war."[289] While this paper had never been approved authoritatively in the General Staff, Cates implied that it represented the real intentions of the Army, and asserted that it was a proposal for the revision by the Defense Department of functions assigned the services by law. On the basis of this and other contentions, Cates, like Denfeld, maintained that the National Security Act was not being followed faithfully.

The testimony of W. Stuart Symington, the Secretary of the Air Force, took up the whole hearing on October 18. Symington was an effective and aggressive witness. His prepared statement was designed to refute the charges made by his opponents that the Air Force handled the approval of its B-36 program improperly, or that the program itself was unjustifiable. Much of what he said was clear and factual refutation of the overstatements of Navy witnesses. Some of what he said begged the basic questions the Navy raised. Never did he admit the substance of any Navy charges.

Symington began his refutation with a denial of the claim (as he termed it) that the Air Force had gone over the head of the Secretary of Defense to authorize purchase of more B-36's. The charge was based upon both the January and April 1949 order changes, but Symington talked about only the January incident, after referring the committee to the whole matter as it was covered in the hearings in August. Denfeld had claimed that when the Air Force announced on January 12, 1949 that thirty-nine additional B-36's would be ordered, every expectation was that production would be cut back, not augmented. Symington claimed that there was no justification for such an expectation, for six months earlier, on June 24, 1948, the Air Force had decided not to cut back the then existing B-36 procurement program. But this was not the point at all. The

issue in June 1948 was whether to cancel the original order of one hundred B-36's. The issue in January 1949 was whether to cancel B-36 production when the original order was completed. Similarly, while Symington gave passing recognition to the fact that the announcement of the additional order of B-36's on January 12, 1949 came before the procedure for getting authorization for such an order was initiated, he failed to give any recognition to the obvious public relations advantage which the Air Force was creating by that act. But, quite justifiably, he made clear to the committee the absurd implications of the Navy's charge that the procedures followed in the additional B-36 procurement orders did not constitute an adherence in good faith to procedures established through unification. Once he had established, as he did, that in the course of clearance, the Joint Chiefs, including Denfeld, had approved the new orders, the only argument left was the public pressure one. Undoubtedly the Air Force did play rather free and easy in its public relations throughout this period, and the January 12 procurement announcement was no exception. But to imply that either Forrestal or Denfeld approved the new order because of public pressure was absurd, as Symington quite rightly asserted.[290]

A continuing theme, from Radford to Denfeld, was that the Air Force was relying chiefly, if not solely, upon the B-36. Symington cited figures to the contrary, including his own testimony before the committee in August. The Air Force, he told the committee, was planning for no more than four groups of B-36's (plus thirty-nine of them in reserve), out of fifty-eight or seventy groups. In the fiscal years 1949 through 1951, this constituted 2.9 per cent of the number of planes, and 16.3 per cent of the cost of all aircraft purchased by the Air Force.[291] He thus disposed of the general charges of the Navy with specific figures which the Navy had ignored, figures which Radford and his two assistants had heard as they sat through the first phase of the hearings in August.

The Navy, it will be remembered, had devoted much attention in the hearings to a characterization of the Air Force view of strategic bombing which they had obtained from a pamphlet called "The Strategic Bombing Myth." Symington had already dealt with this document before the committee in August,[292] and he now quoted himself from the previous hearings. He denied that the Air Force believed it could win wars solely with its strategic air arm, and insisted that, while strategic bombing was destructive of civilian lives, it was not significantly more destructive than other forms of warfare. Since the Navy had continually misconstrued the official Air Force position regarding strategic bombing, Symington later submitted an analysis of the Navy testimony prepared by his staff which attempted to correct the misconstructions wherever they occurred.[293]

Symington further submitted documentation regarding false claims in the Navy testimony. Denfeld had implied, under questioning, that the Harmon Board report on the probable effects of an atomic bomb attack on a possible enemy had concluded, to say the least, that those effects would be of limited importance. Symington submitted a letter which he had solicited from Harmon concerning this allegation which vigorously denied it.[294]

He also submitted a letter from Franklin D'Olier, who had been chairman of the United States Strategic Bombing Survey, which attacked what it claimed were misrepresentations of the report of the Survey, principally made by the pamphlet entitled "The Strategic Bombing Myth," and attempted to correct the record by quoting selectively from the conclusions of the report. D'Olier made no attempt to evaluate the accuracy of Navy witnesses' statements based on the findings of the Survey, and his letter was submitted as evidence for the Air Force. But the quotations from the report which he included in his letter could be counted as much in support of as in opposition to the Navy claims, particularly since the Navy drew a distinction between strategic bombing and tactical bombing, assigning to the latter virtually any precision bombing of selective targets.[295]

Symington's attack upon the false characterization by Navy witnesses of the Air Force's official views regarding the effects and usefulness of strategic air power was obviously his strongest point, and he exploited it to the maximum. The Navy witnesses had inadvertently endorsed the "Myth" pamphlet by their use of it in the hearings. But Symington would offer no such concessions on the Air Force side. Both services had, in fact, been having

trouble with the publication of extreme and partisan views of retired regular and non-active reserve officers. Throughout the spring and summer of 1948 Forrestal had sought to establish a publicity policy which would assure performance of all useful and appropriate functions while preventing the aggravation of interservice feelings by public statements of retired officers. And, in January 1948, when Admiral Nimitz retired as Chief of Naval Operations, his public statements, implying that the Navy should have an important share in strategic bombing, were an important incident in the rousing of Air Force fears. At the very time that the Unification and Strategy hearings were being conducted, General Spaatz, Vandenberg's predecessor as Air Force Chief of Staff, was writing highly provocative statements concerning roles and missions which were published in his column in *Newsweek*. Although Vinson quoted from the most recent of these columns, in which Spaatz advocated a single air arm (hence, the abolition of naval aviation), Symington attributed the extremist statements in behalf of the Air Force to Air Force Reserve officers, and the extremist statements in behalf of the Navy to regular Navy officers, and stated his belief that the former had been led into the expression of those views by the claims of the latter.[296]

On the firmest of ground, Symington reminded the committee of what it had been told in August—that strategic bombing as an instrument of war had been approved by the Joint Chiefs of Staff, and assigned to the Air Force. In concluding his statement he added to his refutation of Navy claims a charge of his own:

To me the most disturbing feature of these attacks against the Air Force and the rest of the Military Establishment is what they have done and are doing to imperil the security of the United States. It was bad enough to have given a possible aggressor technical and operating details of our newest and latest equipment. In my opinion it is far worse to have opened up to him in such detail the military doctrines of how this country would be defended. We have now given the military leaders of any aggressor nations a further advantage in developing their strategic plan by telling them so much about our own.[297]

In the spirited questioning of Symington which followed, the depth of Air Force distrust of the Navy was further revealed. The Secretary indicated that the Air Force had been reluctant to allow Navy aviators to fly the B-36 because of Air Force experience with leaks of distorted information about that aircraft. But perhaps the most striking of attitudes revealed in Symington's testimony was his own view about the origins and nature of the Navy–Air Force dispute. It could be summarized as follows: The Air Force is, by any reasonable standard, blameless. It has merely tried to do its job as assigned it by the Joint Chiefs of Staff under the unification legislation. However, since 1947 the B-36, because it is an intercontinental bomber and capable of competing with the strategic bombing operations of the Navy, has been under continuous attack, largely attributable to Navy sources, and those attacks have always risen in intensity at budget-time each year. They have marred an otherwise quiet and thoughtful consideration of Air Force and Navy roles and missions. Symington thus took a completely uncompromising position. Some people no doubt concluded that he was an unqualified Air Force partisan, the captive of a narrow service viewpoint incapable of understanding to any degree the complex and many-sided nature of the dispute at hand; some undoubtedly decided that he was a civilian Secretary who merely thought it appropriate to defend without qualification the actions of his service before all critics; and some may have concluded that his refusal to admit any qualification was at least partly impelled by his conviction that the Navy representatives would make unfair use of any admission of that sort.

General Hoyt S. Vandenberg, Air Force Chief of Staff, followed his civilian chief the next day as a witness. Less aggressive in his advocacy than Symington, he reiterated the main points that his predecessor had made. Like Symington, he showed that strategic bombing was a concept endorsed by the Joint Chiefs of Staff rather than just an Air Force doctrine. Like Symington, he demonstrated that the Air Force was not putting all its eggs in one basket by overconcentrating on the B-36. Like Symington, he spoke only in general terms of the capabilities of the B-36, emphasizing the continuity of the bomber defense from World War II days.[298] All his major points had already been made by Symington. The Chief of Staff merely reinforced and emphasized them

by providing more detailed and technical data in their support. The two statements were cut from one piece: If Symington had the bolder assertions to lay out, Vandenberg assumed the greater burden of proof.

Under questioning, Vandenberg explained his views on the flush-deck carrier. He did not, he indicated, question the statement of the Chief of Naval Operations concerning its military characteristics. "I accept the military capability of this ship as stated by the Chief of Naval Operations," he explained. "My opposition to building it comes from the fact that I can see no necessity for a ship with those capabilities in any strategic plan against the one possible enemy."[299] He pointed out that the carrier task force had been developed during World War II in the Pacific, but that "carrier aviation performed a significant but not a predominant function in the war against Germany."[300]

Any war we may have to fight in the future [he went on] will obviously be unlike the Pacific war against Japan. It will tend to resemble the war against Germany, though with certain differences. There will be the same problem of killing submarines. And the enemy submarines seem likely to be greater in number and of better performance than were those in World War II. There will be the same problem of protecting Atlantic Ocean supply lines, although the threat to our shipping will come almost wholly from the submarine since the potential enemy has no surface units of the character of the *Bismarck* and the *Tirpitz*. There may or may not be amphibious landings, but if there are they will not be like the landings in North Africa and Normandy and probably unlike most of the landings in the Pacific islands.

Finally, the industrial heart of the potential enemy lies not on any seashore, not on any island, but deep inside the Eurasian land mass. It is to that type of war that we must adapt all of our forces, including carrier aviation.[301]

General Omar N. Bradley, speaking as the Chairman of the Joint Chiefs of Staff, followed Vandenberg as the only other witness on the 19th of October. Longer than any of the Air Force statements, and pitched on a general level of explanation, Bradley began by describing American national objectives in terms of opposition to communism, stressing the ideological nature of that opposition, and including differences in strategic advantages. With these basic strategic considerations in mind, he then stressed the need for long-range military policy, and for its integration with political policy, speaking of the "new relationship between military power and potential accomplishment in the international field."[302] But after this reference to the relationship of military to political factors, he then returned to an analysis of the strategic situation. "We Americans must consider carefully the time and the space factors in the long-range struggle." Hence, "with the many opportunities and kinds of attack left open to an aggressor in total war, our military forces as part of our over-all security must comprise a balanced defense. This is the significant conclusion which we must reach." And by balanced forces, he explained, he meant balance in relationship to the strategic situation and to military plans, not just equal dollar expenditures by the three services.[303] The strategic situation which should determine the size and composition of forces he described as follows: (1) We must be prepared to seize other bases to attack the enemy. (2) We will have to carry the war back to the enemy "by all means at our disposal. I am convinced that this will include strategic bombardment and large-scale land operations." (3) After the initial phases are over, island hopping will be of little use, and large-scale amphibious operations will "never occur again." (4) The first prize for any aggressor is Europe.[304]

Having stated these fundamental suppositions, Bradley proceeded with a direct refutation of some of the Navy charges, and an attack of his own upon the Navy which was the most severe to occur in the hearings. Like Symington and Vandenberg before him, he stated his concern about the security aspects of the hearings:

. . . The careless detractions of the power of this [the atomic] weapon have done national security no good, and may have done our collective security, in these precarious times, untold harm. Frankly, for the good of our Nation, I wish that such testimony, belittling one of our great deterrents to war, had never been given.[305]

Bradley, like Symington and Vandenberg before him, was concerned, it should be noted, not with the secrecy aspects of security, but with the propaganda impact of the Navy charges on national security.

But he had a far more direct attack to make upon the Navy case. On the basis of his ex-

position on strategy, Bradley stated that the role of the Navy was to "assure us control over enemy navies, and the ability to subdue the sterner submarine menace."[306] The Navy's real problem, he indicated, was that its leadership had not, in a time of transition, undertaken to explain the Navy role to its personnel, and thus to reassure them. He made clear that he regarded the main role of the Navy to be the waging of anti-submarine warfare. But, he asserted, its flyers did not think that they were appreciated in this role. Moreover, the Navy had never supported unification:

Despite protestations to the contrary, I believe that the Navy has opposed unification from the beginning, and they have not in spirit as well as deed, accepted it completely to date. As a policy, yes, but as the final and authoritative vehicle for planning our collective defense, no.[307]

He concluded his statement with a ringing charge against the Navy, the tone of which left the committee in distress, the Navy in anger, and the Navy's allegations concerning "true" unification with unexpected supporting evidence. World War II "should have taught all military men," he insisted,

that our military forces are one team—in the game to win regardless of who carries the ball. This is no time for "fancy dans" who won't hit the line with all they have on every play, unless they can call the signals. Each player on this team—whether he shines in the spotlight of the backfield or eats dirt in the line—must be an all-American.

I believe that the public hearing of the grievances of a few officers who will not accept the decisions of the authorities established by law, and charges as to our poor state of preparedness, have done infinite harm to our national defense, our position of leadership in world affairs, the position of our national policy, and the confidence of the people in their Government.[308]

This speech provided a severe, self-inflicted wound to Bradley's high reputation for avoiding service partisanship or personalities for, as might have been expected, "fancy Dans" made the headlines that evening and the next morning. It "shocked the Congressional committee members," one observer noted. Various pointed Congressional compliments the following day to Generals Collins, Eisenhower, and Marshall for their fair-mindedness and moderation "were obvious rebukes to General Bradley."[309] Obviously Bradley had leased a good deal of pent-up partisan ill-temper, and probably deliberately so, but it is most unlikely that he had given careful thought to the highly partisan implications of what he was saying. He had shown his draft to no one before presenting his testimony. As far as the Navy was concerned, the remarks that shocked the committee constituted a downright insult; and Bradley's desire to limit the Navy's role to anti-submarine warfare was a grotesque and deliberate misstatement of their broad war-time functions.

Bradley had testified that, contrary to Denfeld's statements, the Joint Chiefs had not considered the flush-deck carrier prior to April 1949. Following the hearing, Denfeld demanded that a JCS paper dealing with the carrier in May 1948 be released. In the meantime, others had pointed out to Bradley his error. On the following day Bradley returned to make a brief statement to the committee in order to correct this point in his testimony. Because it illustrates so well the misunderstanding possible in the operations of the Joint Chiefs of Staff at the time, the statement is quoted *in toto.*

Mr. Chairman and members of the committee, I have asked to reappear here this afternoon because I believe that one statement which I made yesterday may have created a false impression. In my testimony yesterday, as to an apparent change in my position on the flush-deck carrier, I stated that this matter had not come up before the Joint Chiefs of Staff until April 1949. By that I meant that it had not come up for a formal decision of the Joint Chiefs of Staff prior to that time. As I stated yesterday, I had been given to understand throughout previous informal discussions that the matter had already been approved by the Secretary of Defense, the Bureau of the Budget, and the President, before submission to the Congress. I should have made it plain, however, that my statement pertained to a formal decision, because the matter was, of course, discussed informally at various meetings, particularly in connection with roles and missions.

Specifically, I find that the matter was discussed on May 26, 1948, and the memorandum to the Secretary of Defense, reporting the views of the Joint Chiefs of Staff at their meeting on May 26, would seem to indicate that I went along with the construction of the heavy carrier as a prototype. Again, let me state that this apparent agreement by me at that time was based upon my understanding that it had been approved by those in authority, and I accepted it as a fait accompli. Therefore, I was merely noting, in effect, a decision that had already been made by higher authority. I did not offer opposition to it until I found, in April 1949, that the matter was then open for formal decision.

Apparently, Admiral Denfeld and I interpreted these discussions differently. Our differences of opinion seem to stem from our different interpretations.[310]

It has already been noted that the May 28 vote referred to in this statement was taken only because the meaning of an earlier poll of the Joint Chiefs at Key West on the same subject had been thrown into question on the grounds that the Chiefs were not actually asked their views, but only whether they would accept a decision already made by higher authority.[311] If Bradley's statement is correct that despite these circumstances, on May 28, he was still only accepting a decision made by higher authority, then evidently it was impossible at that time to obtain a straight opinion from the JCS on a policy decision made at a higher level without first revoking that policy.

On the final two days of the hearings (October 20 and 21) seven witnesses besides General Bradley were heard. Two of these witnesses, the Army Chief of Staff, General J. Lawton Collins, and the Secretary of Defense, Louis Johnson, were, in a sense, participants in the controversy. Three of them, General Dwight D. Eisenhower, General George C. Marshall, and former President Herbert Hoover, were non-participants in the current controversy who were called to testify because of their general backgrounds and knowledge of the problems under consideration; of course, both General Marshall and then General Eisenhower had actively engaged in controversy with the Navy from 1944 to 1946 over unification. The other two, General Mark Clark, then Chief of Army Field Forces, and Robert Heller, Chairman of the Advisory Group to the Defense Management Committee, dealt with management details involved in unification, which are of no interest here.

Collins, the only official spokesman for the Army to testify, concerned himself mostly with refuting points made by the Marine Commandant, General Cates. Cates had cited what he claimed to be instances where the Army revealed its desire and intention to eliminate or subordinate the Marine Corps. Collins dealt with the three main ones as follows: (1) The April 1946 suggestion of the Army Chief of Staff (then General Eisenhower) that the Marine Corps be limited to fifty or sixty thousand men was based on the assumption that all services would be three times their pre-war strength, and did not represent a comparative reduction in the Marines.[312] (2) The so-called Collins Plan for unification of the armed forces, proposed before a Congressional hearing on unification in October 1945, did not suggest elimination of the Marine Corps. (3) The recent Army staff paper, referred to by Cates and by Representative Van Zandt in his questioning of Matthews, did in fact propose a consolidation of amphibious units, but not by eliminating the major function of the Corps. The paper proposed four kinds of joint centers under the Joint Chiefs of Staff—airborne, air tactical support, air defense, and amphibious—which would be concerned with the development of doctrines, tactics, techniques, training, and the testing of equipment. According to the proposal, the Chief of Naval Operations would be the executive agent for the joint amphibious center, and it was expected that he would delegate this job to the Commandant of the Marine Corps.

Secretary of Defense Johnson's appearance before the committee was notable for the conciliatory manner in which he and Vinson treated each other, except for a short joust over the budget. Vinson, it will be remembered, had been criticizing him severely throughout the previous days of hearings for cutting the current budget at the same time that he was supporting it through Congress. Johnson admitted that he was reducing the armed forces as well as saving money in their management. He indicated that he still thought that over a billion dollars could be saved through the implementation of the Hoover Commission proposals respecting management of the armed forces. He made no claim as to how much he had saved thus far during the year, and he avoided setting any timetable of savings, although he did refer with approval to his statement, made to the committee in the summer with respect to the Tydings bill, that within a year savings at the rate of one billion dollars a year, and within eighteen months, savings at the rate of one and one-half billion dollars a

year were possible.[313] He then went on to justify the Defense Management Committee on the grounds that the armed services could not be expected to (and indeed would not) effect reductions if left to themselves, and to indicate that the Navy was not the only service to object to the proposed reductions. Johnson's explanation of his expenditure-reducing program was not challenged by Vinson, despite substantial discrepancies in his version of it as against that of the Navy witnesses. Vinson challenged him, however, in their most heated exchange, because he seemed to be ignoring his earlier, less modest, claims about possible money savings in the Defense Department. As Vinson put it,

The point I am making is that you established a policy about a saving, an objective of some $800,000,000, and the Appropriations Committee at that time was writing the appropriation bill. I felt that you should have come up to the Appropriations Committee and told the committee that, after a reevaluation of the appropriations, you found that you probably could make savings, and you should have given the committee an opportunity to have made a good record as well as enabling our distinguished Secretary of Defense to make a good record.[314]

Johnson, in reply, denied that he had ever claimed that he could save $800 million from the 1950 budget, insisted that he had talked of a *rate* of saving by the end of a year under the new unification act, not about how much he would save in that year. Furthermore, he contended, he had made known to Congress his intention both to save and to reduce in the Defense Department, and that he had notified Congress as soon as he could identify by appropriation title any savings he could accomplish.

As had been the case in his other public statements, Johnson was intemperate in discussing the contentions of the Navy witnesses. They had made "many misleading statements" in their characterization of accepted strategic air doctrine, he said. "The war plans which the Joint Chiefs of Staff have unanimously evolved bear only the slightest resemblance to the erroneous picture that was painted by some of your witnesses."[315]

Furthermore, he explained that the functions of the Joint Chiefs of Staff had been misinterpreted. Whether they vote 2-1 or unanimously is not important, he said, for they are advisers to the Secretary of Defense and the President, who do the deciding. (It is doubtful, however, that the JCS at this time—if ever—considered their role solely advisory.) Having set forth this interpretation of JCS responsibilities, Johnson recounted in considerably more detail than had Denfeld the immediate circumstances surrounding the cancellation of the flush-deck carrier the previous April, indicating that, contrary to Denfeld's claims, he was well aware of the views of each member of the Joint Chiefs of Staff before he decided to stop construction.[316] He also gave his views of the circumstances surrounding the resignation of former Secretary of the Navy John L. Sullivan immediately after the carrier cancellation. The press accounts at that time, including Sullivan's published resignation, had quite accurately given the impression that he had quit in protest to the cancellation. Johnson, however, now inserted in the record a letter of resignation signed by Sullivan which was dated March 24, a month earlier than the one published.[317] While this letter was a perfunctory one, sent to the President as a matter of courtesy four days before Johnson replaced Forrestal as Secretary of Defense, Johnson asserted that it had been accepted, and that the reason for its acceptance was because Sullivan was unwilling to support unification. Hence, Johnson implied, Sullivan was already on his way out when the carrier was cancelled. In support of this claim he said that the letter had never been returned to Sullivan.[318] Johnson's conduct in his office suggests that from the beginning he had been determined to augment the powers of the Secretary of Defense, and that he may have preserved such letters of resignation as a source of power over the service Department Secretaries; therefore, the retention of Sullivan's letter offered no evidential support of the contention that Sullivan was to have been dismissed in any case.

Eisenhower was the first of the three non-participants in the immediate controversy to testify. He might have become as involved as any in the charges, for he had been involved in the original unification struggles, and he had also been a kind of informal chairman of the Joint Chiefs of Staff for several months before such an office was authorized by the National Security Act Amendments of 1949, when General Bradley was appointed to it. He had also been involved in the proceedings leading up to the carrier cancellation. But his position as head of the Joint Chiefs had been wholly that of a conciliator. He did not now choose to alter that position. He reminded the committee, referring to all of the witnesses who had appeared, that "We are dealing with distinguished Americans, people who have their country's good at heart and, therefore, we should not be too critical or too ready to call names on either side; above all, we should not be too ready to question motives."[319]

He identified as the source of the friction the unified budget process which forced the services to compete with each other for funds within a budget ceiling. And he suggested that such friction could be reduced if the Armed Services Committees were brought in on the process of budget preparation at its beginning.

General George C. Marshall was the second of the non-participant witnesses, but of course he spoke as a former Army Chief of Staff. He talked of the need for a unified budget, so that in the peacetime squeeze the comparative strength of the armed forces would not be based upon political considerations. In this position, he revealed the fundamental Army approach to unification.[320]

Former President Herbert Hoover was the third non-participant witness, and the final witness of the hearings. Impressed with Johnson's efforts to promote economy and efficiency in the Defense Department, Hoover defended the unification legislation and Johnson's efforts to reorganize and economize. He concluded his statement on a note which had been sounded often in the hearings:

I would like to add one more thought, and that is to emphasize the pressures which now exist upon our economy. It is costing us, in one direction or another, almost 24 billion dollars annually to carry on the cold war. Already we have a budget deficit in sight of 5 or 6 billion dollars for the fiscal year and perhaps more next year. That can mean, if it continues, only one thing, and that is inflation which will damage every worker and every farmer in the United States. In my view our productive economy is already so heavily taxed as to slow up progress in its improvements of methods and the necessary expansion to meet the needs and demands of our increasing population. We cannot continue such burdens forever, and the first service is economy.[321]

Vinson agreed with former President Hoover that Johnson "deserves the full support of this committee and the country in his difficult task."[322]

Whereupon the House Armed Services Committee adjourned, at 12:50 P.M., October 21, 1949, until January 3, 1950.

VI. THE HEARINGS ANALYSED

While the ultimate source of most of the pressures which drove the Navy spokesmen, under the leadership of Admiral Radford, to insist that they be provided with a public forum in which to express their fears about the future of the naval service and the security of the country was ultimately the defense budget policy of the Truman Administration, the object of their criticism was the Air Force, not that policy.

The Director of the Bureau of the Budget had made the Navy choose, in its budgets for fiscal 1949 and fiscal 1950, between new prototypes and the completion of wartime construction, rather than both, as the Navy wished. In both years the President had imposed a budget ceiling far below what the military considered an essential minimum figure. And the supplemental budget of April 1948 was held down to a figure which was one-third of what the services considered essential, and probably somewhat lower than what Congress would have provided, although perhaps it would have increased military appropriations only at the expense of foreign aid.

The carrier cancellation in April 1949 cut into the Navy's vitals because the Navy had been forced by its limited budget to concentrate upon its prototypes development program to the exclusion of the continued construction of established designs. Johnson's action in cancelling the carrier could hardly have been at variance with the President's wishes, as indeed it was not. And the efforts of the Defense Management Committee in the late summer of 1949 to cut naval appropriations constituted only a part of a larger scheme to economize in the military establishment, a scheme which pinched the other two services only a little less severely.

The Navy's major difficulties came from the economy program of the Truman Administration, which kept all three of the services on short rations, measured by their own standards. It is true that the economy measures tended to cut the Navy disproportionately more than they did the other services, but only slightly so. All three services had grounds for alarm on this score. Although the immediate cause of the Navy's break with its civilian leadership was, or appeared to be, the gradually growing budgetary pressures, the more fundamental one was the sense that its future development was being thwarted by the inroads being made upon its air power functions and capabilities.[323] Two factors account for this reaction. The first was a long-standing fear of the Air Force as a rival of naval air power. It can be traced back to the anti-submarine warfare dispute between the Navy and the Army Air Forces which had begun in 1942 and had become a major inter-service dispute by June 1943. By the autumn of 1943 the question of which service should command the aircraft engaged in anti-submarine warfare in the Atlantic had been broadened to involve general proposals for unification of the armed services. Thereafter the Navy, or at least that part of it which was sensitive to inter-service politics and interested in the future of naval air power, feared the challenge of the Air Force and suspected the motives behind the movement for unification of the armed services.

The two objects were not joined together only in Navy fears. In the late 1920's the Army air arm had allied its future hopes of independence with proposals for unification, and in the event its tactics were successful. The controversy over unification, which went on from 1943 until passage of the National Security Act of 1947, had reinforced Navy fears as the fortunes of the Army air arm waxed. Only with carefully drawn compromises, and in view of President Truman's support of unification, did the Navy acquiesce in the defense reorganization of 1947. But it could not put away its fears of the Air Force challenge as readily as did its formal objection to a single executive department for the armed services.

The growing popularity of the Air Force with the public and in Congress, the successes of its public relations programs, the replacement of Forrestal with Louis Johnson, the cancellation of the flush-deck carrier, and the budget pressures against naval aviation in particular all fed the fears of the Navy about its future in aviation—which most of its top leadership were convinced was the basis for its claim to any future.

The immediate pressures upon the Navy came from the Truman Administration's expenditure policies. But it did not follow that naval officers would feel they either could or should attack the Truman Administration. To begin with, they were not advocates of high peacetime federal expenditures. They accepted as inevitable the fact that peacetime military budgets would be stringent, and as a judgment they could not dispute the claim that the American economy could not support a federal budget much larger than the current one. Moreover, for service officers in any official capacity the grounds within which they can advocate a larger military budget are highly circumscribed. Where the strong dogmas of civilian control do not inhibit advocacy, expediency warns that an appeal beyond the executive realm may backfire, and that even if it does not, a larger military budget is an enormous burden in persuasion to assume. The challenge to naval aviation posed, as the Navy saw it, by the Air Force and its aspirations, the disadvantages of criticizing their civilian superiors, and the necessity of accepting the general magnitude of defense expenditures directed the Navy spokesmen to attack the Air Force rather than Secretary Johnson or the Truman Administration.

SUMMARY OF THE TWO CONFLICTING CASES: THE SUBSTANCE OF THE ARGUMENTS

The main arguments of substance were made by Navy and Air Force spokesmen, while the Marine Corps and the Army were concerned almost entirely about whether the Army was trying to eliminate the Marine Corps. Bradley, of course, went further than a defense of Army motives, criticizing the Navy for a lack of cooperation under unification, and a failure of Navy leaders to explain the changing role of their service to its personnel. But he was testifying as JCS Chairman, not as a representative of the Army.

The arguments of the Navy and Air Force varied slightly from time to time, and were at times inconsistent with each other, as will be shown later in this chapter. But the main points of each can be summarized as follows:

The Navy Argument

1. Strategic Bombing: The Air Force. The Air Force has been concentrating all its resources on strategic (i.e., intercontinental area) bombing in the false expectation that in the event of another war it would assure a quick and easy victory. As a result, the Air Force has been neglecting tactical air power and air transport.

Contrary to Air Force claims, strategic bombing could not by itself win the war. Moreover, reliance upon it might actually precipitate a war, and its use could, rather than breaking the enemy's will to fight, actually strengthen it and make him less rational in his employment of force. Instead of being a quick and easy way to win, strategic bombing is warfare by attrition. These assertions are based upon an appraisal of both the accuracy and the power of strategic bombing. The elements which go to make up this appraisal include (1) the power of bombs, (2) the capability of delivering them, and (3) the accuracy of that delivery. Their limited number and power keep atomic bombs from rendering insignificant the factors of delivery and accuracy, both of which remain unsurmounted problems.

Strategic bombing is necessarily inaccurate and hence immoral in its unnecessary waste of human life. It does not have an important effect upon the outcome of war. For instance, it was tactical air power, not strategic bombing, that gave the most help in the allied invasion of Western Europe.

2. The B-36: The Air Force has publicized exaggerated performance claims for the B-36. Instead of being invulnerable, as the Air Force claims, the B-36 is actually a slow-flying and

highly vulnerable target which, in view of the enemy's anticipated radar and fighter achievements, could never reach a defended objective, particularly one deep in Soviet Russia.

3. Unification: The real spirit of unification has been violated by the Air Force, the Army, and the Office of the Secretary of Defense. The Air Force has gone ahead with the mass procurement of the B-36 which had not been properly evaluated by established joint machinery, or approved specifically for large-scale production, nor had the strategic assumptions related to its use (intercontinental strategic bombing) been approved in principle. On the other hand, the cancellation of the flush-deck carrier has deprived the Navy of the right to proceed with further development of its fleet weapons, which was not only an infringement of a right, but a violation of the principle of unification.

In more general terms, the Navy constantly finds itself an unlistened-to minority in the councils of the Defense Department. Along with the Marine Corps, it is gradually being nibbled to death. Its weapons, roles, missions, and budget are constantly under restrictive pressures, the tendency of which is to reduce it to a subordinate position in the defense triumvirate. At the same time the Defense Department seems to have committed itself to a level of forces in the Air Force, the maintenance cost of which will increase so sharply in the next few years that it will force further restrictions of the other services.

4. The Flush-Deck Carrier: It has been completely misunderstood. It is justifiable not for its strategic bombing function but as the next step in the development of the capital ship of the Fleet, made necessary by the increasing weight and size of all aircraft.

5. The Budget: The Air Force program calls for a continuing increase in the Air Force budget, which can only mean a further reduction in future Navy budgets. (No challenge of the over-all defense budget was pressed by the Navy.)

The Air Force Rebuttal

1. Strategic Bombing: The Air Force never has taken the position with respect to strategic bombing that the Navy claims. It does not believe that strategic bombing can alone win wars, but that all services are needed. It does not claim that strategic bombing will yield quick results, but rather that the strategic bombing capability is necessary as a deterrent, and that immediate retaliation in the event of a war would have considerable (though not decisive) effect. The Air Force does not seek to combine all the nation's air forces under one command, as the Navy claims. Nor has the Air Force concentrated unduly upon strategic bombers. The B-36 takes up only a small percentage of the total amount of money and number of aircraft in the Air Force.

Strategic bombing played a highly significant role in both theaters of World War II. Air power will play the most significant role in any future war.

Strategic bombing can be precision bombing. It is not significantly more wasteful of human life than other forms of warfare.

2. The B-36: The Air Force has been forced to release performance data on the B-36 because it has been so smeared by rumors. But the Air Force has never claimed the exaggerations regarding its performance that the Navy attributes to it. It has never claimed that the B-36 is invulnerable, only that it can get through to its target with acceptable losses. The Air Force was aware of all the objections raised by the Navy to the B-36 at the time approval was given for its procurement in quantity. The real experts in strategic bombing nevertheless approve of it.

3. Unification: The B-36 was ordered for procurement with full approval in the Defense Department where appropriate, and that included Navy approval. If the Air Force has been unwilling to provide the Navy with performance details regarding the B-36, it is only because of its poor experience with leaks to the press about the B-36. It was distrustful, but only for cause.

The Navy does not understand that the next war will not be fought just in the same manner as the fighting in the Pacific in the last war. The Navy is well represented in the Defense Department, and is listened to when it knows what it is talking about. It just wants its own way.

4. The Flush-Deck Carrier: Construction of the big new carrier was stopped because it had been justified by the Navy on grounds other than its own primary mission, which is action

against fleets and submarines of the enemy.[324]

5. The Budget: It is true that the Navy budget has been stringently limited. So have the budgets of the other services.

THE CHARACTER OF THE ARGUMENTS OF THE TWO MAJOR PROTAGONISTS

The Navy Case

The Navy had gone to Congress with its troubles and suspicions as a means of stopping tendencies and practices which alarmed it. From the release of the Bogan correspondence by Crommelin to Denfeld's closing statement to the committee ten days later, the Navy enjoyed in some respects the advantage of surprise. But, at the same time, it carried the burden of several handicaps through this public debate. The Navy witnesses spoke without support of their civilian chiefs, hence unauthoritatively. And they talked of intentions, attitudes, and tendencies which could not be documented. These handicaps were unavoidable, inherent in their situation. But others were not.

The major avoidable handicap for the Navy was its lack of thorough preparation. The manner of that preparation has already been described. Captain Arleigh Burke's Op. 23, a division in the Office of the Chief of Naval Operations, was coordinator and aide to the prospective witnesses, but those activities had been limited to supplying them with a highly polemical pamphlet entitled "The Strategic Bombing Myth," some general position papers on the agenda items of the House Armed Services Committee,[325] a very limited amount of help in writing their statements and in research assistance for pertinent data, and a place to meet and compare what they were going to say. The results of their preparation indicated its inadequacies. What the witnesses said showed that their preparatory work had not been carefully coordinated, for the statements were sometimes unfounded, often exaggerated, and not always consistent; and, taken as a whole, they failed to cover some important points in the Navy case. Probably one reason for this independence in their presentations was the Navy approach to staff procedures, which, more than that of the other

services, stresses individual work. But this is no explanation for the errors in presentation which occurred.

The conflicting statements in the Navy presentation were not striking, nor did they evoke much direct attention. But they demonstrated the inadequacy of Navy preparation. Admiral Radford was forced to contradict himself, for while he had said in his prepared statement that the Navy would present facts upon which the committee could base its evaluation of the B-36, he later admitted under questioning that the committee was incompetent to make such an evaluation. While this inconsistency in Radford's position was glossed over with the useful fiction that the Navy was making its presentation about the B-36 only in response to the request of the committee, this shift stood as an indication of the lack of care with which the Navy had worked out a basic premise in its presentation: what it should and would attempt to prove to the committee.

Similarly, Admiral Radford told the committee that instant atomic retaliation would not prevent war, but might actually invite it.[326] But Admiral Nimitz admitted in his written statement, which was read to the committee in his absence, that atomic retaliation capabilities were a deterrent to Soviet aggression.[327] And Admiral Blandy, despite skillful efforts to avoid the subject, left the impression that he could not agree wholly with Captain Trapnell's conservative estimates of atomic bomb effects.

More important than these gaps in the Navy presentation was its failure to present any semblance of convincing proof for most of its major contentions. To be sure, its testimony on the performance characteristics of the B-36, while somewhat incautious, was impressive. But it is significant to note that its B-36 testimony was based upon information readily available to the witnesses, and required little time or effort to assemble. Apart from its attack on the B-36 (which could have only limited significance in view of Radford's agreement that the committee was not qualified to evaluate the evidence), the major portion of the Navy's case consisted of allegations about what the Air Force claimed regarding the performance capabilities of the B-36, the capabilities and strategic significance of strategic bombing, and the extent of Air Force reliance upon both. The allegations could have been established by an examination of Air Force press releases and other publicity emanating from Air Force sources over the previous two or three years. The extent of Air Force concentration upon the B-36 and strategic bombing could have been established, in the first instance, by an analysis of the hearings on B-36 procurement in August, and, further, from public documents on the Air Force budget. Admiral Conolly's testimony introduced evidence based upon some kind of study, evidently done for the hearings, which, quite properly, showed that existing and contemplated commitments to Air Force strength implied future increases in the Air Force budget at an astonishing rate. This was undoubtedly the most striking argument regarding the Air Force budget capable of adequate documentation, for the Air Force was not at that time in fact concentrating its procurement of aircraft as heavily upon B-36 bombers as the Navy charged.

But the most striking omission of available evidence on the part of the Navy was its failure to make use in any way of both the August hearings on B-36 procurement and Air Force publicity. The Air Force had presented in August a story, impressive for its detail, its candidness, and its authoritative corroboration, of the history of B-36 development and procurement. Certain Navy allegations in the October hearings were directly concerned with happenings described in this history. Although Admiral Radford had sat through those hearings, at no time did the Navy relate its testimony to that history, either to refute some of the claims based on it, which it might have done, or to support its own case, which it most assuredly could have done. In a similar manner, Navy statements about what the Air Force claimed about the B-36 in particular and strategic bombing in general remained unrelated to the evidence which lay immediately (but for some clerical labor) at hand, in recent newspaper and periodical files. An examination of such materials over the previous three years would have shown that official Air Force spokesmen were usually careful to say something nice about the other two services in their public speeches; and that publicity releases usually stuck to actual operations capabilities, and did not themselves go on to spell out any extreme implications from strategic bombing. But they could also have shown (1) that the

timing and context of such pronouncements gave much encouragement to strategic bombing enthusiasts to draw the extreme conclusions they wished to; (2) that the Air Force never made any real effort to correct public misapprehensions about air power, or to relate it in a responsible manner to the strength of the other two services; and (3) that public misapprehensions had grown so strong by the spring of 1949 that Army circles were alarmed about them.[328]

The result of these weaknesses in Navy preparation was that the Air Force could dismiss without argument the Navy's allegations about what the Air Force claimed, and rebut Navy charges about its abuse of unification by referring to facts established in August. A focal point of many of the Navy charges, and one also of the inadequacy of its case, was the claim made by Radford and Denfeld that the transfer of funds in January and April of 1949 to B-36 procurement was done by the Air Force before approval was sought from the Defense Department and the JCS. Already in the record of the committee's hearings in August were the details of these two steps, and they showed that a laborious process of clearance was followed, and that it included Forrestal and the Joint Chiefs.

But what the Navy spokesmen did not emphasize was that the Air Force had publicized extensively these increases in B-36 procurement before consideration of them was ever submitted to the clearance procedure. If these facts, as already established, had been combined with the pattern of Air Force publicity at the time, a persuasive claim might have been made about the stresses being created within the Defense Department by the uninhibited public relations program of the Air Force. Since the Navy had taken neither of these steps, its charge was inaccurate, when made, and was wholly crushed in rebuttal by Symington. In a similar manner its claim that the Air Force had approved the flush-deck carrier both at Key West and earlier, and that Bradley had also approved it at Key West, was shown to be inaccurate.

The most glaring inadequacy of the Navy case was the result of its failure to dig into the record of Air Force publicity in order to establish what the Air Force had claimed about air power. Since it was determined to characterize these claims even in the absence of adequate documentation, the Navy used as a substitute for proper documentation the highly partisan pamphlet called "The Strategic Bombing Myth," which was far from being either fair or accurate in its description of Air Force claims, was suspect because of its sponsorship by Navy partisans, and was easily repudiated.[329] Its use in the preparation of the Navy case was a grave error. It led the Navy to misdirect its fire by exaggerating the claims made in behalf of strategic bombing, beyond what either the committee or the Air Force accepted, to an extreme which was supported, at best, only by vague and irresponsible public sentiments. Admiral Ofstie was apparently aware of this misdirection of Navy charges, and he tried in vain to re-aim them:

. . . Much emphasis has been placed upon the instant character of an offensive using atomic bombs. Among laymen this has produced an illusion of power and even a kind of bombrattling jingoism. *Although responsible officials of the Government generally do not themselves subscribe to it,* they must be influenced by the public acceptance of the proposal of instant retaliation.[330]

Further evidence of lack of familiarity with information which was important as background for what the Navy spokesmen had to say was the expressed assumption of many of them that the future of amphibious operations was beyond dispute.[331] Inquiry would undoubtedly have shown this assumption by the Navy to be disputed by the other services at that time.

In short, irrespective of its inherent merits, the Navy's case was weak because its presentation was inadequately prepared and poorly coordinated. It failed to take full advantage of the time allotted because of its concentration on a moot question, the performance capabilities of the B-36. At times the Navy case was conflicting. But mostly it had no solid foundation in relevant facts.

Why it was so poor is not entirely clear, although three reasons provide a partial explanation. First, since what was said had no official sanction, the process of its preparation was suspect. The activities of Op. 23 in preparing Navy statements were never officially admitted, and, as will be seen in detail below, that whole division had come under a cloud.

While the Air Force had been free to carry on extensive preparation for its part in the hearings, without a breath of criticism, the Navy preparation was carried on in the face of a hostile press, and without the knowledge of the Secretary of the Navy, and, hence, under the ever-present threat of being stopped by the Secretary. Under these circumstances, Op. 23 and the Navy spokesmen might have been hard pressed to find the manpower necessary to make adequate preparation.

Second, the failure to use Admiral Denfeld to full advantage in the preparation of the Navy statements was an important source of weakness in the Navy case. The reason for this is evident. It will be remembered that Denfeld had taken no part in Radford's efforts to convince Vinson that the hearings should not be postponed until January 1950, and that until after the hearings had begun Denfeld was opposed to the publication of the Navy statements. At the same time, to all outward appearances his relations with Matthews remained cordial. Under these circumstances, it was hardly to be expected that Denfeld would offer much assistance to Op. 23, or that Radford or Burke would expect him to do so. The results of this failure to use Denfeld were also evident. For instance, Blandy and Kinkaid had evidently not been informed by Denfeld of current doubts in the JCS about the future of amphibious operations, a fact which Denfeld could have supplied if he had read their statements beforehand with the intention of being helpful. As a result, their discussions of strategy assumed a major premise which both the Army and the Air Force denied: that naval warfare in the Pacific during World War II had particular relevance in planning for future conflicts.

Third, until almost the end of its testimony the Navy had good reason to believe that when it was through with its presentation the hearings would end without opportunity for rebuttal. Believing this, its spokesmen may have felt no obligation to be either precise or cautious in what they said, thus leaving themselves open for the rebuttals which followed.

But these explanations do not account wholly for the Navy's poor preparation. Matthews' endorsement was hardly necessary for the proper preparation of the Navy's case; the information which Denfeld could have provided was obtainable elsewhere; and there was no justification for the assumption that the Navy could present in public its case on such a controversial issue without being subject to rebuttal, if not in Congress, then in the press. The Navy, as well as the Air Force, had the whole summer of 1949 to gather data and prepare for its presentation at a hearing scheduled well in advance. To the extent that the errors in the preparation and presentation of the Navy's case are explainable by these circumstances, they were largely avoidable. Probably the most substantial reason for the weakness in the Navy's case was the fact that it wanted to do strategic bombing from its carriers. Thus committed, it could not attack the Air Force very well without criticizing itself.

The Air Force Case

The Air Force rebuttal of Navy charges was carefully limited in its scope and objectives.

1. The Air Force relied heavily upon its previous testimony. It had presented its case very thoroughly in the August hearings, and it had no intention of going over ground already covered so well, particularly since the Navy had not taken direct issue with the information presented at that time. Hence, it cited details brought out in the earlier hearings to disprove general allegations of the Navy, such as that the Air Force had gone over the head of Forrestal in ordering additional B-36's in January and April 1949; that the B-36 had not been properly evaluated; and that the Air Force was over-concentrating on it.

2. The Air Force assumed no burden of responsibility that it could avoid. Avoidance of responsibility was not difficult, in view of the ineffectiveness of the Navy's attack on the Air Force; and on many minor points it was quite justifiable, for the Navy had not been circumspect in many of its charges, and, of course, had levelled many of them against the Defense Department.

This avoidance of issues involved several points. Perhaps the most important issue thus avoided was Air Force public relations, and the charge that the Air Force encouraged belief in quick and easy strategic bombing. In his testimony Symington disavowed any publicity not emanating from official Air Force sources, and then defended the propriety of the official statements. At the same time, he attacked statements from similar unofficial sources on the Navy side, implying Navy responsibility for them. With none of the detailed history of publicity for both services in the record, but with an obvious endorsement by the Navy witnesses of "The Strategic Bombing Myth" pamphlet, by citing it in their testimony, Symington's disavowal of Air Force responsibility for its extremists and charge of Navy responsibility under similar circumstances did not seem unreasonable, though it was inaccurate.

A second issue avoided by the Air Force was the relationship between strategic bombing and the economic, diplomatic, and military alliances which the United States was developing with Western Europe at that time. The Air Force had shown that strategic bombing was approved by the Joint Chiefs of Staff, and that the Air Force did not make the kind of claim that the Navy said it did. Moreover, the broad issues of national security policy were not its direct responsibility. Hence, it paid no attention to this issue.

A third issue avoided was one of the most tangible points made in the Navy case, but one which was not given emphasis either by reference or repetition. Admiral Conolly, it will be remembered, had posed the problem of future budgets, which, even if the Air Force remained at the 48-group level, would have to commit increasing sums to that service. The Air Force avoided any discussion of the long-range budgetary implications of the program which it was currently advocating, and was able to ignore the issue because the Navy had failed to emphasize it. Of course, the Air Force could have made the same criticism of the plans of the other two services as they were developed for the supplementary budget requests of April and May 1948. Yet neither of them was so fully committed to a single, long-range force objective as was the Air Force. By the fall of 1949, it is clear, the Army and the Navy were not fighting singlemindedly for the program objectives they had laid down for themselves the previous spring, while the Air Force continued to do so. Yet they, like the Air Force, avoided discussion of future budgets. The failure of the Navy spokesmen to do so probably indicates that they were more aware of what they had to lose than what they had to gain by raising the question of future military costs.

3. As quickly as it could, the Air Force turned from rebuttal to attack upon the Navy, criticizing it (1) in general, for complaining; (2) for its efforts to take over strategic bombing (this charge largely based upon Symington's claims regarding Navy public relations activities, which have been discussed above);

and (3) for its disclosing, or forcing the disclosure of, secret information of value to the enemy. All three of these points, it should be noted, would have been muted by a detailed presentation from the Navy of the publicity record of the two services over the previous three years.

VII. THE AFTERMATH OF THE HEARINGS

Almost the entire high command of the Navy had taken matters into their own hands and carried their criticisms of the military policy of the President and the Secretary of Defense, as well as of the sister services, to Congress and the public. What were the results of their bold move? The short-run effect was a purge of Admiral Denfeld in order to get a CNO who was not identified with the Navy partisans, and certain demonstrations of hostility against others in that group. A more fundamental effect could be seen in the defense budget.

THE NAVY PURGE

Denfeld's Removal

At the beginning of the October hearings, and after their conclusion, the chairman of the House Armed Services Committee warned the Defense Department not to carry out reprisals against any of the witnesses because of what they had told the committee.[332]

At the opening of the President's press conference on October 27, after Congress had adjourned, President Truman announced that he had received a request from the Secretary of the Navy to authorize the transfer of Admiral Denfeld to other duties, and that he had granted it. The reporters were provided with copies of the correspondence which had passed between Truman and Matthews. The President's note was short and direct. Matthews' letter was longer, and designed to build his case against a possible hostile public reaction to Denfeld's removal.[333] Matthews maintained that Denfeld was being transferred, not because of what he had said in the recent hearings, but because he had endorsed the Bogan letter, and for other unspecified acts of disloyalty. To establish the credence of his story, Matthews mentioned a meeting which he had held with Denfeld on the day the Bogan correspondence was published, at which he told Denfeld his usefulness as CNO was at an end. He reminded the President that he had mentioned to him the following day the possibility of removing Denfeld. With his early consideration of removing Denfeld presumably established, Matthews went on to talk of loyalty:

A military establishment is not a political democracy. Integrity of command is indispensable at all times. There can be no twilight zone in the measure of loyalty to superiors and respect for authority existing between various official ranks. Inability to conform to such requirements for military stability would disqualify any of us for positions subordinate to the Commander in Chief.[334]

Matthews implied that because of Denfeld's lack of loyalty, he himself could not properly perform his duties as Secretary of the Navy. He asked that a new CNO be appointed "at the earliest possible date."

Denfeld learned of his fate from newspaper reports of the President's press conference.[335] Within the Navy itself, as might have been expected, the reaction was highly emotional. The morning after the President's announcement of Denfeld's removal, the latter's office was filled with 300 enlisted Navy men whose spokesman said, "I want you to know that we feel the Navy is shot, that our morale is shot, that we feel very low."[336] The next day, at the Navy-Notre Dame football game, Denfeld was given a standing ovation by the midshipmen; Matthews, who was scheduled to share a box with him, had given up his plans to attend.[337]

If Congress was to do anything about the Denfeld removal, the responsibility lay, first, with the House Armed Services Committee in which the warning against retaliation had occurred; and, second, in the Senate when the appointment of Denfeld's successor was to be approved. But Vinson, while he agreed that Denfeld's dismissal was a reprisal for his testimony before the committee, was more reluctant to become involved in an investigation of the armed services now than he had been in April or September. Although the Republican members of his committee prodded him, he refused to do more than give assurances that the committee report on the October hearings would deal with the matter.[338] One Republican Congressman, W. Sterling Cole, in attempting to apply pressure on Vinson, and at the same time build up a case against the Denfeld removal, sent a telegram to all flag and general officers of the Navy Department (and Marine Corps) on October 28. It read: "In strict confidence please advise if you are in accord with views expressed by Admiral Denfeld before Armed Services Committee." When Matthews heard of the telegram, he granted permission to its recipients to reply to it provided they sent copies of their replies to him. Cole promptly accused him of destroying the ability of Congress to provide for the common defense.[339]

On December 8 Cole announced the results of his inquiry. Of 308 officers whose views he had sought, 55 per cent answered. Of those who answered, 16 per cent said that Navy regulations prohibited them from replying. Of the rest, 82 per cent were "affirmative," and 18 per cent "non-committal."[340] Cole's letter was a bid to the House to fight for Denfeld, but without Vinson's backing it was unsuccessful. It did, however, provide the most tangible evidence of the extent of agreement in the top ranks of the Navy with the position taken by the Navy in the second phase of the B-36 hearings. Meanwhile, on November 1, after a hurried trip from the Mediterranean, a thirty-minute conference with the President at the White House, and an interview at the Pentagon, Admiral Forrest P. Sherman became the first naval aviator to be appointed Chief of Naval Operations in peacetime.[341]

Once again, Denfeld learned of the President's action through private sources—his driver, who had heard it on the radio. Prior to Sherman's confirmation by the Senate on January 24, 1950, his views on unification, roles and missions, and strategy, were watched with great interest. But beyond indicating that he was "100% for the unification law," which he did at a press conference in Matthews' office on the day his appointment was announced,[342] and some references to the importance of naval aviation which were vague enough to make controversy over them impossible, his public statements on matters of controversial interest were negligible. Those who wanted to make an issue over Denfeld's removal could find little basis for doing so in Sherman's utterances.[343]

Millard E. Tydings, the Chairman of the Senate Armed Services Committee, was equally reluctant to get involved in a wrangle over the Denfeld removal, and in the Senate confirmation proceedings on the nomination of Sherman as Chief of Naval Operations, he defended Matthews and gave him every opportunity to present his own view. Despite the fact that Denfeld made evident his willingness to testify, he was not called before the committee. Ultimately, after a dispute had developed over whether Denfeld had been reappointed or not, and hence whether the post for which Sherman had been nominated was in fact vacant, Matthews spent five hours before the committee in executive session, after which Tydings announced that he had settled all problems connected with that mix-up to the committee's satisfaction.[344]

Even now, Denfeld continued to follow a moderate course, although with less and less success. In the end, it seemed that moderation had turned to vacillation; at least, Denfeld's actions—and inaction—gave that impression. Senator McCarthy of Wisconsin used material obtained from Denfeld in an attempt to embarrass Matthews in his efforts to clear the title to the position of Chief of Naval Operations; at the very same time, Denfeld offered to submit his resignation from that post in order to clear up the dispute over his occupancy of it.[345]

Denfeld, it will be remembered, was being transferred from his position as Chief of Naval Operations. He turned down the new assignment offered him, suggesting—presumably in order to embarrass Matthews—that another might be acceptable. When Matthews indicated that he would be offered no other, he retired. For quite different reasons the discord between the Secretary and the Chief of Naval Operations led to a premature ending of the career of one and an inability for any further effective exercise of his office by the other.

Op. 23 and the Promotion of Captain Burke

Op. 23, it will be remembered, was the division in the Office of the Chief of Naval Operations in which the preparation of the Navy's presentation to the House Armed Services Committee was made, and Captain Burke was in charge of it. About the time of Denfeld's removal, Matthews ordered the Navy Inspector General to investigate Op. 23. Although the investigation apparently yielded nothing actually incriminating, a week later, after publication of the fact that a radio address critical of the President and the Secretary of Defense had been reproduced and distributed in the Pentagon by Op. 23, the new Chief of Naval Operations abolished the office.[346]

At the same time, Captain Burke was up for promotion. Denfeld, shortly before his removal, had appointed a selection board to pick captains for promotion to flag rank. When Sherman became Chief of Naval Operations he recommended a new board, dropping three of Denfeld's choices, including Admiral Richard L. Conolly, one of the Navy witnesses in the B-36 hearings. The new board unanimously selected Burke for promotion, but was reconvened and ordered by Matthews to drop Burke's name and add the name of Matthews' own naval aide. Matthews' stated reason for this switch was that Burke would have plenty of chances for promotion while this was the last opportunity for the aide.

When the new promotion list was dispatched to the President at Key West on December 5, it contained twenty-two names, not including Burke's. Ten days later a report of the investigation of Op. 23 and of the removal of Burke's name from the promotion list was published. Burke was one of the ablest officers of his rank in the Navy, and both within and outside of the Navy it was strongly believed that, whatever he had done as head of Op. 23, he had done under orders and should not be blamed. The reaction reached Congress at a time when House Republicans were already expressing concern about the removal of Denfeld, and only added heat to the controversy. The matter was ended amicably on December 29, however, when the President approved a list of twenty-three naval officers for promotion to

flag rank, and Burke's name was included.[347]

By spring 1950, Admirals Blandy and Bogan had joined Admiral Denfeld in retirement, after being offered commands unsatisfactory to them.[348] But for them, retirement was as much an expression of disgust as a sign of reprisal. The only clear instance of a "purge" besides that of Denfeld was suffered by Captain Crommelin, when he was furloughed on April 1, 1950, and ordered to his home in Alabama. But even that action was not a direct result of his role in the hearings, for after he had leaked the Bogan correspondence to the press, he was only reprimanded. It was only after his failure to comply with an order from Sherman on February 22 to stop making public statements criticizing defense officials that he was thus removed from active service.[349]

THE DEFENSE BUDGET

After the hearings Secretary of Defense Johnson proceeded with unabated energy to carry out his economy program for the Defense Department. For current (fiscal 1950) expenditures, he allowed a moderate reduction in the $800-odd million planned reduction which the Defense Management Committee had apportioned to the three services, but the modifications reflected no change of his plans for the Navy. Moreover, plans for Air Force reductions, initiated before the hearings, became clearer as time went on, and turned out to be equally severe. Congress had remained deadlocked over the budget until October 20, and had only reached agreement when the Senate consented to the House increase in Air Force funds with the understanding that the President would not spend the money. As fiscal 1950 unfolded, the hearings seemed to have had no discernible effect upon the budget.

Nor did the preparation of the fiscal 1951 budget within the Executive Branch show any effects from the hearings. The President set the ceiling at $13 billion (apparently including $600 million for stockpiling), certainly no higher than had been expected.[350] The fact that this figure represented an increase of some $545 million may indicate that Johnson had become aware that greater expenditures were both a military necessity and a political possibility as a result of the hearings, or it may indicate nothing at all. Indeed, the absence of any favorable effect upon the budget by the Navy presentation can be seen in the Navy program. While it emphasized the prototype approach which the Navy had been turning to for three years, it included no money for the conversion or construction of aircraft carriers, and only enough new aircraft to keep even with reduced inventories. The major emphasis in the new budget was upon the development of defensive and offensive undersea weapons, including an atomic submarine. The Navy's budget was down about $1 billion from what had been appropriated for the previous year, but its reduction was for the most part only commensurate with that of the other two services. The concentration on submarines meant that naval aviation suffered severely, as had been planned before the hearings.

The effect of the hearings on Congressional attitudes toward defense expenditures could be seen clearly only in the House, for the Korean War disrupted the Senate's view before it had considered the defense budget. In the House, Vinson had introduced a measure for the authorization of a new prototype construction program for the Navy, to cost $500 million and to begin in the following fiscal year (1952). It included the conversion of one fleet carrier, but no new carrier construction, and, like the budget then under consideration, gave strong emphasis to submarine development. But it did represent an increased appreciation of the Navy's weapons-development problem. The bill passed the House on May 24, having been reduced only in the funds to be used for the ships it authorized, and only until the Navy had had a chance to study and report on its existing tonnage authorizations. On the eve of the Korean War the *Army-Navy-Air Force Register* reported that the bill was expected to have smooth sailing in the Senate.[351]

In a modest way the Navy had evidently won some understanding from Congress of its problems. But what was being approved was not what the Navy had asked for in the hearings, a greater participation in the various roles of military aviation, but the only other major task left to it, the further development of naval aviation's role in anti-submarine warfare. Johnson's cancellation of the flush-deck carrier had, until the Korean War, decisively changed the emphasis in the development of Navy weapons and missions, and that change remained un-

modified as North Korea arrayed for battle.

THE COMMITTEE REPORT

The House Armed Services Committee issued on March 1, 1950, a report on its investigation of unification and strategy. The report treated the aviation controversy with perceptive dispassion, showed considerable understanding of the causes of the dispute, recommended some changes in unification policy, exercised great restraint respecting issues with which it was not competent to deal, and made a powerful argument for, and a thoughtful explanation of, the role of Congress in the formulation of national strategic policy. The report's own summary is an extraordinary exposition, although in its preoccupation with Congressional prerogatives, as has so often been the case, it fails to comprehend the position of the Secretary of the Navy, as the politically responsible head of the Navy in his relationship with the professional chief of the Navy. The summary of the committee's report is reprinted here:

1. All testimony presented was based on the committee's agenda and rendered at the committee's request. Personal views of the witnesses were solicited. Criticism of the witnesses for presenting their frank views under these circumstances is unworthy and a disservice to the Nation's defense.

2. The witnesses would have been subject to censure had they failed to present their convictions to the committee on the subjects covered in the committee agenda.

3. The National objectives proposed by General Bradley appear to the committee to be sound, but should not be assumed by the military leaders. The Secretary of Defense should initiate a study in the National Security Council to provide a firm statement of principles upon which the Joint Chiefs of Staff may rely as an official expression of their civilian leaders.

4. The Secretary of Defense should initiate a study in the National Security Council on the relationship to the national objectives of atomic warfare and present strategic planning for the use of atomic weapons, and the appropriate committees of Congress should be fully informed of the decisions reached in order to place the legislative and appropriations problems of national defense in their proper perspective before the Congress.

5. In view of the terrible destructiveness of modern weapons, the Nation can no longer afford lackadaisical planning or complacency as to its

defenses. For an indefinite time, the Nation must maintain sound, modern, alert defensive forces capable of anticipating and dealing with a sudden enemy attack.

6. Intercontinental strategic bombing is not synonymous with air power. The Air Force is not synonymous with the Nation's military air power. Military air power consists of Air Force, Navy and Marine Corps air power, and of this, strategic bombing is but one phase. The national air power consists of the military air power of the various services plus commercial aviation plus the national industrial and manpower resources pertaining to aviation.

7. Navy leaders are not opposed to "strategic air warfare" but do oppose "strategic bombing" if, by the term "strategic bombing," is meant mass aerial bombardment of urban areas.

8. There is possibility of serious damage to the Nation's defense if too much joint planning is concentrated on individual service questions of a highly technical nature during the formative period of unification. The committee has strong doubts that it is a service to the Nation's defense for the military leaders of the respective services to pass judgment jointly on the technical fitness of either new or old weapons each service wishes to develop to carry out its assigned missions.

9. Difficulties between the Air Force and the naval air arm will continue because of fundamental professional disagreements on the art of warfare. Service prejudices, jealousies and thirst for power and recognition have had only a bare minimum of influence on this controversy.

10. The committee expects the services to resolve their professional differences fairly and without rancor and to perform their professional duties not only with efficiency and effectiveness but also with dignity, with decorum, and with full receptivity to one another's professional judgments.

11. A political body cannot of itself reach, through deliberative processes, final answers on professional military questions but must depend upon and encourage a continuation of the process of exploration, study, and coordination among our officers of the several services to preserve a satisfactory doctrine of defense, to have ready applicable plans, and to devise units, suitably equipped, to meet the most probable circumstances of an emergency. The significant thing is to insure that the national defense structure insures adequate consideration of all professional views, especially during these early days of unification.

12. The Committee on Appropriations should make a thorough analysis of present and projected aircraft procurement to verify whether or not the present and planned level of procurement will support the required air power for the nation.

13. A closer relationship should be established between Marine Corps aviators, the Army Field Forces, and the Air Force for the development of sound close air support tactics and techniques. The Secretary of Defense should require the prompt establishment of a joint training center for this purpose.

14. There should be joint training activities between tactical aircraft of the Air Force and Navy to resolve questions of relative performance of these aircraft.

15. All services have been at fault at one time or another in the unification effort. There are no unification Puritans in the Pentagon.

16. Prudent administration of unification, sensitive to the many imponderables of spirit and emotion and service loyalties, can greatly ease service tensions and difficulties over the years that must pass before cross education of the services will truly produce the "one-armed-force" concept. Hasty decisions and brusque dismissals of honestly held service views will aggravate these tensions and difficulties.

17. Cross education of the services holds the ultimate key to the perplexing problems of interservice relations. A much greater concentration of effort is needed in this field.

18. There is no justification whatsoever for barring naval aviation personnel from Strategic Air Command activities of the Air Force. This is not the spirit of unification, despite the provocations that may have occurred in the past to produce this situation.

19. Joint training centers should be established in all areas of greater interservice controversy to remove lack of understanding which breeds suspicion, rivalry, and questioning of motives. This should be done in air matters, amphibious warfare, ground support aviation, air-borne troops.

20. There should be an augmentation of interservice war games to resolve such questions as the Banshee versus the B-36 in order to eliminate or at least reduce the tensions between the services, as well as contributing to their combat readiness.

21. The committee firmly supports unification, but emphasizes that it is a concept requiring definition. Blind support should not be given to "unification" as a word; its meaning should always be examined to determine whether the particular concept being applied or proposed is the proper one.

22. Civilian control of the Nation's armed forces is integrally a part of the Nation's democratic process and tradition; it is strongly supported by the committee. But in supporting civilian control of the armed forces, the committee does not mean (1) preventing free testimony before

congressional committees by members of the armed forces, or (2) the relegation of the United States Congress to a by-stander role in issues pertaining to the national defense.

23. The Joint Chiefs of Staff structure, as now constituted, does not insure at all times adequate consideration for the views of all services. The committee will sponsor legislation to require rotation of the position of chairman of the Joint Chiefs of Staff among the services after a 2-year term, and to add the Commandant of the Marine Corps to the Joint Chiefs of Staff as a member thereof.

24. The committee will ultimately reexamine the entire Joint Chiefs structure to determine whether the structure, as amended as proposed in this report, insures adequate consideration of all service views.

25. The evaluation of the B-36 is properly within the province of the Joint Weapons Systems Evaluation Board; future mass procurement of weapons should not be undertaken until the recommendations of this Board, except in time of emergency, are available to the Joint Chiefs of Staff.

26. The Air Force holds the primary responsibility for conducting strategic bombing. It has maintained that the B-36 bomber is its foremost weapon to carry out that mission and that the B-36 can do its job. The committee holds that the Nation must rely upon the judgment of its professional leaders, in their respective fields in matters of this nature—and that the Nation's leaders in respect to weapons of the Air Force are the leaders of the United States Air Force.

27. The committee deplores the manner of cancellation of the construction of the aircraft carrier *U.S.S. United States,* but because of the pressure of other shipbuilding programs at the present time and the existing budgetary limitations on the Navy Department, will withhold further action—for the present—as regards the construction of this vessel. The committee considers it sound policy, however, for the Nation to follow the advice of its professional leaders in regard to this subject in the same manner as has been heretofore done in respect to the B-36 bomber. In the committee's view, the

Nation's leaders in respect to naval weapons are the leaders of the United States Navy.

28. The appropriate role of the Joint Weapons Systems Evaluation Board is to evaluate weapons after they have been developed, not to instruct the services what types of new weapons they will or will not develop.

29. The committee will sponsor legislation to require, within reasonable limits, consultation by the Secretary of Defense with the Appropriations Committees of the Senate and House of Representatives before appropriated funds are withheld by administrative act.

30. The Appropriations Committee should augment its staff in order to keep in intimate touch with the development of national defense budgets, thereby easing the stresses and strains in the Pentagon and keeping the Congress adequately informed on basic national defense planning as reflected in budgetary plans.

31. The Management Committee of the Department of Defense should be placed under the direction of the Comptroller of the Department of Defense on all fiscal and budgetary matters.

32. The appointment of a career military officer as chairman of a committee composed of civilians on the Assistant Secretary or Under Secretary level is an unfortunate and undesirable precedent which inverts the civilian-control so closely identified with unification.

33. The removal of Admiral Denfeld was a reprisal against him for giving testimony to the House Armed Services Committee. This act is a blow against effective representative government in that it tends to intimidate witnesses and hence discourages the rendering of free and honest testimony to the Congress; it violated promises made to the witnesses, the Secretary of the Navy, and the Secretary of Defense; and it violated the Unification Act, into which a provision was written specifically to prevent action of this nature against the Nation's highest military and naval officers.[352]

Except for item 33, the report was unanimous; dissents on item 33 were included in the published report.[353]

VIII. CONCLUDING REFLECTIONS

The dramatic focus of the B-36 controversy of 1949 was the Congressional hearings held to determine whether charges made against Air Force procurement of its B-36 bombers were correct, and to examine more general issues of Defense Department organization and military strategy. Behind the questions relating to these two subjects formulated by the House Armed Services Committee lay a controversy between the Navy and the Air Force over roles and missions, and the Navy's deep disquiet over the future of its air arm. In effect, the committee had been forced to consider questions which might well have been left to the Executive Branch of the government, and which the committee, or most of its members and certainly its chairman, wished to avoid. The Navy, having lost its confidence in the Office of the President, the Secretary of Defense, and the Secretary of the Navy, had maneuvered the committee into accepting this task, as a kind of court of appeal from its own Secretary, from the Department of Defense, the Bureau of the Budget, and the President. And, as it happened, the hearings occurred shortly after the explosion of the Soviet's first atomic bomb at a time when a general examination of our military strategy was most appropriate. These circumstances suggest several questions which, although they have an intimate connection with the B-36 investigation as an historical incident, are of a general enough character to require treatment apart from the narrative itself.

The questions suggested are: (1) What role was played by Congress in the B-36 investigation, besides the rather obvious neutral role of providing a forum for the expression of conflicting views? (2) What effect, if any, did the experience of the hearings have on Congress, or its Armed Services Committees? (3) To what extent, under the circumstances, was the Navy appeal to Congress successful? (4) What effect

did this appeal have on the problem of service rivalry in general, the roles-and-missions problems, and the Air Force–Navy aviation dispute most particularly? (5) What was accomplished by this public debate over military strategy sponsored by the House Armed Services Committee? Complete answers to these questions would provide a definite statement of the place of the B-36 investigation of 1949 in political and military history. Complete and definitive answers to such questions would be admirable; but completeness and definitiveness are distant goals, never possible of realization. Tentative and incomplete answers are all that can be suggested here.

(1) The role of Congress in investigation. The role of Congress in the aviation controversy throughout 1948 and 1949 was, among other things, to translate issues of strategy into popularly supportable concepts, and to test simultaneously their popularity and their validity. A Congressman has at his disposal some fairly well-established techniques for measuring popularity. His means for testing the validity of military policy are much more limited, particularly at a time when demands for economy, if nothing else, seem to make necessary a unified military budget, while the services had plainly not established unified strategic doctrines to be implemented by the budget, and by which budgets could be meaningfully measured against national policies. The result in Congress was not unique. The military program tended to be measured in terms of its gross quantitative capabilities, rather than against national objectives (which were at best only emerging, and at worst inherently indefinable) on the basis of unified strategic doctrines (which were nonexistent). Gross quantitative capability tended to mean air power rather than sea or land power, and strategic air power at that. Throughout the pre-Korean War period, both before and

after the investigation, the strategic assumption which Congress shared with the general public and much of the Administration was that war meant striking the heart of Russia—and nothing else, or nothing else of any importance.

Beyond this general orientation or bias of Congress in its approach to military policy, for the B-36 investigation the role of Congress is explainable as the role of Carl Vinson, the Chairman of the House Armed Services Committee, former Chairman of the House Naval Affairs Committee, and committee member since World War I. In an age when Congressional hearings can offer distinct publicity advantages to the elected official conducting them, Vinson consistently sought to avoid the holding of these hearings, accepting the duty only when forced to by Van Zandt, ending the first phase promptly by insisting on the identification of Worth as the author of the anonymous document, seeking to postpone the second phase of the hearings, or to limit the subject matter to be considered to something other than the B-36 —to the major questions of organization and strategy. Vinson had spent many years of close working relationships with the military establishment. It is evident that he preferred to have very little publicity on this dispute.

(2) The effect of the hearings on Congress. What effect, if any, did the experience of the hearings have on Congress, or on the House Armed Services Committee? We have already noted that the Navy's determination to appeal to Congress, while it was created most proximately by budget pressures initiated by the Secretary of Defense and the Bureau of the Budget, rested on long-nurtured fears about the future of naval aviation; the pattern of Congressional views and acts about military affairs during 1948 and 1949, favoring, as it often seemed, the Air Force, had tended to reinforce those fears. The effect on Congress as a whole of the experience of the investigation, as has been noted, is not measurable, for budget policies in Congress did not change until the Korean War led to a major alteration in the whole frame of reference of defense policy.

The effect of the controversy on the House Armed Services Committee was more significant. The committee had been established in 1947 as an amalgamation of the Military Affairs and Naval Affairs Committees of the House. But combining the two committees did not assure their real integration. Many of the members of each committee had been closely identified with the service for whose affairs it was responsible. A member's influence on a House committee is normally based on expertness, on the knowledgeability of the member of the details of his subject. Prominent committee members normally have had some years of service on the committee, which not only gives them the status of seniority but which also affords them an opportunity to develop their expertise on the subject with which the committee deals and their contacts with the interested Executive Branch agencies. When the House combined its two services into a common one, these tendencies of expertise and identification were perhaps at their peak. World War II had catapulted the Military and Naval Affairs Committees to great prominence, making committee membership a prize and assuring that committee business was taken seriously. During the war Congress had come to view its relationship to the armed forces, in particular, as more one of aide than overseer; and each of the service committees quite naturally took a strong proprietary interest in the service for which it was responsible to Congress.

When the committees were merged, the question immediately presented itself to the members of the new Armed Services Committee as to what their orientation should be. Unless they were to have two committees in one, service orientations to the service identified with the old committee would have to change. Yet the Office of the Secretary of Defense offered little to inspire the kind of loyalty and sense of duty which committee membership had developed towards the Army or the Navy during recent years. The result was that those who felt obliged to modify the loyalties which they had developed in the old Military or Naval Affairs Committees (and by no means did all the members of the House Armed Services Committee do so) tended to shift from one service to another, to the benefit in almost every case of the Air Force. Both pro-Navy and pro-Army Congressmen turned to the Air Force as their new service orientation on the new House Armed Services Committee. Carl Vinson himself followed this pattern. He had claimed, not without much justification, to be the father of the modern American Navy in the Vinson-Trammel Act of 1938. Following the establishment of the new committee he did not conceal his desire to add a new title: father of the Air Force. His committee thus provided the Air Force with its major ally in Congress. But, following the B-36 investigation, and particularly the Unification and Strategy hearings, the House Armed Services Committee reduced its identification with the Air Force. The committee's report, the conclusions of which are reproduced above, indicated that the committee was determined to be independent of any service viewpoint and that it believed that none of the services had all the answers. Following the hearings the Air Force found it could no longer count on an uncritical acceptance of its 70-group program in the House Armed Services Committee. The experience of the Korean War undoubtedly promoted the substantial integration of one service committee out of its two predecessors in the House. But the process seems to have begun in the early autumn of 1949, and to have been inspired or facilitated by the B-36 investigation.

(3) The success of the Navy appeal to Congress. To the extent that the House Armed Services Committee no longer accepted with so little qualification the strategic doctrines and matériel requests of the Air Force, the Navy achieved some success in its appeal to Congress. There is no doubt that its appeal was made under adverse circumstances, and that many of the adversities were of the Navy's own making. The determination of the Navy witnesses rather than the skill of the Navy presentation was the more convincing evidence for the committee that what was being said deserved attention.

But the Navy appeal was not so successful as to make the House Armed Services Committee an ally of the Navy. At best, it secured a slight shift in committee sympathies.

(4) The effect of the appeal on service rivalry. The effect of the Navy appeal on service rivalry in general was more that of a purgative than an irritant, indicating that the rivalry was due not so much to individual disputes as it was to future long-term expectations of each service. If service rivalry had been caused by frictions over a series of incidents involving public relations, procurement questions, and disputed interpretations of JCS and OSD interpretations, the hearings on the B-36 Investigation and on Unification and Strategy would have heightened that rivalry, for they exposed more disputed interpretations and themselves constituted a ma-

jor contentious incident in public relations. While the hearings did produce some irritants, on the whole their effect was purgative, and after they were over a closer working relationship was developed in the Pentagon among the military chiefs and between a new CNO and his civilian superiors. Navy morale did hit a painfully low level when Denfeld was removed from his position as CNO. But this was precisely the point. The future expectations of the Navy were brought into question by Denfeld's removal, as they had been by cuts in the Navy's budget previously. But the Navy was allowed to state its case in the hearings; what it said had been listened to with much obvious sympathy; the committee report demonstrated that the House Armed Services Committee, at least, was not wedded to a particular service-oriented strategy. Congress did not let the Denfeld purge go unnoticed; rather it described the purge as a breach of faith. The Air Force had found its satisfactions in demonstrating the falsity of the charges about B-36 procurement. Both services could conclude that Congress was not a captive of the other.

The aviation dispute between the Navy and the Air Force was far from settled by the hearings, but the pressures generated by it, since their origins were largely in future expectations, were considerably relieved by the middle ground taken by the House Committee in its report. The complex issue of roles and missions in general was not really dealt with in, by, or through the hearings. The committee refused to deal with that issue because of its supposedly technical nature.

(5) Achievements of the hearings. What, then, was accomplished by this public debate over military strategy sponsored by the House Armed Services Committee? Its primary accomplishment was a demonstration to both the Navy and the Air Force that Congress could not be fooled by either, to the Secretary of Defense that Congress could at least embarrass him in his administration of the Department as a sanction against objectionable policies or procedures, to the committee that it must stand above any single service viewpoint, to the Administration that the defense economy program had political costs as well as gains, and to the public that the nation faced the prospects of nuclear counter-deterrence with divided councils.

BIBLIOGRAPHIC NOTE

The main sources for this study have been Congressional documents and daily newspapers. The core of the Congressional documentation for this subject is two sets of hearings conducted by the House Armed Services Committee during the first session of the 81st Congress, entitled respectively *Investigation of the B-36 Bomber Program* and *The National Defense Program: Unification and Strategy,* and the committee report on the latter, *Unification and Strategy, Report of Investigation,* issued in the second session of the 81st Congress. In addition to these, the *Congressional Record* and a considerable number of hearings and some reports from the House and Senate Armed Services and Appropriations Committees of the 79th, 80th, and 81st Congresses have been used, including the hearings on the *Military Situation in the Far East,* conducted jointly by the Senate Armed Services and Foreign Relations Committees during the second session of the 81st Congress. The biennial reports of the Secretary of Defense and the annual reports of the Secretaries of the Army, Navy, and Air Force were of some value, as were also the Report of the President's Air Policy Commission, *Survival in the Air Age* (Government Printing Office, Washington, 1948); and the Report of the Congressional Aviation Policy Board, entitled *National Aviation Policy* (Senate Rept. 949, 80th Cong., 2d sess.).

The narrative detail has been filled out primarily from newspaper accounts. The *New York Times* has, of course, been the most valuable daily, but I have also drawn from the *Atlanta Constitution,* the *Baltimore Sun,* the *Boston Herald,* the *Christian Science Monitor,* the *Cleveland Plaindealer,* the *Detroit News,* the *Philadelphia Bulletin,* the *Philadelphia Inquirer,* the *New York Herald Tribune,* the *St. Louis Post-Dispatch,* the *San Francisco Chronicle,* the *Washington Daily News,* the *Washing-*ton *Evening Star,* the *Washington Post,* and the *Washington Times-Herald.* Two weekly newspapers, the *Army-Navy-Air Force Register* and the *Army-Navy-Air Force Journal,* were particularly useful, as were the news sections in the periodical *Aviation Week.*

The background of Air Force militancy is traced in a publication of the Documentary Research Division of the Air University, *The Question of Autonomy for the United States Air Arm, 1906-1946,* by R. Earl McClendon (Maxwell Field University, Montgomery, 1948). *The Forrestal Diaries,* edited by Walter Millis (Viking, New York, 1951), is an important source for this subject. The publicity battle between the Air Force and the Navy during 1948 and 1949 can be traced in the daily press and the national weekly and monthly periodicals. Notable among the latter are the *Saturday Evening Post, Collier's,* and the *Reader's Digest.*

A number of people have assisted me by commenting on an early draft of this study or by answering questions which arose in its preparation. Among them are Hanson W. Baldwin, Oswald S. V. Colclough, J. Lawton Collins, Arthur L. Davis, B. Vincent Davis, Louis E. Denfeld, James M. Gillin, Bryce N. Harlow, Phillip C. Holt, H. G. Hopwood, S. P. Huntington, Louis Johnson, Walter Karig, W. John Kenny, Dan A. Kimball, John T. Koehler, W. Barton Leach, Robert LeBaron, Stephen F. Leo, Marx Leva, John H. Ohly, Frank Pace, William F. Schaub, Robert W. Smart, John L. Sullivan, Lyon L. Tyler, James E. Webb, Burke Wilkinson, E. T. Wooldridge, and Eugene Zuckert.

The assistance of three people deserves special mention. W. Barton Leach made available to me a portion of his personal file concerning the B-36 investigation, in addition to his contribution of critical comments. And Murray Green assisted me greatly in locating the published materials on the aviation controversy.

Finally, the critical assistance, suggestions and editorial assistance of Harold Stein have significantly influenced the final outcome of this study. He shares with me, as does no one else, responsibility for it.

NOTES

1. U. S. Air University, Documentary Research Division, *The Question of Autonomy for the United States Air Arm, 1906-1946,* by R. Earl McClendon (Maxwell Field Air Base, Montgomery, 1948), *passim.*

2. *Sundry Legislation,* Hearings before the House Armed Services Committee, 80th Cong., 2d sess., pp. 6889, 6895.

3. *Hearings on Department of the Navy Appropriation Bill for 1949,* House Committee on Appropriations, 80th Cong., 2d sess., p. 1013.

4. This program consisted of six new prototypes (including the new carrier), and three conversions. *Supplementary Hearings on Department of the Navy Appropriation Bill for 1949,* House Committee on Appropriations, 80th Cong., 2d sess., p. 217. It was later increased by fourteen more conversions.

5. In June 1947, Senator Lodge attempted to give legislative sanction to the 70-group program by proposing (unsuccessfully) an amendment to the pending appropriation bill which would have provided for them. *Congressional Record,* XCIII, July 10, 1947, p. 8605; *ibid.,* XCIV, May 24, 1948, pp. 6337-6338.

6. *Military Functions, National Military Establishment Appropriation Bill for 1949,* Hearings before the House Committee on Appropriations, Pt. 2, p. 44; *Military Establishment Appropriation Bill, 1948,* Hearings before the House Committee on Appropriations, pp. 625, 643, 645.

7. *Military Functions . . . ,* House Hearings, p. 44.

8. *Sundry Legislation,* House Hearings, pp. 6860, 6892-6894; *Supplementary Hearings . . . ,* pp. 14, 25; Harlan Trott in *Christian Science Monitor,* June 1, 1948. Trott says that the whole program, including several super carriers, was included in the paper, but that the Air Force Chief, Spaatz, submitted a supplementary statement withholding approval of the carriers.

9. *Military Functions . . . ,* House Hearings, Pt. 3, pp. 18, 1222.

10. *Hearings on Department of the Navy Appropriation Bill for 1949,* House Hearings, p. 40.

11. *The National Defense Program: Unification and Strategy,* Hearings before the House Armed Services Committee, 81st Cong., 1st sess., p. 419 (hereafter cited as *Unification and Strategy* Hearings); *New York Times,* February 6 and 14, 1948.

12. *New York Times,* February 6, 1948. I have chosen to refer to this ship as the "flush-deck carrier" as the least misleading term. "Supercarrier," or even its intended name "U. S. S. United States," seems to imply a different order of magnitude in the size of this vessel compared with its largest predecessor.

13. *Hearings on Department of the Navy Appropriation Bill for 1949,* House Hearings, p. 132.

14. Letter, James E. Webb to author, April 3, 1957.

15. Walter Millis (ed.), *The Forrestal Diaries* (Viking, New York, 1951), pp. 368-377.

16. *Ibid.*

17. *Ibid.,* p. 387.

18. The military establishment estimate was that UMT would ultimately involve an annual expenditure of $4 billion. *Ibid.,* p. 388.

19. *Ibid.,* p. 390; *New York Times,* March 12 and 16, 1948.

20. Sec. 211 (b) (4) (6), Public Law 253, 80th Cong., 1st sess., July 26, 1947; 61 Stat. 495 at 505.

21. Millis, *The Forrestal Diaries,* pp. 392 f.

22. Printed in U. S. Department of the Navy, Office of the Chief of Naval Operations, *OPNAV Instruction 5410.1A,* April 7, 1954.

23. Denfeld testimony in *Hearings on H. R. 6049,* House Armed Services Committee, 80th Cong., 2d sess., p. 6860.

24. *Washington Daily News,* April 25, 1949. Italics added.

25. Millis, *The Forrestal Diaries,* pp. 395 f.

26. *Ibid.,* p. 393.

27. *New York Times,* March 17, 1948.

28. Millis, *The Forrestal Diaries,* p. 397; *Congressional Record,* LXXX, March 17, 1948.

29. Letter, James E. Webb to author, April 13, 1957; *New York Times,* March 31, 1948.

30. Millis, *The Forrestal Diaries,* pp. 397 f.

31. Walter Millis, Harvey C. Mansfield and Harold Stein, *Arms and the State* (The Twentieth

Century Fund, New York, 1958), pp. 205-207.

32. *Military Functions . . .* , House Hearings, Pt. 1, pp. 1 ff. and 116 ff.; Millis, *The Forrestal Diaries,* p. 398.

33. *Universal Military Training,* Hearings before the Senate Armed Services Committee, 80th Cong., 2d sess., pp. 33, 331; Millis, *The Forrestal Diaries,* p. 401.

34. *Military Functions . . .* , House Hearings, Pts. 2 and 3, *passim.*

35. H. Con. Res. 153, *Congressional Record,* XCIV, March 2, 1948, p. 2014; H. R. 5991, *ibid.,* March 24, 1948, p. 3456; H. R. 6158, *ibid.,* April 7, 1948, p. 4217, and H. R. 6247, *ibid.,* April 14, 1948, p. 4474. This last bill, which passed the House on June 14, provided for 70 regular air groups; 22 separate Air Force squadrons; 27 National Guard groups; and 34 Air Reserve groups. It further provided for 70,500 officers, 40,000 of whom could be regulars, 4,800 warrant officers, and 426,700 enlisted men. It authorized 24,000 serviceable aircraft, or 225,000 airframe tons aggregate of serviceable aircraft, leaving to the discretion of the Secretary of the Air Force which of the two standards would be applied. The only 70-group authorization bill to pass the House during this session, H. R. 6247, died in the Senate, sharing its fate with a similar bill introduced in the Senate on the 3rd of June. S. 2792, *Congressional Record,* June 3, 1949, p. 6994.

36. Millis, *The Forrestal Diaries,* p. 412; *Hearings on Supplemental National Defense Appropriation Bill for 1948,* House Committee on Appropriations, 80th Cong., 2d sess., p. 459.

37. Millis, *The Forrestal Diaries,* pp. 414 f.

38. *Ibid.*

39. *Ibid.,* pp. 412, 415-419; *New York Times,* April 21, 1948.

40. *New York Times,* April 27, 1948; *Supplemental National Defense Appropriation Bill for 1948,* Hearings . . . on H. R. 6266, Senate Committee on Appropriations, 80th Cong., 2d sess., pp. 3-4, 12-13.

41. Millis, *The Forrestal Diaries,* p. 418.

42. *New York Times,* April 23, 1948.

43. Millis, *The Forrestal Diaries,* p. 430.

44. Memorandum read by President at military establishment budget meeting in White House, May 13, 1948, quoted in *ibid.,* p. 435.

45. *Ibid.,* p. 438.

46. *Congressional Record,* XCIV, June 19, 1948, p. 9033.

47. For example, *Military Functions . . . ,* House Hearings, Pt. 1, pp. 2-4, 9, 10, 21, 28; Millis, *The Forrestal Diaries,* pp. 400-401, 414-415; *Supplemental National Defense Appropriation Bill for 1948,* Hearings before the House Committee on Appropriations, 80th Cong., 2d

sess., p. 77; *New York Times,* April 26 and 27, 1948; *Army-Navy Journal,* LXXXV, April 24, 1948, pp. 885-887.

48. *New York Times,* April 23, 1948. It should be noted that the Air Force was not always to blame for getting its position on the 70 groups into the record. Sometimes Congressional insistence was responsible. The best example of this came in August 1949, when Symington, anxious to avoid any contentiousness in view of the highly favorable way the B-36 procurement investigation had gone for the Air Force, was forced, despite himself, into reiteration of the Air Force 70-group program. Testimony reprinted in *Congressional Record,* XCV, August 25, 1949, p. 12249.

49. *New York Times,* March 23, 1948; *New York Herald Tribune,* March 26, 1948.

50. *Military Functions . . . ,* House Hearings, Pt. 3, p. 1222; *Supplemental National Defense Appropriation Bill for 1948,* Senate Hearings, p. 82; *Congressional Record,* XCIV, April 15, 1948, p. A2300; *ibid.,* April 30, 1948, p. A2624.

51. Millis, *The Forrestal Diaries,* p. 462.

52. In connection with the Key West press release, see *ibid.,* p. 466.

53. *Atlanta Constitution,* April 14, 1948.

54. W. Stuart Symington, "We've Scuttled Our Air Defenses," *American Magazine,* CXLV, February 1948, pp. 50 ff.; *New York Times,* February 14, 1948.

55. I am indebted to Vincent Davis for help in clarifying this point.

56. *Survival in the Air Age,* A Report by the President's Air Policy Commission, GPO, Washington, 1948; *National Aviation Policy,* Report of the Congressional Aviation Policy Board, S. Rept. 949, 80th Cong., 2d sess., GPO, Washington, 1948. For interest of Congress in these two reports, see *Congressional Record,* XCIV, pp. 1646, 1650, 1986, 2007-2008, 2037, 2575, 2882, 3424, 4181-4182, 4274, 4327, 4565, 5397, 5988. For the interest of the House in the Finletter Commission report see *Military Functions . . . ,* House Hearings, Pt. 2, pp. 20, 43, 44, 47, 48, 52.

57. Drew Pearson in *Philadelphia Bulletin* and *Philadelphia Inquirer* (two articles), April 10, 1948. The Navy issued an official release on May 8, as the dispute with Air Force continued to mount, a somewhat belated report on the details of its combat record against the Japanese air force during World War II. It used as the occasion for this release the 37th anniversary of naval aviation. The material thus published led to lively exchanges in the press and in Congress. Report printed in *Sundry Legislation,* House Hearings, pp. 6873 ff., together with some press reaction to it.

58. *New York Times,* April 10, 1948.

59. *Sundry Legislation,* House Hearings, pp.

6860, 6892-6894.

60. *Hearings on Department of the Navy Appropriation Bill for 1949,* House Hearings, pp. 13 ff.

61. *Sundry Legislation,* House Hearings, pp. 7561 f.; Jim G. Lucas in *Washington Daily News,* May 21, 1948.

62. *Hearings on Department of Navy Appropriations for 1949,* 80th Cong., 2d sess., Senate Hearings, p. 4; *Unification and Strategy* Hearings, p. 360.

63. *Washington Post,* April 26, 1949.

64. *Unification and Strategy* Hearings, p. 567.

65. Twice Gruenther had taken this information to Forrestal. Millis, *The Forrestal Diaries,* pp. 352 and 434.

66. *Ibid.,* p. 432. For future cost of the 70-group Air Force see U. S. Congress, H. Rept. 2169, June 3, 1948, p. 3; and *Military Functions . . . ,* House Hearings, Pt. 3, p. 1229. For future cost of the Army see *ibid.,* p. 1228. For future cost of the Navy see H. Rept. 2169, p. 6.

67. The 70-group authorization bill got through the House, but died in the Senate. H. Rept. 2136, 80th Cong., 2d sess., p. 15.

68. *New York Times,* September 11, 1948. The ceiling was set at $15 billion, but $600 million was for strategic stockpiling; so the ceiling for the military establishment was only $14.4 billion.

69. Millis, *The Forrestal Diaries,* p. 450.

70. Forrestal, speaking before the National Press Club, February 2, 1949, gives the $30 billion figure. *New York Times,* February 3, 1949; Millis, *The Forrestal Diaries,* p. 500; Hanson W. Baldwin in *New York Times,* September 21, 1948.

71. Speech before Reserve Officers Association, New York City, on the eve of the submission of the reduced JCS budget to the President, *New York Times,* December 1, 1948.

72. *National Military Establishment Appropriation Bill for 1950,* Hearings before the House Committee on Appropriations, 81st Cong., 1st sess., Pt. 3, p. 38; and Millis, *The Forrestal Diaries,* p. 450.

73. Millis, *The Forrestal Diaries,* p. 503.

74. *Ibid.,* p. 536.

75. *Ibid.*

76. *Ibid.,* pp. 498-499, 502-506.

77. *Ibid.*

78. *New York Times,* December 2, 1948.

79. *Ibid.* Bradley had been the first member of the Joint Chiefs to agree to Forrestal's request to construct the "intermediate" budget. Millis, *The Forrestal Diaries,* p. 504.

80. Millis, *The Forrestal Diaries,* p. 544; *New York Times,* January 9, 1948; *Annual Report of the Secretary of the Air Force,* Fiscal 1948, pp. 3, 6, 12.

81. *Annual Report of the Secretary of the Air Force,* Fiscal 1949, p. 275.

82. *National Military Establishment Appropriation Bill for 1950,* House Hearings, Pt. 3, p. 4.

83. Millis, *The Forrestal Diaries,* p. 463.

84. *Ibid.,* pp. 463-465.

85. Department of the Air Force, Air Information Division, Press Section, No. 37, for release September 5, 1948. For descriptions of various local Air Force Day celebrations, see *Cleveland Plaindealer,* August 29, and September 16, 1948; *St. Louis Post-Dispatch,* September 12, 1948; *San Francisco Chronicle,* September 18, 1948; *Washington Post,* September 19, 1948.

86. For example, see *San Francisco Chronicle, loc. cit.*

87. *New York Times,* September 27, 1948.

88. The activities of the conference are summarized in Millis, *The Forrestal Diaries,* pp. 476-478.

89. Entire agreement quoted in Hanson W. Baldwin's column, *New York Times,* September 24, 1948.

90. Office of the Secretary of Defense, Press Release, September 1948.

91. *Ibid.*

92. Millis, *The Forrestal Diaries,* pp. 500-502, 508-511.

93. The Brown and Radford statements have never been published. This surmise is based on the following: (1) Shortly thereafter Forrestal asked the JCS some questions which had obviously arisen in the air power dispute. One of them was "What are the chances of effective delivery of the atom bomb?" (2) Forrestal's undelivered letter to Sullivan, *infra.* (3) Symington's published letter to Eberstadt complaining about what was said, *infra,* pp. 488-489. (4) An account in the *New York Herald Tribune,* November 21, 1948.

94. Millis, *The Forrestal Diaries,* p. 514.

95. *New York Times,* November 1, 1948.

96. Millis, *The Forrestal Diaries,* p. 516.

97. Jim G. Lucas in *Washington Daily News,* November 17, 1948.

98. *Baltimore Sun,* November 18, 1948.

99. *Unification and Strategy* Hearings, pp. 352, 263.

100. As the senior editor of the *Reader's Digest* later put it, Huie "has been for years the confidant of Air Force generals, and his articles were prepared with their cooperation." Letter from Merle Crowell (senior editor, the *Reader's Digest*) to Paul R. Watson (Our Navy, Inc.), May 10, 1949. Published in *Investigation of the B-36 Bomber Program,* Hearings before the House Armed Services Committee, 81st Cong., 1st sess., p. 598 (hereafter cited as *B-36 Bomber* Hearings). The

articles appeared in the December 1948, January 1949, March 1949, and April 1949 issues of the *Reader's Digest.* They are reprinted in the *Unification and Strategy* Hearings, pp. 579-597. Later the *Digest* offered the Navy a chance to reply in a single article to the Huie series, but gave it only a week in which to prepare the reply. Fletcher Pratt, a popular writer on naval affairs, was asked to write the article. See Pratt, "Case for the Aircraft Carrier," *Reader's Digest,* May 1949, pp. 53-58. It was not, and could not have been, an effective counter to the anti-Navy publicity of the Huie articles.

In general, the Navy fared better with some of the other popular periodicals. During 1948 the weekly *Saturday Evening Post* published no less than four articles which treated the Navy favorably. During the same year the *Post's* major competitor, *Collier's,* published no articles on the Navy, and one highly favorable to air troop transport, by implication, at least, a criticism of the Air Force emphasis on strategic air power. Thereafter the *Post* published only one article relevant to the unification controversy, a pro-Navy one on June 25, 1949, and *Collier's* none until after the Unification and Strategy hearings had begun in October 1949. In October the *Post* published one article defending the Navy, and in January, March, and April 1950, *Collier's* published four articles presenting various aspects of the Navy's side of the aviation controversy.

Other general periodicals were less favorable to the Navy. *The American Mercury* and *Newsweek,* and, of course, the *Reader's Digest,* were pro-Air Force and anti-Navy from 1947 until at least the end of 1949. *Newsweek's* partisan approach was led by General Carl Spaatz, who had been hired as a columnist upon his retirement from the Air Force. The Luce publications, it should be noted, were not conspicuous for taking sides in the air power controversy, although they did on occasion side with the Air Force.

Furthermore, the Air Force undoubtedly held the advantage with the military matériel trade press, such as *Aviation Weekly.* And it consistently scored better with the daily press, although it would be incorrect to suggest that the prominent American dailies were pressing the Air Force case in the way that *Newsweek* or *Aviation Weekly* did, or even as the *Saturday Evening Post* gave similar voice to the Navy viewpoint.

101. *New York Herald Tribune,* November 27, 1948 and January 2, 1949; *Congressional Record,* XLV, January 1, 1949, p. 19; *ibid.,* January 5, 1949, p. 39. The bill aimed at the flush-deck carrier died in committee.

102. *Washington Post,* September 10, 1948. I am indebted to Vincent Davis for pointing out this pattern in Congressman Vinson's methods.

103. Text printed in *Unification and Strategy* Hearings, p. 481.

104. *New York Times,* January 12, 1949; *Washington Post,* January 13, 1949; *Baltimore Sun,* January 13, 1949; *Unification and Strategy* Hearings, pp. 42, 49, 246, 481 f.

105. *New York Times,* February 20, 1949.

106. *Unification and Strategy* Hearings, p. 399.

107. *New York Times,* January 29 and 30, 1949.

108. *New York Times,* February 9 and 17, 1949; *Washington Times-Herald,* March 23, 1949; *Congressional Record,* XCV, March 22, 1949, p. 2936.

109. *Congressional Record,* XCV, March 30, 1949, pp. 3540-3544; *New York Times,* March 31, 1949.

110. *New York Times,* April 14, 1949.

111. *National Military Establishment Appropriation Bill for 1950,* House Hearings, p. 33.

112. For example, *Hearings . . . on . . . Composition of the Army . . . and the Air Force . . .* (H. R. 1437), House Armed Services Committee, 81st Cong., 1st sess., pp. 155-157.

113. See, e. g., Symington's speech in Boston, February 12, 1949, published in *Unification and Strategy* Hearings, pp. 313-316.

114. *Washington Daily News,* March 3 and 14, 1949; *New York Times,* March 3 and 15, 1949; *Detroit News,* March 4, 1949; *Boston Herald,* March 19, 1949; the accounts of March 3 and 4 covered the B-50 flight, the accounts of March 14-19 the report to the JCS.

115. Harry S. Truman, *Memoirs,* II, *Years of Trial and Hope* (Doubleday, Garden City, 1956), p. 305.

116. *New York Times,* April 6, 1949.

117. *Congressional Record,* XCV, April 14, 1949, pp. A2298-A2301.

118. *Unification and Strategy* Hearings, p. 534.

119. Millis, *The Forrestal Diaries,* pp. 543-553.

120. Johnson denied this claim in *B-36 Bomber* Hearings, p. 491, and Truman made the same denial. But see also Jack Alexander, "Stormy New Boss of the Pentagon," *Saturday Evening Post,* July 30, 1949, pp. 26 ff.

121. *Baltimore Sun,* March 18, 1949; *New York Times,* March 24, 1949; *Washington Daily News,* June 3, 1949.

122. *New York Times,* February 20, 1949.

123. *Unification and Strategy* Hearings, p. 619.

124. Johnson's words, *ibid.*

125. *Ibid.*

126. Denfeld's statement, *ibid.,* p. 360.

127. *Ibid.*

128. *Ibid.,* pp. 529 f.

129. Louis Johnson, "Teamwork for Defense,"

American Magazine, July 1949, p. 130.

130. See Secretary Johnson's testimony in *Military Situation in the Far East,* Hearings before the Joint Committee on Armed Services, 82d Cong., 1st sess., pp. 2636 f.

131. Compare the conflicting versions of Johnson, Denfeld, and Matthews, *Unification and Strategy* Hearings, pp. 360 and 619-620; *Washington Post,* October 14, 1949; Stacy N. Jones, "The Inside Story of the Big Carrier that Wasn't Built," *Liberty,* August 1949, p. 40.

132. *Unification and Strategy* Hearings, pp. 622-623.

133. *Congressional Record,* XCV, April 26, 1949, p. 5053; quoted in *Unification and Strategy* Hearings, p. 621.

134. See, e. g., *Washington Daily News,* April 25, 1949; and *Washington Post,* April 26, 1949.

135. Baldwin in *New York Times,* April 28 and 29, 1949.

136. *Unification and Strategy, Report of Investigation,* House Armed Services Committee, 81st Cong., 2d sess., p. 21. (Hereafter cited as *Unification and Strategy* Report.)

137. *New York Times,* May 18 and 19, 1949; *Washington Star,* May 23, 1949.

138. *B-36 Bomber* Hearings, pp. 562-564.

139. *Ibid.*

140. Worth claimed that Deane wanted information in order to advise Jonathan Daniels on an offer he had been given of the post of Secretary of the Navy, but Daniels has denied that he ever received the offer. *Washington Post,* August 26, 1949.

141. *B-36 Bomber* Hearings, pp. 524-600, *passim.*

142. *Aviation Week,* June 6, 1949, p. 7. Captain John Crommelin, USN, has claimed that at this point he attended a meeting with Worth, Captain Leroy Simpler, a public relations officer, and Lieutenant Samuel Ingram, at which the topic of conversation was "getting a B-36 inquiry going and talking about giving the Worth memorandum to the press." As reported in the *New York Times,* September 11, 1949.

143. *Investigation of the B-36 Bomber Program,* Report of the Committee . . . on H. Res. 234, House Armed Services Committee, 81st Cong., 1st sess., p. 1 (hereafter cited as *B-36 Bomber* Report); *Congressional Record,* XCV, May 26, 1949, pp. 6892-6894.

144. H. Res. 234, 81st Cong., 1st sess.

145. *B-36 Bomber* Report, pp. 1-2.

146. Memorandum for General Fairchild, June 2, 1949; Subject: "Organization of Preparation for B-36 Hearings."

147. *Army-Navy-Air Force Register,* June 18, 1949, pp. 1, 14-15.

148. *Washington Post,* July 8, 1949.

149. The year before, Bradley had avoided appointment as "principal military adviser" to Forrestal. According to Forrestal's understanding of a conversation he had with Gruenther, one reason for Bradley's reluctance was his desire to work for a reduced Navy budget; Millis, *The Forrestal Diaries,* p. 434; but Forrestal's reporting was not always accurate.

150. *Congressional Record,* XCV, August 25, 1949, p. 12249.

151. *Universal Military Training,* Hearings before the Senate Armed Services Committee, 80th Cong., 2d sess., pp. 380-388; reprinted in *Congressional Record,* XCV, August 26, 1949, pp. 12305-12306; *Army-Navy-Air Force Register,* July 23, 1949, p. 19.

152. *B-36 Bomber* Hearings, p. 24.

153. *Washington Daily News,* May 26, 1949; *New York Times,* May 24, 1949.

154. *B-36 Bomber* Hearings, pp. 241, 500. Van Zandt and Vinson did not disclose to him their information.

155. *Ibid.,* p. 233.

156. *Ibid.,* pp. 232-233, 505, 523-524.

157. *Ibid.,* pp. 497-499.

158. *National Security Act Amendments of 1949,* Hearings on S. 1269 and S. 1843, Senate Armed Services Committee, 81st Cong., 1st sess., pp. 110-116, 121-123.

159. *Congressional Record,* XCV, July 12, 1949, pp. 9432 ff.; *New York Herald Tribune,* July 13, 1949; *Washington Star,* July 13, 1949.

160. *New York Herald Tribune,* July 15, 1949; *Washington Post,* July 15, 1949; *Washington Star,* July 15, 1949. On July 18 the President submitted his Reorganization Plan No. 8, 1949, to Congress in order to force action on the Tydings bill. *Congressional Record,* XCV, July 19, 1949, pp. 9668 f; H. Doc. 262, 81st Cong., 1st sess.

161. *Washington Post,* July 27, 1949; *New York Herald Tribune,* August 7, 1949; *Congressional Record,* XCV, August 2, 1949, pp. 10345, 10592; Public Law 216, 81st Cong., 1st sess.

162. Johnson confirmed reports that he had urged the Senate Armed Services Committee to cut back the Air Force to 48 groups in a speech at the National War College, June 21, 1949. *Washington Post,* June 22, 1949.

163. The Appropriations Committee reported out a $433 million reduction, in addition to the $800 million cut for the Air Force, to be made by the Secretary of Defense, since it could not decide for itself what items to reduce. This provision was eliminated on the floor of the Senate after a bitter debate. *Congressional Record,* August 26, 1949, pp. 12308, 12313 and August 29, 1949, pp. 12310-12400.

164. *New York Times,* August 27 and 30, 1949; *Army-Navy-Air Force Register,* September 3, 1949, p. 3; October 22, 1949, p. 7.

165. David Lawrence in *Washington Star,* June 13, 1949.

166. *Army-Navy-Air Force Register,* June 25, 1949, p. 1231; *New York Times,* June 22, 1949; *Philadelphia Inquirer,* June 22, 1949; *Unification and Strategy* Hearings, pp. 9-10.

167. *Ibid.,* p. 122. Johnson had accepted the Senate Armed Services Committee's solution to its budget-cutting problems by directing the Secretary of Defense to cut $433 million more from the budget without specifying where. *Ibid.,* p. 626. Johnson's earnest resolve to save money, as it was displayed in Senate Appropriations Committee hearings (some of which were held in closed sessions that summer) was noted on the floor of the Senate. *Congressional Record,* XCV, August 25, 1949, p. 12249. In these hearings, he specifically supported removal of the $800 million increase in Air Force funds added by the House to the President's estimates. *Ibid.,* August 26, 1949, p. 12301.

168. Hanson W. Baldwin in the *New York Times,* July 28, 1949; *Washington Star,* July 12, 1949.

169. *U. S. News and World Report,* as quoted by David Lawrence in the *Washington Post,* August 9, 1949.

170. Millis, *The Forrestal Diaries,* pp. 135-140.

171. *Foreign Affairs,* XXV, No. 4 (July 1947), pp. 566-582.

172. Interview with Paul H. Nitze, April 27, 1956.

173. Johnson's announcement of the program is printed in *Congressional Record,* XCV, August 25, 1949, p. 12250; see also *Army-Navy-Air Force Register,* August 13, 1949, p. 2.

174. *Unification and Strategy* Hearings, pp. 306, 624-625. For an account of the handling of military expenditures in Congress for fiscal 1950 see Stephen K. Bailey and Howard D. Samuel, *Congress at Work* (Holt, New York, 1953), Chap. 13.

175. Drew Pearson in *Washington Post,* June 3, 1949.

176. *New York Times,* June 2, 1949.

177. *Ibid.,* June 4 and 9, 1949.

178. *Ibid.,* June 22, 1949.

179. See, e. g., an address by Vice Admiral John D. Price, Vice Chief of Naval Operations, at Temple Emmanuel, New York City, on May 22, 1949. *Congressional Record,* XCV, June 10, 1949, p. A3634.

180. Daniel V. Gallery, "Admiral Talks Back to the Airmen," *Saturday Evening Post,* CCXXI, June 25, 1949, pp. 25 ff.

181. *New York Times,* June 25, 1949.

182. Drew Pearson in *Washington Post,* June 17, 1949; *Air Force,* XXXII, August 1949, p. 10.

183. Drew Pearson in *Washington Post,* October 19, 1949; Mark S. Watson in *Baltimore Sun,* October 24, 1949; *Washington Star,* October 30, 1949; Gallery, *loc. cit.*; *B-36 Bomber* Hearings, pp. 524-618 *passim*; interview with Walter Karig, April 3, 1956.

184. Quoted interview with Radford, *Washington Times-Herald,* October 13, 1949; and interview with Karig.

185. *Washington Star,* September 2, 6, 7, 9, and 23, 1949; *Washington Post,* September 7, 8, and 9, 1949; *Baltimore Sun,* September 10 and 23, 1949; *New York Herald Tribune,* September 10, 1949; *New York Times,* September 7 and 12, 1949; *Washington Times-Herald,* September 8, 1949; *Army-Navy-Air Force Register,* September 10, 1949, p. 27.

186. Hanson W. Baldwin in *New York Times,* October 15, 1949.

187. *Ibid.,* September 14, 1949.

188. *Ibid.,* September 11 and 18, 1949.

189. *Ibid.,* September 18 and 19, 1949.

190. *Ibid.,* June 25, 1949.

191. *Ibid.,* September 13, 14, 16 and 18, 1949; *New York Herald Tribune,* September 14, 1949; *Baltimore Sun,* September 13, 1949; *Washington Post,* September 14, 1949; *Washington Star,* September 13, 1949; *Washington Daily News,* September 16, 1949.

192. *New York Times,* September 16, 1949.

193. *Ibid.*

194. Communication quoted in *ibid.,* September 17, 1949.

195. Tris Coffin in *Washington Times-Herald,* October 13, 1949.

196. Martin S. Haydon in *Washington Star,* November 8, 1949.

197. *Washington Post,* September 29, 1949; *Washington Daily News,* October 1, 1949.

198. *New York Times,* October 4, 1949.

199. *Unification and Strategy* Hearings, p. 125; *New York Times,* October 9, 1949.

200. *Ibid.,* October 2, 1949; *Washington Post,* October 2, 1949.

201. Haydon, *loc. cit.*

202. *New York Times,* October 4, 1949.

203. *Ibid.,* October 5, 1949.

204. Letter, Denfeld to Vinson, July 18, 1949; letter, Matthews to Vinson, undated.

205. Press interview with Denfeld, *New York Herald Tribune,* January 19, 1950.

206. Matthews' account, *New York Times* and *Washington Star,* October 28, 1949.

207. *New York Times,* October 5, 1949.

208. *Unification and Strategy* Report, p. 8.

209. Not counting Bradley, who returned briefly to correct the record.

210. *Unification and Strategy* Hearings, pp. 2-3.

211. *Ibid.,* pp. 8-9.

212. *Ibid.*

213. *Ibid.,* p. 22.

214. *New York Times,* October 7, 1949.

215. *Unification and Strategy* Hearings, p. 29.

216. *Ibid.*

217. *New York Times,* October 8, 1949.

218. *Ibid.,* October 7, 1949.

219. *Washington Times-Herald,* October 25, 1949. In the hearings Matthews had indicated that the Navy was proceeding with the court-martial of Crommelin. *Washington Post,* October 7, 1949.

220. *Unification and Strategy* Hearings, p. 116.

221. *New York Times,* October 7, 1949.

222. *Unification and Strategy* Hearings, pp. 51 f.

223. *Ibid.,* pp. 46-48.

224. *Ibid.*

225. *Ibid.,* p. 49.

226. *Ibid.,* p. 68.

227. *Washington Post,* October 8, 1949.

228. *Unification and Strategy* Hearings, pp. 85 f.

229. *Ibid.,* pp. 87 f.

230. *Ibid.,* p. 92.

231. *Ibid.,* p. 110.

232. See p. 504.

233. *Unification and Strategy* Hearings, p. 126.

234. See, e. g., *ibid.,* p. 127.

235. *Ibid.,* p. 128.

236. *Ibid.,* pp. 44, 58.

237. Radford's description, *ibid.,* pp. 43, 133.

238. *Ibid.,* p. 136.

239. *Ibid.,* pp. 141-146. See also Radford's description, *ibid.,* p. 43.

240. *Ibid.,* p. 153. See also Radford's statement, *ibid.,* p. 43.

241. *Ibid.,* pp. 155-157. See also Radford's statement, *ibid.,* pp. 43 f.

242. *Ibid.,* pp. 159, 160. See also Radford's statement, *ibid.,* p. 44.

243. *Ibid.,* p. 161.

244. *Ibid.,* pp. 163-166.

245. *Ibid.,* p. 169.

246. *Ibid.,* pp. 170 f.

247. *Ibid.*

248. *Ibid.,* p. 172.

249. *New York Times,* October 11, 1949; *Washington Times-Herald,* October 10, 1949.

250. William S. White reported in part an interview with Vinson as follows: "He indicated . . . that the inquiry probably would be recessed for some weeks at the end of this week." *New York Times,* October 11, 1949.

251. *Unification and Strategy* Hearings, pp. 177-178.

252. *New York Herald Tribune,* October 12, 1949.

253. *Ibid.*

254. *Ibid.; Congressional Record,* XCV, October 11, 1949, pp. 1183-1184.

255. *Ibid.*

256. *New York Herald Tribune,* October 12, 1949.

257. *Unification and Strategy* Hearings, p. 178.

258. *Ibid.,* pp. 44, 179-183; Memorandum, ACNO (Guided Missiles) for DCNO, Air, December 17, 1947.

259. *Unification and Strategy* Hearings, p. 185.

260. *Ibid.,* pp. 185 f.

261. *Ibid.,* p. 189.

262. *Ibid.,* pp. 189-191.

263. *Ibid.,* pp. 193-201.

264. I am indebted to Vincent Davis for this information about Blandy's professional experience.

265. *Ibid.,* p. 209.

266. *Ibid.,* p. 210.

267. *Ibid.,* p. 245.

268. *Ibid.,* p. 246.

269. *New York Times,* October 13, 1949; *Unification and Strategy* Hearings, pp. 313-316.

270. *Ibid.,* pp. 260 f.

271. *Ibid.,* p. 277.

272. See opinions of Vandenberg and Bradley on cancellation of carrier, April 23, 1949, *supra,* pp. 493-494.

273. *Unification and Strategy* Hearings, p. 291.

274. *Ibid.,* pp. 293-294, 299.

275. *Ibid.,* p. 302.

276. *Ibid.,* p. 303.

277. *Ibid.,* p. 307.

278. *Ibid.,* p. 339.

279. *Ibid.,* p. 346.

280. Bert Andrews in *New York Herald Tribune,* October 16, 1949.

281. *Unification and Strategy* Hearings, p. 350. Italics added.

282. *Ibid.*

283. *Ibid.*

284. *New York Times,* October 15, 16, 1949.

285. *Baltimore Sun,* October 16, 1949.

286. *New York Times,* October 15, 1949.

287. "If the United States should get into another World War, which branch of the armed forces do you think would play the most important part in winning the war—the Army, the Navy or the Air Force?"

Air Force	74%
Army	6%
Navy	4%
Qualified	9%

No opinion _____ 7%
Washington Post, October 15, 1949.

288. *Unification and Strategy* Hearings, p. 369.

289. Allegedly quoting from the Army paper, *ibid.,* p. 372.

290. *Ibid.,* pp. 404 f.

291. *Ibid.,* p. 400.

292. *B-36 Bomber* Hearings, pp. 215 f.

293. *Unification and Strategy* Hearings, p. 403.

294. *Ibid.,* p. 404.

295. The D'Olier letter is printed in the hearings, *ibid.,* pp. 405-407.

296. *Ibid.,* pp. 408-410.

297. *Ibid.,* p. 407.

298. *Ibid.,* pp. 456-457.

299. *Ibid.,* p. 473.

300. *Ibid.,* p. 471.

301. *Ibid.,* p. 472.

302. *Ibid.,* pp. 516-518.

303. *Ibid.,* pp. 519-520.

304. *Ibid.,* p. 521.

305. *Ibid.,* p. 526.

306. *Ibid.,* p. 528.

307. *Ibid.,* p. 535.

308. *Ibid.,* pp. 536-537.

309. Joseph C. Harsch, *Christian Science Monitor,* October 24, 1949.

310. *Unification and Strategy* Hearings, p. 101.

311. See *supra,* p. 481.

312. *Unification and Strategy* Hearings, pp. 546-547.

313. *Ibid.,* p. 514.

314. *Ibid.,* pp. 626-627.

315. *Ibid.,* p. 613.

316. *Ibid.,* pp. 619-621.

317. *Ibid.,* p. 623.

318. *Ibid.,* p. 622.

319. *Ibid.,* p. 565.

320. *Ibid.,* pp. 597-606.

321. *Ibid.,* p. 638.

322. *Ibid.,* p. 639.

323. Vincent Davis has persuaded me of the soundness of this interpretation of Navy motivation.

324. *Unification and Strategy* Hearings, p. 528.

325. Position papers such as "Memorandum: Views of the Navy Department on Question 4 of the Agenda of the House of Representatives Committee on Armed Services Investigation on Matters Pertaining to the B-36 Bomber."

326. *Unification and Strategy* Hearings, p. 52.

327. *Ibid.,* p. 346.

328. See, e. g., the examination given the Air Force commitment to an inflexible strategic bombing doctrine, as revealed in published sources, in Lawrence J. Legere, Jr., "Unification of the Armed Forces" (Ph. D. dissertation, Harvard University, 1950), pp. 408-434.

329. See letter, Franklin D'Olier to Louis Johnson, August 23, 1949, printed in *Unification and Strategy* Hearings, pp. 405-407; Gill Robb Wilson, "The Air World" in *New York Herald Tribune,* September 27, 1949; and William S. White in *New York Times,* October 19, 1949.

330. *Unification and Strategy* Hearings, p. 186. Italics added.

331. For example, the testimony of Blandy and Kinkaid, *ibid.,* pp. 206 and 277.

332. *Unification and Strategy* Hearings, p. 2; *New York Times,* October 24, 1949.

333. Text published October 28, 1949, in *New York Times* and *Washington Star.*

334. *Ibid.*

335. *Washington Star,* October 28, 1949. Denfeld's account of his removal was later published. L. E. Denfeld, "Why I Was Fired," *Collier's,* March 18, 1950, pp. 13 ff.; March 25, 1950, pp. 32 ff.; April 1, 1950, pp. 36 ff.

336. *New York Times,* October 29, 1949.

337. *Baltimore Sun,* October 30, 1949.

338. *New York Times,* October 29 and November 1, 1949.

339. *New York Times,* November 11, 1949; *Washington Post,* November 11, 1949.

340. Mimeographed letter, W. Sterling Cole to All Members, House Committee on Armed Services, December 8, 1949.

341. *New York Herald Tribune,* November 2, 1949.

342. *Ibid.; Washington Post,* November 2, 1949; *New York Times,* November 2, 1949.

343. *Ibid.,* November 5, 1949.

344. *Ibid.,* January 23, 24, 31, 1950.

345. *Army-Navy-Air Force Register,* January 21, 1950, p. 1, January 28, 1950, p. 1.

346. *Washington Daily News,* November 1, 1949; *New York Times,* November 4, 1949.

347. *Washington Star,* October 30 and December 15, 1949; *Washington Post,* November 10 and December 21, 1949; *New York Herald Tribune,* December 16, 1949; *New York Times,* December 30, 1949.

348. *Army-Navy-Air Force Register,* April 1, 1950, p. 7.

349. *Ibid.,* March 18, 1950, pp. 1 ff.

350. *Unification and Strategy* Hearings, p. 609. *Army-Navy-Air Force Register,* January 14, 1950, pp. 1 ff.

351. *Ibid.,* June 24, 1950, p. 1.

352. *Unification and Strategy* Report, pp. 53-56.

353. *Ibid.,* pp. 57-58.

EDITORIAL COMMENTS

The basic issues in the Air Force–Navy (and Army) struggle in 1949 and 1950 centered on three interrelated questions: organization, budget, and strategy. One may not wholly accept Samuel Huntington's ingenious remark that "interservice rivalry was the child of unification"; but clearly unification invited the presidential imposition of a budgetary ceiling on the total military budget; and certainly the ceiling has led to great strains in inter-service relations, and in the process of unification has forced rigidities in strategy, and has sharply limited strategic alternatives.

The psychological, military, and intellectual developments in the last decade have made the substance of the arguments put forth by the services just before the Korean War obsolete; basically and inevitably they were then still fighting World War II: bigger bombers, bigger carriers, more powerful bombs were all thought of in terms of 1941-45 strategic bombing, largely against cities rather than against even the more specific targets in Germany in 1944-45—transportation, oil, etc. Land and sea warfare including amphibious landings were thought of as a modernized version of the victorious sweep against Germany and Japan. The arguments about tactical bombing showed no great change from the arguments in early 1944 about the preparations for D-Day and the perennial Army–Marine Corps disputation. The Navy showed little interest in furthering the possibility of using ships to attack nearby land targets as it had in North Africa, in Italy, in France and across the Pacific, and it dared not speak openly of its burning desire to participate in strategic bombing using atomic bombs.

Finally, the missing elements in military plans and desires were remarkable—at least in hindsight:

First, everyone knew of missiles, and anyone who remembered the V-2 attacks on London knew that missiles could play an important part in warfare. However, the eventual availability and potential use of IRBM's and ICBM's had not yet become a part of strategic thinking. Similarly, the prospects for a more violent explosive, the H-bomb, and for smaller—tactical—A-bombs, were unknown or almost entirely disregarded.

Second, the eventual consequences of the known Russian possession of the basic component of atomic warfare had not yet been thought out. *A fortiori,* the new dangers that would be posed by bomb and missile developments in the hands of the Soviet Union were overlooked.

Third, no thought had been given to limited war. The lack of preparedness that the fighting in Korea illuminated so vividly was of course not entirely caused by lack of forethought; indeed, it is hard to see how the stringent budgetary limitations on both the Army and the Navy would have permitted really adequate preparation. Yet total concentration of strategic planning on all-out war with Russia had both military and diplomatic consequences.

All these three were *lacunae* in official military doctrine. True, the Army had German missile experts, but thought in terms of tactical use; the Air Force, without serious complaint, abandoned some early research on long-range ballistics and reverted to pilotless aircraft—going backward from the V-2 to the V-1! True also that some scholars like Brodie and Borden concerned themselves with strategy in a world in which we had lost our atomic monopoly. And it was likewise true that Kennan in the State Department, mindful of the responsibilities of containment, worried about the problems of limited war. Nevertheless, the Joint Chiefs of Staff jointly and severally, and their civilian Secretaries, concentrated on a type of military planning that was rapidly moving from obsolescent to obsolete.

The budgetary doctrines between VJ-Day and June 25, 1950 were characterized by two aspects with profound consequences. The first was a kind of economic naïveté that was shared by such diverse people as Truman, Forrestal, Johnson and Webb, and Eisenhower, Bradley, Denfeld and Vandenberg—as well as by most congressmen and senators. All of them believed that some—for the United States—modest sum, say, $12.5 or $14 or $15 billion represented an absolute limit for the defense budget; beyond that lay "national bankruptcy."

Whatever "national bankruptcy" may have meant (it was hardly a term that lent itself to precise definition) $15 billion could not have represented any absolute limit. In terms of 1954 dollars, our national defense expenditures in 1949 were $19 billion and our 1960 expenditures $44 billion; whatever our present-day difficulties the more than doubling of defense expenditures has not created national bankruptcy. The far more rational argument, advanced since 1950, that large budgets lead to inflation can point to some obvious factual backing, though there is little clear thinking in public places on what degree of inflation is highly undesirable, nor on what some of the alternative ways of avoiding or minimizing inflation without excessive limitation on military spending may be.

Small budgets forced small military forces both in manpower and in equipment. And small forces meant constricted strategies. The Navy was forced to choose between the flush-deck carriers (and other objects) and submarines; the Air Force, in considerable part, between strategic and tactical forces; the Army between more men with obsolete equipment and fewer men with newer weapons. All the services necessarily cut back on research and development in their attempts to maintain even a limited force-in-being.

Because of this constriction, the services also limited their own thinking; they were unable to explain to the Secretary of Defense and the President their own unreadiness for the wars of the future since they were so deeply concerned with their effort to plan intelligent use of funds that were too small for the wars of the past.

The curious *mystique* about the $12.5 or $14

or $15 billion ceiling in effect prevented much thought on the part of the President and his advisers about the strategic-political consequences of the financial straitjacket. Since everyone (except Forrestal, who toward the end began to revalue the arms-money thesis) felt that the over-all figure was sacred, the debates were all centered on inter-service bickering, in the vain hope that this would break up the tri-partite slicing of the pie. Thus the services were in no position to prepare joint strategic plans since they were totally occupied with mere existence, while the President and his advisers were thinking primarily about funds and inter-service rows.

There was a second aspect of budgeteering at the time (a perennial aspect)—the notion that if the defense funds, no matter how small, were well "managed," "defense" would be quite adequate. The prime exponent of this theory for the conduct of military affairs was, of course, the second Secretary of Defense, Louis Johnson. The consequence was vividly illustrated by Johnson's action on the carrier; as best one can tell, he construed his decision in terms of administrative management and thought the Navy's strategic planning either irrelevant or of negligible importance. Johnson's judgment was based on his intention to lower expenditures to a fixed ceiling—quickly; but his managerial rationale was reinforced by the fact that the three services had no real comprehensive strategic plan (they could not) and no very clear explanation of why one degree of serious inadequacy was worse than another. Johnson noted the fact and exploited it.

Johnson's action in cancelling funds for the super carrier was widely looked on as "courageous" and "in the national interest"— at least this was the attitude of a good many editorial writers; Congressional views were divided, and the general public, although presumably willing to support larger expenditures for defense, was not stirred and was willing to follow the Administration's lead. Those who praised the action and those who were neutral did not include the officers of the Navy: they knew what would happen—and in opposition they too felt they were acting in the national interest. It is wise to note that if what Johnson did was sinful, he was no solitary sinner; in the minds of a great variety of Americans, as has been suggested, a reduction in military expenditures is an act of piety. (Exceptions may, of course, be noted for such matters as near-by navy yards and pet projects like the Marine Corps or B-70's.)

The pains produced by budgetary strictures increased the stresses and strains within the newly created military organization. The fear of annihilation that disrupted Navy morale, for example, was caused, the officers thought, by the misbehavior of their imperialistic rivals in the Air Force who owed their position of power to the National Security Act of 1947. The attribution of troubles to the statute itself was largely a Navy specialty; Army and Air Force alike attributed their own troubles primarily to what they considered the unwillingness of their two sister services to support "unification."

So long as the services were each restricted to $4 or $5 billion a year, the prospects for unification in any meaningful sense were slight. However, as Huntington has also pointed out, the access of comparatively large budgets has relegated the three services to training and similar activities. The major strategic responsibilities now lie in great part with the combined commands and with the functional development groups, with all the Joint Chiefs perhaps more concerned with these than with their own respective forces. Finally, the great debates of the past over roles and missions, the inconclusive compacts at Key West and Newport, are obsolescent. Military forces on land, on the sea, in the air are all prepared to use missiles, and to use atomic bombs and shells. The attempt to establish roles and missions in terms of particular weapons has been largely abandoned. And the efforts to persuade military officers to settle budgetary matters by discussion have been dropped. The Secretary of Defense now has the powers and the accompanying responsibilities whose need Forrestal had not fully realized and Johnson failed to understand at all.

Some of the relationships of strategy to the events in the carrier-bomber controversy have been cited above. One can say, in simplistic terms, that money set strategy, and that the dangers of a rigidly limited strategy were hardly noticeable by men who were either trying to preserve the existence of their organization or to keep the nation from national bankruptcy. In all this welter, Congressman Vinson and his colleagues stand out in sharp relief. They recognized the incompleteness and incoherence of our strategic designs, but they made no attempt to substitute their own judgments for those of the military professionals in a highly technical field. When the Korean attack in June 1950 opened up the effective possibility of new strategic plans and needs, the Vinson committee was receptive and ready.

TO THE YALU AND BACK

MARTIN LICHTERMAN

EXECUTIVE SECRETARY, NEW ENGLAND BOARD OF HIGHER EDUCATION

WINCHESTER, MASSACHUSETTS

CONTENTS

Chronology of Major Events   571

Preface   575

I   Background   576

II   United States and United Nations Intervention   579

III   North from the Beachhead   584

IV   Shifting Objectives: A Review   592

V   The March to the Yalu   598

VI   Rout in the North   606

VII   Reflections on the End-the-War Offensive   611

VIII   The New War: The New Objectives   617

Acknowledgments   631

Bibliographic Note   632

Notes   634

Editorial Comments   640

CHRONOLOGY OF MAJOR EVENTS

Dating events in Korea and Washington during the fighting in Korea is an ambiguous process because the two centers of activity were separated not only by a distance of 7,000 miles but also by the International Date Line. Korean time was fourteen hours in advance of eastern daylight time when the Communists attacked the Republic of Korea. Thus between the hours of 12 midnight and 2:00 P.M. in Korea, that nation was one calendar day ahead of the eastern part of the United States: between 2:00 P.M. and midnight, the same calendar day prevailed in both. The Communist attack, which took place between 4 and 5 A.M.

June 25, 1950 Korean time, thus took place between 2 and 3 P.M. June 24, 1950 Washington time. In this study, Korean time is used for events in Korea and elsewhere in the Far East; e.g., the fall of Pyongyang on October 20 is October 20 KT (Korean time). Similarly, events in Washington and Lake Success are WT (Washington time); e.g., a November 9 meeting of the National Security Council is November 9 WT. Difficulty arises with communication between the two centers; a March 21 cable could be received and replied to on March 20! In the text, the time zone (KT or WT) has been specified in all doubtful cases.

Date			Event
1950	June	25 KT	North Korean aggression begins
		25 WT	1st UN Security Council resolution calling upon North Korea to withdraw
			JCS Directive to MacArthur ordering use of Air and Navy in evacuation of Americans and delivery of supplies to ROK army
		26 WT	Directive to MacArthur ordering air and naval support of ROK army south of 38th parallel
		27 WT	2d UN Security Council resolution recommending assistance to ROK
		27 KT	Fall of Seoul
		29 WT	Directive to MacArthur authorizing limited use of U. S. ground troops in Korea and air and naval action north of the 38th parallel
		30 WT	General US counter-offensive in Korea authorized
	July	7 WT	3d UN Security Council resolution establishing unified command
		8 WT	Appointment of General MacArthur as commander of UN Forces
	August		Vague warnings from Mao Tze-tung and Chou En-lai
		17 WT	Austin's UN speech urging unification of Korea
	Late August		Collins and Sherman agree with MacArthur that the 38th parallel should be crossed if necessary to destroy the North Korean army
	September	7 WT	JCS recommends action north of parallel until North Korean resistance is terminated
		11 WT	Truman approves NSC recommendation for operations north of the 38th parallel contingent on Soviet and Chinese action
		15 WT	Information based on above recommendation sent to MacArthur but with caveats about possible Russian or Chinese intervention

Date		*Event*
	15 KT	Landing at Inchon
	21 WT	Truman press conference discusses crossing the 38th parallel
	25 KT	Chinese warn Indian Ambassador of possible Chinese intervention
	25 KT	Chinese troops move toward Korean border
	27 WT	Evidence of possible Chinese intervention received in Washington
	27 WT	Directive to MacArthur authorizing action north of 38th parallel but limiting action in border provinces to ROK troops
	28 WT	AP story that action north of the 38th parallel is authorized by US to destroy North Korean forces, but occupation policy must await UN action
	28 KT	Liberation of Seoul
	30 WT	Austin's UN speech defending what becomes the Oct. 7 resolution
October	1 WT	MacArthur proposes announcement about crossing the parallel; JCS rejects proposal
	1 WT	Marshall authorizes MacArthur to cross parallel
	1 KT	MacArthur, with JCS approval, demands North Korean surrender
	1 KT	Chou En-lai's speech warning of Chinese intervention
	3 WT	Indian and Yugoslav UN delegates oppose what becomes Oct. 7 resolution
	3 KT	Chou En-lai warns Indian Ambassador of Chinese intervention
	7 WT	First UN General Assembly resolution recommending action to ensure stability and establish a unified, independent and democratic government in all Korea
	8 KT	American troops cross the parallel
	9 KT	No reply from North Koreans to second surrender demand; full-scale drive begins
	9 KT	Surrender warning to North Koreans from MacArthur
	9 KT	First Chinese troops cross the Yalu
	9 WT	JCS directive to MacArthur modifying directive of Sept. 27
	12 KT	Nine Chinese soldiers surrender—under orders to do so
	15 KT	Wake Island meeting of Truman and MacArthur
	20 KT	Liberation of Pyongyang
	24 KT	MacArthur orders use of American troops to spearhead drive to Yalu; JCS questions action
	25 WT	MacArthur replies
	25 WT	Newspapers report that only ROK troops would be used in border provinces
	26 KT	First Chinese soldier captured in combat
	26 KT	ROK battalion reaches Yalu and is surrounded by Chinese troops
	28 KT	US First Cavalry hurries to help ROKs
	31 KT	Chinese regiment identified
November	1 KT	MIG-15 jets cross Yalu; Chinese forces identified south of Changjin Reservoir
	1 KT	General Church orders full speed to Yalu
	1 KT	Tokyo Headquarters spokesmen deny serious Chinese intervention
Early November		State and Defense anxious about troop disposition and suggest caution to MacArthur
	2 KT	Two battalions of US 8th Cavalry overwhelmed
	3 KT	US 24th Division in retreat
	3-5 KT	Chinese attack in east; US First Marine Division sent north
	4 KT	US First Cavalry Division identifies 5 Chinese divisions in its sector
	4 KT	MacArthur recommends against hasty conclusions about Chinese intervention
	4-5 WT	Bradley fears for Walker's right flank
	6 KT	MacArthur communiqué announces UN faces a new enemy
	6 KT	MacArthur informs JCS of plan for airstrike on Antung bridge

Date		Event
	6 WT	Special CINCFE report to UN on Chinese attacks
	6 WT	CIA report on Chinese intentions and capabilities
	7 KT	JCS denies permission for airstrike and asks for report
	7 KT	MacArthur replies with stern warning
	7 KT	MacArthur reports some Chinese intervention and some danger
	7 KT	MacArthur requests authority for hot pursuit of MIG planes
	7 WT	JCS authorizes bombing, with restrictions
	8 WT	JCS recommends effort to obtain political settlement
	8 WT	UN Security Council invites Chinese Communist government to send representatives
	8 KT	Bombing raid on Sinuiju
	9 WT	NSC discusses Korea; no change in MacArthur's instructions
	10 WT	Introduction of 6-nation Security Council resolution giving reassurance and warning
	11 KT	MacArthur denounces British press; troops resume advance
	13 WT	Acheson directs immediate discussion of hot pursuit with allies
	15 WT	Acheson promises to protect Communist interest in power facilities
Sometime in November		British government proposes establishment of military line at or near "waist"
	16 WT	Truman attempts to reassure Communists
	21 KT	US 17th Infantry Regiment reaches the Yalu
	24 KT	MacArthur flies to battle area and announces general attack
	24 KT	MacArthur receives JCS proposals for new military and political measures
	25 KT	MacArthur rejects JCS proposals and presents his own plan
	24 WT	CIA National Intelligence estimate
	26 KT	The Chinese attack
	28 KT	MacArthur's "New War" communiqué
	29 KT	MacArthur's reply to Arthur Krock
29 or 30 WT		Sherman cautions Joy about possible need for ships for evacuation
	30 WT	Truman's comment on use of atomic bomb
December 1 WT		Truman asks for military expansion
	2 KT	Eighth Army makes good its escape
	3 KT	MacArthur requests new instructions
	3 WT	JCS sends MacArthur new instructions
	4 WT	Attlee arrives in Washington; Collins flies to Far East
	5 KT	Pyongyang abandoned
	7 WT	Truman and Attlee agree on new objectives
	11 WT	NSC meets. Truman supports UN resolution, but no new instructions for MacArthur are issued
	13 KT	Xth Corps is evacuated from Hungnam
	14 WT	New UN General Assembly resolution seeking cease-fire
	15 WT	Cease-fire group consults Unified Command
	16 WT	Truman declares national emergency
	18 WT	Truman announces Eisenhower's appointment as SCAPE
	19 KT	MacArthur asks for reinforcements
	22 WT	Chinese reject cease-fire proposal
	29 WT	New directive sent to MacArthur
	30 KT	MacArthur replies with a proposed new policy
	31 KT	New Chinese offensive
1951 January 4 KT		Seoul abandoned
	7 KT	Suwon airbase evacuated
	8-9 KT	UN resistance at Wonju
	9 WT	JCS reply to MacArthur
	10 KT	MacArthur objects to JCS directive
	12 WT	Collins and Vandenberg go to Korea with memorandum

Date		*Event*
	12 WT	New JCS directive
	13 WT	Truman cables MacArthur
	13 WT	UN resolution adopts a peace plan
	17 KT	Generals Collins, Vandenberg, and Smith sure that UN can hold
	17 WT	Chinese Communists reject UN plan
	19 WT	US House of Representatives resolution calling for UN action
	20 KT	MacArthur regains confidence
	25 KT	Operation Killer begins
February	1 WT	UN General Assembly presses resolution condemning China as an aggressor and restating UN objectives in Korea
	12 KT	Unsuccessful Chinese counterattack
	13 WT	Future policy in Korea discussed, not decided
	13 KT	MacArthur publishes protest about restrictions
March	7 KT	Second public protest from MacArthur
	12 KT	Ridgway says re-establishing parallel would be defeat for Communists
	13 WT	US considering boundary near parallel
	15 KT	Seoul liberated again
	15 WT	Further discussion in Washington about recrossing parallel
	15 WT	Truman says crossing parallel is a military problem
	20 WT	Committee of Sixteen agrees on plans
	20 WT	JCS advises MacArthur about Presidential announcement and asks if new directive is needed
	21 WT	MacArthur says no new directive is needed
	24 KT	MacArthur issues his own announcement
April	11 WT	MacArthur relieved of command
	11 WT	Morrison in House of Commons announces that real issue is Chinese willingness to settle, not peace
May		MacArthur hearings; new policy announced
	July 10 KT	Truce talks begin
1953	July 27 KT	Armistice signed

PREFACE

This study is an attempt to describe the series of civil and military decisions relating to our operations in Korea in the fall and winter of 1950-51. The focus of interest is chiefly the limits placed on the advance of our land forces —and the opportunities left open to them— with some secondary consideration of the restrictions placed on our air and naval operations as well. The study is not designed to weigh the merits of these decisions, but to examine the process of arriving at them: the extent to which civil or military authorities determined the policies which governed the actions of the field commanders and the degree of consultation between civil and military leaders, and the balancing of economic, political and military factors. The original decision to intervene militarily against the aggression in Korea, the controversial recall of General of the Army Douglas MacArthur, and the protracted negotiation of an armistice are not within the scope of this study.

I. BACKGROUND

The first genuine commitment concerning the postwar treatment of Korea was made at the Cairo Conference on December 1, 1943, by President Franklin D. Roosevelt, Prime Minister Winston S. Churchill and Generalissimo Chiang Kai-shek who spoke of establishing a free and independent Korea "in due course."[1] At Yalta oblique reference was made to the possibility of a multi-power trusteeship for Korea until she was ready to assume full sovereignty, but no specific commitments were made. In May 1945, when Harry Hopkins was in Moscow for discussions with Joseph Stalin, the Russian leader agreed that there should be a four-nation trusteeship for Korea after the defeat of Japan.[2] President Harry S. Truman and Prime Minister Clement Attlee, with the concurrence of Generalissimo Chiang Kai-shek, announced at Potsdam on July 26 the terms on which they were prepared to accept the Japanese surrender. The terms included a reaffirmation of the Cairo Declaration and on August 8, when the Russians entered the war against Japan, they too declared their adherence to the Potsdam Proclamation.

The dropping of atom bombs on Hiroshima and Nagasaki on August 6 and 9 respectively and the entrance of the Soviets into the Far Eastern conflict on August 8 brought the war to an end sooner than had been anticipated and necessitated immediate decisions on the occupation of Korea. On August 10 the Japanese offered to surrender and two days later the Russians indicated their willingness to accept the appointment of General of the Army Douglas MacArthur as Supreme Commander in Japan. But the Russians were proving to be less cooperative in the negotiations then under way in Moscow with the Chinese over the Far Eastern settlement and with Ambassador Edwin W. Pauley over reparations, and both Ambassador Averell Harriman and Pauley cabled to President Truman urging that the United States occupy as much of Manchuria and Korea as possible before the Russians moved in.[3]

Neither the time nor the troops were available to enable the United States to undertake so ambitious an occupation. On August 11, when the State-War-Navy Coordinating Committee commenced its consideration of a draft of General Order Number 1 to be issued by General MacArthur as Supreme Commander Allied Powers, Japan, outlining the procedures for accepting the surrender of Japanese forces throughout the Far East, the Russians were already in Manchuria and close to Korea while the American troops closest to Korea were on Okinawa. Thus, when Secretary of State James F. Byrnes suggested that Americans receive the surrender as far north as possible, the JCS pointed out that in a race with the Soviets we would do well to get even the tip of the Korean peninsula around Pusan and, furthermore, that our commitments in the Pacific were so vast that we lacked troops to occupy much more than the Pusan area. It was decided that the best we could do—barring Russian opposition —would be to accept the surrender of the Japanese south of the 38th parallel, thus obtaining the ancient Korean capital city of Seoul.[4]

SWNCC was studying the draft of General Order Number 1 on August 11 and 12; but on the 12th, Russian troops were already moving into northeastern Korea. On August 15 the order was forwarded to General MacArthur in Manila and the text communicated to Stalin, who accepted it on August 16 without comment on the 38th parallel. General Order Number 1 was issued by SCAP on September 2, the first American troops landed in South Korea six days later, and on the 9th, Japanese forces south of the 38th parallel surrendered to General Hodges, commander of the U. S. XXIV Corps. As U. S. troops entered Inchon and

Seoul, Russian troops departed.[5] Thus the 38th parallel as a line of demarcation between occupying forces was hastily drawn. It was, in part, purely and simply "a military expedient between two friendly powers," as General John H. Hilldring, Assistant Secretary of State, later declared.[6] Yet, as the record indicates, the decision to accept the surrender of the Japanese troops south of the 38th parallel, rather than stopping around Pusan, carried important political undertones motivated by a growing American suspicion of Russian intentions.[7] At least in the United States, however, the line was generally supposed to be no more than temporary and without any political significance, but future circumstances were to freeze this boundary into a national frontier between two bitterly hostile Korean states.

A Joint Commission consisting of representatives of the U. S. command in the South and the Soviet command in the North was established by the Moscow agreement of December 27, 1945, between the U. S., the U. S. S. R. and the United Kingdom (China also subsequently adhered to the agreement) which was to assist in setting up a provisional Korean government. It was quickly apparent that there was no chance of agreement between the Russians and the Americans on the Joint Commission, the chief point at issue being the procedure to be followed in consulting with various Korean political groups in the course of organizing the provisional government. Even while they argued, the Russians were busily establishing a Communist "people's government" in North Korea and training and equipping a North Korean army, to insure continued Red control after the eventual withdrawal of the Russian occupying force. By May 1947, a complete stalemate had been reached between the U. S. and the U. S. S. R. on all major issues of Korean unification.

In the fall of 1947, the U. S. military leaders had come to the conclusion that it would be desirable to withdraw American troops from Korea as soon as possible. The JCS reported in a memorandum to the Secretary of State dated September 25, 1947, that "from the standpoint of military security, the United States has little strategic interest in maintaining the present troops and bases in Korea . . ." because of our limited military manpower and our vast commitments elsewhere in the world.

It was pointed out by the military leaders that in the event of war in the Far East, the forces in Korea would be a military liability and would require substantial reinforcements to maintain. Moreover, the Korean peninsula would probably be by-passed by the U. S. in any offensive operations conducted on the Asiatic continent and would be more effectively neutralized by air action than by large-scale ground operations. Finally, unless a program of extensive economic, political and cultural rehabilitation was carried out in Korea, progress toward a free and independent nation would end and South Korea would become so disorganized as to make the position of American troops untenable. It was desirable to withdraw before conditions made a precipitous, prestige-shattering evacuation imperative.[8] In light of these recommendations and those presented to President Truman by Lieutenant General Albert C. Wedemeyer, who had been sent in the summer of 1947 by the President to the Far East to study the situation there, it was decided to withdraw when the Russians also withdrew.

In September 1947, therefore, the U. S., recognizing that no progress was being made toward establishing an independent and united Korea and desirous of ending the joint military occupation, submitted the problem of Korea to the General Assembly of the UN.[9] In November 1947, the General Assembly resolved that the Korean people themselves should create a provisional government through free and secret election of representatives and that subsequently foreign troops should be withdrawn from Korea. A UN Temporary Commission on Korea was at the same time created to observe the election and to consult with the elected representatives and the government.

The Temporary Commission visited Seoul in January 1948, but was denied entry into the Soviet zone. The UN instructed the Commission to proceed with the plans to hold elections "in such parts of Korea as are accessible to the Commission."[10] Accordingly, elections for a constituent assembly were held in South Korea under the supervision of the UN Temporary Commission in May 1948; Syngman Rhee's party won a majority of the seats and thus organized a government in July 1948, with Rhee as president. The General Assembly in December accepted the report of the Temporary Commission, voted to establish a new

Commission to continue UN efforts to bring about the peaceful unification of Korea, and recognized the government of the Republic of Korea as the only lawful government in those parts of Korea where the Commission had been able to carry out its duties.

In the meantime a draft constitution for a "Democratic People's Republic of Korea" had been approved at the North Korea People's Council (Assembly) in April 1948, a general election had been held in North Korea on August 25, 1948, to elect representatives of a Supreme People's Assembly, and, finally, on September 9, the Supreme People's Council had declared the establishment of the "Democratic People's Republic of Korea" claiming jurisdiction over all Korea. This government was, of course, recognized immediately by the Soviet Union and its satellites.

The U. S. S. R. informed the U. S. in September that the evacuation of Soviet troops would be completed by December 1948. In the early spring, MacArthur recommended withdrawal, and in March he advised the National Security Council that the training and combat readiness of the ROK troops justified complete U. S. withdrawal.[11] U. S. occupation troops completed their withdrawal from South Korea in June 1949, leaving behind a 500-man Military Advisory Group to help the Republic of Korea organize its military forces. The U. S. gave military equipment—chiefly light weapons—as well as substantial economic aid to the South Koreans.

The UN Commission continued its attempts to bring about peaceful unification of North and South Korea, but as tension between the two sections of Korea mounted in 1949 and early 1950 the Commission was instructed by the General Assembly to make its first task the observing and reporting of developments "which might lead to or otherwise involve military conflict in Korea."[12] The UN Commission had already reported in 1949 that "the border of the 38th parallel was becoming a sea of increasingly frequent exchanges of fire and armed raids, and that this constituted a serious barrier to friendly intercourse among the people of Korea."[13] American policy-makers nevertheless did not believe that the Communists would resort to force on a large scale to achieve their purposes in Korea. At any rate, the U. S. had decided that Korea was not within our defense perimeter and that, now that American troops had been withdrawn, the security of the Republic of Korea would rest on the support of the UN. This policy was hardly new when it was summarized in a speech by Secretary of State Dean Acheson before the National Press Club on January 12, 1950, but the reiteration in an official policy declaration of what was already apparent to observers all over (including the Russians) was to appear in the light of subsequent events as a most unfortunately timed statement, even though Acheson did very carefully say that the UN would come to Korea's aid in case of attack. Had it been clear in January 1950 that the U. S. was prepared to back its moral commitment to the UN with a firm military commitment, the story might have been a different one; but even the Truman Doctrine and the Greek-Turkish aid program were no equivalent of a firm military commitment. Such clarity might have earned rich dividends, but in January 1950 it was outside the range of American political possibilities—at least President Harry S. Truman and his advisers in Washington were not thinking in such terms.

On June 25, 1950 (June 24, WT), the UN Commission reported that between 4 and 5 A.M. North Korean forces had attacked South Korean defenses south of the 38th parallel. Conflict, which was certainly not entirely unpredictable though generally unexpected outside the Iron Curtain, had begun.

II. UNITED STATES AND UNITED NATIONS INTERVENTION

FIRST REACTIONS

The elaborate machinery established in the years following the end of World War II to aid the President in making major decisions in foreign and military policy did not function when the emergency arose in June 1950. The machinery was designed to develop policy, not to issue or recommend a flow of command decisions. Furthermore, the NSC was suffering from the sharp antagonism between the Secretary of State and the Secretary of Defense. In any event, the exigencies of time would hardly have permitted the President to go through the process of summoning the National Security Council into session to ask its advice. Moreover, a hurried meeting of the Council would have served little purpose as the detailed preparatory work by its lower echelons, the passing upward of information and careful analyses which characterized its regular policy papers, was not possible in the face of this unforeseen crisis.[14] Yet the failure to call on the NSC was in one sense only a formality, for its key individual members participated in the decision-making in the several days following the North Korean attack. Indeed, a series of informal meetings took place between the President, the Secretaries of State and Defense, the three service secretaries, the Joint Chiefs of Staff and various assistants, and out of these meetings came the several decisions leading up to the final one to commit American ground forces, decisions that settled immediate actions rather than long-term policy. The National Security Council met several days later and held extensive discussions without arriving at a recommendation. After this the President met with Congressional leaders and announced his decision.[15]

On June 25th, the UN Security Council voted 9-0 (the U. S. S. R. absent)[16] for a resolution presented by the U. S. observing that the Republic of Korea was the lawful government in Korea, stating that a breach of peace had been committed by North Korea and ordering North Korea to cease its action and withdraw north of the 38th parallel. The pertinent parts of the UN resolution stated:

The Security Council

Noting with grave concern the armed attack upon the Republic of Korea by forces from North Korea,

Determines that this action constitutes a breach of the peace,

I. *Calls for* the immediate cessation of hostilities; and

Calls upon the authorities of North Korea to withdraw forthwith with their armed forces to the thirty-eighth parallel;

II. *Requests* the United Nations Commission on Korea

(a) To communicate its fully considered recommendations on the situation with the least possible delay;

(b) To observe the withdrawal of the North Korean forces to the thirty-eighth parallel; and

(c) To keep the Security Council informed on the execution of this resolution;

III. *Calls upon* all Members to render every assistance to the United Nations in the execution of this resolution and to refrain from giving assistance to the North Korean authorities.

Later that day, President Truman at a meeting with some of his cabinet advisers and the Joint Chiefs of Staff ordered General of the Army Douglas MacArthur to use American airplanes and ships to evacuate Americans from Korea. In carrying out these orders MacArthur was authorized to take action by Air and Navy to prevent the Inchon-Kimpo-Seoul area from falling into unfriendly hands. MacArthur was instructed at the same time to deliver ammunition and other supplies to the Korean army by airdrop and other means. Finally, the Seventh Fleet was ordered into the Formosa Strait to prevent the conflict from spreading into that area. This naval force was to repel any attack on the Chinese Nationalist stronghold and prevent attacks on the mainland from Formosa.[17] The next day, Monday, June 26, President Truman, after meeting with the same group of advisers, directed the Secretary of Defense personally to give General MacArthur the President's instructions.[18] MacArthur was to use his air and naval forces to support the Republic of Korea in repelling aggression, but these forces were to be restricted to operations south of the 38th parallel.[19] These instructions, committing American armed forces to aid in repelling the North Korean aggressors, anticipated by several hours the UN Security Council's resolution of June 27 calling upon member nations to repel the attack in Korea and restore peace. President Truman made his announcement at 12 noon and the UN Security Council passed its resolution at 10:45 P.M. by a vote of seven to one; Yugoslavia was in opposition, Egypt and India abstained (their representatives had received no instructions), and the U. S. S. R. was still absent.

The Security Council

Having determined that the armed attack upon the Republic of Korea by forces from North Korea constitutes a breach of the peace,

Having called for an immediate cessation of hostilities, and

Having called upon the authorities of North Korea to withdraw forthwith their armed forces to the 38th parallel, and

Having noted from the report of the United Nations Commission for Korea that the authorities in North Korea have neither ceased hostilities nor withdrawn their armed forces to the 38th parallel and that urgent military measures are required to restore international peace and security,

Having noted the appeal from the Republic of Korea to the United Nations for immediate and effective steps to secure peace and security,

Recommends that the Members of the United Nations furnish such assistance to the Republic of Korea as may be necessary to repel the armed attack and to restore international peace and security to the area.

It has been asserted by some that the U. S. had presented the UN with a *fait accompli,* but it could reasonably be said, as Warren Austin, the U. S. delegate to the Security Council, did indeed state, that our action of June 27 was being taken in complete conformity with the Security Council's resolution of June 25 which had called upon "all Members to render every assistance to the United Nations in execution of [the] resolution." And of course President Truman was also merely hastening his support of the second resolution, whose enactment in a matter of hours was a foregone conclusion. It may be noted that, in the light of President Truman's temperament, he might well have proceeded regardless of a delay in the UN, but he was undoubtedly counting on UN approval and desired it.

Arguments about the timing of U. S. action in relation to the June 27th resolution did not arise at this time—only later in acrimonious legalistic controversies. Of far more substance, however, and largely overlooked at the moment, was the insertion of the clause "to restore peace and security to the area." The clause was, apparently, drafted in the office of the UN General Counsel and added, at his request, by the Department of State to its own draft resolution. The clause invited a notable reinterpretation of the U. S.-UN objective in Korea and later served as ample justification for the crossing of the 38th parallel. It was thus one of the steps by which the U. S.—and the UN—moved from the repelling of aggression to the unification of Korea. The consequences of shifting objectives will be revealed in the later stages of this account.

Regardless of these legal actions, the situation in Korea rapidly worsened as well-trained North Korean divisions overran green ROK troops and hurled them southward in precipitous retreat. Seoul fell on June 27. Two days later General MacArthur flew to Suwon airport to make a personal reconnaissance close to the rapidly deteriorating front. After an eight-hour inspection the General concluded that air and naval support would not be enough to stop the Communists and that American ground troops would have to be used to stiffen South Korean resistance. MacArthur flew back to Tokyo determined to secure from Washington permission to order the necessary ground troops into action. At the same time he concluded that restricting American air operations to the destruction of North Korean military targets south of the 38th parallel sharply limited the effectiveness of his air arm and gave the Communists room to mobilize and maneuver and to move up supplies. Thus, "MacArthur reasoned, he would not be giving the South Korean defenders the 'effective military assistance' that the United Nations had directed him to give. He concluded that his authority to destroy the North Korean military targets was permissive, not restrictive, and that implicit in his directive was the discretion normal to field command."[20]

Without securing authority from Washington to do so, MacArthur went ahead and instructed Lieutenant General George Stratemeyer, the commanding officer of the Far East Air Force, to attack targets north as well as south of the parallel.[21] President Truman's authorization for such action came the following day, but there is no published record of any message from Washington to General MacArthur questioning the General's prior order to his air force.

At the National Security Council meeting on Thursday, June 29, apparently before word had been received of MacArthur's decision to send planes over the parallel, Secretary of Defense Louis Johnson complained of the restriction on air operations and proposed a directive to MacArthur permitting operations north of the line. The Defense Secretary said that the JCS felt that stronger measures were needed— that at least an American foothold must be maintained in South Korea. Thus the draft directive, which had been worked out by the Defense Department and concurred in by the State Department during the earlier part of the day, authorized in addition to air and naval attacks on North Korea the employment in Korea of army service troops of the Signal and Transportation Corps and also the use of combat troops for the limited purpose of protecting a port and an airfield in the Pusan area. The directive said nothing, however, about using our combat troops in the battle area which was then still 200 miles north of Pusan.[22] President Truman objected to the wording of the directive because the final paragraph "permitted the implication that we were planning to go to war against the Soviet Union." Truman's account of this first discussion of operations north of the parallel goes on to say:

I stated categorically that I did not wish to see even the slightest implication of such a plan. I wanted to take every step necessary to push the North Koreans back behind the 38th parallel. But I wanted to be sure that we would not become so deeply committed in Korea that we could not take care of such other situations as might develop.

Secretary [of the Army] Pace expressed the belief that we should be very careful in authorizing operations above the 38th parallel and that we should clearly limit such operations. I agreed, pointing out that operations above the 38th parallel should be designed only to destroy military supplies, for I wanted it clearly understood that our operations in Korea were designed to restore peace there and to restore the border. Secretary Acheson said that the Air Force should not be restricted in its tasks by a rigid application of the 38th parallel as a restraining line, but he wanted to be sure that precautions would be taken to keep the air elements from going beyond the boundaries of Korea.[23]

President Truman's account was written several years after the event and recollection is an uncertain tool. If this is indeed an exact summary of the discussion, it will be seen that the President's views on the appropriate course of action changed in September.

Three o'clock on the morning of Friday, June 30 (WT), not long after his return to Tokyo, General MacArthur held a long telecon conversation with General J. Lawton Collins, Army Chief of Staff, and other high Pentagon officials. ("Telecon" is a device which makes it possible for groups of people separated from each other even by great distances to confer by projecting teletype communications on a large screen.) The Far Eastern Commander was asked to give his estimate of the situation and to make recommendations. MacArthur responded that the situation was desperate and the only possibility of salvaging it would be the immediate introduction of American ground combat forces into the Korean conflict. If authorized to do so, the General planned to send forward a regimental combat team and "to provide for a possible build-up to a two-division strength from the troops in Japan for an early counteroffensive." MacArthur, as later events made clear, seriously underestimated the size of the American force required to repel the Communists; the underestimate may have been based on inadequate intelligence reports on Communist strength in Korea and on a misplaced faith that the ROK troops could be quickly rallied and trained for a counteroffensive. Washington authorities, however, generally shared General MacArthur's estimate of the size of the force needed to face the Communists because they believed that as soon as American troops were committed the Reds would halt.[24] Thus the response to MacArthur's recommendation was favorable. Secretary of the Army Pace was immediately notified of the recommendation, and forwarded it to the President at 4:57 A.M., who then decided to send ground troops into Korea from Japan.[25] This new step was in no sense surprising; as early as the meeting on Sunday, June 25, General Collins had said that the use of American forces might be essential to save the Republic of Korea.[26]

COMMAND OF THE UN FORCES

The story of MacArthur's brilliant and successful tactic of piecemeal commitment of American troops beginning on July 5, when the first American infantrymen made contact with the enemy, need not be recounted here. The two green understrength battalions of the Twenty-first Infantry Regiment of the Twenty-fourth Division, though they were overrun and decimated by the North Koreans, managed to slow down the enemy's attack long enough to throw off his timetable. In the meantime more American troops were ferried over from Japan and Okinawa and others were moved from the U. S. later in the summer to augment the growing, but very much outmanned, UN forces in Korea. Until the end of August, when the first Commonwealth ground troops arrived, only naval and air elements were supplied by any UN members other than the U. S. By the end of 1951, when the Korean operation had become relatively stabilized and peace negotiations were under way, a total of sixteen UN members had armed forces in Korea.[27]

The arrival in Korea of the forces of other UN members made necessary the establishment of some sort of centralized command. In view of the fact that the representative of the Soviet Union might at any time choose to reoccupy his seat (as indeed he did on August 1), the Security Council and its Military Staff Committee clearly could not be given the power to direct operations as the UN Charter prescribed. Thus the Security Council adopted on July 7 a resolution submitted by Sir Gladwyn Jebb of

the United Kingdom which *inter alia* recommended that all members providing military forces pursuant to the resolutions of June 25 and 27 make such forces and other assistance available to a Unified Command under the U. S.; requested the U. S. to designate the commander of such forces; authorized the Unified Command at its discretion to use the UN flag in the course of its operations against the North Koreans concurrently with the flags of the various nations participating; and requested the U. S. to provide the Security Council with reports on the course of action taken under the Unified Command. President Truman on July 8 announced the appointment of General MacArthur as commander of the UN forces and on July 25 General MacArthur established the UN Command with General Headquarters at Tokyo and on the same day made his first report to the Security Council.[28]

The establishment of the UN Command did not basically affect the machinery for directing the operations in Korea. Before July 7, the President of the United States had acted under his powers as Commander-in-Chief of the army and navy of the United States "and he was exercising those powers to try and carry out the purposes laid down in the resolutions [of the Security Council] of the 25th and 27th of June."[29] After the UN Command was established it was, in substance, identical with the Far East Command of the U. S. since General MacArthur was in command of both. MacArthur's chain of command was through the Chief of Staff of the U. S. Army (General Collins), to the Joint Chiefs of Staff (Generals Bradley, Collins and Vandenberg and Admiral Sherman), to the Secretary of Defense (Louis Johnson until September 18, 1950, and then George C. Marshall), to the President. The JCS, it should be noted, also had a direct line to the President as they were by statute the "principal military advisers" to the Chief Executive and, uniquely among the agencies of the Defense Establishment, under his "authority and direction." Usually the Chairman of the Joint Chiefs, General Bradley, rather than the group, briefed the President on military matters and represented the JCS at National Security Council meetings. Ground forces of all participating UN members and the Republic of Korea were attached to the U. S. 8th Army while air and naval forces were attached to the Far Eastern

Air Force and the Seventh Fleet respectively. All these were commanded by General MacArthur from the common headquarters of the UN Command and the Far East Command of the U. S.[30]

Thus the U. S. was in full operational control in Korea and, in theory, had corresponding freedom of action. In reply to interrogation by Senator Guy M. Gillette (D., Ia.) during the Senate Hearings, Acheson said:

Now the military aspects of [the] campaign fall under the command direction, and if it becomes necessary in the military conduct of the war to move here or there or respond to this or that attack, then the command has that authority.[31]

But Secretary Acheson added that the U. S. desired to act in accordance with the resolutions of the Security Council and the General Assembly of the UN and did not contemplate acting unilaterally because ". . . it is very important that in carrying out this campaign we have the enthusiastic and warm support of all those who are taking part in it, and therefore we have endeavored to keep in closest touch, closest consultation with them, and have a continuous exchange of ideas and advice back and forth."[32]

Secretary Acheson's statement that the military aspects of the war fell "under the command direction" leaves certain questions unanswered—above all, how much discretionary authority the theater commander could enjoy. The American army has traditionally granted far wider authority to field commanders than most other armies, notably the British. Yet there is no absolute and definite rule and ambiguities are particularly likely to emerge when "military" actions like bombing have significant "political" implications, or if they affect immediately or potentially the global responsibilities of the armed forces. The ambiguities are naturally increased when a host of allies have or seek to have some voice in deciding the conduct of war.

After the first confused days of the war a fairly regularized procedure was followed in discussing policy and drawing up directives for the Far East Command. The differences between Secretary of Defense Louis Johnson and Secretary of State Dean Acheson for a time delayed the setting up of such procedures, but Johnson was replaced in mid-September by General George C. Marshall and State-Defense relations were generally good thereafter. Secretary Acheson was in close and continuing contact with Marshall and the Joint Chiefs, and Marshall also initiated informal discussions between the "working staffs" of the Defense and State Departments "to get all the facts spread out and to make a proposal for an attitude or decision by the Chiefs of Staff" when they were "involved in something that [had] relationships to the world picture."[33] Directives to MacArthur and his successors were prepared by the Joint Chiefs of Staff (with State Department participation) and forwarded to the Secretary of Defense, who would concur or state his disagreements and then forward the directive to the President for final approval or disapproval. It was customary for Secretary Marshall to give the paper to General Bradley to carry to the White House where he met the President every morning at about 10 o'clock. If the directive was of major importance it was also forwarded to the National Security Council for study and discussion by the senior staff.[34] The Joint Chiefs were not members of the National Security Council but General Bradley or a substitute usually accompanied Secretary Marshall to its meetings.[35] After measures were discussed by the NSC, the President would make his decisions. In the actual dispatch of a directive to the Far East Commander, General Collins acted as executive agent of the JCS. All communications from the State Department to General MacArthur went through the JCS, although Secretary Acheson occasionally wrote letters to the General through "the ordinary processes, sometimes through the mails." Some messages from the State Department went to William Sebald, a foreign service officer serving as political adviser to SCAP, but these messages also went through the Joint Chiefs of Staff.[36]

III. NORTH FROM THE BEACHHEAD

In the early weeks of the Korean War, the UN forces were steadily driven southward, suffering tremendous losses but, by their heroic resistance, badly bloodying the enemy. By the first week in August, only an area of about four thousand square miles around the vital supply port of Pusan in the southeastern corner of Korea was still in UN hands. For more than a month, while the Communists hurled their divisions at the lightly manned UN lines, troops of various UN member nations trickled through Pusan to reinforce its defenders, and at the same time General MacArthur was planning to end the stalemate by an audacious amphibious attack on Inchon, one hundred and fifty miles to the northwest.

The landing at Inchon on September 15, the advisability of which had at first been doubted by the Joint Chiefs until they were persuaded to approve it by the forceful eloquence of General MacArthur, was a brilliant, but not a complete, success. The North Koreans, caught between the Xth Corps which had landed at Inchon and the 8th Army which pushed northward from the old beachhead area around Pusan, retreated precipitously across the 38th parallel into the territory of the People's Democratic Republic. Thus, unfortunately, a large part of the North Korean army escaped the trap. Within two weeks of the Inchon assault there was nothing left to do south of the parallel but mopping-up operations and capturing the scattered Communist guerrilla groups which were left behind by the retreating Red army.

PLANS FOR THE OCCUPATION OF KOREA

The war did not however end—as it might have—with the repelling of the aggressors from the soil of the Republic of Korea. The decision to cross the 38th parallel for the military purpose of destroying the aggressor force had originated before the assault at Inchon. General Collins and Admiral Sherman had discussed the subject with General MacArthur late in August when MacArthur had outlined the Inchon plan. The two representatives of the Joint Chiefs agreed with MacArthur that the initial objective to be obtained by the offensive was the destruction of the North Korean army and that the parallel should not stand in the way of operations to that end. On September 7, the JCS forwarded to the Secretary of Defense their recommendation that the UN forces be permitted to carry on operations both north and south of the parallel until North Korean resistance was terminated.[37] The National Security Council took up the matter in the next few days and then recommended "that General MacArthur was to extend his operations north of the parallel and make plans for the occupation of North Korea, if there was no indication or threat of entry of Soviet or Chinese Communist elements in force."[38] President Truman approved this recommendation on September 11 and the following information was sent to General MacArthur on September 15:

(a) Final decisions cannot be made at this time inasmuch as the course of action best advancing United States national interest must be determined in the light of—
(1) Action by the Soviet Union and the Chinese Communists;
(2) In consultation with friendly members of the United Nations; and
(3) An appraisal of the risk of general war.
(b) The United Nations forces have a legal basis for conducting operations north of the thirty-eighth parallel to compel the withdrawal of the North Korean forces behind the line or to defend against these forces.
(c) The Joint Chiefs of Staff were authorized to direct General MacArthur to plan for the possible occupation of North Korea but to execute such

plans only with the approval of the President.

(d) General MacArthur should undertake no ground operations north of the thirty-eighth parallel in event of occupation of North Korea by Soviet or Chinese Communist forces. In this event, air and naval operations north of the parallel should not be discontinued.

(e) In the event of employment of major Chinese Communist units south of the thirty-eighth parallel, the United States would (1) not permit itself to become engaged in a general war with Communist China; (2) authorize General MacArthur to continue military action as long as it offered a reasonable chance of successful resistance.[39]

This approved JCS recommendation was the foundation for a formal JCS directive of September 27, but MacArthur could foretell the substance of the directive that would follow. As its first line clearly stated, the recommendation was not an order to MacArthur to proceed northward—such an order would not be dispatched for another dozen days—but it was an indication that our policy-makers contemplated going ahead and occupying all of Korea if the Russians and/or the Chinese Communists did not intervene. No further authority could be given to the Far East Commander on September 15 because it was not known whether the hazardous Inchon attack, which was being launched on that very day, would succeed and perhaps because the U. S. government was first seeking assurances from other "friendly members of the United Nations" that they would support operations in North Korea. MacArthur was being apprised of the situation and directed to plan operations north of the 38th parallel.

The critical days in making the decision to cross the 38th parallel came between September 15 and 27. As of the 15th, the Truman Administration was saying that the crossing of the parallel was legally justified for the purpose of forcing the withdrawal of the aggressors, or defending against their forces (this was quite true; the UN resolution actually went further); the occupation of North Korea by the UN army was being contemplated but not yet authorized. By the 27th, when General MacArthur was told to move ahead, the order, though it gave him somewhat greater latitude than did the preliminary directive, was confined to the military objective of destroying the enemy's army.

The fact that the JCS directive of September 27 was couched only in terms of military ob-

jectives did not mean that the U. S. government had given no thought to possible by-product gains, so to speak, of operations in Korea. As early as August 17, soon after the Pusan beachhead had been secured and at a time when military optimism about future actions first had a persuasive ring, Austin made a speech at the Security Council in which the repelling of aggression was listed as merely the first objective of the UN forces, to be followed by actions that would prevent a second invasion, discourage all potential aggressors, and finally permit the UN Commission to carry out the free elections leading to an independent unified democratic Korea. The possibility of achieving the political objective of unifying Korea after the defeat of the North Korean army and the occupation of North Korea was being discussed by State Department officials with UN delegates and in the UN debates themselves. A combination of circumstances during this period made it almost inevitable that the U. S. would press for this policy, which was at most merely an enlargement in detail of what Austin had asserted in August. The phenomenal success of the UN forces in the two weeks after Inchon and the pressures of domestic politics in the U. S. helped persuade the Truman Administration to take advantage of the military situation in Korea to convert the objective of the war from the simple repelling of aggression to the establishment of "a free, independent and unified Korea," the long-range political objective in Korea of both the U. S. and the UN. Similar pressures or desires converged on the governments of our allies, and they too came to the same conclusion. Moreover, in the two weeks after the Inchon landing and the apparent rout of the Communists, public and private soundings of the enemy to make peace were made without any success. Presumably it did not seem to be wise, therefore, in the view of our policy-makers to stop at the 38th parallel with a live and potentially dangerous enemy on the other side who might regroup and re-equip his forces and strike back over the parallel. Finally, enough members of the UN concluded independently, or were persuaded by the U. S., that it was desirable and expedient to advance north of the parallel and to capitalize on the UN military success by uniting Korea.

At his press conference on September 21, President Truman, when asked whether American troops and other UN soldiers in Korea would pursue North Korean Communists across the 38th parallel, said that the UN, not the U. S. government, would make the decision and the U. S. would abide by it. In Congress, Senator William F. Knowland (R., Cal.) agreed that the issue was one for the UN to settle, but warned that a failure to cross the parallel would be appeasement of Russia and would perhaps give the North Koreans a chance to regroup their forces. The California senator was, however, talking about the necessity of crossing the parallel only for the military purpose of defeating the North Korean forces and made no mention of the broad political objective of unifying Korea. Representative Hugh D. Scott, Jr. (R., Pa.), on the same day, accused the State Department of planning "to subvert our military victory in Korea" by calling a UN halt at the 38th parallel.[40] During the next few days, as the UN General Assembly prepared to take up the Korean question, the State Department was carrying on informal conversations with UN officials and delegates to secure backing for formal approval of a move across the parallel. Secretary Acheson was clearly most anxious to make the move, but, as James Reston reported on September 26, he felt that the UN itself must lay down the long-range occupation and political policies to be followed in North Korea. The Secretary of State realized that the UN did not move of its own volition and required direction and leadership. He was present at many of the meetings with diplomats in New York and Washington during these last days of September and early days of October mobilizing support for the American position.[41] There seemed to be general agreement between top officials of the U. S. and other UN members on policies to be followed in Korea if the Russians and Chinese Communists did not intervene. Under this policy the UN forces would be authorized to carry their campaign north of the parallel if the Reds did not cease fire, hand over their arms to the UN forces, and accept UN authority until a free and independent Korea could be established under the supervision of the UN.[42]

Acheson's position was backed by the British, who were urging the UN to adopt a plan to unify Korea under a strong UN supervisory commission, but there was reluctance on the part of some of the countries backing the UN

in Korea to vote for an explicit authorization to General MacArthur to cross the parallel.[43] As late as September 28, the French Foreign Minister Robert Schuman was arguing that "We should do only what is necessary from a military point of view in Korea—no more and no less." "Politically it seems better that we remain in the situation of before the war."[44] In the General Assembly, Lester Pearson, Canada's foreign minister, argued that the UN forces must be given freedom to make certain that the North Koreans were crushed, and the British were reported to be drafting a resolution to permit the crossing of the 38th parallel. American officials, however, pointed out that Assembly approval of the British resolution was not a prerequisite in point of time to a crossing of the parallel by UN forces as the Security Council resolution of June 27 already provided sufficient authority for operations wherever they were necessary to repel the aggressor[45] and "to restore international peace and security to the area."

This was the tack the Administration decided to take. On September 27, while the General Assembly and its Political Committee were discussing the proposed British resolution, the Joint Chiefs transmitted a directive to General MacArthur. The UN Commander was told that his military objective was "the destruction of the North Korean Armed Forces." According to President Truman's account, MacArthur

In attaining this objective . . . was authorized to conduct military operations north of the 38th parallel in Korea, provided that at the time of such operation there had been no entry into North Korea of major Soviet or Chinese Communist forces, no announcement of intended entry, and no threat by Russian or Chinese Communists to counter our operations militarily in North Korea. He was also instructed that under no circumstances were any of his forces to cross the Manchuria or U. S. S. R. borders of Korea, and, as a matter of policy, no non-Korean ground forces were to be used in the provinces bordering on the Soviet Union or in the area along the Manchurian border. Similarly, support of his operations north or south of the thirty-eighth parallel by air or naval action against Manchuria or against U. S. S. R. territory was specifically ruled out.

The directive further instructed the Far East Commander the action he should take in the event of Soviet entry into the conflict or entry by the Chinese Communists. It read:

"In the event of the open or covert employment

of major Chinese Communist units south of the 38th parallel, you should continue the action as long as action by your forces offers a reasonable chance of successful resistance."[46]

In view of subsequent events, it should be particularly noted that the directive stated that "as a matter of policy, no non-Korean ground forces were to be used in the provinces bordering on the Soviet Union or in the area along the Manchurian border." Unfortunately, the geographic limitation was not sharply defined nor was the phrase "as a matter of policy" an ideal choice of language for a prohibition intended to be a firm one. The prohibition was so intended, as the JCS later stated. A notification to CINCFE that went along with the directive stating that "instructions sent to CINCFE were not to be considered final, since they might require modifications in accordance with developments"[47] meant only that such modifications, if there were to be any, would come from Washington.

MacArthur quickly submitted to the Joint Chiefs his plan for operations north of the parallel—an attack along the western coastal corridor by the 8th Army and an amphibious landing by Xth Corps at Wonsan on the east coast. The JCS forwarded their approval on September 29.[48]

To reporters who asked him on September 28 whether MacArthur had been authorized to cross the parallel, President Truman gave a very guarded answer. At one point he said that he could not state publicly whether the UN forces would cross the line. When it was pointed out to the President that State Department spokesmen were asserting that sanction for pursuit of the Reds across the 38th parallel lay in the original Security Council resolution of June 27 under which General MacArthur was acting, the President agreed that the resolution was very broad, but a moment later he said that the UN would have to act first on the matter of the parallel.[49] Obviously, the President was anxious to preserve the military secret—as he earlier indicated. The Associated Press, however, had apparently gotten wind of the decision made on September 27, for its report from Washington, carried in the *New York Times* on September 28, stated that MacArthur had been authorized "to send United Nations troops into North Korea if necessary as a military measure to destroy the power of the fleeing North Korean Army" but that "the longer-range political question of establishing order in North Korea and occupying that area of the peninsula must be decided by the United Nations." The press report added that the decision had been approved by President Truman and "reviewed by Secretary Acheson with the foreign policy chiefs of friendly governments at UN Headquarters in New York."

The decision to cross the 38th parallel for military purposes (though subject to certain qualifications) had thus been made final by the United States by September 27 under its understanding of the authority granted by the Security Council resolution of June 27; and MacArthur had been so advised. By the same date, it was obviously planned to enlarge the scope and objective of the march toward the Yalu so as to include occupation by UN forces and establishment of a free and unified Korea. The enlargement of the objective was the subject of the proposed British resolution in the UN, which was already under discussion on September 27, but not actually passed until October 7. As has been said, the resolution was actually prepared by Acheson but there were obvious advantages in having it introduced by the British, who were in thorough agreement.

On September 28, 1950, just three months after it had fallen to the aggressors from the North, Seoul, capital of the Republic of Korea, was liberated. The jubilant troops of the American and ROK divisions quickly moved through the devastated city rushing northward in pursuit of the shattered and demoralized enemy. The next day UN troops advanced to the 38th parallel where most of the UN forces halted, but some ROK divisions along the easternmost sector of the line pushed probing fingers into the territory of the Democratic People's Republic of North Korea. Ostensibly the UN army had halted awaiting further orders, but, as General MacArthur reported to Secretary of Defense George C. Marshall on September 29, "The logistical supply of our units is the main problem which limits our advance."

In exploiting the defeat of the enemy forces, our own troops may cross the parallel at any time in exploratory probing or exploiting local tactical conditions. My overall strategic plan in North Korea is known to you. I regard all of Korea open for our military operations unless and until the enemy capitulates.[50]

Supplies had to go from Inchon through Seoul or by rail from Pusan northward and General Walton H. Walker, the 8th Army commander, had "the greatest difficulty in getting a sufficient depot of supplies to push the attack north of the Seoul area."[51] The logistical problem was made doubly difficult by the fact that the Xth Corps was heading northeast from Seoul, while the 8th Army was heading northwest from its main base at Pusan.

THE UN AND THE UNIFICATION OF KOREA

At Lake Success, New York, on September 30, there were reports that most diplomats at the UN agreed that General MacArthur, in the absence of specific instructions to the contrary, had the power to decide on the military terms of surrender and the power to decide whether to order a crossing of the parallel.[52] The British Foreign Secretary, Ernest Bevin, told reporters, as he boarded the *Queen Mary* to return to England, that Korea must be dealt with as a whole, implying that the 38th parallel should be ignored.[53] And Warren Austin, the chief of the U. S. delegation to the UN, was paving the way in the General Assembly's First Committee for the passage of what became the October 7 resolution, which was to authorize the use of force to accomplish the political goal of establishing a free and unified Korea. Austin in summarizing the American position, an amplification of what he had proposed on August 17, pointed out that the UN had been defied when the Commission created by the General Assembly had been prevented by the Russian occupation authorities from observing elections in North Korea, and when the occupation forces set up a puppet government which, according to UN findings, ruled only by right of the mere transfer of power from the government of the Soviet Union. The final defiance of the UN had been the aggression by the North Korean regime which endangered the peace and security of all members of the UN. Austin argued that future acts of aggression must be prevented by refusing to permit the aggressor to take refuge behind an imaginary line because the Communists would recreate the condition of a threat to the peace of Korea and of the world. The U. S. delegate agreed that the political aspects of the questions whether the artificial barrier of the 38th parallel should be permanently removed and whether Korea should be united now, must be determined by the UN. But, Austin insisted, on three occasions the General Assembly had recorded its support of the freedom, independence and unity of Korea. Hitherto, these aims could not be carried out because the commissions of the UN had not been permitted to operate north of the parallel. The barrier which divided Korea had no basis in law or reason and was not recognized either by the UN or the Republic of Korea. Moreover, the North Koreans themselves, by armed attack on the Republic of Korea, had denied the reality of any such line. Such a boundary, concluded Austin, should not be erected. The General Assembly should rather set up standards and means by which all Koreans could thereafter live in peace among themselves and with their neighbors.[54]

In the meantime, operations across the parallel had already begun. On October 1 (WT), General MacArthur wired Secretary of Defense Marshall that he planned on October 2 to issue a dramatic announcement on the occasion of the crossing of the 38th parallel, but he received an immediate reply from the JCS stating:

We desire that you proceed with your operations without any further explanation or announcement and let action determine the matter. Our government desires to avoid having to make an issue of the 38th parallel until we have accomplished our mission.[55]

At the same time Secretary Marshall gave CINCFE "tactical and strategic latitude to proceed north of the thirty-eighth parallel."[56] MacArthur thus had authorization to advance.

The instructions to MacArthur to make no mention of the parallel may have been founded on a desire to avoid offense to members of the UN while the October 7 resolution was being discussed. Secrecy was certainly not the objective. On October 1, the American press was carrying a whole collection of stories on the Korean situation: reports that MacArthur had authorized the advance of ROK troops into North Korea; a message from General MacArthur to the Commander-in-Chief of the North Korean forces demanding that he surrender immediately and implying that the UN army would cross into North Korea to supervise the laying down of arms; and the statement by U. S. Delegate Warren Austin (summarized above) to the General Assembly's First Committee also made on September 30 (October 1 in Korea), a few hours before MacArthur issued his surrender demand, that the Reds must not be permitted to take refuge behind the parallel, an "imaginary line" which had no basis in law or logic. "Diplomats here said Mr. Austin's warning," reported the *New York Times* from UN headquarters, "could be taken as clear notice that the United States felt that General MacArthur had the right to order a crossing of the parallel and that, with or without a surrender, United Nations forces would march across the line." The *Herald Tribune* on the same day also headlined a story about a speech by Chou En-lai, Chinese premier, warning that the Chinese would not "supinely tolerate" blows by "savage imperialists."

MacArthur's surrender demand, which, incidentally, had been cleared with Washington a few days before it was issued,[57] made absolutely certain a move northward—either to disarm the Communists, were they to capitulate, or to press the attack, were they to continue their resistance. The surrender message went unheeded by the Communists and within two days ROK divisions had advanced more than fifty miles into Communist territory; the other UN forces had not yet moved north of the line.

The views of Warren Austin concerning the 38th parallel were echoed in the next few days by the delegates from Canada, Great Britain, Australia, Norway, the Philippines and Israel, as the lines were drawn on each side of the debate. Opposition to moving into North Korea was voiced by Andrei Vishinsky, the spokesman of the U. S. S. R., Edward Kardelj of Yugoslavia, and Sir Benegal N. Rau of India. The views of the latter two delegates are of particular interest. The Yugoslav (it should be remembered that this was during a period of Yugoslavia's alienation from the Soviet Union) argued that the sole original objective of the UN in Korea was to repel aggression and the Security Council in June 1950 had "refrained from formulating other concrete objectives." Only now was there talk of crossing the parallel and changing the government of North Korea. "Such a decision," said Kardelj, "would strike a serious blow at the prestige of the United Nations. . . . For the question was whether it was capable of checking aggression without at the same time imposing on a country a specific political and social regime. It was by that test that the United Nations would be judged."[58] The Indian delegate, Sir Benegal N. Rau, took a somewhat different stand. India, he said, favored the unification of Korea, but doubted the wisdom of using force to that end. Advancing into North Korea might increase the area of conflict in the Far East, Rau suggested, and might impair faith in the UN. India therefore recommended that the North Koreans be called upon to cease hostilities immediately so as to permit the UN to take steps to bring about an independent and united Korea. "Should the North Koreans fail to respond," Sir Benegal said, "the situation could be reviewed."[59]

The Yugoslav argument was significant because it attempted to remind the UN that it was departing from its original objective; the argument was a foretaste of the ones that were later used when the UN forces met a strong adversary in Korea. Ultimately, the American policy-makers did decide that forceful unification of Korea would be far too costly or dangerous to justify continuation of the effort (as Rau had suggested) and they returned to the limited objective for which Kardelj had argued. The Indian view reflected the feeling of uneasiness among Indians and increasingly large numbers of other people that the operations in North Korea threatened to erupt into a major Asian and, perhaps, a world conflict.

The Indian objections to UN operations north of the parallel arose also from another source. Not only did the Indian public, which was strongly anti-American in the fall of 1950, feel that Korea was merely the first victim of the great power rivalry between Russia and the U. S., but Indian officialdom took seriously disquieting reports that the Chinese Communists intended to enter the Korean War if non-Korean troops advanced north of the 38th parallel.[60]

The possibility of Chinese and even Russian armed intervention in Korea had been considered by American planners from the opening days of the war. As early as July "brief intimations" were received by Washington that the Chinese might come in and that they were already moving troops northward to the Manchuria-Korea border.[61] Since the main source of intelligence on Red Chinese movements during the summer of 1950 was the Chinese Nationalist government on Formosa, whose reports had frequently in the past proved to be erroneous, there was a tendency to discount them. Nevertheless, as the directives issued to the Far East Command indicate, the theater commander was warned to keep in mind the potential threat of the Chinese. Then, starting in August, Mao Tze-tung and Chou En-lai began a series of public declarations that rang variations on a central theme: they would not "supinely tolerate seeing their neighbors savagely invaded by imperialists." Obviously these pronouncements reflected Chinese distaste for the evident fact that the UN forces were not going to be driven off the peninsula, and, presumably, fear that, in one way or another, the UN forces would burst out from the Pusan perimeter and move north. From late September on, the Chinese leaders, no doubt stirred by the Inchon landings, repeated and intensified their warnings. Beginning about September 27, even more threatening evidence of possible Chinese action was received by the U. S. Yet it was difficult for our policy-makers to perceive that the public threats, even though they were confirmed by intelligence reports, carried any more weight than the numerous other threats made by the Chinese Reds against the "American imperialists" for their activities in Formosa and other parts of the Far East.[62]

From this time on, however, and going into October, there was an entirely new set of reports; these came from the Indian government at New Delhi which had been receiving dispatches from its ambassador to Peiping, Sardar K. M. Panikkar, who had been told by the Chinese leaders that if the UN or U. S. forces crossed the 38th parallel, China would send troops into Korea to defend North Korea.[63] Ambassador Panikkar reported that during July and August, while the Peiping government mounted an increasingly bitter propaganda attack against "the aggressive American forces in Korea," there were no indications that the Chinese intended to intervene with troops in Korea. After the Inchon landings and the rolling back of the North Korean army, however, there were rumors in Peiping of large-scale troop movements into Manchuria and, on September 25, General Nieh Yen-jung, the Chinese acting Chief of Staff, told Panikkar that "the Chinese did not intend to sit back with folded hands and let the Americans come up to their border."[64] The night of September 25 a curfew was clamped on Peiping and all traffic stopped as large formations of troops and trucks moved through the city towards the railroad station to head toward the Manchurian-Korean border. Finally, in the early morning hours of October 3, Panikkar was awakened and called to Premier Chou En-lai's official residence where Chou informed him that the Chinese would intervene if the Americans crossed the parallel. When asked by the Indian Ambassador whether the Chinese intended to enter the war if only South Koreans crossed the parallel, Chou replied emphatically: "The South Koreans did not matter but American intrusion into North Korea would encounter Chinese resistance."[65] Panikkar immediately wired this news to his government and the next morning told Sir John Hutchinson, the British Minister, how matters stood. The warning from Ambassador Panikkar was passed on by the Indian government to the U. S. government on October 3, at the very time that the UN General Assembly's First (Political) Committee was debating the resolution which would authorize the UN forces to occupy North Korea. American policy-makers felt that the Communists were using the threat merely as a bluff to influence the voting on the resolution. For this reason, among others, the U. S. shrugged off the warning and continued to press for the passage of the resolution. Mr. Panikkar's message, however, along with similar reports of possible Chinese actions which had been received by the State Department from Stockholm and Moscow, were forwarded to General MacArthur.[66]

These warnings did not deter the American policy-makers, their active allies, and their other supporters in the UN. On October 7, the General Assembly finally passed the British resolution that had been in preparation for at least ten days; the vote was 47 ayes, 5 noes, and 7 abstentions. The resolution itself was a clear grant of authority, though it partly relied on, and partly superseded, the ambiguous Security Council resolution of June 27. Its pertinent clauses are quoted below; they quite specifically authorized the use of UN troops *throughout* Korea as long as was necessary to ensure "stability" and to aid in the establishment of "a unified, independent and democratic government."

The General Assembly

Having regard to its resolutions of 14 November 1947 (112 (II)), of 12 December 1948 (195 (III)) and of 21 October 1949 (293 (IV)) [these all dealt with the matter of setting up a free, independent and unified Republic of Korea],

Having received and considered the report of the United Nations Commission on Korea,

Mindful of the fact that the objectives set forth in the resolutions referred to above have not been fully accomplished and, in particular, that the unification of Korea has not yet been achieved, and that an attempt has been made by an armed attack from North Korea to extinguish by force the Government of the Republic of Korea,

Recalling the General Assembly declaration of 12 December 1948 that there has been established a lawful government [the Government of the Republic of Korea] having effective control and jurisdiction over that ·part of Korea where the United Nations Temporary Commission on Korea was able to observe and consult and in which the great majority of the people of Korea reside; that this government is based on elections which were a valid expression of the free will of the electorate of that part of Korea and which were observed by the Temporary Commission; and that this is the only such government in Korea,

Having in mind that United Nations armed forces are at present operating in Korea in accordance with the recommendations of the Security Council of 27 June 1950, subsequent to its resolution of 25 June 1950, that the Members of the United Nations furnish such assistance to the Republic of Korea as may be necessary to repel the armed attack and to restore international peace and security to the area,

Recalling that the essential objective of the resolution of the General Assembly referred to above was the establishment of a unified, independent and democratic Government of Korea,

1. *Recommends that*

(a) All appropriate steps be taken to ensure conditions of stability throughout Korea;

(b) All constituent acts be taken, including the holding of elections, under the auspices of the United Nations, for the establishment of a unified, independent and democratic government in the sovereign State of Korea;

(c) All sections and representative bodies of the population of Korea, South and North, be invited to cooperate with the organs of the United Nations in the restoration of peace, in the holding of elections and in the establishment of a unified government;

(d) United Nations forces should not remain in any part of Korea otherwise than so far as necessary for achieving the objectives specified in subparagraphs (a) and (b) above;

(e) All necessary measures be taken to accomplish the economic rehabilitation of Korea;

[The remainder of the resolution outlined the procedures the UN would follow to accomplish the above objectives.]

The key sections of the resolution were 1(a), 1(b), and 1(d); the first two stated the objectives of ensuring stability and establishing a unified government while the third authorized, and limited, the use of UN forces for those purposes.

Early in the morning of October 7 (October 8 in Korea), the first American troops moved over the line, but it was not until the next day, after the North Koreans greeted with silence General MacArthur's second message demanding their surrender, that the UN forces launched a full-scale drive into North Korea. Some critics of American actions in Korea have pointed out that the first American soldiers crossed the parallel at 3:14 A.M. (WT) on October 7, twelve hours before the resolution was passed by the UN General Assembly.[67] In light of what has already been said above about the various directives authorizing the UN commander to cross the parallel the exact timing of his action seems to have no significance. The only issue in terms of UN policy was not the crossing of the parallel, but shifting the UN objective in the war from the repelling of aggression and the restoration of "international peace and security to the area," with or without a change in the *status quo ante bellum,* to securing the political unification of Korea. The possibility of Chinese Communist intervention was not raised as a UN problem at this time except by the Indians. It is possible, although—in light of the general feeling of blind optimism in early October—improbable, that a clearer delineation of military and political objectives might have made UN members more cautious.

IV. SHIFTING OBJECTIVES: A REVIEW

What were the objectives as of October 7? The military objective was the pursuit and destruction of the North Korean armies north and south of the 38th parallel. This objective was subject to three qualifications, all three established by the U. S. government, not by the UN: First, "as a matter of policy" only ROK troops would be used in the border provinces; second, our advance would not proceed unless there had been at the time of the operation no entry of major Soviet or Chinese Communist forces, no announcement of intended entry, and no threat of military action against our forces; and third, no air or naval action would be taken against Manchuria or U. S. S. R. territory. This was the substance of the JCS directive to MacArthur on September 27.

The original objective of both the United States and the UN was merely to get the North Korean forces to cease hostilities and withdraw to the 38th parallel, and this was clearly reflected in the first UN Security Council resolution of June 25 and the initial orders to MacArthur. In this June 25 UN Security Council resolution, all UN members were called on to assist "in the execution of the Resolution."

Within a matter of days, almost hours after passage of this first UN resolution, it became clear that the North Korean forces would not voluntarily withdraw; obviously there was need for force to ensure withdrawal. Clearly, furthermore, the members of the UN Security Council (with Russia absent, Yugoslavia opposed and the uninstructed delegates from India and Egypt abstaining) were in agreement that there should also be a sufficient employment of force to prevent a second aggression. The second UN Security Council resolution, of June 27, read: "such assistance to the Republic of Korea as may be necessary to repel the armed attack *and* to restore international peace and security to the area." [Emphasis

added.] As has been noted above, the last clause was included at the urging of the UN secretariat. Although there seems to have been no careful consideration of possible consequences, presumably the U. S. and other delegates were aware that they were in some fashion enlarging the initial objective.

The restoration of peace and security is a normal enough military objective, but political implications are almost inevitably inherent in the process of attaining the objective. And in this instance, the discarding of the simple geographic purpose opened up new possibilities of a scope certainly not clearly envisaged in the last days of June and certainly not expressed. There was no doubt even then that UN air and naval forces would range north of the parallel in helping to achieve the UN objectives. Probably no one gave much thought in those anxious days to the crossing of the parallel by ground forces—enough, for the moment, if they could keep a toehold around Pusan. Indeed, it is a fair guess that, at that moment, if the North Korean authorities had announced the withdrawal of their forces, this action would have been deemed the equivalent of both the repelling of armed attack and the restoration of peace and security to the area.

The next formal UN action came a little more than three months after the Security Council resolution of June 27—three months of active battle. Even after Inchon, the North Koreans still refused to concede defeat, even in the face of defeat. The UN had indeed repelled aggression, but it had not restored "international peace and security to the area." At the moment, the carrying out of this second objective seemed to present what would probably be a rather simple problem—simple to all, that is, except the Communist nations, and to a few others, notably India and Yugoslavia as well: the UN forces should drive on until the remnants of the North Korean troops were destroyed or disarmed, or, alternatively, until the North Korean authorities sued for peace. How far north the UN armies would advance was left open: as General MacArthur put it, in terms entirely consonant with the JCS instructions of September 27, "until the enemy capitulates."

The JCS directive did contain certain qualifications—qualifications that were almost the equivalent of an admission that international peace and security could not be restored to the area if the Chinese or the Russians intervened or threatened to intervene. But with or without these qualifications (and the qualifications were soon shoved aside), the crossing of the parallel to attain military objectives was fully authorized by the United States government acting in good faith under its perfectly reasonable, and well-nigh universally accepted, interpretation of the Security Council resolution of June 27.

Thus, no reaffirmation by the UN of long-established objectives was necessary. Unfortunately, in the event, the UN enthusiastically welcomed what Austin had advocated in August and what was later described as a "target of opportunity"—a chance to secure the UN's long-dormant political objective of a "unified, independent and democratic government" as a happy by-product of the move to restore peace in the peninsula. Unfortunately, too, in the event, the notions of "target of opportunity" and by-product were not left dangling: the General Assembly resolution of October 7 nailed them to the UN mast. The subsequent failure to achieve this thoroughly political objective by force therefore became not merely regrettable but agonizing.

Since October 1950 there has been much argument that the change of objectives resolved on by the UN was the cause of the dismal events of the next two-and-a-half years. This is an untenable hypothesis. The first Chinese warnings in late August referred solely to troop movements north of the parallel; and by September 25, when the Chinese moved their own troops toward the Korean border, the change of UN objectives was still in embryo, although foreseeable. Chou En-lai's speech of October 1, and his urgent message to Panikkar on October 3, related solely to troop movements—not to air attack, not to naval operations, not to changes in political objectives. (Not, of course, that the warnings were not themselves highly

political!) In other words, so far as one can tell, the Chinese attack would have come just the same if MacArthur had marched forward solely under the June 27 UN resolution and the JCS directive of September 27.

In the bitter aftermath of military defeat, there were a good many arguments, particularly by officials of the State Department, that the large-scale movements of Chinese Communist troops before October 1 would have continued with their crossing of the Yalu and attack on UN forces whatever we did or did not do. The immediate objective of the argument was to justify our position and perhaps also to make sure that the Chinese were branded as aggressors. It has no more factual support than the previous unhappy assurances by many U. S. officials ranging from MacArthur to Acheson that the Chinese threats were bluffs, and, as some asserted, after Inchon, merely intended to prevent passage of the General Assembly resolution.

One last question deserves brief consideration. As has been said, Chou En-lai told Panikkar on October 3 that the Chinese would intervene if American troops crossed the parallel but that "the South Koreans did not matter." Certainly these remarks carried meaning, but the meaning cannot be precisely defined. Presumably the 38th parallel had no sacred significance to the Chinese (they finally settled for a slightly different boundary). Would they have held off their attack if the U. S. troops had stopped at the "waist"? And in what sense did the ROK army "not matter"? Perhaps because the Chinese were sure that with their assistance, direct or indirect, the North Koreans could maintain or regain control over all or much of the territory north of the U. S. forces. What seems incredible is that they would have tolerated a completely "unified, independent and democratic" Korea, however secured; the parallel with Russia's sensitivity about its satellite neighbors needs no laboring. What seems to have escaped attention at the time is that Northern Korea was now transferring its satellite allegiance from Moscow to Peiping.

The above is speculative. What seems quite factual is that the Chinese threats were real threats, and that our political and military leaders and the leaders of all our allies did not take them seriously. The pleas of the two neutrals, India and Yugoslavia, were thrust aside.

The fact that the threats were disregarded or discounted meant that the cautionary provisions of the September 27th JCS directive did not apply. The natural enough next step was the passage of the October 7 resolution which contained no caveats and added a political objective. The political objective was not new, but heretofore the UN had not as a body committed itself to the attaining of Korean unification by force.

The merging of the military and political objectives ultimately became, as has been said, a matter of acute distress and the subject of confusing explanations and accusations. In 1951, Secretary Acheson, testifying in the turbulent atmosphere of the MacArthur hearings, said that the political and military objectives had always been separate. Later, he and some of his colleagues referred to unification as "a target of opportunity"; in other words, if, in the process of destroying Communist resistance unification could also be achieved, that would be fine, but unification had *never* been made something the UN would fight for.[68] The technical correctness of these statements is irrelevant. The world did not see the Korean actions in this light in October 1950. There was no objection raised by American authorities and their allies when MacArthur warned the North Korean commander on October 9 that unless the North Koreans surrendered immediately and cooperated "fully with the UN in establishing a unified independent democratic government of Korea" the UN forces would "at once proceed to take such military action as may be necessary to enforce the decrees of the United Nations."[69] As Leland Goodrich has stated, it is beside the point that the General Assembly had no legislative power and the Unified Command had no authority to execute General Assembly "decrees";[70] and General MacArthur's well-known penchant for orotund eloquence is also immaterial. The UN Commander believed that his U. S. and UN orders authorized and required him to establish a unified Korea, and the world believed that he was right.

In the months following the massive Chinese intervention in the Korean War and the near-catastrophic rout of the UN forces in late November 1950, the decision to cross the 38th parallel was examined and re-examined amidst the most heated debate. As is usually true in such displays of polemic, the facts of the case became obscured, indeed forgotten, in the fog of emotion-charged and electric disputation. It is useful, therefore, to review the critical decision in relation to the charges. One charge was that MacArthur violated orders by crossing the parallel. Actually, at no time during his tenure as UN Commander did General Mac-Arthur and the authorities in Washington, both civil and military, agree so fully on operations in Korea as they did from the time the authorization was given for the Inchon operation until passage of the October 7 resolution or shortly thereafter. In carrying operations into North Korea General MacArthur was following out orders issued in Washington and approved at the UN in Lake Success, New York. He was in no way going beyond the letter of his directives, nor was he acting on his own authority —as numerous critics here and abroad have argued. The UN resolution of June 27, as has been pointed out, could perfectly reasonably be interpreted to authorize action north of the parallel, and was in fact so interpreted by all concerned. The JCS directive of September 27 specifically authorized MacArthur's move. It is true that there were two restrictions on the advance in the directive: One was the limitation on the selection of troops for use in the border provinces—but this problem did not arise until later. The second was the instruction not to advance in the face of a Communist threat—but MacArthur's disregard of the Chinese warnings was fully supported by his superiors in the U. S. government—and by our allies too. The UN resolution of October 7 made no provision for Chinese threats, or even attacks.

A second, frequently repeated charge was that the advance to the north was an American plan foisted on our allies. This charge has no substance either. The October 7 resolution was passed by a 47 to 5 vote of the General Assembly, the five negative votes coming from the Soviet bloc. Seven nations, including Yugoslavia and a portion of the Arab League, and led by India, abstained from voting on the resolution because they felt that all means for securing peace should be exhausted before UN troops crossed the parallel and because they felt that there was a danger that China and Russia might be drawn into the conflict by a move into North Korea. Every nation actually participating in the fighting against the North Koreans voted for the resolution. Secondly, while it is certainly true that the U. S. pressed for the October 7 resolution and made clear that it was determined to move ahead in Korea, it is equally true, as the debates on the draft resolution clearly show, that the U. K., Canada and other Commonwealth nations as well as France and other western powers also took a strong stand that the 38th parallel should not serve as a barrier to protect the North Korean aggressors and that the opportunity had now come to implement the UN's political goals in Korea by the use of armed force. Although the arrangement under which the U. S. government provided political guidance to the UN forces and the lack of direct control by the UN itself were subsequently the subjects of much discord, up to the passage of the October 7 resolution no such complaints were made.

The third and final charge, often repeated, was that military domination of American policy in Korea underlay our crossing of the parallel. This is also patently untrue. All the available evidence leads one to conclude that in arriving at their decision to conduct operations in North Korea, American policy-makers clearly upheld the principle of civil supremacy over the military, for the decision was made by the President and with the concurrence of his civilian advisers, particularly the Secretary of State. Actually the first public statement was made by Ambassador Austin on August 17. The military merely precipitated the decision-making process when General Collins and Admiral Sherman, upon their return from their conference with General MacArthur before the Inchon landing, submitted with their approval to the rest of the Joint Chiefs MacArthur's recommendation that the parallel be crossed to secure the destruction of the North Korean army. The proposal had passed from the JCS to the Secretary of Defense to the President, who, in turn, had discussed it with the National Security Council and had concluded that Mac-Arthur should be authorized to occupy all of North Korea—unless the Russians or Chinese intervened.[71] It was the Secretary of State, Dean Acheson, moreover, who took the lead in pressing for the move into North Korea. Most of the members of the State Department went along with their chief in discounting the danger of Chinese intervention. It appears that only George F. Kennan (who was not on active service, having gone on leave from the Department in July) consistently felt that the risk of crossing the parallel and encountering foreign troops greatly outweighed the advantages, if any.[72] It has also been reported that Secretary of the Air Force Thomas K. Finletter said on October 3 that he was "extremely worried" about the possibility that "China might intervene momentarily in the Korean war."[73] There were thus certain apprehensions and there had been the cautionary note in the directive sent to General MacArthur on September 27 about Communist threats. Finally, there were urgent pleas, for somewhat different reasons, from India and Yugoslavia for the UN troops to hold back. In the afterlight of history, all these matters seem vastly important; consequently, it now seems strange that Secretary Acheson and the Administration pushed ahead with the move into Communist territory. Chou En-lai's very public threat had been in the headlines before the U. S. forces crossed the line. In retrospect, the march to the Yalu can be called a "gamble," but such a term would have been scoffed at in October 1950.

What accounts for this willingness to "gamble" with the possibility of enlarging the conflict in Korea into a war against Chinese or even Russian forces? A combination of factors explains the decision. As has already been stated, Acheson and others apparently believed that the Chinese threat was a bluff to influence the voting in the UN General Assembly. At a press conference at Lake Success on October 4, the Secretary of State said that "there was reason to believe that Communist China would not send troops into North Korea";[74] this belief was common currency in the U. S. government and elsewhere. The Chinese, after all, had been uttering threatening sounds since July, but they had done nothing—not even in early August when intervention (so General MacArthur said) might have meant pushing the outnumbered UN forces off the Pusan beachhead and into the sea. And after the Inchon triumph, the American government (and apparently most of its allies) seem to have considered Ambassador Panikkar rather a spokesman for the Chinese Communists than a dependable reporter of facts—or perhaps merely gullible. In the two weeks after the passage of the October 7 resolution, even though the Chinese continued to hurl out further threats over Peiping radio, the State Department and the military continued to feel that there was little or no chance of Chinese intervention. Nevertheless, on October 9, General MacArthur was sent another directive by the Joint Chiefs stating:

> In light of the possible intervention of Chinese Communist forces in North Korea the following . . . is forwarded for your guidance:
>
> Hereafter in the event of the open or covert employment anywhere in Korea of major Chinese Communist units, without prior announcement, you should continue the action as long as, in your judgment, action by forces now under your control offers a reasonable chance of success. In any case you will obtain authorization from Washington prior to taking any military action against objectives in Chinese territory.[75]

The directive of September 27 had not permitted action north of the parallel if the Chinese made any serious threat of intervention; now on October 9, even actual intervention was not listed as a necessary cause for cessation of the advance. The first cause of the willingness to proceed may therefore be described as a wide failure to evaluate military intelligence correctly.

A second cause of the willingness of the U. S. and its UN associates to hazard operations in North Korea may be found in the optimism produced by MacArthur's triumphant Inchon offensive. Actually, as has been noted, the trap had not been sprung, and many of the North Korean forces had escaped. Yet the UN and the U. S. had been so successful at least in repelling the aggression of the North Koreans that there was inevitably a great temptation to continue the drive in Korea until they had accomplished their long-standing political aims. Actually, Austin's statement of August 17 reflected a feeling that the UN was morally obligated to unify Korea. Moreover, the collapse of North Korean resistance south of the parallel and the rapid deterioration of the Communist army in the three weeks following the Inchon landing seemed to promise a quick victory. Thus our policy-makers may well have believed (as the October 9 JCS directive implies) that even if the Chinese did intervene, all or practically all of Korea could be occupied before the Chinese would be able to throw their weight into the conflict and affect the balance. Once occupied, a democratic government could rule

a unified Korea. Our intelligence about Chinese intentions and capabilities was no doubt imperfect; but it was optimism, not ignorance, that led to the disregard or misinterpretation of all the information that was available.

There is a third explanation of the action, closely related to the optimism about destroying the remains of the North Korean army. Certainly General MacArthur was convinced, as he explained to President Truman at Wake Island,[76] that a Chinese attack would not be dangerous and that the Chinese threat could, therefore, be disregarded. No doubt his faith was shared by others. He, of course, was hardly a dispassionate observer and evaluator of the available information: what finer climax to a resplendent career than the liberation of Korea and the establishment of a unified, democratic, independent government?

Finally, the tremendous pressure of American domestic politics encouraged our decision about Korea. The Truman Administration, and particularly Acheson, had been subjected to heavy and almost unceasing attacks on their Far Eastern policies. The Democrats were facing the approaching mid-term Congressional elections with a certainty of losing some strength in Congress (as the party in power generally does in mid-term elections) and unpopular foreign policies threatened to cost the Democrats their majorities. Secretary Acheson had been frequently attacked as an appeaser of the Chinese Communists and now a failure to capitalize on the success in Korea because of a fear of Chinese counteractions might be politically disastrous. On the other hand, a smashing victory in Korea would greatly enhance the prestige of the Truman Administration. Subsequent events showed how much political dynamite lay in the issues of the Korean War. Certainly neither Truman nor Acheson nor any of the others was consciously making a play for votes, but the pressure did exist and may well have had an impact.

Unwillingness to believe that the Chinese were serious, optimism about the success and beneficial consequences of a march to the north, conviction that a Chinese attack would not be dangerous, a desire to re-establish the Democratic Administration's prestige in its Far Eastern policies—all these pressures were present, and undoubtedly others as well. What weight each carried with the President and with his advisers is unknown. All that is clear is that the dangers were not entirely ignored, but were shoved aside. Finally, it is worth recalling that the decision to advance and to establish a unified Korea was greeted with general (though not universal) approval outside the U. S.; aside from the automatic opposition of the Communist bloc, only India and Yugoslavia publicly questioned the wisdom of the UN resolution.

V. THE MARCH TO THE YALU

Encountering only minor resistance, the UN forces' major offensive into North Korea, which started on October 9, moved rapidly northward. Pyongyang, the Communist capital, fell on October 20 while American paratroopers were dropped thirty miles to the north of the city in an only partly successful attempt to cut off the retreating North Korean troops. Five days earlier, President Truman met with MacArthur at Wake Island. The President did not come to criticize or instruct, rather to establish rapport and to find out if the high hopes of Washington were justified. Actually, General MacArthur was so sanguine of his prospects for an early victory that he assured the President that "formal resistance will end throughout North and South Korea by Thanksgiving" and that it was his "hope to be able to withdraw the 8th Army to Japan by Christmas."[77] Indeed, General MacArthur was so confident that he replied to President Truman's query about the possibilities of Chinese or Soviet intervention that there was "very little" chance of such intervention.

Had they interfered in the first or second months it would have been decisive. We are no longer fearful of their intervention. We no longer stand hat in hand. The Chinese have 300,000 men in Manchuria. Of these probably not more than 100/125,000 are distributed along the Yalu River. Only 50/60,000 could be gotten across the Yalu River. They have no air force. Now we have bases for our Air Force in Korea, if the Chinese tried to get down to Pyongyang there would be the greatest slaughter.[78]

General MacArthur was not alone in his estimate of the situation, for, as Secretary Acheson stated in the Senate Hearings, the State Department, on the 19th of October, came to the conclusion that while the possibility of Chinese intervention could not be completely dismissed, it was unlikely.[79]

At the beginning of the last week of October, just as American newspapers were carrying reports that only ROK troops would push to the Manchurian border and that "foreign (UN)" troops would halt some distance—perhaps as much as forty miles south of the Manchurian line, a disquieting stiffening of Communist resistance occurred.[80] A hint of a reason why the seemingly demoralized North Koreans were now standing their ground and fighting became apparent (or should have become apparent) on October 26, when the first Chinese Communist soldier was captured in combat by the UN forces. For several days, UN intelligence officers had suspected that some Chinese were already participating in the fighting, and it was later learned that the first Chinese had actually crossed the Yalu into Korea as early as October 9. Initially, it was not known, nor was it believed, that the Chinese were fighting as members of their own units, for the first few to be captured wore North Korean uniforms and General MacArthur stated in his communiqués that they may have been volunteers. His staff also assumed that some, or all, were bi-lingual, intermixed Chinese-Koreans from the border provinces on both sides of the Yalu.[81] On October 12, nine Chinese soldiers had walked into the ROK II Corps lines and had surrendered. When interrogated by intelligence officers, the prisoners had said that they had entered Korea with small units of "volunteers" which had been dragooned from Red Chinese Army formations. General MacArthur was undoubtedly supplied with a report of this interrogation just before he went to Wake Island and his opinion that the Chinese would not intervene in force was strengthened when the nine Chinese prisoners were further interrogated by 8th Army intelligence experts in Pyongyang after its capture on October 20. Here the POWs spoke freely of Chinese operations and stated that only 9,000 Chinese were fighting in Korea.

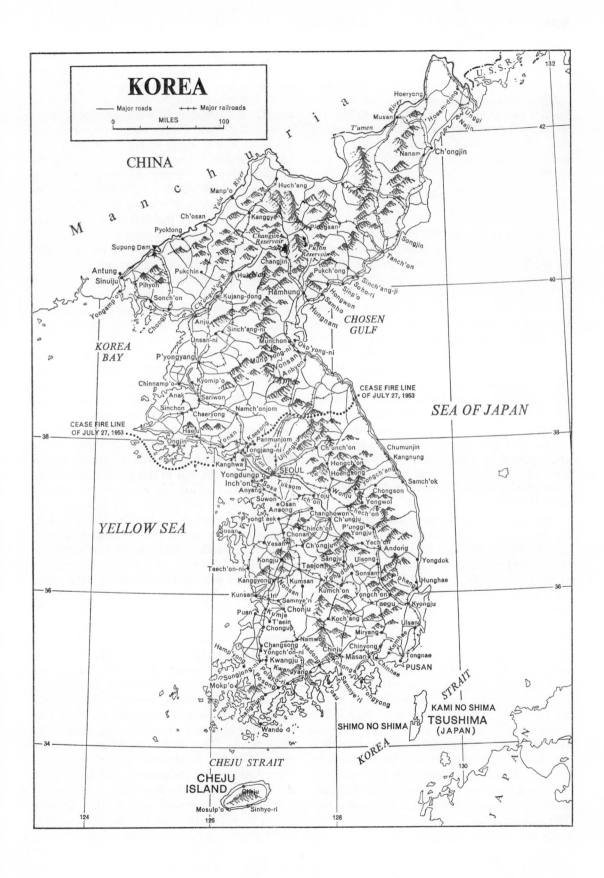

Whatever worries UN commanders had about Chinese intervention were thus put aside—which was exactly what the Chinese Communists intended when they ordered the nine soldiers to cross into the UN lines to be captured. As subsequent events demonstrated, the men who had been captured had been briefed with false information before being sent into the field.[82]

A CHANGE IN PLANS

Although there was thus a tendency at the end of October and the beginning of November for the UN Commander to minimize the degree of Chinese intervention, there was no mistaking the fact that the UN offensive was being slowed down. Thus, on October 24, General MacArthur, without prior notice to the JCS, ordered his field commanders to use American troops to spearhead the drive to the Yalu—in effect countermanding the directive of the JCS of September 27 which ordered him to use only ROK troops in the border provinces. The Far Eastern Commander did, however, add that UN ground forces, other than ROK troops, were to be withdrawn as soon as feasible and replaced by ROK units, but in the meantime all commanders were enjoined to drive forward with all speed and with full utilization of their forces.

The JCS received a copy of the new directive the day it was issued and immediately advised General MacArthur that the directive's instructions came in conflict with previous instructions of the Joint Chiefs, and asked for a report on his reasons "since the action contemplated was a matter of concern to them."[83]

General MacArthur's reply came the next day. The lifting of the restrictions on the use of UN forces in North Korea, the Far Eastern Commander declared, was a matter of military necessity since ROK troops were neither sufficiently strong nor sufficiently well led to be able to handle the situation. MacArthur stated further that he saw no conflict between his order to field commanders and the directives sent to him from Washington, for the message from the Secretary of Defense of September 30 had given him "tactical and strategic latitude" in his operations north of the 38th parallel.[84] The JCS accepted this explanation and did not order any change.

This exchange of cables was significant. It was not the very first time that MacArthur took action on his own reinterpretation of JCS orders; but it was the beginning of a series of discordant differences between the two. Whether or not the Joint Chiefs were convinced that MacArthur was right in his judgment is unknown. At that moment there seemed to be obvious tactical military advantages in using maximum force. This required no elaborate explanation; no such obvious explanation was available as to why the remnants of a routed North Korean army plus some Chinese "volunteers" could repulse an attack by the ROK forces, however green. No explanation of this necessity was offered or, so far as is known, requested. The problem facing the Joint Chiefs was an awkward one: acting with the advice of the State Department and under the direction of the President they had sent directives to MacArthur that represented a partial compromise between a retention of all non-ROK troops south of the parallel and a use of all troops clear to the Yalu. The temptation to mop up quickly was great and the unwillingness to overrule the field commander perhaps even greater. Not only was it the strong tradition in the U. S. Army to give the widest latitude to generals in the field, but in this particular instance the strained relationship of some top military men, including the Secretary of Defense, with General MacArthur—a tension which had its origins as early as the 1930s—tended to make Secretary Marshall and the JCS reluctant to call CINCFE's hand. So far as is known JCS dropped the subject without asking for a ruling by President Truman.

Leaving aside the question of ultimate military effects, the political effects of MacArthur's drive were unfortunate, even though it is perfectly clear that the employment of non-Korean soldiers in the border provinces was not the cause of the Chinese intervention. The Chinese had announced that any non-ROK move north of the parallel would be fought and they may well have intended to attack even unattended ROK troops. They had crossed into North Korea on October 9, eleven days before the UN army had entered Pyongyang, and long before the border area had been reached. (Conceivably they had merely waited until the UN General Assembly took action on the British resolution on October 7, a resolution that called for abolition of North Korea, which was becoming, or perhaps had already become, their satellite rather than a satellite of the Soviet Union.) But the use of American and other non-Korean troops close to Manchuria, just like the use of these troops north of the parallel, gave the Chinese another argument to justify their intervention as a move in defense of their own borders—an argument which, whatever its merits, was most persuasive to millions of uncommitted Asians as well as to many people in Western European nations allied to the U. S. Moreover, the fact that General MacArthur made the decision unilaterally, without consultation with civil authorities, and that the U. S. government had permitted the decision to stand, without consulting the other nations involved in the Korean operation, was most disquieting to the governments of those nations who had promptly learned of MacArthur's actions. This was the first graphic demonstration of the inadequacy of the methods of consultation with other UN members participating in the Korean operation and the lack of participation by those nations in the decisions taken in "the crucial border line between operations and international politics."[85] As the situation in Korea in the fall of 1950 changed from a hopeful one to an increasingly grim one, there would be numerous other demonstrations of the shortcomings of the methods of inter-allied consultation and decision-making.

CHINESE INTERVENTION: THE FIRST ATTACK

The last two days of October saw the UN forces still advancing, but facing increasingly large bodies of Chinese troops. In the far northwest a battalion of the ROK Sixth Division, which had, on October 26, reached the frontier village of Changjin on the Yalu, found itself suddenly surrounded by a flood of Chinese troops who cut the ROKs off from their division far to the south. Only a few survivors of the battalion managed to beat their way back to friendly lines two days later to tell the story of the swarms of new enemy troops pouring into action. In the whole area of the Suiho hydroelectric plant along the Yalu, and just south of the frontier, ROK divisions encountered thousands of Chinese soldiers who hit the ROKs with powerful night attacks hurling

the South Koreans backward in rapid retreat to Unsan, forty-five miles south of the Yalu point reached two days before by the most advanced ROK units. The U. S. First Cavalry Division was hurried northward to Unsan to help the embattled ROKs. On October 31st, a Chinese regiment was identified, the next day Russian-made MIG-15 jets swept across the Yalu from Manchurian bases, made passes at UN planes and then scurried back across the border. On the same day elements of the 124th Division of the Chinese Communist forces were identified just south of the Changjin Reservoir.

On November 1, in spite of these reports about the heavy Chinese attacks, Major General John H. Church, commanding general of the U. S. Twenty-fourth Division, said that the "order of the day is full speed ahead for the Yalu River," and in Tokyo spokesmen at General MacArthur's headquarters refused to attribute the stiffening enemy resistance to the influx of Red Chinese troops.[86]

On November 2, two battalions of the U. S. Eighth Cavalry Regiment were attacked and overwhelmed by bugle-playing, tommy-gun shooting masses of Chinese infantrymen. Only relatively few American soldiers managed to fight their way out of the ambush. On the 3rd, General Church had apparently been forced to change his plans, for the Twenty-fourth Division, the most advanced unit of which had approached within fifteen miles of the Yalu, was now hightailing down the west coast road, retreating fifty miles to avoid Red tank attacks from the north. Elsewhere, in the Xth Corps zone on the east, Chinese suddenly appeared in the region between Hamhung and the Changjin and Pujŏn reservoirs where two important hydroelectric plants were located, and hit ROK troops. The U. S. First Marine Division, which had been engaged in mopping-up operations around Wonsan on the east coast where it had landed on October 15, was trucked northward to give the battered South Koreans muchneeded aid. By November 4, the First Cavalry Division had identified five Chinese Divisions in its sector and, in the east, the First Marines had spotted three more.

Yet even as late as this, there was little evidence that General MacArthur's headquarters was unduly disturbed by the rapidly changing complexion of the war. Indeed, it did not yet appear that the General was ready to agree that the war had changed, for he stated in an intelligence appreciation on November 4 that "while Chinese Communist intervention was a distinct possibility, sufficient evidence was not at hand to warrant immediate acceptance."[87] MacArthur added: "I recommend against any hasty conclusions which might be premature and believe that a final appraisement should await a more complete accumulation of military facts."[88]

"Military facts" were fast accumulating. On November 6, General MacArthur issued a communiqué in Tokyo in which he announced that he had evaded a "possible trap . . . surreptitiously laid" by the Chinese; and he added that while the North Korean forces had been destroyed, the UN army was now faced by a new and fresh army "backed up by a possibility of large enemy reserves and adequate supply."[89] On the same day, or the next, CINCFE sent a special report to the UN stating that UN forces were "in hostile contact with Chinese Communist military units."[90] Far off in Washington General Omar N. Bradley felt that the situation on the 8th Army's eastern flank was so precarious as Chinese poured into the battle on November 4-5 (WT) that "only diplomacy would save Walker's right flank."[91] Yet in MacArthur's estimate of the situation forwarded to Washington on November 7 (KT), the general continued to maintain the view that the Chinese were not making a full-scale intervention, but conceded the possibility that if the enemy build-up continued, they might be able to prevent any further advance and might even force a retreat of the UN army.[92] Washington at this time held the general view that the Chinese objective "was to halt the advance of the UN forces in Korea and to keep a Communist regime in being on Korean soil."[93] There was no flat disagreement, therefore, between the guessing of the theater commander and the policy-makers at home about Chinese intentions. In other words, on this question the men in the Far East and the men in Washington were equally in the dark.

Yet regardless of Chinese intentions, there was still the question of the military consequences of Chinese intervention, limited and total; and here there was a real difference between MacArthur and the military and civilian chiefs in Washington. The men in the Pentagon, the State Department building and the White House executive offices scanned the dispatches from Korea with growing uneasiness as they read of the division of CINCFE's forces into the 8th Army and Xth Corps and the further division of each of these into several unattached columns fanning northward into Korea in the face of increasing contacts with a strengthened enemy and the obstacles presented by logistical shortcomings and difficult terrain made more hazardous by the rapidly oncoming bitter Korean winter. General Bradley was not alone in his anxiety about Walker's right flank, and Xth Corps as well as 8th Army seemed to Washington to be in danger too. There were now more frequent meetings between State and Defense with Lieutenant General Matthew B. Ridgway standing before the situation map and Secretaries Acheson and Marshall along with the JCS and various assistants and deputies gathered around the table all trying desperately to figure out what General MacArthur was doing. The discussions were lengthy and frank, but frustratingly unproductive. Cables of inquiry and suggestions of caution were sent to the Far Eastern Commander and answered with bland assurance. The traditional independence of the theater commander, MacArthur's reputation and particularly his brilliant successes of September and October and the vast distance separating Korea from Washington made the men at home unwilling to hazard any new and forceful directive to the man directing the battle. Secretary Marshall and the Joint Chiefs asked Secretary Acheson to go to the President and recommend an order to CINCFE to halt his advance and consolidate his positions, but said that the military themselves would not make any recommendations. Acheson pointed out that he had discussed the matter with President Truman, but that he could not advise the President on military matters when the military leaders themselves were not ready to advise. Thus, in the end, nothing was done and the drama in Korea hastened to its tragic dénouement.[94]

As enemy soldiers poured across the Yalu from Manchuria, there was, unfortunately, no time for watchful waiting. On November 6, the same day he announced his evasion of the Chinese trap, General MacArthur determined to strike the Chinese at what he thought was the main point where they were funneling troops and supplies into Korea so he ordered a massive bombing strike by the Far East Air Force against the city of Sinuiju and the bridge across the Yalu to Antung, Manchuria. Because the Air Force had been ordered not to bomb within five miles of the Yalu River in order to avoid provocative action against the Chinese, the JCS were wired notice of the intended raid. The message was received on November 6 (WT). The Defense and State Departments immediately conferred on the matter and, while he was still discussing the raid with Under Secretary of Defense Robert Lovett, Secretary Acheson telephoned President Truman in Kansas City where he was staying the day before going to Independence, Missouri, to vote. Acheson told the President that the matter was so important that an immediate decision was necessary. Lovett had informed Acheson that he did not believe that the results to be achieved by the proposed raid would be important enough to risk bombing the Chinese city of Antung or other points in Manchuria. Assistant Secretary of State for Far Eastern Affairs Rusk noted that the U. S. had told the British that we would not take any action which might involve hitting Manchuria without consulting them. Moreover, there was a danger of involving Russia, which was bound by a mutual assistance treaty to come to Chinese aid in the event of an attack on China. The President told Secretary Acheson that he would approve the bombing if "there was an immediate and serious threat to the security of our troops."[95] At 11:40 A.M., November 6 (WT), just an hour and twenty minutes before the B-29s were scheduled to take off from their bases in Japan, the JCS cabled General MacArthur that "consideration was urgently being given to the Korean situation at the Governmental level," but that for the time being no targets within five miles of the Manchurian border were to be bombed. MacArthur was also asked to forward his estimate of the situation and his reasons for ordering the bombing along the Yalu.[96]

There was an immediate and alarming response to the JCS request. This message from MacArthur was sent only about three days after his message recommending that there be no "hasty conclusions" about the dangers of Chinese intervention, and about a day after the moderately apprehensive intelligence report, though that report had no doubt been prepared, and probably even approved, somewhat earlier. General MacArthur's reply was as follows:

7 November 50

Men and material in large force are pouring across all bridges over the Yalu from Manchuria. This movement not only jeopardizes but threatens the ultimate destruction of the forces under my command. The actual movement across the river can be accomplished under the cover of darkness and the distance between the river and our lines is so short that the forces can be deployed against our troops without being subjected to air interdiction. The only way to stop this reinforcement of the enemy is the destruction of these bridges and the subjection of all installations in the north area supporting the enemy advance to the maximum of our air destruction. Every hour that this is postponed will be paid for dearly in American and other United Nations blood. The main crossing at Sinuiju was to be hit within the next few hours and the mission is actually being mounted. Under the gravest protest that I can make, I am suspending this strike and carrying out your instructions. What I had ordered is entirely within the scope of the rules of war and the resolutions and directions I have received from the United Nations and constitutes no slightest act of belligerency against Chinese territory, in spite of the outrageous international lawlessness emanating therefrom. I cannot overemphasize the disastrous effect, both physical and psychological, that will result from the restrictions which you are imposing. I trust that the matter be immediately brought to the attention of the President, as I believe your instructions may well result in a calamity of major proportions for which I cannot accept the responsibility without his personal and direct understanding of the situation. Time is so essential that I request immediate reconsideration of your decision. . . .[97]

This message was read by General Omar Bradley to the President over the telephone and President Truman decided that, in spite of the dangers of provoking retaliatory action by the Chinese, MacArthur be authorized to order the strike against the Yalu area. The Joint Chiefs then wired to MacArthur that they agreed that the destruction of the Yalu bridges would contribute to the security of his forces "unless this action resulted in increased Chinese Communist effort and even Soviet contribution in response to what they might well construe as an attack on Manchuria." The bombing was thus authorized on November 7, but the Far East Commander was explicitly directed not to bomb dams or hydroelectric installations on the Yalu and he was urged to see that every precaution be taken not to violate Manchurian territory "because it is vital in the national interests of the U. S. to localize the fighting in Korea."[98] MacArthur was also asked to report promptly any hostile action from Manchuria and keep the JCS informed of important changes.

Sinuiju was devastated on November 8 by 600 tons of demolition bombs and 85,000 incendiaries dropped by 79 B-29s and 300 fighter-bombers. The railway bridge to Antung, however, was not destroyed because the B-29s were required by their instructions to remain over Korea and were forced to fly high to avoid heavy anti-aircraft fire coming from both sides of the Yalu River. The next day Navy dive-bombers scored direct hits, but did not completely destroy the bridge. In subsequent raids along the Yalu UN planes struck at other bridges and at the communication centers through which traffic from Manchuria was passing. Although the UN aircraft were severely handicapped by being required to strike only at the southern termini of the bridges and by the strict observance of the order that they fly only over Korean territory, the destructive results of the air strikes were very good. Destruction of the bridges, however, had no decisive effect on the Chinese attack. And within a week or two, the Yalu froze over hard enough to permit the Chinese to move even heavy equipment across the ice.

"HOT PURSUIT"

The UN air strikes along the Yalu aggravated another problem. For the first time in the war the complete supremacy of the UN in the air was challenged by enemy jet aircraft. Beginning on November 1, a week before the Sinuiju strike, Russian-built MIG-15 fighters shot across the border from Manchurian bases and attacked UN planes operating south of the river and then darted back into Chinese territory. On November 7, General MacArthur requested that the JCS give him instructions for dealing with "this new and threatening development." MacArthur pointed out:

The distance from the Yalu to the main line of contact is so short that it is almost impossible to deal effectively with the hit and run tactics now being employed. The present restrictions imposed upon my area of operation provide a complete sanctuary for hostile aircraft immediately upon their crossing the Manchurian-North Korean border.[99]

The JCS recommended that our planes be permitted to pursue Communist planes a few miles into Manchuria. The right of "hot pursuit" had been long established in international law and the rules of war and, while it had never been applied in such a situation as this, cogent argument could be made for such application. But the danger of enlarging the scope of the war loomed above all other considerations. In those days, immediately after the Chinese had intervened, there was considerable talk among the allies of the U. S. about setting up a "buffer zone" in the region along the Korean-Manchurian frontier in order to make it clear to the Chinese that the UN effort to pacify Korea involved no threat to Peiping's security. The Department of Defense, accordingly, discussed the question of "hot pursuit" with the State Department. Both departments and the President agreed that our planes should be permitted to pursue the Communist jets, but they felt that it would be desirable first to notify the other nations engaged in the UN operation in Korea that U. S. aircraft might shortly be permitted to engage in "hot pursuit" of enemy aircraft. On November 13, the Secretary of State transmitted a telegram to our envoys to six of the nations who were partners of the U. S. in the Korean action asking the ambassadors to discuss immediately the matter of "hot pursuit" with the Foreign Ministers. The Secretary of State pointed out that the concurrence of the governments involved was not being asked "because we believe the highly limited application of hot-pursuit doctrine in this situation would turn upon military necessity and elementary principles of self-defense, but we think it important that Government [to which you are accredited] be notified of the problem."[100] All six nations responded that they thought that the proposal was dangerous and not desirable and after these views were transmitted by the State Department to the Department of Defense it was determined by the two departments not to go further with the suggestion.[101] As Secretary Acheson indicated on several occasions at the Senate Hearings, the negative position of six "prominent and representative" nations was enough to forestall

American action, because it was highly desirable to maintain unity of action in Korea. In resolving the issues of "hot pursuit" and the bombing of the Yalu bridges, the U. S. government showed that in making "military" decisions, which previously the Unified Command had made alone, it felt that the views of its allies in the Korean enterprise had to be reckoned with, particularly when these other nations believed that the proposed military decisions might have very dangerous political implications.

It may be added that in the matter of "hot pursuit" the decision to honor the Yalu boundary apparently turned out to be one side of an implicit bargain rather than a gift to the Communists, for we too had our own "privileged sanctuary." Later on General MacArthur and many of his supporters in the great debate over ends and means in Korea did not mention the fact that the Communists had also fought under certain self-imposed limitations. And indeed, in a minority report on the Senate Hearings, a group of Republican senators stated in their discussion of limited war: "The enemy in Korea fought with no holds barred. They had no Navy or they would have used it. They had a small air force, which was steadily expanded as the war went on and the full strength of this air force was thrown into battle."[102] This is hardly a tenable position. If the Soviet Union wanted the North Koreans and Chinese to have a navy, they could have supplied it, just as they did furnish an air force and most of the other heavy equipment; the Russians could have permitted or ordered the use of submarines and other vessels in the waters around Korea and between Korea and the U. S. bases in Japan. Moreover, the Communists almost never used their air force against UN ground forces, supply depots, ports, railroads, and bridges or ships. Our ports operated at night fully illuminated and our battleships and carriers ranged up and down the enemy's coast freely attacking North Korean targets without fear of retaliation. It is pointless to speculate here on the enemy's motivation in so limiting his warfare—except perhaps to point out that the Communists, too, may have feared all-out war—but it is important to remember that they *did* fight under limitations that were quite as restrictive as our own.[103]

VI. ROUT IN THE NORTH

U. S. AND UN UNCERTAINTIES

While the UN forces were stubbornly beating off Red Chinese attacks, Western policy-makers were busily attempting to assess the new situation and to seek ways of preventing the spread of the conflict. The Central Intelligence Agency told President Truman that it estimated that the Soviets did not want a general war, but did want the U. S. to become so heavily involved in Asia that the Russians would have a free hand in Europe. CIA at this time judged that there might be as many as 200,000 Chinese Communist troops (presumably trained and organized forces) in Manchuria, who could stop our advance and even force a retreat. While Chinese intentions were uncertain, the CIA believed that the Chinese knew that their intervention put their prestige at stake, and were willing to risk all.[104]

On November 7, while "hot pursuit" was at issue, General MacArthur sent two messages, in which he again took the position that this was not "full-scale intervention," though it might cause "a movement in retrograde." This was MacArthur's justification for announcing his intention to assume the initiative to take "accurate measure . . . of enemy strength." He also used it as justification for requesting the Antung bombing and "hot pursuit."[105]

With all this material in hand, President Truman asked the Joint Chiefs to give him their views. On November 8, they recommended:

1. Every effort should be expended as a matter of urgency to settle the problem of the Chinese Communist intervention in Korea by political means, preferably through the United Nations, to include reasonable assurances to the Chinese Communists with respect to our intent, direct negotiations through our Allies and the Interim Committee [of the United Nations] with the Chinese Communist Government, and by any other available means.

2. Pending further clarification as to the military objectives of the Chinese Communists and the extent of their intended commitments, the missions assigned to the Commander in Chief, United Nations Command, should be kept under review, but should not be changed.[106]

The next day the National Security Council met to discuss these recommendations. General Bradley presented the views of the Joint Chiefs, stating that there were three possible intentions of the Chinese Communists. First, there was the possibility that the Chinese were concerned only with protecting their interests in the Yalu River hydroelectric works by setting up a buffer area. In this case, negotiations might be useful. Second, the Chinese might be seeking to involve the U. S. in a war of attrition where American forces would be so pinned down as to place the U. S. in danger of losing were the Soviets to decide to start a global war. Finally, the Chinese might be planning to drive us completely out of Korea. The Joint Chiefs felt that this last possibility would produce World War III, because the Chinese were incapable of doing it alone and the entry of the Russians would extend the conflict to every point of contact between the East and West. In his opinion, General Bradley stated, we should be able to maintain our lines somewhere in the area of our current positions but there would be a growing question of how much pressure our forces could stand without attacking the Manchurian bases. Such an attack, the Joint Chiefs felt, should be "a decision of the UN" because it went beyond the terms of the resolutions under which the UN forces were operating in Korea.

Secretary of Defense Marshall raised the point that the wide dispersion and thin spread of our eastern front in Korea produced an added risk. General Bradley replied that General MacArthur had spread his troops in order to carry out his directive to occupy all of Korea. Secretary Acheson then asked General Bradley whether there was any line which, from a strictly military point of view, would be better than the present one. Bradley answered that the further back the line was the easier it would be to maintain, but that any backward movement by the UN forces would discourage the South Koreans and might lose us their will to fight. It was agreed therefore, as Secretary Acheson stated when he summarized the discussion, "that General MacArthur's directive should not now be changed and that he should be free to do what he could in a military way, but without bombing Manchuria."[107]

What is surprising about this NSC meeting is that—as far as one can tell—no one present even suggested that the Chinese objective was none of the three alternatives listed by General Bradley, but rather, to use Secretary Acheson's words, "to halt the advance of the UN forces in Korea and to keep a Communist regime in being on Korean soil." A facing up to this possibility might have led to different conclusions.

During the two weeks following the November 9 meeting of the NSC, the hopes of the U. S. and its allies of conciliating the Chinese and preventing their full-scale intervention were encouraged by the fact that after their initial attacks the Chinese broke off action and appeared to have withdrawn. In some cases wounded UN soldiers were given medical care by the Chinese and left in the field to be recovered by their comrades. A handful of American and other UN troops who had been captured by the Chinese were released and permitted to drift back to their own lines. As early as November 8, the UN Security Council, meeting to consider the Chinese intervention, had invited Peiping to send a representative to discuss the Chinese position and, on November 10, the U. S., the U. K., France and three other nations introduced a draft resolution which had the purpose of giving both reassurance and warning to China. The resolution restated that UN forces would leave Korea as soon as unity and independence had been achieved. It also (1) called again upon all states to refrain from assisting the North Koreans and to bring about the recall of any of their nationals who attempted such assistance; (2) affirmed the inviolability of the Chinese-

Korean frontier; (3) called attention to the grave danger of the continued intervention by Chinese Communists; and (4) requested the Commission on Korea to assist in the settlement of frontier disputes between China and Korea.[108] The resolution was not brought to a vote until November 30, after the situation in Korea had again changed radically, at which time the Soviet Union vetoed the measure.

At the UN at Lake Success and at various Western capitals there was much talk about setting up a "buffer zone" in the Korean frontier provinces as further reassurance to the Chinese that the UN action in Korea presented no threat to Chinese interests or security.[109] On November 16, President Truman in his weekly news conference made a formal statement to the Chinese that the U. S. planned no invasion and, indeed, was doing everything within its power to localize the conflict in Korea. This announcement came a day after Secretary Acheson had assured the Chinese Communists that the U. S. would protect their interests in the power facilities along the Manchurian-Korean border.[110] Our allies were relieved by the apparent willingness of the American leaders to talk with the Chinese Communists, but the British feared that "a military impasse is arising in Korea that will force General MacArthur as a military man to let strategic necessities override diplomatic considerations."[111] Whatever the source of the British concern, it was not alleviated when General MacArthur declared that the idea of a buffer zone in Korea was impossible. Indeed, when UN troops in Northwest Korea resumed their advance on November 11, the UN Commander angrily denounced those sections of the English press which had stated that MacArthur had disregarded instructions suggested by the British government and approved by the American State Department to avoid a major clash with the Chinese.[112]

UN FORCES RESUME THEIR DRIVE

After the first Chinese attacks at the end of October and beginning of November and the revelation that whole Chinese divisions were committed, General Walker, who had initially tended to minimize Chinese strength, became considerably more apprehensive. He pulled back his forward elements to reform along the

Chongchon River where the main body of the 8th Army lay, and endeavored to secure more information on enemy strength and troop dispositions before advancing again. Walker also was keenly aware that his troops lacked adequate winter clothing and equipment and that logistical problems were becoming more complicated with each mile the UN forces moved north. Although intelligence reports were meagre, especially since ROK field agents had been demoralized and panicked by the first Chinese intervention, 8th Army felt quite convinced that the Chinese were undertaking a major build-up in the area between Unsan, where the first disastrous clash between the Americans and the Chinese had occurred, and Huichon to the northeast. As S. L. A. Marshall points out, G-3 of the 8th Army gave that area "sombre regard."

Its main idea was right. But its pin-pointing was off about the width of a lead pencil (on the average map) from the ground where the enemy was concentrating. A small difference—but decisive.[113]

Eighth Army Headquarters thus had the uneasy knowledge that important enemy concentrations were nearby, but the exact whereabouts of the enemy were not known and, quite as important, the enemy's intentions were completely obscure. The three interpretations held by the 8th Army of the objectives of the new enemy were: "(a) a limited assist to help the North Koreans hold a defensive base within their own country; (b) a show of force to bluff Eighth Army away from the Manchurian frontier; and (c) a screening movement to cover the advance of armies from behind the Yalu." All three were wrong, because the enemy armies were already in North Korea and close to the UN forces, having moved in as early as the middle of October.[114]

General Walker wanted time to reassemble his forces along the Chongchon, to resupply, winterize and absorb green troops. But CINCFE was impatient and, just as Walker ordered reorganization, orders came down from Tokyo to attack toward the Yalu as soon as possible. The 8th Army commander asked for more time—at least until November 15—pointing out that he was not yet fully reinforced and was facing great supply problems. By mid-November, Walker was still not ready and was still just as disturbed by the order to move ahead toward the Yalu, for there were no re-assuring changes in the intelligence picture.[115]

When the UN offensive was renewed, it edged forward very cautiously at first, both on the 8th Army western front and the Xth Corps eastern front. The advancing troops were amazed to find that they were meeting practically no resistance—the Chinese seemed to have disappeared and only small North Korean units were encountered. Allied morale mounted and caution disappeared as the troops on the northwestern front rolled ahead. In the Xth Corps' sector in the northeast the First Marine Division at first fought a tough battle against the Chinese at the frozen Changjin Reservoir, but then drove ahead on both sides of the huge lake and spoke optimistically of mounting a great attack over the high mountains along the central spine of Korea to outflank the Chinese who were facing the 8th Army in the west. In the meantime, the Seventeenth Infantry of the U. S. Seventh Division sped northward and on the 21st of November it stood on the banks of the Yalu at Hyesan, the first American troops to reach the border. As they looked across the frozen river to Manchuria, at the place which was supposed to be one of the chief crossing points for the Chinese, they saw no enemy troops. The Americans sat and waited for the rest of Xth Corps to catch up with them so that the occupation of northeastern Korea could be completed and the victory which appeared so imminent could be achieved. All the units of 8th Army and Xth Corps competed in the race northward; and they made no serious attempt to form a common line across northern Korea. The two organizations were under the separate commands of Lieutenant General Walton H. Walker, USA, and Major General Edward M. Almond, USMC, with the only liaison between them going through MacArthur's Tokyo headquarters.

On Thanksgiving Day, November 23, spirits were high as American soldiers ate their turkey with all the trimmings and talked of the "end of the war offensive" which was to start the next day. News of the coming offensive had been kept about as secret as a Hollywood premiere, and for several days before the commencement of the drive the allied newspapers had been predicting an attack by the 8th Army and had been describing the allied build-up, estimates of enemy strength and disposition of enemy troops. Early on the morning of the

24th, General MacArthur flew over to the battle area from Tokyo and flew along the Yalu conducting a personal aerial reconnaissance of the terrain. He then landed, just as the drive was about to start, and at an airstrip near the front he released a statement describing his strategy. He said that a "general attack" was under way, which, if successful, "should for all practical purposes end the war." To one of his field commanders the UN Commander said jocularly although confidently that he hoped the operation would get the American GIs home by Christmas. Unfortunately (in light of subsequent events), this remark later received wide circulation and detracted from the General's reputation.

When General MacArthur returned to Tokyo later in the day he found a communication from the JCS advising him "of the growing concern of other members of the United Nations of the possibility of bringing on a general conflict if the United Nations forces advanced and seized the entire North Korean area at the boundary between Korea and Manchuria and the Union of Soviet Socialist Republics." The message went on to say:

The consensus of political and military opinion in Washington was that there should be no change in CINCFE's mission; rather, a course of action should be formulated which would permit establishment of a unified Korea and at the same time reduce the risk of general involvement. On the assumption that the United Nations attack would be successful, exploratory discussions were held to discover what military measures and political actions might be taken to reduce the tension with the Chinese Communists and the Soviet Union and to maintain a solid United Nations front. The following measures were considered:

(a) After advancing to or near the Yalu, CINCFE might hold his forces in terrain dominating the approaches to the valley of the Yalu. These forces should be principally ROK troops. Other United Nations forces should be grouped in positions in readiness;

(b) United Nations forces would continue to make every effort to spare the hydroelectric installations in North Korea;

(c) The United Nations Unification and Rehabilitation Commission would, at a propitious time, enter into negotiations with appropriate representatives of the Chinese Communist Government in order to insure equitable distribution of hydroelectric power;

(d) In the event the Chinese forces did not again attack in force across the Yalu, elections in Korea could proceed in accordance with the action of the United Nations, and;

(e) The ultimate handling of the extremely sensitive northeast provinces would await United Nations procedures.[116]

The Commander-in-Chief, Far East, replied to the Joint Chiefs on the following day while the 8th Army's offensive was still rolling ahead unimpeded by any significant enemy resistance. General MacArthur said that the suggested approaches of the Joint Chiefs would, "in all probability, not only fail to achieve the desired result but would be provocative of the very consequence that we are seeking to avoid."

CINCFE felt it would be utterly impossible for the United Nations forces to stop on the commanding terrain south of the Yalu, as suggested. He also felt that it was necessary to destroy all enemy forces within North Korea if unity and peace in all Korea were to be restored. He also felt that the matter of the hydroelectric power would not be a major factor either to the Chinese Communists or to the Soviets. CINCFE stated that his plan was to consolidate positions along the Yalu River as soon as he was able and then to replace, so far as possible, American forces with those of the Republic of Korea. He would then announce his plans which would include:

(a) The return of the American forces to Japan;

(b) The parole of all POWs to their homes; and

(c) Leaving the matter of unification of Korea and the restoration of the civil processes of government to the people, with the advice and assistance of United Nations authorities.

He felt that as soon as United Nations military objectives had been reached prompt implementation of his plan would effectively appeal to the reason in the Chinese mind.[117]

THE CHINESE ATTACK EXPLODES

The JCS were prevented by circumstances from replying to General MacArthur's rejection of their suggestions, and, indeed, circumstances made the whole question of the deployment of UN troops along the border an academic one. On November 26, the day after MacArthur's reply and only two days after the UN offensive had commenced, 200,000 Communist troops hit the 8th Army. The Chinese poured through the central sector of Korea rolling back the ROK II Corps which held the right flank of the 8th Army line. After the ROKs broke and fell back, the Chinese, gathering up speed, hit the Americans at several different points hurling them back to the south—in speedy retreat if not complete disorder.[118] Before the Chinese temporarily broke off their attack, the 8th Army had retreated about forty miles. The Chinese then swung to the east and west cutting off any possibility of communication between the 8th Army and the Xth Corps.

In the eastern sector the First Marine Division up around the Changjin Reservoir and the Seventeenth Infantry Regiment of the U. S. Seventh Division up at the Yalu—both far in advance of other Xth Corps units—found themselves isolated by swarms of Chinese. An estimated ten Chinese divisions surrounded the Marines and part of the Seventh Division who were fighting to cut their way back to the coast. Two weeks of extremely bitter fighting under the worst conditions of winter weather brought the Marines and their Army comrades to the port of Hungnam from which place the whole Xth Corps was evacuated by the Navy in a magnificent amphibious operation in reverse. More than 100,000 soldiers, 91,000 Korean civilians, 17,500 military vehicles, and 350,000 tons of materiel were evacuated by the 193-ship task force. These troops were shipped south to Pusan and later moved up the Korean peninsula to reinforce the beleaguered 8th Army.

Until December 2, the fate of the 8th Army remained uncertain, since it appeared possible that the Chinese, if they could sustain their attacks, would be able to cut off the retreat of the UN forces. The shortcomings of the Communist logistical system, however, proved to be the salvation of the UN troops. The Chinese, as they were to do on several later occasions, were forced to break off their offensive after five days of heavy fighting, which respite enabled the battered 8th Army to reform its ranks and pull back in better order.

The UN retreat continued all through the black month of December and halfway through January 1951. The Communist capital of Pyongyang, which had become 8th Army's advance headquarters in November, was abandoned after vast stores of supplies were put to the torch on December 5. By mid-December, the UN troops were just north of the 38th parallel and by Christmas they had pulled generally south of the parallel and rested awaiting a new major Communist offensive. The enemy had been strengthened by the reappearance of the North Korean army which had been torn apart by the UN forces in October, but had been reassembled and re-equipped under Chinese supervision in December. Along with the other heavy blows the 8th Army received still another on December 22 when General Walker was killed in a jeep accident. The choice of Lieutenant General Matthew B. Ridgway as successor to Walker proved to be a wise one, for the tough former paratroop commander was just what the dispirited UN forces needed. Within an amazingly brief period of time Ridgway raised the morale of his command and eradicated the "bug-out fever" which had afflicted the soldiers in the December retreat.

VII. REFLECTIONS ON THE END-THE-WAR OFFENSIVE

Extensive post-mortems over the disastrous "end-the-war" offensive have no place here, but a few reflections are pertinent. In the first place, the question arises whether General MacArthur in launching the offensive, which was to carry the UN forces to the Yalu, was carrying out U. S. and UN policy. There is no clear-cut, black-and-white answer to this question. After the first Chinese attack, as has been noted, the leaders in Washington were worried, suggested caution, and requested information; but there were no definite instructions and no clear-cut replies. At the meeting of the National Security Council on November 9, it was decided to let MacArthur's directives stand. During the same period, when MacArthur wanted to bomb Sinuiju and the Antung bridge, he asked for permission, but he did so at the very last moment; and when his request was denied, his reply demanding reconsideration had the flavor of an imperative ultimatum. Later, after there had been an ominous quiet on the front and after our allies' fears had increased, the JCS sent a message on November 24th (KT) that proposed caution and new military and political measures. MacArthur's reply on the following day dealt loftily with both military and political problems, and indicated that he had no intention of delaying his offensive while the U. S. and its allies continued their deliberations. But the message from the Joint Chiefs of Staff was not an order and could not, therefore, be disobeyed.

In his testimony at the Senate Hearings, General Collins stated that the suggested line of halt was further north than General MacArthur had advanced at the time the Chinese made their mass attack, but Collins' denial that MacArthur had ever said that he could not be responsible for the security of his command if a decision was made to halt any place before the border was erroneous. Actually such a dire threat had been made in MacArthur's message of November 7 on the Sinuiju-Antung bridge bombing dispute; and his message of November 25 had said: "utterly impossible for the United Nations forces to stop on the commanding terrain." MacArthur had not communicated very extensively with Washington before proceeding with the attack. Yet the lateness of the Joint Chiefs' message (arriving as it did on the very day when the offensive was to start) indicates that there was still considerable hesitation on the part of the authorities in Washington in their dealings with him. In view of the fact that General MacArthur had once before (in the matter of using non-ROK troops in the border regions) taken things into his own hands and actually disobeyed an order, though not an absolutely precise order, and had on several occasions indicated impatience with the policies laid down in Washington, the Joint Chiefs might well have been more specific in their directives to the theater commander. However, General MacArthur's position as an American military leader was unique. He had tremendous prestige and great support among the American people, particularly in important political circles, and as American pro-consul in occupied Japan had displayed great independence of action. During the first nine months of the Korean War, General MacArthur, as Senator Morse put it in the Hearings, was "looked upon as a military prima donna,"[119] and the relations between MacArthur and the Joint Chiefs were uncomfortable. As Senator Wayne Morse went on to say:

As I listened to the witnesses in this case, and as I study the documents in this case, I somehow get the feelings that the human relationships, the man-to-man relationships, between MacArthur and his group, on one hand, and the Joint Chiefs of Staff and the Secretary of Defense and apparently the President, on the other hand, were relationships that properly would be described, as I described them in a comment or colloquy with General Marshall when he was on the stand, as dealing at arm's length, as showing a lack of what I would describe as a complete teamwork relationship, where there seemed to be the maximum degree of mutual confidence and trust, a feeling that I developed that General MacArthur was somewhat of a strict constructionist, a literalist, and questions in the committee constantly indicating, well, did you give him a mandatory order? Did you specifically say that? Did you specifically direct General MacArthur to do this or that?

The answer is to the effect that we didn't specifically, literally direct it, but a feeling that he ought to have understood what our policy was.

Had there been that mutuality of confidence and trust between the Government on this side and MacArthur's group on the other, a lot of these misunderstandings would not have occurred.[120]

Who or what was responsible for the failure to anticipate the massive Chinese intervention? As in most cases involving a variety of large governmental organizations, no simple answer is valid. It cannot, for example, be asserted that the failure was caused by the obvious lack of effective cooperation between the Pentagon and CINCFE—but it can be said that both would probably have proved wiser if they had been operating in an atmosphere of mutual confidence and harmony. What did the parties at interest know, how much did they learn from their knowledge? We have already mentioned some of the information received by the U. S. about Chinese movements and intentions,[121] but a few more words will be useful. At the Senate Hearings it was stated that General MacArthur was regularly furnished by Washington with summaries of intelligence reports on the Chinese and that the Far Eastern Command, in turn, sent back intelligence reports to Washington. General Collins said that about 90 per cent of our intelligence on the Chinese came from MacArthur's headquarters.[122] MacArthur's intelligence services labored under certain difficulties. When U. S. occupation of Korea ended in 1949 and it looked as if we were going to give up any attempt to defend Korea, our network of native agents disintegrated. A new network was being organized under the Far Eastern Command when the war started in the summer of 1950, and many of its agents were killed or taken prisoner. Eighth Army consequently undertook

to train new agents, thirty to forty of whom were attached to each division's intelligence section to roam behind enemy lines and return with information. Although it took time and effort to train the Korean agents and many of them were terrified by the first reports of Chinese intervention, some valuable information was secured by them and other agents and individuals coming out of China. The 8th Army published to its forces in early October the Chinese Communist order of battle along the Yalu River, a report which turned out to be remarkably accurate.[123] Aerial reconnaissance was limited to Korea itself and handicapped in the first few months of the war by lack of trained crews, production apparatus to process photographs, and skilled interpreters of the photos. Moreover, the Chinese forces, unburdened by heavy equipment, moved at night and were, as it turned out, amazingly skillful in concealing themselves by day. Whatever the shortcomings in gathering intelligence, it is clear that considerable evidence of a large-scale Chinese movement into Korea had piled up by mid-November. CINCFE's own tactical commanders were aware that the mountains harbored a force capable of destroying their scattered columns; MacArthur himself on November 6 in three separate communications (his special communiqué, special report to the UN and request for permission to bomb the Yalu bridges) spoke of the flood of men and materials pouring into North Korea from Manchuria which "not only jeopardize[d] but threaten[ed] the ultimate destruction of the forces under my command." Yet CINCFE and his intelligence staff within a fortnight of this alarm chose to ignore it and to put aside the apprehensions of the tactical commanders, and ordered an advance. Why General MacArthur chose to discount or forget such a jeopardy and such a threat is unclear; why he chose not to prepare at all for such an eventuality is baffling.

To turn from Tokyo to Washington: the State and Defense Departments were in continuous receipt of information from our own and foreign diplomats, from the Central Intelligence Agency and allied intelligence sources, and, finally, from reports sent in by MacArthur. All of these materials were, of course, assembled and evaluated, but there apparently was no very shrewd and incisive conclusion about

Chinese intentions. General Bradley stated in the Hearings that we had no warning that the Chinese would intervene—meaning the massive intervention of November 26 and after—only that they were concentrating in Manchuria and had the capability of entering the war;[124] but in fact, as so frequently happens, a pretty clear warning (at least by November 24, as is indicated below) was available to the leaders. They either overlooked it, distrusted it, or failed to take it very seriously. Since the capabilities rather than the intentions of other states are customarily and traditionally most important to the military, the JCS too failed to make full protective use of the information at hand concerning the Communist build-up. They did warn CINCFE and they did call to the attention of civilian policy-makers the hazards of a continued advance in Korea; but they were not sufficiently sure of their ground to be insistent. They were under no obligation to be bound by the State Department's notion that "it was more likely that [the Chinese] would not come in than that they would," because the Chinese stood to lose more ground in their international position than they might gain.[125] Yet President Truman reports in his *Memoirs* that the Central Intelligence Agency on October 20 delivered a memorandum to him saying that they had reports that the Chinese Communists "would move in far enough to safeguard the Suiho electric plant and other installations along the Yalu River which provided them with power." This, of course, was not a prediction of "massive intervention." But on November 6, CIA again reported to the President that the Chinese might have as many as 200,000 troops in Manchuria (and as was known by then in both Tokyo and Washington, there were additional Chinese troops inside Korea); and, finally, on November 24, the day the UN "last" offensive began, a national intelligence summary of the CIA stated that the Chinese would

. . . "at a minimum" increase their operations in Korea, seek to immobilize our forces, subject them to prolonged attrition, and maintain the semblance of a North Korean state in being. It also stated that the Chinese possessed sufficient strength to force the United Nations elements to withdraw to defensive positions.[126]

All these CIA reports were forwarded to General MacArthur together with other intelligence materials, but apparently he and his ad-

visers disbelieved them or discounted them;[127] on November 24 MacArthur told the press, without manifest concern, that the Chinese had about 30,000 volunteers and 30,000 regulars in Korea. Indeed, it was not until November 28 that he announced that an "entirely new war" had developed in Korea. Until then the sharp alarm he had evinced in the first week of November had evaporated; the "new war" concept was promulgated only after the devastating success of the brilliant Chinese ambush tactics had become apparent to all.

The Chinese have not made their archives available to enable us to determine when they made their decision to intervene and what was the basis for that decision. American policy-makers generally were in agreement after the Chinese attacked that the full-scale intervention of the Chinese was not provoked by the UN offensive of late November. Secretary Acheson summarized this view in a message to William J. Sebald, General MacArthur's political adviser, on December 7, 1950:

View advanced in number of other countries, both Asia and Europe, according to reports reaching Department, that Chinese Communists' onslaught Korea was merely responsive to imagined threat presented by United Nations offensive. This theory doubtless advanced in part as result natural human tendency when faced by unpalatable reality and hard decision to find formula reducing situation to comfortable dimensions and relieving one's self of need facing hard facts. As such, theory possibly impossible extirpate from credulous minds. Nevertheless, Department considers it important when you encounter such explanations you make it clear it is wholly at variance with the fact, it is unanimous considered judgment Joint Chiefs of Staff, supported by information from field commanders, the present Chinese offensive planned and staged over considerable period of time and that what happened is that two offensives collided.

Obviously it is fantastic to suppose that offensive involving half million men could have been prepared impromptu. Owing fact considerable displacement Chinese Communist units began a year ago, involving movement north of Lin Piao's Fourth Field Army, it is impossible to say when concentration for purpose of assault on Korea began, but reports reaching us May and June (prior to North Korean attack upon South Korea) from travelers arriving Hong Kong revealed railway traffic both north and south Hankow clogged with troop trains moving north. Appearance on Korean front of Chinese Communist troops of

Korean ancestry, as individuals and units, began during initial Korean assault and long before return to 38th parallel, indicating Peiping would in any case feel free to assert itself in Korea regardless of military situation.

Department now in receipt of unpublished report by neutral Asian journalist in Communist China written before offensive, which discloses that Communist China had by third week in November completed preparations for mass advance against United Nations forces in Korea designed to drive them back the length of the Peninsula regardless of the risk of general war and had secured pledge of Soviet assistance in event reverse suffered. Report contains eye-witness account of feverish movement of troops in readiness for invasion as early as second week in October of preparations for air raid defense in major north China cities recalling Jap days. This report paralleled from many other sources.[128]

With our forces engaged in desperate retreat, with all too many of our friends totally forgetful of their own support of the October 7 resolution, a calm, full, and dispassionate review of the situation would be too much to expect. Acheson's cable naturally was incomplete and therefore somewhat misleading.

Obviously the original North Korean attack was made in an effort to take over the whole peninsula (even the Communists dropped their fictions on this point early in the game) and it must have had Chinese Communist support or concurrence, for the Chinese government promptly announced its approval. And certainly the Chinese put their troops in position on the Yalu in no impromptu manner; indeed the November onslaughts were not intended as a mere slap in the face. Yet unresolved questions remain.

It will be recalled that on November 24 the CIA had predicted that "at a minimum" the Chinese would seek, *inter alia,* to "maintain the semblance of a North Korean state in being"—a prediction stated in even more decisive terms in Secretary Acheson's phrase "to keep a Communist regime in being on Korean soil." (As has been suggested, Secretary Acheson's testimony delivered eighteen months or so after the event may well have suggested as early November 1950 insights, ideas that emerged in effective form only after later hindsight was available.) In both cases, the statements are understatements. As best one can tell, the Chinese wanted not a "semblance" of

"a Communist regime," but a substantial Communist satellite on their flank.

If this assumption is sound, it would follow that the Chinese warnings about our crossing the parallel were not propaganda or bluffing, but serious. If we had stopped at the parallel, or near the parallel (the precise location of the boundary was never a matter of real concern in the armistice negotiations), might not the Chinese have adopted a defensive rather than an aggressive strategy? And perhaps also if we had stopped at the "waist"—which would still have left room for a substantial satellite country—as the proposal for a neutral zone did not?

Two more questions remain: Would the establishment of a unified non-Communist Republic of Korea have been accepted if the northern march to the Yalu had been carried on solely by ROK troops? If the assumption about the primary Chinese objective is sound, the answer is "certainly not"; but in such case, if the UN forces had stopped, say, at the waist, a Chinese or Chinese-North Korean attack might have halted there too. But we do not know. Is it not quite possible that the Chinese attempt to drive the UN off the peninsula was itself a "target of opportunity" move?

To return to Acheson's cable: it states the obvious when it says that "two offensives collided." But could, and should, the collision have been avoided? Could it have been deflected or reduced, and what were the political and military consequences? More specifically, assuming (as has been said) that the advance of non-ROK troops in the border provinces was not the cause of the intervention by the Chinese Reds, what, then, was the basis for the political criticism of MacArthur's decision? First, that it gave the Chinese a persuasive argument to use in justification of their intervention and served to arouse suspicion of American intentions among the peoples of uncommitted areas of Asia as well as in many West European countries. The Indian delegate to the UN, Sir Benegal N. Rau, stated at a meeting of the First (Political) Committee of the General Assembly on December 12 that General Wu Hsui-chuan, one of the Red Chinese who had come to the UN to discuss the Korean situation, had said in a conversation that China did not want war with the U. S. or the UN "but that the forces of the United

States and the United Nations were carrying on military operations near the Chinese border and thus a war had been forced upon the Chinese people."[129] And this line was parroted by the representatives of various Communist satellite states at the UN.[130] The second source of political criticism was the fact that among our allies the use of the UN forces created painful fears that we were reckless and unable to control MacArthur. The additional fact that this conclusion was in considerable part a distortion of history did not reduce the strain on the Department of State.

In retrospect, it appears that the advance of UN troops into the border provinces was not the primary issue. The real question (posed above) is whether the Chinese would have invaded, or, if they had crossed the Yalu, would have attacked us had we stayed near the 38th parallel or even further north at the Pyongyang-Wonsan line—the narrow "waist" of Korea? Secretary Acheson's cable to Sebald hardly meets this issue. Granted that the massive Chinese offensive of late November was well planned and well staged, would it have been executed had there been no major UN move northward? And the cable to Sebald fails to meet, or confuses, another issue: when the cable speaks of "the imagined threat presented by United Nations offensive," the statement is absolutely true if "offensive" is defined as an attack on China itself, but quite insubstantial if the Chinese defined "offensive" to include destruction of their (or the Russians') North Korean satellite—and this is just what their leaders had been saying since August. Perhaps it should be added that Acheson's views on this point were also held by almost all the American political and military leaders (not only by MacArthur) and were probably no wider of the mark than the views about a neutral zone and so forth held by many of our allies.

Quite aside from these questions, it is relevant to pause for a moment to consider what might have happened if the UN course of conduct had not put aside the potential dangers implicit in the Chinese attacks in early November. Even after the first Chinese intervention at that time, there might have been substantial UN political and military gains had MacArthur withdrawn his Xth Corps from northeast Korea and consolidated it with the 8th Army in a better defense line across Korea. He could then have conducted more extensive reconnaissance, could have sought further intelligence on Chinese movements and continued his aerial bombardment of the enemy build-up areas. He thus would have greatly weakened the Chinese pretext for intervention (though they might easily have devised another), would have made any Communist aggression far more naked and blatant, and would have avoided marching into the trap which he himself proclaimed the Chinese were laying.

Instead General MacArthur chose to gamble —and in this gamble he sought an objective that Washington desired—on pacifying all Korea before the Chinese were fully prepared to make their move or on overawing the Chinese, whose "Oriental psychology" he said he knew so well.

The massive intervention of the Chinese and their rout of the UN forces just at the time when victory appeared imminent badly shook the confidence of our allies in General MacArthur. This is in no way surprising; what is surprising is the unwillingness of the American people and their government to place the blame for the appalling defeat on the shoulders of the commanding general. Even five years later President Truman wrote: "Now, no one is blaming General MacArthur, and I never did, for the failure of the November offensive." Yet, the military dangers implicit in MacArthur's gamble had been perceived with painful clarity by the Joint Chiefs of Staff, who had expressed their concern both to the general and to the Commander-in-Chief, though they had failed to exercise their own powers or to ask the President to exercise his to prevent disaster.

The damage to MacArthur's military reputation led to serious damage to President Truman's position as a world leader—a damage that eventually spread to his reputation as a leader in his own country. He was promptly and severely criticized abroad for his acquiescence in MacArthur's bold offensive and his rejection of the more cautious policy urged by our leading allies. Leading newspapers in Great Britain and elsewhere in Western Europe denounced MacArthur (and by inference President Truman) and urged the UN not to give MacArthur a blank check in Korea.[131] The feeling of bitterness and frustration among our allies was doubtless intensified by the fact that they had never been fully consulted in the making of important decisions in Korea. Some of the UN members—our more important allies—had been consulted from time to time on military developments in Korea; they had concurred, for example, in the decision to cross the parallel: but on the basic issue of a bold advance vs. caution, their advice had not been actively sought or followed; and the rest of our allies had not been consulted at all. Those members of the UN who were participating in the operations in Korea, even though their degree of participation was a fraction of that of the U. S., felt that they ought to have more to say in the making of decisions since they were likely to suffer considerably from the consequences of a mistaken or imprudent one.

Perceiving this malaise among the participating members of the UN, in late November the U. S. began to hold weekly briefings in Washington of the representatives of the nations participating in the Korean operations. At these sessions of what later became known as the "Committee of Sixteen" the participants in the war were kept more fully advised of military developments, but they were not informed in advance of operations being planned by the U. S. and thus they were unable to make known to the U. S. their views on the political consequences which might follow such operations. Occasionally certain governments were given information through other and more confidential channels than the "Committee of Sixteen" in the fashion that they had been consulted on the matter of "hot pursuit" and thus were able to express their views to the U. S. Generally speaking, however, these methods of consultation were inadequate to the purpose of providing collective political guidance to the Unified Command.[132]

VIII.   THE NEW WAR: THE NEW OBJECTIVES

"We face an entirely new war," General MacArthur declared dramatically on November 28, 1950, in a special communiqué to announce the massive Chinese Communist attack. "This situation," the UN Commander continued, "repugnant as it may be, poses issues beyond the authority of the United Nations military council —issues which must find their solutions within the councils of the United Nations and the chancelleries of the world."[133] On the 3rd of December, when the dimensions of the Chinese onslaught had become even clearer, General MacArthur wired Washington for new instructions for dealing with the situation; after predicting that his army would be forced into successive retreats, or to retire to "beachhead bastion positions," he went on to say:

The directives under which I am operating based upon the North Korean Forces as an enemy are completely outmoded by events. The fact must be clearly understood that our relatively small force now faces the full offensive power of the Chinese Communist nation augmented by extensive supply of Soviet materiel. The strategic concept suitable for operations against the North Korean Army which was so successful is not susceptible to continued application against such power. This calls for political decisions and strategic plans in implementation thereof, adequate fully to meet the realities involved.[134]

Upon his return to the U. S. in April 1951, after his recall from command in the Far East, General MacArthur said that his plea for new directives and new "political decisions and strategic plans" fell on deaf ears in Washington, that the Administration did not adjust its policies to the new conditions and that he was consequently forced to operate without specific policies.[135] Actually, this was not the case. General MacArthur confused the Truman Administration's failure to accept his own recommendations for new policies (which would have expanded the conflict to the Chinese mainland) with a failure to adopt any new policies at all. A new military directive was sent to the Far Eastern Commander on December 3rd, the day his request for a new directive had been received. The Joint Chiefs, with the approval of the President, told General MacArthur:

We consider that the preservation of your forces is now the primary consideration. Consolidation of forces into beachhead concurred in.[136]

General Collins, the Army Chief of Staff, was, on the same day, ordered to fly to the Far East to make a personal estimate of the situation.

The general reassessment of Far Eastern policies took more time, but it had commenced at about the same time as the new military directive had been sent to MacArthur. The reassessment (apparently concurred in by all the agencies and most if not all of the senior officials concerned) concluded that China's action in Korea was only a part of a global Communist strategy, *ergo* that the Soviet Union was willing to risk global war. Conclusions of this sort are not subject to proof or disproof: A decade later, however, the Chinese offensive seems more like an action taken in the Chinese national interest (as that interest was defined in Peiping), though quite consistent with Sino-Russian hopes for global Communist domination.

Right or wrong, the conclusion that the Chinese attack opened up the possibility of global war in the immediate future paved the way for a momentous series of actions. On December 1, President Truman asked for a vast expansion of the armed services, and on December 16 he declared a national emergency. Two days later, he announced the appointment of General Eisenhower, then President of Columbia University, as SCAPE (Supreme Commander, Allied Powers, Europe—an appointment agreed on in October but highlighted now as part of a large-scale movement to rebuild the free world's defenses.[137] These actions were followed by many others in which the Korean War became the trigger for a new national and international defense structure, one maintained throughout the rest of the Truman Administration. In retrospect, perhaps, the by-products of the Korean War may seem more important than the Korean actions themselves; but speculation along these lines is irrelevant here.

To return to the immediate Korean problems of the dismal winter of 1950: On November 30, President Truman at a press conference made a statement which permitted the newspapers to give the world the impression that the use of the atomic bomb against the Chinese was being considered by the Administration. Already extremely jittery, Western Europe now became understandably panicky at the prospect of being caught in the middle of an all-out atomic attack on Russia's Chinese allies. In response to public pressure Prime Minister Attlee flew to Washington on December 4 to confer with President Truman. All that emerged publicly from the conference was assurance that the reports that the atomic bomb would be used were false and the reassurance that Western Europe would not be abandoned by the U. S. But privately a significant development occurred, for the groundwork was laid for a shift of objectives in Korea. The President and the Prime Minister agreed that the conflict should remain limited to Korea and that the UN ought to hold out in Korea— even on beachheads—as long as possible. In the December 7 meeting of the two leaders Secretary Acheson pointed out that there was not very much that could be done to Communist China unless we wished to engage in all-out war. The matter of negotiating with the Chinese then arose and Mr. Attlee suggested that perhaps the negotiations could be limited to keeping the Communists behind the 38th parallel.[138] This appears to have been the first serious discussion of returning to the original war aim expressed in the June 25 resolution— repelling aggression in the narrow sense—and dropping the idea of the October 7 resolution of attempting to promote by force of arms the political objective of establishing a unified and independent Korea, or even the military objective of the June 27 resolution of destroying all aggressor troops.

The next step in the public retreat from the objectives of the General Assembly's October 7 resolution (including both unification and destruction of aggressor troops) came on December 14 when the General Assembly adopted a resolution proposed by thirteen Asian and Middle Eastern states requesting that the President of the General Assembly constitute a group of three persons including himself to determine the basis on which a satisfactory cease-fire in Korea might be arranged. General Assembly President Nazrollah Entezam of Iran appointed Lester Pearson of Canada and Sir Benegal N. Rau of India to serve on the group and, on December 15, the Cease-Fire Group consulted representatives of the Unified Command as to what they considered a satisfactory basis for a cease-fire. The details of the suggestions emerging from this consultation do not concern us here. What was important was the willingness, even eagerness, for the most part, of the UN members fighting in Korea to settle on a return to the *status quo ante bellum* —the 38th parallel—as a cease-fire line. On December 11, while the cease-fire resolution was still under consideration at Lake Success, President Truman discussed the resolution with the National Security Council and stated that he did not believe that we should agree to a cease-fire without first arriving at terms. To this Vice President Barkley replied that the U. S. should not be maneuvered into a position where we might be accused of opposing a cease-fire. The President apparently was persuaded to accept this view as the U. S. voted three days later for the resolution. On the other hand, when General Bradley inquired at the NSC meeting if orders should go out to General MacArthur to pull back to the 38th parallel, the President replied in the negative and stated that our present position ought to be held "as tenaciously as possible" until the cease-fire agreement had been arrived at. The present directive to General MacArthur, President Truman added, was still adequate and effective.[139]

Although the Chinese on December 22, emboldened by their successful offensives, rejected the cease-fire proposal except on their own terms, the basis for future negotiations with the 38th parallel as the truce line had been established. In December 1950, Chinese Premier Chou En-lai in a statement ironically reminiscent of statements by Bevin, Austin, MacArthur and many others, and eventually equally ineffectual, declared that the parallel had been "obliterated forever" as a "demarcation line of political geography." This was when the Chinese appeared to be on the way to driving the UN forces to the sea, but by the summer of 1951, after the Chinese had been badly mauled by the UN troops, they were again willing to accept the parallel as a truce line.

EVACUATION DEBATED

The grim picture in December and early January forced consideration of the possibility of evacuating the UN forces from Korea. During the Senate Hearings there was considerable discussion between Administration and anti-Administration forces in a fruitless attempt to ascertain who had first suggested the possibility of withdrawing from Korea. It is pointless to continue the investigation of the question here. This is no matter of "innocence" or "guilt," for, in light of the determination of the U. S. to localize the conflict and the belief of our policy-makers that committing ever larger numbers of troops to the Korean War would merely weaken our European commitments and thus play into Communist hands, our policy-makers could not sensibly avoid making plans for the contingency of a forced withdrawal from the Korean peninsula. The record shows that General MacArthur (for quite different reasons) and the Administration in Washington gave a great deal of attention to the question during this period. The attitudes reflected by this discussion shed light on subsequent developments in our policy in Korea.

The possibility of evacuating the UN forces from Korea was first broached as early as the 29th or 30th of November when Admiral Forrest Sherman notified Vice Admiral C. Turner Joy, the U. S. naval commander in the Far East, that he assumed that shipping would be held in the Far East "because of the obvious possible requirements" of an evacuation.[140] Whether Sherman was thinking of total (or maximum) evacuation to Japan or large-scale evacuation from one Korean port to another (like the Hungnam operation, soon to take place) is not known.

Although General Collins, who had flown to the Far East on December 4, reported that the 8th Army could "take care of itself," the situation in general grew grimmer with the advance of December. It was not only the pressure of the Chinese in Korea that accounted for the gloom, but also what appeared at the time as a very real threat of Soviet moves in Europe or Asia;[141] this was not the first emergence of anxiety, for the limitations in the directive of September 27 show the same concern. On December 19, General MacArthur wired urgently for reinforcements, whereupon Secretary of Defense Marshall and the JCS held a series of discussions with State Department officials. The military leaders thought that it was necessary to consider ways of withdrawing from Korea "with honor" in order to return our troops to Japan, the defense of which was our chief commitment in the Far East. The JCS pointed out that all combat-ready American divisions but one were now committed either in Korea or in Europe so that there were none available as reinforcements for Korea. The State Department opposed the proposal to evacuate Korea, saying that we should not retreat unless we were forced out. Anything less, the Department insisted, would be abandoning the principle that originally prompted our intervention.[142]

Toward the end of December, the Joint Chiefs again took up the matter of drafting a new directive to General MacArthur. A draft of the directive was sent on December 27 by Secretary Marshall to Secretary Acheson and on the evening of that day the draft was discussed by the President, Acheson, Marshall and Bradley. On the 28th, Secretary Marshall, Assistant Secretary of State Dean Rusk and General Bradley conferred on the draft, and, finally, on the morning of the 29th, Rusk and Bradley again discussed the directive.[143] The new order was sent to the Far East Commander that same day and stated:

Chinese Communists now appear, from estimates available, capable of forcing evacuation by forces of UN. By committing substantial United States forces which would place other commitments, including safety of Japan, in serious jeopardy, or by inflicting serious losses on him, enemy might be forced to abandon exercise of his capability. If with present UN strength successful resistance at some position in Korea without our incurring serious losses could be accomplished and apparent military and political prestige of Chinese Communists could be deflated, it would be of great importance to our national interests. In the face of increased threat of general war JCS believe commitment of additional United States ground forces in Korea should not be made, since our view is that major war should not be fought in Korea.

Not considered practicable to obtain at this time significant additional forces from other United Nations. Therefore in light of present situation your basic directive, [to] furnish to ROK assistance as necessary to repel armed attack and restore to the area security and peace, is modified. Your directive now is to defend in successive positions, subject to safety of your troops as your primary consideration, inflicting as much damage to hostile forces in Korea as is possible.

In view of continued threat to safety of Japan and possibility of forced withdrawal from Korea it is important to make advance determination of last reasonable opportunity for orderly evacuation. It appears here that if Chinese Communists retain force capability of forcing evacuation after having driven UN forces to rear it would be necessary to direct commencement of your withdrawal. Request your views on those conditions which should determine evacuation. You should consider your mission of defending Japan and limitation on troops available to you. Definite directive on conditions for initiation of evacuation will be provided when your views are received.[144]

This new directive represented a significant change in policy. It did not even mention unification, the key objective of the UN resolution of October 7; and it specifically "modified" the two more military objectives that had been spelled out in the UN resolution of June 27 and the JCS directive of September 27—repelling aggression and restoring peace and security to the area. As a new goal, it stressed the importance of successful resistance in Korea with "present UN strength," and orderly evacuation if necessary. It made clear that the defense of Japan was more important than the defense of a UN position in Korea, though the maintenance of our position in Korea would be extremely valuable. Finally, the directive emphasized the importance of inflicting as much damage on the aggressors as possible—in other words carrying on as long as possible a war of attrition against the Communists even if evacuation could not be permanently avoided.

MacARTHUR'S PROPOSED NEW POLICY

The Far Eastern Commander replied to the JCS on the same day:

He pointed out that United States naval and air potential was being only partly utilized and that the potential of the Chinese Nationalists on For-

mosa and guerrilla action on the mainland were being ignored.

Further, were the Government to make a political determination to recognize the state of war forced upon the United States by China and to take appropriate retaliatory measures, the United States could—

a. Blockade the coast of China;
b. Destroy through naval gunfire and air bombardment China's industrial capacity to wage war;
c. Secure appropriate reinforcements from the Nationalist garrison on Formosa; and
d. Release existing restrictions upon the Formosa garrison for diversionary action (possibly leading to counter-invasion) against vulnerable areas of the Chinese mainland.

After pointing out the advantages of such action, he stated his consciousness of the fact that this course of action had been rejected in the past for fear of provoking China to a major war effort, but that there was nothing that could be done in any event to aggravate the situation vis-à-vis China. He admitted that Soviet military intervention was a matter of speculation, but gave his opinion that the Soviets would act on the basis of their own estimate with little regard for other factors. His recent request for reinforcement by four divisions had as its purpose the defense of Japan in the contingency of Soviet attack. Further, a forced evacuation from Korea without retaliatory action against China would have a most adverse effect upon the peoples of Asia, including the Japanese, and the eventual result of such action would call for an even greater reinforcement of the forces in the Far East. He understood the demand for European security and concurred in doing everything possible in that sector short of the point of accepting defeat everywhere else. Accepting defeat everywhere else, however, could not fail to insure later defeat in Europe itself. He concurred in the Joint Chiefs of Staff tactical estimate of the Korean situation under the conditions implied; namely, no reinforcements; restrictions on Chinese Nationalist action; no military measures against China; and the concentration of Communist China's military forces in the Korean sector. The tactical plan of successively contracting defense line to the Pusan beachhead would appear to be the only way in which an evacuation could be accomplished. In such an eventuality, it would not be necessary for the Joint Chiefs to make an anticipatory decision.[145]

Although the Joint Chiefs took General MacArthur's reply under immediate consideration, no answer was sent to him until January 9. In the meantime, developments in Korea pointed to an even more imminent withdrawal than had been anticipated. On New Year's Eve the Communists, in greater strength than in their offensive of November 26, launched a new drive against the UN lines north of Seoul.[146] Against these tremendous odds, the 8th Army pulled back and retreated in fairly good order across the Han River, abandoning Seoul for a second time on January 4. As was the case in their previous offensives, the Chinese main attack waned after five days, but two Chinese "armies" (actually roughly the equivalent of two small American army corps) along with some eleven North Korean divisions pursued the 8th Army beyond the Han. Inchon, whose port facilities had been partly rebuilt, was scorched and abandoned, the big Kimpo Air Base was similarly put to the torch by retreating UN troops, and finally, a second air base at Suwon was also evacuated on January 7 in the retreat southward. By January 8, the situation looked very grave as Communists drove a deep wedge into the UN line east of the town of Wonju, forcing the American Second Infantry Division out of the town and threatening to isolate the division and its attached units. Here, however, on January 8-9, the tide began to turn; General Ridgway had been in command only about two weeks, but his leadership was having its impact. "Bug-out fever," the urge to take off for the rear, which had so sorely afflicted UN troops in December, had been replaced by a new will to stand and fight. The Second Division and its attached French and Dutch battalions counter-attacked south of Wonju, driving back into the town which was forty-five miles south of the 38th parallel and the gateway to the mountain passes leading to Taegu and Pusan. The UN forces then suddenly withdrew, luring the Communists back into the town, which was then heavily bombarded by UN planes. The North Korean divisions were badly wounded and their hitting power greatly diminished, whereupon the Second Division along with other UN units was able to make an orderly withdrawal to straighten their lines and to improve their positions for meeting future Communist attacks.

The Wonju victory was minor in itself and the UN Command was well aware that the Communists could be expected to launch another major assault, but Wonju gave confidence to the UN troops when they badly needed it and showed that they could still put up a fight. Nevertheless, as the 8th Army's divisions dug in on a line across the Korean peninsula fifty to sixty miles south of the 38th parallel in preparation for the next enemy attack, they knew that further retreats might be necessary and they established their divisional rear headquarters far to the south of their lines.

On January 9, while the Wonju battle was raging and the news from Korea was still very depressing, the JCS notified General MacArthur, with President Truman's approval, that however much the assaults of the Chinese Communists had changed the situation in Korea "other considerations . . . required us to maintain our present policy in Korea." The measures against China, which MacArthur had recommended in his message of December 30, were still under consideration, but for the present MacArthur was to continue to inflict as much damage as possible on the enemy, and defend successive positions; and since the primary consideration was the safety of his troops and the protection of Japan, "if it should become evident, in his judgment, that evacuation was essential to avoid severe losses of men and matériel, then he was to withdraw to Japan."[147]

General MacArthur's reply on January 10 was deeply disturbing to the President and his advisers, for, as Truman has said in his *Memoirs,* "the Far East Commander was, in effect, reporting that the course of action decided by the National Security Council and by the Joint Chiefs of Staff and approved by me was not feasible."[148] MacArthur asked for clarification of the January 9th directive and pointed out that his present strength was inadequate to the double task of holding a position in Korea and protecting Japan and that a choice of strategies must rest on "the relativity of American interests in the Far East." A beachhead line could, indeed, be held in Korea but not without heavy losses. The General went on pessimistically to describe the condition of his troops who, he said, were embittered by "the shameful propaganda which has falsely condemned their fighting qualities and courage in misunderstood retrograde maneuver," and were tired from the tough fighting. Unless "the political basis upon which they are asked to trade life for time is clearly delineated," the General warned, his soldiers would become so demoralized as to lose their efficiency. MacArthur then made his recommendation to withdraw from Korea unless there were overriding political considerations:

I am in full agreement, as I stated in my message of December 30 [29] in reply to your message of the same date, with your estimate that the conditions and limitations, namely: no reinforcements, no measures permissible against China's continental military potential, continued restrictions upon Chinese Nationalist military action, and the concentration in the Korean-Manchurian sector of China's military force, will eventually render untenable the military position of the command in Korea. In the absence of overriding political considerations, under these conditions the command should be withdrawn from the peninsula just as rapidly as it is feasible to do so. If, on the other hand, the primary political interests of the United States in the Far East lies in holding a position in Korea and thus pinning down a large segment of the Chinese military potential, the military course is implicit in political policy and we should be prepared to accept any attendant hazard to Japan's security and whatever casualties result.

The issue involves a decision of highest national and international importance, far above the competence of a theater commander guided largely by incidents affecting the tactical situation developing upon a very limited field of action, and really boils down to the question of whether or not the United States intends to evacuate Korea. Nor is it a decision which should be left to the initiative of enemy action which would in effect be the determining criterion under a reasonable interpretation of your message. Therefore my query amounts to this: Is it the present objective of the United States political policy to minimize losses by evacuation as soon as it can be accomplished; or to maintain a military position in Korea —indefinitely, for a limited time?

Under the extraordinary limitations and conditions imposed upon the command in Korea, as I have pointed out, its military position is untenable, but it can hold, if overriding political considerations so dictate, for any length of time up to its complete destruction. Your clarification requested.[149]

A gloomier or more disturbing message could hardly have been sent. MacArthur was saying in effect that the only proper military action— given the limitations— would be a prompt withdrawal from Korea; that if a holding operation was desirable for political reasons, eventually it would result in the destruction of his forces and create an attendant hazard for Japan. And, to give a final turn to the screw, he attributed

the conclusion that Korea was absolutely untenable under the circumstances to the JCS and implied that he had merely concurred in their conclusion—a reading of the JCS message of December 29 and his reply of December 30 that must have amazed the Joint Chiefs. It is true that their opening sentence (based largely, of course, on MacArthur's messages and announcements) indicated that the Chinese seemed to have the strength to force us out of Korea, but later in the cable they specifically referred to the *"possibility* of forced withdrawal." [Emphasis supplied.]

MacArthur's cable was clearly not a mere military problem. The JCS promptly started consultations with representatives of the State Department on January 11 and 12, and on the 12th the President called a special meeting of the NSC to discuss MacArthur's pessimistic report and recommendations. A new directive to General MacArthur was discussed and dispatched (quoted below) and it was decided that the President also would send a personal message to the general "bringing him up to date on our foreign policy."[150] The NSC also discussed a memorandum of the JCS listing sixteen points of possible action, which the Joint Chiefs had had under study for some time and had tentatively agreed should be put into operation were the UN forces pushed out of Korea or confined to a narrow perimeter around Pusan with no chance of breaking out. Four of the sixteen points were General MacArthur's often-repeated suggestions for retaliatory action against China and the other twelve included diplomatic, economic and military measures concerning much of the Far East, only a few of which were made public at the Senate Hearings.[151] A copy of the memorandum was carried to General MacArthur for his information by General Collins who, with General Vandenberg, left for Korea on the evening of the 12th to get a first-hand view of the situation. Some of the measures—economic sanctions against China, branding China as an aggressor, enlarging the American military training mission to the Chinese Nationalists and increasing Mutual Defense aid to Formosa—were ultimately carried out, but others were held in abeyance as the military situation in Korea improved during the winter and spring of 1951 and in the opinion of the JCS made the other actions unnecessary. General MacArthur, however, overlooking or forgetting the tentative nature of the proposals, and the fact that these were proposals, and did not constitute an approved or even a recommended policy, assumed, then or later, that the courses of action which were not followed out had been vetoed or disapproved by Secretary Marshall, Secretary Acheson or some other high authority, and bitterly attacked this alleged interference with "military affairs" in his speech to Congress after his recall from Korea and in his testimony before the Senate Committees.

The actual directive sent by the Joint Chiefs to General MacArthur on January 12 was quite different; it stated:

We are forced to the conclusion, based upon all the factors known to us, including particularly those presented by you in your present message, that it is infeasible under existing conditions, including sustained major effort by Communist China, to hold the position in Korea for a protracted period.

It would be to our national interest, however, and also to the interest of the UN, before you issue firm instructions for initiation of evacuation of troops from Korea, to gain some further time for essential military and diplomatic consultations with UN countries participating in Korean effort.

It is important also to future of UN and NATO organizations, to the United States' prestige worldwide, and to efforts to organize anti-Communist resistance in Asia that maximum practicable punishment be inflicted on Communist aggressors and that Korea not be evacuated unless actually forced by military considerations.[152]

The Commander-in-Chief, Far East, was thus authorized to withdraw his command from Korea if and when his troops were pushed back to the old Pusan beachhead and if it appeared to him that the security of his forces was endangered. Presumably the first sentence was drafted to shift the authorship of the prophecy of doom from the JCS to MacArthur—a response, in effect, to MacArthur's attribution of responsibility for the prophecy to the JCS in his cable of January 10.

On the next day, at what appeared to be the darkest moment of the war, President Truman sent a long telegram to General MacArthur to explain to him how and why our national interests and international purposes would be served by continuing our resistance in Korea. Successful resistance, said the President, would demonstrate that the U. S. and the UN would not accept aggression and would rally the free world to meet the world-wide threat of the Soviets. It would give the free world time to organize its defense against the Communists and would lend resolution to those nations who live in the shadow of Communist power and let them know that they need not appease the Communists. Resistance against this Communist aggression would inspire those who may in the future be called upon to fight against a sudden onslaught by Russia or China. It would prick the inflated military and political prestige of Communist China which endangered the resistance of non-Communist Asia, inside and outside of China.

The President went on to point out that our policy must be one that would "consolidate the great majority of the United Nations" and gain support of all the countries whose support we would need in the event the Soviets move against us. Thus we must avoid extending the area of hostilities at least until our own national strength is built up. "Steps which might in themselves be fully justified," Truman stated, "and which might lend some assistance to the campaign in Korea would not be beneficial if they thereby involve Japan or Western Europe in large-scale hostilities."

Finally, the President turned to the possible evacuation of Korea and said that if that eventuality came, then the purposes mentioned above might be served by continued resistance from some of the offshore islands of Korea. "In the worst case," Truman added, "it would be important that, if we must withdraw from Korea, it be clear to the world that that course is forced upon us by military necessity and that we shall not accept the result politically or militarily until the aggression has been rectified."

The conclusion of President Truman's letter was a vivid illustration of the President's total acceptance of the Army notion that Washington must always back the general-in-command. Presumably our military good guidance and good luck in the Spanish-American War and World Wars I and II had blotted out the painful memories of the absolute necessity of Lincoln's turn-over policy until he finally found Grant. What Truman said was: "The entire nation is grateful for your splendid leadership in the difficult struggle in Korea and for the superb performance of your forces under the most difficult circumstances."[153]

NEW UN RESOLUTIONS: TURN OF THE TIDE IN KOREA

The pessimism of early January also pervaded the UN at Lake Success and the cold fear that the war might spread led the majority of members to seek peace in Korea even at the price of appeasement. The General Assembly consequently adopted, on January 13, by a 50-7 vote, a new peace plan which had been proposed by the three-man Cease-Fire Group. The five points called for:

1. An immediate cease-fire in Korea with guarantees against use of the truce as a screen for mounting a new offensive.
2. Action during the truce on a permanent Korean settlement.
3. Withdrawal of "non-Korean" troops by "appropriate stages."
4. United Nations-approved administration of all Korea during the truce.
5. Creation of a special United Nations agency, including Red China, Russia, Britain, and the United States, to settle outstanding Far Eastern issues, including the future of Formosa and Chinese representation in the United Nations.[154]

Despite the fact that the peace plan, with its implicit surrender to China on UN membership and to some extent on Formosa, contradicted American policy, our UN delegate, Warren Austin, was directed by the State Department to vote for it to show that the U. S. desired peace and would go along with its Western allies. A tremendous blast of public and Congressional disapproval followed the UN decision. Even Democrats joined with Republicans in stigmatizing Secretary Acheson as an appeaser or worse.

The Secretary of State, however, maintained his usual aplomb. His confidence in his course was quickly justified when the Chinese reply to the peace proposals was received on January 17. The Chinese made inacceptable demands—just as Acheson had expected—which demonstrated their aggressive intentions and helped the United States in its move to get the UN to brand China as an aggressor. The Chinese demanded among other things immediate seating in the UN and insisted that negotiations on Korea commence before a cease-fire. Acheson termed the Chinese reply a complete rejection of the UN proposal and said that it was now clear that the Chinese intended to continue their defiance of the UN. He instructed the

U. S. delegation to press for a UN resolution branding China as an aggressor. On January 19, the House of Representatives passed a resolution which called on the UN to act and on the next day our delegation at Lake Success introduced the draft resolution naming China an aggressor for rejecting the cease-fire proposal, but significantly at the same time affirming the policy of seeking by peaceful means, the achievement of the UN's political aims in Korea and requesting the President of the General Assembly to appoint a Good Offices Committee to work to that goal.

For ten days, action on the American resolution was delayed as the British, Canadian and Arab-Asian bloc delegates, who had refused to consider the Chinese reply rejection of the peace plan, hopefully endeavored to secure some "clarification" by the Chinese of their stand. All that Peiping would concede was a vague assurance that a cease-fire for a limited period might be agreed upon at the first meeting of the proposed conference, but they continued to insist on admission to the UN and the settling of all outstanding Far Eastern problems as conditions for the conclusion of the war.[155]

While these maneuvers were taking place at Lake Success, the situation on the Korean battlefields was changing. Not only had the Communist drive southward been halted as their vulnerable communications were pounded by UN air power, but the 8th Army had launched local attacks which had gained considerable ground by January 17 and gave promise of future gains. Generals Collins and Vandenberg along with General Walter Bedell Smith, the director of the Central Intelligence Agency, who had flown to Korea to investigate the situation, left on the 17th assured that the UN forces could hold out indefinitely and that there was no longer any reason to consider evacuation. By January 20, General MacArthur had also regained his confidence and announced: "No one is going to drive us into the sea. This command intends to maintain a military position in Korea just as long as the statesmen of the United Nations decide we should do so."[156]

On February 1, the General Assembly, encouraged by the news from the front, passed by a 44-7 vote the American resolution condemning China as an aggressor. Because there was still among members of the Arab-Asian bloc a desire for conciliation and a hope that it could be attained, the U. S. had tempered the resolution to appeal to this group of nations. In its final form the measure, after condemning China, and calling on her to end her aggression and reaffirming the UN's determination to continue its action in Korea against the aggressor, called for a Committee composed of members of the Collective Measures Committee to consider additional measures (economic sanctions for example) to be employed to meet the aggression and to report thereon to the General Assembly. If, however, the Good Offices Committee, which was attempting to secure a truce, reported satisfactory progress in its efforts, the report of the Collective Measures Committee might be deferred. Finally, the resolution retained the affirmation that the UN policy continues to be "to bring about a cessation of hostilities in Korea and the achievement of United Nations objectives in Korea by peaceful means. . . ."

Thus the U. S. and the UN had come a long way back to their original purposes in Korea. The resolution of October 7 was never to be repudiated in so many words; instead, it was conveniently ignored as conditions changed.

The military side of the changing policy for Korea was represented by "Operation Killer," General Ridgway's accurately, though—from a propaganda viewpoint—unfortunately, named strategy of attrition. Ridgway recognized that there was no likelihood of driving the Communists back the length of North Korea and winning a complete military victory over the Chinese under the conditions of limited warfare established by American and UN policy. He was determined therefore to match the enemy's manpower with his own superior firepower and mobility and thus to inflict such damage to the enemy as to force him to agree to a peace settlement. The gaining of ground was therefore incidental to the depletion of enemy manpower. Unfortunately this was a policy which General MacArthur either did not understand or with which he had no sympathy and his unwillingness to accept it was to lead to his recall.

On January 25, the first phase of "Operation Killer" got under way as the 8th Army took the offensive. Excellent coordination between ground and air forces produced heavy enemy casualties and drove the Communists back. By

February 12, when the Communists counterattacked, the UN army had recovered considerable ground and stood close to where it had been in early January. Far more important, the enemy had been bled badly. The Communist offensive at first scored gains, but at Chipyong and Wonju in central Korea it ran aground and was so completely blunted by UN resistance that a general Chinese retreat commenced on February 16.

The process of seriously damaging the Communist army commenced again on February 20 when "Operation Killer" was reopened. This time there seemed to be no stopping of the UN troops. Their progress was cautious and slow but marked by tremendous enemy casualties which were far out of proportion to the UN losses. By March 6, the UN line ran from the south bank of the Han River just below Seoul on the west to a point on the east less than twenty miles south of the 38th parallel. Nine days later Seoul was liberated for the second, and last, time. After the liberation of the Republic of Korea capital, Communist resistance in South Korea collapsed. All along the line the enemy disappeared in flight back across the 38th parallel into North Korea. By the last week of March the UN army was once more confronted by the question of six months before: was the parallel to be crossed?

THE FINAL DECISION

As early as February 13, when the first phase of "Operation Killer" had demonstrated that the UN forces might achieve some success with the strategy of attrition, American policymakers had begun to discuss the question of new political objectives for the Korean War. At that time State Department representatives at a meeting with the JCS said that they preferred "not to express political objectives with respect to Korea until military capabilities there were established."[157] In other words, the State Department did not wish to stick its neck out. The JCS, on the other hand, were of the opinion "that a political decision was required before there could be suitable determination of military courses of action."[158] The army was presumably still operating under the directive of January 12, which had anticipated evacuation of Korea or, at best, barely holding its ground, and now the improved situation seemed to demand a new directive. All that came out of the February 13 discussion, however, was the decision to wait and see what developed on the field of battle. Yet a month later, on March 15, when the JCS and State Department officials again met to discuss objectives in Korea no decision was made even though the UN forces had by then advanced to within fifteen miles of the 38th parallel and considerable discussion had already occurred on the question of recrossing the parallel among our allies and in the press at home and abroad.[159]

The need for an enunciation of policy was made even more imperative by General MacArthur's impatient chafing under the strategy of attrition. On February 13 and again on March 7, he made statements to the press protesting against the restrictions under which he was laboring and which, MacArthur said, gave the enemy "unprecedented military advantage." The type of war the UN troops were being forced to fight could lead to nothing better than a stalemate with endless bloodshed and destruction. MacArthur thus demanded that "vital decisions" "which are neither solely political nor solely military" be made to provide "on the highest international levels an answer to the obscurities which now becloud the unsolved problems raised by Red China's undeclared war in Korea."[160] To Hugh Baillie, the president of the United Press, General MacArthur said that the UN would have to continue the war of maneuver in Korea rather than stop on or near the 38th parallel because there were no natural defenses near the parallel to hold against the Communists. "The terrain is such," the General declared, "that to establish a conventional defense system in reasonable depth would require such a sizable force that if we had it, and could logistically maintain it, we would be able to drive the Chinese Communists back across the Yalu, and proceed to the accomplishment of our mission in the unification of Korea."[161]

The confusion of purposes was compounded by General Matthew B. Ridgway's statement on March 12, just five days after MacArthur spoke of the war as a "stalemate," that the UN would have gained a "tremendous victory if the Korean War were to end on the 38th parallel, because the failure of the Chinese Communists to drive the allies from Korea "would be a defeat of incalculable importance."[162]

Ridgway's view was considerably closer than MacArthur's to what was evolving in Washington and at the UN. The *New York Times* correspondent at Lake Success reported on March 13 in an article that appeared the next day:

United Nations diplomats reported today that the idea of unifying Korea by military victory throughout the country was being quietly dropped.

Cautiously and without commitments the United States is said to be considering the position that the United Nations military job will end somewhere around the thirty-eighth parallel and that the second task—unification—will depend on political jockeying that may last a long time.

United States sources would say for the record that no hard and fast decision had been reached on the question of calling a halt in the vicinity of the parallel. It was predicted that no such announcement would be forthcoming since it would amount to a gift of information to the Chinese Communists.

The report went on to state:

Exactly where to stabilize the line is still regarded as a military matter here. The thirty-eighth parallel is usually mentioned because of its political importance, but it is emphasized that the United Nations Command would have the full right to establish bridgeheads or other military positions north of the parallel if it considered such moves militarily important.[163]

The reports from Washington all indicated that there was agreement between American high-level planners and our allies that caution should be exercised in recrossing the 38th parallel, especially if the Chinese withdrew across it and then gave indications that they might negotiate. It was also agreed that if military exigencies demanded it, the UN Commander had the right to cross the parallel.[164] President Truman told the press on March 15 that the decision to re-cross the line was a tactical matter for the UN Commander.[165]

The press, here and abroad, urged editorially that the political decision on how far the UN forces were to advance should be made quickly so that General MacArthur might be properly instructed.[166] The editorials, too, generally conceded that a certain amount of freedom of maneuver across the parallel must be given to the Far Eastern Commander.

Agreement among the UN members participating in the Korean War on future operations was reached by the 20th of March. The semiweekly talks at the State Department of the Committee of Sixteen under the chairmanship of Dean Rusk, Assistant Secretary of State for Far Eastern Affairs, as well as other diplomatic consultations had resulted in the decision that the UN forces would be permitted to cross the 38th parallel for tactical reasons, but that there would be no attempt again to advance to the Manchurian border. No general advance into North Korea would take place without further consultations among the nations participating in the war. It was also agreed that another strong appeal would be made to Peiping to negotiate.[167]

Kenneth Younger, British Minister of State, in announcing this decision to the House of Commons on Thursday, March 22, stated that the parallel would no longer be considered a line of great political importance and thus would not be imposed as a boundary for the UN forces.[168]

On March 20, having secured agreement among our allies, the State Department went ahead with a statement which it proposed that the President should issue calling again on the Communists to cease fighting. Also on the same day, before the President's announcement was made, the Joint Chiefs sent the following message to General MacArthur advising him of the forthcoming announcement:

State Department planning a Presidential announcement shortly that, with clearing bulk of South Korea of aggressors, United Nations now preparing to discuss conditions of settlement in Korea. United Nations feeling exists that further diplomatic efforts towards settlement should be made before any advance with major forces north of 38th parallel. Time will be required to determine diplomatic reactions and permit new negotiations that may develop. Recognizing that parallel had no military significance, State has asked Joint Chiefs of Staff what authority you should have to permit sufficient freedom of action for next few weeks to provide security for United Nations forces and maintain contact with enemy. Your recommendations desired.

MacArthur replied that his current directive was adequate since with the limitations imposed on him and the size of the force under his command it was not practicable for him to attempt to clear all of North Korea of the enemy.[169]

The President's announcement was discussed again by the Joint Chiefs and the Secretaries of Defense and State and further details were worked out after the receipt of MacArthur's reply. The proposed draft was also approved by representatives in Washington of the other nations having troops in Korea. When the opportune moment would come—and it was expected that it would be within the next few days upon the clearing of South Korea of the aggressors—the President proposed to say:

I make the following statement as Chief Executive of the Government requested by the United Nations to exercise the Unified Command in Korea, and after full consultation with the United Nations Governments contributing combat forces in support of the United Nations in Korea.

United Nations forces in Korea are engaged in repelling the aggressions committed against the Republic of Korea and against the United Nations.

The aggressors have been driven back with heavy losses to the general vicinity from which the unlawful attack was first launched last June.

There remains the problem of restoring international peace and security in the area in accordance with the terms of the Security Council resolution of June 27, 1950. The spirit and principles of the United Nations Charter require that every effort be made to prevent the spread of hostilities and to avoid the prolongation of the misery and loss of life.

There is a basis for restoring peace and security in the area which should be acceptable to all nations which sincerely desire peace.

The Unified Command is prepared to enter into arrangements which would conclude the fighting and ensure against its resumption. Such arrangements would open the way for a broader settlement for Korea, including the withdrawal of foreign forces from Korea.

The United Nations has declared the policy of the world community that the people of Korea be permitted to establish a unified, independent and democratic state.

The Korean people are entitled to peace. They are entitled to determine their political and other institutions by their own choice and in response to their own needs.

The Korean people are entitled to the assistance of the world community in repairing the ravages of war—assistance which the United Nations is ready to give and for which it has established the necessary machinery. Its member nations have already made generous offers of help. What is needed is peace, in which the United Nations can use its resources in the creative tasks of reconstruction.

It is regrettable that those who are opposing the United Nations in Korea have made so little response to the many opportunities which have been and continue to be afforded for a settlement in Korea.

A prompt settlement of the Korean problem would greatly reduce international tension in the Far East and would open the way for the consideration of other problems in that area by the processes of peaceful settlement envisaged in the Charter of the United Nations.

Until satisfactory arrangements for concluding the fighting have been reached, United Nations military actions must be continued.[170]

Here was an open statement to the Communists and to the rest of the world that the U. S. and the UN were willing to negotiate on the basis of something close to the *status quo ante bellum*—as the reference, on one hand, to the June 27 resolution of the Security Council and the careful avoidance, on the other hand, (even though unification was supported in principle), of mention of the October 7 resolution of the General Assembly implied. The opportunity for making the Presidential announcement never came, for, on March 24, General MacArthur, without any previous consultation with Washington, issued an ultimatum to the enemy which, as Truman has stated, "was so entirely at cross purposes with the [announcement] I was to have delivered that it would only have confused the world if my carefully prepared statement had been made." MacArthur declared:

Operations continue according to schedule and plan. We have now substantially cleared South Korea of organized Communist forces. It is becoming increasingly evident that the heavy destruction along the enemy's line of supply, caused by our round-the-clock massive air and naval bombardment, has left his troops in the forward battle area deficient in requirements to sustain his operations. This weakness is being brilliantly exploited by our ground forces. The enemy's human wave tactics have definitely failed him as our own forces have become seasoned to this form of warfare; his tactics of infiltration are but contributing to his piecemeal losses, and he is showing less stamina than our own troops under the rigors of climate, terrain and battle.

Of even greater significance than our tactical successes has been the clear revelation that this new enemy, Red China, of such exaggerated and vaunted military power, lacks the industrial capacity to provide adequately many critical items necessary to the conduct of modern war. He lacks the manufacturing base and those raw materials needed to produce, maintain, and operate even

moderate air and naval power, and he cannot provide the essentials for successful ground operations, such as tanks, heavy artillery and other refinements science has introduced into the conduct of military campaigns. Formerly his great numerical potential might well have filled this gap but with the development of existing methods of mass destruction, numbers alone do not offset the vulnerability inherent in such deficiencies. Control of the seas and the air, which in turn means control over supplies, communications and transportation, are no less essential and decisive now than in the past. When this control exists as in our case, and is coupled with an inferiority of ground fire power such as in the enemy's case, the resulting disparity is such that it cannot be overcome by bravery, however fanatical, or the most gross indifference to human loss.

These military weaknesses have been clearly and definitely revealed since Red China entered upon its undeclared war in Korea. Even under the inhibitions which now restrict the activity of the United Nations forces and the corresponding military advantages which accrue to Red China, it has shown its complete inability to accomplish by force of arms the conquest of Korea. The enemy, therefore, must by now be painfully aware that a decision of the United Nations to depart from its tolerant effort to contain the war to the area of Korea, through an expansion of our military operations to its coastal areas and interior bases, would doom Red China to the risk of imminent military collapse. These basic facts being established, there should be no insuperable difficulty in arriving at decisions on the Korean problem if the issues are resolved on their own merits, without being burdened by extraneous matters not directly related to Korea, such as Formosa or China's seat in the United Nations.

The Korean nation and people, which have been so cruelly ravaged, must not be sacrificed. This is a paramount concern. Apart from the military area of the problem where issues are resolved in the course of combat, the fundamental questions continue to be political in nature and must find their answer in the diplomatic sphere. Within the area of my authority as the military commander, however, it would be needless to say that I stand ready at any time to confer in the field with the commander in chief of the enemy forces in earnest effort to find any military means whereby realization of the political objectives of the United Nations in Korea, to which no nation may justly take exceptions, might be accomplished without further bloodshed.[171]

This extraordinary implied threat by the UN Commander that the UN would expand the area of the war in the Far East unless the

Communists came to terms astounded and shocked the Administration and our allies. The ultimatum was not only unauthorized but in total disregard of directives to military leaders to abstain from any declarations on foreign policy. Coming as it did at the very time that the U. S. was paving the way for a new attempt at making peace it confounded our allies. The State Department was deluged with inquiries from the foreign offices of other nations asking if there was to be a shift in American policy. The State Department disassociated itself with General MacArthur's statement, but the damage was done.

This statement, along with previous expressions of General MacArthur's disagreement with Administration policies plus two more statements which followed close on the heels of the March 24 ultimatum, convinced President Truman and his advisers that the time had come to replace the Far East Commander with a man who understood the aims of the U. S. government and the UN in Korea and who could better carry out orders. Accordingly, on April 11, General McArthur was relieved of all his commands in the Far East and Lieutenant General Matthew B. Ridgway was ordered to assume those commands. On April 14, Lieutenant General James A. Van Fleet, after having been called from the U. S., took over command of the 8th Army as General Ridgway's successor.

General MacArthur's ultimatum and his relief from command did not change the situation in regard to the crossing of the 38th parallel. Nor did these events produce any new announcement of UN policy. On March 24, the day he had issued the controversial ultimatum, General MacArthur also announced that he had ordered UN troops to cross the parallel "if and when security makes it tactically advisable,"[172] and on March 27, Secretary of Defense Marshall publicly confirmed that MacArthur had the authority to go as far beyond the 38th parallel as was necessary for military security. Marshall at the same time strongly indicated that this did not mean that MacArthur was authorized to sweep to the Manchurian border. "Any general advance," the Secretary stated, "is a matter for political decision." This was the first official clarification of how far the UN forces might go without a new directive from the UN.[173] On the other side of the Atlantic,

the British Foreign Secretary, Herbert Morrison, told the House of Commons on April 11, in a speech discussing the recall of General MacArthur, that the U. S., Great Britain and the other participants in the UN action in Korea were continuing their consultations regarding the advance into North Korea and promised that an announcement of UN policy would be issued as soon as it had been agreed upon. He added that the real issue was not the parallel but whether the Communists were willing to negotiate a settlement.[174] It seemed fairly certain, however, that by the end of March, the British, along with most of the allies, and perhaps even the U. S., regarded the October 7 resolution as a dead letter and were convinced that it was desirable to seek a settlement based on the status quo in Korea now that aggression had been repelled. Unification of the peninsula would have to come through political means, but the length and bitterness of the conflict between North and South Korea made the ideal of unification impossible of achievement at an early date—even by force of any available arms.

The 8th Army advanced across the 38th parallel between March 27 and April 1 and by mid-April it had slugged its way about six to eight miles north of the controversial line. From the end of April to the end of May, the UN army and the Communist forces pushed back and forth across the line in more than a month of the most sanguinary fighting. Two great Communist offensives—April 22 to 27 and May 16 to 21—were hurled at the 8th Army in desperate attempts to regain Seoul and a Red foothold in South Korea, but, by the end of May, the enemy was stopped and then thrown into reverse. By June 2, the UN forces stood again several miles north of the parallel at almost the identical position where they had been when the Communist offensive started on April 22. During these bloody weeks the Communists had suffered 200,000 casualties— at least one-third of their estimated strength in Korea.

The promised new political directive never came either from the U. S. government or the UN. Throughout the months of terrible fighting in April and May 1951, indeed, throughout two more long years of war until the armistice was signed on July 27, 1953, no new directive was issued.

Nevertheless, there had been a very real change of policy and it was announced quite publicly by Administration spokesmen at the Senate MacArthur Hearings in May 1951. Secretaries Acheson and Marshall and General Bradley stated at several points during the hearings that we had returned to our original objective in Korea of resisting Communist aggression and that we would seek the unification and independence of Korea by political means rather than by force.

When General Van Fleet, early in June, after his successful crushing of the Communist offensives, proposed to Washington that he capitalize on his victory and continue his offensive up through North Korea, the proposal was vetoed in keeping with the new policy. The September enthusiasm for a drive to the Yalu had evaporated.

On June 1, Trygve Lie, the Secretary-General of the UN, declared that a cease-fire "approximately along" the 38th parallel would fulfill the purpose of the UN—the repulsion of aggression against the Republic of Korea. Secretary of State Acheson, following the recommendation of the NSC and with the approval of President Truman, made a similar statement on June 7. The NSC had taken up the formulation of new objectives in Asia on May 2; the discussion ended May 16.[175]

The State Department in mid-June suggested offering a new cease-fire proposal to the Communists, but the Committee of Sixteen of the representatives of the UN countries fighting in Korea decided against the proposal. The new position of the U. S. was instead made known to the Communists by neutral diplomats in Peiping.

On June 23, Jacob Malik, the chief of the Soviet delegation to the UN, speaking on the weekly UN radio program in New York City, proposed a cease-fire and a beginning of negotiations to bring peace to Korea. After ascertaining in Moscow and at the UN whether the Russians were acting in good faith and with the acquiescence of the Chinese Communists, the U. S. Government ordered General Ridgway on June 29 to communicate with the Communist high command and to arrange armistice talks.

On July 10, 1951, more than a year after the commencement of hostilities in Korea, truce talks commenced at Kaesong, a little town just one mile south of the 38th parallel and five miles above the UN line on the westernmost part of the front. It was to take two years, two weeks, three days and hundreds of thousands more casualties in some of the most desperate fighting of the war, before an armistice was finally signed at Panmunjom on July 27, 1953.

ACKNOWLEDGMENTS

Of great value in supplying additional information and correcting errors in my original draft were interviews with Messrs. Dean Acheson, Dean Rusk, Thomas K. Finletter and George M. Elsey. They were also kind enough to read the original draft.

I am greatly indebted also to the following, who read the original draft of this paper and supplied useful criticism and additional material: Richard D. Challener, Captain Robert S. Gard, Jr., USA, Captain Paul F. Gorman, USA, Philip C. Jessup, George F. Kennan, Colonel G. A. Lincoln, USA, Walter Lippmann, Walter Millis, Richard E. Neustadt, Norman J. Padelford, and Gordon B. Turner. For whatever errors have crept into this study I alone am responsible.

As editor of the whole work of which this is part, Harold Stein has been helpful in suggesting many of the improvements that have been made since the completion of the original draft of this study. In two sections—"Shifting Objectives: A Review" and "Reflections on the End-the-War-Offensive"—a limited portion of the text is rather more the work of the editor than of the author.

—Martin Lichterman

BIBLIOGRAPHIC NOTE

Governmental archives covering such recent and controversial events as the march to the Yalu are customarily and understandably closed to the inquiring scholar. For reasons that were political, not scholarly, a mass of archival materials dealing with the Korean conflict was, however, made public in the course of the MacArthur Hearings: *Military Situation in the Far East,* Hearings Before the Committee on Armed Services and the Committee on Foreign Relations, United States Senate, 82nd Congress, 1st session. It should be noted, however, that a considerable amount of testimony and other material introduced at the hearings was censored by Admiral Arthur C. Davis, the official censor of the hearings, and does not appear in the five volumes printed for public distribution. The *New York Times* reported on June 6, 1951, that Admiral Davis had deleted 1,239,750 words during the first twenty-seven days of the hearings, which ran for a total of forty-three days.

Formal documentation was made public during the actual flow of events in publications of the United States Department of State and, at considerable length, in the publications of the United Nations. The most important of these publications are: U. S. Department of State, Office of Public Affairs, *Korea's Independence,* Publication #2933, Far Eastern Series 18 (Washington, 1947); U. S. Department of State, *Korea, 1945-1948,* Publication #3305, Far Eastern Series 28 (Washington, 1948); U. S. Department of State, *United States Policy in the Korean Crisis,* Far Eastern Series 34 (Washington, 1951); the following United Nations documents: General Assembly Official Records, Fifth Session, Resolutions; General Assembly Official Records, Fifth Session, First Committee Records; General Assembly Official Records, Fifth Session, Plenary Meetings Records; General Assembly Official Records,

Fifth Session, Annexes; Security Council Official Records, Fifth Session; Department of Public Information, Background Paper No. 62, "The Question of Korea, 1947-1949"; Department of Public Information, Background Paper No. 79, "The Question of Korea, 1950-1953." These constitute the primary source material for this study. Additional archival material was made available in Volume II of *Memoirs of Harry S. Truman: Years of Trial and Hope,* though of course President Truman's autobiography is in part of polemical character.

Another important, generally accurate and remarkably comprehensive source of materials is the columns of the *New York Times* and the *New York Herald Tribune* and particularly the articles written by James Reston, Hanson Baldwin, the brothers Alsop, A. M. Rosenthal and Arthur Krock. As Alexander L. George has concluded, "a surprising amount of reliable information about American policy calculations can be obtained from the columns of the better metropolitan dailies." ("American Policy-Making and the North Korean Aggression," *World Politics,* VII, No. 2, January 1955, 210n.)

Finally, use has been made of secondary sources, most of them highly polemical. The chief pro-MacArthur works are: Frazier Hunt, *The Untold Story of Douglas MacArthur* (New York, 1954); Courtney Whitney, *MacArthur: His Rendezvous with History* (New York, 1956); Charles A. Willoughby and John Chamberlain, *MacArthur, 1941-1951* (New York, 1954). Clark Lee and Richard Henschel, *Douglas MacArthur* (New York, 1952) although slanted in favor of General MacArthur is somewhat more objective than the other three works; but of course Whitney's official or semi-official biography contains a good deal of archival material. The chief anti-MacArthur works are: Richard M. Rovere and Arthur M. Schlesinger, Jr., *The General and the President* (New York,

1951) and I. F. Stone, *The Hidden History of the Korean War* (New York, 1952). The latter volume is generally critical of the United States' and United Nations' attempt to repel aggression in Korea and comes close to following the Communist Party line. There are a few useful publications that avoid taking sides in the MacArthur controversy, including: Leland M. Goodrich, "Korea: Collective Measures Against Aggression," *International Conciliation,* No. 494 (October 1953); Leland M. Goodrich and Anne P. Simons, *The United Nations and the Maintenance of International Peace and Security* (Washington, 1955); Leland M. Goodrich, *Korea: A Study of United States Policy in the United Nations* (New York, 1956); Rutherford M. Poats, *Decision in Korea* (New York, 1954). Three papers which were also of considerable use in preparing this study were: Captain (then Lieutenant, USA) Paul F. Gorman, "Limited War: Korea, 1950," a paper written for Professor William Y. Elliott's Government 285 course (Harvard University, Fall 1953); Kenneth Hubbard, "The United States and Great Britain in the Korean Crisis, 1950-1951" (MS., Widener Library, Harvard University Honors Thesis, 1956); and Bayley F. Mason, "The War in Korea: A Case Study in the Problems of Limited War," Harvard Defense Policy Seminar, 1956-57, mimeo.

Before completion of the revision of this study in the summer of 1958, two interesting and useful MSS. were generously made available to the author; both have since been published. The two authors, it may be noted, similarly had whatever advantage came from seeing the semi-final draft of this study: Richard E. Neustadt, *Presidential Power: The Politics of Leadership* (John Wiley, New York, 1960) and Trumbull Higgins, *Korea and The Fall of MacArthur* (Oxford, New York, 1960). Both of these works deal with many of the same events dealt with here but in each case from a different standpoint; in the Neustadt work, the Korean War is only a small part of the whole. Two other studies on the Korean War have also been published since 1958; their perspectives have been even further removed, but both have been useful: Allen S. Whiting, *China Crosses the Yalu: The Decision to Enter the Korean War* (Macmillan, New York, 1960) and John W. Spanier, *The Truman-MacArthur Controversy and the Korean War* (Harvard University Press, Cambridge, 1959). Through the good offices of Richard C. Snyder, two successive unpublished drafts of Glenn D. Paige, *The Korean Decision* [June 24-30, 1950] have also been made available. This constitutes an extraordinarily detailed account of the events in Washington in the first week of the Korean War; what is said in the present study about the early decision is, in contrast, merely a highly condensed summary of the happenings described in Mr. Paige's account.

Walter Millis, in preparing Chapter 7, "Truman and MacArthur," of *Arms and the State,* the first volume in the Twentieth Century Fund project of which this is the second, used an earlier draft of this study, and his chapter has been used in revising what is written here.

All the additional materials used in this study may be found listed in the footnotes.

NOTES

1. Quoted in George W. McCune and Arthur L. Grey, *Korea Today* (Harvard University Press, Cambridge, 1950), p. 42. I have summarized *ibid.*, pp. 42-52.

2. Robert E. Sherwood, *Roosevelt and Hopkins: An Intimate History* (Harper, New York, 1948), p. 903; Harry S. Truman, *Memoirs*, I, *Year of Decisions* (Doubleday, Garden City, 1955), pp. 265, 269.

3. *Ibid.*, pp. 433-434.

4. Interview with Dean Rusk, March 26, 1957; Truman, *Memoirs*, I, pp. 444-445; Bayley F. Mason, "The War in Korea: A Case Study in the Problems of Limited War" (Harvard Defense Policy Seminar, 1956-57), Part I, Appendix 2, p. 22.

5. The chronology on the 38th parallel decision is given in Mason, "The War in Korea," Part I, Appendix 2, pp. 22-23.

6. McCune and Grey, *Korea Today*, p. 44.

7. Leland M. Goodrich, *Korea: A Study of United States Policy in the United Nations* (Council on Foreign Relations, New York, 1956), pp. 13-14. The willingness of the Soviets to accept the division of Korea invites speculation. Possibly the Russian leaders believed that by sharing in the occupation of Korea they improved their chances of similarly sharing in the military government of Japan. It is also possible that the Russians assumed that the Americans were aware (which they were not) that the 38th parallel almost a half century before, in 1903, had been suggested by the Russians to mark the division of Korea into Russian and Japanese spheres of influence and that by selecting this historic line the United States was recognizing a traditional area of Russian control.

8. Harry S. Truman, *Memoirs*, II, *Years of Trial and Hope* (Doubleday, Garden City, 1956), pp. 325-326.

9. The best summary of the attempts of the UN to deal with the problem of Korea in the years between 1947 and the outbreak of the war in Korea, is in Goodrich, *Korea: A Study of U. S. Policy in the United Nations*, Chapters II, III, IV.

10. Instructions of the Interim Committee of the General Assembly, February 26, 1948, quoted in UN, Department of Public Information, *A Korea Chronology* (New York, 1950), p. 4.

11. Truman, *Memoirs*, II, p. 329.

12. *Ibid.*, p. 5.

13. *Military Situation in the Far East*, Hearings before the Senate Committee on Foreign Relations and Committee on Armed Services, 82d Cong., 1st sess., 1951 (hereafter cited as *Hearings*), Part 5, p. 3367.

14. Richard C. Snyder and Edgar S. Furniss, Jr., *American Foreign Policy* (Rinehart, New York, 1954), p. 222. The Joint Chiefs had no war plan to meet the challenge in Korea. President Truman says in his *Memoirs*, II, p. 331, that the CIA had warned of a possible North Korean invasion during the spring of 1950, and there were periodic fears that President Rhee would order his troops to march northward. Yet the JCS had no premonition that the armed services would be asked to defend Korea. They were concerned with total, rather than limited, war, and believed that Korea would not and should not be used as a battleground in a war with Russia. Korea, as Acheson said, lay outside our defense perimeter and the military planning that underlay his statement had been fully accepted.

15. *Ibid.*

16. The U. S. S. R. had been boycotting the Security Council for several months because the Chinese member was a Nationalist and not a Communist.

17. Truman, *Memoirs*, II, p. 334. President Truman states that in using his air force to keep open Kimpo and other airports General MacArthur was instructed that his air forces should stay south of the 38th parallel but the order itself, according to the list of directives, orders and memoranda sent to General MacArthur by the Department of Defense containing restrictions imposed on him in the conduct of the campaign which was supplied to Senator Richard B. Russell, Chairman, Committee on Armed Services, by Secretary of Defense George C. Marshall, mentions no such restriction. *Hearings*, Part 5, Appendix K, p. 3192. The directive issued the next day, however, does include the restriction, so it is probable

that the first directive sent MacArthur did also.

18. Present at the meeting on Sunday were Secretaries Dean Acheson (State), Louis Johnson (Defense), Frank Pace (Army), Frank P. Matthews (Navy), Thomas K. Finletter (Air), Under Secretary of State James Webb, Assistant Secretary of State for Far Eastern Affairs Dean Rusk, Assistant Under Secretary of State John Hickerson, Ambassador Philip Jessup; JCS members General of the Army Omar Bradley (Chairman), General J. Lawton Collins (Army), Admiral Forrest P. Sherman (Navy), General Hoyt S. Vandenberg (Air Force). All but Secretaries Matthews and Rusk were present at the Monday meeting.

19. Truman, *Memoirs,* II, p. 337.

20. Courtney Whitney, *MacArthur: His Rendezvous with History* (Knopf, New York, 1956), p. 326.

21. *Ibid.*; James Reston in *New York Times,* July 9, 1950, as quoted in I. F. Stone, *The Hidden History of the Korean War* (Monthly Review Press, New York, 1952), p. 80.

22. Beverly Smith, Jr., "The White House Story: Why We Went to War in Korea," *Saturday Evening Post,* November 10, 1951, p. 86.

23. Truman, *Memoirs,* II, p. 341.

24. Interview with Dean Rusk, March 27, 1957.

25. Frazier Hunt, *The Untold Story of Douglas MacArthur* (Devin Adair, New York, 1954), p. 452; Whitney, *MacArthur,* pp. 332-333; Richard M. Rovere and Arthur M. Schlesinger, Jr., *The General and the President and the Future of American Foreign Policy* (Farrar, Straus & Young, New York, 1951), pp. 105-106.

26. Truman, *Memoirs,* II, p. 335.

27. These were Australia, Belgium, Canada, Colombia, Ethiopia, France, Greece, Luxembourg, the Netherlands, New Zealand, the Philippines, Thailand, Turkey, the Union of South Africa, the United Kingdom, and the United States. Other members had contributed supplies and services. By the end of August 1952, sixteen members had ground forces in action, eight had naval forces and five air forces; seventeen members altogether were represented. Five other members had offered transport of medical facilities which were being used and six more had made offers which had not been accepted or acceptance of which had been deferred. Altogether considerably less than half the members of the United Nations had contributed or had made offers to contribute to the Korean effort. As of December 1951, of the total United Nations and ROK forces in Korea, the United States had contributed 50.32 per cent of ground, 85.89 per cent of naval, 93.38 per cent of air. The ROK's contributions were 40.10 per cent, 7.45 per cent and 5.65 per cent respectively, and the remainder was contributed by 15 other members

ber nations of the United Nations with the Commonwealth contributing a major share in each category. Leland M. Goodrich and Anne P. Simons, *The United Nations and the Maintenance of International Peace and Security* (Brookings Institution, Washington, 1955), p. 460; Leland M. Goodrich, "Korea: Collective Measures against Aggression," in *International Conciliation* (October 1953), p. 145n; Leland M. Goodrich, "The United Nations and the Korean War: A Case Study," in Andrew Gyorgy and Hubert J. Gibbs, *Problems in International Relations* (Prentice-Hall, New York, 1955), p. 247.

28. On July 15 President Syngman Rhee formally placed ROK forces under General MacArthur's command. U. S. Department of State, *Bulletin,* XXIII (August 7, 1950), p. 206.

29. *Hearings,* Part 3, pp. 1938-1939, Testimony of Secretary Acheson.

30. Goodrich and Simons, *The United Nations and the Maintenance of International Peace and Security,* p. 463. Each service was commanded by a United States commander and the fact of United States operational control was not affected by the subsequent addition to the staff of the United Nations Commander of a Commonwealth Deputy Chief of Staff. Goodrich, "Korea: Collective Measures Against Aggression," p. 162. Allied naval units operating with the Seventh Fleet were employed solely for Korean operations in support of the Security Council resolutions and were kept separate from that part of the Seventh Fleet which was in the vicinity of the Formosa Strait for the defense of Formosa. Prime Minister Attlee made it clear to the House of Commons on July 10, 1950 that the British government had promised "no assistance for the defense of Formosa." *Hansard,* Vol. 477, col. 957, quoted in Kenneth Hubbard, "The United States and Great Britain in the Korean Crisis 1950-1951" (MS., Harvard University Honors Thesis, 1956), p. 38.

31. *Hearings,* Part 3, p. 1940.

32. *Ibid.*

33. *Hearings,* Part 1, p. 379, Testimony of Secretary Marshall.

34. President Truman strengthened the NSC early in August 1950 by appointing a Senior Staff group to do preparatory "spade work." The original Senior Staff included Philip C. Jessup for the State Department; Thomas K. Finletter for Defense; Robert J. Smith, vice chairman of the National Security Resources Board; William McChesney Martin, Assistant Secretary of the Treasury; Rear Admiral Edmund T. Wooldridge for the JCS; Rear Admiral Roscoe Hillenkoetter, director of CIA; and James S. Lay, Jr., executive secretary of the NSC, as its chairman. *New York Times,* August 3, 1950.

35. *Hearings,* Part 2, p. 1067, Testimony of General Omar Bradley.

36. *Hearings,* Part 3, p. 1787, Testimony of Secretary Acheson.

37. *Hearings,* Part 4, pp. 2697-2698, from paragraph 17, page 35 of paraphrased messages furnished by Joint Chiefs of Staff to Congressional Committees (Senate Committees on Armed Services and Foreign Relations).

38. Truman, *Memoirs,* II, p. 359.

39. *Hearings,* Part 1, p. 718, from paragraph 33, page 41 of paraphrased messages furnished by Joint Chiefs of Staff to Congressional Committees (Armed Services and Foreign Relations).

40. *New York Herald Tribune,* September 22, 1950, p. 4.

41. Interview with Dean Acheson, March 28, 1957. The resolution, which was finally passed by the General Assembly on October 7, was drafted by Secretary Acheson, but was introduced by the United Kingdom and seven other nations.

42. *New York Times,* September 26, 1950, p. 1.

43. A. M. Rosenthal in the *New York Times,* September 27, 1950, p. 1. On the same day, David Lawrence wrote in his column: "If . . . the Allied forces are not permitted to go beyond the 38th parallel to disarm the government which has committed the aggression, the Republicans will certainly make capital out of that policy." *New York Herald Tribune,* September 27, 1950, p. 8.

44. *New York Times,* September 29, 1950, quoted in Hubbard, "The U. S. and Great Britain in the Korean Crisis," p. 31.

45. John G. Rogers in *New York Herald Tribune,* September 28, 1950, p. 1.

46. Truman, *Memoirs,* II, p. 360; see also *Hearings,* Part 5, p. 3193, Appendix K.

47. *Hearings,* Part 1, p. 721.

48. Truman, *Memoirs,* II, p. 361.

49. Anthony Leviero in *New York Times,* September 29, 1950, p. 1.

50. Quoted in Whitney, *MacArthur,* p. 398.

51. *Hearings,* Part 1, p. 245, Testimony of General MacArthur.

52. A. M. Rosenthal in the *New York Times,* September 30, 1950, p. 1; see also General Assembly Official Records, First Committee Records, Fifth Session, 347th Meeting (September 30, 1950), p. 11, paragraphs 23, 24, 26; p. 12, paragraph 31.

53. *New York Herald Tribune,* September 30, 1950, p. 2.

54. General Assembly Official Records, First Committee Records, Fifth Session, 347th Meeting (September 30, 1950), p. 13, paragraphs 39, 42, 43.

55. Whitney, *MacArthur,* p. 399; Truman, *Memoirs,* II, p. 361.

56. *Hearings,* Part 1, p. 721. The printed record of this directive of September 30 carries no further mention of limitations on operations of the UN forces. This was merely a confirmation of the directive of September 27.

57. President Truman had let slip at his press conference on September 28 that a surrender broadcast would be made. Stone, *Hidden War,* p. 112; A. P. dispatch in *New York Times,* October 1, 1950.

58. General Assembly, Fifth Session, First Committee, 351st Meeting (October 3, 1950), pp. 38-39, paragraphs 19-21.

59. General Assembly, Fifth Session, First Committee, 350th Meeting (October 3, 1950), p. 33, paragraphs 17-18.

60. Charles H. Heimsath, "Indo-American Relations," in *Journal of International Affairs* (Spring 1952), pp. 154, 157.

61. *Hearings,* Part 2, p. 1234, Testimony of General J. Lawton Collins.

62. Rovere and Schlesinger, *The General and the President,* p. 149.

63. *Hearings,* Part 3, p. 1833, Testimony of Secretary Acheson; K. M. Panikkar, *In Two Chinas: Memoirs of a Diplomat* (G. Allen, London, 1955), pp. 108-110.

64. *Ibid.,* p. 108.

65. *Ibid.,* p. 110.

66. *Hearings,* Part 3, p. 1833, Testimony of Secretary Acheson.

67. See, for example, Stone, *Hidden War,* p. 132. It should be noted that Ambassador Panikkar's memoir states that Chinese troops were already in North Korea by October 9. *In Two Chinas,* p. 112.

68. *Hearings,* Part 3, p. 1729, Testimony of Secretary Acheson; interview with Acheson, March 27, 1957; interview with Dean Rusk, March 26, 1957; letter from Philip C. Jessup, March 13, 1957.

69. *New York Times,* October 9, 1950.

70. Goodrich, *Korea: A Study of United States Policy in the United Nations,* p. 134.

71. See pp. 584-585.

72. Rovere and Schlesinger, *The General and the President,* p. 151; James Reston in *New York Times,* November 16, 1950, p. 6; Walter H. Waggoner in *New York Times,* November 16, 1950, p. 2.

73. Quoted in Clark Lee and Richard Henschel, *Douglas MacArthur* (Holt, New York, 1952), p. 204.

74. *New York Times,* October 5, 1950, p. 4.

75. Truman, *Memoirs,* II, p. 362; *Hearings,* Part 1, p. 720.

76. See below for brief explanation of Wake Island Conference.

77. Text of the Truman-MacArthur Wake Island Conference, as released by the Senate Armed

Services and Foreign Relations Committees, in Rovere and Schlesinger, *The General and the President*, Appendix, pp. 253-254.

78. *Ibid.*, p. 258. It should be noted that this statement, along with the rest of the text of the Wake Island Conference, was pieced together from notes of participants as well as from notes taken by Ambassador Jessup's secretary. General MacArthur refused to accept responsibility for the words and ideas attributed to him although the text of the conference was sent to his headquarters shortly after the conference and was received without comment or complaints. The General has never stated in what respects the record is misleading. Ambassador Philip Jessup has asserted that the record of the Wake Island Conference prepared and edited by General Bradley "was a composite of all the notes; it was accurate and fairly complete but not verbatim." *New York Times*, February 10, 1956, p. 14.

79. *Hearings*, Part 3, p. 1833, Testimony of Secretary Acheson.

80. *New York Times*, October 25, 1950; *New York Herald Tribune*, October 25, 1950. As early as October 13, Marguerite Higgins reported in the *Herald Tribune* rumors that all but ROK troops would halt some distance south of the Manchurian line.

81. *New York Times*, October 28, 1950, p. 5.

82. S. L. A. Marshall, *The River and the Gauntlet: The Defeat of the Eighth Army by the Chinese Communist Forces* (Morrow, New York, 1953), pp. 7-8.

83. *Hearings*, Part 2, p. 1240, Testimony of General Collins.

84. *Ibid.*, p. 1241.

85. *Times* (London), July 2, 1952, p. 7, quoted in Goodrich, "Korea: Collective Measures against Aggression," p. 166.

86. *New York Herald Tribune*, November 1, 1950, p. 1. The day before, this newspaper had a headline reading "Red Chinese Units Open Heavy Attacks on Allies" and reported that at least two divisions of Chinese were already in combat. The press seems to have accepted field intelligence that General MacArthur's headquarters rejected.

87. *Hearings*, Part 3, p. 1833, Testimony of Secretary Acheson.

88. Truman, *Memoirs*, II, p. 373.

89. *Hearings*, Part 3, p. 1834. The Central Intelligence Agency on November 6 (Washington time) also gave President Truman an estimate of the situation in which it stated that there might be as many as 200,000 Chinese Communist troops in Manchuria. Truman, *Memoirs*, II, p. 377.

90. *Hearings*, Part 3, p. 1833, Testimony of Secretary Acheson.

91. Walter Karig, "The War in Korea" in *Battle Report* (Rinehart, New York, 1952), p. 374.

92. *Hearings*, Part 3, p. 1834, Testimony of Secretary Acheson.

93. *Ibid.* This summary note may somewhat (and quite naturally) reflect hindsight; other speculative suggestions in November were bandied about. There was talk about a Chinese desire for prestige, a desire to keep the U. S. involved in Korea, concern for the hydroelectric power stations, and so on. And of course there was perhaps an equal amount of talk about the reasons why there would be no large-scale commitment of Chinese troops.

94. Letter from Dean Acheson, January 30, 1957; interview with Acheson, March 27, 1957; interview with Dean Rusk, March 26, 1957.

95. Truman, *Memoirs*, II, pp. 373-374.

96. *Ibid.*, p. 375.

97. Quoted in *ibid*. The date given in the *Memoirs* is November 6, but Whitney (*MacArthur*, p. 406) says, undoubtedly correctly, that MacArthur was awakened at 2 A.M., November 7 (KT) to receive and reply to the JCS message. There is a similar slight difference in the text of the message: in the next to last sentence, Truman says "proportion," Whitney says "proportions"; the latter is probably correct.

98. Quoted in Truman, *Memoirs*, II, p. 375.

99. Quoted in *ibid.*, p. 377.

100. Quoted in *Hearings*, Part 3, p. 1928, Testimony of Secretary Acheson.

101. The matter was again raised in mid-January 1951, with the same outcome.

102. *Hearings*, Part 5, p. 3585.

103. A very full and most enlightening discussion of the Communists' limited warfare may be found in Captain (then Lieutenant, U. S. Army) Paul F. Gorman, "Limited War: Korea, 1950," a paper written for Professor William Y. Elliott's Government 285 (MS. Thesis, Harvard University, Fall 1953), pp. 40 ff.

104. Truman, *Memoirs*, II, pp. 376-378.

105. *Ibid.*, p. 377.

106. *Ibid.*, pp. 378-379.

107. This report of the NSC meeting is a paraphrase of President Truman's account. *Ibid.*, pp. 378-380.

108. Summarized in Norman J. Padelford, "The United Nations and Korea: A Political Résumé" in *International Organization* (November 1951), p. 694.

109. See Secretary Acheson's Testimony, *Hearings*, Part 3, pp. 1957-1958. A group of Labour members of the British Parliament proposed in Commons that the United Nations forces halt their advance rather than continue with the proposed occupation of all of Korea and the Marquis of Salisbury, Conservative leader in the House of

Lords, suggested that a line short of the border be immediately announced by the UN beyond which troops would not advance. Rutherford M. Poats, *Decision in Korea* (McBride Co., New York, 1954), p. 95. In mid-December, the Labour Government revealed that it had, indeed, proposed to the U. S. government sometime in November that a buffer zone be established and that a line at the narrow "waist" of North Korea, or at the best military position in advance of it, be fortified. The proposal was based on the belief that the Chinese intervention in early November had been based on misplaced fears that their source of hydro-electric power was threatened and that the intervention had been undertaken with no more than limited objectives. The proposal would thus allow time to determine whether or not an opportunity existed to settle Chinese fears. As late as November 29, Anthony Eden as spokesman for the Conservatives urged the Labour Government to confer with the U. S. on such a proposal and stated that he still favored the fortified line across the North Korean "waist." Hubbard, "U. S. and Great Britain in the Korean Crisis," pp. 51, 56.

110. *New York Times,* November 17, 1950, p. 1.

111. Raymond Daniell in *New York Times,* November 16, 1950, p. 7.

112. *New York Herald Tribune,* November 12, 1950, p. 1.

113. Marshall, *The River and the Gauntlet,* p. 13.

114. *Ibid.,* pp. 13-14.

115. *Ibid.,* p. 15.

116. Paraphrase of message, item 60, page 64, of "Joint Chiefs of Staff Report for Senate Committees on Korean Operations," quoted in *Hearings,* Part 2, p. 1229, Testimony of General Collins. It should be noted that less than a week later, when word leaked out that General MacArthur had been told to stop short of the Yalu, Arthur Krock of the *New York Times* wired to the General asking him if he had ever received such instructions. General MacArthur replied on November 29: "I have received no suggestion from any authoritative source that in the execution of its mission, the command should stop at the Thirty-Eighth Parallel, at Pyongyang, or at any other line short of the international boundary." *New York Times,* December 1, 1950, p. 1.

117. Paraphrase of message, item 60, page 64 of "Joint Chiefs of Staff Report for Senate Committees on Korean Operations," quoted in *Hearings,* Part 2, p. 1230, Testimony of General Collins.

118. No details of the Chinese attack are given here. The best account of the event (and an excellent one) can be found in Marshall, *The River and the Gauntlet.*

119. *Hearings,* Part 2, p. 1314.

120. *Hearings,* Part 2, p. 1314.

121. See above, pp. 589-590, 595-596, 598-603, 606-609.

122. *Hearings,* Part 2, p. 1234. It has been claimed that CINCFE controlled his own intelligence and did not allow other U. S. intelligence agencies, including the CIA, to operate in his command. When this question was raised during the Hearings, General MacArthur vigorously denied that the CIA had been kept out of his theater. General Marshall, however, was rather hazy in his testimony on the matter and implied that there had been some conflict between the CIA and MacArthur's G-2; *Hearings,* Part 1, pp. 86, 122-123, 241-242, 350.

123. Marshall, *The River and the Gauntlet,* pp. 3, 4, 7.

124. *Hearings,* Part 2, p. 759.

125. *Ibid.,* Part 3, p. 2101, Testimony of Secretary Acheson.

126. Truman, *Memoirs,* II, pp. 372, 376, 381.

127. General Courtney Whitney in his biography of his commanding officer states that the CIA "formally reported on the day [General Walton] Walker launched the Eighth Army's drive to the Yalu, November 24, that 'there is no evidence that the Chinese Communists plan major offensive operations in Korea,'" *MacArthur,* p. 392. Perhaps this was Whitney's idiosyncratic interpretation of the CIA report quoted in the text.

128. Quoted in Whitney, *MacArthur,* p. 447.

129. General Assembly, Fifth Sess., First Committee, 415th Meeting (December 12, 1950), p. 433, paragraph 3.

130. *Ibid.,* p. 434, paragraph 12.

131. James Reston in *New York Times,* November 30, 1950, p. 1; summary of foreign press reports in *New York Herald Tribune,* November 30, 1950, p. 1.

132. This account is a summary of Goodrich, "Korea: Collective Measures against Aggression," pp. 167-168.

133. *Hearings,* Part 5, Appendix, p. 3495.

134. Quoted in Truman, *Memoirs,* II, p. 393.

135. "Address of General MacArthur to Joint Meeting of the Congress, April 19, 1951," in *Hearings,* Part 5, Appendix, p. 3614.

136. Truman, *Memoirs,* II, p. 393.

137. *Ibid.,* pp. 257-258.

138. *Ibid.,* pp. 406-407.

139. *Ibid.,* pp. 417-418.

140. *Hearings,* Part 2, p. 1617, Testimony of Admiral Sherman.

141. Evidence of the bad case of nerves that the U. S. and its allies experienced in December is the story of the air alert which reached Washington during the Truman-Attlee Conference. Radar in

the far north had picked up "blips" of large numbers of unidentified planes and it was believed for a brief breathless moment that a Russian "sneak" attack over the North Pole was on its way. It was soon ascertained that the "blips" were caused by atmospheric conditions, not enemy planes, but our policy-makers suffered several tense moments. Truman, *Memoirs*, II, p. 405.

142. *Ibid.*, p. 432.

143. *Hearings*, Part 3, pp. 2243-2244, Testimony of Secretary Acheson.

144. Quoted in *Hearings*, Part 3, pp. 2179-2180.

145. Paraphrase quoted *ibid.*, pp. 2180-2181.

146. MacArthur's intelligence calculated that a total of 443,406—276,173 Chinese and 167,233 North Koreans—faced the UN forces of around 250,000 men, and that the Chinese were believed to have in Manchuria another 650,000 reinforcements and 250,000 more Chinese soldiers were on the way to Manchuria; Poats, *Decision in Korea*, p. 127. It is doubtful that the Chinese or the North Koreans themselves could have supplied figures down to the last digit as was done by MacArthur's G-2 for the Red troops actually in Korea, though perhaps their figures for troops in China would have been rounded at tens of thousands rather than hundreds of thousands. The *New York Times* reported that the enemy force in Korea totalled "over 400,000." January 7, 1951, Section 4, p. 1.

147. Truman, *Memoirs*, II, pp. 433-434.

148. *Ibid.*, p. 434; the phrase "decided by the National Security Council" carries the implication that the NSC is an operating agency; it is, of course, a statutory interdepartmental committee, advisory to the President. But the habit of attributing decisional power to the NSC is, unhappily, endemic.

149. Quoted in *Hearings*, Part 2, p. 906, Testimony of General Bradley.

150. Truman, *Memoirs*, II, p. 435.

151. *Hearings*, Part 1, pp. 333-334, Testimony of Secretary Marshall.

152. Paraphrase quoted in *Hearings*, Part 2, p. 907, Testimony of Secretary Marshall.

153. Quoted in Truman, *Memoirs*, II, pp. 435-436.

154. Poats, *Decision in Korea*, p. 135.

155. Padelford, "The United Nations and Korea: A Political Résumé," pp. 697-699.

156. Quoted in Poats, *Decision in Korea*, p. 137.

157. "Joint Chiefs of Staff Report for the Senate Committees on Korean Operations," p. 93, paragraph 17, quoted in *Hearings*, Part 2, p. 920.

158. *Ibid.*

159. *Times* (London), for example, said at the beginning of March that the solid achievements of the UN forces in Korea "give a new urgency to the question whether or not the 38th parallel should be crossed again. . . ." This, the *Times* declared, should be discussed now while there is an opportunity to look ahead and weigh the consequences. "What seems to be advisable is a definite understanding that the parallel and its immediate neighborhood shall be the limit of military occupation until it can be seen whether the Chinese are ready, on that basis, for an unacknowledged cease-fire that might in time become more precise and lead to a settlement." Quoted in *New York Herald Tribune*, March 4, 1951, section 2, p. 2.

The British hope that there would be no major penetration of the 38th parallel was criticized by some Americans. David Lawrence said that such a halt would encourage the Communists and would be appeasement. *Herald Tribune*, March 6, 1951, p. 6.

160. *New York Times*, February 14, 1951, March 8, 1951, quoted in *Hearings*, Part 5, Appendix, pp. 3539-3540.

161. *New York Herald Tribune*, March 16, 1951, p. 8.

162. *Ibid.*, March 13, 1951, p. 1.

163. A. M. Rosenthal in *New York Times*, March 14, 1951, p. 1.

164. *Ibid.*, March 16, 1951, p. 1; *New York Herald Tribune*, March 17, 1951, p. 3.

165. *New York Times*, March 16, 1951, p. 1.

166. See, for example, editorials in *Washington Post*, March 17, 22, 1951; *Manchester Guardian* quoted in *New York Herald Tribune*, March 18, 1951, section 2, p. 6.

167. Ned Russell in *New York Herald Tribune*, March 21, 1951, p. 1; A. M. Rosenthal in *New York Times*, March 22, 1951, p. 3.

168. *New York Herald Tribune*, March 23, 1951, p. 1.

169. Truman, *Memoirs*, II, pp. 438-439.

170. Quoted in *ibid.*, pp. 439-440.

171. Quoted in *ibid.*, pp. 440-441.

172. *New York Times*, March 25, 1951, p. 1.

173. *New York Herald Tribune*, March 28, 1951, p. 1.

174. *Ibid.*, April 12, 1951, p. 12.

175. Truman, *Memoirs*, II, p. 455.

EDITORIAL COMMENTS

Everyone knows that war is a dangerous undertaking; but most of us forget that it is dangerous not only in its tragic physical destructiveness, but also in its frequently appalling unpredictability; it is unpredictable in the question of who will win, of what the victory will consist, and unpredictable too with respect to what will happen to the initial objectives as the fighting progresses.

In the Anglo-French and Israeli attack on Egypt in 1956, the two large European powers lost all, the two small powers, victor and vanquished alike, ended up as substantial gainers: Egypt, badly beaten in battle, kept the Suez Canal and acquired great prestige, while Israel, forced to withdraw to its boundaries, secured UN protection along the border of the Gaza strip and freedom of transit in the Gulf of Aqaba. Our Spanish-American War began either as a revenge for the sinking of the *Maine* or as a movement to liberate Cuba, but when the fighting ended, we held two protectorates in the Caribbean and one in the far Pacific— indeed in the Philippines we found ourselves fighting a war with the Filipinos. And, to cite one more example, we began the Civil War to preserve the Union; in midstream we found ourselves engaged in a war to free the slaves, an objective that Lincoln would never have requested or been granted in 1861.

Seen in the light of history, the Korean War and particularly its central feature, the march to the Yalu and back, are not surprising in terms of shifting objectives, of changing estimates of the nature of probable victory, but only in the fact that the final UN objective was the same as the first, the final victory what was originally hoped for, and perhaps expected, and no more. Yet even this limited war—and even the expanded objectives were never unlimited —had grotesque and utterly unanticipated consequences: an enormous expansion of U. S.

military force, for example, and a transfer of the North Korean satellite from Russian to Chinese control. But such unpredictability is almost a predictable factor. The forces generated by war are normally visible and definable, but their ultimate resting place is never knowable *ante,* only *ex post facto.*

The progressive shifts from repelling aggression to restoring peace and security, to overseeing free elections, to the unification of a "democratic" Korea (perfectly valid long-standing objectives, but only designed for attainment by political, not military, means) were thus not surprising. What was unusual was the final decision to revert to "repelling aggression" as a satisfactory, the only satisfactory, solution of the protracted struggle. This final decision, bitterly criticized, was arrived at simultaneously after long discussions by officers of the State Department and of the armed services. They agreed fully, though the fulcrum of emphasis for the two overlapping rationales differed. Both, of course, like the President, were deeply concerned with domestic political outcries, ever increasing. Beyond this, to the diplomats the most instant concern was with the almost strident complaints of our allies and of the neutrals like India; to the military the pressing desire was to strengthen our defenses in Europe and to avoid the drain of the fighting in Korea. To some extent, their urgent desire for an end to the war in Korea and their insistence on a continuing limitation on our involvement there, were based on the false assumption that this was the beginning of total war; as this assumed probability began to fade, it was assumed that the Communists were trying to draw us into a trap, to make us waste our resources on the Korean peninsula. In retrospect, it seems far more likely that the Communist objective was aggrandizement—no more, no less. Nevertheless, our basic decision to give priority to European defense is still a cornerstone of our military policy.

To say that the intellectual approaches of the officers of the State Department and the military had different emphases is not to say that they did not understand and concur in each other's views. Acheson and his subordinates wished to back up strategy by diplomacy, Marshall and the JCS sought diplomatic aid in achieving strategic objectives. Both groups made their positions clear to the President, and he fully accepted their advice. What he also faced, knowingly, and more sharply than they, were the domestic political consequences.

The consequences would have been unpleasant in any event; their impact was greatly enhanced by MacArthur's actions. It is unnecessary here to discuss the wisdom of MacArthur's policy. What must be noted is that MacArthur's moves constituted a civil-military issue only in the special technical context of his relations with his formal Commander in Chief; he was just as much at odds with the Joint Chiefs of Staff and Secretary Marshall as he was with the President. The long debate concerned basic policy: to use vulgar phrases, Asia Firsters vs. Europe Firsters, Go-It-Aloners vs. Stay-with-our-Allies-Men, and so on. And the noisy but evanescent outcry in MacArthur's favor really reflected dismay over the dismal events in Korea, the stirrings of violent partisan political warfare, and general distaste with the Truman Administration; it did not represent any substantial support of MacArthur's proposal to enlarge the fighting. Limited war proved to be bitterly distasteful, but the American people showed no desire to end the limitations by means which might open up the possibility of total war.

One other aspect of the MacArthur controversy is the American concept of the independence of the theater commander. Apparently the Joint Chiefs of Staff believed that the march to the Yalu was in great danger of running into trouble, but their cables to MacArthur did no more than suggest and question, nor did they ever ask the President to intervene. One need not adopt the British tradition where Churchill felt free to send out daily, almost hourly, suggestions, instructions, requests to Auchinleck, for example, to believe that the JCS did not live up to the inherent responsibilities of their office when they failed to translate

their justifiable fears into specific admonitions or into specific requests for presidential intervention.

The President was also affected by his own somewhat similar attitude toward theater commanders when it did not occur to him to relieve MacArthur after MacArthur's own *hubris* led to disastrous defeat. As has been noted in the text, six years later Truman was still equating Eisenhower's 30-mile setback in the Battle of the Bulge with MacArthur's 250-mile pellmell retreat from the Yalu.

On the larger constitutional issue, however, Truman was patient, but eventually firm and decisive. Ernest May has suggested that the framers of the Constitution expected the Commander in Chief to "determine where [war] was to be fought . . . to make the choices between primary and secondary theaters. He was to assume responsibility for naming the officers to direct operations in each of these theaters and hence for their choice of subsidiary aims." These are indeed the responsibilities that Truman accepted and executed. No President could have been a more fully constitutional Commander in Chief.

One further aspect of the Korean affair deserves note: coalition war. From 1939 to 1941 we were laying the plans for a coalition in preparing for war; from 1941 to 1945 we were active participants in a coalition waging full-scale war; beginning about 1949 we again entered into coalition to prevent war, or win it if necessary; and in June 1950 we formed a coalition to carry out limited war.

Efficient and effective coalition warfare is a highly sophisticated art, and a deliberately limited war with seventeen participating nations, with two providing well over 95 per cent of the troops, and one providing the great bulk of the equipment and supplies, nine-tenths of the non-ROK forces and all the immediate military direction, is a formidably difficult task. So far as conduct of a war is concerned a CCS with six members is infinitely more manageable than a Committee of Sixteen. One is inclined to sympathize with MacArthur who resented the presence of our allies. Yet all the advice of the Committee was filtered through the State Department and the Department of Defense and reached MacArthur officially from the JCS via the Army Chief of Staff. Furthermore, MacArthur did not have to deal with military representatives of allies acting in positions of prominence and power, as Eisenhower did with Montgomery (and as, one might perhaps say, MacArthur did from 1942 to 1945 with some of our own admirals).

MacArthur's public condemnation of the British, implying the British government, and indicated disdain for most of the other allies really turned on the large question of strategy for limited war. He assumed rightly that almost all our allies were anxious to keep the war limited; he assumed also that his own government unwillingly and supinely acceded to the wishes of the allies. This was not true, except for the special case of "hot pursuit." In fact, to put the matter crudely, leaving aside the Republic of Korea which presented its own special problems, dealing with our fifteen allies was usually no more than a conventional diplomatic problem. There were some hesitations when the troops passed the 38th parallel, more when they approached the Yalu. And the defeat by the Chinese led to recrimination and debate. New and acceptable policies were adopted, and the coalition stayed together.

What motivated Marshall and Acheson and Truman were considerations that MacArthur had no interest in. They had to be sure they could count on the active participation of England and France in NATO, they had to do their best to bolster the position of India in Southwest Asia, and to retain her friendship; and they necessarily had deep concern for our other NATO allies and for the impact of our behavior on the rest of the world. It was for reasons such as these, which MacArthur brushed aside, that Truman and his aides insisted on retaining the participation of the allies in the Korean War even though their presence was of little immediate military import. And finally, the deliberate tying-in of the Korean conflict into UN meant that UN acceptance of our policy was essential if UN was to be preserved and strengthened. On this point, Truman was fully committed, by public statement and by personal conviction.

THE AMERICAN DECISION TO
REARM GERMANY

LAURENCE W. MARTIN

ASSOCIATE PROFESSOR OF EUROPEAN DIPLOMACY

SCHOOL OF ADVANCED INTERNATIONAL STUDIES AND RESEARCH ASSOCIATE,

WASHINGTON CENTER OF FOREIGN POLICY RESEARCH

THE JOHNS HOPKINS UNIVERSITY

CONTENTS

The American Decision to Rearm Germany   645

Bibliographic Note   661

Notes   662

Editorial Comments   664

THE AMERICAN DECISION TO REARM GERMANY

During hearings on the extension of the Mutual Defense Assistance Act on June 5, 1950, the Secretary of State, Dean Acheson, assured members of the House Foreign Affairs Committee that the United States would continue to maintain the demilitarization of Germany. Indeed, he went so far as to say: "There is no discussion of doing anything else. That is our policy and we have not raised it or revalued it."[1] The same day, the Secretary of Defense, Louis Johnson, told the Senate Armed Services and Foreign Relations Committees that "there has been no detailed discussion or adoption of any plan for an overall Commander" of NATO forces and that "an overall Commander we deem neither advisable nor necessary."[2] Neither Acheson nor Johnson made any mention of any proposal to increase American ground forces in Europe.

Just three months later, in September, when Acheson met with the British and French Foreign Secretaries at the Waldorf in New York, prior to a session of the North Atlantic Council, he informed them that the United States was now willing to provide NATO with a Supreme Commander and substantial reinforcements of American ground forces. To the distress of the two Europeans, they discovered that these offers that they so ardently desired were tightly linked to a policy which called for the rearmament of Germany.[3] This, it appeared, was the basis upon which the United States was willing to continue and indeed expand its vigorous exertions in support of NATO.

There had been a great change in American policy. This about-turn was precipitated by the Communist invasion of the Republic of Korea. But the Korean War was not the only reason for Acheson's position in New York, nor did it explain how he had arrived at the particular combination of proposals which he advanced at that time. His new policy can only be under-

stood as the result of several developments, some well established, some recent, in the American approach to the future of Germany and the defense of Europe. These trends, set in motion by earlier Russian truculence, had entered a critical phase even before the Korean outbreak, under the stimulus of the Russian A-bomb detonation in September 1949.

The future of Germany has a strong claim to rank as one of the gravest and most dangerous unresolved diplomatic questions of post-war years. If Europe is to be tranquil presumably it must provide a stable place in the balance of power for Germany and its people. Efforts to work out a settlement for the whole of Germany which would be acceptable to the four occupying powers met constant frustration in the descending chill of the Cold War. As prospects waned that East and West could agree on methods to deal with the Germans as a common danger, Germany increasingly assumed the aspect of a prize to be won. American policy for the occupation, as laid down in 1946 in directive JCS 1067, was progressively pruned of its punitive aspects, until JCS 1779, issued in July 1947, formally embodied a new and milder policy. By 1948 deadlock among the occupying powers had hardened beyond immediate hope of solution, and the Western Three, with France uneasily bringing up the rear, began to merge their zones and organize them on a long-term basis. Successful resistance to the Berlin Blockade (April 1948-May 1949) gave added impetus to this process, and the inauguration of the Bonn Republic in 1949 marked a decisive stage in Germany's road back to sovereignty.[4]

Also in 1949, on April 4, the signing of the North Atlantic Pact made explicit another development of American policy toward Europe. The European Recovery Program had already demonstrated that the United States government was convinced that it had a vital interest in the economic and political stability and independence of Europe. American participation in NATO acknowledged the futility of building up Europe via the Marshall Plan only to have it lie open to Soviet conquest. If there seemed little prospect of finding the wherewithal to muster forces which would be a real match for Russia, it might at least be possible to reconstitute sufficient semblance of military power in the Continental democracies to bolster their confidence in the face of Soviet encroachments. Furthermore, a solid even if not invincible force would constitute a shield to be employed along with the sword of SAC.

The North Atlantic Treaty did not obligate the United States to maintain troops of its own permanently in Europe, but it was no longer possible for those responsible for American security to avoid a careful consideration of the prospects for defending Western Europe. The very creation of NATO reflected a conviction that Europe's defenses were far from adequate and could be made so only by close coordination of European efforts, supplemented by American support. Congress demonstrated the importance it attached to a cooperative effort by specifying in the Mutual Defense Assistance Act (October 6, 1949) that the bulk of the supplies provided by the program were not to be shipped until the President was satisfied that there existed a concept for "an integrated defense of the North Atlantic Area." This concept was approved by the North Atlantic Council on January 6, 1950 and approval was accepted by President Truman as satisfactory; he then gave the signal on January 27 for full-scale deliveries to begin.

As American policy toward both Germany and NATO unfolded, the United States government repeatedly avowed its unalterable opposition to any relaxation of German disarmament. In April 1949, during hearings on the North Atlantic Treaty, Acheson had explained to the Senate Foreign Relations Committee that "the disarmament and demilitarization of Germany must be complete and absolute" and that "a discussion of including West Germany in the pact is not possible."[5] The Occupation Statute of April 8, 1949, which set up machinery for the control of the emergent Bonn Republic, provided for the continued existence of a Military Security Board to en-

force demilitarization. Even in November 1949, the so-called Petersberg Agreement, which granted Germany an even greater measure of autonomy, affirmed the obligation of the German government itself to prevent rearmament. But, for all this, the closer Germany came to sovereignty and the greater the attention paid to the task of defending Western Europe, the more difficult it became to leave out of calculation the military potential of a major European nation.

Apparently as early as 1947 the Joint War Plans Branch of what was then the Operations and Plans Division of the U. S. Army (G-3) gave some consideration to the future place of Germany and Japan in the strategic balance. These early speculations, the first of many at lower levels, were highly tentative and did not indicate a serious expectation that there would soon be any important changes in the official American policy of keeping Germany disarmed. But certainly when, in 1948, the Brussels Pact established Western Union and the United States had to define its relation to the new grouping, the Joint Chiefs of Staff were alert to the importance of a possible German armed force. The question was, of course, a delicate one, for Western Union was intended to meet the danger of German as well as Russian aggression. At a meeting of the National Security Council on May 20, 1948, the Secretary of the Army, Kenneth Royall, stressed the trepidation with which the JCS would regard a commitment to the defense of Europe and their anxiety to make sure that any agreements entailing such an engagement should leave open the possibility of a later accession of Germany and Spain. The State Department, however, was eager to associate the United States with Europe's efforts as quickly and with as few reservations as possible and thought it inopportune to run the risks of discord which would be incurred by taking up the issues mentioned by Royall. President Truman personally forbade any dealings with the Spanish regime. In the end, the NSC decided or recommended (in line, naturally, with President Truman's attitudes) that although Germany and Spain certainly presented questions for the future, these should not be broached at the moment. Consequently, on June 6, 1948, in talks with the ambassadors of the Brussels Powers in Washington, the Under Secretary of State, Robert Lovett, told them that America considered it too early to raise the problem of a Spanish or German part in the defense effort.[6]

Speculation on the military future of Germany was not confined to government officials and in the summer and autumn of 1948 the first serious discussion of German rearmament took place in the American and European press. Mutual American and Soviet charges that the other was plotting to revive the Wehrmacht enlivened public interest. As these propaganda sallies suggest, most of the public discussion presented German rearmament as a potential danger to be avoided rather than as a worthy object of national policy.[7]

This debate, like that in the NSC, proceeded on the assumption that the question was one for the fairly remote future, and in the winter of 1948 the topic dropped out of sight. But by the autumn of 1949 several causes combined to renew and intensify interest in Germany's military status. Negotiation of the Petersberg Agreement served to draw special attention to the speed of German progress toward recovery and independence. Within NATO, efforts to devise a concept for European defense in order to inaugurate the Mutual Defense Assistance Program and serve as a basis for drawing up a Medium Term Defense Plan more than ever convinced military leaders on both sides of the Atlantic that the Western powers labored under a gross deficiency of forces-in-being and of resources, particularly manpower, for filling the gap. Political and economic instability in France, coupled with the strength of the French Communist Party, combined to sap faith in France as an ally. There was, therefore, an increasing interest in Germany as the only obvious untapped reservoir of industry and manpower. The formidable military reputation of the Germans reinforced this interest, the more so as Western strategists sought from the very first to establish their defense line as far to the East as possible. Such a strategy seemed imperative in a modern war of movement (World War II was still thought of as a "modern" war) and was also the plan which best accorded with the fervent European desire to be defended rather than liberated. Even a line on the Rhine was unacceptable to those members of NATO, such as Holland and Denmark, who would find themselves on the wrong side. A "forward strategy" to meet this situation required the use

of German territory for maneuvering, increased the need for fighting men, and suggested the importance of ensuring that the German population would identify themselves with the cause of the NATO forces and thus prove cooperative if hostilities began.[8] The terms of reference given to the Regional Planning Groups of NATO by the Standing Group, early in 1950, instructed them to make use of German territory but made no mention of a possible German contribution to the defending forces.[9] In point of fact, there were insufficient forces at that time to hold any line at all, forward or rearward.

Probably the most influential single advocate of German military revival whose views had recently been made public was Field Marshal Viscount Montgomery, who had an excellent opportunity to survey the situation from his WEU headquarters at Fontainebleau. In several informal statements made during a visit to America in November 1949, he declared that the forces planned at the moment were totally incapable of holding the Rhine, much less the Elbe, and that the only plausible solution lay in the use of German manpower.[10] At about the same time General Lucius D. Clay, the recently retired American Military Governor in Germany came out in favor of a limited German contribution to a composite European force.[11] Visiting Paris, Senator Elmer Thomas of Oklahoma suggested that "several divisions of German troops should be armed by the United States, without Germany being permitted to manufacture arms."[12] Press reports appeared to the effect that American and European staff officers were convinced of the need for German armed forces.[13]

John J. McCloy, the American High Commissioner in Germany, was privately another proponent of German rearmament, at least in the form of a strong federal police to counter the para-military police force which East Germany was building up to a projected strength of 360,000. In addition to being acutely alarmed by the East German police, McCloy believed that Germany could be made a stable element in Europe only on a basis of full equality, and that equality included the right to maintain defense forces. Early in December, Chancellor Konrad Adenauer invigorated public discussion and pointed up the two-way relation between rearmament and German independence by declaring that if German troops were to be raised, they must serve not as mercenaries but as a contribution on equal terms to a European Army. Although the Chancellor referred to such a development as "one for the remote future," his remarks indicated that Germany herself would impose conditions before falling in with any schemes for remilitarization.[14] This hint received less attention than it deserved.

However firmly the military leaders of NATO might already have decided by the end of 1949 that a realistic plan for the defense of Europe demanded a formidable increase in forces, the State Department was very much aware that an effort to solve the problem by rearming Germany would have political repercussions both at home and abroad which might more than outweigh its military advantages. Apart from any fears of renewed German aggression which Americans might harbor, European and especially French hostility to a German military renaissance raised the possibility that an effort to associate Germany with NATO plans might undermine the whole edifice of Western defense. The reassurance of a NATO from which Germany was excluded had, indeed, done much to reconcile the French to the formation of the Bonn Republic.[15] Other arguments for caution were the possibility of provoking Russian countermeasures and the danger of driving the satellites of Eastern Europe deeper into Soviet arms; this latter danger was particularly acute with Poland, partly because of the Poles' profound hatred of the Germans, partly because of the problems caused by the creation of the Oder-Neisse line. Remilitarization might also impair hopes of achieving the ultimate reunification of Germany. Obviously Acheson and Henry Byroade, Director of the State Department's Bureau of German Affairs, were familiar with all these arguments and perhaps with others too. They remained convinced that the risks of German rearmament in the immediate future were too great; presumably their judgment was accepted, indeed almost certainly encouraged, or even required by President Truman. The Secretary was therefore necessarily willing to settle for a relaxation of the process of dismantling and the restrictions on German industry which ran counter to the purposes of the Marshall Plan. This became the official American position and on November 16 and 17, 1949, Acheson and the President responded to the flurry of public speculation by disavowing any

intention of letting the Germans rearm. Johnson and General Omar Bradley, Chairman of the JCS, then in Europe, echoed these denials a few days later.[16]

This decision against modifying the demilitarization of Germany implied, if it was to be realistic, a determination to close the gaps in European defenses from other sources. A general conviction that the acute threat of war lay at least four or five years ahead lent plausibility to this policy. Efforts to develop a Medium Term Defense Plan and to muster the forces to execute it without German assistance occupied American and NATO planners throughout the spring of 1950. The grave difficulties they encountered actually reinforced their interest in the possibility of using German troops.

Any speculation within the American government as to the possibility of using German troops would, of course, remain highly confidential so long as the official policy of the United States remained precisely the opposite. As it happened, while American spokesmen were quite truthfully denying, in November 1949, that there was any change in their policy concerning German rearmament, the United States Army was already beginning a vigorous effort to bring about the creation of German divisions. Apparently the initiative stemmed from the Joint War Plans Branch, whose periodic contemplation of the gaps in American defenses had once more prompted them to identify Germany as a possible source of relief. This time the idea was at last taken up seriously within the Plans Division of G-3, under Brigadier General C. V. R. Schuyler; the burden of detailed planning fell upon the International Branch of the Plans Division.[17] General Alfred Gruenther, Deputy Chief of Staff, and General Bradley watched the whole operation closely.

Under these auspices a plan emerged which called for the direct incorporation in NATO of German ground forces organized conventionally in divisions. To meet anticipated objections that these forces might become instruments of renewed German aggression, the Army plan contained provisions, relatively unrefined, for retaining control, perhaps by restricting the types of weapons which the Germans might acquire or produce. Both the Army staff and, later on, the JCS seem to have been quite sanguine as to the readiness of the Germans themselves to take up arms.

Because deficiencies in ground forces provided the most powerful incentive toward German rearmament, the plan was chiefly of interest to the Army. But after it had been thoroughly worked out by the Army staff and signed by Gruenther as Deputy Chief of Staff, it was laid before the Army's opposite numbers in the Navy and Air Force. These services had markedly less interest in the project. The Air Force indicated that it would welcome additional tactical air forces in Europe and that any German effort in the air should take that form. Naval planners displayed somewhat greater interest in a German contribution toward meeting a serious deficiency of minesweepers and antisubmarine vessels, particularly in the Baltic.

These discussions lasted well into 1950. On several occasions while working on the plan, Lieutenant Colonel J. G. K. Miller consulted with Byroade, with whom he had been acquainted during the latter's career as an Army officer. Actually the Director of the Bureau of German Affairs was himself a graduate of West Point, had a wide acquaintance in the Pentagon as a result of his own experience as a professional soldier, and was still a colonel in the Army on active service, merely on loan to the State Department at this time. These circumstances facilitated a freer exchange of views between the two institutions than might otherwise have occurred. For in general, the Pentagon and the State Department were somewhat at "arm's length" during this period. Many members of each organization doubted the wisdom and discretion of the other. More important, Secretary Johnson's own explicit distrust and animus were such that he had forbidden any of his subordinates to engage in binding discussions with members of the State Department without his own explicit permission, and strongly discouraged any discussion at all. Personal relations between the two Secretaries were painfully unpleasant. Under these circumstances the discreet and informal exchanges of views which took place during the formulation of a national policy on German rearmament performed an unusually important service in preventing a serious breakdown in communication.

In the consultations which took place early in 1950, Byroade counselled delay, certainly until completion of the complicated legal process of restoring Germany to full sovereignty. Nevertheless, the Army planners elected to push

their scheme forward, and after receiving the assent of the other services, submitted the plan to the JCS for approval. This approval was given by April 30, 1950. Apparently, the JCS postponed their request for Presidential approval.

Work on the Army's plan had proceeded against the background of an urgent reassessment of all aspects of American security, prompted by Russia's unexpectedly rapid success in exploding an atomic bomb, announced by President Truman on September 23, 1949. The President had then promptly ordered a comprehensive scrutiny of national defense by an interdepartmental team.[18] The results of the survey formed the basis for a massive state paper, NSC-68. This paper never won full acceptance as a guide for American policy and it did not give prominence to possible German assistance. Indeed, in its recommendations for strengthening the free world, the paper urged concentration first on the United States, secondly on America's allies, and only as a final stage upon Germany and Japan. But NSC-68 undoubtedly reflected a much sharpened fear of the Russian danger and a generally held belief that the Western alliance must rapidly increase its armed forces.

To the JCS this belief meant that there was an urgent need for developing conventional forces capable of meeting a conventional Russian attack before loss of the United States' overwhelming nuclear superiority neutralized her atomic deterrent. Though there was already hope of securing new types of weapons to compensate for inferiority in numbers, the prospect was not thought to obviate the need for a large increase in ground forces; some military leaders, aware that a decision to use nuclear weapons would not be theirs alone, felt compelled to strive toward a satisfactory defense based on conventional forces until they were specifically authorized to do otherwise. In two speeches which he delivered in the spring of 1950, Bradley gave a clue to the foundations of planning within the JCS. On April 14, at Chicago, he warned that NATO plans were in danger of outrunning the readiness of governments to provide the necessary forces. A month later, on May 19, in San Francisco, the General expounded the need to establish adequate ground forces before Russia succeeded in her efforts to achieve an atomic deadlock.[19]

These statements were made in the light of the sobering studies which occupied the attention of NATO in the early months of 1950. The North Atlantic Council was scheduled to meet in London on May 15 to review the efforts of the Regional Planning Groups to work out a Medium Term Defense Plan; prior to the meeting, the "Big Three" Foreign Ministers planned to discuss the future of Germany. Earlier, Winston Churchill had directed renewed public attention to the possibility of rearming Germany by declaring in the House of Commons on March 16 that he was in favor of incorporating German troops in a European army. This suggestion drew heated condemnation from the British Foreign Minister, Ernest Bevin, on March 28, and early in April, Acheson and McCloy had reiterated American opposition to German rearmament.[20] In conformity with these professions the communiqué issued by the Big Three after their pre-Council meeting ended on May 13 (just before the North Atlantic Council meeting) announced the intention of gradually integrating Germany with the "European community" but made no mention of creating any German forces, even for the purpose of balancing the East German police. These para-military forces were then arousing sufficient anxiety to prompt the three Western occupying powers to deliver a joint protest to the Soviet Union a week later.[21]

In the May 1950 meeting which followed the Big Three session, the North Atlantic Council took up the plans which had been prepared by the Regional Groups and approved by the Defense Committee on April 1. It immediately became clear that military requirements exceeded the efforts which their governments were willing to make. The forces budgeted for would not even meet the needs of the Medium Term Defense Plan, in itself the concoction rather of faith than experience. Confidence in NATO's capacity to fulfill its task was ebbing and the American representatives were somewhat isolated in their eagerness to stimulate greater exertions. The United States itself shared with the other NATO participants a widespread reluctance to undertake greater economic and military burdens.

Defects in organization had aggravated the difficulties. In particular, the strategists and the financial and economic experts were hampered by inadequate knowledge of each other's needs and capabilities. The French were especially eager to secure a pooling of expenses. Whatever its larger merits, this was a device which would have increased French influence, or veto power, and would also have meant financial assistance for France. In April the Prime Minister, Georges Bidault, had also proposed an Atlantic High Council for Peace to provide coordination. The North Atlantic Council did not address itself to this proposal but it made a partial move in the same direction by establishing a Council of Deputies, to be in continuous session. The Deputies' first task would be to continue the effort to obtain national commitments adequate to fulfill the defense plan. In another attempt to secure greater efficiency the Council also decided to seek "balanced collective forces" instead of merely coordinating self-contained national armed forces.[22]

The Council did not discuss a possible German contribution. Inside the American delegation, however, Germany's future military role commanded considerable attention, for the JCS, having made up their minds in favor of rearming Germany, took the bold course of cabling to their representative on the American delegation, instructing him to place their proposal before Acheson with a view to taking it up with the other NATO powers for immediate action. This dramatic action prompted debate among the State Department representatives. Within their own circle, members of the Bureau of German Affairs conceded that the question of rearmament must be faced before long. Perry Laukhuff, Director of the Division of German Political Affairs, inclined toward a close association of Germany with NATO, whereby she could make a contribution short of rearmament. But the risks still weighed heavily, the more so as the mere presence of American troops bound by the obligations of the North Atlantic Treaty was widely regarded as sufficient deterrent for the near future. Acheson himself was acutely aware of the need for greater efforts to strengthen the defense structure against the day of nuclear parity, but he, and Byroade even more so, were also among those most sensitive to the diplomatic hazards which an effort to rearm Germany would encounter. In any case, the Secretary firmly believed that he should not raise the matter even informally with the allies during the meetings in London until it had been subjected to thorough consideration within the

United States government. He also knew that the President would have to be persuaded and he therefore refused to adopt the JCS suggestion. There the matter rested on May 18, 1950, when the Council adjourned.

The tenor of JCS thinking and its divergence from that of the State Department finally became public and explicit on June 6, 1950, when Bradley testified before the House Foreign Affairs Committee during its hearings on the extension of the Mutual Defense Assistance Act. Acheson, as has been noted, had assured the committee on the previous day that, although NATO defenses were "totally inadequate," there was no thought of permitting German rearmament. By contrast, Bradley announced that the highest American military opinion was settled in favor of rearming Germany. Endorsing Acheson's pessimistic estimate of existing forces, the Chairman of the JCS declared:

From a strictly military point of view, I do believe the defense of Western Europe would be strengthened by the inclusion of Germany . . . because we do know that they have great production facilities that we could use and we know that they are very capable soldiers and airmen and sailors. . . . From a strictly military point of view I think we must all admit that the security of Western Europe would be strengthened if they were included in it.

But he added in response to questions:

There are political considerations that enter into it with relation to ourselves and other countries of Europe. I do not feel qualified to say just how much they augment the purely military picture.

The extent of German military participation, he continued cannily, is "something entirely out of military hands. It must be decided on a higher level and with all the angles considered."[23]

Early in June 1950, then, high-ranking American diplomats, concerned though they were about the unsatisfactory state of Europe's defenses, remained convinced that to remedy the situation by attempting to rearm Germany would entail disproportionate diplomatic damage, especially to Western European cooperation and morale, and would run counter to European economic rehabilitation, which had been given clear priority in the original MDAP. On the other hand, military leaders, presented with a mission which they believed beyond the resources available to them, had concluded that strategic realism called for the creation of German armed forces. However, in view of the general conviction that the acute danger of Soviet aggression lay several years off, the difference over German rearmament could be regarded as one for speculation rather than active resolution.[24]

At this point the North Koreans crossed the 38th parallel. Their attack cast the German question in a new and lurid light. The Communists' demonstration of strength and their resort to hostilities even, as it seemed, at the risk of large-scale nuclear war compelled military leaders and diplomats alike to reappraise the requirements for deterring Soviet aggression. In the words of General Bradley, it was apparent "that communism is willing to use arms to gain its ends. This is a fundamental change and it has forced a change in our estimate of the military needs of the United States."[25] The weight carried by strategic and military factors in national policy greatly increased. The decline in the attention paid to ground forces was abruptly reversed. Both the scale and the timing of NATO's effort had to be reconsidered.

The Administration at once made a survey of other possible danger points, resulting in the production of yet another paper, NSC-76. It did not require extended cogitation, however, to perceive that Korea might hold special implications for Germany. The German and Korean situations lent themselves to a deceptively neat analogy. Both countries were divided and in the Communist half of each there were indigenous armed forces.[26] Acheson, who regarded the commitment of Communist troops to combat as a major turning point, recalled a speech in which Georgi Malenkov, late in 1949, had listed Korea, Yugoslavia, and Berlin as three unsatisfactory situations due for early correction. There was much nervousness in West Germany itself, and though somewhat reassured by the promptness with which America took up the challenge in Korea, Chancellor Adenauer hastened to demand greater provision for the defense of his country.[27] As it was, against an East German police force already numbering some 60,000 men, supported by 27 Soviet divisions in Germany and 75 more available for speedy concentration, NATO could muster only 12 divisions, ill-equipped, uncoordinated, and deployed with no thought of combat. Against about 1,000 combat aircraft in the NATO forces the Russians were believed to dispose of more than 6,000.[28]

Korea might be the occasion for the advance or collapse of United States' policy toward Europe. The new sense of urgency might reconcile Congress and the American electorate to greater efforts and steel Europeans for sterner sacrifices. But if a feeling of hopelessness developed instead, and the next meeting of the North Atlantic Council, set for New York in September, failed to mark a decisive step forward, the flimsy defensive structure might crumble. Very soon after the Korean outbreak there were signs that the stimulus might indeed be more than offset by pessimism. Some Europeans believed that an attempt to build up NATO forces would provoke a preventive attack by the Russians long before Western defenses had been adequately strengthened. Even those who were willing to make the attempt thought it essential for the United States to provide aid on a majestic scale and participate in the early provision of a shield behind which preparations might proceed. The possibility of an undue diversion of American attention to Asia was most alarming.

President Truman's Administration tried to surmount these obstacles and press forward in Europe as best it could among the distractions of the Korean campaign. In the midst of a complete reshaping of American defense policy, Acheson continued to regard Europe as the key to the world situation and to work toward bolstering European morale. The NATO Standing Group set about revising the Medium Term Defense Plan. In July the President requested greatly expanded appropriations for American armed forces and an additional $4 billion for the MDAP—a sum that had been worked out earlier, but was considered politically impracticable before Korea. At the same time the United States requested the other members of NATO to supply, by the first week in August, estimates of their own increased defense programs.[29] On July 25, the North Atlantic Deputies, with an American, Charles Spofford, as Chairman, began their work under conditions of unexpected urgency.

Earlier speculation made it impossible for such an intensive review of Europe's defense to ignore the possibility of German assistance. Both the urgency of the need for more troops and the climate of political possibility had changed fundamentally since the issue of German rearmament had last been shelved. The JCS now had all the more reason for misgivings about the gap between their capabilities and their commitments. Korea magnified the danger in Europe and simultaneously drained off resources to Asia.

But there still remained a great many questions to settle before selecting German rearmament as a solution. Were the Germans in a mood to rearm and what price were they likely to exact? How long would it take to create the organization and amass the supplies necessary for the establishment of effective German units? The whole Western alliance was desperately short of military equipment and Germany lacked the barest framework of a military establishment. On this account alone it might well be several years before any sizable German force could take the field.

If these difficulties did not present an unanswerable objection to German rearmament in themselves, there remained the question of whether the advantages would be offset by consequent diplomatic embarrassments. In particular, would the other occupying powers (by now, occupiers in form only) and members of NATO give their consent? France would certainly resist the formation of an independent German army, and German statesmen had made it quite clear that they would never accept an inferior status for their troops. Could these attitudes be reconciled? These questions and the answers to them would intertwine with each other and be colored by the reconsideration of strategic doctrine which ought to attend the prospect of nuclear parity, the development of tactical atomic weapons and the inception of limited conventional warfare, as in Korea, all of which presaged the military revolution of mid-century. The problem was one of those major issues of national security which cannot be separated into its military and diplomatic components but must be dealt with as a coherent whole. American foreign policy could not rest solidly upon an inadequate military base. But an attempt to rearm Germany which alienated essential allies or assumed a German readiness to cooperate which failed to materialize, could only weaken American defenses.

In response to this challenge, the JCS refurbished their earlier plan to set up German divisions under somewhat tenuous restrictions as to equipment and higher staff organization. The JCS presented a revised proposal in the NSC in July, as part of a plan to advance NATO from the concept of "balanced collective forces" to that of a "ready force" unified under a permanent fighting command. The speed with which they did so suggested a belief that the need for rapid action was too great to permit extended exploration of all the possible implications of the proposal in its new context. The Joint Chiefs and their advisers knew well enough that a considerable interval must elapse before German troops put in an appearance. Impatience to make a start on the long process of rearmament was indeed one of the prime arguments in favor of an early decision to begin. But the insistence with which the JCS were shortly to demand acceptance of precisely their formula gives rise to the speculation that the military leaders could not wholly divest themselves of a feeling that the very decision to create German divisions would somehow improve the immediate strategic situation. For the moment, however, the Joint Chiefs had to bide their time. The State Department again successfully resisted the suggestion of rearming Germany; and the commander in chief was more likely to support his Secretary of State than his Secretary of Defense.

Within the State Department, Acheson and his staff were nonetheless engaged upon their own reassessment of Germany's part in the design for NATO. They shared the view that Korea had inaugurated a new epoch requiring fresh departures in American policy and they were also aware that the JCS would not long be content to let the matter of German rearmament rest. But although there was general recognition of the danger and of the need for action, there was no unanimity on what to do. The attractiveness of German rearmament varied according to the outlook of the beholder upon the general problem of European security. A bold and hazardous attempt to rush the Germans into uniform appealed to those who were oppressed by a sense of imminent danger and who responded most sensitively to the advice and pressure of the JCS. Others believed that because a lengthy period must elapse before German troops could make a significant contribution to NATO's fighting strength, German rearmament must be regarded as a long-term proposition. On this assumption it was reasonable to take the time to deliberate carefully on the best way to proceed. This argument

was reinforced by the consideration that a hasty approach which aggravated political and diplomatic difficulties might well prove the least expeditious path to reach the goal of German units in a well-integrated NATO force. The anxiety produced in Europe by Korea, the desire of the Germans for protection, and the eagerness of the French and others for financial assistance should therefore be used as a basis on which to seek a method of German rearmament tolerable to all concerned. There was, of course, no guarantee that this procedure would ultimately produce German troops without damaging NATO, but to its proponents it seemed the safest course.

At any rate it was clear that a decision could not be long delayed if Germany was to play a part in the next wave of NATO planning. In July, Byroade relieved Laukhuff and his deputy of their normal duties so that they could devote their whole attention to an examination of the case for rearming Germany and the manner in which it might best be accomplished. Their object was a program which would yield appreciable assistance to NATO while doing the least damage to the solidarity of the alliance or to hopes of a democratic and peaceable Germany. The paper which emerged from this study concluded that the altered circumstances following Korea did justify an effort to develop German armed forces as direct contributions to NATO, subject to restrictions of the kind embodied in the Army's scheme.

After he had initiated this inquiry, Byroade learned that McCloy, still extremely wary of the East German para-military police and an early advocate of giving West Germany some means of self-defense,[30] had sent his legal adviser, Robert Bowie, a professor on leave from the Harvard Law School and experienced in governmental service, and Colonel H. A. Gerhardt, an Army officer assigned to service with the State Department, to work on a similar investigation. The prospect of German rearmament naturally aroused great interest in McCloy's headquarters, and there too a variety of opinions emerged. From the vantage point of Bonn it was not easy to minimize the resistance to rearmament within Germany itself. A general mood of disillusionment with military affairs gripped the country. Some Germans opposed rearmament on the grounds that it would provoke a Russian attack or destroy all hope of peaceful reunification. All democratic leaders were uneasy lest the revival of a German army should undermine the new democracy which was just finding its feet. Moreover, those who were willing to swallow their doubts made it clear that they would never accept restrictions which would imply an inferior status for German soldiers.

To meet some of these difficulties Bowie became a proponent of a plan for a European Army, which had been advanced in various quarters during the previous year. This might provide a control over German forces capable of allaying French fears without imposing inferiority on Germany. Such a structure might prove more stable than unilateral restrictions which the Germans would doubtless seek to throw off as they gained strength and bargaining power. It might also prove an effective safeguard against the danger that a rearmed Germany would one day attempt to solve its grievances in the East by force. A European Army had a special appeal, of course, to those who were proponents of European integration in general.

By no means all of McCloy's advisers endorsed these views. Colonel Gerhardt, for example, though he shared an awareness of the difficulties presented by the Germans themselves, was, as were most of his fellow officers, inclined to believed that a European Army would pose immense problems of organization which would disrupt NATO and do more to delay the creation of effective German units than the political and diplomatic friction generated by an effort to rearm Germany on a national basis.

The pros and cons of various schemes were vigorously debated by McCloy and his staff during the early summer of 1950; McCloy himself did not come down firmly on one side or the other, but at the end of July he was sufficiently convinced of the need for caution to approve two long cables to Byroade, stressing the pitfalls within Germany and pointing out the merits of the European Army as a scheme which might in the long run prove to be the most expeditious way to secure military contributions from Germany. These communications apparently aroused little enthusiasm in Washington. But when Byroade learned of the work being done by Bowie and Gerhardt, he arranged for the two to return to Washington and continue their work in his office. Byroade wished Gerhardt to pay special attention to the technical military aspects of rearmament, for which there was relatively little competence in the State Department. As an officer still on active service, Gerhardt also possessed the advantage of being able to remain comparatively inconspicuous while conducting consultations in the Pentagon.

All these efforts were designed to lay down lines for guidance when the German question came up again, as it was bound to do, for formal decision by the Administration, including, ultimately, the President. The views of the Pentagon were well known and the State Department also expected Congress to raise the matter in connection with appropriations for the MDAP. Many Congressmen were demanding evidence that the European nations were doing all they should to match American contributions, and that everything possible was being done to lighten the burdens of the United States.[31] It was, of course, an election year and Acheson's conduct of affairs came under heavy, even savage, attack. As a public indication of the train of thought within his department, the Secretary of State admitted, on August 2, that he was reconsidering the place of Germany and Japan in defense planning. But he went on to emphasize the delicacy of the topic and the importance of settling it in harmony with America's allies.[32] As Acheson later said, "A unified defense of Europe was not possible unless Western Germany, the keystone geographically and militarily, were a part of it . . . but there . . . was a difference of opinion on how to bring this about."[33]

The objections to German rearmament retained much of their old force, but every day it became clearer, or should have, that the Germans would have conditions of their own and would use their new-found strategic value to exact further concessions of independence and equality. Perhaps one of the strongest arguments for acting quickly, if at all, was to forestall a sharp rise in the German price.[34] Most Frenchmen remained bitterly opposed to giving Germany an armed force and some members of the State Department who were most closely concerned with France represented French views with what many of their colleagues felt to be excessive vigor. There undoubtedly was a real danger in presenting France with a dilemma at which governments would fall and the nation sink deeper into paralysis.

The need for settling upon definite American

proposals for NATO's next step forward was now very pressing. In Europe, the revised Defense Plan advanced the dates by which combat forces ought to be in readiness.[35] The new dates lent special significance to the replies which NATO countries returned early in August to the American requests for an estimate of their expanded defense program. These answers expressed willingness to make substantially greater efforts but nevertheless fell short of the hopes entertained in Washington. The Europeans made it plain that they were "gravely concerned with the financial and economic difficulties involved." Their replies also stressed the importance of having American ground combat forces permanently stationed in Europe as a pledge that the United States would be constant in support of NATO and would commit itself to a strategy of defense rather than liberation.[36] European reluctance to act decisively without guarantees from America was in fact one of Spofford's greatest handicaps as he labored with the Deputies in London to match proposed forces to strategic requirements. As time passed and tension in the Far East eased slightly, the initial stimulus of Korea began to wear off and yield to a feeling of aimlessness and futility. On August 9 Spofford flew back to Washington to add his voice to those urging bold American action to allay European fears, leaving the Deputies to continue their discussions right up to the New York conference of the North Atlantic Council without mentioning German rearmament.

Two French memoranda received in August did much to bring matters to a head within the State Department. The first, dated August 5, accompanied the French estimate of their revised military effort and indicated that their increased exertions were conditioned on satisfaction of French desires for more financial aid, more ground forces from other members of NATO, and the adoption of a unified command. On August 17 the French government addressed a second note to the United States, posing several specific questions: did the United States think that countries outside the Continent—including America—should furnish permanent ground forces? Should such forces be integrated or operate as self-contained formations? Should there be a simplified structure for collectively financing the joint military effort?[37]

Spurred by the French, prodded by the JCS

and impelled by its own recognition of the need to reinvigorate NATO, the State Department moved hastily toward definite proposals to place before the North Atlantic Council meeting, now only a few weeks away. In drafting these proposals Byroade and Gerhardt frequently went over to the Pentagon to consult with Gruenther and his subordinates and with Bradley himself, who was now working closely with Gruenther on the German question. The State Department representatives, of course, preferred to deal with Bradley, so Johnson remained in the background.

The proposals which the State Department set before the Pentagon called for continued financial aid on condition of vigorous European cooperation; and for reinforcements of about four to six divisions to be sent to join our occupation troops in Germany which then constituted the American ground forces in Europe. These measures were predicated on a radical reorganization of NATO. Balanced collective forces, agreed upon in May, were to give way to an integrated force organized under a single command even in peacetime. A Supreme Commander, it was thought, was the best means of breaking the tangle of planning and renewing the advance of NATO preparations. Thus American financial aid and troop reinforcements were linked with integrated forces and a Supreme Commander.

Summing up the position of the JCS and the Army in a meeting with Colonel Gerhardt, General Schuyler wholeheartedly endorsed the object of strengthening NATO so that it could make a stand on an easterly line. American strategists believed that to hold at the Rhine or farther east would require at least 25 to 35 more divisions than were currently contemplated.[38] Schuyler willingly conceded that some of the additional divisions should be American, as and when such units were formed. The JCS had already made known their opinion that NATO forces should be welded together under a unified command. But integration called for a Supreme Commander, an individual who would of necessity be American. The Europeans wanted an American and the JCS would in any case accept no officer of any other nation. Appointment of an American Commander would decisively commit the prestige of United States armed forces to land action in Europe. It was from this commitment, in fact, that many of the diplomatic advantages of the appointment would stem. The JCS had concluded, however, that the totally inadequate forces then planned for NATO would condemn the American Commander and his troops to complete disaster if war broke out. They therefore regarded it as essential that the American proposals at New York include the formation of German divisions to make up the necessary strength—a strength that could not practically be obtained solely from the United States itself and its NATO allies.

This insistence, of course, caused no surprise in the State Department. Acheson and Byroade were still alert to the risks involved even though they agreed on the necessity of an ultimate contribution of German military manpower to NATO; the question remained of how to bring this about.[39] But by now apparently even the most chary reckoned that a cautious rearmament policy, agreed on with the Pentagon, was preferable to a radical program which might be pushed through by the JCS if military deficiencies became even more pressing in days to come. By August 18, at the latest, the State Department had definitely informed the JCS of its readiness to endorse German rearmament, presumably in the form desired by the JCS. In effect this was a decision in favor of a speedy, frontal assault on the problem of a German armed force.

General Schuyler promised that the JCS would regard the new policy as an urgent matter for action within forty-eight hours. If all responsible authorities could quickly agree upon a comprehensive policy for approval by the President, it might yet be possible to give two weeks notice, the respectable minimum, to the foreign ministers of the other NATO countries. But the expected recommendation from the JCS to the President via the Secretary of Defense failed to materialize.

Several considerations probably contributed to this hesitancy. The proposed reinforcements required careful scrutiny in view of the over-all shortage of American forces. Some officers favored the alternative of allocating disposable formations, as they became available, to a central strategic reserve.[40] But the most serious misgivings still concerned the prospect of a long and hazardous commitment to a collective defense effort which would not even be under the sole control of the United States. This

objection carried great weight with those who believed—as Johnson asserted with exceptional vigor—that the Europeans were not making adequate exertions on their own behalf. The kind of understanding sought by the State Department, leaving the details and the timing uncertain, really sidestepped the issue facing the JCS. For the JCS wanted categorical assurances that they could count on German assistance in the shape they desired and that they would be able to make an immediate start on raising and equipping the German units. This was, of course, more than any agency of the United States government could guarantee, for it depended largely on the will of other nations. But, impressed by the danger that the State Department's proposals might involve them in a hopeless enterprise, the JCS decided (no doubt with Johnson's hearty approval) to insist that the American proposals to NATO be made strictly conditional upon iron-clad commitments by the Europeans to their own contributions, and in particular, upon unequivocal acceptance of an immediate start on German rearmament in a form technically acceptable to American strategists.[41]

Some form of German rearmament was now receiving increased support in public from various quarters. The European Consultative Assembly, meeting in the second week of August, voted in favor of a European Army, and Churchill later explained that this should include German units. A number of Congressmen were expressing impatience for the United States to secure German assistance, and in August Senator Kenneth Wherry, a veteran critic of Acheson, strongly criticized the Secretary of State on the floor of the Senate for obstructing a German contribution to the defense effort.[42] On August 23, Adenauer, encouraged by McCloy, again demanded stronger protection for Germany and intimated German willingness to play a part.[43]

Decision was now a matter of extreme urgency. With the New York meeting of the NATO Council only two weeks away, Acheson urged the President to insist upon an agreed policy. On August 26, at a White House meeting chiefly concerned with a controversial message sent by General MacArthur to the Veterans of Foreign Wars, Truman demanded joint State-Defense recommendations on five related points: should the United States (1) accept a joint North Atlantic production authority, (2) continue military aid to Europe, (3) commit additional forces to Europe, (4) provide an American chief for a combined force, and (5) develop German armed forces. The President requested an answer by September 1, a date later extended to September 5.[44]

Faced with this ultimate crisis, a delegation of three from the State Department, including George W. Perkins, Assistant Secretary of State for European Affairs, and Paul Nitze, Chief of the Policy Planning Staff, went over to the Pentagon and worked out an answer to the President's request in three days of discussion with a representative of the Joint Chiefs, a representative of the Army, and Colonel Royden E. Beebe, USAF, director of the Office of North Atlantic Treaty Affairs in the Office of the Secretary of Defense. This written agreement bound reinforcements, a Supreme Commander, and German rearmament closely together in a "single package"—a package in which German rearmament was added to the State Department's own package of financial aid-reinforcements-integration-Supreme Command.

The agreement on German rearmament did not go very far in dealing with the technical details involved, although there was mention of some limitations on the kinds of weapons the Germans might possess, on the arms they might manufacture, and the staff organization they might establish. Probably the unified command also seemed to be an effective control. The plan was quite definite, however, in calling for an immediate start on the formation of German units large enough for operational requirements, which, in the eyes of the JCS, meant divisions directly incorporated in the NATO force.[45] Removing all doubt on this point had been the chief concern of the Pentagon representatives at the joint discussions.

This final formula tied German rearmament to the State Department package much more rigidly than the State Department had intended. Indeed, Acheson later concluded that he had erred in agreeing to the package formula, and to its presentation at New York;[46] but it is difficult to see how the New York meetings could have been satisfactory if the JCS had refused to accept the State Department package without German rearmament. The bargain meant a great deal to the JCS, who looked on

it as a solemn compact. At the subsequent New York conferences Acheson and other members of the American delegation became convinced that the chief concern of the JCS representative, Rear Admiral Thomas Hinckley Robbins, Jr., was to see that there was no attempt to implement the new policy other than as a "single package," and they nicknamed him "One Package Robbins." To the JCS the package was a reasonable gamble: a short-term liability incurred in the pursuit of greater gains in the long run. The "package" was an attempt to guarantee that the long-run gains did in fact follow and in the shape desired by the JCS. There was, it may be noted, no decision as to what the United States would do if the other NATO powers rejected the American proposals.

After the President received the reply to his request for recommendations, he spent several days discussing it with his advisers, including Averell Harriman, who was serving as an adviser to the President on civil-military affairs. By September 9 Truman approved the new policy, though he later made it clear that his approval was based on policy, not on liking. Apparently the plan never formally came before the NSC for discussion, though it had, of course, been drawn up by a process in which many members of the NSC had participated.

The President's endorsement of the agreement between the State Department and the Pentagon made it possible for Acheson to proceed with the new policy, but it did not relieve him of responsibility for deciding when to do so. There were patently grave objections to springing a surprise at the New York meetings, now only four days away. But for several reasons Acheson decided not to delay. He believed it would be impossible to suppress knowledge of the recent decisions; already much speculation was appearing in the press. Moreover, the French questions in their memoranda of August 5 and 17 were so specific that they had to receive a definite answer. But the dominant consideration in the Secretary's mind was his reluctance to conceal America's position from her allies and thereby to conduct a crucial conference on a false basis, foredooming the results to obsolescence at a time when delay might be fatal.[47] Acheson therefore determined to present the new United States policy to his British and French colleagues and to lay it before the North Atlantic Council.

On September 9, the same day that he approved the package plan, the President made public his intention to send "substantial" reinforcements to Europe. He intimated that the actual dispatch of the troops would depend on the other members of NATO making equivalent efforts but he gave no hint of German rearmament, which was, of course, still a matter for tripartite decision. Word that the United States intended to raise the question of German rearmament at New York was telegraphed to Bevin and Robert Schuman, the French Foreign Minister. Bevin was already at sea and Schuman was on the point of departure. It had been so widely reported that the United States was revising its policy on Germany that the telegrams could scarcely have come as a complete shock to the two men. But the fact that they had to send for new instructions within hours of their arrival suggests how little they had anticipated the form or the inflexibility (as it seemed) of Acheson's proposals.

The most detailed intimation of American intentions which the visiting foreign ministers received came from newspapers. A supposedly "off the record" remark dropped by McCloy to a gathering of reporters on Saturday, September 9, to the effect that Germany could conceivably provide ten divisions, was reflected in an article by Ferdinand Kuhn in the *Washington Post* on Sunday, September 10. This article contained an extremely accurate description of the Administration's new policy; it was widely noted and caused sharp reactions.

The Council meetings began on Wednesday, September 13, in a stormy atmosphere. A preliminary talk of the British and French Foreign Ministers with Acheson was later referred to by a member of one of their delegations as "the bomb in the Waldorf." After such an unceremonious introduction it was perhaps remarkable that the American plan won agreement even if only in principle from every one of the NATO countries except France. To the end of the New York meetings, however, the French representative staunchly refused to accept even the principle of German rearmament.

As a result of their discussions in the pre-NATO Council meeting, the three occupying powers were able to agree that the creation of a German national army, pure and simple, free of all restrictions, "would not serve the best interests of Germany and Europe." Further

than that they could not go. While disclaiming any intention to "impose specific conditions" Acheson insisted that he could not proceed without a definite commitment from the Europeans both on their own contributions and on German rearmament. The French would not budge. Then, after protracted argument in the North Atlantic Council, and an adjournment on September 18 to permit the various Defense Ministers to attend, France remained adamant. On September 26, when the conference reconvened—and ended, it issued an official communiqué which announced agreement on the creation "at the earliest date" of an integrated force under a Supreme Commander. As for Germany, the communiqué could only declare that the "Conference was in agreement that Germany should be enabled to contribute to the build-up of the defense of Western Europe, and noting that the occupying powers were studying the matter, requested the Defense Committee to make recommendations at the earliest possible date as to the methods by which Germany could most usefully make its contribution."[48]

The stormy meetings had ended in relative calm; there had been progress; and the avoidance of a decision about Germany was inevitable. As Schuman pointed out privately to Acheson, his own agreement on German rearmament would have been meaningless because he could not have obtained the consent of his government, and *it* could not have obtained the consent of the Deputies. The progress was in substantial part attributable to General Marshall, who succeeded Johnson as Secretary of Defense while the conference was still in session; he decided to move ahead with unified command and collective defense while giving Acheson freedom to start on a new diplomatic tack to secure German rearmament.[49]

Three more months of delicate negotiations, skillfully conducted within the Council of Deputies by Spofford, were required to gain French consent to the principle of allowing Germany to raise an armed force. During this interval France produced the Pleven Plan for a European Army in a European Defense Community. A meeting of the North Atlantic Council at Brussels in December finally proclaimed unanimous agreement that "German participation would strengthen the defense of Europe" and "on the part which Germany should play."[50] Even then there was no indication as to what the part should be or when Germany would begin to play it. No such doubt surrounded the institution of an integrated force, for, in fulfillment of the intention expressed in September, at the Brussels meeting, the Council there and then appointed General Dwight D. Eisenhower as Supreme Commander. President Truman immediately placed American troops in Europe under the new command. But as to Germany, it was plain that a great deal still remained unsettled. The Council could only invite the occupying powers to "explore the matter" with the German government, while also taking note of the French intention to call a conference to consider formation of a European Army along lines of the Pleven Plan. Thus began the ill-fated pursuit of a European Defense Community.[51]

German rearmament presented the United States with an intricate problem of great consequence. The Communist invasion of the Republic of Korea hastened the decision, but German resurgence, Russian success in nuclear development and the gaping holes in Western defenses had already made the military destiny of Germany a subject for active debate within the American Administration. And once NATO was taken as an active instrument of policy and not just an alliance with a vague and uncertain future, the logic of German rearmament would become irrefutable. As it was, Korea accelerated several established trends toward a decisive change in policy. Naturally enough the Joint Chiefs were first to raise the question of German rearmament formally in the National Security Council. By August 1950, the difference between the Pentagon and the State Department had dwindled to one of method and timing. But insofar as success depended on the active cooperation of other nations it was of the essence that the new policy be presented to them in an acceptable form and at a favorable moment.

There is no way of knowing whether the State Department would have been willing to proceed from an acceptance of the notion of German rearmament to prompt diplomatic action without prodding by the Joint Chiefs. It seems quite clear that the United States eventually put the question of the basic reorganization and strengthening of NATO to its allies earlier and more closely linked with German rearmament than would have been the case had the diplomats been left to their own devices. Despite Bradley's protestations that German rearmament was a question for a "higher level," the JCS did much more than present the military position. In effect, they prevented the Secretary of State from adopting one possible diplomatic approach, and thereby enforced the adoption of another. This JCS action was taken, however, only within the context of a foreign policy which laid upon them burdensome military commitments which they were quite incapable of fulfilling with the resources made available to them.

Conceivably, had the JCS felt justified in reposing greater confidence in the State Department's judgment, discretion, and appreciation of military problems, they might have been willing to allow the Secretary of State to employ a more subtle and pliable strategy in seeking to procure German troops; and a different Secretary of Defense could almost certainly have been persuaded to follow Acheson's lead. Contrariwise, had members of the State Department possessed a more sympathetic ear for the professional anxieties of the Pentagon they might have turned to the task of reaching a definite position on the JCS proposal for German rearmament early enough to avoid the abruptness with which the United States placed its plans before the other members of NATO. Poor personal relations between the Secretaries of State and Defense apparently aggravated the difficulty of securing a free and open exchange of views between their respective Departments, but a number of informal consultations by people like Nitze and General Beebe (and General Burns, who served almost as a direct link between Johnson and Acheson), between the State Department and the Pentagon at various levels from the JCS downward, helped to lubricate the process of arriving at an agreed policy. In fact, once the issue was firmly grappled in August 1950, agreement on such a momentous and complex problem in about a month was no mean achievement for the American government.

As it turned out, the package laboriously wrapped up in Washington came untied in New York. The policy had not provided against a firm rebuff by other members of NATO. When it came to the point, the United States was not prepared to withhold reinforcements or a

Supreme Commander, still less to pull out of Europe if France would not accept the Joint Chiefs' plan for Germany. French resistance compelled the United States to accept drawn-out negotiations on the German question while it pressed ahead with the other elements in its program. The speedy improvement in relations between the Secretaries of State and Defense and their departments which followed General George C. Marshall's succession to Johnson on September 12, 1950, greatly facilitated the adoption of a more leisurely approach to Germany's rearmament.

Thus, after all the anxious calculation and bargaining in Washington, the French did indeed take alarm and did become obstructive. Long after the United States had given Ameri-can reinforcements to NATO and endowed it with a Supreme Commander, there were no German troops and disappointingly few of any other nationality. By the time German troops appeared in any numbers the strategic concept within which the United States had decided to rearm Germany was completely altered and nuclear weapons were assigned the role of compensating for the West's deficiency in conventional forces. Whether this development was desirable, whether different American tactics in 1950 could have allayed French fears and expedited German rearmament, and whether this would have well served the national interest of the United States, or indeed made any substantial difference, are questions which will provide grounds for many years of debate.

BIBLIOGRAPHIC NOTE

There is no abundance of printed material on "The American Decision to Rearm Germany." The subject is sufficiently recent and sufficiently controversial to make government archives inaccessible; but it was not of sufficient domestic political importance to lend itself to extensive hearings like those that followed General MacArthur's relief, so replete with factual information and opinions of all sorts.

There are a few relevant hearings before the interested Congressional committees, and these are cited in footnotes. So too are a few scholarly books and articles. At the time this study was made, only a pair of books were of major importance: Lord Ismay's *NATO: The First Five Years* and the second volume of President Truman's *Memoirs: Years of Trial and Hope.* A third has come out recently: Dean Acheson's *Sketches from Life of Men I Have Known,* which amplifies with vivid detail the information about the "package deal" he had so kindly given the author of this study. A number of U. S. government publications and a few British have been useful. There are also valuable materials scattered in various magazine and newspaper articles. The reporting in the *Washington Post* deserves special mention. And, as might be expected, the *New York Times* has provided what can almost be called a documentary account of the whole development.

Fortunately the memories of the living, still fresh though naturally not infallible, are sources of information available to scholars denied access to the archives bearing upon such recent events. This account is based in large part on information generously provided by participants in the events, including Mr. Dean G. Acheson, Major General Royden E. Beebe, USAF, General Lucius D. Clay, USA, Dr. F. J. A. Kraemer, Mr. Perry Laukhuff, Mr. Robert A. Lovett, Mr. John J. McCloy, Lieutenant Colonel J. G. K. Miller, USA, Mr. Charles Spofford and numerous others whose names must be withheld for various reasons. For related reasons, it has not been possible to cite particular interviews and correspondence in footnotes.

NOTES

1. *To Amend the Mutual Defense Assistance Act of 1949,* Hearings before the House Foreign Affairs Committee, 81st Cong., 2d sess., June 5, 1950, p. 22.

2. *Mutual Defense Assistance Program,* Hearings before the Senate Committee on Foreign Relations and Committee on Armed Services, 81st Cong., 2d sess., June 5, 1950, p. 30.

3. Royal Institute of International Affairs, *WEU and the Atlantic Alliance* (London, 1956), p. 26; Harry S. Truman, *Memoirs,* II, *Years of Trial and Hope* (Doubleday, Garden City, 1956), pp. 253 ff.

4. JCS 1067, JCS 1779, and other documents illustrating this process may be conveniently found in Department of State, *Germany, 1947-1949, The Story in Documents,* European and British Commonwealth Series, No. 9, Washington, [1950].

5. *North Atlantic Treaty,* Hearings before the Senate Foreign Relations Committee, 81st Cong., 1st sess., April 27, 1949, pp. 57, 61.

6. Truman, *Memoirs,* II, pp. 244-249. The alteration in our policy toward Spain is recounted in Theodore J. Lowi's "Bases in Spain," in this volume.

7. Cf. *Der Deutsche Soldat in der Armee von Morgen,* Muenchen, Isar-Verlag, 1954 (Hrsg. in Zsarbeit mit d. Institut für Europaische Politik und Wirtschaft, . . . veroffentlichen des Instituts für Staatslehre und Politik e. V., Mainz), Chapter 1, *passim;* Eric Willenz, *Early Discussions Regarding a Defense Contribution in Germany (1948-1950)* (Rand Research Memorandum 968, October 15, 1952); *U.S. News and World Report,* July 30, August 6, 1948.

8. For public reflections of this thinking, see C. Z. Sulzberger, *New York Times,* December 1, 1949; also *U.S. News and World Report,* November 2, 1949.

9. William Reitzel, *et al., United States Foreign Policy, 1945-1955* (Brookings Institution, Washington, 1956), p. 288.

10. *New York Times,* November 29, 30, December 6, 29, 1949; Lewis J. Edinger, *West German Armament,* Documentary Research Division, Research Studies Institute, Air University, 1955

(Air University, Documentary Research Study, AU-254-54-RSI), p. 7, note 1.

11. *New York Times,* November 21, 1949; C. G. Onslow, *World Politics,* July 1951, pp. 450-485.

12. *New York Times,* November 23, 1949.

13. *Ibid.,* November 15, December 1, 1949.

14. *Ibid.,* December 10, 1949.

15. Council on Foreign Relations, *The United States in World Affairs,* 1949, p. 136. For expressions of French fears, see the *New York Times,* November 23, 1949, and *News From France,* 5th Year, No. 1, January 15, 1950.

16. Office of U. S. High Commissioner for Germany, *First Quarterly Report,* 1950, p. 41; *New York Times,* November 17, 18, 23, and 27, 1949. Even then Bradley added that once Germany was on a sound basis economically and politically, "we can consider the Germans' military attitude."

17. During 1950 the old "Plans Group" became the "Plans Division" and the larger entity, the "Operations and Plans Division," became the "Office of the Assistant Chief of Staff, G-3." The newer usage is employed here.

18. Truman, *Memoirs,* II, pp. 309-311.

19. *Foreign Policy Bulletin,* April 21, 1950; *New York Times,* April 15, May 20, 1950.

20. *Parliamentary Debates,* Fifth Series, *472,* pp. 1288-1290; *473,* pp. 324-325; *New York Times,* April 5 and 6, 1950.

21. U. S. High Commissioner for Germany, *3d Quarterly Report,* 1950, pp. 79-80; *4th Quarterly Report,* 1950, p. 11, Communiqué in Cmd. 7977, Misc. 10, 1950, *London Conference.*

22. Lord Ismay, *NATO: The First Five Years, 1949-1954* (Paris, 1955), pp. 28-29.

23. *To Amend the Mutual Defense Assistance Act of 1949,* House Hearings, June 6, 1950, pp. 54-55.

24. Cf. statements of Generals Lemnitzer, Bradley and Marshall in *To Amend the Mutual Defense Assistance Act of 1949,* House Hearings, pp. 39 ff., 46-47, 99. It is interesting to note that General Bradley emphasized in an article published in the *Washington Post,* September 24, 1950, that the

United States "must never have a foreign policy that sends our armed forces to world tasks beyond their capabilities."

25. *Supplemental Appropriation Bill for 1951; Department of Defense; Mutual Defense Assistance Program,* Hearings before the House Appropriations Committee, 81st Cong., 2d sess., July 25, 1950.

26. For the analogy see, for instance, U. S. High Commissioner for Germany, *Report on Germany,* September 21, 1949-July 31, 1952, p. 170.

27. *New York Times,* July 4, 1950. McCloy was asked to advise the German government of the possibility that U. S. troops might be forced to evacuate Korea; he was also told to prepare a list of important Germans whom we should help to escape from Germany, if their country was overrun. News about the list leaked out and McCloy was overwhelmed by enthusiastic Germans who wanted to be enrolled!

28. Ismay, *NATO:The First Five Years,* p. 29.

29. *Ibid.,* p. 31.

30. On July 22 McCloy had declared publicly that it "would be hard to deny the Germans the right to defend themselves." *New York Times,* July 23, 1950.

31. For example, Senator Cain, *New York Times,* August 3, 1950; Representative Sikes, *Supplemental Appropriation Bill for 1951,* House Hearings, August 2-3, 1950, pp. 295, 329.

32. *Ibid.*

33. Dean Acheson, *Sketches from Life of Men I Have Known* (Harper, 1961), pp. 25-26.

34. Cf. Truman, *Memoirs,* II, p. 255.

35. The Deputies were informed by the Standing Group, August 2, 1950; *New York Times,* August 5, 1950.

36. Ismay, *NATO: The First Five Years,* p. 31; *U. S. in World Affairs,* 1950, pp. 259-261.

37. A text of the first note was published at the time. There is an accurate summary of the second in James Reston, *New York Times,* February 20, 1952.

38. Edinger, *West German Armament,* p. 9; Truman, *Memoirs,* II, pp. 254 ff.

39. For an indication of continued misgivings, *cf.* a broadcast by Byroade on August 20, Department of State *Bulletin,* September 18, 1950, and for growing reconciliation with the idea of rearmament, *cf.* Acheson's endorsement of a speech by John Sherman Cooper on August 19, 1950, in which Cooper declared: "It is inevitable and moral that Germany be given the opportunity to defend herself." *New York Times,* August 20, 23, 1950.

40. Cf. *Washington Post,* August 28, 1950.

41. Cf. *ibid.,* August 31, September 17, 1950; *Newsweek,* September 18, 1950.

42. *Congressional Record,* 81st Cong., 2d sess., 1950, *Senate,* p. 12743. See also exchanges between Acheson and Wherry in hearings on the MDAP appropriations. Appropriations Committee, Senate, *Supplemental Appropriations for 1951,* August 30, 1950, pp. 264 ff.

43. *New York Times,* August 24, 1950; Wilenz, *Early Discussions Regarding a Defense Contribution in Germany,* p. 14.

44. *Washington Post,* September 5, 1950.

45. Ten divisions was the figure generally mentioned. Cf. Henry Cabot Lodge, *New York Times,* September 9, 1950.

46. Acheson, *Sketches from Life,* pp. 26-27.

47. Cf. Acheson's remarks, *Supplemental Appropriations for 1951,* Senate Hearings, August 30, 1950, p. 278.

48. Ismay, *NATO: The First Five Years,* pp. 185-186.

49. Acheson, *Sketches from Life,* pp. 41-43, 27; his account also tells of the support Bevin gave him, presumably after persuading the British Cabinet to go along by assuring them that the French would not agree. The "package" episode is vividly described on pp. 25-27 of the chapter on Bevin and pp. 41-43 of the chapter on Schuman.

50. Ismay, *NATO: The First Five Years,* pp. 186-187.

51. *Ibid.*

EDITORIAL COMMENTS

The policy underlying the American decision to rearm Germany is in an important sense a continuation of the policy underlying the few humanitarian aspects of JCS 1067 and more strikingly its successive revisions both in form and in application. The Morgenthau tidal wave for a draconic post-war German policy reached its farthest penetration in Quebec on September 15, 1944; thereafter there were wavelets and ripples, but the basic undertow away from a Carthaginian peace was constant. By July 1947, when JCS 1779 was issued, the United States, with its two western companion occupying powers, was ready to relax its role as occupier and move rapidly to re-establish Western Germany's place in the family of nations—more importantly in the Western world.

The scars of deep wounds do not suddenly disappear. By the summer of 1950, Western Germany was indeed accepted as a nation, yet the latent fears of a third German aggression remained; life with an unarmed Germany was comforting, particularly because the Western world was still adjusting painfully to the necessity of facing an aggressive Russia. Even after the Soviet atomic explosion in September 1949, the view that the small and unorganized forces of NATO plus the atomic deterrent would meet all defense needs without greater contributions by the NATO powers—and without the addition of German forces—was so appealing that the many voices of Cassandra found no effective audience in Europe. The goad to action was the Communist invasion of the Republic of Korea on June 25, 1950.

After the invasion of Korea, the President became willing to ask for and the Congress was willing to supply the greatly enlarged military appropriations that reflected in some degree the necessities set forth by NSC-68. The useful working relations between the officers of the armed forces and of the State Department forced into existence by President Truman over Secretary Johnson's veto in order to produce NSC-68 could now be utilized to help design and create a NATO shield that would be more than a mere symbol. In the case of the most troublesome of the NATO problems—the rearmament of Germany, for some time a JCS objective—the quiet discussions between the military and the State Department were eased by the presence in the staff of the State Department in Washington of HICOG officers assigned to Washington by McCloy himself. Johnson was less likely to show active distrust of such men than of Foreign Service officers or other State Department officials; and the slow process of mutual understanding and accommodation between officials of the two departments—subsequently eagerly encouraged by Marshall—continued its progress.

As well as one can tell, after June 1950, there was no issue of substantive objectives between the chief representatives of the two departments. Accepting as the fundamental objective the effective build-up of NATO, Acheson and Bradley agreed that NATO should be reorganized, that it should receive a substantial reinforcement of American troops, that NATO forces should be integrated, that there should be a single American commander, that our European allies should increase their contributions—and that there still would be a need for more, i.e., German, soldiers. But all this agreement did not settle the issues of how and when.

The Army attitude was characterized by a pursuit of the perpetual military *ignis fatuus:* as stated by Bradley, we "must never have a foreign policy that sends our armed forces to world tasks beyond their capabilities." (Why keep our soldiers in Berlin?) Hence, in the judgment of the Pentagon, there were to be no American reinforcements until the European build-up was complete, or at least until there was assurance that the combined forces would meet the requirements before Russian atomic power equalled ours. On the latter basis, the necessary assurance was viewed as an immediate promise by our allies of the necessary European increments, including German forces, before we took up our share of the NATO burden, i.e., before we increased our forces, before we participated in integration, before we put the American commander in charge.

Acheson was more than willing to pursue what he had already begun—to support our own moves, to urge England, France and the other NATO powers to increase their share of the burden. He also agreed that the logic of military arithmetic required German soldiers, and by the summer of 1950 he was willing to set their recruitment as a goal; but he was unwilling to try to force German armament by threats on our allies, on independent powers who might well look to our fixed European commitment as a necessary preliminary to a re-examination, indeed reversal, of the agreed German policy, greatly modified in 1947, but still based on the permanent pacification of Germany.

The insistent demands of the military for all-or-none, for the single package, produced a setting not unlike the situation in 1942 when Roosevelt not only overruled the Joint Chiefs but sharply criticized them for seeking to "pick up their marbles" and abandon Europe for the Pacific. But President Truman lacked President Roosevelt's position of power. Although German rearmament was distasteful to him, he wanted wholehearted Army and public support for a new and stronger NATO and approved what seemed to be necessary to achieve it.

So it was that the package deal between the two departments was duly made, all neatly tied, and shepherded by an admiral to the NATO meetings in New York. And no doubt Acheson did strive earnestly to carry out his side of the bargain, a bargain he thought unwise. The fact that all the NATO allies but France agreed, even in principle, is evidence of exceedingly energetic negotiation.

The near-miss in the Waldorf did not make the Army happy. The Europeans naturally seized with joy all the American contributions to the package, expressed a willingness to do more and left the question of German forces unanswered. Indeed, the question could not have been answered at the time. No French government could have agreed to German rearmament even in principle without at least the long, hopeless pursuit of EDC or an equivalent. Acheson's premonitions about excess haste showed good judgment. Probably American diplomacy was saved from a disastrous defeat only by Marshall's replacement of Johnson as Secretary of Defense. Marshall quickly agreed to proceed with collective defense while permitting Acheson to pursue the more time-consuming circumambulatory processes of diplomacy to secure European agreement on German rearmament. One can only wonder what the course of action would have been if Marshall had succeeded Johnson in June rather than October; perhaps Marshall would have agreed from the beginning with the agenda that the military had to accept in the end.

BASES IN SPAIN

THEODORE J. LOWI

ASSISTANT PROFESSOR OF GOVERNMENT

CORNELL UNIVERSITY

CONTENTS

Introduction   669

I   Consensus: Background and Setting   671

II   The Opposition Forms   673
    Pentagon Politics   673
    Politics and the Administration   674
    The Spanish Lobby: Charles Patrick Clark   675

III   The Battle: First Phase   677
    Administrative Recovery   677
    The Line Officers   677
    The Junketeers   679
    Congress Takes the Lead   680

IV   The Battle: Second Phase   683
    Money in Search of Policy   683

V   The Battle: Final Phase   687
    Griffis to Madrid   687
    Truman—Minus Acheson   688
    Truman Reluctantly Half Consents   691
    Enter Sherman   691
    The New Policy Is Announced   692

VI   Repercussions   694
    The $450 Million Question   694
    Plus Ça Change   695

VII   Epilogue   698

    Bibliographic Note   700

    Notes   701

    Editorial Comments   703

INTRODUCTION

On August 25, 1953 Senator Pat McCarran was presented the Grand Cross of the Order of Isabella La Catolica by the Spanish Ambassador, José Felix de Lequerica, "for his efforts to improve Spanish-American relations." On September 26, 1953 the first military-economic agreement between Spain and the United States was signed in Madrid.

McCarran's decoration symbolized a critical factor in five years of Spanish-American relations: the role of Congress in bringing about an important shift in foreign and military policy. Congress, led by Senator McCarran, brought the entire spectrum of political techniques successfully to bear on the Truman Administration. Large sums of money were voted gratuitously to Spain; strong public pronouncements were registered in favor of Generalissimo Franco and Spain; the spokesmen of the Administration were consistently badgered in public hearings; officers and civilian officials of all branches of the armed services were encouraged in hearings and meetings to publicize the tactical and strategical importance of Spain; and the issue was surcharged with the growing fears of the Communist threat. With the support of key members of the two houses of Congress, the Spanish issue was placed upon the policy agenda and was kept there until action was taken. Much of the internal politics of the moves toward securing the Spanish bases remains unknown because much of the vital discussion took place in the privacy of the National Security Council and the Joint Chiefs of Staff and within the interested services themselves. Thomas K. Finletter, who served during this period as Secretary of the Air Force, characterized the Spanish problem as "something special, like a separate stairway."

Secretary Finletter was among many top executives who did not participate in the discussions. Others like him were not informed of the basic shift in policy until the announcement in the newspapers. George Kennan and his State Department Policy Planning Staff were themselves ignorant of the impending policy change, although the PPS had been heavily involved in the earlier discussions concerning the renewal of ambassadorial exchange with Spain.

The Administration bargained with the points which, until 1948, had proved to have great weight in justifying the policy of avoiding close or friendly relations with Spain. President Truman and Secretary of State Acheson emphasized the Fascist origin and nature of the Spanish government and the delicate balance of the Western Alliance which might be upset with the slightest hint that the United States was inclined to European defense behind the Pyrenees. Our story is an account of how the Truman-Acheson policy was finally changed.

Perhaps most significant from the civil-military point of view is Congress' use of a military rationale with or without the support of the Defense Department in an attempt to precipitate a decision by the executive branch on a problem of foreign as well as military policy. In 1948 the idea of any military affiliation with Spain claimed the support of a very small number of government officials. In addition to the Congressional bloc, there were several admirals on active sea duty. Those of the Secretaries in the National Military Establishment from the Secretary of Defense on down who may have favored bases in Spain were bound to a great extent by the opposition of President Truman and Secretary Acheson, and they avoided the issue publicly by answering Congressional and newspaper queries with equivocation. But the line admirals and others of the lower echelons were not so tightly bound to official policy. They grew to be in effect the channels of communication between the pro-bases elements in the Defense Department and those in Congress. The officers provided Congress with data and cogent arguments, and Congress, in turn, provided them with protection and encouragement.

Thus the issues and the sides to the controversy emerged rather clearly during the two years or more in which it was carried on. But it would be misleading simply to conclude that one side was victorious and that the decision reflected that victory. During this period the entire fabric of international relations had changed. Anti-communism had replaced anti-totalitarianism as the most popular as well as the most realistic issue of the day. And economic recovery—the Marshall Plan, which was concerned solely with the rebuilding of the civil economy—had been replaced or augmented by military containment, the conse-

quences of which had been fully realized in Korea. Within this new context emerged a substantial, then irresistible, Spanish bloc made up of elements hitherto small and fragmented.

Acheson aligned himself with bases in Spain late in 1950. To him, the Spanish question had been "magnified by controversy to a position among our present day foreign policy problems which is disproportionate to its intrinsic importance."[1] Without Acheson, President Truman remained for many months practically alone against his entire Administration. Long after the new Spanish policy had been established with Presidential approval, the President continued to express his distaste for it. Reluctantly the President had acquiesced in a series of actions which, taken cumulatively, amounted to a decision.

I. CONSENSUS: BACKGROUND AND SETTING

At the close of World War II, the victorious allies cast uncharitable eyes toward Spain and its military dictator, General Franco. Franco's equivocal neutrality had kept his country out of the war, but his opportunistic flirtations with the Axis had wounded the allies far too deeply for the salve of his latter-day cooperative overtures, and the bitter memories of the tragic Spanish civil war were still vivid.

President Roosevelt expressed the feelings of all the allies on March 10, 1945, in a letter to Norman Armour, the United States Ambassador to Spain. (The style of the letter suggests that it was drafted in the State Department, but there is no reason to doubt that the President knew what he was signing.)

. . . Having been helped to power by Fascist Italy and Nazi Germany, and having patterned itself along totalitarian lines the present regime in Spain is naturally the subject of distrust. . . . Most certainly we do not forget Spain's official position with and assistance to our Axis enemies at a time when the fortunes of war were less favorable to us, nor can we disregard the activities, aims, organizations, and public utterances of the Falange, both past and present. These memories cannot be wiped out by actions more favorable to us now that we are about to achieve our goal of complete victory . . .

The fact that our Government maintains formal diplomatic relations with the present Spanish regime should not be interpreted by anyone to imply approval of that regime and its sole party, the Falange, which has been openly hostile to the United States and which has tried to spread its fascist party ideas in the Western Hemisphere. Our victory over Germany will carry with it the extermination of Nazi and similar ideologies.

As you know, it is not our practice in normal circumstances to interfere in the internal affairs of other countries unless there exists a threat to international peace. The form of government in Spain and the policies pursued by that Government are quite properly the concern of the Spanish people. I should be lacking in candor, however, if I did not tell you that I can see no place in the community of nations for governments founded on fascist principles.[2]

A year later, on March 4, 1946, the governments of France, the United Kingdom and the United States, after an extended series of discussions on Spanish relations, issued a joint statement. In language almost identical with that of Roosevelt's quoted above (in this case the draftsmen were likewise professional diplomats), the three governments went further to say that:

It is hoped that leading patriotic and liberal-minded Spaniards may soon find means to bring about a peaceful withdrawal of Franco, the abolition of the Falange, and the establishment of an interim or caretaker government under which the Spanish people may have an opportunity freely to determine the type of government they wish to have and to choose their leaders. An interim government which would be and would remain dedicated to these ends should receive the recognition and support of all freedom-loving peoples.[3]

The new United Nations followed suit. At the San Francisco Conference, ending in June 1945, a resolution was adopted according to which membership could not be extended to those "States whose regimes have been installed with the help of military forces which have waged war against the United Nations, so long as those regimes are in power."[4] At the Potsdam Conference on July 17, 1945 President Truman joined with Churchill and Stalin to state affirmatively that they would not support a request by Spain for admission to the United Nations.[5]

It was not so clear, however, just how far beyond a United Nations blackball the United States was willing to go in order to encourage reform in Spain. In letters dated April 8 and 9, 1946, to the Secretary General, the Polish delegate requested that the Security Council declare the Franco regime a threat to international security under Articles 34 to 37 of the UN Charter. Pursuant to this, Poland submitted a resolution calling on UN members to sever all relations with Spain.[6]

Throughout the summer of 1946 the Polish resolution, along with a spate of others more mildly phrased, passed among the subcommittees to the Council and back again to committees. Finally, on October 30, the United States, through its delegate, Senator Tom Connally, made its commitment in a statement before the Political and Security Committee of the General Assembly:

I would like to summarize [very briefly] the position of the United States with respect to the Spanish question.

1. We are [unalterably] opposed to Franco and welcome any democratic change in Spain which protects basic human rights and freedoms.

2. We shall take part in any necessary action against the Franco regime, under the United Nations Charter, if and when this regime becomes a threat to international peace and security.

3. Pending such an eventuality, we are opposed to coercive measures by the United Nations, such as a severance of diplomatic relations or the imposition of economic sanctions, because they would either aid Franco by uniting the Spanish people against outside interference or would precipitate the Spanish people themselves into the disaster of civil war with unknown but inevitably costly consequences.

4. We shall join in continuing to oppose the admission of the Franco regime, not only to the United Nations but to any international agencies set up at the initiative of the United Nations.

5. Finally, we believe that the Spanish people should determine their own destiny. Following the withdrawal of the Franco regime, it is our hope that they will establish a provisional government and hold a free election.[7]

Then, on December 12, 1946, the General Assembly adopted a resolution compromising the American with the Polish point of view. Taking notice of the origin and nature of the Franco regime, and further noting the conduct of the regime during the war in spite of repeated allied protests, the General Assembly recommended that (1) Spain be debarred from membership in the United Nations and all its agencies, (2) all members immediately recall their ambassadors and ministers plenipotentiary, and (3) the Security Council consider further measures to be taken to remedy the situation if a more liberal government were not established in "a reasonable time."[8]

The United States had had no ambassador in Spain ever since the withdrawal of Norman Armour in December 1945. To implement the new resolution, the United States simply left the American Embassy in Madrid in the hands of the *chargé d'affaires,* Paul Culbertson.

The United States resisted further attempts to strengthen the original resolution. A November 1947 resolution calling for a reaffirmation of the original ambassadorial ban—to stop the gradual flow of ambassadors back to Spain— was not passed, primarily because of the abstention of the United States. The United States backed a second resolution which expressed the confidence of the General Assembly in the Security Council's judgment to take measures against Spain when ever such action might be required.

The story of the Spanish bases begins in 1948, when such a notion seemed almost preposterous. The road that the bases idea travelled during the next three years was as rough as the ordinary Spanish highway. But with Spanish perseverance, the idea lingered, grew and finally reached general acceptance in the form of American dollars.

II. THE OPPOSITION FORMS

In 1948 the Washington merry-go-round was spinning far from blithely to the tune of atoms, Marshall Plan, unification, the second session of the 80th Congress and the Presidential election—a Republican victory was forecast by many leading Democrats. To understand how and where Spain fitted into an over-crowded agenda, it is necessary to look at the inner workings of those agencies which participate in the making of foreign policy in all its aspects, political, economic and military.

PENTAGON POLITICS

Secretary of Defense James V. Forrestal was beset with overwhelming tasks. A Wall Streeter who had come to Washington for temporary duty in 1940 as one of the "anonymous" assistants to President Roosevelt, he soon became Assistant Secretary of the Navy, then succeeded Frank Knox as Secretary of the Navy in 1944 and became the first Secretary of Defense in 1947. The task of mediating the three services, unreconciled to unification, was proving to be more than a man-sized task, and Forrestal was torn by his desire to pacify factions and still develop a new, balanced defense force. As to policy, reflected in budgetary terms, Forrestal was also torn between the necessities of a possible third World War, the demands of preventing it, and the characteristic post-war budgetary cuts demanded by President and Congress.

The basic issue was often expressed in terms of the peacetime "defense force in being." In the past it had been national policy to slant the peacetime defense budget in favor of the Navy and to depend on emergency measures to rebuild a deteriorated Army and Air Force in the event of war. The once natural geographic reasons for this pattern of allocation were hotly questioned after World War II.

Using the words of the Finletter Commission:

Our present Air Force is divided into 55 groups. From evidence received from the Secretary of the Air Force, its Chief of Staff and many of its ranking generals, as well as informed authorities outside of the Military Establishment, we conclude that the 55-group force, if engaged in action in this present phase (1) could not carry out the missions assigned to it because it is lacking in the essential air units for effective combat action. . . .

Even more alarming is the statement made by the Air Force that the funds presently available will not permit the maintenance of the present inadequate Air Force, and that if its appropriations are not increased the establishment must be cut back to approximately 40 groups, with reductions starting in July 1948.

None of this must be permitted. There is a minimum force in being below which we must not go if we are to protect our country and its vital interests. We have concluded that the mini-mum force necessary at the present time is an Air Force composed of 12,400 modern planes, organized into 70 combat groups and 22 special squadrons, supplemented by 27 National Guard groups and 34 groups of Air Reserve. All of these forces, with the exception of the Air Reserve must be equipped, trained and ready for im-mediate action in the event of war.

We should build this force as rapidly as pos-sible, and once it is achieved, never permit it to drop below this level. Nor should we permit it to become impotent and ineffective because of failure to keep it modernized with the very best planes and equipment available.[9]

This seventy-group Air Force would include an enlarged strategic air arm with 100 B-36 "intercontinental" bombers.

Spain held a low priority—if any at all—on the Air Force agenda; for the Air Force was generally cool at this time to the idea of a string of foreign bases. Intercontinental striking power—especially intercontinental delivery of the atomic bomb—would obviate further and increased dependence upon foreign bases. At least, it would be politically hazardous to press simultaneously for funds for bases and for B-36's. The Air Force leaders certainly wanted the B-36's first.

The Department of the Army, on the other hand, was preoccupied primarily with the *ignis fatuus* of universal military training and the achievement of a total force of 822,000 men instead of the 782,000 provided for in the Forrestal plans for the coming fiscal year. To add to the confusion, the Joint Chiefs of Staff unanimously reported on April 14, 1948 that an 837,000-man Army would be required under the new concept of a *balanced* military establishment to make the Army commensurate with a seventy Air-group program. Additional complications piled up at this time when JCS began to consider what our relations should be with the Western European Union, recently established by the Brussels Pact. The Army particularly was reluctant to assume any responsibility for the defense of Europe unless any agreements with the European powers at least left open the possibility of using the military potentialities of both Germany and Spain. Later, after the creation of NATO, the Army lost its interest in Spain (though not in Germany). NATO's military aspects became primarily an Army project involving decisions on the number and placement of military personnel in Western Europe. In brief, Army's task in Europe was to build a defense of the entire continent from Western Germany to the sea, not even to consider defense behind the Pyrenees; the possibility of using Spanish troops was either forgotten or shoved aside.[10]

In the meantime, the Navy Department was cool toward UMT; and it feared the "empire-building" tendencies of the Air Force and the Air Force's lack of emphasis on foreign bases. During 1948 there was a running quarrel between the Air Force and the Navy over "operational control" of atomic bombs. For the Navy to "perform some of its primary missions," some provisions were required for the delivery of atomic bombs, thus pointing to the need for the proposed giant carrier capable of launching atomic bombers.

Naval personnel were particularly aware of weaknesses in the Mediterranean and its Atlantic entrances. Great Britain held the most important bases in the area, those in Gibraltar, Malta and Egypt. If the United States Navy was to have a predominant position in the inland sea and the approaches to it, it must have bases of its own. With the build-up of the Sixth Fleet, the Navy greatly feared being bottled-up in or sealed-out of the Mediterranean. Moreover, the Navy could hardly bargain with Great Britain over control of the Mediterranean fleet under the North Atlantic Treaty if the Navy had no bases of its own in either the nearby Atlantic or the Mediterranean. Consequently, the Navy looked warmly upon Cadiz, El Ferrol and the North African coast line.

Secretary Forrestal's own leanings were strongly toward the admirals. Because of his service as Secretary of the Navy, Forrestal had taken office as Secretary of Defense holding many of Navy's fears of unification, which were reflected in the National Security Act of 1947 itself, though the responsibilities of office soon changed his mind, as the amendments of 1949 demonstrate. He counted as absurd an imbalance in favor of the Air Force. This, he contended, would mean a plan based on a massive air offensive from Great Britain. Such a position might lead to war rather than prevent it, Forrestal felt.[11]

Furthermore, Forrestal was very much concerned about Middle East oil supplies. Although his appraisal of the importance of this oil was to change drastically later, in 1948 he felt that no precaution should be overlooked in "securing the Mediterranean line of communications."[12]

POLITICS AND THE ADMINISTRATION

At the State Department, the problems were of just as large and complex an order. In a letter to Secretary of State Marshall dated October 31, 1948, Forrestal addressed a number of questions in hopes of getting Marshall's guidance in accommodating the Defense Department's allocations to President Truman's $15 billion ceiling. Specifically, the questions were: "(a) Has there been an improvement in the international picture which would warrant a substantial reduction in the military forces we had planned . . .? (b) Has the situation worsened since last spring and should we, therefore, be considering an augmentation . . .? (c) Is the situation about the same . . .?"[13]

On November 1, Under Secretary of State

Lovett called Forrestal to inquire as to the speed with which Forrestal desired an answer. The Secretary of Defense's plea was for November 15 with respect to how strongly he should urge upon the President his, Forrestal's, recommendation for a $2.5 billion addition to the President's budget ceiling.[14]

Marshall's answer came a week later from Paris. It evaded the real issue of defense requirements—or, at least, gave Forrestal no help—by stating simply that the international situation had not changed in the past eight months. Marshall insisted that the important task was to rearm Western Europe.[15] The Marshall Plan was just reaching fruition and NATO was a-borning; the energies of the State Department would be devoted to working with them.

Marshall had often urged rescission of the UN ban on ambassadorial exchange with Spain. While in Europe, he had actively sought a change of heart in the British and French governments through their Foreign Ministers, Bevin and Schuman. However, bases and Ambassadors were entirely separate in the mind of General Marshall. In view of the hostility of the NATO nations toward Spain, and in view of their fear of a policy of defense behind the Pyrenees, it would have been folly to press for Spanish participation in the Marshall Plan even though the Plan itself did not include military aid.

In Washington, preparations were being made for a Presidential election. Prospects were not good for the Democrats. Many members of the Truman Administration had practically conceded defeat. President Truman was an implacable foe of Franco Spain, but for the moment he held his peace. He also secured— and quite possibly sought—some domestic political advantage from a bit of diplomatic maneuvering with Spain that could cause no harm and might even be useful. On March 30, 1948, Myron C. Taylor, President Truman's representative to the Vatican, stopped in Madrid en route to Rome. Taylor had instructions to inform General Franco by what means he could gain the acceptance of the Western governments; but it was asserted by some that the intention of the visit was to demonstrate to American Catholics that the Truman Administration was in a conciliatory mood toward Spain.[16]

THE SPANISH LOBBY: CHARLES PATRICK CLARK

In 1948 the Spanish Foreign Ministry began a full-scale assault on the Administration's policies. Overwhelming economic problems were forcing drastic revisions in the Spanish view of the outside world. Since the loss of its once vast overseas empire, Spain had not known decent living standards. The ups and downs of various types of political regimes made little difference in its economic plight.

Spain had made no progress in recovering from its devastating civil war, the proving grounds for both Nazi and Soviet military might. Here, almost ten years later, the Spanish worker was poorer by more than twice, figured by any accurate statistical standard. After 1945 Spain had been scourged by severe drought which had curtailed crops and dangerously shortened the hydroelectric power available for industry. Spain was plagued by three of the severest afflictions known to modern states: inflation, increasing population, and decreasing productivity.

In 1948 it was painfully obvious that Spain was to be the only country in Western Europe without some form of aid from the United States. In relative terms, Spain was, in effect, not only going to miss out on the big bonanza; it would be damaged by the projected European Recovery Program. The political vicissitudes of an American election year, however, encouraged General Franco to try to improve Spain's position.

The upshot of all this: the Spanish Lobby.

Responsibility was given to Señor Don José Felix de Lequerica, an able, experienced diplomat. During the early months of 1948, Lequerica, with the title Inspector of Ministries, became in effect chief of the Spanish delegation in Washington.

The Spanish Foreign Ministry through its roving Ambassador-without-portfolio sought the aid of interested congressmen in getting the right person to represent its interests. The services of one Charles Patrick Clark were retained. Clark, not yet forty, was already an old-timer in Washington circles. An honor graduate of Georgetown, he had served on the staffs of several Congressional committees and government agencies. His major distinction, as he would take pains to point out, was his service with the Truman Committee Investigating the National Defense Program.

It is impossible to evaluate or measure exactly the influence of interest groups and skilled public relations men in such a complicated milieu, but it is no coincidence that the Spanish cause began to improve almost immediately after Clark became a part of it. He mobilized effectively the groups that coalesced to form the Spanish Lobby.

After 1948 pro-Spanish support came primarily from five separable but overlapping groups. The first might be called the Catholic group, made up of some of the most ardent Spanish supporters, such as McCarran, McCarthy, O'Konski, Keogh and others. Very close and partially identical to the Catholic group was the extreme anti-Communist group, which viewed Spain as the most zealous anti-Communist nation in Europe and probably the only "reliable" ally in the cause. The third was the pro-Spanish-bases group composed of Admirals Conolly, Cassady, Gardner, *et al.,* and Secretary Sullivan and his successor, Secretary Matthews. Although most of these men were Catholics, they would no doubt have sought Iberian bases regardless of religion. As the months passed, these men were joined by hosts of senators, congressmen and bureaucrats. The fourth group can be called simply the anti-Trumanists, led by Senator Taft. Growing anti-Administration feeling brought to the support of bases in Spain such men as Senators McKellar, Brewster, Bridges and so on. The fifth group was economic, the vanguard of which was southern cotton. Taken together, these elements gave the "Spanish Lobby" a surprisingly bipartisan, supra-sectional, supra-religious and supra-economic appearance.

In March 1948 their first big opportunity arose. The first Economic Cooperation Act implementing the Marshall Plan was on the floor of the House of Representatives. Representative Alvin O'Konski (Republican of Wisconsin) introduced an amendment making Spain one of the participating nations. In a surprising show of support, the House adopted the amendment 149-52, almost 3-1. Later the amendment was killed in House-Senate conference. Undoubtedly, the sudden burst of support for Spain was due in part to the pressures of an election year. But the surprisingly large vote gave warning in all circles that a basic reappraisal of the entire Spanish question might be necessary.

The Spanish Lobby had missed its opportunity in the 80th Congress, but the fight had just begun. On September 30, 1948 Senator Chan Gurney (Republican of South Dakota) held an hour's interview in Madrid with Franco. Gurney, Chairman of the Senate Committee on Armed Services, was one of the powerful members of Congress on military legislation. Senator Gurney was accompanied by the United States *chargé d'affaires* in Spain, Paul Culbertson, and several United States military officers. However, when the time came for the interview, Culbertson was left in the waiting room while private discussions were held between Gurney and Franco. When he emerged from the interview, the Senator said that he favored "complete re-establishment of all relations between Spain and the United States."[17]

On October 5, Senator Gurney, back in Washington, held conferences with Secretary Forrestal and the three service Secretaries: Royall, Army; Sullivan, Navy; and Symington, Air Force.

III. THE BATTLE: FIRST PHASE

ADMINISTRATIVE RECOVERY

The sudden burst of Spanish support in 1948 can be attributed in part to election-year fever, the lenient attitude of Secretaries Marshall and Forrestal toward Spain, and the formation of the Spanish Lobby. The 1948 election had temporarily weakened the anti-Spanish bloc—which was still a majority. With respect to the Spanish cause the most important post-election change was the replacement of Marshall by Dean Acheson as Secretary of State. Acheson, while serving as Under Secretary of State, had been instrumental in the formulation of the Truman Doctrine and the Marshall Plan which followed it. As Secretary, he promptly worked for the establishment of NATO. He was particularly sensitive to the problems of European economic and military cooperation, and he was in sympathy with the Spanish policy expressed in 1945 and 1946. In 1949, as the new Secretary of State, Acheson helped revivify the established Spanish policy in the executive branch because, or primarily because, a change might adversely affect NATO and ERP.

Acheson's earliest expression on Spain came on May 5, 1949, before the subcommittee of the Senate Committee on Appropriations, meeting for hearings on State Department requests for the next fiscal year. First, with respect to ambassadors, Acheson said, we were bound to honor the United Nations ban as long as it stood. Second, we never had severed diplomatic relations with Spain. The lack of an ambassador was, Acheson pointed out, a trivial point. Third, as to money: Spain was welcome to apply to the Export-Import Bank like any other nation. Fourth, the rest was up to Spain and the Western allies; Spain would have to liberalize its government and be accepted unanimously by the allies before we could enter into closer relations.[18]

On May 11, one week later, Secretary Acheson further strengthened his position by stating that the UN ban on ambassadors was not in itself so important but that it had "become a symbol" to all of the Western democracies.[19]

Although Acheson had the President's full backing, the primary reason for the President's opposition was simpler, more direct and considerably more eloquent: Franco had come to power on the coattails of the Axis and was continuing to follow Fascist patterns of religious and political persecution. Consequently, in response to a July 1949 attempt in Congress to include Spain under the Marshall Plan, President Truman went beyond his Secretary of State and said simply that the United States opposed the step because relations between the two countries were "not friendly."[20] The situation had not been stated so bluntly since the immediate post-war period. Senator Taft in exasperation called on the Administration to "shake loose from its communist-front philosophy" and grant full recognition to Spain.[21]

THE LINE OFFICERS

Meanwhile, another source of support for Spain was building up, the significance of which was not appreciated at the time. As was said before, the Navy had been in stiff competition with the British for predominance in the Mediterranean and the nearby Atlantic; and the fight for control was increased in 1949 as a consequence of the organization of the fleets under a single NATO command. This fight expressed itself in a need for bases independent of the British and strategically located with respect to both oceans. A glance at the map is enough to appreciate Spain's strategic allure to the Navy. Floating facilities or mooring rights in Spain bespoke of few political difficulties as far as the Navy was concerned. No construction would be necessary and no United

States military personnel would have to be stationed on the Spanish mainland.

Admiral Richard L. Conolly, Commander of the United States Naval Forces in the Eastern Atlantic and Mediterranean, took the first forthright step toward breaking the Spanish ice. Between 1947 and 1949, Admiral Conolly made repeated requests for permission to take units of the fleet to pay courtesy calls on Spanish ports. These requests were blocked by the State Department until September 1949, when the President (presumably on Acheson's recommendation) authorized an informal visit which Conolly himself described as "informal but official." American warships entered a Spanish port for the first time since the civil war on September 3, 1949. There they remained, at El Ferrol, for five days. When Admiral Conolly called on General Franco, who was at his summer headquarters nearby, he was accompanied by: four Admirals including George R. Henderson; Major General Robert W. Harper; Air Force Brigadier General William L. Ritchie; and the United States Naval Attaché in Madrid, Captain Preston V. Mercer.[22] Captain Mercer, who served under Culbertson, the *chargé d'affaires,* had often openly criticized the policy of the United States government toward Spain.[23]

Conolly's visit was authorized as a test of Franco's intentions and as a feeler of American and European public opinion. No specifics were discussed, and no commitments were made. Conolly and Franco exchanged civilities and discussed problems of mutual interest.

Admiral Conolly returned to the United States in October. He conferred with the White House and with the interested members of Congress. The President was not displeased with Conolly's report, which included the fact that Spain was eager to cooperate with the Western powers. However, when Conolly departed, the core of the President's opposition to Spain still remained.[24] Before the House Armed Services Committee Conolly made a strong plea for naval bases in Spain. "The strategic importance of the Iberian Peninsula is uniquely evident," Conolly reported. Furthermore, "the more friends you have on your flank the better."[25]

The State Department's leaders stood firm. They feared that any friendship with Spain would imperil the Western Alliance, soon to be NATO. They had predicted that Conolly's visit was going to cause great furor at home and abroad. But when the news of Conolly's trip broke, little of this took place. The tempest turned out to be a spring squall. Although much of the press of the West was unfavorable, it had little of the expected invective and denunciation.

The visit of Conolly and company to Spain was not the only evidence of revolt by the line against the President's anti-Spanish policy. Other naval units were soon to follow, the first one being shortly after the Conolly visit when a task force of the Sixth Fleet paid a call at Barcelona. And Admiral Sherman, whose role in this story became highly significant in 1951, requested permission to include Spain in his tour of Europe shortly after his appointment as Chief of Naval Operations in November 1949. The request was not approved. In these activities, Conolly and Sherman had the open support of Admirals Cassady, Carney and Gardner. The Sixth Fleet had turned its big guns on Washington.

Rumblings were also heard from the Air Force. Nine months before Conolly's well-publicized visit, Major General William H. Tunner, chief of the Berlin airlift, paid an inconspicuous visit to Madrid. Following his visit, General Tunner was host in Wiesbaden to a party of Spanish officials including Lieutenant General Apolinar Saenza de Burnaga, Spanish Under Secretary for Aviation.[26]

The exchange of visits between General Tunner and the Spanish officers was part of a more general movement in the Air Force to revise strategies. Like the Navy, the Air Force had developed a pattern of collaboration with the British in the use of RAF bases, primarily on the British Isles. In 1948 arrangements were made for still greater direct use of the British bases. At the same time, there were misgivings that such arrangements would not entirely fulfill the fundamental means of defense against aggression: (1) the general policy of containment; (2) the military axiom of having as many friends on the flank as possible; (3) dispersion of the acutely concentrated base locations of all our services; and (4) closer proximity all the time to the Soviet Union. Secretary Forrestal encouraged the reappraisal in his fear that overconcentration courted hot war and that lack of suitable bases could mean loss of access to countries of the Middle East.

Two countries were considered well suited for air bases: Spain and French Morocco. Both countries would require economic and military bolstering, plus the outright construction of military installations. But, whereas the Navy considered mooring rights in Spain a simple matter, the Air Force could foresee insuperable problems of politics and utilization. Morocco, on the other hand, while in essentially the same radius as Spain, was both outside liberal America's realm of attention and (at that time) inside the legal shadow of the French Union. For the time being, the Air Force passed over Spain and landed in North Africa, although the makings of Spanish support did not disappear.

THE JUNKETEERS

By the fall of 1949, Spain had indeed achieved a new status in governmental circles. This is indicated by the sheer number of Congressional junketeers whose itineraries included Madrid.

Charles Patrick Clark led the way. Both his visit and the Congressional visits were a direct result of Admiral Conolly's. It shows how closely all parties were attuned to possible changes in the official stand. And there were grounds for hope that Conolly's visit reflected a new predisposition on the part of the Administration.

Clark spent several weeks in Spain during September and October. He travelled extensively and had access to the normally secretive Spaniards. On his return, Clark wrote a lengthy report "as requested" to his former boss, the President. This report, dated November 10, 1949, concerned freedom of worship in Spain, specifically as applied to Protestants.[27]

Of the several authorities Clark cited, the most interesting was Max H. Klein. On the basis of his twenty-seven years as President of the American Chamber of Commerce in Spain, Klein attempted to answer the many adverse reports which had been appearing in American newspapers and journals. In part, Mr. Klein said: "Protestantism is not a problem in Spain. . . . Confining myself to Barcelona, where I usually live, I can be quite definite in saying that the Protestant community is not persecuted and they are free to worship according to their beliefs. In the past years I have

several times attended services at the Protestant Chapel and have many friends who attend them regularly without the slightest difficulty." Klein went on to say that "Spaniards are great individualists and are apt to be very undisciplined. There is just one issue on which they are practically all agreed and that is their religion. Why should we attempt to destroy that unity?"

One significant fact omitted in this report was that Klein himself was a Catholic.

Ending his report to the President, Clark said:

The writer, in discussing the question of religious freedom, with General Franco, stated that he might have the pleasure of visiting with the President on his return, and, if he should, he would like to take back an expression of General Franco's feeling regarding the religious situation, as well as other matters. The writer would prefer to discuss the Chief of State's message orally. The writer arrived at certain conclusions which he would also prefer to give orally.

The meeting with the President never occurred. But Clark's report and conclusions gained currency in many other circles, predominantly Congressional.

At the time when Clark was making his survey, many prominent senators and congressmen visited Spain. On September 14, Senator McCarran departed for Spain. He announced to the press that it was his intention to discuss the loan question with Franco.[28] On September 15, President Truman issued a sharp statement that McCarran went as a private citizen and did not represent anyone in the Administration.[29]

Following closely on Senator McCarran's heels were Representative James J. Murphy, a New York Democrat, and seven associates. After an interview with the Spanish leader, Murphy said that General Franco impressed him as a "very, very lovely and lovable character."[30] Senator Brewster (Republican of Maine), with Representatives James P. Richards (Democrat of South Carolina), Eugene J. Keogh (Democrat of New York), Noble J. Gregory (Democrat of Kentucky) and W. R. Poage (Democrat of Texas) arrived at the same time.

On November 1, 1949, an important subcommittee of the Senate Appropriations Committee arrived in Frankfurt for a five-week tour: Senators Chavez (Democrat of New Mexico),

Stennis (Democrat of Mississippi), Thye (Republican of Minnesota), McClellan (Democrat of Arkansas), Robertson (Democrat of Virginia) and Thomas (Democrat of Oklahoma). Chavez declared that Spain should receive military and economic aid to "bulwark Western Europe's security." On return from Spain the committee unanimously agreed that full diplomatic relations should be restored as soon as possible and that some form of economic aid should be granted.[31]

From the standpoint of the Administration, however, matters were getting out of hand. This public courtship of Spain was tending to give the wrong impression. Thus, on December 3, several Administration supporters in the House Foreign Affairs Committee departed for Spain. On December 11, Representative Joseph L. Pfeifer (Democrat of New York) told the press that where Spanish-American relations are concerned, " . . . it is a matter not simply for the United States to settle. It is in the last analysis a question for Spain and the Spanish people to settle." (Secretary Acheson's words.) He also warned that Spaniards had given undue weight to the pronouncements of certain individual members of Congress, and that no individual could speak for the entire body. This report was concurred in by Thomas Gordon (Democrat of Illinois) and Clement Zablocki (Democrat of Wisconsin).[32]

The Spanish press denounced the Pfeifer statement as "offensive and impertinent." And for good reason, in the context of 1949. The major effect of Congressional activity of 1948 and 1949 had been to obstruct and frustrate the President's personal animus and the Administration's general coolness toward an unreconstructed Spanish regime. Why should Franco yield to the remonstrances of Myron Taylor, Paul Culbertson, Dean Acheson, *et al.,* if he had the encouragement of growing numbers in Congress, from Senators Gurney and McCarran on down?

CONGRESS TAKES THE LEAD

The Congressional stage was set. On January 18, 1950, in the opening days of the 81st Congress' 2nd session, Senator Connally, at his request, received clarification of the Spanish policy from Acheson. The contents of this letter will be considered in some detail in a later section. For its importance to the legislative process, certain points must be mentioned here.

Acheson explained that our policy of withdrawal of ambassadors from Spain "as a means of political pressure was a mistaken departure from established practice." However, he reaffirmed the Administration's opposition to making money available to Spain to use as it saw fit. Spain would not be discriminated against at the Export-Import Bank, which loaned solely on the basis of need, the merit of the purpose and the prospect of repayment. At the same time, and entirely aside from the present view of the Spanish regime, the United States, said Acheson, was in favor of rescinding the UN ban on ambassadors. As long as the Resolution stood, however, the United States was obliged to comply with it.[33]

In a sense the Spanish cause had taken the legendary one step forward and two steps backward. While the Administration was willing to restore Spain to full diplomatic status, it had reaffirmed its opposition to extending the generosity of the United States to Franco. To give Spain access to American money only through the Export-Import Bank meant in effect no access at all. Spain was unable to offer guarantees of any kind in return for loans. Even its supporter Argentina had curtailed economic assistance in the face of Spanish insolvency.

Owen Brewster delivered the first lengthy attack of the session on the Spanish policy on March 10, 1950. It was clear by now that the emotional or ideological factor—most notably in the President himself—was the chief barrier to be overcome, and Brewster concentrated his fire in that direction. In his speech Brewster stressed, first of all, Spain's important role in World War II, especially in keeping the western end of the Mediterranean open. On the religious problem he quoted Max Klein at length.[34] By this time, Mr. Klein's name, as an authority on Protestantism in Spain, had become almost a household word.

The lengthiest exposition in Spain's favor came from South Carolinian James Richards. Chairman of the House Foreign Affairs Committee. Richards reaffirmed his faith in Acheson and the Administration in general, and Yalta and China in particular: "At no time in the history of any other government has greater vision or initiative been shown."

"There is, however, to my mind, at least one

glaring weakness and inconsistency in the foreign policy of the United States. I refer to our attitude toward Spain," he went on to say.

Richards made an earnest attack upon the basic premises of the Administration's policy. For each of the President's points concerning Spain's degraded economic and political practices, Richards offered counterpoints showing the countries where the United States did not bother to inquire into such matters before entering into full relations.[35] On the general problem of religious freedom, Richards drew upon the researches of Brewster and Representative Abraham Multer (Democrat of New York)—a close friend of Charles Patrick Clark who had earlier delivered a speech on the Jewish problem in Spain. All in turn had drawn heavily on Clark's report.

Speeches notwithstanding, it was Senator McCarran who led the way for positive action again in this session. On April 27, he got the support of 35 of his colleagues for his amendment to the Economic Cooperation Act authorizing a loan to Spain for $50 million. No doubt there was less support for the amendment because—unlike previous attempts—it had specified a certain amount of money; but even so, there was every reason for optimism. For, although a second attempt to put Spain into the Marshall Plan had been defeated, support for Spain had grown; and, moreover, the State Department had weakened on an important point—the UN ban. This was viewed as the preliminary but inseparable stage to full economic, political and military rapprochement with Spain.

At the very moment when the pro-Spanish forces were being organized for another attempt, the Korean War broke out. After the initial surprise had passed, the Spanish bloc made preparations. In July, less than a month after the North Korean invasion, McCarran called a secret or somewhat secret meeting in his office at the Senate Office Building. This meeting was attended by a few senators and a small group of military representatives from the Pentagon. No names were disclosed "for obvious reasons," Senator McCarran reported.[36]

McCarran announced to the slightly uneasy officeful that he planned to introduce another bill in Congress for a Spanish loan. This time it would be for $100 million. Following these introductory remarks, the Senator turned the

meeting over to the military officers who repeated generously the strategic arguments which had already been furnished congressmen for the ever-growing number of floor speeches.[37] It must be emphasized here that these and other individual contacts between members of Congress and the Pentagon occurred without the express sanction or disapproval of the Defense Department Secretaries.

Whatever opposition remained in Congress after the Korean outbreak was fully dispersed during the following few weeks. For, hot on the heels of Korea came an urgent demand from the Administration for aid to Tito, and the passage of the Yugoslav Emergency Relief Assistance Act. In spite of important distinctions between the Yugoslav and Spanish situations, which the State Department took special pains to point out, the simplest and most immediate impression was that of inconsistency. If you can aid one dictator without approving of his political methods, nothing is to prevent you from aiding another on the same basis.

On August 1, 1950, the first Spanish loan was pushed through the Senate. It was a painful defeat for the Administration. The vote was overwhelmingly favorable, 65-15. Even the Democratic leadership in the Senate defected to the majority. In a meeting of the Democratic Policy Committee just prior to the vote, Senator Connally, *et al.,* had made the decision to capitulate. Scott Lucas (Democrat of Illinois), majority leader, attempted to explain this move to the press on August 4. "We had to make a deal. I don't care what any Senator or anyone else says. I'm a realist, and when I'm licked, I don't hesitate to admit it."[38]

It had been a shrewd maneuver. First of all, the bill had been attached as an amendment to the United States' first General (Omnibus) Appropriations bill, which would have to be accepted or rejected *in toto* by the President. Secondly, it had been arranged so that none of the proposed ECA funds would be used. The loans were to be made by the Export-Import Bank and administered by the ECA; but the money was completely above and beyond the ECA appropriations. Thus it was designed to remove all cause for alarm by the allies who had expressed fears that Spanish aid could come only at their sacrifice.

On August 3, after considerable pressure had been applied, a motion was entertained to reconsider the Spanish loan amendment. By the same vote, 65-15, the motion was tabled—a scant few hours after Truman had denounced the loan.[39] The President's denunciation had had no effect.

Throughout August the fate of the Spanish loan lay in the hands of the House-Senate Conference where this minor item was only one of many differences between the House and Senate versions of the Omnibus Appropriations bill. On August 24th, the Conference report was presented to the House. The House Conferees had accepted the principle of the Spanish loan, at a reduced sum of $62.5 million. In return, the Senate had accepted the House demand for a cut in the Point Four appropriation from President Truman's request of $26.9 million to $15 million and the elimination of the United Nations Children's Fund altogether.

In response, the President sent a strong appeal for restoration of the full amount for Point Four. Floor leader McCormack did not read the President's message; he inserted it in the record with no comment. However, its terms were carried out in a new Conference Committee compromise. On August 25th, with unusual dispatch, the House approved a $34.1 billion omnibus appropriation by a vote of 165-90. The bill included the Spanish loan and

the full $26.9 million Point Four appropriation. No Administration leader spoke against the "mandatory" loan to Spain; no Republican leader spoke out against full restoration of the Point Four Program. The Senate approved the Conference report on August 28th with a minor amendment, and later that day both houses approved the final version by voice vote. The Spanish loan had ridden in on the coattails of Point Four.[39a]

On September 6 President Truman signed H.R. 7786, the General Appropriations bill. But he gave warning in his accompanying statement that he would withhold the Spanish funds indefinitely. He refused to consider the loan "mandatory": it was no more than an "authorization." "Money will be loaned to Spain whenever mutually advantageous arrangements can be made with respect to security, terms of repayment, purposes for which the money is to be spent, and other appropriate factors, and *whenever such loans will serve the interest of the United States in the conduct of foreign relations.*"[40]

With this statement, the President had set the stage for the final phases of the fight for bases in Spain. Before we would relinquish money liberally to Spain, we would have to have a plan for a *quid pro quo.*

IV. THE BATTLE: SECOND PHASE

MONEY IN SEARCH OF POLICY

Until the official policy of the United States government changed, Congressional measures would be of relatively small importance. Truman's statement that the loan was considered an "authorization" and not a "mandate" confirmed the fears of the Spanish Lobby that after all was said and done in Congress, the route to Spain had to pass through the doors of the executive branch. Consequently, the fight for financial aid to Spain was only one phase of the battle with the Administration.

Secretary Acheson was the focal point of the barrage. And pressure on Acheson for a change of policy had begun over a year before the monetary victory. Spain was one of the several reasons for the growing unpopularity of Acheson with Congress.

The attack on Acheson was led by his constant assailants, Senators McCarran and McKellar. On May 5, 1949 the subcommittee of the Senate Committee on Appropriations met for hearings on State Department requests for the next fiscal year. The matter of ambassadors arose first, and the cross-examination shows how neatly appropriations hearings can be turned to substantive questions of policy:

Sen. McCarran: Mr. Secretary, during the course of these hearings there will come up in this bill the matter of diplomatic items. I should like to ask you why it is that this country refuses to recognize Spain.

* * *

Sen. McKellar: Mr. Chairman, I may say that I feel exactly as you do about our nonrecognition of Spain. Spain is a Christian nation and we have had friendly relations with her. She has been a good customer of ours. She has usually paid her debts. I see no reason why we should not have friendly relations with Spain.

* * *

Sec. Acheson: Senator, I tried to state a moment ago that, acting under this recommendation of the General Assembly, we have not appointed an ambassador.

Sen. McCarran: Are we to be enslaved to the U.N.? I never voted with that in mind.

Sen. McKellar: Neither did I.

* * *

Sen. McCarran. Let me say to you Mr. Secretary that so far as I am personally concerned as chairman of this subcommittee I am not in favor of your policy with reference to Spain and until that policy is changed I am going to examine your appropriations with a fine tooth comb.[41]

The Senators' cross-examination then went on to the question of Spain's place in the United States security program.

Sen. Saltonstall: If nonrecognition of Spain is the policy of the Department of State now, I assume it is based on our security because of the attitude of other nations in Europe toward Spain and our wanting to work along with them. Is that a fair statement?

Secretary Acheson: Senator, I think we ought to be very clear that there is no policy of nonrecognition of Spain.

Senator Saltonstall: I emphasized the word "security."

Secretary Acheson: So far as security is concerned, you are entirely right. Spain is a very important element in the security of the United States, and that is why it is so important and why we have been doing our best to bring about what I call a reintegration of Spain in the west.

In order to bring Spain into a system of collective security in the west, it must be by common agreement. You cannot get Spain into a thing such as the North Atlantic Treaty without some resolution of these difficulties with the other countries. There has to be common desire and common understanding.

Senator McKellar: I am in hopes that you will be diplomatically friendly to Spain hereafter. I think it ought to be done. Spain is a great country as far as we are concerned, and just as important as any other western European country so far as our defense is concerned, and so far as our protection is concerned, and I hope you will look into it and change it. I am sure you will.

Senator McCarran: He did not answer you in the affirmative, Senator.

Senator McCarran: [A few minutes later after several other topics had been covered.] . . . Is not the Iberian Peninsula on which Spain exists essential to the full success of the North Atlantic Pact?

Secretary Acheson: It is very important. The pact can be successful without it; it can be stronger with it. I do not think we ought to pretend there is any mystery about this. As I said at the outset, this is the result of history. Now it is no secret that the Spanish regime was a fascist regime. At the end of the war, it was the idea that this type of authoritarian government was out. However, it has gone on in Spain.

What the western Europeans want is some movement toward the relaxation of those oppressive measures, which is not an unreasonable thing to want and which could be accomplished very easily. If you could bring together the western Europeans and Spain on some basis of mutual adjustment, the problem would very largely be solved.[42]

The highest military authorities were coming in for their share of Congressional inquiry also. However, in their case it was another problem. The Congressional committees were attempting to marshal a large body of professional opinion in support of Spain. But the military chiefs were by no means willing to make a public commitment to that effect. It was hoped that these hearings would provide the military supporters of Spain at least one politically important channel to present views which, until the very last, were unpopular among the chief formulators of foreign policy —the State Department, the National Security Council with the exception of the Secretary of Defense, and the White House.

Secretary Johnson, who headed the Department of Defense until September 1950, was the chief force behind military planning on Spain. But in 1950 it was still a behind-the-scenes job, and in answering Senator Cain's question on what Spain's role would be in case of war, Johnson replied: "I know that everyone does not agree with my ideas about Spain. I still have the same ideas. I would like to discuss them with you in executive session."[43]

In 1951 the military leaders were still elusive. Thus the Army Chief of Staff:

Senator Wherry: Do you feel you have a

proper defense of western Europe without having Spain brought into the family of nations?

General Collins: I think it would materially aid, and again I am speaking from a military point of view.

Senator Wherry: Military experts have also stated it was very necessary to have Spain friendly to the North Atlantic Treaty community. And I was asking your opinion, if you felt that an adequate defense could be built without Spain.

General Collins: Yes, sir; I believe it could be. The alternative would be if Spain were an enemy. If Spain were an enemy the lines of communication through the Mediterranean would be dreadfully threatened but we did operate through the Mediterranean with Spain neutral, during the last war.[44]

A few days later the Chief of Naval Operations was on the stand.

Senator Connally: Of course, Admiral, we want all the help, all the assistance, and all the co-operation we can get, don't we?

Admiral Sherman: Yes. But we do not want to make commitments on which the disadvantages may outweigh the advantages.

Senator Wherry: If those questions could be settled, whatever they are, political, military, or otherwise, do you feel if they would be invited into the North Atlantic community of nations, they would be of tremendous assistance? I say, if the questions could be settled, whatever they are.

Admiral Sherman: In certain cases there are other problems so I cannot answer to that without reservations which require elaboration in executive session.[45]

Secretary of Defense Marshall was in a particularly difficult position in view of his support before the 1948 Presidential elections for improved relations with Spain:

Senator Russell: What are your views on agreement with Turkey or with Spain, or other nations that might be in a position to contribute to the defense of Western Europe?

Secretary Marshall: As to Spain, that is quite a delicate international diplomatic question today. For the Defense Department I would not care to make any comment at this time.

Senator Russell: I thought perhaps since you have served as Secretary of State you would be able to comment from that standpoint. We have had the Secretary of State before us and he has replied that there are a good many military questions involved, and you say it is a question of diplomacy. I had thought, perhaps since you had served in both capacities you might give us the answer.

Secretary Marshall: When I walked out of the door of the State Department I ceased to be Secretary of State very definitely, and a great deal of water has gone over the dam since then.[46]

However, as a consequence of these probings, the sides of the controversy emerged all the more clearly. How long were the "delicate international diplomatic questions," so phrased by Secretary of Defense Marshall, to take precedence over singularly pressing desires to push the boundaries of our defense further away from our shores? On the one side were those who feared that, although Spain would undoubtedly add to Western military strength, this might be more than neutralized by an eventual loss of morale and unity amongst the allies; and there were also some who feared that bases in Spain might prove no more solid than castles in Spain.

On the other side was a Congressional majority, arguing that whatever was lost of the morale of the allies would be more than compensated by the collaboration of the most reliable of anti-Communists, and that Spanish bases would be firm bastions. In the uncomfortable middle remained Marshall, Matthews, Bradley, Collins, Sherman and many other top officials in the Pentagon. The President's obduracy had bound them, and some of them were probably uncertain about the net advantages of a new Spanish policy; and they necessarily had at least to refuse to be open parties to Congressional polemics. Instead, they spoke of the desirability of Spanish affiliation only in terms of a "military point of view," and they shunned the larger question of evaluating the over-all effect of Spain's inclusion in the Western Alliance.

President Truman's answer to the "mandatory loan" had, however, left the door to policy change ever so slightly ajar. It must be shown that aid to Spain would indeed be beneficial to the United States, and already a majority in Congress believed that such was the case. They continued to press the Administration.

On June 30, 1950, Senator Cain (Republican of Washington) had exclaimed:

To my mind, it is impossible to separate Spain from a study of the North Atlantic Pact. Those responsible for strategic planning do not hide the fact that they believe Spain is essential to the reliability and effectiveness of the North Atlantic Pact.

To all intents and purposes Spain is a huge airfield of 195,000 square miles surrounded by water. Its sea coast has many ports and natural first class naval bases.[47]

And after the loan was put through, the Spanish bloc did not sit back to enjoy victory. On the day of the Senate victory two senior Senators, one from each side of the aisle, spoke for a military arrangement on just such a mutually beneficial basis as Truman spoke of a month later. Senator Styles Bridges (Republican of New Hampshire) demanded: "If Spain wants to be included in arms aid, there is no reason why we shouldn't negotiate for some bases which we could use if there is a Russian attack in Europe."[48]

Senator Millard Tydings (Democrat of Maryland) warned: "To go through with this plan [Mutual Security] without putting Spain in the picture, with her great national army, and with her great antipathy to communism, is to lose one of the great assets of national defense without which the picture is not complete."[49]

The vanguard of the Spanish bloc was joined in March 1951 by the Senate Committees on Foreign Relations and Armed Services. In a joint report on Assignment of Ground Forces to Europe, the Committees concluded:

. . . Spain has 350,000 men under arms; Yugoslavia, 330,000; and Greece, 150,000. . . .

It is fair . . . to say that the addition of over a million armed men, who would fight for their freedom, would contribute immeasurably to the security of Western Europe and be an additional deterrent to Soviet Aggression.[50]

(The Committee arrived at its total of "over a million armed men" by adding, say, 200,000 U. S. soldiers, sailors and airmen to the oddly assorted 830,000 in the Greek, Yugoslav and Spanish armed forces.)

And on April 4, 1951, following the recommendation of the Foreign Relations and Armed Services Committees, the Senate, in its resolution authorizing dispatch of troops to Europe in support of NATO, asked that consideration be given to revision of European defense plans to provide for the utilization of Spanish military and other resources.

But Senator McCarran was not content to depend upon debate and hearings and resolutions. If the Administration was stalling for time, more direct measures were called for. Let us return to McCarran's meeting with the senators and military officers in July 1950, alluded to briefly above. After announcing his plan for the $100 million loan bill, he went on to outline his program for the future. The loan was only a starter. Later, he promised, he was going to begin a drive to bring Spain into NATO. The Senator went further to say that the ultimate intent was to send not merely a hundred million dollars, but as many millions as necessary to make Spain's army one of the strongest in Europe. And if bringing Spain into the Atlantic Alliance "involves too much international malarky," he hoped to lift the quarantine by sending the economic and military aid and letting "the NATO nations catch up and approve later."[51]

The meeting served a twofold purpose. He had turned the gathering over to the military in order to persuade the senators. At the same time the meeting encouraged supporters in the Pentagon to come out in the open. McCarran did not identify the officers except to say that they were of the "lower echelons."[52]

As McCarran himself reported, he realized that "political decisions belong to the State Department and the White House, and the President had made it clear he wanted no relations with Spain. This left the technical men in a spot. They could not openly advocate a policy which frightened their superiors, let alone contradict the President, yet their blueprints did just that. Unofficially, the lower echelon made known its views. The meeting in my office was just one of many in Washington."[53] And it may be noted that McCarran's article describing the meeting was not published until April 1951 when Spain was once again in the limelight.

Nor was the Defense Department alone singled out for pressure. Later, in May 1951, only weeks before the President's crucial decision, McCarran held another meeting. The Senator was very much concerned that after almost a year a very small amount of the 1950 mandatory $62.5 million loan had gotten into Spanish hands. If the State Department was delaying until a decision could be made as to what we could get in return for the money, McCarran wanted that decision immediately. To this meeting came: Carlisle Humelsine, Deputy Under Secretary of State; William B. Dunham, Spanish Desk, State Department (Mr. Dunham returns to our story in a moment); Herbert E. Gaston, Chairman of the Board, Export-Import Bank; Paul R. Porter of the ECA; and, demonstrating that the Senator's private State Department was in operation, Ambassador Lequerica.

In the presence of Lequerica, McCarran questioned the officials about the Spanish situation and demanded action. The fiery Senator was later roundly denounced in the press and in government circles for his breach of protocol. (Not since Representative Sol Bloom and Lord Halifax had cooperated in getting aid for embattled Britain in 1940, reported the press, had such methods been used.) McCarran conceded that he had "gone a little out of line," but he felt that it had been necessary to get to the truth. It was not as Chairman of the Judiciary Committee but as sponsor of the loan that he had called the meeting, he explained.[54]

Wherever there was support for Spanish bases, or aid for Spain more generally, McCarran and his colleagues sought to encourage it. While the highest Pentagon personnel were still forced to hedge on the subject, there was no such reticence on the part of their underlings, who shared the knowledge but not the responsibility. And if the officials under State Department control could not be goaded into action, they could at least be embarrassed. Word of these and other meetings drifted down the corridors around Washington, and many were beginning to get the cue.

V. THE BATTLE: FINAL PHASE

In the preceding section of this study, the Congressional battle has been carried forward to the spring and summer of 1951. It is now necessary to return to executive branch developments during the same period.

The early skirmishes of 1950 left President Truman and Secretary Acheson with two immediate adjustments. First, the 1946 United Nations ban on exchange of ambassadors with Spain was to be lifted. The Administration was committed to some form of action on this by dint of Acheson's letter to Senator Connally in January 1950. Lifting the UN ban was of great importance in the fight for bases. As a practical matter, full and equal diplomatic status must exist before an important treaty can be given serious consideration. The official UN position was critical in the battle for bases because it had been an important part of Acheson's argument against changing the situation at all. The second adjustment concerned the unwanted authorization for loans to Spain, enacted in September 1950.

Both were sensitive matters. Up until this point official policy had been one of inaction, watchful waiting for the time when Spain's internal politics would take a turn for the better, or for the time when our Western allies cast toward Spain a more favorable eye. In this context, any positive move would surely have repercussions in Washington and among the fearful allies.

GRIFFIS TO MADRID

As November 1950 arrived there was no doubt that the General Assembly would lift its ban on ambassadors. The delegates from the various nations no longer felt any obligation to uphold the ban. It was freely admitted that the ban had been a failure. Most of the states which had espoused the original 1946 resolution had long since disregarded it and had sent their ambassadors back to Madrid. This included most of the Latin American states that had deferred to the United States only so long as the position of the United States was clearly back of the ban. Thus, when, in January 1950, Acheson had recommended rescission of the ban, it only remained for the General Assembly to convene in the fall.

The concerted four-year effort of Spain for restoration of full international status reached its climax on October 31, 1950. On that day the Special Political Committee of the General Assembly passed a resolution that would repeal those portions of the original resolution relating to the exchange of ambassadors with Spain. The vote was 37-10 with 12 abstaining, well over the required two-thirds majority of those voting yes or no.

The General Assembly approved the action of the Special Political Committee on November 4 by 38-10 with 12 abstentions. On both occasions the United States voted with the majority. And on both occasions the resolutions were sponsored by Bolivia, Costa Rica, the Dominican Republic, El Salvador, Honduras, Nicaragua, Peru and the Philippines.

It was not an unqualified success for Spain. While the ambassadorial ban had been erased from the record, some important parts of the original resolution remained. The preamble which linked Franco to Nazism and Fascism was not affected. And the third recommendation calling upon the Security Council to consider measures "to remedy the situation" if another government has not been established "within a reasonable time," still stood.

Furthermore, the Assembly's action was not a request that members send ambassadors to Madrid. It was simply a suggestion that those nations wishing to do so could in good grace resume full diplomatic relations.

No one was sure what the United States would do. No one, including the Secretary of State, could be sure just when the United States would respond to the UN action. Fighting was still going on inside the Administration. On October 7 the State Department officially released a volume of German documents disclosing the relations of the Axis with Spain during the late 1930's. Among other things these documents showed that some $200 millions of Nazi money had been invested in the Franco regime. A similar set of documents on Franco's World War II role had been released in 1946 on the day the original UN Spanish resolution had been approved.

Ineffective though this October 7 attempt seems to have been, it did indicate that under no circumstances would the Administration adopt an all-is-forgiven position. The Department was out to prove what it had often emphasized about Spain: Exchanging ambassadors with a country did not imply approval of its form of government. And it also indicated that there still existed a strong determination to maintain a climate of opinion unfavorable to a full political or military embrace.

On the eve of the General Assembly vote, November 2, President Truman told those assembled at his press conference that it would be a "long, long, time" before we would decide to send an ambassador to Spain and that reporters would have a "long time to think about it."[55]

Two weeks later, November 16, the President was again confronted by the question of ambassadorial exchange with Spain. When reminded by one reporter that he had said it would be a long, long time, the President replied, "That's right." This time, however, he did make the qualification that although he was reluctant about any appointment, he could be convinced that it was necessary, but that he "was not in that frame of mind right now."[56]

Nevertheless, the "long, long time" turned out to be only slightly more than a month. On December 27 the President announced the nomination of Stanton Griffis as Ambassador to Spain. Griffis, born in Boston in 1887, brought a wide and varied experience to the post. A New York financier, he had served as Ambassador to Egypt, Poland and Argentina. In 1948 he had headed the United Nations Relief for Palestine Refugees.

Griffis also brought a strongly pro-Spanish attitude to his new post. Almost three years before his appointment, upon transferral from Poland to Egypt, he had confided to Forrestal that he would have preferred Spain. He said that he found it "difficult to understand how we can talk about the control of the Mediterranean at one end and ignore the other points, now that we have no ambassador in Spain."[57]

In order to stop any false impressions coming out of the surprise action, the President on the day following Griffis' nomination issued a statement. He insisted that the nomination of Griffis did not represent a change of policy toward Spain. The Administration had been deliberating the move since the Acheson-Connally letter of January 1950, the President reported. The exchange of ambassadors was simply a more orderly way of doing business.

TRUMAN—MINUS ACHESON

The Secretary of State had had a long and uncomfortable ride over the years 1949 and 1950. Congressional harassment had often moved beyond the penumbra of propriety. And many of his peers and close advisers had differed with him privately and publicly on Spain. Secretary Johnson did not hesitate to forward the pro-Spanish point of view on Capitol Hill and in the NSC meetings. Even as early as October 31, 1947, George Kennan, by 1950 Chief of the State Department's Policy Planning Staff, had expressed his opposition to unfriendly relations with Spain. The Mediterranean, he said to Forrestal, could not be considered without considering Spain and the question of transit through the straits of Gibraltar.[58]

By the fall of 1950, Secretary Acheson was juxtaposed precariously between Congress and its military sympathizers—with the unanswerable argument that money was available as a *quid pro quo*—and the President, who still bore the justifiable grudges coming out of the past fifteen years and the weather-beaten but hardy conviction that the wishes of the Western allies must be honored.

Acheson's letter to Senator Connally on January 18, 1950 had touched off the beginning of the State Department's shift in Spanish policy. Included in this letter along with his admission that the UN ban had been an unsuccessful departure from accepted diplomatic practice was a lengthy discussion of the general position of the United States toward Spain. In speaking of the UN ban he volunteered the further information that "Experience since that time has served to confirm our doubts about these recommendations. They were intended as a gesture of disapproval and as an attempt to bring about a change in the Spanish Government. In retrospect it is now clear, however, that this action has not only failed in its intended purpose but has served to strengthen the position of the present regime. The Spanish reaction has been no different from that to be expected from any proud people."

Of even greater significance were his comments on the present outlook of the State Department.

The policy of the United States toward Spain is based on the recognition of certain essential facts. First, there is no sign of an alternative to the present Government. Second, the internal position of the present regime is strong, and enjoys the support of many who, although they might prefer another form of government or chief of state, fear that chaos and civil strife would follow a move to overthrow the Government. Third, Spain is a part of Western Europe which should not be permanently isolated from normal relations with that area.

Acheson then went on to specify the conditions which he felt must be fulfilled before normal relations could be achieved. "Spain is still unacceptable to many of the Western European nations. We believe that this is a matter in which the Western European nations must have a leading voice." The cooperative projects such as the European Recovery Plan and the Council of Europe, Acheson emphasized, were not a negative reaction to Communism. They were part of a "positive program to support and strengthen democratic freedoms, politically, economically and militarily. In that context, the participation of the present Spanish Government, unless and until there has been some indication of evolution toward more democratic government in Spain, would weaken rather than strengthen the collective effort to safeguard and strengthen democracy."[59]

Acheson's attitude emerges from this communication in two separate points. First, we cannot hope for any changes of government. Rather, we should deplore the prospect, for it might possibly reduce Spain again to the shambles of civil war from which it has not recovered after more than a decade. Second, however, we should not enter into closer economic and military relations with Spain until certain political conditions were fulfilled: until the Spanish government had introduced some liberal economic and political features into Spanish life and until the Western allies could set aside their fears of defense behind the Pyrenees.

In the months following the Acheson-Connally letter, little or no action was taken on Spain by the State Department. Congress had taken the initiative on Spain; debate, hearings and oratory filled the air and there were good prospects of a loan. More important, however, the attention of the Department was deeply engaged in another direction, pending participation in and completion of what was to be known as "NSC 68," a monumental attempt to re-evaluate the principles and objectives of American and Western security and to provide a general plan for attaining such objectives or to provide a context within which policy decisions could be more realistically made. The trigger that set off the interdepartmental forces that worked on NSC 68 was the Soviet atomic bomb in September 1949.

What was the nature of world tensions and conflicts: Simply a struggle to fill the so-called power vacuums created by World War II? The prelude to World War III? How capable were we to prevent war? How well-fitted were we to fight in case of war? NSC 68 concluded that, if our basic aims were to develop a world system of politically independent, militarily and economically secure, cooperating states, we were not in good shape at all.

There was a common belief that in the event of a Soviet invasion, the entire European continent could be conquered in a matter of days. NATO was suffering; the NATO governments were reluctant to provide the shares agreed upon, and the representatives in the NATO councils were jealous of rights and prerogatives. NATO was not an encouraging prospect in the summer of 1950. NSC 68 had set 1952 as the "period of maximum danger," when the Soviet Union and its satellites would be most capable of defeating our purpose.

The Korean war, coming only a few weeks after the circulation of NSC 68, did not change the appraisal of NSC 68. It intensified the efforts of the executive branch to fulfill its aims, provided a practical reason for requesting more defense expenditures, and put Congress into a more propitious mood.

Thus, world events had favored the Spanish cause. For it was under these circumstances that the $62.5 million "mandatory" loan for Spain was attached to the Omnibus Appropriations bill on August 1, 1950.

The Administration's attitude toward the Spanish loan was set forth in the previous section. The money would be delayed until it could be used to the benefit of the United States. Money, ambassadors, bases, were all tied inextricably together. The forthcoming exchange of ambassadors with Spain was an important preliminary for any desirable future action. What might this action be? What would be the actual costs and gains of closer ties with Spain?

To help decide these and other questions, a joint policy committee was formed, including staff of the Departments of State and Defense. Working closely together on the Spanish "policy paper" were William Dunham of the State Department's Spanish desk and James Wilson from the office of the Assistant Secretary of Defense for International Security Affairs. Working relations between the State Department and the Pentagon had taken a turn much for the better as a consequence of the replacement of Louis Johnson by General Marshall as Secretary of Defense in September 1950. There had been much enmity between Johnson and Acheson, whereas there was cordiality between Acheson and Marshall.

Although the details of this paper have never been revealed, its balance of favor was admittedly strongly in the direction of military arrangements in some form with Spain preferably outside NATO. Work continued on the paper through the fall of 1950, and it was later turned over to another interdepartmental group, the Senior Staff of the NSC, in the persons of Frank Nash and Paul Nitze. Nash later became Assistant Secretary of Defense for International Affairs, and Nitze went on to succeed George Kennan as Chief of the State Department's Policy Planning Staff.

The Korean crisis and the events which followed closely after it had served to increase desire for a change in our relations with Spain within the Administration. The middle echelons in both the Department of State and the Department of Defense, represented by Dunham and Wilson, Nash and Nitze, had begun to shift. In the higher ranks there were such men as John Floberg, Assistant Secretary of the Navy for Air, and Secretary of the Navy Matthews who were now arguing for a shift in policy. Although Air Force Secretary Finletter remained adamantly opposed (because he had no confidence that Spanish bases would remain available after war began), his Chief of Staff Vandenberg favored Spanish bases, and Vandenberg became one of the first official United States visitors to Spain after negotiations had begun. And one of the key figures in the final shift was Chief of Naval Operations Sherman.

In November 1950 the Spanish policy paper awaited Secretary Acheson's approval, which had to be given prior to presentation formally to the NSC. For Secretary Acheson it was a problem of his own values, those of the President and those of the Western allies.

In November, even the exchange of ambassadors was not to come "for a long, long time" as far as President Truman was concerned. To discuss anything beyond that would have been unseasonable and impertinent. Consequently, the policy paper did not come before the NSC until January 1951, shortly after Griffis' nomination. In presenting the paper, Acheson had accepted the full import of its conclusions. A major purpose of the exchange of ambassadors would be to search out the situation for a possible military arrangement. The Spanish Government had expressed a strong desire for such an arrangement, but it was not known just what concessions they would be willing to make.

However, one last question the policy paper could not answer: To what extent would France and England now react against an agreement with Spain, preferably outside NATO? For, although more and more members of the executive were moving toward a pro-Spanish bases view, the Korean situation might actually have increased the fears of the allies that if war did come the United States would defend Europe from behind the Pyrenees. This was the task of Ambassador Griffis and his colleagues in Paris and London.

Griffis departed for Spain in early February 1951. On February 7 Secretary Acheson appeared before the Senate Foreign Relations

Committee. When directly asked just what our policy was with respect to Spain, Acheson replied that the United States had sent "a most able ambassador to Spain" with the hope that "the relations of this country, and I hope of the other countries, with Spain, are now entering a new phase."[60]

Further than this, the Department and Acheson remained close-mouthed. The Secretary made no comments after Griffis' first conversations with General Franco. Fairly detailed reports of the Griffis-Franco talks reached the press, and the State Department remained silent. Among the topics covered were the rights of Protestants and military collaboration. On the former Franco promised to issue a manifesto to the civil governors of every province, instructing them to see that there was no infringement of Protestant rights. On the latter Franco said that Spain did not desire to become a member of NATO, but that he would be delighted to make a bilateral agreement with the U. S. which would bind Spain to all the obligations of NATO membership—if it received proper military aid.

Shortly after these events, instructions were given to the ambassadors in Paris and London to discuss with those governments the possible role of Spain in general European defense.

What remained? The President must yield, and the pressure for doing so was well-nigh overwhelming.

TRUMAN RELUCTANTLY HALF CONSENTS

One factor which colors the entire Spanish story is the President's strong opposition to negotiations with Spain. Changing his position was painful for him. It required him to take a stand counter to his emotions, and his action would in effect contradict a host of his own public statements.

Apparently, when President Truman said in November 1950 that exchange of ambassadors would not come for a long, long time, he meant it. On their first encounter, prior to the December 27 announcement, Griffis told the President that he would be happy to accept the appointment if he were allowed a few weeks' vacation. To this the President said: "That's great and exactly what I want. I don't want you to go for the present—so soon after what I said a few weeks ago. I have been a little overruled and worn down by the [State] Department."[61]

The President went on further to say: "I don't know what your religion is, I do not even know if you have any, but I am a Baptist and I believe that in any country man should be permitted to worship his God in his own way. The situation in Spain is intolerable. Do you know that a Baptist who dies in Spain must even be buried in the middle of the night?"[62]

Obviously, President Truman had not relied upon the findings of Charles Patrick Clark and the travelling congressmen of the year before. And it is also fairly apparent that political and religious factors—and, to a lesser extent, NATO morale—were the central considerations in the President's mind. As far as the President was concerned, the improvement of civil liberties was to be Griffis' first task, and the prerequisite to a change of policy.

At the January NSC meeting at which the policy paper was presented, the President left the meeting still in substantial disagreement with the recommendations which had been accepted by Secretaries Acheson and Marshall.[63]

ENTER SHERMAN

Admiral Forrest P. Sherman had been appointed Chief of Naval Operations in the fall of 1949—a fitting climax to a brilliant career. Admiral Sherman practically symbolized the drive for unification of the military services. As Deputy Chief of Naval Operations from 1945 to 1947 he, with General Lauris Norstad —two airmen—had negotiated and bargained the basis of the original unification act. In the summer of 1949, as a result of President Truman's attempt to increase the authority of the Secretary of Defense, and as a result of Secretary of Defense Johnson's cancellation of the super-carrier contract, the Navy rose in open revolt against unification. This revolt, led primarily by Admiral Arthur Radford, ended in the resignation of Navy Secretary John L. Sullivan and the replacement of Admiral Louis E. Denfeld by Sherman as CNO. Sherman had soberly dissented from Radford's prophecy that full unification coupled with favoritism toward the Air Force signalled the doom of the Navy's peacetime mission and imperilled its wartime fitness. Sherman's independent position was rewarded by the task of overcoming the hostilities of an embittered, bickering service, which, by the time of his death, he had managed to do.

Admiral Sherman was a well-known advocate of closer relations with Spain. Following his work on unification, Sherman served for two years in command of the Sixth Fleet. Sherman had been convinced that the presence of the Sixth Fleet, sailing at the very edge of the Western sphere of influence, had had a deterrent effect on Russian moves in the Mediterranean.

In 1949 Sherman requested permission from the President on several occasions to visit Madrid, where his son-in-law, Lieut. Commander John Fitzpatrick, was assistant naval attaché. In 1950, while on an official visit to Portugal as Chief of Naval Operations, Sherman renewed his request for permission to go to Spain. This time the State Department replied that they would approve a visit in civilian clothes, but that any official mission was out of the question.

Of Sherman's colleagues on the Joint Chiefs of Staff, Chairman Bradley particularly remained cool to the Spanish idea. According to former Secretary of Defense Johnson, Bradley's position changed in response to Sherman's forceful argument. An important consideration on Bradley's part was that Sherman would probably replace him as chairman on his retirement.

From this time forth, the Spanish policy was a "piece of unification which worked," with Sherman as its spokesman.[64] President Truman met frequently and religiously with his Joint Chiefs. He often called them to the White House in between their regular weekly meetings.

Once Acheson removed his own name from the roster of opposition, Sherman stepped up his urging on the President. How vigorously and often Admiral Sherman broached the subject of Spain with the President will never be fully known. But there is no doubt that Sherman working with Secretary of Defense Marshall provided the critical force to change the President's mind. Reluctantly, the President did change it.

History is sometimes recorded in odd places, and we get some account of Admiral Sherman's activity from his talks with Louis Johnson at the Army-Navy Club. On several occasions over lunch, Sherman discussed Spain

with his friend Johnson (now returned to his private law practice), who had urged Sherman's appointment as Chief of Naval Operations. Sherman, by late spring 1951, had been encouraged in his talks with Truman that on his forthcoming tour of Europe he would finally be authorized to call on the Spanish government. In early July, Johnson saw Sherman for the last time. Within two weeks Sherman was to depart for the long-planned European tour. Sherman told Johnson that he still hoped for word from "the President on Spain."

On the morning of July 16, 1951, Sherman departed for Europe. To Johnson he wrote. "I have delayed answering your letter to let my plans clarify. They have now done so and I am taking off this morning for Spain, France, England and Italy."[65]

THE NEW POLICY IS ANNOUNCED

Later, on the same day, July 16, 1951, Admiral Sherman descended on Madrid, substantially to the surprise of everyone, including Ambassador Griffis. Defense Department press releases for the July 15-19 newspapers had explained that Sherman was on a week's tour to familiarize himself with European military conditions in preparation for the September meeting of the NATO defense ministers. Spain was mentioned in these reports, but this aspect of the journey was not stressed.[66]

On July 18 Acheson confirmed all hopes and fears. His statement is quoted at length here because it is strongly indicative of what had gone on in secret for so many months:

Admiral Sherman's interview with General Franco on Monday has caused widespread speculation in the press both here and abroad. The facts are as follows:

Military authorities are in general agreement that Spain is of strategic importance to the general defense of Western Europe. As a natural corollary to this generally accepted conclusion, tentative and exploratory conversations have been undertaken with the Spanish Government with the sole purpose of ascertaining what Spain might be willing and able to do which would contribute to the strengthening of the common defense against possible aggression.

We have been talking with the British and French Governments for many months about the possible role of Spain in relation to the general defense of Western Europe. We have not been able to find a common position on this subject with these governments for reasons of which we are aware and understand. However, for strategic reasons outlined above, the United States has initiated these exploratory conversations.

Any understanding which may ultimately be reached will supplement our basic policy of building the defensive strength of the West. It has been and is our firm intention to see to it that if Western Europe is attacked it will be defended—and not liberated. The presence of American armed forces in Western Europe bears witness to this intent as does the appointment, at the request of our NATO allies, of General Eisenhower as Supreme Commander.

We are sending vast amounts of military and other aid to these Allies for whom a clear priority has been established. There will be no change in this procedure. In other words, the North Atlantic Treaty is fundamental to our policy in Europe and the closest possible cooperation with our NATO Allies will remain the keystone of this policy.[67]

Truman delayed comment until his press conference on the day following Acheson's statement. With characteristic frankness, the President acknowledged that the Administration had officially changed its policy toward Spain. The President further affirmed that the policy had been shifted as a "result of advice by the Department of Defense."[68]

VI. REPERCUSSIONS

Strategic considerations had prevailed. In the words of Secretary of State Acheson, the military authorities were in general agreement. However, this did not simplify the future of the Spanish bases. Part of that future is reflected in Secretary Acheson's statement. As he saw it, the real problem in 1951 was the same as it had been in 1948, to rearm and unify Europe. The essence of the Acheson statement was its reassurance to the NATO countries that aid to Spain would in no way interfere with the commitment of the United States to NATO. The Secretary also attempted to settle the issue of the Pyrenees: We would continue to station American troops in Europe, and, as a corollary, we would defend Europe at its farthest eastern point in the free world.

Strategic considerations were also victorious over the President. The advice of the Defense Department to which he so openly refers may not have been contrary to his better judgment by July 1951; but it had certainly gone against strong emotions. At a press conference on February 7, 1952, just as negotiations were getting underway, the President stated flatly— to the great embarrassment of the State Department and the mission in Spain—that he was still "not fond of" General Franco.[69] Thus a new policy had been inaugurated without the full concurrence of the Western allies or the whole-hearted approval of President Truman.

On July 1951, as has been said, Admiral Sherman descended on Madrid. A week later, in Naples, the Admiral died. Within that week, Sherman, in the presence of his son-in-law, Lieut. Commander John Fitzpatrick, Ambassador Griffis, and an interpreter, managed to clarify the positions of the two countries well enough to get planning underway. When the conversations came to an end, it appeared that Franco was willing to negotiate; but the Generalissimo, in all fairness, asserted that base privileges would be of little use unless military arrangements were accompanied by economic aid sufficient to make the bases efficient (which could hardly come as an overwhelming surprise to the Americans).

As evidenced by subsequent events, Franco also agreed to allow American economic and military experts to study the situation preparatory to negotiations. For, now that we had made the decision to negotiate with the Spanish ruler, we had to decide what we wanted and how much we were willing to pay for it.

THE $450 MILLION QUESTION

Consequently, before the climactic month of July 1951 had passed, Assistant Secretary of State George A. Perkins outlined the plan before Senate hearings on the Mutual Security bill.

. . . [We] will start off by talking with the Spaniards about our ability to use certain facilities in Spain, not to establish bases at the present time, but that we would have the right to use some of their air and naval facilities.

In doing that it is probably going to be necessary to make some improvements in some of those facilities to make them useful for our purposes. . . . [70]

On August 20, a Temporary Military Survey Team was dispatched from Washington. This team, composed of high-ranking personnel from all three armed services, was headed by Air Force Major General James W. Spry. Spry had been transferred from the command of the Atlantic Division of the Military Air Transport Service. Attached to the team were two Army generals and a lieutenant general, a rear admiral and a captain from the Navy, and an Air Force colonel. In all, there were seventy on the team, counting the aides of lesser rank.

Three days later, the Temporary Economic Study Group departed for Spain. Professor Sydney C. Sufrin, representing the ECA, headed this group. Sufrin was on leave from his directorship of the Business and Economic Research Center at Syracuse University. He was accompanied by two officials of the Export-Import Bank and a small staff. The two groups set to work immediately, with the full cooperation of the Spanish authorities. In November and December 1951, respectively, the military and economic reports were completed, and the two groups returned to Washington. The texts of these reports were never made public. The military report was kept so close to the Pentagon that copies of it were not made available to many highly placed State Department officials until late in January.[71] The general substance of the economic report was made fully available to the press.

Professor Sufrin's feelings on the economic situation in Spain were mixed. His general conclusion was that the Spanish economy was "being held together by baling wire and hope." The railroads were in "terrible shape" and the iron and steel industry was in "dreadful shape." But the situation was not hopeless.[72] If there was to be a substantial increase in Spain's role in Western defense, Sufrin argued, it would be necessary to support Spain with large loans, possibly $450 million over a three-year period. Sufrin warned against a large immediate investment. An enormous dose overnight, he said, would be inflationary, and there were simply not enough trained people in Spain to build an efficient operation on a large scale. In return, Sufrin argued that Spain must make some long-run, drastic political and social reforms if the general standard of living was to rise. If private investors were to be encouraged, he said, they would have to be given assurances that ownership and income rights would not be violated.[73]

The Spry report, apparently, was an even more pessimistic document. While it reaffirmed the strategic value of selected air and naval bases, it pointed to one unanswered question: Would land bases, once established in Spain, always remain available to the United States? As we shall see, this was a question that two years of negotiations and five years of construction did not answer.[74]

PLUS ÇA CHANGE

The over-all effect of the two surveys was to put the military departments back essentially to their former positions. The Air Force and the Army waded back from what appeared to them to be quicksand. Many were dismayed at the apparent obstacles. The Army held to NATO, where base utilization rights were more certain. In the Air Force, Secretary Finletter continued to propound his view that Spanish air bases were impractical and undependable. According to his view, the effectiveness of bases is drastically reduced to the extent that delays in direct use of them are encountered in cases of emergency. As long as these difficulties could be foreseen, Finletter was content to rely on the North African bases, which were being built at a feverish pace, as a supplement to NATO.

But the Navy was undaunted. After a call at Valencia on January 10, 1952, Vice Admiral Gardner, in command of the Sixth Fleet, gleefully proclaimed that the use of Spanish bases would "undoubtedly facilitate the tasks of NATO in the Mediterranean." Spain's part in the Western defense would be a great strengthening factor.[75]

At the same time, Vice Admiral Cassady proclaimed that "Spain stands out as a bastion of defense, a vital link in the lifeline of a free and peaceful Europe." Admiral Cassady said that he considered one of his "primary missions" to further closer understanding between Spain and the Sixth Fleet. Pursuant to this mission, Admiral Cassady six months later presented to the Spaniards a portrait of Admiral Farragut (of Spanish ancestry) who, in Cassady's words, ". . . brought to America the finest traditions of Spanish dash and gallantry."[76]

The State Department was still faced with the embarrassing problem of what to do with the $100 million allocated to Spain in the Mutual Security Act of 1951 (and another $25 million in the 1952 MSA). If only because other departments had backed up slightly, the State Department appeared to be in the lead.

Spain's friend, Ambassador Griffis, announced his resignation and retirement on January 21, 1952, much to the dismay of the Spanish. Griffis stated to the press on that occasion that his main task, "to develop the beginning phase of Spanish-American relation-ships and understanding, has been completed." The second phase, he thought, was that of fol-lowing through the work done by Sherman, Spry and Sufrin for full collaboration. "The decision," said Griffis, "hinges on the Depart-ment of Defense."[77]

In Griffis' place, Lincoln MacVeagh, who had served a good many years in various am-bassadorial posts, most recently as Ambassador to Portugal, was appointed.

On March 12, 1952, amidst President Tru-man's professions of unfriendliness, the Navy's proclamations of cordiality and a general feel-ing of impatience and confusion, Secretary Acheson announced the formal opening of negotiations:

Preparations have now been completed for ne-gotiations with the Spanish Government regarding the use of military facilities in Spain.

. . . After thorough study of the reports of these survey groups, the Department of State, with the Department of Defense and the Mutual Security Agency, have made preparations for ne-gotiations with the Spanish Government. These negotiations will involve the use by the United States of military facilities in Spain and, in that connection, the use of the $100 million already voted by the Congress for aid to Spain.

Negotiations will be opened with the Spanish Government immediately after the arrangements of Ambassador McVeagh [sic]. Military advisers have been appointed to assist the Ambassador. They will be headed by Maj. Gen. August W. Kissner, U. S. Air Force . . .[78]

The Kissner "advisory group," which was to do the everyday negotiating, included a sec-ond Air Force officer and one representative each from the Navy and the Army. A three-man economic advisory group also accompanied Am-bassador MacVeagh. This group was headed by George F. Train of the Mutual Security Agency, who had been with MacVeagh in Portugal on an ECA mission.

For the time being, the responsibility no longer rested on the Secretary of State. And, in view of the supercharged atmosphere, the Spanish problem was one burden which could without regrets be delegated. The Spanish bases became an Air Force project; and, in view of the difficulties of that part of the negotiations that dealt with the air bases, the transfer of responsibility is not surprising.

The Secretary of State chose Kissner and delegated the responsibility primarily to the Air Force virtually without warning to Secretary of the Air Force Finletter. As in the matter of Sherman's mission and Spry's appointment, the Kissner group was formed without the advice and counsel of Finletter.

No sooner had negotiations got underway than they bogged down: another Presidential election was at hand. Spring and summer of 1952 brought forth a series of contrasting state-ments: now agreements had been made, then there was no program. The Spanish press was utterly confused.

After he took office in 1953, President Eisenhower made only one change in the Spanish negotiating team, the replacement of Ambassador MacVeagh by James C. Dunn. With thirty years experience, Dunn had served in many posts in the Foreign Service and had been Assistant Secretary of State. His most re-cent assignment before taking the post at Madrid was Ambassador to France.

There was no doubt that the Eisenhower Ad-ministration was more eagerly resolved to con-summate a deal with Spain than its predeces-sor had been. The pace quickened soon after the inauguration:

March 14, 1953. General Vandenberg, Air Force Chief of Staff, arrived in Spain for con-ferences with the United States military mis-sion.

April 9. Ambassador Dunn held an unusual-ly long conference with Franco and Foreign Minister Artajo. Afterwards, Dunn made the first official statement of the Eisenhower Ad-ministration. With a new cordiality, Dunn in-dicated in no uncertain terms that the new Administration laid more importance on the bases than had the Truman Administration. "We want the bases," the Ambassador said. Dunn affirmed the intention of the United States "to strengthen the cordial relations ex-isting between our countries," and the belief that these relations were "an important bul-wark" in the defense of Western Europe.[79]

May 1. Ambassador Dunn with Train and Kissner returned to Washington to confer with top officials including President Eisenhower. Following these conferences, the State Depart-ment announced that the outlook was good, so good that an agreement could be expected before summer.

August 20. In the heat of summer, General

Kissner returned to Washington for talks before the signing of an agreement. This time there seemed to be no doubt that something definite would be accomplished. In early September Ambassador Dunn flew to Washington for talks with President Eisenhower and returned to Madrid with the President's personal approval of the text of the agreement.

Two years after the Sherman visit and nineteen months after the beginning of negotiations, a bases-agreement was signed. On September 26, 1953, Ambassador Dunn and Foreign Minister Artajo signed three bilateral agreements. The first concerned the construction and use of military facilities by the United States in Spain; the second covered economic assistance; and the third dealt with military assistance. In sum, the United States agreed to provide:

$141 million for military end-item assistance
 85 million for "defense support" assistance

——

$226 million total[80]

In return, Spain agreed to authorize the United States, *"subject to terms and conditions to be agreed,* to develop . . . jointly with Spain such areas and facilities in Spain *as may be agreed upon by competent authorities of both governments."* One final stipulation by Spain was that all areas and facilities were to remain under Spanish jurisdiction, and that the manner of utilization of such facilities in the event of war *"will be mutually agreed upon."*[81]

After nineteen months of negotiations, the question of utilization of the bases in case of emergency had not been solved. Either General Franco had simply worn the American negotiators down in a war of determination; or the bases themselves appeared of such importance to the United States that doubtful use was better than no use at all; or, perhaps, the Eisenhower Administration wished to avoid the embarrassment of a failure to reach agreement.

Thus it came to pass that on August 25, 1953, when consummation was in sight, Senator Pat McCarran was presented the Grand Cross of the Order of Isabella la Catolica by Ambassador José Felix de Lequerica "for his efforts to improve Spanish-American relations."

VII. EPILOGUE

With the bases-agreement signed and sealed the military services returned to the planning stage for another six months. Unpredictable Spanish weather—which was to delay building operations for two succeeding winters—and lack of skilled workers were later to make the plans that emerged appear ludicrously optimistic. But by 1954 the Korean crisis had passed. The base-program got underway in an atmosphere of relative calm, unlike the circumstances surrounding the Moroccan bases. And the Americans carried out their tasks with utmost delicacy to avoid any suggestion that a second Napoleonic empire was occupying Spain. For the first time since Napoleon, Spain had qualified her territorial neutrality, a concession to which the Americans were instructed to show great deference.

On September 23, 1956, Secretary of the Air Force Donald Quarles landed at Torrejon Airdrome with Ambassador John Davis Lodge to open officially the first United States installation in Spain, an emergency air base fifteen miles northeast of Madrid. Although this event was conspicuously unheralded in the press, it was an important milestone.

In the spring of 1957, when a first draft of this study was completed, four years had passed since the Spanish-American treaty was signed. An ambitious program was in the works. The pivot point of the program was the naval base at Rota, near Cadiz on the Atlantic. This was to be the headquarters of the Sixth Fleet which had recently been relying on Villefranche, France, and Naples. This base, the largest of the installations, was then expected to cost over $120 million, of the total of $400 million allotted for base construction. Completion of this base was expected by the fall of 1958, although a nucleus base was to be in operation before that.[82]

The air bases run along a diagonal 500 miles northeast from Rota. Three of the bases were to be built for large bombers of the Strategic Air Command. An oil pipeline would connect all of these installations with a "tank farm" in Rota. Other marginal features included ammunition and supply dumps and a program of improving Spain's own airstrips.[83]

Over $280 million in economic aid had been made available between 1953 and 1957, and an additional $250 million in surplus commodities had been sold to Spain for Spanish currency.[84]

The United States flag does not fly over any of the bases, and every American base is under nominal command of a Spanish officer. That our rights to these bases were tenuous was discovered by Air Force Secretary Talbott on November 2, 1953, greatly to his surprise. On a visit to Spain at that time he remarked to the press that the United States would stock its bases in Spain with atomic bombs.[85] A furious Spanish reaction had all of Washington scurrying about. On November 3, President Eisenhower summoned the Secretaries of State and Defense to the White House to demand that they get their departments together on public statements. After the meeting Secretary of State Dulles told the press that the United States had no plan to store atomic bombs in Spain. Later, Secretary of Defense Wilson stated that he was "completely in line with the Secretary of State on this matter."[86] Talbott later insisted that he meant only that "we will eventually . . . have atomic bombs in Spain. This will be subject to the approval of the Spanish government."[87]

On another occasion, early in 1954, Secretary Talbott again discovered the strict limits of the Spanish agreement. At a press conference attended by himself, Secretary Wilson and others, when asked by a reporter whether the Spanish bases provided for wartime or only peacetime use, Talbott replied, "Well, who's going to stop us? There are certain agreements on the use of the bases, but when the balloon goes up, we are going to use them."[88] Later the Secretary had to explain gingerly: "I wish to clarify the statement attributed to me at Mr. Wilson's press conference this afternoon. The United States has every intention of living up to its agreements made between the United States and those foreign countries that have granted air bases to our country."[89]

These political rhubarbs illustrated beyond any doubt that the Spaniards had not signed a treaty giving us inalienable rights. In an emergency, Spain alone can decide whether the emergency affects her. The basic program was to be completed by June 1958, five years after the signing of the ten-year pact. In 1963 either party can withdraw if a year's notice is given.

Nevertheless, the Eisenhower Administration considered the Spanish arrangement well worth the trouble. The Eisenhower policy toward Spain contrasted sharply with that of 1950 and 1951, when Truman instructed Ambassador Griffis to insist on the liberalization of the Spanish regime toward the exercise of elementary individual rights. On November 1, 1955, Secretary of State John Foster Dulles, after a special trip to Madrid to visit Franco, described the feeling of the United States as one of "frankest cordiality and reciprocal understanding," "American friendship for Spain," and "the spirit of collaboration."[90]

BIBLIOGRAPHIC NOTE

The published sources for this study are not voluminous. The State Department *Bulletin* and various press releases of both State and Defense Departments contain essential material, as do the various hearings before a number of congressional committees and the *Congressional Record* itself. There are important details on the early stages in President Truman's *Memoirs,* Vol. II, *Years of Trial and Hope* and in *The Forrestal Diaries,* edited by Walter Millis. Some material on the later stages has been gleaned from Stanton Griffis' *Lying in State* and Herbert L. Matthews' *The Yoke and the Arrows.*

A far more important source than any of these has been the newspapers: the *Washington Post,* the *Christian Science Monitor,* the *New York Herald Tribune,* and, above all, the nonpareil—the *New York Times.*

For obvious reasons, no archival materials were accessible. In lieu thereof, the writer had the great good fortune to receive generous aid from participants in these events. An expression of deep gratitude is due the following, without whose gracious assistance this story could not have been written: Louis A. Johnson; Robert A. Lovett; Thomas K. Finletter; John Floberg; James Clement Dunn; Stanton Griffis; Frank Nash; Paul Nitze; James Wilson; William Dunham; Admiral Richard L. Conolly; Charles Patrick Clark; Senator John Sparkman and Representative Albert Rains. Responsibility for the interpretation and treatment of their remarks, however, is entirely the author's.

NOTES

1. Raymond Dennett *et al.* (eds.), *Documents on American Foreign Relations*, XII, 1950, World Peace Foundation (Boston, 1951), p. 617.

2. *A Decade of American Foreign Policy*, Senate Committee on Foreign Relations, 81st Cong., 2d sess., Sen. Doc. No. 123 (1950), p. 886.

3. *A Decade of American Foreign Policy*, p. 887.

4. *Yearbook of the United Nations*, 1946-47, pp. 20-21.

5. *Documents on American Foreign Relations*, 1945-46, p. 935.

6. *Yearbook of the United Nations*, 1946-47, pp. 345-351.

7. *Documents on American Foreign Relations*, 1945-46, pp. 889-890.

8. *Ibid.*, pp. 890-891.

9. Quoted in: *Assignment of Ground Forces of the United States to Duty in the European Area*, Hearings before the Senate Committee on Foreign Relations and Committee on Armed Services (1951), p. 224.

10. Truman, *Memoirs*, II, pp. 244-249, gives an account of an NSC meeting on May 20, 1948 in which it was decided to postpone our decisions about Germany and Spain. For a full account of how policy with respect to Germany was altered, see Laurence W. Martin, "The American Decision to Rearm Germany," in this volume.

11. Walter Millis, *The Forrestal Diaries* (Viking Press, New York, 1951), pp. 504-505. For detailed accounts of the bargaining positions of the service and Forrestal's own views, see pp. 462-468, 476-479, and 492-530.

12. *Ibid.*, pp. 356 and 358. According to Millis, Forrestal opposed the $15 billion budget ceiling primarily because it would not be possible without at least $18.5 billion to hold the Mediterranean (pp. 498-499). He also stressed the "overriding importance of access to Middle East oil reserves . . ." in the Cabinet meeting of January 16, 1948, and insisted that it would be "stupid" to allow the Palestine situation to develop in such a way as to do "permanent injury to our relations with the Moslem world. . . ."

13. *Ibid.*, p. 509.

14. *Ibid.*, p. 511.

15. *Ibid.*

16. *New York Times*, March 30, 1948, p. 4.

17. *Ibid.*, October 6, 1948, p. 1.

18. *Departments of State, Justice, Commerce and the Judiciary*, Hearings before the Subcommittee of the Senate Committee on Appropriations (1949), pp. 90-93.

19. *New York Times*, May 12, 1949, p. 1.

20. *Ibid.*, July 15, 1949, p. 6.

21. *Ibid.*, May 12, 1949, p. 10.

22. *Ibid.*, September 4, 1949, p. 4.

23. *Ibid.*, March 31, 1949, p. 4. In April 1949, Mercer, at the last minute, decided to accompany Culbertson back to the United States. This gave rise to widespread speculation that the State Department was making a full-scale review of the Spanish policy. Acheson, preoccupied with NATO, did not take occasion to scotch this rumor until his May statements discussed above.

24. From an interview with Admiral Conolly.

25. *New York Times*, October 13, 1949, p. 1.

26. *New York Times*, January 14, 1949, p. 8.

27. Courtesy of Charles Patrick Clark: The succeeding quotations are taken directly from the report, which was a long letter addressed to the President with accompanying material. Copies were loaned to the writer by Mr. Clark.

28. *New York Times*, September 16, 1949, p. 3.

29. *Ibid.*

30. *Ibid.*, October 1, 1949, p. 16, and October 27, 1949, p. 15.

31. *Ibid.*, November 2, 1949, p. 9; *New York Herald Tribune*, November 28, 1949.

32. *Ibid.*, December 12, 1949, p. 14.

33. Department of State *Bulletin*, XXII, January 30, 1950, pp. 156-160.

34. *Congressional Record*, 81st Cong., 2d sess., Vol. 96, Pt. 3, March 10, 1950, pp. 3176-3180.

35. *Ibid.*, June 13, 1950, pp. 8556-8562.

36. Pat McCarran, "Why Shouldn't the Spanish Fight for Us?" *Saturday Evening Post*, April 28, 1951, p. 25.

37. *Ibid.*

38. *New York Herald Tribune*, August 4, 1950, p. 16.

39. *Ibid.,* p. 1.

39a. *Ibid.,* August 29, 1950, p. 1.

40. *New York Times,* September 7, 1950, pp. 1, C-36.

41. *Departments of State, Justice, Commerce and the Judiciary,* Senate Hearings, pp. 90-93.

42. *Ibid.,* pp. 96-108.

43. *Mutual Defense Assistance Program,* Hearings before the Senate Committee on Foreign Relations and Committee on Armed Services, 81st Cong., 2d sess., 1950, p. 46.

44. *Assignment of Ground Forces,* Senate Hearings, pp. 187-188.

45. *Ibid.,* pp. 212-213.

46. *Ibid.,* p. 47.

47. *Congressional Record,* 81st Cong., 2d sess., Vol. 96, Pt. 7, June 30, 1950, p. 9531.

48. *New York Herald Tribune,* August 3, 1950, p. 26.

49. *Congressional Record,* 81st Cong., 2d sess., Vol. 96, Pt. 9, August 1, 1950, p. 11454.

50. *Assignment of Ground Forces of the United States to Duty in the European Area,* Sen. Rept. No. 175, March 14, 1951, p. 20.

51. McCarran, "Why Shouldn't the Spanish Fight for Us?" pp. 136-138.

52. *Ibid.*

53. *Ibid.*

54. *Washington Post,* June 1, 1951, p. 1.

55. *New York Times,* November 3, 1950, p. 1.

56. *Ibid.,* November 17, 1950, p. 1.

57. *Forrestal Diaries,* p. 445.

58. *Ibid.,* p. 328.

59. Department of State *Bulletin,* XXII, pp. 156-160.

60. *Assignment of Ground Forces,* Senate Hearings, p. 87.

61. Stanton Griffis, *Lying in State* (Doubleday, Garden City, 1952), p. 269.

62. *Ibid.*

63. NSC senior staffmen Nash and Nitze attested to this in interviews.

64. As described by John Floberg.

65. Courtesy of Louis Johnson.

66. *New York Times,* especially July 15, 1951, p. 1; July 17, p. 1; and July 19, p. 6.

67. Department of State Press Release 639, July 18, 1951.

68. *New York Times,* July 20, 1951, p. 4.

69. *Ibid.,* February 8, 1952, p. 1.

70. *Mutual Security Act of 1951,* Hearings before the Senate Committee on Foreign Relations and Committee on Armed Services, July and August 1951, p. 161.

71. *New York Times,* January 4, 1952, p. 1; and from confidential interviews.

72. *Christian Science Monitor,* January 8, 1952, p. 14; also *New York Times,* January 4, 1952, p. 1.

73. Foreign Policy Association, Headline Series No. 95, *passim.*

74. *New York Times,* January 4, 1952, p. 1.

75. *Ibid.,* January 11, 1952, p. 4.

76. *New York Times,* June 28, 1952, p. 13.

77. *Ibid.,* January 22, 1952, p. 14.

78. Department of State *Bulletin,* March 17, 1952, p. 450.

79. *New York Times,* April 10, 1952, p. 11.

80. Department of State *Bulletin,* October 5, 1953, p. 435.

81. *Ibid.,* p. 436. Emphasis added.

82. Herbert L. Matthews, *The Yoke and the Arrows* (George Braziller, New York, 1957), pp. 126-128. For a detailed account see Chapter VII.

83. *Ibid.*

84. *Ibid.,* p. 133.

85. *New York Times,* November 3, 1953, p. 1.

86. *Ibid.,* November 4, 1953, p. 1.

87. *Ibid.,* p. 4.

88. *Ibid.,* January 27, 1954, p. 1.

89. *Ibid.*

90. Matthews, *The Yoke and the Arrows,* p. 135.

EDITORIAL COMMENTS

As in the contemporary American decision to rearm Germany, our process of deciding to establish bases in Spain reflected the pangs of a reversal of policy required because the aftermath of a victorious war turned out to be an unhappy peace, uncertain and dangerous, with new perils replacing the old. In 1945 men's hopes looked forward to a re-educated, disarmed and pacific Germany, and to a democratic successor to Franco's Falangist Spanish government. By 1948, it was clear to many Americans, certainly to the informed, that our existing German and Spanish policies, based on war-time or immediate post-war assumptions, were outmoded; questions now arose as to what the new policies should be, by what means they should be adopted, and what timing was called for. There were certain similarities in both situations: in both, the most immediate, or most visible, objective was strengthening the defense of NATO by extra-NATO means; in both, some degree of re-entry of a former enemy or hostile neutral into the comity of the free world seemed an essential prerequisite; and in both cases it was President Truman who was least anxious to change and who finally gave in only with reluctance.

Characteristically in our unique democratic republic, our independent legislature, whether by action of individual senators or congressmen, or of informal groups, or of formal committees, or of Senate and House engaged in actual legislation, inevitably participates in the making of many decisions about civil-military affairs. What was unusual about legislative participation in deciding the issues about our relations with Spain and our proposed bases there was the high degree of congressional involvement, the extraordinary leadership exerted by one Senator and the successful lobbying carried on by the Spaniards (and the Senator) working through a traditional lobby and a paid lobbyist and through a group of officers of the Navy and Air Force who earnestly desired bases in Spain. Most military-political legislation follows the lead given by the administration, with Congress criticizing and modifying; in this case, Congress gave the lead, granted undesired legislative authority and appropriated unrequested funds. Eventually the policy set by Congress was adopted by the administration.

Senator McCarran's establishment of a private State Department with Sr. Lequerica acting as its Secretary and helping to discipline the unfortunate officials of the conventional Department is no unique episode in American history. A half century earlier Henry Adams had written: "Since the first day the Senate existed, it had always intrigued against the Secretary of State"; and, again, "the interference of the German and Russian legations, and of the Clan-na-Gael, with the press and the Senate was innocently undisguised." The relations of the Senate concerning foreign policy—and the House too—with the State Department—and the White House—have been vastly better since World War II than they were at the turn of the century, or perhaps ever before, but differences still occur and on occasion the foreign policy is led more by the Congress than by the President. What is more unusual and more relevant for this study is the role of the military in helping the Congress set a policy the Commander in Chief disapproved.

A system of government in which testimony by officers of the armed forces before legislative committees is not only permitted but required will obviously encourage public advocacy by its generals and admirals. Usually, however, the object of advocacy is or, more exactly, seems to be "strictly military" like flush-deck carriers and B-36 bombers. When it is clearly broader, like German rearmament, the officer-witness, such as Bradley, will preserve the amenities by warning that he can speak only of the "military aspect" of the policy issue and will avoid a flat discountenancing of his immediate superior in the Department of Defense and of the chief officers of other agencies like the Department of State and of course the White House.

In this tradition, the senior officers of the services and their civilian superiors were duly discreet when the controversy about the Spanish bases began. As time moved on, eager assistance was given McCarran by younger officers who felt protected by the publicly inarticulate but real concurrence of the Air Force generals and the Navy admirals. They also assumed correctly that, with one exception, they had at least the sympathy of the civilian secretaries. The exception was Thomas Finletter, Secretary of the Air Force. He had been an early and effective proponent of an Air Force base program, but when he expressed his lack of faith in Spanish bases, he and the Air Force generals came to a parting of the ways. The parting was particularly distressing because the generals made use of the military hierarchy leading to the JCS and thence to the Secretary of Defense and the President and thereby conveniently evaded their service Secretary. At that time, the downgrading of the service Secretaries inherent in the same reorganization process which has led to a JCS with a chairman, and an ever-stronger chairman, and which contemporaneously has augmented the powers of the Secretary of Defense and his ever-increasing staff was not yet understood, even though the inevitability of the process had already been demonstrated in England. By now, the specialized and limited role of the service Secretaries is widely accepted.

The Army fairly consistently stayed clear of too much involvement in the argument about Spanish bases. Presumably they understood and sympathized with the needs and desires of their sister services, but at best a buildup of trans-Pyrenean troops was a far less urgent objective than a strengthening of ground forces as near the Iron Curtain as possible.

The concern of the Air Force at this period for bases in Spain was understandable. Finletter's doubts lacked persuasive power and the need for a greater dispersion of our aircraft and particularly at bases within medium bomber range of Russia was evident to all. Forecasting the reactions of most nations to our air bases is a chancy matter, as our induced withdrawal from our Moroccan bases after a mere decade illustrates. Furthermore, the Air Force officers were particularly concerned after the outbreak of fighting in Korea for bases that could—as they thought—be obtained promptly and put to use with planes of the kind that were already in service: long-term problems had to wait. Thus, as has been said, the concern of the Air Force officers was indeed understandable. What merits attention is the procedure they used.

In large part, the procedures of the Air Force officers centered on by-passing Secretary Finletter, for he never abandoned his opposition to the Spanish bases. For this purpose, they used directly (or indirectly, using their assistants in some cases) their continuing relations with various power centers: the Secretary of Defense, especially while Johnson was in office, for he was greatly sympathetic with their position and not always too guarded in supporting what he and they jointly wanted regardless of the President's desires; the Navy, both officers and successive civilian secretaries, showing that bitter antagonists can form *ad hoc* alliances for shared objectives; Senator McCarran and his congressional allies; and, in some shadowy form, the various nongovernmental groups and factions that helped to constitute the Spanish lobby.

Like the Air Force, but more energetic, more constant, more determined was the Navy; and here the problem of circumventing the civilian secretary never existed. The Navy had, of course, a special need for Spanish bases that greatly magnified their very real desire to strengthen naval defenses against Russia. The special need was, of course, for bases as a weapon in the war it had been waging with the British since the War of 1812. Top-level control of the NATO naval forces in the Eastern Atlantic and the Mediterranean was (to put the matter in over-simplified form) the prize, and victory in the struggle could best be achieved by bases in Spain to counter the British bases at Gibraltar and Malta. Under these circumstances, it is not surprising that the successive visits that led to negotiation with Spain were, with one fruitless exception, Navy visits with Air Force officers accompanying the admirals.

The rapid movement of events in the modification of U. S. policy towards Spain within the Truman Administration during Truman's last years in office, and thereafter, reflected the change in American views of our place in the world caused by successive crises: the coup in Czechoslovakia, the Berlin blockade and airlift, the Communist invasion of the Republic of Korea. The rate of change was never uniform; it was speeded up by revelations of Soviet espionage, by blatant misbehavior by Soviet officials, by the unpreventable disasters in China, Tibet, Indo-China and elsewhere; it was slowed down by such matters as summitry and the spirit of Camp David. The distance we have traversed in a decade and a half is illustrated by Churchill's 1946 Fulton speech—what so many deemed terrifying then seems almost platitudinous now.

The adjustment of policy to the adjustment of attitudes in a very large democracy is never automatic, indeed almost never easy. The problem is made more difficult by the ever-present need to take into account the views of its allies. One of the delaying and modifying elements concerning both German rearmament and Spanish bases was the divergence of viewpoints between our NATO allies and ourselves, and in the Korean case the varying views that carried weight came from the fifteen other nations participating in the Korean War. These are issues of both military and foreign policy, or rather issues whose resolution will affect both diplomats and military officers. In these debates notably different occupational attitudes become evident. The military, hoping for bases in Spain, were inclined to disregard our allies, to assume that they would eventually give in, and to press for prompt agreement with the Spanish government. Their hopes for prompt settlement and definitive action proved fruitless. Senator McCarran and his congressional allies could maneuver an appropriation for Spanish aid through Congress in spite of the strong opposition of a frustrated president; and, after the outbreak of fighting in Korea, the Departments of State and Defense (with help from many quarters) could secure changes in U. S. policy. But negotiations with General Franco and his government could not be speeded up by anyone, and the building of the bases proved to be a matter of years, not months.

The diplomats whose major tool is persuasion operate usually with a different tempo from the military. They were sure in this case—when they became convinced fairly early that Spanish bases were desirable—that the UN could be persuaded to change its resolution on Spain, that our NATO allies could be convinced of the rationality of Spanish bases; they were equally sure undiplomatic tactics would be fruitless. In the event, they seem to have been right. General Franco could not be rushed any more than could our allies, and the Spanish reaction to any apparent U. S. military assumption of absolute right was an equally absolute "No!" as Secretary Talbott learned to his chagrin.

The contrasts in occupational habits were not contrasts between India ink and pure white. General Bradley, benefiting from three years of tuition by General Eisenhower in the diplomatic responsibilities of military leaders, carefully left room for diplomatic tactics in his pursuit of military ends. And Secretary Acheson was more than willing to use the methods of diplomacy to help the military achieve their goal. Nevertheless, the State Department relies on words, Defense on things; even where they share the same objectives, the routes and time schedules they choose frequently differ.

Truman during the four turbulent years in which our Spanish policy was a fairly frequent though relatively unimportant irritation looked on the problem with a rather different perspective from the others. Oddly enough, his chief concern seems to have been moral—the morality of the U. S. citizen horrified by Franco's anti-democratic outbursts, by the second-class citizenship imposed on Protestants in Spain, and over-all perhaps by a deep-rooted dislike for dictatorship. The whole affair hardly shows Truman in the two constitutional responsibilities he carried out with such vigor on greater issues—Commander in Chief and the leader in foreign policy. If our Spanish policy had been a policy of anything like the magnitude of European recovery or the defense of Korea, Truman's response and leadership would have been different. As it happened, his response was sluggish and leadership lay in other hands. Indeed, the fact of congressional leadership over presidential opposition gave the issue a seeming importance that far exceeded its real significance. By now, the existence of the Spanish bases is no more than a relatively inconspicuous element in our world-wide military program.